T0137907

Lecture Notes in Computer Science 13411

More information about this series at https://link.springer.com/bookseries/558

Ittay Eyal · Juan Garay (Eds.)

Financial Cryptography and Data Security

26th International Conference, FC 2022
Grenada, May 2–6, 2022
Revised Selected Papers

 Springer

Editors
Ittay Eyal (iD)
Technion - Israel Institute of Technology
Haifa, Israel

Juan Garay (iD)
Texas A&M University
College Station, TX, USA

ISSN 0302-9743   ISSN 1611-3349 (electronic)
Lecture Notes in Computer Science
ISBN 978-3-031-18282-2   ISBN 978-3-031-18283-9 (eBook)
https://doi.org/10.1007/978-3-031-18283-9

This Springer imprint is published by the registered company Springer Nature Switzerland AG
The registered company address is: Gewerbestrasse 11, 6330 Cham, Switzerland

Preface

The 26th International Conference on Financial Cryptography and Data Security (FC 2022) was held on the beautiful island of Grenada from May 2 to May 6, 2022. The conference is organized annually by the International Financial Cryptography Association (IFCA) and is a major international forum for research, advanced development, education, exploration, and debate regarding information assurance, with a specific focus on financial and commercial contexts. The conference aims to attract works focusing on both fundamental and real-world deployments on all aspects surrounding commerce security.

The conference was supposed to take place earlier, from February 14 to February 18, 2022, but due to uncertainties related to COVID-19, the conference's Steering Committee decided to postpone it. This turned out to be a prophetic decision as by the beginning of May many travel restrictions had been lifted, resulting in a lively and well-attended conference, a much-needed experience after the long COVID-19 hiatus.

These proceedings include the 36 papers that were selected by the Program Committee (PC), out of a total of 159 received submissions. Submissions were assigned to at least three reviewers, while submissions by PC members were assigned at least four reviews. The double blind review process and ensuing discussion among PC members were lively and engaging, to the extent that 15 of the accepted papers were conditionally accepted and shepherded by selected PC members. Five of the accepted manuscripts are short papers and one is a Systematization of Knowledge (SoK) contribution. In addition, we received four poster submissions, out of which three were accepted, but, due to travel impediments, only one was displayed during the Welcome Reception and Poster Session on Monday evening.

This year the Program Committee consisted of 64 members, and we made every attempt for its composition to reflect our proficiency, diversity, and inclusion goals. We are deeply grateful to the members of the PC for their dedication and thorough work, as well as to the many external reviewers who joined the review process in their areas of expertise.

FC 2022 celebrated 25 years of the FC conference program (postponed from last year's 25th FC that was online only due to COVID-19). The program was enriched by a special anniversary program and included a "Looking back at 25 years of FC history" presentation assembled by Kazue Sako and delivered by Sven Dietrich; a "Perspectives from FC since 2015" anniversary talk by Patrick McCorry; FC 25th anniversary vignettes collected by the anniversary coordinators; and a FC 25th anniversary retrospective panel—past impact and going forward, with panelists Don Beaver, Andrew Miller, and Hinde ten Berge, moderated by Sven Dietrich.

The main conference program, which lasted four days, was followed by a series of one-day workshops and a tutorial on more specialized topics: AMHIS 2022 (1st Workshop on Approaches to Modelling Heterogeneous Interacting Systems), CoDecFin 2022 (3rd Workshop on Coordination of Decentralized Finance), DeFi 2022 (2nd Workshop on Decentralized Finance), Voting 2022 (7th Workshop on Advances in

Secure Electronic Voting), WTSC 2022 (6th Workshop on Trusted Smart Contracts), and the "Quantum Computing Essentials for Financial Cryptographers" tutorial given by Or Sattath.

We are grateful to General Chairs Sergi Delgado Segura and Rafael (Ray) Hirschfeld for their predisposition, availability and efforts. In fact, it is hard to think of an aspect of the event's organization—from managing the conference's website, and collecting and uploading the talks' videos to YouTube, to coordinating all the fluctuating dates, updates, and related logistics with the Radisson Grenada Beach Resort hotel where the conference took place—which Ray wasn't on top of, and which resulted in such a well-planned and enjoyable event—thanks, Ray!

We are also grateful to the conference Platinum sponsors (Casper, CipherTrace, Harmony, Novi, and Ripple); to the Gold Sponsors (Chainalysis, IBM Research, Interlay, and Zilliqa); to the Silver Sponsors (IOHK, Manta Ray Labs, NTT Research, Protocol Labs, Smart Contract Research Forum, and the Zcash Foundation); and to the Sponsors in Kind (Grenada Tourism Authority and Worldpay), as well as the Uniswap Grant Program.

Finally, we thank all the authors who submitted papers to this conference, and all the conference attendees who made this event a truly intellectually stimulating one through their active participation.

August 2022   Ittay Eyal
                                                                                                    Juan Garay

Organization

General Chairs

Sergi Delgado Segura   Talaia Labs, UK
Rafael Hirschfeld   Unipay Technologies, The Netherlands

Program Committee Chairs

Ittay Eyal   Technion, Israel
Juan Garay   Texas A&M University, USA

Steering Committee

Joseph Bonneau   New York University, USA
Rafael Hirschfeld   Unipay Technologies, The Netherlands
Andrew Miller   University of Illinois at Urbana-Champaign, USA
Monica Quaintance   Zenia Systems, USA
Burton Rosenberg   University of Miami, USA

Program Committee

Ittai Abraham   VMware Research, Israel
Christian Badertscher   IOHK, Switzerland
Foteini Baldimtsi   George Mason University, USA
Jeremiah Blocki   Purdue University, USA
Rainer Böhme   University of Innsbruck, Austria
Joseph Bonneau   New York University, USA
Christian Cachin   University of Bern, Switzerland
L. Jean Camp   Indiana University, USA
Srdjan Capkun   ETH Zurich, Switzerland
Hubert Chan   University of Hong Kong, China
Jing Chen   Stony Brook University, USA
Michele Ciampi   University of Edinburgh, UK
Jeremy Clark   Concordia University, Canada
Vanesa Daza   Pompeu Fabra University, Spain
Stefan Dziembowski   University of Warsaw, Poland
Karim Eldefrawy   SRI International, USA
Matthias Fitzi   IOHK, Switzerland

Contents

ZKP

Old-School Consensus

Mostly Payment Networks

Incentives

Not Proof of Work

Performance

Measurements

Tokenomics

Maximizing Extractable Value
from Automated Market Makers

Massimo Bartoletti[1], James Hsin-yu Chiang[2(✉)], and Alberto Lluch Lafuente[2]

[1] Università degli Studi di Cagliari, Cagliari, Italy
[2] Technical University of Denmark, DTU Compute, Copenhagen, Denmark
jchi@dtu.dk

Abstract. Automated Market Makers (AMMs) are decentralized applications that allow users to exchange crypto-tokens without the need for a matching exchange order. AMMs are one of the most successful DeFi use cases: indeed, major AMM platforms process a daily volume of transactions worth USD billions. Despite their popularity, AMMs are well-known to suffer from transaction-ordering issues: adversaries can influence the ordering of user transactions, and possibly front-run them with their own, to extract value from AMMs, to the detriment of users. We devise an effective procedure to construct a strategy through which an adversary can *maximize* the value extracted from user transactions.

Keywords: Miner extractable value · Front-running · Decentralized finance

1 Introduction

Decentralized finance (DeFi) is emerging as an alternative to traditional finance, boosted by blockchains, crypto-tokens and smart contracts [18]. *Automated Market Makers (AMMs)*—one of the main DeFi applications—allow users to exchange crypto-tokens without the need to find another party wanting to participate in the exchange. Major AMM platforms like e.g. Uniswap, Curve Finance, and SushiSwap, hold dozens of billions of USD and process hundreds of millions worth of transactions daily [1,5,8].

AMMs are sensitive to *transaction-ordering attacks*, where adversaries who can influence the ordering of transactions in the blockchain exploit this power to *extract value* from user transactions [14,16,17,21]. We illustrate this kind of attacks through a minimal example. Assume a Uniswap-like AMM holding 100 units of a crypto-token τ_0 and 100 units of another token τ_1, and assume that both tokens have the same price in the reference currency (say, USD 1,000). Now, suppose that user A wants to swap 20 units of τ_0 in her wallet for at least 15 units of τ_1. This requires to append to the blockchain a transaction of the form A : $\mathsf{swap}^0(20 : \tau_0, 15 : \tau_1)$, where the prefix A indicates the wallet involved in the transaction, swap is the called AMM function, and the superscript 0 indicates the swap direction, i.e. deposit $20 : \tau_0$ to receive back at least $15 : \tau_1$ (a superscript 1 would indicate the opposite direction). In a *constant-product* AMM platform

I. Eyal and J. Garay (Eds.): FC 2022, LNCS 13411, pp. 3–19, 2022.
https://doi.org/10.1007/978-3-031-18283-9_1

like Uniswap, the actual amount of τ_1 transferred to A must be such that the product between the AMM reserves remains constant before and after a swap.

Now, suppose that an adversary M (possibly a miner) observes A's transaction in the txpool, and appends to the blockchain the following *sandwich*:

$$\mathsf{M}: \mathsf{swap}^0(5.9 : \tau_0, 5.5 : \tau_1) \quad \mathsf{A}: \mathsf{swap}^0(20 : \tau_0, 15 : \tau_1) \quad \mathsf{M}: \mathsf{swap}^1(25.9 : \tau_0, 20.6 : \tau_1)$$

where the last transaction is in the opposite direction, i.e.M sends $20.6 : \tau_1$ to receive at least $25.9 : \tau_0$. As a result, A only yields the *minimum* amount of $15 : \tau_1$ in return for $20 : \tau_0$. This implies that USD 5,000 have been gained by M and lost by A. This has been called *Miner Extractable Value* (MEV) [14].

Recent works study this and other kinds of attacks to AMMs [14,17,20,21]: however, all these approaches are preeminently *empirical*, as they focus on the definition of heuristics to extract value from AMMs, and on their evaluation in the wild. To the best of our knowledge, a general solution to obtain *optimal* MEV is still missing, even in the special case of constant-product AMMs.

To exemplify a case where prior approaches fail to extract optimal MEV, consider the following set of user transactions, containing a swap of τ_0 for τ_1, a deposit of units of τ_0 and τ_1, and a redeem of units of minted (liquidity) tokens:

$$\{ \quad \mathsf{A}: \mathsf{swap}^0(40 : \tau_0, 35 : \tau_1), \ \mathsf{A}: \mathsf{dep}(30 : \tau_0, 40 : \tau_1), \ \mathsf{A}: \mathsf{rdm}(10 : (\tau_0, \tau_1)) \quad \}$$

Here, both the swap and the dep transactions would be rejected. For instance, the constant-product invariant dictates that $40 : \tau_0$ sent by the user swap in the initial AMM state $(100 : \tau_0, 100 : \tau_1)$ will return exactly $28.6 : \tau_1$; since the swap transaction requires $35 : \tau_1$, it would be discarded. The known heuristics here fail to extract any value. Even considering only the swap, the sandwich would not be profitable for M, since it requires the *same* direction for M's and A's swap (offer τ_0 to obtain τ_1), making A's swap not enabled. Further, the known heuristics only operate on swap actions, neglecting user deposits and redeems. This paper proposes a layered construction to extract the *maximum value* from all user transactions, through a multi-layer sandwich that we call *Dagwood sandwich*. In our example, M's strategy would be to fire the following three-layer sandwich:

$$\mathsf{M}: \mathsf{swap}^1(11 : \tau_0, 13 : \tau_1) \quad \mathsf{A}: \mathsf{swap}^0(40 : \tau_0, 35 : \tau_1)$$
$$\mathsf{M}: \mathsf{swap}^1(42 : \tau_0, 38 : \tau_1) \quad \mathsf{A}: \mathsf{dep}(30 : \tau_0, 40 : \tau_1)$$
$$\mathsf{M}: \mathsf{swap}^0(18 : \tau_0, 21 : \tau_1)$$

The first transaction is a swap in the opposite direction (i.e., pay τ_1 to get τ_0) w.r.t. the subsequent user swap, unlike in the classical sandwich heuristic. M's second swap enables A's deposit; the final swap is an arbitrage move [9]. The user redeem is dropped, since it would negatively contribute to M's profit. By firing the transaction sequence above, M can extract approx. USD 5,700 from A, improving over swap-only attacks, that would only extract USD 5,000.

Contributions. To the best of our knowledge, this work is the first to formalise the *MEV game* for AMMs (Sect. 3), and the first to effectively construct optimal solutions which attack all types of transactions supported by constant-product AMMs (Sect. 4). We discuss in Sect. 6 the applicability of our technique in the wild. The proofs of our statements are in [10].

2   Automated Market Makers

We assume a set $\mathbb{T}_0$ of **atomic token types** (ranged over by $\tau, \tau', \ldots$), representing native cryptocurrencies and application-specific tokens. We denote by $\mathbb{T}_1 = \mathbb{T}_0 \times \mathbb{T}_0$ the set of **minted token types**, representing shares in AMMs. In our model, tokens are *fungible*, i.e. individual units of the same type are interchangeable. In particular, amounts of tokens of the same type can be split into smaller parts, and two amounts of tokens of the same type can be joined. We use v, v', r, r' to range over nonnegative real numbers ($\mathbb{R}_0^+$), and we write $r : \tau$ to denote r units of token type $\tau \in \mathbb{T} = \mathbb{T}_0 \cup \mathbb{T}_1$.

We model the **wallet** of a user A as a term $A[\sigma]$, where the partial map $\sigma \in \mathbb{T} \rightharpoonup \mathbb{R}_0^+$ represents A's token holdings, and write $A[\_]$ if the wallet balance is clear from context. We denote with $\mathrm{dom}\,(\sigma)$ the domain of σ. An **AMM** is a pair of the form $(r_0 : \tau_0, r_1 : \tau_1)$, representing the fact that the AMM is holding r_0 units of τ_0 and r_1 units of τ_1. We denote by $res_{\tau_0,\tau_1}(\Gamma)$ the *reserves* of τ_0 and τ_1 in Γ, i.e. $res_{\tau_0,\tau_1}(\Gamma) = (r_0, r_1)$ if $(r_0 : \tau_0, r_1 : \tau_1)$ is in Γ.

A **state** is a composition of wallets and AMMs, represented as a term:

$$A_1[\sigma_1] \mid \cdots \mid A_n[\sigma_n] \mid (r_1 : \tau_1, r_1' : \tau_1') \mid \cdots \mid (r_k : \tau_k, r_k' : \tau_k')$$

where: (i) all A_i are distinct, (ii) the token types in an AMM are *distinct*, and (iii) distinct AMMs cannot hold exactly the same token types. Note that two AMMs can have a common token type τ, as in $(r_1 : \tau_1, r : \tau) \mid (r' : \tau, r_2 : \tau_2)$, thus enabling indirect trades between token pairs not directly provided by any AMM. We use $\Gamma, \Gamma', \ldots$ to range over states. For a base term Q (either wallet or AMM), we write $Q \in \Gamma$ when $\Gamma = Q \mid \Gamma'$, for some Γ', where we assume that two states are equivalent when they contain the same base terms.

We define the **supply** of a token type τ in a state Γ as the sum of the balances of τ in all the wallets and the AMMs occurring in Γ. Formally:

$$sply_\tau(A[\sigma]) = \begin{cases} \sigma(\tau) & \text{if } \tau \in \mathrm{dom}\,(\sigma) \\ 0 & \text{otherwise} \end{cases} \qquad sply_\tau(r_0 : \tau_0, r_1 : \tau_1) = \begin{cases} r_i & \text{if } \tau = \tau_i \\ 0 & \text{otherwise} \end{cases}$$

and the supply of τ in $\Gamma \mid \Gamma'$ is the summation $sply_\tau(\Gamma) + sply_\tau(\Gamma')$.

We model the interaction between users and AMMs as a transition system between states. A transition $\Gamma \xrightarrow{\mathsf{T}} \Gamma'$ represents the evolution of the state Γ into Γ' upon the execution of the **transaction** T. The possible transactions are:

- A : $\mathsf{dep}(v_0 : \tau_0, v_1 : \tau_1)$, which allows A to **deposit** $v_0 : \tau_0$ and $v_1 : \tau_1$ to an AMM, receiving in return units of the minted token (τ_0, τ_1).
- A : $\mathsf{swap}^d(v_0 : \tau_0, v_1 : \tau_1)$ with $d \in \{0,1\}$, which allows A to **swap** tokens, i.e. transfer $v_d : \tau_d$ to an AMM, and receive in return *at least* $v_{1-d} : \tau_{1-d}$.

– A : $\mathsf{rdm}(v : \tau)$, which allows to A **redeem** v units of minted token $\tau = (\tau_0, \tau_1)$ from an AMM, receiving in return units of the atomic tokens τ_0 and τ_1.

We now formalise the one-step relation $\xrightarrow{\ \mathsf{T}\ }$ through rewriting rules, inspired by [9]. We use the standard notation $\sigma\{v/x\}$ to update a partial map σ at point x: namely, $\sigma\{v/x\}(x) = v$, while $\sigma\{v/x\}(y) = \sigma(y)$ for $y \neq x$. For a partial map $\sigma \in \mathbb{T} \rightharpoonup \mathbb{R}_0^+$, a token type $\tau \in \mathbb{T}$ and a partial operation $\circ \in \mathbb{R}_0^+ \times \mathbb{R}_0^+ \rightharpoonup \mathbb{R}_0^+$, we define the partial map $\sigma \circ v : \tau$ (updating τ's balance in σ by v) as follows:

$$\sigma \circ v : \tau = \begin{cases} \sigma\{\sigma(\tau) \circ v/\tau\} & \text{if } \tau \in \mathrm{dom}\,\sigma \text{ and } \sigma(\tau) \circ v \in \mathbb{R}_0^+ \\ \sigma\{v/\tau\} & \text{if } \tau \notin \mathrm{dom}\,\sigma \end{cases}$$

Deposit. Any user can create an AMM for a token pair (τ_0, τ_1), provided that such an AMM is not already present in the state. This is achieved by the transaction A : $\mathsf{dep}(v_0 : \tau_0, v_1 : \tau_1)$, through which A transfers $v_0 : \tau_0$ and $v_1 : \tau_1$ to the new AMM. In return, A receives an amount of units of a new token type (τ_0, τ_1), which is minted by the AMM. We formalise this behaviour by the rule:

$$\frac{\sigma(\tau_i) \geq v_i > 0 \ (i \in \{0,1\}) \quad \tau_0 \neq \tau_1 \quad \tau_0, \tau_1 \in \mathbb{T}_0 \quad (\_ : \tau_0, \_ : \tau_1), (\_ : \tau_1, \_ : \tau_0) \notin \Gamma}{\mathsf{A}[\sigma] \mid \Gamma \xrightarrow{\ \mathsf{A}:\mathsf{dep}(v_0:\tau_0,v_1:\tau_1)\ } \mathsf{A}[\sigma - v_0 : \tau_0 - v_1 : \tau_1 + v_0 : (\tau_0, \tau_1)] \mid (v_0 : \tau_0, v_1 : \tau_1) \mid \Gamma} \text{[DEP0]}$$

Once an AMM is created, any user can deposit tokens into it, as long as doing so preserves the ratio of the token holdings in the AMM. When a user deposits $v_0 : \tau_0$ and $v_1 : \tau_1$ to an existing AMM, it receives in return an amount of minted tokens of type (τ_0, τ_1). This amount is the ratio between the deposited amount v_0 and the redeem rate of (τ_0, τ_1) in the current state Γ. This redeem rate is the ratio between the amount r_0 of τ_0 stored in the AMM, and the total supply $sply_{(\tau_0,\tau_1)}(\Gamma)$ of the minted token in the state.

$$\frac{\sigma(\tau_i) \geq v_i > 0 \ (i \in \{0,1\}) \quad r_1 v_0 = r_0 v_1 \quad v = \frac{v_0}{r_0} \cdot sply_{(\tau_0,\tau_1)}(\Gamma)}{\Gamma = \mathsf{A}[\sigma] \mid (r_0 : \tau_0, r_1 : \tau_1) \mid \Gamma' \xrightarrow{\ \mathsf{A}:\mathsf{dep}(v_0:\tau_0,v_1:\tau_1)\ }} \text{[DEP]}$$
$$\mathsf{A}[\sigma - v_0 : \tau_0 - v_1 : \tau_1 + v : (\tau_0, \tau_1)] \mid (r_0 + v_0 : \tau_0, r_1 + v_1 : \tau_1) \mid \Gamma'$$

The premise $r_1 v_0 = r_0 v_1$ ensures that the ratio between the reserves of τ_0 and τ_1 in the AMM is preserved, i.e. $\frac{r_1+v_1}{r_0+v_0} = \frac{r_1}{r_0}$.

Swap. Any user A can swap units of τ_0 in her wallet for units of τ_1 in an AMM $(r_0 : \tau_0, r_1 : \tau_1)$, or *vice versa* swap units of τ_1 in the wallet for units of τ_0 in the AMM. This is achieved by the transaction A : $\mathsf{swap}^d(v_0 : \tau_0, v_1 : \tau_1)$, where $d \in \{0,1\}$ is the *swap direction*. If $d = 0$ ("left" swap), then v_0 is the amount of τ_0 transferred from A's wallet to the AMM, while v_1 is a *lower bound* on the amount of τ_1 that A will receive in return. Conversely, if $d = 1$ ("right" swap), then v_1 is the amount of τ_1 transferred from A's wallet, and v_0 is a lower bound on the received amount of τ_0. The actual amount v of received units of τ_{1-d} must satisfy the **constant-product invariant** [19], as in Uniswap [7], SushiSwap [6] and other common AMMs implementations:

$$r_0 \cdot r_1 = (r_d + v_d) \cdot (r_{1-d} - v)$$

Formally, for $d \in \{0, 1\}$ we define:

$$\frac{\sigma(\tau_d) \geq v_d > 0 \qquad v = \frac{r_{1-d} \cdot v_d}{r_d + v_d} \qquad 0 < v_{1-d} \leq v}{A[\sigma] \mid (r_0 : \tau_0, r_1 : \tau_1) \mid \Gamma \xrightarrow{A:swap^d(v_0:\tau_0, v_1:\tau_1)}} \text{[SWAP]}$$

$$A[\sigma - v_d : \tau_d + v : \tau_{1-d}] \mid (r_0 : \tau_0, r_1 : \tau_1) + v_d : \tau_d - v : \tau_{1-d} \mid \Gamma$$

where we define the update of the units of τ in an AMM, for $\circ \in \{+, -\}$, as:

$$(r_0 : \tau_0, r_1 : \tau_1) \circ v : \tau = \begin{cases} (r_0 \circ v : \tau_0, r_1 : \tau_1) & \text{if } \tau = \tau_0 \text{ and } r_0 \circ v \in \mathbb{R}_0^+ \\ (r_0 : \tau_0, r_1 \circ v : \tau_1) & \text{if } \tau = \tau_1 \text{ and } r_1 \circ v \in \mathbb{R}_0^+ \end{cases}$$

Redeem. Users can redeem units of a minted token (τ_0, τ_1) for units of the underlying atomic tokens τ_0 and τ_1. Each unit of (τ_0, τ_1) can be redeemed for equal fractions of τ_0 and τ_1 remaining in the AMM:

$$\frac{\sigma(\tau_0, \tau_1) \geq v > 0 \qquad v_0 = v \frac{r_0}{sply_{(\tau_0,\tau_1)}(\Gamma)} \qquad v_1 = v \frac{r_1}{sply_{(\tau_0,\tau_1)}(\Gamma)}}{\Gamma = A[\sigma] \mid (r_0 : \tau_0, r_1 : \tau_1) \mid \Gamma' \xrightarrow{A:rdm(v:(\tau_0,\tau_1))}} \text{[RDM]}$$

$$A[\sigma + v_0 : \tau_0 + v_1 : \tau_1 - v : (\tau_0, \tau_1)] \mid (r_0 - v_0 : \tau_0, r_1 - v_1 : \tau_1) \mid \Gamma'$$

A key property of the transition system is *determinism*, i.e. if $\Gamma \xrightarrow{T} \Gamma'$ and $\Gamma \xrightarrow{T} \Gamma''$, then the states Γ' and Γ'' are equivalent. We denote with $type(T)$ the type of T (i.e., dep, swap, rdm), and with $usr(T)$ the user issuing T. For a sequence of transactions $\lambda = T_1 \cdots T_n$, we write $\Gamma \xrightarrow{\lambda} \Gamma'$ whenever there exist intermediate states $\Gamma_1, \ldots \Gamma_{n-1}$ such that $\Gamma \xrightarrow{T_1} \Gamma_1 \xrightarrow{T_2} \cdots \xrightarrow{T_{n-1}} \Gamma_{n-1} \xrightarrow{T_n} \Gamma'$. When this happens, we say that λ is *enabled* in Γ, or just $\Gamma \xrightarrow{\lambda}$. A state Γ is *reachable* if there exist some Γ_0 only containing wallets with atomic tokens and some λ such that $\Gamma_0 \xrightarrow{\lambda} \Gamma$.

3　The MEV Game

The model in the previous section defines how the state of AMMs and wallets evolves upon a sequence of transactions, but it does not specify how this sequence is formed. We specify this as a single-player, single-round game where the only player is an adversary M who attempts to maximize its MEV. Accordingly, we call this the **MEV game**. The *initial state* of the game is given by a reachable state Γ (not including M's wallet) and by a finite multiset $\mathcal{X}$ of user transactions, representing the pool of pending transactions (also called **txpool**). The *moves* of M are pairs (σ, λ), where σ is M's initial balance, and λ is a sequence formed by (part of) the transactions in $\mathcal{X}$, and by any number of M's transactions. We require that the sequence λ in a move is enabled in Γ. The MEV game assumes the following (see Sect. 6 for a discussion thereof):

1. Users balances in Γ are sufficiently high to not interfere with the validity of any specific ordering of actions in $\mathcal{X}$.

2. The balance σ of M does not include minted tokens.
3. The length of the sequence λ is unbounded.
4. Prices of atomic tokens are fixed throughout the game execution.

Besides the above, some further assumptions are implied by our AMM model:

5. AMMs only hold atomic tokens (this is a consequence of [DEP0]).
6. Swap actions do not require fees (this is a consequence of [SWAP]).
7. There are no transaction fees.
8. Interval constraints on received token amounts are modelled in swaps only.

A *solution* to the game is a move that maximizes M's *gain*, i.e. the change in M's net worth after performing the sequence λ from Γ. Intuitively, the net worth of a user is the overall *value* of tokens in her wallet. To define it, we need to associate a **price** to each token. We assume that the prices of atomic tokens are given by an oracle $P \in \mathbb{T}_0 \to \mathbb{R}_0^+$: naturally, the MEV game solution will need to be recomputed should the price of atomic tokens be updated. The price $P_\Gamma(\tau_0, \tau_1)$ of a minted token (τ_0, τ_1) in a state Γ is defined as follows:

$$P_\Gamma(\tau_0, \tau_1) = \frac{r_0 \cdot P(\tau_0) + r_1 \cdot P(\tau_1)}{sply_{(\tau_0, \tau_1)}(\Gamma)} \quad \text{if } res_{\tau_0, \tau_1}(\Gamma) = (r_0, r_1) \tag{1}$$

Minted tokens are priced such that the net worth of a user is preserved when she deposits or redeems minted tokens in her wallet. We assume that the reserves in an AMM are never reduced to zero in an execution, in order to preserve equality of minted token prices between two states with equal reserves, thereby facilitating proofs and analysis. While our semantics of AMMs allows reserves to be emptied, we note that this does not occur in practice, as it would halt the operation of the respective AMM pair. We define the **net worth** of a user A in a state Γ such that $A[\sigma] \in \Gamma$ as follows:

$$W_A(\Gamma) = \sum_{\tau \in \text{dom}(\sigma)} \sigma(\tau) \cdot P_\Gamma(\tau) \tag{2}$$

and we denote by $G_A(\Gamma, \lambda)$ the **gain** of user A upon performing a sequence of transactions λ enabled in state Γ (if λ is not enabled, the gain is zero):

$$G_A(\Gamma, \lambda) = W_A(\Gamma') - W_A(\Gamma) \quad \text{if } \Gamma \xrightarrow{\lambda} \Gamma' \tag{3}$$

A **rational player** is a player which, for all initial states $(\Gamma, \mathcal{X})$ of the game, always chooses a move (σ, λ) that maximizes the function $G_M(M[x] \mid \Gamma, y)$ on variables x and y. We define the **miner extractable value** in $(\Gamma, \mathcal{X})$ as the gain obtained by a rational player by applying such a solution (σ, λ), i.e.:

$$MEV(\Gamma, \mathcal{X}) = G_M(M[\sigma] \mid \Gamma, \lambda)$$

Lemma 1 states that firing transactions preserves the *global* net worth, i.e. the gains of some users are balanced by equal overall losses of other users.

Lemma 1. $\sum_A G_A(\Gamma, \mathsf{T}) = 0$.

By using a simple inductive argument, we can extend Lemma 1 to sequences of transactions: if $\Gamma \xrightarrow{\lambda} \Gamma'$, then the summation of the gains $G_A(\Gamma, \lambda)$ over all users (including M) is 0. Hence, the MEV game is zero-sum. The following lemma ensures that deposit and redeem actions do not directly affect the net worth of the user who performs them.

Lemma 2. If $type(\mathsf{T}) \in \{\mathsf{dep}, \mathsf{rdm}\}$, then $G_{usr(\mathsf{T})}(\Gamma, \mathsf{T}) = 0$.

Finally, we note that prices of a minted token in two states are equal if the reserve ratio in the two states are as well.

Lemma 3. Let $\Gamma \xrightarrow{\lambda} \Gamma'$, and let $res_{\tau_0, \tau_1}(\Gamma) = (r_0, r_1)$, $res_{\tau_0, \tau_1}(\Gamma') = (r_0', r_1')$. Then, $P_\Gamma(\tau_0, \tau_1) = P_{\Gamma'}(\tau_0, \tau_1)$ if and only if $r_0/r_1 = r_0'/r_1'$.

4 Solving the MEV Game

By Lemma 1, a move which minimizes the gain of all users but M must maximize M's gain, and therefore is a solution to the MEV game. More formally, we have:

Corollary 1. $G_\mathsf{M}(\Gamma, \lambda)$ is maximized iff $G_A(\Gamma, \lambda)$ is minimized for all $A \neq \mathsf{M}$.

The net worth W_A of a user A can be decomposed in two parts: W_A^0, which accounts for the atomic tokens, and W_A^1, which accounts for the minted tokens:

$$W_A^0(\Gamma) = \sum_{\tau \in \mathbb{T}_0} \sigma_A(\tau) \cdot P(\tau) \qquad W_A^1(\Gamma) = \sum_{\tau \in \mathbb{T}_1} \sigma_A(\tau) \cdot P_\Gamma(\tau) \qquad (4)$$

This provides M with two levers to reduce the users' gain: token balances, and the price of minted tokens. To use the first lever, M needs to exploit user actions in the txpool $\mathcal{X}$ of the MEV game. For the second lever, since the prices of atomic tokens ($\tau \in \mathbb{T}_0$) are fixed, M can only influence the price of minted tokens ($\tau \in \mathbb{T}_1$). This can be achieved by performing actions on the respective AMMs.

In the rest of the section we devise an *optimal* strategy to exploit these two levers. Intuitively, our strategy constructs a multi-layer *Dagwood Sandwich*[1], containing an *inner layer* for each exploitable user action in $\mathcal{X}$, which M *front-runs* by a swap transaction to enable it (if necessary), and a *final layer* of swaps by M to minimize the prices of all minted tokens.

The construction of the final layer of the Dagwood sandwich is shown in Sect. 4.1, while the construction of the inner layers is presented in Sect. 4.2.

4.1 Price Minimization

Lemma 4 below states that, in any state, M can minimize the price of a minted token by using a single swap, at most. In particular, this minimization can always be performed in the final layer of the Dagwood sandwich.

---

[1] We name it after Dagwood Bumstead, a comic strip character who is often illustrated while producing enormous multi-layer sandwiches.

Lemma 4. *There exists a function* P^{min} *such that if* $\mathsf{M}[\sigma] \mid \Gamma \rightarrow^* \mathsf{M}[\sigma'] \mid \Gamma'$
then: (i) $P_{\Gamma'}(\tau_0, \tau_1) \geq P_\Gamma^{min}(\tau_0, \tau_1)$; *(ii) there exist* σ'' *and* λ *consisting at most of
a swap by* M *such that* $\mathsf{M}[\sigma''] \mid \Gamma' \xrightarrow{\lambda} \mathsf{M}[\_] \mid \Gamma''$ *and* $P_{\Gamma''}(\tau_0, \tau_1) = P_\Gamma^{min}(\tau_0, \tau_1)$.

In order to construct the swap transaction which minimizes the price of a minted token (τ_0, τ_1) in Γ, we need some auxiliary definitions. For each swap direction $d \in \{0, 1\}$, we define the **canonical swap values** as:

$$w_d^d(\tau_0, \tau_1, \Gamma) = \sqrt{\frac{P(\tau_{1-d})}{P(\tau_d)} \cdot r_0 \cdot r_1} - r_d \qquad w_{1-d}^d(\tau_0, \tau_1, \Gamma) = \frac{r_{1-d} \cdot w_d^d(\tau_0, \tau_1, \Gamma)}{r_d + w_d^d(\tau_0, \tau_1, \Gamma)}$$

Intuitively, w_d^d is the amount of tokens *deposited* in a swap of direction d: it is defined such that, after the swap, the AMM reaches an equilibrium, where the ratio of the AMM reserves is equal to the (inverse) ratio of the token prices. Instead, w_{1-d}^d is the amount of tokens *received* after the swap, i.e. it is the unique value for which the swap invariant is satisfied.

If both $w_0^0(\tau_0, \tau_1, \Gamma) \leq 0$ and $w_1^1(\tau_0, \tau_1, \Gamma) \leq 0$, then the price of the minted token (τ_0, τ_1) is already minimized. Otherwise, if $w_d^d(\tau_0, \tau_1, \Gamma) > 0$ for some d (and there may exist at most one d for which this holds), then we define the **price minimization transaction** $\mathsf{X}^d(\tau_0, \tau_1, \Gamma)$ as:

$$\mathsf{M} : \mathsf{swap}^d(\ w_0^d(\tau_0, \tau_1, \Gamma) : \tau_0,\ w_1^d(\tau_0, \tau_1, \Gamma) : \tau_1\ ) \tag{5}$$

Theorem 1 constructs the final layer of the Dagwood sandwich. We show that this layer is the solution of the MEV game on an empty txpool. This is because if M cannot leverage user transactions, the solution is just to minimize the price of all minted tokens. The solution is obtained by sequencing price minimization transactions on all AMMs. Since the price of a minted token is a function of the reserves of the corresponding AMM, this can be done in any order.

Theorem 1. *Let* $\Gamma = \|_{i \in I}(r_{i,0} : \tau_{i,0}, r_{i,1} : \tau_{i,1}) \mid \Gamma_w$, *where* Γ_w *only contains wallets. For all* $j \in I$ *and* $d \in \{0, 1\}$, *let* $v_j^d = w_d^d(\tau_{j,0}, \tau_{j,1}, \Gamma)$, *and let:*

$$\sigma_j = \begin{cases} v_j^d : \tau_{j,d} & \text{if } v_j^d > 0 \\ 0 & \text{if } v_j^0, v_j^1 \leq 0 \end{cases} \qquad \lambda_j = \begin{cases} \mathsf{X}^d(\tau_{j,0}, \tau_{j,1}, \Gamma) & \text{if } v_j^d > 0 \\ \varepsilon & \text{if } v_j^0, v_j^1 \leq 0 \end{cases}$$

Then, $(\sigma_1 \cdots \sigma_n, \lambda_1 \cdots \lambda_n)$ *is a solution to the game* $(\Gamma, \mathcal{X})$ *for an empty* $\mathcal{X}$.

4.2   Constructing the Inner Layers

Consider a solution (σ, λ) to the game $(\mathsf{A}[\sigma_\mathsf{A}] \mid \Gamma, \mathcal{X})$, and let:

$$\mathsf{M}[\sigma] \mid \mathsf{A}[\sigma_\mathsf{A}] \mid \Gamma \xrightarrow{\lambda} \mathsf{M}[\sigma'] \mid \mathsf{A}[\sigma_\mathsf{A}'] \mid \Gamma'$$

By decomposing the net worth as in (4), we find that A's gain for λ is:

$$G_\mathsf{A}(\mathsf{M}[\sigma] \mid \mathsf{A}[\sigma_\mathsf{A}] \mid \Gamma, \lambda) = W_\mathsf{A}^0(\Gamma') - W_\mathsf{A}^0(\Gamma) + W_\mathsf{A}^1(\Gamma') - W_\mathsf{A}^1(\Gamma)$$
$$= \sum_{\tau \in \mathbb{T}_0} \left(\sigma_\mathsf{A}'(\tau) - \sigma_\mathsf{A}(\tau)\right) \cdot P(\tau) + \sum_{\tau \in \mathbb{T}_1} \left(\sigma_\mathsf{A}'(\tau) \cdot P_{\Gamma'}(\tau) - \sigma_\mathsf{A}(\tau) \cdot P_\Gamma(\tau)\right)$$

Since λ is a solution, by Lemma 4 we can replace $P_{\Gamma'}(\tau)$ with $P_{\Gamma}^{min}(\tau)$:

$$= \sum_{\tau \in \mathbb{T}_0} \left(\sigma_A'(\tau) - \sigma_A(\tau)\right) \cdot P(\tau) + \sum_{\tau \in \mathbb{T}_1} \left(\sigma_A'(\tau) \cdot P_{\Gamma}^{min}(\tau) - \sigma_A(\tau) \cdot P_{\Gamma}(\tau)\right) \quad (6)$$

Note that all token prices in (6) are already defined in state Γ. Thus, A's gain can be minimized by considering only the effect on the token balance σ_A', which we can rewrite as $\sigma_A + \Delta_0 + \Delta_1 + \cdots$ where Δ_i is the effect on user A's balance induced by the i'th transaction in λ: this transaction is necessarily one initially authorized by A. We will show that Δ_i is *fixed* for any user transaction when executed in an inner solution layer: the position of an inner layer in solution λ does not affect its optimality.

The following theorem states that solutions to the MEV game can be constructed incrementally, by layering the local solutions for each individual transaction in the txpool. Intuitively, we choose a transaction T from $\mathcal{X}$, we solve the game for $(\Gamma, [\mathsf{T}])$, we compute the state Γ' obtained by executing this solution, and we inductively solve the game in the $(\Gamma', \mathcal{X}')$, where $\mathcal{X}'$ is $\mathcal{X}$ minus T.

Theorem 2. *With respect to the MEV game in $(\Gamma, \mathcal{X})$:*

1. *If $\mathcal{X}$ is empty, the solution is the final layer constructed for $(\Gamma, [])$ in Sect. 4.1.*
2. *Otherwise, if $\mathcal{X} = [\mathsf{T}] + \mathcal{X}'$, let (σ, λ) be the inner layer constructed for $(\Gamma, [\mathsf{T}])$, let $\mathsf{M}[\sigma] \mid \Gamma \xrightarrow{\lambda} \mathsf{M}[\_] \mid \Gamma'$, and let (σ', λ') be the solution for $(\Gamma', \mathcal{X}')$. Then, the solution to $(\Gamma, \mathcal{X})$ is $(\sigma + \sigma', \lambda\lambda')$.*

We now describe how to define the inner layers of the Dagwood sandwich, i.e. the base case of the inductive construction given by Theorem 2. Each inner layer includes a user transaction from the txpool, possibly front-run by M such that executing the layer leads the user's net worth to a local minimum. We define below the construction of these inner layers for each transaction type.

Swap Inner Layer. Swap actions only affect the balance of *atomic* tokens. To minimize the gain of A after a swap, M must make A receive exactly the *minimum* amount of requested tokens. The effect of the swap on A's *atomic net worth* is:

$$W_A^0(\Gamma') - W_A^0(\Gamma) = -v_d \cdot P(\tau_d) + v_{1-d} \cdot P(\tau_{1-d}) \qquad \text{if } \Gamma \xrightarrow{A:\mathsf{swap}^d(v_0:\tau_0, v_1:\tau_1)} \Gamma'$$

If the change in A's atomic net worth is negative, A's transaction is included in the layer. Although this transaction minimizes A's atomic net worth, it simultaneously affects the price of the minted token (τ_0, τ_1). This is not an issue, since the final layer of the Dagwood sandwich minimizes the prices of *all* minted tokens. Thus, the change of minted token prices due to the swap inner layer will *not* affect the user gain in the full Dagwood sandwich, as evident from (6). Note that the amount of tokens exchanged in a swap is chosen by the user, so the actual position of the layer in the Dagwood sandwich is immaterial (Theorem 2).

We now define the transaction used by M to front-run A's swap, ensuring that A receives the least amount of tokens from the swap. For $\Gamma = (r_0 : \tau_0, r_1 : \tau_1) \mid \cdots$ and $T = A : \mathsf{swap}^{d_A}(v_0 : \tau_0, v_1 : \tau_1)$, let the **swap front-run reserves** be:

$$\mathsf{SF}r_{d_A}(\tau_0, \tau_1, \Gamma, T) = \frac{\left| \sqrt{v_0^2 \cdot v_1^2 + 4 \cdot v_0 \cdot v_1 \cdot r_0 \cdot r_1} \right| - v_0 \cdot v_1}{2 \cdot v_{1-d_A}}$$

$$\mathsf{SF}r_{1-d_A}(\tau_0, \tau_1, \Gamma, T) = \frac{r_0 \cdot r_1}{\mathsf{SF}r_{d_A}(\tau_0, \tau_1, \Gamma, T)}$$

These values define the reserves of (τ_0, τ_1) in the state Γ' reached from $M[\sigma] \mid \Gamma$ with M's transaction. Intuitively, if the swap front-run reserves do *not* coincide with the reserves r_0, r_1 in Γ, then M's transaction is needed to enable A's swap. We define the **swap front-run direction** d_M as:

$$d_M = \begin{cases} d_A & \text{if } \mathsf{SF}r_{d_A}(\tau_0, \tau_1, \Gamma, T) > r_{d_A} \\ 1 - d_A & \text{if } \mathsf{SF}r_{1-d_A}(\tau_0, \tau_1, \Gamma, T) > r_{1-d_A} \end{cases}$$

We define the **swap front-run values** (i.e., the parameters of M's swap) as:

$$\mathsf{SF}w_{d_M}(\tau_0, \tau_1, \Gamma, T) = \begin{cases} \mathsf{SF}r_{d_A}(\tau_0, \tau_1, \Gamma, T) - r_{d_A} & \text{if } d_M = d_A \\ r_{d_A} - \mathsf{SF}r_{d_A}(\tau_0, \tau_1, \Gamma, T) & \text{if } d_M = 1 - d_A \end{cases}$$

$$\mathsf{SF}w_{1-d_M}(\tau_0, \tau_1, \Gamma, T) = \begin{cases} r_{1-d_M} - \mathsf{SF}r_{1-d_M}(\tau_0, \tau_1, \Gamma, T) & \text{if } d_M = d_A \\ \mathsf{SF}r_{1-d_M}(\tau_0, \tau_1, \Gamma, T) - r_{1-d_M} & \text{if } d_M = 1 - d_M \end{cases} \tag{7}$$

We combine these values to craft the **swap front-run transaction**:

$$\mathsf{SFX}(\tau_0, \tau_1, \Gamma, T) = M : \mathsf{swap}^{d_M}(\mathsf{SF}w_0(\tau_0, \tau_1, \Gamma, T) : \tau_0, \mathsf{SF}w_1(\tau_0, \tau_1, \Gamma, T) : \tau_1)$$

The inner layer is included in the Dagwood sandwich if it reduces A's net worth, i.e. if $-v_d \cdot P(\tau_d) + v_{1-d} \cdot P(\tau_{1-d}) < 0$. The swap front-run transaction is omitted if the reserves in Γ coincide with the swap front-run reserves. The balance of M in the (local) game solution is $\mathsf{SF}w_{d_M}(\tau_0, \tau_1, \Gamma, T) : \tau_{d_M}$. Note that, the amount of tokens exchanged by the swapping user in (6) is fixed by $(-v_d, +v_{1-d})$, and the effect of a swap inner layer does not depend on its position along the Dagwood sandwich (Theorem 2).

Example 1. We recast our first example in Sect. 1 as a MEV game, assuming a txpool $\mathcal{X} = \{A : \mathsf{swap}^0(40 : \tau_0, 35 : \tau_1)\}$. The initial state is $\Gamma = (100 : \tau_0, 100 : \tau_1) \mid \Gamma_w$, where Γ_w is made of user wallets, among which $A[40 : \tau_0]$, and $P(\tau_0) = P(\tau_1) = 1,000$. We construct the Dagwood sandwich. Since A's swap yields a reduction in A's atomic net worth, $35 \cdot P(\tau_1) - 40 \cdot P(\tau_0) = -5,000$, then A's transaction is included in the inner layer. To check if A's swap must be front-run by M, we first compute the swap front-run reserves:

$$\mathsf{SF}r_0(\tau_0, \tau_1, T, \Gamma) = \frac{\sqrt{40^2 \cdot 35^2 + 4 \cdot 40 \cdot 35 \cdot 100^2} - 40 \cdot 35}{2 \cdot 35} \approx 88.8$$

$$\mathsf{SF}r_1(\tau_0, \tau_1, T, \Gamma) = \frac{100^2}{89} \approx 112.7$$

Since these values differ from the reserves in the initial game state, M must front-run A's transaction. The direction d_M of M's swap is 1, as $SFr_1(\tau_0, \tau_1, \Gamma, T) > r_1$. The swap front-run values (7) are given by:

$$SFw_0(\tau_0, \tau_1, \Gamma, T) = 100 - 88.8 \approx 11.2 \quad SFw_1(\tau_0, \tau_1, \Gamma, T) = 112.7 - 100 \approx 12.7$$

Therefore, the swap inner layer is made of two transactions:

$$M : \text{swap}^1(11.2 : \tau_0, 12.7 : \tau_1) \quad A : \text{swap}^0(40 : \tau_0, 35 : \tau_1)$$

and M's balance of the (local) game solution is $12.7 : \tau_1$. To construct the final layer, we consider the state $\Gamma'' = (128.8 : \tau_0, 77.7 : \tau_1) \mid \cdots$, shown in Fig. 1. In Γ'', the canonical swap values are given by:

$$w_0^1(\tau_0, \tau_1, \Gamma'') = \frac{128.8 \cdot 22.3}{77.7 + 22.3} \approx 28.7$$

$$w_1^1(\tau_0, \tau_1, \Gamma'') = \sqrt{\tfrac{1}{1} \cdot 128.8 \cdot 77.7} - 77.7 \approx 22.3$$

Since $w_1^1(\tau_0, \tau_1, \Gamma'') > 1$, the direction d of the price minimization swap is 1. Therefore, the final layer is made of a single swap on the pair (τ_0, τ_1):

$$M : \text{swap}^1(28.7 : \tau_0, 22.3 : \tau_1))$$

where M's required balance is $22.3 : \tau_1$. Summing up, the Dagwood sandwich is constructed by appending the final layer to the inner layer, and M's required balance is $\sigma = 12.7 : \tau_1 + 22.3 : \tau_1 = 35 : \tau_1$. The MEV obtained by M through the Dagwood sandwich is $(11.2 - 12.7) \cdot 1,000 + (28.7 - 22.3) \cdot 1,000 \approx 5,000$. □

Deposit Inner Layer. By Lemma 2, deposits preserve the user's net worth. Thus, executing $T = A : \text{dep}(v_0 : \tau_0, v_1 : \tau_1)$ in Γ does not bring any gain to A:

$$G_A(\Gamma, T) = -v_0 \cdot P(\tau_0) - v_1 \cdot P(\tau_1) + v \cdot P_\Gamma(\tau_0, \tau_1) = 0 \tag{8}$$

where v is the amount of minted tokens (τ_0, τ_1) given to A upon the deposit. By Lemma 4, $P_\Gamma(\tau_0, \tau_1) \geq P_\Gamma^{min}(\tau_0, \tau_1)$. By using this inequality in (8), we have:

$$- v_0 \cdot P(\tau_0) - v_1 \cdot P(\tau_1) + v \cdot P_\Gamma^{min}(\tau_0, \tau_1) \leq 0$$
$$\Longleftrightarrow v \cdot P_\Gamma^{min}(\tau_0, \tau_1) \leq v_0 \cdot P(\tau_0) + v_1 \cdot P(\tau_1)$$

$$M[35 : \tau_1] \mid \Gamma = (100 : \tau_0, 100 : \tau_1) \mid \cdots$$

$$\xrightarrow{\text{SFX}(\tau_0, \tau_1, \Gamma, T)} M[11.2 : \tau_0, 22.3 : \tau_1] \mid \Gamma' = (88.8 : \tau_0, 112.7 : \tau_1) \mid \cdots$$

$$\xrightarrow{T = A:\text{swap}^0(40:\tau_0, 35:\tau_1)} M[11.2 : \tau_0, 22.3 : \tau_1] \mid \Gamma'' = (128.8 : \tau_0, 77.7 : \tau_1) \mid \cdots$$

$$\xrightarrow{X(\tau_0, \tau_1, \Gamma'')} M[40 : \tau_0, 0 : \tau_1] \mid \Gamma''' = (100 : \tau_0, 100 : \tau_1) \mid \cdots$$

Fig. 1. A Dagwood sandwich exploiting a single user swap.

By (6) it follows that including T in a game solution λ reduces A's net worth, since the decrease of A's net worth in atomic tokens is *not* always offset by the increase of net worth in minted tokens. Additionally, the minted token price $P_\Gamma(\tau_0, \tau_1)$ in (8) when the user deposit occurs is determined by deposit parameters v_0, v_1 alone: let $\Gamma \to^* \Gamma'$ be such that the given user deposit T is *enabled* in both Γ and Γ'. By [DEP], this implies $v_0/v_1 = r_0/r_1 = r_0'/r_1'$ where $(r_0, r_1) = res_{\tau_0, \tau_1}(\Gamma)$ and $(r_0', r_1') = res_{\tau_0, \tau_1}(\Gamma')$. Then, by Lemma 3, $P_\Gamma(\tau_0, \tau_1) = P_{\Gamma'}(\tau_0, \tau_1)$, as the reserve ratios in Γ and Γ' are equal. Thus, the amount of minted tokens v received by the depositing user in (6) is fixed by (v_0, v_1), and the effect of a deposit inner layer does not depend on its position along the Dagwood sandwich (Theorem 2).

Similarly to the construction of the swap inner layer, M may need to front-run transaction $\mathsf{T} = \mathsf{A} : \mathsf{dep}(v_0 : \tau_0, v_1 : \tau_1)$ to enable it. For $\Gamma = (r_0 : \tau_0, r_1 : \tau_1) \mid \cdots$, we define the **deposit front-run reserves** as:

$$\mathsf{DF}r_0(\tau_0, \tau_1, \Gamma, \mathsf{T}) = \left| \sqrt{v_0/v_1} \cdot r_0 \cdot r_1 \right| \qquad \mathsf{DF}r_1(\tau_0, \tau_1, \Gamma, \mathsf{T}) = \left| \sqrt{v_1/v_0} \cdot r_0 \cdot r_1 \right|$$

which satisfy $\mathsf{DF}r_0(\tau_0, \tau_1, \Gamma, \mathsf{T}) \cdot v_1 = \mathsf{DF}r_1(\tau_0, \tau_1, \Gamma, \mathsf{T}) \cdot v_0$, as required by [DEP]. Given a swap direction d_M, we define the **deposit front-run values** as:

$$\mathsf{DF}w_{d_\mathsf{M}}(\tau_0, \tau_1, \Gamma, \mathsf{T}) = \mathsf{DF}r_{d_\mathsf{M}}(\tau_0, \tau_1, \Gamma, \mathsf{T}) - r_{d_\mathsf{M}}$$

$$\mathsf{DF}w_{1-d_\mathsf{M}}(\tau_0, \tau_1, \Gamma, \mathsf{T}) = r_{1-d_\mathsf{M}} - \mathsf{DF}r_{1-d_\mathsf{M}}(\tau_0, \tau_1, \Gamma, \mathsf{T})$$

If $\mathsf{DF}w_{d_\mathsf{M}}(\tau_0, \tau_1, \Gamma, \mathsf{T}) > 0$ and $\mathsf{DF}w_{1-d_\mathsf{M}}(\tau_0, \tau_1, \Gamma, \mathsf{T}) > 0$ holds for a swap direction d_M, then we define the **deposit front-run transaction** as:

$$\mathsf{DFX}(\tau_0, \tau_1, \Gamma, \mathsf{T}) = \mathsf{M} : \mathsf{swap}^{d_\mathsf{M}}(\mathsf{DF}w_0(\tau_0, \tau_1, \Gamma, \mathsf{T}) : \tau_0, \mathsf{DF}w_1(\tau_0, \tau_1, \Gamma, \mathsf{T}) : \tau_1)$$

If the reserve ratio in the initial state does not coincide with the ratio of deposited funds, i.e. $v_0/v_1 \neq r_0/r_1$, then the deposit inner layer is $\mathsf{DFX}(\tau_0, \tau_1, \Gamma, \mathsf{T}) \, \mathsf{T}$, and the balance required by M is $\mathsf{DF}w_{d_\mathsf{M}}(\tau_0, \tau_1, \Gamma, \mathsf{T}) : \tau_{d_\mathsf{M}}$. Otherwise, the deposit inner layer is made just by T, and the required balance is zero.

Redeem Inner Layer. By Lemma 2, redeem actions preserve the user's net worth, i.e. A's gain is zero when firing $\mathsf{T} = \mathsf{A} : \mathsf{rdm}(v : (\tau_0, \tau_1))$ in Γ:

$$G_\mathsf{A}(\Gamma, \mathsf{T}) = -v \cdot P_\Gamma(\tau_0, \tau_1) + v_0 \cdot P(\tau_0) + v_1 \cdot P(\tau_1) = 0$$

Unlike for the deposit inner layer, redeem transactions *increase* the users' gain when executed in the game solution. This is apparent when substituting in the above equation $P_\Gamma(\tau_0, \tau_1) = P_\Gamma^{min}(\tau_0, \tau_1)$ (as per Lemma 4) to express the user gain *contribution* (6) of the redeem action.

$$-v \cdot P_\Gamma^{min}(\tau_0, \tau_1) + v_0 \cdot P(\tau_0) + v_1 \cdot P(\tau_1) \geq 0$$

Therefore, user redeem actions always *reduce* M's gain, and so they are *not* included in the solution. Therefore, the redeem inner layer is always empty.

$$M[18 : \tau_0, 50.5 : \tau_1] \mid \Gamma = (100 : \tau_0, 100 : \tau_1) \mid \cdots$$

$$\xrightarrow{\text{SFX}(\tau_0, \tau_1, \Gamma, T)} M[29.3 : \tau_0, 37.8 : \tau_1] \mid \Gamma' = (88.8 : \tau_0, 112.7 : \tau_1) \mid \cdots$$

$$\xrightarrow{T=A:\text{swap}^0(40:\tau_0, 35:\tau_1)} M[29.3 : \tau_0, 37.8 : \tau_1] \mid \Gamma'' = (128.8 : \tau_0, 77.7 : \tau_1) \mid \cdots$$

$$\xrightarrow{\text{DFX}(\tau_0, \tau_1, \Gamma'', T')} M[71.4 : \tau_0, 0 : \tau_1] \mid \Gamma''' = (86.6 : \tau_0, 115.5 : \tau_1) \mid \cdots$$

$$\xrightarrow{T'=A:\text{dep}(30:\tau_0, 40:\tau_1)} M[71.4 : \tau_0, 0 : \tau_1] \mid \Gamma'''' = (116.6 : \tau_0, 155.5 : \tau_1) \mid \cdots$$

$$\xrightarrow{\text{X}(\tau_0, \tau_1, \Gamma'''')} M[53.4 : \tau_0, 20.8 : \tau_1] \mid (134.6 : \tau_0, 134.6 : \tau_1) \mid \cdots$$

Fig. 2. A Dagwood sandwich exploiting a user swap, deposit and redeem (dropped).

Example 2. We now recast the full example in Sect. 1 as a MEV game, considering all three user transactions in the txpool:

$$\mathcal{X} = \{ \, A : \text{swap}^0(40 : \tau_0, 35 : \tau_1) \, , \, A : \text{dep}(30 : \tau_1, 40 : \tau_1) \, , \, A : \text{rdm}(10 : (\tau_0, \tau_1)) \, \}$$

The game solution is shown in Fig. 2: note that we can reuse the swap inner layer from Example 1, since the initial state and user swap action are identical. Thus, we continue by constructing the deposit inner layer for user deposit T' in state $\Gamma'' = (128.8 : \tau_0, 77.7 : \tau_1)$. Here, the deposit front-run reserves are:

$$\text{DFr}_0(\tau_0, \tau_1, \Gamma'', T') = \left| \sqrt{30/40 \cdot 128.8 \cdot 77.7} \right| = 86.6$$

$$\text{DFr}_1(\tau_0, \tau_1, \Gamma'', T') = \left| \sqrt{40/30 \cdot 128.8 \cdot 77.7} \right| = 115.5$$

Since the ratio of the deposit front-run reserves does not coincide with the reserve ratio in Γ'' ($86.6/115.5 \neq 128.8/77.7$), the deposit front-run by M is necessary to enable the user deposit action. By choosing a swap direction $d_M = 1$, we obtain the positive deposit front-run values, which confirm the choice of the direction:

$$\text{DF}w_0(\tau_0, \tau_1, \Gamma'', T') = 128.8 - 86.6 \approx 42.2 \quad \text{DF}w_1(\tau_0, \tau_1, \Gamma'', T') = 115.5 - 77.7 \approx 37.8$$

Therefore, M's deposit front-run transaction is:

$$\text{DFX}(\tau_0, \tau_1, \Gamma'', T') = M : \text{swap}^1(42.2 : \tau_0, 37.8 : \tau_1)$$

which requires a balance $\sigma(\tau_1) \geq 37.8$. The deposit inner layer is obtained by prepending this transaction to A's deposit. The redeem inner layer is empty, as shown before. By (5), the final layer to minimize the price of minted tokens is:

$$M : \text{swap}^1(18.0 : \tau_0, 20.8 : \tau_1)$$

Summing up, the full Dagwood sandwich (see also Fig. 2) is:

$$\mathsf{SFX}(\tau_0, \tau_1, \Gamma, \mathsf{T}) \ \ \mathsf{T} \ \ \mathsf{DFX}(\tau_0, \tau_1, \Gamma'', \mathsf{T}') \ \ \mathsf{T}' \ \ \mathsf{X}(\tau_0, \tau_1, \Gamma'''')$$

which requires an initial balance $\sigma = \{18.0 : \tau_0, 12.7 + 37.8 : \tau_1\}$ by M. By inspection of the Dagwood sandwich execution in Fig. 2, it can be seen that the miner has obtained a gain of approximately 5,700.   □

5   Related Work

Daian et al. [14] study the effect of transaction reordering obtained through *priority gas auctions*. These are games between users who compete to include a bundle of transactions in the next block, bidding on transaction fees to incentivize miners to include their own bundle. Notably, [14] finds empirical evidence of the fact that the gain derived from transaction reorderings in decentralized exchanges (DEX) exceeds the gain given by block rewards and transaction fees in Ethereum. The same work also proposes a game model of priority gas auctions, showing a Nash equilibrium for players to take turns bidding, compatibly with behavior observed in the wild on Ethereum. Our mining game differs from that in [14], since we assume a greedy adversary wanting to maximize its gain at the expense of all the other users, exploiting arbitrages on AMMs.

Zhou et al. [21] provide a theoretical framework to study the front-running on AMMs. Two sandwich heuristics are studied: the *front-run & back-run swap* sandwich, and the novel *front-run redeem & back-run swap and deposit*. The swap semantics used in [21] is simplified, compared to ours, since no minimum amount of received tokens is enforced by the AMM, users only perform swaps and hold no minted tokens (depositing and swapping agents are decoupled). Further, extractable value from arbitrage is considered separately. In comparison, we emphasize that we propose a solution to attack all main user action types offered by leading AMMs, thereby extracting value from user submitted swaps and deposits. Our model also accurately model minted tokens: their value is dynamically affected by miner and user swaps during the execution of the attack. Thus, our game solution extracts the maximum value in a more concrete setting, considering the victim transactions of both aforementioned attacks in [21], and leaving no arbitrage opportunities unexploited.

More general ordering and injection of transactions by a rational agent is generally referred to as *front-running*. Eskandari et al. [16] provide a taxonomy for various front-running attacks in blockchain applications and networks. This taxonomy is expanded in [17] with liquidations, sandwich attacks and arbitrage actions between DEX.

Some works investigate the problem of detecting front-running attacks on public blockchains. For example, in [17], Qin et al. introduce front-running detection heuristics which are deployed to empirically study the presence of such attacks on public DeFi applications. On the other hand, various fair ordering schemes have been proposed to mitigate front-running or exploitation of miner-extractable value. However, simple commit-and-reveal schemes still leak information such as account balances. Breidenbach et al. [12] propose "submarine commitments", which rely on k-anonymity to prevent any leaks from user commitments. Baum *et al.* [11] introduce a order-book based DEX which delegates the matching of orders to an out-sourced, off-chain multi-party computation committee. Private user orders are not revealed to other participants, such that no front-running can occur in each privately-computed order matching round. Ciampi *et al.* [13] introduce a market maker protocol in which the strictly sequential trade history between an off-chain market maker and traders are verifiable as a hash-chain. Any subsequent reordering by the AMM is publicly provable: collateral from the market maker incentivizes honest, fair-ordering behaviour. Such work aims to provide alternative, front-running resistant designs with AMM-like functionality. In contrast, our work is intended to formalize the behaviour of current, mainstream AMMs in the presence of a rational adversary.

The DeFi community is developing tools to enable agents to extract value from smart contracts: e.g., flashbots [2] is a project aiming to develop Ethereum implementations which support transaction bundles: Rather than front-running individual transactions by adjusting their fees, an agent can communicate a sequence or *bundle* of transactions to the miner, asking its inclusion in the next block. Our game solutions could be implemented to solve for such bundles.

6   Conclusions

We have addressed the problem of adversaries extracting value from AMMs interactions to the detriment of users. We have constructed an *optimal* strategy that adversaries can use to extract value from AMMs, focussing on the widespread class of constant-product AMMs. Our results apply to any adversary with the power to reorder, drop or insert transactions: besides miners, this includes *roll-up aggregators*, like e.g. Optimism and StarkWare [3,4]. Notably, our work shows that it is possible to extract value from *all* types of AMM transactions, while previous works focus on extracting value from token swaps, only.

In practice, value is also extracted from AMMs by colluding mining and non-mining agents: for the Ethereum blockchain, agents can send *transaction bundles* [2] to mining pools for block inclusion, in return for a fee. Our technique naturally applies to this setting, where the actions of the miner are simply replaced by actions by the agent submitting the transaction bundle.

We now discuss the simplifying assumptions (1–8) listed in Sect. 3. (1) User balances do not limit the order in which transactions in the *txpool* can be executed. In practice, in some cases it would be possible to perform a sequence of actions by exploiting the funds received from previous actions. We leave ordering constraints imposed by limited wallet balances for future work. (2) The adversary holds no minted tokens prior to executing the game solution. Yet, the adversary can exploit an (unbounded) initial balance of atomic tokens to acquire minted tokens as part of the game solution by performing deposits. The optimality of the Dagwood sandwich illustrates that this is not necessary. (3) The size of the *Dagwood sandwich* is unbounded. In practice, a typical block of transactions will include other transactions besides those directed to AMMs, and so the adversary can find enough space for its sandwiches by dropping non-AMM transactions. During times of block-congestion, a constraint on the length of the Dagwood sandwich will apply: we conjecture that solving such an optimization is NP-hard, and regard this as an relevant question for future work. (4) Prices of atomic tokens are fixed for the duration of the game: the Dagwood sandwich will need to be recomputed should prices change. (5) AMMs only hold atomic tokens. This is common in practice, but we note that extending the mining game to account for arbitrary nesting of minted tokens by AMM pairs is an interesting direction of future research. (6) No AMM swap fees and (7) no transaction fees are modelled: the adversary's gain resulting from the Dagwood sandwich is an upper bound to profitability as fees tend to zero. Yet, fees affect this gain, so they should be taken into account to construct an optimal strategy. Furthermore, transaction fees may make it convenient for a miner to include user redeem transactions in the sandwich, while these are never exploited by our strategy. (8) Besides fees, we abstract from the intervals that users can express to constrain the amount of tokens received upon deposits and redeems (we only model these constraints for swaps). This is left for future work.

In this paper we have considered AMMs which implement the constant-product swap invariant, like e.g. Uniswap and SushiSwap. A relevant research question is how to solve the MEV game under different swap invariants, e.g. those used by Curve Finance and SushiSwap. Uniform frameworks which address this problem have been proposed in [9,15] where swap invariants are abstracted as functions subject to a given set of constraints.

Acknowledgements. Massimo Bartoletti is partially supported by Conv. Fondazione di Sardegna & Atenei Sardi project F75F21001220007 *ASTRID*. James Hsin-yu Chiang is supported by the PhD School of DTU Compute.

References

1. Curve statistics (2020). https://www.curve.fi/dailystats
2. Flashbots (2021). https://github.com/flashbots/pm
3. Optimism website (2021). https://optimism.io/
4. Starkware website (2021). https://starkware.co/
5. SushiSwap statistics (2021). https://analytics.sushi.com/
6. SushiSwap token pair implementation (2021). https://github.com/sushiswap/sushiswap/blob/94ea7712daaa13155dfab9786aacf69e24390147/contracts/uniswapv2/UniswapV2Pair.sol
7. Uniswap token pair implementation (2021). https://github.com/Uniswap/uniswap-v2-core/blob/4dd59067c76dea4a0e8e4bfdda41877a6b16dedc/contracts/UniswapV2Pair.sol
8. Uniswap V2 statistics (2021). https://v2.info.uniswap.org/
9. Bartoletti, M., Chiang, J.H., Lluch-Lafuente, A.: A theory of automated market makers in DeFi. In: Damiani, F., Dardha, O. (eds.) COORDINATION 2021. LNCS, vol. 12717, pp. 168–187. Springer, Cham (2021). https://doi.org/10.1007/978-3-030-78142-2_11

10. Bartoletti, M., Chiang, J.H., Lluch-Lafuente, A.: Maximizing extractable value from automated market makers. CoRR abs/2106.01870 (2021). https://arxiv.org/abs/2106.01870

11. Baum, C., David, B., Frederiksen, T.K.: P2DEX: privacy-preserving decentralized cryptocurrency exchange. In: Sako, K., Tippenhauer, N.O. (eds.) ACNS 2021. LNCS, vol. 12726, pp. 163–194. Springer, Cham (2021). https://doi.org/10.1007/978-3-030-78372-3_7

12. Breidenbach, L., Daian, P., Tramèr, F., Juels, A.: Enter the Hydra: towards principled bug bounties and exploit-resistant smart contracts. In: USENIX Security Symposium, pp. 1335–1352. USENIX Association (2019)

13. Ciampi, M., Ishaq, M., Magdon-Ismail, M., Ostrovsky, R., Zikas, V.: FairMM: a fast and frontrunning-resistant crypto market-maker. Cryptology ePrint Archive, Report 2021/609 (2021). https://eprint.iacr.org/2021/609

14. Daian, P., et al.: Flash boys 2.0: frontrunning in decentralized exchanges, miner extractable value, and consensus instability. In: IEEE Symposium on Security and Privacy, pp. 910–927. IEEE (2020). https://doi.org/10.1109/SP40000.2020.00040

15. Engel, D., Herlihy, M.: Composing networks of automated market makers. In: Advances in Financial Technologies (AFT), pp. 15–28. ACM (2021). https://doi.org/10.1145/3479722.3480987

16. Eskandari, S., Moosavi, S., Clark, J.: SoK: transparent dishonesty: front-running attacks on blockchain. In: Bracciali, A., Clark, J., Pintore, F., Rønne, P.B., Sala, M. (eds.) FC 2019. LNCS, vol. 11599, pp. 170–189. Springer, Cham (2020). https://doi.org/10.1007/978-3-030-43725-1_13

17. Qin, K., Zhou, L., Gervais, A.: Quantifying blockchain extractable value: how dark is the forest? (2021). https://arxiv.org/abs/2101.05511

18. Werner, S.M., Perez, D., Gudgeon, L., Klages-Mundt, A., Harz, D., Knottenbelt, W.J.: SoK: decentralized finance (DeFi). CoRR abs/2101.08778 (2021)

19. Zhang, Y., Chen, X., Park, D.: Formal specification of constant product market maker model & implementation (2018). https://github.com/runtimeverification/verified-smart-contracts/blob/uniswap/uniswap/x-y-k.pdf

20. Zhou, L., Qin, K., Cully, A., Livshits, B., Gervais, A.: On the just-in-time discovery of profit-generating transactions in DeFi protocols. In: IEEE Symposium on Security and Privacy, pp. 919–936. IEEE (2021). https://doi.org/10.1109/SP40001.2021.00113

21. Zhou, L., Qin, K., Torres, C.F., Le, D.V., Gervais, A.: High-frequency trading on decentralized on-chain exchanges. In: IEEE Symposium on Security and Privacy, pp. 428–445. IEEE (2021). https://doi.org/10.1109/SP40001.2021.00027

Kicking-the-Bucket: Fast Privacy-Preserving Trading Using Buckets

Mariana Botelho da Gama[1], John Cartlidge[2], Antigoni Polychroniadou[3],
Nigel P. Smart[1](✉), and Younes Talibi Alaoui[1]

[1] imec-COSIC, KU Leuven, Leuven, Belgium
{mariana.botelhodagama,nigel.smart,younes.talibialaoui}@kuleuven.be
[2] University of Bristol, Bristol, UK
john.cartlidge@bristol.ac.uk
[3] J. P. Morgan AI Research, New York, USA
antigoni.polychroniadou@jpmorgan.com

Abstract. We examine bucket-based and volume-based algorithms for privacy-preserving asset trading in a financial dark pool. Our bucket-based algorithm places orders in quantised buckets, whereas the volume-based algorithm allows any volume size but requires more complex validation mechanisms. In all cases, we conclude that these algorithms are highly efficient and offer a practical solution to the commercial problem of preserving privacy of order information in a dark pool trading venue.

1 Introduction

The majority of major stock exchanges are now electronic order-driven markets, where investors submit orders to buy or sell a quantity of stock at a particular price. Orders that are not immediately filled (i.e., those that do not immediately result in a trade) are publicly displayed in a limit order book (LOB), which presents a price-ordered view of the instantaneous demand and supply in the market. With each order in the book acting as an advertisement of an investor's willingness to commit to a particular trade, the LOB is an efficient method for finding counterparties with whom to trade. However, sometimes it is beneficial for an investor to hide their trading intention. In particular, when attempting to trade in large volume (i.e., when wanting to buy or sell a large quantity of stock), exposing one's intention will likely lead to adverse price movement as the information contained in the large order causes other investors to re-evaluate market price. This effect is known as *price impact*, or *market impact*, and it can be extremely costly to a large-volume investor. To reduce impact, an investor will often "salami slice" one large order into multiple smaller orders and drip feed these into the market slowly over time. So common is this approach that many exchanges offer an "iceberg" order type that automates a similar process. When an iceberg order is submitted, only a small proportion of the full order volume (the "tip of the iceberg") is displayed in the order book at any given

© International Financial Cryptography Association 2022
I. Eyal and J. Garay (Eds.): FC 2022, LNCS 13411, pp. 20–37, 2022.
https://doi.org/10.1007/978-3-031-18283-9_2

time, while the bulk of the remaining order remains hidden ("submerged" out of view). However, while the use of icebergs to disguise order volumes can help limit the effects of market impact, icebergs are exposed to the risk that other investors will anticipate the hidden iceberg volume from information leaking from the visible tip.

To counter this, some trading venues hide all pre-trade order information. Commonly referred to as "dark pools" to contrast with the "lit" order books of an exchange, these trading venues ensure that all order information is non-displayed. As other investors have no access to the information in a dark pool, so market impact can be significantly reduced, or avoided entirely. Hidden away from viewing eyes, orders in a dark pool tend to take longer to fill than equivalent orders submitted to an exchange. However, in most cases, the potential savings available to large volume institutional investors will significantly outweigh the desire for trading urgency. That is, volume investors are usually prepared to wait as long as the final deal they make is fair. As a result, dark pool trading has risen in popularity, with more than 15% of all US equities, and more than 8% of all EU equities, trading on dark pools in 2017 [17]. Yet, dark pools persistently suffer from negative reputation as some operators have taken advantage of their privileged access to the non-displayed orders in their systems. Indeed, between 2011–2018, dark pool operators paid more than $217 million to the SEC in penalty settlements for misusing customer order information or operating the dark pool in a way that disadvantaged their customers [9]. In the shadowy world of the dark pool, it is easier for a market manipulator to hide. As such, it is perhaps unsurprising that many investors have a fear of the dark.

There is now a strong commercial drive from financial institutions, such as JPMorgan [2,4], to offer investors a secure dark pool trading venue. To be commercially viable, such a platform would require guaranteed order privacy, the ability to handle imbalanced order-flows from around 1000 active investors or more, and periodic order matching at regular intervals, where execution price is determined by some reference value such as the mid-point of the National Best Bid and Offer (NBBO). To address this problem, we consider algorithms for implementing fast privacy-preserving trading protocols such that *nobody*, not even the system operator, can access (and therefore misuse) order information. These algorithms are designed to stop fraudulent behaviour but can also benefit honest dark pool operators as they offer customers a guarantee that does not rely solely on trust. Using multi-party computation (MPC) based protocols, the investors secret share their orders across several entities who emulate the dark pool operator. As long as these entities do not collude, nobody can access the system information. In [8], Cartlidge et al. used MPC to present a proof-of-concept implementation of three dark pool trading mechanisms, showing that "volume matching" can be viably executed in a privacy-preserving manner with order throughput similar to that required by a real world dark pool trading venue. Further, in [9], Cartlidge et al. demonstrated how to use MPC to run multiple auctions in parallel, offering simultaneous trading across thousands of stocks such that the identity of the stock being traded is also hidden and secure.

The throughput per MPC engine is however significantly lower than that of the volume matching from [8] due to the use of a more complex matching algorithm.

In this paper, we build upon the work from [8] and introduce two matching algorithms using MPC: (i) "bucket match", and (ii) a "volume match" with a more efficient clearing phase. For both mechanisms, we trade one financial instrument (i.e., one stock) such that orders are matched according to volume only and price is determined by some external reference value. In *bucket match*, buy and sell orders placed in the same auction must have the same volume, which is determined by the bucket size. To hide the volume that each investor wishes to buy or sell (or the fact that the investor is even interested in trading a given stock), orders with zero volume may also be submitted. Multiple auctions with different sized buckets can be run in parallel, after which unfilled orders remaining in the different bucket lists may be matched against each other. In *volume match*, there is no bucketing and investors may submit orders of any volume they wish (including zero volume orders), similar to the volume trading algorithm presented in [8]. However, we extend the previous volume trading protocol by simplifying the clearing phase. Namely, all the orders in the direction with less total volume are opened simultaneously, instead of being checked one by one before opening. We also increase privacy by no longer revealing the direction of an order (i.e., it is not possible to tell whether the order is to buy or to sell). Both algorithms were implemented with the Scale-Mamba Framework [1] using Shamir Secret Sharing based MPC, which provides security with abort against active adversaries for an honest majority. We empirically evaluate the case where three MPC parties emulate the dark pool operator.

Related Work: Work in secure privacy-preserving auction mechanisms can be roughly categorised into two broad categories: those involving a public bulletin board (e.g., a blockchain), for verifying auction correctness, or as a secure communication channel between parties; and those where MPC is used to implement an auction or dark pool using a set of operators. We briefly review these, below.

In 2021, Ngo et al. [15] introduced a framework for secure financial trading that uses a public bulletin board (e.g., a permissionless blockchain) hidden behind an anonymous network (e.g., Tor) for privacy-preserving communication between investors. The authors introduce witness-key-agreement (WKA), a cryptographic scheme that allows counterparties to securely agree on a secret using publicly committed information that meets some desired relation. Parties negotiate securely by publishing partial zk-SNARK proofs on the public bulletin board to reach a trade agreement. This process emulates a secure distributed over-the-counter (OTC) dark pool, such that trade price and volume is negotiated directly between counterparty pairs. Therefore, there is no need for an auctioneer (or dark pool operator) to match orders. The runtimes for each protocol step are below 15 s, the average block generation time in Ethereum.

Also in 2021, Galal and Youssef [12] introduced a publicly verifiable and secrecy preserving periodic auction protocol that makes use of a smart contract deployed on the Ethereum blockchain. Investors first commit to their orders in the smart contract using Bulletproofs to generate an aggregate range proof. The auction (or dark pool) operator then privately receives orders from investors, each encrypted with the operator's public key. The operator decrypts orders and calculates clearing price and volume for the auction, before publishing a proof of correctness to the smart contract. The smart contract serves as a secure bulletin board and enables public verification of the submitted zero-knowledge proofs. Constantinides and Cartlidge [10] introduced a similar smart contract for validating the honesty of the operator. Again, orders are submitted in encrypted form to the smart contract, the operator matches orders off-chain in unencrypted form, and the result of the auction is published to the smart contract. This enables investors to verify whether their own orders were handled correctly, while preserving the privacy of all unexecuted orders. In addition, since the smart contract logic only handles order flow and is independent of the matching logic, the operator can use any double auction matching rules without altering the smart contract.

In 2019, Bag et al. [3] presented a protocol to perform a first-price sealed-bid auction without a central "auctioneer" entity. Decentralised bidders engage in the protocol to determine the winning bidder with the highest bid. The protocol consists of a committing phase, where every bidder sends an order commitment to a public bulletin board, then a second phase where bidders jointly compute the highest bid without leaking the other bids. This computation is performed using a modified version of the Anonymous Veto network protocol proposed in [13]. Following this, the winning bidder can come forward to prove they had the highest bid, and everyone else can verify their claim. The computation and communication have a linear complexity on the bit length of the bids throughout all phases; and the verification phase has linear complexity on the number of parties. While this protocol has efficient time complexity, it is not obvious how it could be extended to a double auction, where buyers and sellers are matched.

In 2006, Parkes et al. [16] proposed a secure protocol to perform a sealed-bid auction using homomorphic encryption, where only one auctioneer carries out the auction. The auctioneer publishes his/her public key, and the auction is performed by bidders committing to their bids and then sending the commitments to the auctioneer. Bidders then submit their bids to the auctioneer who verifies first if the bids are consistent with the commitments, before running the auction on clear bid data. Subsequently, the auctioneer posts the winner of the auction along with proofs that the computation was performed according to the specified protocol. One thing to note here is that, while the protocol prevents the auctioneer from cheating, the unmet orders are revealed to the public and so the trading intentions of these bidders are leaked. This work was extended in 2007 [18] to cope with continuous double auctions (where orders to buy and sell can be submitted and matched at any time), by checking whether orders can be matched with existing orders as soon as they are entered. In 2009 [19], protocols were further extended to enable trading in baskets of securities; and in 2012 [20], rule-based trading was introduced. The works of [2,4] offer a privacy preserving double auction mechanism and a volume matching mechanism, respectively, without any leakage based on fully homomorphic encryption using a single operator.

In 2006, seminal work by Bogetoft et al. [6] introduced an MPC protocol to perform a one-shot double auction among a set of auctioneers, such that investors secret share their orders with the auctioneers and orders are obliviously addressed using Shamir Secret Sharing with passive security. This work was deployed in 2008 [5], to secure the Danish sugar beet auction between farmers and the company Danisco, the only sugar beet processor in Denmark. In this auction, farmers provide the amount of sugar beet they are willing to sell for every potential price. Similarly, buyers provide the amounts they are willing to buy for every potential price. The clearance price is then calculated as the point that supply equals demand. The auction was successfully run by three auctioneers, namely, Danisco; DKS, the sugar beet growers' association; and SIMAP, the research team. Since then, the auction has taken place every year.

In 2015, Jutla [14] introduced an MPC based protocol for periodic double auctions, with five entities playing the role of the auctioneers; four brokers and one regulating authority. Investors first submit orders during an open-auction period. Orders are then cleared at a single price and unmet orders remain in the auction for the following rounds. Making the assumption that the strategies of investors do not have to be kept secret, Jutla suggests that a passively secure protocol is sufficient, as long as the auctioneers wait a reasonable amount of time (e.g., one month) before releasing transcripts of the computations for audit. Jutla does not report an implementation of the protocol, but claims that the MPC technology at that time (in 2015) would be capable of executing the day's first auction in 30 min and subsequent auctions every 15 min; with additional 5 min breaks between auctions, to allow bidders to digest results.

Cartlidge et al. [8] proposed an MPC based protocol for performing auctions in dark pools, where a set of $l = 2$ or $l = 3$ auctioneers can emulate the dark pool operator. Cartlidge et al. considered three common matching mechanisms: (i) a continuous double auction, where buyers and sellers can submit orders at any time and a limit order book is used for matching; (ii) a periodic double auction, where the clearance price is determined by maximising quantity matched; and (iii) a volume matching algorithm, which simply matches buy and sell volume and price is taken from some reference exchange. Investors submit orders by secret sharing them among the auctioneers, thus auctioneers learn nothing about the orders, except for the direction of the order (i.e., whether the order is to sell or to buy), as this information is sent to auctioneers on clear data. The protocols proposed are actively secure with abort and were implemented using the Scale-Mamba framework [1], with $l = 2$ using the SPDZ protocol [11], and $l = 3$ using Shamir Secret Sharing based MPC. The runtimes reported show that the volume matching is the fastest algorithm, capable of processing a throughput of around 1000 orders per second for the case where $l = 3$, and around 2000 orders per second for the case where $l = 2$. The throughput for the other two algorithms was found to be insufficient for real-world applicability. Namely, the continuous double auction algorithm which can be commonly found in lit markets was considered unsuitable for evaluation in an MPC system for dark pools.

In 2020, Cartlidge et al. [9] introduced a follow-up work to secure a system inspired by the London Stock Exchange Group's Turquoise Plato Uncross algorithm (TPU for short). The TPU manages dark pool trading across 4500 different instruments, thus Cartlidge et al. considered running the auction on multiple engines, where each engine addresses a sub-set of instruments, so as to cope with the amount of orders that TPU receives in real life. The challenge consisted of distributing instruments across engines without leaking the instruments that each engine is dealing with, as this would reveal information about the trading activity of each instrument. Cartlidge et al. [9] concluded that assigning 16 instruments to each engine (and thus 281 engines are needed)[1] would cope with the real world throughput that TPU needs to address. The worst case throughput for each of these engines is of around 8 orders per second for $l = 2$, and around 5 orders per second for $l = 3$. Note that, as mentioned before, this is indeed significantly lower than the throughput of the volume matching in [8] presented above.

2 Our Proposed Auction Algorithms

Both of the proposed algorithms follow the scheduled cross methodology, where the matching occurs at fixed points in time and is based on volume only. Trade price is determined by reference to an external lit market value, thus the orders for both algorithms do not contain price information. Each order contains the identity of the investor who submitted it, the direction of the order (i.e., whether it is a buy or a sell order), and, in the volume match case, the volume to be traded. A separate auction is run for each tradable instrument (i.e., each stock). The output of each auction consists of a list of all filled orders (although some orders might be partially filled, as will be explained at the end of this section).

A textual description of the bucket match and the volume match in the clear can be found below.

Bucket Match: We consider an auction in which orders can only be executed in a given number y of bucket sizes. For each $j \in [1, \ldots, y]$ we define the fixed bucket size as unit^j, and the algorithm maintains a list L^j of the orders with list L^j containing only buy and sell orders of size unit^j. Order i in list j is of the form $[\mathsf{id}_i^j, \mathsf{direction}_i^j]$, where id_i^j is the identity of the investor, and $\mathsf{direction}_i^j$ is the direction of the order, i.e., whether the order is a sell ($\mathsf{direction}_i^j = 1$) or buy order ($\mathsf{direction}_i^j = 0$). Therefore, if an investor wishes, for instance, to sell a volume v, the investor has to submit g^j *distinct* orders to list j, where $g^j \geq 0$, such that $v = \sum_{j=1}^{j=y} g^j \cdot \mathsf{unit}^j$, with the direction of each of these orders indicating that they consist of sell orders, i.e., $\mathsf{direction}_i^j = 1$ for all orders.

Orders are placed in their lists in order of arrival, and orders that arrived first will be matched first. The clearing of all orders is then run at periodic intervals.

---

[1] Plus one engine that serves as an entry gateway for orders; therefore a total of 282 engines required.

Unless the number of sell orders is identical to the number of buy orders in a given list, there will be leftover unmatched orders after this same list is cleared. After every list is cleared, we can check the direction of the leftover orders from each of them. If there are leftover orders with different directions (e.g., leftovers from L^1 are buy orders, and leftovers from L^2 are sell orders), then there will be another clearing period where the leftover orders of all lists are matched among each other. Recall that orders from different lists have different volume and hence we must now take into consideration their unit volume, in addition to their direction.

For ease of exposition, we will consider in our work only the cases of $y = 1$ and $y = 2$; i.e., we will either have one bucket size or two bucket sizes. As a shorthand, we will refer to these as *bucket-1* and *bucket-2*, respectively; *bucket-z* will refer to the general case of multiple lists, i.e., where $y > 1$.

Volume Match: In this algorithm, the auction runs over one list L that contains orders of different sizes. Order i is thus of the form [id_i, direction_i, volume_i], where id_i is the identity of the investor, direction_i is the direction of the order, and volume_i is the volume of the order. Note that, in this situation, if one wishes to trade a volume v, it is enough to submit a single order of volume v (though it is also possible to split the volume into multiple smaller orders). The procedure is then similar to the bucket match case, except that here we consider only one list and therefore the cross-list matching does not take place.

Table 1. Intuitive comparison of bucket match with 1 list, multiple lists, and volume match.

Algorithm	Total orders	Additional computation	Leakage potential	Loss in volume submitted
Bucket-1	Most	–	Low	Low
Bucket-z	Medium	Cross-list matching	Cross-list match leakage	Low
Volume	Least	Input correctness check	Lowest	No loss

Intuitive Comparison: Bucket-1 will tend to receive more orders than bucket-z or volume match, as multiple orders must be submitted for trading large volumes. Therefore, as more orders need to be processed, runtimes for bucket-1 are likely to be longer. Bucket-z solves this problem by introducing multiple bucket sizes, thus allowing orders of different volumes. However, it will usually require an additional cross-list matching period to find all possible matches between different bucket sizes. Moreover, we would like the volume of unmatched orders to remain secret, which might not be possible when matching orders of different volumes. If an order can only be partially matched, the leftover volume will become public. Therefore, bucket-z has potential for greater leakage than bucket-1. Regarding the total submitted volume, note that one cannot always submit the exact volume they wish, since all orders must fit the predefined bucket size(s). Thus, investors might need to submit a lower total volume than intended.

Volume match allows orders to be submitted with any volume, so there is additional uncertainty about the volume of unopened orders. There is also no need to implement an additional cross-list matching period, therefore preventing the leakage of leftover volume of partially matched orders. However, checking the correctness of input orders will be slower than in bucket-1 and bucket-z, with the runtime growing linearly with the number of input bits representing the volume.

3   Secure Implementations of the Algorithms

To ensure privacy of the orders we implement the above auction algorithms on top of a generic multi-party computation (MPC) system. For an overview of the MPC requirements see the full version of this paper [7].

3.1   Setup

The setup consists of a number of servers $S = \{S_1, \ldots, S_l\}$ emulating the auctioneer, where the orders entering the auction will be secret shared among these servers.

3.2   Bucket Match

We aim to hide as much about the intention of the investors as possible, especially for unmet orders. Thus we allow investors to enter 'dummy' orders, i.e., orders which are neither buy or sell. We will discuss later the precise number of dummy orders which should be entered, and how this number affects the privacy and performance of the auction. Note that investors can submit dummy orders to stocks they do not wish to trade, thus hiding their trading activity in each stock.

For $i = 1, \ldots, n$, each order i will of be the form $\mathsf{ord}_i^j = [\langle \mathsf{id}_i^j \rangle, \langle b_i^j \rangle, \langle s_i^j \rangle]$, where b_i^j and s_i^j are bits indicating the direction of the order, that is, a sell order will have $b_i^j = 0$, $s_i^j = 1$ and a buy order will have $b_i^j = 1$, $s_i^j = 0$. To allow dummy orders, orders can also contain $b_i^j = 0$ and $s_i^j = 0$. Every order for which $(b_i^j, s_i^j) \notin \{(0,0), (0,1), (1,0)\}$ will be rejected. Each list j will contain n^j orders, among which m^j are dummy. For instance, if an investor j wants to sell a volume V, they need to enter the orders $\{\mathsf{ord}_1^1, \ldots, \mathsf{ord}_{g^1}^1, \ldots, \mathsf{ord}_1^y, \ldots, \mathsf{ord}_{g^y}^y\}$ such that $V = \sum_{j=1}^{j=y} \sum_{i=1}^{i=g^j} (s_i^j - b_i^j) \cdot \mathsf{unit}^j$.

To ensure that the conditional operation $\langle c \rangle > 0$ can be executed we need to ensure that $c \in [-2^{k-1}, \ldots, 2^{k-1}]$. For the case of one list we simply need to ensure that the total number of orders n is less than 2^{k-1}. For the case of more than one list we need to ensure that $n \cdot \mathsf{unit}^y < 2^{k-1}$.

Bucket-1 Match: For ease of exposition we first examine the case when we have only one bucket size, i.e. $y = 1$. The formal description of the algorithm is given in Fig. 1. We distinguish 3 phases:

1. The input phase, where orders are entered into the auction and a check is run to discard invalid orders. In the input orders for this algorithm, the buy and sell entries b and s must be bits. Additionally, at least one of these two entries must be zero. To verify this, we draw three numbers $\alpha, \beta, \gamma \in \mathbb{F}_p$ at random and calculate

$$\langle t \rangle = \alpha \cdot (\langle b \rangle \cdot \langle b \rangle - \langle b \rangle) + \beta \cdot (\langle s \rangle \cdot \langle s \rangle - \langle s \rangle) + \gamma \cdot (\langle b \rangle \cdot \langle s \rangle).$$

   Afterwards, we open $\langle t \rangle$ and check whether $t = 0$. The first two terms are zero only if b and s are bits, except with probability $1/p$. The last term is zero only if either $b = 0$ or $s = 0$, except with probability $1/p$. If more than one term is different from zero, their sum will be zero with probability $1/p$.
2. The clearing phase one, where we open the orders in the direction that will be completely cleared. First, we need to check which list has largest total volume. To do so, we first calculate

$$\langle c \rangle \leftarrow \sum_{i=1}^{n} \langle b_i \rangle - \langle s_i \rangle.$$

   Then, we perform the comparison $\langle c \rangle > 0$ and open the output. If c is greater than zero, there are more buy orders than sell orders and so we open the $\langle s_i \rangle$ share of every order i. Otherwise, we open the $\langle b_i \rangle$ shares. The $\langle id \rangle$ of non-dummy orders is also opened. Opening $\langle s_i \rangle$ (or $\langle b_i \rangle$) will reveal whether order i is a sell order (or buy order, respectively). However, because of the existence of dummy orders, revealing that order i is not a sell order (or buy order, respectively) does not imply that it is an order in the opposite direction. We are then left with a mix of dummy and non-dummy orders, without knowing which are which.
3. The clearing phase two, where we open the orders in the direction that will be only partially cleared. The orders are opened one by one, and the $\langle id \rangle$ of non-dummy orders is also opened. For each opened order, we check whether the opposite direction has been completely cleared. When that is the case, we exit the algorithm.

Bucket-2 Match: We now examine the case with two bucket sizes, i.e., $y = 2$. The size of the first bucket is unit[1] and the size of the second bucket is unit[2]. The formal description of the algorithm is given in the full version. We distinguish the following phases of the algorithm:

1. The input phase, the clearing phase one and the clearing phase two are exactly as in the bucket match with one bucket size. Each of the two lists is cleared individually, and then we check whether the leftover orders from both lists have different directions. If so, we can proceed to matching orders from different lists. If all the orders have the same direction, we exit the algorithm. Note that, while we know the direction of the leftover orders, we do not know which of them might be dummy orders.

Bucket-1: match on one list

Input phase: On input $\text{ord}_i = [\langle \text{id}_i \rangle, \langle s_i \rangle, \langle b_i \rangle]$, where $\text{id}_i, s_i, b_i \in \mathbb{F}_p$:

1. $\alpha_i, \beta_i, \gamma_i \leftarrow \mathcal{F}_{\text{Rand}}()$.
2. $\langle t_i \rangle \leftarrow \alpha_i \cdot (\langle b_i \rangle \cdot \langle b_i \rangle - \langle b_i \rangle) + \beta_i \cdot (\langle s_i \rangle \cdot \langle s_i \rangle - \langle s_i \rangle) + \gamma_i \cdot (\langle b_i \rangle \cdot \langle s_i \rangle)$
3. $t_i \leftarrow \text{Open}(\langle t_i \rangle)$
4. If $t_i = 0$ then add ord_i to a list L, otherwise reject ord_i.

Clearing phase one: On input $L = [\text{ord}_1, \dots, \text{ord}_n]$, the list of orders that will be cleared on the same round

1. $\langle c \rangle \leftarrow \sum_{i=1}^{n} \langle b_i \rangle - \langle s_i \rangle$
2. $\langle d \rangle \leftarrow (\langle c \rangle > 0)$
3. $d \leftarrow \text{Open}(\langle d \rangle)$
4. If $d = 1$
   - I. For all i, execute $s_i \leftarrow \text{Open}(\langle s_i \rangle)$
   - II. For all i such that $s_i = 1$, execute $\text{id}_i \leftarrow \text{Open}(\langle \text{id}_i \rangle)$.
   - III. $\sigma \leftarrow \sum_{i=1}^{n} s_i$
   - IV. Move all orders with $s_i = 0$ to a list L^b
5. Else
   - I. For all i, execute $b_i \leftarrow \text{Open}(\langle b_i \rangle)$
   - II. For all i such that $b_i = 1$, execute $\text{id}_i \leftarrow \text{Open}(\langle \text{id}_i \rangle)$.
   - III. $\sigma \leftarrow \sum_{i=1}^{n} b_i$
   - IV. Move all orders with $b_i = 0$ to a list L^s

Clearing phase two: On input a List $L^b = [\text{ord}_1, \dots, \text{ord}_o]$ (or $L^s = [\text{ord}_1, \dots, \text{ord}_o]$), and the sum σ:

1. $c \leftarrow 0$
2. For i in $\{1, \dots, o\}$
   - I. $b_i \leftarrow \text{Open}(\langle b_i \rangle)$ if $d = 1$ (or $s_i \leftarrow \text{Open}(\langle s_i \rangle)$ if $d = 0$)
   - II. If $b_i = 1$ (or $s_i = 1$)
     - i. $\text{id}_i \leftarrow \text{Open}(\langle \text{id}_i \rangle)$
     - ii. $c \leftarrow c + 1$
     - iii. If $c = \sigma$ then **break**.

Output the set of completely opened orders from L^b (resp. L^s).

Fig. 1. Bucket-1: match on one list

2. The clearing phase three, where we open the orders in the direction that will be completely cleared. First, we need to check which direction has largest total volume. To do so, we first calculate

$$\langle c \rangle \leftarrow \sum_{i=1}^{n'^2} \langle \text{dir}_i^2 \rangle \cdot \text{unit}^2 - \sum_{i=1}^{n'^1} \langle \text{dir}_i^1 \rangle \cdot \text{unit}^1,$$

where dir^j is b^j if the leftovers from list j are buy orders, or s^j if the leftovers from list j are sell orders. Then, we perform the comparison $\langle c \rangle > 0$ and open the output. If c is greater than zero, there is more volume in direction dir^2 and so we open all the $\langle \text{dir}^1 \rangle$ shares. Otherwise, we open the $\langle \text{dir}^2 \rangle$ shares. The $\langle \text{id} \rangle$ of non-dummy orders is also opened.

3. The clearing phase four, where we open the orders in the direction that will be only partially cleared. The orders are opened one by one, and the $\langle id \rangle$ of non-dummy orders is also opened. For each opened order, we check whether the opposite direction has been completely cleared. When that is the case, we exit the algorithm.

Note, the last opened order from the clearing phase four will not be necessarily completely matched. The unmatched volume from this last order will therefore be leaked. This source of leakage is further discussed in Sect. 4

3.3   Volume Match

Similarly to the bucket match, we will hide here the direction of orders and we will allow dummy orders. Each order i will be of the form $\text{ord}_i = [\langle id_i \rangle, \langle v_i \rangle, \langle \text{dir}_i^b \rangle, \langle \text{dir}_i^s \rangle]$, where v_i is the volume of the order, $\text{dir}_i^b = 0$ if ord_i is a sell order, $\text{dir}_i^s = 0$ if ord_i is a buy order, and $\text{dir}_i^b = \text{dir}_i^s = 0$ if ord_i is a dummy order. The list of orders from all the investors will contain n orders, m of which are dummy orders. If an investor wants to sell volume V, they need to enter orders $\text{ord}_1, \ldots, \text{ord}_g$ such that $V = \sum_{i=1}^{i=g}(v_i \cdot (\text{dir}_i^s - \text{dir}_i^b))$

The formal description of this algorithm is presented in the full version. Again we distinguish 3 phases of the algorithm:

1. The input phase, where orders are entered into the auction and a check is run to discard invalid orders. To ensure investors enter values v_i that are valid non-negative numbers less than some bound B (which we assume is an exact power of two, i.e. $B = 2^\ell$), they enter the value as a sequence of ℓ bits, $v_{i,j}$, for $j = 0, \ldots, \ell - 1$. Additionally, they enter two bits dir_i^b and dir_i^s that indicate the direction of the order. All these values are checked to be bits, using the same check used in the bucket matching algorithm, and then the actual values of the volume in each direction are formed from $v_i^b = \text{dir}_i^b \cdot \sum_{j=0}^{\ell-1} v_{i,j} \cdot 2^j$ and $v_i^s = \text{dir}_i^s \cdot \sum_{j=0}^{\ell-1} v_{i,j} \cdot 2^j$. We still need to check that at least one of dir_i^b or dir_i^s is zero, so we calculate

$$\langle t_i \rangle = \langle \text{dir}_i^b \rangle \cdot \langle \text{dir}_i^s \rangle,$$

open $\langle t_i \rangle$ and check whether $t_i = 0$. Clearly, that happens if and only if either $\text{dir}_i^b = 0$ or $\text{dir}_i^s = 0$. To ensure the comparison $\langle c \rangle > 0$ can be evaluated correctly we simply need to pick parameters so that $n \cdot B < 2^{k-1}$.
2. The clearing phase one, where we open the orders in the direction that will be completely cleared. First, we need to check which list has largest total volume. To do so, we first calculate

$$\langle c \rangle \leftarrow \sum_{i=1}^{n} \langle v_i^b \rangle - \langle v_i^s \rangle.$$

Then, we perform the comparison $\langle c \rangle > 0$ and open the output. If c is greater than zero, the total buy volume is greater than the total sell volume and so we open the $\langle v_i^s \rangle$ share of every order i. Otherwise, we open the $\langle v_i^b \rangle$ shares. The $\langle \mathsf{id} \rangle$ of non-dummy orders is also opened. We then calculate the total volume σ of the opened orders. Suppose the $\langle v_i^s \rangle$ shares were opened. For every $v_i^s = 0$, we calculate the cumulative buy volume of the first i orders, $\langle w_i \rangle = \sum_{h=1}^{i} \langle v_h^b \rangle$. If the $\langle v_i^b \rangle$ shares were opened, the cumulative sell volume is calculated instead. This cumulative volume will be used in the next clearing phase to avoid leaking the unmatched volume of the last opened order.

3. The clearing phase two, where we open the orders in the direction that will be only partially cleared. First, we run a binary search on the cumulative volume calculated previously to find the highest index u such that $\langle w_u \rangle < \sigma$. Then, the first u orders are opened, as well as the $\langle \mathsf{id} \rangle$ of non-dummy orders. At this point, we still did not completely clear the orders opened during clearing phase one. However, if we open ord_{u+1}, part of its volume will remain unmatched and there will be an information leakage. To avoid this, we simply subtract the volume $\sigma - \langle w_u \rangle$ we still need from ord_{u+1} and open $\langle \mathsf{id}_{u+1} \rangle$. This way, only the volume that will indeed be cleared is revealed, with the leftover volume of this last order remaining secret.

4   Leakage

There are two possible sources of information leakage in the described algorithms: (i) leakage from partially unmatched orders; and (ii) leakage from opening orders. Each of these sources is discussed below. All the analyses are equivalent when the buy orders have the largest total volume, thus we consider always the case when the total sell volume is more than the total buy volume.

Leakage from Partially Matched Orders: This type of leakage can happen in both the volume match and the bucket-2 match, since in both of these algorithms there are orders with different volumes. In the bucket-1 match, every non-dummy order has exactly the same volume, so every opened order is completely matched and this type of leakage never happens.

In the volume match, orders from the direction with largest total volume are opened until the next order to be opened would finish clearing the other direction. We will then remove the volume we need to finish the clearing from this next order without opening its volume share. This means that the last order might still have some leftover volume, though it is also possible that all its volume was matched. Since it was at least partially matched, we need to reveal the investor who submitted the order so that the trade can be processed. We will therefore know that this investor might still have some volume left to trade and, if that is the case, we also know the direction of the order. The leftover volume in this last order and whether it is positive or not will however remain unknown.

In the bucket-2 match, the clearing phases one and two are the same as the bucket-1 match, and hence there is no leakage. As for clearing phases three and four, since the orders in each direction will have different volumes, the situation is similar to the volume match. Let unit^1 and unit^2 be the bucket sizes of the buy and the sell orders, respectively, in the clearing phases three and four. Considering $\text{unit}^1 = k \cdot \text{unit}^2$ for some $k \in \mathbb{N}$, if the sell orders have larger total volume, then there will be no leakage. If the buy orders have larger total volume, the unmatched volume will be $\text{leak} = h \cdot \text{unit}^2$, for $h \in \{0, ..., k-1\}$.

In case $\gcd(\text{unit}^1, \text{unit}^2) = k$, for some $k \notin \{\text{unit}^1, \text{unit}^2\}$, then the unmatched volume will be either $\text{leak} \in \{0, k, 2k, ..., \text{unit}^1 - k\}$, when the buy orders have largest total volume, or $\text{leak} \in \{0, k, 2k, ..., \text{unit}^2 - k\}$, when the sell orders have largest total volume.

Note that for this algorithm the maximum leakage that can occur from unmatched orders is known, and the investors can plan how to divide their orders into the two lists according to this information.

Leakage from Opening Orders: Consider the bucket-1 match and suppose there are no dummy orders in a given auction. Let the sell orders be the ones with largest total volume, and hence the buy orders are the first ones to be opened. For each $\langle b_i \rangle$ that is revealed to be $b_i = 0$, we learn that this must be a sell order of unit volume. This means that as soon as we finish the clearing phase one, all the information about the orders' volume has been revealed.

Suppose now that the probability of having a dummy order is p_d, with the total number of dummy orders being $m = p_d \cdot n$. Let the buy orders be the first ones to be opened, and let the number of buy orders be $B = p_b \cdot (n - m)$ (note that here we must have $p_b \leq 1/2$ since there are less buy orders than sell orders). After clearing phase one, we will have $n - B$ orders which might be either dummies or sells, and the probability of finding a sell order is $\frac{n-B-m}{n-B}$. For each newly opened sell order, we learn whether an order is a sell or a dummy. Let i be the number of opened sell orders, and j the number of opened dummies, then the probability of the next opened order being a sell is:

$$\text{Pr}(\text{``order is sell''}) = \frac{n - B - m - i}{n - B - (i + j)}.$$

Assuming an even distribution of dummy orders within the buy orders.

By the end of clearing phase two, we should have opened a total of B sell orders plus m' dummy orders. At this moment, even if p_d is unknown, an adversary might use the information about previously opened orders and consider $p_d' = m'/(2B + m')$. The expected amount of leftover sell orders will then be $(n - 2B - m') \cdot (1 - p_d')$. Note that, since we are in the bucketed case, knowing the amount of leftover sells implies knowing the total leftover sell volume.

In the bucket-2 match, the situation for the clearing phases one and two is identical to the bucket-1 match. For clearing phases three and four, we also know exactly the volume of each buy and sell order (even if this volume is different for buys and sells). However, note that these orders have a different format, i.e., they only contain the ID and either the sell or the buy volume, and so opening one of the directions does not leak information about the other. Therefore, the leakage associated with the opening of each of these lists will be the same as if we were continuing the clearing phase two openings.

The case for the volume match is similar, except that since each non-dummy order might have any positive volume, the uncertainty about the volume of unopened orders increases.

Summary: The bucket-1 match has no leakage from partially matched orders, but there is some leakage from opening orders. In order to mitigate this effect, the investors must submit more dummy orders. The bucket-2 match does have leakage from partially matched orders (although this does not necessarily occur), in addition to the leakage from opening orders, which is similar to bucket-1 match. Once again, submitting dummy orders reduces this last type of leakage. Note also that when we have two lists, usually less non-dummy orders need to be submitted, so we can increase the proportion of dummy orders without getting worse runtimes than when using one list only.

Runtimes for different amounts of dummy orders are presented in the full version. Note that for the chosen bucket sizes, bucket-2 match with 9 dummy orders per non-dummy order has faster runtimes than bucket-1 match with 5 dummy orders per non-dummy order. However, using bucket-2 match means we might get leakage from partially matched orders, depending on the balance between buy and sell orders in each list.

Volume match results in the least leakage. The leakage from partially matched orders corresponds only to the direction of a (possibly empty) order. The leakage from opening orders is minor when compared to bucket match, because of the uncertainty introduced by fact that orders can have any possible volume. This means that even if investors submit only 1 (or fewer) dummy order per non-dummy order, the leakage will remain low.

5   Runtimes

To provide runtimes of our algorithms, we model the situation where T investors participate in the auction, each of whom has one volume to submit drawn from the distribution $(\mathcal{N}(0,1) + 5) \cdot 10^6$, and places the *same* order in three different auctions, each of which utilizes one of our three algorithms presented, namely volume match, bucket-1 match, and bucket-2 match. We varied T in $\{10, 100, 1000, 10000\}$, as well as the number of dummy orders submitted per non-dummy order (which we call d) in $\{0, 1, 5, 9\}$. Buy, sell, and dummy orders (when they exist) are evenly distributed in the lists of orders. We also assume that there is an *order imbalance* such that $2/5$ of the investors are buyers and $3/5$ are sellers.

This order imbalance was suggested through discussions with JPMorgan, a tier one US investment bank who operate in this space and have observed a tendency of investors to have a buy:sell imbalance in the ratio of 2:3. This conforms with evidence that informed investors tend to trade in the same direction (e.g., [21]). Here we model a sell imbalance ($3/5$ of investors are sellers), however buy imbalances (where $3/5$ of investors are buyers) also occur, depending on the mood of the market. For the protocols we have presented, results are symmetric such that a buy:sell imbalance of 2:3 has the same run time as a buy:sell imbalance of 3:2. If the imbalance is different or if there is no imbalance at all, the number of matched orders will be affected (assuming the submitted volume is drawn from the same distribution). This will influence the running time of the clearing phases, where we might need to reveal more or less id's. However, most of the total running time comes from the input phase and so a different order imbalance will not have a significant impact.

As a simplification, we computed runtimes for the situation where there is only one auction trading one stock. However, a real world venue would allow trading in many stocks, so many auctions would be required. For instance, if the venue is trading 5000 different stocks then 5000 auctions are required. These auctions can be run sequentially, in which case the runtime for all auctions to complete is 5000 times the runtime of a single auction. Alternatively, multiple MPC engines can be used to run auctions in parallel. In the extreme case, where we have 5000 engines (i.e., one engine per stock), all auctions run in parallel and hence the total runtime for all auctions to complete is the same as the runtime for a single auction.

Setting: We used Scale-Mamba with Shamir secret sharing between $l = 3$ parties. All the parties run identical machines with an Intel i-9900 CPU and 128 GB of RAM. The ping time between the machines is 1.003 ms.

Online Phase of Volume Match: The average time for input phase depends on the bound B that is set for the volume of the orders. Recall that the orders' volumes are entered as a sequence of bits, and we must confirm that every one of them really is a bit. Therefore, the more bits we allow for the input volume, the longer it will take to run this check. Here we assume that the volume of each order can have at most 32 bits, and we obtain an average time for the input phase of 0.00062 s (0.62 ms) per order, with a standard deviation of 0.00005 s (0.05 ms).

Runtimes are provided in the full version, where we also provide a comparison of this version of volume matching to that described in [8]). One can notice that clearing phase 1 is faster than clearing phase 2. This is mainly due to the fact that the operation of opening directions can be vectorized for the case of clearing phase 1, as we are opening the direction of all orders, while for the case of clearing phase 2, this operation has to be sequential, as we do not know for how many orders we should open the direction.

Online Phase of Bucket-1 Match: The average time of the input phase is 0.00013 s (0.13 ms) per order, with a standard deviation of 0.00001 s (0.01 ms). Note that the order format check is similar to the one used for the volume match, but here the volume of each order consists of a single bit, resulting in a faster input phase.

However, unlike what happens in the volume match, every order must now have the same fixed volume. This means that each investor must submit different non-dummy orders that sum up to the desired volume. When this volume is not a multiple of the chosen bucket size unit, we round the volume down to the closest multiple. Thus, we will generally have more orders than in the volume match, depending on the exact value of unit. If unit is small, more orders will be needed and the total submitted volume will be closer to the volume match case. If we choose unit to be large, we will not need as many orders, but the investors will submit significantly less volume than in the volume match case. The average number of orders and the average total submitted volume for different bucket sizes can be found in the full version.

In our case, 99.7% of the investors will submit a volume between $2 \cdot 10^6$ and $8 \cdot 10^6$. If we choose e.g. unit $= 10^6$, the volume submitted by each investor will be rounded down to the closest multiple of 10^6. This will result in an average submitted volume of $4.49 \cdot 10^6$, as opposed to the average volume of $5 \cdot 10^6$ obtained in the volume match, where no rounding is needed. We will also have around 4.5 orders for each order in the volume match case.

We present in the full version the runtimes corresponding to the bucket match for one list with unit $= 10^6$. One can make the same remark as the volume match for the runtimes. That is, clearing phase 1 is faster than clearing phase 2 due to the fact that we can vectorise computation for the case of clearing phase 1.

Online Phase of Bucket-2 Match: Let unit^k denote the bucket size associated with list L^k. We assume that unit^1 (the small bucket) is smaller than unit^2 (the big bucket).

Similar to bucket-1 match, the volume to be traded in bucket-2 match will be divided into multiple orders according to the bucket sizes. If the volume cannot be fully obtained with a combination of the two buckets, we round it down to the closest possible combination. We assume that the investors will divide their volume such that they use as many big buckets as possible. The average number of orders in each list and the average total submitted volume for different bucket sizes can be found in the full verion.

Summary: If clearing phases 3 and 4 of bucket-2 match are not executed then all three algorithms have roughly the same leakage, which in each case is extremely small and relies on estimating unmatched order volume by observing historical dummy ratios. In practice, this level of information leakage is negligible if investors use a randomised dummy order submission strategy. Assuming a 3:2 imbalance in orders to sell or buy, this implies that bucket-2 (or, more generally, bucket-z) is to be preferred as it has the quickest input phase. However, the precise trade off between the simple cost of input checking in bucket-z versus the more complicated cost of input checking in the volume matching algorithm depends on the exact distribution of dummy orders that investors submit in a real environment. Compared with volume match, bucket-z match is likely to incentive the placement of more dummy orders to disguise the fact that each real order has a known volume equal to the bucket size. Once this number of additional dummy orders grows above some threshold, then volume match becomes more efficient than bucket-z match. For example, with T = 1000 investors, with a 9:1 ratio of dummy to real orders in bucket-2 match and a 1:1 ratio of dummy to real orders in volume match, volume match has an input phase of 1.24 s and a clearing phase of 0.06 s, whereas bucket-2 match has a longer input phase of 2.8 s and a longer parallel clearing phase of 0.27 s. However, in either scenario that bucket-z or volume match is quickest, the runtimes demonstrate that these algorithms can securely input and clear more than a thousand orders per second, and are therefore clearly capable of handling the throughput requirements of a real world dark pool trading venue.

Acknowledgments. This work has been supported in part by ERC Advanced Grant ERC-2015-AdG-IMPaCT, by the FWO under an Odysseus project GOH9718N, and by CyberSecurity Research Flanders with reference number VR20192203. Additionally, the first author is supported by the Flemish Government through FWO SBO project SNIPPET S007619N. The second author is sponsored by Refinitiv.

This paper was prepared in part for information purposes by the Artificial Intelligence Research group of JPMorgan Chase & Co and its affiliates ("JPMorgan"), and is not a product of the Research Department of JPMorgan. JPMorgan makes no representation and warranty whatsoever and disclaims all liability, for the completeness, accuracy or reliability of the information contained herein. This document is not intended as investment research or investment advice, or a recommendation, offer or solicitation for the purchase or sale of any security, financial instrument, financial product or service, or to be used in any way for evaluating the merits of participating in any transaction, and shall not constitute a solicitation under any jurisdiction or to any person, if such solicitation under such jurisdiction or to such person would be unlawful.

References

1. Aly, A., et al.: SCALE-MAMBA v1.12: Documentation (2021). https://homes.esat. kuleuven.be/~nsmart/SCALE/Documentation.pdf
2. Asharov, G., Balch, T.H., Polychroniadou, A., Veloso, M.: Privacy-preserving dark pools. In: Seghrouchni, A.E.F., Sukthankar, G., An, B., Yorke-Smith, N. (eds.) Proceedings of the 19th International Conference on Autonomous Agents and Multiagent Systems, AAMAS 2020, Auckland, New Zealand, 9–13 May 2020, pp. 1747–1749. International Foundation for Autonomous Agents and Multiagent Systems (2020)
3. Bag, S., Hao, F., Shahandashti, S.F., Ray, I.G.: SEAL: sealed-bid auction without auctioneers. Cryptology ePrint Archive, Report 2019/1332 (2019). https://eprint. iacr.org/2019/1332
4. Balch, T., Diamond, B.E., Polychroniadou, A.: SecretMatch: inventory matching from fully homomorphic encryption. In: Balch, T. (ed.) ICAIF 2020: The First ACM International Conference on AI in Finance, New York, NY, USA, 15–16 Oct 2020, pp. 1–17. ACM (2020). https://doi.org/10.1145/3383455.3422569
5. Bogetoft, P., et al.: Multiparty computation goes live. Cryptology ePrint Archive, Report 2008/068 (2008). http://eprint.iacr.org/2008/068
6. Bogetoft, P., Damgård, I., Jakobsen, T., Nielsen, K., Pagter, J., Toft, T.: A practical implementation of secure auctions based on multiparty integer computation. In: Di Crescenzo, G., Rubin, A. (eds.) FC 2006. LNCS, vol. 4107, pp. 142–147. Springer, Heidelberg (2006). https://doi.org/10.1007/11889663_10

7. da Gama, M.B., Cartlidge, J., Polychroniadou, A., Smart, N.P., Talibi Alaoui, Y.: Kicking-the-bucket: fast privacy-preserving trading using buckets. Cryptology ePrint Archive, Report 2021/1549 (2021). https://eprint.iacr.org/2021/1549

8. Cartlidge, J., Smart, N.P., Alaoui, Y.T.: MPC joins the dark side. In: Galbraith, S.D., Russello, G., Susilo, W., Gollmann, D., Kirda, E., Liang, Z. (eds.) ASIACCS 19, pp. 148–159. ACM Press (2019). https://doi.org/10.1145/3321705.3329809

9. Cartlidge, J., Smart, N.P., Talibi Alaoui, Y.: Multi-party computation mechanism for anonymous equity block trading: a secure implementation of Turquoise Plato Uncross. Intell. Syst. Acc. Finance Manage. **28**, 239–267 (2020)

10. Constantinides, T., Cartlidge, J.: Block Auction: A general blockchain protocol for privacy-preserving and verifiable periodic double auctions. In: 2021 IEEE International Conference on Blockchain (Blockchain) (2021)

11. Damgard, I., Keller, M., Larraia, E., Pastro, V., Scholl, P., Smart, N.P.: Practical covertly secure MPC for dishonest majority - or: breaking the SPDZ limits. Cryptology ePrint Archive, Report 2012/642 (2012). http://eprint.iacr.org/2012/642

12. Galal, H., Youssef, A.: Publicly verifiable and secrecy preserving periodic auctions. In: Workshop on Trusted Smart Contracts (WTSC) (2021). https://fc21.ifca.ai/wtsc/WTSC21paper2.pdf

13. Hao, F., Zieliński, P.: A 2-round anonymous veto protocol. In: Christianson, B., Crispo, B., Malcolm, J.A., Roe, M. (eds.) Security Protocols 2006. LNCS, vol. 5087, pp. 202–211. Springer, Heidelberg (2009). https://doi.org/10.1007/978-3-642-04904-0_28

14. Jutla, C.S.: Upending stock market structure using secure multi-party computation. Cryptology ePrint Archive, Report 2015/550 (2015). http://eprint.iacr.org/2015/550

15. Ngo, N., Massacci, F., Kerschbaum, F., Williams, J.: Practical witness-key-agreement for blockchain-based dark pools financial trading. In: Financial Cryptography and Data Security 2021 (2021). https://fc21.ifca.ai/papers/113.pdf

16. Parkes, D.C., Rabin, M.O., Shieber, S.M., Thorpe, C.A.: Practical secrecy-preserving, verifiably correct and trustworthy auctions, pp. 70–81. Association for Computing Machinery, New York, NY, USA (2006). https://doi.org/10.1145/1151454.1151478

17. Petrescu, M., Wedow, M.: Dark pools in European equity markets: emergence, competition and implications. European Central Bank: Occasional Paper Series, No. 193 (2017). https://www.ecb.europa.eu/pub/pdf/scpops/ecb.op193.en.pdf

18. Thorpe, C., Parkes, D.C.: Cryptographic securities exchanges. In: Dietrich, S., Dhamija, R. (eds.) FC 2007. LNCS, vol. 4886, pp. 163–178. Springer, Heidelberg (2007). https://doi.org/10.1007/978-3-540-77366-5_16

19. Thorpe, C., Parkes, D.C.: Cryptographic combinatorial securities exchanges. In: Dingledine, R., Golle, P. (eds.) FC 2009. LNCS, vol. 5628, pp. 285–304. Springer, Heidelberg (2009). https://doi.org/10.1007/978-3-642-03549-4_18

20. Thorpe, C., Willis, S.R.: Cryptographic rule-based trading. In: Keromytis, A.D. (ed.) FC 2012. LNCS, vol. 7397, pp. 65–72. Springer, Heidelberg (2012). https://doi.org/10.1007/978-3-642-32946-3_6

21. Zhu, H.: Do Dark Pools Harm Price Discovery? Rev. Finan. Stud. **27**(3), 747–789 (2013)

Speculative Multipliers on DeFi: Quantifying On-Chain Leverage Risks

Zhipeng Wang[✉], Kaihua Qin, Duc Vu Minh, and Arthur Gervais

Imperial College London, London, UK
{zhipeng.wang20,kaihua.qin,duc.vu-minh20,a.gervais}@imperial.ac.uk

Abstract. Blockchains and DeFi have consistently shown to attract financial speculators. One avenue to increase the potential upside (and risks) of financial speculation is leverage trading, in which a trader borrows assets to participate in the financial market. While well-known over-collateralized loans, such as MakerDAO, only enable leverage multipliers of $1.67\times$, new under-collateralized lending platforms, such as Alpha Homora (AH), unlock leverage multipliers of up to $8\times$ and attracted over 1.2B USD of locked value at the time of writing.

In this paper, we are the first to formalize a model for under-collateralized DeFi lending platforms. We analytically exposit and empirically evaluate the three main risks of a leverage-engaging borrower: *(i)* impermanent loss (IL) inherent to Automated Market Makers (AMMs), *(ii)* arbitrage loss in AMMs, and *(iii)* collateral liquidation. Based on our analytical and empirical results of AH over a timeframe of 9 months, we find that a borrower may mitigate the IL through a high leverage multiplier (e.g., more than $4\times$) and a margin trading before supplying borrowed assets into AMMs. We interestingly find that the arbitrage and liquidation losses are proportional to the leverage multiplier. In addition, we find that 72.35% of the leverage taking borrowers suffer from a negative APY, when ignoring the governance token incentivization in AH. Finally, when assuming a maximum $\pm 10\%$ move among two stablecoins, we pave the way for more extreme on-chain leverage multipliers of up to $91.9\times$ by providing appropriate system settings.

1 Introduction

Over 44% of the total locked DeFi value is dedicated to lending and borrowing services. Financial debt has therefore manifested its importance within the decentralized financial ecosystem. The very first DeFi debt protocols focused on so-called *over-collateralized loans*—wherein a borrower must collateralize more financial value than the lent debt amounts to [4,15,16]. Common over-collateralized loan systems require the collateral value not to decline below 150% of the total debt value. While over-collateralized loans grant the borrower a wide degree of flexibility in using the borrowed' assets, they remain capital-inefficient

© International Financial Cryptography Association 2022
I. Eyal and J. Garay (Eds.): FC 2022, LNCS 13411, pp. 38–56, 2022.
https://doi.org/10.1007/978-3-031-18283-9_3

and limit the borrowers leverage multipliers below 2×[1]—that is the multiplier by which traders can increase their financial up- or downside of a loan.

In *under-collateralized loans*, however, speculate-afine traders can gamble with leverage multipliers beyond 2×, which we subsequently refer to as leverage trading. While the borrowed assets remain under the tight control of immutable on-chain smart contracts, existing on-chain leverage platform, such as Alpha Homora [1] grants the borrowers the ability to speculate with a leverage of up to 8×. To the best of our knowledge, this is the first work to explore the practices and possibilities of secure under-collateralized on-chain leverage. We formalize an on-chain leverage model, measure existing lending practices and assess the risks quantitatively as we summarize in our contributions:

On-chain Leverage Model: To the best of our knowledge, we are the first to provide a model for on-chain lending platforms with a leverage factor beyond 2×. We formalize the generic users and components to encompass future leverage designs. We show that with reasonable system settings, an on-chain lending system can achieve a leverage multiplier of up to 91.9×.

On-chain Leverage Analytics: Over a timeframe of 9 months, we analyze on-chain data analytics of Alpha Homora (AH), with 1.2B USD of locked value, the largest on-chain leverage platform in DeFi. We find that lenders consistently benefit from a positive APY, while 72.35% of the leverage taking borrowers suffer from a negative APY, when ignoring the governance token incentivization in AH.

Leverage Risk Quantification: We identify three risks causing borrower losses: *(1)* impermanent loss (IL) inherent to Automated Market Makers, *(2)* asset arbitrage, and *(3)* collateral liquidation. We find that out of the 10,430 positions analyzed over 9 months for leverage trading in AH, 1,139 suffer from IL, 149 are susceptible to asset arbitrage and 270 suffered from collateral liquidation. We find that a borrower may mitigate the risk of IL by simultaneously (1) employing a high leverage multiplier (e.g., more than 4×) and (2) performing a margin trade to swap the borrowed assets to collateralized tokens before supplying assets into AMMs.

2 Background

In the following, we provide essential notions of DeFi to further understand the novelties presented in this paper.

2.1 DeFi

Decentralized Finance, also known as DeFi, is a financial ecosystem which runs autonomously on smart-contracts-enabled blockchains and has grown to a total locked value (TVL) of over 100B USD at the time of writing. Many DeFi protocols are inspired by traditional centralized finance (CeFi) systems, such as

---

[1] For instance, 1.67×, in the case of MakerDAO, where the collateral value shall not decline below 150% of the debt value.

lending and borrowing platforms, asset exchanges, derivatives, and margin trading systems. However, compared to CeFi, DeFi offers distinct features to its users, such as complete transparency and non-custodial asset control. DeFi also enables novel financial primitives that do not exist in traditional CeFi, such as flash loans [27]. Flash loans enable borrowers with nearly zero upfront collateral to borrow instantly billions of USD. Such financial enablers grant arbitrageur traders significant power through the atomic execution of arbitrage transactions across the many composable DeFi markets. For a more thorough background on DeFi, we refer the interested reader to the related works [24, 28].

2.2 Price Oracles

While DeFi is being built, the decentralized finance paradigm remains deeply connected to CeFi. Because blockchains are isolated databases, and cannot access off-chain data, DeFi gathers external data from third-party services, commonly referred to as oracles. Price oracles allow feeding e.g. stock or other asset price information to smart contracts and can therefore act as a bridge between DeFi and the external world [17]. Oracles can be classified as centralized and decentralized oracles based on the number of external sources. Two major decentralized DeFi oracle providers are Chainlink [8] and the Band Protocol [23].

2.3 Automated Market Maker

The prevalent price-finding and order matching mechanism in centralized exchanges (CEXs) is the limit order-book model (LOB), which matches buyers' bids to sellers' ask prices [24]. In decentralized exchanges (DEXs) [29, 31], the Automated Market Maker (AMM) evolved to replace LOB due to its suitability for low-throughput blockchains [36]. An AMM consists of a liquidity pool which receives and emits financial assets through the control of a pre-defined algorithm, in its simplest form a constant product formula. A pool is funded by liquidity providers (LP), who receive LP tokens matching the accounting share of their pool ownership. Liquidity takers (LT) request a trade with the pool by providing one asset X plus a transaction fee [9] while receiving another asset Y in return. The transaction fees are paid to the LPs, proportionally to the LP pool shares.

Impermanent Loss. Liquidity providers have the choice of either depositing their assets to a liquidity pool, or holding the assets in their wallets. If the accumulative value of the tokens in a liquidity pool drops below the hypothetical value of simply holding the assets in a wallet, there exists an impermanent loss (IL), also known as divergence loss. From the moment of an LP deposit, the accumulative asset value decline may occur, when the tokens in a liquidity pool diverge in price from each other [6, 9]. If the token values revert to the price ratio at the time of the LP deposit, the IL is reverted. An IL is therefore only *realized*, when an LP exits a liquidity pool in a state where there exists an IL.

Arbitrage. Arbitrage is the process of profiting by selling/buying assets among multiple markets, leveraging price differences. Arbitrage increases the DeFi market efficiency and is typically considered benign. Previous works [10, 34, 36] have shown that DeFi arbitrage bots monitor blockchain state changes and execute arbitrages among AMMs to make profits.

2.4   Financial Leverage

Leverage is the practice of taking on debt, i.e., to borrow assets for a subsequent financial operation [5]. One such operation is to perform a momentary exchange of assets, which is commonly referred to as margin trading. Another operation would be to take the lent assets and provide these towards a financial instrument, such as a DeFi liquidity pool, as we investigate within this work.

Leverage, in general, can amplify trader profits, as well as losses. Aggressive traders are known to be willing to undertake such risks in pursuit of higher returns [30]. The degree of amplification is determined by the leverage multiplier, which is defined as the ratio of the total assets to the equity (or cash) that a trader holds. The leverage multiplier can be freely adjusted by the trader, i.e., by providing or removing ad hoc collateral from the leverage position. A multiplier of 1× means that the total assets that the trader has access to are equivalent to the trader's equity, i.e., the trader does not borrow any assets. A leverage factor beyond 1× is achieved as soon as the trader can borrow assets to perform a subsequent financial operation. Centralized cryptocurrency trading platforms have readily introduced leverage trading, e.g., Prime XBT [33], OkEX [19], BitMEX [7], and Poloniex [22], offering leverage multipliers *from* 2.5× *to* 100× [20].

2.5   Leverage in DeFi

Because of the lack of Know-Your-Customer (KYC) verifications and the blockchain's pseudonymity, DeFi users cannot safely resort to credit to exert leverage. Therefore, DeFi borrowing is usually fully collateralized or over-collateralized and (with 29B USD of total locked value) widely applied in several lending platforms such as MakerDAO [16], Compound [15] and Aave [4]. MakerDAO for instance, allows traders to open collateralized debt positions by providing various cryptocurrencies as a then locked security deposit. In exchange for locking these assets, the trader can then mint a stablecoin DAI, which can be freely used, as long as the collateral value does not decline below a certain threshold. Specifically, MakerDAO requires that the collateral value does not decline below 150% of the granted debt position. As such, MakerDAO enables maximum leverage of $2.5/1.5 \approx 1.67\times$, while in this work we investigate protocols that enable higher leverage multipliers. If the collateral value declines below 150% in MakerDAO, the debt position becomes liquidatable as we elaborate further in the following.

2.6   Liquidations

If the value of debt collateral in a lending system declines below a custom threshold, then the debt position may be opened for liquidation. The Health Factor

(HF) is a common metric to measure the health of a debt position, whereas an HF smaller than 1 indicates that a debt position is liquidatable [25]. A liquidation is then an event in which a liquidator repays outstanding debts of a position and, in return, receives a portion of the collateral of the position as a reward. Liquidations in DeFi are widely practiced, and related works have quantified that over the years 2020 and 2021, liquidators realized a financial profit of over 800M USD while performing liquidations [25].

3 On-Chain Leverage System

We proceed to outline the actors and components of on-chain leverage systems as shown in Fig. 1.

Lending Pool. A lending pool is a multi-asset management pool that allows capital-providing entities to earn interest on their capital as well as capital-taking entities to trade with a multiple of the capital they hold. Essentially, three actors interact with a lending pool: **Lenders, Borrowers** as well as **Liquidators**.

Lender. Lenders supply assets (e.g., ETH, USDT) to the lending pool to earn from the lending interest rate. The lending interest rate is paid by the borrowing interest rate that leveraged yield farmers contribute for borrowing assets.

Borrower. Borrowers supply assets as collateral to the lending pool to then open leveraged positions, while paying borrowing interests. To avoid liquidations, borrowers can provide additional collateral or partially repay their position. In addition, borrowers can supply the borrowed assets to liquidity providing pools to earn trading fees, or stake LP tokens to liquidity mining pools to earn profits.

Liquidator. Leveraged positions are subject to liquidation when the debt becomes unhealthy [25]. A liquidator can repay the debt and benefit from a liquidation spread.

Price Oracle. The lending pool obtains the asset prices of various cryptocurrencies through external price oracles, which can then inform the smart contract whether a position is liquidatable.

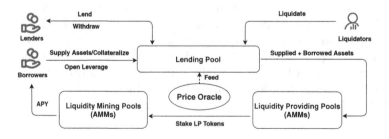

Fig. 1. High-level system diagram of on-chain leverage platforms. The solid arrows ($\rightarrow$) represent the movement of cryptocurrencies, and the dash arrows ($-\rightarrow$) represent the transmission of data.

Table 1. Notation summary

Notations	Definitions	Notations	Definitions
$\mathcal{LV}$	leverage platform	$\mathtt{Coll}_t(\mathbf{P}_{\mathsf{id}}^{\mathsf{C}})$	amount of collateral cryptocurrency
$\mathbf{P}_{\mathsf{id}} = (\mathsf{C}, \mathsf{B})$	debt position	$\mathtt{Borr}_t(\mathbf{P}_{\mathsf{id}}^{\mathsf{B}})$	amount of borrowing cryptocurrency
$x\,\mathsf{X}$	x amount of cryptocurrency X	$p_t^{\mathsf{B}\to\mathsf{C}}$	price of B in the unit C at time t
$\mathsf{DebtRatio}_t(\mathbf{P}_{\mathsf{id}})$	debt ratio	(B, C)	how much credit a position gains when collaterizing $1\,\mathsf{C}$ and borrowing $1\,\mathsf{B}$
$\mathsf{LM}_t(\mathbf{P}_{\mathsf{id}})$	leverage multiplier	m	the initial leverage multiplier when opening a position
$\mathsf{Loss}^{\mathsf{IL}}$	impermanent loss	$\mathsf{Return}_{\mathsf{cp}}^{\mathsf{IL},\mathsf{Mg}}$	the return from impermanent loss and margin trading
$\mathsf{Loss}^{\mathsf{AR}}$	arbitrage loss	$\mathsf{Return}_{\mathsf{cp}}^{\mathsf{Mg}}$	the return from margin trading without impermanent loss
$\mathsf{Loss}^{\mathsf{LQ}}$	liquidation loss	LS	liquidation spread, which determines the rewards for a liquidator after repaying the debt

3.1 Formal Leverage Model

In the following, we formalize the leverage model. We also provide a table to summarize the notations used in this paper (cf. Table 1).

We denote an on-chain leverage platform as $\mathcal{LV} = \langle \mathbb{C}, \mathbb{B}, \mathbb{P}, \mathbb{F} \rangle$, where $\mathbb{C}$ denotes the set of collateral cryptocurrencies; $\mathbb{B}$ denotes the set of debt cryptocurrencies available for borrowing; $\mathbb{P}$ denotes the set of debt positions. A position is denoted as $\mathbf{P} = (\mathsf{C}, \mathsf{B})$, where $\mathsf{C} \in \mathbb{C}$ is a collateral cryptocurrency and $\mathsf{B} \in \mathbb{B}$ is a debt cryptocurrency. $\mathbb{F}$ denotes the set of farming cryptocurrencies that borrowers can receive after providing their borrowing cryptocurrencies into farming pools. In practice, borrowers can *(1)* supply their borrowing cryptocurrencies to liquidity providing pools to earn trading fees, and *(2)* stake LP tokens to liquidity mining pools to earn profits. For simplicity, in our model, we regard steps *(1)* and *(2)* as block box and only consider borrowers' final returns.

Each debt position $\mathbf{P} = (\mathsf{C}, \mathsf{B})$ has a unique id, denoted as $\mathbf{P}_{\mathsf{id}}$. We define $\mathtt{Coll}_t(\mathbf{P}_{\mathsf{id}}^{\mathsf{C}})$ and $\mathtt{Borr}_t(\mathbf{P}_{\mathsf{id}}^{\mathsf{B}})$ as the amount of collateral and borrowing cryptocurrencies of a position $\mathbf{P}_{\mathsf{id}}$ respectively in $\mathcal{LV}$ at time t (in practice, time t is measured in block timestamp). In a leverage platform, the prices of cryptocurrencies are available through a price oracle (cf. Sect. 2.2). We denote x amount of cryptocurrency X with $x\,\mathsf{X}$. We denote $p_t^{\mathsf{B}\to\mathsf{C}}$ as the price of B in the unit C at time t, i.e., $1\,\mathsf{B} = p_t^{\mathsf{B}\to\mathsf{C}}\,\mathsf{C}$.

$\mathcal{LV}$ maintains the state of every position $\mathbf{P}_{\mathsf{id}} \in \mathbb{P}$, and the state is quantified by the debt ratio $\mathsf{DebtRatio}_t(\mathbf{P}_{\mathsf{id}}) = \frac{\mathtt{Borr}_t(\mathbf{P}_{\mathsf{id}}^{\mathsf{B}})}{\mathtt{Coll}_t(\mathbf{P}_{\mathsf{id}}^{\mathsf{C}})} \cdot (\mathsf{B}, \mathsf{C}) \cdot p_t^{\mathsf{B}\to\mathsf{C}} \cdot 100\%$, where (B, C) is a fixed parameter set by the platform $\mathcal{LV}$, which determines how much credit $\mathbf{P}_{\mathsf{id}}$ receives when collaterizing $1\,\mathsf{C}$ and borrowing $1\,\mathsf{B}$. When $\mathsf{DebtRatio}_t(\mathbf{P}_{\mathsf{id}})$ exceeds 100% due to, for example, the fluctuations of price $p_t^{\mathsf{B}\to\mathsf{C}}$, $\mathbf{P}_{\mathsf{id}}$ becomes available for liquidations.

A position $\mathbf{P}_{\mathsf{id}}$ is over-collateralized, if $\mathtt{Coll}_t(\mathbf{P}_{\mathsf{id}}^{\mathsf{C}}) > \mathtt{Borr}_t(\mathbf{P}_{\mathsf{id}}^{\mathsf{B}}) \cdot p_t^{\mathsf{B}\to\mathsf{C}}$, and under-collateralized otherwise. Debt positions in a leverage platform $\mathcal{LV}$ are typically under-collateralized. We finally define the leverage multiplier to measure to what degree borrowers can expand their assets in a position $\mathbf{P}_{\mathsf{id}}$, i.e.,
$\mathsf{LM}_t(\mathbf{P}_{\mathsf{id}}) = \frac{\mathtt{Borr}_t(\mathbf{P}_{\mathsf{id}}^{\mathsf{B}}) \cdot p_t^{\mathsf{B}\to\mathsf{C}} + \mathtt{Coll}_t(\mathbf{P}_{\mathsf{id}}^{\mathsf{C}})}{\mathtt{Coll}_t(\mathbf{P}_{\mathsf{id}}^{\mathsf{C}})}.$

3.2   AMM Model

AMM exchanges are to date the most prevalent markets where leverage borrowers deposit borrowed assets to realize revenue through the collection of trading fees. Hence, the borrowers' returns and risks are fundamentally influenced by the underlying AMM mechanisms. To ease our subsequent analysis, we proceed to outline an AMM (cf. Sect. 2.3) model. We assume the existence of an AMM **A** allowing the exchange between a pair of cryptocurrencies X and Y. x_t and y_t denote the amount of X and Y respectively supplied in **A** at time t. x_t and y_t satisfy a conservation function $f(x_t, y_t, \boldsymbol{k}) = 0$, where $\boldsymbol{k}$ is invariant over time. The spot price of X with respect to Y in **A** at time t is defined as $p_t = \frac{\partial f}{\partial y_t} / \frac{\partial f}{\partial x_t}$. We assume that at time t, a trader swaps δx X to δy Y. Following the conservation function, δx and δy should satisfy $f(x_t, y_t, \boldsymbol{k}) = 0$ and $f(x_t + \delta x, y_t - \delta y, \boldsymbol{k}) = 0$.

Liquidity providers (LPs) provide liquidity to **A** by depositing asset X and Y. Due to the price movement between X and Y, x_t and y_t may change over time. Hence, the amount of X and Y that a LP is allowed to redeem varies with respect to p_t, denoted by $g_t^X(p_t)$ and $g_t^Y(p_t)$.

Constant Product AMMs. For a constant product AMM **A**, the conservation function is $f(x_t, y_t, k) = x_t \cdot y_t - k = 0$, which stipulates that the product of x_t and y_t remains constant after an asset exchange and generally defines the AMM's bonding curve. The spot price in **A** is derived with $p_t = \frac{y_t}{x_t}$.

Exchange. When a trader purchases Y from **A** with δx X, we can derive the output amount of Y with $\delta y = y_t - \frac{x_t \cdot y_t}{x_t + \delta x}$. Note that the realized exchange rate $\frac{\delta y}{\delta x}$ is lower than the spot price p_t, as the executed price depends on the trade volume along the AMM bonding curve. We refer to the difference between the expected price (i.e., the spot price) and the actual exchange rate as slippage [36].

Liquidity Supply. Liquidity providers supply X and Y to a pool **A** while typically not changing the pool's spot price. The ratio between the supplied X and Y in a single deposit at time t therefore follows $\frac{\Delta y}{\Delta x} = \frac{y_t}{x_t}$.

4   Analytical Evaluation

While leverage is a speculative tool to increase the borrowers' profit, this upside increases the potential monetary risks as we outline in the following. The primary risks we identify are *(i)* impermanent loss, *(ii)* arbitrage and *(iii)* liquidation.

4.1   Impermanent Loss Risk

As widely understood, the impermanent loss (IL) [6,9] is caused by diverging asset prices within a liquidity pool (cf. Sect. 2.3). In the following, we investigate the financial risks created through the IL. Notably, we find that the return from margin trading through leverage may positively outweigh IL (cf. Fig. 3).

Generic Formulas for IL. We assume that at time t_0, the price $p_{t_0}^{B \to C}$ in an AMM **A** is p_0, i.e., $1\,B = p_0\,C$. A borrower supplies $g_{t_0}^C(p_0)\,C + g_{t_0}^B(p_0)\,B$ to **A**.

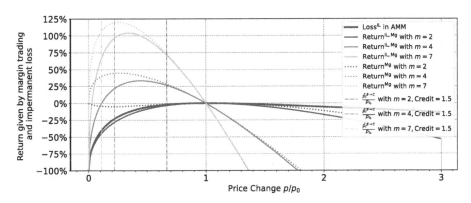

Fig. 2. Resulting return from impermanent loss in constant product AMMs and margin trading in on-chain leverage systems such as Alpha Homora. We find that the return from margin trading through leverage may positively outweigh the impermanent loss if the leverage multiplier is sufficiently high. For example, at a leverage of 7×, we find that upon a price change of 0.64, the return given by margin trading is 94.43%, while the impermanent loss amounts to -2.44%.

We further assume that, at time $t_0 + \Delta$, the price changes to p and the borrower removes all supplied tokens from **A**. Due to the price movement, the assets that the borrower is allowed to redeem become $g^C_{t_0+\Delta}(p)\,$C and $g^B_{t_0+\Delta}(p)\,$B. We can then derive the borrower's impermanent loss in **A** with Eq. 1.

$$\mathsf{Loss}^{\mathsf{IL}} = \frac{g^C_{t_0+\Delta}(p) \cdot 1 + g^B_{t_0+\Delta}(p) \cdot p}{g^C_{t_0}(p_0) \cdot 1 + g^B_{t_0}(p_0) \cdot p} - 1 \tag{1}$$

IL in Constant Product AMMs. We assume that at time t_0, a borrower collateralizes $c\,$C in the leverage platform $\mathcal{LV}$, sets the leverage multiplier as m to borrow $g^C_{t_0}(p_0)\,$C $+ g^B_{t_0}(p_0)\,$B, and then provides the assets to a constant product AMM **A**. Because **A** typically requires to receive a specific proportion of supplied assets for returning LP tokens, $g^C_{t_0}(p_0)$ and $g^B_{t_0}(p_0)$ need to satisfy $\frac{g^C_{t_0}(p_0)}{g^B_{t_0}(p_0)} = p_0$. We can then derive that $g^C_{t_0}(mc, p_0) = \frac{mc}{2}$ and $g^B_{t_0}(mc, p_0) = \frac{mc}{2p_0}$.

We further assume that the percentage of the total liquidity that the borrower owns in **A** is invariant over time. Then at time $t_0 + \Delta$, the borrower can redeem $g^C_{t_0+\Delta}(mc, p)\,$C $= \frac{mc}{2\sqrt{p_0}}\sqrt{p}\,$C and $g^B_{t_0+\Delta}(mc, p)\,$B $= \frac{mc}{2\sqrt{p \cdot p_0}}\,$B. Then according to Eq. 1, the borrower's impermanent loss in **A** is $\mathsf{Loss}^{\mathsf{IL}}_{\mathsf{cp}} = \frac{2\sqrt{\frac{p}{p_0}}}{1+\frac{p}{p_0}} - 1$.

Speculation Through Margin Trading. If we only consider the impermanent loss in **A**, the borrower will always suffer from $\mathsf{Loss}^{\mathsf{IL}}$. However, a borrower can choose to mitigate the IL though a margin trading as follows: *(1)* the borrower collateralizes $c\,$C, and sets the leverage multiplier as $m(m > 2)$ to borrow $\frac{(m-1)c}{p_0}\,$B; *(2)* the borrower then swaps $(\frac{m}{2} - 1)\frac{c}{p_0}\,$B to $(\frac{m}{2} - 1)c\,$C and supplies $\frac{mc}{2}\,$C $+ \frac{mc}{2p_0}\,$B into **A**; *(3)* the borrower removes all assets in **A** and repays the

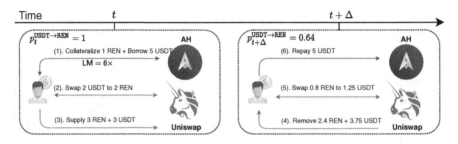

Fig. 3. Example of positive return from margin trading and IL: We assume that, at time t, the price between two tokens USDT and REN is $p_t^{\text{USDT}\to\text{REN}} = 1$ in Uniswap [31], which is a constant product AMM exchange. A borrower, namely Bob, *(1)* collateralizes 1 REN in AH and sets a 6× leverage multiplier to borrow 5 USDT. *(2)* Bob then swaps 2 USDT to 2 REN, and *(3)* supplies 3 USDT and 3 REN to Uniswap. If at time $t + \Delta$, the price $p_{t+\Delta}^{\text{USDT}\to\text{REN}}$ becomes 0.64, Bob then holds 2.4 REN and 3.75 USDT in Uniswap. Bob suffers from an IL of $\frac{3.75\times0.64+2.4}{3\times0.64+3} - 1 = -2.44\%$. *(4)* Finally, Bob removes all assets from Uniswap and *(5)* swaps 0.8 REN to 1.25 USDT (now Bob has $1.25 + 3.75 = 5$ USDT), and *(6)* repays the debt with 5 USDT. Bob's final return is $2.4 - 0.8 - 1 = 0.6$ REN, a profit realized through leverage and margin trading.

debt at time $t + \Delta$. We can then derive the borrower's resulting return from impermanent loss and margin trading with Eq. 2.

$$\text{Return}_{\text{cp}}^{\text{IL,Mg}} = \frac{\frac{mc}{2\sqrt{p_0}}\sqrt{p}\cdot 1 + \frac{mc}{2\sqrt{p\cdot p_0}}\cdot p - \frac{(m-1)c}{p_0}\cdot p}{c} - 1 = m\left(\sqrt{\frac{p}{p_0}} - \frac{p}{p_0}\right) + \frac{p}{p_0} - 1 \tag{2}$$

We notice that, because the borrower performs a margin trade to swap the borrowed token B (i.e., *shorts* the debt B) to the collateralizing token C (i.e., *longs* the collateral C) before supplying assets into **A**, the decline of p may help the borrower to increase the financial return. We can further derive the return from margin trading without IL: $\text{Return}_{\text{cp}}^{\text{Mg}} = \text{Return}_{\text{cp}}^{\text{IL,Mg}} - \text{Loss}_{\text{cp}}^{\text{IL}} = m\left(\sqrt{\frac{p}{p_0}} - \frac{p}{p_0}\right) + \frac{p}{p_0} - \frac{2\sqrt{\frac{p}{p_0}}}{1+\frac{p}{p_0}}$. This return may outweigh the impermanent loss $\text{Loss}_{\text{cp}}^{\text{IL}}$, when the leverage m satisfies $m > \frac{1-\frac{p}{p_0}}{\sqrt{\frac{p}{p_0}} - \frac{p}{p_0}}$.

In Fig. 2, we set the leverage of a position to be 2×, 4× and 7×. We then visualize the return $\text{Return}_{\text{cp}}^{\text{IL,Mg}}$ of such position by capturing a hypothetical price change $\frac{p}{p_0}$ in the range of 0 to 3. Under a leverage setting of 4 or 7, we observe that the borrower may receive a positive return, if $\frac{1}{9} < \frac{p}{p_0} < 1$. We provide an example to show our results in practice (cf. Fig. 3).

4.2 Arbitrage Risk

A liquidity pool typically requires receiving a specific proportion of supplied assets before returning the accounting LP tokens. The LP therefore may need to exchange parts of its assets prior to providing the liquidity. Because liquidity provisions may involve significant liquidity amounts, the prior swap of assets may cause a slippage which can be exploited by DeFi arbitrageurs [10,34,36].

Although arbitrage is regarded as benign for the whole DeFi ecosystem (cf. Sect. 2.3), borrowers on a leverage platform can suffer from a loss when swapping their assets in AMMs, which may generate profitable opportunities for arbitrageurs. In the following, we formalize the financial risks originating through arbitrage loss.

Generic Formulas for Arbitrage Loss. We assume that there are two constant product AMMs $\mathbf{A}_1$ and $\mathbf{A}_2$ allowing exchanges between cryptocurrencies B and C. At time t, $\mathbf{A}_1$ and $\mathbf{A}_2$ have the same spot price $p_t^{B \to C} = p_t(x_t, y_t)$. A borrower swaps δx C to δy B in $\mathbf{A}_1$. We can then derive that the new spot price $p_{t+\delta}^{B \to C}$ in $\mathbf{A}_1$ is $p_{t+\delta}^{B \to C} = p_{t+\delta}(x_t + \delta x, y_t - \delta y + \delta y)$.

We assume that the spot price in $\mathbf{A}_2$ does not change from time t to $t + \delta$. If $p_{t+\delta}^{B \to C} < p_t^{B \to C}$, an arbitrageur can undertake the following actions to make profits: (1) The arbitrageur first swaps δy_2 B to $\delta y_2 \cdot p_t^{B \to C}$ C in $\mathbf{A}_2$; (2) The arbitrageur then swaps $\delta y_2 \cdot p_t^{B \to C}$ C to $\frac{\delta y_2 \cdot p_t^{B \to C}}{p_{t+\delta}^{B \to C}}$ B in $\mathbf{A}_1$. We can then derive the arbitrageur's final profits is $\mathsf{Loss}^{AR} = \delta y_2 \cdot \left(\frac{p_t^{B \to C}}{p_{t+\delta}^{B \to C}} - 1 \right)$ B, which also equals to the loss of the borrower who supplies δx C to $\mathbf{A}_1$.

Arbitrage Risk in Constant Product AMMs. If $\mathbf{A}_1$ and $\mathbf{A}_2$ are both constant product AMMs, then $p_t^{B \to C} = \frac{y_t}{x_t}$. If the borrower performs a margin trading, then $\delta x = (\frac{m}{2} - 1)c$, and $p_{t+\delta}^{B \to C} = \frac{y_t - \delta y + \delta y}{x_t + \delta x} = \frac{y_t}{x_t + \delta x}$. We can derive the arbitrage loss as $\mathsf{Loss}_{cp}^{AR} = \delta y_2 \cdot \left(\frac{x_t + \delta x}{x_t} - 1 \right)$ B $= \frac{(\frac{m}{2} - 1)c \cdot \delta y_2}{x_t}$ B.

We find that the arbitrage loss Loss_{cp}^{AR} is proportional to δx, the amount of C supplied by the borrower, and δy_2, the amount of B swapped by the arbitrageur. Hence, to reduce the arbitrage loss Loss_{cp}^{AR}, the borrower can simply supply assets to the liquidity pool through multiple (temporally distributed) transactions by dividing the entire volume into smaller chunks suffering from less slippage. Note that generating several transactions will involve additional blockchain fees.

4.3 Liquidation Risk

As discussed in Sect. 3, a position is liquidatable when the debt becomes unhealthy, i.e., $\mathsf{DebtRatio}_{t+\Delta}(\mathbf{P}_{id}) > 100\%$, due to a price change of $p_t^{B \to C}$. In the following, we explore what price changes may cause liquidations and associated financial risks in leverage systems.

We denote the leverage multiplier at time t as m. To capture how the price affects a position's health, we compute the liquidation threshold price $\hat{p}_l^{B \to C}$ at which the position is eligible for liquidation (cf. Eq. 3).

$$\mathsf{DebtRatio}_{t+\Delta}(\mathbf{P}_{id}) \leq 1 \iff \frac{\hat{p}_l^{B \to C}}{p_{t_0}} \leq \frac{1}{(\mathsf{B, C}) \cdot (m - 1)} \qquad (3)$$

In Fig. 2, we choose $(B,C) = 1.5$ and show the liquidation thresholds of $\hat{p}_l^{B\to C}$ given a leverage $2\times$, $4\times$ and $7\times$. We find that the threshold $\hat{p}_l^{B\to C}$ is inversely proportional to the chosen leverage. Moreover, the threshold $\hat{p}_l^{B\to C}$ is unrelated to the resulting return from impermanent loss and margin trading, i.e., even if the return is positive under a leverage $4\times$ or $7\times$, the position can still be liquidatable when $\frac{p_t^{B\to C}}{p_{t_0}} > \frac{1}{9}$.

In addition, according to Sect. 2.6, the financial loss from a liquidation for a position $\mathbf{P}_{id}$ at time t can be derived as $\mathsf{Loss}^{LQ} = \frac{\mathrm{Borr}_t(\mathbf{P}_{id}^B) \cdot \mathsf{LS} \cdot c_l \cdot p_t^{B\to C}}{\mathrm{Coll}_t(\mathbf{P}_{id}^C)} = (m-1) \cdot$ $\mathsf{LS} \cdot c_l \cdot \frac{p_t^{B\to C}}{p_{t_0}}$, where $\mathsf{LS} \in (0,1]$ is a parameter for the liquidation spread set by the leverage platform $\mathcal{LV}$, with which a liquidator can receive profits by repaying the debt[2]; $c_l \in (0,1]$ is a parameter that the liquidator chooses to determine what percentage of the debt shall be repaid.

4.4 Maximum Reasonable On-Chain Leverage

In the following, we investigate how to achieve a larger maximum on-chain leverage multiplier, by changing the system parameters of a DeFi leverage platform. Note that the maximum leverage multiplier discussed in this section is limited to the liquidation risk.

We consider two conditions regarding liquidations: *(1)* To avoid an instant liquidation when opening a position, the debt ratio should be less than 1 after setting the initial leverage, i.e., $\mathsf{DebtRatio}_t(\mathbf{P}_{id}) \leq 1$ (cf. Eq. 3); *(2)* To incentivize liquidators, a position should have sufficient collateral to repay for a liquidation, i.e., $\mathsf{Loss}^{LQ} \leq 1$ (cf. Sect. 4.3). By combining the two conditions, we derive the maximum leverage multiplier $m_{\max}$ in Eq. 4.

$$m_{\max} = \frac{1}{\max(\mathsf{LS}, (B,C)) \cdot \max(\frac{p_t}{p_{t_0}})} + 1 \qquad (4)$$

We notice that three parameters play herein an important role: *(1)* (B,C), a parameter determining the credit that a position gains when collaterizing $1\,C$ and borrowing $1\,B$ (cf. Sect. 3.1). *(2)* LS, the liquidation spread on the system (cf. Sect. 4.3). *(3)* $\frac{p_t}{p_{t_0}}$, the price change with respect to the initial price when opening a position, which varies over time. Both (B,C) and LS are configurable system parameters, while $\frac{p_t}{p_{t_0}}$ indicates the price volatility.

Given (B,C), LS and $\max(\frac{p_t}{p_{t_0}})$, we plot the distribution of $m_{\max}$ in Fig. 4. We discuss three cases for choosing $m_{\max}$ for stablecoins:

- **Case 1:** If $\max(\frac{p_t}{p_{t_0}}) = 1.1$, choosing $\max(\mathsf{LS}, (B,C)) = 0.11$, then $m_{\max} = 9.3\times$. In this case, we assume that *the price change $\frac{p_t}{p_{t_0}}$ always remains below* 1.1. This is a reasonable assumption for stablecoins in practice. For instance,

---

[2] For example, in Alpha Homora V2, if a liquidator repays all debt of a position, the liquidator will receive 5% of debts as rewards, i.e., $\mathsf{LS} = 5\%$.

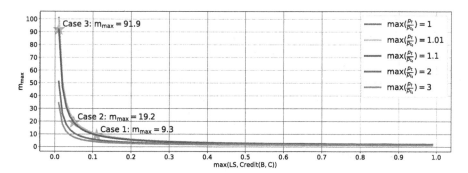

Fig. 4. Distribution of the maximum leverage multiplier $m_{\max}$ over $\max(\mathtt{LS}, (\mathtt{B}, \mathtt{C}))$, when $\max(\frac{p_L}{p_{t_0}})$ is fixed.

the prices of $\mathtt{USDT}$ and $\mathtt{USDC}$ range between 0.99 USD and 1.01 USD in 2020 [18, 24]. Moreover, the two system parameters $(\mathtt{B}, \mathtt{C})$ and $\mathtt{LS}$ satisfy the following constraints: *(1)* $(\mathtt{B}, \mathtt{C})$ *is less than* 0.11, which is a practical number adopted on AHv2 [3] when $\mathtt{B}$ and $\mathtt{C}$ are stablecoins. *(2) The liquidation spread $\mathtt{LS}$ on the system is at most* 11%, which is larger than the $\mathtt{LS}$ on AHv2 (i.e., 5%).

- **Case 2:** If $\max(\frac{p_L}{p_{t_0}}) = 1.1$, choosing $\max(\mathtt{LS}, (\mathtt{B}, \mathtt{C})) = 0.05$, then $m_{\max} = 19.2\times$. In this case, $(\mathtt{B}, \mathtt{C})$ is equal to the $\mathtt{LS}$ on AHv2.
- **Case 3:** If $\max(\frac{p_L}{p_{t_0}}) = 1.1$, choosing $\max(\mathtt{LS}, (\mathtt{B}, \mathtt{C})) = 0.01$, then $m_{\max} = 91.9\times$. In this case, $\mathtt{LS}$ decreases to 1%. However, as $m_{\max}$ increases, liquidators' final rewards do not drop (cf. Sect. 4.3) and they will still be incentivized to liquidate unhealthy positions in practice.

Furthermore, according to Fig. 4, to achieve a large leverage multiplier for non-stablecoins (e.g., cryptocurrencies with a high price volatility $\frac{p_L}{p_{t_0}} > 1.1$), the leverage system needs to choose small $(\mathtt{B}, \mathtt{C})$ and $\mathtt{LS}$.

5   Empirical Evaluation

This section outlines our empirical evaluation of user behavior and risks in Alpha Homora, the biggest leverage platform to date.

Measurement Setup. We crawl the on-chain events of AH's smart contracts [14] (e.g., `borrow`, `repay` and `liquidate` events) and related blockchain states (e.g., oracle prices, the supply interest rates of a lending pool on a specific block height, etc.) from Ethereum block 11,007,158 (7th October, 2020, the inception of AH) to 13,010,057 (12th August, 2021). We use an Ethereum full archive node, on an AMD Ryzen Threadripper 3990X with 64 cores, 256 GB of RAM, and 2 × 8 TB NVMe SSD in Raid 0 configuration. Note that we capture both AHv1 [2] and AHv2 [3], while AHv2 debuted at block 11,515,006 (24th December, 2020).

We observe a total of 5,110 `borrow`, 3,616 `repay`, and 122 `liquidate` events in AHv2. In AHv1, we find 14,466 `work` (emitted during borrows and repays) and 148 `kill` (liquidation) events. We normalize the prices of different tokens to ETH by calling the smart contract of the platform's on-chain price oracles at the block when an event was triggered. Note that we do not rely on any third-party API or external oracle for our data, and solely use the publicly available on-chain data which eases the reproducibility of our results.

5.1   User Behavior in On-Chain Leverage Platforms

We proceed to empirically analyze the user behavior for borrowers and lenders in Alpha Homora. We identify that 3,800 borrowers opened 10,430 leverage positions in AH (i.e., 7,081 in AHv1 and 3,349 in AHv2). In addition, because lending on AH is basically the same as on other lending protocols [4,12,15], which have been investigated thoroughly in related works [21,25], we focus on AH borrowers in this section and analyze lenders in our full paper [32].

Borrower Leverage Multiplier. In AH, borrowers can collateralize their assets and then open a leverage position by setting the leverage multiplier while borrowing assets from the lending pool. For each leverage position, we crawl the amount of collateralized and borrowed assets from the `transfer` and `borrow` events in AH, at the time when opening the position. Given a position' collateral and debt, we can calculate the leverage multiplier.

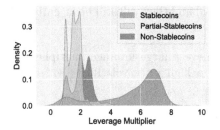
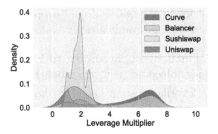

Fig. 5. Distribution of leverage over tokens. Stablecoins attract higher leverage settings. Partial-stablecoin means that borrowers collateralize stable and non-stable coins simultaneously.

Fig. 6. Platform leverage distribution. The stablecoin platform Curve appears to attract higher leverage settings.

We find that 65% of the 3,349 borrower positions in AHv2 select a leverage multiplier smaller than 3.0, the average leverage multiplier is 3.07×. In AHv1, the maximum and average leverage multiplier of the 7,071 positions are 3× and 2.01×, respectively.

Contrary to AHv1, which only supports borrowing ETH, in AHv2, a borrower can collateralize (resp. borrow) 43 (resp. 12) tokens and then provide liquidity to Uniswap, Sushiswap, Curve, and Balancer. We plot the leverages' distribution when borrowers collateralize stable and non-stable coins (cf. Fig. 5) and when borrowers provide liquidity to the four platforms (cf. Fig. 6). We observe that borrowers in AHv2 tend to choose a high leverage multiplier while collateralizing stablecoins or providing liquidity to Curve. This can be explained by the fact that stablecoin pools (which Curve specializes in) are less volatile and hence less likely to experience a liquidation event. We find that stablecoin pools are being used with an average leverage of 5.39×, which is 344.70% higher than the average leverage on non-stablecoin pools.

A borrower can choose to dynamically adjust the leverage of a position, by adding or removing collateral. In Fig. 7 we visualize the distribution of 2,581 closed positions in AHv2 over their adjustment frequency and initial leverage (upon position creation). We find that 348 positions are adjusted more than once and the higher the initial leverage, the less likely this position will be adjusted. Moreover, we observe that 67.92% (i.e., 1,753) of the positions are open for less than two weeks (cf. Fig. 8).

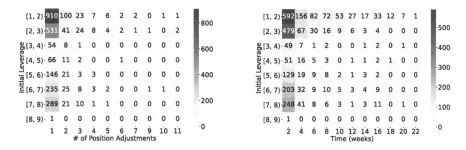

Fig. 7. Debt position distribution over leverage multiplier and adjustment frequency.

Fig. 8. Debt position distribution over leverage multiplier and duration.

Borrower APY. In the following, we analytically derive the borrower interest rates on closed debt positions with only 1 adjustment, i.e. which went through the entire cycle of opening a position with collateral, without modifying the leverage intermediately, and ultimately closing the debt. By focusing on closed positions we achieve a holistic image of the borrowers' return and behavior over the entire life-cycle of a leveraged debt position.

To calculate the APY of a borrower, we crawl the initial collateral deposit and the collateral return amounts, as well as the position opening and closure timestamps. Given this data, we can infer the financial return or APY of a closed position. Note that we convert all assets to USD (cf. Fig. 9) at the position opening and closure moments. Beware that we do ignore the additional potential revenue from Alpha token yield farming, as these are custom temporary protocol participation incentives [32].

Figure 9 visualizes the relationship between the BorrowAPY and the leverage multipliers. The average APY of a maximum of 1-day long positions is −585.70%.

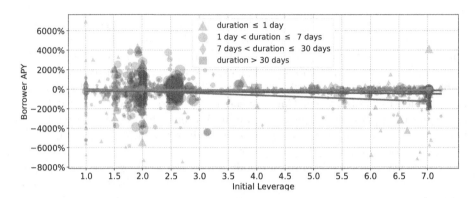

Fig. 9. Distribution of debt positions over BorrowAPY and leverage multipliers. The marker size in the figure is proportional position's collateral value. The linear regression lines are for the APY of the positions with the same duration (i.e., the same color). We find that any leverage setting is prone to negative and positive APY.

From the regression lines, we infer that the longer a position is open (i.e., more than 7 days), the more likely the borrower achieves an APY of 0%. By separating the DeFi platforms to which the borrowers supply borrowed assets, we observe that BorrowAPY varies across platforms [32].

Notably, we find that for 72.35% of the closed positions, the borrowers achieve a negative APY, i.e., lose assets despite leverage. Therefore, we can conclude that, in practice, platform subsidies (i.e., governance token rewards such as Alpha tokens) are an essential incentive mechanism for borrowers using leverage.

5.2   Empirical Analysis of Risks

In the following, we provide an empirical analysis of three risks for borrowers in Alpha Homora, and compare our results with Sect. 4.

Impermanent Loss. We investigate the AH borrowers' IL when supplying assets into constant product AMMs. We find that 1,139 closed positions in AHv2 interact with Sushi- or Uniswap. For each position, we crawl the spot price in the liquidity pool when a borrower deposits and withdraws assets. We observe that all 1,139 positions suffer from impermanent loss, with a price change $\frac{p}{p_0}$ from 0.63 to 1.62. Interestingly, we find that if the borrowers perform a margin trade (cf. Sect. 4.1) before supplying assets into the liquidity, 44.95% (i.e., 512) positions can benefit from a positive return, which compensates IL (cf. Fig. 10).

Arbitrage Loss. We find that borrowers suffer an arbitrage loss in 149 AH positions, when swapping and supplying assets in Uni- or Sushiswap. To further investigate the arbitrage loss, we crawl the cryptocurrency X's amount x_t in the pool, the borrowers' collateral c, and the arbitrageur's swapped assets δy_2. We find that for the positions in AHv2 suffering from arbitrage losses, the average leverage multiplier is $5.25 \pm 1.95 \times$, and the average collateral is 2.03 ± 4.21M USD,

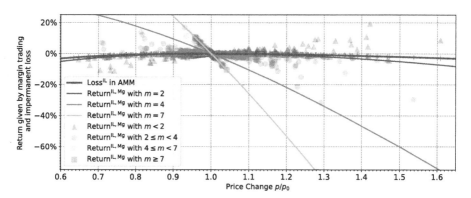

Fig. 10. Distribution of IL for AHv2 positions interacting with Uni- and Sushiswap. The continuous lines show our analytical results, while the points represent the empirical measurements. Note that the difference between our results can be explained by the fact our analytical results assume a constant leverage factor.

which are 61.04% and 21.06% higher than the average leverage multiplier and collateral in AHv2, respectively. Interestingly, we find that the position with id 61 suffered from the most important arbitrage loss, i.e., 81.67% (1.66M USD) of the collateral was lost due to the arbitrage [32].

To show an arbitrageur's expected return, given a borrower's collateral and leverage, we visualize the relationship between $\frac{\text{Loss}_{\text{cp}}^{\text{AR}}}{\delta y_2}$ and $\frac{c}{x_t}$ in Fig. 11. We find that arbitrageurs achieve less profits than our analytical results when the leverage multiplier is large (i.e., $m > 4$). This is probably because the borrowers do not perform a margin trading to swap $(\frac{m}{2} - 1)c\text{X}$ (cf. Sect. 4.2).

Liquidation Loss. We identify 50 unique liquidators performing 270 liquidations in AH to repay 4,352.52 ETH of debt in total. To show the liquidation loss, we crawl a position's collateral before and after the liquidation. Figure 12 visualizes the relationship between liquidation loss and the initial leverage multiplier. We find that the average leverage for the 122 liquidated positions in AHv2 is 2.01×, and the maximal liquidation loss is 10.63%. We observe that, due to the change of p_t, 73.77% positions suffer from a higher liquidation loss than the analytical results (cf. Sect. 4.3) when LS = 5%, and $c_l = 1$ (i.e., the liquidator repays all the debt).

6 Related Work

In this section, we proceed to discuss existing work related to this paper.

Liquidations in DeFi. A growing body of literature has studied liquidations on borrowing and lending platforms in DeFi. Qin *et al.* [25] measure various risks that liquidation participants are exposed to on four major Ethereum lending pools (i.e., MakerDAO [16], Aave [4], Compound [15], and dYdX [12]), and quantify the instabilities of existing lending protocols. Darlin *et al.* [11] analyze the optimal bidding strategies for auction liquidations.

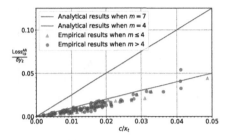

Fig. 11. Distribution of arbitrage loss for 149 debt positions in AH. Arbitrageurs achieve fewer profits than our analytical results when $m > 4$.

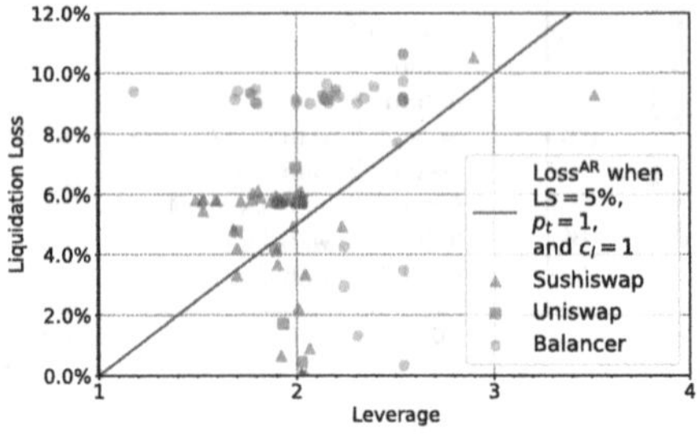

Fig. 12. Distribution of liquidation loss for 122 debt positions in AHv2. We observe that liquidations on Balancer cause higher loss (i.e., 8.51% on average).

Blockchain Extractable Value. Eskandir *et al.* [13] are the first to propose a front-running taxonomy for permissionless blockchains. Daian *et al.* [10] follow up by introducing the concept of Miner Extractable Value (MEV) on blockchains. Zhou *et al.* [36] formalize sandwich attacks on AMM exchanges, which involve front- and back-running victim transactions on DEXs. Qin *et al.* [26] quantify how much value was sourced from blockchain extractable value (BEV), such as sandwich attacks, liquidations, and decentralized exchange arbitrage [35].

7   Conclusion

In this work, we are to the best of our knowledge the first to provide a deep dive into under-collateralized DeFi lending protocols. While under-collateralization reduces the flexibility of the borrowed funds, with up to 8× leverage multipliers, such designs grant speculators more powerful tools to indulge in riskier on-chain trading. We qualitatively and quantitatively analyze the risks caused by impermanent loss, arbitrage, and liquidation. We find that 72.35% of the closed debt positions suffer from a negative APY, when ignoring the rewards of Alpha token in AH. We also find empirical evidence that stablecoin leverage is on average 344.70% higher than non-stable coin leverage. We finally show that with reasonable system settings, an on-chain leverage system can achieve a leverage multiplier of up to 91.9×.

Acknowledgments. We thank the anonymous reviewers and Stephanie Hurder for providing valuable comments and feedback which helped us to strengthen the paper. We are moreover grateful to Nimiq for partially funding this work.

References

1. Alpha homora (2021). https://alphafinancelab.gitbook.io/alpha-finance-lab/alpha-products/alpha-homora
2. Alpha homora v1 (2021). https://homora.alphafinance.io/
3. Alpha homora v2 (2021). https://homora-v2.alphafinance.io/
4. Aave: Aave Protocol (2020). https://github.com/aave/aave-protocol
5. Adrian, T., Shin, H.S.: Liquidity and leverage. J. Financ. Intermed. **19**(3), 418–437 (2010)
6. Aigner, A.A., Dhaliwal, G.: Uniswap: impermanent loss and risk profile of a liquidity provider. arXiv preprint arXiv:2106.14404 (2021)
7. BitMEX: Bitmex (2021). https://www.bitmex.com/
8. Breidenbach, L., et al.: Chainlink 2.0: next steps in the evolution of decentralized oracle networks (2021)
9. Cousaert, S., Xu, J., Matsui, T.: SoK: yield aggregators in DeFi. In: 2022 IEEE International Conference on Blockchain and Cryptocurrency (ICBC), pp. 1–14. IEEE (2022)
10. Daian, P., et al.: Flash boys 2.0: frontrunning, transaction reordering, and consensus instability in decentralized exchanges. In: IEEE Symposium on Security and Privacy (SP) (2020)
11. Darlin, M., Papadis, N., Tassiulas, L.: Optimal bidding strategy for maker auctions. arXiv preprint arXiv:2009.07086 (2020)
12. dYdX: dYdX (2020). https://dydx.exchange/
13. Eskandari, S., Moosavi, M., Clark, J.: SoK: transparent dishonesty: front-running attacks on blockchain (2019)
14. Alpha Finance: AHV contract addresses (2021). https://immunefi.com/bounty/alphafinance/
15. Compound Finance: Compound finance (2019). https://compound.finance/
16. The Maker Foundation: Makerdao (2019). https://makerdao.com/en/
17. Liu, B., Szalachowski, P., Zhou, J.: A first look into DeFi oracles, pp. 39–48 (2021)
18. Moin, A., Sekniqi, K., Sirer, E.G.: SoK: a classification framework for stablecoin designs. In: Bonneau, J., Heninger, N. (eds.) FC 2020. LNCS, vol. 12059, pp. 174–197. Springer, Cham (2020). https://doi.org/10.1007/978-3-030-51280-4_11
19. OkEX: Okex (2021). https://www.okex.com/
20. Trading Crypto with Leverage & the Top 6 Providers (2019). https://blog.goodaudience.com/trading-crypto-with-leverage-the-top-6-providers-31d4db6d3e00
21. Perez, D., Werner, S.M., Xu, J., Livshits, B.: Liquidations: DeFi on a knife-edge. In: Borisov, N., Diaz, C. (eds.) FC 2021. LNCS, vol. 12675, pp. 457–476. Springer, Heidelberg (2021). https://doi.org/10.1007/978-3-662-64331-0_24
22. Poloniex: Poloniex (2021). https://poloniex.com/
23. Band Protocol: Band protocol (2019). https://bandprotocol.com/
24. Qin, K., Zhou, L., Afonin, Y., Lazzaretti, L., Gervais, A.: CeFi vs. DeFi-comparing centralized to decentralized finance. In: 2021 Crypto Valley Conference on Blockchain Technology (CVCBT). IEEE (2021)
25. Qin, K., Zhou, L., Gamito, P., Jovanovic, P., Gervais, A.: An empirical study of DeFi liquidations: incentives, risks, and instabilities. In: Proceedings of the 21st ACM Internet Measurement Conference, pp. 336–350. ACM (2021)
26. Qin, K., Zhou, L., Gervais, A.: Quantifying blockchain extractable value: how dark is the forest? In: 2022 IEEE Symposium on Security and Privacy (SP). IEEE (2022)

27. Qin, K., Zhou, L., Livshits, B., Gervais, A.: Attacking the DeFi ecosystem with flash loans for fun and profit. In: Borisov, N., Diaz, C. (eds.) FC 2021. LNCS, vol. 12674, pp. 3–32. Springer, Heidelberg (2021). https://doi.org/10.1007/978-3-662-64322-8_1

28. Schär, F.: Decentralized finance: on blockchain-and smart contract-based financial markets. Available at SSRN 3571335 (2020)

29. SushiSwap: SushiSwap (2020). https://sushi.com/

30. Thurner, S., Farmer, J.D., Geanakoplos, J.: Leverage causes fat tails and clustered volatility. Quant. Finance **12**(5), 695–707 (2012)

31. Uniswap: Uniswap (2020). https://uniswap.org/

32. Wang, Z., Qin, K., Minh, D.V., Gervais, A.: Speculative multipliers on DeFi: quantifying on-chain leverage risks. Financ. Cryptogr. Data Secur. (2022). https://www.ifca.ai/fc22/preproceedings/71.pdf

33. Prime XBT: Prime XBT (2021). https://primexbt.com/

34. Zhou, L., Qin, K., Cully, A., Livshits, B., Gervais, A.: On the just-in-time discovery of profit-generating transactions in DeFi protocols. In: 2021 IEEE Symposium on Security and Privacy (SP), pp. 919–936 (2021)

35. Zhou, L., Qin, K., Gervais, A.: A2MM: mitigating frontrunning, transaction reordering and consensus instability in decentralized exchanges. arXiv preprint arXiv:2106.07371 (2021)

36. Zhou, L., Qin, K., Torres, C.F., Le, D.V., Gervais, A.: High-frequency trading on decentralized on-chain exchanges. In: 2021 IEEE Symposium on Security and Privacy (SP), pp. 428–445. IEEE (2021)

MPC (Mostly)

Explainable Arguments

Lucjan Hanzlik[1]($\boxtimes$) and Kamil Kluczniak[1,2]

[1] CISPA Helmholtz Center for Information Security, Saarbrücken, Germany
{lucjan.hanzlik,kamil.kluczniak}@cispa.saarland
[2] Stanford University, Stanford, USA
kamil.kluczniak@stanford.edu

Abstract. We introduce an intriguing new type of argument systems with the additional property of being explainable. Intuitively by explainable, we mean that given any argument under a statement, and any witness, we can produce the random coins for which the Prove algorithm outputs the same bits of the argument.

This work aims at introducing the foundations for the interactive as well as the non-interactive setting. We show how to build explainable arguments from witness encryption and indistinguishability obfuscation. Finally, we show applications of explainable arguments. Notably we construct deniable chosen-ciphertext secure encryption. Previous deniable encryption scheme achieved only chosen plaintext security.

1 Introduction

Deniability, first introduced by Dolev, Dwork, and Naor [30], is a notion that received a considerable amount of attention because of its application to authentication protocols. This property allows the user to argue against a third party that it did not take part in a protocol execution. The usual argument made by the user to the third party is that the server could simulate a valid communication transcript without actually interacting with the user.

A variant of deniability was considered in the case of encryption schemes [15,16,63], where a public Expl algorithm allows anyone to open any ciphertext to any message without the secret key. Since we can publicly open ciphertexts, the random coins cannot serve as proof that a particular message is encrypted.

A similar concept was recently introduced to ring signatures [58] and called unclaimability. The property states that no one can claim to be the signer of a particular ring signature σ. The premise is similar. There exists an Expl algorithm that allows any of the ring members to generate random coins that can be used to receive the same σ.

Deniability and unclaimability are related notions. In the former, we consider the server malicious because it tries to gain an undeniable proof of an interaction. In the latter, the malicious party is a different user that tries to make it impossible for honest users to explain an interaction/signature. Interestingly, the deniability and unclaimability definitions studied in the literature only consider scenarios where the party producing a transcript/signature/ciphertext is honest, but may eventually become corrupt in the future.

© International Financial Cryptography Association 2022
I. Eyal and J. Garay (Eds.): FC 2022, LNCS 13411, pp. 59–79, 2022.
https://doi.org/10.1007/978-3-031-18283-9_4

1.1   Contribution

We introduce a new property for argument systems called explainability. Explainability informally resembles deniability and unclaimability. We consider interactive and non-interactive variants of such systems. We show that achieving strong explainability is hard and requires very strong primitives like witness encryption (WE) and indistinguishability obfuscation (iO). Our contribution can be summarized as follows.

New Definitions. We introduce a new property for argument systems that we call explainability, i.e., the ability for anyone with a valid witness wit to compute the random coins coins that "explain" a given argument arg. By "explain," we mean that the witness and coins result in the same argument string arg = Prove(stmt, wit; coins) or the same transcript of an interaction, given the same instance of the verifier. Thus if one can explain an argument for all witnesses and all coins, then such argument/transcript cannot serve as proof that a particular witness was used. We accounted for certain subtle differences between interactive and non-interactive arguments. In both cases, we consider *malicious prover* explainability, where a prover tries to create a proof that other provers cannot explain with a different but valid witness. In this case, we require the protocol to be unique, in the sense that it is infeasible for a malicious prover to produce two different arguments (or transcripts) that the verifier accepts given the same statement and random coins. For the interactive case, we also consider a *malicious verifier* (similar to deniability) that can abort the protocol execution or send corrupt messages to make it impossible for provers with a different witness to explain the current interaction. Since, in the non-interactive case, there is no interaction with a verifier, we consider a scenario where the common reference string (if used) is maliciously generated. We refer to this case as *malicious setup explainability*. Additionally, we call a (non-)interactive argument system fully explainable, when it is explainable even if both the setup/verifier and the prover are malicious.

Implications. To study the power of explainable arguments we prove several interesting implications of explainable arguments.

- We show that when an argument system is malicious verifier explainable, then it is also witness indistinguishable.
- We show that non-interactive malicious prover explainable arguments and one-way functions imply witness encryption (WE). This result serves us as evidence that constructing such arguments is difficult and requires strong cryptographic primitives.

Constructions of Interactive Explainable Arguments. We introduce new properties for witness encryption that we call *robustness* and *plaintext awareness*. Informally, robustness ensures that decryption is independent of which witness is used. In other words, there do not exist two valid witnesses for which a ciphertext decrypts to a different message (or $\perp$). Plaintext awareness ensures that an encrypter must know the plaintext it encrypted. We then show how to leverage robust witness encryption to construct interactive explainable arguments. The resulting protocol is round-optimal, predictable, and can be instantiated to yield an optimally laconic argument. Given the witness encryption is plaintext aware, we can show that the protocol is zero-knowledge. Finally, assuming the witness encryption is extractably secure, we can show that our protocol is a proof of knowledge.

Constructions of Non-interactive Explainable Arguments. We show how to construct malicious setup and malicious prover explainable arguments from indistinguishability obfuscation. While malicious prover explainable arguments can trivially be build using techniques from Sahai and Waters [63], the case of malicious setup explainable arguments is more involved and requires us to use dual-mode witness indistinguishable proofs. Furthermore, we show how to build fully explainable arguments, additionally assuming NIZK.

Why Study Explainable Arguments? Argument systems are fundamental primitives in cryptography. While some privacy properties like zero-knowledge already give a strong form of deniability, our notion of explainability is much stronger as it considers the extreme case where the provers' coins are leaked or are chosen maliciously. For example, using our explainable arguments, we can show explainable interactive anonymous authentication schemes, where anonymity is defined similarly as in ring-signature schemes (see full paper [45]). Notably, we can construct CCA-1 secure encryption with deniability as defined by Sahai and Waters [63], from CPA secure deniable encryption and our explainable arguments assuming random oracles. Our deniable encryption is a variant of the Naor-Yung transform [56], but only rely on witness indistinguishability instead of zero-knowledge which allows us to instantiate this transformation using our explainable arguments.

Malicious Verifier/Setup Explainability. We consider adversaries that are substantially more powerful than what is usually studied in the literature, e.g., in deniable authentication schemes or ring-signatures. In particular, in our case, the user can deny an argument even when the adversary asks to reveal the user's random coins used to produce the argument. Immediate real-world examples of such powerful adversaries are rogue nation-state actors that might have the right to confiscate a user's hardware and apply effectual forensics techniques to obtain the random seeds as evidence material against the user. We believe that the threat posed by such potent adversaries may prevent the use of e.g., ring-signatures by whistleblowers, as the anonymity notions provided might be insufficient.

Malicious Prover Explainability. The main application we envision for malicious prover explainability is internet voting. An essential part of a sound and fair voting scheme is to prevent the selling of votes by malicious voters. We note that the "selling votes" issue isn't limited to actual bribery but, perhaps more critically, addresses the issue of forcing eligible voters to vote on a particular candidate. In this case, an authoritarian forces others to deliver evidence that they voted on a particular option or participate in a specific digital event. An authoritarian here may be an abusive family member, corrupt supervisor, or employer. Our strong unclaimability notion is essential to handle such drastic cases, mainly because users might be coerced or bribed to use specific coins in the protocol.

1.2   Related Work

Explainability of the verifier was used by Bitansky and Choudhuri [8] as a step in proving the existence of deterministic-prover zero-knowledge proofs. In their definition they used the fact that the choices of a verifier can be "explained" by outputting random coins that will lead to the same behaviour. This later can be used to transform the system to be secure even against a malicious verifier. In contrary, we consider the explainability of the prover. While arguments with our type of explainability have not been studied before, there exists some related concepts. Here we give an overview of the related literature.

Deniable Authentication. Dolev, Dwork, and Naor [30] first introduced the concept of deniability. The first formal definition is due to Dwork, Naor, and Sahai [32]. Deniability was studied in numerous works [25,48,55] in the context of authentication protocols. The concept was later generalized to authenticated key exchange and was first formally defined by Di Raimondo, and Genaro [26]. Since then deniable key exchange protocols got much attention from the community [11,24,27,28,46,49,51,65–69]. In such protocols, deniability is informally defined as a party's ability to simulate the transcript of interaction without actually communicating with another party. Since each party can generate a transcript itself, the transcript cannot be used as proof to a third party that the interaction took place. At a high level, deniability is very similar to zero-knowledge, but it is important to mention that Pass [59] showed some subtle differences between both notions.

Deniable Encryption. Deniable encryption was first introduced by Canetti, Dwork, Naor, and Ostrovsky [15]. Here we deal with a "post" compromise situation, where an honest encrypter may be forced to "open" a ciphertext. In other words, given a ciphertext, it should be possible to show a message and randomness that result in the given ciphertext. Deniable encryption was intensively studied [1,7,20–22,41,57,63]. Very recently, Canetti, Park, and Poburinnaya [16] generalize deniable encryption to the case where multiple parties are compromised and show constructions also assuming indistinguishability obfuscation.

Ring Signatures. Early forms of deniability were the main motivation for the work of Rivest, Shamir, and Tauman [61], which introduces the concept of ring signatures. This early concept took into account a relaxed form of deniability where only the secret key of a user may leak. Very recently [58] extended ring signatures with additional deniability properties. For example, they show a signer deniable ring signature where any signer may generate random coins that, together with its secret key, will result in the given signature. However, they require to assume the prover is honest at the moment of signature generation. In our argument setting, we do not make such assumptions.

We are the first to study arguments with unclaimability and deniability properties that allow denying executing a protocol even when the prover is forced to reveal all its random coins or where the prover chooses its coins maliciously. Previous works mostly address a post-compromise setting, whereas some of our explainability notions take into account malicious prover. We believe that our primitives may find applications in protocols as a means of providing consistency checks or anonymous authentication of the votes. For example, the protocols from [17,62] rely on a trusted party to verify a voter's signature. That party knows the user's vote. Using our explainable arguments, we can build (see full paper) a simple anonymous authentication protocol without degrading receipt freeness of the voting scheme, and in effect, remove the trust assumption in terms of privacy.

Receipt Freeness and Coertion Resistance in Voting Schemes. Some of our definitions and potential application are tightly connected to voting schemes. In particular, our definition of malicious prover explainability poses the same requirements, at a high level, for an argument system as receipt freeness or coercion resistance in voting schemes [6,47,54,64]. Since we focus on a single primitive, our definitions are much simpler in comparison to complex voting systems. For example, the definition from [17] involves numerous oracles, and defines a set of parties, and assumes trusted parties. Our definition for malicious prover explainability is simple and says that it is infeasible to produce two different arguments under the same statement that verify incorrectly.

Outline of the Paper. In Sect. 3 we give definitions of explainable argument systems. In Sect. 4 we construct non-interactive explainable arguments. In Sect. 5 we introduce robust witness encryption, and apply it to build interactive explainable arguments. Finally, in Sect. 6, we show how to apply explainable arguments to construct deniable CCA-secure encryption. In the full paper [45], we recall all definitions for the primitives in the preliminaries section, show an explainable anonymous authentication protocol, and all security proofs.

2 Preliminaries

Notation. We denote execution of an algorithm Alg on input x as $a \leftarrow \mathsf{Alg}(x)$ were the output is assigned to a. Unless said otherwise, we will assume that algorithms are probabilistic and choose some random coins internally. In some cases, however, we will write $\mathsf{Alg}(.; r)$ to denote that Alg proceeds deterministically on input a seed $r \in \{0,1\}^s$ for some integer s. We denote an execution of a protocol between parties V and P, by $\langle \mathsf{Prove}(.) \rightleftharpoons \mathsf{Verify}(.) \rightarrow x \rangle = \mathsf{trans}$, where x is the output of Verify after completion of the protocol, and trans is the transcript of the protocol. A transcript trans contains all messages send between Prove and Verify and the input of Verify. We write $\mathsf{View}(\mathsf{Prove}(.) \rightleftharpoons \mathsf{Verify}(.))$ to denote the view of Verify. The view contains the transcript, all input to Verify including its random coins and its internal state. W say that a function $\mathsf{negl} : \mathbb{N} \mapsto \mathbb{R}^+$ is negligible if for every constant $c > 0$ there exists a integer $N_c \in \mathbb{N}$ such that for all $\lambda > N_c$ we have $\mathsf{negl}(\lambda) < \lambda^{-c}$.

Standard Definitions. We use a number of standard cryptographic tools throughout the paper, including: pseudorandom generators and Goldreich-Levin hardcore bits [39], existential unforgeable and unique signature schemes [37,42], zero-knowledge (ZK) and witness-indistinguishable (WI) argument systems, non-interactive ZK arguments from non-falsifiable assumptions [35], dual-mode witness-indistinguishable proofs [43], CCA1 secure and publicly deniable encryption [63], witness encryption [36] and extractable witness encryption [40], indistinguishability obfuscation [3], and punctured pseudorandom functions [13,14,50].

3   Explainable Arguments

In this section, we introduce the security notions for explainable arguments.

3.1   Interactive Explainable Arguments

In an interactive argument system, the prover uses a witness wit for statement stmt to convince the verifier that the statement is true. The communication between the prover and the verifier creates a transcript trans that contains all the exchanged messages. An interactive explainable argument system allows a prover with a different witness wit^* to generate random coins coins for which $\mathsf{Prove}(\mathsf{stmt}, \mathsf{wit}^*; \mathsf{coins})$ interacting with the same instance of the verifier (i.e., the verifier uses the same random coins) creates the same transcript trans. In other words, this means that any prover with a valid witness can provide random coins that would explain the interaction in trans. More formally.

Definition 1 (Interactive Explainable Arguments). *An interactive argument system $\Pi_{\mathcal{R}} = (\mathsf{Prove}, \mathsf{Verify})$ for language $L_{\mathcal{R}}$ is an interactive explainable argument system if there exists an additional Expl algorithm:*

- $\mathsf{Expl}(\mathsf{stmt}, \mathsf{wit}, \mathsf{trans})$: *takes as input a statement stmt, any valid witness wit (i.e. $\mathcal{R}(\mathsf{stmt}, \mathsf{wit}) = 1$) and transcript trans, and outputs $\mathsf{coins} \in \mathbf{Coin}_{\mathsf{Prove}}$ (i.e. coins that are in the space of the randomness used in Prove),*

which satisfies the correctness definition below.

Definition 2 (Correctness). *For all security parameter* λ, *for all statements* stmt $\in L_{\mathcal{R}}$, *for all* wit, wit* *such that* $\mathcal{R}(\text{stmt}, \text{wit}) = \mathcal{R}(\text{stmt}, \text{wit}^*) = 1$, *we have*

$$\langle \text{Verify}(\text{stmt}) \rightleftharpoons \text{Prove}(\text{stmt}, \text{wit}) \rangle =$$
$$\langle \text{Verify}'(\text{stmt}; \text{trans}) \rightleftharpoons \text{Prove}(\text{stmt}, \text{wit}^*; \text{coins}_E) \rangle = \text{trans},$$

where $\text{coins}_E \leftarrow \text{Expl}(\text{stmt}, \text{wit}^*, \text{trans})$ *and* $\text{coins}_E \in \mathbf{Coin}_{\text{Prove}}$ *and* Verify' *sends its messages as in* trans *as long as* Prove *answers as is* trans. *If the output of* Prove *do not match* trans, *then* Verify' *aborts and outputs* $\bot$.

Remark 1. Note that a naive way to implement the Expl algorithm would be to set coins_E and make the Prove algorithm to "replay" the messages. However, this is obviously a scheme that would not be desirable, since an adversary could easily distinguish such coins from honest ones. Therefore we require that $\text{coins}_E \in \mathbf{Coin}_{\text{Prove}}$ to ensure that coins_E can be given as input to an honest Prove algorithm.

The above definition constitutes a correctness definition for explainable arguments and assumes that all parties are honest. Informally, we require that given a witness and a transcript of an interaction between a verifier and a prover (with a possibly different witness), Expl generates coins such that a honest prover returns the same messages given that the verifier send its messages as in trans.

Below we describe explainability of a malicious verifier. Roughly speaking, this property says that a transcript produced during an execution with a malicious verifier, and a honest prover P, should be explainable. The goal of a verifier, is to send such messages to the prover P, that P sends such responses that no other prover (with a different witness) would send. If the adversary succeeds then the transcript (possibly with P's random coins) can be used as a proof to a third party, that P indeed took part in the communication. Remind that P may be forced to reveal its random coins after completing the protocol.

Definition 3 (Malicious Verifier Explainability). *For a security parameter* λ, *we define the advantage* $\text{Adv}_{\mathcal{A}}^{\text{MVExpl}}(\lambda)$ *of an adversary* $\mathcal{A} = (\mathcal{A}_1, \mathcal{A}_2, \mathcal{A}_3)$ *as*

$$1 - \Pr[\langle \mathcal{A}_3(\text{stmt}; \text{coins}_{\mathcal{A}}) \rightleftharpoons \text{Prove}(\text{stmt}, \text{wit}^*; \text{coins}_P) \rangle = \text{trans}], \quad where$$

$$(\text{stmt}, \text{wit}, \text{wit}^*, \text{st}) \leftarrow \mathcal{A}_1(\lambda),$$
$$\text{trans} = \langle \text{coins}_{\mathcal{A}} \leftarrow \mathcal{A}_2(\text{stmt}; \text{st}) \rightleftharpoons \text{Prove}(\text{stmt}, \text{wit}) \rangle,$$
$$\text{coins}_P \leftarrow \text{Expl}(\text{stmt}, \text{wit}^*, \text{trans}),$$
$$\text{wit} \neq \text{wit}^*, \quad \mathcal{R}(\text{stmt}, \text{wit}) = \mathcal{R}(\text{stmt}, \text{wit}^*) = 1,$$

where the probability is taken over the random coins of Prove. *Furthermore,* $\mathcal{A}_3$ *sends the same messages to* Prove *as in* trans *as long as the responses from the prover are as in* trans.

We say that an interactive argument system is malicious verifier explainable *if for all adversaries* $\mathcal{A} = (\mathcal{A}_1, \mathcal{A}_2, \mathcal{A}_3)$ *such that* $\mathcal{A}_1, \mathcal{A}_2, \mathcal{A}_3$ *are PPT algorithms there exists a negligible function* negl(.) *such that* $\mathsf{Adv}_{\mathcal{A}}^{\mathsf{MVExpl}}(\lambda) \leq \mathsf{negl}(\lambda)$. *We say that the argument system is* malicious verifier statistically explainable *if the above holds for an unbounded adversary* $\mathcal{A}$.

Let us now consider a scenario where proving ownership of an argument is beneficial to the prover, but at the same time, the system requires the proof to be explainable. A malicious prover tries to prove the statement in a way that makes it impossible for others to "claim" the generated proof. For this property, it is easy to imagine a malicious prover that sends such messages to the verifier, that the verifier accepts, and no other honest prover would ever send such messages. In practice, we may imagine that an adversary runs a different implementation of the prover, for which the distribution of the sent messages deviate from the distribution of the original implementation. Later to "claim" the transcript that adversary may prove that the transcript is indeed the result of the different algorithm, not the honest one. Note that such a "claim" is sound if an honest prover would never produce such messages. To prevent such attacks, we require that there is only one (computationally feasible to find) valid way a prover can respond to the messages from an honest verifier.

Definition 4 (Uniqueness/Malicious Prover Explainability). *We define the advantage* $\mathsf{Adv}_{\mathcal{A}}^{\mathsf{MPExpl}}(\lambda)$ *of an adversary* $\mathcal{A} = (\mathcal{A}_1, \mathcal{A}_2, \mathcal{A}_3)$ *as*

$$1 - \Pr\left[\begin{array}{c} \langle 1 = \mathsf{Verify}(\mathsf{stmt}; \mathsf{coins}_V) \rightleftharpoons \mathcal{A}_2(\mathsf{st}_1) \rightarrow \mathsf{st}_2 \rangle \\ \neq \langle 1 = \mathsf{Verify}(\mathsf{stmt}; \mathsf{coins}_V) \rightleftharpoons \mathcal{A}_3(\mathsf{st}_2) \rangle \end{array} \right],$$

where $\mathsf{st}_1, \mathsf{stmt} \leftarrow \mathcal{A}_1(\lambda)$ *and the probability is taken over the coins* coins_V.

We say that an interactive argument system is malicious prover explainable *if for all PPT adversaries* $\mathcal{A}$ *there exists a negligible function* negl(.) *such that* $\mathsf{Adv}_{\mathcal{A}}^{\mathsf{MPExpl}}(\lambda) \leq \mathsf{negl}(\lambda)$. *We say that the system is* malicious prover statistically explainable *if the above holds for an unbounded* $\mathcal{A}$.

Theorem 1. *If* (Prove, Verify, Expl) *is a malicious verifier (statistical) explainable argument system then it is also (statistical) witness indistinguishable.*

Definition 5. *We say that an interactive argument system is* fully explainable *if it is malicious prover explainable and malicious verifier explainable.*

3.2 Non-interactive Explainable Arguments

Here we present definitions for non-interactive explainable arguments. Similar to the interactive case, we begin by defining what it means that a system is explainable.

Definition 6 (Non-Interactive Explainable Arguments). *A non-interactive argument system* $\Pi_{\mathcal{R}} = $ (Setup, Prove, Verify) *for language* $L_{\mathcal{R}}$ *is a non-interactive explainable argument system if there exists an additional* Expl *algorithm:*

– Expl(crs, stmt, wit, arg): *takes as input a statement* stmt, *any valid witness* wit *and an argument* arg, *and outputs random coins* coins

which satisfies the correctness definition below.

Definition 7 (Correctness). *For all security parameter* λ, *for all statements* stmt $\in L_{\mathcal{R}}$, *for all* wit, wit* *such that* $\mathcal{R}(\text{stmt}, \text{wit}) = \mathcal{R}(\text{stmt}, \text{wit}^*) = 1$, *for all random coins* coins$_P \in \mathbf{Coin}_{\text{Prove}}$, *we have*

$$\text{Prove}(\text{crs}, \text{stmt}, \text{wit}; \text{coins}_P) = \text{Prove}(\text{crs}, \text{stmt}, \text{wit}^*; \text{coins}_E)$$

where coins$_E$ $\leftarrow$ Expl(crs, stmt, wit*, arg), coins$_E$ $\in$ $\mathbf{Coin}_{\text{Prove}}$ *and* crs $\leftarrow$ Setup(λ).

Now we define malicious setup explainability. Note that a malicious verifier cannot influence the explainability of an argument because there is no interaction with the prover. Hence, the malicious verifier from the interactive setting is replaced with an untrusted setup. An adversary might generate parameters that result in the Expl algorithm to output coins yielding a different argument or even failing on certain witnesses. In some sense, we can think of the adversary as wanting to subvert the common reference string against deniability of certain "targeted" witnesses.

Definition 8 (Malicious Setup Explainability). *We define the advantage* $\text{Adv}_{\mathcal{A}}^{\text{MSExpl}}(\lambda)$ *of an adversary* $\mathcal{A}$ *by the following probability*

$$1 - \Pr\left[\text{arg}^* = \text{arg} : \begin{array}{c} (\text{stmt}, \text{wit}, \text{wit}^*, \text{crs}) \leftarrow \mathcal{A}(\lambda) \\ \text{wit} \neq \text{wit}^* \\ \mathcal{R}(\text{stmt}, \text{wit}) = \mathcal{R}(\text{stmt}, \text{wit}^*) = 1 \\ \text{arg} \leftarrow \text{Prove}(\text{crs}, \text{stmt}, \text{wit}); \\ \text{coins}_P \leftarrow \text{Expl}(\text{crs}, \text{stmt}, \text{wit}^*, \text{arg}); \\ \text{arg}^* \leftarrow \text{Prove}(\text{crs}, \text{stmt}, \text{wit}^*; \text{coins}_P) \end{array}\right],$$

where the probability is taken over the random coins of the prover Prove. *We say that a non-interactive argument is* malicious setup explainable *if for all PPT adversaries* $\mathcal{A}$ *there exists a negligible function* negl(.) *such that* $\text{Adv}_{\mathcal{A}}^{\text{MSExpl}}(\lambda) \leq$ negl(λ). *We say the that a non-interactive argument is* malicious setup statistically explainable *if the above holds for an unbounded adversary* $\mathcal{A}$. *Moreover, we say that a non-interactive argument is perfectly malicious setup explainable if* $\text{Adv}_{\mathcal{A}}^{\text{MSExpl}}(\lambda) = 0$.

Theorem 2. *If there exists a malicious setup explainable non-interactive argument, then there exists a two-move witness-indistinguishable argument, where the verifier's message is reusable. In other words, given a malicious setup explainable non-interactive argument, we can build a private-coin ZAP.*

Malicious prover explainability is defined similarly as in the case of interactive arguments. For the non-interactive setting, it is simpler to formalize the definition, as we simply require the adversary to return two arguments that verify correctly, but their canonical representation is different.

Definition 9 (Uniqueness/Malicious Prover Explainability). *We define the advantage of an adversary $\mathcal{A}$ against malicious prover explainability of* ExArg *as* $\mathsf{Adv}_{\mathcal{A}}^{\mathsf{MPExpl}}(\lambda) = \Pr[\arg_1 \neq \arg_2]$ *where* crs $\leftarrow$ Setup(λ) *and* $(\mathsf{stmt}, \arg_1, \arg_2) \leftarrow \mathcal{A}(\lambda)$ *are such that* Verify(crs, stmt, $\arg_1$) = Verify(crs, stmt, $\arg_2$), *and the probability is over the random coins of* Setup. *We say that a non-interactive argument is* malicious prover explainable *if for all PPT adversaries $\mathcal{A}$ there exists a negligible function* negl(.) *such that* $\mathsf{Adv}_{\mathcal{A}}^{\mathsf{MPExpl}}(\lambda) \leq$ negl(λ). *We say that a non-interactive argument is* malicious prover statistically explainable *if the above holds for an unbounded adversary $\mathcal{A}$. Moreover, we say that an argument system is a* perfectly malicious prover explainable *if* $\mathsf{Adv}_{\mathcal{A}}^{\mathsf{MPExpl}}(\lambda) = 0$.

For full explainability, we combine both malicious prover and malicious verifier explainability.

Definition 10 (Full Explainability). *We define the advantage of an adversary $\mathcal{A}$ against full explainability of* ExArg *by the following probability*

$$\mathsf{Adv}_{\mathcal{A}}^{\mathsf{FExpl}}(\lambda) = \Pr[\arg_1 \neq \arg_2]$$

where (stmt, crs, $\arg_1, \arg_2$) $\leftarrow \mathcal{A}(\lambda)$ *is such that* Verify(crs, stmt, $\arg_1$) = Verify(crs, stmt, $\arg_2$). *We say that a non-interactive argument is* full explainable *if for all PPT adversaries $\mathcal{A}$, there exists a negligible function* negl(.) *such that* $\mathsf{Adv}_{\mathcal{A}}^{\mathsf{FExpl}}(\lambda) \leq$ negl(λ). *We say that the non-interactive argument is* full statistically explainable *if the above holds for an unbound adversary $\mathcal{A}$. Moreover, we say that an argument system is* perfectly full explainable *if* $\mathsf{Adv}_{\mathcal{A}}^{\mathsf{FExpl}}(\lambda) = 0$.

Theorem 3. *If* ExArg *is a fully explainable argument, then* ExArg *is a malicious setup and malicious prover explainable argument.*

Theorem 4. *Given that one-way functions and malicious prover selectively sound non-interactive (resp. two-move) arguments for* NP *exist, then there exists a witness encryption scheme for* NP.

4   Non-interactive Explainable Arguments

In this section, we show that it is possible to construct malicious setup explainable non-interactive argument systems from falsifiable assumptions. We also show a fully explainable argument assuming non-interactive zero-knowledge. As both schemes are nearly identical and differ only in several lines, we will denote the lines or specific algorithms with ∘ for the malicious setup explainable argument, and with †, we denote the code specific for the fully explainable argument.

Scheme 1 (Non-interactive Explainable Argument). Let $\nabla = \circ$ for the malicious setup explainable argument, and $\nabla = \dagger$ for the fully explainable argument. Let DMWI be a dual-mode proof, NIWI be a non-interactive witness indistinguishable proof, Com be an equivocal commitment scheme, Sig be a unique signature scheme, and PRF be a punctured pseudorandom function. We construct the non-interactive argument system ExArg$^{\nabla}$ = (Setup, Prove, Verify) as follows.

Circuit for ProgProve$_\circ^1$ and ProgProve$_\dagger^1$	Circuit for ProgVerify
Hardwired: pp, crs$_{\mathsf{DMWI}}$, K	**Hardwired:** K
Input: (stmt, wit)	**Input:** (stmt)
1°: **if** DMWI.Verify(crs$_{\mathsf{DMWI}}$, stmt, wit) $= 0$	$1:$ sk$_s \leftarrow$ PRF.Eval$(K,$ stmt$)$
$1^\dagger$: **if** $R($stmt, wit$) = 0$	$2:$ vk$_s \leftarrow$ Sig.Setup$($sk$_s)$
$2:$ **return** $\bot$.	$3:$ **return** vk$_s$
$3:$ **else**	
$4:$ sk$_s \leftarrow$ PRF.Eval$(K,$ stmt$)$	
$5:$ arg $\leftarrow$ Sig.Sign$($sk$_s,$ stmt$)$	
$6:$ **return** arg	

Fig. 1. Circuits for ProgProve$_\circ^1$, ProgProve$_\dagger^1$ and ProgVerify. Note that ProgProve differ only in line 1.

Setup$(\lambda, \mathsf{L}_\mathcal{R})$:

1. Choose $K \leftarrow$ PRF.Setup(λ) and crs$_{\mathsf{DMWI}} \leftarrow$ DMWI.Setup$(\lambda,$ modeSound; coins$_S)$, where coins$_S$ are random coins.

2. $O_{\mathsf{Prove}} \leftarrow$ Obf$(\lambda,$ ProgProve$_\nabla^1[$pp, crs$_{\mathsf{DMWI}}, K]$; coins$_P)$, where ProgProve$_\nabla^1$ is given by Fig. 1 and coins$_P$ are random coins.

3°. Define statement stmt$_{\mathsf{Setup}}^\circ$ as

$$\left\{ \begin{array}{l} \exists_{i \in [2], K, \mathsf{coins}_P} O_{\mathsf{Prove}} \leftarrow \mathsf{Obf}(\lambda, \mathsf{ProgProve}_\circ^i[\mathsf{pp}, \mathsf{crs}_{\mathsf{DMWI}}, K]; \mathsf{coins}_P) \ \vee \\ \exists_{\mathsf{mode}, \mathsf{coins}_S} \mathsf{crs}_{\mathsf{DMWI}} \leftarrow \mathsf{DMWI.Setup}(\lambda, \mathsf{mode}; \mathsf{coins}_S) \wedge \mathsf{mode} = \mathsf{modeWI} \end{array} \right\}.$$

$3^\dagger$. Define statement stmt$_{\mathsf{Setup}}^\dagger$ as

$$\{\exists_{K, \mathsf{coins}_P} O_{\mathsf{Prove}} \leftarrow \mathsf{Obf}(\lambda, \mathsf{ProgProve}_\dagger^1[\mathsf{pp}, \mathsf{crs}_{\mathsf{DMWI}}, K]; \mathsf{coins}_P)\}.$$

4. Set wit$_{\mathsf{Setup}} = (1, K,$ coins$_P)$.

5°. $\pi \leftarrow$ NIWI.Prove(stmt$_{\mathsf{Setup}}^\circ$, wit$_{\mathsf{Setup}}$).

$5^\dagger$. $\pi \leftarrow$ NIZK.Prove(stmt$_{\mathsf{Setup}}^\dagger$, wit$_{\mathsf{Setup}}$).

6. Compute $O_{\mathsf{Verify}} \leftarrow$ Obf$(\lambda,$ ProgVerify$[K])$ and output crs $=$ $(O_{\mathsf{Prove}}, O_{\mathsf{Verify}},$ pp, etd, crs$_{\mathsf{DMWI}}, \pi)$.

Prove(crs, stmt, wit; r):

1°. Set stmt$_{\mathsf{Setup}}^\circ$ as in the setup algorithm.

$1^\dagger$. Set stmt$_{\mathsf{Setup}}^\dagger$ as in the setup algorithm.

2°. If NIWI.Verify(stmt$_{\mathsf{Setup}}^\circ, \pi) = 0$ return $\bot$.

$2^\dagger$. If NIZK.Verify(stmt$_{\mathsf{Setup}}^\dagger, \pi) = 0$ return $\bot$.

3°. Run wit$' \leftarrow$ DMWI.Prove(crs$_{\mathsf{DMWI}}$, stmt, wit; r) and arg $\leftarrow O_{\mathsf{Prove}}($stmt, wit$')$.

$3^\dagger$. Run arg $\leftarrow O_{\mathsf{Prove}}($stmt, wit$)$.

4. Run vk$_s \leftarrow O_{\mathsf{Verify}}($stmt$)$.

5. If Sig.Verify(vk_s, arg, stmt) $\neq 1$ return $\perp$.
6. Otherwise, return arg.

Verify(crs, stmt, arg):
  1. Run $\mathsf{vk}_s \leftarrow O_{\mathsf{Verify}}(\mathsf{stmt})$.
  2. Output Sig.Verify(vk_s, sig, msg)

Expl(crs, stmt, wit, arg):
  1. Output 0.

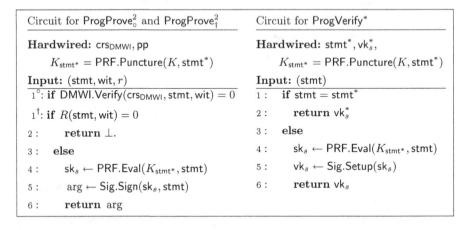

Circuit for $\mathsf{ProgProve}_\circ^2$ and $\mathsf{ProgProve}_\dagger^2$	Circuit for $\mathsf{ProgVerify}^*$
Hardwired: $\mathsf{crs}_{\mathsf{DMWI}}$, pp $\quad K_{\mathsf{stmt}^*} = \mathsf{PRF.Puncture}(K, \mathsf{stmt}^*)$	**Hardwired:** $\mathsf{stmt}^*, \mathsf{vk}_s^*$, $\quad K_{\mathsf{stmt}^*} = \mathsf{PRF.Puncture}(K, \mathsf{stmt}^*)$
Input: (stmt, wit, r)	**Input:** (stmt)
1°: **if** $\mathsf{DMWI.Verify}(\mathsf{crs}_{\mathsf{DMWI}}, \mathsf{stmt}, \mathsf{wit}) = 0$	1 : **if** stmt = stmt^*
$1^\dagger$: **if** $R(\mathsf{stmt}, \mathsf{wit}) = 0$	2 : **return** vk_s^*
2 : **return** $\perp$.	3 : **else**
3 : **else**	4 : $\mathsf{sk}_s \leftarrow \mathsf{PRF.Eval}(K_{\mathsf{stmt}^*}, \mathsf{stmt})$
4 : $\mathsf{sk}_s \leftarrow \mathsf{PRF.Eval}(K_{\mathsf{stmt}^*}, \mathsf{stmt})$	5 : $\mathsf{vk}_s \leftarrow \mathsf{Sig.Setup}(\mathsf{sk}_s)$
5 : $\mathsf{arg} \leftarrow \mathsf{Sig.Sign}(\mathsf{sk}_s, \mathsf{stmt})$	6 : **return** vk_s
6 : **return** arg	

Fig. 2. Circuits for $\mathsf{ProgProve}_\circ^2$, $\mathsf{ProgProve}_\dagger^2$ and $\mathsf{ProgVerify}^*$ used in the soundness proof of the non-interactive argument.

Theorem 5. *Let* ExArg° *be the system given by Scheme 1. The system* ExArg° *is computationally sound (in the selective setting) assuming indistinguishability obfuscation of* Obf, *pseudorandomness in punctured points of* PRF, *mode indistinguishability of the* DMWI *scheme, and unforgeability of the signature scheme (Fig. 2).*

Theorem 6. *Given that the signature scheme* Sig *is unique,* NIWI *is perfectly sound,* DMWI *is a dual-mode proof, and all primitives are perfectly correct, the argument system* ExArg° *is malicious setup explainable.*

Theorem 7. *Let* $\mathsf{ExArg}^\dagger$ *be the system given by Scheme 1. The system* $\mathsf{ExArg}^\dagger$ *is computationally sound (in the selective setting), assuming indistinguishability obfuscation of* Obf, *pseudorandomness in punctured points of* PRF, *zero-knowledge of the* NIZK *scheme and unforgeability of the signature scheme.*

Theorem 8. *Given that the signature scheme* Sig *is unique,* NIZK *is sound, and all primitives are perfectly correct, argument system* $\mathsf{ExArg}^\dagger$ *is fully explainable.*

Corollary 1. *The scheme is witness indistinguishable against a malicious setup.*

Proof. Witness indistinguishability follows from explainability of the argument system and Theorem 2.

Theorem 9. *Let* ExArg^∇ *be the system given by Scheme 1 for* $\nabla = \circ$ *or* $\nabla = \dagger$. ExArg^∇ *is zero-knowledge in the common reference string model.*

5 Robust-Witness Encryption and Interactive Explainable Arguments

We introduce robust witness encryption and show a generic transformation from any standard witness encryption scheme to a robust witness encryption scheme.

Definition 11 (Robust Witness Encryption). *We call a witness encryption scheme* $\mathsf{WE} = (\mathsf{Enc}, \mathsf{Dec})$ *a robust witness encryption scheme if it is correct, secure and robust as defined below:*

Robustness: *A witness encryption scheme* $(\mathsf{Enc}, \mathsf{Dec})$ *is robust if for all PPT adversaries* $\mathcal{A}$ *there exists a negligible function* $\mathsf{negl}(.)$ *such that*

$$\Pr\left[m_0 \neq m_1 : \begin{array}{c} \mathcal{R}(\mathsf{stmt}, \mathsf{wit}_0) = \mathcal{R}(\mathsf{stmt}, \mathsf{wit}_1) = 1 \wedge \\ (\mathsf{stmt}, \mathsf{ct}, \mathsf{wit}_0, \mathsf{wit}_1) \leftarrow \mathcal{A}(\lambda); \\ m_0 \leftarrow \mathsf{Dec}(\mathsf{stmt}, \mathsf{wit}_0, \mathsf{ct}) \\ m_1 \leftarrow \mathsf{Dec}(\mathsf{stmt}, \mathsf{wit}_1, \mathsf{ct}) \end{array} \right] \leq \mathsf{negl}(\lambda),$$

We call the scheme perfectly robust if the above probability is always zero.

Below we define plaintext awareness [5], but tailored to the case of witness encryption.

Definition 12 (Plaintext Aware Witness Encryption). *Let* $\mathsf{WE} = (\mathsf{Enc}, \mathsf{Dec})$ *be a witness encryption scheme. We extend the scheme with an algorithm* Verify *that on input a ciphertext* ct *and a statement* stmt *outputs a bit indicating whether the ciphertext is in the ciphertext space or not. Additionally we define an algorithm* Setup *that on input the security parameter* λ *outputs a common reference string* crs, *and an algorithm* Setup^* *that additionally outputs* τ. *We say that the witness encryption scheme for a language* $L \in \mathbf{NP}$ *is plaintext aware if for all PPT adversaries* $\mathcal{A}$, *there exists a negligible function* $\mathsf{negl}(.)$ *such that*

$$| \Pr[\mathcal{A}(\mathsf{crs}) = 1 : \mathsf{crs} \leftarrow \mathsf{Setup}(\lambda)]$$
$$- \Pr[\mathcal{A}(\mathsf{crs}) = 0 : (\mathsf{crs}, \tau) \leftarrow \mathsf{Setup}^*(\lambda)]| \leq \mathsf{negl}(\lambda),$$

and there exists a PPT extractor Ext *such that*

$$\Pr\left[\mathsf{msg} \leftarrow \mathsf{Ext}(\mathsf{stmt}, \mathsf{ct}, \tau) : \begin{array}{c} (\mathsf{crs}, \tau) \leftarrow \mathsf{Setup}^*(\lambda); \\ (\mathsf{ct}, \mathsf{stmt}) \leftarrow \mathcal{A}(\mathsf{crs}); \\ \mathsf{Verify}(\mathsf{stmt}, \mathsf{ct}) = 1 \end{array} \right] \leq 1 - \mathsf{negl}(\lambda)$$

where for all witnesses wit *such that* $\mathcal{R}(\mathsf{stmt}, \mathsf{wit}) = 1$ *we have* $\mathsf{msg} = \mathsf{Dec}(\mathsf{ct}, \mathsf{wit})$, *and the probability is taken over the random coins of* Setup *and* Setup^*.

Scheme 2 (Generic Transformation). Let $\mathsf{WE} = (\mathsf{Enc}, \mathsf{Dec})$ be a witness encryption scheme and $\mathsf{NIZK} = (\mathsf{NIZK.Prove}, \mathsf{NIZK.Verify})$ be a proof system. We construct a robust witness encryption scheme WE_{rob} as follows.

$\mathsf{Enc}_{rob}(\lambda, \mathsf{stmt}, \mathsf{msg})$:

1. Compute $\mathsf{ct}_{\mathsf{msg}} \leftarrow \mathsf{WE.Enc}(\lambda, \mathsf{stmt}, \mathsf{msg})$
2. Let $\mathsf{stmt}_{\mathsf{NIZK}}$ be defined as
   $\{\exists_{\mathsf{msg}}\ \mathsf{ct}_{\mathsf{msg}} \leftarrow \mathsf{WE.Enc}(\lambda, \mathsf{stmt}, \mathsf{msg})\}$
3. Compute $\pi \leftarrow \mathsf{NIZK.Prove}(\mathsf{stmt}_{\mathsf{NIZK}}, \mathsf{wit})$ using witness $\mathsf{wit} = (\mathsf{msg})$
4. Return $\mathsf{ct} = (\mathsf{ct}_{\mathsf{msg}}, \pi)$.

$\mathsf{Dec}_{rob}(\mathsf{stmt}, \mathsf{wit}, \mathsf{ct})$:

1. Set the statement $\mathsf{stmt}_{\mathsf{NIZK}}$ as
   $\{\exists_{\mathsf{msg}}\ \mathsf{ct}_{\mathsf{msg}} \leftarrow \mathsf{WE.Enc}(\lambda, \mathsf{stmt}, \mathsf{msg})\}$
2. If $\mathsf{NIZK.Verify}(\mathsf{stmt}_{\mathsf{NIZK}}, \pi) = 0$, then return $\bot$. Otherwise return $\mathsf{WE.Dec}(\mathsf{stmt}, \mathsf{wit}, \mathsf{ct}_{\mathsf{msg}})$

Theorem 10 (Security and Extractability). *Scheme 2 is a (extractably) secure witness encryption if* WE *is a (extractably) secure witness encryption, and* NIZK *is zero-knowledge (in the common reference string or RO model).*

Theorem 11 (Robustness and Plaintext Awareness). *Scheme 2 is robust if the witness encryption scheme* WE *is perfectly correct, and the* NIZK *proof system is perfectly sound (in the common reference string or RO model). If the* NIZK *proof system is a proof of knowledge (in the common string or RO model), then Scheme 2 is plaintext aware.*

5.1   Fully Explainable Arguments from Robust Witness Encryption

In this subsection, we will tackle the problem of constructing fully explainable arguments. The system is described in more detail by Scheme 3.

Scheme 3 (Interactive Explainable Argument). The argument system consists of Prove, Verify and Expl, where the protocol between Prove and Verify is specified as follows. Prove takes as input a statement stmt and a witness wit, and Verify takes as input stmt. First Verify chooses $r \leftarrow_\$ \{0,1\}^\lambda$, computes $\mathsf{ct} \leftarrow \mathsf{Enc}_{rob}(\lambda, \mathsf{stmt}, r)$ and sends ct to Prove. Then Prove computes $\mathsf{arg} \leftarrow \mathsf{Dec}_{rob}(\mathsf{stmt}, \mathsf{wit}, \mathsf{ct})$ and sends arg to Verify. Finally, Verify returns iff $\mathsf{arg} = r$. The explain algorithm Expl is as follows.

Expl(stmt, wit, trans): On input the statement stmt, the witness wit and a transcript trans, output $\bot$.

Theorem 12 (Soundness). *Scheme 3 is an argument system for* NP *language L assuming the witness encryption scheme* WE *for L is secure. Furthermore, if the underlying witness encryption scheme* WE *scheme is extractable, then Scheme 3 is an argument of knowledge.*

Theorem 13 (Zero-Knowledge). *Scheme 3 is zero-knowledge given the underlying witness encryption scheme* WE *is plaintext aware.*

Theorem 14 (Explainability). *Scheme 3 is fully explainable assuming the used witness encryption scheme is robust (or plaintext aware) and correct.*

Remark 2. Scheme 3 is predictable in the sense that the verifier can "predict" the value of the prover's arguments/proof [33]. Furthermore, the protocol is optimally laconic [12], as the verifier can encrypt single bits.

Theorem 15. *Let* WE *be a (non-robust) perfectly correct witness encryption scheme for* NP. *Let* Π *be an interactive public-coin zero-knowledge proof protocol for* NP. *Then there exists a malicious verifier explainable (and witness-indistinguishable) argument for* NP.

6 Applications

In this section, we show how to apply explainable arguments. We focus on constructing a CCA1 secure publicly deniable encryption scheme using as a building block malicious verifier explainable arguments. Our transformation is based on the one from Naor and Yung [56] but we replace the NIZK proof system with a NIWI. In the full version we show how to build a deniable anonymous credential scheme from malicious prover explainable arguments. Here we note that the anonymous credential system is a straightforward application of malicious prover explainable arguments and standard signature schemes.

The main idea behind the Naor and Yung construction is to use two CPA secure ciphertexts ct_1, ct_2 and a NIZK that both contain the same plaintext. The soundness property ensures that a decryption oracle can use either of the secret keys (since the decrypted message would be the same) and zero-knowledge allows the security reduction to change the challenged ciphertext, i.e. change the two CPA ciphertexts. We note that in our approach we replace NIZK with NIWI, that to the best of our knowledge has not been do before.

Scheme 4 (Generic Transformation from CPA to CCA). Let $\mathcal{E} =$ (KeyGen$_{cpa}$, Enc$_{cpa}$, Dec$_{cpa}$) be a CPA secure encryption scheme, (NIWI.Setup, NIWI.Prove, NIWI.Verify) be a non-interactive witness-indistinguishable proof system. Additionally we define the following statement stmt$_{cpa}$ be defined as

$$\{((\exists_{msg}\ ct_1 \leftarrow Enc_{cpa}(pk_1, msg) \wedge ct_2 \leftarrow Enc_{cpa}(pk_2, msg)) \vee$$
$$(\exists_{\alpha,\beta}\mathcal{H}_{\mathbb{G}}(ct_1, ct_2) = (g^\alpha, g^\beta, g^{\alpha\cdot\beta}))\},$$

where $\mathcal{H}_{\mathbb{G}}$ is defined as above.

KeyGen$_{cca1}(\lambda)$:
   1. generate CPA secure encryption key pairs $(pk_1, sk_1) \leftarrow$ KeyGen$_{cpa}(\lambda)$ and $(pk_2, sk_2) \leftarrow$ KeyGen$_{cpa}(\lambda)$,
   2. generate a common reference string crs $\leftarrow$ NIWI.Setup(λ),
   3. set $pk_{cca1} = (pk_1, pk_2, crs)$ and $sk_{cca1} = sk_1$.
Enc$_{cca1}(pk_{cca1}, msg)$:

1. compute ciphertexts $ct_1 \leftarrow Enc_{cpa}(pk_1, msg)$ and $ct_2 \leftarrow Enc_{cpa}(pk_2, msg)$,
2. compute NIWI proof $\Pi \leftarrow$ NIWI.Prove$(crs, stmt_{cpa}, (msg)$,
3. return ciphertext $ct = (ct_1, ct_2, \Pi)$.

$Dec_{cca1}(sk_{cca1}, ct)$:
1. return $\bot$ if NIWI.Verify$(crs, stmt_{cpa}, \Pi) = 0$,
2. return $msg \leftarrow Dec_{cpa}(sk_1, ct_1)$.

Theorem 16. *Scheme 4 is an encryption scheme secure against non-adaptive chosen ciphertext attacks (CCA1) in the random oracle model assuming the encryption scheme $\mathcal{E}$ is an encryption scheme secure against chosen plaintext attacks and* NIWI *is a sound and witness indistinguishable proof system.*

Theorem 17. *Scheme 4 is an publicly deniable encryption scheme secure against non-adaptive chosen ciphertext attacks (CCA1) in the random oracle model assuming the encryption scheme $\mathcal{E}$ is an publicly deniable encryption scheme secure against chosen plaintext attacks and* NIWI *is a malicious setup explainable argument system.*

7   Conclusions

In this paper, we introduce new security definitions for interactive and non-interactive argument systems that formally capture a property called explainability. Such arguments can be used to construct CCA1 deniable encryption and deniable anonymous authentication. We also introduced a new property for witness encryption called robustness which can be of independent interest. An interesting open question is whether such arguments systems can be constructed from simpler primitives or we need such strong primitives because malicious prover explainability implies uniqueness of the proof.

Acknowledgements. This work has been partially funded/supported by the German Ministry for Education and Research through funding for the project CISPA-Stanford Center for Cybersecurity (Funding numbers: 16KIS0762 and 16KIS0927).

References

1. Apon, D., Fan, X., Liu, F.-H.: Deniable attribute based encryption for branching programs from LWE. In: Hirt, M., Smith, A. (eds.) TCC 2016-B, Part II. LNCS, vol. 9986, pp. 299–329. Springer, Heidelberg (2016). https://doi.org/10.1007/978-3-662-53644-5_12
2. Babai, L., Moran, S.: Arthur-merlin games: a randomized proof system, and a hierarchy of complexity classes. J. Comput. Syst. Sci. **36**(2), 254–276 (1988)
3. Barak, B., et al.: On the (im)possibility of obfuscating programs. In: Kilian, J. (ed.) CRYPTO 2001. LNCS, vol. 2139, pp. 1–18. Springer, Heidelberg (2001). https://doi.org/10.1007/3-540-44647-8_1
4. Barak, B., Ong, S.J., Vadhan, S.: Derandomization in cryptography. In: Boneh, D. (ed.) CRYPTO 2003. LNCS, vol. 2729, pp. 299–315. Springer, Heidelberg (2003). https://doi.org/10.1007/978-3-540-45146-4_18

5. Bellare, M., Rogaway, P.: Optimal asymmetric encryption. In: De Santis, A. (ed.) EUROCRYPT 1994. LNCS, vol. 950, pp. 92–111. Springer, Heidelberg (1995). https://doi.org/10.1007/BFb0053428

6. Benaloh, J.C., Tuinstra, D.: Receipt-free secret-ballot elections (extended abstract). In: 26th ACM STOC, pp. 544–553. ACM Press, May 1994

7. Bendlin, R., Nielsen, J.B., Nordholt, P.S., Orlandi, C.: Lower and upper bounds for deniable public-key encryption. In: Lee, D.H., Wang, X. (eds.) ASIACRYPT 2011. LNCS, vol. 7073, pp. 125–142. Springer, Heidelberg (2011). https://doi.org/10.1007/978-3-642-25385-0_7

8. Bitansky, N., Choudhuri, A.R.: Characterizing deterministic-prover zero knowledge. In: Pass, R., Pietrzak, K. (eds.) TCC 2020, Part I. LNCS, vol. 12550, pp. 535–566. Springer, Cham (2020). https://doi.org/10.1007/978-3-030-64375-1_19

9. Bitansky, N., Paneth, O.: ZAPs and non-interactive witness indistinguishability from indistinguishability obfuscation. In: Dodis, Y., Nielsen, J.B. (eds.) TCC 2015, Part II. LNCS, vol. 9015, pp. 401–427. Springer, Heidelberg (2015). https://doi.org/10.1007/978-3-662-46497-7_16

10. Blum, M., Feldman, P., Micali, S.: Non-interactive zero-knowledge and its applications (extended abstract). In: 20th ACM STOC, pp. 103–112. ACM Press, May 1988

11. Bohli, J.-M., Steinwandt, R.: Deniable group key agreement. In: Nguyen, P.Q. (ed.) VIETCRYPT 2006. LNCS, vol. 4341, pp. 298–311. Springer, Heidelberg (2006). https://doi.org/10.1007/11958239_20

12. Boneh, D., Ishai, Y., Sahai, A., Wu, D.J.: Quasi-optimal SNARGs via linear multi-prover interactive proofs. In: Nielsen, J.B., Rijmen, V. (eds.) EUROCRYPT 2018, Part III. LNCS, vol. 10822, pp. 222–255. Springer, Cham (2018). https://doi.org/10.1007/978-3-319-78372-7_8

13. Boneh, D., Waters, B.: Constrained pseudorandom functions and their applications. In: Sako, K., Sarkar, P. (eds.) ASIACRYPT 2013, Part II. LNCS, vol. 8270, pp. 280–300. Springer, Heidelberg (2013). https://doi.org/10.1007/978-3-642-42045-0_15

14. Boyle, E., Goldwasser, S., Ivan, I.: Functional signatures and pseudorandom functions. In: Krawczyk, H. (ed.) PKC 2014. LNCS, vol. 8383, pp. 501–519. Springer, Heidelberg (2014). https://doi.org/10.1007/978-3-642-54631-0_29

15. Canetti, R., Dwork, C., Naor, M., Ostrovsky, R.: Deniable encryption. In: Kaliski, B.S. (ed.) CRYPTO 1997. LNCS, vol. 1294, pp. 90–104. Springer, Heidelberg (1997). https://doi.org/10.1007/BFb0052229

16. Canetti, R., Park, S., Poburinnaya, O.: Fully deniable interactive encryption. In: Micciancio, D., Ristenpart, T. (eds.) CRYPTO 2020, Part I. LNCS, vol. 12170, pp. 807–835. Springer, Cham (2020). https://doi.org/10.1007/978-3-030-56784-2_27

17. Chaidos, P., Cortier, V., Fuchsbauer, G., Galindo, D.: BeleniosRF: a non-interactive receipt-free electronic voting scheme. In: Weippl, E.R., Katzenbeisser, S., Kruegel, C., Myers, A.C., Halevi, S. (eds.) ACM CCS 2016, pp. 1614–1625. ACM Press, October 2016

18. Chakraborty, S., Prabhakaran, M., Wichs, D.: Witness maps and applications. In: Kiayias, A., Kohlweiss, M., Wallden, P., Zikas, V. (eds.) PKC 2020, Part I. LNCS, vol. 12110, pp. 220–246. Springer, Cham (2020). https://doi.org/10.1007/978-3-030-45374-9_8

19. Cramer, R., Shoup, V.: Signature schemes based on the strong RSA assumption. In: Motiwalla, J., Tsudik, G. (eds.) ACM CCS 1999, pp. 46–51. ACM Press, November 1999

20. Dachman-Soled, D.: On the impossibility of sender-deniable public key encryption. Cryptology ePrint Archive, Report 2012/727 (2012). https://eprint.iacr.org/2012/727

21. Dachman-Soled, D.: A black-box construction of a CCA2 encryption scheme from a plaintext aware (sPA1) encryption scheme. In: Krawczyk, H. (ed.) PKC 2014. LNCS, vol. 8383, pp. 37–55. Springer, Heidelberg (2014). https://doi.org/10.1007/978-3-642-54631-0_3

22. De Caro, A., Iovino, V., O'Neill, A.: Deniable functional encryption. In: Cheng, C.-M., Chung, K.-M., Persiano, G., Yang, B.-Y. (eds.) PKC 2016, Part II. LNCS, vol. 9614, pp. 196–222. Springer, Heidelberg (2016). https://doi.org/10.1007/978-3-662-49384-7_8

23. De Santis, A., Micali, S., Persiano, G.: Non-interactive zero-knowledge proof systems. In: Pomerance, C. (ed.) CRYPTO 1987. LNCS, vol. 293, pp. 52–72. Springer, Heidelberg (1988). https://doi.org/10.1007/3-540-48184-2_5

24. Di Raimondo, M., Gennaro, R.: New approaches for deniable authentication. In: Atluri, V., Meadows, C., Juels, A. (eds.) ACM CCS 2005, pp. 112–121. ACM Press, November 2005

25. Di Raimondo, M., Gennaro, R.: New approaches for deniable authentication. J. Cryptol. $22(4)$, 572–615 (2009)

26. Di Raimondo, M., Gennaro, R., Krawczyk, H.: Deniable authentication and key exchange. In: Juels, A., Wright, R.N., Capitani di Vimercati, S.D. (eds.) ACM CCS 2006, pp. 400–409. ACM Press, October/November 2006

27. Dodis, Y., Fiore, D.: Interactive encryption and message authentication. In: Abdalla, M., De Prisco, R. (eds.) SCN 2014. LNCS, vol. 8642, pp. 494–513. Springer, Cham (2014). https://doi.org/10.1007/978-3-319-10879-7_28

28. Dodis, Y., Katz, J., Smith, A., Walfish, S.: Composability and on-line deniability of authentication. In: Reingold, O. (ed.) TCC 2009. LNCS, vol. 5444, pp. 146–162. Springer, Heidelberg (2009). https://doi.org/10.1007/978-3-642-00457-5_10

29. Dodis, Y., Yampolskiy, A.: A verifiable random function with short proofs and keys. In: Vaudenay, S. (ed.) PKC 2005. LNCS, vol. 3386, pp. 416–431. Springer, Heidelberg (2005). https://doi.org/10.1007/978-3-540-30580-4_28

30. Dolev, D., Dwork, C., Naor, M.: Non-malleable cryptography (extended abstract). In: 23rd ACM STOC, pp. 542–552. ACM Press, May 1991

31. Dwork, C., Naor, M.: Zaps and their applications. In: 41st FOCS, pp. 283–293. IEEE Computer Society Press, November 2000

32. Dwork, C., Naor, M., Sahai, A.: Concurrent zero-knowledge. In: 30th ACM STOC, pp. 409–418. ACM Press, May 1998

33. Faonio, A., Nielsen, J.B., Venturi, D.: Predictable arguments of knowledge. In: Fehr, S. (ed.) PKC 2017, Part I. LNCS, vol. 10174, pp. 121–150. Springer, Heidelberg (2017). https://doi.org/10.1007/978-3-662-54365-8_6

34. Feige, U., Lapidot, D., Shamir, A.: Multiple noninteractive zero knowledge proofs under general assumptions. SIAM J. Comput. $29(1)$, 1–28 (1999)

35. Fiat, A., Shamir, A.: How to prove yourself: practical solutions to identification and signature problems. In: Odlyzko, A.M. (ed.) CRYPTO 1986. LNCS, vol. 263, pp. 186–194. Springer, Heidelberg (1987). https://doi.org/10.1007/3-540-47721-7_12

36. Garg, S., Gentry, C., Sahai, A., Waters, B.: Witness encryption and its applications. In: Boneh, D., Roughgarden, T., Feigenbaum, J. (eds.) 45th ACM STOC, pp. 467–476. ACM Press, June 2013

37. Gennaro, R., Halevi, S., Rabin, T.: Secure hash-and-sign signatures without the random oracle. In: Stern, J. (ed.) EUROCRYPT 1999. LNCS, vol. 1592, pp. 123–139. Springer, Heidelberg (1999). https://doi.org/10.1007/3-540-48910-X_9

38. Goldreich, O.: Basing non-interactive zero-knowledge on (enhanced) trapdoor permutations: the state of the art. In: Goldreich, O. (ed.) Studies in Complexity and Cryptography. Miscellanea on the Interplay between Randomness and Computation. LNCS, vol. 6650, pp. 406–421. Springer, Heidelberg (2011). https://doi.org/10.1007/978-3-642-22670-0_28

39. Goldreich, O., Levin, L.A.: A hard-core predicate for all one-way functions. In: 21st ACM STOC, pp. 25–32. ACM Press, May 1989

40. Goldwasser, S., Kalai, Y.T., Popa, R.A., Vaikuntanathan, V., Zeldovich, N.: How to run turing machines on encrypted data. In: Canetti, R., Garay, J.A. (eds.) CRYPTO 2013, Part II. LNCS, vol. 8043, pp. 536–553. Springer, Heidelberg (2013). https://doi.org/10.1007/978-3-642-40084-1_30

41. Goldwasser, S., Klein, S., Wichs, D.: The edited truth. In: Kalai, Y., Reyzin, L. (eds.) TCC 2017, Part I. LNCS, vol. 10677, pp. 305–340. Springer, Cham (2017). https://doi.org/10.1007/978-3-319-70500-2_11

42. Goldwasser, S., Ostrovsky, R.: *Invariant* signatures and non-interactive zero-knowledge proofs are equivalent. In: Brickell, E.F. (ed.) CRYPTO 1992. LNCS, vol. 740, pp. 228–245. Springer, Heidelberg (1993). https://doi.org/10.1007/3-540-48071-4_16

43. Groth, J., Ostrovsky, R., Sahai, A.: Non-interactive zaps and new techniques for NIZK. In: Dwork, C. (ed.) CRYPTO 2006. LNCS, vol. 4117, pp. 97–111. Springer, Heidelberg (2006). https://doi.org/10.1007/11818175_6

44. Groth, J., Ostrovsky, R., Sahai, A.: Perfect non-interactive zero knowledge for NP. In: Vaudenay, S. (ed.) EUROCRYPT 2006. LNCS, vol. 4004, pp. 339–358. Springer, Heidelberg (2006). https://doi.org/10.1007/11761679_21

45. Hanzlik, L., Kluczniak, K.: Explainable arguments. Cryptology ePrint Archive, Report 2021/xxxx (2021, to appear). https://ia.cr/2021/xxxx

46. Hanzlik, L., Kluczniak, K., Kutyłowski, M., Krzywiecki, Ł: Mutual restricted identification. In: Katsikas, S., Agudo, I. (eds.) EuroPKI 2013. LNCS, vol. 8341, pp. 119–133. Springer, Heidelberg (2014). https://doi.org/10.1007/978-3-642-53997-8_8

47. Hirt, M., Sako, K.: Efficient receipt-free voting based on homomorphic encryption. In: Preneel, B. (ed.) EUROCRYPT 2000. LNCS, vol. 1807, pp. 539–556. Springer, Heidelberg (2000). https://doi.org/10.1007/3-540-45539-6_38

48. Jakobsson, M., Sako, K., Impagliazzo, R.: Designated verifier proofs and their applications. In: Maurer, U. (ed.) EUROCRYPT 1996. LNCS, vol. 1070, pp. 143–154. Springer, Heidelberg (1996). https://doi.org/10.1007/3-540-68339-9_13

49. Jiang, S., Safavi-Naini, R.: An efficient deniable key exchange protocol (extended abstract). In: Tsudik, G. (ed.) FC 2008. LNCS, vol. 5143, pp. 47–52. Springer, Heidelberg (2008). https://doi.org/10.1007/978-3-540-85230-8_4

50. Kiayias, A., Papadopoulos, S., Triandopoulos, N., Zacharias, T.: Delegatable pseudorandom functions and applications. In: Sadeghi, A.-R., Gligor, V.D., Yung, M. (eds.) ACM CCS 2013, pp. 669–684. ACM Press, November 2013

51. Krzywiecki, L., Kluczniak, K., Kozieł, P., Panwar, N.: Privacy-oriented dependency via deniable sigma protocol. Comput. Secur. **79**, 53–67 (2018)

52. Lysyanskaya, A.: Unique signatures and verifiable random functions from the DH-DDH separation. In: Yung, M. (ed.) CRYPTO 2002. LNCS, vol. 2442, pp. 597–612. Springer, Heidelberg (2002). https://doi.org/10.1007/3-540-45708-9_38

53. Micali, S., Rabin, M.O., Vadhan, S.P.: Verifiable random functions. In: 40th FOCS, pp. 120–130. IEEE Computer Society Press, October 1999

54. Moran, T., Naor, M.: Receipt-free universally-verifiable voting with everlasting privacy. In: Dwork, C. (ed.) CRYPTO 2006. LNCS, vol. 4117, pp. 373–392. Springer, Heidelberg (2006). https://doi.org/10.1007/11818175_22

55. Naor, M.: Deniable ring authentication. In: Yung, M. (ed.) CRYPTO 2002. LNCS, vol. 2442, pp. 481–498. Springer, Heidelberg (2002). https://doi.org/10.1007/3-540-45708-9_31

56. Naor, M., Yung, M.: Public-key cryptosystems provably secure against chosen ciphertext attacks. In: 22nd ACM STOC, pp. 427–437. ACM Press, May 1990

57. O'Neill, A., Peikert, C., Waters, B.: Bi-deniable public-key encryption. In: Rogaway, P. (ed.) CRYPTO 2011. LNCS, vol. 6841, pp. 525–542. Springer, Heidelberg (2011). https://doi.org/10.1007/978-3-642-22792-9_30

58. Park, S., Sealfon, A.: It wasn't me! Repudiability and claimability of ring signatures. In: Boldyreva, A., Micciancio, D. (eds.) CRYPTO 2019, Part III. LNCS, vol. 11694, pp. 159–190. Springer, Cham (2019). https://doi.org/10.1007/978-3-030-26954-8_6

59. Pass, R.: On deniability in the common reference string and random oracle model. In: Boneh, D. (ed.) CRYPTO 2003. LNCS, vol. 2729, pp. 316–337. Springer, Heidelberg (2003). https://doi.org/10.1007/978-3-540-45146-4_19

60. Peikert, C., Shiehian, S.: Noninteractive zero knowledge for NP from (plain) learning with errors. In: Boldyreva, A., Micciancio, D. (eds.) CRYPTO 2019, Part I. LNCS, vol. 11692, pp. 89–114. Springer, Cham (2019). https://doi.org/10.1007/978-3-030-26948-7_4

61. Rivest, R.L., Shamir, A., Tauman, Y.: How to leak a secret. In: Boyd, C. (ed.) ASIACRYPT 2001. LNCS, vol. 2248, pp. 552–565. Springer, Heidelberg (2001). https://doi.org/10.1007/3-540-45682-1_32

62. Ryan, P.Y.A., Rønne, P.B., Iovino, V.: Selene: voting with transparent verifiability and coercion-mitigation. In: Clark, J., Meiklejohn, S., Ryan, P.Y.A., Wallach, D., Brenner, M., Rohloff, K. (eds.) FC 2016. LNCS, vol. 9604, pp. 176–192. Springer, Heidelberg (2016). https://doi.org/10.1007/978-3-662-53357-4_12

63. Sahai, A., Waters, B.: How to use indistinguishability obfuscation: deniable encryption, and more. In: Shmoys, D.B. (ed.) 46th ACM STOC, pp. 475–484. ACM Press, May/June (2014)

64. Sako, K., Kilian, J.: Receipt-free mix-type voting scheme. In: Guillou, L.C., Quisquater, J.-J. (eds.) EUROCRYPT 1995. LNCS, vol. 921, pp. 393–403. Springer, Heidelberg (1995). https://doi.org/10.1007/3-540-49264-X_32

65. Unger, N., Goldberg, I.: Improved strongly deniable authenticated key exchanges for secure messaging. Proc. Priv. Enhanc. Technol. **2018**(1), 21–66 (2018)

66. Unger, N., Goldberg, I.: Deniable key exchanges for secure messaging. In: Ray, I., Li, N., Kruegel, C. (eds.) ACM CCS 2015, pp. 1211–1223. ACM Press, October 2015

67. Vatandas, N., Gennaro, R., Ithurburn, B., Krawczyk, H.: On the cryptographic deniability of the signal protocol. In: Conti, M., Zhou, J., Casalicchio, E., Spognardi, A. (eds.) ACNS 2020, Part II. LNCS, vol. 12147, pp. 188–209. Springer, Cham (2020). https://doi.org/10.1007/978-3-030-57878-7_10

68. Yamada, S., Attrapadung, N., Santoso, B., Schuldt, J.C.N., Hanaoka, G., Kunihiro, N.: Verifiable predicate encryption and applications to CCA security and anonymous predicate authentication. In: Fischlin, M., Buchmann, J., Manulis, M. (eds.) PKC 2012. LNCS, vol. 7293, pp. 243–261. Springer, Heidelberg (2012). https://doi.org/10.1007/978-3-642-30057-8_15
69. Yao, A.C.-C., Zhao, Y.: Deniable internet key exchange. In: Zhou, J., Yung, M. (eds.) ACNS 2010. LNCS, vol. 6123, pp. 329–348. Springer, Heidelberg (2010). https://doi.org/10.1007/978-3-642-13708-2_20

MPCCache: Privacy-Preserving Multi-Party Cooperative Cache Sharing at the Edge

Duong Tung Nguyen and Ni Trieu[✉]

Arizona State University, Tempe, AZ, USA
{duongnt,nitrieu}@asu.edu

Abstract. We present MPCCache, an efficient **M**ulti-**P**arty **C**ooperative **Cache** sharing framework, which allows multiple network operators to determine a set of common data items with the highest access frequencies to be stored in their capacity-limited shared cache while guaranteeing the privacy of their individual datasets. The technical core of our MPCCache is a new construction that allows multiple parties to compute a specific function on the intersection set of their datasets, without revealing both the private data and the intersection itself to any party.

We evaluate our protocols to demonstrate their efficacy and practicality. The numerical results show that MPCCache scales well to large datasets and achieves a few hundred times faster compared to a baseline scheme that optimally combines existing MPC protocols.

1 Introduction

The explosive growth of data traffic due to the proliferation of wireless devices and bandwidth-hungry applications leads to an ever-increasing capacity demand across wireless networks to enable scalable wireless access with high quality of service (QoS). This trend will likely continue for the near future due to the emergence of new applications like augmented/virtual reality, 4K/8K UHD video, and tactile Internet [13]. Thus, it is imperative for mobile operators to develop cost-effective solutions to meet the soaring traffic demand and diverse requirements of various services in the next generation communication network.

Enabled by the drastic reduction in data storage cost, edge caching has appeared as a promising technology to tackle the aforementioned challenges in wireless networks [3]. In practice, many users in the same service area may request similar content such as highly-rated Netflix movies. Furthermore, most user requests are associated with a small amount of popular content. Hence, by proactively caching popular content at the network edge (e.g., at base stations, edge clouds) in advance during off-peak times, a portion of requests during peak hours can be served locally right at the edge instead of going all the way through the mobile core and the Internet to reach the origin servers. The new edge caching paradigm can significantly reduce duplicate data transmission, alleviate the backhaul capacity requirement, mitigate backbone network congestion, increase network throughput, and improve user experience [1,3,13,37].

© International Financial Cryptography Association 2022
I. Eyal and J. Garay (Eds.): FC 2022, LNCS 13411, pp. 80–99, 2022.
https://doi.org/10.1007/978-3-031-18283-9_5

Motivation. With edge caching, the advantages brought by cooperation become clear. Each operator can maintain a private cache and share a shared cache with others. Although the benefits of edge caching have been studied extensively in the previous literature along with many real-world deployments [1,3,37], most of the existing works on cooperative edge caching consider cooperation among edge caches owned by a single operator only [27,37,38]. The potential of cache cooperation among multiple operators has been overlooked. For cooperative cache sharing, the data privacy of individual Telcos is important. For example, if TelcoA knows the access pattern of subscribers of TelcoB, TelcoA can learn characteristics of TelcoB's subscribers and design incentive schemes and services to attract these subscribers to switch to TelcoA. Therefore, it is imperative to study various mechanisms that provide the benefits of cache sharing without compromising privacy.

Contributions. We introduce an MPCCache scheme to tackle the cooperative content caching problem at the network edge where multiple semi-honest parties (i.e., network operators) can jointly cache common data items in a shared cache. The problem is to identify the set of common items with the highest access frequency to be cached in the shared cache while respecting the privacy of each individual party. To the best of our knowledge, we are among the first to realize and formally examine the multi-party cooperative caching problem by exploiting the non-rivalry of cached data items, and tackle this problem through the lens of secure multi-party computation. We introduce an efficient construction that outputs only the result of a specific function computed securely on the intersection set, (i.e., find k best items in the intersection set) without revealing the private data of individual parties as well as the intersection itself to any party, and works for the multi-party setting with more than two parties. In addition, we propose an efficient top-k algorithm that achieves an approximate $\frac{\log^2(m)}{\left(\log(k)+2\right)\log(k)} \times$ improvement compared with the prior top-k algorithms, where m is the size of the dataset.

We demonstrate the practicality of our protocol with experimental numbers. For instance, for the setting of 8 parties each with a data-set of 2^{16} records, our decentralized protocol requires 5 min to compute k-priority common items for $k = 2^8$. We also propose an optimized server-aid MPCCache construction, which is scalable for large datasets and a number of parties. With 16 parties, each has 2^{20} records, our optimized scheme takes only 8 min to compute the k-priority common items for $k = 2^8$. MPCCache aims at proactive caching where caches are refreshed periodically (e.g., hourly). Therefore, the running time of MPCCache is practical in our application.

In addition to cooperative cache sharing as our main motivation, we believe that the proposed techniques can find applications in other areas as well.

2   Related Work and Technical Overview of MPCCache

Consider a single party with a set of items S. Each item includes an identity x (i.e., a file name, a content ID) and its associated value v. For each set S,

PARAMETERS: n parties $P_{i \in [n]}$, each has m_i items, a threshold k, where k is much smaller than the intersection size.

FUNCTIONALITY:

- Wait for an input $S_i = \{(x_1^i, v_1^i), \ldots, (x_{m_i}^i, v_{m_i}^i)\} \subset (\{0,1\}^\kappa, \{0,1\}^\theta)$ from P_i
- Let $I = \bigcap_{i \in [n]} \{x_1^i, \ldots, x_{m_i}^i\}$ to be the intersection set. For each $x^\star \in I$, compute the sum $v^\star$ of associated values, i.e., $v^\star = \sum_{i=1}^n v_{j_i}^i$ where $(x^\star, v_{j_i}^i) \in S_i$
- Give parties $\{x_1^\star, \ldots, x_k^\star\}$ where $v_1^\star, \ldots, v_k^\star$ are k largest numbers among $v_1^\star, \ldots, v_{|I|}^\star$.

Fig. 1. The MPCCache functionality

an element (x, v) is said to belong to a set of *k-priority* elements of S if its associated value v is one of the k-largest values in S. Note that the value of each content item may represent the number of predicted access frequency of the content or the benefit (valuation) of the operator for the cached content. Each network operator has its own criteria to define the value for each content that can be stored in the shared edge cache space. How to define the value for each content is beyond the scope of this work. In this work, we assume that the parties are truthful by using their true valuations for each content item in their databases. It is because the access frequency of each party to each cached file is measurable and known. Additionally, some economic penalty schemes can be used to enforce truthfulness as mentioned in the full version of the paper [25].

Since the cache is shared among the operators, they would like to store only common content items in the cache. Here, a common item refers to an item (based on identity) that is owned by every party. The common items with the highest values will be placed in the shared cache. The value of a common item is defined as the sum of the individual values of the operators for the item. Concretely, we consider the cooperative caching problem in the multi-party setting where each party P_i has a set $S_i = \{(x_1^i, v_1^i), \ldots, (x_{m_i}^i, v_{m_i}^i)\}$. Without loss of generality, we assume that all parties have the same set size m. An item $(x^\star, v^\star)$ is defined to belong to the set of the k-*priority common* elements if it satisfies the two following conditions: (1) $x^\star$ is the *common* identity of all parties; (2) $(x^\star, v^\star)$ are the *k-priority* elements of $S^\star = \{(x_1^\star, v_1^\star), \ldots, (x_{|I|}^\star, v_{|I|}^\star)\}$, where $v_i^\star$ is the sum of the values associated with these common identities from each party, and $I = \bigcap_{i \in [n]} \{x_1^i, \ldots, x_{m_i}^i\}$ is the intersection set with its size $|I|$. In the setting, we consider the input datasets of each P_i contain proprietary information, thus none of the parties are willing to share its data with the other. We describe the ideal functionality of MPCCache in Fig. 1. For simplicity, we remove under-script of the common item $x^\star$ and clarify that a pair $(x^\star, v_{j_i}^i) \in S_i$ belongs to P_i.

A closely related work to MPCCache is a private set intersection (PSI). Recall that the functionality of PSI enables n parties with respective input sets $X_{i \in [n]}$ to compute the intersection itself $\bigcap_{i \in [n]} X_i$ without revealing any information about the items which are not in the intersection. However, MPCCache requires to evaluate a top-K computation on the top of the intersection $\bigcap_{i \in [n]} X_i$ while also keeping the intersection secret from parties. The work [8,21,29,32] proposed optimized circuits for computing on the intersection by deciding which items of the parties need to be compared. However, their constructions only work for the two-party setting. Most of the existing multi-party PSI constructions [10,17,20,24,33] output the intersection itself. Only very few works [18,23] studied some specific functions on the intersection. While [18] does not deal with the intersection set of all parties (in particular, an item in the output set in [18] *is not necessarily a common item of all parties*), [23] finds common items with the highest preference (rank) among all parties. [23] can be extended to support MPCCache which is a general case of the rank computation. However, the extended protocol is very expensive since if an item has an associated value v, [23] represents the item by replicating it v times. For ranking, their solution is reasonable with small v but for our MPCCache it is not suitable since v can be a very large value. We describe a detailed discussion in the full version of the paper [25]. The work of [31] proposes MPCircuits, a customized MPC circuit. One can extend MPCircuits to identify the secret share of the intersection and use generic MPC protocols to compute a top-k function on the secret-shared intersection set. However, the number of secure comparisons inside MPCircuits is large and depends on the number of parties. A concurrent and independent work by Chandran et al. [7] is the state-of-the-art multi-party circuit-PSI, but only supports a weaker adversary, who may corrupt at most $t < n/2$ the parties. Moreover, in terms of theoretical complexity comparisons, [7] is expensive than ours. We explicitly compare our proposed MPCCache with the MPCircuits and [7] in Sect. 6.3.

Our decentralized MPCCache construction contains two main phases. The first one is to obliviously identify the common items (i.e., items in the intersection set) and aggregate their associated values of the common items in the multi-party setting. In particular, if all parties have the same $x^\star$ in their set, they obtain secret shares of the sum of the associated values $v^\star = \sum_{i=1}^n v_{j_i}^i$ where $(x^\star, v_{j_i}^i) \in S_i$. Otherwise, $v^\star$ equals to zero and it should not be counted as a k-priority element. A more detailed overview of the approach is presented in Sect. 4. It is worth mentioning that the first phase does not leak the intersection set to any party. The second phase takes these secret shares which are either the zero value or the correct sum of the associated values of common items, and outputs k-priority items. To privately choose the k-priority elements that are secret shared by n parties, one could study top-k algorithms.

In MPC setting, a popular method for securely finding the top-k elements is to use an oblivious sort (i.e., parties jointly sort the dataset in decreasing order of the associated values, and pick the k largest values). The most practical algorithm is Batcher's network [4], which computational and communication complexity are $O(m \log^2(m))$ and $O(\ell m \log^2(m))$, respectively, where m is the size of the dataset and ℓ is the bit-length of the element (see the full version of the paper [25] for more detail). To output the index of the k largest values, we also need to keep track of their indexes, therefore, the total communication complexity of oblivious Batcher's network is $O((\ell + \log(m))m \log^2(m))$. Another approach to compute k-priority elements is to use an oblivious heap that allows to get a maximum element from the heap (ExtractMax). This solution requires to call ExtractMax k times, which leads to a number of rounds of the interaction of at least $O(k \log(m))$.

In MPCCache, the size of an edge cache k is usually much smaller than the size of the dataset m. In addition, it is also much smaller than the caching facility at the core of the network operator. Since we are motivated by applications where $k \ll m$, we propose a new protocol with computational and communication overhead of $O(m \log^2(k))$ of secure comparisons and $O((\ell + \log(m))m \log^2(k))$ bits, respectively. Our protocol requires $O(\log(m))$ rounds. Concretely, we show an approximate $\dfrac{\log^2(m)}{\left(\log(k)+2\right)\log(k)} \times$ improvement compared with the prior work.

Recently, [9] presents an *approximate* top-K selection with complexity of $O(m+k^2)$ comparisons and $O((\ell+\log(m))(m+k^2))$ bits. One could integrate their algorithm in the second phase of our scheme to achieve better performance. In applications where *exact* top-K selection is required, our k-priority is preferable.

Our decentralized protocol supports the full corrupted majority, which means that if any subset of parties is corrupted, they learn nothing except the protocol output. In this paper, we also present the optimization for MPCCache in the non-colluding semi-honest setting in which we assume to know two non-colluding parties. This model can be considered as the server-aided model where clients obliviously distribute (secret share) their private database to two non-colluding servers. Our optimized server-aided MPCCache construction achieves almost the same cost as that of our two-party decentralized protocol.

3   Cryptographic Preliminaries

In this work, the computational and statistical security parameters are denoted by κ, λ, respectively. We use [.] notation to refer to a set, and $[i, j]$ to denote the set $\{i, \ldots, j\}$. The additive secret sharing of a value x is defined as $[\![x]\!]$.

Secret Sharing. To additively secret share $[\![x]\!]$ an ℓ-bit value x of the party P_i to other parties, he first chooses $x^i \leftarrow \mathbb{Z}_{2^\ell}$ uniformly at random such that $x = \sum_{j=1}^{n} x^j \mod 2^\ell$, and then sends each x^j to the party P_j. For ease of composition, we omit the mod. To reconstruct an additive shared value $[\![x]\!]$, all parties P_j sends $[\![x]\!] = x^j$ to the party P_i, who locally reconstructs the secret value by computing $x \leftarrow \sum_{i=1}^{n} x^j$. In this work, we also use Boolean sharing in the binary field. Boolean sharing can be seen as additive sharing in the field $\mathbb{Z}_2$.

Oblivious Key-Value Store (OKVS). An OKVS [14] is a data structure in which a sender, holding a set of key-value mapping $\Gamma = \{(k_i, v_i), i \in [n]\}$ with pseudo-random v_i, wishes to give that mapping over to a receiver who can evaluate the mapping on any input but without revealing the keys k_i. Formally, an OKVS consists of two algorithms: $\mathsf{Encode}(\Gamma) \to \mathcal{T}$ is a randomized algorithm that takes as input a set of n key-value pairs $\Gamma = \{(k_i, v_i)_{i \in [n]}\}$ from the domain $\mathcal{K} \times \mathcal{V}$, outputs a table $\mathcal{T}$; and $\mathsf{Decode}(k, \mathcal{T}) \to v$ is a deterministic algorithm that takes as input a table $\mathcal{T}$, a key k and outputs a value v.

The correctness of the OKVS is that if for all key-value pairs $A \subseteq \mathcal{K} \times \mathcal{V}$ with distinct keys and pseudo-random values, $\mathsf{Encode}(A) = \mathcal{T}$ and $(k, v) \in A$ then $\mathsf{Decode}(k, \mathcal{T}) = v$. An OKVS is secure if the values v_i are chosen uniformly then the output of Encode hides the choice of the keys k_i.

Garbled Circuit. An ideal functionality GC [5,16,36] is to take the inputs x_i from party P_i, and computes a function f on them without revealing the parties' inputs. We use Yao [36] and BMR-style protocols [5,6] for two-party and multi-party GC, respectively. In our protocol, we use f as "less than" and "equality" where inputs are secretly shared amongst all parties. For example, a "less than" GC takes the parties' secret shares $[\![x]\!]$ and $[\![y]\!]$ as input, and output the shares of 1 if $x < y$ and 0 otherwise. We denote the GC by $[\![z]\!] \leftarrow \mathcal{GC}([\![x]\!], [\![y]\!], f)$.

Oblivious Sort and Merge. The main building block of the sorting algorithm is Compare-Swap operation that takes the secret shares of two values x and y, then compares and swaps them if they are out of order. It is typical to measure the complexity of oblivious sort/merge based on the number of Compare-Swap.

Oblivious Sort: We denote the oblivious sorting by $\{[\![x_i]\!]_{i \in [m]}\} \leftarrow \mathcal{F}_{\mathsf{obv\text{-}sort}}(\{[\![x_i]\!]_{i \in [m]}\})$ which takes the secret share of m values and returns their refresh shares in which all $x_{i \in [m]}$ are sorted in decreasing order. As discussed in [25], Batcher's network for oblivious sort requires $\frac{1}{4}m \log^2(m)$ Compare-Swap operations.

Oblivious Merge: Given two sorted sequences, each of size m, we also need to merge them into a sorted array, which is part of the Batcher's oblivious merge sort. It is possible to divide the input sequences into their odd and even parts, and then combine them into an interleaved sequence. This oblivious merge requires $\frac{1}{2}m \log(m)$ Compare-Swap operations and has a depth of $\log(m)$. We denote the oblivious merge by $\{[\![z_1]\!], \ldots, [\![z_{2m}]\!]\} \leftarrow \mathcal{F}_{\mathsf{obv\text{-}merge}}(\{[\![x_1]\!], \ldots, [\![x_m]\!]\}, \{[\![y_1]\!], \ldots, [\![y_m]\!]\})$.

4   Our Decentralized MPCCache Construction

Recall that our MPCCache construction contains two main parts. The first phase allows parties to securely generate shares of the sum of the associated values under a condition. More precisely, if all parties have x in their sets then the sum of their obtained shares is equal to the sum of the associated values for the common x. Otherwise, the sum of the shares is zero. These shares are forwarded as input to the second phase, which ignores the zero sum and returns only k-priority common items. For the second phase, we first present the $\mathcal{F}_{\mathsf{k\text{-}prior}}$ functionality of computing k-*priority* elements in Fig. 2, and use it as a black box in our MPCCache construction. We describe our $\mathcal{F}_{\mathsf{k\text{-}prior}}$ construction in Sect. 4.3.

4.1   A Special Case of Our First Phase

We start with a special case. Suppose that each party $P_{i \in [n]}$ has only one item (x^i, v^i) in its set S_i. Our first phase must satisfy the following conditions:

PARAMETERS: Set size m, and n parties
FUNCTIONALITY:
- Wait for secret shares $\{[\![v_1]\!], ..., [\![v_m]\!]\}$ from the ith party.
- Give all parties k indexes $\{i_1, ..., i_k\}$ such that $\{v_{i_1}, ..., v_{i_k}\}$ are largest values among $\{v_1, ..., v_m\}$.

Fig. 2. The k-priority functionality ($\mathcal{F}_{\text{k-prior}}$)

(1) If all x^i are equal, the parties obtain secret shares of the sum of the associated values as $v^\star = \sum_{i=1}^n v^i$.
(2) Otherwise, the parties obtain secret shares of zero.
(3) The protocol is secure in the semi-honest model, against any number of corrupt, colluding parties.

The requirement (3) implies that all corrupt parties should learn nothing about the input of honest parties. To satisfying (3), the protocol must ensure that parties do not learn which of the cases (1) or (2) occurs.

We assume that there is a leader party (say P_1) who interacts with other parties to output (1). The protocol works as follows. For (x^i, v^i), $P_{i \neq 1}$ chooses a secret $s^i \in \{0,1\}^\theta$ uniformly at random, and defines $w^i \overset{\text{def}}{=} v^i - s^i$ (for ease of composition we omit the mod). He then computes a one-time pad as $\mathsf{OTP}(x^i, w^i) = x^i \oplus w^i$ (for simplicity, we assume that the domain size of x^i and w^i are equal; it is also possible to use $H(x^i)$ instead of the original item x^i, where $H : \{0,1\}^\star \to \{0,1\}^\star$ is a collision-resistant hash function). The $P_{i \neq 1}$ then sends the ciphertext to the leader P_1. Using his item x^1, the P_1 decrypts the received ciphertext and obtains w^i if $x^1 = x^i$, random otherwise. Clearly, if all parties have the same x^1, P_1 receives $w^i = v^i - s^i$ from $P_{i \neq 1}$. Now, P_1 computes $s^1 \overset{\text{def}}{=} v^1 + \sum_{i=2}^n w^i$. It easy to verify that $\sum_{i=1}^n s^i = (v^1 + \sum_{i=2}^n w^i) + \sum_{i=2}^n s^i = v^1 + \sum_{i=2}^n (w^i + s^i) = \sum_{i=1}^n v^i = v^\star$. By doing so, each P_i has an additive secret share s^i of $v^\star$ as required in (1).

In case that not all x^i are equal, the sum of all the shares $\sum_{i=1}^n s^i$ is a random value since P_1 receives a random (incorrect) w^i from some party/parties. To satisfy (2), we use GC to turn the random sum $\sum_{i=1}^n s^i$ to zero. However, for (3), the random sum and the correct sum are indistinguishable from the view of all parties. One might make use of GC by computing n equality comparisons to check whether all x^i is equal. If yes, the circuit gives refreshed shares of the correct sum, otherwise shares of zero. This solution requires $O(n)$ equality comparisons inside MPC. We aim to minimize the number of equality tests.

We improve the above solution using zero-sharing [2,20,22]. An advantage of the zero-sharing is that the party can non-interactively generate a Boolean share of zero after a one-time setup. Let's denote the zero share of P_i to be z^i. We have $\bigoplus_{i=1}^n z^i = 0$. Similar to the protocol described above to achieve (1): Instead of (x^i, v^i), the P_i uses (x^i, z^i) as input, and receives a Boolean secret share t^i. If all x^i are equal, the XOR of all obtained shares is equal to the XOR of all associated values z^i. In other words, $\bigoplus_{i=1}^n t^i = \bigoplus_{i=1}^n z^i = 0$. Otherwise, $\bigoplus_{i=1}^n t^i$

is random. These obtained shares are used as an `if` condition to output either (1) or (2). Concretely, parties jointly execute a garbled circuit to check whether $\bigoplus_{i=1}^{n} t^i = 0$. If yes (*i.e.* parties have the same item), the circuit re-randomizes the shares of $v^\star$, otherwise, generates the shares of zero. The zero-sharing based solution requires only one equality comparison inside MPC.

We now describe a detailed construction to generate zero-sharing [20] and how to compute t^i, w^i more efficiently.

a) Zero-sharing key setup: one key is shared between every pair of parties. For example, the key k_{ij} is for a pair (P_i, P_j) where $i, j \in [n], i < j$. It can be done as P_i randomly chooses $k_{i,j} \leftarrow \{0,1\}^\kappa$ and sends it to P_j. Let's denote a set of the zero-sharing keys of P_i as $K_i = \{k_{i,1}, \ldots, k_{i,(i-1)}, k_{i,(i+1)}, \ldots, k_{i,n}\}$.

b) Generating zero share: Given a PRF $F : \{0,1\}^\kappa \times \{0,1\}^* \rightarrow \{0,1\}^*$, a set of keys K_i and a value x, each P_i locally computes a zero share of x as $z^i = \bigoplus_{j=1}^{n} F(k_{i,j}, x)$. Clearly, each term $F(k_{i,j}, x)$ appears exactly twice in the expression $\bigoplus_{i=1}^{n} z^i$. Thus, $\bigoplus_{i=1}^{n} z^i = 0$. We define $f^z(K_i, x) \stackrel{\text{def}}{=} \bigoplus_{j=1}^{n} F(k_{ij}, x)$ for P_i to generate the zero share of x.

c) Computing s^1 and t^1: the $P_{i \neq 1}$ chooses random s^i and t^i. For an input (x^i, v^i) and a zero share $z^i \leftarrow f^z(K_i, x^i)$, he computes $w^i \stackrel{\text{def}}{=} v^i - s^i$ and $y^i \stackrel{\text{def}}{=} z^i \oplus t^i$ and sends the one-time pad $\mathsf{OTP}(x^i, y^i \| w^i)$ to the leader P_1 (assume that the length of x^i and $y^i \| w^i$ are equal). Using his item x^1 as a decryption key, P_1 obtains the correct $y^i \| w^i$ if $x^1 = x^i$, random otherwise. P_1 computes $s^1 \stackrel{\text{def}}{=} v^1 + \sum_{i=2}^{n} w^i$ and $t^1 \stackrel{\text{def}}{=} (\bigoplus_{i=2}^{n} y^i) \oplus z^1$. At this point, each P_i has secret shares s^i and t^i such that $\sum_{i=1}^{n} s^i = v^\star$ and $\bigoplus_{i=1}^{n} t^i = 0$ if all x^i are equal.

4.2   A General Case of Our First Phase

So far, we only consider the simple case where each party has only one item. In this section, we show how to efficiently extend our protocol to support the general case where $m > 1$. At the high-level idea, we use hashing scheme to map the common items into the same bin and then reply on OKVS to compress each bin into a share so that the parties can evaluate MPCCache bin-by-bin efficiently.

Similar to many PSI constructions [19,28], we use two popular hashing schemes: Cuckoo and Simple. The leader P_1 uses Cuckoo hashing [26] with $\widetilde{k} = 3$ hash functions to map his $\{x_1^1, \ldots, x_m^1\}$ into $\beta = 1.27m$ bins. He then pads his bin with dummy items so that each bin contains exactly one item. This step is to hide his actual Cuckoo bin size. On the other hand, each $P_{i \neq 1}$ use the same $\widetilde{k}$ Cuckoo hash functions to place its $\{x_1^i, \ldots, x_m^i\}$ into β bins (so-called Simple hashing), each item is placed into $\widetilde{k}$ bins with high probability. The $P_{i \neq 1}$ also pads his bin with dummy items so that each bin contains exactly $\gamma = 2\log(m)$ items. According to [12,28], the parameters $\beta, \widetilde{k}, \gamma$ are chosen so that with the probability $1 - 2^{-\lambda}$ every Cuckoo bin contains at most one item and no Simple bin contains more than γ items. More detail is described in the full version of the paper [25].

For each bin b^{th}, P_1 and $P_{i \neq 1}$ can run a special-case protocol described in Sect. 4.1. In particular, let $B_i[b]$ denote the set of items in the bth bin of P_i. All parties locally generate zero shares $z_j^i \leftarrow f^z(K_i, x_j^i)$. The $P_{i \neq 1}$ locally chooses random values s_b^i and t_b^i. For each $(x_j^i, v_j^i) \in B_i[b]$, $P_{i \neq 1}$ computes $w_j^i \overset{\text{def}}{=} v_j^i - s_b^i$ and $y_j^i \overset{\text{def}}{=} z_j^i \oplus t_b^i$ and sends the one-time pad ciphertext $\mathsf{OTP}(x_j^i, y_j^i || w_j^i)$ to the leader P_1. Using his item $x_b^1 \in B_1[b]$ as a decryption key, P_1 obtains $\hat{y}_j^i || \hat{w}_j^i$ which equals $y_j^i || w_j^i$ if $x_b^1 = x_j^i$, random otherwise. Since there are γ values $\hat{y}_j^i || \hat{w}_j^i$, each for a pair in $B_i[b]$, obtained from $P_{i \neq 1}$, the P_1 has γ^{n-1} possible ways to choose $j_i \in [\gamma]$ and compute his share $s_b^1 \overset{\text{def}}{=} v_b^1 + \sum_{i=2}^n \hat{w}_{j_i}^i$ and $t_b^1 \overset{\text{def}}{=} \bigoplus_{i=2}^n \hat{y}_{j_i}^i \oplus z_b^1$. Thus, this solution requires γ^{n-1} equality comparisons to check all combinations of whether $\bigoplus_{i=1}^n t_b^i = 0$ to determine whether x_b^1 is common.

To improve the above computation, we rely on an OKVS data structure in order that P_1 learns from $P_{i \neq 1}$ only one pair $\{\hat{y}^i, \hat{w}^i\}$ per bin, instead of γ pairs per bin. More precisely, for each bin b, the party $P_{i \neq 1}$ creates a set of points $\Gamma_b^i = \{(x_j^i, y_j^i || w_j^i) \mid x_j^i \in B_i[b]\}$, encodes it as $\mathsf{Encode}(\Gamma_b^i) \to \mathcal{T}_b^i$ and sends the OKVS table $\mathcal{T}_b^i$ to the leader P_1. Thanks to the oblivious property of OKVS, we no longer need the one-time pad encryption. Using x_b^1, the P_1 decodes $\mathcal{T}_b^i$ and obtains $\hat{y}_b^i || \hat{w}_b^i \leftarrow \mathsf{Decode}(x_b^1, \mathcal{T}_b^i)$. Note that, if $x_b^1 \in B_{i \neq 1}[b]$, $\hat{y}_b^i || \hat{w}_b^i$ equals to a $y_{j_i}^i || w_{j_i}^i$ that was encoded in $\mathcal{T}_b^i$, and otherwise, random.

In summary, if all parties have x_b^1 in their b^{th} bin, the leader P_1 receives $\hat{w}_b^i = v_{j_i}^i - s_b^i$ and $\hat{y}_b^i = z_j^i \oplus t_b^i$ from the corresponding OKVS execution involving $P_{i \neq 1}$. The leader computes $s_b^1 \overset{\text{def}}{=} v_b^1 + \sum_{i=2}^n \hat{w}_b^i$. If all parties have x_b^1, we have $\sum_{i=1}^n s_b^i$ is equal to the sum of the associated values corresponding with the identity x_b^1. Similarly, when defining $t_b^1 \overset{\text{def}}{=} (\bigoplus_{i=2}^n \hat{y}_b^i) \oplus z_b^1$, we have $\bigoplus_{i=1}^n t_b^i = 0$ if all parties have x_b^1. Consider a case that some parties $P_{i \neq 1}$ might not hold the item $x_b^1 \in B_1[b]$ that P_1 has, the corresponding OKVS with these parties gives P_1 random $\hat{y}_b^i || \hat{w}_b^i$. Thus $t_b^1 \overset{\text{def}}{=} (\bigoplus_{i=2}^n \hat{y}_b^i) \oplus z_b^1$ is random, so is $\bigoplus_{i=1}^n t_b^i$.

Similar to Sect. 4.1, we use GC to check whether $\bigoplus_{i=1}^n t_b^i = 0$ for the bin b, and outputs either refreshed shares of $\sum_{i=1}^n s_b^i$ or shares of zero. Since P_1 only has one s_b^1, the protocol only needs to execute one comparison circuit per bin, thus the number of equality tests needed is linear in the number of the bins.

Even though $P_{i \neq 1}$ uses the same offset s_b^i, t_b^i per bin, all w_j^i and y_j^i are random (assume that v_j^i is randomly distributed). In addition, the OKVS only gives P_1 one pair per bin. Therefore, as long as the OKVS used is secure, so is our first phase of MPCCache construction. We formalize and prove secure our first phase which is presented, together with proof of our MPCCache security in Sect. 4.4.

4.3   Our Second Phase: *k-priority* Construction

In this section, we measure the complexity of our *k-priority* protocol based on the number of secure Compare-Swap operations. As discussed in Sect. 2, one could use oblivious sorting to sort the input set and then take the indexes of k biggest values. This approach requires about $\frac{1}{4} m \log^2(m)$ Compare-Swap operations and the depth of $\log(m)$. In the following, we describe our simple construction which costs $\left(\frac{1}{4} \log(k) + \frac{1}{2} \right) m \log(k) - \frac{1}{2} k \log(k)$ Compare-Swap with the same depth. The proposed algorithm achieves an approximate $\frac{\log^2(m)}{\left(\log(k) + 2 \right) \log(k)} \times$ improvement.

PARAMETERS:
- Set size m, a bit-length θ, security parameter λ, and n parties $P_{i\in[n]}$
- A zero-sharing key setup, GC, and k-priority primitives
- An OKVS data structure with Encode and Decode algorithms.
- A Cuckoo and Simple hashing with 3 hash functions, β bins, and max bin size γ.

INPUT OF PARTY $P_{i\in[n]}$: A set $S_i = \{(x_1^i, v_1^i), \ldots, (x_m^i, v_m^i)\} \subset (\{0,1\}^*, \{0,1\}^\theta)^m$

PROTOCOL:

I. **Pre-processing**.
1. Each party P_i interacts with other parties $\{P_1, \ldots, P_{i-1}, P_{i+1}, P_n\}$ to generate a zero-sharing key K_i and locally computes zero shares as $z_j^i \leftarrow f_i^z(K_i, x_j^i), \forall j \in [m]$.
2. A leader P_1 hashes $\{x_1^1, \ldots, x_m^1\}$ into β bins using the Cuckoo hashing scheme. Let $B_1[b]$ denote the item in the bth bin (or a dummy item if this bin is empty).
3. Each party $P_{i\in[2,n]}$ hashes items $\{x_1^i, \ldots, x_m^i\}$ into β bins using Simple hashing. Let $B_i[b]$ denote the set of items in the bth bin of this party.

II. **Online**.
1. For each bin $b \in [\beta]$:
   a) Each party $P_{i\in[2,n]}$ chooses $t_b^i \leftarrow \{0,1\}^{\lambda+\log(n)}$ and $s_b^i \leftarrow \{0,1\}^\theta$ at random, and generates a set of key-value pairs $\Gamma_b^i = \{(x_j^i, y_j^i \| w_j^i) \mid x_j^i \in B_i[b]\}$ where $y_j^i \stackrel{\text{def}}{=} z_j^i \oplus t_b^i$ and $w_j^i \stackrel{\text{def}}{=} v_j^i - s_b^i$. The party then pads Γ_b^i with dummy pairs to γ.
   b) Each party $P_{i\in[2,n]}$ encodes Γ_b^i as $\mathsf{Encode}(\Gamma_b^i) \to \mathcal{T}_b^i$ and sends $\mathcal{T}_b^i$ to P_1 who computes $\mathsf{Decode}(x_b^1, \mathcal{T}_b^i)$ and obtains $\hat{y}_b^i \| \hat{w}_b^i$. Note that $\hat{y}_b^i = z_{j_i}^i \oplus t_b^i$ and $\hat{w}_b^i = v_{j_i}^i - s_b^i$ for $x_b^1 = x_{j_2}^2 = \ldots = x_{j_n}^n$. Otherwise, $\hat{y}_b^i, \hat{w}_b^i$ are random.
   c) P_1 computes $t_b^1 \stackrel{\text{def}}{=} (\bigoplus_{i=2}^n \hat{y}_b^i) \oplus z_b^1$ and $s_b^1 \stackrel{\text{def}}{=} v_b^1 + \sum_{i=2}^n \hat{w}_b^i$ where z_b^1 and v_b^1 are zero share and the associated value corresponding to x_b^1, respectively.
   d) Parties jointly invoke a GC instance:
      - Input from P_i is t_b^i and s_b^i.
      - Output to P_i is an additive share $[\![u_b]\!]$ where $u_b = \sum_{i=1}^n s_b^i$ if $\bigoplus_{i=1}^n t_b^i = 0$, otherwise $u_b = 0$.
      Note that if x_b^1 is common, u_b is equal to the sum of its associated values of the common item identity x_b^1.
2. Parties invoke a k-priority functionality with input $[\![u_b]\!], \forall b \in [\beta]$, and obtain k indexes of the k-priority common identities.

Fig. 3. Our decentralized MPCCache construction.

The main idea of our construction is that parties divide the input set into $\lceil \frac{m}{k} \rceil$ groups, each has k items except possibly the last group which may have less than k items (without loss of generality, we assume that m is divisible by k). Parties then execute an oblivious sorting invocation within each group to sort these values of this group in decreasing order. Unlike the recent work [9] for *approximate* top-K selection where it selects the maximum element within each group for further computation, we select the top-K elements of two neighbor groups. Concretely, the oblivious merger is built on top of each two sorted neighbor groups. We select only a set of the top-K elements from each merger and recursively merge two selected sets until reaching the final result.

Sorting each group requires $\frac{1}{4}k\log^2(k)$ Compare-Swap invocations, thus, for $\frac{m}{k}$ groups the total Compare-Swap operations needed is $\frac{m}{k}\left(\frac{1}{4}k\log^2(k)\right)$. The oblivious odd-even mergers are performed in a binary tree structure. The merger of two sorted neighbor groups, each has k items, is computed at each node of the tree. Unlike the sorting algorithm, we truncate this resulted array, maintain the secret shares of only k largest sorted numbers among these two groups, and throw out the rest of k numbers. By doing so, instead of $2k$, only k items are forwarded to the next odd-even merger. The number of Compare-Swap required for each merger does not blow up, and is equal to $\frac{1}{2}k \log(k)$. After $(\frac{m}{k} - 1)$ recursive oblivious merger invocations, parties obtain the secret share of the k largest values among the input set. In summary, our secure k-priority construction requires $\left(\frac{1}{4}\log(k) + \frac{1}{2}\right)m\log(k) - \frac{1}{2}k\log(k)$ Compare-Swap operations.

The above discussion gives parties the secret shares of k largest values. To output their indexes, before running our k-priority protocol we attach the index with its value using the concatenation $||$. Namely, we use $(\ell + \lceil\log(m)\rceil)$-bit string to represent the input. The first ℓ bits to store the additive share $[\![v_i]\!]$ and the last $\lceil\log(m)\rceil$ bits to represent the index i. Therefore, within a group the oblivious sorting takes $\{[\![v_i]\!]||i, ..., [\![v_{i+k-1}]\!]||(i+k-1)\}$ as input, use the shares $[\![v_j]\!], \forall j \in [i, i+k-1]$ for the secure comparison. The algorithm outputs the secret shares of the indexes, re-randomizes the shares of the values and swaps them if needed. The output of the modified oblivious sorting is $\{[\![v_{i_1}||i_1]\!], ..., [\![v_{i_k}||i_k]\!]\}$ where the output values $\{v_{i_1}, ..., v_{i_k}\} \subset \{v_i, ..., v_{i+k-1}\}$ are sorted. Similarly, we modify the oblivious merger structure to maintain the indexes. At the end of the protocol, parties obtain the secret share of the indexes of k largest values, which allows them jointly reconstruct the secret indexes.

Figure 4 presents our k-priority construction which security proof is given in the full version of the paper [25].

4.4   Putting All Together: MPCCache

We formally describe our semi-honest MPCCache construction in Fig. 3. From the preceding description, the cuckoo-simple hashing maps the same items into the same bin. Thus, for each bin #b, if parties have the same $x_b^1 \in B_1[b]$, they obtain the secret share of the sum of all corresponding associated values. Otherwise, they receive the secret share of zero (in practice, the sum of all parties' associated values for items in the intersection is not equal to zero). In our protocol, the equation $\bigoplus_{i=1}^{n} t_b^i = 0$ determines whether the item x_b^1 is common. We choose the bit-length of the zero share to be $\lambda + \log(n)$ to ensure that the probability of the false positive event for this equation is overwhelming $(1 - 2^{-\lambda})$.

The second step of the online phase takes the shares from parties, and returns the indexes of k-priority common elements. Since k must be less than or equal to the intersection size, the obtained results will not contain an index whose value is equal to zero. In other words, the output of our protocol satisfies the MPCCache conditions since the identity is common and the sum of the values associated corresponding to this identity is k-largest.

The security of our decentralized MPCCache is based on OKVS and $\mathcal{F}_{\text{k-prior}}$ primitives. Its formal proof is given in the full version of the paper [25].

PARAMETERS:
- Number of parties n, set size m, and a k value
- An ideal oblivious sort $\mathcal{F}_{\text{obv-sort}}$ and oblivious merge $\mathcal{F}_{\text{obv-merge}}$ primitives described in Section 3.
- A truncation function trunc which returns first k elements in the list as $\{x_1, \ldots, x_k\} \leftarrow \text{trunc}(\{x_1, \ldots, x_{2k}\})$

INPUT OF PARTY P_i: secret share values $S_i = \{[\![v_1]\!], ..., [\![v_m]\!]\}$

PROTOCOL:

1. Parties divide the input set S_i into $\frac{m}{k}$ groups, each has k items.
2. For each group $i \in [\frac{m}{k}]$ consisted of $\{[\![v_i]\!], ..., [\![v_{i+k-1}]\!]\}$ from party P_j, they jointly execute an oblivious sort $G[i] \leftarrow \mathcal{F}_{\text{obv-sort}}(\{[\![v_i]\!] || i, ..., [\![v_{i+k-1}]\!] || (i+k-1)\})$, where $G[i] \stackrel{\text{def}}{=} \{[\![v_{i_1}]\!] || i_1], ..., [\![v_{i_k}]\!] || i_k]\}$
3. Parties recursively invoke oblivious merges as follows. Assuming that $\frac{m}{k} = 2^d$.

   Procedure LevelMerge $(G[0, \ldots, d], d)$
   | **if** $d = 1$ **then**
   | | **return** $\{[\![v_{i_1}]\!] || i_1], ..., [\![v_{i_k}]\!] || i_k]\}$
   | **else**
   | | $L = \text{LevelMerge}(G[0, \ldots, \frac{d}{2} - 1], \frac{d}{2})$
   | | $R = \text{LevelMerge}(G[\frac{d}{2}, \ldots, d - 1], \frac{d}{2})$
   | | $M \leftarrow \mathcal{F}_{\text{obv-merge}}(L, R)$
   | | where $M \stackrel{\text{def}}{=} \{[\![v_{i_1}]\!] || i_1], ..., [\![v_{i_k}]\!] || i_{2k}]\}$
   | | $\{[\![v_{i_1}]\!] || i_1], ..., [\![v_{i_k}]\!] || i_k]\} \leftarrow \text{trunc}(M)$
   | **end**
   end

4. Parties jointly reconstruct the share $\{[\![v_{i_1}]\!] || i_1], ..., [\![v_{i_k}]\!] || i_k]\}$, and output $\{i_1, \ldots, i_k\}$.

Fig. 4. Our secure k-*priority* construction

5 Our Server-Aided MPCCache

In this section, we show an optimization to improve the efficiency of MPCCache. We assume that P_1 and P_2 are two non-colluding servers, and we call other parties as users. The optimized protocol consists of two phases. In the first one, each user interacts with the servers so that each server holds the same secret value, chosen by all users, for the common identifies that both servers and all users have. The servers also obtain the additive secret share of the sum of all the associated values corresponding to these common items. In a case that an identity x_j^e of the server $P_{e \in \{1,2\}}$ is not common, this server receives a random value. This phase can be considered as each user distributes a share of zero and a share of its associated value under a "common" condition. Note that, if even two servers collude they only learn the intersection items and nothing else, which provides a stronger security guarantee than the standard server-aided setting mentioned in the full version [25]. Our second phase involves only the servers' computation, which can be done by our 2-party decentralized MPCCache described in Sect. 4.4.

PARAMETERS:
- Set size m, a bit-length θ, security parameter λ, and n parties $P_{i\in[n]}$.
- A two-party decentralized MPCCache, and an OKVS with Encode and Decode.

INPUT OF PARTY $P_{i\in[n]}$: A set of key-value pairs $S_i = \{(x_1^i, v_1^i), \ldots, (x_m^i, v_m^i)\}$

PROTOCOL:

I. **Centralization.**
  1. Each user $P_{i\in[3,n]}$ chooses random $z_j^i \leftarrow \{0,1\}^{\lambda+\log(n)}$ and $s_j^i \leftarrow \{0,1\}^\theta$, and generates two sets $\Gamma^{e,i} = \{(x_j^i, z_j^i || w_j^{e,i})\}$, where $w_j^{1,i} \stackrel{\text{def}}{=} s_j^i$ and $w_j^{2,i} \stackrel{\text{def}}{=} v_j^i - s_j^i$.
  2. Each user $P_{i\in[3,n]}$ encodes $\Gamma^{e,i}$ as $\mathsf{Encode}(\Gamma^{e,i}) \rightarrow \mathcal{T}^{e,i}$ and sends $\mathcal{T}^{e,i}$ to $P_{e\in\{1,2\}}$ who computes $\mathsf{Decode}(x_j^e, \mathcal{T}^{e,i})$ and obtains $\hat{z}_j^{e,i} || \hat{w}_j^{e,i}$.
  3. For $j \in [m]$, each $P_{e\in\{1,2\}}$ computes $y_j^e \stackrel{\text{def}}{=} \bigoplus_{i=3}^n \hat{z}_j^{e,i}$ and $s_j^e \stackrel{\text{def}}{=} v_j^e + \sum_{i=3}^n \hat{z}_j^{e,i}$.

II. **Server-working.** Two servers $P_{e\in\{1,2\}}$ invoke an instance of MPCCache where P_e's input is a set $\{(y_1^e, s_1^e), \ldots, (y_m^e, s_m^e)\}$ and learns k-priority common items.

Fig. 5. Our server-aided MPCCache construction.

More concretely, in the first phase, each user $P_{i\in[3,n]}$ chooses random $z_j^i \leftarrow \{0,1\}^{\lambda+\log(n)}$ and $s_j^i \leftarrow \{0,1\}^\theta$, and then defines $w_j^{1,i} \stackrel{\text{def}}{=} s_j^i$, and $w_j^{2,i} \stackrel{\text{def}}{=} v_j^i - s_j^i$. Next, $P_{i\in[3,n]}$ generates two sets of key-value points $\Gamma^{e,i} = \{(x_j^i, z_j^i || w_j^{e,i})\}, \forall e \in \{1,2\}$, computes $\mathcal{T}^{e,i} = \mathsf{Encode}(\Gamma^{e,i})$, and sends $\mathcal{T}^{e,i}$ to the server P_e. Let's $\hat{z}_j^{e,i} || \hat{w}_j^{e,i} \leftarrow \mathsf{Decode}(x_j^e, \mathcal{T}^{e,i})$ be an output of the OKVS decoding computed by $P_{e\in\{1,2\}}$. If two servers have the same item $x_k^1 = x_{k'}^2$ which is equal to the item x_j^i of the user P_i, we have $\hat{z}_k^{1,i} = \hat{z}_{k'}^{2,i} = z_j^i$ and $\hat{w}_k^{1,i} + \hat{w}_{k'}^{2,i} = v_j^i$ (since $\hat{w}_k^{1,i} = s_j^i$ and $\hat{w}_{k'}^{2,i} = v_j^i - s_j^i$). Each server $P_{e\in\{1,2\}}$ defines $y_j^e \stackrel{\text{def}}{=} \bigoplus_{i=3}^n \hat{z}_j^{e,i}$ as an XOR of all the obtained values $\hat{z}_j^{e,i}$ corresponding to each item $x_{j\in[m]}^e$. For two indices k and k', we have $y_k^1 = \bigoplus_{i=3}^n \hat{z}_j^{1,i} = \bigoplus_{i=3}^n \hat{z}_j^{2,i} = y_{k'}^2$ if all parties has $x_k^1 = x_{k'}^2$ in their set. This property allows servers obliviously determinate the common items (i.e., checking whether $y_k^1 = y_{k'}^2, \forall k, k' \in [m]$). Moreover, let $s_j^e \stackrel{\text{def}}{=} v_j^e + \sum_{i=3}^n \hat{w}_j^{e,i}$. For two indices k and k', s_k^1 and $s_{k'}^2$ are secret shares of the sum of the associated values for the common item $x_k^1 = x_{k'}^2$. In summary, after this first phase, each server $P_{e\in\{1,2\}}$ has a set of points $\{(y_1^e, s_1^e), \ldots, (y_m^e, s_m^e)\}$ where $y_k^1 = y_{k'}^2$ if all parties have the same identity $x_k^1 = x_{k'}^2$, and $s_k^1 + s_{k'}^2$ is equal to the sum of the associated values of the common item x_k^1. Therefore, we reduce the problem of n-party MPCCache to the problem of a two-party case where each server $P_{e\in\{1,2\}}$ has a set of points $\{(y_1^e, s_1^e), \ldots, (y_m^e, s_m^e)\}$ and wants to learn the k-priority common items. We formally describe the optimized MPCCache protocol is in Fig. 5.

Recall that $y_j^e = \bigoplus_{i=3}^n \hat{z}_j^{e,i}, \forall e \in \{1,2\}, j \in [m]$. Let i be the highest index of a user $P_{i\in[3,n]}$ who did not have the identity x_k^1 in their input set. That user does not insert a pair $\{x_k^1, \texttt{something}\}$ to his set $\Gamma^{e,i}$ for the OKVS in Step (I.1). Thus, P_1 obtains a random $\hat{z}_k^{1,i}$ in Step (I.3). The protocol is correct except in the event of a false positive—i.e., $y_k^1 = y_{k'}^2$ for some x_k^1 not in the intersection.

By setting $\ell = \lambda + 2\log_2(n)$, a union bound shows that the probability of *any* item being erroneously included in the intersection is $2^{-\lambda}$.

The security proof of our server-aided MPCCache protocol is essentially similar to that of the decentralized protocol, which is presented in the full version [25].

Discussion. From our two-server-aided framework, our protocol can be extended to support a small set of servers (e.g., t servers, $t < n$). More precisely, in the centralization phase, each user $P_{i \in [t+1,n]}$ secretly shares their associated value $v^i_{j \in [m]}$ to the servers $P_{e \in [t]}$ via OKVS. Each server aggregates the share of the associated value corresponding to their item. The obtained results are forwarded to the server-working phase in which $P_{e \in [t]}$ jointly run MPCCache to learn k-priority common items. The main cost of our server-aided construction is dominated by the second phase. Hence, the performance of t-server-aided scheme is similar to that of decentralized MPCCache performed by t parties. We are interested in two-server aided architecture since we can take advantage of efficient two-party secure computation for the k-priority and GC. Moreover, the two-server setting is common in various cryptography schemes (e.g. private information retrieval [11], distributed point function [15], private database query [34]).

6   Implementation

We implement building blocks of MPCCache and do experiments on a single Linux machine that has Intel Core i7 1.88 GHz CPU and 16 GB RAM, where each party is implemented as a separate process. Computing cache sharing usually runs in the fast and low-latency edge network, especially with 5G technologies [1,3,13,37] as the servers of operators are typically placed closer to each other (e.g., in edge clouds in the same area such as New York City). Thus, we evaluate MPCCache over a simulated 10 Gbps network with 0.2 ms round-trip latency. We assume there is an authenticated secure channel between each pair of parties. Our MPCCache is very amenable to parallelization. Specifically, our algorithm can be parallelized at the level of bins. In our evaluation, however, we use a single thread to perform the computation between two parties.

All evaluations were performed with an identity and its associated value input length 128 bits and $\theta = 16$ bits, respectively, $\lambda = 40$, and $\kappa = 128$. We use OKVS code from [14], garbled circuit from [35]. To understand the scalability of our scheme, we evaluate it on the range of the number parties $n \in \{4, 6, 8, 16\}$. Note that the dataset size m of each party is expected to be not too large (e.g., billions). First, the potential of MPCCache is in 5G where each shared cache is deployed for a specific region. Second, each operator chooses only frequently-accessed files as an input to MPCCache because the benefit of caching less-accessed files is small. Therefore, we benchmark our MPCCache on the set size $m \in \{2^{12}, 2^{14}, 2^{16}, 2^{18}, 2^{20}\}$. To understand the performance effect of the k values discussed in Sect. 4.3, we use $k \in \{2^6, 2^7, 2^8, 2^9, 2^{10}\}$ in our k-priority experiments, and compare its performance to the most common oblivious sort protocol [30,35] which is based on Batcher's network (ref. Sect. 2).

Table 1. The total runtime (minute) and communication per item (KB) of our k-priority construction and the state-of-the-art oblivious sort, where m is the dataset size.

m	Running time					Communication				
	Ours k-priority				Sort [30,35]	Ours k-priority				Sort [30,35]
	$k=2^7$	$k=2^8$	$k=2^9$	$k=2^{10}$		$k=2^7$	$k=2^8$	$k=2^9$	$k=2^{10}$	
2^{12}	0.012	0.014	0.016	0.018	0.014	8.008	10.11	12.38	14.72	18.43
2^{14}	0.049	0.056	0.068	0.087	0.071	8.05	10.21	12.6	15.2	25.09
2^{16}	0.199	0.238	0.294	0.35	0.382	8.061	10.23	12.65	15.32	32.77
2^{18}	0.786	0.996	1.217	1.449	1.964	8.063	10.24	12.67	15.35	41.47
2^{20}	2.984	3.798	4.697	5.527	9.844	8.064	10.24	12.67	15.36	51.2

Table 2. The total runtime (minute) of our MPCCache constructions to find k-priority common items, where the number of parties n, each with dataset size m.

Parameters		Server-aided					Decentralized				
m	n	$k=2^6$	$k=2^7$	$k=2^8$	$k=2^9$	$k=2^{10}$	$k=2^6$	$k=2^7$	$k=2^8$	$k=2^9$	$k=2^{10}$
2^{12}	4	0.036	0.036	0.039	0.041	0.04	0.15	0.14	0.16	0.16	0.16
	6	0.036	0.036	0.039	0.041	0.04	0.23	0.22	0.24	0.23	0.27
	8	0.037	0.037	0.039	0.041	0.04	0.31	0.29	0.32	0.33	0.33
2^{16}	4	0.502	0.526	0.564	0.62	0.68	2.08	2.23	2.3	2.75	2.72
	6	0.502	0.531	0.569	0.625	0.68	3.09	3.06	3.71	3.65	3.96
	8	0.53	0.53	0.57	0.63	0.68	4.47	4.24	4.59	5.01	5.41
2^{20}	4	7.59	7.69	7.73	8.02	8.07	31.51	31.71	31.74	33.59	36.24
	6	7.7	7.92	7.81	8.1	8.17	46.07	46.35	46.37	46.69	46.96
	8	7.76	7.97	8.18	8.32	8.37	60.73	61.83	62.24	63.76	64.66

Table 3. The total runtime (minute) and communication cost per item (KB) of our server-aided MPCCache with $k=2^8$ for the number of parties n, each with set size m.

#party n	Role	Running time (minute)					Communication (KB)				
		$m=2^{12}$	$m=2^{14}$	$m=2^{16}$	$m=2^{18}$	$m=2^{20}$	$m=2^{12}$	$m=2^{14}$	2^{16}	$m=2^{18}$	$m=2^{20}$
4	User	0.002	0.003	0.088	0.324	1.202	0.58	0.66	0.73	0.81	0.88
	Server	0.039	0.146	0.564	2.089	7.732	24.47	26.34	28.06	29.74	31.41
6	User	0.002	0.004	0.093	0.342	1.271	1.17	1.32	1.46	1.61	1.76
	Server	0.039	0.147	0.569	2.1	7.813	24.77	26.67	28.43	30.14	31.85
8	User	0.002	0.004	0.095	0.35	1.291	1.75	1.97	2.19	2.42	2.64
	Server	0.039	0.147	0.571	2.12	7.781	25.06	27	28.79	30.54	32.28
16	User	0.02	0.058	0.24	0.912	3.374	4.09	4.61	5.12	5.64	6.15
	Server	0.047	0.167	0.598	2.155	7.833	26.23	28.32	30.26	32.15	34.04

6.1 k-priority Performance

Our k-priority requires $\left(\frac{1}{4}\log(k) + \frac{1}{2}\right)m\log(k) - \frac{1}{2}k\log(k)$ Compare-Swap instances. We use GC [5,36] to perform secure comparisons. Table 1 presents the running time and communication cost of our k-priority for the different k values. The cost is measured in KB per item as we would like to show an improved performance factor of our proposed protocol compared to the state-of-the-art oblivious sort as well as a performance change when increasing k. Thus, for

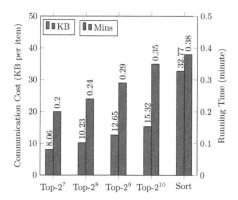

Fig. 6. The total running time (red bar) in minute and communication cost (blue bar) per item in KB of our k-priority and oblivious sort for Top-k and data set size $m = 2^{16}$. (Color figure online)

$m = 2^{18}$ and $k = 2^7$, our approach shows 5.15× and 2.5× improvements in terms of communication and computational costs, respectively.

To see more clearly the performance change for different k values, we present the performance of our k-priority protocol using a bar chart in Fig. 6, and show that there is a minor change in the running time when increasing k.

6.2   MPCCache Performance

Table 2 presents the total running time for the decentralized and server-aided MPCCache. The main difference between these constructions is in the steps of GC equality checks and k-priority. While the decentralized scheme requires all participants to jointly compute these steps, in the server-aided framework only two specific servers perform the computation. Thus, the former model is expensive than the latter one but provides a stronger security guarantee where any subset of corrupted parties learns nothing about the dataset of honest parties.

The numbers reported in Table 2 are for an end-to-end server-aided MPC-Cache execution, which includes the user's waiting time for the servers's computation. As discussed Sect. 5, the server-aided protocol is asymmetric with respect to the servers $P_{e \in \{1,2\}}$ and other users. Table 3 presents the performance of different roles of the participants. Because the user only distributes its dataset to two servers in the centralization phase, his workload is very light. The performance of our server-aided MPCCache on the user's side does not depend much on the number of parties due to the parallelizability with a separate secure channel between user and server. The server's work is heavy due to equality checks and k-priority. Table 3 shows that our protocol scales to a large number of parties.

6.3   Comparison with Prior Work

We compare our protocols with recent related works [7,31]. One can extend MPCircuits [31] to address the multi-party cooperative cache sharing problem by following similar steps of MPCCache: the first phase is to compute the secret share of the intersection. The second phase uses generic MPC protocols or our k-priority to compute the top-k function on the obtained results. Recall that MPCircuits only allows to compute secret-shared intersection items themselves. It is based on a binary tree structure as [31] observed that the set intersection of n sets can be expressed as a consecutive set intersection of two sets until reaching the final result. Therefore, the intersection of two sets is computed at each node of the tree, and the final intersection of all sets is computed at the root of the tree. Using three operations as sort, merge, and compare, the complexity of their garbled circuit is $O(n^2 m\ell \log(m)^2)$ where ℓ is the bit-length of the element identity. To keep track θ-bit associated value of the identity, the MPCircuits-based solution requires a complexity of $O(n^2 m(\ell + \theta) \log^2(m))$. In contrast, with the lightweight OKVS, our solution requires only a single equality comparison per bin. Thus, the complexity of our circuit is $O(nm(|z|+\theta))$, where z is a bit-length of the zero share which is equal to min $(\ell, \lambda + \log(n))$. It is easy to see that the first phase of our solution is about $n \log^2(m) \times$ better than that of MPCircuit-based approach. For example, with $n = 8$ and $m = 2^{20}$ our solution shows about an $3,200\times$ improvement.

To hide the intersection set size, the output of the MPCircuits-based computation at the root of the tree consists of mn secret shares of all intersection and non-intersection items. As a result, the second phase of the baseline solution takes mn secret shares as an input of each party. On the other hand, our MPCCache only takes $\beta = 1.27m$ secret shares, each per bin.

A concurrent and independent work [7] is designed for a generic circuit-PSI which only supports an honest majority (e.g., the number of colluding parties is up to $t < n/2$). Their protocol is similar to MPCCache and consists of two main phases. However, the first phase of [7] requires expensive steps (e.g., multiplication on secret-shared values) to compute the shares of intersection (Step 6 &7, [7, Figure 6]). Moreover, each participant (e.g. client) of [7] has a computation/communication complexity $O(nm)$ and requires to participate in the mostly full computation process. In contrast, in our server-aided protocol, the client does not involve in the entire MPCCache computation process, thus, has commutation/communication complexity $O(tm)$ which is independent of n. According to [7, Table 4] for $m = 2^{20}, n = 5, t = 2$ their client expects to finish the first phase in 25.48 s while ours requires only 13.02 s, an $1.96\times$ improvement[1]. The improvement factor is higher when the ratio n/t is larger.

For the second phase, [7] is not customized for the top-K computation. Based on the theoretical analysis in Sect. 6.1 and numerical experiment in Sect. 4.3, we expect that the second phase of MPCCache is about 1.7–3.3× faster than [7].

---

[1] [7]'s implementation is not yet publicly available. Its benchmark machine is stronger than ours, which is in favor of their protocol.

Acknowledgements. The second author is partially supported by NSF awards #2101052, and #2115075.

References

1. AT&T Edge Cloud (AEC) - White Paper (2017). https://about.att.com/ecms/dam/innovationdocs/Edge_Compute_White_Paper%20FINAL2.pdf
2. Araki, T., Furukawa, J., Lindell, Y., Nof, A., Ohara, K.: High-throughput semi-honest secure three-party computation with an honest majority. In: Weippl, E.R., Katzenbeisser, S., Kruegel, C., Myers, A.C., Halevi, S. (eds.) ACM CCS 2016, pp. 805–817. ACM Press, October 2016
3. Bastug, E., Bennis, M., Debbah, M.: Living on the edge: the role of proactive caching in 5G wireless networks. IEEE Commun. Mag. **52**(8), 82–89 (2014)
4. Batcher, K.E.: Sorting networks and their applications. In: Spring Joint Computer Conference (1968)
5. Beaver, D., Micali, S., Rogaway, P.: The round complexity of secure protocols. In: STOC (1990)
6. Ben-Efraim, A., Lindell, Y., Omri, E.: Optimizing semi-honest secure multiparty computation for the internet. In: CCS 2016 (2016)
7. Chandran, N., Dasgupta, N., Gupta, D., Obbattu, S.L.B., Sekar, S., Shah, A.: Efficient linear multiparty PSI and extensions to circuit/quorum PSI. ePrint (2021)
8. Chandran, N., Gupta, D., Shah, A.: Circuit-PSI with linear complexity via relaxed batch OPPRF. ePrint (2021)
9. Chen, H., Chillotti, I., Dong, Y., Poburinnaya, O., Razenshteyn, I., Riazi, M.S.: SANNS: scaling up secure approximate k-nearest neighbors search. In: USENIX Security (2020)
10. Cheon, J.H., Jarecki, S., Seo, J.H.: Multi-party privacy-preserving set intersection with quasi-linear complexity. IEICE Trans. **95**(8), 1366–1378 (2012)
11. Corrigan-Gibbs, H., Kogan, D.: Private information retrieval with sublinear online time. In: Canteaut, A., Ishai, Y. (eds.) EUROCRYPT 2020. LNCS, vol. 12105, pp. 44–75. Springer, Cham (2020). https://doi.org/10.1007/978-3-030-45721-1_3
12. Demmler, D., Rindal, P., Rosulek, M., Trieu, N.: PIR-PSI: scaling private contact discovery. In: Privacy Enhancing Technologies Symposium (PETS) (2018)
13. ETSI: Multi-access edge computing (2019). https://www.etsi.org/technologies/multi-access-edge-computing
14. Garimella, G., Pinkas, B., Rosulek, M., Trieu, N., Yanai, A.: Oblivious key-value stores and amplification for private set intersection. In: Malkin, T., Peikert, C. (eds.) CRYPTO 2021. LNCS, vol. 12826, pp. 395–425. Springer, Cham (2021). https://doi.org/10.1007/978-3-030-84245-1_14
15. Gilboa, N., Ishai, Y.: Distributed point functions and their applications. In: Nguyen, P.Q., Oswald, E. (eds.) EUROCRYPT 2014. LNCS, vol. 8441, pp. 640–658. Springer, Heidelberg (2014). https://doi.org/10.1007/978-3-642-55220-5_35
16. Goldreich, O., Micali, S., Wigderson, A.: How to play any mental game or a completeness theorem for protocols with honest majority. In: Aho, A. (edr.) 19th ACM STOC, pp. 218–229. ACM Press, May 1987
17. Hazay, C., Venkitasubramaniam, M.: Scalable multi-party private set-intersection. In: Fehr, S. (ed.) PKC 2017. LNCS, vol. 10174, pp. 175–203. Springer, Heidelberg (2017). https://doi.org/10.1007/978-3-662-54365-8_8
18. Jónsson, K.V., Kreitz, G., Uddin, M.: Secure multi-party sorting and applications. ePrint (2011)

19. Kolesnikov, V., Kumaresan, R., Rosulek, M., Trieu, N.: Efficient batched oblivious PRF with applications to private set intersection. In: Weippl, E.R., Katzenbeisser, S., Kruegel, C., Myers, A.C., Halevi, S. (eds.) ACM CCS 2016, pp. 818–829. ACM Press, October 2016

20. Kolesnikov, V., Matania, N., Pinkas, B., Rosulek, M., Trieu, N.: Practical multi-party private set intersection from symmetric-key techniques. In: Thuraisingham, B.M., Evans, D., Malkin, T., Xu, D. (eds.) ACM CCS 2017, pp. 1257–1272. ACM Press, October 2017

21. Lepoint, T., Patel, S., Raykova, M., Seth, K., Trieu, N.: Private join and compute from PIR with default. In: Tibouchi, M., Wang, H. (eds.) ASIACRYPT 2021. LNCS, vol. 13091, pp. 605–634. Springer, Cham (2021). https://doi.org/10.1007/978-3-030-92075-3_21

22. Mohassel, P., Rindal, P.: ABY^3: a mixed protocol framework for machine learning. In: Lie, D., Mannan, M., Backes, M., Wang, X. (eds.) ACM CCS 2018, pp. 35–52. ACM Press, October 2018

23. Neugebauer, G., Meyer, U., Wetzel, S.: SMC-muse: a framework for secure multi-party computation on multisets. In: INFORMATIK 2013 - Informatik angepasst an Mensch, Organisation und Umwelt (2013)

24. Nevo, O., Trieu, N., Yanai, A.: Simple, fast malicious multiparty private set intersection. In: ACM Conference on Computer and Communications Security (CCS) (2021)

25. Nguyen, D.T., Trieu, N.: MPCCache: privacy-preserving multi-party cooperative cache sharing at the edge. Cryptology ePrint Archive, Report 2021/317 (2021). https://ia.cr/2021/317

26. Pagh, R., Rodler, F.F.: Cuckoo hashing. J. Algorithms **51**(2), 122–144 (2004)

27. Paschos, G.S., Iosifidis, G., Tao, M., Towsley, D., Caire, G.: The role of caching in future communication systems and networks. IEEE J. Sel. Areas Commun. **36**(6), 1111–1125 (2018)

28. Pinkas, B., Schneider, T., Segev, G., Zohner, M.: Phasing: private set intersection using permutation-based hashing. In: Jung, J., Holz, T. (eds.) USENIX Security 2015, pp. 515–530. USENIX Association, August 2015

29. Pinkas, B., Schneider, T., Tkachenko, O., Yanai, A.: Efficient circuit-based PSI with linear communication. In: Ishai, Y., Rijmen, V. (eds.) EUROCRYPT 2019. LNCS, vol. 11478, pp. 122–153. Springer, Cham (2019). https://doi.org/10.1007/978-3-030-17659-4_5

30. Poddar, R., Kalra, S., Yanai, A., Deng, R., Popa, R.A., Hellerstein, J.M.: Senate: a maliciously-secure MPC platform for collaborative analytics. In: USENIX (2021)

31. Riazi, M.S., Javaheripi, M., Hussain, S.U., Koushanfar, F.: MPCircuits: optimized circuit generation for secure multi-party computation. In: HOST, pp. 198–207 (2019)

32. Rindal, P., Schoppmann, P.: VOLE-PSI: Fast OPRF and circuit-PSI from vector-OLE. ePrint (2021)

33. Sang, Y., Shen, H.: Privacy preserving set intersection based on bilinear groups. In: ACSC 2008 (2008)

34. Wang, F., Yun, C., Goldwasser, S., Vaikuntanathan, V., Zaharia, M.: Splinter: practical private queries on public data. In: NSDI (2017)

35. Wang, X., Malozemoff, A.J., Katz, J.: EMP-toolkit: efficient MultiParty computation toolkit (2016). https://github.com/emp-toolkit

36. Yao, A.C.-C.: How to generate and exchange secrets (extended abstract). In: 27th FOCS, pp. 162–167. IEEE Computer Society Press, October 1986

37. Yao, J., Han, T., Ansari, N.: On mobile edge caching. IEEE Commun. Surv. Tutor. **21**(3), 2525–2553 (2019)
38. Zhang, K., Leng, S., He, Y., Maharjan, S., Zhang, Y.: Cooperative content caching in 5G networks with mobile edge computing. IEEE Wirel. Commun. **25**(3), 80–87 (2018)

Multi-party Updatable Delegated Private Set Intersection

Aydin Abadi[1]([✉]), Changyu Dong[2], Steven J. Murdoch[1], and Sotirios Terzis[3]

[1] University College London, London, UK
{aydin.abadi,s.murdoch}@ucl.ac.uk
[2] Newcastle University, Newcastle upon Tyne, UK
changyu.dong@newcastle.ac.uk
[3] University of Strathclyde, Glasgow, UK
sotirios.terzis@strath.ac.uk

Abstract. With the growth of cloud computing, the need arises for Private Set Intersection protocols (PSI) that can let parties outsource the storage of their private sets and securely delegate PSI computation to a cloud server. The existing delegated PSIs have two major limitations; namely, they cannot support (1) efficient updates on outsourced sets and (2) efficient PSI among multiple clients. This paper presents "Feather", the *first* lightweight delegated PSI that addresses both limitations simultaneously. It lets clients independently prepare and upload their private sets to the cloud once, then delegate the computation an unlimited number of times. We implemented Feather and compared its costs with the state of the art delegated PSIs. The evaluation shows that Feather is more efficient computationally, in both update and PSI computation phases.

1 Introduction

Private Set Intersection (PSI) is an interesting protocol that lets parties compute the intersection of their private sets without revealing anything about the sets beyond the intersection [23]. PSI has various applications. For instance, it has been used in COVID-19 contact tracing schemes [21], remote diagnostics [17], and Apple's child safety solution to combat "Child Sexual Abuse Material" (CSAM) [14]. PSI has been considered by the "Financial Action Task Force" (FATF) as one of the vital tools for enabling collaborative analytics between financial institutions to strengthen "Anti-Money Laundering" (AML) and "Countering the Financing of Terrorism" (CFT) compliance [22].

Traditionally, PSIs have been designed for the setting where parties locally maintain their sets and jointly compute the sets' intersection. Recently, it has been a significant interest in the *delegated* PSIs that let parties outsource the storage of their sets to cloud computing which later can compute the intersection without being able to learn the sets and their intersection. One of the reasons for this trend is that the cloud is becoming mainstream among individuals, businesses, and financial institutes. For instance, IDC's 2020 survey suggests that the banking industry is not only adopting but also accelerating the adoption of

© International Financial Cryptography Association 2022
I. Eyal and J. Garay (Eds.): FC 2022, LNCS 13411, pp. 100–119, 2022.
https://doi.org/10.1007/978-3-031-18283-9_6

the cloud, based on its benefits proven in the market [41]. The cloud can serve as a hub that allows for large-scale storage and data analysis by pooling clients' data together, without the need for them to locally maintain the data, which lets them discover new knowledge that could provide fresh insights to their business.

However, there are two major limitations to the existing delegated PSIs; namely, *they cannot efficiently support (1) updates on outsourced private sets, and (2) PSI among multiple clients.* Particularly, they have been designed for static sets and do not let parties efficiently update their outsourced sets. For application areas involving large private sets frequently updated, like fintech (e.g., stock market trend analysis [42]), e-commerce (e.g., consumer behaviour prediction [43]), or e-health (e.g., cancer research on genomic datasets [11]), the cost of securely updating outsourced sets using these schemes is prohibitive; in particular, it is linear with the entire set's size, $O(c)$. Another limitation is that they cannot scale to multiple clients without sacrificing security or efficiency. Specifically, in the most efficient delegate PSI in [1], the cloud has to perform a high number of random polynomials' evaluations which leads to a performance bottleneck, when the number of clients is high. A PSI that supports more than two parties creates opportunities for much richer analytics than what is possible with two-party PSIs. For example, it can benefit (i) companies that wish to jointly launch an ad campaign and identify the target audience, (ii) multiple ISPs which have private audit logs and want to identify network attacks' sources, or (iii) the aforementioned Apple's solution in which different CSAM datasets are provided by distinct child safety organizations [9].

Our Contributions. In this paper, we:

- present Feather, the first multi-party delegated PSI that lets a client efficiently update its outsourced set by accessing only a tiny fraction of this set. The update in Feather imposes $O(d^2)$ computation cost, where d is a hash table's bin size, i.e., $d = 100$.
- implement Feather and make its source code public, in [2].
- perform a rigorous cost analysis of Feather. The analysis shows that (a) updates on a set of 2^{20} elements are over 1000 times, and (b) PSI's computations are over 2 times faster than the fastest delegated PSI. Moreover, during the PSI computation when two clients participate, Feather's cloud-side runtime is over 26 times faster than the cloud's runtime in the fastest delegated PSI and this gap would grow when the number of clients increases. In Feather, it only takes 4.7 s to run PSI with 1000 clients, where each client has 2^{11} elements.

Feather offers other features too; for instance, the cloud *learns nothing* about the sets and their intersection, each client can *independently* prepare its set, and can delegate the PSI computation an *unlimited* number of times. We define and prove Feather's security in the simulation-based paradigm.

2 Related Work

Since their introduction in [23], various PSIs have been designed. PSIs can be broadly divided into *traditional* and *delegated* ones. In *traditional* PSIs data owners interactively compute the result using their local data. So far, the protocol of Kolesnikov *et al.* in [36] is the fastest two-party PSI secure against a semi-honest/passive adversary. It relies on symmetric key operations and has a computation complexity linear with the set size, i.e., $O(c)$, where c is a set size. Recently, Pinkas *et al.* in [39] proposed an efficient PSI that is secure against a stronger (i.e., active) adversary, and has $O(c \log c)$ computation complexity. Recently, researchers propose two threshold PSIs in [14] that let the Apple server learn the intersection of CSAM and a user's set only if the intersection cardinality exceeds a threshold. These two PSIs involve $O(c)$ asymmetric key operations. Also, there have been efforts to improve the communication cost in PSIs, through homomorphic encryption and polynomial representation [10,16,19,26]. Recently, a new PSI has been proposed that achieves a better balance between communication and computation costs [18]. Also, researchers designed PSIs that let multiple (i.e., more than two) parties efficiently compute the intersection. The multi-party PSIs in [28,37] are secure against passive adversaries while those in [12,25,45] were designed to remain secure against active ones. To date, the protocols in [37] and [25] are the most efficient multi-party PSIs designed to be secure against passive and active adversaries respectively. The computation complexities of [37] and [25] are $O(c\xi^2 + c\xi)$ and $O(c\xi)$ respectively, where ξ is the number of clients. However, Abadi *et al.* [5] showed that the latter is susceptible to several attacks. The former uses inexpensive symmetric key primitives and performs well with a small number of clients, i.e., up to 15. But, as we will discuss, it imposes high costs when the number of clients is high.

Delegated. PSIs use cloud computing for computation and/or storage, while preserving the privacy of the computation inputs and outputs from the cloud. They can be divided further into protocols that support *one-off* and *repeated* delegation of PSI computation. The former like [30,33,46] cannot reuse their outsourced encrypted data and require clients to re-encode their data locally for each computation. The most efficient such protocol is [30], which has been designed for the two-party setting and its computation complexity is $O(c)$. In contrast, the latter (i.e., repeated PSI delegation ones) let clients outsource the storage of their encrypted data to the cloud only once, and then with the data owners' consent run any number of computations.

Looking more closely at the repeated PSI delegation protocols, the ones in [38,40,47] are not secure, as illustrated in [1,6]. In contrast, the PSIs in [1,6,7,44] are secure. Those in [6,7,44] involve $O(c)$ asymmetric key operations. In these schemes, the entire set is represented as a polynomial outsourced to the cloud. The protocol in [1] is more efficient than the ones in [6,7,44] and involves only $O(c)$ symmetric key operations. It uses a hash table to improve the performance. However, all these four protocols have been designed for the two-party setting and only support static datasets. Even though the authors in [1,6,7] explain how their two-party protocols can be modified to support multi-party, the extensions are computationally expensive; they also (a) impose a bottleneck to the cloud, and (b) do not provide any empirical evaluation for their modified protocols. In these PSIs, for parties to update their sets and avoid serious data leakage, they need to locally re-encode their entire outsourced set that incurs high costs.

3 Preliminaries

In this section, we outline the primitives used in this paper.

3.1 Pseudorandom Functions and Permutation

Informally, a pseudorandom function is a deterministic function that takes a key of length Λ and an input; and outputs a value indistinguishable from that of a truly random function. In this paper, we use two pseudorandom functions: $\text{PRF} : \{0,1\}^\Lambda \times \{0,1\}^* \to \mathbb{F}_p$ and $\text{PRF}' : \{0,1\}^\Lambda \times \{0,1\}^* \to \{0,1\}^\Psi$, where $|p| = \Omega$ and Λ, Ψ, Ω are the security parameters. In practice, a pseudorandom function can be obtained from an efficient block cipher [32].

A pseudorandom permutation, $\pi(k, \vec{v})$, is a deterministic function that permutes the elements of a vector, $\vec{v}$, pseudorandomly using a secret key k. In practice, Fisher-Yates shuffle algorithm [35] can permute a vector of m elements in time $O(m)$. Formal definitions of pseudorandom function and permutation can be found in [32].

3.2 Hash Tables

A hash table is an array of bins each of which can hold a set of elements. It is accompanied with a hash function. To insert an element, we first compute the element's hash, and then store the element in the bin whose index is the element's hash. In this paper, we set the table's parameters appropriately to ensure the number of elements in each bin does not exceed a predefined capacity. Given the maximum number of elements c and the bin's maximum size d, we can determine the number of bins, h, by analysing hash tables under the balls into the bins model [13]. In the paper's full version [4], we explain how the hash table parameters are set.

3.3 Horner's Method

Horner's method [20] is an efficient way of evaluating polynomials at a given point, e.g., x_0. In particular, given a degree-n polynomial of the form: $\tau(x) = a_0 + a_1 x + a_2 x^2 + ... + a_n x^n$ and a point: x_0, one can efficiently evaluate the polynomial at the point iteratively from inside-out, in the following fashion:

$$\tau(x_0) = a_0 + x_0(a_1 + x_0(a_2 + ... + x_0(a_{n-1} + x_0 a_n)...)))$$

Evaluating a degree-n polynomial naively requires n additions and $\frac{(n^2+n)}{2}$ multiplications, whereas using Horner's method the evaluation requires only n additions and n multiplications. We use this method throughout the paper.

3.4 Bloom Filter

A Bloom filter [15] is a compact data structure that allows us to efficiently check an element membership. It is an array of m bits (initially all set to zero), that represents n elements. It is accompanied with k independent hash functions. To insert an element, all the hash values of the element are computed and their corresponding bits in the filter are set to 1. To check an element membership, all its hash values are re-computed and checked whether all are set to 1 in the filter. If all the corresponding bits are 1, then the element is probably in the filter; otherwise, it is not. In Bloom filters it is possible that an element is not in the set, but the membership query indicates it is, i.e., false positives. In this work, we ensure the false positive probability is negligible, e.g., 2^{-40}. In the paper's full version [4], we explain how the Bloom filter parameters can be set.

3.5 Representing Sets by Polynomials

Freedman *et al.* in [23] put forth the idea of using a polynomial to represent a set elements. In this representation, set elements $S = \{s_1, ..., s_d\}$ are defined over a field, $\mathbb{F}_p$, and set S is represented as a polynomial of form: $\rho(x) = \prod_{i=1}^{d}(x - s_i)$, where $\rho(x) \in \mathbb{F}_p[X]$ and $\mathbb{F}_p[X]$ is a polynomial ring. Often a polynomial of degree d is represented in the "coefficient form" as: $\rho(x) = a_0 + a_1 \cdot x + ... + a_d \cdot x^d$. As shown in [34], for two sets $S^{(A)}$ and $S^{(B)}$ represented by polynomials $\rho^{(A)}$ and $\rho^{(B)}$ respectively, their product, i.e., polynomial $\rho^{(A)} \cdot \rho^{(B)}$, represents the set union, while their greatest common divisor, i.e., $gcd(\rho^{(A)}, \rho^{(B)})$, represents the set intersection. For two degree-d polynomials $\rho^{(A)}$ and $\rho^{(B)}$, and two degree-d random polynomials $\gamma^{(A)}$ and $\gamma^{(B)}$, it is proven in [34] that:

$$\theta = \gamma^{(A)} \cdot \rho^{(A)} + \gamma^{(B)} \cdot \rho^{(B)} = \mu \cdot gcd(\rho^{(A)}, \rho^{(B)}), \tag{1}$$

where μ is a uniformly random polynomial, and polynomial θ contains only information about the elements in $S^{(A)} \cap S^{(B)}$, and contains no information about other elements in $S^{(A)}$ or $S^{(B)}$. To find the intersection, one extracts θ's roots, which contain the roots of (i) random polynomial μ and (ii) the polynomial that represents the intersection, i.e., $gcd(\rho^{(A)}, \rho^{(B)})$. To distinguish errors (i.e., roots of μ) from the intersection, PSIs in [1,6,34] use a padding technique. In this technique, every element u_i in the set universe $\mathcal{U}$, becomes $s_i = u_i || \mathsf{G}(u_i)$, where G is a cryptographic hash function with sufficiently large output size. Given a field's arbitrary element, $s \in \mathbb{F}_p$, and G's output size, we can parse s into a and b, such that $s = a||b$ and $|b| = |\mathsf{G}(.)|$. Then, we check $b \stackrel{?}{=} \mathsf{G}(a)$. If $b = \mathsf{G}(a)$, then s is an element of the intersection; otherwise, it is not.

Polynomials can also be represented in the "point-value form". Specifically, a polynomial $\mathbf{p}(x)$ of degree d can be represented as a set of m $(m > d)$ point-value pairs $\{(x_1, y_1), ..., (x_m, y_m)\}$ such that all x_i are distinct non-zero points and $y_i = \rho(x_i)$ for all i, $1 \leq i \leq m$. Polynomials in point-value form have been used previously in PSIs [1,26]. A polynomial in this form can be converted into coefficient form via polynomial interpolation, e.g., via Lagrange interpolation [8].

Usually, PSIs that rely on this representation assume that all x_i are picked from $\mathbb{F}\backslash\mathcal{U}$. Also, one can add or multiply two polynomials, in point-value form, by adding or multiplying their corresponding y-coordinates.

4   Feather: Multi-party Updatable Delegated PSI

In this section, we first outline Feather's model, followed by an overview of its three protocols: setup, update, and PSI computation. Then, we elaborate on each protocol.

4.1   An Overview of Feather's Definition

Similar to most PSIs, we consider the semi-honest adversaries; similar to the PSIs in [1, 7, 29], we assume that the adversaries do not collude with the cloud. However, all but one clients are allowed to collude with each other. Similar to the security model of searchable encryption [27, 31], in our security model we let some information, i.e., the query and access patterns, be leaked to the cloud to achieve efficiency. Informally, we say the protocol is secure as long as the cloud does not learn anything about the computation inputs and outputs beyond the allowed leakage and clients do not learn anything beyond the intersection about the other clients' set elements. We formalise Feather's security in the simulation-based paradigm. We require the clients' and cloud's view during the execution of the protocol can be simulated given their input and output (as well as the leakage). We refer readers to the paper's full version [4] for a formal definition.

4.2   An Overview of Feather's Protocols

At a high level, Feather works as follows. In the setup, the cloud publishes a set of public parameters. Any time a client wants to outsource the storage of its set, it uses the parameters to create a hash table. It inserts its set's elements to the hash table's bins, encodes the bins' content such that the encoded bins leak no information. Next, it assigns random-looking metadata to each bin, and shuffles the bins and the metadata. It sends the shuffled hash table and metadata to the cloud. When the client wants to insert/delete an element to/from its outsourced set, it figures out to which bin the element belongs and asks the cloud to send only that bin to it. Then, the client locally updates that bin's content, encodes the updated bin, and sends it to the cloud. In the PSI computation phase, the result recipient client, i.e., client B, interacts with other clients' to have their permission. Those clients that want to participate in the PSI computation send a set of messages to the cloud and client B. Using the clients' messages, the cloud connects the clients' permuted bins with each other and then obliviously computes the sets intersection. It sends the result to client B which, with the assistance of other clients' messages, extracts the result.

In Feather, we use various techniques to attain scalability and efficiency. For instance, by analysing the most efficient delegated PSI in [1], we identified a *performance bottleneck* that prevents this PSI to scale in the multi-party setting.

Specifically, we observed that in this scheme, the cloud has to perform a high number of random polynomials' evaluations on the clients' behalf. To avoid this bottleneck, in Feather, each client locally evaluates its random polynomials and sends the result to the cloud, yielding a significant performance improvement on the cloud side. To attain efficiency, we (i) substitute previous schemes' padding technique with an efficient error detecting mechanism, (ii) use an efficient polynomial evaluation (i.e., Horner's) method, and (iii) utilise a novel combination of permuted hash tables, permutation mapping, labels, and resettable counters.

4.3   Feather Setup

In this section, we first explain the efficient error detecting technique and then present Feather's setup protocol.

An Efficient Error Detecting Technique. As we described in Sect. 3.5, often in the PSIs that use the polynomial representation, during the setup, each set element is padded (with some values). This lets the result recipient distinguish actual set elements from errors. A closer look reveals that the minimum bit-size of the padding is $t + \epsilon$ (due to the union bound), where 2^t is the total number of roots and $2^{-\epsilon}$ is the maximum probability that at least one invalid root has a set element structure, e.g., $\epsilon \geq 40$. So, this padding scheme increases element size, and requires a larger field. This has a considerable effect on the performance of (all arithmetic operations in the field and) polynomial factorisation whose complexity is bounded by (i) the polynomial's degree and (ii) the logarithm of the number of elements in the field, i.e., $O(n^a \log_2 2^{|p|})$ or $O(n^a |p|)$, where $1 < a \leq 2$, n is polynomial's degree and $|p|$ is the field bit size [24].

We observed that to improve efficiency, the padding scheme can be replaced by Bloom filters. The idea is that each client generates a Bloom filter which encodes all its set elements, blinds, and then sends the blinded Bloom filter (BB) along with other data to the cloud. For PSI computation, the result recipient gets the result along with its *own* BB. After it extracts the result, i.e., polynomials' roots, it checks if the roots are already in the Bloom filter and only accepts those in it. The use of BB reduces an element size and requires a smaller field which improves the performance of all arithmetic operations in the field. Here, we highlight only the improvement during the factorisation, as it dominates the protocol's cost. After the modification, the factorisation complexity is reduced from $O(n^a(|p|+t+\epsilon))$ to $O(n^a|p|)$. For instance, for e elements, $e \in [2^{10}, 2^{20}]$, and the error probability 2^{-40}, we get a factor of 1.5-2.5 lower runtime, when $|p| \in [40, 100]$. In general, this improvement is at least a factor of 2, when $|p| \leq t + \epsilon$. The smaller element and field size *reduces the communication and cloud-side storage costs too.*

Feather Setup Protocol. Now, we present the setup protocol in Feather. Briefly, first the cloud generates and publishes a set of public parameters. Then, each client builds a hash table using these parameters. It maps its set elements into the hash table's bins and represents each bin's elements as a blinded polynomial. It assigns a Bloom filter to each bin such that a bin's Bloom filter encodes that bin's set elements. Next, it blinds each filter and assigns a unique label to each bin. It pseudorandomly permutes the (i) bins (containing the blinded polynomials), (ii) blinded Bloom filters, and (iii) labels. It sends the permuted: bins, blinded Bloom filters, and labels to the cloud. It can delete its local set at this point. Below, we present the setup protocol.

Cloud Setup: Sets c as an upper bound of sets' size and sets a hash table parameters, i.e., table's length: h, hash function: H, and bin's capacity: d. It picks pseudorandom functions PRF (used to generate labels and masking) and PRF' (used to mask Bloom filters), and a pseudorandom permutation, π. It picks a vector $\vec{x} = [x_1, .., x_n]$ of $n = 2d + 1$ distinct non-zero values. It publishes the parameters.

Client Setup: Let client $I \in \{A_1, ...A_\xi, B\}$ have set: $S^{(I)}, |S^{(I)}| < c$. Client I:

1. ***Gen. a hash table and Bloom filters:*** Builds a hash table $HT^{(I)}$ and inserts its elements into it, i.e., $\forall s_i^{(I)} \in S^{(I)}: H(s_i^{(I)}) = j$, then $s_i^{(I)} \to HT_j^{(I)}$. If needed, it pads every bin to d elements (using dummy values). Then, for every j-th bin, it generates a polynomial representing the bin's elements: $\prod_{l=1}^{d}(x - e_l^{(I)})$, and evaluates each polynomial at every element $x_i \in \vec{x}$, where $e_l^{(I)}$ is either a set element or a dummy value. This yields a vector of n y-coordinates: $y_{j,i}^{(I)} = \prod_{l=1}^{d}(x_i - e_l^{(I)})$, for that bin. It allocates a Bloom filter: $B_j^{(I)}$ to bin $HT_j^{(I)}$, and inserts only the set elements of the bin in the filter.

2. ***Blind Bloom filters:*** Blinds every Bloom filter, by picking a secret key: $bk^{(I)}$, extracting h pseudorandom values and using each value to blind each Bloom filter; i.e., $\forall j, 1 \le j \le h : BB_j^{(I)} = B_j^{(I)} \oplus PRF'(bk^{(I)}, j)$, where $\oplus$ denotes XOR. Thus, a vector of blinded Bloom filters is computed: $\vec{BB}^{(I)} = [BB_1^{(I)}, ..., BB_h^{(I)}]$.

3. ***Blind bins:*** To blind every $y_{j,i}^{(I)}$, it assigns a key to each bin by picking a master secret key $k^{(I)}$, and generating h pseudorandom keys: $\forall j, 1 \le j \le h$: $k_j^{(I)} = PRF(k^{(I)}, j)$. Next, it uses each $k_j^{(I)}$ to generate n pseudorandom values $z_{j,i}^{(I)} = PRF(k_j^{(I)}, i)$. Then, for each bin, it computes n blinded y-coordinates as follows: $\forall i, 1 \le i \le n : o_{j,i}^{(I)} = y_{j,i}^{(I)} + z_{j,i}^{(I)}$. Thus, d elements in each $HT_j^{(I)}$ are represented as $\vec{o}_j^{(I)} : [o_{j,1}^{(I)}, ..., o_{j,n}^{(I)}]$.

4. ***Gen. labels:*** Assigns a pseudorandom label to each bin, by picking a fresh key: $lk^{(I)}$ and then computing h values, i.e., $\forall j, 1 \le j \le h : l_j^{(I)} = PRF(lk^{(I)}, j)$.

5. ***Shuffle:*** Pseudorandomly permutes the labeled hash table. To do that, it picks a fresh key, $pk^{(I)}$, and then calls π as follows: $\vec{o}^{(I)} = \pi(pk^{(I)}, \vec{o}^{(I)})$, $\vec{l}^{(I)} = \pi(pk^{(I)}, \vec{l}^{(I)})$, where $\vec{o}^{(I)} = [\vec{o}_1^{(I)}, ..., \vec{o}_h^{(I)}]$ and $\vec{l}^{(I)}$ contains the labels generated in step 4. Also, it pseudorandomly permutes $\vec{BB}^{(I)}$ as: $\vec{BB}^{(I)} = \pi(pk^{(I)}, \vec{BB}^{(I)})$.

6. ***Gen. resettable counters:*** Builds and maintains a vector: $\vec{c}^{(I)}$ of counters $c_i^{(I)}$ initially zero, where each counter $c_i^{(I)}$ keeps track of the number of times a bin $HT_i^{(I)}$ in the outsourced hash table is retrieved by the client for an update. They will let the client efficiently regenerate the most recent blinding factors.

Outsourcing: Every client I sends the permuted labeled hash table: $(\overrightarrow{o}^{(I)}, \overrightarrow{l}^{(I)})$ along with the permuted blinded Bloom filters: $\overrightarrow{BB}^{(I)}$ to the cloud.

4.4   Feather Update Protocol

In this section, we present the update protocol in Feather. Briefly, for client I to insert/delete an element, $s^{(I)}$, to/from its outsourced set, it asks the cloud to send to it a bin and that bin's blinded Bloom filter. To do that, it first determines to which bin the element belongs. It recomputes the bin's label and sends the label to the cloud which sends the bin and related blinded Bloom filter to it. Then, the client uses the counter and a secret key to remove the most recent blinding factors from the bin's content, applies the update, re-encodes the bin and filter. Next, it refreshes their blinding factors and sends the updated bin along with the updated filter to the cloud.

The efficiency of Feather's update protocol stems from three factors: (a) the ability of a client to (securely) update only a bin of its outsourced hash table, that leads to very low complexities, (b) the use of an efficient error detecting technique that yields communication and computation costs reduction, and (c) the use of the local counters that yields client-side storage cost reduction. Now, we explain the update protocol in detail.

1. ***Fetch a bin and its Bloom filter:*** Recomputes the label of the bin to which element $s^{(I)}$ belongs, by generating the bin's index: $H(s^{(I)}) = j$, and computing the label: $l_j^{(I)} = PRF(lk^{(I)}, j)$. It sends $l_j^{(I)}$ to the cloud which sends back the bin: $\overrightarrow{o}_j^{(I)}$, and the blinded Bloom filter: $BB_j^{(I)}$.
2. ***Unblind:*** Removes the blinding factors from $\overrightarrow{o}_j^{(I)}$ and $BB_j^{(I)}$ as follows.
   a. ***Regen. blinding factors:*** To regenerate the blinding factors of the bin and its Bloom filter, it first regenerates the key for that bin, as $k_j^{(I)} = PRF(k^{(I)}, j)$. Then, it uses $k_j^{(I)}$, $bk^{(I)}$, and $c_j^{(I)}$ to regenerate the bin's masking values:
      - If the bin has never been fetched (i.e., $c_j^{(I)} = 0$), then it computes

      $$b_j^{(I)} = PRF'(bk^{(I)}, j) \text{ and } \forall i, 1 \leq i \leq n : z_{j,i}^{(I)} = PRF(k_j^{(I)}, i)$$

      - Otherwise (i.e., $c_j^{(I)} \neq 0$), it computes:

      $$b_j^{(I)} = PRF'(PRF'(bk^{(I)}, j), c_j^{(I)}) \text{ and } \forall i, 1 \leq i \leq n : z_{j,i}^{(I)} = PRF(PRF(k_j^{(I)}, c_j^{(I)}), i)$$

   b. ***Unblind:*** Removes the blinding factors from the bin and its blinded Bloom filter, as follows. $B_j^{(I)} = BB_j^{(I)} \oplus b_j^{(I)}$, $\forall i, 1 \leq i \leq n : y_{j,i}^{(I)} = o_{j,i}^{(I)} - z_{j,i}^{(I)}$. The result is a Bloom filter: $B_j^{(I)}$ and a vector: $\overrightarrow{y}_j^{(I)} = \{y_{j,1}^{(I)}, ..., y_{j,n}^{(I)}\}$.
3. ***Update the counter:*** Increments the corresponding counter: $c_j^{(I)} = c_j^{(I)} + 1$.
4. ***Update the bin's content:***
   - If update: **element insertion**

* if the element, to be inserted, is not in the bin's Bloom filter, then it uses the n pairs of $(y_{j,i}^{(l)}, x_i)$ to interpolate a polynomial: $\psi_j(x)$ and considers valid roots of $\psi_j(x)$ as the set elements in that bin. Then, it generates a polynomial: $\prod_{m=1}^{d}(x - s_m'^{(l)})$, where its roots consist of valid roots of $\psi_j(x)$, $s^{(l)}$, and some random elements to pad the bin. Next, it evaluates the polynomial at every $x_i \in \vec{x}$. This yields $\vec{u}_j^{(l)} = [u_{j,1}^{(l)}, ..., u_{j,n}^{(l)}]$. It discards $\mathsf{B}_j^{(l)}$ and builds a fresh one: $\mathsf{B}_j'^{(l)}$ encoding $s^{(l)}$ and valid roots of $\psi_j(x)$.

* otherwise, i.e., if $s^{(l)} \in \mathsf{B}_j^{(l)}$, it sets $\vec{u}_j^{(l)} = \vec{y}_j^{(l)}$ and $\mathsf{B}_j'^{(l)} = \mathsf{B}_j^{(l)}$, where $\vec{y}_j^{(l)}$ and $\mathsf{B}_j^{(l)}$ were computed in step 2.b. Note, in this case the element already exists in the set; therefore, the element is not inserted.

- If update: **element deletion**
  * if the element, to be deleted, is not in the bin's Bloom filter, then it sets $\vec{u}_j^{(l)} = \vec{y}_j^{(l)}$ and $\mathsf{B}_j'^{(l)} = \mathsf{B}_j^{(l)}$, where $\vec{y}_j^{(l)}$ and $\mathsf{B}_j^{(l)}$ were computed in step 2.b. It means the element does not exist in the set, so no deletion is needed.
  * otherwise, if $s^{(l)} \in \mathsf{B}_j^{(l)}$, it uses pairs $(y_{j,i}^{(l)}, x_i)$ to interpolate a polynomial: $\psi_j(x)$. It constructs a polynomial: $\prod_{m=1}^{d}(x - s_m'^{(l)})$, where its roots contains valid roots of $\psi_j(x)$, excluding $s^{(l)}$, and some random elements to pad the bin (if required). Then, it evaluates the polynomial at every $x_i \in \vec{x}$. This yields $\vec{u}_j^{(l)} = [u_{j,1}^{(l)}, ..., u_{j,n}^{(l)}]$. Also, it discards $\mathsf{B}_j^{(l)}$ and builds a fresh one: $\mathsf{B}_j'^{(l)}$ that encodes valid roots of $\psi_j(x)$ excluding $s^{(l)}$.

5. **Blind**: Blinds the updated bin: $\vec{u}_j^{(l)}$ and Bloom filter: $\mathsf{B}_j'^{(l)}$ as follows.
   a. generates fresh blinding factors:

   $$b_j^{(l)} = \mathsf{PRF}'(\mathsf{PRF}'(bk^{(l)}, j), c_j^{(l)}), \quad \forall i, 1 \le i \le n : z_{j,i}^{(l)} = \mathsf{PRF}(\mathsf{PRF}(k_j^{(l)}, c_j^{(l)}), i)$$

   b. blinds the bin's content and Bloom filter, using the fresh blinding factors.

   $$\mathsf{BB}_j^{(l)} = \mathsf{B}_j'^{(l)} \oplus b_j^{(l)} \quad and \quad \forall i, 1 \le i \le n : o_{j,i}^{(l)} = u_{j,i}^{(l)} + z_{j,i}^{(l)}$$

6. **Send update query**: Sends $\vec{o}_j^{(l)} = [o_{j,1}^{(l)}, ..., o_{j,n}^{(l)}], \mathsf{BB}_j^{(l)}, l_j^{(l)}$, and "Update" to the cloud which replaces the bin's and Bloom filter's contents with the new ones.

4.5 Feather PSI Computation Protocol

In this section, we present the PSI computation protocol in Feather. Note, to let the cloud compute PSI correctly, clients need to tell it how to combine the bins of their hash tables (each of which permuted under a different key) without revealing the bins' original order to the cloud. Also, as the blinding values of some of the bins get refreshed (when updated), each client needs to efficiently regenerate the most recent ones in PSI delegation and update phases. To address those issues, we use two novel techniques: *permutation mapping*, and *resettable counter*, respectively. Now, we outline how the clients delegate the computation to the cloud. When client B wants the intersection of its set and clients $A_\sigma \in \{A_1, ..., A_\xi\}$ sets, it sends a message to each client A_σ to obtain its permission. If client A_σ agrees, it generates two sets of messages (with the help of the counter), one for client B and one for the cloud. It sends messages that include unblinding vectors to client B, and a message that includes a permutation map to the cloud. The vectors help client B to unblind the cloud's response. The map lets the cloud associate client A_σ's bins to client B's bins. The cloud uses the clients' messages and the outsourced datasets to compute the result that contains a set of blinded polynomials. It sends them to client B which unblinds them and retrieves the intersection. Below, we present the PSI computation protocol in more detail.

1. **Computation Delegation:** It is initiated by B which is interested in the intersection.

   a. **Gen. a permission query:** Client B performs as follows.

      i. ***Regen. blinding factors:*** regenerates the most recent blinding factors: $\vec{z}^{(B)} = [\vec{z}_1^{(B)}, ..., \vec{z}_h^{(B)}]$ (as explained in step 2.a. of the update). Then, it shuffles the vector: $\pi(pk^{(B)}, \vec{z}^{(B)})$.

      ii. ***Mask blinding factors:*** to mask the shuffled vector, it picks a fresh temporary key: $tk^{(B)}$, uses it to allocate a key to each bin, i.e., $\forall g, 1 \leq g \leq h : tk_g^{(B)} = \text{PRF}(tk^{(B)}, g)$. Then, using each key, it generates fresh pseudorandom values and uses them to blind the vector's elements, as below:

      $$\forall g, 1 \leq g \leq h, \ \forall i, 1 \leq i \leq n : r_{g,i}^{(B)} = z_{a,i}^{(B)} + \text{PRF}(tk_g^{(B)}, i)$$

      Let $\vec{r}_g^{(B)} = [r_{g,1}^{(B)}, ..., r_{g,n}^{(B)}]$. Note, $\vec{z}_a^{(B)}$ at index a ($1 \leq a \leq h$) in $\vec{z}^{(B)}$ moved to index g after it was shuffled in the previous step.

      iii. ***Send off secret values:*** sends $lk^{(B)}, pk^{(B)}, \vec{r}^{(B)} = [\vec{r}_1^{(B)}, ..., \vec{r}_h^{(B)}]$, and its id: $\text{ID}^{(B)}$, to every client A_σ. Also, it sends $tk^{(B)}$ to the cloud.

   b. **Grant the computation:** Each client $A_\sigma \in \{A_1, ..., A_\xi\}$ performs as follows.

      i. ***Gen. a mapping:*** computes a mapping vector that will allow the cloud to match client A_σ's bins to client B's ones. To do so, it first generates $\vec{M}_{A_\sigma \to B}$ whose elements, m_g, are computed as follows.

      $$\forall g, 1 \leq g \leq h : \ l_g^{(A_\sigma)} = \text{PRF}(lk^{(A_\sigma)}, g), l_g^{(B)} = \text{PRF}(lk^{(B)}, g), m_g = (l_g^{(A_\sigma)}, l_g^{(B)})$$

      It permutes the elements of $\vec{M}_{A_\sigma \to B}$. This yields mapping vector $\vec{\vec{M}}_{A_\sigma \to B}$.

      ii. ***Regen. blinding factors:*** regenerates the most recent blinding factors: $\vec{z}^{(A_\sigma)} = [\vec{z}_1^{(A_\sigma)}, ..., \vec{z}_h^{(A_\sigma)}]$ where each $\vec{z}_g^{(A_\sigma)}$ contains n blinding factors. After that, it pseudorandomly permutes the vector as: $\pi(pk^{(A_\sigma)}, \vec{z}^{(A_\sigma)})$.

      iii. ***Gen. random masks and polynomials:*** assigns n fresh random values: $a_{g,i}^{(A_\sigma)}$ and two random degree-d polynomials: $\omega_g^{(A_\sigma)}, \omega_g^{(B_\sigma)}$ to each bin: HT_g.

iv. **Gen. mask removers:** generates $\vec{q}^{(A_\sigma)}$ that will assist client B to remove the blinding factors from the result provided by the cloud. To do that, it first multiplies each element at position g in $\pi(pk^{(A)}, \vec{z}^{(A)})$ and in $\vec{r}^{(B)}$, by $\omega_g^{(A_\sigma)}$ and $\omega_g^{(B_\sigma)}$, respectively, i.e., $\forall g, 1 \le g \le h$ and $\forall i, 1 \le i \le n$:

$$v_{g,i}^{(A_\sigma)} = \omega_{g,i}^{(A_\sigma)} \cdot z_{j,i}^{(A_\sigma)} \quad \text{and} \quad v_{g,i}^{(B_\sigma)} = \omega_{g,i}^{(B_\sigma)} \cdot r_{g,i}^{(B_\sigma)} = \omega_{g,i}^{(B_\sigma)} \cdot (z_{a,i}^{(B)} + \mathsf{PRF}(tk_g^{(B)}, i))$$

Then, given permutation keys: $pk^{(A_\sigma)}$ and $pk^{(B_\sigma)}$, for each value $v_{g,i}^{(A_\sigma)}$ it finds its matched value: $v_{e,i}^{(B_\sigma)}$, such that the blinding factors $z_{j,i}^{(A_\sigma)}$ and $z_{j,i}^{(B)}$ of the two values belong to the same bin, HT_j. Specifically, for each $v_{g,i}^{(A_\sigma)} = \omega_{g,i}^{(A_\sigma)} \cdot z_{j,i}^{(A_\sigma)}$ it finds $v_{e,i}^{(B_\sigma)} = \omega_{e,i}^{(B_\sigma)} \cdot (z_{j,i}^{(B)} + \mathsf{PRF}(tk_e^{(B)}, i))$. Next, it combines and blinds the matched values, i.e., $\forall g, 1 \le g \le h$ and $\forall i, 1 \le i \le n$:

$$q_{e,i}^{(A_\sigma)} = -(v_{g,i}^{(A_\sigma)} + v_{e,i}^{(B_\sigma)}) + a_{g,i}^{(A_\sigma)} = -(\omega_{g,i}^{(A_\sigma)} \cdot z_{j,i}^{(A_\sigma)} + \omega_{e,i}^{(B_\sigma)} \cdot (z_{j,i}^{(B)} + \mathsf{PRF}(tk_e^{(B)}, i))) + a_{g,i}^{(A_\sigma)}$$

v. **Send values:** sends $\vec{q}^{(A_\sigma)} = [\vec{q}_1^{(A_\sigma)}, ..., \vec{q}_h^{(A_\sigma)}]$ to client B, where each $\vec{q}_e^{(A_\sigma)}$ contains $q_{e,i}^{(A_\sigma)}$. It sends to the cloud $\mathsf{ID}^{(B)}$, $\mathsf{ID}^{(A_\sigma)}$, $\vec{M}_{A_\sigma \to B}$, the blinding factors: $a_{g,i}^{(A_\sigma)}$, "**Compute**", and random polynomials' y-coordinates, i.e., all $\omega_{g,i}^{(A_\sigma)}$, $\omega_{g,i}^{(B_\sigma)}$.

2. **Cloud-side Result Computation:** The cloud uses each mapping vector: $\vec{M}_{A_\sigma \to B}$ to match the bins of clients A_σ and B. Specifically, for each e-th bin in $\vec{o}^{(B)}$ it finds g_σ-th bin in $\vec{o}^{(A_\sigma)}$, where both bins would have the same index, e.g., j, before they were permuted. Next, it generates the elements of $\vec{t}_e$, i.e., $\forall e, 1 \le e \le h$ and $\forall i, 1 \le i \le n$:

$$t_{e,i} = \left(\sum_{\sigma=1}^{\xi} \omega_{e,i}^{(B_\sigma)}\right) \cdot (o_{e,i}^{(B)} + \mathsf{PRF}(tk_e^{(B)}, i)) - \sum_{\sigma=1}^{\xi} a_{g_\sigma,i}^{(A_\sigma)} + \sum_{\sigma=1}^{\xi} \omega_{g_\sigma,i}^{(A_\sigma)} \cdot o_{g_\sigma,i}^{(A_\sigma)}$$

where $o_{g_\sigma,i}^{(A_\sigma)} \in \vec{o}_{g_\sigma}^{(A_\sigma)} \in \vec{o}^{(A_\sigma)}$. It sends to B its blinded Bloom filters: $\vec{\mathsf{BB}}^{(B)}$ and result $\vec{t} = [\vec{t}_1, ..., \vec{t}_h]$, where each $\vec{t}_e$ has values $t_{e,i}$.

3. **Client-side Result Retrieval:** Client B unblinds the permuted Bloom filters using the key $bk^{(B)}$. This yields a vector of permuted Bloom filters $\hat{\mathsf{B}}^{(B)}$. Then, it uses the elements of vectors $\vec{q}^{(A_\sigma)}$ to remove the blinding from the result sent by the cloud, i.e., $\forall e, 1 \le e \le h$ and $\forall i, 1 \le i \le n$:

$$f_{e,i} = t_{e,i} + \sum_{\sigma=1}^{\xi} q_{e,i}^{(A_\sigma)} = \left(\sum_{\sigma=1}^{\xi} \omega_{e,i}^{(B_\sigma)}\right) \cdot (u_{j,i}^{(B)}) + \sum_{\sigma=1}^{\xi} \omega_{g_\sigma,i}^{(A_\sigma)} \cdot u_{j,i}^{(A_\sigma)}$$

Given vectors $\vec{f}_e$ and $\vec{x}$, it interpolates h polynomials: $\phi_e(x)$, for all e. Then, it extracts the roots of each polynomial. It considers the roots encoded in $\mathsf{B}_e^{(B)} \in \hat{\mathsf{B}}^{(B)}$ as valid, and the union of all valid roots as the sets' intersection.

Theorem 1. *If* PRF *and* $\mathsf{PRF'}$ *are pseudorandom functions, and* π *is a pseudorandom permutation, then Feather is secure in the presence of (a) a semi-honest cloud, or (b) semi-honest clients where all but one clients collude with each other.*

Proof Outline. In the following, we provide an overview of the proof and we refer readers to the paper's full version, for an elaborated one. We conduct the security analysis for three cases where one of the parties is corrupt at a time. In *corrupt cloud* case, we show that given the leakage function output, i.e. query and access patterns, we can construct a simulator that produces a view indistinguishable from the one in the real model. The proof includes (1) simulating each client's outsourced data, (2) simulating clients queries (in PSI and update) by using query pattern (and access pattern in the update), and (3) arguing that the simulated values are indistinguishable from their counter-party in the real model, mainly based on the indistinguishability of pseudorandom functions and permutation outputs. In *corrupt client B* case, the proof includes (1) simulating each authoriser client's input and query, (2) simulating cloud's result, and (3) arguing that the simulated values are indistinguishable from their counter-party in the real model and it cannot learn anything beyond the intersection; the argument is based on the indistinguishability of randomised polynomials (in Sect. 3.5) and the indistinguishability of pseudorandom functions and permutation output. In *corrupt client A_σ* case, the proof comprises (1) simulating client B's queries and (2) arguing that the simulated values are indistinguishable from those in the real model, according to the indistinguishability of pseudorandom functions output.

In the paper's full version, we provide several remarks on Feather's protocols and explain why naive solutions cannot offer Feather's features. In the full version, we present various extensions of Feather that outline how to: (a) reduce authorizers' storage space, (b) reset the counters, (c) further delegate grating the computation to a semi-honest third-party, and (d) further reduce communication cost.

5   Asymptotic Cost Analysis

In this section, we analyse and compare the complexities of Feather with those of delegated and traditional PSIs that support multi-client in the semi-honest model. Table 1 summarizes the results. We do not take the update cost of the traditional multi-party PSIs, i.e., in [28, 37], into account, as they are designed

Table 1. Comparison of the multi-party PSIs. Note, c: set cardinality upper bound, $\xi + 1$: total number of clients, $d = 100$, and all costs are in big O.

Property	Feather	[1]	[6]	[7]	[44]	[37]	[28]
Repeated delegated PSI	✓	✓	✓	✓	✓	✗	✗
Supporting multi-party	✓	✓	✓	✓	✓	✓	✓
Mainly symmetric key primitives	✓	✓	✗	✗	✗	✓	✓
Total PSI comm. complexity	$c\xi$	$c\xi$	$c\xi$	$c\xi$	$c\xi$	$c\xi^2$	$c\xi^2$
Total PSI cmp. complexity	$c\xi + c$	$c\xi + c$	$c\xi + c^2$	$c\xi + c^2$	$c\xi + c^2$	$c\xi^2 + c\xi$	$c\xi^2 + c\xi$
Update comm. complexity	d	c	c	c	c	–	–
Update comp. complexity	d^2	c	c	c	c	–	–

for the cases where parties maintain locally their set elements and do not (need to) support data update. We present a full analysis in the paper's full version.

5.1   Communication Complexity

In PSI Computation. Below, we analyse the protocols' communication cost during the PSI computation. Briefly, in Feather, client B's cost is $O(c\xi)$, each client A_σ's cost is $O(c)$, and the cloud's cost is $O(c)$. Thus, Feather's total communication cost during the computation of PSI is $O(c\xi)$. The cost of each PSI in $[1,6,7,44]$ is $O(c\xi)$, where the majority of the messages in $[6,7,44]$ are the output of a public-key encryption scheme, whereas those in $[1]$ and Feather are random elements of a finite field, that have much shorter bit-length. Also, each scheme's complexity in $[28,37]$ is $O(c\xi^2)$.

In Update. In Feather, for a client to update its set, it sends to the cloud two labels, a vector of $2d+1$ elements, and a Bloom filter. So, in total its complexity is $O(d)$. The cloud sends a vector of $2d+1$ elements and a Bloom filter to the client that costs $O(d)$. Therefore, the update in Feather imposes $O(d)$ communication cost. The protocols in $[1,6,7,44]$ offer no efficient update mechanism. Therefore, for a client to securely update its set, it has to download and locally update the entire set, which costs $O(c)$.

5.2   Computation Complexity

In PSI Computation. Next, we analyse the schemes computation complexity during the PSI computation. First, we analyse Feather's complexity. In short, client B's and cloud's complexity is $O(c\xi + c)$ while each client A_σ's complexity is $O(c)$. During the PSI computation, the main operations that the parties perform are modular addition, multiplication, and polynomial factorization. Thus, Feather's complexity during the PSI computation is $O(c\xi + c)$. In the delegated PSIs in $[6,7,44]$, the cost is dominated by asymmetric key operations and polynomial factorization. These protocols' cost is $O(c\xi + c^2)$. Moreover, the cost of running PSI in the delegated PSI in $[1]$ is $O(c\xi + c)$. Now, we turn our attention to the traditional PSIs in $[28,37]$. Each PSI in $[28,37]$ has $O(c\xi^2 + c\xi)$ complexity and involves mainly symmetric key operations.

In Update. In Feather, to update an element, a client (i) performs $O(d)$ modular additions and multiplications, (ii) interpolates a polynomial that costs $O(d)$, (iii) extracts a bin's elements that costs $O(d^2)$, and (iv) evaluates a polynomial which costs $O(d)$. So, the client's total cost is $O(d^2)$. To update a set element in the PSIs in $[6,44]$, a client has to encode the element as a polynomial, evaluate the polynomial on $2c + 1$ points, and perform $O(c)$ multiplications. The cloud performs the same number of multiplications to apply the update. So, each protocol's update complexity is $O(c)$. In $[7]$, the client has to download the entire set, remove blinding factors, and apply the change locally that costs

$O(c)$. Although the PSI in [1] use a hash table, if a client updates a single bin, then the cloud would learn which elements are updated (with a non-negligible probability); Because the bins are in their original order and each bin's address is the hash value of an element in that bin. Thus, in [1], for a client to securely update its set, it has to locally re-encode the entire set that costs $O(c)$.

6 Concrete Cost Evaluation

In this section, we first explain how we choose the optimal parameters of a hash table. Then, we provide a concrete evaluation of three protocols: Feather and the PSIs in [1,37]. The reason we only consider [1,37] is that [37] is the fastest *traditional multi-party* PSI while [1] is the fastest *delegated* PSI among the PSIs studied in Sect. 5. We consider protocols in the semi-honest model.

6.1 Choice of Parameters

In Feather, with the right choice of the hash table's parameters, the cloud can keep the overall costs optimal. In this section, we briefly show how these parameters can be chosen. As before, let c be the upper bound of the set cardinality, d be the bin size, and h be the number of bins. Recall, in Feather the overall cost depends on the product, hd, i.e., the total number of elements, including set elements and random values stored in the hash table. Also, the computation cost is dominated by factorizing h polynomials of degree $n = 2d + 1$. For the cloud to keep the costs optimal, given c, it uses Inequality 2 (in the full version) to find the right balance between parameters d and h, in the sense that the *cost of factorizing a polynomial of degree n is minimal, while hd is* close to c. At a high level, to find the right parameters, we take the following steps. First, we measure the average time, t, taken to factorize a polynomial of degree n, for different values of n. Then, for each c, we compute h for different values of d. Next, for each d we compute ht, after that for each c we look for minimal d whose ht is at the lowest level. After conducting the above experiments, we can see that the cloud can set $d = 100$ for all values of c. In this setting, hd is at most $4c$ and only with a negligibly small probability, 2^{-40}, a bin receives more than d elements. We present a full analysis in the paper's full version.

6.2 Concrete Communication Cost Analysis

In PSI Computation. Below, we compare the three PSIs' concrete communication costs during the PSI computation. Briefly, Feather has 8–496 times lower cost than the PSI in [37], while it has 1.6–2.2 times higher cost than the one in [1], for 40-bit elements. The PSI's cost in [37] grows much faster than Feather's and the scheme in [1], when the number of clients increases. Feather has a slightly higher cost than the one in [1], as Feather lets each client A_σ send to the cloud $2hn$ y-coordinates of random polynomials yielding a significant computation *improvement*. Table 2 compares the three PSIs' cost. Table 5, in the paper's full version, provides a detailed analysis of Feather's communication cost.

In Update. In Feather, a client downloads and uploads only one bin, that makes its cost of update 0.003 MB for all set sizes, when each element bit-size is 40. In [1], for a client to securely update its data, it has to download the entire set, locally update and upload it. Via this approach, the update's total communication cost, in MB, is in the range $[0.13, 210]$ when the set size is in the range $[2^{10}, 2^{20}]$ and each element bit-size is 40. Thus, Feather's communication cost is from 45 to 70254 times lower than [1].

6.3 Concrete Computation Cost Analysis

In this section, we provide an empirical computation evaluation of Feather using a prototype implementation developed in C++. Feather's source code can be found in [2]. We compare the concrete computation cost of Feather with the two protocols in [1,37]. All experiments were run on a macOS laptop, with an Intel $i5@2.3$ GHz CPU, and 16 GB RAM. In the paper's full version, we provide full detail about the system's parameters used in the experiment.

Table 2. Concrete communication cost comparison (in MB)

Protocols	Elem. size	Set's cardinality			Number of clients				
		2^{12}	2^{16}	2^{20}	3	4	10	15	100
[37]	40, 64-bit	✓			24	45	300	679	30278
			✓		407	762	5015	11341	505658
				✓	6719	12571	82697	186984	8335520
[1]	40-bit	✓			0.8	1	2	4	29
			✓		18	25	62	93	625
				✓	300	400	1001	1501	10011
	64-bit	✓			1.3	1.7	4	6	43
			✓		28	37	94	141	941
				✓	452	602	1506	2260	15069
Feather	40-bit	✓			1	2	5	8	61
			✓		30	44	123	189	1311
				✓	494	705	1973	3028	20979
	64-bit	✓			2	3	9	14	97
			✓		48	69	196	301	2096
				✓	773	1111	3138	4828	33549

In PSI Computation. We first compare the runtime of Feather and the PSI in [1] in a two-client setting, as the latter was designed and implemented in this setting. Briefly, Feather is 2–2.5 times faster than the PSI in [1]. The cloud-side runtime in Feather is 26–34 times faster than the one in [1]. Because Feather lets each client compute and send y-coordinates of random polynomials to the cloud, so the cloud does not need to re-evaluate them. Tables 6 and 7, in the full version, compare these PSIs' runtime in the setup and PSI computation respectively. Briefly, for a small number of clients, the performance of the PSI in [37] is better than Feather, e.g., about 40–4 times when the number of clients is 3–15. But, the performance of the one in [37] gets *significantly* worse when the number of clients is large, e.g., 100–150; as its cost is quadratic with the number of clients. Thus, Feather outperforms the PSI in [37] when the number of clients is large. We provide a more detailed analysis in the full version. We also conducted experiments when a very large number of clients participate in Feather, i.e., up to 16000 clients. To provide a concrete value here, in Feather it takes 4.7 s to run PSI with 1000 clients where each client has 2^{11} elements. Table 9, in the full version, provides more detail.

In Update. Now, we compare the runtime of Feather and the PSI in [1] during the update. As the PSI in [1] does not provide a way for an update, we developed a prototype implementation of it that lets clients securely update their sets. The implementation's source code is in [3]. The update runtime of Feather is much faster than that of in [1]. The update runtime of the latter scheme, for 40-bit elements, grows from 0.07 to 27 s when the set size increases from 2^{10} to 2^{20}; whereas in Feather, the update runtime remains 0.023 s for all set sizes. Hence, the update in Feather is 3–1182 times faster than the one in [1]. Table 3 provides the update's runtime detailed comparison.

Table 3. The update runtime comparison between Feather and [1] (in sec.).

Protocols	Elem. size	2^{10}	2^{11}	2^{12}	2^{13}	2^{14}	2^{15}		2^{16}	2^{17}	2^{18}	2^{19}	2^{20}
[1]	40-bit	0.07	0.09	0.13	0.21	0.37	0.68		1.72	3.41	6.88	13.75	27.2
	64-bit	0.08	0.11	0.14	0.22	0.38	0.69		1.76	3.43	7.12	13.94	28.15
Feather	40-bit					← 0.023 →							
	64-bit					← 0.035 →							

7 Conclusion

Private set intersection (PSI) is an elegant protocol with numerous applications. Nowadays, due to cloud computing's growing popularity, there is a demand for an efficient PSI that can securely operate on multiple outsourced sets that are updated frequently. In this paper, we presented Feather. It is the first efficient delegated PSI that lets multiple clients (i) securely store their private sets in the cloud, (ii) efficiently perform data updates, and (iii) securely compute PSI on the outsourced sets. We implemented Feather and performed a rigorous cost analysis. The analysis indicates that Feather's performance during the update is over 10^3 times, and during PSI computation is over 2 times faster than the most efficient delegated PSI. Feather has low communication costs too.

Recently, it has been shown that the most efficient multi-party PSI in [25] supposed to be secure against active adversaries, suffers from serious issues. Hence, to fill the void, future research could investigate how to enhance Feather so it remains secure against *active* adversaries while preserving its efficiency.

Acknowledgments. Aydin Abadi was supported in part by REPHRAIN: The National Research Centre on Privacy, Harm Reduction and Adversarial Influence Online, under UKRI grant: EP/V011189/1. Steven J. Murdoch was supported by REPHRAIN and The Royal Society under grant UF160505. This work was also partially funded by EPSRC Doctoral Training Grant studentship and EPSRC research grants EP/M013561/2 and EP/N028198/1.

References

1. Abadi, A., Terzis, S., Metere, R., Dong, C.: Efficient delegated private set intersection on outsourced private datasets. IEEE Trans. Dependable Secure Comput. **16**(4), 608–624 (2018)

2. Abadi, A.: The implementation of multi-party updatable delegated private set intersection (2021). https://github.com/AydinAbadi/Feather/tree/master/Feather-implementation

3. Abadi, A.: The implementation of the update phase in efficient delegated private set intersection on outsourced private datasets (2021). https://github.com/AydinAbadi/Feather/tree/master/Update-Simulation-code

4. Abadi, A., Dong, C., Murdoch, S.J., Terzis, S.: Multi-party updatable delegated private set intersection-full version. In: FC (2022)

5. Abadi, A., Murdoch, S.J., Zacharias, T.: Polynomial representation is tricky: maliciously secure private set intersection revisited. In: Bertino, E., Shulman, H., Waidner, M. (eds.) ESORICS 2021. LNCS, vol. 12973, pp. 721–742. Springer, Cham (2021). https://doi.org/10.1007/978-3-030-88428-4_35

6. Abadi, A., Terzis, S., Dong, C.: O-PSI: delegated private set intersection on outsourced datasets. In: Federrath, H., Gollmann, D. (eds.) SEC 2015. IAICT, vol. 455, pp. 3–17. Springer, Cham (2015). https://doi.org/10.1007/978-3-319-18467-8_1

7. Abadi, A., Terzis, S., Dong, C.: VD-PSI: verifiable delegated private set intersection on outsourced private datasets. In: Grossklags, J., Preneel, B. (eds.) FC 2016. LNCS, vol. 9603, pp. 149–168. Springer, Heidelberg (2017). https://doi.org/10.1007/978-3-662-54970-4_9

8. Aho, A.V., Hopcroft, J.E.: The Design and Analysis of Computer Algorithms. Pearson Education India (1974)

9. Apple Inc.: Security threat model review of Apple's child safety features (2021). https://www.apple.com/child-safety/pdf/Security_Threat_Model_Review_of_Apple_Child_Safety_Features.pdf

10. Badrinarayanan, S., Miao, P., Raghuraman, S., Rindal, P.: Multi-party threshold private set intersection with sublinear communication. In: Garay, J.A. (ed.) PKC 2021. LNCS, vol. 12711, pp. 349–379. Springer, Cham (2021). https://doi.org/10.1007/978-3-030-75248-4_13

11. Baldi, P., Baronio, R., De Cristofaro, E., Gasti, P., Tsudik, G.: Countering gattaca: efficient and secure testing of fully-sequenced human genomes. In: CCS (2011)

12. Ben-Efraim, A., Nissenbaum, O., Omri, E., Paskin-Cherniavsky, A.: PSImple: practical multiparty maliciously-secure private set intersection. IACR Cryptology ePrint Archive (2021)

13. Berenbrink, P., Czumaj, A., Steger, A., Vöcking, B.: Balanced allocations: the heavily loaded case. In: STOC (2000)

14. Bhowmick, A., Boneh, D., Myers, S., Talwar, K., Tarbe, K.: The Apple PSI system (2021). https://www.apple.com/child-safety/pdf/Apple_PSI_System_Security_Protocol_and_Analysis.pdf
15. Bloom, B.H.: Space/time trade-offs in hash coding with allowable errors. Commun. ACM **13**(7), 422–426 (1970)
16. Branco, P., Döttling, N., Pu, S.: Multiparty cardinality testing for threshold private set intersection. IACR Cryptology ePrint Archive (2020)
17. Brickell, J., Porter, D.E., Shmatikov, V., Witchel, E.: Privacy-preserving remote diagnostics. In: CCS (2007)
18. Chase, M., Miao, P.: Private set intersection in the internet setting from lightweight oblivious PRF. In: Micciancio, D., Ristenpart, T. (eds.) CRYPTO 2020. LNCS, vol. 12172, pp. 34–63. Springer, Cham (2020). https://doi.org/10.1007/978-3-030-56877-1_2
19. Chen, H., Laine, K., Rindal, P.: Fast private set intersection from homomorphic encryption. In: ACM CCS (2017)
20. Dorn, W.S.: Generalizations of Horner's rule for polynomial evaluation. IBM J. Res. Dev. **6**(2), 239–245 (1962)
21. Duong, T., Phan, D.H., Trieu, N.: Catalic: delegated PSI cardinality with applications to contact tracing. In: Moriai, S., Wang, H. (eds.) ASIACRYPT 2020. LNCS, vol. 12493, pp. 870–899. Springer, Cham (2020). https://doi.org/10.1007/978-3-030-64840-4_29
22. Financial Action Task Force (FATF): Stocktake on data pooling, collaborative analytics and data protection (2021). https://www.fatf-gafi.org/publications/digitaltransformation/documents/data-pooling-collaborative-analytics-data-protection.html
23. Freedman, M.J., Nissim, K., Pinkas, B.: Efficient private matching and set intersection. In: Cachin, C., Camenisch, J.L. (eds.) EUROCRYPT 2004. LNCS, vol. 3027, pp. 1–19. Springer, Heidelberg (2004). https://doi.org/10.1007/978-3-540-24676-3_1
24. von zur Gathen, J., Panario, D.: Factoring polynomials over finite fields: a survey. J. Symb. Comput. **31**(1–2), 3–17 (2001)
25. Ghosh, S., Nilges, T.: An algebraic approach to maliciously secure private set intersection. In: Ishai, Y., Rijmen, V. (eds.) EUROCRYPT 2019. LNCS, vol. 11478, pp. 154–185. Springer, Cham (2019). https://doi.org/10.1007/978-3-030-17659-4_6
26. Ghosh, S., Simkin, M.: The communication complexity of threshold private set intersection. In: Boldyreva, A., Micciancio, D. (eds.) CRYPTO 2019. LNCS, vol. 11693, pp. 3–29. Springer, Cham (2019). https://doi.org/10.1007/978-3-030-26951-7_1
27. Hahn, F., Kerschbaum, F.: Searchable encryption with secure and efficient updates. In: ACM CCS (2014)
28. Inbar, R., Omri, E., Pinkas, B.: Efficient scalable multiparty private set-intersection via garbled bloom filters. In: Catalano, D., De Prisco, R. (eds.) SCN 2018. LNCS, vol. 11035, pp. 235–252. Springer, Cham (2018). https://doi.org/10.1007/978-3-319-98113-0_13
29. Kamara, S., Mohassel, P., Raykova, M.: Outsourcing multi-party computation. ePrint (2011)
30. Kamara, S., Mohassel, P., Raykova, M., Sadeghian, S.: Scaling private set intersection to billion-element sets. In: Christin, N., Safavi-Naini, R. (eds.) FC 2014. LNCS, vol. 8437, pp. 195–215. Springer, Heidelberg (2014). https://doi.org/10.1007/978-3-662-45472-5_13

31. Kamara, S., Papamanthou, C.: Parallel and dynamic searchable symmetric encryption. In: Sadeghi, A.-R. (ed.) FC 2013. LNCS, vol. 7859, pp. 258–274. Springer, Heidelberg (2013). https://doi.org/10.1007/978-3-642-39884-1_22
32. Katz, J., Lindell, Y.: Introduction to Modern Cryptography. CRC Press (2007)
33. Kerschbaum, F.: Outsourced private set intersection using homomorphic encryption. In: ASIACCS (2012)
34. Kissner, L., Song, D.: Privacy-preserving set operations. In: Shoup, V. (ed.) CRYPTO 2005. LNCS, vol. 3621, pp. 241–257. Springer, Heidelberg (2005). https://doi.org/10.1007/11535218_15
35. Knuth, D.E.: The Art of Computer Programming, Volume II: Seminumerical Algorithms, 2nd edn. Addison-Wesley (1981)
36. Kolesnikov, V., Kumaresan, R., Rosulek, M., Trieu, N.: Efficient batched oblivious PRF with applications to private set intersection. In: CCS (2016)
37. Kolesnikov, V., Matania, N., Pinkas, B., Rosulek, M., Trieu, N.: Practical multiparty private set intersection from symmetric-key techniques. In: CCS (2017)
38. Liu, F., Ng, W.K., Zhang, W., Giang, D.H., Han, S.: Encrypted set intersection protocol for outsourced datasets. In: IC2E (2014)
39. Pinkas, B., Rosulek, M., Trieu, N., Yanai, A.: PSI from PaXoS: fast, malicious private set intersection. In: Canteaut, A., Ishai, Y. (eds.) EUROCRYPT 2020. LNCS, vol. 12106, pp. 739–767. Springer, Cham (2020). https://doi.org/10.1007/978-3-030-45724-2_25
40. Qiu, S., Liu, J., Shi, Y., Li, M., Wang, W.: Identity-based private matching over outsourced encrypted datasets. IEEE Trans. Cloud Comput. 6(3), 747–759 (2018)
41. Silva, J.: Banking on the cloud: results from the 2020 cloudpath survey (2020). https://www.idc.com/getdoc.jsp?containerId=US45822120
42. Tsai, C.F., Hsiao, Y.C.: Combining multiple feature selection methods for stock prediction: union, intersection, and multi-intersection approaches. Decis. Support Syst. 50(1), 258–269 (2010)
43. Citrin, A.V., Sprott, D.E., Silverman, S.N., Stem Jr., D.E.: Adoption of internet shopping: the role of consumer innovativeness. Ind. Manag. Data Syst. 100(7), 294–300 (2000)
44. Yang, X., Luo, X., Wang, X.A., Zhang, S.: Improved outsourced private set intersection protocol based on polynomial interpolation. Concurr. Comput. 30(1), e4329 (2018)
45. Zhang, E., Liu, F., Lai, Q., Jin, G., Li, Y.: Efficient multi-party private set intersection against malicious adversaries. In: CCSW (2019)
46. Zhao, Y., Chow, S.S.M.: Can you find the one for me? Privacy-preserving matchmaking via threshold PSI. IACR Cryptology ePrint Archive (2018)
47. Zheng, Q., Xu, S.: Verifiable delegated set intersection operations on outsourced encrypted data. In: IC2E (2015)

Privacy

The Effect of False Positives: Why Fuzzy Message Detection Leads to Fuzzy Privacy Guarantees?

István András Seres[1]([✉]), Balázs Pejó[2], and Péter Burcsi[1]

[1] Eötvös Loránd University, Budapest, Hungary
`seresistvanandras@gmail.com`
[2] CrySyS Lab, HIT/VIK/BME, Budapest, Hungary

Abstract. Fuzzy Message Detection (FMD) is a recent cryptographic primitive invented by Beck et al. (CCS'21) where an untrusted server performs coarse message filtering for its clients in a recipient-anonymous way. In FMD—besides the true positive messages—the clients download from the server their cover messages determined by their false-positive detection rates. What is more, within FMD, the server cannot distinguish between genuine and cover traffic. In this paper, we formally analyze the privacy guarantees of FMD from three different angles.

First, we analyze three privacy provisions offered by FMD: recipient unlinkability, relationship anonymity, and temporal detection ambiguity. Second, we perform a differential privacy analysis and coin a relaxed definition to capture the privacy guarantees FMD yields. Finally, we simulate FMD on real-world communication data. Our theoretical and empirical results assist FMD users in adequately selecting their false-positive detection rates for various applications with given privacy requirements.

Keywords: Fuzzy Message Detection · Unlinkability · Anonymity · Differential privacy · Game theory

1 Introduction

Fuzzy Message Detection (FMD) [3] is a promising, very recent privacy-enhancing cryptographic primitive that aims to provide several desired privacy properties such as recipients' anonymity. In recipient-anonymous communication systems, not even the intended recipients can tell which messages have been sent to them without decrypting all messages. The main practical drawback for the users in a recipient-anonymous scheme such as messaging and payment systems is to *efficiently and privately* detect the incoming messages or transactions. Decrypting all traffic in the system leads to a private but inevitably inefficient and bandwidth-wasting scan. This challenge is tackled by FMD, which allows the users to outsource the detection of their incoming traffic to an untrusted server in an efficient and privacy-enhanced way. It is assumed that messages/transactions are posted continuously to a potentially public board, e.g., to a permissionless

© International Financial Cryptography Association 2022
I. Eyal and J. Garay (Eds.): FC 2022, LNCS 13411, pp. 123–148, 2022.
https://doi.org/10.1007/978-3-031-18283-9_7

public blockchain. It is expected that users are intermittently connected and resource-constrained. In the FMD scheme, whenever users are online, they download their genuine transactions as well as false-positive transactions according to their custom-set false-positive detection rate. The cryptographic technique behind FMD guarantees that true and false-positive messages are indistinguishable from the server's point of view. Thus, the false-positive messages act as cover traffic for genuine messages.

The FMD protocol caught the attention of many practitioners and privacy advocates due to the protocol's applicability in numerous scenarios. In general, it supports privacy-preserving retrieval of incoming traffic from store-and-forward delivery systems. We highlight two applications currently being implemented by multiple teams and waiting to be deployed in several projects [4,8,23,32].

– **Anonymous messaging.** In a recipient-anonymous messaging application, the senders post their recipient-anonymous messages to a store-and-forward server. If the server employs FMD, recipients can detect their incoming (and false-positive) messages in an efficient and privacy-enhanced way. Recently, the Niwl messaging application was deployed utilizing FMD [23].
– **Privacy-preserving cryptocurrencies & stealth payments.** In privacy-preserving cryptocurrencies, e.g., Monero [29], Zcash [33], or in a privacy-enhancing overlay, payment recipients wish to detect their incoming payments without scanning the whole ledger. At the time of writing, several privacy-enhancing overlays for Ethereum (e.g., Zeth [32], Umbra [4]) as well as for standalone cryptocurrencies (e.g., Penumbra [8]) are actively exploring the possibility of applying FMD in their protocols.

Contributions. Despite the rapid adoption and interest in the FMD protocol, as far as we know, there is no study analyzing the provided privacy guarantees. Consequently, it is essential to understand the privacy implications of FMD. Furthermore, it is an open question how users need to choose their false-positive detection rates to achieve an efficiency-privacy trade-off suitable for their scenario. In this work, we make the following contributions.

– **Information-Theoretical Analysis.** We assess and quantify the privacy guarantees of FMD and the enhanced k-anonymity it provides in the context of anonymous communication systems. We focus on three notions of privacy and anonymity: relationship anonymity, recipient unlinkability, and temporal detection ambiguity. We demonstrate that FMD does not provide relationship anonymity when the server knows the senders' identity. What is more, we also study relationship anonymity from a game-theoretic point of view, and show that in our simplified model at the Nash Equilibrium the users do not employ any cover traffic due to their selfishness. Concerning recipient unlinkability and temporal detection ambiguity, we show that they are only provided in a meaningful way when the system has numerous users and users apply considerable false-positive detection rates.
– **Differential Privacy Analysis.** We adopt differential privacy (DP) [11] for the FMD scenario and coin a new definition, called Personalized Existing

Edge Differential Privacy (PEEDP). Moreover, we analyze the number of incoming messages of a user with (ε, δ)-differential privacy. The uncovered trade-off between the FMD's false-positive rates and DP's parameters could help the users to determine the appropriate regimes of false-positive rates, which corresponds to the level of tolerated privacy leakage.

- **Simulation of FMD on Real-World Data.** We quantitatively evaluate the privacy guarantees of FMD through open-source simulations on real-world communication systems. We show that the untrusted server can effortlessly recover a large portion of the social graph of the communicating users, i.e., the server can break relationship anonymity for numerous users.

Outline. In Sect. 2, we provide some background on FMD, while in Sect. 3, we introduce our system and threat model. In Sect. 4, we analyze the privacy guarantees of FMD while in Sect. 5 we study FMD using differential privacy. In Sect. 6, we conduct simulations on real-world communication networks, and finally, in Sect. 7, we conclude the paper.

2 Fuzzy Message Detection

The FMD protocol seeks to provide a reasonable privacy-efficiency trade-off in use cases where *recipient anonymity* needs to be protected. Users generate detection keys and send them along with their public keys to the untrusted server. Senders encrypt their messages with their recipient's public key and create flag ciphertexts using the intended recipient's public key. Detection keys allow the server to test whether a flag ciphertext gives a match for a user's public key. If yes, the server stores the message for that user identified by its public key. In particular, matched flag ciphertexts can be false-positive matches, i.e., the user cannot decrypt some matched ciphertexts. Users can decrease their false-positive rate by sending more detection keys to the server. Above all, the FMD protocol ensures *correctness*; whenever a user comes online, they can retrieve their genuine messages. The *fuzziness* property enforces that each other flag ciphertext is tested to be a match approximately with probability p set by the recipient.

Besides recipient anonymity, FMD also aims to satisfy *detection ambiguity*, which requires that the server cannot distinguish between true and false-positive matching flag ciphertexts provided that ciphertexts and detection keys are honestly generated. Hence, whenever a user downloads its matched messages, false-positive messages serve as cover traffic for the genuine messages. For formal security and privacy definitions of FMD and concrete instantiations, we refer the reader to Appendix A and ultimately to [3]. To improve readability, in Table 1, we present the variables utilized in the paper: we refer to the downloaded (genuine or cover) flag ciphertext as a fuzzy tag.

Privacy-Efficiency Trade-Off. If user u's false-positive rate is $p(u)$, it received $in(u)$ messages and the total number of messages in the system is M, then the server will store $tag(u) \approx in(u) + p(u)(M - in(u))$ messages for u. Clearly, as the number of messages stored by the server increases, so does the strength

Table 1. Notations used throughout the paper.

Variable	Description
U	Number of honest users (i.e., recipients and senders)
M	Number of all messages sent by honest users
$p(u)$	False-positive detection rate of recipient u
$tag(u)$	Number of fuzzy tags received by u (i.e., genuine and false positive)
$tag_v(u)$	Number of fuzzy tags received by u from v
$in(u)$	Number of genuine incoming messages of u
$out(u)$	Number of sent messages of u

of the anonymity protection of a message. Note the trade-off between privacy and bandwidth efficiency: larger false-positive rate $p(u)$ corresponds to stronger privacy guarantees but also to higher bandwidth as more messages need to be downloaded from the server.[1] Substantial bandwidth can be prohibitive in certain use cases, e.g., for resource-constrained clients. Even though in the original work of Beck et al. [3] their FMD instantiations support a restricted subset of $[2^{-l}]_{l \in \mathbb{Z}}$ as false-positive rates, in our privacy analysis, we lift these restrictions and assume that FMD supports any false-positive rate $p \in [0,1]$.

Provided Privacy Protection. The anonymity protection of FMD falls under the "hide-in-the-crowd" umbrella term as legitimate messages are concealed amongst cover ones. More precisely, each legitimate message enjoys an enhanced version of the well-known notion of k-anonymity [36].[2] In more detail, the anonymity guarantee of the FMD scheme is essentially a "dynamic", "personalized", and "probabilistic" extension of k-anonymity. It is dynamic because k could change over time as the overall number of messages could grow. It is personalized because k might differ from user to user as each user could set their own cover detection rates differently. Finally, it is probabilistic because achieved k may vary message-wise for a user due to the randomness of the amount of selected fuzzy messages.

To the best of our knowledge, as of today, there has not been a formal anonymity analysis of the "enhanced k-anonymity" achieved by the FMD protocol. Yet, there is already a great line of research demonstrating the weaknesses and the brittle privacy guarantees achieved by k-anonymity [10,25]. Intuitively, one might hope that enhanced k-anonymity could yield strong(er) privacy and anonymity guarantees. However, we show both theoretically and empirically and by using several tools that this enhanced k-anonymity fails to satisfy standard anonymity notions used in the anonymous communication literature.[3]

---

[1] Similar scenario was studied in [5] concerning Bloom filters.

[2] Note that Beck et al. coined this as *dynamic k-anonymity*, yet, we believe it does not capture all the aspects of their improvement. Hence, we renamed it with a more generic term.

[3] For an initial empirical anonymity analysis, we refer the reader to the simulator developed by Sarah Jamie Lewis [24].

3   System and Threat Model

System Model. In a typical application where the FMD scheme is applied, we distinguish between the following four types of system components where the users can simultaneously be senders and recipients.

1. **Senders:** They send encrypted messages to a message board. Messages are key-private, i.e., no party other than the intended recipient can tell which public key was used to encrypt the message. Additionally, senders post flag ciphertexts associated with the messages to an untrusted server. The goal of the flag ciphertexts is to allow the server and the recipients to detect their messages in a privacy-enhanced manner.
2. **Message Board:** It is a database that contains the senders' messages. In many applications (e.g., stealth payments), we think of the message board as a public bulletin board; i.e., everyone can read and write the board. It might be implemented as a blockchain or as a centrally managed database, e.g., as would be the case in a messaging application. In either case, we assume that the message board is always available and that its integrity is guaranteed.
3. **Server:** It stores the detection keys of recipients. Additionally, it receives and stores flag ciphertexts from senders and tests the flag ciphertexts with the recipient's detection keys. It forwards matching flag ciphertexts and their associated data (messages, transactions, etc.) to recipients whenever they query it. Typically, flag ciphertexts match numerous recipients' public keys.[4]
4. **Recipients:** The recipient obtains matching flag ciphertexts from the server. An application-dependent message is attached as associated data to each flag ciphertext, e.g., e-mail, payment data, or instant message. The number of matching ciphertexts is proportional to the recipient's false-positive detection rate and all the messages stored by the untrusted server.

Threat Model. Our focus is on the privacy and anonymity guarantees provided by FMD. Hence, we assume that the FMD scheme is a secure cryptographic primitive, i.e., the cryptographic properties of FMD (correctness, fuzziness, and detection ambiguity) hold. Senders and recipients are assumed to be honest. Otherwise, they can be excluded from the messages' anonymity sets. We consider two types of computationally-bounded attackers that can compromise user's privacy in an FMD scheme. The adversaries' goal is to learn as much information as possible about the relationship between senders, recipients, and messages.

- **Server:** Naturally, the server providing the FMD service can endanger the user's privacy since it has continuous access to every relevant information related to message detection. Specifically, the server knows the users' false-positive rates. It can analyze each incoming message, flag ciphertext, and their corresponding anonymity sets.

---

[4] In this work, we stipulate that a single server filters the messages for all users, i.e., a single server knows all the recipients' detection keys.

- • *Sender-oracle.* The server may know the sender of each message, i.e., a sender-oracle might be available in FMD. For instance, it is mandatory for the untrusted server if it only serves registered users. We assumed solely in Sect. 4.2 that such sender-oracle is available. If FMD is integrated into a system where senders apply anonymous communication (e.g., use Tor to send messages and flag ciphertexts to the server), then sender-oracle is not accessible to the FMD server.
- – **Eavesdropper:** A local passive adversary might observe the amount of data each user downloads from the server. Specifically, an eavesdropper could inspect the number of flag ciphertexts each user has received. Even though this attacker type does not have continual intrusion to the server's internal state, as we will show, it can still substantially decrease FMD user's privacy, e.g., if $p(u)$ is known, then the number of genuine incoming messages of users does not enjoy sufficiently high privacy protection (see Sect. 5).

4   Privacy Guarantees in FMD

In this section, we analyze and quantify various privacy and anonymity guarantees provided by the FMD scheme. Specifically, in Sects. 4.1, 4.2, and 4.3, we measure recipient unlinkability, assess relationship anonymity, and estimate detection ambiguity, respectively. Note that for the latter two property we provide experimental evaluations in Sect. 6, and we formulate a game in Appendix D concerning relationship anonymity. We denote the security parameter with λ, and if an (probabilistic) algorithm A outputs x, then we write $A \to x$ ($A \xrightarrow{\$} x$). The Binomial distribution with success probability p and number of trials n is denoted as $\mathsf{Binom}(n, p)$, while a normal distribution with mean μ and variance σ^2 is denoted as $\mathcal{N}(\mu, \sigma^2)$.

4.1   Recipient Unlinkability

In anonymous communication systems, recipient unlinkability is the cornerstone of anonymity guarantees. It ensures that it is hard to distinguish whether two different messages were sent to the same recipient or different ones. Whenever recipient unlinkability is not attained, it facilitates possibly devastating passive attacks, i.e., if an adversary can infer which messages are sent to the same recipient, then the adversary can effortlessly launch intersection attacks, see Appendix E. In the absence of recipient unlinkability, it is also possible to efficiently map every message to its genuine recipient by 1) clustering the messages that are sent to the same recipient and 2) see the intersection of the users who downloaded the flag ciphertexts sent to the same recipient.

We consider a definition of recipient unlinkability similar to the one introduced in [2]. Informally, in the recipient unlinkability game, we examine two recipients u_0, u_1 and a sender u_2. The challenger C generates uniformly at random $c \xleftarrow{\$} \{0, 1\}$ and instructs u_2 to send message m_α to u_c. Afterwards, C draws a uniformly random bit $b \xleftarrow{\$} \{0, 1\}$. If $b = 0$, then instructs u_2 to send a message m_β to u_c. Otherwise u_2 sends m_β to u_{1-c}. Adversary $\mathcal{A}$ examines the network, the flag ciphertexts and all communications and outputs b' indicating whether the two messages were sent to the same recipient.

Definition 1 (Recipient unlinkability (RU)). *An anonymous communication protocol Π satisfies recipient unlinkability if for all probabilistic polynomial-time adversaries $\mathcal{A}$ there is a negligible function $\mathsf{negl}(\cdot)$ such that*

$$\Pr[\mathcal{G}^{RU}_{\mathcal{A},\Pi}(\lambda) = 1] \leq \frac{1}{2} + \mathsf{negl}(\lambda), \tag{1}$$

where the privacy game $\mathcal{G}^{RU}_{\mathcal{A},\Pi}(\lambda)$ is defined in Fig. 6 in Appendix B.

We denote the set of users who downloaded message m by *fuzzy(m)*, i.e., they form the anonymity set of the message m. We estimate the advantage of the following adversary $\mathcal{A}$ in the $\mathcal{G}^{RU}_{\mathcal{A},\Pi}(\lambda)$ game: $\mathcal{A}$ outputs 0 if $fuzzy(m_\alpha) \cap fuzzy(m_\beta) \neq \emptyset$ and outputs 1 otherwise. Note that $\mathcal{A}$ always wins if the same recipient was chosen by the challenger (i.e., $b = 0$) because it is guaranteed by the correctness of the FMD scheme that $u_c \in fuzzy(m_\alpha) \cap fuzzy(m_\beta)$. Therefore, we have that $\Pr[\mathcal{G}^{RU}_{\mathcal{A},\Pi}(\lambda) = 1|b = 0] = 1$. If two different recipients were chosen by the challenger in the $\mathcal{G}^{RU}_{\mathcal{A},\Pi}(\lambda)$ game (i.e., $b = 1$), then $\mathcal{A}$ wins iff. $fuzzy(m_\alpha) \cap fuzzy(m_\beta) = \emptyset$. The advantage of the adversary can be computed as follows.

$$\Pr[\mathcal{G}^{RU}_{\mathcal{A},\Pi}(\lambda) = 1|b = 1] = \Pr[\cap_{m \in \{m_\alpha, m_\beta\}} fuzzy(m) = \emptyset | b = 1]$$

$$= \sum_{i=1}^{U} \sum_{\substack{V \subseteq U \\ |V|=i \\ \alpha \in V}} \Pr[fuzzy(m_\alpha) = V] \cdot \Pr[(V \cap fuzzy(m_\beta) = \emptyset] \tag{2}$$

$$= \sum_{i=1}^{U} \sum_{\substack{V \subseteq U \\ |V|=i \\ \alpha \in V}} \left(\prod_{u_l \in V \setminus \{u_0\}} p(u_l) \cdot \prod_{u_l \in U \setminus V} (1 - p(u_l)) \right) \cdot \left(\prod_{u_l \in V} (1 - p(u_l)) \right).$$

We simplify the adversarial advantage in Eq. 2 by assuming that $\forall i : p(u_i) = p$ and that the sizes of the anonymity sets are fixed at $\lfloor pU \rfloor$. Moreover, computer-aided calculations show that the following birthday paradox-like quantity can be used as a sufficiently tight lower bound[5] for the recipient unlinkability adversarial advantage, whenever $p(u_i)$ are close to each other.

$$\prod_{j=1}^{\lfloor pU \rfloor} \frac{U - \lfloor pU \rfloor - j}{U} = \prod_{j=1}^{\lfloor pU \rfloor} \left(1 - \frac{\lfloor pU \rfloor + j}{U} \right) \approx \prod_{j=1}^{\lfloor pU \rfloor} e^{-\frac{\lfloor pU \rfloor + j}{U}} \tag{3}$$

$$= e^{-\frac{\sum_j (\lfloor pU \rfloor + j)}{U}} = e^{-\frac{3\lfloor pU \rfloor^2 + \lfloor pU \rfloor}{2U}} \leq \Pr[\mathcal{G}^{RU}_{\mathcal{A},\Pi}(\lambda) = 1|b = 1].$$

---

[5] This lower bound is practically tight since the probability distribution of the adversary's advantage is concentrated around the mean $\lfloor pU \rfloor$ anyway.

The approximation is obtained by applying the first-order Taylor-series approximation for $e^x \approx 1 + x$, whenever $|x| \ll 1$. We observe that the lower bound for the adversary's advantage in the recipient unlinkability game is a negligible function in U for a fixed false-positive detection rate p. Thus, in theory, the number of recipients U should be large in order to achieve recipient unlinkability asymptotically. In practice, the classical birthday-paradox argument shows us that the two anonymity sets intersect with constant probability if $p = \theta\left(\frac{1}{\sqrt{U}}\right)$. Our results suggest that a deployment of the FMD scheme should *concurrently* have a large number of users with high false-positive rates in order to provide recipient unlinkability, see Fig. 1a for the concrete values of Eq. 3.

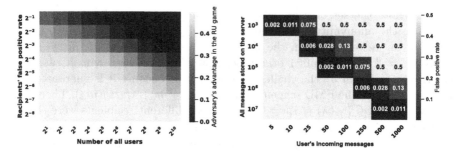

(a) Approximate values of the recipient unlinkability adversarial advantage in the $\mathcal{G}_{RU}^{\mathcal{A},\Pi}(\lambda)$ game according to Equation 3.

(b) Smallest false-positive rates to obtain temporal detection ambiguity against the utilized statistical tests.

Fig. 1. Recipient unlinkability and temporal detection ambiguity guarantees provided by the FMD scheme for various parameter settings.

4.2   Relationship Anonymity

Relationship anonymity ensures that the adversary cannot determine the sender and the recipient of a communication at the same time. Intuitively, recipients applying low false-positive rates receive only a handful of fuzzy tags from peers they are not communicating with. Therefore, multiple fuzzy tags between a sender and a recipient can eradicate their relationship anonymity, given that the server knows the number of messages a sender issued. We assume the server knows the sender of each message, which holds whenever the untrusted server has access to a sender-oracle, see Sect. 3.

The number of fuzzy tags between a *non-communicating pair* of receiver u_1 and sender u_2 follows $\mathsf{Binom}(\mathsf{out}(u_2), p(u_1))$. If $tag_{u_2}(u_1)$ is saliently far from the expected mean $\mathsf{out}(u_2)p(u_1)$, then the untrusted server can deduce with high confidence that a relationship exists between the two users. We approximate the binomial distribution above with $\mathcal{N}^* := \mathcal{N}(\mathsf{out}(u_2)p(u_1), \mathsf{out}(u_2)p(u_1)(1 -$

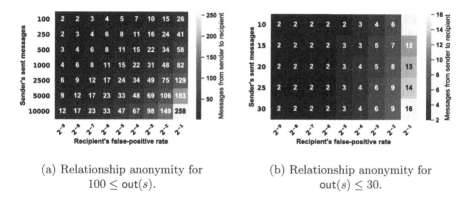

(a) Relationship anonymity for $100 \le \mathsf{out}(s)$.

(b) Relationship anonymity for $\mathsf{out}(s) \le 30$.

Fig. 2. The minimum number of messages between a pair of users that statistically reveal the relationship of the communicating users (significance level 1%).

$p(u_1)))^6$ so we can apply Z-tests to determine whether u_2 and u_1 had exchanged messages. Concretely, we apply two-tailed Z-test[7] for the hypothesis $H : tag_{u_2}(u_1) \sim \mathcal{N}(\mathsf{out}(u_2)p(u_1), \mathsf{out}(u_2)p(u_1)(1 - p(u_1)))$. If the hypothesis is rejected, then users u_2 and u_1 are deemed to have exchanged messages.

Each recipient u_1 downloads on average $tag_{u_2}(u_1) \approx p(u_1)(out(u_2) - in_{u_2}(u_1)) + in_{u_2}(u_1)$ fuzzy messages from the messages sent by u_2, where $in_{u_2}(u_1)$ denotes the number of genuine messages sent by u_2 to u_1. We statistically test with Z-tests (when $100 \le \mathsf{out}(u_2)$) and t-tests (when $\mathsf{out}(u_2) \le 30$) whether $tag_{u_2}(u_1)$ could have been drawn from the $\mathcal{N}^*$ distribution, i.e., there are no exchanged messages between u_1 and u_2. The minimum number of genuine messages $in_{u_2}(u_1)$ that statistically expose the communication relationship between u_1 and u_2 is shown for various scenarios in Fig. 2. We observe that the relationship anonymity of any pair of users could be broken by a handful of exchanged messages. This severely limits the applicability of the FMD scheme in use cases such as instant messaging. To have a meaningful level of relationship anonymity with their communicating peer, users should either apply substantial false-positive rates, or the server must not be able to learn the sender's identity of each message. The latter could be achieved, for instance, if senders apply an anonymous communication system to send messages or by using short-lived provisional pseudo IDs where no user would send more than one message.

Game Theoretic Analysis. Incentive compatibility has the utmost importance in decentralized and privacy-enhancing technologies. Therefore, we present a game-theoretic study of the FMD protocol concerning relationship anonymity. We believe applying game theory to FMD by itself is a fruitful and over-arching

---

[6] Note that this approximation is generally considered to be tight enough when $\mathsf{out}(u_2)p(u_1) \ge 5$ and $\mathsf{out}(u_2)(1 - p(u_1)) \ge 5$.

[7] For senders with only a few sent messages ($\mathsf{out}(u_2) \le 30$), one can apply t-tests instead of Z-tests.

direction. Our goal, besides conducting a preliminary analysis, is to raise interest and fuel future research towards this direction. The formalization of the game as well as the corresponding theorems and proofs can be found in Appendix D.

4.3 Temporal Detection Ambiguity

The FMD scheme is required to satisfy the security notion of *detection ambiguity* devised by Beck et al. [3]. Namely, for any message that yields a match for a detection key, the server should not be able to decide whether it is a true or a false-positive match. This definition is formalized for a single incoming message in isolation. Yet, the detector server can *continuously* observe the stream of incoming messages.[8] Consequently, the server might be able to assess whether the user has received a message in *a certain time interval*. To capture this time-dependent aspect, we relax detection ambiguity and coin the term *temporal detection ambiguity*. Informally, no adversary should be able to tell in a given time interval having access to all incoming flag ciphertexts whether a user received an incoming true-positive match. We provide the formal definition in Appendix B, and we empirically study temporal detection ambiguity on real communication data in Sect. 6. In Sect. 5, we measure the level of privacy protection the number of incoming messages enjoys from a differential privacy angle.

Any message that enters the communication system yields a match to a detection key according to its set false-positive rate. Specifically, the number of false-positive matches acquired by user u's detection key follows a $\mathsf{Binom}(M - \mathrm{in}(u), p(u))$ distribution. Similarly to Sect. 4.2, if M is large, then we can approximate the number of false-positive matches with a $\mathcal{N}(p(u)M, p(u)(1 - p(u))M)$ distribution and use statistical tests to assess that the number of downloaded messages by a recipient is statistically far from the expected number of downloaded messages. More precisely, the adversary can statistically test whether $tag(u)$ could have been drawn from $\mathcal{N}(p(u)M, p(u)(1 - p(u))M)$ (the approximation of $\mathsf{Binom}(M, p(u))$). We observe that in an epoch, a user should have either large false-positive rates or a small number of incoming messages to provide temporal detection ambiguity, shown in Fig. 1b.

5   Differential Privacy Analysis

Differential privacy (DP) [11] is a procedure for sharing information about a dataset by publishing statistics of it while withholding information about single data points. DP is formalized in Definition 2; the core idea is to ensure that an arbitrary change on any data point in the database has a negligible effect on the query result. Hence, it is infeasible to infer much about any data point.

Definition 2 (Differential Privacy [11]). *An algorithm A satisfies ε-differential privacy if for all $S \subseteq Range(A)$ and every input pair D and D′ differing in a single element Eq. 4 holds.*

---

[8] As an illustrative example collected from a real communication system, see Fig. 3b.

$$\Pr(A(D) \in S) \le e^{\varepsilon} \cdot \Pr(A(D') \in S). \tag{4}$$

Personalized Existing Edge DP. A widely used relaxation of the above definition is (ε, δ)-DP, where Eq. 4 is extended with a small additive term δ at the right end. There are over 200 modifications of DP [9], we combined several to make it suitable for FMD. Concretely, we create a novel definition called *Personalized Existing Edge DP (PEEDP)* (formally defined in Definition 3)[9] by combining four existing notions. We utilize *edge-DP* [17] which applies DP to communication graphs: D and D' are the original communication graphs with and without a particular edge respectively, and S is a set of graphs with fuzzy edges included. Furthermore, we apply *personalized DP* [18], which allocates different level of protection to incoming messages, as in FMD the users' false positive rates could differ.

Hiding the presence or absence of a message is only possible by explicitly removing real messages and adding fuzzy ones to the communication graph, which is indistinguishable from real ones. This setting (i.e., protecting existence and not value) corresponds to *unbounded DP* [20]. Hence, as also noted in [3], without a false negative rate (which would directly contradict correctness), FMD cannot satisfy DP: fuzzy messages can only hide the presence of a message not the absence. To tackle this imbalance, we utilize *asymmetric DP* [37] which only protects some of the records determined by policy P. It only differs from Definition 2 in the relationship of D and D' as Eq. 4 should only hold for *every input pair D and D' where later is created by removing in D a single sensitive record defined by P*. By combining all these DP notions, we can formulate our PEEDP definition.

Definition 3 ($\bar{\varepsilon}$-Personalized Existing Edge Differential Privacy). *An algorithm A satisfies $\bar{\varepsilon}$-PEEDP (where $\bar{\varepsilon}$ is an element-wise positive vector which length is equal with the amount of nodes in D) if Eq. 5 holds for all $S \subseteq Range(A)$ and every input graphs D and D' where later is created by removing in D a single incoming edge of user u.*

$$\Pr(A(D) \in S) \le e^{\bar{\varepsilon}_u} \cdot \Pr(A(D') \in S). \tag{5}$$

Once we formalized a suitable DP definition for FMD, it is easy to calculate the trade-off between efficiency (approximated by $p(u)$) and privacy protection (measured by ε_u). This is captured in Theorem 1 (proof can be found in Appendix C).

Theorem 1. *If we assume the distribution of the messages are IID then FMD satisfy $\left[\log \frac{1}{p(u)}\right]_{u=1}^{U}$-PEEDP.*

---

[9] We elaborate more on various DP notions in Appendix C.

Therefore, detection rates $p(u) = \{0.5^0, 0.5^1, 0.5^2, 0.5^4, 0.5^8\}$ in FMD correspond to $\varepsilon_u = \{0.000, 0.693, 1.386, 2.773, 5.545\}$ in $\bar{\varepsilon}$-PEEDP. Clearly, perfect protection (i.e., $\varepsilon_u = 0$) is reached only when all messages are downloaded (i.e., $p(u) = 1$). On the other hand, the other ε values are much harder to grasp: generally speaking, privacy-parameter below one is considered strong with the classic DP definition. As PEEDP only provides a relaxed guarantee, we can postulate that the privacy protection what FMD offers is weak.

Protecting the Number of Incoming Messages. In most applications, e.g., anonymous messaging or stealth payments, we want to protect the number of incoming messages of the users, $in(u)$. Intuitively, the server observes $tag(u) \sim in(u) + \mathsf{Binom}(M - in(u), p(u))$ where (with sufficiently large M) the second term can be thought of as Gaussian-noise added to mask $in(u)$, a common technique to achieve (ε, δ)-DP. Consequently, FMD does provide $(\varepsilon_u, \delta_u)$-DP[10] for the number of incoming messages of user u, see Theorem 2 (proof in Appendix C).

Theorem 2. *If we assume the distribution of the messages is IID than the FMD protocol provides $(\varepsilon_u, \delta_u)$-DP for the number of incoming messages $in(u)$ of user u where $\delta_u = \max_u(p(u), 1 - p(u))^{M - in(u)}$ and*

$$\varepsilon_u = \log\left[\max_u\left(\frac{p(u) \cdot (M - 2 \cdot in(u))}{(1 - p(u)) \cdot (in(u) + 1)}, \frac{(1 - p(u)) \cdot (M - in(u))}{p(u)}\right)\right].$$

Table 2. Exemplary settings to illustrate the trade-off between the false-positive rate $p(u)$ and the privacy parameters of (ε, δ)-differential privacy for protecting the number of incoming messages.

M	100	100	100	**200**	1 000 000	1 000 000	1 000 000	**2 000 000**
$in(u)$	10	10	**20**	10	100	100	**1000**	100
$p(u)$	0.5^4	**0.5^2**	0.5^4	0.5^4	0.5^8	**0.5^4**	0.5^8	0.5^8
ε_u	7.2	5.6	7.1	8.0	19.4	16.5	19.4	20
δ_u	3e−3	6e−12	6e−3	5e−6	1e−1700	1e−28027	1e−1699	1e−3400

To illustrate our results, we provide some exemplary settings in Table 2 and show how the false positive rate $p(u)$ translates into ε_u and δ_u. It is visible that increasing the detection rate does increase the privacy protection (i.e., lower ε_u and δ_u), and increasing the overall and incoming messages result in weaker privacy parameter ε_u and δ_u respectively. These results suggest, that even the number of incoming messages does not enjoy sufficient (differential) privacy protection in FMD, as the obtained values for ε_u are generally considered weak.

---

[10] Note that this is also a personalized guarantee as in [18].

6   Evaluation

We evaluate the relationship anonymity and temporal detection ambiguity guarantees of FMD through simulations on data from real communication systems.[11] We chose two real-world communication networks that could benefit from implementing and deploying FMD on top of them.

- **College Instant Messaging (IM)** [30]. This dataset contains the instant messaging network of college students from the University of California, Irvine. The graph consists of 1899 nodes and 59 835 edges that cover 193 days of communication.
- **EU Email** [31]. This dataset is a collection of emails between members of a European research institution. The graph has 986 nodes and 332 334 edges. It contains the communication patterns of 803 days.

Users are roughly distributed equally among major Information Privacy Awareness categories [35], thus for each node in the datasets, we independently and uniformly at random chose a false-positive rate from the set $\{2^{-l}\}_{l=1}^{7}$. Note that the most efficient FMD scheme only supports false-positive rates of the form 2^{-l}. Moreover, for each message and user in the system, we added new "fuzzy" edges to the graph according to the false-positive rates of the messages' recipients. The server is solely capable of observing the message-user graph with the added "fuzzy" edges that serve as cover traffic to enhance the privacy and anonymity of the users. We run our experiments 10-fold where on average, there are around 16 and 48 million fuzzy edges for the two datasets, i.e., a randomly picked edge (the baseline) represents a genuine message with $\ll 1\%$.

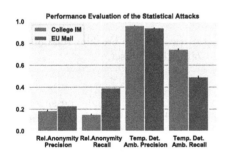
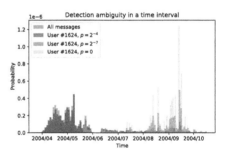

(a) The precision and recall of the statistical tests breaking relationship anonymity and temporal detection ambiguity, cf. Section 4.2 and 4.3.

(b) Temporal probability distribution of receiving a fuzzy tag for various false-positive detection rates. The exemplary user is taken from the College IM dataset.

Fig. 3. Privacy guarantees of FMD in simulations on real communication systems.

---

[11] The simulator can be found at https://github.com/seresistvanandras/FMD-analysis.

6.1   Uncovering the Relationship Graph

The server's goal is to uncover the original social graph of its users, i.e., to expose the communicating partners. The relationship anonymity of a sender and a receiver can be easily uncovered by the statistical test introduced in Sect. 4.2 especially if a user is receiving multiple messages from the same sender while having a low false-positive rate. We found that statistical tests produce a 0.181 and 0.229 precision with 0.145 and 0.391 recall on average in predicting the communication links between all the pairs of nodes in the College IM and EU Email datasets, respectively, see Fig. 3a. The results corresponding to the EU Email dataset are higher due to the increased density of the original graph. These results are substantial as they show the weak anonymization power of FMD in terms of relationship anonymity.

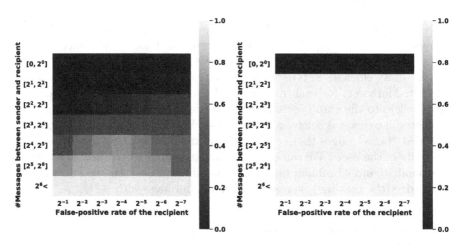

Fig. 4. Recall (left) and precision (right) of the statistical tests in breaking relationship anonymity (see Sect. 4.2) in simulations on the College IM dataset.

Specifically, communication relationships where merely a single message has been exchanged remain undetected by the applied statistical tests, cf. Fig. 4. However, note that for every other pairs of users, neither of the analyzed datasets yields false positives by the used statistical tests. These simulation results demonstrate that relationship anonymity is effectively maintained against statistical attacks if each user sends only a single message from the server's point of view. This can be achieved by cryptographic tools or anonymous communication systems, e.g., Tor. On the other hand, recurrent communication relationships reveal the relationship of communicating peers. Thus, relationship anonymity is breached with perfect precision, cf. Fig. 4. Simulation results confirm our intuition as well. Namely, statistical tests produce higher recall for nodes with lower false-positive detection rates, while they are less effective for communicating pairs that exchanged very few messages.

6.2 Breaking Temporal Detection Ambiguity

We empirically quantify whether users can deny that they received an incoming (true positive) message. We consider 25 000 randomly selected messages with the corresponding fuzzy edges as one epoch. The server tried to assess using statistical tests (see Sect. 4.3) that a user has received an incoming message. The intuition is that users receive messages heterogeneously concerning time. Hence, surges in incoming traffic might not be adequately covered by fuzzy edges for users with low false-positive rates. Thus, these messages could be tight to the receiver with high probability, see Fig. 3b for an illustrative example. Indeed, Fig. 3a suggests that, in general, deniability can be broken effectively with high precision and recall. On the other hand, Fig. 3b also shows that higher false-positive rates could provide enough cover traffic for messages within these conspicuous epochs, which is in line with the findings presented in Fig. 1b.

7 Conclusion

In this paper, we present a privacy and anonymity analysis of the recently introduced Fuzzy Message Detection scheme. Our analysis is thorough as it covers over three directions. Foremost, an information-theoretical analysis was carried out concerning recipient unlinkability, relationship anonymity, and temporal detection ambiguity. It is followed by a differential privacy analysis which leads to a novel privacy definition. Finally, we gave an exhaustive simulation based on real-world data. Our findings facilitate proper parameter selection and the deployment of the FMD scheme into various applications. Yet, we also raise concerns about the guarantees what FMD provides and questions whether it is adequate/applicable for many real-world scenarios.

Limitations and Future Work. Although far-reaching, our analysis only scratches the surface of what can be analyzed concerning FMD, and substantial work and important questions remain as future work. Thus, a hidden goal of this paper is to fuel discussions about FMD so it can be deployed adequately for diverse scenarios. Concretely, we formulated a game only for one privacy property and did not study the Price of Stability/Anarchy. Concerning differential privacy, our assumption about the IID nature of the edges in a communication graph is non-realistic. At the same time, the time-dependent aspect of the messages is not incorporated in our analysis via Pan-Privacy.

Acknowledgements. We thank our shepherd Fan Zhang and our anonymous reviewers for helpful comments in preparing the final version of this paper. We are grateful to Sarah Jamie Lewis for inspiration and publishing the data sets. We thank Henry de Valence and Gabrielle Beck for fruitful discussions. Project no. 138903 has been implemented with the support provided by the Ministry of Innovation and Technology from the NRDI Fund, financed under the FK_21 funding scheme. The research reported in this paper and carried out at the BME has been supported by the NRDI Fund based on the charter of bolster issued by the NRDI Office under the auspices of the Ministry for Innovation and Technology.

A   FMD in More Details

The fuzzy message detection scheme consists of the following five probabilistic polynomial-time algorithms (Setup, KeyGen, Flag, Extract, Test). In the following, let $\mathcal{P}$ denote the set of attainable false positive rates.

Setup(1^λ) $\xrightarrow{\$}$ pp. Global parameters pp of the FMD scheme are generated, i.e., the description of a shared cyclic group.

KeyGen$_{pp}$(1^λ) $\xrightarrow{\$}$ (pk, sk). This algorithm is given the global public parameters and the security parameter and outputs a public and secret key.

Flag(pk) $\xrightarrow{\$}$ C. This randomized algorithm given a public key pk outputs a flag ciphertext C.

Extract(sk, p) $\rightarrow$ dsk. Given a secret key sk and a false positive rate p the algorithm extracts a detection secret key dsk iff. $p \in \mathcal{P}$ or outputs $\perp$ otherwise.

Test(dsk, C) $\rightarrow$ $\{0, 1\}$. The test algorithm given a detection secret key dsk and a flag ciphertext C outputs a detection result.

An FMD scheme needs to satisfy three main security and privacy notions: correctness, fuzziness and detection ambiguity. For the formal definitions of these, we refer to [3]. The toy example presented in Fig. 5 is meant to illustrate the interdependent nature of the privacy guarantees achieved by the FMD scheme.

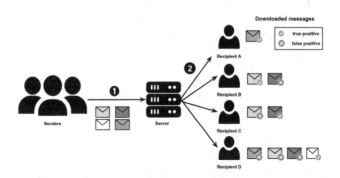

Fig. 5. A toy example of the FMD scheme. ① Several senders post anonymous messages to the untrusted server. ② Whenever recipients come online, they download messages that correspond to them (some false positive, some true positive). Recipient A, B, C and D have a false positive rate $0, \frac{1}{3}, \frac{1}{3}, 1$, respectively. Note that the server can map the messages that belong to A and D. However, the messages of Recipient B and C are 2-anonymous.

B Formal Definitions of Security and Privacy Guarantees

The recipient unlinkability $\mathcal{G}_{\mathcal{A},\Pi}^{RU}(\lambda)$ game

1. Adversary $\mathcal{A}$ selects target recipients u_0, u_1 and a target sender u_2.
2. Challenger $\mathcal{C}$ instructs sender u_2 to send a message to u_c for $c \xleftarrow{\$} \{0,1\}$.
3. $\mathcal{C}$ uniformly at random generates a challenge bit $b \xleftarrow{\$} \{0,1\}$. If $b = 0$, $\mathcal{C}$ instructs u_2 to send a message to u_c. Otherwise, instructs u_2 to send a message to u_{1-c}.
4. $\mathcal{A}$ observes network traffic and flag ciphertexts and outputs b'.
5. Output 1, iff. $b = b'$, otherwise 0.

Fig. 6. The security game for the anonymity notion of recipient unlinkability.

Definition 4 (Temporal Detection Ambiguity). *An anonymous communication protocol Π satisfies temporal detection ambiguity if for all probabilistic polynomial-time adversaries $\mathcal{A}$ there is a negligible function $\mathsf{negl}(\cdot)$ such that*

$$\Pr[\mathcal{G}_{\mathcal{A},\Pi}^{TDA}(\lambda) = 1] \leq \frac{1}{2} + \mathsf{negl}(\lambda), \tag{6}$$

where the temporal detection ambiguity game $\mathcal{G}_{\mathcal{A},\Pi}^{TDA}(\cdot)$ is defined below (Fig. 7).

The temporal detection ambiguity $\mathcal{G}_{\mathcal{A},\Pi}^{TDA}(\lambda)$ game

1. Adversary $\mathcal{A}$ selects a target recipient u_0.
2. Challenger $\mathcal{C}$ uniformly at random generates a challenge bit $b \xleftarrow{\$} \{0,1\}$. If $b = 0$, $\mathcal{C}$ picks $k \xleftarrow{\$} [1,2,\ldots,U]$ and instructs sender u_k to send a message to u_0. Otherwise, the challenger does nothing.
3. The anonymous communication protocol Π remains functional for a certain period of time, i.e., users keep sending messages using Π.
4. $\mathcal{A}$ observes network traffic and flag ciphertexts and outputs b'.
5. Output 1, iff. $b = b'$, otherwise 0.

Fig. 7. The security game for the privacy notion of temporal detection ambiguity

C   Differential Privacy Relaxations and Proofs

Our novel DP notion called PEEDP (short for Personalized Existing Edge DP) is an instance of d-privacy [7], which generalizes the neighbourhood of datasets (on which the DP inequality should hold) to an arbitrary metric d defined over the input space. Yet, instead of a top-down approach where we are presenting a complex metric to fit our FMD use-case, we follow a bottom-up approach and show the various building blocks of our definition. PEEDP is a straight forward combination of unbounded DP [20], edge-DP [17]), asymmetric DP [37], and personalized DP [18]. Although Definition 3 is appropriate for FMD, it does not capture the FMD scenarios fully as neither time-dependent nature of the messages nor the dependencies and correlations between them are taken into account.

The first issue can be tackled by integrating other DP notions into PEEDP which provide guarantees under continuous observation (i.e., stream-data), such as pan-privacy [14]. Within this streaming context several definitions can be considered: user-level [13] (to protect the presence of users), event-level [12] (to protect the presence of messages), and w-event level [19] (to protect the presence of messages within time windows).

The second issue is also not considered in Theorem 1 as we assumed the messages are IID, while in a real-world applications this is not necessarily the case. Several DP notions consider distributions, without cherry-picking any we refer the readers to two corresponding surveys [9,38]. We leave it as a future work to tweak our definition further to fit into these contexts.

Proof (of Theorem 1). Due to the IID nature of the messages it is enough to show that Eq. 5 holds for an arbitrary communication graph D with arbitrary message m of an arbitrary user u. The two possible world the adversary should not be able to differentiate between $D = D'/\{m\}$, i.e., whether the particular message exists or not. Due to the asymmetric nature of Definition 3 (i.e., it only protects the existence) Eq. 7 does not need to be satisfied. On the other hand, if the message exists than Eq. 8 and 9 must be satisfied where $S_1 = \{$message m is downloaded by user $u\}$ and $S_2 = \{$message m is not downloaded by user $u\}$.

$$\Pr(A(D') \in S) \leq e^{\varepsilon_u} \cdot \Pr(A(D) \in S) \tag{7}$$

$$\Pr(A(D) \in S_1) \leq e^{\varepsilon_u} \cdot \Pr(A(D') \in S_1) \tag{8}$$

$$\Pr(A(D) \in S_2) \leq e^{\varepsilon_u} \cdot \Pr(A(D') \in S_2) \tag{9}$$

If we reformulate the last two equations with the corresponding probabilities we get $1 \leq e^{\varepsilon_u} \cdot p(u)$ and $0 \leq e^{\varepsilon_u} \cdot (1 - p(u))$ respectively. While the second holds trivially the first corresponds to the formula in Theorem 1.   □

Proof (of Theorem 2). The users' number of incoming messages are independent from each other hence we can focus on a single user u. The proof follows the idea from [21][12]: we satisfy Eq. 4 (with $+\delta$ at the end) when $A(D) = tag(u) \sim D + \mathsf{Binom}(M - in(u), p(u))$ for $D = in(u)$ and $D' = in(u) \pm 1$, i.e., we show that the following Equation holds.

$$\Pr(A(D) = tag(u) \in S | D = in(u), M, p(u)) \leq$$
$$e^{\varepsilon} \cdot \Pr(A(D') = tag'(u) \in S | D' = in(u) \pm 1, M' = M \pm 1, p(u)) + \delta$$
$$\Rightarrow \qquad \Pr(in(u) + \mathsf{Binom}(M - in(u), p(u)) \in S) \leq$$
$$e^{\varepsilon} \cdot \Pr(in(u) \pm 1 + \mathsf{Binom}(M \pm 1 - (in(u) \pm 1), p(u)) \in S) + \delta$$

First, we focus on δ and provide a lower bound originating from the probability on the left when $\Pr(\cdot) \leq e^{\varepsilon} \cdot 0 + \delta$. This corresponds to two cases as seen in the Equation below: when $D' = in(u) + 1$ with $S = \{in(u)\}$ and when $D' = in(u) - 1$ with $S = \{M\}$. The corresponding lower bounds (i.e., probabilities) correspond to the event when user u does not download any fuzzy messages and when user u does downloads all messages respectively. Hence, the maximum of these are indeed a lower bound for δ.

$$\Pr(A(in(u)) = in(u)) \leq e^{\varepsilon} \cdot \Pr(A(in(u) + 1) = in(u)) + \delta \Rightarrow (1 - p(u))^{M - in(u)} \leq \delta$$
$$\Pr(A(in(u)) = M) \leq e^{\varepsilon} \cdot \Pr(A(in(u) - 1) = M) + \delta \Rightarrow p(u)^{M - in(u)} \leq \delta$$

Now we turn towards ε and show that $(\varepsilon, 0)$-DP holds for all subset besides the two above, i.e., when $S = \{in(u) + y\}$ with $y = [1, \ldots, M - in(u) - 1]$. First, we reformulate Eq. 4 as seen below.

$$\frac{\Pr(in(u) + \mathsf{Binom}(M - in(u), p(u)) \in S)}{\Pr(in(u) \pm 1 + \mathsf{Binom}(M - in(u), p(u)) \in S)} \leq e^{\varepsilon}$$

Then, by replacing the binomial distributions with the corresponding probability formulas we get the following two equations for $D' = in(u) + 1$ and $D' = in(u) - 1$ respectively.

$$\frac{\binom{M - in(u)}{y} \cdot p(u)^y \cdot (1 - p(u))^{M - in(u) - y}}{\binom{M - in(u)}{y - 1} \cdot p(u)^{y-1} \cdot (1 - p(u))^{M - in(u) - y + 1}} = \frac{M - in(u) - y + 1}{y} \cdot \frac{p(u)}{1 - p(u)} \leq e^{\varepsilon}$$

$$\frac{\binom{M - in(u)}{y} \cdot p(u)^y \cdot (1 - p(u))^{M - in(u) - y}}{\binom{M - in(u)}{y + 1} \cdot p(u)^{y+1} \cdot (1 - p(u))^{M - in(u) - y - 1}} = \frac{y + 1}{M - in(u) - y} \cdot \frac{1 - p(u)}{p(u)} \leq e^{\varepsilon}$$

Consequently, the maximum of these is the lower bound for e^{ε}. The first formula's derivative is negative, so the function is monotone decreasing, meaning that its maximum is at $y = in(u) + 1$. On the other hand, the second formula's derivative is positive so the function is monotone increasing, hence the maximum

---

[12] We present the proof for singleton sets, but it can be extended by using the following formula: $\frac{A+C}{B+D} < \max(\frac{A}{B}, \frac{C}{D})$.

is reached at $y = M - in(u) - 1$. By replacing y with these values respectively one can verify that the corresponding maximum values are indeed what is shown in Theorem 2.   □

D Game-Theoretical Analysis

Here—besides a short introduction of the utilized game theoretic concepts— we present a rudimentary game-theoretic study of the FMD protocol focusing on relationship anonymity introduced in Sect. 4. First, we formalize a game and highlight some corresponding problems such as the interdependence of the user's privacy. Then, we unify the user's actions and show the designed game's only Nash Equilibrium, which is to set the false-positive detection rates to zero, rendering FMD idle amongst selfish users. Following this, we show that a higher utility could been reached with altruistic users and/or by centrally adjusting the false-positive detection rates. Finally, we show that our game (even with non-unified actions) is a potential game, which have several nice properties, such as efficient Nash Equilibrium computation.

- **Tragedy of Commons** [15]: users act according to their own self-interest and, contrary to the common good of all users, cause depletion of the resource through their uncoordinated action.
- **Nash Equilibrium** [27]: every player makes the best/optimal decision for itself as long as the others' choices remain unchanged.
- **Altruism** [34]: users act to promote the others' welfare, even at a risk or cost to ourselves.
- **Social Optimum** [16]: the user's strategies which maximizes social welfare (i.e., the overall accumulated utilities).
- **Price of Stability/Anarchy** [1,22]: the ratio between utility values corresponding to the best/worst NE and the SO. It measures how the efficiency of a system degrades due to selfish behavior of its agents.
- **Best Response Mechanism** [28]: from a random initial strategy the players iteratively improve their strategies

Almost every multi-party interaction can be modeled as a game. In our case, these decision makers are the users using the FMD service. We assume the users bear some costs C_u for downloading any message from the server. For simplicity we define this uniformly: if f is the cost of retrieving any message for any user than $C_u = f \cdot tag(u)$. Moreover, we replace the random variable $tag(u) \sim in(u) + \mathsf{Binom}(M - in(u), p(u))$ with its expected value, i.e., $C_u = f \cdot (in(u) + p(u) \cdot (M - in(u)))$.

Besides, the user's payoff should depend on whether any of the privacy properties detailed in Sect. 4 are not satisfied. For instance, we assume the users suffer from a privacy breach if relationship anonymity is not ensured, i.e., they uniformly lose L when the recipient u can be linked to any sender via any message between them. In the rest of the section we slightly abuse the notation u as in contrast to the rest of the paper we refer to the users as $u \in \{1, \ldots, U\}$ instead of $\{u_0, u_1, \dots\}$. The probability of a linkage via a particular message for user u is $\alpha_u = \prod_{v \in \{1,\dots,U\}/u}(1 - p(v))$. The probability of a linkage from any incoming message of u is $1 - (1 - \alpha_u)^{in(u)}$.[13] Based on these we define the FMD-RA Game.

Definition 5. *The FMD-RA Game is a tuple $\langle \mathcal{N}, \Sigma, \mathcal{U} \rangle$, where the set of players is $\mathcal{N} = \{1, \dots, U\}$, their actions are $\Sigma = \{p(1), \dots, p(U)\}$ where $p(u) \in [0, 1]$ while their utility functions are $\mathcal{U} = \{\varphi_u(p(1), \dots, p(U))\}_{u=1}^{U}$ such that for $1 \leq u \leq U$:*

$$\varphi_u = -L \cdot \left(1 - (1 - \alpha_u)^{in(u)}\right) - f \cdot (in(u) + p(u) \cdot (M - in(u))). \quad (10)$$

It is visible in the utility function that the bandwidth-related cost (second term) depends only on user u's action while the privacy-related costs (first term) depend only on the other user's actions. This reflects well that relationship anonymity is an interdependent privacy property [6] within FMD: by downloading fuzzy tags, the users provide privacy to others rather than to themselves. As a consequence of this tragedy-of-commons [15] situation, a trivial no-protection Nash Equilibrium (NE) emerges. Moreover, Theorem 3 also states this NE is unique, i.e., no other NE exists.

Theorem 3. *Applying no privacy protection in the FMD-RA Game is the only NE: $(p^*(1), \dots, p^*(U)) = (0, \dots, 0)$.*

Proof. First we prove that no-protection is a NE. If all user u set $p(u) = 0$ than a single user by deviates from this strategy would increased its cost. Hence no rational user would deviate from this point. In details, in Eq. 10 the privacy related costs is constant $-L$ independently from user u's false-positive rate while the download related cost would trivially increase as the derivative of this function (shown in Eq. 11) is negative.

$$\frac{\partial \varphi_u}{\partial p(u)} = -f \cdot (M - in(u)) < 0 \quad (11)$$

Consequently, $p^* = (p^*(1), \dots, p^*(U)) = (0, \dots, 0)$ is indeed a NE. Now we give an indirect reasoning why there cannot be any other NEs. Lets assume $\hat{p} = (\hat{p}(1), \dots, \hat{p}(U))$ is a NE. At this state any player could decrease its cost by reducing its false positive-rate which only lower the download related cost. Hence, $\hat{p}$ is not an equilibrium. □

This negative result highlights that in our simplistic model, no rational (selfish) user would use FMD; it is only viable when altruism [34] is present. On the other hand, (if some condition holds) in the Social Optimum (SO) [16], the users do utilize privacy protection. This means a higher total payoff could be achieved (i.e., greater social welfare) if the users cooperate or when the false-positive rates

---

[13] It is only an optimistic baseline as it merely captures the trivial event when no-one downloads the a message from any sender v besides the intended recipient u.

are controlled by a central planner. Indeed, according to Theorem 4 the SO≠NE if, for all users, the cost of the fuzzy message downloads is smaller than the cost of the privacy loss. The exact improvement of the SO over the NE could be captured by the Price of Stability/Anarchy [1,22], but we leave this as future work.

Theorem 4. *The SO of the FMD-RA Game is not the trivial NE and corresponds to higher overall utilities if $f \cdot (M - \max_u(in(u))) < L$.*

Proof. We show that the condition in the theorem is sufficient to ensure that SO≠NE by showing that greater utility could be achieved with $0 < p'(u)$ than with $p(u) = 0$. To do this we simplify out scenario and set $p(u) = p$ for all users. The corresponding utility function is presented in Eq. 12 while in Eq. 13 we show the exact utilities when p is either 0 or 1.

$$\varphi_u(p) = -L \cdot (1 - (1 - (1 - p)^{U-1})^{in(u)}) - f \cdot (in(u) + p \cdot (M - in(u))) \quad (12)$$
$$\varphi_u(0) = -L - f \cdot in(u) \qquad \varphi_u(1) = -f \cdot M \quad (13)$$

One can check with some basic level of mathematical analysis that the derivative of Eq. 12 is negative at both edge of $[0, 1]$ as $\frac{\partial \varphi_u(p)}{\partial p}(0) = \frac{\partial \varphi_u(p)}{\partial p}(1) = -f \cdot (M - in(u))$. This implies that the utility is decreasing at these points. Moreover, depending on the relation between the utilities in Eq. 13 (when $p = 0$ and $p = 1$), two scenario is possible as we illustrate in Fig. 8. From this figure it is clear that when $\varphi_u(0) < \varphi_u(1)$ (or $f \cdot (M - in(u)) < L$) for all users that the maximum of their utilities cannot be at $p = 0$. □

Potential Game. We also show that FMD-RA is a potential game [26]. This is especially important, as it guaranteed that the Best Response Dynamics terminates in a NE.

Definition 6 (Potential Game). *A Game $\langle \mathcal{N}, \mathcal{A}, \mathcal{U} \rangle$ (with players $\{1, \ldots, U\}$, actions $\{a_1, \ldots, a_U\}$, and utilities $\{\varphi_1, \ldots, \varphi_U\}$) is a Potential Game if there exist a potential function Ψ such that Eq. 14 holds for all players u independently of the other player's actions.*[14]

$$\varphi_u(a_u, a_{-u}) - \varphi_u(a'_u, a_{-u}) = \Psi(a_u, a_{-u}) - \Psi(a'_u, a_{-u}) \quad (14)$$

Theorem 5. *FMD-RA is a Potential Game with potential function shown in Eq. 15.*

$$\Psi(p(1), \ldots, p(U)) = -f \cdot \sum_{u=1}^{U} p(u) \cdot (M - in(u)) \quad (15)$$

---

[14] a_{-u} is a common notation to represent all other players action except player u. Note that $p(-u)$ stands for the same in relation with FMD.

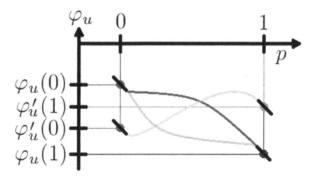

Fig. 8. Illustration of the utility functions: the yellow curve's maximum must be between zero and one since the gray dot is below the green where the derivative is negative. (Color figure online)

Proof. We prove Eq. 14 by transforming both side to the same form. We start with the left side: the privacy related part of the utility does only depend on the other user's action, therefore this part falls out during subtraction. On the other hand the download related part accumulates as shown below.

$$\varphi_u(p(u), (p(-u)) - \varphi_u(p(u)', p(-u)) =$$
$$-f \cdot (in(u) + p(u) \cdot (M - in(u))) - (-f \cdot (in(u) + p(u)' \cdot (M - in(u)))) =$$
$$-f \cdot p(u) \cdot (M - in(u)) - (-f \cdot p(u)' \cdot (M - in(u)))$$

Coincidentally, we get the same result if we do the subtraction on the right side using the formula in Eq. 15 as all element in the summation besides u falls out (as they are identical because they do not depend on user u's action).   □

E   Attacks on Privacy

We show several possible attacks against the FMD scheme, that might be fruitful to be analyzed in more depth.

Intersection Attacks. The untrusted server could possess some background knowledge that it allows to infer that some messages were meant to be received by *the same recipient*. In this case, the server only needs to consider the intersection of the anonymity sets of the "suspicious" messages. Suppose the server knows that l messages are sent to the same user. In that case, the probability that a user is in the intersection of all the l messages' anonymity sets is drawn from the $\mathsf{Binom}(U, p^l)$ distribution. Therefore, the expected size of the anonymity set after an intersection attack is reduced to $p^l U$ from pU.

Sybil Attacks. The collusion of multiple nodes would decrease the anonymity set of a message. For instance, when a message is downloaded by K nodes out of U, and N node is colluding, then the probability of pinpointing a particular message to a single recipient is $\frac{\binom{N+1}{K}}{\binom{U}{K}}$. This probability clearly increases as more node is being controlled by the adversary. On the other hand, controlling more nodes does trivially increase the controller's privacy (not message-privacy but user-privacy) as well. However, formal reasoning would require a proper definition for both of these privacy notions.

Neighborhood Attacks. Neighborhood attacks had been introduced by Zhou et al. in the context of deanonymizing individuals in social networks [39]. An adversary who knows the neighborhood of a victim node could deanonymize the victim even if the whole graph is released anonymously. FMD is susceptible to neighborhood attacks, given that relationship anonymity can be easily broken with statistical tests. More precisely, one can derive first the social graph of FMD users and then launch a neighborhood attack to recover the identity of some users.

References

1. Anshelevich, E., Dasgupta, A., Kleinberg, J., Tardos, E., Wexler, T., Roughgarden, T.: The price of stability for network design with fair cost allocation. SIAM J. Comput. **38**(4), 1602–1623 (2008)
2. Backes, M., Kate, A., Manoharan, P., Meiser, S., Mohammadi, E.: AnoA: a framework for analyzing anonymous communication protocols. In: 2013 IEEE 26th Computer Security Foundations Symposium, pp. 163–178. IEEE (2013)
3. Beck, G., Len, J., Miers, I., Green, M.: Fuzzy message detection. IACR eprint (2021)
4. Solomon, M., DiFrancesco, B.: Privacy preserving stealth payments on the Ethereum blockchain (2021)
5. Bianchi, G., Bracciale, L., Loreti, P.: "Better than nothing" privacy with bloom filters: to what extent? In: Domingo-Ferrer, J., Tinnirello, I. (eds.) PSD 2012. LNCS, vol. 7556, pp. 348–363. Springer, Heidelberg (2012). https://doi.org/10.1007/978-3-642-33627-0_27
6. Biczók, G., Chia, P.H.: Interdependent privacy: let me share your data. In: Sadeghi, A.-R. (ed.) FC 2013. LNCS, vol. 7859, pp. 338–353. Springer, Heidelberg (2013). https://doi.org/10.1007/978-3-642-39884-1_29
7. Chatzikokolakis, K., Andrés, M.E., Bordenabe, N.E., Palamidessi, C.: Broadening the scope of differential privacy using metrics. In: De Cristofaro, E., Wright, M. (eds.) PETS 2013. LNCS, vol. 7981, pp. 82–102. Springer, Heidelberg (2013). https://doi.org/10.1007/978-3-642-39077-7_5
8. de Valence, H.: Determine whether penumbra could integrate fuzzy message detection (2021)
9. Desfontaines, D., Pejó, B.: SoK: differential privacies. Proc. Priv. Enhanc. Technol. **2**, 288–313 (2020)
10. Domingo-Ferrer, J., Torra, V.: A critique of k-anonymity and some of its enhancements. In: 2008 Third International Conference on Availability, Reliability and Security, pp. 990–993. IEEE (2008)
11. Dwork, C.: Differential privacy. In: Bugliesi, M., Preneel, B., Sassone, V., Wegener, I. (eds.) ICALP 2006. LNCS, vol. 4052, pp. 1–12. Springer, Heidelberg (2006). https://doi.org/10.1007/11787006_1

12. Dwork, C.: Differential privacy in new settings. In: Proceedings of the Twenty-First Annual ACM-SIAM Symposium on Discrete Algorithms. SIAM (2010)
13. Dwork, C., Naor, M., Pitassi, T., Rothblum, G.N.: Differential privacy under continual observation. In: Proceedings of the Forty-Second ACM Symposium on Theory of Computing. ACM (2010)
14. Dwork, C., Naor, M., Pitassi, T., Rothblum, G.N., Yekhanin, S.: Pan-private streaming algorithms. In: ICS (2010)
15. Hardin, G.: The tragedy of the commons: the population problem has no technical solution; it requires a fundamental extension in morality. Science **162**(3859), 1243–1248 (1968)
16. Harsanyi, J.C., Selten, R., et al.: A General Theory of Equilibrium Selection in Games. MIT Press, Cambridge (1988)
17. Hay, M., Li, C., Miklau, G., Jensen, D.: Accurate estimation of the degree distribution of private networks. In: 2009 Ninth IEEE International Conference on Data Mining, pp. 169–178. IEEE (2009)
18. Jorgensen, Z., Yu, T., Cormode, G.: Conservative or liberal? Personalized differential privacy. In: 2015 IEEE 31st International Conference on Data Engineering, pp. 1023–1034. IEEE (2015)
19. Kellaris, G., Papadopoulos, S., Xiao, X., Papadias, D.: Differentially private event sequences over infinite streams. Proc. VLDB Endow. **7**(12), 1155–1166 (2014)
20. Kifer, D., Machanavajjhala, A.: No free lunch in data privacy. In: Proceedings of the 2011 ACM SIGMOD International Conference on Management of Data, pp. 193–204 (2011)
21. Korolova, A., Kenthapadi, K., Mishra, N., Ntoulas, A.: Releasing search queries and clicks privately. In: Proceedings of the 18th International Conference on World Wide Web, pp. 171–180 (2009)
22. Koutsoupias, E., Papadimitriou, C.: Worst-case equilibria. In: Meinel, C., Tison, S. (eds.) STACS 1999. LNCS, vol. 1563, pp. 404–413. Springer, Heidelberg (1999). https://doi.org/10.1007/3-540-49116-3_38
23. Lewis, S.J.: Niwl: a prototype system for open, decentralized, metadata resistant communication using fuzzytags and random ejection mixers (2021)
24. Lewis, S.J.: A playground simulator for fuzzy message detection (2021)
25. Machanavajjhala, A., Kifer, D., Gehrke, J., Venkitasubramaniam, M.: L-diversity: privacy beyond k-anonymity. ACM Trans. Knowl. Discov. Data (TKDD) **1**(1), 3-es (2007)
26. Monderer, D., Shapley, L.S.: Potential games. Games Econ. Behav. **14**(1), 124–143 (1996)
27. Nash, J.F., et al.: Equilibrium points in n-person games. Proc. Natl. Acad. Sci. **36**(1), 48–49 (1950)
28. Nisan, N., Schapira, M., Valiant, G., Zohar, A.: Best-response mechanisms. In: ICS, pp. 155–165. Citeseer (2011)
29. Noether, S.: Ring signature confidential transactions for monero. IACR Cryptology ePrint Archive 2015/1098 (2015)
30. Panzarasa, P., Opsahl, T., Carley, K.M.: Patterns and dynamics of users' behavior and interaction: network analysis of an online community. J. Am. Soc. Inf. Sci. Technol. **60**(5), 911–932 (2009)
31. Paranjape, A., Benson, A.R., Leskovec, J.: Motifs in temporal networks. In: Proceedings of the Tenth ACM International Conference on Web Search and Data Mining, pp. 601–610 (2017)
32. Rondelet, A.: Fuzzy message detection in Zeth (2021)

33. Sasson, E.B., et al.: Zerocash: decentralized anonymous payments from bitcoin. In: 2014 IEEE Symposium on Security and Privacy, pp. 459–474. IEEE (2014)
34. Simon, H.A.: Altruism and economics. Am. Econ. Rev. **83**(2), 156–161 (1993)
35. Soumelidou, A., Tsohou, A.: Towards the creation of a profile of the information privacy aware user through a systematic literature review of information privacy awareness. Telematics Inform. **61**, 101592 (2021)
36. Sweeney, L.: k-anonymity: a model for protecting privacy. Int. J. Uncertain. Fuzziness Knowl.-Based Syst. **10**(05), 557–570 (2002)
37. Takagi, S., Cao, Y., Yoshikawa, M.: Asymmetric differential privacy. arXiv preprint arXiv:2103.00996 (2021)
38. Zhang, T., Zhu, T., Liu, R., Zhou, W.: Correlated data in differential privacy: definition and analysis. Concurr. Comput. Pract. Exp. **34**(16), e6015 (2020)
39. Zhou, B., Pei, J.: The k-anonymity and l-diversity approaches for privacy preservation in social networks against neighborhood attacks. Knowl. Inf. Syst. **28**(1), 47–77 (2011). https://doi.org/10.1007/s10115-010-0311-2

Differential Privacy in Constant Function Market Makers

Tarun Chitra[1]([✉]), Guillermo Angeris[2], and Alex Evans[3]

[1] Gauntlet Networks, Inc., Dallas, USA
tarun@gauntlet.network
[2] Stanford University, Stanford, USA
angeris@stanford.edu
[3] Bain Capital, Boston, USA
aevans@baincapital.com

Abstract. Constant function market makers (CFMMs) are the most popular mechanism for facilitating decentralized trading. While these mechanisms have facilitated hundreds of billions of dollars of trades, they provide users with little to no privacy. Recent work illustrates that privacy cannot be achieved in CFMMs without forcing worse pricing and/or latency on end users. This paper quantifies the trade-off between pricing and privacy in CFMMs. We analyze a simple privacy-enhancing mechanism called *Uniform Random Execution* and prove that it provides (ϵ, δ)-differential privacy. The privacy parameter ϵ depends on the curvature of the CFMM trading function and the number of trades executed. This mechanism can be implemented in any blockchain system that allows smart contracts to access a verifiable random function. Our results provide an optimistic outlook on providing partial privacy in CFMMs.

1 Introduction

Constant function market makers (CFMMs) have become the most widely used decentralized product. In 2021, these market makers were facilitating over a billion dollars of daily (spot) volume, comparable to centralized exchanges such as Binance, Coinbase, or FTX. These market makers allow those looking for passive yield on a portfolio of assets to be automatically matched with traders looking to execute a swap against their assets. CFMMs work by ensuring that an invariant known as the trading function is kept constant before and after a trade is executed. The trading function, which is a function of the liquidity provided by those seeking passive yield, controls the price displayed by the CFMM that traders can execute a trade at. In order to ensure that liquidity providers (LPs) do not always lose money, as they are effectively buying the currency whose value is going down in exchange for one that is going up, a trading fee is applied to each transaction. Prior work [AC20, AAE+21, AEC20] has investigated necessary and sufficient conditions for the trading function and choice of fee to lead to profitable outcomes for LPs.

Privacy in CFMMs. One major problem with CFMMs is their lack of privacy. At a high-level, privacy in CFMMs boils down to preventing an adversary from

I. Eyal and J. Garay (Eds.): FC 2022, LNCS 13411, pp. 149–178, 2022.
https://doi.org/10.1007/978-3-031-18283-9_8

discerning trade sizes as a function of public prices and the knowledge of a feasible trade. Additionally, the dramatic increase in maximal extractable value (MEV) and front-running on Ethereum makes transaction-level privacy increasingly important [QZLG20, QZG21, ZQT+20, AEC21a]. Mechanisms that reduce the amount of information that an adversary has about user transactions can help reduce MEV and increase privacy. However, we do note that there are subtle distinctions between mechanisms that reduce MEV versus mechanisms that increase privacy (which we address in Sect. 3.1) In this paper, we study mechanisms purely in terms of privacy, but are motivated to study the problem in the hope that some form of privacy might address MEV.

Prior work [AEC21b] has shown that given any feasible trade and the (usually public) prices before and after executed trades, one can uniquely identify the size of the trade. This is a natural (although somewhat indirect) consequence of the concavity of the trading function [AC20, AAE+21]. This work implies that, even with modern cryptography such as zero-knowledge proofs (ZKPs), one will need to modify the CFMM mechanism to blind user's trade sizes. In other words, simply hiding balances via ZKPs of reserves (which has been proposed and implemented in multiple protocols [CXZ20, Pow21]) is not sufficient for transaction-level privacy.

Proposed Solutions. The two main options presented in [AEC21b] for recovering privacy involve either modifying prices (*e.g.*, adding noise to quoted prices) or batching transactions.[1] Both of these changes often degrade the user experience: both options force traders to bear worse price impact while the latter option also means that users face higher latency for trade confirmation. Assuming that these are the only options available, a natural question to ask is: how well can we control the trade-off between worsened price and latency and improved transaction privacy? One might formulate this rather general question as the following:

- What is the minimum number of swaps, $n(\delta)$, that must be batched such that an adversary is unable to infer the true trade sizes, beyond a precision of δ?
- How much worse is the worst price offered to any one user via such a mechanism?

Answers to the former question are analogous to sample complexity bounds from learning theory, whereas answers to the latter question measure the 'cost of privacy'.

Differential Privacy. One method for answering questions of this form is through the lens of differential privacy [DR+14]. Differentially private algorithms aim to hide individual user data (*e.g.*, trades) while simultaneously preserving aggregate statistics (*e.g.*, prices or averages). Many differentially private mechanisms work by adding targeted randomness to each individual users' data. As a simple illustration, suppose for which we have a sequence of values $x_1, \ldots, x_n$ and we want

---

[1] There are two live batching CFMMs in production, CowSwap on Ethereum [Mar21] and Penumbra which relies on a specialized ZKP chain [dV21].

to report the mean $\mu = \frac{1}{n}\sum_i x_i$. One can (in expectation) preserve the mean μ by adding i.i.d., mean zero noise to each x_i, before computing and reporting the new mean, $\tilde{\mu}$. Intuitively, as the variance of the added noise becomes large, it is harder to recover the original value of x_i, prior to the added noise, but the new reported mean $\tilde{\mu}$ is likely to be far away from the true mean μ.

In this sense, differentially private algorithms induce a natural trade-off between the privacy and accuracy of a query, much like the trade-off between price impact and privacy in CFMMs. We note that the methods from differential privacy have been used at scale and in production at the US Census [Dwo19], Google [ACG+16], and Apple [CJK+18]. Our threat model for the adversary (Sect. 3.1) involves an adversary trying to estimate an ordered vector of trades given prices. In this scenario, we can view the set of trades to be executed as "private" user data while the accuracy of the query is the deviation in price that users have to pay for privacy. Differential privacy is a natural way to study the expected worst case behavior of such an estimation process, similar to its usage within machine learning.

We note that achieving differential privacy, even with non-private noise, can help reduce expected MEV profits. Moreover, as differential privacy has often been used in machine learning to improve algorithmic fairness, we posit (without proof) that differentially private DeFi algorithms inherit fairness guarantees [DHP+12]. These fairness guarantees are distinct of those from cryptographic fair ordering [KZGJ20], as they provide explicit guarantees on the trade-off between (economic) utility, privacy, and fairness [CGKM19,XYW19].

Uniform Random Execution. To achieve differential privacy in CFMMs, we construct a black-box algorithm called *Uniform Random Execution* (URE). This algorithm can be viewed as the inverse of batching, as it breaks up and splits large trades before subsequently randomly permuting the trade ordering. Randomness is used for both splitting up large trades and for permuting the split up trades. Blockchains with smart contract capabilities that include CFMM ordering as part of consensus rules can execute the URE (*e.g.,* Celo [KOR19], Terra [MSS20], Penumbra [dV21], Osmosis [AO21]). In particular, any blockchain with a verifiable random function (VRF) [MRV99] that provides public randomness and consensus rules for executing trades in a particular order suffices for URE.

Summary. Our analysis of the differential privacy of URE utilizes a novel representation of a sequence of trades as a binary tree. The tree is constructed such that the height of the tree provides a lower bound on the worst case price impact. On the other hand, number of leaves of the tree controls how easy it is for one to invert the precise trades executed. Representing continuous objects (sequences of real-valued trades) as a random discrete data structure allows us to utilize traditional tools from differential privacy. We show that the trade tree controls the maximum price impact of a sequence of trades by utilizing curvature of a CFMM [AEC20, §2]. Curvature represents bounds on market impact cost and liquidity and is crucial for relating the trade tree to worst-case price impact. Subsequently, we analyze the impact of splitting up and randomly permuting trades on the trade tree and then compute bounds on the price impact associated to these actions.

In order to achieve differential privacy, we first prove that splitting up trades can be executed in a differentially private manner (Claim 2). To split a trade, we sample a random distribution π and the split up a single trade according to π. After splitting up the trades, we then show that randomly permuting the trades leads to an (ϵ, δ)-differentially private algorithm. We use composition laws [DR+14, KOV15] to combine these two results and show that the URE is differentially private. Note that ϵ and δ depend on the CFMM's curvature and on the on the number of trades executed.

2   Preliminaries

We will cover preliminaries on CFMMs and differential privacy. For more details, please refer to review articles on CFMMs [AAE+21] and differential privacy [DR+14].

2.1   Constant Function Market Makers

A *constant function market maker* is a contract that holds some amount of *reserves* $R, R' \geq 0$ of two assets and has a *trading function* $\psi : \mathbf{R}^2 \times \mathbf{R}^2 \to \mathbf{R}$. Traders can then submit a *trade* (Δ, Δ') denoting the amount they wish to tender (if negative) or receive (if positive) from the contract. The contract then accepts the trade if

$$\psi(R, R', \Delta, \Delta') = \psi(R, R', 0, 0),$$

and pays out (Δ, Δ') to the trader.

Curvature. We briefly summarize the main definitions and results of [AEC20] here. Suppose that the trading function ψ is differentiable (as most trading functions in practice are), then the marginal price for a trade of size Δ is

$$g(\Delta) = \frac{\partial_3 \psi(R, R', \Delta, \Delta')}{\partial_4 \psi(R, R', \Delta, \Delta')}.$$

Here ∂_i denotes the partial derivative with respect to the ith argument, while Δ' is specified by the implicit condition $\psi(R, R', \Delta, \Delta') = \psi(R, R', 0, 0)$; *i.e.*, the trade (Δ, Δ') is assumed to be valid. Additionally, the reserves R, R' are assumed to be fixed. The function g is known as the *price impact* function as it represents the final marginal price of a positive sized trade. When there are fees, one can show that $g^{fee}(\Delta) = \gamma g(\gamma \Delta)$ where $1 - \gamma$ denotes the percentage fee. We say that a CFMM is μ-*stable* if it satisfies

$$g(0) - g(-\Delta) \leq \mu \Delta$$

for all $\Delta \in [0, M]$ for some positive M. This is a linear upper bound on the maximum price impact that a bounded trade (bounded by M) can have. Similarly, we say that a CFMM is κ-liquid if it satisfies

$$g(0) - g(-\Delta) \geq \kappa \Delta$$

for all $\Delta \in [0, K]$ for some positive K. Simple methods for computing some μ and κ in common CFMMs are presented in [AEC20, §1.1].

Two-Sided Bounds. We can define similar upper and lower bounds for $g(\Delta) - g(0)$, with constants μ' and κ', which hold when the trades Δ are in intervals $[0, M'], [0, K']$, respectively. For the remainder of this paper, we will refer to μ-stability as the upper bound for both $g(0) - g(-\Delta)$ and $g(\Delta) - g(0)$, and similarly for κ-liquidity. More specifically, given μ, μ', we say that a CFMM is symmetrically μ''-stable if

$$|g(\Delta) - g(0)| \leq \mu|\Delta|,$$

when $-M \leq \Delta \leq M'$, and symmetrically κ'' stable if

$$|g(\Delta) - g(0)| \geq \kappa|\Delta|.$$

when $-K \leq \Delta \leq K'$. From the above, it suffices to pick $\mu'' = \min\{\mu, \mu'\}$ and $\kappa'' = \min\{\kappa, \kappa'\}$.

For the remainder of this paper, we will focus on using CFMM curvature parameters to bound the impact cost realized, which in turn controls how easily an adversary can invert a trade size from prices.

2.2 Differential Privacy

Differential privacy is a framework for classifying how well a randomized algorithm $\mathcal{A}$ anonymizes individual data points.

Definition 1. *A randomized algorithm $\mathcal{A}$ is (ϵ, δ)-differentially private if for all $S, S' \in \mathbf{Dom}\,\mathcal{A}$ with $d(S, S') \leq 1$ we have for all measurable $B \subset \mathbf{Range}\,\mathcal{A}$*

$$\mathbf{Prob}[\mathcal{A}(S) \in B] \leq e^{\epsilon}\,\mathbf{Prob}[\mathcal{A}(S') \in B] + \delta$$

In this definition, ϵ can be thought of as a uniform upper bound on the Kullback-Leibler divergence over the distribution induced by any pair of neighboring data sets. Traditionally, S, S' are thought of as discrete and the metric d corresponds to the Hamming metric. In this case, the intuition behind the definition is the following: changing one entry of the variable S' does not change the output distribution 'too much,' making it difficult to tell apart S from S' by looking only at the results of algorithm $\mathcal{A}$. In this paper, we will assume d is the L^1 norm [DR+14, NRS07]. We provide further details on differential privacy in Appendix A.

3   Problem Construction

In the discussions of [AEC21b, §3], two ways of providing approximate privacy are presented:

1. *Randomizing price*: the protocol can randomly perturb the price quoted by the CFMM, in manner resistant to adversaries (while also not destroying liquidity provider returns).
2. *Batching orders*: picking a number of orders n to batch prior to execution.

Neither of these proposed solutions are perfect and [AEC21b] provides no adversarial model for assessing them. Here we first formulate a simple adversarial threat model for these solutions and then introduce URE. To construct URE, we first describe a simpler method called *Simple Uniform Random Execution* (SURE) which achieves differential privacy under restrictive conditions on trade sizes. We then prove that the URE achieves differential privacy by modifying SURE using extra randomness whose entropy is parametrized by the number of trades to execute and the curvature. For the remainder of the paper, we will assume that there are only two assets traded (in order to utilize curvature bounds) while n will refer to the number of trades executed.

3.1   Threat Model

Adversary Definition and Attack. We assume a simple model of an adversary that generalizes [AEC21b]. The adversary, who we will call Eve, attempts to discover the quantities traded by a set of agents referred to as Traders. Eve is unable to see the exact quantities the Traders use to trade with the CFMM, but knows when the Traders transactions $\Delta_1, \ldots, \Delta_n$ are executed as a block. Eve does not know the order in which the trades are executed and her goal is to estimate the ordering and sizes of the trades. Her only ability is to interact with the CFMM in the state before the traders' transactions are executed and the state after their transactions are executed. Explicitly, Eve's goal is to produce a vector $(\tilde{\Delta}_1, \ldots, \tilde{\Delta}_n)$ such that $\|(\tilde{\Delta}_1, \ldots, \tilde{\Delta}_n) - (\Delta_1, \ldots, \Delta_n)\|_1$ is small with high probability. Differential privacy provides a precise way of characterizing the probability of such a scenario occurring.

When a user submits a transaction to a blockchain, they send a transaction via a peer-to-peer network that reaches a miner or validator. In both proof-of-stake and layer 2 chains, the validator who chooses the final execution order of transactions is known as a *sequencer*. For the remainder of this paper, any reference to the sequencer will assume that the sequencer is honest (e.g. they execute a given ordering when received from an MEV auction). Unless the blockchain uses a fully homomorphic virtual machine (which does not currently exist), the sequencer necessarily sees a user's transaction in order to execute a valid state transition. Fair-ordering systems [KZGJ20, KDL+21] attempt to decentralize this sequencing operation, albeit with extra assumptions on validator behavior. Our threat model does not prevent the sequencer from discovering Traders' trades and front-running them as we assume that Eve is not the (honest) sequencer.

Action Space. We assume that Eve has access to two queries:

- marginalPrice(): Computes the marginal price of the CFMM at its current reserves
- isValid(Δ): Takes a trade $\Delta \in \mathbf{R}$, returns True if the trade is valid and False otherwise

We will denote the set of valid trades at reserves $R \in \mathbf{R}_+^n$ as $\mathcal{A}_\varphi(R)$ and note that it can effectively be thought of as the epigraph of the trading function φ [AC20].

3.2   Simple Uniform Random Execution

One of the simplest ways to introduce entropy into a CFMM is to randomly permute the set of trades to be executed. We will first describe the *simple uniform random execution* (SURE) mechanism that simply permutes observed trades. Formally, suppose that we are given a vector of valid trades

$$\Delta_1 \in \mathcal{A}_\varphi(R), \Delta_i \in \mathcal{A}_\varphi\left(R + \sum_{j=1}^{i-1} \Delta_j\right)$$

For brevity, we will refer to above condition as $\mathcal{A}_\varphi(\Delta)$ for a trade vector Δ. The SURE mechanism draws a random permutation $\pi \sim_{\mathsf{Unif}} S_n$ and constructs a sequence of trades $\Delta_i^\pi = \Delta_{\pi(i)}$, which arise from permuting the order in which the trades are executed. Consider the marginal prices of the original trades $p_1, \ldots, p_n$ and the permuted prices $p_1^\pi, \ldots, p_n^\pi$. Note that $p_n = p_{\pi(n)}$ if and only if the CFMM is path-independent (*e.g.*, feeless). Our goal is two-fold: first, we aim to bound the maximum deviation between the true price p and the permuted prices p^π. That is, we want to compute

$$\mathcal{E}_{SURE} = \mathop{\mathbf{E}}_{\pi \sim S_n} \left[\max_{i \in [n]} |p^\pi(i) - p(i)|\right]$$

This deviation effectively corresponds to a bound on the worst quoted price that a trader can receive (relative to their original order price). Secondly, we want to capture a notion of how difficult it is for an adversary to learn the values of π chosen given only the prices p_n^π.

Before analyzing the SURE mechanism for some classes of trades, let's look at some simple examples. If all of the trades Δ_i are unique—e.g., $\nexists i, j \in [n]$ such that $\Delta_i = \Delta_j$—then computing Δ_i given p^π is in some sense be difficult to invert to a precision higher than $\kappa \min_{i,j} |\Delta_i - \Delta_j|$. This is because if π is a single adjacent transposition $(i\ i+1)$, then $g(\sum_{j=1}^i \Delta_i) - g(\sum_{j=1}^{i-1} \Delta_j) \geq \kappa \min(\Delta_i, \Delta_{i-1}) \geq \kappa \min_{i,j} |\Delta_i - \Delta_j|$. Moreover, we should expect that SURE should work better when $\sum_{i=1}^n \mathsf{sgn}(\Delta_i) \approx 0$. This is because the probability of having a long run of trades in the same direction is very low. For instance, if Δ_i is a Rademacher random variable (*e.g.*, uniformly drawn from $\{-1, 1\}$) then the expected maximum length of a run is $\Theta(\log n)$ [ER75, Theorem 1].

On the other hand, if there is a set $S \subset [n]$ with $|S| = \Omega(n)$ such that for all $i, j \in S, \Delta_i = \Delta_j$, then it will be much easier to invert the set of trades. There is a loss of entropy in the output trade sequences as there will be many permutations $\pi, \pi', \pi \neq \pi'$ such that $\Delta^\pi = \Delta^{\pi'}$. Let's consider an explicit numerical example. Let $\Delta_1 = 100$ and $\Delta_i = 1$ for all $i \in \{2, \ldots, n\}$. Even though we are sampling from $n!$ permutations, there are only n output sequences that SURE outputs: $\Delta_j^\pi = \Delta_{\pi(1)} = 100$ in the jth position for $j \in [n]$. Suppose we consider a permutation π with $\pi(1) = j$. For any trade in position i with $\pi(i) < j$, the trade gets significantly better execution than they did initially. This is because their trade is executed before the trade of size 100 is executed, giving them significantly less impact. Therefore, SURE requires the trade distribution to have sufficient entropy and the distribution of trade sizes to not be too concentrated in order to work.

We will first analyze SURE on a subset of allowable input trades. This subset will be defined via simple constraints on $\min_{i,j} |\Delta_i - \Delta_j|$. We later relax these by splitting up large trades in a manner that ensure that the trade size distribution satisfies these constraints with high probability. To analyze SURE, we will start by obtaining upper and lower bounds on the worst case expected price discrepancy, $\mathbf{E}[\max_i |p^\pi(i) - p(i)|]$. This analysis will provide insight into what subset of admissible trades provide provable bounds on price discrepancy and identifiability.

Maximum of the Price Process and Random Binary Trees. Suppose the price impact function g is κ-liquid and μ-stable on an interval $[-M, M]$. By definition this implies that for all $i \in [n]$

$$\sum_{j=1}^{i} \kappa \Delta_{\pi(j)} - \mu \Delta_j \leq p^\pi(i) - p(i) \leq \sum_{j=1}^{i} \mu \Delta_{\pi(j)} - \kappa \Delta_j$$

This means that we have

$$\kappa \max_i \left| \sum_{j=1}^{i} \Delta_{\pi(j)} - \frac{\mu}{\kappa} \Delta_j \right| \leq \max_i |p^\pi(i) - p(i)| \leq \mu \max_i \left| \sum_{j=1}^{i} \Delta_{\pi(j)} - \frac{\kappa}{\mu} \Delta_j \right| \tag{1}$$

Therefore, bounds on partial sums of permuted trades will allow us to bound the worst case price impact of SURE. Define the partial sum

$$\rho_i(\mathbf{\Delta}, \pi) = \sum_{j=1}^{i} \Delta_{\pi(j)} - \frac{\mu}{\kappa} \Delta_j \tag{2}$$

Now consider the binary search tree $T(\rho(\mathbf{\Delta}, \pi))$ whose root is $\rho_1(\mathbf{\Delta}, \pi)$. Each element $\rho_j(\mathbf{\Delta}, \pi)$ is inserted sequentially to construct the tree (see Fig. 1 for an example).

This representation of the partial sums as a tree provides a natural geometric description of the maximum price deviation. In particular, $\max_i \rho_i(\mathbf{\Delta}, \pi)$ is

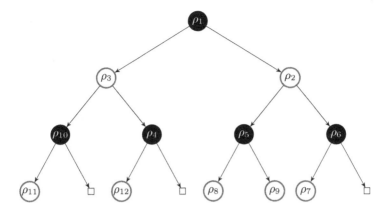

Fig. 1. Depiction of the tree $T(\rho(\mathbf{\Delta}, \pi))$ where $\rho_i = \rho_i(\mathbf{\Delta}, \pi)$ and $\rho_{11} < \rho_{10} < \rho_3 < \rho_{12} < \rho_4 < \rho_1 < \rho_8 < \rho_5 < \rho_9 < \rho_2 < \rho_7 < \rho_6$

necessarily a leaf node in this tree. This means that the maximum deviation $\max_{i,j} |\rho_i(\mathbf{\Delta}, \pi) - \rho_j(\mathbf{\Delta}, \pi)|$ is at most 2 times the height of the tree as the distance from ρ_1 to any element is maximized by the height. This provides the following bounds using (1)

$$\max_i |p^\pi(i) - p(i)| \le \mu \left(|\rho_1(\mathbf{\Delta}, \pi)| + \max_j \left| \Delta_{\pi(j)} - \frac{\kappa}{\mu} \Delta_j \right| \cdot 2 \cdot \mathsf{height}(T(\rho(\mathbf{\Delta}, \pi))) \right) \tag{3}$$

$$\max_i |p^\pi(i) - p(i)| \ge \kappa \left| \rho_1(\mathbf{\Delta}, \pi) + \min_j \left(\Delta_{\pi(j)} - \frac{\mu}{\kappa} \Delta_j \right) \cdot 2 \cdot \mathsf{height}(T(\rho(\mathbf{\Delta}, \pi))) \right| + O(1) \tag{4}$$

Note that the second bound comes from bounded support of curvature:

$$\max_j |\rho_j(\mathbf{\Delta}, \pi)| \ge |\rho_j(\mathbf{\Delta}, \pi)| = \left| \rho_1(\mathbf{\Delta}, \pi) + \sum_{i=1}^{j} \left(\Delta_{\pi(j)} - \frac{\mu}{\kappa} \Delta_j \right) \right|$$

$$\ge \left| \rho_1(\mathbf{\Delta}, \pi) + \min_j \left(\Delta_{\pi(j)} - \frac{\mu}{\kappa} \Delta_j \right) \cdot 2 \cdot \mathsf{height}(T(\rho(\mathbf{\Delta}, \pi))) \right| + O(1)$$

Moreover, the number of leaves in the tree represent the number of left-to-right local maxima of ρ_j. Note, furthermore, that by using curvature and the tree structure, we have reduced the maximum price deviation problem (a continuous problem) into a combinatorial one regarding a random tree. If the tree is roughly balanced (*e.g.*, height is $O(\log n)$) and there are $\Omega(n)$ leave nodes then it is unlikely that a small change to the permutation π by a transposition will change the maximum value. We will formalize this by studying the behavior of the random variable $T(\mathbf{\Delta})$, which draws a permutation π randomly and sets $T(\mathbf{\Delta}) = T(\rho(\mathbf{\Delta}, \pi))$.

To study the behavior of $T(\mathbf{\Delta})$, we need to analyze the expected height of a random binary tree. It is known that the height of a random binary tree with distinct elements (*e.g.*, such that every permutation is equiprobable) has height $\Theta(\log n)$ with high probability:

Theorem 1 (Theorem 1   [Ree03]). *Let* Δ *have unique elements. Then* $\mathbf{E}[\text{height}(T(\Delta))] = \alpha \log n - \beta \log \log n$ *and* $\mathbf{Var}[\text{height}(T(\Delta))] = O(1)$

If we can guarantee that the elements of $T(\Delta)$ are distinct (*e.g.*, such that every permutation of Δ is equiprobable) then combining this result with (3) yields

$$\mathbf{E}[\max_i |p^\pi(i) - p(i)|] \leq \mu \left(\mathbf{E}[\rho_1(\Delta, \pi)] + 2 \max_{i,j} \left| \Delta_i - \frac{\kappa}{\mu} \Delta_j \right| \cdot \mathbf{E}[\text{height}(T(\Delta))] \right)$$

$$\leq \mu \left(\mathbf{E}[\rho_1(\Delta, \pi)] + 2 \max_{i,j} \left| \Delta_i - \frac{\kappa}{\mu} \Delta_j \right| (\alpha \log n - \beta \log \log n) \right)$$

$$\leq 3\mu \left(\max_{i,j} \left| \Delta_i - \frac{\kappa}{\mu} \Delta_j \right| \right) (\alpha \log n - \beta \log \log n + 1) \qquad (5)$$

where we used the upper bounds $\max_j \left| \Delta_{\pi(j)} - \frac{\kappa}{\mu} \Delta_j \right| \leq \max_{i,j} \left| \Delta_i - \frac{\kappa}{\mu} \Delta_j \right|$ and

$$\mathbf{E}[\rho_1(\Delta, \pi)] = \frac{1}{n} \sum_{j=1}^{n} \left| \Delta_j - \frac{\kappa}{\mu} \Delta_1 \right| \leq \max_{i,j} \left| \Delta_i - \frac{\kappa}{\mu} \Delta_j \right|$$

Similarly, note that $\mathbf{E}[\rho_1(\Delta, \pi)] \geq \min_j \left(\Delta_{\pi(j)} - \frac{\mu}{\kappa} \Delta_j \right)$ so we have

$$\mathbf{E}[\max_i |p^\pi(i) - p(i)|] \geq \kappa \left| \min_j \Delta_{\pi(j)} - \frac{\mu}{\kappa} \Delta_j \right| (2 \mathbf{E}[\text{height}(T(\Delta)) + O(1)])$$

$$\geq 2\kappa \left| \min_{i,j} \Delta_i - \frac{\mu}{\kappa} \Delta_j \right| (\alpha \log n - \beta \log \log n + O(1))$$

Therefore, provided that the following two conditions hold

$$\Delta_{\min} = \left| \min_{i,j} \Delta_i - \frac{\mu}{\kappa} \Delta_j \right| = \Omega(1) \qquad \Delta_{\max} = \left| \max_{i,j} \Delta_i - \frac{\kappa}{\mu} \Delta_j \right| = O(1) \qquad (6)$$

we have $\mathcal{E}_{SURE} = \mathbf{E}[\max_i |p^\pi(i) - p(i)|] = \Theta(\log n)$. Such a bound is ideal as it ensures that there is always a minimum price discrepancy of $\Omega(\kappa \log n)$ so that an adversary cannot determine a trade size with precision greater than $\Omega(\kappa)$. On the other hand, the upper bound on price deviation means that the mechanism will not cause too great of a price impact for users.

Note that the usage of Theorem 1 is prefaced on every permutation of the elements of $\rho_j(\Delta, \pi)$ being equiprobable. One simple example of when this isn't true is from the threshold trades, $\Delta = (T, 1, \ldots, 1) \in \mathbf{R}^T$ when $\mu \geq 100\kappa$. When this is true, neither of the conditions (6) hold and moreover, the conditions of Theorem 1 do not hold. This means that SURE only works when (a) all permutations of partial sums are unique and (b) when $\mu \leq (\max_i \Delta_i)\kappa$. In the next section, we will achieve (a) by adding noise dependent on Δ, μ, κ to the trades and (b) by splitting trades.

3.3   Uniform Random Execution

We have seen the SURE mechanism works well at providing privacy while minimizing price discrepancy when (6) holds, when elements of $\boldsymbol{\Delta}$ are unique, and when $\frac{\mu}{\kappa}$ is not too large. However, we're not guaranteed that both of these conditions hold in general as illustrated by the example at the end of the last section. This section will focus on using randomization to ensure that a) (6) holds with high probability and b) the elements of $\boldsymbol{\Delta}$ are unique. We will do this by performing two actions: splitting large trades to ensure the maximum condition holds and adding noise to trades to ensure that trades are not too close in size. Applying these two actions to $\boldsymbol{\Delta}$ and subsequently executing SURE is termed the *Uniform Random Execution* mechanism. There are three parameters that control the URE mechanism:

- $c_{\min}$: Lower bound on $\Delta_{\min}$
- $s \in \mathbf{R}_+$: Split threshold that controls the average chunk size for a big trade
- $k \in \mathbf{N}$: Multiple of $(1 + s)\Delta_{\min}$ that requires splitting

Lower Bounding the Minimum by Adding Laplace Noise. Our goal is to construct random variables $\xi_1, \ldots, \xi_n$ drawn i.i.d. from a distribution that can depend on a particular $\boldsymbol{\Delta}$ but guarantees that $\tilde{\boldsymbol{\Delta}} = \boldsymbol{\Delta} + \xi$ satisfies the left hand side of (6) with high probability. In particular, we would like to control $\mathbf{Prob}\left[\left|\min_{i,j} \tilde{\Delta}_i - \frac{\kappa}{\mu}\tilde{\Delta}_j\right| > c_{\min}\right]$ for a constant $c_{\min} > 0$. We desire the following condition to hold bounded above by $\delta \in (0,1)$:

$$
\begin{aligned}
\mathbf{Prob}\left[\left|\min_{i,j} \tilde{\Delta}_i - \frac{\kappa}{\mu}\tilde{\Delta}_j\right| \leq c_{\min}\right] &= \mathbf{Prob}\left[\left|\min_{i,j} \Delta_i + \xi_i - \frac{\kappa}{\mu}(\Delta_j + \xi_j)\right| \leq c_{\min}\right] \\
&\leq \mathbf{Prob}\left[-\left|\min_{i,j} \Delta_i - \frac{\kappa}{\mu}\Delta_j\right| + \left|\min_{i,j} \xi_i - \frac{\kappa}{\mu}\xi_j\right| \leq c_{\min}\right] \\
&= \mathbf{Prob}\left[\left|\min_{i,j} \xi_i - \frac{\kappa}{\mu}\xi_j\right| \leq c_{\min} + \left|\min_{i,j} \Delta_i - \frac{\kappa}{\mu}\Delta_j\right|\right] \leq \delta
\end{aligned}
\tag{7}
$$

In Appendix C, we prove the following claim:

Claim 1. There exists $a \in \mathbf{R}$ dependent on $\boldsymbol{\Delta}, \mu, \kappa$ and $\xi_i \sim \mathsf{Lap}(a, |a|)$ such that (7) holds

This mechanism can be naturally modified to inherit the ϵ-privacy guarantees of the Laplace mechanism [DR+14, §3.2]. Note that the dependence of the noise parameter a on $\boldsymbol{\Delta}$ is similar to smoothed sensitivity in differential privacy [NRS07]. We note that this added noise ensures both that the lower bound of (6) holds and ensures that the elements of $\boldsymbol{\Delta} + \xi$ are unique so that Theorem 1 holds.

Upper Bounding the Maximum by Splitting Trades. One way to reduce the upper bound on error in (5) is to split up a trade Δ_i. This reduces $\Delta_{\max}$ and as explained in Appendix G, also increases the privacy of SURE. More precisely, we split Δ_i into Δ'_i, Δ''_i with $\Delta_i = \Delta'_i + \Delta''_i$ and then consider the pricing error associated to $p(\boldsymbol{\Delta}')$ where $\boldsymbol{\Delta}' = (\Delta_1, \ldots, \Delta_{i-1}, \Delta'_i, \Delta''_i, \Delta_{i+1}, \ldots, \Delta_n)$. This process can be iterated until all trades meet a particular criteria. Instead of splitting trades in two, we instead split trades into $m(\Delta_i)$ pieces, where $m(\Delta_i)$ is defined as

$$m(\Delta_i) = \max\left(1, \left\lceil \frac{|\Delta_i|}{(1+s)\Delta_{\min}} \right\rceil\right)$$

That is, the mechanism splits the trade into $m(\Delta_i)$ pieces who sizes are roughly $(1+s)\Delta_{\min}$. Let $\mathbf{1}^m = (1, \ldots, 1)$. For any trade Δ_i with $m(\Delta_i) > 1$, we draw $\pi \sim \mathsf{Dir}(\mathbf{1}^{m(\Delta_i)})$ and split Δ_i into trades $\Delta_{i,j} = \Delta_i \pi_j$. Since $\sum_{j=1}^n \pi_j = 1$, this provides a natural mechanism for splitting trades in a single step. As the Dirichlet distribution is sub-Gaussian when using uniform weights [MA17] and as the expected order statistics of a Dirichlet process decay exponentially [BJP12], $\mathbf{Prob}[\Delta_{i,j} - (1+s)\Delta_{\min} > k\Delta_{\min}]$ also decays exponentially in k. This ensures that we have very few chunks that are significantly greater than $(1+s)\Delta_{\min}$, which ensures that with high probability $\max_i \Delta_i < (1+s+k)\Delta_{\min}$. As described in Appendices D and G, this condition ensures that SURE is effective with high probability. We note that the precise price impact of splitting trades (as a function of curvature) is analyzed in [AEC20].

3.4   Differential Privacy

We are now in a position to prove that the URE mechanism satisfies (ϵ, δ)-differential privacy, where $\epsilon = O(\mu \log n + \max_i \Delta_i)$. Our proof proceeds in two steps. First, we prove the following claim in the Appendix E.

Claim 2 (Splitting is differentially private). Suppose that we have a sequence of admissible trades $\boldsymbol{\Delta} \in \mathbf{R}^n$ and after adding noise we have $\tilde{\boldsymbol{\Delta}}$ with $\tilde{\Delta}_{\min} > 0$. For each $k \in \mathbf{N}$ define $S_k = \{j : \tilde{\Delta}_j > k\tilde{\Delta}_{\min}\}$. If $\eta^* = \max_j \frac{\Delta_j}{\tilde{\Delta}_{\min}} = O(n)$ and there exists $k > 0$ such that $|S_k| = O(1)$, then there exists an (ϵ, δ)-differentially private algorithm $\mathsf{Split}(\Delta)$ for splitting trades in $\tilde{\Delta}$ such that $\mathsf{height}(T(\mathsf{Split}(\tilde{\Delta}))) = O(\log n)$ where $\epsilon = O(\eta^*)$

This claim ensures that under mild conditions on the maximum trade size, we can generate a partial sum trade tree of height $O(\log n)$. Note that we can get the claim's conditions to be satisfied by varying s, the scale parameter, which leads to a privacy-utility trade-off. Second, we show that when a partial sum trade tree has height $O(\log n)$, permuting the trades provides $(O(\mu \log n), \delta)$-differential privacy for the maximum price impact (Claim 3). We combine these two differentially private algorithms using standard composition theorems (see Appendix), resulting in a differentially private CFMM.

Claim 3 (SURE is differentially private). Suppose that we have a sequence of admissible trades $\boldsymbol{\Delta} \in \mathbf{R}^n$ such that $\mathsf{height}(T(\boldsymbol{\Delta})) = O(\log n)$ and all trade sizes are unique. Then randomly permuting the trades Δ^π can be made into a $(\mu \log n, \delta)$-differential private algorithm for the minimum and maximum price impact

While the full proof of the theorem is in the appendix, we sketch the steps of the proof below. First, we show that if a set of trades satisfies (6), then we can achieve differential privacy. We do this by first bounding the local sensitivity [DR+14] of the price impact vector $p_j(\pi, \Delta)$ as a function of Δ. This is done by reducing the problem to analyzing two different price trees (Appendix B). We make an analogue of smooth sensitivity [NRS07] that rounds a vector of trades to an integer lattice whose length is $\Delta_{\min}$. These steps ensure that the maximum difference in price impact between neighboring sets of trades will be $O(\mu \log n)$. This immediately leads to achieving (ϵ, δ)-differential privacy, where $\epsilon = O(\mu \log n)$.

Using the composition property of differential privacy, we are able to compose these two mechanisms to achieve $(\mu \log n + \max_i \Delta_i, \delta)$-differential privacy where $\delta = F^{-1}(O\left(\frac{1}{\epsilon}\right))$ and F^{-1} is the inverse Laplace CDF. While the constants can likely be improved, this suggests that permuting and splitting up trades is a simple and viable mechanism for adding differential privacy to CFMMs. Finally, note that in Appendix F we provide a convex program that can split up trades more efficiently than the Dirichlet mechanism of Theorem 3.4. This is likely useful to practitioners where randomness is a constrained resource (e.g., on a blockchain).

4   Worst-Case Bounds and Path Deficiency

In this section, we'll explore if we can do better than the URE mechanism by analyzing the curvature of the mechanism and generalizing the previous work using Generic Chaining. Our goal will be to consider classes of mechanisms, $\mathcal{F}$, that can provide (ϵ, δ)-differential privacy for CFMMs and attempt to compute worst-case bounds. We first provide some necessary conditions that elements of such a class have to satisfy. We will also show that extending the results of Sect. 3.4 to the path-deficient (positive fee) case involves proving bounds over a class of functions $\mathcal{F}$. Finally, we'll investigate connections to private PAC learning which suggest that one cannot do significantly better than the URE unless curvature is dynamically adjusted.

4.1   Mechanism Curvature

Instead of directly working with a mechanism, can we say something about the set of all mechanisms that ensure that $|p^m(i) - p^t(i)| > \delta$ where $p^m(i)$ is the ith price of the mechanism and $p^t(i)$ is the non-private or true price? Using a curvature definition analogous to those of [AEC20], we can provide a simple bounds related to this question.

Note that bounds of the form $|p_i^m - p_i^t| > \delta$ involve bounding changes between two different price processes. Suppose that we define "curvatures" of the form

$$\kappa_t |\Delta_i| < |p^t(i) - p^t(i-1)| < \mu_t |\Delta_i|$$
$$\kappa_m |\Delta_i| < |p^m(i) - p^m(i-1)| < \mu_m |\Delta_i|$$
$$\kappa_{mt} |\Delta_i| < |p^m(i) - p^t(i)| < \mu_{mt} |\Delta_i|$$

First, let's look at the difference between the mechanism price at time i and the true price at time $i - 1$:

$$|p^m(i) - p^t(i)| = |(p^m(i) - p^t(i)) - (p^t(i-1) - p^t(i))|$$
$$\geq |p^m(i) - p^t(i)| - |p^t(i) - p^t(i-1)|$$
$$\geq (\kappa_m - \mu_{mt})|\Delta_i|$$

This says that we can ensure that the predictive value of previous price information on a trade cannot be resolved more than a multiplicative amount of $\kappa_m - \mu_{mt}$ times the trade size. In particular, $\kappa_m > \alpha + \mu_{mt}$ ensures that an adversary never has more than a precision α of information about the trade size. This provides a necessary condition in terms of mechanism curvature for a class $\mathcal{F}$ of mechanisms to provide differential privacy bounds.

4.2   Path Deficiency

Any CFMM that has non-zero fees (e.g., $\gamma = 1 - f < 1$) is path-deficient and has strictly negative expected value for round trip trades [AEC20]. Such CFMMs have price path $p^t(i)$ that are explicitly dependent on the trade ordering. Note that almost all CFMMs that are used in practice have non-zero fees to attract liquidity, so this is an important scenario to study. Previous work on path-deficient CFMMs has focused on analyzing how a particular price process (such as a geometric brownian motion) interacts with the expected returns from fees [EAC21]. Moreover, [AEC20, §2] illustrated that when fees are present $g^f(\Delta) = \gamma g(\gamma \Delta)$, where g^f is the price impact function with fees and g is the feeless price impact function. This suggests that we can analyze the path-dependent case by uniformly bounding the geometric parameters of Sect. 3.2 (e.g., height and number of leaves) as a function of the fee.

Suppose that given a trade vector $\boldsymbol{\Delta}$, we have a bound of the form

$$\mathop{\mathbf{E}}_{\pi \in S_n} \left[\max_{i \in [n]} |p_f^\pi(\boldsymbol{\Delta}) - p^\pi(\boldsymbol{\Delta})| \right] = O(\gamma^k) \tag{8}$$

In Appendix I, we compute a lower bound that allows one to prove such a bound for Uniswap (the most commonly used CFMM). Then we can bound the deviation in height between the set of trade and price trees (see Appendix B) as a function of γ and transfer path-independent returns to the path-deficient case with extra polylogarithmic terms in γ. Two ways of proving bounds of the form (8) are using generic chaining [Tal21, Ch. 3] and smoothed analysis [HRS20]. We discuss how this analysis can be applied to CFMMs in Appendix H.

4.3 Private PAC Learning and Adversarial Bounds

A number of recent results have shown that differentially private PAC learning and online learning are closely related. In particular, the finiteness of an integer-valued complexity measure known as the Littlestone dimension controls whether a particular algorithm can be learned in both an online and differentially private manner [ALMM19,BLM20]. The Littlestone dimension of a class of functions $\mathcal{F}$ from $X \to Y$, $\mathsf{LDim}(\mathcal{F})$, is defined as the maximum depth $d \in \mathbf{N}$ of a tree made up of sequences $x_1, \ldots, x_d \in X$ such that there exists $f \in \mathcal{F}$ with $f(x_i) = y_i$ for every possible $y_i \in Y$. Consider the set $\mathcal{F}^\pi(\Delta)$ which is the set of all trees constructable from any permutation $\pi \in S_n$ for a fixed $\Delta \in \mathbf{R}^n$. The results of Sect. 3.2 show that $\mathsf{LDim}(\mathcal{F}^\pi(\Delta)) = \Omega(\mu \log n)$. State-of-the-art results for blackbox constructions of online learners [GL21] show that the regret of a differentially private online learning algorithm is $O(2^{2^{\mathsf{LDim}(\mathcal{F})}})$. This implies that the best online learners can do again the URE, in a blackbox manner, is $O(2^{n^\mu})$. This means that any algorithm that has non-zero curvature is unlikely to do asymptotically better then the URE. If it were possible to construct a polynomial time algorithm to privately PAC learn trades, then there would be significantly degraded privacy guarantees for users. However, this would require a mechanism for which $\mathsf{LDim}(\mathcal{F}^\pi) = O(\log \log n)$, which appears unlikely except for constant-sum market makers that have $\mu = 0$. One other piece of evidence that Littlestone dimension is the correct complexity measure for CFMM privacy comes from the fact that the worst case instances for Littlestone dimension and CFMMs are thresholds (*cf.*, Sect. 3.2 and [ALMM19]).

5   Differentially (Non)-private MEV Reduction

In previous sections, we assumed an honest sequencer who implements a differentially private mechanism for CFMM trades. We had explored this in the hopes that privacy might hinder MEV. Interestingly, it may be possible to prevent MEV by instantiating the "sequencer" and our mechanism on a public blockchain with access to a verifiable random function [MRV99], which exists on chains such as Polkadot [BCC+20] and Cosmos [Buc16].[2] While this would not necessarily be differentially private—the noise is from public but unpredictable random coins—it could still prevent MEV. And the cost to users of doing so is modeled by the price impact analysis of Sect. 3.2. We see a similarity between this and results in machine learning relating differential privacy and fairness [DHP+12].

In practice, the majority of front-running and sandwich attacks are executed via maximal extractable value (MEV) auctions [BDKJ21]. These auctions separate the roles of sequencing (choosing an execution ordering) from *searching*,

---

[2] We note, however, that the precise design in this paper is not immediately implementable—there are a number of practical and technical hurdles to overcome. These include, but are not limited to, determining how to allow applications to use randomness generated by consensus and figuring out how transaction submission and the pending transaction queue are affected by random orderings.

which is the process of finding the optimal front-run or sandwich transactions to maximize profit. Searchers bid for priority of transaction placement—they place a trade of size X before another user's trade of size Y in order to front-run them. Sequencers collect these bids and construct a final transaction ordering based on which bids generate the maximum profit for them. Within this context, we can view the searchers as Eve (Sect. 3.1)—they do not know the final ordering and they can only affect it by placing a bid with the sequencer. Note, however, that when consensus-provided randomness is used to dictate the transaction order and sizing (e.g. via a verifiable random function), searchers match the description of Eve as they have a negligible edge over a coin flip in determining the order of trades. Even if searchers colluded with the sequencer to try to force a particular ordering, they would need to successfully execute a grinding attack against the VRF. In this paper, we implicitly have assumed that a VRF for which grinding attacks are hard to execute is used by the base protocol.

This observation demonstrates that our threat model is one in which searchers (not sequencers) are thwarted by the mechanisms of the subsequent sections. Given that >50% of CFMM extractable value from front-running is executed via the largest MEV auction, Flashbot [DOS], our model more closely models the real agents who are front-running users.

6   Conclusion

In this paper, we demonstrated that there exists a novel, practical mechanism for providing differential privacy to users of constant function market makers. This mechanism, unlike previous methods such as batching, has provable guarantees on the worst case price impact and strong privacy guarantees. As a number of new blockchain protocols implement CFMMs directly in their consensus mechanism, the randomness needed to execute this algorithm will become more plentiful and easier to source. Our analysis used novel techniques combining results from stochastic processes, concentration inequalities, and differential privacy. The results in this paper can likely be improved by providing tighter bounds on the minimal amount of noise needed to achieve (ϵ, δ)-differential privacy. Moreover, numerical studies of the utility loss (e.g., worsened price impact) would justify practical usage of URE on networks such as Osmosis [AO21] and Penumbra [dV21]. Finally, we note that differential privacy has been explored in path-independent prediction markets [FW17], where similar bounds to the ones found in this paper exist. These bounds utilize different proof techniques as prediction market makers do not directly translate to CFMMs (cf., [AC20, §3.2]). We note that a consequence of using this mechanism is that it likely provides better fairness for end users. Unlike fair ordering solutions [KZGJ20, KDL+21], our results provide economic guarantees on fairness for a particular application. Future work involves demonstrating that fairness is inherently present when a DeFi protocol can guarantee differential privacy.

Acknowledgements. The authors want to thank Ian Miers, Yi Sun, GaussianProcess, Tim Roughgarden, Kobi Gurkan, Dev Ojha, Henry de Valence, and the anonymous reviewers for helpful comments and feedback.

A   Differential Privacy Results

We implicitly use a number of differential privacy results on composition and provide them here for convenience. First we note the serial composition theorem:

Theorem 2 (Composition Theorem 3.16 [DR+14]). *Let $\mathcal{A}_1, \ldots \mathcal{A}_n$ be a sequence of (ϵ_i, δ_i) algorithms such that $\mathbf{Range}\,\mathcal{A}_i \subseteq \mathbf{Dom}\,\mathcal{A}_{i+1}$. Then the composition $\mathcal{A}_n \circ \cdots \circ \mathcal{A}_1$ is $(\sum_{i=1}^{n} \epsilon_i, \sum_{i=1}^{n} \delta_i)$-differentially private*

Secondly, we note the parallel composition theorem

Theorem 3. *Let $\mathcal{A}_1, \ldots, \mathcal{A}_n$ be algorithms whose domains (databases) are independent and each algorithm is (ϵ_i, δ_i)-differentially private. Then $(\mathcal{A}_1, \ldots, \mathcal{A}_n)$ is $\max_i \epsilon_i$ differentially private*

Finally, we note that the serial composition rule can be improved from $(\sum_i \epsilon_i, \sum_i \delta_i)$ to $(n\epsilon^2 + \epsilon\sqrt{n \log(1/\tilde{\delta})}, n\delta + \tilde{\delta})$ where $\tilde{\delta} = O(n\delta)$ if $\epsilon_i = \epsilon, \delta_i = \delta$ for all i [KOV15]. We will not need to use this result, only the generic composition rules. However, it is possible that one can improve our constants using results such as this.

B   Price Tree Height Is Close to Trade Tree Height

Suppose that we have an admissible trade vector $\boldsymbol{\Delta} = (\Delta_1, \ldots, \Delta_n) \in \mathcal{A}_\varphi$. Given $\pi \in S_n$, we can write a sequence of prices in terms of the price impact function:

$$p_j(\pi) = g\left(\sum_{i=1}^{j} \Delta_{\pi(i)}\right)$$

We generate a random binary tree from the price vector by uniformly sampling $j \sim [n]$ and making $p_j(\pi)$ the root before inserting the remaining prices sequentially as per π. Under this framework, we have

$$\mathop{\mathbf{E}}_{\pi \sim S_n}\left[\max_j p_j(\pi)\right] \le \mathop{\mathbf{E}}_{j \sim [n]}[p_j(\pi)] + \max_i |p_i(\pi) - p_{i-1}(\pi)| \mathop{\mathbf{E}}_{\pi \sim S_n}[\text{height}(T(p_j(\pi)))]$$

$$\le \mathop{\mathbf{E}}_{j \sim [n]}[p_j(\pi)] + \mu(\max_i \Delta_i) \mathop{\mathbf{E}}_{\pi \sim S_n}[\text{height}(T(p_j(\pi)))]$$

We can later remove this constraint by adding a small amount of noise to each entry, which will make the entries unique a.s. Note that the height of the tree generated by P_j represents the number of trades in the longest sequential deviation from the mean price. Let's consider when the trade tree and price tree differ in branching. On average, this occurs when the jth price $p_{\pi(j)}$ is a left branch whereas the $j+1$st price $p_{\pi(j+1)}$ is a right branch, but both trades $\varDelta_{\pi(j)}, \varDelta_{\pi(j+1)}$ are left branches. When this happens, the price tree has an average height that is 1 less than the trade tree.

We will first illustrate this when the first two elements of the permutation after the pivot (which is random) differ from the expected pivot value. Explicitly, suppose that we have

$$p_{\pi(2)} - \frac{1}{n} \sum_{i=1}^{n} p_{\pi(i)} < 0 \qquad\qquad p_{\pi(3)} - \frac{1}{n} \sum_{i=1}^{n} p_{\pi(i)} > 0$$

Using curvature bounds, the first equation gives

$$0 \geq p_{\pi(2)} - \frac{1}{n} \sum_{i=1}^{n} p_{\pi(i)} \geq \kappa \varDelta_{\pi(2)} - \frac{\mu}{n} \sum_{i=1}^{n} \varDelta_i$$

Similarly, the second equation gives

$$0 \leq p_{\pi(3)} - \frac{1}{n} \sum_{i=1}^{n} p_{\pi(i)} \leq \mu \varDelta_{\pi(3)} - \frac{\kappa}{n} \sum_{i=1}^{n} \varDelta_i$$

which when combined gives

$$\varDelta_{\pi(2)} \leq \frac{\mu}{\kappa} \left(\frac{1}{n} \sum_{i=1}^{n} \varDelta_i \right) = \eta_+ \qquad\qquad (9)$$

$$\varDelta_{\pi(3)} \geq \frac{\kappa}{\mu} \left(\frac{1}{n} \sum_{i=1}^{n} \varDelta_i \right) = \eta_- \qquad\qquad (10)$$

Let ρ_i be as in (2) and let $\overline{\varDelta} = \frac{1}{n} \sum_{i=1}^{n} \varDelta_i$. On the other hand, suppose that $\rho_2(\pi) - \overline{\varDelta}(\pi), \rho_3(\pi) - \overline{\varDelta}(\pi)$ are both greater than zero (e.g., they are both left nodes of their parent). This implies that $\varDelta_{\pi(2)} + \varDelta_{\pi(3)} \geq \frac{1}{n} \sum_{i=1}^{n} \varDelta_i$. This means that we can only end up in a state where $\mathsf{height}(T(\rho_j(\pi))) > \mathsf{height}(T(p_j(\pi)))$ if the trades are within the interval $[\eta_-, \eta_+]$. For instance, when the drift $\frac{1}{n} \sum_{i=1}^{n} \varDelta_i = 0$, then interval has size zero (its a mean-reverting set of trades) and we never enter this error condition. This matches intuition: if there's a lot of drift in the trades, then we shouldn't expect our price and trade vectors to 'sort' the same way. In particular, the higher the curvature of the CFMM, the less drift we can tolerate because large trades cause more noticeable price impact. The length of the interval $[\eta_-, \eta_+]$ is

$$\left(\frac{\mu}{\kappa} - \frac{\kappa}{\mu} \right) \left(\frac{1}{n} \sum_{i=1}^{n} \varDelta_i \right)$$

Note that we can recurse the above argument as we go down the tree and get a set of intervals $I_1 = [\eta_-(1), \eta_+(1)], I_2 = [\eta_-(2), \eta_+(2)], \dots, I_n = [\eta_-(n), \eta_+(n)]$. Performing the same calculation as above yields

$$\eta_-(i) = \frac{\kappa}{\mu}\left(\frac{1}{n-i}\sum_{i=i}^{n}\Delta_{\pi(i)}\right) \qquad \eta_+(i) = \frac{\mu}{\kappa}\left(\frac{1}{n-i}\sum_{i=i}^{n}\Delta_{\pi(i)}\right)$$

Given that the maximum interval size is μM is the max trade size for which curvature is valid), we can use this to bound the probability p_j that vertex j has a height difference between the trade and price trees. This probability is upper bounded by ratio of the length of I_j and the interval length μM, e.g., $p_j \leq \frac{|I_j|}{\mu M}$. We can upper bound the interval length by the maximum mean-drift subsequence:

$$|I_j| \leq \left(\frac{\mu}{\kappa} - \frac{\kappa}{\mu}\right)\left(\max_{J\subset[n]}\frac{1}{|J|}\sum_{j\in J}\Delta_j\right)$$

Define $R^*(\Delta) = \max_{J\subset[n]}\frac{1}{|J|}\sum_{j\in J}\Delta_j$. Finally, performing a union bound gives an upper bound on the probability p_{diff} of the heights of the trade tree and price tree different

$$p_{\text{diff}} \leq \sum_{j=1}^{n}p_j = n\left(\frac{1}{M\kappa} - \frac{\kappa}{\mu^2 M}\right)R^*(\Delta) \tag{11}$$

If this quantity is sufficiently small (e.g., we have tight curvature bounds), then bounds on the trade tree transfer to the price tree with high probability. For the rest of the paper, we will assume that (11) is sufficiently small. We note that fee adjustments and curvature adjustments are intricately related [AEC20, §3] and in practice, this can be enforced by dynamic updates to a CFMM curve.

C   Proof of Claim 1

Suppose that $\xi_i \sim_{iid} \mathsf{Lap}(a,b)$. We need to analyze the distribution of $\xi_i - \frac{\mu}{\kappa}\xi_j$. Recall that if $X \sim \mathsf{Lap}(a,b)$ then $kX \sim \mathsf{Lap}(ka,|k|b)$. Therefore we are trying to bound the distribution of $Z(a,b) = X + Y$ where $X \sim \mathsf{Lap}(a,b)$, $Y \sim \mathsf{Lap}\left(-\frac{\mu}{\kappa}a, \frac{\mu}{\kappa}b\right)$. In particular, given $\delta < 0$ we want to choose a, b such that

$$F_Z(k) \leq \mathbf{Prob}[X + Y \leq k] \leq \delta$$

where $k = c_{\min} + \left|\min_{i,j}\Delta_i - \frac{\kappa}{\mu}\Delta_j\right|$. Nadarajah [Nad07, Theorem 1] explicitly computes the CDF $F_{Z(a,b)}(k)$ and shows that it is monotone, continuous, and differentiable in a, b except at one value of k for all a, b. Moreover, it is supported on the entire real line. Therefore, $\exists a^*$ such that $F_{Z(a^*,|a^*|)}(k) = \delta$.

D   Proof of Claim 2

Our proof works by differentially privately sampling a probability distribution $\pi \sim \text{Dir}(1)$ multiple times using the mechanism of [GWH+21]. The Dirichlet mechanism on k nodes $\mathcal{M}_D^{(k)}(\pi)$ samples a Dirichlet distribution centered at π, where $\pi \in P_k = \{x \in \mathbf{R}^k : \sum_i x_i = 1, x_i \geq 0\}$. One can think of it as sampling an increment $d\pi$, adding it to π and renormalizing. First, we reproduce a theorem on differentially private Dirichlet sampling.

Theorem 4 ([GWH+21], Theorem 1, Corollary 1). *The Dirichlet mechanism $\mathcal{M}_D^{(k)}(\pi)$ achieves (ϵ, δ)-differential privacy where $\epsilon = O(k(1 + \log(o(k)))$ and $\delta = 1 - \min_\pi \mathbf{Prob}[\mathcal{M}_D^k(\pi) - \pi > \Omega(\epsilon)]$*

Define the vector $\eta(\boldsymbol{\Delta})$ as follows:

$$\eta(\boldsymbol{\Delta}) = \left(\left\lceil \frac{\Delta_1}{\Delta_{\min}} \right\rceil, \ldots, \left\lceil \frac{\Delta_n}{\Delta_{\min}} \right\rceil \right)$$

Each coordinate represents rounding each trade to an integer lattice with width $\Delta_{\min}$. Define $S_k = \{i : \eta(\boldsymbol{\Delta}) > k\}$ and $S_k^c = [n] - S_k$. For each $j \in S_k$, privately sample $\pi \sim \text{Dir}(1)$ where $\mathbf{1} = (1, \ldots, 1) \in \mathbf{R}^{\eta(\boldsymbol{\Delta})_j}$. Let $\hat{\Delta}_{j,k} = \Delta_j \pi_k$ with $\sum_k \hat{\Delta}_{j,k} = \Delta_j$. We can view each Dirichlet sample π as providing a mechanism for splitting the trade Δ_j. Our goal is to find $k \in \mathbf{N}$ such that the following two conditions hold

1. $\text{height}(T(\Delta_{S_k^c})) = \Theta(\log n)$
2. $\text{height}(T(\hat{\Delta}_{j,k})) = \Theta(\log \eta_j)$ with high probability

We can show that the latter condition holds with high probability when the distribution sampled is Dirichlet centered at the centroid $(\frac{1}{n}, \ldots, \frac{1}{n})$. Constructing a partial sum tree from a Dirichlet sample is the same as drawing a sample from a Poisson-Dirichlet branching random walk [ABF13]. These walks satisfy $\mathbf{Prob}[|\text{height}(T(\hat{\Delta}_{j,k})) - c \log \eta(\boldsymbol{\Delta})_j| \geq k] = O(e^{-k})$ for a universal constant c [ABF13, Corollary 1.3]. Therefore, the probability that all of the Dirichlet constructed trees $T(\hat{\Delta}_{j,k})$ have height greater than $c \log \eta(\boldsymbol{\Delta})_j$ is

$$\mathbf{Prob}\left[\exists j \in S_k | \text{height}(T(\hat{\Delta}_{j,k})) - c \log \eta_j | \geq c' \log \eta_j \right] \leq \left(\frac{|S_k|}{\eta_j^{c'}} \right)$$

which directly follows from the independent sampling from the private Dirichlet distribution and inclusion-exclusion. Therefore, with probability $p^* = 1 - \frac{|S_k|}{\delta_j^{c'}}$, we have the maximum height of a tree constructed from all $|S_k|$ vectors $\hat{\Delta}_{j,k}$ is

$$\sum_{j \in S_k} \log \eta_j \leq |S_k| \max_j \log \eta_j$$

which under our assumptions is $O(\log n)$. Our claim about differential privacy then follows immediately from Theorem 4.

E   Proof of Claim 3

We will prove differential privacy by using the smooth sensitivity framework of [NRS07]. First, we will recall definitions and introduce preliminaries on this framework before specializing it to SURE. Smooth sensitivity places an upper bound on the local sensitivity of a function f, which is defined as

$$LS_f(x) = \max_{d(x,y)\leq 1} |f(x) - f(y)|$$

Note that unlike the global sensitivity, which is used in the generic Laplace mechanism [DR+14], the local sensitivity depends on the particular input x. Often times, it is too difficult to get uniform bounds on local sensitivity and instead it is easier to use a smooth proxy. A β-smooth upper bound $S : \mathbf{Dom}\, f \to \mathbf{R}$ for $LS_f(x)$ satisfies $S(x) \geq LS_f(x)$ for all $x \in \mathbf{Dom}\, f$ and $S(x) \leq e^\beta S(y)$ for all $x, y \in \mathbf{Dom}\, f$ with $d(x, y) = 1$. We are now in a position to recall two results of Nissim, et al.:

Theorem 5 ([NRS07], **Lemma 2.6**). *Let h be an (α, β)-admissible noise probability density function and let $Z \sim h$. For a function $f : D^n \to \mathbf{R}^d$, let S be a β-smooth upper bound in the local sensitivity of f, then $\mathcal{A}(x) = f(x) + \frac{S(x)}{\alpha} Z$ is (ϵ, δ)-differentially private.*

Theorem 6 ([NRS07], **Lemma 2.9**). *For $\epsilon, \delta \in (0, 1)$, the d-dimensional Laplace distribution, $h(z) = 2^{-d} e^{-\|z\|_1}$ is (α, β)-admissible with $\alpha = \frac{\epsilon}{2}$, $\beta = \frac{\epsilon}{2\rho_{\delta/2}(\|Z\|_1)}$ where $\rho_\delta(Y)$ is the $1 - \delta$ quantile of Y.*

Combined, these results illustrate that if we can construct a β-smooth upper bound, we can immediately construct a Laplace mechanism that achieves (ϵ, δ)-differential privacy. Section 3 of [NRS07] provides a mechanism for computing a β-smooth upper bound by first defining the sensitivity at distance k,

$$LS_f^k(x) = \max_{\substack{y\in\mathbf{Dom}\, f \\ d(x,y)\leq k}} LS_f(x)$$

A β-smooth upper bound on local sensitivity is defined as,

$$S_{f,\beta}(x) = \max_{k\in\{0,1,\ldots,n\}} e^{-k\beta} LS_f^k(x)$$

Therefore, we need to construct a function f that represents price impact and compute an analogue of local sensitivity.

For a differentially private CFMM, we want to minimize the worst case price impact in a neighborhood of a trade $\mathbf{\Delta}$. We define $f(\mathbf{\Delta})$ as

$$f(\mathbf{\Delta}) = \max_{j\in[n]} p_j(\Delta)$$

Now we need to modify the definition of local sensitivity to account for trade admissibility and discretization. Normally, local sensitivity is defined for discrete spaces where the distance d is taken to be the Hamming metric. We can discretize our trade space in terms of $\Delta_{\min}$. Recall that we ensure that $\Delta_{\min} > 0$ by adding Laplace noise to all trades (whose parameter will be tuned in accordance with the above theorem). Note that moving to such a discretization simply changes our choice of β. Using this definition, we can define the local trade sensitivity as

$$TS_f^k(\Delta) = \sup_{\substack{\Delta' \in \mathbf{Dom} \, f \cap \mathcal{A}(R) \\ d(\Delta, \Delta') \leq k\Delta_{\min}}} |f(\Delta) - f(\Delta')|$$

where $\mathcal{A}(R)$ is the set of admissible trades. From the results of Sect. 3.2, we know that $TS_f^k(\Delta) = O(k\mu(\max_i \Delta) \log n)$ since the depth of the tree quantifies the largest price impact. In particular, each element Δ_i' such that $|\Delta_i - \Delta_i'| > \Delta_{\min}$ can cause price impact of at most $\mu(\max_i \Delta) \log n$ and we can add these independently over the at most k coordinates that have prices changed by more than $\Delta_{\min}$. We can define an analogous smooth sensitivity bound,

$$\tilde{S}_{f,\beta}(x) = \max_\ell e^{-\ell\beta} TS_f^\ell(\Delta) = \max_\ell e^{-\ell\beta} \ell\mu(\max_i \Delta) \log n$$

This is minimized when $\ell = \frac{1}{\beta}$, giving

$$\tilde{S}_{f,\beta}(x) = \frac{\mu}{e\beta}(\max_i \Delta) \log n$$

Therefore, provided that a) the partial sum tree has height $O(\log n)$ b) the noise added ensures that $\Delta_{\min} > 0$, and c) the noise is rescaled by $\frac{2\tilde{S}_{f,\beta}(x)}{\epsilon}$, we achieve differential privacy.

Note that in particular, our bound depends on $\max_i \Delta$ and the curvature upper bound. By splitting trades using Claim 2, we reduce $\max_i \Delta$ and can ensure that the noise added is reasonable. Moreover, as we saw, without splitting trades, we run into issues with trades of the form $(T, 1, \ldots, 1)$. Note that algorithms that try to learn where the trade T occurs (after applying a permutation π) is equivalent to privately learning threshold functions [BNSV15, ALMM19].

F   Convex Trade Splitting

When we are considering CFMM arbitrage, it can be shown that a necessary condition for stability is path-deficiency. Path deficiency ensures that no rational trader (*e.g.*, profit optimizing) is incentivized to split a desired trade size Δ into two trades $\Delta_1 + \Delta_2 = \Delta$. However, if a trader also desires privacy, splitting up trades can become necessary. To see why, consider a trader who makes a trade of size T and a sequence of trades $\Delta = (T, 1, \ldots, 1) \in \mathbf{R}^{T+1}$. Using curvature, we know that the price impact is at least κT after a trade of size T and of size κ after each trade of size 1. This means that an adversary can easily discern where my trade is, even if Δ is randomly permuted due to the T times larger price impact. Therefore, splitting up the trade of size T into trades close to size 1 will make it hard for an adversary to reconstruct the total trade size.

Our goal is to split up trades such that the probability of an adversary detecting the position of a single trade is small relative to the curvature. Suppose that a trade Δ_1 is split into trades $\Delta'_1, \ldots, \Delta'_j$ and let $\tilde{\Delta} = (\Delta'_1, \ldots, \Delta'_j, \Delta_2, \ldots, \Delta_n)$ A splitting adversary is a binary classifier $\ell(\Delta, \mathbf{\Delta})$ that returns 1 if $\Delta \in \{\Delta'_1, \ldots, \Delta'_j\}$ and 0 otherwise. We say that a splitting mechanism is (δ, ϵ) indistinguishable if

$$\mathbf{Prob}\left[\left|\frac{1}{n}\sum_{i=1}^{n}\ell(\tilde{\Delta}_i, \tilde{\mathbf{\Delta}}^\pi) - \frac{j}{n}\right| < \epsilon\right] < \delta$$

over some suitable set of splitting classifiers. The inequalities in Appendix G can directly be used to prove that this holds for the L^2 norm.

However, path-deficiency implies that splitting trades will cost a user an extra fee. This trade-off between best execution price and privacy can be explored via a simple, convex objective function that trades off price impact vs. improved privacy via splitting. Recall that the L^2 norm strictly decreases under splitting, e.g.,

$$\|(\Delta_1, \ldots, \Delta_n)\|_2^2 = \sum_{i=1}^{n}\Delta_i^2 = \Delta_1^2 + \sum_{i=2}^{n}\Delta_i^2$$

$$= a\Delta_1^2 + (1-a)\Delta_1^2\sum_{i=2}^{n}\Delta_i^2 > a^2\Delta_1^2 + (1-a)^2\Delta_1 + \sum_{i=2}^{n}\Delta_i^2$$

$$= \|(a\Delta_1, (1-a)\Delta_1, \ldots, \Delta_n)\|_2^2$$

where $a \in (0, 1)$ represents the splitting fraction.

This property allows us to quantify the privacy benefit to splitting trades, as the more minimal the L^2 norm, the less noise that is needed to ensure that the random binary tree has height $\Theta(\log n)$ and $\Omega(n)$ leaves. In particular, the Cauchy and Gaussian mechanisms for differential privacy utilize distributions whose variances are proportional to the L^2 norm.

Given that we want to minimize price impact while maximizing the amount of trade splitting necessary for indistinguishable, we construct a convex optimization problem. Define the function f as:

$$f(\Delta_1, \ldots, \Delta_n) = \sum_{i=1}^{n}\gamma g\left(\gamma\sum_{j=1}^{i}\Delta_i\right) + \eta\sum_{i=1}^{n}\Delta_i^2$$

The first term in f represents an upper bound on the price impact and the second term represents the L^2 splitting term. Our goal is to minimize f over sequences of trades $(\Delta_1, \ldots, \Delta_k) \in \sqcup_{i=1}^{\infty}\mathbf{R}^i$ such that $\sum_{i=1}^{k}\Delta_i = \Delta^*$, e.g.,

$$\begin{aligned} \text{minimize} \quad & f(\Delta_1, \ldots, \Delta_n) \\ \text{subject to} \quad & \Delta_1 + \cdots + \Delta_n = \Delta^* \end{aligned} \tag{12}$$

Using curvature bounds, we can construct a simple descent algorithm to solve this. Firstly, note that the definition of curvature yields

$$\kappa\gamma^2 \sum_{i=1}^{n}\sum_{j=1}^{i} \Delta_i \le f(\Delta_1,\ldots,\Delta_n) - \eta \sum_{i=1}^{n}\Delta_i^2 \le \mu\gamma^2 \sum_{i=1}^{n}\sum_{j=1}^{i}\Delta_i$$

Furthermore, note that we can rewrite the double sum as

$$\sum_{i=1}^{n}\sum_{j=1}^{i}\Delta_i = \sum_{i=1}^{n}(n-i+1)\Delta_i$$

Next, note that we can upper bound the split function, $f(a\Delta_1, (1-a)\Delta_1, \ldots, \Delta_n)$ as

$$f(a\Delta_1, (1-a)\Delta_1, \ldots, \Delta_n) \le \mu\gamma^2 \left((n+1)a\Delta_1 + n(1-a)\Delta_1 + \sum_{i=2}^{n}(n-i+2)\Delta_i \right)$$

$$+ \eta \left(a^2\Delta_1^2 + (1-a)^2\Delta_1^2 + \sum_{i=2}^{n}\Delta_i^2 \right)$$

$$= \mu\gamma^2 \left((n+a)\Delta_1 + \sum_{i=2}^{n}(n-i+1)\Delta_i + \Delta^* \right)$$

$$+ \eta \left(a^2\Delta_1^2 + (1-a)^2\Delta_1^2 + \sum_{i=2}^{n}\Delta_i^2 \right)$$

Combining these gives the following

$$f(\Delta_1,\ldots,\Delta_n) - f(a\Delta_1, (1-a)\Delta_1, \ldots, \Delta_n) \ge \gamma^2(\kappa-\mu)\sum_{i=2}^{n}(n-i+1)\Delta_i - \Delta^*$$

$$- \mu\gamma^2(n+a)\Delta_1 + \eta\Delta_1^2(1-a^2-(1-a)^2)$$

$$(13)$$

Maximize the right-hand side in a provide a mechanism for deciding whether to split trade Δ_1. Optimizing over a yields

$$a^* = \max\left(\frac{1}{2} - \frac{\mu\gamma^2}{4\eta\Delta_1}, 0 \right)$$

If we substitute a^* into (1) and the right-hand side is position, we split the trade Δ_1 into two trades of size $a^*\Delta_1$ and $(1-a^*)\Delta_1$.

G Splitting Trades: Concentration

Chatterjee proved a concentration bound using Stein's method that provides intuition as to why splitting trades improves the effectiveness of SURE. Theorem 7 shows that the variance of concentration around the mean for a randomly permuted sum is linear in the expected value.

Theorem 7 ([Cha07], **Proposition 1.1**). *Let $\{a_{i,j}\}_{1 \leq i,j \leq n}$ be a collection of numbers from $[0,1]$. Let $X = \sum_{i=1}^{n} a_{i,\pi(i)}$ where $\pi \sim S_n$ uniformly. Then*

$$\mathbf{Prob}[|X - \mathbf{E}[X]| \geq t] \leq 2 \exp\left(-\frac{t^2}{4\,\mathbf{E}[X] + 2t}\right) \tag{14}$$

Note that unlike Bernstein-like inequalities there is no direct dependence on n. Moreover, unlike Talagrand-like inequalities [Tal21], we do not have terms dependent on ϵ-nets. If we let $t = k\,\mathbf{E}[X]$, we have

$$\exp\left(-\frac{t^2}{4\,\mathbf{E}[X] + 2t}\right) = \exp\left(-\frac{k^2\,\mathbf{E}[X]}{2k + 4}\right) \leq \exp(-k\,\mathbf{E}[X])$$

For positive trade sizes, this implies that if we can split big trades into smaller trades (which reduces in turn reduces $\mathbf{E}[X]$) we can achieve the sufficient condition. More specifically, suppose that $a_{i,j} = \Delta_j - \frac{\kappa}{\mu}\Delta_i$. Then $X = \sum_{i=1}^{n} a_{i,\pi(i)}$ is the upper bound from (6) and the theorem claims that reducing the maximum will reduce the variance of SURE's utility.

We also note that better asymptotic results exist for non-negative sums:

Theorem 8 ([Alb19], **Corollary 2.2**). *Let a_{ij} be a connection of any real numbers and $\pi \sim S_n$ as uniform random permutation. Let $Z_n = \sum_{i=1}^{n} a_{i,\pi(i)}$. Then for all $x > 0$*

$$\mathbf{Prob}(|Z_n - \mathbf{E}[Z_n]| \geq t) \leq 16e^{1/16} \exp\left(\frac{-t^2}{256(\mathbf{Var}[Z_n] + \max_{i,j}|a_{ij}|t)}\right)$$

This bound explicitly includes a maximum term, directly justifying the improvement to SURE provided by splitting trades.

H   Path Dependency and Generic Chaining

Suppose that we want to try to find the worst case price deviation given that we have fees, $\gamma < 1$. If we define $X_j = p^\pi(i) - p(i)$, then we want to study the extremal behavior of this process, albeit without being able to directly bound price impact using methods from Sect. 3.2. We will be most interested in the behavior of the random variable $X^* = \max_j X_j$, which quantifies the worse execution price received by a user under this mechanism. To do this, we will utilize the theory of empirical processes. Roughly speaking, one can show that for a metric space (T, d), $\mathbf{E} \sup_{t \in T} X_t = \Theta(\mathrm{Diam}(T)\sqrt{\log \mathrm{card}T})$ by looking at simple bounds for empirical processes [Tal14, Tal21]. Our goal is to define a metric space T_γ that depends on fees and such that S_n acts faithfully on T_γ. We want the action to be faithful because that will be equivalent to the condition of unique elements of the form $|\Delta_i - \frac{\mu}{\kappa}\Delta_j|$ We can then attempt to bound, using chaining arguments, the worst case price deviation.

Chaining bounds rely on tail bounds on increments, *e.g.*, showing that for some metric d on our space T_γ, we have the following two conditions:

$$\forall u > 0, \ \mathbf{Prob}[|X_s - X_t| \geq u] \leq 2\exp\left(-\frac{u^2}{2d(s,t)^2}\right) \tag{15}$$

$$\exists u > 0, \ \sum_{s \in T} \mathbf{Prob}[X_s \geq u] \geq 1 \tag{16}$$

In our case, we need to construct a metric space that takes advantage of our trading function curvature and the randomness induced by the choice of permutation.

Our goal is to construct a metric on S_n that depends on both φ. We need to construct metric $d_{\varphi,\rho_0,\boldsymbol{\Delta}} : S_n \times S_n \to \mathbf{R}_+$ that we can use to find a formula like Eq. (15). A natural metric to construct is the raw price differences:

$$d_{\varphi,\rho_0,\boldsymbol{\Delta}}(\pi_1, \pi_2) = \sum_{i=1}^n |p_{\pi_1(i)}^t - p_{\pi_2(i)}^t|$$

Note that if we took an infimum over one of the two permutations, we arrive at the Wasserstein distance. Suppose we have $d_{\varphi,\rho_0,\boldsymbol{\Delta}}(\pi_1, \pi_2) \leq f(\varphi, \rho_0, \boldsymbol{\Delta})d(\pi_1, \pi_2)$ for some natural metric on the symmetric group (*e.g.*, Mallows metric [Dia88]). Moreover, suppose there exists $\kappa > 0$ such that $\mathbf{Prob}[X_s \geq \sqrt{\log n}\,(\kappa + \sum_i \Delta_i)] \geq 1$. Then we have the lower bound [Tal21, Eq. 2.15]

$$C\left(\kappa + \sum_i \Delta_i\right)\sqrt{\log n} \leq \mathbf{E}\sup_{t \in T} X_t \leq C'\left(\kappa + \sum_i \Delta_i\right)\mathrm{Diam}_d(T)\sqrt{\log n}$$

One simple idea for a metric upper bound is:

$$d^{ub}(\pi_1, \pi_2) = \mu \sum_{i=1}^n |\Delta_{\pi_1(i)} - \Delta_{\pi_2(i)}|$$

Under this metric, we need to show that

$$\mathbf{Prob}[|X_\pi - X_{\pi'}| \geq u] \leq 2\exp\left(-\frac{u^2}{2d(\pi, \pi')^2}\right)$$

This is effectively direct from Azuma's inequality since Δ_i is in a bounded ball (in order for us to use curvature). Next, we need to show $\mathbf{Prob}[X_s \geq \sqrt{\log n}\,(\kappa + \sum_i \Delta_i)] \geq 1$. For each permutation $\pi \in S_n$, we can construct a binary tree T_π from the partial sums $S_i \sum_i \Delta_{\pi(i)}$, where $S_i < S_j$ implies S_i is in the left subtree of S_j (and vice versa). Assume, first, that each S_i is unique. Then, it can be shown that the expected height and the tail bounds for the height of this subtree satisfies [ABC20, Ree03]

$$\mathbf{Prob}[h(T_\pi) \geq \sqrt{\log n}] \geq \frac{c}{n}$$

Our conjecture is that $\kappa h(T_\pi) \le X_s \le \mu h(T_\pi)$ which would immediately imply $\sum_{\pi \in S_n} \mathbf{Prob}[X_\pi \ge u] \ge 1$. Unfortunately to find bounds of this form with fees, one needs to find universal bounds on $g(\Delta) - \gamma g(\gamma \Delta)$. We illustrate such bounds for Uniswap in Appendix I.

I Path Dependency in Uniswap

Getting bounds such as (15) relies on bounding how far away the path-dependent case strays from the path independent case. For a fixed Δ, p_n^{pi} only depends on $\sum_i \Delta_i$ for path-independent, whereas $p_n^{pd}(\pi)$ does depend on the path $\Delta_{\pi(1)}, \ldots, \Delta_{\pi(n)}$. However, if we can uniformly bound $\max_{\pi \in S_n} |p_n^{pd}(\pi) - p_n^{pi}|$ as a function of fees and curvature.

For Uniswap, we have $g_{uni}(\Delta) = \frac{k}{(R-\Delta)^2}$. This gives a difference between the impact of a single path independent trade and a single path dependent trade as (see [AEC20] for the formulae):

$$g(\Delta) - \gamma g(\gamma \Delta) = k \left(\frac{1}{(R-\Delta)^2} - \frac{\gamma}{(R-\gamma\Delta)^2} \right) = \frac{k}{(R-\Delta)^2} \left(1 - \frac{\gamma(R-\Delta)^2}{(R-\gamma\Delta)^2} \right)$$

$$= g(\Delta) \left(1 - \frac{\gamma(R-\Delta)^2}{R^2} \frac{1}{(1 - \frac{\gamma\Delta}{R})^2} \right)$$

$$\le g(\Delta) \left(1 - \frac{\gamma(R-\Delta)^2}{R^2} \left(1 - \frac{c\gamma\Delta}{R} \right) \right)$$

$$= g(\Delta) \left(1 - \frac{\gamma(R-\Delta)^2}{R^2} - \frac{c\gamma\Delta(R-\Delta)}{R^3} \right)$$

$$= g(\Delta) \left(1 - \gamma \left(\frac{R-\Delta}{R} \right)^2 \left(R - \left(1 + \frac{c}{R} \right) \Delta \right) \right)$$

where we assume that $\frac{\gamma\Delta}{R} < 1$ and use the geometric series (so $c < 1$). When $R \gg 1$ and $R - \Delta \le kR$ for some $k < 1$, this gives us the bound

$$\frac{g(\Delta) - \gamma g(\gamma \Delta)}{g(\Delta)} \le 1 - \gamma \frac{(R-\Delta)^3}{R^2} \le 1 - \gamma k^3 R$$

References

[AAE+21] Angeris, G., Agrawal, A., Evans, A., Chitra, T., Boyd, S.: Constant function market makers: multi-asset trades via convex optimization (2021)

[ABC20] Addario-Berry, L., Corsini, B.: The height of mallows trees. arXiv preprint arXiv:2007.13728 (2020)

[ABF13] Addario-Berry, L., Ford, K.: Poisson-Dirichlet branching random walks. Ann. Appl. Probab. **23**(1), 283–307 (2013)

[AC20] Angeris, G., Chitra, T.: Improved price oracles: constant function market makers. In: Proceedings of the 2nd ACM Conference on Advances in Financial Technologies, pp. 80–91. ACM, New York, October 2020

[ACG+16] Abadi, M., et al.: Deep learning with differential privacy. In: Proceedings of the 2016 ACM SIGSAC Conference on Computer and Communications Security, pp. 308–318 (2016)

[AEC20] Angeris, G., Evans, A., Chitra, T.: When does the tail wag the dog? Curvature and market making. arXiv preprint arXiv:2012.08040 (2020)

[AEC21a] Angeris, G., Evans, A., Chitra, T.: A note on bundle profit maximization (2021)

[AEC21b] Angeris, G., Evans, A., Chitra, T.: A note on privacy in constant function market makers. arXiv preprint arXiv:2103.01193 (2021)

[Alb19] Albert, M.: Concentration inequalities for randomly permuted sums. In: Gozlan, N., Latała, R., Lounici, K., Madiman, M. (eds.) High Dimensional Probability VIII. PP, vol. 74, pp. 341–383. Springer, Cham (2019). https://doi.org/10.1007/978-3-030-26391-1_17

[ALMM19] Alon, N., Livni, R., Malliaris, M., Moran, S.: Private PAC learning implies finite Littlestone dimension. In: Proceedings of the 51st Annual ACM SIGACT Symposium on Theory of Computing, pp. 852–860 (2019)

[AO21] Agrawal, S., Ojha, D.: Vision for osmosis, May 2021

[BCC+20] Burdges, J., et al.: Overview of polkadot and its design considerations. arXiv preprint arXiv:2005.13456 (2020)

[BDKJ21] Babel, K., Daian, P., Kelkar, M., Juels, A.: Clockwork finance: automated analysis of economic security in smart contracts. arXiv preprint arXiv:2109.04347 (2021)

[BJP12] Broderick, T., Jordan, M.I., Pitman, J.: Beta processes, stick-breaking and power laws. Bayesian Anal. **7**(2), 439–476 (2012)

[BLM20] Bun, M., Livni, R., Moran, S.: An equivalence between private classification and online prediction. In: 2020 IEEE 61st Annual Symposium on Foundations of Computer Science (FOCS), pp. 389–402. IEEE (2020)

[BNSV15] Bun, M., Nissim, K., Stemmer, U., Vadhan, S.: Differentially private release and learning of threshold functions. In: 2015 IEEE 56th Annual Symposium on Foundations of Computer Science, pp. 634–649. IEEE (2015)

[Buc16] Buchman, E.: Tendermint: Byzantine fault tolerance in the age of blockchains. Ph.D. thesis (2016)

[CGKM19] Cummings, R., Gupta, V., Kimpara, D., Morgenstern, J.: On the compatibility of privacy and fairness. In: Adjunct Publication of the 27th Conference on User Modeling, Adaptation and Personalization, pp. 309–315 (2019)

[Cha07] Chatterjee, S.: Stein's method for concentration inequalities. Probab. Theory Relat. Fields **138**(1), 305–321 (2007)

[CJK+18] Cormode, G., Jha, S., Kulkarni, T., Li, N., Srivastava, D., Wang, T.: Privacy at scale: local differential privacy in practice. In: Proceedings of the 2018 International Conference on Management of Data, pp. 1655–1658 (2018)

[CXZ20] Chu, S., Xia, Q., Zhang, Z.: Manta: Privacy preserving decentralized exchange. IACR Cryptology ePrint Archive 2020/1607 (2020)

[DHP+12] Dwork, C., Hardt, M., Pitassi, T., Reingold, O., Zemel, R.: Fairness through awareness. In: Proceedings of the 3rd Innovations in Theoretical Computer Science Conference, pp. 214–226 (2012)

[Dia88] Diaconis, P.: Metrics on groups, and their statistical uses. In: Group Representations in Probability and Statistics, pp. 102–130. Institute of Mathematical Statistics (1988)

[DOS] Daian, P., Obadia, A., Setters, L.: MeV explore

[DR+14] Dwork, C., Roth, A., et al.: The algorithmic foundations of differential privacy. Found. Trends Theor. Comput. Sci. **9**(3–4), 211–407 (2014)

[dV21] de Valence, H.: Sealed-bid batch auctions (2021)

[Dwo19] Dwork, C.: Differential privacy and the US census. In: Proceedings of the 38th ACM SIGMOD-SIGACT-SIGAI Symposium on Principles of Database Systems, p. 1 (2019)

[EAC21] Evans, A., Angeris, G., Chitra, T.: Optimal fees for geometric mean market makers. arXiv preprint arXiv:2104.00446 (2021)

[ER75] Erdos, P., Révész, P.: On the length of the longest head-run. Top. Inf. Theory **16**, 219–228 (1975)

[FW17] Frongillo, R., Waggoner, B.: Bounded-loss private prediction markets. arXiv preprint arXiv:1703.00899 (2017)

[GL21] Golowich, N., Livni, R.: Littlestone classes are privately online learnable. arXiv preprint arXiv:2106.13513 (2021)

[GWH+21] Gohari, P., Bo, W., Hawkins, C., Hale, M., Topcu, U.: Differential privacy on the unit simplex via the Dirichlet mechanism. IEEE Trans. Inf. Forensics Secur. **16**, 2326–2340 (2021)

[HRS20] Haghtalab, N., Roughgarden, T., Shetty, A.: Smoothed analysis of online and differentially private learning. arXiv preprint arXiv:2006.10129 (2020)

[KDL+21] Kelkar, M., Deb, S., Long, S., Juels, A., Kannan, S.: Themis: fast, strong order-fairness in byzantine consensus. Cryptology ePrint Archive (2021)

[KOR19] Kamvar, S., Olszewski, M., Reinsberg, R.: Celo: a multi-asset cryptographic protocol for decentralized social payments. DRAFT version 0.24 (2019). https://storage.googleapis.com/celowhitepapers/Celo AMultiAssetCryptographicProtocolforDecentralizedSocialPayments.pdf

[KOV15] Kairouz, P., Oh, S., Viswanath, P.: The composition theorem for differential privacy. In: International Conference on Machine Learning, pp. 1376–1385. PMLR (2015)

[KZGJ20] Kelkar, M., Zhang, F., Goldfeder, S., Juels, A.: Order-fairness for Byzantine consensus. In: Micciancio, D., Ristenpart, T. (eds.) CRYPTO 2020. LNCS, vol. 12172, pp. 451–480. Springer, Cham (2020). https://doi.org/10.1007/978-3-030-56877-1_16

[MA17] Marchal, O., Arbel, J.: On the sub-Gaussianity of the Beta and Dirichlet distributions. Electron. Commun. Probab. **22**, 1–14 (2017)

[Mar21] Martinelli, F.: The crypto cinematic universe crossover event of the summer: balancer-gnosis-protocol (BGP), April 2021

[MRV99] Micali, S., Rabin, M., Vadhan, S.: Verifiable random functions. In: 40th Annual Symposium on Foundations of Computer Science (Cat. No. 99CB37039), pp. 120–130. IEEE (1999)

[MSS20] Moin, A., Sekniqi, K., Sirer, E.G.: SoK: a classification framework for stablecoin designs. In: Bonneau, J., Heninger, N. (eds.) FC 2020. LNCS, vol. 12059, pp. 174–197. Springer, Cham (2020). https://doi.org/10.1007/978-3-030-51280-4_11

[Nad07] Nadarajah, S.: The linear combination, product and ratio of Laplace random variables. Statistics **41**(6), 535–545 (2007)

[NRS07] Nissim, K., Raskhodnikova, S., Smith, A.: Smooth sensitivity and sampling in private data analysis. In: Proceedings of the Thirty-Ninth Annual ACM Symposium on Theory of Computing, pp. 75–84 (2007)

[Pow21] Powers, B.: SecretSwap is the secret network's answer to DeFi privacy, February 2021

[QZG21] Qin, K., Zhou, L., Gervais, A.: Quantifying blockchain extractable value: how dark is the forest? arXiv preprint arXiv:2101.05511 (2021)

[QZLG20] Qin, K., Zhou, L., Livshits, B., Gervais, A.: Attacking the DeFi ecosystem with flash loans for fun and profit. arXiv preprint arXiv:2003.03810 (2020)

[Ree03] Reed, B.: The height of a random binary search tree. J. ACM (JACM) **50**(3), 306–332 (2003)

[Tal14] Talagrand, M.: Upper and Lower Bounds for Stochastic Processes: Modern Methods and Classical Problems, vol. 60. Springer, Heidelberg (2014). https://doi.org/10.1007/978-3-642-54075-2

[Tal21] Talagrand, M.: Upper and Lower Bounds for Stochastic Processes: Modern Methods and Classical Problems, 2nd edn. Preprint (2021)

[XYW19] Xu, D., Yuan, S., Wu, X.: Achieving differential privacy and fairness in logistic regression. In: Companion Proceedings of the 2019 World Wide Web Conference, pp. 594–599 (2019)

[ZQT+20] Zhou, L., Qin, K., Torres, C.F., Le, D.V., Gervais, A.: High-frequency trading on decentralized on-chain exchanges. arXiv preprint arXiv:2009.14021 (2020)

Anonymous Tokens with Public Metadata and Applications to Private Contact Tracing

Tjerand Silde[1]([⊠])[iD] and Martin Strand[2][iD]

[1] Department of Mathematical Sciences, Norwegian University of Science and Technology – NTNU, Trondheim, Norway
tjerand.silde@ntnu.no
[2] Norwegian Defence Research Establishment – FFI, Kjeller, Norway
martin.strand@ffi.no

Abstract. Anonymous single-use tokens have seen recent applications in private Internet browsing and anonymous statistics collection. We develop new schemes in order to include public metadata such as expiration dates for tokens. This inclusion enables planned mass revocation of tokens without distributing new keys, which for natural instantiations can give 77 % and 90 % amortized traffic savings compared to Privacy Pass (Davidson *et al.*, 2018) and DIT: De-Identified Authenticated Telemetry at Scale (Huang *et al.*, 2021), respectively. By transforming the public key, we are able to append public metadata to several existing protocols essentially without increasing computation or communication.

Additional contributions include expanded definitions, a more complete framework for anonymous single-use tokens and a description of how anonymous tokens can improve the privacy in dp^3t-like digital contact tracing applications. We also extend the protocol to create efficient and conceptually simple tokens with both public and private metadata, and tokens with public metadata and public verifiability from pairings.

Keywords: Anonymous tokens · Public metadata · Contact tracing

1 Introduction

Anonymous credentials have been an active research area since the 1980's [21,22], involving schemes such as blind signatures, partially blind signatures, anonymous tokens, attribute-based credentials, group signatures, ring signatures etc. This enables more complex systems for e.g., electronic cash or electronic voting, but also, to protect the privacy of the users in chat applications like Signal.

Recent work by Davidson *et al.* [28] presents a very practical protocol, named Privacy Pass [27], for anonymous single-use tokens. This protocol allows users to browse anonymously, e.g., using Tor, without having to solve a CAPTCHA every time they visit a website. Privacy Pass gives the user a set of randomized tokens whenever they solve a CAPTCHA, which they then later can redeem instead of

© International Financial Cryptography Association 2022
I. Eyal and J. Garay (Eds.): FC 2022, LNCS 13411, pp. 179–199, 2022.
https://doi.org/10.1007/978-3-031-18283-9_9

solving a new CAPTCHA. This improves the usability of anonymous browsing. It also gives protection against spam, prevents DDoS attacks and provides fraud resistance without the need for cross-site tracking or fingerprinting. However, the only way to expire or revoke batches of unspent tokens is by replacing the private-public key pair in a trusted way, which is impractical [26].

Privacy Pass has gained a lot of attention, and is currently being integrated to improve privacy in several applications, e.g., for private file storage[1] and for basic attention tokens (BATs) in the Brave browser[2]. It can also be used for private click measurement when making a purchase or signing up for a service[3].

Facebook uses partially blind signatures for combating fraud [38], and they have developed an extension of Privacy Pass called DIT: De-Identified Authenticated Telemetry at Scale [36], which is used for privately collecting client-side telemetry from WhatsApp. DIT requires daily key-rotation to prevent DoS attacks, which led to the development of an attribute-based verifiable oblivious pseudorandom function for transparent key-rotation.

The IETF is currently standardizing Privacy Pass [37], while Trust Token [46] is currently being standardized by the World Wide Web Consortium. Both standardization processes mention private and public metadata, in addition to public verifiability, as desirable extensions to the Privacy Pass protocol. Public metadata allows for more efficient key-rotation, and opens for applications using public labeling and public anonymity sets, while private metadata allows for allow/deny lists, rate-limiting, or trust-indication. Public verifiability allows for outsourcing signing or verification of tokens.

Kreuter et al. [41] gave the first construction of anonymous tokens with private metadata, while we give the first construction with public metadata. Our construction can also be combined with private metadata or public verifiability.

Privacy Pass guarantees anonymity for all tokens generated by the same key. The addition of any metadata reduces the anonymity set. We have designed the protocol in such a way that the user and the signer must agree on the metadata. Any application should restrict its use of metadata to generic, predefined values that would otherwise have triggered a change of keys, e.g., expiry dates. Client software should validate that the metadata is in accordance to the policy, and reject any malformed tokens. Furthermore, private metadata bits also reduces the anonymity set. Our protocol can easily be extended to include more than one private metadata bit, but this must be done with great care, as it opens for secretly tracking smaller sets of individual users.

Independently of this work, Tyagi et al. [45] have proposed a similar construction to include public metadata, along with a novel hardness assumption and a reduction to a more conventional problem, to be used in partially oblivious pseudo-random functions. We discuss their work further in Sects. 1.4 and 3.

---

[1] PrivateStorage: medium.com/least-authority/the-path-from-s4-to-privatestorage-ae9d4a10b2ae.

[2] Brave: github.com/brave/brave-browser/wiki/Security-and-privacy-model-for-ad-confirmations.

[3] Private Click Measurement: privacycg.github.io/private-click-measurement.

1.1   Our Contribution

Our contribution in this paper is threefold: first, we present new definitions and a new framework for anonymous tokens – extending the work by Kreuter *et al.* [41] – to also consider public metadata and/or public verifiability. Secondly, we present three efficient protocols for anonymous tokens with efficient batched revocation: 1) Privacy Pass [28] with public metadata, 2) Kreuter *et al.* [41] with public and private metadata, and 3) a Privacy Pass inspired protocol using pairings to satisfy public verifiability while including public metadata. Thirdly, we present contact tracing as a new and important application for anonymous single-use tokens, and discuss the implementation of Privacy Pass used in the Norwegian contact tracing app Smittestopp to improve users' privacy.

Updated Definitions and New Framework. Several works have asked for efficient batched revocation of anonymous tokens without key-rotation [26,28]. Additionally, there is a need for anonymous tokens with public verifiability [46], so that token generation can be delegated, and verification can be performed locally for token redemption. We provide updated definitions for all of these cases: designated verifier anonymous tokens with or without public and/or private metadata and public verifier anonymous tokens with and without public metadata. Details can be found in Sect. 2.

Anonymous Tokens with Public Metadata. We present the first anonymous tokens protocols with efficient batched revocation, meaning that the protocol only requires one round of communication based on lightweight primitives and that we avoid key-rotation. The key insight in our protocol is conceptually very simple: all parties locally update the public key based on the hash of the public metadata, and then execute the protocols with respect to the new key pair. The main challenge is to sign tokens in a way that does not allow the user to forge tokens initially signed under metadata md to be valid under metadata md' instead. Let k be the secret key and let $d = \mathsf{H}(\mathsf{md})$ be the hash of the metadata. Our solution, inspired by Zhang *et al.* [48], is to use the inverse $e = (d + k)^{-1}$ as the new signing key. This allows us to replace the secret keys in the previous protocols in a modular way.

Furthermore, to avoid subliminal channels, the signer needs to prove that the signed token is computed correctly. This is easily solved for Privacy Pass [28]. In the original protocol they use a zero-knowledge protocol to prove, given generator G, public key $K = [k]G$, blinded token T' and signed token $W' = [k]T'$, the equality of discrete logarithms $\log_G K = k = \log_{T'} W'$ to ensure correctness. In our updated protocol, including metadata md, updated public key $U = [d]G + K$ and signed token $W' = [e]T'$, we prove the equality of discrete logarithms $\log_G U = d + k = \log_{W'} T'$ to ensure correctness.

However, it is not as easy to ensure correctness in the extended version of the protocol by Kreuter *et al.* [41] including both public and private metadata. We solve this by combining an OR-proof with two AND-proofs to make sure that the correct key is used. Further improvement is an open problem.

Next, we give a protocol based on pairings. The protocol is an adapted version of the partially blind signatures by Zhang *et al.* [48], where we tweak it into the same structure as Privacy Pass. We note that the communication in the protocol is the same, but in addition to get a more streamlined protocol structure, we also allow for more efficient instantiation in practice using the BLS12-381 pairing [5]. Ideally, we would like to avoid pairings altogether, but this seems necessary in practice. See more details about the protocols in Sect. 3.

Finally, we detail the communication efficiency of the protocols in Sect. 4, and compare our constructions with the current state of the art with respect to efficient batched revocation in Table 1. We show that our protocols are much more efficient in practice. We also make a concrete comparison with DIT [36] for collecting telemetry-data from WhatsApp, and show that our protocol in Fig. 4 would decrease the size of the signed token in a natural setting by 90 %, saving the Facebook servers up to 1.7 TB of communication every day.

More Private Contact Tracing. Many countries have recently developed contact tracing apps as one of the measurements to battle the ongoing pandemic. These apps are inherently storing sensitive information about the user, e.g., the users' location graph and social graph. To avoid large, centralized databases with such sensitive information about a large portion of a country's adult population, most apps are based on the decentralized Google/Apple Exposure Notification System (ENS). However, there are still privacy issues with regards to uploading the randomized exposure keys to the central server, as the user would have to identify themselves to ensure that only people who have tested positive for COVID-19 are able to upload keys. We implemented Privacy Pass into the Norwegian contact tracing app to improve the users' privacy. We present more details about the contact tracing infrastructure and improvements in Sect. 5.

1.2   Comparison to Anonymous Credentials

There is a long line of research on more generalized anonymous credentials with features such as multi-show, multi-attributes, and revocability – in addition to the mandatory unlinkability and unforgeability – that allow one to encode expiration dates as attributes.

However, generalized anonymous credentials often depends on stronger assumptions, e.g., strong RSA [12,13,15,16,18], strong Diffie-Hellman [3] or DL assumptions in bilinear groups [17,33]. Some schemes only depend on DDH [4,19,20,43], but these schemes require larger messages in general. In conclusion, generalized anonymous credentials inherently impose larger parameters, more rounds of communication and less efficient protocols in practice, resulting in thousands of bits on communication over multiple rounds.

Finally, more general and complex anonymous credentials make these schemes less suited for use in simpler single-use systems with many users, which is the case in our setting. We want to minimize the rounds of communication and data being sent, in addition to minimizing the local computation and the local state. Hence, we only compare to one-round single-use efficiently revocable anonymous credentials with minimal communication in Sect. 4.

1.3 Related Work

Our work achieving designated verification and public metadata extends a long line of publications. Freedman *et al.* [30] introduced oblivious pseudo-random functions, and Jarecki *et al.* [39,40] gave an efficient instantiation based on DDH in the random oracle model. Papadopoulos *et al.* [42] gave a verifiable PRF from elliptic curves, and Burns *et al.* [11] gave an oblivious PRF from elliptic curves. Privacy Pass combined these results with an extended version of the Chaum-Pedersen zero-knowledge protocol [23] given by Henry and Goldberg [34,35] to prove knowledge of batches of elements having the same discrete logarithm, and Kreuter *et al.* [41] added private metadata to Privacy Pass. In a concurrent work, Tyagi *et al.* [45] recently extended this line of works to partially oblivious PRFs.

To achieve public verifiability we use parings, inspired by the seminal work of Boneh *et al.* [10] for short and efficient signatures and a series of constructions of (partially) blind signatures based on pairings [7,8,14,24,25,31,32,48].

1.4 Chronology

As we report on both an implementation and new protocols, we believe it can be helpful to lay out the chronology of this work to separate the contributions.

Mid-October 2020, the authors were made aware of a potential privacy weakness in Norway's upcoming second COVID-19 contact tracing app Smittestopp. The first iteration had been stopped by the Norwegian Data Protection Agency in June, due to privacy concerns following from lack of data minimization. The new app had a set launch date in December.

The issue was that the verification service would collect IDs in order to automatically verify the infection status, and then send a token to the app which could then be used for uploading exposure keys. This token would create a hard link between an ID-based service and the rest of the system, in which the users are assumed to be anonymous.

Within a few days, we suggested using Privacy Pass in order to remove this link. Due to lack of capacity, our proposal was acknowledged, but we were asked to provide the code. We teamed up with Henrik Walker Moe to implement Privacy Pass in C#, and our implementation was eventually accepted into Smittestopp along with an improvised solution to rotate keys every three days.

Motivated by this process and the last-minute improvisation, we expanded the original Privacy Pass protocol to deal with the issues of key-rotation and revocation. Our initial manuscript was posted on ePrint February 24th, 2021. We were then made aware of a complication to the security proof, which was originally from the work by Zhang *et al.* [48]. A correct proof was posted on ePrint by Tyagi *et al.* [45] June 24th, 2021. The primary separation between these two manuscripts are that we were the first to present this protocol along with its variations, while Tyagi *et al.* present a correct proof. We also present the protocols in a way that is compatible to previous work. In this sense, these works complement each other.

The new protocol has not been implemented in Smittestopp. This is due to lack of further development of the app, and we do not expect any major changes to be accepted into the codebase at this stage.

2   Definitions for Anonymous Tokens

Anonymous tokens as used in Privacy Pass are conceptually simple: both issuance and verification require the private key, and the final token is uniquely determined by the token seed t and the private key. Kreuter *et al.* [41] extended this notion by adding a private bit in the token. We further extend the definition in two different directions: we want to add public metadata, and we want to make the token publicly verifiable. Now, private bits do not make immediate sense in the context of a publicly verifiable token scheme, but public metadata can be relevant in both settings.

The metadata can for instance be used to indicate an expiry date, replacing the need for frequent key rotation in certain applications [36]. We model it as a value that the user and issuer must agree upon, which should restrict the issuer from using arbitrary, identifiable values.

Lending terminology from programming, we would like the definition to provide backwards compatibility, and handle the notational incompatibility between private and public verifiability. To this end, we imitate the notion of [optional arguments] from programming. The notation vk|sk is meant as "at least one of the public or the secret key". We align our definitions as close as possible to those by Kreuter *et al.* [41].

Definition 1 (Anonymous tokens). *An anonymous token scheme with zero or more of **private metadata bit**, **public metadata**, or **public verifiability** consists of the following algorithms:*

- $(\text{crs}, \text{td}) \leftarrow \text{AT.Setup}(1^\lambda)$, *the setup algorithm that takes as input the security parameter λ in unary form, and returns a common reference string crs and trapdoor td. All the remaining algorithms take crs as their first input.*
- $(\text{pp}, \text{sk}, [\text{vk}]) \leftarrow \text{AT.KGen}(\text{crs})$, *the key generation algorithm that generates a signing key sk and optionally a verification key vk along with public parameters pp. All the remaining algorithms take pp as their second input.*
- $\sigma \leftarrow \langle \text{AT.User}(\text{pp}, [\text{vk}], t, [\text{md}]), \text{AT.Sign}(\text{sk}, [\text{md}], [b]) \rangle$, *the token issuance protocol, which involves interactive algorithms AT.User and AT.Sign. The user algorithm takes as input values the public parameters and the token seed $t \in \{0,1\}^\lambda$, and potentially the verification key vk and the public metadata md. The signing algorithm takes the private key sk and potentially metadata md and the private bit b. At the end of the interaction, the issuer outputs nothing, while the user outputs σ, or $\perp$ to indicate error.*

- $bool \leftarrow \mathsf{AT.Vf}(\mathsf{vk}|\mathsf{sk}, t, [\mathsf{md}], \sigma)$, *the verification algorithm that takes as input either the public verification key* vk *or the private key* sk, *a token seed* t, *metadata* md *and the signature* σ. *It returns true if the token was valid.*
- $[\mathsf{ind} \leftarrow \mathsf{AT.ReadBit}(\mathsf{sk}, t, [\mathsf{md}], \sigma)]$, *the private bit extraction algorithm that takes as input the private key* sk *and token* $(t, [\mathsf{md}], \sigma)$. *It returns an indicator* $\mathsf{ind} \in \{\perp, 0, 1\}$ *which is either the private bit, or* $\perp$.

The notation of the above definition should be interpreted in a global sense. If one – for example – wants to use public metadata, it should be included everywhere it is mentioned. This listing then defines the following six notions:

1. With designated verification:
   (a) Anonymous single-use tokens
   (b) Anonymous single-use tokens with private metadata bit
   (c) Anonymous single-use tokens with public metadata
   (d) Anonymous single-use tokens with public and private metadata
2. With public verification:
   (a) Anonymous single-use tokens
   (b) Anonymous single-use tokens with public metadata

Examples of 1a and 1b are well known from previous work [28,41]. A previous example of 2b is known as a partially blind signature scheme [2]. We will provide new examples of the last four (2a is implicit in 2b) in Sect. 3 and in the full version of this paper. We collectively refer to all of these as anonymous tokens.

We follow the convention of dividing the interactive protocol $\langle \mathsf{AT.User}, \mathsf{AT.Sign} \rangle$ into the non-interactive algorithms $\mathsf{AT.User}_0$, $\mathsf{AT.Sign}_0$ and $\mathsf{AT.User}_1$.

An anonymous token scheme must satisfy the following properties:

Definition 2 (Token correctness). *An anonymous token scheme* AT *is correct if any honestly generated token verifies. For any honestly generated* crs, $(\mathsf{pp}, \mathsf{sk}, [\mathsf{vk}])$, t *and* $[\mathsf{md}]$,

$$\Pr[\mathsf{AT.Vf}(\mathsf{vk}, t, [\mathsf{md}], \langle \mathsf{AT.User}(\mathsf{pp}, [\mathsf{vk}], t, \mathsf{md}),$$
$$\mathsf{AT.Sign}(\mathsf{sk}, [\mathsf{md}], [b])\rangle) = 1] = 1 - \mathsf{negl}(\lambda).$$

We split correctness of the private metadata bit into a separate definition in order to reduce notational clutter. This definition only applies in the private-key setting, and the parameters have been fixed accordingly.

Definition 3 (Correct private bit). *An anonymous token scheme* AT *is correct with respect to private metadata if the correct bit is retrieved successfully:*

$$\Pr[\mathsf{AT.ReadBit}(\mathsf{sk}, t, \langle \mathsf{AT.User}(\mathsf{pp}, t, [\mathsf{md}]),$$
$$\mathsf{AT.Sign}(\mathsf{sk}, [\mathsf{md}], b)\rangle) = b] = 1 - \mathsf{negl}(\lambda).$$

No adversary should be able to redeem other tokens than those that have been correctly issued. The *one-more unforgeability* notion has become the common notion for anonymous credentials. It allows the adversary to claim ℓ tokens from the issuer, and the adversary should not be able to redeem $\ell + 1$ tokens. We require the tokens to be unique with respect to the value of the seed t.

Definition 4 (One-more unforgeability). *An anonymous token scheme* AT *is one-more unforgeable if for any* PPT *adversary* $\mathcal{A}$, *and any* $\ell \geq 0$:

$$\mathsf{Adv}^{\mathrm{omuf}}_{\mathsf{AT},\mathcal{A},\ell}(\lambda) := \Pr[\mathrm{OMUF}_{\mathsf{AT},\mathcal{A},\ell}(\lambda) = 1] = \mathsf{negl}(\lambda),$$

where $\mathrm{OMUF}_{\mathsf{AT},\mathcal{A},\ell}$ *is the game defined in Fig. 1.*

Next, we want to provide user anonymity. The right notion for this is unlinkability, which guarantees that even colluding issuers and verifiers are unable to link tokens. Arbitrary metadata is a strong way of creating a link, and we omit this problem by only considering fixed public metadata for this notion. Notice that the adversary may query the user oracles for any public metadata md, but that we expect the post-processing to implicitly fail if md $\neq$ md'. This is in line with for example expiry dates, which would otherwise have been solved in practice using key rotation, and the definition is (as usual) also using a fixed key. Private metadata is outside the control of the user, and gives one bit leakage. We fix it for this game. Note that the adversary controls the keys, and that we therefore do not need to provide access to signing and verification oracles.

Definition 5 (Unlinkability). *An anonymous token scheme* AT *is* κ-*unlinkable if for any* PPT *adversary* $\mathcal{A}$, *fixed* b, md, *and any* $m > 0$,

$$\mathsf{Adv}^{\mathrm{unlink}}_{\mathsf{AT},\mathcal{A},m,[b],[\mathrm{md}]}(\lambda) := \Pr\left[\mathrm{UNLINK}_{\mathsf{AT},\mathcal{A},m,[b],[\mathrm{md}]}(\lambda) = 1\right] \leq \frac{\kappa}{m} + \mathsf{negl}(\lambda),$$

where $\mathrm{UNLINK}_{\mathsf{AT},\mathcal{A},m}$ *is the game defined in Fig. 2.*

We finally consider the private metadata bit. We give the adversary access to two signing oracles: One uses the adversary's chosen private bit, the other is using a fixed bit for the game. The adversary can also query a verification oracle. At the end, the adversary outputs its guess for the fixed challenge bit.

Game $\mathrm{OMUF}_{\mathsf{AT},\mathcal{A},\ell}(\lambda)$	Oracle $\mathrm{SIGN}(\mathsf{msg}, [\mathsf{md}], [b])$
$(\mathsf{crs}, \mathsf{td}) \leftarrow \mathsf{AT.Setup}(1^\lambda)$	$q_{b,\mathsf{md}} := q_{b,\mathsf{md}} + 1$
$(\mathsf{pp}, \mathsf{sk}, [\mathsf{vk}]) \leftarrow \mathsf{AT.KGen}(\mathsf{crs})$	$\mathbf{return}\ \mathsf{AT.Sign}_0(\mathsf{sk}, \mathsf{msg}, [\mathsf{md}], [b])$
$\mathbf{for}\ (b \in \{0,1\}, \mathsf{md}), q_{b,\mathsf{md}} := 0$	Oracle $\mathrm{VERIFY}(t, [\mathsf{md}], \sigma)$
$(t_i, \mathsf{md}_i, \sigma_i)_{i \in [\ell+1]} \leftarrow \mathcal{A}^{\mathrm{SIGN,VERIFY,READ}}(\mathsf{crs}, \mathsf{pp})$	$\mathbf{return}\ \mathsf{AT.Vf}(\mathsf{sk}|\mathsf{vk}, t, [\mathsf{md}], \sigma)$
$\mathbf{return}\ (\forall b \in \{0,1\}\ \forall \mathsf{md}, q_{b,\mathsf{md}} \leq \ell\ \mathbf{and}$	
$\quad \forall i \neq j\ \mathbf{in}\ [\ell+1]\ (t_i, \mathsf{md}_i, \sigma_i) \neq (t_j, \mathsf{md}_j, \sigma_j)$	Oracle $\mathrm{READ}(t, \sigma)$
$\mathbf{and}\ \exists (b, \mathsf{md}) \in \{0,1\} \times \{\mathsf{md}\} : \forall i \in [\ell+1],$	$\mathbf{return}\ \mathsf{AT.ReadBit}(\mathsf{sk}, t, [\mathsf{md}], \sigma)$
$\quad \mathsf{AT.ReadBit}(\mathsf{sk}, t_i, \sigma_i) = b\ \mathbf{and}$	
$\quad \mathsf{AT.Vf}(\mathsf{sk}|\mathsf{vk}, t_i, [\mathsf{md}], \sigma_i) = \mathbf{true})$	

Fig. 1. One-more unforgeability with metadata.

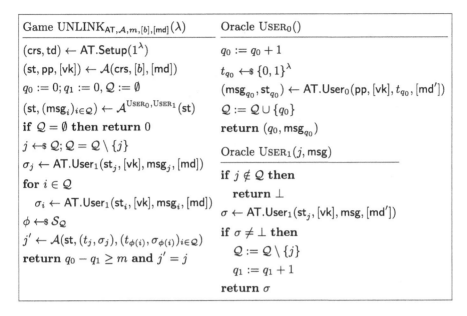

Fig. 2. Public-key unlinkability with fixed metadata. If X is a set, then $\mathcal{S}_X$ is the symmetric group of X.

Definition 6 (Private metadata bit). *An anonymous token scheme* AT *provides private metadata bit if for any* PPT *adversary* $\mathcal{A}$,

$$\mathsf{Adv}^{\mathrm{pmb}}_{\mathsf{AT},\mathcal{A}}(\lambda) := \left| \Pr[\mathrm{PMB}^0_{\mathsf{AT},\mathcal{A}}(\lambda)] - \Pr[\mathrm{PMB}^1_{\mathsf{AT},\mathcal{A}}(\lambda)] \right| = \mathsf{negl}(\lambda),$$

where $\mathrm{PMB}^\beta_{\mathsf{AT},\mathcal{A}}$ *is the game defined in Fig. 3.*

3   Anonymous Token Protocols

The Privacy Pass protocol [28] and its siblings [36,41] are based on Verifiable Oblivious Pseudo-Random Functions (VOPRF). Here, a user holds some secret input x and the signer holds a secret key k and they evaluate the function F obliviously such that the user learns $F(x, k)$ but nothing about k, and the signer learns nothing about the input x nor the output $F(x, k)$. Additionally, the user is ensured that the function is evaluated by the correct secret key.

We give three protocols for Anonymous Tokens (AT) with 1) public metadata, 2) public and private metadata, and 3) public metadata and public verifiability, respectively, constructed from the same framework.

At the core of our protocols lies a verifiable key transformation. Let $d := \mathsf{H}_m(\mathsf{md})$ and the curve point $U := [d]G + K$, where G is a public generator and K is the public key with a corresponding private key k. Let $e = (d + k)^{-1}$ be the new signing key and $W' = [e]T'$. Notice the relation

$$\mathsf{KT} : \log_G([d]G + K) = (d + k) = \log_{W'} T'. \tag{1}$$

Game $\mathrm{PMB}^{\beta}_{\mathsf{AT},\mathcal{A}}(\lambda)$	Oracle SIGN(msg, [md])
$(\mathsf{crs},\mathsf{td}) \leftarrow \mathsf{AT.Setup}(1^{\lambda})$	$\mathbf{return}\ \mathsf{AT.Sign}_0(\mathsf{sk},\mathsf{msg},[\mathsf{md}],\beta)$
$(\mathsf{pp},\mathsf{sk}) \leftarrow \mathsf{AT.KGen}(\mathsf{crs})$	Oracle SIGN'(msg, [md], b)
$\beta' \leftarrow \mathcal{A}^{\text{SIGN},\text{SIGN}',\text{VERIFY}}(\mathsf{crs},\mathsf{pp})$	$\mathbf{return}\ \mathsf{AT.Sign}_0(\mathsf{sk},\mathsf{msg},[\mathsf{md}],b)$
$\mathbf{return}\ \beta'$	Oracle VERIFY(t, [md], σ)
	$\mathbf{return}\ \mathsf{AT.Vf}(\mathsf{sk},t,[\mathsf{md}],\sigma)$

Fig. 3. Game for private metadata bit for anonymous tokens.

We give background on elliptic curves and detail zero-knowledge proofs for equal discrete logarithms, AND-proofs and OR-proofs in the full version of this paper.

3.1 Secure Key Transformation

We argue that the key-transformation from k to e is secure against one-more unforgeability attacks. Several papers has been written using this transformation. Boneh and Boyen [9] shows that this transformation is secure against a non-adaptive attacker for arbitrary metadata md when used for signatures. Furthermore, Dodis and Yampolskiy [29] shows that this transformation is secure against active attackers when the set of possible metadata values is small, and give applications to PRFs. However, these works only prove security with respect to a fixed generators, while our construction signs arbitrary new generators in each execution of the protocol. Recently, Tyagi et al. [45] proved that this transformation is secure against an active attacker with respect to arbitrary generators and arbitrary set of metadata. They reduce the security of the transform to a new one-more gap strong inversion Diffie-Hellman problem (see the full version of this paper). They also show that this new problem is equivalent to the simpler q-DL assumption. We summarize these results in a lemma.

Lemma 1. *Let* AT *be a scheme with keys* $(\mathsf{pk},\mathsf{vk})$ *with security property P within adversarial advantage* $\mathsf{Adv}^{\mathrm{P}}_{\mathsf{AT},\mathcal{A}}(\lambda)$, *and assume we can prove the relation in Eq. 1 within adversarial advantage* $\mathsf{Adv}^{\mathrm{rel}}_{\mathsf{KT},\mathcal{A}}(\lambda)$. *Then $\mathcal{A}$ has advantage* $\mathsf{Adv}^{\mathrm{P}}_{\mathsf{AT},\mathcal{A}}(\lambda) +$ $\mathsf{Adv}^{\mathrm{rel}}_{\mathsf{KT},\mathcal{A}}(\lambda)$ *against property P in the scheme* AT *with transformed keys* $(\{e = (\mathsf{md} + \mathsf{sk})^{-1}, [e]G\})$.

3.2 Anonymous Tokens with Public Metadata

In Fig. 4 we present an extension of Privacy Pass [28] with public metadata. The protocol is designated verifier, as the secret key is needed to verify tokens.

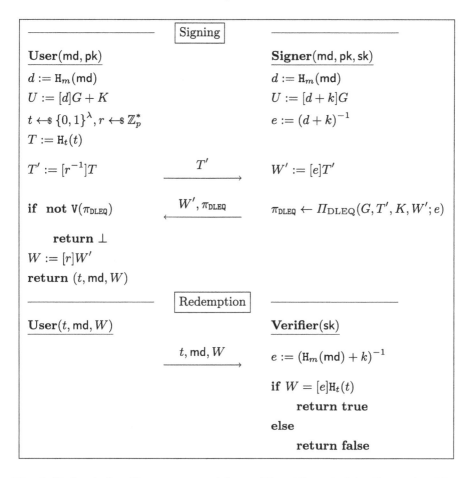

Fig. 4. Designated verifier anonymous tokens with public metadata. Our protocol is a direct extension of Privacy Pass [28].

Setup and Key Generation. Let λ be the security parameter, let p be a prime and let E be an elliptic curve group of order p with generator G. Let $\mathrm{H}_t : \{0,1\}^* \to E$ and $\mathrm{H}_m : \{0,1\}^* \to \mathbb{Z}_p$ be hash functions, and assume that group elements and integers can be encoded uniquely as strings. Furthermore, let metadata md be an element of a public set of valid strings. Finally, let $\mathrm{sk} := k \leftarrow_\$ \mathbb{Z}_p^*$ be the signing key, and let $\mathrm{pk} := K := [k]G$ be the public key. We consider $G, E, p, \mathrm{H}_t, \mathrm{H}_m$ and K to be implicit knowledge in Fig. 4.

Signing and Verification. The anonymous tokens protocol in Fig. 4 uses the Π_{DLEQ}-protocol defined in the full version of this paper. The signer computes a proof $\pi_{\mathrm{DLEQ}} := (c, z)$ of equality of discrete logarithms by instantiating the protocol $\Pi_{\mathrm{DLEQ}}(G, T', K, W'; e)$. Given the public parameters G and K, and $U := [d]G + K$, this is a proof that $\log_G U = d + k = \log_{W'} T'$. This proves that $W' = [e]T'$, where $e := (d + k)^{-1}$, is computed correctly with respect to d and K. To verify, the user instantiates the verification algorithm, denoted by $V(\pi_{DLEQ})$.

Theorem 1 (Completeness). *The anonymous token protocol with public metadata in Fig. 4 is complete according to Definition 2.*

Proof. The completeness follows from expanding W:

$$W = [r]W' = [r][e]T' = [r][e][r^{-1}]T = [e]H_t(t).$$

$\square$

Theorem 2 (Unforgeability). *The anonymous token protocol with public metadata in Fig. 4 achieve one-more unforgeability with respect to Definition 4.*

Proof. Using the key transformation as described in Lemma 1, the security of the protocol reduces to the security of the one-more gap strong inversion Diffie-Hellman game. The security follows from Tyagi *et al.* [45, Theorem 1].

$\square$

Theorem 3 (Unlinkability). *Fix metadata md. Within the set defined by all tokens using md, the anonymous token protocol with public metadata in Fig. 4 achieve unlinkability with respect to Definition 5.*

Proof. This proof is identical to [28, Theorem 1]: As we sample $r \leftarrow_s \mathbb{Z}_p$ uniformly at random, it follows that our protocol is unconditionally unlinkable. Since T is a generator of E, then $T' = [r^{-1}]T$ is uniformly random and contain no information about t nor T. As the signer only sees T', and the verifier only receive t, and they are independent, there is no link between the view of the signer and the view of the verifier.

$\square$

3.3   Tokens with Private Metadata and Public Verification

Using the same framework, we present anonymous tokens with public and private metadata and anonymous tokens with public metadata and public verification in the full version of this paper. We provide security proofs for both protocols.

4   Performance and Comparison

In this section, we briefly describe the most efficient anonymous single-use token protocols with public metadata in the literature, for example, to enable batched revocation. We only consider protocols with one round of communication. We compare the protocols with our schemes in Table 1. To streamline the comparison, we assume that all parties know the public metadata, for example that md is the current date, and assume that this implicit knowledge is not sent. We instantiate the schemes with $\lambda = 128$ bits of security. Finally, we present a concrete example to show that we can replace DIT with our protocol in Fig. 4 to improve both communication size and computational efficiency.

4.1 Anonymous Single-Use Tokens with Public Metadata

Privacy Pass. Our protocol in Fig. 4 is inspired by Privacy Pass [28], and they have identical structure and communication. The main difference is the change of private key used for signing, and the updated zero-knowledge proof with respect to the new public key, both depending on the public metadata. The zero-knowledge proofs are of the same size, and it follows that the communication sizes are equal. However, Privacy Pass does not allow public metadata unless we have one public key for each valid string of metadata, and hence, to allow for 2^N possible messages md, Privacy Pass must publish 2^N public keys.

DIT: De-Identified Authenticated Telemetry at Scale. DIT [36] is also inspired by Privacy Pass [28], but uses an attribute-based VOPRF to generate new public keys on the fly. To allow for 2^N strings of public metadata, there are two main differences: 1) the public key consists of $N + 2$ group elements, and 2) the token consists of an additional N group elements and zero-knowledge proofs to ensure that the correct public key is used in the signature.

Tokens from RSA. Abe and Fujisaki [1] presents a partially blind signature scheme based on RSA. The public exponent e must be at least two bits longer than the public metadata, and we fix this to be of length 130 bits. The user updates the public key to $e_{md} = e \cdot \tau(md)$, for a public formatting function τ, when they blind the message, and the signer updates the secret key $d_{md} = (e \cdot \tau(md))^{-1} \mod N$ when signing. Otherwise, the partially blind signature scheme [1] is similar to the blind signature by Chaum [21].

Tokens with Private Metadata. Kreuter *et al.* [41] presents an extension of Privacy Pass [28] to include private metadata. They publish two public keys, and the signer proves in zero-knowledge that the token is signed with one of the corresponding private keys. To ensure metadata privacy, each token is randomized based on a fresh seed s that is given to the user, and hence, the signature consists of a seed, a group element, and a proof. The token consists of the initial seed t in addition to two group elements. Like Privacy Pass, this protocol must publish a new pair of public keys for each valid string of metadata.

4.2 Comparison

We present a comparison of schemes in Table 1, where we focus on communication complexity. We note that both RSA and pairing based cryptography is usually slower than elliptic curve cryptography, in addition to requiring larger parameters. We also note that the updated keys in our protocols are only dependent on the secret key and the metadata, and can often be pre-computed. We conclude that when allowing for batched token-revocation, our protocols are more efficient than the state of the art in all categories.

   While RSA and elliptic curve cryptography are primitives implemented in all mainstream cryptographic libraries, there are few trustworthy implementations of pairings. Even though there exists a few implementations[4], they are mostly for academic use, maybe except for the implementation in Rust used by Zcash[5]. We refer to [45, Table 1] for a comparison in computation between some protocols.

Table 1. Size given in bits. We compare the schemes for 128 bits of security, allowing for 2^N strings md of metadata. Token seed t is of size 128 bits, and metadata md is implicit knowledge. Privacy Pass, DIT, Kreuter *et al.* and our protocols in Sect. 3 are instantiated with curve x25519 [6], our pairing-based protocol is instantiated with BLS12-381 [47], and Abe and Fujisaki is instantiated with RSA-3072.

Public Metadata (PM)	PubKey	Request	Signature	Token
Privacy Pass [28]	$257 \cdot 2^N$	257	769	385
DIT [36]	$257 \cdot (N + 2)$	257	$769 \cdot (N + 1)$	385
Our scheme (Fig. 4)	257	257	769	385
PM + Private Metadata	PubKey	Request	Signature	Token
Kreuter *et al.* [41]	$514 \cdot 2^N$	257	1921	642
Our Scheme	1028	257	3203	642
PM + Public Verifiability	PubKey	Request	Signature	Token
Abe and Fujisaki [1]	3202	3072	3072	3200
Our scheme	763	382	382	510

4.3   Telemetry Collection in WhatsApp

DIT [36] was designed to allow users of WhatsApp to anonymously report telemetry data to Facebook. We present a concrete comparison to our protocols in Table 2. Here, we assume that Facebook wants to update their public keys only once a year, rotate signing keys every day, and only sign one token per user each day. We fix a year and encode public metadata as strings "YYYY-MM-DD".

Privacy Pass [28] is very efficient in terms of communication, but requires one public key per day. Hence, the public key is of size 93805 bits over a year of 365 days, that is, approximately 12 KB. An alternative method to download all keys and store them until usage is to use a Merkle-tree for key-transparency and give paths corresponding to the current public key as a part of each signature. Then, the public key consists of the root of size 256 bits, while each signature consists of $\lceil \log_2(365) \rceil = 9$ hashes of 256 bits in addition to the public key, the token, and the zero-knowledge proof. We give both instantiations in the table, and denote the alternative protocol as Privacy Pass+.

Our scheme in Fig. 4 has the smallest overall communication complexity of all schemes. It offers much smaller keys than Privacy Pass, and much smaller signatures than Privacy Pass+ and DIT, saving up to 90 % in communication. If all 2 billion users of WhatsApp report their telemetry every day, our scheme in Fig. 4 would save more than 1.7 TB of communication for the Facebook servers on a daily basis compared to the current implementation of DIT.

---

[4] Pairings: hackmd.io/@zkteam/eccbench.

[5] Zcash: github.com/zkcrypto/bls12_381.

Our pairing-based scheme offers similar improvements to communication, in addition to public verifiability using pairings, but at the cost of less standardized cryptography and less efficient computation.

Table 2. Size given in bits. We compare Privacy Pass, DIT, and the protocols in Sect. 3 with daily key-rotation in a year, signing one token at a time.

Protocol	PubKey	Request	Signature	Token
Privacy Pass [28]	93805	257	769	385
Privacy Pass+	256	257	3330	385
DIT [36]	2313	257	7690	385
Our scheme (Fig. 4)	257	257	769	385
Our scheme (Pairings)	763	382	382	510

5 Application to Contact Tracing

As nations started adopting digital contact tracing during the COVID-19 pandemic, privacy experts warned that such systems could enable the collection of people's contact graphs. The dp^{3}t protocol [44] was eventually adopted as the *de facto* method for digital contact tracing through its implementation and deployment in iOS and Android as the Exposure Notification System (ENS).

We provide a brief overview of the basic dp^{3}t idea in order to put our contribution into context. The protocol is instantiated on each participating phone, which generates a random key (Temporary Exposure Key, TEK) every day. The TEK is used to generate new Rotating Proximity Identifiers (RPI) every 10–20 min, which is then broadcast from the phone using Bluetooth Low Energy (BLE). Other phones in the proximity store any RPI they hear.

If Alice tests positive for COVID-19 she can upload her TEKs (now renamed to diagnosis keys, DK) along with her BLE transmission strength to a health authority bulletin board. Bob's phone regularly checks the board to see if there is a sufficiently large overlap between published the DKs and the RPIs stored locally, and with sufficiently low difference between transmission strength and received strength. If this is the case, then Bob is given a suitable alert to let him know that he most likely has been in close vicinity of an infected individual, and should follow any advice given by the health authorities.

The process of uploading TEKs should depend on some sort of authorization. The dp^{3}t documentation describes a simplified model where a doctor receives the test results, and sends the patient an SMS with a short upload code. Now, this process may take precious person-hours during a pandemic. Some countries have therefore opted to connect their exposure notification with already existing centralized registries of positive test results, e.g., Norway, Denmark, and Estonia.

When starting the upload process, the user is prompted to log in to some government service ("verification"). Once the user has identified herself, the service makes a query to the relevant health registry. The service returns an access

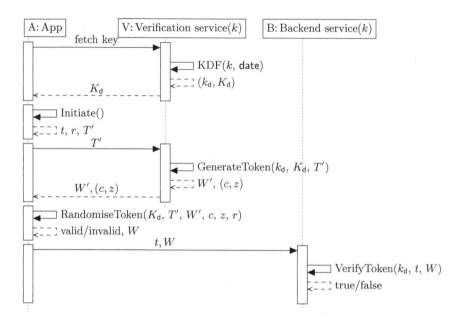

Fig. 5. A sequence diagram of anonymous tokens in the Norwegian app Smittestopp.

token to the app if there exists a recent positive test, which is then used to upload the keys to "backend". Unfortunately, this token may create an identifiable link from the meant-to-be-anonymous database of DKs, and unique identities in the health registry. Using anonymous single-use tokens, one can break this link (up to traffic analysis, e.g., logging timings and network addresses).

The Norwegian Institute of Public Health (NIPH) wanted the tokens to be timestamped in order to avoid users posting severely delayed keys: this would have allowed an attacker to get well again, move back out among other people, and only then upload to the backend service. Notice that merely tying the token to keys – e.g., by using a hash of the TEKs as the token seed t – would not avoid this attack, as those could have been generated and stored until the time of the attack. As a result, it was decided that the keys should be rotated regularly.

The original Privacy Pass protocol was reimplemented as a reusable C# package, to ease the integration into the Norwegian contact tracing app Smittestopp. The verification and backend services keep a master secret key k, and generate daily keys from some $\mathsf{KDF}(k, \mathsf{date})$. The public key is posted from the verification service. The full integration of anonymous tokens is described in Fig. 5.

We finally note that this key distribution method suffers from a potential attack by a dishonest verification service that could serve special public keys to track individuals. It is, however, detectable by the users if they share their view of the public keys with each other to ensure consistency. The current solution was accepted by all involved stakeholders due to limited time and a weighting of the practical risk against the potential reward. The challenges with respect to key-rotation and key-sharing strongly motivated the authors' work in Sect. 3.

6   Conclusion

In this work, we have updated the definitions for anonymous single-use tokens to also include public metadata, and we have constructed three protocols that satisfy these definitions. Additionally, we combine public metadata with either private metadata or public verifiability, and show that all instantiations are efficient in practice. For situations with frequent key-rotation, we show that our protocols can save up to 90 % in communication over the state of the art. Furthermore, our protocols fit nicely into the Privacy Pass framework, which makes it easy to incorporate our contributions in the ongoing standardization processes by IETF and W3C, solving an open problem.

We also provide a description of how anonymous one-time tokens can be used to improve the user's privacy in contact tracing applications, and implemented this into the solution used in Norway. The app has more than one million users at the time of writing[6]. As the Norwegian app is built on top of the same code base as the Danish app, we consider it to be easy to extend the adaption of anonymous tokens to their app, and most likely others as well.

We would also like to suggest new use-cases for anonymous tokens. For example, anonymous tokens can improve the privacy of users traveling with public transport. Bus or train companies may require patrons to verify their period tickets for each journey, perhaps primarily to analyze traffic data. However, this can easily reveal the routes of single users while traveling in-between their home and workplace, but also to the abortion clinic, their church or to a public demonstration etc. If all travelers with valid tickets are given a series of tokens (e.g., with public metadata being the date or week or month the ticket is valid), then these can be redeemed when boarding. This way, the companies get the statistics they are interested in, without invading the user's privacy. In general, any systems with leveled authenticated login but anonymous actions can make use of our protocols, e.g., systems with electronic locks that only care if the user has certain privileges or not. We also note that Tyagi *et al.* [45] detail applications of a construction similar to ours to reduce key management complexity in the OPAQUE password authenticated key exchange protocol, and to ensure stronger security for password breach alerting services.

Finally, we would like to see improvements in three directions. Firstly, the zero-knowledge proofs used by the anonymous tokens protocol with public and private metadata are much larger than the ones by Kreuter *et al.* [41], in contrast to our protocol with public metadata in Fig. 4 achieving the exact same communication cost as Privacy Pass [28]. In particular, we would like to reduce the number of proofs and extra group elements in the protocol for private metadata. Secondly, we would like to provide protocols free of zero-knowledge proofs, to reduce the communication and computational cost, as provided in [41, Section 7].

---

[6] Smittestopp: fhi.no/om/smittestopp/nokkeltall-fra-smittestopp, last accessed 2022-07-11.

References

1. Abe, M., Fujisaki, E.: How to date blind signatures. In: Kim, K., Matsumoto, T. (eds.) ASIACRYPT 1996. LNCS, vol. 1163, pp. 244–251. Springer, Heidelberg (1996). https://doi.org/10.1007/BFb0034851

2. Abe, M., Okamoto, T.: Provably secure partially blind signatures. In: Bellare, M. (ed.) CRYPTO 2000. LNCS, vol. 1880, pp. 271–286. Springer, Heidelberg (2000). https://doi.org/10.1007/3-540-44598-6_17

3. Akagi, N., Manabe, Y., Okamoto, T.: An efficient anonymous credential system. In: Tsudik, G. (ed.) FC 2008. LNCS, vol. 5143, pp. 272–286. Springer, Heidelberg (2008). https://doi.org/10.1007/978-3-540-85230-8_25

4. Baldimtsi, F., Lysyanskaya, A.: Anonymous credentials light. In: Sadeghi, A.R., Gligor, V.D., Yung, M. (eds.) ACM CCS 2013, pp. 1087–1098. ACM Press (2013). https://doi.org/10.1145/2508859.2516687

5. Barreto, P.S.L.M., Lynn, B., Scott, M.: Constructing elliptic curves with prescribed embedding degrees. In: Cimato, S., Persiano, G., Galdi, C. (eds.) SCN 2002. LNCS, vol. 2576, pp. 257–267. Springer, Heidelberg (2003). https://doi.org/10.1007/3-540-36413-7_19

6. Bernstein, D.J.: Curve25519: high-speed elliptic curve cryptography (2005). https://cr.yp.to/ecdh.html

7. Blazy, O., Pointcheval, D., Vergnaud, D.: Compact round-optimal partially-blind signatures. In: Visconti, I., De Prisco, R. (eds.) SCN 2012. LNCS, vol. 7485, pp. 95–112. Springer, Heidelberg (2012). https://doi.org/10.1007/978-3-642-32928-9_6

8. Boldyreva, A.: Threshold signatures, multisignatures and blind signatures based on the gap-diffie-hellman-group signature scheme. In: Desmedt, Y.G. (ed.) PKC 2003. LNCS, vol. 2567, pp. 31–46. Springer, Heidelberg (2003). https://doi.org/10.1007/3-540-36288-6_3

9. Boneh, D., Boyen, X.: Short signatures without random oracles. In: Cachin, C., Camenisch, J.L. (eds.) EUROCRYPT 2004. LNCS, vol. 3027, pp. 56–73. Springer, Heidelberg (2004). https://doi.org/10.1007/978-3-540-24676-3_4

10. Boneh, D., Lynn, B., Shacham, H.: Short signatures from the weil pairing. In: Boyd, C. (ed.) ASIACRYPT 2001. LNCS, vol. 2248, pp. 514–532. Springer, Heidelberg (2001). https://doi.org/10.1007/3-540-45682-1_30

11. Burns, J., Moore, D., Ray, K., Speers, R., Vohaska, B.: EC-OPRF: oblivious pseudorandom functions using elliptic curves. Cryptology ePrint Archive, Report 2017/111 (2017). https://eprint.iacr.org/2017/111

12. Camenisch, J., Groß, T.: Efficient attributes for anonymous credentials. In: Ning, P., Syverson, P.F., Jha, S. (eds.) ACM CCS 2008, pp. 345–356. ACM Press (2008). https://doi.org/10.1145/1455770.1455814

13. Camenisch, J., Hohenberger, S., Lysyanskaya, A.: Compact e-cash. In: Cramer, R. (ed.) EUROCRYPT 2005. LNCS, vol. 3494, pp. 302–321. Springer, Heidelberg (2005). https://doi.org/10.1007/11426639_18

14. Camenisch, J., Kohlweiss, M., Soriente, C.: An accumulator based on bilinear maps and efficient revocation for anonymous credentials. In: Jarecki, S., Tsudik, G. (eds.) PKC 2009. LNCS, vol. 5443, pp. 481–500. Springer, Heidelberg (2009). https://doi.org/10.1007/978-3-642-00468-1_27

15. Camenisch, J., Lysyanskaya, A.: An efficient system for non-transferable anonymous credentials with optional anonymity revocation. In: Pfitzmann, B. (ed.) EUROCRYPT 2001. LNCS, vol. 2045, pp. 93–118. Springer, Heidelberg (2001). https://doi.org/10.1007/3-540-44987-6_7

16. Camenisch, J., Lysyanskaya, A.: A signature scheme with efficient protocols. In: Cimato, S., Persiano, G., Galdi, C. (eds.) SCN 2002. LNCS, vol. 2576, pp. 268–289. Springer, Heidelberg (2003). https://doi.org/10.1007/3-540-36413-7_20

17. Camenisch, J., Lysyanskaya, A.: Signature schemes and anonymous credentials from bilinear maps. In: Franklin, M. (ed.) CRYPTO 2004. LNCS, vol. 3152, pp. 56–72. Springer, Heidelberg (2004). https://doi.org/10.1007/978-3-540-28628-8_4

18. Camenisch, J., Van Herreweghen, E.: Design and implementation of the idemix anonymous credential system. In: Atluri, V. (ed.) ACM CCS 2002, pp. 21–30. ACM Press (2002). https://doi.org/10.1145/586110.586114

19. Chase, M., Meiklejohn, S., Zaverucha, G.: Algebraic MACs and keyed-verification anonymous credentials. In: Ahn, G.J., Yung, M., Li, N. (eds.) ACM CCS 2014, pp. 1205–1216. ACM Press (2014). https://doi.org/10.1145/2660267.2660328

20. Chase, M., Perrin, T., Zaverucha, G.: The signal private group system and anonymous credentials supporting efficient verifiable encryption. In: Ligatti, J., Ou, X., Katz, J., Vigna, G. (eds.) ACM CCS 2020, pp. 1445–1459. ACM Press (2020). https://doi.org/10.1145/3372297.3417887

21. Chaum, D.: Blind signatures for untraceable payments. In: Chaum, D., Rivest, R.L., Sherman, A.T. (eds.) Advances in Cryptology, pp. 199–203. Springer, Boston, MA (1983). https://doi.org/10.1007/978-1-4757-0602-4_18

22. Chaum, D.: Blind signature system. In: Chaum, D. (ed.) Advances in Cryptology, p. 153. Springer, Boston, MA (1983). https://doi.org/10.1007/978-1-4684-4730-9_14

23. Chaum, D., Pedersen, T.P.: Wallet databases with observers. In: Brickell, E.F. (ed.) CRYPTO 1992. LNCS, vol. 740, pp. 89–105. Springer, Heidelberg (1993). https://doi.org/10.1007/3-540-48071-4_7

24. Chen, X., Zhang, F., Mu, Y., Susilo, W.: Efficient provably secure restrictive partially blind signatures from bilinear pairings. In: Di Crescenzo, G., Rubin, A. (eds.) FC 2006. LNCS, vol. 4107, pp. 251–265. Springer, Heidelberg (2006). https://doi.org/10.1007/11889663_21

25. Chow, S.S.M., Hui, L.C.K., Yiu, S.M., Chow, K.P.: Two improved partially blind signature schemes from bilinear pairings. In: Boyd, C., González Nieto, J.M. (eds.) ACISP 2005. LNCS, vol. 3574, pp. 316–328. Springer, Heidelberg (2005). https://doi.org/10.1007/11506157_27

26. Davidson, A.: Supporting the latest version of the privacy pass protocol (2021). https://blog.cloudflare.com/supporting-the-latest-version-of-the-privacy-pass-protocol. Accessed 01 Dec 2021

27. Davidson, A., Goldberg, I., Sullivan, N., Tankersley, G., Valsorda, F.: Privacy pass: a privacy-enhancing protocol and browser extension. https://privacypass.github.io. Accessed 01 Dec 2021

28. Davidson, A., Goldberg, I., Sullivan, N., Tankersley, G., Valsorda, F.: Privacy pass: bypassing internet challenges anonymously. PoPETs **2018**(3), 164–180 (2018). https://doi.org/10.1515/popets-2018-0026

29. Dodis, Y., Yampolskiy, A.: A verifiable random function with short proofs and keys. In: Vaudenay, S. (ed.) PKC 2005. LNCS, vol. 3386, pp. 416–431. Springer, Heidelberg (2005). https://doi.org/10.1007/978-3-540-30580-4_28

30. Freedman, M.J., Ishai, Y., Pinkas, B., Reingold, O.: Keyword search and oblivious pseudorandom functions. In: Kilian, J. (ed.) TCC 2005. LNCS, vol. 3378, pp. 303–324. Springer, Heidelberg (2005). https://doi.org/10.1007/978-3-540-30576-7_17

31. Fuchsbauer, G., Hanser, C., Kamath, C., Slamanig, D.: Practical round-optimal blind signatures in the standard model from weaker assumptions. In: Zikas, V., De Prisco, R. (eds.) SCN 2016. LNCS, vol. 9841, pp. 391–408. Springer, Cham (2016). https://doi.org/10.1007/978-3-319-44618-9_21

32. Fuchsbauer, G., Hanser, C., Slamanig, D.: Practical round-optimal blind signatures in the standard model. In: Gennaro, R., Robshaw, M. (eds.) CRYPTO 2015. LNCS, vol. 9216, pp. 233–253. Springer, Heidelberg (2015). https://doi.org/10.1007/978-3-662-48000-7_12

33. Hanzlik, L., Slamanig, D.: With a little help from my friends: constructing practical anonymous credentials. In: Proceedings of the 2021 ACM SIGSAC Conference on Computer and Communications Security, CCS 2021, Association for Computing Machinery (2021). https://doi.org/10.1145/3460120.3484582

34. Henry, R.: Efficient Zero-Knowledge Proofs and Applications. Ph.D. thesis, University of Waterloo (2014). http://hdl.handle.net/10012/8621

35. Henry, R., Goldberg, I.: Batch proofs of partial knowledge. In: Jacobson, M., Locasto, M., Mohassel, P., Safavi-Naini, R. (eds.) ACNS 2013. LNCS, vol. 7954, pp. 502–517. Springer, Heidelberg (2013). https://doi.org/10.1007/978-3-642-38980-1_32

36. Huang, S., et al.: Dit: de-identified authenticated telemetry at scale. Technical report, Facebook Inc. (2021). https://research.fb.com/wp-content/uploads/2021/04/DIT-De-Identified-Authenticated-Telemetry-at-Scale_final.pdf

37. Internet Engineering Task Force: Privacy pass datatracker (2021). https://datatracker.ietf.org/wg/privacypass. Accessed 01 Dec 2021

38. Iyengar, S., Taubeneck, E.: Fraud resistant, privacy preserving reporting using blind signatures (2021). https://github.com/siyengar/private-fraud-prevention. Accessed 01 Dec 2021

39. Jarecki, S., Kiayias, A., Krawczyk, H.: Round-optimal password-protected secret sharing and T-PAKE in the password-only model. In: Sarkar, P., Iwata, T. (eds.) ASIACRYPT 2014. LNCS, vol. 8874, pp. 233–253. Springer, Heidelberg (2014). https://doi.org/10.1007/978-3-662-45608-8_13

40. Jarecki, S., Krawczyk, H., Xu, J.: OPAQUE: an asymmetric PAKE protocol secure against pre-computation attacks. In: Nielsen, J.B., Rijmen, V. (eds.) EUROCRYPT 2018. LNCS, vol. 10822, pp. 456–486. Springer, Cham (2018). https://doi.org/10.1007/978-3-319-78372-7_15

41. Kreuter, B., Lepoint, T., Orrù, M., Raykova, M.: Anonymous tokens with private metadata bit. In: Micciancio, D., Ristenpart, T. (eds.) CRYPTO 2020. LNCS, vol. 12170, pp. 308–336. Springer, Cham (2020). https://doi.org/10.1007/978-3-030-56784-2_11

42. Papadopoulos, D., et al.: Making NSEC5 practical for DNSSEC. Cryptology ePrint Archive, Report 2017/099 (2017). https://eprint.iacr.org/2017/099

43. Paquin, C., Zaverucha, G.: U-prove cryptographic specification v1.1 revision 3 (2013). https://www.microsoft.com/en-us/research/project/u-prove

44. Troncoso, C., et al.: Decentralized privacy-preserving proximity tracing. https://arxiv.org/abs/2005.12273 (2020)

45. Tyagi, N., Celi, S., Ristenpart, T., Sullivan, N., Tessaro, S., Wood, C.A.: A fast and simple partially oblivious PRF, with applications. In: Dunkelman, O., Dziembowski, S. (eds.) EUROCRYPT 2022, Part II. LNCS, vol. 13276, pp. 674–705. Springer, Heidelberg (2022). https://doi.org/10.1007/978-3-031-07085-3_23

46. World Wide Web Consortium: Trust Token API Explainer (2021). https://github.com/WICG/trust-token-api. Accessed 01 Dec 2021

47. Yonezawa, S., Chikara, S., Kobayashi, T., Saito, T.: Pairing-Friendly Curves (2021). https://tools.ietf.org/id/draft-yonezawa-pairing-friendly-curves-02.html. Accessed 01 Dec 2021
48. Zhang, F., Safavi-Naini, R., Susilo, W.: Efficient verifiably encrypted signature and partially blind signature from bilinear pairings. In: Johansson, T., Maitra, S. (eds.) INDOCRYPT 2003. LNCS, vol. 2904, pp. 191–204. Springer, Heidelberg (2003). https://doi.org/10.1007/978-3-540-24582-7_14

ZKP

SnarkPack: Practical SNARK Aggregation

Nicolas Gailly[1]([✉]), Mary Maller[2]([✉]), and Anca Nitulescu[1]([✉])

[1] Protocol Labs, San Francisco, USA
{nikkolasg,anca}@protocol.ai
[2] Ethereum Fondation, Zug, Switzerland
mary.maller@ethereum.org

Abstract. Zero-knowledge SNARKs (zk-SNARKs) are non-interactive proof systems with short and efficiently verifiable proofs that do not reveal anything more than the correctness of the statement. zk-SNARKs are widely used in decentralised systems to address privacy and scalability concerns.

A major drawback of such proof systems in practice is the requirement to run a trusted setup for the public parameters. Moreover, these parameters set an upper bound to the size of the computations or statements to be proven, which results in new scalability problems.

We design and implement SnarkPack, a new argument that further reduces the size of SNARK proofs by means of aggregation. Our goal is to provide an off-the-shelf solution that is practical in the following sense: (1) it is compatible with existing deployed SNARK systems, (2) it does not require any extra trusted setup.

SnarkPack is designed to work with Groth16 scheme and has logarithmic size proofs and a verifier that runs in logarithmic time in the number of proofs to be aggregated. Most importantly, SnarkPack reuses the public parameters from Groth16 system.

SnarkPack can aggregate 8192 proofs in 8.7 s and verify them in 163 ms, yielding a verification mechanism that is exponentially faster than other solutions. SnarkPack can be used in blockchain applications that rely on many SNARK proofs such as Proof-of-Space or roll-up solutions.

1 Introduction

Arguments of Knowledge. Decentralised systems make extensive use of protocols that enable a prover to post a statement together with a *short* proof, such that any verifier can publicly check that the statement (e.g., correctness of a computation, claims of storage etc.) is true while expending fewer resources, e.g. less time than would be required to re-execute the computation.

SNARKs are such proofs that allow one party to demonstrate knowledge of a satisfying witness to some NP statement and have verification time and proof size independent of the size of this witness. If these proofs also conceal anything else about the witness we refer to them as zk-SNARKs. In the last decade,

© International Financial Cryptography Association 2022
I. Eyal and J. Garay (Eds.): FC 2022, LNCS 13411, pp. 203–229, 2022.
https://doi.org/10.1007/978-3-031-18283-9_10

there has been a series of works on constructing SNARKs [BCI+13, GGPR13, PHGR13, BCTV14, Gro16] with constant-size proofs that rely on trusted setups.

SNARKs are becoming very popular in real-world applications such as delegated computation or blockchain systems: as examples of early practical use case, Zerocash [BCG+14] showed how to use zk-SNARKs in distributed ledgers to achieve payment systems with strong privacy guarantees. The Zerocash protocol, with some modifications, is now commercially deployed in several cryptocurrencies, e.g. Zcash.

More recent zk-SNARK use cases are Aztec and zkSync, two projects boosting the scalability and privacy of Ethereum smart contracts[1]. Another example of SNARK application is the Filecoin System[2] that implements a decentralized storage solution for the internet.

The rapid and massive adoption of SNARK schemes has created new scalability challenges for blockchain systems: the generation of trusted setups requires complicated ceremonies, proving large statements has significant overhead, and verifying multiple proofs is expensive even with batching.

Trusted Setup Ceremony. All the constant-size zk-SNARK schemes have a common major disadvantage in practice: they rely on some public parameters, the structured reference string (SRS), that are generated by a trusted setup. In theory, this setup is run by a trusted third party, while in practice, such a string can be generated by a so called "ceremony", a multi-party computation between participants who are believed not to collude as shown in [ABL+19, BGM17, BCG+15]. Generating such a trusted setup is a cumbersome task. These ceremonies are expensive in terms of resources, they must follow specific rules, and they are generally hard to organise: hundreds of participants with powerful machines need to join efforts to perform a multi-party computation over multiple months.

Groth16. The construction by Groth [Gro16] is the state-of-the-art for pairing-based zk-SNARKs. Groth16 requires the computation to be expressed as an arithmetic circuit and relies on some trusted setup to prove the circuit satisfiability. Due to its short proof size (3 group elements) and verifier's efficiency, Groth16 has become a de facto standard in blockchain projects. This results in a great number of available implementations, code auditing, and multiple trusted setup ceremonies run by independent institutions.

Motivation. Importantly, the trusted setup in SNARK schemes sets an upper bound on the size of computations that can be proven (number of constraints in the circuit description). Because modern applications have an increased demand for the size of circuits, Groth16 is starting to face scalability problems. A simple solution would be to split the computation in different pieces and prove them independently in smaller circuits, but this increases the number of proofs to be added to a single statement and the verification time.

---

[1] Aztec, https://zk.money; zksync, https://zksync.io; https://ethereum.org.

[2] Filecoin, https://filecoin.io.

We address this problem by demonstrating a method to reduce the overhead in communication and verification time for multiple proofs without the need of further larger trusted setup ceremonies.

Filecoin System. One example is Filecoin [Lab18] proof-of-space blockchain. To onboard storage in the network, Filecoin miners post a Groth16 proof that they correctly computed a Proof-of-Space [Fis19]. Each proof guarantees that the miner correctly "reserves" 32 GB of storage to the network and consists of 10 different SNARKs. The chain currently processes a large number of proofs each day: approximately 500,000 Groth16 proofs, representing 15 PiB of storage.

Contribution. We explore reducing proof size and verifier time for SNARKs even further by examining techniques to aggregate proofs without the requirement for additional trusted setups.

We design SnarkPack, an argument that allows to aggregate n Groth16 zkSNARKs with a $O(\log n)$ proof size and verifier time. Our scheme is based on a trusted setup that can be constructed from two different existing ceremonies (e.g. the "powers of tau" for Zcash [Zca18] and Filecoin [Fil20]).

Being able to rely on the security of well-known trusted setups for which the ceremonies have been largely publicly advertised is a great practical advantage and makes SnarkPack immediately useful in real-world applications.

Our techniques are generic and can also apply to other pairing-based SNARKs. The roadmap is similar, since all such SNARK constructions require the generation of "powers of tau" for the setup ceremony and then have a few pairing check equations in the verification algorithm. However, we choose to focus on Groth16 proofs and tailor optimisations for this case, since it is the most popular scheme among practitioners. Therefore, SnarkPack is the first practical system that can be used in blockchain applications to reduce the on-chain work by employing verifiable outsourcing to process a large number of proofs off-chain. This applies broadly to any system that needs to delegate batches of state updates to an untrusted server.

Related Work. Prior works have built similar schemes for recursion or aggregation of proofs, but they all have critical shortcomings when it comes to implementing them in real-world systems.

Bünz et al. [BMM+19] presented a scheme for aggregating Groth16 proofs that requires a specific trusted setup to construct the structured reference string (SRS) necessary to verify such aggregated proofs. Our result is conceptually similar to that of Bünz et al. while benefiting from many optimizations. We focus specifically on aggregating proofs generated using the same Groth16 SRS which is the common use case, as opposed to the generic result in [BMM+19] that allows aggregation of proofs from different SRSes. Our result can be extended to support this latter case as well.

While our techniques built on top of inner pairing arguments with logarithmic verifier previously introduced by [DRZ20], we build new such schemes that avoid the need of a different trusted setup ceremony (other than the existing SNARK setup). Our approach for aggregation is preferable to [BMM+19] in practical use cases.

Other approaches to aggregation rely on recursive composition. In more detail, [BCG+20] propose a new SNARK for the circuit that contains n copies of the Groth16 verifier's circuit. However, constructing arithmetic circuits for pairings is expensive (e.g., computing a pairing on the BLS12-377 curve requires ≈ 15000 constraints as shown in [BCG+20]). The advantage of using such expensive schemes for aggregation is their transparent setup.

However, the costs are significant compared with our scheme: they compute FFTs, which require time $O(n \log n)$, the verifier performs $O(n)$ cryptographic operations as opposed to $O(n)$ field operations in our scheme and they require special cycles of curves.

SnarkPack has the best of both worlds: it benefits from the power of structured public parameters to avoid expensive computations, while it does not require additional trust assumptions, as it relies on already available trusted setup transcripts for the underlying Groth16 scheme.

Technical Overview. To explain how SnarkPack works, we need to consider 3 multiplicative cyclic groups $\mathbb{G}_1, \mathbb{G}_2, \mathbb{G}_T$ of order p equipped with the bilinear map, also called "pairing" $e : \mathbb{G}_1 \times \mathbb{G}_2 \to \mathbb{G}_T$ such that $\forall a, b \in \mathbb{Z}_p : e(g^a, h^b) = e(g, h)^{ab}$.

Groth16 proofs $\pi = (A, B, C)$ for statements $u = \mathbf{a}$ consist of 3 group elements $A, C \in \mathbb{G}_1$ and $B \in \mathbb{G}_2$. The high-level idea of Groth16 aggregation is quite simple: Since Groth16 verification consists in checking a pairing equation between the proof elements $\pi = (A, B, C)$, instead of checking that n different pairing equations are simultaneously satisfied, it is sufficient to prove that only one inner pairing product of a random linear combination of these initial equations defined by a verifier's random challenge $r \in \mathbb{Z}_p$ holds. In a bit more detail, Groth16 verification asks to check an equation of the type $e(A_i, B_i) = Y_i \cdot e(C_i, D)$ for $Y_i \in \mathbb{G}_T, D \in \mathbb{G}_2$ where Y_i is a value computed from each statement $u_i = \mathbf{a}_i$, $D \in \mathbb{G}_2$ is a fixed verification key and $\pi_i = (A_i, B_i, C_i)_{i=0}^{n-1}$ are proof triples.

The aggregation will instead check a single randomized equation:

$$\prod_{i=0}^{n-1} e(A_i, B_i)^{r^i} = \prod_{i=0}^{n-1} Y_i^{r^i} \cdot e\left(\prod_{i=0}^{n-1} C_i^{r^i}, D \right).$$

We denote by $Y'_{prod} := \prod_{i=0}^{n-1} Y_i^{r^i}$ so this can be rewritten as:

$$Z_{AB} = Y'_{prod} \cdot e(Z_C, D), \quad \text{where } Z_{AB} := \prod_{i=0}^{n-1} e(A_i, B_i)^{r^i} \text{ and } Z_C := \prod_{i=0}^{n-1} C_i^{r^i}.$$

What is left after checking that this unified equation holds is to verify that the elements Z_{AB}, Z_C are consistent with the initial proof triples in the sense that they compute the required inner product. This is done by applying an argument that proves two different inner pairing product relations:

– TIPP: the target inner pairing product takes some initial committed vectors $\mathbf{A} \in \mathbb{G}_1, \mathbf{B} \in \mathbb{G}_2$ and shows that $Z_{AB} = \prod_{i=0}^{n-1} e(A_i, B_i)$;
– MIPP: the multi-exponentiation inner product takes a committed vector $\mathbf{C} \in \mathbb{G}_1$ and a vector $\mathbf{r} \in \mathbb{Z}_p$ and shows that $Z_C = \prod_{i=0}^{n-1} C_i^{r^i}$.

New Commitment Schemes. The key ingredient for SnarkPack is the efficient realisation of the two specialised inner pairing product arguments following the ideas initially proposed by [DRZ20] and generalised to other inner products by [BMM+19]. These require a special commitment scheme that allows a party to commit to vectors of group elements in both source groups $\mathbb{G}_1$ and $\mathbb{G}_2$ with further homomorphic and collapsing properties.

We therefore introduce two new Pair Group Commitment schemes described in Sect. 3 that enable to commit to vectors $\mathbf{A}, \mathbf{C} \in \mathbb{G}_1, \mathbf{B} \in \mathbb{G}_2$. Our commitments are doubly-homomorphic with respect to the message space and key space and they have a collapsing property. Both schemes have constant-size commitments and are proved to be binding based on assumptions that hold in the generic group model. Our second scheme has the advantage that it allows a party to commit to two vectors from two different groups with no size overhead. We think these schemes can be of independent interest in protocols that need to commit to source-group elements.

Reusing Groth16 Trusted Setup. The advantage of our commitment schemes is that they can reuse existing public setups for Groth16 to generate their structured commitment keys.

The public parameters required for the generation of the commitment keys can be extracted from two *compatible* copies of Groth16 SRS.

For a given bilinear group $(p, \mathbb{G}_1, \mathbb{G}_2, \mathbb{G}_T)$, Groth16 SRS consist (among other elements) of consecutive powers of some random evaluation point τ in both groups $\mathbb{G}_1$ and $\mathbb{G}_2 : \{g^{\tau^i}\}_i \in \mathbb{G}_1^d, \{h^{\tau^i}\}_i \in \mathbb{G}_2^d$. We will call these "powers of tau".

The generation of SnarkPack public parameters (the commitment keys) comes naturally from two ceremonies for Groth16 setup (also known as "powers of tau") for the same generators g and h and different powers $a = \tau_1$ and $b = \tau_2$: $g, h, g^{\tau_1}, \ldots, g^{\tau_1^n}, h^{\tau_1}, \ldots, h^{\tau_1^n}$, one up to n and the other $g^{\tau_2} \ldots, g^{\tau_2^m}, h^{\tau_2}, \ldots, h^{\tau_2^m}$ up to $m \geq n$.

Our assumptions rely on the fact that cross powers (e.g. $g^{\tau_1 \tau_2}$) are not known to the prover. Since the two SRSes we use are the result of two independent ceremonies, it is unlikely that such terms can be learned since τ_1 and τ_2 were destroyed after the SRS generation.

In practice, we fortunately have at least two ceremonies that satisfy the requirements for same group generators and different powers: Such values can be obtained from the powers of tau transcript of Zcash [Zca18] and Filecoin [Lab18]. The SRS created goes up to $n = 2^{19}$ for τ_1 and $m = 2^{127}$ for τ_2.

Implementation. In ?? we provide benchmarks and optimisation details for our implementation in Rust, and evaluate its efficiency against batching. SnarkPack is exponentially more efficient than aggregation via batching: it takes $163\,ms$ to verify an aggregated proof for 8192 proofs (including unserialization) versus $621\,ms$ when doing batch verification. The former is of $40\,kB$ in size. The aggregator can aggregate 8192 proofs in $8.7\,s$.

2   Preliminaries

Bilinear Groups. A bilinear group is given by a description $\mathsf{gk} = (p, \mathbb{G}_1, \mathbb{G}_2, \mathbb{G}_T)$ such that

- p is prime, so $\mathbb{Z}_p = \mathbb{F}$ is a field.
- $\mathbb{G}_1 = \langle g \rangle, \mathbb{G}_2 = \langle h \rangle$ are cyclic groups of prime order p.
- $e : \mathbb{G}_1 \times \mathbb{G}_2 \to \mathbb{G}_T$ is a bilinear asymmetric map (pairing), which means that $\forall a, b \in \mathbb{Z}_p : e(g^a, h^b) = e(g, h)^{ab}$.

Vectors. For n-dimensional vectors $\mathbf{a} \in \mathbb{Z}_p^n, \mathbf{A} \in \mathbb{G}_1^n, \mathbf{B} \in \mathbb{G}_2^n$, we denote the i-th entry by $a_i \in \mathbb{Z}_p, A_i \in \mathbb{G}_1, B_i \in \mathbb{G}_2$ respectively. Let $\mathbf{A} \| \mathbf{A}' = (A_0, \dots, A_{n-1}, A_0', \dots, A_{n-1}')$ be the concatenation of vectors $\mathbf{A}, \mathbf{A}' \in \mathbb{G}_1^n$. We write $\mathbf{A}_{[:\ell]} = (A_0, \dots, A_{\ell-1}) \in \mathbb{G}_1^\ell$ and $\mathbf{A}_{[\ell:]} = (A_\ell, \dots, A_{n-1}) \in \mathbb{G}_1^{n-\ell}$ to denote slices of vectors $\mathbf{A} \in \mathbb{G}_1^n$ for $0 \le \ell < n - 1$.

We write group operations as multiplications. We define:

- $\mathbf{A}^x = (A_0^x, \dots, A_{n-1}^x) \in \mathbb{G}_1^n$ for $x \in \mathbb{Z}_p$ and a vector $\mathbf{A} \in \mathbb{G}_1^n$.
- $\mathbf{A}^\mathbf{x} = (A_0^{x_0}, \dots, A_{n-1}^{x_{n-1}}) \in \mathbb{G}_1^n$ for vectors $\mathbf{x} \in \mathbb{Z}_p^n, \mathbf{A} \in \mathbb{G}_1^n$.
- $\mathbf{A} * \mathbf{x} = \prod_{i=0}^{n-1} A_i^{x_i}$ for vectors $\mathbf{x} \in \mathbb{Z}_p^n, \mathbf{A} \in \mathbb{G}_1^n$.
- $\mathbf{A} * \mathbf{B} := \prod_{i=0}^{n-1} e(A_i, B_i)$ for group vectors $\mathbf{A} \in \mathbb{G}_1^n, \mathbf{B} \in \mathbb{G}_2^n$.
- $\mathbf{A} \circ \mathbf{A}' := (A_0 A_0', \dots, A_{n-1} A_{n-1}')$ for vectors $\mathbf{A}, \mathbf{A}' \in \mathbb{G}_1^n$.

Relations. We use the notation $\mathcal{R}$ to denote an efficiently decidable binary relation. For pairs $(u, w) \in \mathcal{R}$ we call u the statement and w the witness. We write $\mathcal{R} = \{(u; w) : p(u, w)\}$ to describe an NP relation.

Common and Structured Reference String. The common reference string (CRS) model, introduced by Damgård [Dam00], captures the assumption that a trusted setup exists. Schemes proven secure in the CRS model are secure given that the setup was performed correctly. We will use the terminology "Structured Reference String" (SRS) since all our crs strings are structured.

Background on Groth16. We recall here some necessary elements from [Gro16] construction. The definition of zk-SNARKs is given in Appendix A.1. A detailed description of the Groth16 protocol can be found in Appendix C. The main highlights follow:

Setup. For a given bilinear group $\mathsf{gk} = (p, \mathbb{G}_1, \mathbb{G}_2, \mathbb{G}_T)$, the SRS contains, among other elements, consecutive powers of some random evaluation point s in both groups $\mathbb{G}_1, \mathbb{G}_2 : \{g^{s^i}\}_{i=0}^{d-1} \in \mathbb{G}_1^d$, and $\{h^{s^i}\}_{i=0}^{d-1} \in \mathbb{G}_2^d$.

Prove. A Groth16 proof π for a statement $u := \mathbf{a} = \{a_j\}_{j=0}^t$ (with $a_0 = 1$) and a witness $w := \{a_j\}_{j=t+1}^m$ consists in 3 group elements $\pi = (A, B, C)$, where $A, C \in \mathbb{G}_1$ and $B \in \mathbb{G}_2$.

Verify. For the verification algorithm, Groth16 uses only a part of its structured reference string which we will call verification key vk:

$$\mathsf{vk} := \left(P = g^\alpha, Q = h^\beta, \left\{S_j = g^{\frac{\beta v_j(s) + \alpha w_j(s) + y_j(s)}{\gamma}}\right\}_{j=0}^t, H = h^\gamma, D = h^\delta\right).$$

Groth16 verification consists in checking a pairing equation between the proof elements $\pi = (A, B, C)$ using the verification key:

$$e(A, B) = e(g^\alpha, h^\beta) \cdot e(\prod_{j=0}^t S_j^{a_j}, h^\gamma) \cdot e(C, h^\delta).$$

Assumptions. We introduce two new assumptions necessary to prove our schemes are secure. Formal proofs that these assumptions hold in the Generic Group Model can be found in Appendix B.1.

Assumption 1 (ASSGP). *The (q, m)-Auxiliary Structured Single Group Pairing assumption holds for the bilinear group generator $\mathcal{G}$ if for all PPT adversaries $\mathcal{A}$ we have, on the probability space $\mathsf{gk} = (p, \mathbb{G}_1, \mathbb{G}_2, \mathbb{G}_T) \leftarrow \mathcal{G}(1^\lambda)$, $g \leftarrow_\$ \mathbb{G}_1, h \leftarrow_\$ \mathbb{G}_2$ and $a, b \leftarrow_\$ \mathbb{Z}_p$ the following probability is negligible in λ:*

$$\Pr\left[\begin{array}{c} (A_0, \ldots, A_{q-1}) \neq 1_{\mathbb{G}_1} \\ \wedge \prod_{i=0}^{q-1} e(A_i, h^{a^i}) = 1_{\mathbb{G}_T} \\ \wedge \prod_{i=0}^{q-1} e(A_i, h^{b^i}) = 1_{\mathbb{G}_T} \end{array} \middle| \begin{array}{c} g \leftarrow_\$ \mathbb{G}_1, h \leftarrow_\$ \mathbb{G}_2, a, b \leftarrow_\$ \mathbb{Z}_p \\ \sigma = (g^{a^i}, g^{b^i}, h^{a^i}, h^{b^i})_{i=0}^{2q-1} \\ \mathsf{aux} \leftarrow (g^{a^i}, g^{b^i}, h^{a^i}, h^{b^i})_{i=2q}^m \\ \mathbf{A} \leftarrow \mathcal{A}(\mathsf{gk}, \sigma, \mathsf{aux}) \end{array}\right].$$

Assumption 2 (ASDGP). *The (q, m)-ASDGP assumption holds for the bilinear group generator $\mathcal{G}$ if for all PPT adversaries $\mathcal{A}$ we have, on the probability space $\mathsf{gk} = (p, \mathbb{G}_1, \mathbb{G}_2, \mathbb{G}_T) \leftarrow \mathcal{G}(1^\lambda)$, $g \leftarrow_\$ \mathbb{G}_1, h \leftarrow_\$ \mathbb{G}_2$ and $a, b \leftarrow_\$ \mathbb{Z}_p$ the following probability is negligible in λ:*

$$\Pr\left[\begin{array}{c} (\mathbf{A} \neq 1_{\mathbb{G}_1} \vee \mathbf{B} \neq 1_{\mathbb{G}_2}) \wedge \\ \prod_{i=0}^{q-1} e(A_i, h^{a^i}) \prod_{i=q}^{2q-1} e(g^{a^i}, B_i) = 1_{\mathbb{G}_T} \\ \wedge \\ \prod_{i=0}^{q-1} e(A_i, h^{b^i}) \prod_{i=q}^{2q-1} e(g^{b^i}, B_i) = 1_{\mathbb{G}_T} \end{array} \middle| \begin{array}{c} g \leftarrow_\$ \mathbb{G}_1, h \leftarrow_\$ \mathbb{G}_2, a, b \leftarrow_\$ \mathbb{Z}_p \\ \sigma = (g^{a^i}, g^{b^i}, h^{a^i}, h^{b^i}) \\ \mathsf{aux} = (g^{a^i}, g^{b^i}, h^{a^i}, h^{b^i})_{2q}^m \\ (\mathbf{A}, \mathbf{B}) \leftarrow \mathcal{A}(\mathsf{gk}, \sigma, \mathsf{aux}) \end{array}\right].$$

We can similarly define the dual assumptions, by swapping $\mathbb{G}_1$ and $\mathbb{G}_2$ in the definition above.

3   Pair Group Commitment Schemes

In this section we introduce a new commitment scheme to group elements in a bilinear group. In order to use them in our aggregation protocol, we require the following properties from the commitment schemes:

- *Computationally Binding Commitment:* as per Definition 4
- *Constant Size Commitment:* the commitment value is independent of the length of the committed vector
- *Doubly-Homomorphic:* homomorphic both in the message space and in the key space

$$\mathsf{CM}(\mathsf{ck}_1 + \mathsf{ck}_2; M_1 + M_2) = \mathsf{CM}(\mathsf{ck}_1; M_1) + \mathsf{CM}(\mathsf{ck}_1; M_2) +$$
$$\mathsf{CM}(\mathsf{ck}_2; M_1) + \mathsf{CM}(\mathsf{ck}_2; M_2).$$

- *Collapsing Property:* double-homomorphism implies a distributive property between keys and messages that allows multiple messages to be collapsed via a deterministic function Collapse defined as follows:

$$\mathsf{Collapse}\left(\mathsf{CM}\begin{pmatrix} \mathsf{ck}_1\|\mathsf{ck}_1' & M_1\|M_1 \\ \mathsf{ck}_2\|\mathsf{ck}_2' & M_2\|M_2 \\ \mathsf{ck}_3 & M_3 \end{pmatrix}\right) = \mathsf{CM}\begin{pmatrix} \mathsf{ck}_1 + \mathsf{ck}_1' & M_1 \\ \mathsf{ck}_2 + \mathsf{ck}_2' & M_2 \\ \mathsf{ck}_3 & M_3 \end{pmatrix}$$

There are a few candidates for such schemes, but none of them are adapted for fulfilling our goals. The commitment schemes proposed by [DRZ20,BMM+19] work under some new assumption that asks for the commitment keys to be structured in a specific way. In order to use this commitment, we need to run a new trusted setup to generate a commitment key. It would be impossible to consider existing Groth16 setups, since those give away elements that break the binding of the commitment scheme.

Our main goal is to find a commitment scheme that uses a structured reference string similar to the one from many popular SNARK implementations, e.g. Groth16.

The commitment scheme proposed by Lai et al. [LMR19] is likely to satisfy these properties, but it is shown to be binding only for unstructured random public parameters; however, in order to obtain a log-time verification Inner Pairing Product Argument scheme, we would need some structure for the commitment keys. We adapt the commitments from [LMR19] to work with structured keys and prove the binding property for an adversary that has access to these structured public parameters under our new assumptions ASSGP and ASDGP.

To optimise the commitment sizes, we define two different variants of the commitment scheme: one that takes a vector of elements of a single group $\mathbb{G}_1$, and one that takes two vectors of points in $\mathbb{G}_1$ and $\mathbb{G}_2$, respectively.

Single Group Version CM_s. This version is useful for the MIPP relation. It takes one vector $\mathbf{A} \in \mathbb{G}_1^n$ and outputs two target group elements $(T_A, U_A) \in \mathbb{G}_T^2$ as a commitment.

$\mathsf{KG}_s(1^\lambda) \to \mathsf{ck}_s = (\mathbf{v}_1, \mathbf{v}_2)$ Sample $a, b \leftarrow_\$ \mathbb{Z}_p$ and set
$$\mathbf{v}_1 = (h, h^a, \dots, h^{a^{n-1}}), \qquad \mathbf{v}_2 = (h, h^b, \dots, h^{b^{n-1}}).$$
$\mathsf{CM}_s(\mathsf{ck}_s = (\mathbf{v}_1, \mathbf{v}_2), \mathbf{A} = (A_0, \dots, A_{n-1})) \to (T_A, U_A)$:
1. $T_A = \mathbf{A} * \mathbf{v}_1 = e(A_0, h) \cdot e(A_1, h^a) \dots e(A_{n-1}, h^{a^{n-1}})$
2. $U_A = \mathbf{A} * \mathbf{v}_2 = e(A_0, h) \cdot e(A_1, h^b) \dots e(A_{n-1}, h^{b^{n-1}})$

Lemma 1. *Under the hardness of (n, m)-ASSGP assumption for $m > 2n$, this commitment scheme is computationally binding as per Definition 4.*

Proof. Suppose there exists a PPT adversary $\mathcal{A}$ that breaks the binding property of the commitment scheme. Then, given the output $((T_A, U_A); \mathbf{A}, \mathbf{A}^*)$ of the adversary $\mathcal{A}$, we have that $(T_A, U_A) = (T_{A^*}, U_{A^*})$:

$$e(A_0, h)e(A_1, h^a) \dots e(A_{n-1}, h^{a^{n-1}}) = e(A_0^*, h)e(A_1^*, h^a) \dots e(A_{n-1}^*, h^{a^{n-1}})$$

$$e(A_0, h)e(A_1, h^b) \dots e(A_{n-1}, h^{b^{n-1}}) = e(A_0^*, h)e(A_1^*, h^b) \dots e(A_{n-1}^*, h^{b^{n-1}})$$

By applying the homomorphic properties of the commitment scheme to these equations we get:

$$e(A_0/A_0^*, h)e(A_1/A_1^*, h^a) \dots e(A_{n-1}/A_{n-1}^*, h^{a^{n-1}}) = 1$$

$$e(A_0/A_0^*, h)e(A_1/A_1^*, h^b) \dots e(A_{n-1}/A_{n-1}^*, h^{b^{n-1}}) = 1$$

where the vector $(A_0/A_0^*, A_1/A_1^*, \dots A_{n-1}/A_{n-1}^*) \neq 1_{\mathbb{G}_1}$. This breaks the (n, m)-ASSGP assumption.

Double Group Version CM_d. This version is useful for the TIPP relation. It takes two vectors $\mathbf{A} \in \mathbb{G}_1^n, \mathbf{B} \in \mathbb{G}_2^n$ and outputs two target group elements $(T_{AB}, U_{AB}) \in \mathbb{G}_T^2$ as a commitment.

$\mathsf{KG}_d(1^\lambda) \to \mathsf{ck}_d = (\mathbf{v}_1, \mathbf{v}_2, \mathbf{w}_1, \mathbf{w}_2)$: Sample $a, b \leftarrow_\$ \mathbb{Z}_p$ and set
$$\mathbf{v}_1 = (h, h^a, \dots, h^{a^{n-1}}), \qquad \mathbf{w}_1 = (g^{a^n}, \dots, g^{a^{2n-1}}),$$
$$\mathbf{v}_2 = (h, h^b, \dots, h^{b^{n-1}}), \qquad \mathbf{w}_2 = (g^{b^n}, \dots, g^{b^{2n-1}}).$$
$\mathsf{CM}_d(\mathsf{ck}_d, \mathbf{A}, \mathbf{B}) \to (T_{AB}, U_{AB})$:
1. $T_{AB} = (\mathbf{A} * \mathbf{v}_1)(\mathbf{w}_1 * \mathbf{B})$
2. $U_{AB} = (\mathbf{A} * \mathbf{v}_2)(\mathbf{w}_2 * \mathbf{B})$

Lemma 2. *Under the hardness of (n, m)-ASDGP assumption for $m > 2n$, this commitment scheme is computationally binding.*

Proof. The proof is analogous to the one of Lemma 1. Since the commitment is homomorphic, breaking the binding is equivalent to finding a non-trivial opening to 1. Thus it breaks the assumption.

Inner Pairing Product Commitments. It is straightforward to check that the two versions of pairing commitment schemes CM_s and CM_d are compatible with inner product arguments, in the sense that they satisfy all the necessary properties: constant size, doubly-homomorphic, and the identity is a collapse function defined $\mathsf{Collapse}_{id}(C) = C$.

Reusing Groth16 SRS. The two commitment schemes have the advantage that they can reuse two compatible (independent) SNARK setup ceremonies for their structured keys generation and therefore can be easily deployed without requiring a new trusted setup.

The SRSes required for the generation of the public commitment keys should satisfy some properties: We ask for the two ceremonies to use the same basis/generators in the same bilinear group $g \in \mathbb{G}_1, h \in \mathbb{G}_2$, but two different randomnesses $a, b, \in \mathbb{Z}_p, a \neq b$ for the exponents. The setups consists of consecutive powers $\{g^{a^i}, h^{a^i}\}_{i=0}^{m}$ and $\{g^{b^i}, h^{b^i}\}_{i=0}^{n}$.

Importantly, even if the two setups have different dimensions $m \neq n$, this does not affect the binding of the commitments. The extra elements available to the adversaries are taken into account in the auxiliary input aux in the two assumptions, by setting the parameters accordingly.

4   MT-IPP Scheme

This new protocol will be used to prove two inner pairing product relations that are essential to SNARK aggregation: the multiexponentiation inner product (MIPP) between vectors $\mathbf{C}$ and $\mathbf{r}$ and the target inner pairing product (TIPP) between vectors $\mathbf{A}, \mathbf{B}$, for vectors $\mathbf{A}, \mathbf{C} \in \mathbb{G}_1$ and $\mathbf{B} \in \mathbb{G}_2$.

In order to optimize the aggregation construction, we design a new protocol MT-IPP that "fuses" together proofs for MIPP and TIPP relations. The formal relations $\mathcal{R}_{\text{mipp}}$ and $\mathcal{R}_{\text{tipp}}$ are stated in Appendix D.1.

We recall the two inner product maps for bilinear group gk $= (p, \mathbb{G}_1, \mathbb{G}_2, \mathbb{G}_T, e)$ and the combined relation for MT-IPP:

1. Multiexponentiation inner product map $\mathbb{G}_1^n \times \mathbb{F}^n \to \mathbb{G}_1$: $\mathbf{C} * \mathbf{r} = \prod C_i^{r_i}$
2. Target inner pairing product map $\mathbb{G}_1^n \times \mathbb{G}_2^n \to \mathbb{G}_T$: $\mathbf{A} * \mathbf{B} := \prod e(A_i, B_i)$
3. Relation for both MIPP and TIPP:

$$\mathcal{R}_{\text{mt}} := \left\{ \begin{array}{c} ((T_{AB}, U_{AB}), (T_C, U_C), \\ Z_{AB}, Z_C, r; \mathbf{A}, \mathbf{B}, \mathbf{C}) \end{array} : \begin{array}{c} (\text{CM}_s(\mathbf{C}), Z_C, r; \mathbf{C}) \in \mathcal{R}_{\text{mipp}} \\ \wedge \\ (\text{CM}_d(\mathbf{A}, \mathbf{B}), Z_{AB}, r; \mathbf{A}, \mathbf{B}) \in \mathcal{R}_{\text{tipp}} \end{array} \right\}$$

Construction. Our MT-IPP makes black-box use of the two Pair Group Commitments schemes $\text{CM}_s = (\text{KG}_s, \text{CM}_s)$ and $\text{CM}_d = (\text{KG}_d, \text{CM}_d)$ from Sect. 3 and KZG Polynomial Commitment KZG.PC $= (\text{KZG.KG}, \text{KZG.CM}, \text{KZG.Open}, \text{KZG.Check})$ from Appendix A.4.

The scheme consists of 3 algorithms: MT-IPP $=$ (MT.Setup, MT.Prove, MT.Verify):

MT.Setup$(1^\lambda, \mathcal{R}_{\text{mt}}) \to \text{crs}_{\text{mt}}$:
1. Run: $\text{ck}_s := (\mathbf{v}_1, \mathbf{v}_2) \leftarrow \text{CM}_s(1^\lambda)$, $\text{ck}_d := (\mathbf{v}_1, \mathbf{v}_2, \mathbf{w}_1, \mathbf{w}_2) \leftarrow \text{CM}_d(1^\lambda)$.
2. Set commitment keys for KZG.PC scheme:

$$\text{ck}_{1v} := \{h^{a^i}\}_{i=0}^{n-1}, \quad \text{vk}_{1v} := g^a \qquad \text{ck}_{1w} := \{g^{a^i}\}_{i=0}^{2n-1}, \quad \text{vk}_{1w} := h^a$$

$$\text{ck}_{2v} := \{h^{b^i}\}_{i=0}^{n-1}, \quad \text{vk}_{2v} := g^b \qquad \text{ck}_{2w} := \{g^{b^i}\}_{i=0}^{2n-1}, \quad \text{vk}_{2w} := h^b$$

3. Define $\mathsf{ck}_{\mathsf{kzg}} := (\mathsf{ck}_{j\sigma})$, $\mathsf{vk}_{\mathsf{kzg}} := (\mathsf{vk}_{j\sigma})$ for $j = 1, 2$; $\sigma = v, w$.
4. Fix $\mathsf{Hash}_{com} \colon \mathbb{G}_T^4 \to \mathbb{Z}_p$ and its description hk_{com}.
5. Fix $\mathsf{Hash}_{x_0} \colon \mathbb{Z}_p^2 \times \mathbb{G}_T \times \mathbb{G}_1 \to \mathbb{Z}_p$ and its description hk_{x_0}.
6. Fix $\mathsf{Hash} \colon \mathbb{Z}_p \times \mathbb{G}_T^{12} \to \mathbb{Z}_p$ and its description hk.
7. Fix $\mathsf{Hash}_z \colon \mathbb{Z}_p \times \mathbb{G}_2^2 \times \mathbb{G}_1^2 \to \mathbb{Z}_p$ and its description hk_z.
8. Set $\mathsf{crs}_{\mathsf{mt}} := (\mathsf{hk}_{com}, \mathsf{hk}_{x_0}, \mathsf{hk}, \mathsf{hk}_z, \mathsf{ck}_s, \mathsf{ck}_d, \mathsf{ck}_{\mathsf{kzg}}, \mathsf{vk}_{\mathsf{kzg}})$.

$\mathsf{MT.Prove}(\mathsf{crs}_{\mathsf{mt}}, (T_{AB}, U_{AB}), (T_C, U_C), Z_{AB}, Z_C, r; \mathbf{A}, \mathbf{B}, \mathbf{C}) \to \pi_{\mathsf{mt}}$:
  – Loop "split & collapse" for step i
    1. $n' = n_{i-1}/2$ where $n_0 = n = 2^\ell$
    2. If $n' < 1$: *break*
    3. Set $\mathbf{B}' := \mathbf{B}^\mathbf{r}$, $\mathbf{w}_1' := \mathbf{w}_1^{\mathbf{r}^{-1}}$, $\mathbf{w}_2' := \mathbf{w}_2^{\mathbf{r}^{-1}}$.
    4. Compute L/R inner products:

$$(Z_L)_{AB} = \mathbf{A}_{[n':]} * \mathbf{B}'_{[:n']} \quad \text{and} \quad (Z_R)_{AB} = \mathbf{A}_{[:n']} * \mathbf{B}'_{[n':]}$$

$$(Z_L)_C = \mathbf{C}_{[n':]}^{\mathbf{r}_{[:n']}} \quad \text{and} \quad (Z_R)_C = \mathbf{C}_{[:n']}^{\mathbf{r}_{[n':]}}$$

    5. Compute left cross commitments:

$$(T_L, U_L)_{AB} = \mathsf{CM}_d((\mathbf{v}_1, \mathbf{w}_1'; \mathbf{v}_2, \mathbf{w}_2'); \mathbf{A}_{[n':]}||\mathbf{0}, \mathbf{0}||\mathbf{B}'_{[:n']}))$$

$$(T_L, U_L)_C = \mathsf{CM}_s((\mathbf{v}_1, \mathbf{v}_2), \mathbf{C}_{[n':]}||\mathbf{0})$$

    6. Compute right cross commitments:

$$(T_R, U_R)_{AB} = \mathsf{CM}_d((\mathbf{v}_1, \mathbf{w}_1'; \mathbf{v}_2, \mathbf{w}_2'); \mathbf{0}||\mathbf{A}_{[:n']}, \mathbf{B}'_{[n':]}||\mathbf{0})$$

$$(T_R, U_R)_C = \mathsf{CM}_s((\mathbf{v_1}, \mathbf{v_2}), \mathbf{0}||\mathbf{C}_{[:n']})$$

    7. Compute hash to the vector commitments

$$h_{com} = \mathsf{Hash}_{com}((T_{AB}, U_{AB}), (T_C, U_C)).$$

    8. Compute challenge x_i: $x_0 = \mathsf{Hash}_{x_0}(r, h_{com}, Z_{AB}, Z_C)$.

$$x_i = \mathsf{Hash}\,(x_{i-1}; (Z_L, Z_R)_{AB}, (Z_L, Z_R)_C, (T_L, U_L; T_R, U_R)_{AB},$$
$$(T_L, U_L; T_R, U_R)_C)$$

    9. Compute Hadamard products on vectors

$$\mathbf{A} := \mathbf{A}_{[:n']} \circ \mathbf{A}_{[n':]}^{x_i}, \quad \mathbf{B}' := \mathbf{B}'_{[:n']} \circ \mathbf{B}'^{x_i^{-1}}_{[n':]}, \quad \mathbf{C} := \mathbf{C}_{[:n']} \circ \mathbf{C}_{[n':]}^{x_i}$$

    10. Compute Hadamard products on keys $\mathbf{v}_1, \mathbf{v}_2$ and $\mathbf{w}_1', \mathbf{w}_2'$:

$$(\mathbf{v}_1, \mathbf{v}_2) := (\mathbf{v}_{1[:n']} \circ \mathbf{v}_{1[n':]}^{x^{-1}}, \mathbf{v}_{2[:n']} \circ \mathbf{v}_{2[n':]}^{x^{-1}})$$

$$(\mathbf{w}_1', \mathbf{w}_2') := (\mathbf{w}_{1[:n']}' \circ \mathbf{w}_{1[n':]}'^{x}, \mathbf{w}_{2[:n']}' \circ \mathbf{w}_{2[n':]}'^{x})$$

11. Set $n_i = n'$

- Compute proofs $(\pi_{v_j}, \pi_{w_j})_{j=1,2}$ of correctness of final commitment keys $(v_1, v_2) \in \mathbb{G}_2^2$; $(w_1', w_2') \in \mathbb{G}_1^2$ (This step is detailed in Appendix E):

    1. Define $f_v(X) = \prod_{j=0}^{\ell-1}(1 + x_{\ell-j}^{-1} X^{2^j})$ and
    $f_w(X) = X^n \prod_{j=0}^{\ell-1} \left(1 + x_{\ell-j} r^{-2^j} X^{2^j}\right)$

    2. Draw challenge $z = \mathsf{Hash}_z(x_\ell, v_1, v_2, w_1, w_2)$

    3. Prove that $v_1 = g^{f_v(a)}$, $v_2 = h^{f_v(a)}$, $w_1 = g^{f_w(a)}$, $w_2 = h^{f_w(b)}$ are KZG commitments of $f_v(X)$ by opening evaluations in z

    $$\pi_{v_j} \leftarrow \mathsf{KZG.Open}(\mathsf{ck}_{jv}; v_j, z, f_v(z); f_v(X)) \text{ for j=1,2}$$
    $$\pi_{w_j} \leftarrow \mathsf{KZG.Open}(\mathsf{ck}_{jw}; w_j, z, f_w(z); f_w(X)) \text{ for j=1,2}$$

- Given the final elements A, B', C and $(v_1, v_2), (w_1', w_2')$ at the end of the loop after split & collapsing $\mathbf{A}, \mathbf{B'} = \mathbf{B^r}, \mathbf{C}$ and $\mathbf{v_1}, \mathbf{v_2}, \mathbf{w_1'}, \mathbf{w_2'}$, set

$$\pi_{\mathsf{mt}} = \big(A, B', C, (\mathbf{Z_L}, \mathbf{Z_R})_{AB}, (\mathbf{Z_L}, \mathbf{Z_R})_C, (\mathbf{T_L}, \mathbf{U_L})_{AB}, (\mathbf{T_R}, \mathbf{U_R})_{AB},$$
$$(\mathbf{T_L}, \mathbf{U_L})_C, (\mathbf{T_R}, \mathbf{U_R})_C, (v_1, v_2), (w_1', w_2'), (\pi_{v_j}, \pi_{w_j})_{j=1,2}\big)$$

$\mathsf{MT.Verify}(\mathsf{crs_{mt}}, \mathsf{statement}; \pi_{\mathsf{mt}}) \rightarrow b$:

1. Parse $\mathsf{statement} = ((T_{AB}, U_{AB}), (T_C, U_C), Z_{AB}, Z_C, r)$

2. Compute hash to the commitments

$$h_{com} = \mathsf{Hash}_{com}((T_{AB}, U_{AB}), (T_C, U_C))$$

3. Reconstruct challenges $\{x_i\}_{i=1}^\ell$:
$x_0 = \mathsf{Hash}_{x_0}(r, h_{com}, Z_{AB}, Z_C)$

$$x_i = \mathsf{Hash}\big(x_{i-1}, (\mathbf{Z_L}[i], \mathbf{Z_R}[i])_{AB}, (\mathbf{Z_L}[i], \mathbf{Z_R}[i])_C,$$
$$(\mathbf{T_L}[i], \mathbf{T_R}[i], \mathbf{U_L}[i], \mathbf{U_R}[i])_{AB}, (\mathbf{T_L}[i], \mathbf{T_R}[i], \mathbf{U_L}[i], \mathbf{U_R}[i])_C\big)$$

4. Construct products and commitments recursively, $i = 1 \rightarrow \ell$:
    - $(Z_i)_{AB} = \mathbf{Z_L}[i]_{AB}^{x_i} \cdot (Z_{i-1})_{AB} \cdot \mathbf{Z_R}[i]_{AB}^{x_i^{-1}}$
    - $(T_i)_{AB} = \mathbf{T_L}[i]_{AB}^{x_i} \cdot (T_{i-1})_{AB} \cdot \mathbf{T_R}[i]_{AB}^{x_i^{-1}}$
    - $(U_i)_{AB} = \mathbf{U_L}[i]_{AB}^{x_i} \cdot (U_{i-1})_{AB} \cdot \mathbf{U_R}[i]_{AB}^{x_i^{-1}}$
    where $(Z_0)_{AB} = Z_{AB}, (T_0)_{AB} = T_{AB}, (U_0)_{AB} = U_{AB}$
    - $(Z_i)_C = \mathbf{Z_L}[i]_C^{x_i} \cdot (Z_{i-1})_C \cdot \mathbf{Z_R}[i]_C^{x_i^{-1}}$
    - $(T_i)_C = \mathbf{T_L}[i]_C^{x_i} \cdot (T_{i-1})_C \cdot \mathbf{T_R}[i]_C^{x_i^{-1}}$,
    - $(U_i)_C = \mathbf{U_L}[i]_C^{x_i} \cdot (U_{i-1})_C \cdot \mathbf{U_R}[i]_C^{x_i^{-1}}$
    where $(Z_0)_C = Z_C, (T_0)_C = T_C, (U_0)_C = U_C$

5. Compute final vector value from r: $r' = \prod_{i=0}^{\ell-1}(1 + x_{\ell-i}^{-1} r^{2^i})$

6. Verify final values $(T_\ell, U_\ell, Z_\ell)_{AB}, (T_\ell, U_\ell, Z_\ell)_C$:
    (a) $(Z_\ell)_{AB} \overset{?}{=} e(A, B')$
    (b) $(Z_\ell)_C \overset{?}{=} C^{r'}$

(c) Check if $(T_\ell)_{AB} \overset{?}{=} e(A, v_1)e(w_1', B')$ and $(U_\ell)_{AB} \overset{?}{=} e(A, v_2)e(w_2', B')$

(d) Check if $(T_\ell)_C \overset{?}{=} e(C, v_1)$ and $(U_\ell)_C \overset{?}{=} e(C, v_2)$

7. Verify final commitment keys v_1, v_2, w_1', w_2' as detailed in Appendix E

   (a) Reconstruct KZG challenge point: $z = \mathsf{Hash}_z(A, B', C, x_\ell, v_1, v_2, w_1', w_2')$

   (b) Reconstruct commitment polynomials: $f_v(X) = \prod_{j=0}^{\ell-1}\left(1 + x_{\ell-j}^{-1}X^{2^j}\right), f_w(X) = X^n \prod_{j=0}^{\ell-1}\left(1 + x_{\ell-j}r^{-2^j}X^{2^j}\right)$

   (c) Run verification for openings of evaluations in z for $j = 1, 2$:

$$b_{1j} \leftarrow \mathsf{KZG.Check}(\mathsf{vk}_{jv}; v_j, z, f_v(z); \pi_{v_j}),$$
$$b_{2j} \leftarrow \mathsf{KZG.Check}(\mathsf{vk}_{jw}; w_j, z, f_w(z); \pi_{w_j})$$

Theorem 3. *If* $\mathsf{CM}_s, \mathsf{CM}_d$ *are computationally binding commitments as per Definition 4, the hash functions are modelled as random oracles, and* $\mathsf{KZG.PC}$ *has computational knowledge binding as per Definition 6, then the protocol* $\mathsf{MT\text{-}IPP}$ *has completeness and computational knowledge soundness (Definition 1) against algebraic adversaries in the random oracle model.*

Proof. An adversary breaking soundness of the MT-IPP scheme, either convinces the verifier of incorrect final keys v_1, v_2, w_1', w_2' or breaks computational binding of one of $\mathsf{CM}_s, \mathsf{CM}_d$.

Since both $\mathsf{CM}_s, \mathsf{CM}_d$ are computationally binding, what is left to show is the completeness and soundness of the proof of correctness of the final commitment keys. The validity of the final commitment keys is shown using the $\mathsf{KZG.PC}$ scheme. The complete analysis for this step follows in Appendix E.

5   SnarkPack: Aggregation Scheme

In this section we describe SnarkPack, our new efficient protocol for Groth16 aggregation. The relation proven by SnarkPack can be stated as follows:

Relation for Aggregation. More formally, we introduce the relation for aggregating n Groth16 proof vectors $\mathbf{A}, \mathbf{C} \in \mathbb{G}_1^n, \mathbf{B} \in \mathbb{G}_2^n$ with respect to a fixed verification key vk:

$$\mathcal{R}_{\mathsf{AGG}} := \left\{ (\mathbf{u} = \{\mathbf{a}_i\}_{i=0}^{n-1}; \pi = \{(\mathbf{A}, \mathbf{B}, \mathbf{C})\}) : \mathsf{Verify}(\mathsf{vk}, u_i, \pi_i) = 1, \forall i \right\}$$

where $u_i = \mathbf{a}_i = \{a_{i,j}\}_{j=0}^t, \pi_i = (A_i, B_i, C_i) \in \mathbb{G}_1 \times \mathbb{G}_2 \times \mathbb{G}_1$ for $i = 0, \dots n-1$.

The resulting argument for aggregation consists in 3 algorithms SnarkPack = (SP.Setup, SP.Prove, SP.Verify) that work as follows:

$\mathsf{SP.Setup}(1^\lambda, \mathcal{R}_{\mathsf{AGG}}) \rightarrow (\mathsf{crs}_{\mathsf{agg}}, \mathsf{vk}_{\mathsf{agg}})$

1. Generate commitment key for CM_d:

$$ck_d = (\mathbf{v}_1, \mathbf{v}_2, \mathbf{w}_1, \mathbf{w}_2) \leftarrow CM_d.KG(1^\lambda)$$

2. Set commitment key for CM_s : $ck_s = (\mathbf{v}_1, \mathbf{v}_2)$
3. Call $crs_{mt} \leftarrow MT.Setup(1^\lambda, \mathcal{R}_{mt})$
4. Fix hash function $Hash_r : \mathbb{Z}_p^{t \cdot n} \times \mathbb{G}_T^4 \rightarrow \mathbb{Z}_p$ given by its description hk_r
5. Set aggregation public parameters: $crs_{agg} = (vk, crs_{mt}, hk_r)$

$SP.Prove(crs_{agg}, \mathbf{u}, \pi = (\mathbf{A}, \mathbf{B}, \mathbf{C})) \rightarrow \pi_{agg}$

1. Parse proving key $crs_{agg} := (vk, crs_{mt}, ck_s, ck_d, hk)$
2. Parse $ck_s = (\mathbf{v}_1, \mathbf{v}_2)$, $ck_d = (\mathbf{v}_1, \mathbf{v}_2, \mathbf{w}_1, \mathbf{w}_2)$
3. Commit to $\mathbf{A}$ and $\mathbf{B}$:

$$CM_d((\mathbf{v_1}, \mathbf{v_2}, \mathbf{w_1}, \mathbf{w_2}); \mathbf{A}, \mathbf{B}) = (T_{AB}, U_{AB})$$

4. Commit to $\mathbf{C}$: $CM_s((\mathbf{v_1}, \mathbf{v_2}); \mathbf{C}) = (T_C, U_C)$
5. Hash these commitments $h_{com} = Hash_{com}((T_{AB}, U_{AB}), (T_C, U_C))$
6. Derive random challenge $r = Hash_r(\mathbf{u}, h_{com})$ and set $\mathbf{r} = \{r^i\}_{i=0}^{n-1}$
7. Compute $Z_{AB} = \mathbf{A}^\mathbf{r} * \mathbf{B}$
8. Compute $Z_C = \mathbf{C}^\mathbf{r} = \prod_{i=0}^{n-1} C_i^{r_i}$.
9. Run MT proof for inner products Z_{AB}, Z_C, r:

$$\pi_{mt} = MT.Prove(crs_{mt}, (T_{AB}, U_{AB}), (T_C, U_C), Z_{AB}, Z_C, r; \mathbf{A}, \mathbf{B}, \mathbf{C}, \mathbf{r})$$

10. Set $\pi_{agg} = ((T_{AB}, U_{AB}), (T_C, U_C), Z_{AB}, Z_C, \pi_{mt})$

$SP.Verify(vk_{agg}, \mathbf{u}, \pi_{agg}) \rightarrow b$

1. Parse SNARK instances $\mathbf{u} = \{a_{i,j}\}_{i=0,\dots n-1; j=0,\dots t}$
2. Parse verification key $vk_{agg} := (vk, crs_{mt}, hk)$
3. Hash the commitments $h_{com} = Hash_{com}((T_{AB}, U_{AB}), (T_C, U_C))$
4. Parse $vk := (P = g^\alpha, Q = h^\beta, \{S_j\}_{j=0}^t, H = h^\gamma, D = h^\delta)$
5. Derive random challenge $r = Hash_r(\mathbf{u}, h_{com})$
6. Set statement $= (\mathbf{u}, (T_{AB}, U_{AB}), (T_C, U_C), Z_{AB}, Z_C, r)$
7. Check MT proof $b_1 \leftarrow MT.Verify(crs_{mt}, statement, \pi_{mt})$
8. Compute $Z_{S_j} = S_j^{\sum_{i=0}^{n-1} a_{ij}r^i}$ for all $j = 0 \dots t$
9. Check Groth16 final equation to the decision bit b_2:

$$Z_{AB} \overset{?}{=} e(P^{\sum_{i=0}^{n-1} r^i}, Q)e(\prod_{j=0}^{t} Z_{S_j}, H)e(Z_C, D)$$

10. Set decision bit $b = b_1 \wedge b_2$

Assumptions. We introduce two new assumptions necessary to prove our schemes are secure. Formal proofs that these assumptions hold in the Generic Group Model can be found in Appendix B.1.

Assumption 4 (ASSGP). *The (q, m)-Auxiliary Structured Single Group Pairing assumption holds for the bilinear group generator $\mathcal{G}$ if for all* PPT *adversaries $\mathcal{A}$ we have, on the probability space* $\mathsf{gk} = (p, \mathbb{G}_1, \mathbb{G}_2, \mathbb{G}_T) \leftarrow \mathcal{G}(1^\lambda)$, $g \leftarrow_\$ \mathbb{G}_1, h \leftarrow_\$ \mathbb{G}_2$ *and* $a, b \leftarrow_\$ \mathbb{Z}_p$ *the following probability is negligible in λ:*

$$\Pr\left[\begin{array}{l}(A_0, \ldots, A_{q-1}) \neq 1_{\mathbb{G}_1} \\ \wedge \ \prod_{i=0}^{q-1} e(A_i, h^{a^i}) = 1_{\mathbb{G}_T} \\ \wedge \ \prod_{i=0}^{q-1} e(A_i, h^{b^i}) = 1_{\mathbb{G}_T}\end{array}\middle|\begin{array}{l}g \leftarrow_\$ \mathbb{G}_1, h \leftarrow_\$ \mathbb{G}_2, a, b \leftarrow_\$ \mathbb{Z}_p \\ \sigma = (g^{a^i}, g^{b^i}, h^{a^i}, h^{b^i})_{i=0}^{2q-1} \\ \mathsf{aux} \leftarrow (g^{a^i}, g^{b^i}, h^{a^i}, h^{b^i})_{i=2q}^{m} \\ \mathbf{A} \leftarrow \mathcal{A}(\mathsf{gk}, \sigma, \mathsf{aux})\end{array}\right].$$

Assumption 5 (ASDGP). *The (q, m)-ASDGP assumption holds for the bilinear group generator $\mathcal{G}$ if for all* PPT *adversaries $\mathcal{A}$ we have, on the probability space* $\mathsf{gk} = (p, \mathbb{G}_1, \mathbb{G}_2, \mathbb{G}_T) \leftarrow \mathcal{G}(1^\lambda)$, $g \leftarrow_\$ \mathbb{G}_1, h \leftarrow_\$ \mathbb{G}_2$ *and* $a, b \leftarrow_\$ \mathbb{Z}_p$ *the following probability is negligible in λ:*

$$\Pr\left[\begin{array}{c}(\mathbf{A} \neq 1_{\mathbb{G}_1} \vee \mathbf{B} \neq 1_{\mathbb{G}_2}) \wedge \\ \prod_{i=0}^{q-1} e(A_i, h^{a^i}) \prod_{i=q}^{2q-1} e(g^{a^i}, B_i) = 1_{\mathbb{G}_T} \\ \wedge \\ \prod_{i=0}^{q-1} e(A_i, h^{b^i}) \prod_{i=q}^{2q-1} e(g^{b^i}, B_i) = 1_{\mathbb{G}_T}\end{array}\middle|\begin{array}{l}g \leftarrow_\$ \mathbb{G}_1, h \leftarrow_\$ \mathbb{G}_2, a, b \leftarrow_\$ \mathbb{Z}_p \\ \sigma = (g^{a^i}, g^{b^i}, h^{a^i}, h^{b^i}) \\ \mathsf{aux} = (g^{a^i}, g^{b^i}, h^{a^i}, h^{b^i})_{2q}^{m} \\ (\mathbf{A}, \mathbf{B}) \leftarrow \mathcal{A}(\mathsf{gk}, \sigma, \mathsf{aux})\end{array}\right].$$

We can similarly define the dual assumptions, by swapping $\mathbb{G}_1$ and $\mathbb{G}_2$ in the definition above.

Acknowledgements. We would like to thank Benedikt Bunz, Pratyush Mishra, and Psi Vesely for valuable discussions on this work, as well as Ben Fisch and Nicola Greco for the initial intuition of using inner pairing product proofs for aggregating Filecoin SNARK-based proofs. We are also grateful to dignifiedquire for his contributions to the Rust codebase.

A   Cryptographic Primitives

A.1   SNARKs

Let $\mathcal{R}$ be an efficiently computable binary relation which consists of pairs of the form (u, w). A Proof or Argument System for $\mathcal{R}$ consists in a triple of PPT algorithms $\Pi = (\mathsf{Setup}, \mathsf{Prove}, \mathsf{Verify})$ defined as follows:

$\mathsf{Setup}(1^\lambda, \mathcal{R}) \rightarrow \mathsf{crs}$: takes a security parameter λ and a binary relation $\mathcal{R}$ and outputs a common (structured) reference string crs.

$\mathsf{Prove}(\mathsf{crs}, u, w) \rightarrow \pi$: on input crs, a statement u and the witness w, outputs an argument π.

$\mathsf{Verify}(\mathsf{crs}, u, \pi) \rightarrow 1/0$: on input crs, a statement u, and a proof π, it outputs either 1 indicating accepting the argument or 0 for rejecting it.

We call Π a Succinct Non-interactive ARgument of Knowledge (SNARK) if further it is complete, succinct and satisfies *Knowledge Soundness* (also called *Proof of Knowledge*).

Non-black-box Extraction. The notion of *Knowledge Soundness* requires the existence of an extractor that can compute a witness whenever the prover $\mathcal{A}$ produces a valid argument. The extractor we defined bellow is non-black-box and gets full access to the prover's state, including any random coins. More formally, a SNARK satisfies the following definition:

Definition 1 (SNARK). $\Pi = (\mathsf{Setup}, \mathsf{Prove}, \mathsf{Verify})$ *is a SNARK for an NP language* $L_\mathcal{R}$ *with corresponding relation* $\mathcal{R}$, *if the following properties are satisfied.*

Completeness. *For all* $(x, w) \in \mathcal{R}$, *the following holds:*

$$\Pr \left(\mathsf{Verify}(\mathsf{crs}, u, \pi) = 1 \left| \begin{array}{l} \mathsf{crs} \leftarrow \mathsf{Setup}(1^\lambda, \mathcal{R}) \\ \pi \leftarrow \mathsf{Prove}(\mathsf{crs}, u, w) \end{array} \right. \right) = 1$$

Knowledge Soundness. *For any* PPT *adversary* $\mathcal{A}$, *there exists a* PPT *extractor* $\mathsf{Ext}_\mathcal{A}$ *such that the following probability is negligible in* λ:

$$\Pr \left(\begin{array}{l} \mathsf{Verify}(\mathsf{crs}, u, \pi) = 1 \\ \wedge \, \mathcal{R}(u, w) = 0 \end{array} \left| \begin{array}{l} \mathsf{crs} \leftarrow \mathsf{Setup}(1^\lambda, \mathcal{R}) \\ ((u, \pi); w) \leftarrow \mathcal{A} \| \chi_\mathcal{A}(\mathsf{crs}) \end{array} \right. \right) = \mathsf{negl}(\lambda).$$

Succinctness. *For any* u *and* w, *the length of the proof* π *is given by* $|\pi| = \mathsf{poly}(\lambda) \cdot \mathsf{polylog}(|u| + |w|)$.

Zero-Knowledge. A SNARK is zero-knowledge if it does not leak any information besides the truth of the statement. More formally:

Definition 2 (zk-SNARK). *A SNARK for a relation* $\mathcal{R}$ *is a zk-SNARK if there exists a* PPT *simulator* $(\mathcal{S}_1, \mathcal{S}_2)$ *such that* $\mathcal{S}_1$ *outputs a simulated common reference string* crs *and trapdoor* td; $\mathcal{S}_2$ *takes as input* crs, *a statement* u *and* td, *and outputs a simulated proof* π; *and, for all* PPT *(stateful) adversaries* $(\mathcal{A}_1, \mathcal{A}_2)$, *for a state* st, *the following is negligible in* λ:

$$\left| \Pr \left(\begin{array}{l} (u, w) \in \mathcal{R} \, \wedge \\ \mathcal{A}_2(\pi, \mathsf{st}) = 1 \end{array} \left| \begin{array}{l} \mathsf{crs} \leftarrow \mathsf{Setup}(1^\lambda) \\ (u, w, \mathsf{st}) \leftarrow \mathcal{A}_1(1^\lambda, \mathsf{crs}) \\ \pi \leftarrow \mathsf{Prove}(\mathsf{crs}, u, w) \end{array} \right. \right) - \right.$$
$$\left. \Pr \left(\begin{array}{l} (u, w) \in \mathcal{R} \, \wedge \\ \mathcal{A}_2(\pi, \mathsf{st}) = 1 \end{array} \left| \begin{array}{l} (\mathsf{crs}, \mathsf{td}) \leftarrow \mathcal{S}_1(1^\lambda) \\ (u, w, \mathsf{st}) \leftarrow \mathcal{A}_1(1^\lambda, \mathsf{crs}) \\ \pi \leftarrow \mathcal{S}_2(\mathsf{crs}, \mathsf{td}, u) \end{array} \right. \right) \right| = \mathsf{negl}(\lambda).$$

A.2   Commitment Schemes

A non-interactive commitment scheme allows a sender to create a commitment to a secret value. It may later open the commitment and reveal the value or some information about the value in a verifiable manner. More formally:

Definition 3 (Non-interactive Commitment). *A non-interactive commitment scheme is a pair of algorithms* $\mathsf{Com} = (\mathsf{KG}, \mathsf{CM})$:

$\mathsf{KG}(1^\lambda) \to \mathsf{ck}$: *given a security parameter λ, it generates a commitment public key ck. This ck implicitly specifies a message space M_{ck}, a commitment space C_{ck} and (optionally) a randomness space R_{ck},. This algorithm is run by a trusted or distributed authority.*

$\mathsf{CM}(\mathsf{ck}; m) \to C$: *given ck and a message m, outputs a commitment C. This algorithm specifies a function $\mathsf{Com}_{\mathsf{ck}} : M_{\mathsf{ck}} \times R_{\mathsf{ck}} \to C_{\mathsf{ck}}$. Given a message $m \in M_{\mathsf{ck}}$, the sender (optionally) picks a randomness $\rho \in R_{\mathsf{ck}}$ and computes the commitment $C = \mathsf{Com}_{\mathsf{ck}}(m, \rho)$*

For deterministic commitments we simply use the notation $C = \mathsf{CM}(\mathsf{ck}; m) := \mathsf{Com}_{\mathsf{ck}}(m)$, while for randomised ones we write $C \leftarrow_\$ \mathsf{CM}(\mathsf{ck}; m) := \mathsf{Com}_{\mathsf{ck}}(m, \rho)$.

A commitment scheme is asked to satisfy one or more of the following properties:

Binding Definition. It is computationally hard, for any PPT adversary $\mathcal{A}$, to come up with two different openings $m \neq m^* \in M_{\mathsf{ck}}$ for the same commitment C. More formally:

Definition 4 (Computationally Binding Commitment). *A commitment scheme $\mathsf{Com} = (\mathsf{KG}, \mathsf{CM})$ is computationally binding if for any PPT adversary $\mathcal{A}$, the following probability is negligible:*

$$\Pr\left[\begin{array}{c} m \neq m^* \\ \wedge\ \mathsf{CM}(\mathsf{ck}; m) = \mathsf{CM}(\mathsf{ck}; m^*) = C \end{array} \middle| \begin{array}{c} \mathsf{ck} \leftarrow \mathsf{KG}(1^\lambda) \\ (C; m, m^*) \leftarrow \mathcal{A}(\mathsf{ck}) \end{array} \right]$$

Hiding Definition. A commitment can be hiding in the sense that it does not reveal the secret value that was committed.

Definition 5 (Statistically Hiding Commitment). *A commitment scheme $\mathsf{Com} = (\mathsf{KG}, \mathsf{CM})$ is statistically hiding if it is statistically hard, for any PPT adversary $\mathcal{A} = (\mathcal{A}_0, \mathcal{A}_1)$, to first generate two messages $\mathcal{A}_0(\mathsf{ck}) \to m_0, m_1 \in M_{\mathsf{ck}}$ such that $\mathcal{A}_1$ can distinguish between their corresponding commitments C_0 and C_1 where $C_0 \leftarrow_\$ \mathsf{CM}(\mathsf{ck}; m_0)$ and $C_1 \leftarrow_\$ \mathsf{CM}(\mathsf{ck}; m_1)$.*

$$\Pr\left[b = b' \middle| \begin{array}{c} \mathsf{ck} \leftarrow \mathsf{KG}(1^\lambda) \\ (m_0, m_1) \leftarrow \mathcal{A}_0(\mathsf{ck}) \\ b \leftarrow \{0,1\},\ C_b \leftarrow_\$ \mathsf{CM}(\mathsf{ck}; m_b) \\ b' \leftarrow \mathcal{A}_1(\mathsf{ck}, C_b) \end{array} \right] = \mathsf{negl}(\lambda).$$

A.3   Polynomial Commitments

Polynomial commitments (PCs) first introduced by [KZG10] are commitments for the message space $\mathbb{F}^{\leq d}[X]$, the ring of polynomials in X with maximum degree $d \in \mathbb{N}$ and coefficients in the field $\mathbb{F} = \mathbb{Z}_p$, that support an interactive argument of knowledge $(\mathsf{KG}, \mathsf{Open}, \mathsf{Check})$ for proving the correct evaluation of a committed polynomial at a given point without revealing any other information about the committed polynomial.

A polynomial commitment scheme over a field family $\mathcal{F}$ consists in 4 algorithms $\mathsf{PC} = (\mathsf{KG}, \mathsf{CM}, \mathsf{Open}, \mathsf{Check})$ defined as follows:

$\mathsf{KG}(1^\lambda, d) \to (\mathsf{ck}, \mathsf{vk})$: given a security parameter λ fixing a field $\mathcal{F}_\lambda$ family and a maximal degree d samples a group description gk containing a description of a field $\mathbb{F} \in \mathcal{F}_\lambda$, and commitment and verification keys $(\mathsf{ck}, \mathsf{vk})$. We implicitly assume ck and vk each contain gk.

$\mathsf{CM}(\mathsf{ck}; f(X)) \to C$: given ck and a polynomial $f(X) \in \mathbb{F}^{\leq d}[X]$ outputs a commitment C.

$\mathsf{Open}(\mathsf{ck}; C, x, y; f(X)) \to \pi$: given a commitment C, an evaluation point x, a value y and the polynomial $f(X) \in \mathbb{F}[X]$, it output a prove π for the relation:

$$\mathcal{R}_{\mathsf{kzg}} := \left\{ (\mathsf{ck}, C, x, y; f(X)) : \begin{array}{c} C = \mathsf{CM}\,(\mathsf{ck}; f(X)) \\ \wedge\ \deg(f(X)) \leq d \\ \wedge\ y = f(x) \end{array} \right\}$$

$\mathsf{Check}(\mathsf{vk}, C, x, y, \pi) \to 1/0$: Outputs 1 if the proof π verifies and 0 if π is not a valid proof for the opening (C, x, y).

A polynomial commitment satisfy an extractable version of binding stated as follows:

Definition 6 (Computational Knowledge Binding). *For every* PPT *adversary* $\mathcal{A}$ *that produces a valid proof* π *for statement* C, x, y, *i.e. such that* $\mathsf{Check}(\mathsf{vk}, C, x, y, \pi) = 1$, *there is an extractor* $\mathsf{Ext}_\mathcal{A}$ *that is able to output a pre-image polynomial* $f(X)$ *with overwhelming probability:*

$$\Pr\left[\begin{array}{c} \mathsf{Check}(\mathsf{vk}, C, x, y, \pi) = 1 \\ \wedge\ C = \mathsf{CM}(\mathsf{ck}; f(X)) \end{array} \;\middle|\; \begin{array}{c} \mathsf{ck} \leftarrow \mathsf{KG}(1^\lambda, d) \\ (C, x, y, \pi; f(X)) \leftarrow (\mathcal{A}\|\mathsf{Ext}_\mathcal{A})(\mathsf{ck}) \end{array} \right] = 1 - \mathsf{negl}(\lambda).$$

A.4 KZG Polynomial Commitment

We describe the KZG Polynomial Commitment from [KZG10] which allows to check correctness of evaluation openings.

We recall the scheme $\mathsf{KZG.PC} = (\mathsf{KZG.KG}, \mathsf{KZG.CM}, \mathsf{KZG.Open}, \mathsf{KZG.Check})$ defined over bilinear groups $\mathsf{gk} = (p, \mathbb{G}_1, \mathbb{G}_2, \mathbb{G}_T)$ with $\mathbb{G}_1 = \langle g \rangle, \mathbb{G}_2 = \langle h \rangle$:

$\mathsf{KZG.KG}(1^\lambda, n) \to (\mathsf{ck}, \mathsf{vk}_h)$: Set keys $\mathsf{ck}_g = \{g^{\alpha^i}\}_{i=0}^{n-1}, \mathsf{vk}_h = h^\alpha$.

$\mathsf{KZG.CM}(\mathsf{ck}_g; f(X)) \to C_f$: For $f(X) = \sum_{i=0}^{n-1} f_i X^i$, computes $C_f = \prod_{i=0}^{n-1} g^{f_i \alpha^i} = g^{f(\alpha)}$.

$\mathsf{KZG.Open}(\mathsf{ck}_g; C_f, x, y; f(X)) \to \pi$: For an evaluation point x, a value y, compute the quotient polynomial

$$q(X) = \frac{f(X) - y}{X - x}$$

and output prove $\pi := C_q = \mathsf{KZG.CM}(\mathsf{ck}_g; q(X))$.

$\mathsf{KZG.Check}(\mathsf{vk}_h = h^\alpha, C_f, x, y, \pi) \to 1/0$: Check if

$$e(C_f \cdot g^{-y}, h) = e(C_q, \mathsf{vk}_h \cdot h^{-x}).$$

The $\mathsf{KZG.PC}$ scheme works similarly for a pair of keys of the form $\mathsf{ck}_h = \{h^{\alpha^i}\}_{i=0}^{n-1}, \mathsf{vk}_g = g^\alpha$, by just swapping the values in the final pairing equation check to match the correct basis.

B   Assumptions in GGM

B.1   ASSGP Assumption in GGM

Assumption 6 (ASSGP).   *The (q, m)-Auxiliary Structured Single Group Pairing assumption holds for the bilinear group generator $\mathcal{G}$ if for all   PPT adversaries $\mathcal{A}$ we have, on the probability space $\mathsf{gk} = (p, \mathbb{G}_1, \mathbb{G}_2, \mathbb{G}_T) \leftarrow \mathcal{G}(1^\lambda)$, $g \leftarrow_s \mathbb{G}_1, h \leftarrow_s \mathbb{G}_2$ and $a, b \leftarrow_s \mathbb{Z}_p$ the following*

$$\Pr\left[\begin{array}{c} \mathbf{A} \neq 1_{\mathbb{G}_1} \\ \wedge \ \prod_{i=0}^{q-1} e(A_i, h^{a^i}) = 1_{\mathbb{G}_T} \\ \wedge \ \prod_{i=0}^{q-1} e(A_i, h^{b^i}) = 1_{\mathbb{G}_T} \end{array} \middle| \begin{array}{c} g \leftarrow_s \mathbb{G}_1, h \leftarrow_s \mathbb{G}_2, a, b \leftarrow_s \mathbb{Z}_p \\ \sigma \leftarrow [g^{a^i}, g^{b^i}, h^{a^i}, h^{b^i}]_{i=0}^{2q-1} \\ \mathsf{aux} \leftarrow [g^{a^i}, g^{b^i}, h^{a^i}, h^{b^i}]_{i=2q}^{m} \\ \mathbf{A} \leftarrow \mathcal{A}(\mathsf{gk}, \sigma, \mathsf{aux}) \end{array} \right] = \mathsf{negl}(\lambda)$$

We can similarly define the dual assumption, by swapping $\mathbb{G}_1$ and $\mathbb{G}_2$ in the definition above.

Lemma 3. *The (q, m)-ASSGP assumption holds in the generic group model.*

Proof. Suppose $\mathcal{A}$ is an adversary that on input $(\mathsf{gk}, \sigma, \mathsf{aux})$, outputs $(A_0, \ldots, A_{q-1}) \in \mathbb{G}_1^q$ such that $\prod_{i=0}^{q-1} e(A_i, h^{a^i}) = 1_{\mathbb{G}_T}$ and $\prod_{i=0}^{q-1} e(A_i, h^{b^i}) = 1_{\mathbb{G}_T}$. Then its GGM extractor outputs $\alpha_i(X, Y) = \sum_{j=0}^{m}(x_j X^j + y_j Y^j + c_j)$ for $0 \leq i < q$ then we have:

$$\alpha_0(X, Y) + X\alpha_1(X, Y) + X^2\alpha_2(X, Y) + \cdots + X^{q-1}\alpha_{q-1}(X, Y) = 0 \quad (1)$$
$$\alpha_0(X, Y) + Y\alpha_1(X, Y) + Y^2\alpha_2(X, Y) + \cdots + Y^{q-1}\alpha_{q-1}(X, Y) = 0 \quad (2)$$

Then we have:

$$\alpha_0(X, Y) = -X\alpha_1(X, Y) - X^2\alpha_2(X, Y) - \cdots - X^{q-1}\alpha_{q-1}(X, Y) \quad (3)$$
$$\alpha_0(X, Y) = -Y\alpha_1(X, Y) - Y^2\alpha_2(X, Y) - \cdots - Y^{q-1}\alpha_{q-1}(X, Y) \quad (4)$$

If we substract (4) and (3) we got

$$0 = (X - Y)\alpha_1(X, Y) + \cdots + (X^{q-1} - Y^{q-1})\alpha_{q-1}(X, Y) \quad (5)$$
$$-(X - Y)\alpha_1(X, Y) = (X^2 - Y^2)\alpha_2(X, Y) + \cdots + (X^{q-1} - Y^{q-1})\alpha_{q-1}(X, Y) \quad (6)$$

Now we can divide by $(X - Y)$ and obtain:

$$-\alpha_1(X, Y) = (X + Y)\alpha_2(X, Y) + (X^2 + XY + Y^2)\alpha_3(X, Y) + \cdots +$$
$$+ (X^{q-2} + YX^{q-3} + \cdots + Y^{q-3}X + Y^{q-2})\alpha_{q-1}(X, Y) \quad (7)$$

Substitute the expression of $-\alpha_1(X, Y)$ in Eq. (3) and remark that all $X^i\alpha_i(X, Y)$ terms are vanishing:

$$\alpha_0(X, Y) = XY[\alpha_2(X, Y) + (X + Y)\alpha_3(X, Y) + \cdots + (X^{q-3} + \cdots + Y^{q-3})\alpha_{q-1}(X, Y)] \quad (8)$$

This implies that either $\alpha_0(X, Y)$ is a multiple of XY or $\alpha_0(X, Y) = 0$. By the GGM assumption, we have that $\alpha_0(X, Y) = 0$. We continue by replacing $\alpha_0(X, Y) = 0$ in Eq. (8):

$$0 = \alpha_2(X, Y) + \cdots + (X^{q-3} + X^{q-4}Y + \cdots + Y^{q-3})\alpha_{q-1}(X, Y)$$
$$-\alpha_2(X, Y) = (X + Y)\alpha_3(X, Y) + \cdots + (X^{q-3} + \cdots + Y^{q-3})\alpha_{q-1}(X, Y) \quad (9)$$

Substitute the expression of $-\alpha_2(X, Y)$ in Eq. (4) and remark that all $Y^i\alpha_i(X, Y)$ terms are vanishing:

$$0 = -Y\alpha_1(X, Y) - Y^2[(X + Y)\alpha_3(X, Y) + \cdots + (X^{q-3} + X^{q-4}Y +$$
$$\cdots + Y^{q-3})\alpha_{q-1}(X, Y)] - Y^3\alpha_3(X, Y) - \cdots - Y^{q-1}\alpha_{q-1}(X, Y) \quad (10)$$

$$Y\alpha_1(X, Y) = Y^2 X\alpha_3(X, Y) \cdots + (X^{q-3}Y^2 \cdots + XY^{q-2})\alpha_{q-1}(X, Y)$$
$$Y\alpha_1(X, Y) = Y^2 X[\alpha_3(X, Y) \cdots + (X^{q-4} \cdots + Y^{q-4})\alpha_{q-1}(X, Y)] \quad (11)$$

This implies that either $\alpha_1(X, Y)$ is a multiple of XY or $\alpha_1(X, Y) = 0$. By the GGM assumption, we have that $\alpha_1(X, Y) = 0$. We continue by replacing $\alpha_1(X, Y) = 0$ in Eq. (11):

$$0 = \alpha_3(X, Y) + \ldots (X^{q-4} + X^{q-5}Y \cdots + Y^{q-4})\alpha_{q-1}(X, Y)$$
$$-\alpha_3(X, Y) = (X^2 + XY + Y^2)\alpha_4(X, Y) + \ldots \quad (12)$$

And so on... till we show that $\alpha_i(X, Y) = 0 \ \forall i = 0 \ldots q - 1$. We conclude that the adversarly produced vector $(A_0, \ldots, A_{q-1}) = \mathbf{1}_{\mathbb{G}_1}$.

B.2   ASDGP Assumption in GGM

Assumption 7 (ASDGP). *The (q, m)-ASDGP assumption holds for the bilinear group generator $\mathcal{G}$ if for all PPT adversaries $\mathcal{A}$ we have, on the probability space $\mathsf{gk} = (p, \mathbb{G}_1, \mathbb{G}_2, \mathbb{G}_T) \leftarrow \mathcal{G}(1^\lambda)$, $g \leftarrow_\$ \mathbb{G}_1, h \leftarrow_\$ \mathbb{G}_2$ and $a, b \leftarrow_\$ \mathbb{Z}_p$ the following probability is negligible in λ:*

$$\Pr\left[\begin{array}{c} (\mathbf{A} \neq \mathbf{1}_{\mathbb{G}_1} \vee \mathbf{B} \neq \mathbf{1}_{\mathbb{G}_2}) \wedge \\ \prod_{i=0}^{q-1} e(A_i, h^{a^i}) \prod_{i=q}^{2q-1} e(g^{a^i}, B_i) = \mathbf{1}_{\mathbb{G}_T} \\ \wedge \\ \prod_{i=0}^{q-1} e(A_i, h^{b^i}) \prod_{i=q}^{2q-1} e(g^{b^i}, B_i) = \mathbf{1}_{\mathbb{G}_T} \end{array} \middle| \begin{array}{c} g \leftarrow_\$ \mathbb{G}_1, h \leftarrow_\$ \mathbb{G}_2, a, b \leftarrow_\$ \mathbb{Z}_p \\ \sigma = (g^{a^i}, g^{b^i}, h^{a^i}, h^{b^i}) \\ \mathsf{aux} = (g^{a^i}, g^{b^i}, h^{a^i}, h^{b^i})_{2q}^m \\ (\mathbf{A}, \mathbf{B}) \leftarrow \mathcal{A}(\mathsf{gk}, \sigma, \mathsf{aux}) \end{array}\right]$$

Lemma 4. *The (q, m)-ASDGP assumption holds in the generic group model.*

Proof. Suppose $\mathcal{A}$ is an adversary that on input $(\mathsf{gk}, \sigma, \mathsf{aux})$, outputs $\mathbf{A} = (A_0, \ldots, A_{q-1})$ and $\mathbf{B} = (B_0, \ldots, B_{q-1})$ such that:

$$\prod_{i=0}^{q-1} e(A_i, h^{a^i}) \prod_{i=q}^{2q-1} e(g^{a^i}, B_i) = \mathbf{1}_{\mathbb{G}_T} \text{ and } \prod_{i=0}^{q-1} e(A_i, h^{b^i}) \prod_{i=q}^{2q-1} e(g^{b^i}, B_i) = \mathbf{1}_{\mathbb{G}_T}.$$

Then its GGM extractor outputs $\alpha_i(X,Y) = \sum_{j=0}^{m}(x_j X^j + y_j Y^j + c_j)$ and $\beta_i(X,Y) = \sum_{j=0}^{m}(x_j X^j + y_j Y^j + c_j)$ for $0 \le i < q$ such that:

$$\alpha_0(X,Y) + X\alpha_1(X,Y) + \cdots + X^{q-1}\alpha_{q-1}(X,Y) +$$
$$+X^q\beta_0(X,Y) + \cdots + X^{2q-1}\beta_{q-1}(X,Y) = 0 \qquad (13)$$

$$\alpha_0(X,Y) + Y\alpha_1(X,Y) + \cdots + Y^{q-1}\alpha_{q-1}(X,Y) +$$
$$+Y^q\beta_0(X,Y) + \cdots + Y^{2q-1}\beta_{q-1}(X,Y) = 0 \qquad (14)$$

By substracting (14) and (13) we got

$$0 = (X-Y)\alpha_1(X,Y) + \cdots + (X^{q-1}-Y^{q-1})\alpha_{q-1}(X,Y) + (X^q-Y^q)\beta_q(X,Y) + \cdots \qquad (15)$$

Now we can factor $(X - Y)$ and then divide by it and obtain:

$$-\alpha_1(X,Y) = (X+Y)\alpha_2(X,Y) + (X^2 + XY + Y^2)\alpha_3(X,Y) + \cdots +$$
$$+ (X^{2q-2} + YX^{2q-3} + \cdots + Y^{2q-3}X + Y^{2q-2})\beta_{2q-1}(X,Y) \qquad (16)$$

Substitute $-\alpha_1(X,Y)$ in Eq. (13) and remark that all $X^i\alpha_i(X,Y)$, $X^{q+i}\beta_{q+i}(X,Y)$ terms are vanishing:

$$\alpha_0(X,Y) = X\left[\sum_{i=2}^{q-1}\left(\sum_{j=0}^{i-1}X^{i-j-1}Y^j\right)\alpha_i(X,Y) + \sum_{i=q}^{2q-1}\left(\sum_{j=0}^{i-1}X^{i-j-1}Y^j\right)\beta_i(X,Y)\right] -$$
$$- \sum_{i=2}^{q-1}X^i\alpha_i(X,Y) - \sum_{i=q}^{2q-1}X^i\beta_i(X,Y)$$

$$\alpha_0(X,Y) = X\left[\sum_{i=2}^{q-1}\left(\sum_{j=1}^{i-1}X^{i-j-1}Y^j\right)\alpha_i(X,Y) + \sum_{i=q}^{2q-1}\left(\sum_{j=1}^{i-1}X^{i-j-1}Y^j\right)\beta_i(X,Y)\right]$$

$$\alpha_0(X,Y) = XY\left[\sum_{i=2}^{q-1}\left(\sum_{j=1}^{i-1}X^{i-j-1}Y^{j-1}\right)\alpha_i(X,Y) + \sum_{i=q}^{2q-1}\left(\sum_{j=1}^{i-1}X^{i-j-1}Y^{j-1}\right)\beta_i(X,Y)\right] \qquad (17)$$

This implies that either $\alpha_0(X,Y)$ is a multiple of XY or $\alpha_0(X,Y) = 0$.
  By the GGM assumption, we have that $\alpha_0(X,Y) = 0$.
  We continue by replacing $\alpha_0(X,Y) = 0$ in Eq. (17):

$$-\alpha_2(X,Y) = \sum_{i=3}^{q-1}\left(\sum_{j=1}^{i-1}X^{i-j-1}Y^{j-1}\right)\alpha_i(X,Y) + \sum_{i=q}^{2q-1}\left(\sum_{j=1}^{i-1}X^{i-j-1}Y^{j-1}\right)\beta_i(X,Y) \qquad (18)$$

  Substitute the expression of $-\alpha_2(X,Y)$ in Eq. (13) or (14) and remark that all terms $X^i\alpha_i(X,Y), X^i\beta_i(X,Y)$ (respectively $Y^i\alpha_i(X,Y), Y^i\beta_i(X,Y)$) terms are vanishing.
  And so on till we show that $\alpha_i(X,Y) = 0 \;\forall i = 0\ldots q-1$ and $\beta_i(X,Y) = 0 \;\forall i = q\ldots 2q-1$.
  We conclude that the adversarly produced vectors $(A_0,\ldots,A_{q-1}) = \mathbf{1}_{\mathbb{G}_1}$, $(B_0,\ldots,B_{q-1}) = \mathbf{1}_{\mathbb{G}_2}$.

C   Groth16 Scheme

Let C be an arithmetic circuit over $\mathbb{Z}_p$, with m wires and d multiplication gates. Groth16 scheme proves circuit satisfiability, using a Quadratic Arithmetic Program (QAP) characterisation. Briefly, a QAP as introduced by [GGPR13] is translating a circuit into an equivalent arithmetic relation that holds only if the circuit has a solution.

Groth.Setup($1^\lambda, \mathcal{R}$)

$\alpha, \beta, \gamma, \delta \leftarrow_\$ \mathbb{Z}_p^*, \quad s \leftarrow_\$ \mathbb{Z}_p^*,$

$$\text{crs} = \Big(\text{QAP}, g^\alpha, g^\beta, g^\delta, \{g^{s^i}\}_{i=0}^{d-1}, \Big\{ g^{\frac{\beta v_j(s) + \alpha w_j(s) + y_j(s)}{\gamma}} \Big\}_{j=0}^{t}, \Big\{ g^{\frac{\beta v_j(s) + \alpha w_j(s) + y_j(s)}{\delta}} \Big\}_{j>t},$$

$$\Big\{ g^{\frac{s^i t(s)}{\delta}} \Big\}_{i=0}^{d-2}, h^\beta, h^\gamma, h^\delta, \{h^{s^i}\}_{i=0}^{d-1} \Big)$$

$$\text{vk} := \Big(P = g^\alpha, Q = h^\beta, \Big\{ S_j = g^{\frac{\beta v_j(s) + \alpha w_j(s) + y_j(s)}{\gamma}} \Big\}_{j=0}^{t}, H = h^\gamma, D = h^\delta \Big)$$

$\text{td} = (s, \alpha, \beta, \gamma, \delta)$

return (crs, td)

Groth.Prove(crs, u, w)

$u = (a_1, \ldots, a_t), \ a_0 = 1$

$w = (a_{t+1}, \ldots, a_m)$

$v(x) = \sum_{j=0}^{m} a_j v_j(x)$

$v_{mid}(x) = \sum_{j \in I_{mid}} a_j v_j(x)$

$w(x) = \sum_{j=0}^{m} a_j w_j(x)$

$w_{mid}(x) = \sum_{j \in I_{mid}} a_j w_j(x)$

$y(x) = \sum_{j=0}^{m} a_j y_j(x)$

$y_{mid}(x) = \sum_{j \in I_{mid}} a_j y_j(x)$

$h(x) = \frac{(v(x) w(x) - y(x))}{t(x)}$

$f_{mid} = \frac{\beta v_{mid}(s) + \alpha w_{mid}(s) + y_{mid}(s)}{\delta}$

$r, u \leftarrow_\$ \mathbb{Z}_p^*$

$a = \alpha + v(s) + r\delta, \qquad b = \beta + w(s) + u\delta$

$c = f_{mid} + \frac{t(s) h(s)}{\delta} + ua + rb - ur\delta$

return ($\pi = (A = g^a, B = h^b, C = g^c)$)

Groth.Verify(vk, u, π)

$\pi = (A, B, C)$

$v_{io}(x) = \sum_{i=0}^{t} a_i v_i(x)$

$w_{io}(x) = \sum_{i=0}^{t} a_i w_i(x)$

$y_{io}(x) = \sum_{i=0}^{t} a_i y_i(x)$

$f_{io} = \frac{\beta v_{io}(s) + \alpha w_{io}(s) + y_{io}(s)}{\gamma}$

Check

$e(A, B) = e(g^\alpha, h^\beta) \cdot e(g^{f_{io}}, h^\gamma) \cdot e(C, h^\delta)$

Groth.Sim(td, u)

$a, b \leftarrow_\$ \mathbb{Z}_p^*$

$c = \frac{ab - \alpha\beta - \beta v_{io}(s) + \alpha w_{io}(s) + y_{io}(s)}{\delta}$

return ($\pi = (A = g^a, B = h^b, C = g^c)$)

Fig. 1. Groth16 Construction from QAP.

Let $Q = (t(x), \{v_k(x), w_k(x), y_k(x)\}_{k=0}^m)$ be a Quadratic Arithmetic Program (QAP) which computes C. We denote by $I_{io} = \{1, 2, \ldots t\}$ the indices corresponding to the public input and public output values of the circuit wires and by $I_{mid} = \{t+1, \ldots m\}$, the wire indices corresponding to the private input and non-input, non-output intermediate values (for the witness).

We describe Groth = (Setup, Prove, Verify) scheme in [Gro16] that consists in 3 algorithms as per Fig. 1.

D Building Blocks for Aggregation

SRS. We need elements from two independent compatible Groth16 SRS:

- Common bilinear group description for both SRS: $\mathsf{gk} = (p, \mathbb{G}_1, \mathbb{G}_2, \mathbb{G}_T)$
- Common group generators for both SRS: $g \in \mathbb{G}_1, h \in \mathbb{G}_2$
- First SRS with random evaluation point $a \in \mathbb{Z}_p$ for:

$$\mathbf{v}_1 = (h, h^a, \ldots, h^{a^{n-1}}) \text{ and } \mathbf{w}_1 = (g^{a^n}, \ldots, g^{a^{2n-1}})$$

- Second SRS with random evaluation point $b \in \mathbb{Z}_p$ for:

$$\mathbf{v}_2 = (h, h^b, \ldots, h^{b^{n-1}}) \text{ and } \mathbf{w}_2 = (g^{b^n}, \ldots, g^{b^{2n-1}})$$

Pair Group Commitments. To instantiate our aggregated scheme, we use two new pairing commitment schemes. These schemes need to satisfy special properties (as discussed in Sect. 3) and they require structured commitment keys $\mathsf{ck}_s, \mathsf{ck}_d$ of the form $\mathsf{ck}_s = (\mathbf{v}_1, \mathbf{v}_2), \mathsf{ck}_d = (\mathbf{v}_1, \mathbf{w}_1, \mathbf{v}_2, \mathbf{w}_2)$. We then commit to vectors $\mathbf{A} \in \mathbb{G}_1^n, \mathbf{B} \in \mathbb{G}_2^n$ as follows:

1. Single group version $\mathsf{CM}_s(\mathbf{A}) := \mathsf{CM}_s(\mathsf{ck}_s; \mathbf{A}) = (T_A, U_A)$ where

$$T_A = \mathbf{A} * \mathbf{v}_1 = e(A_0, h)e(A_1, h^a)\ldots.e(A_{n-1}, h^{a^{n-1}})$$
$$U_A = \mathbf{A} * \mathbf{v}_2 = e(A_0, h)e(A_1, h^b)\ldots.e(A_{n-1}, h^{b^{n-1}})$$

2. Double group version $\mathsf{CM}_d(\mathbf{A}, \mathbf{B}) := \mathsf{CM}_d(\mathsf{ck}_d; \mathbf{A}, \mathbf{B}) = (T_{AB}, U_{AB})$ where

$$T_{AB} = (\mathbf{A} * \mathbf{v}_1)(\mathbf{w}_1 * \mathbf{B}), \quad U_{AB} = (\mathbf{A} * \mathbf{v}_2)(\mathbf{w}_2 * \mathbf{B})$$

IPP Protocols. One of the key building blocks for our aggregation protocol are *generalized inner product arguments*, called GIPA or IPP protocols. These protocols, as designed in [BMM+19], enable proving the correctness of a large class of inner products between vectors of group and/or field elements committed using (possibly distinct) doubly-homomorphic commitment schemes.

For our aggregation protocol, we need to instantiate two specialised cases of IPP – multi-exponentiation inner product (MIPP) and an target inner pairing product (TIPP) – using our new commitment schemes under structured references string, and thus, we obtain logarithmic verifier time.

D.1   Relation for MT-IPP

Here we define the relation proven using the merged MT-IPP argument. This is a conjunction of the two relations MIPP and TIPP:

MIPP Relation. The multiexponentiation product relation:

$$\mathcal{R}_{\mathsf{mipp}} := \{((T_C, U_C), Z_C, r; \mathbf{C}, \mathbf{r}) : Z_C = \mathbf{C} * \mathbf{r} \;\wedge$$
$$(T_C, U_C) = \mathsf{CM}_s(\mathsf{ck}_s; \mathbf{C}) \wedge \mathbf{r} = (r^i)_{i=0}^{n-1}\}.$$

TIPP Relation. The target inner pairing relation:

$$\mathcal{R}_{\mathsf{tipp}} := \{((T_{AB}, U_{AB}), Z_{AB}, r; \mathbf{A}, \mathbf{B}) : Z_{AB} = \mathbf{A} * \mathbf{B^r} \;\wedge$$
$$(T_{AB}, U_{AB}) = \mathsf{CM}_d(\mathsf{ck}_d; \mathbf{A}, \mathbf{B}) \;\wedge\; \mathbf{r} = (r^i)_{i=0}^{n-1}\},$$

where $(T_{AB}, U_{AB}) \in \mathbb{G}_T^2$, $Z_{AB} = \mathbf{A} * \mathbf{B^r} \in \mathbb{G}_T$, $\mathbf{A} \in \mathbb{G}_1^n$, $\mathbf{B} \in \mathbb{G}_2^n$, $r \in \mathbb{Z}_p$.

MT-IPP Relation. The merged MT-IPP relation:

$$\mathcal{R}_{\mathsf{mt}} := \left\{ \begin{array}{c} ((T_{AB}, U_{AB}), (T_C, U_C), \\ Z_{AB}, Z_C, r; \mathbf{A}, \mathbf{B}, \mathbf{C}) \end{array} : \begin{array}{c} (\mathsf{CM}_d(\mathbf{A}, \mathbf{B}), Z_{AB}, r; \mathbf{A}, \mathbf{B}) \in \mathcal{R}_{\mathsf{tipp}} \\ \wedge \\ (\mathsf{CM}_s(\mathbf{C}), Z_C, r; \mathbf{C}) \in \mathcal{R}_{\mathsf{mipp}} \end{array} \right\}$$

for vectors $\mathbf{A}, \mathbf{C} \in \mathbb{G}_1$ and $\mathbf{B} \in \mathbb{G}_2$.

E   Final Commitment Keys

In this section, we will detail one step of the MT-IPP protocol: Checking the correctness of the final commitment key, obtained after all "split & collapse" steps.

Recall that our scheme MT-IPP achieves logarithmic proof size using a specially structured commitment scheme that allows the prover to use one new challenge x_j in each round of recursion to transform the commitments homomorphically. Because of this, the verifier must also perform a linear amount of work in rescaling the commitment keys $(\mathsf{ck}_s, \mathsf{ck}_d)$. To avoid having the verifier rescale the commitment keys, our scheme apply the same trick as [DRZ20, BMM+19]: we do this by outsourcing the work of rescaling the commitment keys to the prover.

Then what is left is to convince a verifier that this rescaling was done correctly just by checking a succinct proof on the final keys.

Proof for Final Key. In our MT-IPP scheme, the prover will compute the final commitment keys v_1, v_2, w_1', w_2' (the result of many rounds of rescaling/collapsing $\mathbf{v}_1, \mathbf{v}_2, \mathbf{w}_1', \mathbf{w}_2'$ until the end of the loop) and then prove that they are well-formed.

This is possible due to the structure in the commitment keys. For ease of presentation, we will show how this proof works for a generic vector $\mathbf{v}$, where $\mathbf{v} = (v_1, v_2, \ldots, v_{2\ell}) = (g, g^\alpha, g^{\alpha^2}, \ldots g^{\alpha^{n-1}})$. The other checks for the keys v_1, v_2 and w_1, w_2 work in an analogously fashion.

Let us first define the relation to be proven, i.e. the correctness of the final commitment key $v \in \mathbb{G}_1$ given the initial key $\mathbf{v}$:

$$\mathcal{R}_{\mathsf{ck}} := \left\{ (\mathsf{gk}, v, f(X), \mathsf{ck}_g = (\{g^{\alpha^i}\}_{i=0}^{2n-2}, \mathsf{vk}_h = h^\alpha)) : v = g^{f(\alpha)} \right\}$$

The argument for the relation $\mathcal{R}_{\mathsf{ck}}$ allows the verifier to check well-formedness of the final structured commitment key. The idea is simple: the final commitment key $\mathbf{v}$ is interpreted as a KZG polynomial commitment that the prover must open at a random point z. The verifier produces the challenge point $z \in \mathbb{Z}_p$ and the prover provides a valid KZG opening proof of $f(z)$ for the commitment v. The interaction can be removed using Fiat-Shamir heuristic via a collision-resistant hash to generate the challenge z. The proof of security of such a protocol is given in [BMM+19] in the algebraic group model. In a nutshell, an algebraic adversary that convinces a verifier of incorrect keys can extract a valid $2n$-SDH instance by breaking knowledge-binding of KZG.PC polynomial commitment scheme.

We will use a polynomial commitment scheme (Definition A.3) that allows for openings of evaluations on a point and proving correctness of these openings. The concrete scheme is called KZG.PC and works for both groups $\mathbb{G}_1$ and $\mathbb{G}_2$ as described in Appendix A.4. The verification requires an evaluation of the corresponding polynomial and four pairing checks.

Polynomial Formula. We will show now, hot to define the correct polynomials to be committed under KZG.PC scheme in order to show that the final commitment keys were honestly generated.

Recall the structure of the 4 vectors $\mathbf{v}_1, \mathbf{v}_2 \in \mathbb{G}_2$ and $\mathbf{w}_1, \mathbf{w}_2 \in \mathbb{G}_1$ used for the commitment keys $\mathsf{ck}_s, \mathsf{ck}_d$:

$$\mathbf{v}_1 = (h, h^a, \ldots, h^{a^{n-1}}), \qquad \mathbf{w}_1 = (g^{a^n}, \ldots, g^{a^{2n-1}}), \qquad \mathbf{w}_1' := \mathbf{w}_1^{\mathbf{r}^{-1}}$$
$$\mathbf{v}_2 = (h, h^b, \ldots, h^{b^{n-1}}), \qquad \mathbf{w}_2 = (g^{b^n}, \ldots, g^{b^{2n-1}}), \qquad \mathbf{w}_2' := \mathbf{w}_2^{\mathbf{r}^{-1}}$$

We will show the formulae for the polynomials the two polynomials $f_v(X)$ and $f_w(X)$ that we used in our scheme MT-IPP for v_1, v_2 and for w_1', w_2' are correct.

For ease of presentation, we state and prove the formula for a generic vector $\mathbf{v} = (v_1, v_2, \ldots, v_{2^\ell}) = (g, g^\alpha, g^{\alpha^2}, \ldots g^{\alpha^{2^\ell - 1}})$ of length $n = 2^\ell$ to which we apply the same rescaling as for the commitment keys $\mathsf{ck}_s, \mathsf{ck}_d$. The specific formulae for $\mathbf{v}_1, \mathbf{v}_2, \mathbf{w}_1', \mathbf{w}_2'$ are easy to deduce once we have a formula for $\mathbf{v}$.

Consider a challenge x_j for round j, where the total number of rounds is ℓ. Note that at each round j we split the sequence $v_1, v_2, \ldots, v_n$ in half and we use x_j to rescale first half and the second half of the vector recursively until we end up with a single value v.

We claim that the formula for some initial key $\mathbf{v} = (v_1 = g, v_2 = g^\alpha, \ldots, v_n = g^{\alpha^{n-1}})$ and for a vector of challenges $x_1 \ldots x_{\ell-1}, x_\ell$ is:

$$v = g^{\prod_{j=0}^{\ell-1}(1+x_{\ell-j}\alpha^{2^j})}.$$

We will prove the general formula by induction:

Step 1. Check the formula for $\ell = 1$ (initial commitment key $\mathbf{v}$ has two elements v_1, v_2):

$$v = v_1 v_2^{x_1} = g^{1+x_1\alpha} = g^{\Pi_{j=0}^0 (1+x_{\ell-j}\alpha^{2^j})}.$$

Step 2. Suppose the statement is true for $\ell - 1$. We prove it for ℓ.

On the first round, we have a challenge x_1 and we rescale the commitment key $\mathbf{v}$ which has length $n = 2^\ell$ as follows:

$$\mathbf{v}' = \mathbf{v}_{[:2^{\ell-1}]} \circ \mathbf{v}_{[2^{\ell-1}:]}^{x_1},$$

$$\mathbf{v}' = (g \cdot g^{x_1\alpha^{2^{\ell-1}}}, g^\alpha \cdot g^{x_1\alpha^{2^{\ell-1}+1}}, g^{\alpha^2} \cdot g^{x_1\alpha^{2^{\ell-1}+2}}, \ldots).$$

We can write this differently as $\mathbf{v}' = (v_1 v_1^{x_1\alpha^{2^{\ell-1}}}, \ldots v_{2^{\ell-1}} v_{2^{\ell-1}}^{x_1\alpha^{2^{\ell-1}}})$.
This gives us a nicely written commitment key after first round

$$\mathbf{v}' = (v_1^{1+x_1\alpha^{2^{\ell-1}}}, v_2^{1+x_1\alpha^{2^{\ell-1}}}, \ldots v_{2^{\ell-1}}^{1+x_1\alpha^{2^{\ell-1}}}) = \mathbf{v}_{[:2^{\ell-1}]}^{1+x_1\alpha^{2^{\ell-1}}}.$$

We can apply the induction assumption for step $\ell - 1$ to $\mathbf{v}_{[:2^{\ell-1}]}$ which is a commitment key of length $2^{\ell-1}$. This means the final key for $\mathbf{v}$ is:

$$v = \left(g^{\Pi_{j=0}^{\ell-2}\left(1+x_{\ell-j}\alpha^{2^j}\right)}\right)^{(1+x_1\alpha^{2^{\ell-1}})} = g^{\Pi_{j=0}^{\ell-1}(1+x_{\ell-j}\alpha^{2^j})}.$$

Remark than in more generality, this can be written as:

$$v = v_1^{\Pi_{j=0}^{\ell-1}(1+x_{\ell-j}\alpha^{2^j})}$$

Therefore, if we start with an initial key $\mathbf{w} = (w_1 = g^{\alpha^n}, w_2^{\alpha^{n+1}} \ldots, w_n = g^{\alpha^{2n-1}})$, the final key w can be written as:

$$w = w_1^{\Pi_{j=0}^{\ell-1}(1+x_{\ell-j}\alpha^{2^j})} = g^{\alpha^n \Pi_{j=0}^{\ell-1}(1+x_{\ell-j}\alpha^{2^j})}$$

References

ABL+19. Abdolmaleki, B., Baghery, K., Lipmaa, H., Siim, J., Zajac, M.: UC-secure CRS generation for SNARKs. In: Buchmann, J., Nitaj, A., Rachidi, T. (eds.) AFRICACRYPT 2019. LNCS, vol. 11627, pp. 99–117. Springer, Cham (2019). https://doi.org/10.1007/978-3-030-23696-0_6

BCG+14. Ben-Sasson, E., et al.: Decentralized anonymous payments from Bitcoin. Cryptology ePrint Archive, Report 2014/349 (2014). https://eprint.iacr.org/2014/349

BCG+15. Ben-Sasson, E., Chiesa, A., Green, M., Tromer, E., Virza, M.: Secure sampling of public parameters for succinct zero knowledge proofs, pp. 287–304 (2015)

BCG+20. Bowe, S., Chiesa, A., Green, M., Miers, I., Mishra, P., Wu, H.: ZEXE: enabling decentralized private computation. In: 2020 IEEE Symposium on Security and Privacy (SP), pp. 947–964 (2020)

BCI+13. Bitansky, N., Chiesa, A., Ishai, Y., Paneth, O., Ostrovsky, R.: Succinct non-interactive arguments via linear interactive proofs. In: Sahai, A. (ed.) TCC 2013. LNCS, vol. 7785, pp. 315–333. Springer, Heidelberg (2013). https://doi.org/10.1007/978-3-642-36594-2_18

BCTV14. Ben-Sasson, E., Chiesa, A., Tromer, E., Virza, M.: Succinct non-interactive zero knowledge for a von Neumann architecture, pp. 781–796 (2014)

BGM17. Bowe, S., Gabizon, A., Miers, I.: Scalable multi-party computation for zk-SNARK parameters in the random beacon model. Cryptology ePrint Archive, Report 2017/1050 (2017). https://eprint.iacr.org/2017/1050

BMM+19. Bünz, B., Maller, M., Mishra, P., Tyagi, N., Vesely, P.: Proofs for inner pairing products and applications. Cryptology ePrint Archive, Report 2019/1177 (2019). https://eprint.iacr.org/2019/1177

Dam00. Damgård, I.: Efficient concurrent zero-knowledge in the auxiliary string model. In: Preneel, B. (ed.) EUROCRYPT 2000. LNCS, vol. 1807, pp. 418–430. Springer, Heidelberg (2000). https://doi.org/10.1007/3-540-45539-6_30

DRZ20. Daza, V., Ràfols, C., Zacharakis, A.: Updateable inner product argument with logarithmic verifier and applications. In: Kiayias, A., Kohlweiss, M., Wallden, P., Zikas, V. (eds.) PKC 2020. LNCS, vol. 12110, pp. 527–557. Springer, Cham (2020). https://doi.org/10.1007/978-3-030-45374-9_18

Fil20. Filecoin. Filecoin powers of tau ceremony attestations (2020). https://github.com/arielgabizon/perpetualpowersoftau

Fis19. Fisch, B.: Tight proofs of space and replication (2019). https://web.stanford.edu/~bfisch/tight_pos.pdf

GGPR13. Gennaro, R., Gentry, C., Parno, B., Raykova, M.: Quadratic span programs and succinct NIZKs without PCPs. In: Johansson, T., Nguyen, P.Q. (eds.) EUROCRYPT 2013. LNCS, vol. 7881, pp. 626–645. Springer, Heidelberg (2013). https://doi.org/10.1007/978-3-642-38348-9_37

Gro16. Groth, J.: On the size of pairing-based non-interactive arguments. In: Fischlin, M., Coron, J.-S. (eds.) EUROCRYPT 2016. LNCS, vol. 9666, pp. 305–326. Springer, Heidelberg (2016). https://doi.org/10.1007/978-3-662-49896-5_11

KZG10. Kate, A., Zaverucha, G.M., Goldberg, I.: Constant-size commitments to polynomials and their applications. In: Abe, M. (ed.) ASIACRYPT 2010. LNCS, vol. 6477, pp. 177–194. Springer, Heidelberg (2010). https://doi.org/10.1007/978-3-642-17373-8_11

Lab18. Protocol Labs. Filecoin (2018). https://filecoin.io/filecoin.pdf

LMR19. Lai, R.W.F., Malavolta, G., Ronge, V.: Succinct arguments for bilinear group arithmetic: practical structure-preserving cryptography, pp. 2057–2074 (2019)

PHGR13. Parno, B., Howell, J., Gentry, C., Raykova, M.: Pinocchio: nearly practical verifiable computation, pp. 238–252 (2013)

Zca18. Zcash. Zcash Powers of Taus ceremony attestation (2018). https://github.com/ZcashFoundation/powersoftau-attestations

On Interactive Oracle Proofs for Boolean R1CS Statements

Ignacio Cascudo[1] and Emanuele Giunta[1,2,3(✉)]

[1] IMDEA Software Institute, Madrid, Spain
{ignacio.cascudo,emanuele.giunta}@imdea.org
[2] Universidad Politécnica de Madrid, Madrid, Spain
[3] Scuola Superiore di Catania, Catania, Italy

Abstract. The framework of interactive oracle proofs (IOP) has been used with great success to construct a number of efficient transparent zk-SNARKS in recent years. However, these constructions are based on Reed-Solomon codes and can only be applied *directly* to statements given in the form of arithmetic circuits or R1CS over *large* enough fields $\mathbb{F}$.

This motivates the question: what is the best way to apply these IOPs to statements that are naturally written as R1CS over *small* fields, and more concretely, the *binary* field $\mathbb{F}_2$? While one can just see the system as one over an extension field $\mathbb{F}_{2^e}$ containing $\mathbb{F}_2$, this seems wasteful, as it uses e bits to encode just one "information" bit. In fact, in FC21 the work BooLigero devised a way to apply the well-known Ligero while being able to encode $\sqrt{e}$ bits into one element of $\mathbb{F}_{2^e}$.

In this paper, we introduce a new protocol for $\mathbb{F}_2$-R1CS which among other things relies on a more efficient embedding which (for practical parameters) allows to encode $\geq e/4$ bits into an element of $\mathbb{F}_{2^e}$. Our protocol makes then *black box use* of *lincheck* and *rowcheck* protocols for the larger field. Using the lincheck and rowcheck introduced in Aurora and Ligero respectively we obtain $1.31 - 1.65\times$ smaller proofs for Aurora and $3.71\times$ for Ligero. We also estimate the reduction of prover time by a factor of $24.7\times$ for Aurora and between $6.9 - 32.5\times$ for Ligero without interactive repetitions.

Our methodology uses the notion of reverse multiplication friendly embeddings introduced in the area of secure multiparty computation, combined with a new IOPP to test linear statements modulo a subspace $V \leq \mathbb{F}_{2^e}$ which may be of independent interest.

1 Introduction

A zero-knowledge proof is a protocol in which a *prover* convinces a *verifier* that a statement is true, while conveying no other information apart from its truth.

Research partially supported by the Spanish Government under project SecuRing (PID2019-110873RJ-I00/MCIN/AEI/10.13039/501100011033), by Madrid regional government as part of the program S2018/TCS-4339 (BLOQUES-CM) co-funded by EIE Funds of the European Union, and by a research grant from Nomadic Labs and the Tezos Foundation.

I. Eyal and J. Garay (Eds.): FC 2022, LNCS 13411, pp. 230–247, 2022.
https://doi.org/10.1007/978-3-031-18283-9_11

Zero-knowledge proofs have been among the most useful and studied primitives in cryptography since their advent in the 80s. Their popularity has increased even more in recent times, propelled by new applications motivated by blockchain technologies. This context has highlighted the relevance of a particular flavour of zero-knowledge proof, known as zero-knowledge succinct non-interactive argument of knowledge, or zk-SNARK.

The flexibility and efficiency of zk-SNARKs allow to provide practical arguments of knowledge for relations that lack any kind of algebraic structure, for instance the preimage relation for a one-way function. However, it is well known [Wee05] that under standard complexity assumptions, succinct non-interactive arguments do not exist unless some kind of setup is assumed, such as a common reference string. This either requires a trusted third party or the execution of heavy MPC protocols if the setup relies on secret randomness.

For this reason, *transparent* SNARKs have been proposed, whose setup involves only publicly generated randomness. Many constructions of transparent setup SNARKs have been proposed in recent years, both based on asymmetric [BCC+16], [WTS+18], [BBB+18], [BFS20] and symmetric [AHIV17], [BBHR18b], [BCR+19], [COS20], [Set20], [BFH+20] cryptographic techniques.

In this work we focus on this latter type of constructions and remark that all cited works in this category are built in (variants of) the Interactive Oracle Proof framework presented in [BCS16] and independently in [RRR16] as "interactive PCP". Moreover they all address directly or indirectly the NP-complete rank 1 constraint system satisfiability problem. An easier to state variant asks to prove, given $A, B, C \in \mathbb{F}^{m,n}$ and $\mathbf{b} \in \mathbb{F}^m$, the existence of a vector $\mathbf{z} \in \mathbb{F}^n$ such that $A\mathbf{z} * B\mathbf{z} = C\mathbf{z} + \mathbf{b}$, where $*$ is the component-wise multiplication of vectors in $\mathbb{F}^m$.

An IOP is an interactive proof where the verifier has oracle access to some strings provided by the prover. Its relation to zk-SNARKs stems from the results in [BCS16] where it was shown that any IOP can be efficiently compiled into a non-interactive argument in the random oracle model by using Merkle trees [Mer90]. Moreover the transformation, which can be seen as a generalization of the reduction in [Mic94] from PCP, preserves zero knowledge and knowledge soundness. In particular, IOPs can be used to construct zk-SNARKs.

Unfortunately, the IOP constructions above cannot be *directly* instantiated for every field choice as they extensively use Reed-Solomon codes, that requires the existence of enough points in $\mathbb{F}$ and, even worse, the soundness error is often greater than $|\mathbb{F}|^{-1}$ due to polynomial identity tests which implies $|\mathbb{F}| > 2^\lambda$ with λ security parameter. This leaves out, for example, the case of R1CS over $\mathbb{F}_2$. This case is actually interesting as some hash functions and encryption schemes can be interpreted as boolean circuits with relative ease, and then translated to a R1CS. A straight-forward way to overcome this problem, mentioned in [AHIV17], is to simply embed $\mathbb{F}_2$ in a larger field $\mathbb{F}_{2^e}$, for large enough e (where at least $e > \lambda$) and add constraints of the kind $z_i^2 = z_i$ for $i = 1, \ldots, n$ to ensure that the witness entries belongs to $\mathbb{F}_2$,[1] and then execute the protocol for R1CS over the larger field.

However this approach seems wasteful, as elements of $\mathbb{F}_{2^e}$ which in principle could encode up to e bits of information are used to represent only one element of $\mathbb{F}_2$. Also, operations over $\mathbb{F}_{2^e}$ are more expensive than those over $\mathbb{F}_2$. Finally one needs the aforementioned additional constraints on the witness, which increase the size of the system.

Since $\mathbb{F}_{2^e}$ is an e-dimensional vector space over $\mathbb{F}_2$, one attempt to improve this would be to interpret vectors in $\mathbb{F}_2^e$ as elements over the larger field $\mathbb{F}_{2^e}$. While this would work for systems that only involve additions (XORs), it fails in general when multiplications (ANDs) are needed too.[2] The technical issue is that for $e > 1$, the ring $\mathbb{F}_2^e$, considered with component-wise addition and multiplication, cannot be embedded via a ring homomorphism into $\mathbb{F}_{2^e}$ (nor any other finite field) since $\mathbb{F}_2^e$ contains zero divisors while fields do not.

A better approach was presented in BooLigero [GSV21] for the case of Ligero [AHIV17]. Their technique allows to encode e bits into roughly $\sqrt{e}$ field elements in $\mathbb{F}_{2^e}$, so that one can use Ligero over $\mathbb{F}_{2^e}$ to treat $\sqrt{e}$ times larger statements over $\mathbb{F}_2$ than the "naïve" method, with roughly the same R1CS size. This however motivates the following question: *can we find embeddings of $\mathbb{F}_2^k$ into $\mathbb{F}_{2^e}$ with a larger embedding rate k/e which allow to produce more efficient IOPs for R1CS over $\mathbb{F}_2$ given an IOP for R1CS over $\mathbb{F}_{2^e}$?*

1.1 Our Contributions

In this work we answer the above question in the affirmative using a more efficient embedding that allows us to encode $k \geq e/4$ bits into an element of $\mathbb{F}_{2^e}$. We then present a construction of an IOP for $\mathbb{F}_2$-R1CS satisfiability which makes black-box use of any IOP satisfying mild assumptions for R1CS over larger fields. This leads us to reducing Aurora's argument size up to $1.31 - 1.65\times$ and Ligero's argument size up to $3.71\times$.

More concretely, we can use any *Reed Solomon encoded IOP*, a variant of IOP introduced in [BCR+19], that provides two commonly used sub-protocols: a *generalised lincheck*, which tests linear relations of the form $A_1\mathbf{x}_1 + \ldots + A_n\mathbf{x}_n = \mathbf{b}$ when the verifier has only oracle access to Reed Solomon codewords encoding $\mathbf{x}_i$, and a *rowcheck*, which tests quadratic relations $\mathbf{x} * \mathbf{y} = \mathbf{z}$ when the verifier has oracle access to encodings of $\mathbf{x}, \mathbf{y}, \mathbf{z}$. This includes Ligero[3], Aurora [BCR+19][4]

---

[1] This is necessary as, for example, $x^2 + x + 1 = 0$ is satisfiable over $\mathbb{F}_4$ but not over $\mathbb{F}_2$, despite the fact that the constraint only involves constants over $\mathbb{F}_2$. Note that interpreting field multiplication as logical AND, the above constrain is equivalent to $x \cdot (x - 1) = 1$, i.e. both x and its negation are true.

[2] This not only includes coordinate-wise products of secret vectors, but also the linear operations $A\mathbf{x}$ in the R1CS system, where A is a public matrix over the larger field.

[3] See [BCR+19] for how to see Ligero as an IOP with these characteristics.

[4] We cannot however apply our techniques to IOPs with preprocessing, see comment in Sect. 1.3.

and Ligero++ [BFH+20] up to minor manipulations to transform their lincheck, see the full version [CG21].

In a nutshell, our embedding technique relies primarily on two components: first, the use of reverse multiplication friendly embeddings (RMFE), introduced in the MPC literature in [CCXY18] and independently in [BMN18] and used in several subsequent works [DLN19, CG20, PS21, DGOT21, ACE+21]. Such algebraic device maps a vector from $\mathbb{F}_2^k$ into an element of a larger field $\mathbb{F}_q = \mathbb{F}_{2^e}$ in a manner such that field additions and products of two encodings in $\mathbb{F}_q$ still encode the component-wise additions and products of the originally vectors from $\mathbb{F}_2^k$, even though the map is not a ring homomorphism. For $k < 100$ we can get RMFEs with $e \approx 3.3k$ (or $e = 4k$ if we insist on e being a power of 2). Second, the notion of *modular lincheck*, an IOPP which we introduce in Sect. 3.3 and that we believe is of independent interest, to test linear relations modulo an $\mathbb{F}_2$ vector space V contained in $\mathbb{F}_q$, i.e. equations of the form $A\mathbf{x} = \mathbf{b} \mod V^n$ (meaning that each coordinate of the vector $A\mathbf{x} - \mathbf{b}$ is in V).

In conclusion for each of the aforementioned schemes we compare known adaptations to $\mathbb{F}_2$-R1CSs with our general reduction both in terms of argument size and prover complexity. Regarding the proof size we estimate it numerically, see our Python implementation at [Git21]. Regarding prover time we estimate it asymptotically, predicting an improvement factor of 24.7× for Aurora and between $6.9 - 32.5\times$ for Ligero without interactive repetitions.

1.2   Techniques

Reverse Multiplication Friendly Embeddings. A $(k, e)_p$-RMFE is a pair of $\mathbb{F}_p$-linear maps $\varphi : \mathbb{F}_p^k \to \mathbb{F}_{p^e}$ and $\psi : \mathbb{F}_{p^e} \to \mathbb{F}_p^k$ satisfying $\mathbf{x} * \mathbf{y} = \psi(\varphi(\mathbf{x}) \cdot \varphi(\mathbf{y}))$ for all $\mathbf{x}, \mathbf{y} \in \mathbb{F}_p^k$, where $*$ denotes the component-wise product. The properties automatically imply that φ is injective, hence the name *embedding*. Note that φ is not necessarily a ring homomorphism, i.e. $\varphi(\mathbf{x} * \mathbf{y}) \neq \varphi(\mathbf{x}) \cdot \varphi(\mathbf{y})$ in general. In this paper we extend the notation blockwise to $\Phi : (\mathbb{F}_p^k)^n \to \mathbb{F}_{p^e}^n$ given by $\Phi(\mathbf{x}_1, \ldots, \mathbf{x}_n) = (\varphi(\mathbf{x}_1), \ldots, \varphi(\mathbf{x}_n))$ and $\Psi : \mathbb{F}_{p^e}^n \to (\mathbb{F}_p^k)^n$ given by $\Psi(x_1, \ldots, x_n) = (\psi(x_1), \ldots, \psi(x_n))$. These satisfy then $\mathbf{x} * \mathbf{y} = \Psi(\Phi(\mathbf{x}) * \Phi(\mathbf{y}))$ for all $\mathbf{x}, \mathbf{y} \in (\mathbb{F}_p^k)^n = \mathbb{F}_p^{kn}$, where the component-wise product on the right side is on $\mathbb{F}_{p^e}^n$.

From $\mathbb{F}_2$ -R1CS to a System of Statements Over $\mathbb{F}_q$. A key ingredient of our result is how to translate the system $A_1\mathbf{w} * A_2\mathbf{w} = A_3\mathbf{w} + \mathbf{b}$ over $\mathbb{F}_2$ into an equivalent set of relations over $\mathbb{F}_q$ that can be efficiently checked. Even with the RMFE in hand, this is not trivial because φ (consequently Φ) is neither a ring homomorphism nor surjective.

Defining $\mathbf{x}_i = A_i\mathbf{w}$, we can split the above statement into the three *linchecks* $A_i\mathbf{w} = \mathbf{x}_i$ and the *rowcheck* $\mathbf{x}_1 * \mathbf{x}_2 = \mathbf{x}_3 + \mathbf{b}$. The prover will start by embedding $\widetilde{\mathbf{w}} = \Phi(\mathbf{w}) \in \mathbb{F}_q^{n/k}$ and $\widetilde{\mathbf{x}}_i = \Phi(\mathbf{x}_i)$. We then need to deal with the following:

First of all, because Φ is not surjective, we need additional constraints to ensure $\widetilde{\mathbf{w}}, \widetilde{\mathbf{x}}_i$ lie in the image of Φ. We can write these in the form $I_{n/k} \cdot \widetilde{\mathbf{w}} \in (\text{Im } \varphi)^{n/k}$ and $I_{m/k} \cdot \widetilde{\mathbf{x}}_i \in (\text{Im } \varphi)^{m/k}$ (where I_ℓ is the ℓ by ℓ identity matrix).

Then, because Φ is not a ring homomorphism, we can *not* simply translate $\mathbf{x}_1 * \mathbf{x}_2 = \mathbf{x}_3 + \mathbf{b}$ into $\widetilde{\mathbf{x}}_1 * \widetilde{\mathbf{x}}_2 = \widetilde{\mathbf{x}}_3 + \Phi(\mathbf{b})$, as this is not true in general. Instead, we need to use the RMFE "product recovery map" ψ. Setting $\mathbf{t} = \widetilde{\mathbf{x}}_1 * \widetilde{\mathbf{x}}_2$, we show that the rowcheck statement is equivalent to the modular linear relation $\mathbf{t} - u \cdot \widetilde{\mathbf{x}}_3 = u \cdot \Phi(\mathbf{b}) \mod (\text{Ker } \psi)^{m/k}$ where $u = \varphi(\mathbf{1}) \in \mathbb{F}_q$, $\mathbf{1}$ is the all-one vector and Ker denotes the kernel.

Similarly, we show that each lincheck $A_i \mathbf{w} = \mathbf{x}_i$ can be translated into $\widetilde{A_i} \widetilde{\mathbf{w}} - \widetilde{I_m} \widetilde{\mathbf{x}}_i \in (\text{Ker } S \circ \psi)^m$, where $\widetilde{A_i}, \widetilde{I_m}$ are the result of applying Φ to A_i, I_m row-wise and S is the map summing the k components of a vector in $\mathbb{F}_2^k$.

Modular Linear Test. The sketched characterization above implies that providing a way to test linear modular relations over $\mathbb{F}_q$ yields the desired IOP as the prover could provide oracle access to encodings of $\widetilde{\mathbf{w}}, \widetilde{\mathbf{x}}_1, \widetilde{\mathbf{x}}_2, \widetilde{\mathbf{x}}_3, \mathbf{t}$ and then convince the verifier that all those constraints are satisfied. To test $\mathbf{x} = \mathbf{0} \mod V^n$, a standard approach would consist in proving that a random linear combination of its coordinates belongs to V. However, we are dealing with a $\mathbb{F}_2$-vector space, and this translates into a soundness error of $1/2$. In order to decrease it to $2^{-\lambda}$, we could check λ independent linear combinations, which involves λn random bits. In Sect. 3.3 we describe how to reduce the required random bits to $\Theta(\lambda)$ by using a certain family of almost universal linear hash functions, and achieve zero knowledge by adding a masking term.

Optimizations. The above techniques require a total of 8 modular linchecks and a rowcheck. In Sect. 4, we introduce several modifications, the main of which is to reduce the number of modular linchecks to just 3. The observation is that we can test several equations of the form $A\mathbf{x}_i = \mathbf{b}_i \mod V^{n_i}$ (with common V) all at once by checking $\sum R_i(A\mathbf{x}_i - \mathbf{b}_i) \in V^\lambda$ for appropriately chosen matrices R_i. Additionaly, we compress messages sent by the prover using the structure of these vector spaces V, which comes from our use of an RMFE.

1.3   Other Related Work

Our work provides a significant reduction of the proof size with respect to BooLigero [GSV21]. Applying our construction to Ligero for an $\mathbb{F}_2$-R1CS consisting of 2^{20} constraints we measure proofs $3.71\times$ shorter than plain Ligero and $3.03\times$ smaller than BooLigero. We also stress that in contrast to [GSV21] we present a general reduction that can be applied to a larger class of protocols.

Regarding the use of RMFE, to the best of our knowledge only the recent work [DGOT21] applied this tool in the IOP framework (see their Appendix A). However, their use is restricted to their own protocol, which follows the MPC-in-the-head paradigm introduced in [IKOS07], and cannot be applied directly to other existing IOPs such as Aurora. Furthermore, this optimisation is only considered in the multi-instance case while in our work we manage to integrate the RMFE also for a single instance.

We also remark that even though our construction captures essentially any IOPs that provides a lincheck and a rowcheck, it still cannot be applied out of the box to zk-SNARKS with preprocessing such as Fractal [COS20] or Spartan [Set20]. The reason is that we use the given linchecks to test a randomised relation depending on the random coins of the verifier. This significantly affects the usefulness of any pre-computation. We believe however that this issue can be overcome in a non black-box way with different techniques, a problem that we leave for future work.

2 Preliminaries

The set $\{1, \ldots, n\}$ is called $[n]$. Vectors are denoted with boldface font. $\mathbf{v} * \mathbf{w}$ denotes the coordinate-wise product of two vectors of the same length, and $\|\mathbf{v}\|$ is the Hamming weight of $\mathbf{v}$. $\mathbf{1}_k$ is the vector of k 1's. Matrices are denoted with capital letters, $A^\top$ is the transpose of A and I_n is the n by n identity matrix. Given q a prime power, $\mathbb{F}_q$ is a field of q elements. When $q = p^e$, $\mathbb{F}_p$ can be seen as a subset of $\mathbb{F}_q$ and $\mathbb{F}_q$ can be treated as an $\mathbb{F}_p$ vector space of dimension e. $V \le \mathbb{F}_q$ means that V is an $\mathbb{F}_p$-vector subspace of $\mathbb{F}_q$. $a = b \mod V$ means that $a - b \in V$, and for vectors of length m, $\mathbf{a} = \mathbf{b} \mod V^m$ iff $a_i = b_i \mod V$ for all $i \in [m]$. Given an $\mathbb{F}_p$-linear map $L : V \to W$ its kernel is $\operatorname{Ker} L = \{\mathbf{x} \in V : L(\mathbf{x}) = 0\}$ and its image is $\operatorname{Im} L = \{\mathbf{y} \in W : \mathbf{y} = L(\mathbf{x}) \text{ for some } \mathbf{x} \in V\}$. Given a polynomial $\widehat{f} \in \mathbb{F}_q[x]$ and $L \subseteq \mathbb{F}_q$ we denote $\widehat{f}_{|L} = (\widehat{f}(\alpha))_{\alpha \in L}$ its evaluation over L. The Reed-Solomon code over L of rate $\rho \in [0, 1]$ is the set $\mathrm{RS}_{\mathbb{F}_q, L, \rho} := \{\widehat{f}_{|L} : \widehat{f} \in \mathbb{F}_q[x], \ \deg \widehat{f} < \rho|L|\}$. We will typically encode vectors $\mathbf{v}$ of length $m < \rho|L|$ as codewords from $\mathrm{RS}_{\mathbb{F}_q, L, \rho}$ by sampling a $f \in \mathrm{RS}_{L, \rho}$ such that $\widehat{f}_{|H} = \mathbf{v}$. $\mathbb{F}_q^H$ denotes the set of vectors over $\mathbb{F}_q$ with coordinates indexed by H and $\mathbb{F}_q^{H_1 \times H_2}$ is the set of matrices with rows and columns indexed by H_1 and H_2 respectively. Finally $\mathrm{FFT}(\mathbb{F}, n)$ denotes the number of field operations required to perform a fast Fourier transform over a set of size n, see [GM10].

2.1 Reverse Multiplication Friendly Embedding

We now recall the notion of reverse multiplication friendly embedding from [CCXY18]. Its purpose is to 'reconcile' the coordinate-wise multiplicative structure of a ring $\mathbb{F}_p^k$ and the finite field structure of an extension $\mathbb{F}_{p^e}$ of $\mathbb{F}_p$.

Definition 1. *Given a prime power p and $k, e \in \mathbb{N}$ a **Reverse Multiplication-Friendly Embedding**, denoted $(k, e)_p$-RMFE, is a pair of $\mathbb{F}_p$-linear maps $\varphi : \mathbb{F}_p^k \to \mathbb{F}_{p^e}$, $\psi : \mathbb{F}_{p^e} \to \mathbb{F}_p^k$ such that for all $\mathbf{x}, \mathbf{y} \in \mathbb{F}_p^k$, it holds that*

$$\mathbf{x} * \mathbf{y} = \psi(\varphi(\mathbf{x}) \cdot \varphi(\mathbf{y})).$$

That is, one can embed $\mathbb{F}_p^k$ into $\mathbb{F}_{p^e}$ via a linear map φ so that the product in $\mathbb{F}_{p^e}$ of the images of any two vectors $\mathbf{x}, \mathbf{y}$ carries information about their component-wise product $\mathbf{x} * \mathbf{y}$, and this can be recovered applying ψ to that field product. However, φ is in general not a ring homomorphism and therefore $\psi \ne \varphi^{-1}$. For notational convenience, we extend both φ and ψ to maps Φ, Ψ as follows. Given vectors $\mathbf{x} = (\mathbf{x}_1, \ldots, \mathbf{x}_n) \in (\mathbb{F}_p^k)^n$ and $\mathbf{z} = (z_1, \ldots, z_n) \in (\mathbb{F}_{p^e})^n$ we define

$$\Phi(\mathbf{x}) := (\varphi(\mathbf{x}_1), \ldots, \varphi(\mathbf{x}_n)) \in (\mathbb{F}_{p^e})^n, \qquad \Psi(\mathbf{z}) := (\psi(z_1), \ldots, \psi(z_n)) \in (\mathbb{F}_p^k)^n.$$

The following properties of these extended functions will be key in Sect. 3.1 to transform a $\mathbb{F}_2$-R1CS system into a system of equations over $\mathbb{F}_{2^e}$. Note in particular (3) and (4) characterize respectively coordinatewise and inner products over $\mathbb{F}_p$ in terms of the corresponding operations over $\mathbb{F}_{p^e}$. The lemma follows quite directly from the definitions and a proof appears in the full version [CG21].

Lemma 1. *The following holds for all positive $n \in \mathbb{N}$:*

1. *The maps φ and Φ are injective. The maps ψ and Ψ are surjective.*
2. *For all $\mathbf{x}, \mathbf{y} \in (\mathbb{F}_p^k)^n$, $\mathbf{x} * \mathbf{y} = \Psi(\Phi(\mathbf{x}) * \Phi(\mathbf{y}))$ where the $*$ product in the right-hand side is component-wise in $(\mathbb{F}_{p^e})^n$, i.e. in each component we use the field product in $\mathbb{F}_{p^e}$.*
3. *Let $u = \varphi(\mathbf{1}_k) \in \mathbb{F}_{p^e}$.[5] Then for all $\mathbf{x} \in (\mathbb{F}_p^k)^n$ we have $\mathbf{x} = \Psi(u \cdot \Phi(\mathbf{x}))$.*
4. *Let $S : \mathbb{F}_p^k \to \mathbb{F}_p$ be given by $S(x_1, x_2, \ldots, x_k) = x_1 + x_2 + \cdots + x_k$. Then for all $\mathbf{x}, \mathbf{y} \in (\mathbb{F}_p^k)^n$, the inner product $\mathbf{x}^\top \mathbf{y}$ can be written as*

$$\mathbf{x}^\top \mathbf{y} = S \circ \psi(\Phi(\mathbf{x})^\top \Phi(\mathbf{y}))$$

As for the existence of RMFEs, in our case of interest $p = 2$ one can obtain the following parameters by concatenation of polynomial interpolation techniques [CCXY18, CG20] (for asymptotics and other results see the full version [CG21]):

Lemma 2. *For all $r \leq 33$, there exists a $(3r, 10r)_2$-RMFE. For all $a \leq 17$ there exists a $(2a, 8a)_2$-RMFE. For all $b \leq 65$ there exists a $(3b, 12b)_2$-RMFE.*

This yields RMFEs with parameters $(48, 192)$, $(48, 160)$ and $(32, 128)$, setting $r = a = b = 16$, that we will concretely use to evaluate our reduction.

2.2 R1CS, Lincheck and Rowcheck

We now recall the main relations used in recent IOP-based[6] SNARKs like [BCR+19, AHIV17]. The first one is the *rank 1 constraints system*, or R1CS, that defines an NP-complete language closely related to arithmetic circuit satisfiability. Here we present an equivalent affine version that requires for $A_1, A_2, A_3 \in \mathbb{F}^{m,n}$ and $\mathbf{b} \in \mathbb{F}^m$ to exhibit a vector $\mathbf{w} \in \mathbb{F}^n$ such that $A_1\mathbf{w} * A_2\mathbf{w} = A_3\mathbf{w} + \mathbf{b}$. Formally

Definition 2. *We define the affine R1CS relation as the set*

$$\mathcal{R}_{\mathsf{R1CS}} = \{((\mathbb{F}, m, n, A_1, A_2, A_3, \mathbf{b}), \mathbf{w}) : A_i \in \mathbb{F}^{m,n}, A_1\mathbf{w} * A_2\mathbf{w} = A_3\mathbf{w} + \mathbf{b}\}.$$

---

[5] Note that u is not necessarily equal to 1.
[6] See [BCS16, BCR+19] for the rigorous definition , or the full version [CG21] for a simplified explanation.

Instead of directly providing a proof system for R1CS, two intermediate relations, *lincheck* and *rowcheck*, are defined and for which [BCR+19] constructs RS-encoded IOPPs.[7] These are then used as building blocks to produce a RS-encoded IOP for the R1CS relation, which in turn can be combined with a low degree test, such as FRI [BBHR18a] or [BGKS20], to make a standard IOP for R1CS. The complexity of this reduction depends on the so-called *max rates*, two parameters related to the degrees of polynomials and the relations which are tested

The lincheck relation requires that the witnesses $f_1, f_2 \in \mathsf{RS}_{L,\rho}$ encode over $H_1, H_2 \subseteq \mathbb{F}_q$ two vectors $\mathbf{x}_1, \mathbf{x}_2$ (i.e. $\widehat{f}_{i|H_i} = \mathbf{x}_i$) which satisfy a given linear constraint $M\mathbf{x}_1 = \mathbf{x}_2$. The rowcheck relation requires that witnesses $f_1, f_2, f_3 \in \mathsf{RS}_{L,\rho}$ encode over $H \subseteq \mathbb{F}_q$ three vectors $\mathbf{x}_1, \mathbf{x}_2, \mathbf{x}_3$ such that $\mathbf{x}_1 * \mathbf{x}_2 = \mathbf{x}_3$. For efficiency reasons, depending on the concrete instantiations of Aurora and FRI, in both definitions below L, H_1, H_2, H are taken to be $\mathbb{F}_2$-affine subspaces of $\mathbb{F}_q$.

Definition 3. *We define $\mathcal{R}_{\mathsf{Lin}}$ as the set of tuples $((\mathbb{F}_q, L, H_1, H_2, \rho, M), (f_1, f_2))$ such that $L, H_i \subseteq \mathbb{F}_q$ are affine subspaces, $H_i \cap L = \varnothing$ for $i \in \{1, 2\}$, $f_i \in \mathsf{RS}_{L,\rho}$, $M \in \mathbb{F}_q^{H_1 \times H_2}$ and the linear relationship $\widehat{f}_{1|H_1} = M \cdot \widehat{f}_{2|H_2}$ holds.*

Definition 4. *We define $\mathcal{R}_{\mathsf{Row}}$ as the set of tuples $((\mathbb{F}_q, L, H, \rho), (f_1, f_2, f_3))$ such that $L, H \subseteq \mathbb{F}_q$ are disjoint affine subspaces, $f_i \in \mathsf{RS}_{L,\rho}$ for $i \in \{1, 2, 3\}$ and the quadratic relationship $\widehat{f}_{1|H} * \widehat{f}_{2|H} = \widehat{f}_{3|H}$ holds.*

RS-encoded IOPPs $(\mathsf{P}_{\mathsf{Lin}}, \mathsf{V}_{\mathsf{Lin}})$ and $(\mathsf{P}_{\mathsf{Row}}, \mathsf{V}_{\mathsf{Row}})$ for the two relations above are provided in [BFH+20,BCR+19] and in [AHIV17] up to minor adaptations in the second case. We will need a generalisation of $\mathcal{R}_{\mathsf{Lin}}$ that tests relations of the form $M_1\mathbf{x}_1 + \ldots + M_h\mathbf{x}_h = \mathbf{b}$ (for $h = 2$, $M_1 = -I$ and $\mathbf{b} = \mathbf{0}$ we get back the standard lincheck).

Definition 5. *$\mathcal{R}_{\mathsf{Lin}_h}$ is the set of tuples $((\mathbb{F}_q, L, H_0, H_i, \rho, M_i, \mathbf{b})_{i=1}^h, (f_i)_{i=1}^h)$ such that $L, H_0, H_i \leq \mathbb{F}_q$, $L \cap H_0 = L \cap H_i = \varnothing$ for all $i \in \{1, \ldots, h\}$, $f_i \in \mathsf{RS}_{L,\rho}$, $M_i \in \mathbb{F}_q^{H_0 \times H_i}$ and the linear relationship $\sum_{i=1}^h M_i \cdot \widehat{f}_{i|H_i} = \mathbf{b}$ holds.*

The lincheck protocol presented in Aurora can be generalised to capture this variant, as shown in the full version of this paper.

3   Simplified Construction

In the rest of the paper we aim at describing an efficient RS-encoded IOP for $\mathbb{F}_2$-R1CS. As the only tools we assume are a lincheck and a rowcheck over a large enough field, our first step in Sect. 3.1 is to characterise $\mathbb{F}_2$-R1CS in terms of one quadratic relation over $\mathbb{F}_q$ and a set of linear relations modulo some vector

---

[7] Reed-Solomon IOPs are IOPs where soundness is guaranteed only when the messages sent by the prover are oracles to codewords of a Reed-Solomon code. Reed-Solomon IOPPs (proofs of proximity) additionally provide oracle access to the witness, also a set of Reed-Solomon codewords, to the verifier.

space $V \leq \mathbb{F}_q$. An RS-encoded IOPP to test the latter conditions is provided in Sect. 3.3. Finally a simple solution that uses naively the above IOPP is provided in Section 3.4. Even if suboptimal, we see this as a useful stepping stone to better present the efficient version in Sect. 4.2.

3.1   Characterisation of R1CS

In the following we assume (φ, ψ) to be a $(k, e)_2$-RMFE, where $q = 2^e$, and recall that Φ, Ψ denote the block-wise application of φ and ψ, cf. Sect. 2.1.

Theorem 1. *Let* $A_1, A_2, A_3 \in \mathbb{F}_2^{m,n}$, $\mathbf{b} \in \mathbb{F}_2^m$ *with* m, n *multiples of* k. *Then there exists* $\mathbf{w} \in \mathbb{F}_2^n$ *such that* $((\mathbb{F}_2, m, n, A_1, A_2, A_3, \mathbf{b}), \mathbf{w}) \in \mathcal{R}_{\text{R1CS}}$ *if and only if there exist* $\widetilde{\mathbf{w}} \in \mathbb{F}_q^{n/k}$ *and* $\widetilde{\mathbf{x}}_1, \widetilde{\mathbf{x}}_2, \widetilde{\mathbf{x}}_3, \mathbf{t} \in \mathbb{F}_q^{m/k}$ *satisfying*

$$\widetilde{\mathbf{x}}_1 * \widetilde{\mathbf{x}}_2 = \mathbf{t} \tag{1}$$

$$\widetilde{\mathbf{w}} = \mathbf{0} \quad \mathrm{mod} \ (\mathrm{Im} \, \varphi)^{n/k} \tag{2}$$

$$\widetilde{\mathbf{x}}_i = \mathbf{0} \quad \mathrm{mod} \ (\mathrm{Im} \, \varphi)^{m/k} \qquad \forall i \in \{1, 2, 3\} \tag{3}$$

$$\widetilde{A}_i \widetilde{\mathbf{w}} - \widetilde{I}_m \widetilde{\mathbf{x}}_i = \mathbf{0} \quad \mathrm{mod} \ (\mathrm{Ker} \, S \circ \psi)^m \qquad \forall i \in \{1, 2, 3\} \tag{4}$$

$$\mathbf{t} - u\widetilde{\mathbf{x}}_3 = u\widetilde{\mathbf{b}} \quad \mathrm{mod} \ (\mathrm{Ker} \, \psi)^{m/k} \tag{5}$$

where $\widetilde{\mathbf{b}} = \Phi(\mathbf{b}) \in \mathbb{F}_q^{m/k}$, $u = \varphi(1_k) \in \mathbb{F}_q$, $\widetilde{A}_i \in \mathbb{F}_q^{m,n/k}$ *is the matrix obtained by applying* Φ *row-wise to* A_i, *and* $\widetilde{I}_m \in \mathbb{F}_q^{m,m/k}$ *is the matrix obtained by applying* Φ *row-wise to the identity matrix* $I_m \in \mathbb{F}_2^{m,m}$. *Moreover if* $\mathbf{w}$ *is a witness for the R1CS then* $\widetilde{\mathbf{w}} = \Phi(\mathbf{w})$, $\widetilde{\mathbf{x}}_i = \Phi(A_i \mathbf{w})$, $\mathbf{t} = \widetilde{\mathbf{x}}_1 * \widetilde{\mathbf{x}}_2$ *satisfy the conditions above.*

The proof appears in the full version [CG21], but we remark Eqs. (2), (3) are equivalent to saying $\widetilde{\mathbf{w}} = \Phi(\mathbf{w})$, $\widetilde{\mathbf{x}}_i = \Phi(\mathbf{x}_i)$ for some $\mathbf{w}$, $\mathbf{x}_i$; Eqs. (1) and (5) encode $\mathbf{x}_1 * \mathbf{x}_2 = \mathbf{x}_3 + \mathbf{b}$ (the rowcheck) and the latter is derived using properties (2) and (3) in Lemma 1; while Eqs. (4) encode $A_i \mathbf{w} = \mathbf{x}_i$ (the lincheck) and are derived from property (4) in Lemma 1.

3.2   Linear Hashing

We now adapt linear checks to small fields. A common technique to test $A\mathbf{x} = \mathbf{b}$ over $\mathbb{F}_q$ is to sample a random vector $\mathbf{r} \in \mathbb{F}_q^m$ and check $\mathbf{r}^\top A\mathbf{x} = \mathbf{r}^\top \mathbf{b}$. Alternatively one can set $\mathbf{r} = (1, r, \dots, r^{m-1})$ for $r \xleftarrow{\$} \mathbb{F}_q$ to save randomness. The soundness errors of these approaches are respectively $1/q$ and $(m-1)/q$, which are too large if q is small as in our case. Therefore they need to be adapted. With this aim in mind, let $\vartheta : \mathbb{F}_2^\lambda \to \mathbb{F}_{2^\lambda}$ be an isomorphism of $\mathbb{F}_2$-linear spaces[8]. For any $\alpha \in \mathbb{F}_{2^\lambda}$ define $R_\alpha^{(m)} : \mathbb{F}_2^{\lambda m} \to \mathbb{F}_2^\lambda$ such that

$$R_\alpha^{(m)}(\mathbf{x}_1, \dots, \mathbf{x}_m) = \vartheta^{-1}(\alpha \vartheta(\mathbf{x}_1) + \dots + \alpha^m \vartheta(\mathbf{x}_m)).$$

---

[8] Observe here we do not worry about their multiplicative structures.

Seeing this function as a matrix in $\mathbb{F}_2^{\lambda,\lambda m}$, we can apply it to vectors in $\mathbb{F}_q^{\lambda m}$, i.e., if $R_\alpha^{(m)} = (r_{i,j}) \in \mathbb{F}_2^{\lambda,\lambda m}$ and $\mathbf{x} = (x_j)_{j=1}^{\lambda m} \in \mathbb{F}_q^{\lambda m}$ then $R_\alpha^{(m)}\mathbf{x} = \left(\sum_{j=1}^{\lambda m} r_{i,j}x_j\right)_{i=1}^{\lambda}$. This family of linear functions satisfies the following properties.

Proposition 1. *Let $V \leq \mathbb{F}_q$ be an $\mathbb{F}_2$ vector subspace, $\mathbf{y} \in \mathbb{F}_q^{\lambda}$, $\mathbf{x} \in \mathbb{F}_q^{\lambda m} \setminus V^{\lambda m}$ and $\alpha \sim U(\mathbb{F}_{2^\lambda})$, then* $\Pr\left[R_\alpha^{(m)}\mathbf{x} = \mathbf{y} \mod V^\lambda\right] \leq 2^{-\lambda} \cdot m$

Proposition 2. *Let $V \leq \mathbb{F}_q$ be an $\mathbb{F}_2$ vector subspace, $\mathbf{y} \in \mathbb{F}_q^{\lambda}$, $\mathbf{x}_i \in \mathbb{F}_q^{\lambda m_i}$ for $i \in [h]$ such that $\mathbf{x}_j \notin V^{\lambda m_j}$ for some j. Then $\alpha_i \sim U(\mathbb{F}_{2^\lambda})$ implies*

$$\Pr\left[R_{\alpha_1}^{(m_1)}\mathbf{x}_1 + \ldots + R_{\alpha_h}^{(m_h)}\mathbf{x}_h = \mathbf{y} \mod V^\lambda\right] \leq 2^{-\lambda} \cdot \max\{m_i : i \in [h]\}.$$

3.3 Modular Lincheck

In this section we provide an RS-encoded IOPP that generalises the Lincheck to linear relations of the form $M_1\mathbf{x}_1 + \ldots + M_h\mathbf{x}_h = \mathbf{b}$ modulo an $\mathbb{F}_2$ vector space $V \leq \mathbb{F}_q$, where the verifier has oracle access to an encoding of $\mathbf{x}_i$ for each i.

Definition 6. *The Modular Lincheck relation is the set $\mathcal{R}_{\mathsf{Mlin}_h}$ of all tuples $((\mathbb{F}_q, L, H_0, H_i, \rho, M_i, \mathbf{b}, V)_{i=1}^h, (f_i)_{i=1}^h)$ such that $L, H_0, H_i \subseteq \mathbb{F}_q$ are affine $\mathbb{F}_2$-spaces with $L \cap H_i = \varnothing$, $\rho \in [0,1)$, $M_i \in \mathbb{F}_q^{H_0 \times H_i}$, $f_i \in \mathsf{RS}_{L,\rho}$ and $\sum_{i=1}^h M_i\widehat{f}_{i|H_i} = \mathbf{b} \mod V^{H_0}$.*

Consider the simpler statement $\mathbf{x} = \mathbf{0} \mod V^H$, i.e. $\mathbf{x} \in V^H$, and the following proof: the verifier samples a random $R \sim U(\mathbb{F}_2^{H_0' \times H})$, and receives $\mathbf{v} = R\mathbf{x}$ from the prover; the verifier then checks $\mathbf{v} \in V^{H_0'}$ and then runs a lincheck to test $\mathbf{v} = R\mathbf{x}$. In order to make this zero knowledge, we add a masking codeword g sampled from $\mathsf{Mask}(L, \rho, H_0', V) = \{f \in \mathsf{RS}_{L,\rho} : \widehat{f}_{|H_0'} \in V^{H_0'}\}$ so that the sender first sends an oracle to g, receives R, and sends $\mathbf{v} = R\mathbf{x} + \widehat{g}_{|H_0'}$ in plain. In the general case we replace $\mathbf{x}$ with $\sum_{i=1}^h M_i\widehat{f}_{i|H_i} - \mathbf{b}$ and, for efficiency reasons, the random matrix R with R_α obtaining the protocol in Fig. 1.

From the above observations, the protocol has the following properties, where soundness comes from Proposition 2. See the full paper for a rigorous proof.

Theorem 2. *Protocol 1 is an RS-encoded IOPP for the relation $\mathcal{R}_{\mathsf{Mlin}_h}$ that upon setting $|H_0'| = \lambda$ has the following parameters:*

Rounds	$= 2$
Proof Length	$= 3|L|$ *elements of* $\mathbb{F}_q$
Randomness	$= \lambda + 2\log q$ *bits*
Soundness Error	$= \lceil m/\lambda \rceil 2^{-\lambda} + \lambda q^{-1}$
Prover Time	$= \mathsf{FFT}(\mathbb{F}_q, |L|) + \sum_{i=1}^h \|M_i\| + \|\mathbf{b}\| + \lambda \sum_{i=1}^n |H_i| + T_{\mathsf{Lin}_{h+1}}^{\mathsf{P}}$
Verifier Time	$= \lambda \dim V + \sum_{i=1}^h \|M_i\| + \|\mathbf{b}\| + T_{\mathsf{Lin}_{h+1}}^{\mathsf{V}}$
Max Rates	$= \left(\rho + \lambda|L|^{-1}, \rho + (\lambda + |H|)|L|^{-1}\right)$

where $H = \mathsf{span}(H_1, \ldots, H_h, H_0')$ and $T_{\mathsf{Lin}_{h+1}}^{\mathsf{P}}, T_{\mathsf{Lin}_{h+1}}^{\mathsf{V}}$ denotes the costs of running respectively $\mathsf{P}_{\mathsf{Lin}_{h+1}}$ and $\mathsf{V}_{\mathsf{Lin}_{h+1}}$.

$$\mathsf{P}_{\mathsf{Mlin}_h}((\mathsf{pp}, M_i, \mathbf{b}, V, f_i)_{i=1}^h) \qquad\qquad \mathsf{V}_{\mathsf{Mlin}_h}^{f_1,\dots,f_h}((\mathsf{pp}, M_i, \mathbf{b}, V)_{i=1}^h)$$

Agree on $H_0' \subseteq \mathbb{F}_q : H_0' \cap L = \varnothing$	Agree on $H_0' \subseteq \mathbb{F}_q : H_0' \cap L = \varnothing$
$M_{h+1} \leftarrow I_{H_0'},\ H_{h+1} \leftarrow H_0'$	$M_{h+1} \leftarrow I_{H_0'},\ H_{h+1} \leftarrow H_0'$
$\rho' \leftarrow \rho + |H_0'||L|^{-1}$	$\rho' \leftarrow \rho + |H_0'||L|^{-1}$
$\mathsf{pp}' \leftarrow (\mathbb{F}_q, L, H_0', H_i, \rho')_{i=1}^{h+1}$	$\mathsf{pp}' \leftarrow (\mathbb{F}_q, L, H_0', H_i, \rho')_{i=1}^{h+1}$

$$f_{h+1} \xleftarrow{\$} \mathsf{Mask}(L, \rho', H_0', V) \qquad \xrightarrow{\;f_{h+1}\;}$$

$$\xleftarrow{\;\alpha\;} \qquad \alpha \xleftarrow{\$} \mathbb{F}_{2^\lambda}$$

$$\mathbf{v} \leftarrow R_\alpha \left[\sum_{i=1}^h M_i \widehat{f}_{i|H_i} - \mathbf{b} \right] + \widehat{f}_{h+1|H_0'} \qquad \xrightarrow{\;\mathbf{v}\;}$$

$$\qquad\qquad\qquad\qquad\qquad\qquad\qquad \text{If } \mathbf{v} \notin V^{H_0'} \text{ return } \bot$$

$$M' \leftarrow ((R_\alpha M_i)_{i=1}^h, I_{H_0'}) \qquad\qquad M' \leftarrow ((R_\alpha M_i)_{i=1}^h, I_{H_0'})$$

Execute: Execute:

$$\mathsf{P}_{\mathsf{Lin}_{h+1}}(\mathsf{pp}', M', R_\alpha\mathbf{b} + \mathbf{v}, (f_i)_{i=1}^{h+1}) \qquad \mathsf{V}_{\mathsf{Lin}_{h+1}}^{f_1,\dots,f_{h+1}}(\mathsf{pp}', M', R_\alpha\mathbf{b} + \mathbf{v})$$

Fig. 1. RS-encoded IOPP for $\mathcal{R}_{\mathsf{Mlin}_h}$ with $\mathsf{pp} = (\mathbb{F}_q, L, H_0, (H_i)_{i=1}^h, \rho)$

3.4   An RS-Encoded IOP for R1CS from Modular Lincheck

Given RS-encoded IOPP for Modular Lincheck and Rowcheck we briefly sketch how to build a simple RS-encoded IOP for $\mathbb{F}_2$-R1CS. By Theorem 1 we know that a given system, defined by $A_1, A_2, A_3 \in \mathbb{F}_2^{m,n}$, $\mathbf{b} \in \mathbb{F}_2^m$ is satisfied if and only if there exists $\widetilde{\mathbf{x}}_1, \widetilde{\mathbf{x}}_2, \widetilde{\mathbf{x}}_3, \mathbf{t} \in \mathbb{F}_q^{m/k}$ and $\widetilde{\mathbf{w}} \in \mathbb{F}_q^{n/k}$ that satisfy Eqs. 1–5.

Thus we let the prover initially compute the extended witness $\mathbf{x}_i = A_i\mathbf{w}$, apply block-wise the RMFE to get $\widetilde{\mathbf{x}}_i = \Phi(\mathbf{x}_i)$, $\widetilde{\mathbf{w}} = \Phi(\mathbf{w})$ and finally set $\mathbf{t} = \widetilde{\mathbf{x}}_1 * \widetilde{\mathbf{x}}_2$. Next, it picks two affine subspaces $H_1, H_2 \subseteq \mathbb{F}_q$ of sizes $m/k, n/k$ and sample five codewords $f_{\widetilde{\mathbf{x}}_i}, f_{\mathbf{t}}, f_{\widetilde{\mathbf{w}}}$ such that $\widehat{f}_{\widetilde{\mathbf{x}}_i|H_1} = \widetilde{\mathbf{x}}_i$, $\widehat{f}_{\mathbf{t}|H_1} = \mathbf{t}$ and $\widehat{f}_{\widetilde{\mathbf{w}}|H_2} = \widetilde{\mathbf{w}}$.

Finally it provides oracle access to these codewords to the verifier and they both run:

- One rowcheck to test $\widetilde{\mathbf{x}}_1 * \widetilde{\mathbf{x}}_2 = \mathbf{t}$.
- Four modular lincheck to test $I_{m/k} \cdot \widetilde{\mathbf{x}}_i \in (\mathrm{Im}\,\varphi)^{H_1}$ and $I_{n/k} \cdot \widetilde{\mathbf{w}} \in (\mathrm{Im}\,\varphi)^{H_2}$.
- Three modular lincheck to test that $\tilde{A}_i \cdot \widetilde{\mathbf{w}} - \tilde{I}_m \cdot \widetilde{\mathbf{x}}_i \in (\mathrm{Ker}\,S \circ \psi)^m$.
- One modular lincheck to check $I_{m/k} \cdot \mathbf{t} - (uI_{m/k}) \cdot \widetilde{\mathbf{x}}_3 = u\widehat{\mathbf{b}} \mod (\mathrm{Ker}\,\psi)^{H_1}$.

Correctness and soundness of the above protocol follows from Theorem 1, while Zero Knowledge against β queries can be achieved setting the rate of $f_{\widetilde{\mathbf{x}}_i}, f_{\mathbf{t}}$ to $\frac{m/k+\beta}{|L|}$ and the rate of $f_{\widetilde{\mathbf{w}}}$ to $\frac{n/k+\beta}{|L|}$.

4 Efficient Construction

4.1 Batching Modular Linchecks and Packing Vectors

The protocol above requires a total of 8 modular Linchecks. In this section we show how to reduce the number of required modular linchecks to three, by batching proofs of relations modulo the same vector space: we aim at designing an RS-encoded IOPP for a relation of the form: $\forall i \in [h], A_i \mathbf{x}_i = \mathbf{b}_i \mod V^{m_i}$.

We propose the following: as before the prover begins by sending a codeword that encodes a masking term $\mathbf{y} \sim U(V^\lambda)$. The verifier then chooses h matrices $R_{\alpha_1}, \ldots, R_{\alpha_h}$ and the prover replies by sending $\mathbf{v} = \sum_{i=1}^h R_{\alpha_i}(A_i \mathbf{x}_i - \mathbf{b}_i) + \mathbf{y}$. Finally the verifier checks if $\mathbf{v} \in V^\lambda$ and both parties executes a lincheck to test the above relation. Informally security follows as in the single modular lincheck from Sect. 3.3, except that for soundness we use Proposition 2.

To further improve the complexities, we now show how to reduce the size of vectors sent in plain by the prover in the (batched) modular lincheck. Recalling $u = \varphi(\mathbf{1}_k)$ we point out $\operatorname{Ker} \psi$ and $u \cdot \operatorname{Im} \varphi$ intersect only in 0, because $\psi(u \cdot \varphi(\mathbf{v})) = \mathbf{1}_k * \mathbf{v} = \mathbf{v}$. Therefore $\mathbb{F}_q$ is the direct sum of $\operatorname{Ker} \psi$ and $(u \cdot \operatorname{Im} \varphi)$. Then given $\mathbf{x} \in (\operatorname{Im} \varphi)^n$ and $\mathbf{y} \in (\operatorname{Ker} \psi)^n$, we just need to send $\mathbf{z} = u\mathbf{x} + \mathbf{y}$. Given $\mathbf{z}$ one can extract $\mathbf{x} = \Phi(\Psi(\mathbf{z}))$ and $\mathbf{y} = \mathbf{z} - u\mathbf{x}$, where the former equation is justified by observing that, if we call $\mathbf{v} \in \mathbb{F}_2^{kn}$ such that $\mathbf{x} = \Phi(\mathbf{v})$, then $\Phi(\Psi(\mathbf{z})) = \Phi(\Psi(u\mathbf{x} + \mathbf{y})) = \Phi(\Psi(u \cdot \Phi(\mathbf{v}))) = \Phi(\mathbf{v}) = \mathbf{x}$, where the second equality following from $\mathbf{y} \in (\operatorname{Ker} \psi)^n$ and the third one from Lemma 1.

4.2 An Efficient RS-Encoded IOP for R1CS

With the two ideas presented so far we can now improve the protocol sketched in Sect. 3.4. We batch linchecks in three groups, testing equations modulo $\operatorname{Im} \varphi$, $\operatorname{Ker} S \circ \psi$ and $\operatorname{Ker} \psi$ respectively. Moreover we observe that the masking terms of these tests can be aggregated. To do so we choose three disjoint affine subspaces H'_1, H'_2, H'_3 of size λ and sample g from the set $\mathsf{BMask}\,(L, \rho, H'_1, H'_2, H'_3, \varphi, \psi)$ defined as

$$\left\{ f \in \mathsf{RS}_{L,\rho} : \widehat{f}_{|H'_1} \in (\operatorname{Im} \varphi)^{H'_1} , \ \widehat{f}_{|H'_2} \in (\operatorname{Ker} S \circ \psi)^{H'_2} , \ \widehat{f}_{|H'_3} \in (\operatorname{Ker} \psi)^{H'_3} \right\}.$$

In the following protocol we let $\rho_1 = (m/k + \beta)|L|^{-1}$, $\rho_2 = (n/k + \beta)|L|^{-1}$ and $\rho_3 = (3\lambda + \beta)|L|^{-1}$ be the three rates used (Fig. 2).

Theorem 3. *Protocol 2 is an RS-encoded IOP for the relation $\mathcal{R}_{\mathsf{R1CS}}$ which, using Aurora's lincheck and rowcheck, achieves the following parameters*

Rounds	$= 3$
Proof Length	$= 8\|L\|$ *elements of* $\mathbb{F}_q$
Randomness	$= 8\lambda + 5\log q$ *bits*
Soundness Error	$= \max(\lceil m/\lambda \rceil, \lceil n/k\lambda \rceil) \cdot 2^{-\lambda} + \lambda q^{-1}$
Prover Time	$= O(\|L\| \log(m+n) + \sum_{i=1}^3 \|A_i\| + \|\mathbf{b}\|) + 35 \cdot \mathrm{FFT}(\mathbb{F}_q, \|L\|)$
Verifier Time	$= O(\sum_{i=1}^3 \|A_i\| + \|\mathbf{b}\| + n + m)$
Max Rates	$= \left(\frac{\max(m/k, n/k, 3\lambda) + 2\beta}{\|L\|}, \frac{\max(2m/k, 2n/k, 3\lambda) + 2\beta}{\|L\|} \right)$

$\mathsf{P}_{\mathsf{R1CS}}(\mathbb{F}_q, m, n, A_1, A_2, A_3, \mathbf{b}, \mathbf{w})$	$\mathsf{V}_{\mathsf{R1CS}}(\mathbb{F}_q, m, n, A_1, A_2, A_3, \mathbf{b})$
$u := \varphi(\mathbf{1}_k)$	$u := \varphi(\mathbf{1}_k)$
$\widetilde{I}_m \leftarrow (\Phi(\mathbf{e}_j)^\top)_{j=1}^m$	$\widetilde{I}_m \leftarrow (\Phi(\mathbf{e}_j)^\top)_{j=1}^m$
$\widetilde{A}_i \leftarrow (\Phi(\mathbf{a}_{i,j})^\top)_{j=1}^m$	$\widetilde{A}_i \leftarrow (\Phi(\mathbf{a}_{i,j})^\top)_{j=1}^m$
$\widetilde{\mathbf{b}} \leftarrow \Phi(\mathbf{b}),\ \widetilde{\mathbf{w}} \leftarrow \Phi(\mathbf{w})$	$\widetilde{\mathbf{b}} \leftarrow \Phi(\mathbf{b})$

$$\widetilde{\mathbf{x}}_i \leftarrow \Phi(A_i\mathbf{w}),\ \mathbf{t} \leftarrow \widetilde{\mathbf{x}}_1 * \widetilde{\mathbf{x}}_2$$

$$f_{\widetilde{\mathbf{w}}} \overset{\$}{\leftarrow} \{f \in \mathsf{RS}_{L,\rho_2} : \widehat{f}_{|H_2} = \widetilde{\mathbf{w}}\}$$

$$f_{\widetilde{\mathbf{x}}_i} \overset{\$}{\leftarrow} \{f \in \mathsf{RS}_{L,\rho_1} : \widehat{f}_{|H_1} = \widetilde{\mathbf{x}}_i\}$$

$$f_{\mathbf{t}} \overset{\$}{\leftarrow} \{f \in \mathsf{RS}_{L,\rho_1} : \widehat{f}_{|H_1} = \mathbf{t}\}$$

$$g \overset{\$}{\leftarrow} \mathsf{BMask}\,(L, \rho_3, H'_1, H'_2, H'_3, \varphi, \psi) \qquad \xrightarrow{\ f_{\widetilde{\mathbf{w}}},\, f_{\widetilde{\mathbf{x}}_i},\, f_{\mathbf{t}},\, g\ }$$

$$\qquad\qquad\qquad\qquad\qquad\qquad (\alpha_i)_{i=1}^4 \overset{\$}{\leftarrow} \mathbb{F}_{2^\lambda}$$

$$\xleftarrow{\ \alpha_i,\, \gamma_i,\, \delta\ } \qquad (\gamma_i)_{i=1}^3 \overset{\$}{\leftarrow} \mathbb{F}_{2^\lambda},\ \delta \overset{\$}{\leftarrow} \mathbb{F}_{2^\lambda}$$

$M_1 \leftarrow ((R_{\alpha_i})_{i=1}^4, I_\lambda)$	Compute M_1
$M_2 \leftarrow (\sum_{j=1}^3 R_{\gamma_j}\widetilde{A}_j, (-R_{\gamma_i}\widetilde{I}_m)_{i=1}^3, I_\lambda)$	Compute M_2
$M_3 \leftarrow (R_\delta, -uR_\delta, I_\lambda)$	Compute M_3

$$\mathbf{v}_1 \leftarrow \sum_{i=1}^3 R_{\alpha_i}\widetilde{\mathbf{x}}_i + R_{\alpha_4}\widetilde{\mathbf{w}} + \widehat{g}_{|H'_1}$$

$$\mathbf{v}_2 \leftarrow \sum_{i=1}^3 R_{\gamma_i}(\widetilde{A}_i\widetilde{\mathbf{w}} - \widetilde{I}_m\widetilde{\mathbf{x}}_i) + \widehat{g}_{|H'_2}$$

$$\mathbf{v}_3 \leftarrow R_\delta\mathbf{t} - uR_\delta(\widetilde{\mathbf{x}}_3 + \widetilde{\mathbf{b}}) + \widehat{g}_{|H'_3}$$

$$\mathbf{v}_0 \leftarrow \mathbf{v}_3 + u\mathbf{v}_1 \qquad\qquad \xrightarrow{\ \mathbf{v}_0,\, \mathbf{v}_2\ }$$

$$\qquad\qquad\qquad\qquad\qquad\qquad \text{If } \mathbf{v}_2 \notin (\mathrm{Ker}\, S \circ \psi)^{H'_0}$$

$$\qquad\qquad\qquad\qquad\qquad\qquad\quad \text{Return } \bot$$

$$\qquad\qquad\qquad\qquad\qquad\qquad\quad \mathbf{v}'_1 \leftarrow \Phi(\Psi(\mathbf{v}_0))$$

$$\qquad\qquad\qquad\qquad\qquad\qquad\quad \mathbf{v}'_3 \leftarrow \mathbf{v}_0 - u\mathbf{v}_1$$

Run: $\mathsf{P}_{\mathsf{Lin}_5}(M_1, \mathbf{v}_1, (f_{\widetilde{\mathbf{x}}_i})_{i=1}^3, f_{\widetilde{\mathbf{w}}}, g)$	Run: $\mathsf{V}_{\mathsf{Lin}_5}^{(f_{\widetilde{\mathbf{x}}_i})_{i=1}^3, f_{\widetilde{\mathbf{w}}}, g}(M_1, \mathbf{v}'_1)$
$\mathsf{P}_{\mathsf{Lin}_5}(M_2, \mathbf{v}_2, f_{\widetilde{\mathbf{w}}}, (f_{\widetilde{\mathbf{x}}_i})_{i=1}^3, g)$	$\mathsf{V}_{\mathsf{Lin}_5}^{f_{\widetilde{\mathbf{w}}}, (f_{\widetilde{\mathbf{x}}_i})_{i=1}^3, g}(M_2, \mathbf{v}_2)$
$\mathsf{P}_{\mathsf{Lin}_3}(M_3, uR_\delta\widetilde{\mathbf{b}} + \mathbf{v}_3, f_{\mathbf{t}}, f_{\widetilde{\mathbf{x}}_3}, g)$	$\mathsf{V}_{\mathsf{Lin}_3}^{f_{\mathbf{t}}, f_{\widetilde{\mathbf{x}}_3}, g}(M_3, uR_\delta\widetilde{\mathbf{b}} + \mathbf{v}'_3)$
$\mathsf{P}_{\mathsf{Row}}(\mathbb{F}_q, L, H_1, \rho_1, f_{\widetilde{\mathbf{x}}_1}, f_{\widetilde{\mathbf{x}}_2}, f_{\mathbf{t}})$	$\mathsf{V}_{\mathsf{Row}}^{f_{\widetilde{\mathbf{x}}_1}, f_{\widetilde{\mathbf{x}}_2}, f_{\mathbf{t}}}(\mathbb{F}_q, L, H_1, \rho_1)$

Fig. 2. RS-encoded IOP for R1CS. We fix a linear order on H_0, H_1, H_2 and assume $\widetilde{A}_i \in \mathbb{F}_q^{H_0 \times H_2}$, $\widetilde{I}_m \in \mathbb{F}_q^{H_0 \times H_1}$. Note the first two steps can be precomputed knowing the input size, and that $\mathbf{v}_0, \mathbf{v}_2$ are sent directly, i.e. without providing oracle access

Observe this means can take $|L| \cdot \rho \approx \max(2m/k, 2n/k, 3\lambda) + 2\beta$ for a fixed rate $\rho \approx 1/8$.

5   Comparisons

In this section we compare our construction with [AHIV17, BCR+19, GSV21, BFH+20] when proving satisfiability of an R1CS over $\mathbb{F}_2$. In all cases we assume [BCS16] is used to compile IOP into NIZK. Our focus will be on the proof size, which we compute through a parameter optimiser, available at [Git21], based on [lib20], the open source implementation of Aurora and R1CS-Ligero. We also consider prover efficiency, which we only estimate theoretically. Regarding verifier time instead we do not expect significant improvements or overhead, as asymptotic costs are the same with roughly the same constants.

Aurora - Proof Size: Compiling Aurora [BCR+19] to a NIZK, proof size is dominated by the replies to oracle queries. Calling $|L|$ the block length of the Reed Solomon code in use, each of these replies requires $O(\log^2 |L|)$ hash values. As we use Reed Solomon codewords that encode vectors k times smaller w.r.t. Aurora with naïve embedding, the block length in our work is roughly k times smaller. We therefore estimate the proof size to be reduced by a term $O(\log k \log |L|)$. Concrete proof sizes are shown in Fig. 3 where results on the left are obtained using proven soundness bounds, while on the right optimistic (but not proven) bounds are used, see the full version for more details. The improvement factor for 2^{20} constraints with a $(48, 192)_2$-RMFE and 128 security bits amounts in the first case to 1.65, in the second case to 1.31.

Aurora - Prover Time: Using again the fact that the block length is reduced by a factor of k with a $(k, e)_2$-RMFE observe that

- In the RS-encoded IOP, the cost is dominated by the $18 \cdot \text{FFT}(\mathbb{F}_q, |L|)$. In our case we perform 35 fast Fourier transforms over a set k times smaller, leading to an improvement factor of $18k/35$.
- In the low degree test, prover complexity is upper bounded by $6|L|$ arithmetic operations [BBHR18a]. Hence our construction improves by a factor k.
- In the BCS transform, computing the Merkle tree from an oracle of size $|L|$ requires $2|L| - 1$ hashes. Using column hashing our construction requires the same amount of trees as in plain Aurora. Moreover, calling f_i FRI's i-th oracle, the length of f_i is $|L| \cdot 2^{-i\eta}$ for a constant η, i.e. it scales linearly in $|L|$. Therefore our protocol requires k times less hash function evaluations.

In conclusion, we estimate that deploying a $(48, 192)_2$-RMFE leads to a $18k/35 \approx 24.7\times$ speed up asymptotically.

Ligero and BooLigero - Proof Size: Applying our construction to R1CS-Ligero [BCR+19], whose proof size is $\Theta(\sqrt{n})$, over a field $\mathbb{F}_{2^{160}}$ we can obtain shorter proof by a factor $\sqrt{k} \approx 6.9$ as we would invoke every sub-protocol on

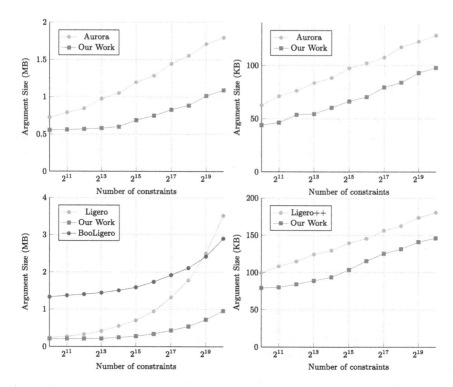

Fig. 3. Argument Size w.r.t. the number of constraints for 128 security bit for: Aurora with proven soundness bounds (up, left) and with optimistic bounds (up, right), Ligero/BooLigero *with interactive repetitions and smaller fields* (down, left) and Ligero++ (down, right). Our work uses a $(48, 192)_2$-RMFE in the first two cases, and a $(48, 160)_2$-RMFE for the others.

input k times shorter. However in [AHIV17] an optimisation through interactive repetitions working over smaller fields is presented. As this version is harder to analyse asymptotically, we estimate its cost comparing it with BooLigero and our construction using a $(48, 160)_2$-RMFE (Fig. 3, down left).

Ligero and BooLigero - Prover Time: For simplicity we only compare our construction to Ligero without repetitions, as in this case operations are performed over the same extension of $\mathbb{F}_2$, for a R1CS over $\mathbb{F}_2$ with n variables and n constraints. Recall that $|L| = \Theta(\sqrt{n})$ and each vector is divided in m blocks of length ℓ, both growing asymptotically as $\sqrt{n}$. As in Aurora we split the prover time in three terms:

– In the IOP, costs are dominated asymptotically by $21m \cdot \mathrm{FFT}(\mathbb{F}_q, |L|)$. In our cases we would need $31m'$ fast Fourier transform but with $m' \sim m/\sqrt{k}$ and over a set $\sqrt{k}$ times smaller, leading to an improvement factor of $21k/31$

- As Ligero performs a direct low degree test no extra computation is performed for testing proximity
- In the BCS transform, using column hashing only one tree with $2|L| - 1$ nodes has to be computed. Hence in our construction this step is performed $\sqrt{k}$ times faster.

In conclusion we expect an improvement factor between 6.9–32.5 with a $(48, 160)_2$-RMFE. We leave prover time comparison with the more efficient version of Ligero that allows repetitions as future work.

Ligero++: As [BFH+20] combines Ligero with an inner product argument, which can be realised adapting Aurora's sumcheck to achieve poly-logarithmic argument size, we expect a prover time reduction comparable to those in plain Ligero and Aurora. The same applies to the proof size that, for completeness, we also estimate through our parameter optimiser, Fig. 3, achieving a median improvement factor of $1.26\times$.

References

[ACE+21] Abspoel, M., Cramer, R., Escudero, D., Damgård, I., Xing, C.: Improved single-round secure multiplication using regenerating codes. IACR Cryptol. ePrint Arch. **2021**, 253 (2021)

[AHIV17] Ames, S., Hazay, C., Ishai, Y., Venkitasubramaniam, M.: Ligero: lightweight sublinear arguments without a trusted setup. In: Thuraisingham, B.M., Evans, D., Malkin, T., Xu, D. (eds.) ACM CCS 2017, pp. 2087–2104. ACM Press (2017)

[BBB+18] Bünz, B., Bootle, J., Boneh, D., Poelstra, A., Wuille, P., Maxwell, G.: Bulletproofs: short proofs for confidential transactions and more. In: 2018 IEEE Symposium on Security and Privacy, pp. 315–334. IEEE Computer Society Press (2018)

[BBHR18a] Ben-Sasson, E., Bentov, I., Horesh, Y., Riabzev, M.: Fast reed-solomon interactive oracle proofs of proximity. In: Chatzigiannakis, I., Kaklamanis, C., Marx, D., Sannella, D. (eds.) ICALP 2018, vol. 107 of LIPIcs, pp. 14:1–14:17. Schloss Dagstuhl (2018)

[BBHR18b] Ben-Sasson, E., Bentov, I., Horesh, Y., Riabzev, M.: Scalable, transparent, and post-quantum secure computational integrity. Cryptology ePrint Archive, Report 2018/046 (2018). https://eprint.iacr.org/2018/046

[BCC+16] Bootle, J., Cerulli, A., Chaidos, P., Groth, J., Petit, C.: Efficient zero-knowledge arguments for arithmetic circuits in the discrete log setting. In: Fischlin, M., Coron, J.-S. (eds.) EUROCRYPT 2016. LNCS, vol. 9666, pp. 327–357. Springer, Heidelberg (2016). https://doi.org/10.1007/978-3-662-49896-5_12

[BCR+19] Ben-Sasson, E., Chiesa, A., Riabzev, M., Spooner, N., Virza, M., Ward, N.P.: Aurora: transparent succinct arguments for R1CS. In: Ishai, Y., Rijmen, V. (eds.) EUROCRYPT 2019. LNCS, vol. 11476, pp. 103–128. Springer, Cham (2019). https://doi.org/10.1007/978-3-030-17653-2_4

[BCS16] Ben-Sasson, E., Chiesa, A., Spooner, N.: Interactive oracle proofs. In: Hirt, M., Smith, A. (eds.) TCC 2016. LNCS, vol. 9986, pp. 31–60. Springer, Heidelberg (2016). https://doi.org/10.1007/978-3-662-53644-5_2

[BFH+20] Bhadauria, R., et al.: Ligero++: a new optimized sublinear IOP. In: Ligatti, J., Ou, X., Katz, J., Vigna, G. (eds.) ACM CCS 2020, pp. 2025–2038. ACM Press (2020)

[BFS20] Bünz, B., Fisch, B., Szepieniec, A.: Transparent SNARKs from DARK compilers. In: Canteaut, A., Ishai, Y. (eds.) EUROCRYPT 2020. LNCS, vol. 12105, pp. 677–706. Springer, Cham (2020). https://doi.org/10.1007/978-3-030-45721-1_24

[BGKS20] Ben-Sasson, E., Goldberg, L., Kopparty, S., Saraf, S.: DEEP-FRI: sampling outside the box improves soundness. In: Vidick, T. (ed.) ITCS 2020, vol. 151, pp. 5:1–5:32. LIPIcs (2020)

[BMN18] Block, A.R., Maji, H.K., Nguyen, H.H.: Secure computation with constant communication overhead using multiplication embeddings. In: Chakraborty, D., Iwata, T. (eds.) INDOCRYPT 2018. LNCS, vol. 11356, pp. 375–398. Springer, Cham (2018). https://doi.org/10.1007/978-3-030-05378-9_20

[CCXY18] Cascudo, I., Cramer, R., Xing, C., Yuan, C.: Amortized complexity of information-theoretically secure MPC revisited. In: Shacham, H., Boldyreva, A. (eds.) CRYPTO 2018. LNCS, vol. 10993, pp. 395–426. Springer, Cham (2018). https://doi.org/10.1007/978-3-319-96878-0_14

[CG20] Cascudo, I., Gundersen, J.S.: A secret-sharing based MPC protocol for boolean circuits with good amortized complexity. In: Pass, R., Pietrzak, K. (eds.) TCC 2020. LNCS, vol. 12551, pp. 652–682. Springer, Cham (2020). https://doi.org/10.1007/978-3-030-64378-2_23

[CG21] Cascudo, I., Giunta, E.: On interactive oracle proofs for boolean r1cs statements. Cryptology ePrint Archive, Report 2021/694 (2021). https://ia.cr/2021/694

[COS20] Chiesa, A., Ojha, D., Spooner, N.: FRACTAL: post-quantum and transparent recursive proofs from holography. In: Canteaut, A., Ishai, Y. (eds.) EUROCRYPT 2020. LNCS, vol. 12105, pp. 769–793. Springer, Cham (2020). https://doi.org/10.1007/978-3-030-45721-1_27

[DGOT21] Delpech, C., Guilhem, S., Orsini, E., Tanguy, T.: Limbo: efficient zero-knowledge mpcith-based arguments. To appear in Proceedings of ACM CCS 2021. Available at Cryptology ePrint Archive, Report 2021/215 (2021). https://eprint.iacr.org/2021/215

[DLN19] Damgård, I., Larsen, K.G., Nielsen, J.B.: Communication lower bounds for statistically secure MPC, with or without preprocessing. In: Boldyreva, A., Micciancio, D. (eds.) CRYPTO 2019. LNCS, vol. 11693, pp. 61–84. Springer, Cham (2019). https://doi.org/10.1007/978-3-030-26951-7_3

[Git21] zk-SNARKs argument size comparison (2021). https://github.com/emanuelegiunta/snarks_comparison

[GM10] Gao, S., Mateer, T.: Additive fast fourier transforms over finite fields. IEEE Trans. Inf. Theory **56**(12), 6265–6272 (2010)

[GSV21] Gvili, Y., Scheffler, S., Varia, M.: Booligero: improved sublinear zero knowledge proofs for boolean circuits. To appear in phProceedings of Financial Crypto 2021. Available at Cryptology ePrint Archive (2021). https://eprint.iacr.org/2021/121.pdf

[IKOS07] Ishai, Y., Kushilevitz, E., Ostrovsky, R., Sahai, A.: Zero-knowledge from secure multiparty computation. In: Johnson, D.S., Feige, U. (eds.) 39th ACM STOC, pp. 21–30. ACM Press (2007)

[lib20] Libiop (2020). https://github.com/scipr-lab/libiop

[Mer90] Merkle, R.C.: A certified digital signature. In: Brassard, G. (ed.) CRYPTO 1989. LNCS, vol. 435, pp. 218–238. Springer, New York (1990). https://doi.org/10.1007/0-387-34805-0_21

[Mic94] Micali, S.: CS proofs (extended abstracts). In: 35th FOCS, pp. 436–453. IEEE Computer Society Press (1994)

[PS21] Polychroniadou, A., Song, Y.: Constant-overhead unconditionally secure multiparty computation over binary fields. In: Canteaut, A., Standaert, F.-X. (eds.) EUROCRYPT 2021. LNCS, vol. 12697, pp. 812–841. Springer, Cham (2021). https://doi.org/10.1007/978-3-030-77886-6_28

[RRR16] Reingold, O., Rothblum, G.N., Rothblum, R.D.: Constant-round interactive proofs for delegating computation. In: Wichs, D., Mansour, Y. (eds.) 48th ACM STOC, pp. 49–62. ACM Press (2016)

[Set20] Setty, S.: Spartan: efficient and general-purpose zkSNARKs without trusted setup. In: Micciancio, D., Ristenpart, T. (eds.) CRYPTO 2020. LNCS, vol. 12172, pp. 704–737. Springer, Cham (2020). https://doi.org/10.1007/978-3-030-56877-1_25

[Wee05] Wee, H.: On round-efficient argument systems. In: Caires, L., Italiano, G.F., Monteiro, L., Palamidessi, C., Yung, M. (eds.) ICALP 2005. LNCS, vol. 3580, pp. 140–152. Springer, Heidelberg (2005). https://doi.org/10.1007/11523468_12

[WTS+18] Wahby, R.S., Tzialla, I., Shelat, A., Thaler, J., Walfish, M.: Doubly-efficient zksnarks without trusted setup. In: 2018 IEEE Symposium on Security and Privacy (SP), pp. 926–943. IEEE (2018)

Zero Knowledge Proofs Towards Verifiable Decentralized AI Pipelines

Nitin Singh[(✉)], Pankaj Dayama, and Vinayaka Pandit

IBM Research Lab, Bangalore, India
{nitisin1,pankajdayama,pvinayak}@in.ibm.com

Abstract. We are witnessing the emergence of decentralized AI pipelines wherein different organisations are involved in the different steps of the pipeline. In this paper, we introduce a comprehensive framework for verifiable provenance for decentralized AI pipelines with support for confidentiality concerns of the owners of data and model assets. Although some of the past works address different aspects of provenance, verifiability, and confidentiality, none of them address all the aspects under one uniform framework. We present an efficient and scalable approach for verifiable provenance for decentralized AI pipelines with support for confidentiality based on *zero-knowledge proofs* (ZKPs). Our work is of independent interest to the fields of *verifiable computation* (VC) and *verifiable model inference*. We present methods for basic computation primitives like read only memory access and operations on datasets that are an order of magnitude better than the state of the art. In the case of verifiable model inference, we again improve the state of the art for decision tree inference by an order of magnitude. We present an extensive experimental evaluation of our system.

1 Introduction

In this paper we consider a *decentralized* AI pipeline with multiple independent organizations wherein one set of organizations specialize in curating high quality datasets based on independent data sources, another set of organizations specialise in training models from the curated datasets, and another set of organizations deploy the trained models and provide them as a service to the *model consumers*. A typical decentralized AI pipeline is shown in Fig. 1. The core *assets* like datasets and models represent significant intellectual property for their respective owners. Therefore, it is essential for the *asset owners* to ensure the confidentiality of their assets beyond the intended usage. On the other hand, since the model consumers are likely to use them for driving major decisions, they would like to ensure *auditability* and *integrity* of the models by (i) verifying the provenance and performance of the models on benchmark datasets[1] and (ii) ensuring that the predictions from the deployed service match with that of the verified model. In summary, decentralized AI pipelines need to provide end to end provenance while ensuring the confidentiality of different assets.

---

[1] Provenance of the model training step is not considered in this paper.

© International Financial Cryptography Association 2022
I. Eyal and J. Garay (Eds.): FC 2022, LNCS 13411, pp. 248–275, 2022.
https://doi.org/10.1007/978-3-031-18283-9_12

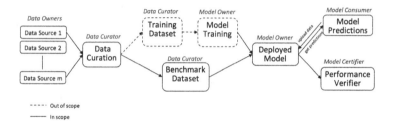

Fig. 1. Typical decentralized AI pipeline.

Consider an example of deciding on mortgage applications using an AI service. A data service provider, SP, provides high quality training and benchmark datasets by curating historical mortgage data from reputationally trusted financial institutes. A specialized fintech company, FC, trains and deploys an AI model as a service for the given task. Further, it makes a public claim on the model performance on benchmark dataset. Note that establishing provenance of model training carried out by FC is not addressed in this work. A financial institute, CONS, wanting to use AI in mortgage approval process would want to independently verify the claim made by FC before deciding to subscribe to the service. If CONS is satisfied after the verification process, it might use the deployed service to make decision on mortgage applications. At this time, CONS and individual mortgage applicants should be able to independently verify that the predictions from the deployed service match with that of the verified model. The reputationally trusted data owners and FC would like to protect the confidentiality of their assets except from those actors who are entitled to access them. We would like to highlight a special and important requirement of FC: to prevent model reengineering attacks, the FC would like to ensure that the model verifier does not get to learn the predictions of the models on individual instances during the process of verification.

We present significant progress towards describing efficient and scalable approach to provide public verifiability for common operations in an AI pipeline, while preserving confidentiality of involved data and model assets. In the paper we have highlighted few primitive operations, but more operations on both data and models can be added as state of the art improves. While it is difficult to match the expressiveness of what is possible via plain-text computations, our methods can nevertheless provide provenance over simpler pipelines.

1.1 Related Work

While there is no prior work that addresses all the aspects of verifiable distributed AI pipeline as introduced in this paper, there are past works that address different aspects of the overall requirements. The provenance requirement is addressed in [19,21], the model verification or certification requirement is addressed in [15,22], and the verifiable inference from private model requirement is addressed in [11,14,18,23,28]. Our work is of independent interest to the field of *Verifiable*

Computation (VC) as it provides more efficient methods for useful computational primitives like *Read Only Memory* (ROM) access and operations on datasets. We briefly review and contrast the relevant literature with our work.

Provenance Models for AI: There has recently been considerable interest in the provenance of AI assets. For instance, [19,21] provide good motivation and DLT based architecture for establishing provenance of AI assets. The provenance is enabled by recording the cryptographic hash of each asset on the tamper-proof ledger, and recording any operations on them as transactions. While this provides auditability and lineage of an asset, its verification necessarily involves revealing the assets, thereby violating the confidentiality requirements in our setting. We build on the tools from verifiable computation to enable verifiability of assets and operations on them while supporting all the stated confidentiality requirements.

Model Certification for AI: Training and testing AI models for fairness and bias is an area of active research. Recently, efforts have been made to leverage methods from *secure multiparty computation* (MPC) to enable fair training and certification of AI models while ensuring privacy of sensitive data of the participants [15,22]. These methods require a trusted party (e.g. a regulator) to certify the claims on the models and therefore, do not support the public verifiability requirement in our setting.

Verifiable Model Inference: The problem of verifying the predictions from private AI models, with different privacy requirements, has been considered in the literature. For instance, verifiable execution of neural networks has been considered in [14,18,23,27] and verification of predictions from decision trees has been considered in [28]. These works cannot be extended for end to end pipeline verification as they cannot handle verification of operations on datasets. In our work, apart from providing verification for the entire AI pipeline, we improve upon the work of [28] by making the verification of the decision tree inference more scalable as described in Sect. 1.2.

Reusable Gadgets for VC: On the technical front, our work complements persistent efforts such as [16,25] to enable more computations efficiently in the VC setting. The problem of efficiently supporting addressable memory inside VC circuits has received considerable attention [3,5,16,25,31] as many computations are best expressed using the abstraction of memory. Methods in aforementioned efforts support arbitrary *zero knowledge Succinct Arguments of Knowledge* (zkSNARKs). We provide a more efficient variant of prior methods, leveraging a zkSNARK with *commit and prove* capability (see Sect. 3). However, this is not a major hinderance as many efficient zkSNARKs can be modified to be commit and prove with negligible overhead (see [8]). Our efficient abstractions for read only memory (ROM) and datasets can be incorporated into zkSNARK circuit compilers such as ZokRates [10], when suitably targeted for a commit and prove backend. In particular, supporting datasets as first class primitives in zkSNARK compilers will make them more attractive for privacy preserving data science applications. Finally we mention that the work on *Verifiable Outsourced*

Databases (e.g. [29,30]) is not directly applicable here as (i) current implementations do not address data confidentiality and (ii) they do not support reusable representation of datasets across computations.

1.2   Our Contributions

We present the first efficient and scalable system for decentralized AI pipelines with support for confidentiality concerns of the asset owners (as described in Table 2) and public verifiability. Our work represents major system level innovations in the areas of model certification ([15] - lacks public verifiability, provenance), provenance architectures for AI artifacts ([19,21] - lack privacy), and confidentiality preserving model inference ([14,23,28] - lack provenance). A number of technical contributions enable this system level novelty and they are summarized as follows.

- Improved method for read-only memory access in arithmetic circuits with an order of magnitude gain in efficiency over the existing methods (see Table 3). The improved memory access protocol is crucially used in realizing efficient circuits for data operations (inner-join) and decision tree inference.
- A method for consistent modeling of datasets in arithmetic circuits with complete privacy. In addition, we design efficient circuits to prove common operations on datasets. We make several optimizations over the basic approach of using zkSNARKs resulting in at least an order of magnitude gain in efficiency (see Table 4). On commodity hardware, our implementation scales well to prove operations on datasets with up to 1 million rows in a few minutes. The verification takes few hundred milliseconds.
- We present an improved protocol for privacy preserving verifiable inference from decision tree. Our method yields up to ten times smaller verification circuits by avoiding expensive one-time hashing of the tree used in [28]. Further leveraging our method for read-only memory access, we also incur fewer multiplication gates per prediction (see Sect. 5 for more details). Comparative performance under different settings is summarized in Table 5.
- We implement our scheme using Adaptive-Pinocchio [24] to experimentally evaluate the efficacy of our scheme. We report the results in Sect. 6. Our scheme can also be instantiated with other CP-SNARKs.

Our implementation uses pre-processing zkSNARKs [5,9,13,20] which pre-process a circuit description to make subsequent proving and verification more efficient. Our circuits can also be used with generic zkSNARKs such as those in [2,4,7], suitably augmented with commit and prove capability.

2   Verifiable Provenance in Decentralized AI Pipelines

A typical AI pipeline consists of different steps, such as accessing raw datasets from multiple sources, performing aggregation and transformations in order to curate training and testing datasets for the AI task on hand, developing the AI

Table 1. Performance of our dataset operations. For concrete numbers we took number of rows $N = 100K$ and bit-width of elements $b = 32$.

Operation	Complexity (asymptotic)	Complexity (concrete)	Prov. time (s)	Ver. time (ms)
Aggregation	$O(N)$	2.1 mil	37	400
Filter	$O(N)$	0.7 mil	12	400
Order-By	$O(bN)$	3.1 mil	50	400
Inner-Join	$O(bN)$	6.5 mil	80	400

model, and deploying it in production. We are interested in settings in which the AI pipeline is decentralized, i.e., different steps of the pipeline are carried out by different independent actors. We assume five different type of actors: data owners(DO), data curators(DC), model owners(MO), model certifiers(MCERT), and model consumers(MCONS). For brevity of exposition, we assume that the number of data curators, model owners, model certifiers, and model consumers is just one. However, all the concepts and results extend in a straight forward manner to the general setting involving multiple entities of each type.

We assume that there is a task T for which the process of building an AI pipeline is undertaken in a decentralized setting. The salient features of our provenance and certification framework is summarized as follows.

There are m data owners $DO_1, DO_2, \ldots, DO_m$ who share their respective raw datasets $D_1, D_2, \ldots, D_m$ privately with the data curator DC and also make a public commitment of the datasets. The data curator curates a dataset $D_b = f(D_1, D_2, \ldots, D_m)$ for the purpose of benchmarking the performance of an AI model for the task T and makes a public commitment of D_b. We assume the model owner, MO, has a pre-trained AI model M and wants to offer it as a service. MO makes a public commitment of the model. MO buys the benchmark dataset D_b from DC. MO wishes to convince potential consumers of the utility of the model M by making performance claim $accuracy = score(M, D_b)$ when M is used for getting predictions on the dataset D_b. The model certifier, MCERT, should be able to independently verify the provenance of all the steps and the claimed performance of the model M. MCERT also ensures that the timestamp of the public commitment of model M is earlier than the timestamp of public commitment of D_b to ensure that the model M cannot be overfitted to the dataset D_b. MCERT certifies the model M only after verifying the correctness of the claim. The model consumer, MCONS, subscribes to the model M only upon its successful certification. Suppose MCONS supplies a valid input data D' to the service provided by MO and gets a prediction Y'. We require that MCONS should be able to independently verify that the prediction Y' matches with the prediction of the committed model M on the instance D'.

We observe that the outlined requirements ensure that the decentralized AI pipeline is transparent. The key question we address in this paper is that of providing such a transparency while satisfying the confidentiality requirements of all the actors. We assume that none of the actors in the set up have any incentive to collude with the others, but, can act maliciously. The privacy requirements and security model of different actors is summarized in Table 2.

Table 2. Summary of privacy requirements and trust assumptions in our setting.

Participant	Confidentiality requirement	Security model
DOs	P1: Only DC can access their plaintext data	S1: Trusted to provide the correct data
DC	P2: Only MO can access curated plaintext data	S2: Not trusted with the correct computation
MO	P3: No one can access the plaintext model P4: During the certification, MCERT cannot get access to prediction of M for any instance in the dataset D_b	S3: Not trusted to make the right performance claim or use the certified model for providing predictions
MCERT	NA	S4: Trusted to certify the model only after end to end provenance is verified
MCONS	P5: No one other than model owner (optional) can access its data in clear	NA

We present a provenance framework which ensures trust in the AI pipeline by proving each computation step using zero-knowledge proofs, thus meeting all the confidentiality requirements captured in Table 2. Below, we present a concrete example of an AI pipeline for establishing fairness of an AI model, where we clearly highlight involvement of various actors.

2.1 Decentralized Model Fairness

Increasingly, AI models are required to be fair (i.e. non-discriminating) with respect to protected attributes (e.g. Gender). There are several metrics which are used to evaluate a model for fairness. For the sake of illustration, we choose the popular metric called *predictive parity*, which requires a model to have similar accuracy for different values of the protected attribute. In our specific example, our goal is to show that for binary classification model M we have:

$$\left| \Pr[M(\boldsymbol{x}) = y \mid \mathsf{Gender}(\boldsymbol{x}) = \mathsf{M}] - \Pr[M(\boldsymbol{x}) = y \mid \mathsf{Gender}(\boldsymbol{x}) = \mathsf{F}] \right| \leq \varepsilon$$

where $(\boldsymbol{x}, y) \sim \mathcal{D}$ for representative distribution $\mathcal{D}$. We may estimate the above metric emperically on a test data T consisting of samples $\{(\boldsymbol{x}_i, y_i)\}_{i=1}^n$. For concreteness, let M be a decision tree model developed by model owner MO to be used by financial institutions for approving home mortgage loan applications. Let D_1 and D_2 be two *private* datasets consisting of loan applications, which are owned by financial instituions DO$_1$ and DO$_2$ respectively. A data curator DC curates the dataset T by concatenating (row-wise) datasets D_1, D_2 and further generates datasets T_M, T_F consisting of applications with *male* and *female* applicants respectively. Finally the model owner MO obtains datsets T_M and T_F and computes the accuracy of its model on the respective datasets. In Fig. 2, the top left code block shows the operations executed by different actors in the pipeline without verifiability. The remaining code blocks show operations performed by actors in a verifiable pipeline. The asset owners publicly commit their private assets (bottom left) and generate proofs to attest correctness of their operations on assets (top right). Finally, a verifier (e.g. auditor) uses published commitments and proofs to establish the correctness of steps performed by respective actors in the pipeline (bottom right).

Fig. 2. Example pipeline for certifying financial model for fairness.

3 Overview

This section provides overview of the technical challenges in instantiating our solution. More detailed technical contributions appear in Sects. 4 and 5.

3.1 Building Blocks

Cryptographic Primitives: We use zkSNARKs as the main cryptographic tool to verify correctness of data operations and model inference while maintaining confidentiality of the respective assets. A zkSNARK consists of a triple of algorithms $(\mathsf{G}, \mathsf{P}, \mathsf{V})$ where (i) G takes description of a computation as an arithmetic circuit C and outputs public parameters $\mathsf{pp} \leftarrow \mathsf{G}(1^\lambda, C)$, (ii) P takes pp and a satisfying instance $(\boldsymbol{x}, \boldsymbol{w})$ for C and outputs a proof $\pi \leftarrow \mathsf{P}(\mathsf{pp}, \boldsymbol{x}, \boldsymbol{w})$ while (iii) V takes pp, statement $\boldsymbol{x}$ and a proof π and outputs $b \leftarrow \mathsf{V}(\mathsf{pp}, \boldsymbol{x}, \pi)$. The proof π reveals no knowledge of the witness $\boldsymbol{w}$, while an accepting proof π implies that prover knows a satisfying assignment $(\boldsymbol{x}, \boldsymbol{w})$ with overwhelming probability. A *commit and prove* zkSNARK (CP-SNARK) allows proving knowledge of witness $\boldsymbol{w}$ as before, where part of $\boldsymbol{w}$ additionally opens a public commitment c, i.e. $\boldsymbol{w} = (\boldsymbol{u}, \boldsymbol{z})$ and $\mathsf{Open}(c) = \boldsymbol{u}$. A CP-SNARK specifies a commitment scheme Com and like a zkSNARK, it provides algorithms G, P and V for generating public parameters, generating proofs and verifying proofs respectively. Additionally, a CP-SNARK allows one to generate proofs over data committed using Com with negligible overhead in proof generation and verification.

Notation: We use the notation $[n]$ to denote the set of natural numbers $\{1, \ldots, n\}$. We often use the array notation $\boldsymbol{x}[i]$ to denote the ith component of the vector $\boldsymbol{x}$, with 1 as the starting index. We will denote the concatenation of vectors $\boldsymbol{x}$ and $\boldsymbol{y}$ as $[\![\boldsymbol{x}, \boldsymbol{y}]\!]$. All our arithmetic circuits, vectors and matrices are over a finite field $\mathbb{F}$ of prime order.

Circuits for Dataset Operations: To use zkSNARKs, we express operations on datasets as arithmetic circuits. At a high level, arithmetic circuits representing data operations accept *datasets* as their inputs and outputs. Since establishing provenance of an asset in an AI pipeline requires verifying operations over several related assets, we require *uniform* representation of datasets across arithmetic circuits, which would allow a dataset to be used as inputs/outputs in different circuits. The second design constraint we enforce is that arithmetic circuits to be *universal*, i.e., the same circuit can be used to verify operations on all datasets within a known size bound. We need universal circuits for two primary reasons: (i) the sizes of datasets are considered confidential and must not be inferable from the circuits being used, and (ii) the circuits can be *pre-processed* to yield efficient verification as it is a frequent operation in our applications.

Dataset Representation in Circuits: As we use the same circuit to represent operations over datasets of varying sizes, we first describe a *uniform* representation of datasets which can be used within the arithmetic circuits. Let N denote a known upper bound on the size of input/output datasets. We view a dataset as a collection of its column vectors (of size at most N). We encode a vector of size at most N as $N + 1$ size vector $[\![s, \boldsymbol{X}]\!]$ where $\boldsymbol{X} = (\boldsymbol{X}[1], \ldots, \boldsymbol{X}[N])$ In this encoding s denotes the size of the vector, $\boldsymbol{X}[1], \ldots, \boldsymbol{X}[s]$ contain the s entries of the vector, while $\boldsymbol{X}[i]$ for $i > s$ are set to 0^2. Similarly, a dataset is encoded by encoding each of its columns separately.

Dataset Commitment: Let Com be a vector commitment scheme associated with a CP-SNARK CP. We additionally assume that Com is homomorphic. To commit a vector $\boldsymbol{x}$, we first compute its encoding $\overline{\boldsymbol{x}}$ as a vector of size $N + 1$, and then compute $c = \mathsf{Com}(\overline{\boldsymbol{x}}, r)$ as its commitment. Here r denotes the commitment randomness. To commit a dataset $\boldsymbol{D}$ with columns $\boldsymbol{x}_1, \ldots, \boldsymbol{x}_M$, we commit each of its columns to obtain $\boldsymbol{c} = (c_1, \ldots, c_M)$, where $c_i = \mathsf{Com}(\boldsymbol{x}_i)$ as the commitment. Using our circuits with the CP-SNARK CP allows us to efficiently prove operations over committed datasets.

3.2 Optimizations

We now highlight optimizations that are pivotal to the scalability of our system:

Mitigating Commitment Overhead: To prove statements over committed values using general zkSNARKs, one generally needs to compute the commitment as part of the arithmetic circuit expressing the computation. This introduces substantial overhead, when the amount of data to be committed is large. To avoid this,

---

^{2} This introduces no ambiguity if 0 is legitimately part of the vector, as s specifies the content of the vector.

we use a CP-SNARK and its associated commitment scheme. We instantiate our system using Adaptive-Pinnochio [24], as the CP-SNARK. Adaptive-Pinnochio augments the popular Pinnochio [20] zkSNARK with commit and prove capability. The resulting scheme incurs $\leq 5\%$ overhead in proof generation time over Pinnochio, while verification continues to be efficient (≤ 400 ms) in practice. We expect similar savings with other CP-SNARK schemes, and thus our constructs are agnostic to the choice of CP-SNARK.

Circuit Decomposition: For some operations, verification is more efficient when decomposed as two or more circuits, than when encoded as a monolithic circuit. Let $C(x, u, w)$ be an arithmetic circuit which checks some property on (x, u) where u additionally opens the commitment c. Our decomposition takes the form $C(x, u, w) \equiv C_1(x, u, w_0, w_1) \wedge C_2(x, u, w_0, w_2)$ where $w = (w_0, w_1, w_2)$ denotes a suitable partition of witness wires. Using a CP-SNARK we let the prover provide an additional commitment c_0 for the witness wires w_0 which are common to both the sub-circuits. In our decompositions, we let C_1 encode relation that is easily verified by an arithmetic circuit and let C_2 encode the relation which has substantially cheaper probabilistic verification circuit, i.e., there exists a circuit $\widetilde{C}_2(\alpha, x, u, w_0, w_2)$ which takes additional random challenge α and has identical output to C_2 with overwhelming probability (over random choices of α). In our constructions, the latter circuit verifies either the *simultaneous permutation* property or *consistent memory access* property which we introduce below. These are inefficient to check deterministically using arithmetic circuits but admit efficient probabilistic circuits.

3.3   Simultaneous Permutation

We say that tuples $(u_1, \ldots, u_k)$ and $(v_1, \ldots, v_k)$ of vectors in $\mathbb{F}^N$ satisfy the *simultaneous permutation* relation if there exists a permutation σ of $[N]$ such that $v_i = \sigma(u_i)$ for all $i \in [k]$. We now describe protocol to check the relation over committed vectors: i.e., given commitments $\mathsf{cu}_1, \ldots, \mathsf{cu}_k, \mathsf{cv}_1, \ldots, \mathsf{cv}_k$ the prover shows knowledge of vectors $u_1, \ldots, u_k$ and $v_1, \ldots, v_k$ corresponding to the commitments which satisfy the relation. To achieve this, the verifier first sends a challenge $\beta_1, \ldots, \beta_k$ and challenges the prover to show that β-linear combinations of the vectors $u = \sum_{i=1}^{k} \beta_i u_i$, $v = \sum_{i=1}^{k} \beta_i v_i$, corresponding to commitments $\mathsf{cu} = \sum_{i=1}^{k} \beta_i \mathsf{cu}_i$, $\mathsf{cv} = \sum_{i=1}^{k} \beta_i \mathsf{cv}_i$ are permutations of each other. This is accomplished via a further challenge $\alpha \leftarrow \mathbb{F}$ and subsequently chekcing $\prod_{i=1}^{N}(\alpha - u[i]) = \prod_{i=1}^{N}(\alpha - v[i])$. We describe the formal protocol and its analysis in Appendix C.1. The last computation can be expressed in an arithmetic circuit using $O(N)$ multiplication gates which is concretely more efficient compared to deterministic circuits for checking permutation relation using routing networks [6, 26].

3.4   Consistent Memory Access

We define *consistent memory access* relation for a triple of vectors L, U and V where $L \in \mathbb{F}^n$ and $U, V \in \mathbb{F}^m$ for some integers m, n. We say that (L, U, V)

Table 3. Comparison of Circuit Complexity for different ROM approaches. ZK and CP denote zkSNARK and CP-SNARK protocols. m and n denote number of reads and memory size respectively.

	Circuit complexity	Circuit complexity ($m = n = 10000$)	Backend
Linear scan	$2mn$	200 mill	ZK
Routing networks [6, 26]	$(m + n)(3\log(m + n) + 3\log m)$	5.7 mill	ZK
Buffet [25]	$m(21 + 2\log n + 10\log m)$	1.9 mill	ZK
xJSNARK [16]	$m(2\sqrt{n} + \log n)$	2.1 mill	ZK
Our work	$5(m + n)$	0.1 mill	CP

satisy the relation if $V[i] = L[U[i]]$ for all $i \in [m]$. We think of $\boldsymbol{L}$ as *read only memory* (ROM) which is accessed at locations given by $\boldsymbol{U}$ with $\boldsymbol{V}$ being the corresponding values. We adapt the techniques in [3,5,25,31] to take advantage of CP-SNARKs in our construction. Next, we present a protocol to check the relation given commitments to $\boldsymbol{L}, \boldsymbol{U}$ and $\boldsymbol{V}$. The verification proceeds as:

1. First $m + n$ sized vectors $\boldsymbol{u}$ and $\boldsymbol{v}$ are computed as follows: For the vector $\boldsymbol{u}$ we require $\boldsymbol{u}[i] = i$ for $i \in [n]$ and $\boldsymbol{u}[i + n] = \boldsymbol{U}[i]$ for $i \in [m]$. For the vector $\boldsymbol{v}$ we require $\boldsymbol{v}[i] = \boldsymbol{L}[i]$ for $i \in [n]$ and $\boldsymbol{v}[i + n] = \boldsymbol{V}[i]$ for $i \in [m]$ (see Fig. 3).
2. The prover also supplies auxiliary vectors $\tilde{\boldsymbol{u}}$ and $\tilde{\boldsymbol{v}}$ of size $m + n$, where $\tilde{\boldsymbol{u}}$ and $\tilde{\boldsymbol{v}}$ are purportedly obtained from $\boldsymbol{u}$ and $\boldsymbol{v}$ via the same permutation.
3. Finally, we ensure that the vector $\tilde{\boldsymbol{u}}$ is sorted and that the vector $\tilde{\boldsymbol{v}}$ differs in adjacent positions only if the same is true for those positions in vector $\tilde{\boldsymbol{u}}$.

The constraints on the first n entries of vectors $\boldsymbol{u}$ and $\boldsymbol{v}$ in step (1) can be thought of as "loading" constraints that load the entries of $\boldsymbol{L}$ against corresponding address in memory, while constraints on the last m entries can be thought of as "fetching" constraints that fetch the appropriate value against the specified memory location. The steps (2) and (3) ensure that the value fetched for a given location is same as the value loaded against it during the initial loading steps. We decompose above checks across two circuits. The first arithmetic circuit $\mathsf{C}_{\mathsf{ROM},m,n}$ ensures steps (1) and (3) while the second circuit checks that vectors $\tilde{\boldsymbol{u}}, \tilde{\boldsymbol{v}}$ are obtained by applying the same permutation to vectors $\boldsymbol{u}, \boldsymbol{v}$ respectively. The circuit $\mathsf{C}_{\mathsf{ROM},m,n}$ can be realized using $O(m + n)$ multiplication gates. Generally, verifying that a vector such as $\tilde{\boldsymbol{u}}$ is sorted in step (3) incurs logarithmic overhead due to the need for bit decomposition of each element. However, we can leverage the fact that $\tilde{\boldsymbol{u}}$ is a (sorted) rearrangement of $\boldsymbol{u}$, which includes all elements of $[n]$ by construction. Thus, monotonicity of $\tilde{\boldsymbol{u}}$ is established provided (i) $\tilde{\boldsymbol{u}}[n] = 1$, (ii) $\tilde{\boldsymbol{u}}[m + n] = n$ and $\tilde{\boldsymbol{u}}[i + 1] - \tilde{\boldsymbol{u}}[i] \in \{0, 1\}$ for all $1 \le i \le m + n - 1$, which together require $O(m + n)$ gates to verify. Finally, we invoke the protocol for "Simultaneous Permutation" property in Sect. 3.3 to check compliance of step (2). We illustrate the verification circuit and the decomposition in Fig. 3. The formal protocol and analysis appears in Appendix C.2. Overall we incur $O(m+n)$

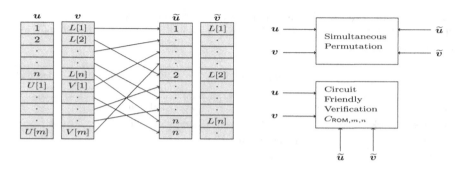

Fig. 3. Consistent memory access

gates, which is more efficient than encoding entire relation in one circuit. In that case one uses routing networks which incur $O((m+n)\log(m+n))$ gates and are concretely much more expensive. We can optimize further when the same access pattern is used for accessing different ROMs as described below.

Multiplexed Memory Access. For access pattern $U \in \mathbb{F}^m$ and ROMs $L_j \in \mathbb{F}^n$ for $j \in [k]$, we can show the correctness of lookup values $V_j[i] = L_j[U[i]]$, $i \in [M], j \in [k]$ using just one instance of protocol discussed in this section. To achieve this, the verifier sends a random challenge $\alpha_1, \ldots, \alpha_k$ to the prover. The prover then shows that (L, U, V) satisfy correct memory access where $L = \alpha_1 L_1 + \cdots + \alpha_k L_k$ and $V = \alpha_1 V_1 + \cdots + \alpha_k V_k$ for uniformly sampled $\alpha_1, \ldots, \alpha_k$. Note that due to the homomorphism of the commitment scheme, both the prover and the verifier can compute the commitments for L, U and V.

3.5 Our Techniques in Perspective

Commit and prove functionality in conjunction with zero knowledge proofs has been used in recent works addressing privacy in machine learning, most notably in [18,27,28]. In [18] and [28], CP-SNARKs are used to "link" proofs of correctness for different parts of the circuit (similar to Circuit Decomposition in our setting) to prove inference from a private neural network and a decision tree respectively. In [27], public commitments are linked to set of *authenticated inputs* between a prover and a verifier in a two party protocol. Subsequently the prover produces a ZK proof showing correctness of neural network inference over authenticated inputs. In contrast, our usage of CP-SNARKs is more pervasive. We first optimize key relations (simultaneous permutation, consistent memory access) for CP-SNARKs and then design our dataset representation in a way that allows us to represent operations on them in terms of aforementioned relations.

4 Privacy Preserving Dataset Operations

We now describe protocols for common dataset operations such as `aggregation`, `filter`, `order-by`, `inner-join` etc. These operations serve to illustrate our key techniques, which can be further applied to yeild protocols for much more comprehensive list of dataset operations. We use the fact that most of the operations distribute nicely as identical computations over different pairs of columns. Throughout this section, N denotes the upper bound on the sizes of input/output datasets.

Aggregation: Aggregation operation takes two datasets as inputs and outputs their row-wise concatenation. We first describe arithmetic circuit to verify the concatenation of vectors. The circuit accepts three vectors in their uniform representation as discussed in Sect. 3.1. Let x, y, z be three vectors of size at most N represented as $[\![s, X]\!]$, $[\![t, Y]\!]$ and $[\![w, Z]\!]$ respectively where X, Y, Z are vectors of size N. The verification involves ensuring that the first w entries of Z contain the first s entries of X and the first t entries of Y. Figure 4 illustrates the setting for $s = 3$, $t = 4$, $w = 7$ and $N = 9$. To aid the verification, the prover provides N-length binary vectors ρ_s, ρ_t and ρ_w as auxiliary inputs. The vector ρ_s is 1 in its first s entires, and 0 elsewhere. Similar relation is satisfied by ρ_t and ρ_w. The correctness of aggregation now reduces to showing that there is a permutation that simultaneously maps $[\![\rho_s, \rho_t]\!]$ to $[\![\rho_w, 0]\!]$ and $[\![X, Y]\!]$ to $[\![Z, 0]\!]$. Figure 4 also shows how the verification is decomposed: The first circuit checks that (i) $w = s + t$, (ii) vectors ρ_s, ρ_t, ρ_t are correctly provided and (iii) ensures $u_1 = [\![\rho_s, \rho_t]\!]$, $v_1 = [\![X, Y]\!]$, $u_2 = [\![\rho_w, 0]\!]$ and $v_2 = [\![Z, 0]\!]$. The second circuit checks the "simultaneous permutation" property on the pairs (u_1, v_1) and (u_2, v_2). Both the circuits can be realized using $O(N)$ multiplication gates. Using a CP-SNARK we can verify the correctness of aggregation of vectors over commitments.

We now leverage the above construction to verify aggregation operation over datasets. Let D_x, D_y and D_z be datasets each with k columns given by $(x_i)_{i=1}^{k}, (y_i)_{i=1}^{k}$ and $(z_i)_{i=1}^{k}$ respectively. The reduction technique involves the verifier sampling random $\alpha_1, \ldots, \alpha_k$ satisfying $\alpha_1 + \cdots + \alpha_k = 1$. Next, we use the above circuit construction with a CP-SNARK to prove that vectors $x = \sum_{i=1}^{k} \alpha_i x_i$,$y = \sum_{i=1}^{k} \alpha_i y_i$ and $z = \sum_{i=1}^{k} \alpha_i z_i$ satisfy the concatenation property. We give complete protocol and proof of the reduction in the Appendix C.3.

Filter: Filter operation involves a dataset and a selection predicate as inputs and subsequently outputs a dataset consisting of subset of rows satisfying the predicate. We divide the computation in two parts (i) Applying selection predicate to rows of the dataset to obtain a binary vector f which we call as *selection vector* and (ii) Applying selection vector to the source dataset to obtain the target dataset. The latter computation can be verified with techniques similar to those used in `aggregation` operation. For the first computation, we describe an efficient circuit for predicates of the form $\wedge_{i=1}^{k}(x_i == v_i)$ where $x_1, \ldots, x_k$ are the columns of the dataset. Once again the verifier chooses random $\alpha_1, \ldots, \alpha_k$ with $\sum_{i=1}^{k} \alpha_i = 1$ and challenges the prover to show that the selection vector f satisfies $f = (x == v)$ where $x = \sum_{i=1}^{k} \alpha_i x_i$ and $v = \sum_{i=1}^{k} \alpha_i v_i$. The relation $f = (x == v)$ can be verified using a circuit with $O(N)$ gates. Due to the homomorphism of the commitment scheme, the verifier can compute the commitment

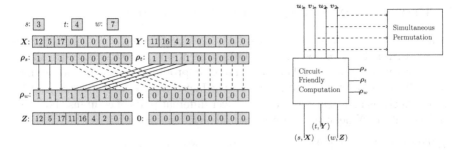

Fig. 4. Circuit for verifying vector concatenation

for vector x given the commitments to columns of the dataset. For more general range queries of the form $\wedge_{i=1}^{k}(\ell_i < x_i \leq r_i)$, we can compute selection vector f_i for each column, and then compute the final selection vector $f = \wedge_{i=1}^{k} f_i$.

Order By: Order-By relation involves permuting the rows of the dataset so that a specified column is in sorted order. The verification can be naturally expressed as columns of source and target dataset satisfying simultaneous permutation relation, where additionally the specified column is sorted. We can check the monotonicity of a column using a circuit with $O(bN)$ gates where b is the bit-width of the range of values in the column. We skip the details.

Inner-Join: Inner join operation concatenates pairs of rows of input datasets which have identical value for the designated columns (joining columns). We consider the inner-join operation under the restriction that the joining columns have distinct values. As a first step, we order both the input datasets so that the joining columns are sorted. We can use the verification protocol for `order-by` operation to ensure correctness of this step. We therefore assume that joining columns are sorted, and take distinct values. Let D_1 and D_2 be two datasets which are joined on columns x and y to yield the dataset D. We write D as juxtaposition of columns $[D_1', z, D_2']$ where D_i' denotes the columns coming from D_i while z denotes the column obtained as intersection of x and y. We first design sub-circuit for *private set intersection* (PSI) to compute the size w of the resulting dataset. We then let the prover provide auxiliary selection vectors f_1 and f_2 of size w. Finally, using the circuit for `filter` relation, we verify that f_1 applied to D_1 yields dataset $D_L = [D_1', z]$ and f_2 applied to D_2 yields the dataset $D_R = [D_2', z]$. The overall circuit complexity is $O(bN)$ where b is the bit-width of the range of values in x and y with set-intersection computation dominating the overall cost.

5   Privacy Preserving Model Inference: Decision Trees

In this section we present a zero knowledge protocol for verifiable inference from decision trees (and random forests). Decision trees are popular models in machine learning due to their interpretability. A decision tree recursively partitions the feature space (arranged as a tree), and finally assigns a label to each leaf segment. The problem of proving correct inference from a decision tree was considered recently in [28], where authors present a privacy preserving method for an adversary to commit to a decision tree and later prove inference from the tree on public test data. We present a new construction based on *consistent memory access*, which improves upon the prior construction by reducing the number of multiplication gates in the inference circuit. We also provide zero knowledge protocol for establishing the accuracy of a decision tree on test data. We consider variants with test data being public or private. The latter scenario is helpful while verifying performance of a private model on reputationally trusted private dataset.

Decision Tree Representation: We parameterize a binary decision tree with following parameters: the maximum number of nodes (N), the maximum length of a decision path (h) and maximum number of features used as predictors (d). We assume that the nodes in the decision tree have unique identifiers from the set $[N]$, while features are identified using indices in set $[d]$. We naturally represent a decision tree $\mathcal{T}$ as a lookup table with five columns, i.e., $\mathcal{T} = (\boldsymbol{V}, \boldsymbol{T}, \boldsymbol{L}, \boldsymbol{R}, \boldsymbol{C})$, where each column vector is of size N. For a decision tree with $t \leq N$ nodes, we encode as follows: For $i \in [t]$:

- $\boldsymbol{V}[i]$ denotes the identifier for the splitting feature for i^{th} node.
- $\boldsymbol{T}[i]$ denotes the threshold value for the splitting feature for i^{th} node.
- $\boldsymbol{L}[i]$ and $\boldsymbol{R}[i]$ denote the identifiers for the left and right child of ith node. In case of a leaf node, this value is set to i itself.
- $\boldsymbol{C}[i]$ denotes the label associated with the ith node, when it is a leaf node. For non-leaf nodes this may be set arbitrarily.

We commit to a decision tree, by committing to each of the vectors. We define $\mathsf{cm}_{\mathcal{T}} = (\mathsf{cm}_V, \mathsf{cm}_T, \mathsf{cm}_L, \mathsf{cm}_R, \mathsf{cm}_C)$ as the commitment to $\mathcal{T}$.

Decision Tree Inference: We model the test data D as $n \times d$ matrix, consisting of n d-dimensional samples. Let $\boldsymbol{D}$ be the vector of size dn obtained by flattening D in row major order. The algorithm below computes decision paths $\boldsymbol{p}_i = (\boldsymbol{p}_i[1], \ldots, \boldsymbol{p}_i[h])$ for each sample $i \in [n]$. The prediction vector $\boldsymbol{q}$ contains class labels corresponding to leaf nodes $\boldsymbol{p}_i[h]$ for $i \in [n]$.

1. For $i = 1, \ldots, n$ do:
   - Set $\boldsymbol{p}_i[1] = 1$: root is the first node on every decision path.
   - For $j = 1, \ldots, h$ determine next node as follows:
     (a) Compute splitting feature: $\boldsymbol{f}_i[j] = \boldsymbol{V}[\boldsymbol{p}_i[j]]$.
     (b) Compute threshold value: $\boldsymbol{t}_i[j] = \boldsymbol{T}[\boldsymbol{p}_i[j]]$.
     (c) Compute left and right child id: $\boldsymbol{l}_i[j] = \boldsymbol{L}[\boldsymbol{p}_i[j]], \boldsymbol{r}_i[j] = \boldsymbol{R}[\boldsymbol{p}_i[j]]$.
     (d) Compute label: $\boldsymbol{c}_i[j] = \boldsymbol{C}[\boldsymbol{p}_i[j]]$.
     (e) Compute $\hat{\boldsymbol{f}}_i[j] = d * i + \boldsymbol{f}_i[j]$.
     (f) Compute value of splitting feature: $\boldsymbol{v}_i[j] = D[i, \boldsymbol{f}_i[j]] = \boldsymbol{D}[\hat{\boldsymbol{f}}_i[j]]$.
     (g) Compute next node: $\boldsymbol{p}_i[j+1] = \boldsymbol{l}_i[j]$ if $\boldsymbol{v}_i[j] \leq \boldsymbol{t}_i[j]$ and $\boldsymbol{r}_i[j]$ otherwise.
   - Compute label for the sample: $\boldsymbol{q}[i] = \boldsymbol{c}_i[h]$.

Verification of the above algorithm involves verifying (i) hn memory accesses on the tables of $\mathcal{T}$ in steps (a)-(d), which share the access pattern $\boldsymbol{p}_i[j]$, (ii) verifying hn memory accesses on $\boldsymbol{D}$ (of size dn) in step (f) and (iii) hn comparisons as part of step (g). Using the optimization in Sect. 3.4, the first verification incurs $O(N + hn)$ multiplication gates, while the second verification incurs $O(dn + hn)$ multiplication gates. Using standard techniques, verification of (iii) can be made using $O(whn)$ multiplication gates, where w is the bit-width of feature values. Thus, overall circuit complexity of our solution is $O(N + n(d + h + wh))$. We compare our solution with the method for zero-knowledge decision tree (zkDT) inference presented in [28]. Broadly, the method in [28] establishes the correctness of inference as three checks:

- Consistency of input decision tree with public commitment: This involves $O(N)$ evaluations of the hash function $\mathcal{H}$ used for commitment and thus incurs $c(\mathcal{H}) \cdot N$ multiplication gates. Here $c(\mathcal{H})$ denotes the size of circuit required to evaluate $\mathcal{H}$.
- Consistency of feature vector with decision path: The verification of this step leverages a "Multiset Check" ([28, Section 4.1]) which costs $O(d \log h)$ multiplication gates per sample.
- Correct evaluation of decision tree function: It involves h comparisons for each sample, which incurs hw mutliplication gates, where w is the bit-width of feature values.

Above steps result in an overall circuit complexity of $c(\mathcal{H})N + n(3d \log h + hw)$ for zkDT. Our solution improves upon the approach in [28] by reducing the cost of the first two checks. Using a CP-SNARK, we avoid the cost of computing the commitment within the verification circuit, while using our optimized protocols for memory access allows us to accomplish the second check with an average cost of $O(h + d)$ gates per sample ($O(dn + hn)$ overall), which compares favorably with per sample cost of $O(d \log h)$ incurred by zkDT for $h = \Theta(d)$. The concrete improvement obtained using our approach depends on which of the three checks dominate the cost for specific parameter settings. We compare the cost of the two approaches for some representative parameter settings in Table 5.

Decision Tree Accuracy: The above circuit for decision tree inference can be easily modified to yield the circuit for proving accuracy of a decision tree on test data. In this case, the prediction vector is kept private, and tallied against ground truth to compute accuracy. Since our system also includes verifiability of model performance (accuracy) on *private* benchmark datasets, we briefly describe the modifications required to achieve the same. Let D be a private dataset with columns $(\boldsymbol{x}_1, \ldots, \boldsymbol{x}_d)$ with commitments to columns being public. Since, we can no longer compute the flattened vector $\boldsymbol{D}$ as before, we cannot verify the lookup $\boldsymbol{v}_i[j] = \boldsymbol{D}[\hat{\boldsymbol{f}}_i[j]]$. Instead we use polynomial interpolation to pre-process D. For i^{th} row $D[i, \cdot]$ of the original data (a vector of size d), we interpolate a polynomial p_i of degree $d-1$ such that $p(j) = D[i, j]$. We obtain the pre-processed dataset D' whose i^{th} row consists of coefficients of p_i. The data owner makes a commitment to D' instead of D. The lookup $\boldsymbol{v}_i[j] = D'[i, j] = p_i(j)$ now involves evaluating a $d-1$ degree polynomial which incurs d multiplication gates. The overall circuit complexity for accuracy over private datasets is therefore $O(N + hn + hnw + hnd)$.

Table 4. Measuring the efficacy of our optimizations on 100K× 10 datasets.

	No optimization	Partial optimization	Full optimization
`Aggregation`	19.3 mil	1.6 mil	0.21 mil
`Filter`	12.5 mil	0.7 mil	0.07 mil
`Inner-Join`	22.1 mil	4.4 mil	0.65 mil

Table 5. Comparison of Circuit Complexity for decision tree inference.

Test data size (n)	T1 = (1000,50,20)		T2 = (10000,35,25)	
	Our Work	zkDT [28]	Our Work	zkDT [28]
100	0.11 mil	3.1 mil	0.16 mil	30.1 mil
1000	1 mil	4.3 mil	1.2 mil	31 mil
10000	9.5 mil	16.5 mil	11.5 mil	41 mil

6 Experimental Evaluation

In this section we report the concrete performance of our system primitives. For our implementation, we used Adaptive Pinocchio [24] as the underlying CPSNARK, which we implemented using the `libsnark` [17] library. We also used the `libsnark` library for our circuit descriptions. Our experiments were performed on Ubuntu Linux 18.04 cloud instances with 8 Intel Xeon 2.10 GHz virtual cpus with 32 GB of RAM. The experiments were run with finite field arithmetic libraries and FFT libraries compiled to exploit multiple cores. We often use circuit complexity (multiplication gates in the circuit) as the "environment neutral" metric for comparing different approaches (the proving times scale quasi-linearly with circuit complexity).

Performance of Dataset Operations: Table 1 contains summary of asymptotic as well as concrete efficiency of our dataset operations. All the operations scale linearly with the number of rows (with marginal additive dependence on the number of columns). The numbers for proof generation and verification were generated for representative dataset size of $100K \times 10$. While proof generation is an expensive operation by general standards, it is practical enough for infrequent usage. We also tabulate the efficacy of our optimizations in Table 4. For the unoptimized case, we do not use CP-SNARKs and instead compute commitments using circuit-friendly MiMC hash [1]. For partially optimized case, we use native commitment scheme of CP-SNARK for commitments, but use monolithic circuits to encode the operations. To express permutations in monolithic circuits, we use gadgets for routing networks [6, 26] available in [17]. The fully optimized version delegates permutation checking and memory access check to probabilistic circuits as discussed in Sect. 3.2. In the first case, hashing dominates the circuit complexity resulting in 50–100 times larger circuits. Decomposing the circuits instead of monolithic circuits also results in an order of magnitude savings.

Table 6. Concrete proving and verification time for decision tree inference.

Test data size (n)	T1 = (1000,50,20)		T2 = (10000,35,25)	
	Prov.Time(s)	Ver.Time(ms)	Prov.Time(s)	Ver.Time(ms)
100	1	400	1	400
1000	5	400	6	400
10000	170	400	200	400

Performance of Decision Tree Inference: We use two decision trees $T1$ and $T2$ to benchmark performance of our decision tree inference implementation. We also use the same trees to compare our method with the one presented in [28]. We synthetically generate the tree $T1$ with 1000 nodes, 50 features and depth as 20, which roughly corresponds to the largest tree used in [28]. The tree $T2$ is trained on a curated version of dataset [12] for Home Mortgage Approval. We identify 35 features from the dataset to train binary decision tree. We train $T2$ with 10000 nodes and depth 25. We verify the inference from the two trees for batch sizes of 100 (small), 1000 (medium) and 10000 (large). Using our method to generate proof of predictions takes from few seconds (on small data) to few minutes (on large data), as seen in Table 6. The circuit complexity and the proving time scale almost linearly for our method. We also compare the multiplication gates incurred by arithmetic circuits in our method with that in [28] in Table 5. Our efficiency is an order of magnitude better for smaller data sizes, as we do not incur one time cost for hashing the tree. For larger batch sizes, our method is still about 1.5-4× more efficient. As the batch sizes get large, comparisons dominate the circuit complexity in both the approaches. We report the circuit complexity for proving the accuracy for decision trees on private datasets and public datasets. Table 7 shows that the overhead for proving accuracy on private datasets ranges from 50–80%.

Performance of Memory Access: We also independently benchmark the performance of our memory abstraction technique and compare it to existing methods in Table 3. Leveraging CP-SNARKs and probabilistic reductions we essentially incur *constant* number of gates per access. We compare different approaches both in terms of asymptotic complexity and concrete complexity for parameter settings representative of their usage in our work. Our concrete efficiency is an order of magnitude better than the alternatives considered.

Table 7. Circuit Complexity for decision tree accuracy for public and private benchmark datasets.

Test data size (n)	T1 = (1000,50,20)		T2 = (10000,35,25)	
	Public	Private	Public	Private
100	0.11 mil	0.18 mil	0.16 mil	0.23 mil
1000	1 mil	1.75 mil	1.2 mil	1.8 mil
10000	9.5 mil	17.4 mil	11.5 mil	18 mil

A   Preliminaries

We briefly summarise some key cryptographic notions that we use throughout the paper. For more details on the notions discussed below, we refer the reader to [8, Section 2].

A.1   Commitment Scheme

Definition 1. *A commitment scheme* Com = (Setup, Commit, VerCommit) *is a tuple of algorithms with message space $\mathcal{D}$, commitment space $\mathcal{C}$ and opening space $\mathcal{O}$ which satisfies* correctness, hiding *and* binding *as described below:*

- Setup(1^λ) $\to$ ck *takes security parameter λ and outputs commitment key* ck.
- Commit(ck, u) $\to$ (c, o) *takes commitment key* ck *and $u \in \mathcal{D}$ and outputs commitment $c \in \mathcal{C}$ and opening $o \in \mathcal{O}$.*
- VerCommit(ck, c, u, o) $\to$ b *takes commitment key* ck, *commitment c, message u and opening o and outputs $b \in \{0, 1\}$.*

Correctness: *A valid commitment always verifies correctly, i.e. for* ck $\leftarrow$ Setup(1^λ), $(c, o) \leftarrow$ Commit(ck, u), *with probability 1, we have* VerCommit(ck, c, u, o) = 1.

Binding: *It is infeasible for a polynomial time adversary to provide two openings to the same commitment.*

Hiding: *Commitments to any two messages are indistinguishable.*

A.2   Zero Knowledge Arguments

We define the notion of pre-processing *zero-knowledge Succinct Arguments of Knowledge* (zkSNARKs).

Definition 2. *A zkSNARK for a family of* NP *relations $\{\mathcal{R}_\lambda\}_{\lambda \in \mathbb{N}}$ is a tuple of algorithms* (G, P, V) *where:*

- G($1^\lambda, R$) $\to$ (pp, td) *takes security parameter and the relation $R \in \mathcal{R}_\lambda$ and outputs public parameters* pp = (pk, vk) *and a trapdoor* td. *In the above* pk *is called the* evaluation key *and* vk *is called the* verification key.
- P(pk, $\boldsymbol{x}, \boldsymbol{w}$) $\to$ π *takes the evaluation key, public input vector $\boldsymbol{x}$, witness vector $\boldsymbol{w}$ and outputs a proof π.*
- V(vk, $\boldsymbol{x}, \pi$) $\to$ b *takes the verification key, public input vector $\boldsymbol{x}$, a proof π and outputs $b = 1$ (accept) or $b = 0$ (reject).*

A zkSNARK $\mathcal{S}$ = (G, P, V) satisfies the following properties:

Completeness: *For all* $(R, \boldsymbol{x}, \boldsymbol{w})$ *such that* $R \in \mathcal{R}_\lambda$ *and* $R(\boldsymbol{x}, \boldsymbol{w}) = 1$, *the following probability is 1.*

$$\Pr[\pi \leftarrow \mathsf{P}(\mathsf{pk}, \boldsymbol{x}, \boldsymbol{w}); \mathsf{V}(\mathsf{vk}, \boldsymbol{x}, \pi) = 1]$$

Knowledge Soundness: *Let* $\mathcal{RG}$ *denote a* relation generator *and* $\mathcal{Z}$ *denote a (benign) auxiliary input generator. Then the zkSNARK* $\mathcal{S}$ *is called* knowledge sound *for* $(\mathcal{RG}, \mathcal{Z})$ *if for all efficient provers* P^*, *there exists an extractor* E^{P^*} *such that the following probability is negligible:*

$$\Pr \left[\begin{array}{c} (R, aux_R) \leftarrow \mathcal{RG}, \mathsf{pp} \leftarrow \mathsf{G}(1^\lambda, R) \\ Z \leftarrow \mathcal{Z}(\mathsf{pp}, R, aux_R) \\ (\boldsymbol{x}, \pi) \leftarrow P^*(R, aux_R, \mathsf{pp}, Z) \\ \boldsymbol{w} \leftarrow E^{P^*}(R, aux_R, \mathsf{pp}, Z) \end{array} \middle| \begin{array}{c} \mathsf{V}(\mathsf{pp}, \boldsymbol{x}, \pi) \wedge \\ \neg R(\boldsymbol{x}, \boldsymbol{w}) \end{array} \right]$$

Zero Knowledge: *We say that* $\mathcal{S}$ *satisfies zero-knowledge for relation generator* $\mathcal{RG}$ *if there exists simulator* $S = (S_1, S_2)$ *such that the following hold:*

– Key Indistinguishability: *For all efficient adversaries* $\mathcal{A}$ *we have:*

$$\Pr \left[(R, aux_R) \leftarrow \mathcal{RG}(1^\lambda), \mathsf{pp} \leftarrow \mathsf{G}(1^\lambda, R) \middle| \mathcal{A}(R, aux_R, \mathsf{pp}) = 1 \right]$$

$$\approx \Pr \left[\begin{array}{c} (R, aux_R) \leftarrow \mathcal{RG}(1^\lambda), \\ (\mathsf{pp}, \mathsf{td}) \leftarrow S_1(R, aux_R) \end{array} \middle| \mathcal{A}(R, aux_R, \mathsf{pp}) = 1 \right]$$

– Proof Indistinguishability: *For all efficient adversaries* $\mathcal{A}$ *and all* $R \in \mathcal{R}_\lambda$, $(\boldsymbol{x}, \boldsymbol{w})$ *such that* $R(\boldsymbol{x}, \boldsymbol{w}) = 1$ *we have:*

$$\Pr \left[\begin{array}{c} (R, aux_R) \leftarrow \mathcal{RG}(1^\lambda), \\ \mathsf{pp} \leftarrow \mathsf{G}(R, aux_R), \\ \pi \leftarrow \mathsf{P}(\mathsf{pp}, \boldsymbol{x}, \boldsymbol{w}) \end{array} \middle| \mathcal{A}(\mathsf{pp}, aux_R, \pi) = 1 \right]$$

$$\approx \Pr \left[\begin{array}{c} (R, aux_R) \leftarrow \mathcal{RG}(1^\lambda), \\ (\mathsf{pp}, \mathsf{td}) \leftarrow S_1(R, aux_R), \\ \pi \leftarrow S_2(\mathsf{pp}, \boldsymbol{x}, \mathsf{td}) \end{array} \middle| \mathcal{A}(\mathsf{pp}, aux_R, \pi) = 1 \right]$$

A.3   Commit and Prove SNARKs

Informally, a *commit and prove* SNARK (CP-SNARK) is a SNARK that can prove knowledge of *witness* where part of the witness opens a commitment c. In other words, a CP-SNARK for relation R allows one to prove knowledge of $\boldsymbol{w} = (\boldsymbol{u}, \boldsymbol{z})$ such that $R(\boldsymbol{x}, \boldsymbol{w}) = 1$ and c is a commitment for $\boldsymbol{u}$. The commitments can be used in several proofs to prove composite statements. We summarise the formal notion of CP-SNARKs as defined in [8].

Definition 3 (CP-SNARK). *Let* Com *be a commitment scheme with input space* $\mathcal{D}$, *opening space* $\mathcal{O}$ *and commitment space* $\mathcal{C}$. *Let* $\{R_\lambda\}_{\lambda \in \mathbb{N}}$ *be a family of relations* R *over* $\mathcal{D}_x \times \mathcal{D}_u \times \mathcal{D}_w$ *where* $\mathcal{D}_u$ *splits as* $\mathcal{D}_1 \times \cdots \times \mathcal{D}_\ell$ *for some* $\ell \geq 1$ *such that* $\mathcal{D}_i \subseteq \mathcal{D}$ *for* $i = 1, \ldots, \ell$. *A commit and prove zkSNARK* (CP) *for* Com *and* $\{R_\lambda\}_{\lambda \in \mathbb{N}}$ *is a zkSNARK for family of relations* $\{R_\lambda^{\mathsf{Com}}\}_{\lambda \in \mathbb{N}}$ *where:*

- *every $R \in R^{\mathsf{Com}}$ is represented by (ck, R) where $\mathsf{ck} \in \mathsf{Setup}(1^\lambda)$ and $R \in R_\lambda$.*
- *R is over the pairs $(\boldsymbol{x}, \boldsymbol{w})$ where $\boldsymbol{x} = (x, (c_j)_{j \in [\ell]}) \in \mathcal{D}_x \times \mathcal{C}^\ell$ is the statement and $\boldsymbol{w} = ((u_j)_{j \in [\ell]}, (o_j)_{j \in [\ell]}, \omega) \in \mathcal{D}_1 \times \cdots \times \mathcal{D}_\ell \times \mathcal{O}^\ell \times \mathcal{D}_\omega$ is the witness. The relation R holds iff:*

$$\bigwedge_{j \in [\ell]} \mathsf{VerCommit}(\mathsf{ck}, c_j, u_j, o_j) = 1 \wedge R(x, (u_j)_{j \in [\ell]}, \omega) = 1$$

Further, we say that CP *is knowledge sound for relation generator $\mathcal{RG}$ and auxiliary input generator $\mathcal{Z}$ if it satisfies knowledge soundness $(\mathcal{RG}^{\mathsf{Com}}, \mathcal{Z})$ where $\mathcal{RG}^{\mathsf{Com}}$ denotes the relation generator which samples (ck, R, aux) as $\mathcal{RG}(1^\lambda) \to (R, aux)$ and $\mathsf{Setup}(1^\lambda) \to \mathsf{ck}$.*

We elaborate slightly on the intuition behind the above definition. Typically a zkSNARK for relation $R \subseteq \mathcal{D}_x \times \mathcal{D}_\omega$ proves knowledge of $\boldsymbol{w} \in \mathcal{D}_\omega$ for a given statement $\boldsymbol{x} \in \mathcal{D}_x$ such that $R(\boldsymbol{x}, \boldsymbol{w}) = 1$. With a CP-SNARK, we additionally wish to prove that part of the witness $\boldsymbol{w}$ opens a commitment c, i.e. $\boldsymbol{w} = (\boldsymbol{u}, z)$ where c is a commitment for $\boldsymbol{u}$. Generalizing this further, we can decompose the committed part of the witness $\boldsymbol{u}$ into ℓ slots, where witness corresponding to each slot opens a specified commitment.

B   Security Analysis

We describe our protocols as interactive protocols with (semi) honest verifiers. One can obtain non-interactive arguments of knowledge (SNARKs) in the Random Oracle model from them via Fiat-Shamir heuristic. We first define a secure protocol for proving a relation R under commitments using the commitment scheme Com. We will write a relation R as $R(\boldsymbol{x}, \boldsymbol{u}, \boldsymbol{w})$ where $\boldsymbol{x}$ denotes the public input (plain-text), $\boldsymbol{u}$ denotes the committed witness while $\boldsymbol{w}$ denotes the "free" (uncommitted witness). The vector $\boldsymbol{u}$ purportedly opens a public commitment c.

Definition 4 (Secure Protocol). *A secure protocol for a relation R and commitment scheme* Com *consists of tripe $\Pi = (\mathcal{G}, \mathcal{P}, \mathcal{V})$ consisting of generator algorithm $\mathcal{G}$, a* PPT *prover $\mathcal{P}$ and a* PPT *verifier $\mathcal{V}$ which work as follows:*

1. *$\mathcal{G}(\mathsf{ck}, R, 1^\lambda) \longrightarrow \mathsf{pp}$: Given a commitment key $\mathsf{ck} \leftarrow \mathsf{Com.Setup}(1^\lambda)$ and R, $\mathcal{G}$ outputs public parameters pp.*
2. *Given public parameters pp for relation R and a pair $(\boldsymbol{x}, c)$ consisting of statement $\boldsymbol{x}$ and a public commitment c, $\mathcal{P}$ and $\mathcal{V}$ interact via an alternating sequence of messages, at the end of which $\mathcal{V}$ outputs $0\,(\mathtt{Reject})$ or $1\,(\mathtt{Accept})$.*

Further, a secure protocol Π satisfies completeness, soundness *and* zero-knowledge *which we define shortly.*

Let $\Pi(\mathsf{pp}, \boldsymbol{x}, c; \boldsymbol{u}, \boldsymbol{w}, 0)$ denote the output $(0/1)$ of interaction between $\mathcal{P}$ and $\mathcal{V}$ on common input $(\boldsymbol{x}, c)$ and $\mathcal{P}$'s private inputs as $\boldsymbol{u}, \boldsymbol{w}, o$. Similarly, let $\Pi.\mathsf{Vw}(\boldsymbol{x}, c; \boldsymbol{u}, \boldsymbol{w}, o)$ denote $\mathcal{V}$'s view in the interaction. We use $\Pi_{\mathcal{A}}(\mathsf{pp}, \boldsymbol{x}, c)$ to denote the output of interaction between an adversarial prover $\mathcal{A}$ and $\mathcal{V}$ on common input (x, c). Next, we define the security properties satisfied by a secure protocol Π.

Completeness: We call Π to be complete if for all $\mathsf{ck} \in \mathsf{Com.Setup}(1^\lambda)$ and $(x, u, w) \in R$ we have:

$$\Pr\left[\mathsf{pp} \leftarrow \mathcal{G}(\mathsf{ck}, R, 1^\lambda), c = \mathsf{Com.Commit}(\mathsf{ck}, u, o), \Pi(x, c; u, w, o) = 1\right] = 1$$

Soundness: We call Π to have soundness if for all PPT adversaries $\mathcal{A}$, there exists and efficient extractor $\mathcal{E}$ such that the following probability is negligible:

$$\Pr\left[\begin{matrix} \mathsf{ck} \leftarrow \mathsf{Com.Setup}(1^\lambda), \mathsf{pp} \leftarrow \mathcal{G}(\mathsf{ck}, R, 1^\lambda), \\ (x, c) \leftarrow \mathcal{A}(\mathsf{pp}, z), (u, w, o) \leftarrow \mathcal{E}^{\mathcal{A}}(\mathsf{pp}, z) \end{matrix} \middle| \begin{matrix} \Pi_{\mathcal{A}}(\mathsf{pp}, x, c) = 1 \\ \wedge \neg \tilde{R}(x, c, u, w, o) \end{matrix}\right]$$

Here $\tilde{R}(x, c, u, w, o) \equiv R(x, u, w) \wedge \mathsf{Com.VerCommit}(\mathsf{ck}, c, u, o)$.

Zero Knowledge: We say that Π is zero-knowledge if there exists efficient simulator $\mathcal{S} = (\mathcal{S}_1, \mathcal{S}_2)$ such that for all $\mathsf{ck} \in \mathsf{Com.Setup}(1^\lambda)$, (x, c, u, w, o) such that $(x, u, w) \in R$ and $c = \mathsf{Com.Commit}(\mathsf{ck}, u, o)$, the following are statistically indistinguishable:

$$\left[\mathsf{pp} \leftarrow \mathcal{G}(\mathsf{ck}, R) \mid (\mathsf{pp}, \Pi.\mathsf{Vw}(\mathsf{pp}, x, c; u, w, o))\right]$$
$$\approx \left[(\mathsf{pp}, \mathsf{td}) \leftarrow \mathcal{S}_1(1^\lambda, R) \mid (\mathsf{pp}, \mathcal{S}_2(\mathsf{td}, \mathsf{pp}, \mathsf{ck}, x, c))\right]$$

First, we exhibit a trivial secure protocol that can be obtained from a CP-SNARK for a relation.

Lemma 1. *Let* $\mathsf{CP} = (\mathsf{G}, \mathsf{P}, \mathsf{V})$ *be a CP-SNARK for relation* R *and commitment scheme* Com. *Then* $\Pi = (\mathcal{G}, \mathcal{P}, \mathcal{V})$ *as described below is a secure protocol for relation* R *and commitment scheme* Com.

- $\mathcal{G}(\mathsf{ck}, R, 1^\lambda) \longrightarrow \mathsf{pp}$ *where* $\mathsf{pp} \leftarrow \mathsf{G}(\mathsf{ck}, R, 1^\lambda)$.
- *On common input* (x, c) *and* $\mathcal{P}$'s *input* (u, w, o), $\mathcal{P}$ *and* $\mathcal{V}$ *interact as follows:*
  1. $\mathcal{P}$ *computes:* $\pi \leftarrow \mathsf{P}(\mathsf{pp}, x, u, w, o)$.
  2. $\mathcal{P} \rightarrow \mathcal{V}$: $\mathcal{P}$ *sends* π *to* $\mathcal{V}$.
  3. $\mathcal{V}$ *outputs* $\mathsf{V}(\mathsf{pp}, x, c, \pi)$.

The proof of the above is trivial and follows directly from the properties of CP-SNARK CP. We now formally define the probabilistic relation decomposition and provide a secure protocol for decomposed relation in by gluing the secure protocols for the constituent relations.

Definition 5 (Probabilistic Relation Decomposition). *Let $R(\boldsymbol{x}, \boldsymbol{u}, \boldsymbol{w})$ be a relation. We say that relations (R_1, R_2) are a probabilistic decomposition of R if there exists a canoical partitioning of $\boldsymbol{w}$ as $\boldsymbol{w}_0 \| \boldsymbol{w}_1 \| \boldsymbol{w}_2$ and a challenge space $\mathcal{C}$ such that for $\alpha \leftarrow \mathcal{C}$:*

$$\Pr[R_1(\boldsymbol{x}, \boldsymbol{u}, \boldsymbol{w}_0, \boldsymbol{w}_1) \wedge R_2(\alpha, \boldsymbol{x}, \boldsymbol{u}, \boldsymbol{w}_0, \boldsymbol{w}_2) = 1 \mid R(\boldsymbol{x}, \boldsymbol{u}, \boldsymbol{w}) = 1] = 1$$
$$\Pr[R_1(\boldsymbol{x}, \boldsymbol{u}, \boldsymbol{w}_0, \boldsymbol{w}_1) \wedge R_2(\alpha, \boldsymbol{x}, \boldsymbol{u}, \boldsymbol{w}_0, \boldsymbol{w}_2) = 1 \mid R(\boldsymbol{x}, \boldsymbol{u}, \boldsymbol{w}) = 0] = \mathsf{negl}$$

Lemma 2 (Glueing Lemma). *Let (R_1, R_2) be a probabilistic relation decomposition of the relation R and let Π_1 and Π_2 be secure protocols for (R_1, Com) and (R_2, Com) respectively, where Com is a commitment scheme. Then the protocol $\Pi = (\mathcal{G}, \mathcal{P}, \mathcal{V})$ as described below is a secure protocol for (R, Com).*

- $\mathcal{G}(\mathsf{ck}, R, 1^\lambda) \longrightarrow \mathsf{pp}$: *The algorithm $\mathcal{P}$ invokes generator algorithms for the consituent relations as $\mathsf{pp}_1 \leftarrow \Pi_1.\mathcal{G}(\mathsf{ck}, R_1, 1^\lambda)$, $\mathsf{pp}_2 \leftarrow \Pi_2.\mathcal{G}(\mathsf{ck}, R_2, 1^\lambda)$ and returns $\mathsf{pp} = (\mathsf{pp}_1, \mathsf{pp}_2)$.*
- *On common input $(\boldsymbol{x}, c)$ and private prover inputs $(\boldsymbol{u}, \boldsymbol{w}, o)$, $\mathcal{P}$ and $\mathcal{V}$ interact as follows:*
  1. *$\mathcal{P}$ computes: $\mathcal{P}$ partitions $\boldsymbol{w}$ as $\boldsymbol{w}_0 \| \boldsymbol{w}_1 \| \boldsymbol{w}_2$. Next $\mathcal{P}$ samples $o_w \leftarrow \mathcal{O}$ and computes $c_w = \mathsf{Com.Commit}(\mathsf{ck}, \boldsymbol{w}_0, o_w)$.*
  2. *$\mathcal{P} \rightarrow \mathcal{V}$: $\mathcal{P}$ sends c_w to $\mathcal{V}$.*
  3. *$\mathcal{P}$ and $\mathcal{V}$ execute the secure protocol Π_1 with common input $(\boldsymbol{x}, (c, c_w))$ and prover's $(\Pi_1.\mathcal{P})$ inputs as $((\boldsymbol{u}, \boldsymbol{w}_0), \boldsymbol{w}_1, (o, o_w))$. Let b_1 denote the output of the protocol Π_1.*
  4. *$\mathcal{V} \rightarrow \mathcal{P}$: $\mathcal{V}$ samples $\alpha \leftarrow \mathcal{C}$ and sends α to $\mathcal{P}$.*
  5. *$\mathcal{P}$ and $\mathcal{V}$ execute the secure protocol Π_2 with common input $((\alpha, \boldsymbol{x}), (c, c_w))$ and prover's $(\Pi_2.\mathcal{P})$ inputs as $((\boldsymbol{u}, \boldsymbol{w}_0), \boldsymbol{w}_2, (o, o_w))$. Let b_2 denote the output of the protocol Π_1.*
  6. *$\mathcal{V}$ outputs $b_1 \wedge b_2$.*

Proof. We skip the proof of completeness of protocol Π, as it is straightforward to verify. To show soundness, let $\mathcal{A}$ be a PPT adversary such that $\Pi_{\mathcal{A}}(\mathsf{pp}, \boldsymbol{x}, c) = 1$. Let c_w be the first message (commitment) sent by $\mathcal{A}$ to $\mathcal{V}$. From the protocol description of Π, we have:

$$\Pi_{\mathcal{A}}(\mathsf{pp}, \boldsymbol{x}, c) = \Pi_{1,\mathcal{A}}(\mathsf{pp}_1, \boldsymbol{x}, (c, c_w)) \wedge \Pi_{2,\mathcal{A}}(\mathsf{pp}_2, (\alpha, \boldsymbol{x}), (c, c_w)).$$

Thus $\mathcal{A}$ is also an adversary for secure protocols Π_1 and Π_2. Soundness of Π_1 and Π_2 implies existence of extractors $\mathcal{E}_1$ and $\mathcal{E}_2$ such that $((\boldsymbol{u}, \boldsymbol{w}_0), \boldsymbol{w}_1, o) \leftarrow \mathcal{E}_1^{\mathcal{A}}(\mathsf{pp}_1, z)$ and $((\boldsymbol{u}', \boldsymbol{w}_0', \boldsymbol{w}_2, (o', o_w')) \leftarrow \mathcal{E}_2^{\mathcal{A}}(\mathsf{pp}_2, z)$. We define extractor $\mathcal{E}$ which invokes the above extractors and outputs $(\boldsymbol{u}, \boldsymbol{w}, o)$ for $\boldsymbol{w} = \boldsymbol{w}_0 \| \boldsymbol{w}_1 \| \boldsymbol{w}_2$. With overwhelming probability we have

$$R_1(\boldsymbol{x}, \boldsymbol{u}, \boldsymbol{w}_0, \boldsymbol{w}_1) \wedge \mathsf{Com.VerCommit}(\mathsf{ck}, (c, c_w), (\boldsymbol{u}, \boldsymbol{w}_0), (o, o_w))$$
$$R_2(\alpha, \boldsymbol{x}, \boldsymbol{w}_0', \boldsymbol{w}_2) \wedge \mathsf{Com.VerCommit}(\mathsf{ck}, (c, c_w), (\boldsymbol{u}', \boldsymbol{w}_0'), (o', o_w'))$$

By the binding property of Com, we also have $\boldsymbol{u}' = \boldsymbol{u}$, $\boldsymbol{w}_0' = \boldsymbol{w}_0$, $o' = o$ and $o_w' = o_w$ and $\mathsf{Com.VerCommit}(\mathsf{ck}, (c, c_w), (\boldsymbol{u}, \boldsymbol{w}_0), (o, o_w)) = 1$ with overwhelming probability. Finally, since $R_1(\boldsymbol{x}, \boldsymbol{u}, \boldsymbol{w}_0, \boldsymbol{w}_1) \wedge R_2(\alpha, \boldsymbol{x}, \boldsymbol{u}, \boldsymbol{w}_0, \boldsymbol{w}_2) = 1$, we must have $R(\boldsymbol{x}, \boldsymbol{u}, \boldsymbol{w}) = 1$ for $\boldsymbol{w} = \boldsymbol{w}_0 || \boldsymbol{w}_1 || \boldsymbol{w}_2$ with probability negligibly close to 1. This proves that $\mathcal{E}$ extracts a valid witness with overwhelming proability.

We now show that Π is zero-knowledge. Let $ck \leftarrow \mathsf{Com.Setup}(1^\lambda)$ and let $(\boldsymbol{x}, c, \boldsymbol{u}, \boldsymbol{w}, o)$ be such that $(\boldsymbol{x}, \boldsymbol{u}, \boldsymbol{w}) \in R$ and $c = \mathsf{Com.Commit}(ck, \boldsymbol{u}, o)$. We show the existence of simulator $\mathcal{S} = (\mathcal{S}_1, \mathcal{S}_2)$ such that:

$$\big[\mathsf{pp} \leftarrow \mathcal{G}(ck, R) \,|\, \big(\mathsf{pp}, \Pi.\mathsf{Vw}(\mathsf{pp}, \boldsymbol{x}, c; \boldsymbol{u}, \boldsymbol{w}, o)\big)\big]$$
$$\approx \big[(\mathsf{pp}, \mathsf{td}) \leftarrow \mathcal{S}_1(1^\lambda, R) \,|\, \big(\mathsf{pp}, \mathcal{S}_2(\mathsf{td}, \mathsf{pp}, ck, \boldsymbol{x}, c)\big)\big]$$

Let $\widetilde{\mathcal{S}} = (\widetilde{\mathcal{S}}_1, \widetilde{\mathcal{S}}_2)$ and $\widehat{\mathcal{S}} = (\widehat{\mathcal{S}}_1, \widehat{\mathcal{S}}_2)$ be the simulators for secure protocols Π_1 and Π_2 respectively. The simulator $\mathcal{S}$ works as follows:

- $\mathcal{S}_1(1^\lambda, R) \longrightarrow (\mathsf{pp}', \mathsf{td}')$: On input R and security parameter, $\mathcal{S}_1$ invokes simulators for R_1, R_2 to obtain $(\mathsf{pp}'_1, \mathsf{td}'_1) \leftarrow \widetilde{\mathcal{S}}_1(1^\lambda, R_1)$, $(\mathsf{pp}'_2, \mathsf{td}'_2) \leftarrow \widehat{\mathcal{S}}_1(1^\lambda, R_2)$ respectively. It sets $\mathsf{pp}' = (\mathsf{pp}'_1, \mathsf{pp}'_2)$ and $\mathsf{td}' = (\mathsf{td}'_1, \mathsf{td}'_2)$.
- $\mathcal{S}_2$ works as follows: It samples $\alpha \leftarrow \mathcal{C}$, $\tilde{o} \leftarrow \mathcal{O}_\lambda$ and computes $\tilde{c}_w = \mathsf{Com.Commit}(ck, \boldsymbol{0}, \tilde{o})$. Then it invokes simulators $\widetilde{\mathcal{S}}_2$ and $\widehat{\mathcal{S}}_2$ as:
  - $V'_1 \leftarrow \widetilde{\mathcal{S}}_2(\mathsf{td}'_1, \mathsf{pp}'_1, \boldsymbol{x}, (c, \tilde{c}_w))$,
  - $V'_2 \leftarrow \widehat{\mathcal{S}}_2(\mathsf{td}'_2, \mathsf{pp}'_2, (\alpha, \boldsymbol{x}), (c, \tilde{c}_w))$.
- Finally it outputs $(\alpha, \tilde{c}_w, V'_1, V'_2)$.

The required indistinguishability follows via hybrids shown below. For ease of notation let V_1 denote $\Pi_1(\mathsf{pp}_1, \boldsymbol{x}, (c, c_w); (\boldsymbol{u}, \boldsymbol{w}_0), \boldsymbol{w}_1, (o, o_w))$ and V_2 denote $\Pi_2(\mathsf{pp}_2, (\alpha, \boldsymbol{x}), (c, c_w); (\boldsymbol{u}, \boldsymbol{w}_0), \boldsymbol{w}_2, (o, o_w))$. Then we have:

$$\langle \mathsf{pp}, \Pi.\mathsf{Vw}(\mathsf{pp}, \boldsymbol{x}, c; \boldsymbol{u}, \boldsymbol{w}, o)\rangle \tag{1}$$
$$= \langle \mathsf{pp}_1, \mathsf{pp}_2, \alpha, c_w, V_1, V_2\rangle \tag{2}$$
$$\approx \langle \mathsf{pp}'_1, \mathsf{pp}_2, \alpha, c_w, \widetilde{\mathcal{S}}_2(\mathsf{td}'_1, \mathsf{pp}'_1, \boldsymbol{x}, (c, c_w)), V_2\rangle \tag{3}$$
$$\approx \langle \mathsf{pp}'_1, \mathsf{pp}'_2, \alpha, c_w, \widetilde{\mathcal{S}}_2(\mathsf{td}'_1, \mathsf{pp}'_1, \boldsymbol{x}, (c, c_w)), \widehat{\mathcal{S}}_2(\mathsf{td}'_2, \mathsf{pp}'_2, (\alpha, \boldsymbol{x}), (c, c_w))\rangle \tag{4}$$
$$\approx \langle \mathsf{pp}'_1, \mathsf{pp}'_2, \alpha, \tilde{c}_w, V'_1, V'_2\rangle \tag{5}$$

In the above the indistinguishability of (2) and (3) follows from the zero knowledge property of Π_1. Similarly zero knowledge of Π_2 implies indistinguishability of (3) and (4). Finally, the indistinguishability of (4) and (5) follows from the hiding property of Com. This completes the proof.

C   Secure Protocols

In this section, we give secure protocols for the different relations discussed in this paper such as simultaneous permutation, consistent memory access, various dataset operations and decision tree inference.

C.1 Simultaneous Permutation

For a fixed N, recall that k-tuples $(\boldsymbol{u}_1, \ldots, \boldsymbol{u}_k)$ and $(\boldsymbol{v}_1, \ldots, \boldsymbol{v}_k)$ of vectors in $\mathbb{F}^N$ satisfy simultaneous permutation relation if there exists a permutation σ of $[N]$ such that $\sigma(\boldsymbol{u}_i) = v_i$ for all $i \in [N]$. Let R_σ denote the relation over $(\alpha, \boldsymbol{u}, \boldsymbol{v})$ with $\alpha \in \mathbb{F}$ and $\boldsymbol{u}, \boldsymbol{v} \in \mathbb{F}^N$ such that $\prod_{i=1}^{N}(\alpha - \boldsymbol{u}[i]) = \prod_{i=1}^{N}(\alpha - \boldsymbol{v}[i])$. Let Π_σ denote the trivial secure protocol obtained from CP-SNARK for (R_σ, Com) (using Lemma 1), where we also assume Com is homomorphic.

Lemma 3. *The protocol $\Pi_{\mathrm{perm}} = (\mathcal{G}, \mathcal{P}, \mathcal{V})$ in Fig. 5 is a secure protocol for simultaneous permutation relation and commitment scheme* Com.

Proof. By standard rewinding technique, with overwhelming probability the extractor $\mathcal{E}$, for an accepting adversarial prover $\mathcal{A}$ can extract vectors $\{\boldsymbol{u}_i, \boldsymbol{v}_i\}_{i=1}^{k}$ such that $\boldsymbol{u}_i$ opens commitment cu_i and $\boldsymbol{v}_i$ opens commitment cv_i for all $i \in [k]$. This is accomplished by running the subprotocol Π_σ for k different linear combinations of commitments given by the challenge $(\beta_1, \ldots, \beta_k)$, and using the extractor for Π_σ to obtain openings for respective linear combinations of vectors. Since the challenges are linearly independent with overwhelming probability, we can solve the system of equations to obtain openings for individual commitments cu_i and cv_i for all $i \in [k]$. By homomorphism of Com, the vectors $\boldsymbol{u} = \sum_{i=1}^{k} \beta_i \boldsymbol{u}_i$ and $\boldsymbol{v} = \sum_{i=1}^{k} \beta_i \boldsymbol{v}_i$ open commitments cu and cv respectively. Again soundness of Π_σ implies with overwhelming probability $(\alpha, \boldsymbol{u}, \boldsymbol{v}) \in R_\sigma$. Since α was drawn uniformly at random, we conclude that there is a permutation π such that $\pi(\boldsymbol{u}) = \boldsymbol{v}$ with probability almost 1. Finally, since $\beta_1, \ldots, \beta_k$ were drawn uniformly at random $\pi(\sum_{i=1}^{k} \beta_i \boldsymbol{u}_i) = \sum_{i=1}^{k} \beta_i \boldsymbol{v}_i$, with overwhelming probability we must have $\pi(\boldsymbol{u}_i) = \boldsymbol{v}_i$ for all $i \in [k]$. This shows the soundness of Π_{perm}. We skip the proof of zero-knowledge for Π_{perm} as it follows from the same property for Π_σ.

$\mathcal{G}(1^\lambda) \longrightarrow \mathsf{pp}$: Obtains pp as $\mathsf{pp} \leftarrow \Pi_\sigma.\mathcal{G}(1^\lambda, R_\sigma)$.
Inputs: On common input $\mathsf{c}_u = (\mathsf{cu}_i)_{i=1}^{k}$, $\mathsf{c}_v = (\mathsf{cv}_i)_{i=1}^{k}$ and $\mathcal{P}$'s inputs consisting of $\{\boldsymbol{u}_i, \boldsymbol{v}_i, o_i, \omega_i\}_{i=1}^{k}$, permutation π of $[N]$; $\mathcal{P}$ and $\mathcal{V}$ interact as follows:

1. $\mathcal{V} \to \mathcal{P}$: $(\alpha, \beta_1, \ldots, \beta_k) \leftarrow \mathbb{F}^{k+1}$.
2. $\mathcal{P}$ and $\mathcal{V}$ compute: $\mathsf{cu} = \sum_{i=1}^{k} \beta_i \mathsf{cu}_i$, $\mathsf{cv} = \sum_{i=1}^{k} \beta_i \mathsf{cv}_i$.
3. $\mathcal{P}$ computes: $\boldsymbol{u} = \sum_{i=1}^{k} \beta_i \boldsymbol{u}_i$, $\boldsymbol{v} = \sum_{i=1}^{k} \beta_i \boldsymbol{v}_i$, $o = \sum_{i=1}^{k} \beta_i o_i$, $\omega = \sum_{i=1}^{k} \beta_i \omega_i$.
4. $\mathcal{P}$ and $\mathcal{V}$ execute the protocol Π_σ with $(\alpha, \mathsf{cu}, \mathsf{cv})$ as the common input and $(\boldsymbol{u}, \boldsymbol{v}, o, \omega)$ as prover's inputs. Let b be the output of the protocol Π_σ.
5. $\mathcal{V}$ outputs b.

Fig. 5. Protocol Π_{perm} for simultaneous permutation

C.2   Consistent Memory Access

in this section, we formalize the secure protocol for consistent memory access relation discussed in Sect. 3.4.

Lemma 4. *There exists a secure protocol Π_{cma} for consistent memory access relation defined in Sect. 3.4.*

Proof. We consider the relation R_{cma} explained in Sect. 3.4 for consistent memory access as:

$$R_{\text{cma}}(\cdot, [\![L, U, V]\!], [\![u, v, \tilde{u}, v, \tilde{w_1}, w_2]\!])$$

In the above, there are no public inputs, the committed witness consists of L, U and V which denote the read only memory, access pattern and values respectively. The uncommitted witness consists of auxiliary inputs $(u, v, \tilde{u}, \tilde{v})$ and other witness w_1 and w_2 required to prove the relation. The description in Sect. 3.4 partitions the above as:

$$\mathsf{C}_{\text{ROM},m,n}(\cdot, [\![L, U, V, w_0]\!], w_1) \wedge R_\sigma(\cdot, w_0, w_2) \tag{6}$$

where $w_0 = [\![u, v, \tilde{u}, \tilde{v}]\!]$. The secure protocol Π_{ROM} can be obtained using a CP-SNARK for circuit $\mathsf{C}_{\text{ROM},m,n}$ via Lemma 1. Invoking Glueing Lemma (Lemma 2) with Π_{ROM} and protocol Π_{perm} for simultaneous permutation relation, we obtain the secure protocol Π_{cma}.

C.3   Aggregation Operation

We now provide a secure protocol for showing correctness of aggregation operation on datasets as described in Sect. 4. In Sect. 4 we described a protocol for checking correct concatenation of vectors under commitments, and then reduced the verification of dataset aggregation to that of verifying concatenation of vectors (obtained via linear combination of columns of dataset). We also justify the aforementioned reduction. We assume Π_{concat} is a secure protocol for checking concatenation of vectors, which we assume is described by the relation R_{concat}. The secure protocol $\Pi_{\text{agg}} = (\mathcal{G}, \mathcal{P}, \mathcal{V})$ for verifying aggregation of datasets appears in Fig. 6. Let D_x, D_y and D_z be datasets with columns given by $(x_i)_{i=1}^k$, $(y_i)_{i=1}^k$ and $(z_i)_{i=1}^k$ respectively. Similarly let $(\mathsf{cx}_i)_{i=1}^k$, $(\mathsf{cy}_i)_{i=1}^k$ and $(\mathsf{cz}_i)_{i=1}^k$ denote public commitments to the columns of D_x, D_y and D_z respectively. As in Sect. 4, let N denote the upper bound on the sizes of datasets and vectors.

Lemma 5. *The protocol Π_{agg} in Fig. 6 is a secure protocol for aggregation relation on datasets and commitment scheme* Com.

Proof. The completeness and zero-knowledge properties of the protocol are proved in a manner similar to earlier protocols. Here we prove the soundness of the probabilistic reduction from aggregation relation on datasets to concatenation relation on vectors, which implies soundness of the overall protocol. With overwhelming probability, a successful adversary $\mathcal{A}$ knows vectors

---

$\mathcal{G}(1^\lambda) \longrightarrow$ pp: Obtains pp as pp $\leftarrow \Pi_{\text{concat}}.\mathcal{G}(1^\lambda, R_{\text{concat}})$.

Inputs: On common input $(\mathsf{cx}_i)_{i=1}^k$, $(\mathsf{cy}_i)_{i=1}^k$ and $(\mathsf{cz}_i)_{i=1}^k$ and $\mathcal{P}$'s inputs consisting of $\{\boldsymbol{x}_i, \boldsymbol{y}_i, \boldsymbol{z}_i, o_i, \omega_i, \delta_i\}_{i=1}^k$; $\mathcal{P}$ and $\mathcal{V}$ interact as follows:

1. $\mathcal{V} \rightarrow \mathcal{P}$: $(\beta_1, \ldots, \beta_k) \leftarrow \mathbb{F}^{k+1}$ satisfying $\sum_{i=1}^k \beta_i = 1$.
2. $\mathcal{P}$ and $\mathcal{V}$ compute: $\mathsf{cx} = \sum_{i=1}^k \beta_i \mathsf{cx}_i$, $\mathsf{cy} = \sum_{i=1}^k \beta_i \mathsf{cy}_i$ and $\mathsf{cz} = \sum_{i=1}^k \beta_i \mathsf{cz}_i$.
3. $\mathcal{P}$ computes: $\boldsymbol{x} = \sum_{i=1}^k \beta_i \boldsymbol{x}_i$, $\boldsymbol{y} = \sum_{i=1}^k \beta_i \boldsymbol{y}_i$, $\boldsymbol{z} = \sum_{i=1}^k \beta_i \boldsymbol{z}_i$. Similarly it also obtains o, ω and δ as β-linear combinations of $\{o_i\}_{i=1}^k$, $\{\omega_i\}_{i=1}^k$, $\{\delta_i\}_{i=1}^k$ respectively.
4. $\mathcal{P}$ and $\mathcal{V}$ execute the protocol Π_{concat} with $(\mathsf{cx}, \mathsf{cy}, \mathsf{cz})$ as the common input and $(\boldsymbol{x}, \boldsymbol{y}, \boldsymbol{z}, o, \omega, \delta)$ as prover's inputs. Let b be the output of the protocol Π_{concat}.
5. $\mathcal{V}$ outputs b.

Fig. 6. Protocol Π_{agg} for dataset aggregation

$(\boldsymbol{x}_i)_{i=1}^k$, $(\boldsymbol{y}_i)_{i=1}^k$ and $(\boldsymbol{z}_i)_{i=1}^k$ such that their respective β-linear combinations $\boldsymbol{x}, \boldsymbol{y}$ and $\boldsymbol{z}$ satisfy the concatenation relation. As in Sect. 4, we write $\boldsymbol{x}_i = [\![s_i, \boldsymbol{X}_i]\!]$, $\boldsymbol{y}_i = [\![t_i, \boldsymbol{Y}_i]\!]$ and $\boldsymbol{z}_i = [\![w_i, \boldsymbol{Z}_i]\!]$ for $i \in [k]$. Similarly, let $\boldsymbol{x} = [\![s, \boldsymbol{X}]\!]$, $\boldsymbol{y} = [\![t, \boldsymbol{Y}]\!]$ and $\boldsymbol{z} = [\![w, \boldsymbol{Z}]\!]$. Note that we must have:

$$s = \sum_{i=1}^k \beta_i s_i, \quad t = \sum_{i=1}^k \beta_i t_i, \quad w = \sum_{i=1}^k \beta_i w_i$$

$$\boldsymbol{X} = \sum_{i=1}^k \beta_i \boldsymbol{X}_i, \quad \boldsymbol{Y} = \sum_{i=1}^k \beta_i \boldsymbol{Y}_i, \quad \boldsymbol{Z} = \sum_{i=1}^k \beta_i \boldsymbol{Z}_i$$

Now, from description in Sect. 4, the vectors $\boldsymbol{x}, \boldsymbol{y}$ and $\boldsymbol{z}$ satisfy the concatenation relation if there exists a permutation of $[2N]$, which we denote by permutation matrix Λ such that $\Lambda \cdot [\![\boldsymbol{\rho}_s, \boldsymbol{\rho}_t]\!] = [\![\boldsymbol{\rho}_w, \mathbf{0}]\!]$, $\Lambda \cdot [\![\boldsymbol{X}, \boldsymbol{Y}]\!] = [\![\boldsymbol{Z}, \mathbf{0}]\!]$ where vectors $\boldsymbol{\rho}_s, \boldsymbol{\rho}_t$ and $\boldsymbol{\rho}_w$ are in $\{0,1\}^N$ such that $\boldsymbol{\rho}_s$ is 1 in precisely the first s positions, $\boldsymbol{\rho}_t$ is 1 in precisely the first t positions and $\boldsymbol{\rho}_w$ is 1 in precisely the first w positions where further $w = s + t$. The relation thus also implicity requires that $s, t, w \in [N]$. We now claim that $s_i = s$, $t_i = t$ and $w_i = w$ for all $i \in [k]$. Otherwise it is easily seen that s is distributed uniformly in $\mathbb{F}$ (and likewise for t and w) for uniformly sampled $\beta_1, \ldots, \beta_k$ (subject to sum being 1), and thus $s \in [N]$ with negligible probability $N/|\mathbb{F}|$. Similar reasoning also implies that with overwhelming probability we have $\Lambda \cdot [\![\boldsymbol{X}_i, \boldsymbol{Y}_i]\!] = [\![\boldsymbol{Z}_i, \mathbf{0}]\!]$ for all $i \in [k]$. Combined with the fact that $\Lambda \cdot [\![\boldsymbol{\rho}_s, \boldsymbol{\rho}_t]\!] = [\![\boldsymbol{\rho}_w, \mathbf{0}]\!]$, it implies that the same permutation Λ maps the first s entries of column $\boldsymbol{x}_i$ and first t entries of column $\boldsymbol{y}_i$ to the first $w = s + t$ entries of the column $\boldsymbol{z}_i$ for all $i \in [k]$. Thus D_z corresponds to aggregation of datasets D_x and D_y.

Protcols and Proofs for Other Operations: We have provided circuit descriptions for other operations such as `filter`, `order-by`, `inner-join` and also ML operations such as inference and accuracy from decision trees. These circuits can be used with CP-SNARKs to yeild secure protocols for those operations using techniques similar to presented protocols (essentially using Lemmas 1 and 2), alongwith reduction technique when applicable.

References

1. Albrecht, M., Grassi, L., Rechberger, C., Roy, A., Tiessen, T.: MiMC: efficient encryption and cryptographic hashing with minimal multiplicative complexity. In: Cheon, J.H., Takagi, T. (eds.) ASIACRYPT 2016. LNCS, vol. 10031, pp. 191–219. Springer, Heidelberg (2016). https://doi.org/10.1007/978-3-662-53887-6_7
2. Ames, S., Hazay, C., Ishai, Y., Venkitasubramaniam, M.: Ligero: lightweight sublinear arguments without a trusted setup. In: Proceedings of the ACM SIGSAC Conference on Computer and Communications Security (CCS), pp. 2087–2104 (2017)
3. Ben-Sasson, E., Chiesa, A., Genkin, D., Tromer, E., Virza, M.: SNARKs for C: verifying program executions succinctly and in zero knowledge. In: Canetti, R., Garay, J.A. (eds.) CRYPTO 2013. LNCS, vol. 8043, pp. 90–108. Springer, Heidelberg (2013). https://doi.org/10.1007/978-3-642-40084-1_6
4. Ben-Sasson, E., Chiesa, A., Riabzev, M., Spooner, N., Virza, M., Ward, N.P.: Aurora: transparent succinct arguments for R1CS. In: Ishai, Y., Rijmen, V. (eds.) EUROCRYPT 2019. LNCS, vol. 11476, pp. 103–128. Springer, Cham (2019). https://doi.org/10.1007/978-3-030-17653-2_4
5. Ben-Sasson, E., Chiesa, A., Tromer, E., Virza, M.: Succinct non-interactive zero knowledge for a von neumann architecture. In: Proceedings of the 23rd USENIX Security Symposium, pp. 781–796 (2014)
6. Beneš, V.: Mathematical Theory of Connecting Networks and Telephone Traffic. Elsevier Science, ISSN (1965)
7. Bünz, B., Bootle, J., Boneh, D., Poelstra, A., Wuille, P., Maxwell, G.: Bulletproofs: short proofs for confidential transactions and more. In: Proceedings of the IEEE Symposium on Security and Privacy (SP), pp. 315–334 (2018)
8. Campanelli, M., Fiore, D., Querol, A.: Legosnark: modular design and composition of succinct zero-knowledge proofs. In: Proceedings of the ACM SI)GSAC Conference on Computer and Communications Security (CCS), pp. 2075–2092 (2019)
9. Chiesa, A., Ojha, D., Spooner, N.: FRACTAL: post-quantum and transparent recursive proofs from holography. In: Canteaut, A., Ishai, Y. (eds.) EUROCRYPT 2020. LNCS, vol. 12105, pp. 769–793. Springer, Cham (2020). https://doi.org/10.1007/978-3-030-45721-1_27
10. Eberhardt, J., Tai, S.: Zokrates - scalable privacy-preserving off-chain computations. In: Proceedings of the IEEE International Conference on Internet of Things (iThings), pp. 1084–1091 (2018)
11. Feng, B., Qin, L., Zhang, Z., Ding, Y., Chu, S.: ZEN: efficient zero-knowledge proofs for neural networks. IACR Cryptol. ePrint Arch. **2021**, 87 (2021)
12. ffiec. Home mortgage disclosure act. https://ffiec.cfpb.gov/data-publication/snapshot-national-loan-level-dataset/2018. Accessed 14 Sept 2021
13. Gennaro, R., Gentry, C., Parno, B., Raykova, M.: Quadratic span programs and succinct NIZKs without PCPs. In: Johansson, T., Nguyen, P.Q. (eds.) EUROCRYPT 2013. LNCS, vol. 7881, pp. 626–645. Springer, Heidelberg (2013). https://doi.org/10.1007/978-3-642-38348-9_37
14. Ghodsi, Z., Gu, T., Garg, S.: Safetynets: verifiable execution of deep neural networks on an untrusted cloud. In: Proceedings of the Annual Conference on Neural Information Processing Systems (NeurIPS), pp. 4672–4681 (2017)

15. Kilbertus, N., Gascón, A., Kusner, M.J., Veale, M., Gummadi, K.P., Weller, A.: Blind justice: Fairness with encrypted sensitive attributes. In: Proceedings of the 35th International Conference on Machine Learning (ICML), pp. 2635–2644 (2018)
16. Kosba, A.E., Papamanthou, C., Shi, E.: xjsnark: a framework for efficient verifiable computation. In: Proceedings of the IEEE Symposium on Security and Privacy (SP), pp. 944–961 (2018)
17. Lab, S.: libsnark: A C++ library for zkSNARK proofs, howpublished. https:// github.com/scipr-lab/libsnark. Accessed 14 Sept 2021
18. Lee, S., Ko, H., Kim, J., Oh, H.: vcnn: verifiable convolutional neural network. IACR Cryptol. ePrint Arch. **2020**, 584 (2020)
19. Lüthi, P., Gagnaux, T., Gygli, M.: Distributed ledger for provenance tracking of artificial intelligence assets. CoRR, abs/2002.11000 (2020)
20. Parno, B., Howell, J., Gentry, C., Raykova, M.: Pinocchio: nearly practical verifiable computation. In: Proceedings of the IEEE Symposium on Security and Privacy (SP), pp. 238–252 (2013)
21. Sarpatwar, K.K., et al.: Towards enabling trusted artificial intelligence via blockchain. In: Extended papers from the Second International Workshop on Policy-based Autonomic Data Governance, vol. 11550, pp. 137–153 (2018)
22. Segal, S., Adi, Y., Pinkas, B., Baum, C., Ganesh, C., Keshet, J.: Fairness in the eyes of the data: certifying machine-learning models. In: Proceedings of the AAAI/ACM Conference on AI, Ethics, and Society (AIES), pp. 926–935 (2021)
23. Tramèr, F., Boneh, D.: Slalom: fast, verifiable and private execution of neural networks in trusted hardware. In: Proceedings of the 7th International Conference on Learning Representations (ICLR) (2019)
24. Veeningen, M.: Pinocchio-based adaptive zk-SNARKs and secure/correct adaptive function evaluation. In: Joye, M., Nitaj, A. (eds.) AFRICACRYPT 2017. LNCS, vol. 10239, pp. 21–39. Springer, Cham (2017). https://doi.org/10.1007/978-3-319-57339-7_2
25. Wahby, R.S., Setty, S.T.V., Ren, Z., Blumberg, A.J., Walfish, M.: Efficient RAM and control flow in verifiable outsourced computation. In: Proceedings of the 22nd Annual Network and Distributed System Security Symposium (NDSS) (2015)
26. Waksman, A.: A permutation network. J. ACM **15**(1), 159–163 (1968)
27. Weng, C., Yang, K., Xie, X., Katz, J., Wang, X.: Mystique: efficient conversions for zero-knowledge proofs with applications to machine learning. In: 30th USENIX Security Symposium (USENIX Security 2021), pp. 501–518 (2021)
28. Zhang, J., Fang, Z., Zhang, Y., Song, D.: Zero knowledge proofs for decision tree predictions and accuracy. In: Proceedings of the ACM SIGSAC Conference on Computer and Communications Security (CCS), pp. 2039–2053 (2020)
29. Zhang, Y., Genkin, D., Katz, J., Papadopoulos, D., Papamanthou, C.: VSQL: verifying arbitrary SQL queries over dynamic outsourced databases. In: Proceedings of the IEEE Symposium on Security and Privacy (SP), pp. 863–880 (2017)
30. Zhang, Y., Genkin, D., Katz, J., Papadopoulos, D., Papamanthou, C.: A zero-knowledge version of vsql. IACR Cryptol. ePrint Arch. **2017**, 1146 (2017)
31. Zhang, Y., Genkin, D., Katz, J., Papadopoulos, D., Papamanthou, C.: vram: Faster verifiable RAM with program-independent preprocessing. In: 2018 IEEE Symposium on Security and Privacy, SP 2018, Proceedings, San Francisco, California, USA, 21–23 May 2018, pp. 908–925 (2018)

Old-School Consensus

Be Aware of Your Leaders

Shir Cohen[1,2,3]([✉]), Rati Gelashvili[1,2], Lefteris Kokoris Kogias[1,2,4], Zekun Li[1,2],
Dahlia Malkhi[1,2], Alberto Sonnino[1,2], and Alexander Spiegelman[1,2]

[1] Novi Research, Menlo Park, USA
[2] Novi Research, London, UK
[3] Technion, Haifa, Israel
shirco@cs.technion.ac.il
[4] IST Austria, Klosterneuburg, Austria

Abstract. Advances in blockchains have influenced the State-Machine-Replication (SMR) world and many state-of-the-art blockchain-SMR solutions are based on two pillars: *Chaining* and *Leader-rotation*. A pre-determined round-robin mechanism used for Leader-rotation, however, has an undesirable behavior: crashed parties become designated leaders infinitely often, slowing down overall system performance. In this paper, we provide a new Leader-Aware SMR framework that, among other desirable properties, formalizes a *Leader-utilization* requirement that bounds the number of rounds whose leaders are faulty in crash-only executions.

We introduce Carousel, a novel, reputation-based Leader-rotation solution to achieve Leader-Aware SMR. The challenge in adaptive Leader-rotation is that it cannot rely on consensus to determine a leader, since consensus itself needs a leader. Carousel uses the available on-chain information to determine a leader locally and achieves Liveness despite this difficulty. A HotStuff implementation fitted with Carousel demonstrates drastic performance improvements: it increases throughput over 2x in faultless settings and provided a 20x throughput increase and 5x latency reduction in the presence of faults.

Keywords: SMR · Leader-election · Chain-quality

1 Introduction

Recently, Byzantine agreement protocols in the eventually synchronous model such as Tendermint [5], Casper FFG [6], and HotStuff [22], brought two important concepts from the world of blockchains to the traditional State Machine Replication (SMR) [12] settings, *Leader-rotation* and *Chaining*. More specifically, these algorithms operate by designating one party as *leader* of each round to propose the next block of transactions that extends a *chained* sequence of blocks. Both properties depart from the approach used by classical protocols such as PBFT [7], Multi-Paxos [13] and Raft [17] (the latter two in benign settings). In those solutions, a stable leader operates until it fails and then it is replaced by a new leader. Agreement is formed on an immutable sequence of indexed (rather than chained) transactions, organized in slots.

© International Financial Cryptography Association 2022
I. Eyal and J. Garay (Eds.): FC 2022, LNCS 13411, pp. 279–295, 2022.
https://doi.org/10.1007/978-3-031-18283-9_13

Leader-rotation is important in a Byzantine setting, since parties should not trust each other for load sharing, reward management, resisting censoring of submitted transactions, or ordering requests fairly [11]. The advantage of Chaining is that it simplifies the leader handover since in the common case the chain eliminates the need for new leaders to catch up with outcomes from previous slots.

In the permissioned SMR settings [1], most existing Leader-rotation mechanisms use a round-robin approach to rotate leaders [8,21,22]. This guarantees that honest parties get a chance to be leaders infinitely often, which is sufficient to drive progress and satisfy *Chain-quality* [10]. Roughly speaking, the latter stipulates that the number of blocks committed to the chain by honest parties is proportional to the honest nodes' percentage. The drawback of such a mechanism is that it does not bound the number of faulty parties which are designated as leaders during an execution. This has a negative effect on latency even in crash-only executions, as each crashed leader delays progress. Similarly to XFT [14], we seek to improve the performance in such executions. Unlike XFT, we also maintain Chain-quality to thwart Byzantine attacks.

In this paper, we propose a leader-rotation mechanism, Carousel, that enjoys both worlds. Carousel satisfies non-zero Chain-quality, and at the same time, bounds the number of faulty leaders in crash-only executions after the global stabilization time (GST), a property we call *Leader-utilization*. The Carousel algorithm leverages Chaining to execute purely locally using information available on the chain, avoiding any extra communication. To capture all requirements, we formalize a *Leader-Aware SMR* problem model, which alongside Agreement, Liveness and Chain-quality, also requires Leader-utilization. We prove that Carousel satisfies the Leader-Aware SMR requirements.

The high-level idea to satisfy Leader-utilization is to track active parties via the records of their participation (e.g. signatures) at the committed chain prefix and elect leaders among them. However, if done naively, the adversary can exploit this mechanism to violate Liveness or Chain-quality. The challenge is that there is no consensus on a committed prefix to determine a leader, since consensus itself needs a leader. Diverging local views on committed prefixes may be effectuated, for instance, by having a Byzantine leader reveal an updated head of the chain to a subset of the honest parties. Hence, Carousel may not have agreement on the leaders of some rounds, but nevertheless guarantees Liveness and Leader-utilization after GST.

To focus on our leader-rotation mechanism, we abstract away all other SMR components by defining an SMR framework. Similarly to [20], we capture the logic and properties of forming and certifying blocks of transactions in each round in a *Leader-based round (LBR)* abstraction, and rely on a Pacemaker abstraction [4,15,16] for round synchronization. We prove that when instantiated into this framework, Carousel yields a Leader-Aware SMR protocol. Specifically, we show (1) for Leader-utilization: at most $O(f^2)$ faulty leaders may be elected in crash-only executions (after GST); and (2) for Chain-quality: one out of $O(f)$ blocks is authored by an honest party in the worst-case. Note that in practice

Chain-quality guarantees are much better since the worst case scenario requires the adversary to posses an unrealistic power.

We provide an implementation of Carousel in a HotStuff-based system and an evaluation that demonstrates a significant performance improvement. Specifically, we get over 2x throughput increase in faultless settings, and 20x throughput increase and 5x latency reduction in the presence of faults. Our mechanism is adopted in the most recent version of DiemBFT [21], a deployed HotStuff-based system.

2 Model and Problem Definition

We consider a message-passing model with a set of n parties $\Pi = \{p_1, \ldots, p_n\}$, out of which $f < \frac{n}{3}$ are subject to failures. A party is *crashed* if it halts prematurely at some point during an execution. If it deviates from the protocol it is *Byzantine*. An *honest* party never crashes or becomes Byzantine. We say that an execution is *crash-only* if there are no Byzantine failures therein.

For the theoretical analysis we assume an eventually synchronous communication model [9] in which there is a global stabilization time (GST) after which the network becomes synchronous. That is, before GST the network is completely asynchronous, while after GST messages arrive within a known bounded time, denoted as δ.

As we later describe, we abstract away much of the SMR implementation details by defining and using primitives. Therefore, our Leader-rotation solution is model agnostic and the adversarial model depends on the implementation choices for those primitives.

2.1 Leader-Aware SMR

In this section we introduce some notation and then define the Leader-Aware SMR problem. Roughly speaking, Leader-Aware SMR captures the desired properties of the Leader-rotation mechanism in SMR protocols that are leader-based.

An SMR protocol consists of a set of parties aiming to maintain a growing chain of *blocks*. Parties participate in a sequence of rounds, attempting to form a block per round. In Leader-Aware SMR, each round is driven by a leader. We capture these rounds via the Leader-based round (LBR) abstraction defined later.

A block consists of transactions and the following meta-data:

- A (cryptographic) link to a *parent* block. Thus, each block implicitly defines a chain to the genesis block.
- A round number in which the block was formed.
- The author id of the party that created the block.
- A certificate that (cryptographically) proves that $2f + 1$ parties endorsed the block in the given round and with the given author. We assume that it is possible to obtain the set of $2f + 1$ endorsing parties[1].

---

[1] This can be achieved by multi-signature schemes which are practically as efficient as threshold signatures [3].

Note that having a round number and the author id as a part of the block is not strictly necessary, but they facilitate formalization of properties and analysis. For example, an *honest block* is defined as a block authored by an honest party and a *Byzantine block* is a block authored by a Byzantine party.

We assume a predicate `certified`$(B, r) \in \{true, false\}$ that locally checks whether the block has a valid certificate, i.e. it has $2f + 1$ endorsements for round r. If `certified`$(B, r) = true$ we say that B is a *certified* block of round r. When clear from context, we say that B is *certified* without explicitly mentioning the round number.

An SMR protocol does not terminate, but rather continues to form blocks. Each block B determines its *implied* chain starting from B to the genesis block via the parent links. We use notation $B \longrightarrow B'$, saying B' *extends* B, if block B is on B''s implied chain. Honest parties can *commit* blocks in some rounds (but usually not all). A committed block indirectly commits its implied chain. An SMR protocol must satisfy the following:

Definition 1 (Leader-Aware SMR).

- **Liveness:** *An unbounded number of blocks are committed by honest parties.*
- **Agreement:** *If an honest party p_i has committed a block B, then for any block B' committed by any honest party p_j either $B \longrightarrow B'$ or $B' \longrightarrow B$.*
- **Chain-quality:** *For any block B committed by an honest party p_i, the proportion of Byzantine blocks on B's implied chain is bounded.*
- **Leader-Utilization:** *In crash-only executions, after GST, the number of rounds r for which no honest party commits a block formed in r is bounded.*

The first two properties are common to SMR protocols. While most SMR algorithms satisfy the above mentioned Liveness condition, a stronger Liveness property can be defined, requiring that each honest party commits an unbounded number of blocks. This property can be easily be achieved by an orthogonal forwarding mechanism, where each honest leader that creates a block explicitly sends it to all other parties. A notion of Chain-quality that bounds the adversarial control over chain contents was first suggested by Garay et al. [10]. We introduce the Leader-utilization property to capture the quality of the Leader-rotation mechanism in crash-only executions. Note that although it is tempting to define leader utilization for Byzantine executions as well, it seems impossible to do so without failure detectors. Byzantine parties can decide not to form a block whenever they become leaders. This reduces to the question – can we bound the number of adversarial leaders? the answer is, unfortunately, no.

3   Leader-Aware SMR: The Framework

In order to isolate the Leader-rotation problem in Leader-Aware SMR protocols, we abstract away the remaining logic into two components. First, similar to [19,20] we capture the logic to form and commit blocks by the *Leader-based round (LBR)* abstraction (Sect. 3.1). We follow [4,16] and capture round synchronization by the Pacemaker abstraction (Sect. 3.2). These two abstractions can be instantiated with known implementations from existing SMR protocols.

In Sect. 3.3 we define the core API for Leader-rotation and combine it with the above components to construct an SMR protocol. In Sect. 4 we present a Leader-rotation algorithm that can be easily computed based on locally available information and makes the construction a Leader-Aware SMR.

3.1 Leader-Based Round (LBR)

The LBR abstraction exposes to each party p_i an API to invoke $LBR(r, \ell)$, where $r \in \mathbb{N}$ is a round number and ℓ is the leader of round r according to party p_i. Intuitively, a leader-based round captures an attempt by parties to certify and commit a block formed by the leader[2] – which naturally requires sufficiently many parties to agree on the identity of the leader. We assume that non-Byzantine parties can only endorse a block B with round number r and author ℓ by calling $LBR(r, \ell)$.

Every LBR invocation returns within $\Delta_l > c\delta$ time, where c depends on the specific LBR implementation (i.e., each round requires a causal chain of c messages to complete). That is, Δ_l captures the inherent timeouts required for eventually synchronous protocols. We say that round r has $k \leq n$ *LBR-synchronized(ℓ)* invocations if k honest parties invoke $LBR(r, \ell)$ after GST and within $\Delta_l - c\delta$ time of each other with the same party ℓ[3].

The return value of an LBR invocation in round r is always a block with a round number $r' \leq r$. The intention is for LBR invocations to return gradually growing committed chains. Occasionally, there is no progress, in which case the invocations are allowed to return a committed block whose round r' is smaller than r. Formally, the output from LBR satisfies the following properties:

Definition 2 (LBR)

– **Endorsement:** *For any block B and round r, if* certified$(B, r) = true$, *then the set of endorsing parties of B contains $2f + 1$ parties.*[4]
– **Agreement:** *If B and B' are certified blocks that are each returned to an honest party from an LBR invocation, then either $B \longrightarrow B'$ or $B' \longrightarrow B$.*
– **Progress:** *If there are $k \geq 2f + 1$ LBR-synchronized(ℓ) invocations at round r and ℓ is honest, then they all return a certified B with round number r authored by ℓ.*
– **Blocking:** *If a non-Byzantine party ℓ never invokes $LBR(r, \ell)$, then no $LBR(r, \ell)$ invocation may return a certified block formed in round r.*

---

[2] Existing SMR protocols may have separate rounds (and even leaders) for forming and committing blocks, but this distinction is not relevant for the purposes of the paper and LBR abstraction is defined accordingly.

[3] LBR-synchronized requires that the corresponding execution intervals have a shared intersection lasting $\geq c\delta$ time.

[4] Note that Endorsement implies that although LBR can be invoked for round r with more than one leader l, there is at most one author for a block in r.

– **Reputation:** *If a non-Byzantine party p never invokes LBR for round r, then any certified block B with round number r does not contain p among its endorsers.*

The LBR definition intends to capture just the key properties required for round abstraction in SMR protocols but leaves room for various interesting behavior. For example, if the progress preconditions are not met at round r, then some honest parties may return a block B for round r while others do not. Moreover, in this case the adversary can *hide* certified blocks from honest parties and reveal them at any point via the LBR return values.

3.2   The Pacemaker

The Pacemaker [4,15,16] component is a commonly used abstraction, which ensures that, after GST, parties are synchronized and participate in the same round long enough to satisfy the LBR progress. We assume the following:

Definition 3 (Pacemaker). *The Pacemaker eventually produces* new_round(r) *notifications at honest parties for each round r. Suppose for some round r all* new_round(r) *notifications at non-Byzantine parties occur after GST, the first of which occurs at time T_f, and the last of which occurs at time T_l. Then no non-Byzantine party receives a* new_round(r + 1) *notification before $T_l + \Delta_p$ and $T_l - T_f \leq \delta$. The Pacemaker can be instantiated with any parameter $\Delta_p > 0$.*

To combine the LBR and Pacemaker components into an SMR protocol in Sect. 3.3 we fix $\Delta_p = \Delta_l$. Note that by using the above definition, the resulting protocol is not responsive since parties wait Δ_p before advancing rounds. This can easily be fixed by using a more general Pacemaker definitions from [4,15,16]. However, we chose the simplified version above for readability purposes since the Pacemaker is orthogonal to the thesis of our paper.

3.3   Leader-Rotation - The Missing Component

In Algorithm 1 we show how to combine the LBR and Pacemaker abstractions into a leader-based SMR protocol. The missing component is the Leader-rotation mechanism, which exposes a choose_leader(r, B) API. It takes a round number $r \in \mathbb{N}$ and a block B and returns a party $p \in \Pi$. The choose_leader procedure is locally computed by each honest party at the beginning of every round.

The Agreement property of Algorithm 1 follows immediately from the Agreement property of LBR, regardless of choose_leader implementation. In Appendix A we prove that Algorithm 1 satisfies liveness as long as all honest parties follow the same choose_leader procedure and that this procedure returns the same honest party at all of them infinitely often. In the next section we instantiate Algorithm 1 with Carousel: a specific choose_leader implementation to obtain a Leader-Aware SMR protocol. That is, we prove that Algorithm 1 with Carousel satisfies liveness, Chain-quality, and Leader-utilization.

Algorithm 1. Constructing SMR: code for party p_i

```
1: commit_head ← genesis
2: upon new_round (r) do
3:     leader ← choose_leader (r, commit_head)
4:     B ← LBR(r,leader)
5:     if commit_head ⟶ B then
6:         commit B    ▷ all blocks in B's implied chain that were not yet committed.
7:         commit_head ← B
```

4 Carousel: A Novel Leader-Rotation Algorithm

In this section, we present Carousel– our Leader-rotation mechanism. The pseudo-code is given in Algorithm 2, which combined with Algorithm 1 allows to obtain the first Leader-Aware SMR protocol.

We use reputation to avoid crashed leaders in crash-only executions. Specifically, at the beginning of round r, an honest party checks if it has committed a block B with round number $r - 1$. In this case, the endorsers of B are guaranteed to not have crashed by round $r - 1$. For Chain-quality purposes, the f latest authors of committed blocks are excluded from the set of endorsers, and a leader is chosen deterministically from the remaining set.

If an honest party has not committed a block with round number $r-1$, it uses a round-robin fallback scheme to elect the round r leader. Notice that different parties may or may not have committed a block with round number $r - 1$ before round r. In fact, the adversary has multiple ways to cause such divergence, e.g. Byzantine behavior, crashes, or message delays. As a result, parties can disagree on the leader's identity, and potentially compromise liveness. We prove, however, that Carousel satisfies liveness, as well as leader utilization and Chain-quality. Specifically, we show that (1) the number of rounds r for which no honest party commits a block formed in r is bounded by $O(f^2)$; and (2) at least one honest block is committed every $5f + 2$ rounds. The argument is non-trivial since, for example, we need to show that the adversary cannot selectively alternate the fallback and reputation schemes to control the Chain-quality.

4.1 Correctness

Leader-Utilization. In this section, we are concerned with the protocol efficiency against crash failures. We consider time after GST, and at most f parties that may crash during the execution but follow the protocol until they crash (i.e., non-Byzantine). We say that a party p crashes in round r if $r + 1$ is the minimal number for which p does not invoke LBR in line 4. Accordingly, we say that a party is *alive* at all rounds before it crashes. In addition, we say that a round r occurs after GST if all new_round (r) notifications at honest parties occur after GST.

We start by introducing an auxiliary lemma which extends the LBR Progress property for crash-only executions. Since in a crash-only case faulty parties follow

Algorithm 2. Leader-rotation: code for party p_i

```
 8:  procedure choose_leader(r, commit_head)
 9:      last_authors ← ∅
10:      if commit_head.round_number ≠ r − 1 then
11:          return (r mod n)                          ▷ round-robin fallback
12:      active ← commit_head.endorsers
13:      block ← commit_head
14:      while |last_authors| < f ∧ block ≠ genesis do
15:          last_authors ← last_authors ∪ {block.author}
16:          block ← block.parent
17:      leader_candidates ← active \ last_authors
18:      return leader_candidates.pick_one()      ▷ deterministically pick from the set
```

the protocol before they crash, honest parties cannot distinguish between an honest leader and an alive leader that has not crashed yet. Hence, the LBR Progress property hold even if the leader crashes later in the execution. Formal proof of the following technical lemma, using indistinguishability arguments, appears in Appendix A.

Lemma 1. *In a crash-only execution, let r be a round with $k \geq 2f + 1$ LBR-synchronized(ℓ) invocations, such that ℓ is alive at round r, then these k invocations return a certified B with round number r authored by ℓ.*

Furthermore, if no party crashes in a given round and the preconditions of the adapted LBR Progress conditions are met a block is committed in that round and another alive leader is chosen.

Lemma 2. *If the preconditions of Lemma 1 hold and no party crashes in round r, then $k \geq 2f + 1$ honest parties commit a block for round r and return the same leader ℓ' at line 3 of round $r + 1$ and ℓ' is alive at round r.*

Proof. By Lemma 1, k honest parties return from $LBR(r, \ell)$ with a certified block B with round number r authored by ℓ. Then, since $commit\_head \longrightarrow B$, they all commit B at line 6 of round $r+1$. By the LBR Reputation property, the set of B's endorsers does not include parties that crashed in rounds $< r$. Since no party crashes in round r, B's endorsers are all alive in round r. Since these $2f + 1$ parties each committed block B with round number r, in choose_leader in Algorithm 1, they all use the reputation scheme (line 18) to choose the leader of round $r + 1$, that we showed is alive at round r.

Next, we utilize the latter to prove that in a round with no crashes, it is impossible for a minority of honest parties to return with a certified block from an LBR instance. Namely, either no honest party returns a block, or at least $2f + 1$ of them do.

Lemma 3. *In a crash-only execution, let r be a round after GST in which no party crashes. If one honest party returns from LBR with a certified block B with round number r, then $2f + 1$ honest parties return with B.*

Proof. Assume an honest party returns a certified block B with round number r after invoking $LBR(r, \ell)$. By the LBR Blocking property, ℓ itself must have invoked $LBR(r, \ell)$ and by assumption it was *alive* at round r. By the LBR Endorsement property, the set of endorsing parties of B contains $2f + 1$ parties. Since we consider a crash-only execution, it follows by assumption that $2f + 1$ party called $LBR(r, \ell)$. Due to the use of Pacemaker, these calls are LBR-synchronized(ℓ) invocations. Finally, by Lemma 1 all these calls return a certified B with round number r authored by ℓ.

We prove that in a window of $f + 2$ rounds without crashes, there must be a round with the sufficient conditions for a block to be committed for that round.

Lemma 4. *In a crash-only execution, let R be a round after GST such that no party crashes between rounds R and $R + f + 2$ (including). There exists a round $R \leq r \leq R + f + 2$ for which there are $2f + 1$ LBR-synchronized(ℓ) invocations with a leader ℓ that is* alive *at round r.*

Proof. First, let us consider the LBR invocations for round R. By Lemma 3, if one honest party returns with a block B with round number R, then $2f + 1$ honest parties return with B, commit it and update *commit_head* accordingly (line 7). In this case, there are $2f+1$ `choose_leader`$(R+1, B)$ invocations, which all return at line 18. Otherwise, no party return a block with round number R, and thus they all return at line 11. By the code and since a block implies a unique chain, in both cases $2f + 1$ honest parties return the same leader ℓ in `choose_leader`$(R + 1, B)$ (either by reputation or round-robin). By the Pacemaker guarantees and since $R + 1$ occurs after GST, there are at least $2f + 1$ LBR-synchronized(ℓ) invocations. If ℓ is alive at round $R + 1$, we are done. Otherwise, ℓ must have been crashed before round R by the alive definition and lemma assumptions. Thus, by the LBR Blocking property no honest party commits a block for round R and they all choose the same leader for the following round at line 11. The lemma follows by applying the above argument for $R + f + 2 - R + 1 = f + 1$ rounds.

Finally, we bound by $O(f^2)$ the total number of rounds in a crash-only execution for which no honest party commits a block:

Lemma 5. *Consider a crash-only execution. After GST, the number of rounds r for which no honest party commits a block formed in r is bounded by $O(f^2)$.*

Proof. Consider a crash-only execution and let $R_1, R_2, \ldots R_k$ the rounds after GST in which parties crash ($k \leq f$). For ease of presentation we call a round for which no honest party commits a block formed in r a *skipped* round. We prove that the number of skipped rounds between R_i and R_{i+1} for $1 \leq i < k$ is bounded. If $R_{i+1} - R_i < f + 4$, then there are at most $f + 4$ rounds and hence at most $f + 4$ skipped rounds. Otherwise, we show that at most $f + 2$ rounds are skipped between rounds R_i and R_{i+1}.

First, by Lemma 4, there exists a round $R_i < R_i + 1 \leq r \leq R_i + 1 + f + 2 < R_{i+1}$ for which there are $2f + 1$ LBR-synchronized(ℓ) invocations with a leader

ℓ that is *alive* at round r. By Lemma 2, since no party crashes in round r, $2f + 1$ honest parties return the same leader ℓ' at line 3 of round $r + 1$ and ℓ' is alive at round r. Since no party crashes at round $r + 1$ as well (because $R_{i+1} - R_i \geq f + 4$), ℓ' is alive at round $r + 1$. By the Pacemaker guarantees and since we consider rounds after GST, we conclude that there are at least $2f + 1$ LBR-synchronized(ℓ') invocations for round $r + 1$. By Lemma 2 applied again for round $r + 1$, $2f + 1$ honest parties commit a block for round $r + 1$. Thus, round $r + 1$ is not *skipped*. We repeat the same arguments until round R_{i+1}, and conclude that in each of these rounds a block is committed. Hence, the rounds that can possibly be skipped between R_i and R_{i+1} are $R_i \leq r' < r$. Thus there are $O(f)$ skipped round between R_i and R_{i+1}. For R_k we use similar arguments but since no party crashes after R_k, we apply Lemma 2 indefinitely. We similarly conclude that there are $O(f)$ skipped rounds after R_k. All in all, since $k \leq f$, we get $O(f^2)$ skipped rounds.

We immediately conclude the following:

Corollary 1. *Algorithm 1 with Algorithm 2 satisfies Leader-utilization.*

Chain-Quality. For the purposes of the Chain-quality proof, we say that a block is committed when some honest party commits it. We say that a block B with round number r is *immediately committed* if an honest party commits B in round r. When we refer to a leader elected in of Algorithm 2 from the round-robin mechanism we mean line 11, and when we refer to a leader elected from the reputation mechanism, we mean line 18.

We begin by showing that each round assigned with an honest round-robin leader implies a committed block in that round or the one that precedes it (not necessarily an honest block).

Lemma 6. *Let r be a round after GST such that $p_i = (r \bmod n)$ is honest. Then, either a Byzantine block with round number $r - 1$ or an honest block with round number $r - 1$ or r is immediately committed.*

Proof. If a block is immediately committed with round number $r - 1$ then we are done. Otherwise, no honest party commits a block with round number $r - 1$ in round $r - 1$, and they all elect the round r leader ℓ using the round-robin mechanism. By the assumption, ℓ is honest.

By the Pacemaker, all honest invocations of $LBR(r, \ell)$ in line 4 are LBR-synchronized(ℓ). Since there are at least $2f + 1$ honest parties, by the LBR Progress property, all honest invocations return the same certified block B with round number r authored by ℓ. Then, the honest parties commit B at line 6.

If there are two consecutive rounds assigned with honest round-robin leaders and in addition the last f committed blocks are Byzantine, then an honest block follows, as proven in the following lemma.

Lemma 7. *Let r' be a round after GST such that $p_i = (r' \mod n)$ and $p_j = (r' + 1 \mod n)$ are honest. Suppose f blocks with round numbers in $[r, r')$ with different Byzantine authors are committed. For a block B with round number r' or $r' + 1$ that is immediately committed, there is an honest block with round number $[r, r' + 1]$ on B's implied chain.*

Proof. By the LBR endorsement assumption and property, the author of block B should be either a reputation-based, or a round-robin leader of round r' or $r' + 1$. If it is a round-robin leader, then by the lemma assumption, the leader is honest and since B is the head of its implied chain, the proof is complete. Thus, in the following we assume that B's author is a reputation-based leader. By the SMR Agreement property and the lemma assumption, B's implied chain contains f blocks with different Byzantine authors and rounds numbers in $[r, r')$. By the code of the reputation-based mechanism, either all f Byzantine authors are excluded from the *leader_candidates* which implies that B has an honest author, or that there is an honest block with round number in $[r, r')$ on B's implied chain.

Lastly, the following lemma proves that in any window of $5f + 2$ rounds an honest block is committed.

Lemma 8. *Let r be a round after GST. At least one honest block is committed with a round number in $[r, r + 5f + 2]$.*

Proof. Suppose for contradiction that no honest block with round number in $[r, r + 5f + 2]$ is committed. There are at least f rounds r' in $[r, r + 3f + 1)$, such that rounds $r' - 1$ and r' are allocated an honest leader by the round-robin mechanism. By Lemma 6, a block with round number $r' - 1$ or r' is immediately committed. Due to Lemma 6 and the contradiction assumption, for any such round r', a Byzantine block with round number $r' - 1$ is immediately committed. Since $r' - 1$ has an honest round-robin leader, the block must be committed from the reputation mechanism.

It follows that f Byzantine blocks with round numbers in $[r, r + 3f + 1)$ are immediately committed from the reputation mechanism, and consequently, they all must have different authors. Note that there exists $r' \in [r + 3f + 1, r + 5f + 2)$ (in a window of $2f + 1$ rounds), such that the round-robin mechanism allocates honest leaders to rounds r' and $r' + 1$. By Lemma 6, a block B with round number r' or $r' + 1$ is immediately committed. Lemma 7 concludes the proof.

We conclude the following:

Corollary 2. *Algorithm 1 with Algorithm 2 satisfies Chain-quality and Liveness.*

Taken jointly, Corollary 1, Corollary 2, and the Agreement property proved in Sect. 3.3 yield the following theorem:

Theorem 1. *Algorithm 1 with Algorithm 2 implements Leader-Aware SMR.*

5   Implementation

We implement Carousel on top of a high-performance open-source implementation of HotStuff[5] [22]. We selected this implementation because it implements a Pacemaker [22], contrarily to the implementation used in the original Hot-Stuff paper[6]. Additionally, it provides well-documented benchmarking scripts to measure performance in various conditions, and it is close to a production system (it provides real networking, cryptography, and persistent storage). It is implemented in Rust, uses Tokio[7] for asynchronous networking, ed25519-dalek[8] for elliptic curve based signatures, and data-structures are persisted using RocksDB[9]. It uses TCP to achieve reliable point-to-point channels, necessary to correctly implement the distributed system abstractions. By default, this Hot-Stuff implementation uses traditional round-robin to elect leaders; we modify its `LeaderElector` module to use Carousel instead. Implementing our mechanism requires adding less than 200 LOC, and does not require any extra protocol message or cryptographic tool. We are open-sourcing Carousel[10] along with any measurements data to enable reproducible results[11].

6   Evaluation

We evaluate the throughput and latency of HotStuff equipped Carousel through experiments on Amazon Web Services (AWS). We then show how it improves over the baseline round-robin leader-rotation mechanism. We particularly aim to demonstrate that Carousel (i) introduces no noticeable performance overhead when the protocol runs in ideal conditions (that is, all parties are honest) and with a small number of parties, and (ii) drastically improves both latency and throughput in the presence of crash-faults. Note that evaluating BFT protocols in the presence of Byzantine faults is still an open research question [2].

   We deploy a testbed on AWS, using `m5.8xlarge` instances across 5 different AWS regions: N. Virginia (us-east-1), N. California (us-west-1), Sydney (ap-southeast-2), Stockholm (eu-north-1), and Tokyo (ap-northeast-1). Parties are distributed across those regions as equally as possible. Each machine provides 10 Gbps of bandwidth, 32 virtual CPUs (16 physical core) on a 2.5 GHz, Intel Xeon Platinum 8175, 128 GB memory, and run Linux Ubuntu server 20.04.

   In the following sections, each measurement in the graphs is the average of 5 independent runs, and the error bars represent one standard deviation. Our baseline experiment parameters are 10 honest parties, a block size of 500 KB, a transaction size of 512 B, and one benchmark client per party submitting

---

[5] https://github.com/asonnino/hotstuff.
[6] https://github.com/hot-stuff/libhotstuff.
[7] https://tokio.rs.
[8] https://github.com/dalek-cryptography/ed25519-dalek.
[9] https://rocksdb.org.
[10] https://github.com/asonnino/hotstuff/tree/leader-reputation.
[11] https://github.com/asonnino/hotstuff/tree/leader-reputation/data.

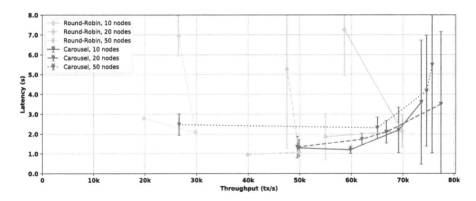

Fig. 1. Comparative throughput-latency performance of HotStuff equipped with Carousel and with the baseline round-robin. WAN measurements with 10, 20, 50 parties. No party faults, 500 KB maximum block size and 512 B transaction size.

transactions at a fixed rate for a duration of 5 min. We then crash and vary the number of parties through our experiments to illustrate their impact on performance. The leader timeout value is set to 5 s for runs with 10 and 20 parties and increased to 10 s for runs with 50 parties. When referring to *latency*, we mean the time elapsed from when the client submits the transaction to when the transaction is committed by one party. We measure it by tracking sample transactions throughout the system.

6.1   Benchmark in Ideal Conditions

Figure 1 depicts the performance of HotStuff with both Carousel and the baseline round-robin running with 10, 20, and 50 honest parties. For runs with a small number of parties (e.g., 10), the performance of the baseline round-robin Hot-Stuff is similar to HotStuff equipped with Carousel. We observe a peak throughput around 70,000 tx/s with a latency of around 2 s. This illustrates that the extra code required to implement Carousel has negligible overhead and does not degrade performance when the total number of parties is small. When increasing the system's size (to 20 and 50 parties), HotStuff with Carousel greatly outperforms the baseline: the bigger the system's size, the bigger the performance improvement. With 50 nodes, the throughput of our mechanism-based HotStuff increases by over 2x with respect to the baseline, and remains comparable to the 10-parties testbed. After a few initial timeouts, Carousel has the benefit to focus on electing performant leaders. Leaders on more remote geo-locations that are typically slower are elected less often, the protocol is thus driven by the most performant parties. Similar ideas were presented in [18] in the context of distributed data storage, where a leader placement was optimized based on replicas' locations. In our experiments, latency is similar for both implementations and around 2–3 s.

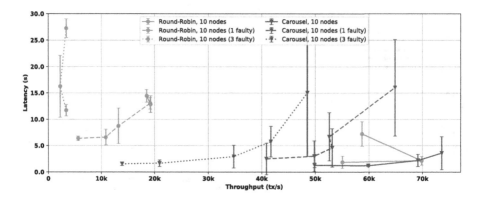

Fig. 2. Comparative throughput-latency performance of HotStuff equipped with Carousel and with the baseline round-robin. WAN measurements with 10 parties. Zero, one and three party faults, 500 KB maximum block size and 512 B transaction size.

6.2 Performance Under Faults

Figure 2 depicts the performance of HotStuff with both Carousel and the baseline round-robin when a set of 10 parties suffers 1 or 3 crash-faults (the maximum that can be tolerated). The baseline round-robin HotStuff suffers a massive degradation in throughput as well as a dramatic increase in latency. For three faults, the throughput of the baseline HotStuff drops over 30x and its latency increases 5x compared to no faults. In contrast, HotStuff equipped with Carousel maintains a good level of throughput: our mechanism does not elect crashed leaders, the protocol continues to operate electing leaders from the remaining active parties, and is not overly affected by the faulty ones. The reduction in throughput is in great part due to losing the capacity of faulty parties. When operating with 3 faults, Carousel provides a 20x throughput increase and about 5x latency reduction with respect to the baseline round-robin.

Figure 3 depicts the evolution of the performance of HotStuff with both Carousel and the baseline round-robin when gradually crashing nodes through time. For roughly the first minute, all parties are honest; we then crash 1 party (roughly) every minute until a maximum of 3 parties are crashed. The input transaction rate is fixed to 10,000 tx/s throughout the experiment. Each data point is the average over intervals of 10 s. For roughly the first minute (when all parties are honest), both systems perform ideally, timely committing all input transactions. Then, as expected, the baseline round-robin HotStuff suffers from temporary throughput losses when a crashed leader is elected. Similarly, its latency increases with the number of faulty parties and presents periods where no transactions are committed at all. In contrast, HotStuff equipped with Carousel delivers a stable throughput by quickly detecting and eliminating crashed leaders. Its latency is barely affected by the faulty parties. This graph clearly illustrates how Carousel allows HotStuff to deliver a seamless client experience even in the presence of faults.

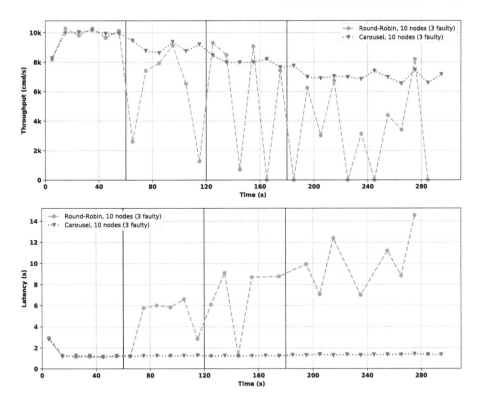

Fig. 3. Comparative performance of HotStuff equipped with Carousel and with the baseline round-robin when gradually crashing nodes through time. The input transactions rate is fixed to 10,000 tx/s; 1 party (up to a maximum of 3) crashes roughly every minute. WAN measurements with 10 parties, 500 KB maximum block size and 512 B transaction size.

7   Conclusions

Leader-rotations mechanisms in chaining-based SMR protocols were previously overlooked. Existing approaches degraded performance by keep electing faulty leaders in crash-only executions. We captured the practical requirement of leader-rotation mechanism via a Leader-utilization property, use it define the Leader-Aware SMR problem, and described an algorithm that implements it. That is, we presented a locally executed algorithm to rotate leaders that achieves both: Leader-utilization in crash-only executions and Chain-quality in Byzantine ones. We evaluated our mechanism in a Hotstuff-based open source system and demonstrated drastic performance improvements in both throughput and latency compared to the round-robin baseline.

Appendix A   Correctness

Lemma 9. *If* choose_leader *returns the same honest party at all honest parties for infinitely many rounds, then each honest party commits an unbounded number of blocks.*

Proof. If choose_leader returns the same honest party at all honest parties for infinitely many rounds, then there are infinitely many rounds after GST for which it does so. Let r be such a round. By the Pacemaker guarantees, all honest parties make LBR-synchronized(ℓ) invocations with the same honest leader ℓ returned from the choose_leader procedure. By the LBR Progress property, they all return a certified block B and commit it at line 6.

Lemma 1. *In a crash-only execution, let r be a round with $k \geq 2f + 1$ LBR-synchronized(ℓ) invocations, such that ℓ is alive at round r, then these k invocations return a certified B with round number r authored by ℓ.*

Proof. Let π_1 be a crash-only execution, such that round r has $k \geq 2f + 1$ LBR-synchronized(ℓ) invocations with a leader ℓ that is alive at round r. If ℓ is honest, then the LBR Progress property concludes the proof.

Otherwise, ℓ is faulty and by definition it crashes in round $> r$. Let π_2 be a crash-only execution that is identical to π_1 until ℓ crashes, and the rest of π_2 is an arbitrary execution where the honest parties in π_1 remain honest but ℓ never crashes and is also honest. Thus, in π_2 the preconditions of the LBR Progress property hold and all k LBR-synchronized(ℓ) invocations return a certified B with round number r authored by ℓ.

An $LBR(r, \ell)$ invocation by any party p completes within Δ_l time, and starts immediately after Pacemaker's new_round(r) notification at p (because choose_leader is computed locally and takes 0 time). By Pacemaker's guarantees, no party receives new_round($r+1$) notification until $\Delta_p = \Delta_l$ time after the last new_round($r+1$) notification at some party, hence all $LBR(r, \ell)$ invocations must complete before any party receives a new_round($r + 1$) notification.

π_1 and π_2 are identical until ℓ crashes, which must happen after ℓ receives its new_round($r + 1$) notification from the Pacemaker. This is because ℓ is alive in round r and follows the protocol, invoking LBR in round $r + 1$ after receiving the new_round($r + 1$) notification. As a result, π_1 and π_2 are indistinguishable to all $LBR(r, \ell)$ invocations, and the k LBR-synchronized(ℓ) invocations in π_1 return certified block B with round number r authored by ℓ as in π_2, as desired.

References

1. Androulaki, E., et al.: Hyperledger fabric: a distributed operating system for permissioned blockchains. In: Proceedings of the Thirteenth EuroSys Conference, pp. 1–15 (2018)
2. Bano, S., et al.: Twins: Bft systems made robust. In: 25th International Conference on Principles of Distributed Systems (OPODIS 2021). Schloss Dagstuhl-Leibniz-Zentrum für Informatik (2022)

3. Boneh, D., Drijvers, M., Neven, G.: The modified BLS multi-signature construction (2018). http://www.crypto.stanford.edu/~dabo/pubs/papers/BLSmultisig.html
4. Bravo, M., Chockler, G., Gotsman, A.: Making byzantine consensus live. In: 34th International Symposium on Distributed Computing (DISC 2020). Schloss Dagstuhl-Leibniz-Zentrum für Informatik (2020)
5. Buchman, E.: Tendermint: Byzantine fault tolerance in the age of blockchains. Ph.D. thesis (2016)
6. Buterin, V., Griffith, V.: Casper the friendly finality gadget
7. Castro, M., Liskov, B., et al.: Practical byzantine fault tolerance. In: OSDI 99, pp. 173–186 (1999)
8. Chan, B.Y., Shi, E.: Streamlet: textbook streamlined blockchains. In: Proceedings of the 2nd ACM Conference on Advances in Financial Technologies, pp. 1–11 (2020)
9. Dwork, C., Lynch, N., Stockmeyer, L.: Consensus in the presence of partial synchrony. J. ACM (JACM) **35**(2), 288–323 (1988)
10. Garay, J., Kiayias, A., Leonardos, N.: The bitcoin backbone protocol: analysis and applications. In: Oswald, E., Fischlin, M. (eds.) EUROCRYPT 2015. LNCS, vol. 9057, pp. 281–310. Springer, Heidelberg (2015). https://doi.org/10.1007/978-3-662-46803-6_10
11. Kelkar, M., Zhang, F., Goldfeder, S., Juels, A.: Order-fairness for byzantine consensus. In: Micciancio, D., Ristenpart, T. (eds.) CRYPTO 2020. LNCS, vol. 12172, pp. 451–480. Springer, Cham (2020). https://doi.org/10.1007/978-3-030-56877-1_16
12. Lamport, L.: Time, clocks, and the ordering of events in a distributed system. In: Communications of the ACM, vol. 21, pp. 558–565 (1978)
13. Lamport, L., et al.: Paxos made simple. ACM Sigact News **32**(4), 18–25 (2001)
14. Liu, S., Viotti, P., Cachin, C., Quéma, V., Vukolić, M.: {XFT}: practical fault tolerance beyond crashes. In: 12th USENIX Symposium on Operating Systems Design and Implementation ({OSDI} 16), pp. 485–500 (2016)
15. Naor, O., Baudet, M., Malkhi, D., Spiegelman, A.: Cogsworth: byzantine View Synchronization. Cryptoeconomic Syst. **1**(2), 22 Oct 2021
16. Naor, O., Keidar. I.:. Expected linear round synchronization: the missing link for linear byzantine smr. In: 34th International Symposium on Distributed Computing (DISC 2020). Schloss Dagstuhl-Leibniz-Zentrum für Informatik (2020)
17. Ongaro, D., Ousterhout, J.: In search of an understandable consensus algorithm. In: 2014 USENIX Annual Technical Conference (USENIX ATC 14), pp. 305–319 (2014)
18. Sharov, A., Shraer, A., Merchant, A., Stokely, M.: Take me to your leader! online optimization of distributed storage configurations. In: Proceedings of the VLDB Endowment, vol. 8(12) (2015)
19. Spiegelman, A.: In search for an optimal authenticated byzantine agreement. In: 35th International Symposium on Distributed Computing (2021)
20. Spiegelman, A., Rinberg, A., Malkhi, D.: Ace: abstract consensus encapsulation for liveness boosting of state machine replication. In: 24th International Conference on Principles of Distributed Systems (OPODIS 2020). Schloss Dagstuhl-Leibniz-Zentrum für Informatik
21. The Diem Team. Diembft v4: State machine replication in the diem blockchain. http://www.developers.diem.com/docs/technical-papers/state-machine-replication-paper.html
22. Yin, M., Malkhi, D., Reiter, M.K., Gueta, G.G., Abraham, I.: Hotstuff: Bft consensus with linearity and responsiveness. In: Proceedings of the 2019 ACM Symposium on Principles of Distributed Computing, pp. 347–356 (2019)

Jolteon and Ditto: Network-Adaptive Efficient Consensus with Asynchronous Fallback

Rati Gelashvili[1], Lefteris Kokoris-Kogias[1,2], Alberto Sonnino[1], Alexander Spiegelman[1], and Zhuolun Xiang[1,3(✉)]

[1] Novi Research, Novi, USA
{gelash,asonnino,sashaspiegelman}@fb.com
[2] IST Austria, Klosterneuburg, Austria
ekokoris@ist.ac.at
[3] University of Illinois at Urbana-Champaign, Champaign, USA
xiangz1@illinois.edu

Abstract. Existing committee-based Byzantine state machine replication (SMR) protocols, typically deployed in production blockchains, face a clear trade-off: (1) they either achieve linear communication cost in the steady state, but sacrifice liveness during periods of asynchrony, or (2) they are robust (progress with probability one) but pay quadratic communication cost. We believe this trade-off is unwarranted since existing linear protocols still have asymptotic quadratic cost in the worst case. We design Ditto, a Byzantine SMR protocol that enjoys the best of both worlds: optimal communication on and off the steady state (linear and quadratic, respectively) and progress guarantee under asynchrony and DDoS attacks. We achieve this by replacing the view-synchronization of partially synchronous protocols with an asynchronous fallback mechanism at no extra asymptotic cost. Specifically, we start from HotStuff, a state-of-the-art linear protocol, and gradually build Ditto. As a separate contribution and an intermediate step, we design a 2-chain version of HotStuff, Jolteon, which leverages a quadratic view-change mechanism to reduce the latency of the standard 3-chain HotStuff. We implement and experimentally evaluate all our systems to prove that breaking the robustness-efficiency trade-off is in the realm of practicality.

1 Introduction

The popularity of blockchain protocols generated a surge in researching how to increase the efficiency and robustness of consensus protocols used for agreement (Table 1). On the efficiency front, the focus has been on decreasing the communication complexity in the steady state, first to quasilinear [19] and ultimately to linear [15,32]. These protocols work in the eventually synchronous model and require a leader to aggregate proofs. However, handling leader failures or unexpected network delays requires quadratic communication and if the network is asynchronous, there is no liveness guarantee. On the robustness side, recent protocols [4,25,30] make progress by having each replica act as the leader and

I. Eyal and J. Garay (Eds.): FC 2022, LNCS 13411, pp. 296–315, 2022.
https://doi.org/10.1007/978-3-031-18283-9_14

Table 1. Theoretical comparison of our protocol implementations. For HotStuff and our protocols, sync $O(n)$ assumes synchrony and no faults. Message complexity measures the cost per committed block (that contains hash digests of transactions). Rounds measure the block-commit latency. $E(r)$ means r rounds in expectation.

	Message complexity	Rounds	Liveness
HotStuff [32]	sync $O(n)$	7	Not live if async
VABA [4]	$O(n^2)$	$E(16.5)$	Always live
Jolteon	sync $O(n)$	5	Not live if async
Ditto	sync $O(n)$, async $O(n^2)$	sync 5, async $E(10.5)$	Always live

decide on a leader retroactively. This requires quadratic communication even under good network conditions when the adversary is strongly adaptive [2].

We believe that in practice, we need the best of both worlds. An efficient steady state is beneficial for any production system, but for blockchains to support important (e.g. financial) infrastructure, robustness against asynchrony is also key. First, unpredictable network delays are a common condition when running in a geo-distributed network environment, e.g. over the Internet. Second, the possibility of targeted DDoS attacks on the leaders of leader-based protocols motivates the leaderless nature of the asynchronous solutions. Thus, we ask:

Are there efficient blockchain systems that have a linear steady state and are robust against asynchrony?

This is an important question, posed as early as [21], and studied from a theoretical prospective [27,29], but the existing blockchain systems still forfeit robustness for efficiency [15,19,32]. In this paper, we answer the above question with the first practical system, Ditto, tailor-made to directly apply to the prominent HotStuff/DiemBFT [31,32] family of protocols.

Contribution (i): Jolteon. As an intermediate step to build Ditto, we first present Jolteon, a protocol that's a hybrid of HotStuff [32] and classical PBFT [8]. Jolteon abandons the linear view-change [32] of HotStuff/DiemBFT, since the protocol anyway has a quadratic pacemaker [31]. In particular, Jolteon preserves the linearity of HotStuff under good network conditions while reducing the steady state block-commit latency by 30% using a 2-chain commit rule. This decrease in latency comes at the cost of a quadratic view-change. As the pacemaker is already quadratic, as expected, this does not affect performance in our experiments.

Contribution (ii): Ditto. We design Ditto, which combines the optimistic (good network conditions) linear steady state with pessimistic (worst-case network conditions) liveness guarantees with no extra asymptotic communication cost. Ditto is based on the key observation that when there is asynchrony or failures, the protocols with linear steady state still pay the quadratic cost, same as state-of-the-art asynchronous protocols (e.g., VABA [4] or Dumbo [25]) that provide significantly more robustness. Specifically, Ditto replaces the pacemaker of Jolteon/HotStuff/DiemBFT (a quadratic module that deals with view synchronization) with an asynchronous fallback. In other words, instead of synchronizing views that will anyway fail due to asynchrony or faults, we fall back to an asynchronous protocol that guarantees progress. Furthermore, Ditto switches between the steady state and the fallback *without overhead* (e.g. additional rounds), and maintains *pipelined/chained operations* similar to HotStuff.

Contribution (iii): Implementation and Evaluation. Since Jolteon outperforms the original HotStuff in every scenario, we use it as the basis for Ditto design and implementation. As shown experimentally under good network conditions both Jolteon and Ditto outperform HotStuff. Importantly, Ditto's performance is almost identical to Jolteon in this good case whereas during attack Ditto performs almost identically to our optimized implementation of VABA [4]. In addition, the throughput of Ditto is 50% better than VABA in the steady state and much better than HotStuff and Jolteon under faulty (dead) leaders (30–50% better) or network instability (they drop to 0). Finally, after discussions with the Diem Engineering team, they deployed Jolteon and are currently considering the use of Ditto if attacks or instability of the network happen too often.

2 Preliminaries

We consider a permissioned system that consists of an adversary and n replicas numbered $1, 2, \ldots, n$, where each replica has a public key certified by a public-key infrastructure (PKI). The replicas have all-to-all reliable and authenticated communication channels controlled by the adversary. We say a replica multicasts a message if it sends the message to all replicas. We consider an adversary that can adaptively corrupt up to f replicas, referred as *Byzantine*. The rest of the replicas are called *honest*. The adversary controls the message delivery times, but we assume messages among honest replicas are eventually delivered.

An execution of a protocol is *synchronous* if all message delays between honest replicas are bounded by Δ; is *asynchronous* if they are unbounded; and is *partially synchronous* if there is a global stabilization time (GST) after which they are bounded by Δ [11]. Without loss of generality, we let $n = 3f + 1$ where f denotes the assumed upper bound on the number of Byzantine faults, which is the optimal worst-case resilience bound for asynchrony, partial synchrony [11], or asynchronous protocols with fast synchronous path [5].

Cryptographic Primitives and Assumptions. We assume standard digital signature and public-key infrastructure (PKI), and use $\langle m \rangle_i$ to denote a message m signed by replica i. For simplicity, we assume every message in the protocol is signed by its sender. We also assume an adaptively secure threshold signature scheme such as [22], where a set of signature shares for message m from t (the threshold) distinct replicas can be combined into one threshold signature of the same length for m. We use $\{m\}_i$ to denote a threshold signature share of a message m signed by replica i. We also assume a collision-resistant cryptographic hash function $H(\cdot)$ that can map an input of arbitrary size to an output of fixed size. Any deterministic agreement protocol cannot tolerate even a single fault under asynchrony due to FLP [12]. Our asynchronous fallback protocol generates distributed randomness using the adaptively secure common coin of [23]: the generated randomness of a view is the hash of the unique threshold signature (of threshold $f + 1$) on the view number.

For simplicity of presentation, we assume the above cryptographic schemes are ideal and a trusted dealer equips replicas with these cryptographic materials. The dealer assumption can be lifted using any asynchronous distributed key generation protocol such as [3,9,10,20]. For brevity, we will also omit the cryptographic object sizes (of signature and hash digest) in the complexity measurement in this paper.

BFT SMR. A Byzantine fault-tolerant state machine replication protocol [1] commits client transactions as a log akin to a single non-faulty server, and provides the following two guarantees:

- Safety. Honest replicas commit same transactions at the same log position.
- Liveness. Each transaction is eventually committed by all honest replicas.

We assume that each client transaction will be repeatedly proposed by honest replicas until it is committed[1]. In other words, any transaction will not be censored by Byzantine leaders forever. For most of the paper, we omit the client from the discussion and focus on replicas. SMR protocols usually implement many instances of single-shot Byzantine agreement, but there are various approaches for ordering. We focus on the chaining approach, used in HotStuff [32] and DiemBFT [31], in which each proposal references the previous one and each commit commits the entire prefix of the chain.

Terminology. We present some terminologies used throughout the paper.

- *Round Number and View Number.* The protocol proceeds in rounds and views and each replica keeps track of the current round number and view number, both initialized as 0. Each view can have several rounds and it is incremented by 1 after each asynchronous fallback. Each round r has a designated leader L_r that proposes a new block (defined below) of transactions in round r.
- *Block Format.* A block is formatted as $B = [id, qc, r, v, txn]$ where qc is the quorum certificate (defined below) of B's parent block in the chain, r is the round number of B, v is the view number of B, txn is the digest of a batch of new transactions, and $id = H(qc, r, v, txn)$ is the unique hash digest of qc, r, v, txn. We will use $B.x$ to denote the element x of B.
- *Quorum Certificate.* A *quorum certificate (QC)* of some block B is a threshold signature of a message that includes $B.id, B.r, B.v$, produced by combining the signature shares $\{B.id, B.r, B.v\}$ from a quorum of $n - f = 2f + 1$ replicas. We say a block is *certified* if there exists a QC for the block. Blocks are chained by QCs to form a blockchain, or block-tree if there are forks. The round and view

---

[1] For example, clients can send their transactions to all replicas, and the leader can propose transactions that are not yet included in the blockchain, in the order that they are submitted. With rotating leaders of HotStuff/DiemBFT and random leader election of the asynchronous fallback, the assumption can be guaranteed.

Let L_r be the leader of round r. Each replica keeps the highest voted round r_{vote}, the highest locked round r_{lock} [a], current round number r_{cur}, and the highest quorum certificate qc_{high} (the current view number v_{cur} is not used and remains 0 throughout). Replicas initialize $r_{vote} = 0$, $r_{lock} = 0$, $r_{cur} = 1$, qc_{high} as the QC of the genesis block of round 0, and enter round 1.

Steady State Protocol for Replica i

– **Propose.** Upon entering round r, the leader L_r multicasts a signed block $B = [id, qc_{high}, r, v_{cur}, txn]$.
– **Vote.** Upon receiving the first valid block $B = [id, qc, r, v, txn]$ from L_r in round r, execute *Advance Round, Lock,* and then *Commit* (defined below). If $r = r_{cur}$, $v = v_{cur}$, $r > r_{vote}$ and $qc.r \geq r_{lock}$, vote for B by sending the threshold signature share $\{id, r, v\}_i$ to L_{r+1}, and update $r_{vote} \leftarrow r$.
– **Lock.** (2-chain lock rule) Upon observing any valid qc [b], let qc' be the QC contained in the block certified by qc (i.e., qc' is the parent of qc), the replica updates $r_{lock} \leftarrow \max(r_{lock}, qc'.r)$, and $qc_{high} \leftarrow \max(qc_{high}, qc)$.
– **Commit.** (3-chain commit rule) If there exist three adjacent certified blocks B, B', B'' in the chain with consecutive round numbers, i.e., $B''.r = B'.r+1 = B.r + 2$, the replica commits B and all its ancestors.

Pacemaker Protocol for Replica i

– **Advance Round.** The replica updates current round $r_{cur} \leftarrow \max(r_{cur}, r)$ iff
  • the replica receives or forms a round-$(r-1)$ quorum certificate qc, or
  • the replica receives or forms a round-$(r-1)$ timeout certificate tc.
– **Timer and Timeout.**
  • Upon entering round r, the replica sends the round-$(r-1)$ TC to L_r if it has the TC, and resets its timer to count down for a predefined time interval (timeout τ).
  • When the timer expires, the replica stops voting for round r_{cur} and multicasts a signed timeout message $\langle\{r_{cur}\}_i, qc_{high}\rangle$ where $\{r_{cur}\}_i$ is a threshold signature share.
  • Upon receiving a valid timeout message or TC, execute *Advance Round, Lock,* and then *Commit.*
  • Upon receiving 2f+1 timeouts, form a TC.

---

[a] Corresponds to the *preferred round* in [31].
[b] May be formed from votes (by a leader) or contained in a proposal or a timeout messsage.

Fig. 1. DiemBFT in our terminology.

numbers of QC for block B are denoted by $QC.r$ and $QC.v$, which equals $B.r$ and $B.v$, respectively. A QC or a block of view number v and round number r has rank $rank = (v, r)$, and QCs or blocks are compared lexicographically by their rank (i.e. first by the view number, then by the round number). We use qc_{high} to denote the highest ranked quorum certificate.

– *Timeout Certificate.* A timeout message of round r by a replica contains the replica's threshold signature share on r, and its qc_{high}. A timeout certificate (TC) is formed by a quorum of $n - f = 2f + 1$ timeout messages, containing a threshold signature on a round number r produced by combining $2f + 1$ signature shares $\{r\}$ from the `timeout` messages, and $2f + 1$ qc_{high}'s. A valid TC should only contain qc_{high} with round numbers $< TC.r$, and this will be checked implicitly when a replica receives a TC.

We say a message (block, QC or TC) is valid, if it follows the definition and is properly signed.

Performance Metrics. We consider *communication complexity* per committed block. For the theoretical analysis, we consider the standard latency metric called *block-commit latency*, i.e., the number of rounds for all honest replicas to commit a block since it is proposed by an honest leader (under synchrony and honest leaders). For the empirical analysis, we measure the *end-to-end latency*, i.e., the time to commit a transaction since it is sent by a client.

Description of DiemBFT. The DiemBFT protocol (or LibraBFT) [31] is a production version of HotStuff [32] with a synchronizer implementation (Pacemaker). We describe the full protocol of DiemBFT in Fig. 1, and give a brief description below.

There are two components of DiemBFT, a *Steady State protocol* that makes progress when the round leader is honest, and a *Pacemaker protocol* that advances round numbers either due to the lack of progress or due to the current round being completed.

- *Propose.* The leader L_r, upon entering round r, proposes a block B that extends a block certified by the highest QC it knows about.

When receiving the first valid round-r block from L_r, any replica tries to advance its current round number, and update its highest QC. It also checks for commit, updates its locked round and votes for the block according to the following rules.

- *3-chain commit.* A block can be committed if it is the first block among 3 adjacent certified blocks with consecutive round numbers.
- *2-chain lock.* For any two adjacent certified blocks observed, update the locked round number to be the highest of the first block's round number.
- *Voting.* Replica votes for a block if the block has round and view number same as the replica, and round number higher than last voted block's round, and contains a QC of round no less than replica's locked round number. The replica votes for B by sending a threshold signature share to the next leader.

Then, when the next leader L_{r+1} receives $2f + 1$ such votes, it forms a QC of round r, enters round $r + 1$, proposes the block for that round, and the above process is repeated.

- *Quadratic view-synchronization.* When the timer of some round r expires before entering round $r+1$, the replica stops voting for round r and multicast a timeout containing a threshold signature share for r and its highest QC.

When any replica receives $2f + 1$ such timeout messages, it forms a TC of round r, enters round $r + 1$ and sends the TC to the (next) leader L_{r+1}. When any replica receives a timeout or a TC, it tries to advance its current round number given the high-QCs (in the timeout or TC) or the TC, updates its highest locked round and its highest QC given the high-QCs, and checks if any block can be committed using the same rules above.

3   Jolteon Design

In this section, we describe how we turn DiemBFT into Jolteon – a 2-chain version of DiemBFT (commit via 2-chain rule). We present the full protocol of Jolteon in Fig. 2, and highlight the intuition and major changes compared to DiemBFT below. As mentioned previously, the quadratic cost of view-synchronization in leader-based consensus protocols, due to faulty leaders or asynchronous periods, is inherent. While the linearity of HotStuff's view-change is a theoretical milestone, its practical importance is limited by this anyway quadratic cost of synchronization after bad views.

Table 2. Theoretical comparison between DiemBFT and Jolteon.

	Latency	Steady state	View-change	View-synchronization
DiemBFT	7 messages	Linear	Linear	Quadratic
Jolteon	5 messages	Linear	Quadratic	Quadratic

With this insight in mind, Jolteon uses a quadratic view-change protocol that allows a linear 2-chain commit rule in the steady state (see the **Commit** rule in Fig. 2). The idea is inspired by PBFT [8] with each leader proving the safety of its proposal. In the steady state each block extends the block from the previous round and providing the QC of the parent is enough to prove safety, hence the steady state protocol remains linear. However, after a bad round caused by asynchrony or a bad leader, proving the safety of extending an older QC requires the leader to prove that nothing more recent than the block of that QC is committed. To prove this, the leader uses the TC formed for view-changing the bad round. Recall that a TC for round r contains $2f + 1$ replicas' qc_{high} sent in timeout messages for round r. The leader attaches the TC to its proposal in round $r + 1$ and extends the highest QC among the QCs in the TC.

When a replica gets a proposal B, it first tries to advance its round number, then updates its qc_{high} with $B.qc$ and checks the 2-chain commit rule for a possible commit. Then, before voting, it verifies that at least one of the following two conditions is satisfied:

- $B.r = B.qc.r + 1$ or;
- $B.r = B.tc.r + 1$ and
  $B.qc.r \geq \max\{qc_{high}.r \mid qc_{high} \in B.tc\}$

In other words, either B contains the QC for the block of the previous round; or it contains at least the highest QC among the $2f + 1$ QCs in the attached TC, which was formed to view-change the previous round.

Safety Intuition. If the first condition is satisfied then B directly extends the block from the previous round. Since at most one QC can be formed in a round, this means that no forks are possible, and voting for B is safe.

The second condition is more subtle. Note that by the 2-chain commit rule, if a block B' is committed, then there exists a certified block B'' s.t. $B'.round+1 = B''.round$. That is, at least $f+1$ honest replicas vote to form the QC for B'' and thus set their qc_{high} to be the QC for block B' ($qc_{B'}$). By quorum intersection and since replicas never decrease their qc_{high}, any future (higher round) TC contains a qc_{high} that is at least as high as $qc_{B'}$. The second condition then guarantees that honest replicas only vote for proposals that extend the committed block B'. Due to lack of space, the full proof is given in the full version [14].

Replicas keep the same variables as DiemBFT in Figure 1.

Steady State Protocol for Replica i

Changes from DiemBFT in Figure 1 are marked in blue.

- **Propose.** Upon entering round r, the leader L_r multicasts a signed block $B = [id, qc_{high}, tc, r, v_{cur}, txn]$, where $tc = tc_{r-1}$ if L_r enters round r by receiving a round-$(r-1)$ tc_{r-1}, and $tc = \perp$ otherwise.
- **Vote.** Upon receiving the first valid block $B = [id, qc, tc, r, v, txn]$ from L_r, execute *Advance Round*, *Lock*, and then *Commit* (defined below). If $r = r_{cur}$, $v = v_{cur}$, $r > r_{vote}$ and ((1) $r = qc.r + 1$, or (2) $r = tc.r + 1$ and $qc.r \geq \max\{qc_{high}.r \mid qc_{high} \in tc\}$), vote for B by sending the threshold signature share $\{id, r, v\}_i$ to L_{r+1}, and update $r_{vote} \leftarrow r$.
- **Lock.** (1-chain lock rule) Upon seeing a valid qc (formed by votes or contained in proposal or timeouts), the replica updates $qc_{high} \leftarrow \max(qc_{high}, qc)$.
- **Commit.** (2-chain commit rule) If there exists two adjacent certified blocks B, B' in the chain with consecutive round numbers, i.e., $B'.r = B.r + 1$, the replica commits B and all its ancestors.

Pacemaker Protocol for Replica i

Identical to DiemBFT in Figure 1.

Fig. 2. Jolteon.

Efficiency. Table 2 compares the efficiency of DiemBFT and Jolteon from a theoretical point of view. Both protocols have linear communication complexity per round and per decision in steady state (under synchrony and honest leaders), due to the leader-to-all communication pattern and the threshold signature scheme[2]. The complexity of the Pacemaker to synchronize views (view-synchronization in Table 2), for both protocols, under asynchrony or failures is quadratic due to the all-to-all timeout messages. The complexity of proposing

---

[2] The implementation of DiemBFT does not use threshold signatures, but for the theoretical comparison here we consider a version of DiemBFT that does.

a block after a bad round that requires synchronization (view-change communication in Table 2) is linear for DiemBFT and quadratic for Jolteon. This is because in DiemBFT such a proposal only includes qc_{high}, whereas in Jolteon it includes a TC containing $2f + 1$ qc_{high}. The block-commit latency *under synchrony and honest leaders* is 7Δ and 5Δ for DiemBFT and Jolteon, respectively, due to the 3-chain (2-chain) commit. Each 1-chain requires two rounds (leader proposing and replicas voting), plus the new leader multicast the last QC of the chain that allows replicas to learn and commit the new block.

Limitations. During periods of asynchrony, or when facing DDoS attacks on the leaders, both protocols have *no liveness guarantees* – the leaders' blocks cannot be received on time. As a result, replicas keep multicasting timeout messages and advancing round numbers without certifying or committing any blocks. This is fundamentally unavoidable [29]: communication complexity of any deterministic partially synchronous Byzantine agreement protocol is unbounded before GST.

Fortunately, in the next section, we show that it is possible to boost the liveness guarantee of DiemBFT and Jolteon, by replacing the view-synchronization mechanism with a fallback protocol that guarantees progress even under asynchrony. Furthermore, the asynchronous fallback can be efficient. The protocol we propose in the next section has quadratic communication cost for fallback, which is the cost DiemBFT and Jolteon pay to synchronize views.

4   Ditto Design

To strengthen the liveness guarantees of existing partially synchronous BFT protocols such as DiemBFT [31] and Jolteon, we propose an Asynchronous Fallback protocol. It has quadratic communication complexity (same as Jolteon view-change and the Pacemaker of DiemBFT) and always makes progress even under asynchrony or DDoS attacks on the leader. We call the composition of Jolteon with Asynchronous Fallback Ditto. Ditto has linear communication cost for the synchronous path, quadratic cost for the asynchronous path, and preserves liveness robustly in asynchronous network conditions. The steady state protocol (sync. path) is presented in Fig. 4, and the asynchronous fallback protocol (async. path) is presented in Fig. 5. The proofs for Ditto can be found in the full version [14].

Protocol Intuition. Our solution consists of a steady state protocol, which is similar to that of Jolteon, and an asynchronous fallback protocol, which replaces the view-change of Jolteon. An illustration of our protocol is shown in Fig. 3. The idea behind our fallback protocol is that, after entering the fallback, all replicas will act as leaders to build their

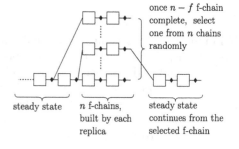

Fig. 3. The protocol intuition.

fallback chains. Once enough fallback chains grow to a certain height, a random leader election occurs to select one fallback chain, allowing the replicas to return to steady state and continue with the chosen chain. It can be shown that with constant probability, a fallback chain with enough blocks is selected, such that at least one new block on this fallback chain is committed by all replicas.

Since this protocol has two paths, a synchronous fast path and an asynchronous fallback path, it is critical to ensure safety and liveness when the protocol switches from one path to another. On a high level, our protocol ensures safety by always following commit and voting rules from `Jolteon`. While in the fallback path, the fallback chain selected by leader election is very similar to a steady state chain, hence we let all replicas update their local states with respect to the fallback chain when exiting the fallback, as if `Jolteon` had made progress. As for liveness, our protocol guarantees that either the sync path (same as `Jolteon`) makes progress, or enough replicas timeout the synchronous path and enter the fallback, and the fallback always finishes.

Additional Terminology for `Ditto`

- *Fallback-block and Fallback-chain.* For the fallback, we define another type of block named *fallback-block (f-block)*, denoted as $\overline{B}$. In contrast, the steady state block is called the *regular block*. An f-block $\overline{B}$ adds two additional fields to a regular block B, formatted as $\overline{B} = [B, height, proposer]$ where $height \in \{1, 2\}$ is the position of the f-block in the fallback-chain and *proposer* is the replica that proposes the block. We will use $\overline{B}_{h,i}$ to denote a height-h f-block proposed by replica i. A fallback-chain (f-chain) consists of f-blocks.
- *Fallback-QC.* A fallback quorum certificate (f-QC) $\overline{qc}$ for an f-block $\overline{B}_{h,i}$ is a threshold signature for the message $(\overline{B}.id, \overline{B}.r, \overline{B}.v, h, i)$, produced by combining the signature shares $\{\overline{B}.id, \overline{B}.r, \overline{B}.v, h, i\}$ from a quorum of replicas $(n - f = 2f + 1$ replicas). An f-block is certified if there exists an f-QC for the f-block. f-QCs or f-blocks are first ranked by view numbers and then by round numbers. In contrast, the QC of regular blocks is called *regular QC*.
- *Fallback-TC.* A fallback timeout certificate (f-TC) $\overline{tc}$ is a threshold signature for a view number v, produced by combining the signature shares $\{v\}$ from a quorum of replicas $(n - f = 2f + 1$ replicas). f-TCs are ranked by views.
- *Leader Election and Coin-QC.* We use the adaptively secure common coin [23] for leader election. For any given view, each replica signs the view number with threshold signature as the coin share. Then any $f + 1$ valid coin shares of the same view from distinct replicas can form a unique threshold signature (called coin-QC or qc_{coin}) on the view number. The hash of the unique threshold signature above is used as randomness to elect leader L among n replicas with probability $1/n$. The probability of the adversary to predict the outcome of the election is at most $1/n + negl(k)$.
- *Endorsed Fallback-QC and Endorsed Fallback-block.* Once a replica has a qc_{coin} of view v that elects replica L as the fallback-chain leader, we say any f-QC of view v by replica L is endorsed (by qc_{coin}), and the f-block certified by the f-QC is also endorsed (by qc_{coin}). Any endorsed f-QC is handled

Let L_r be the leader of round r. Each replica keeps the highest voted round r_{vote}, current round number r_{cur}, the highest quorum certificate qc_{high}, and a boolean value **async**. Replicas initialize $r_{vote} = 0$, $r_{cur} = 1$, qc_{high} as the QC of the genesis block of round 0, **async** $= false$ and enter round 1.

Steady State Protocol for Replica i

Changes from Jolteon in Figure 2 are marked in blue.

- **Propose.** Upon entering round r, the leader L_r multicasts a block $B = [id, qc_{high}, qc_{coin}, r, v_{cur}, txn]$, where qc_{coin} is the coin-QC of view v_{cur-1} if B is the first proposal in view v_{cur}, otherwise $qc_{coin} = \bot$.

- **Vote.** Upon receiving the first valid proposal $B = [id, qc, qc_{coin}, r, v, txn]$ from L_r, execute *Exit Fallback if $qc_{coin} \neq \bot$*; otherwise execute *Advance Round, Lock,* and then *Commit*. If $r = r_{cur}$, $v = v_{cur}$, $r > r_{vote}$, $r = qc.r+1$, $qc.rank \geq qc_{high}.rank$, and **async** $= false$, vote for B by sending the threshold signature share $\{id, r, v\}_i$ to L_{r+1}, and update $r_{vote} \leftarrow r$.

- **Lock.** (1-chain lock rule) Upon seeing a valid qc (formed by votes or contained in proposal or timeouts), the replica updates $qc_{high} \leftarrow \max(qc_{high}, qc)$.

- **Commit.** (2-chain commit rule) If there exists two adjacent blocks B, B' with the *same view number* in the chain, each can be a certified block or an endorsed fallback-block, the replica commits B and all its ancestors.

Round Synchronization for Replica i

- **Advance Round.** Upon receiving a valid qc, the replica updates its current round $r_{cur} \leftarrow \max(r_{cur}, qc.r + 1)$.

- **Timer and Timeout.** Upon entering a new round or a new view, the replica resets its timer to τ. When the timer expires, the replica updates **async** $\leftarrow true$, and multicasts a **timeout** message $\langle \{v_{cur}\}_i, qc_{high}\rangle_i$ where $\{v_{cur}\}_i$ is a threshold signature share. Upon receiving a valid **timeout** message, execute *Advance Round, Lock,* and then *Commit*.

Fig. 4. Steady State of Ditto

as a regular QC in any steps of the protocol such as *Lock, Commit, Advance Round*. An endorsed f-QC ranks higher than any regular QC with the same view number. As cryptographic evidence of endorsement, the first block in a new view includes the coin-QC of the previous view.

Description of Steady State. The steady state protocol is given in Fig. 4. Compared to Jolteon, the leader no longer provides TC in the block as the proof of view-synchronization. Instead, it attaches the coin-QC formed by the fallback of the previous view, which proves the fallback already finishes and replicas should enter the new view. Each replica additionally keeps a boolean value **async** to record if it is in the fallback, during which the replica will not vote regular blocks. The 1-chain lock rule and 2-chain commit rule still apply, but the two blocks in the 2-chain can be certified regular block or endorsed fallback-block from the same view.

During a fallback of view v, replicas record all the f-QCs of view v by any replica j, and keeps a voted round number $\bar{r}_{vote}[j]$ and a voted height number $\bar{h}_{vote}[j]$.

Async. Fallback Protocol for Replica i

- **Enter Fallback.** Upon receiving or forming an f-TC $\bar{tc}$ of view $v \geq v_{cur}$, update **async** $\leftarrow true$, $v_{cur} \leftarrow v$, $\bar{r}_{vote}[j] \leftarrow 0$, $\bar{h}_{vote}[j] \leftarrow 0$ for $\forall j \in [n]$, and multicast $\bar{tc}$ and a height-1 f-block $\overline{B}_{1,i} = [id, qc_{high}, qc_{high}.r + 1, v_{cur}, txn, 1, i]$.

- **Fallback Vote.** Upon receiving an f-block $\overline{B}_{h,j}$ from replica j, if $h > \bar{h}_{vote}[j]$, **async** $= true$, and
  - if $h = 1$ and $\overline{B}_{h,j} = [id, qc, r, v, txn, 1, j]$ such that $qc.rank \geq qc_{high}.rank$, $r = qc.r + 1$, and $v = v_{cur}$; or
  - if $h = 2$, and $\overline{B}_{h,j} = [id, \overline{qc}, r, v, txn, 2, j]$ such that $\overline{qc}$ is a valid f-QC, $v = v_{cur}$, $r = \overline{qc}.r + 1$, $r > \bar{r}_{vote}[j]$ and $\overline{qc}.height = 1$,

  set $\bar{r}_{vote}[j] \leftarrow r, \bar{h}_{vote}[j] \leftarrow h$ and send $\{id, r, v, h, j\}_i$ back to replica j.

- **Fallback Propose.** Upon the first height-h f-block $\overline{B}_{h,j}$ (*proposed by any replica j*) is certified by some f-QC $\overline{qc}$ and **async** $= true$,
  - if $h = 1$, replica i multicasts $\overline{B}_{2,i} = [id, \overline{qc}, \overline{B}_{1,j}.r + 1, v, txn, 2, i]$.
  - if $h = 2$, replica i signs and multicasts $\overline{qc}$;

- **Leader Election.** Upon receiving $n - f$ distinct signed height-2 f-QCs of view v_{cur} and **async** $= true$, sign and multicast a coin share for view v_{cur}.

- **Exit Fallback.** Upon receiving or forming a coin-QC qc_{coin} (consisting of $f + 1$ coin shares) of view $\geq v_{cur}$ for the first time, multicast qc_{coin}. Let replica L be the fallback-chain leader elected by qc_{coin}. If **async** $= true$, update $r_{vote} \leftarrow \bar{r}_{vote}[L]$. Update **async** $\leftarrow false$, $v_{cur} \leftarrow qc_{coin}.v + 1$. Execute *Advance Round*, *Lock*, and then *Commit*.

Fig. 5. Asynchronous Fallback of `Ditto`

Description of Asynchronous Fallback. Now we give a brief description of the Asynchronous Fallback protocol (Fig. 5), which replaces the Pacemaker protocol in the `Jolteon` protocol (Fig. 2). Just like in `Jolteon`, when the timer expires, the replica tries to initiate the fallback (the equivalent of view-change) by broadcasting a timeout message containing the highest QC and a signature share of the current view number. When receiving or forming a fallback-TC from $2f + 1$ timeout messages, the replica enters the fallback path: It updates its current view number v_{cur}, initializes the voted round number $\bar{r}_{vote}[j] = 0$ and the voted height number $\bar{h}_{vote}[j] = 0$ for each replica j. Finally, the replica starts building its fallback-chain by broadcasting the f-TC and proposing the first f-block which extends the qc_{high}, has height 1, round number $qc_{high}.r + 1$, and view number v_{cur}. Any f-block (irrelevant of height) gets verified by all replicas who vote on it (updating their voted round and height number for the fallback) by sending signature shares back to the proposer of the f-block. Replicas build their fallback-chain *not by necessarily extending their own chain but by adopting the first certified block of matching height they received* (in v_{cur}). This boosting strategy guarantees that no honest replica's chain is left behind in the middle of the fallback, hence at least $2f + 1$ chains will reach height-2 and their leader-replica will broadcast a height-2 f-QC.

Finally, when the replica receives $2f + 1$ height-2 f-QCs, it knows that $2f + 1$ f-chains are complete and starts the leader election by releasing a coin share for the current view number. When $f + 1$ shares are released the leader of the view is determined through the formation of a coin-QC qc_{coin}. The fallback is then terminated, and the replica updates $async = false$ to exit the fallback and enters the next view, acting as if the chain of the elected leader is the only known chain. Looking at this chain the replica updates all relevant variables and commits any blocks that have 2-chain support. Given that we waited for $2f + 1$ long-enough chains, with 2/3 probability the replicas will commit a block.

5 Implementation

We implement `Jolteon`, `Ditto`, and 2-chain VABA on top of a high-performance open-source implementation of HotStuff[3] [32]. We selected this implementation because it implements a Pacemaker [32], contrary to the implementation used in the original HotStuff paper[4]. Additionally, it provides well-documented benchmarking scripts to measure performance in various conditions, and it is close to a production system (it provides real networking, cryptography, and persistent storage). It is implemented in Rust, uses Tokio for asynchronous networking, ed25519-dalek for elliptic curve based signatures, and data-structures are persisted using RocksDB. It uses TCP to achieve reliable point-to-point channels, necessary to correctly implement the distributed system abstractions. We additionally use `threshold_crypto` to implement random coins, Our implementations are between 5,000 and 7,000 LOC, and a further 2,000 LOC of unit tests. We are open sourcing our implementations of `Jolteon`, and `Ditto` and 2-chain VABA We are also open sourcing all AWS orchestration scripts, benchmarking scripts, and measurements data to enable reproducible results[5].

2-chain VABA: As a by-product of `Ditto`, we improve the block-commit latency of VABA [4] from expected 16.5 rounds to expected 10.5 rounds, through chaining and adopting the 2-chain commit rule. We refer to the improved version as 2-chain VABA and the analysis can be found in the full version [14]. The 2-chain VABA implementation is obtained by disabling the synchronous path of `Ditto`.

`Ditto` **with Exponential Backoff:** To improve the latency performance of `Ditto` under long periods of asynchrony or leader attacks, we adopt an exponential backoff mechanism for the asynchronous fallback as follows. We say a replica executes the asynchronous fallback consecutively x times if it only waits for the timer to expire for the first fallback, and skips waiting for the timer and immediately sends timeout for the rest $x - 1$ fallbacks. Initially, replicas only execute

---

[3] https://github.com/asonnino/hotstuff/tree/3-chain.

[4] https://github.com/hot-stuff/libhotstuff.

[5] https://github.com/asonnino/hotstuff/tree/async.

asynchronous fallback consecutively $x = 1$ time. However, if a replica, within the timeout, does not receive from the steady state round-leader immediately after the fallback, it will multiply x by a constant factor (5 in our experiments); otherwise, the replica resets $x = 1$. For instance, during long periods of asynchrony or leader attacks, the number of consecutively executed fallbacks would be exponentially increasing $(1, 5, 25, ...)$; while during periods of synchrony and honest leaders, the number of consecutively executed fallbacks is always 1.

6   Evaluation

We evaluate the throughput and latency of our implementations through experiments on Amazon Web Services (AWS). We particularly aim to demonstrate (i) that Jolteon achieves the theoretically lower block-commit latency than 3-chain DiemBFT under no contention and (ii) that the theoretically larger message size during view-change does not impose a heavier burden, making Jolteon no slower than 3-chain DiemBFT under faults (when the view-change happens frequently). Additionally we aim to show that Ditto adapts to the network condition, meaning that (iii) it behaves similarly to Jolteon when the network is synchronous (with and without faults) and (iv) close to our faster version of VABA (2-chain) when the adversary adaptively compromises the leader.

We deploy a testbed on AWS, using m5.8 × large instances across 5 different AWS regions: N. Virginia (us-east-1), N. California (us-west-1), Sydney (apsoutheast-2), Stockholm (eu-north-1), and Tokyo (ap-northeast1). They provide 10 Gbps of bandwidth, 32 virtual CPUs (16 physical core) on a 2.5 GHz, Intel Xeon Platinum 8175, and 128 GB memory and run Ubuntu server 20.04.

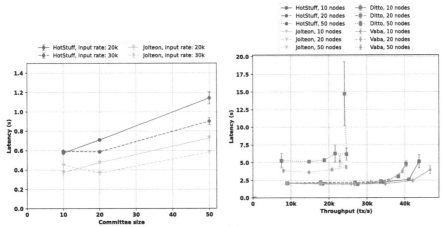

(a) Comparative block-commit latency for 3-chain DiemBFT (HotStuff) and Jolteon. WAN measurements with 10, 20, or 50 replicas. No replica faults, 500KB mempool batch size and 512B transaction size.

(b) Comparative throughput-latency performance for 3-chain DiemBFT (HotStuff), Jolteon, Ditto, and 2-chain VABA. WAN measurements with 10, 20, or 50 replicas. No replica faults, 500KB mempool batch size, and 512B transaction size. Leader constantly under DoS attack.

Fig. 6. Evaluations of Jolteon and Ditto.

This type of machines are well in the price range of commodity servers and fairly common for prototype testbeds of distributed systems.

We measure throughput and end-to-end latency as the performance metrics. Throughput is computed as the average number of committed transactions per second, and end-to-end latency measures the average time to commit a transaction from the moment it is submitted by the client. Compared with the block-commit latency in our theoretical analysis, end-to-end latency also includes the queuing delay of the transaction when the clients' input rate is high which helps identify the capacity limit of our system.

In all our experiments, the transaction size is set to be 512 B and the mempool batch size is set to be 500 KB. We deploy one benchmark client per node submitting transactions at a fixed rate for a duration of 5 min (to ensure we report steady state performance). We set the timeout to be 5 seconds for experiments with 10 and 20 nodes, and 10 seconds for 50 nodes, so that the timeout is large enough for not triggering the pacemaker of Jolteon and fallback of Ditto. In the following sections, each measurement in the graphs is the average of 3 runs, and the error bars represent the standard deviation.

To find the peak performance of our system, we keep increasing the transaction submission rate of the clients until the capacity of the system is saturated. As a result, the latency-throughput measurements in the figures share similar patterns: the throughput of the system first increases with stable latency (dominated by the network delay) before the saturation point; then the throughput stops increasing and the latency increases significantly (due to high queuing delay) as the transaction submission rate exceeds the system's maximum capacity.

Due to space limit, more evaluations can be found in the full version [14].

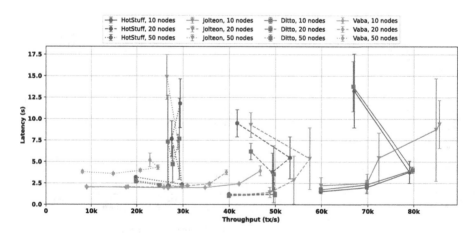

Fig. 7. Comparative throughput-latency performance for 3-chain DiemBFT (Hot-Stuff), Jolteon, Ditto, and 2-chain VABA WAN measurements with 10, 20, or 50 replicas. No replica faults, 500 KB mempool batch size and 512 B transaction size.

6.1 Evaluation of `Jolteon`

In this section, we compare `Jolteon` with our baseline 3-chain DiemBFT implementation in two experiments. First in Fig. 6a we run both protocol with a varying system size (10, 20, 50 nodes). In order to remove any noise from the mempool, this graph does not show the end-to-end latency for clients but the time it takes for a block to be committed. As the Figure illustrated `Jolteon` consistently outperforms 3-chain DiemBFT by about $200-300$ms of latency which is around one round-trip across the world and both systems scale similarly. In Fig. 7 this effect is less visible due to the noise of the mempool (end-to-end latency of around 2 secs), but `Jolteon` is still slightly faster than 3-chain DiemBFT in most experiments.

6.2 Evaluation of `Ditto`

Synchronous and Fault-Free Executions. When all replicas are fault-free and the network is synchronous, we compare the performances of the four protocol implementations in Fig. 7. As we can observe from the figure, the synchronous path performance of `Ditto` is very close to that of `Jolteon`, when the quadratic asynchronous fallback of `Ditto` and the quadratic pacemaker of `Jolteon` is not triggered. On the other hand, the performance of 2-chain VABA is worse than `Jolteon` and `Ditto` in this setting, due to its quadratic communication pattern – instead of every replica receiving the block metadata and synchronizing the transaction payload with only one leader per round in `Jolteon` and `Ditto`, in VABA every replica will receive and synchronize with $O(n)$ leaders per round.

Attacks on the Leaders. Figure 6b presents the measurement results. When the eventual synchrony assumption does not hold, either due to DDoS attacks on the leaders or adversarial delays on the leaders' messages, 3-chain DiemBFT and `Jolteon` will have no liveness, i.e., the throughput of the system is always 0. The reason is that whenever a replica becomes the leader for some round, its proposal message is delayed and all other replicas will timeout for that round. On the other hand, `Ditto` and 2-chain VABA are robust against such adversarial delays and can make progress under asynchrony. The performance of the 2-chain VABA protocol implementation is not affected much by delaying a certain replica's proposal. Therefore, we use it as a baseline to compare with our `Ditto` protocol implementation. Our results, confirm our theoretical assumption as the asynchronous fallback performance of `Ditto` is very close to that of 2-chain VABA under 10 or 20 nodes, and slightly worse than 2-chain VABA under 50 nodes. This extra latency cost is due to the few timeouts that are triggered during the exponential back-off.

Take Away. To conclude, there is little reason not to use `Ditto` as our experiments confirm our theoretical bounds. `Ditto` adapts to the network behavior and achieves almost optimal performance. The only system that sometimes outperforms `Ditto` is 2-chain VABA during intermittent periods of asynchrony as it does not pay the timeout cost of `Ditto` when deciding how to adapt. This, however, comes at a significant cost when the network is good and in our opinion legitimizes the superiority of `Ditto` when run over the Internet.

7   Related Work

Eventually Synchronous BFT. BFT SMR has been studied extensively in the literature. A sequence of efforts [6–8,15,19,32] have been made to reduce the communication cost of the BFT SMR protocols, with the state-of-the-art being HotStuff [32] that has $O(n)$ cost for decisions, a 3-chain commit latency under synchrony and honest leaders, and $O(n^2)$ cost for view-synchronization. `Jolteon` presents another step forward from HotStuff as we realize the co-design of the pacemaker with the commit rules enables removing one round without sacrificing the linear steady state. Two concurrent theoretical works propose a 2-chain variation of the HotStuff as well [17,28]. However, the work of Rambaud et al. [28] relies on impractical cryptographic primitives to preserve a linear view-change (assuming still a quadratic pacemaker) whereas neither protocol provides a comprehensive evaluation to showcase that the extra view-change costs (which also applies in [17]) does not cause significant overheads. Most importantly, both protocols fail to realize the full power of 2-chain protocols missing the fact the view-change can become robust and DDoS resilient.

Asynchronous BFT. Several recent proposals focus on improving the communication complexity and latency, including HoneyBadgerBFT [26], VABA [4], Dumbo-BFT [16], Dumbo-MVBA [25], ACE [30], Aleph [13], and DAG-Rider [18]. The state-of-the-art protocols for asynchronous SMR have $O(n^2)$ cost per decision [30], or amortized $O(n)$ cost per decision after transaction batching [13,16,18,25]. As mentioned in Sect. 5, our design and implementation separate transaction dissemination (mempool) from the critical path of consensus to fairly evaluate the consensus protocols.

BFT with Optimistic and Fallback Paths. To the best of our knowledge, [21] is the first asynchronous BFT protocol with an efficient steady state. Their asynchronous path has $O(n^3)$ communication cost while their steady state has $O(n^2)$ cost per decision, which was later extended [27] to an amortized $O(n)$. A recent paper [29] further improved the communication complexity of asynchronous path to $O(n^2)$ and the cost of the steady state to $O(n)$. The latency of these protocols is not optimized, e.g. latency of the protocol in [29] is $O(n)$. Moreover, these papers are theoretical in nature and far from the realm of practicality. Finally, a concurrent work named the Bolt-Dumbo Transformer (BDT) [24], proposes a BFT SMR protocol with both synchronous and asynchronous paths and provides implementation and evaluation. BDT takes the straightforward solution of composing three separate consensus protocols as black boxes. Every round starts with 1) a partially synchronous protocol (HotStuff), times-out the leader and runs 2) an Asynchronous Binary Agreement in order to move on and run 3) a fully asynchronous consensus protocol [16] as a fallback. Although BDT achieves asymptotically optimal communication cost for both paths this is simply inherited by the already known to be optimal back boxes. On the theoretical side, their design is beneficial since it provides a generally composable framework, but this generality comes at a hefty practical cost. BDT has a latency cost of 7 rounds (vs 5 of `Ditto`) at the fast path and of 45 rounds (vs 10.5 of `Ditto`) at the fallback, making it questionably practical. Finally, not opening the black-boxes stopped BDT from reducing the latency of HotStuff although it also has a quadratic view-change.

8   Conclusion

We first design a 2-chain version of HotStuff, named `Jolteon`, which leverages a quadratic view-change mechanism to reduce the latency of the standard 3-chain HotStuff. We then present `Ditto`, a practical byzantine SMR protocol that enjoys the best of both worlds: optimal communication on and off the steady state (linear and quadratic, respectively) and progress guarantees under the worst case asynchrony and DDoS attacks. We implement and experimentally evaluate all our systems to validate our theoretical analysis.

Acknowledgments. We thank our shepherd Aniket Kate and the anonymous reviewers at FC 2022 for their helpful feedback. This work is supported by the Novi team at Facebook. We also thank the Novi Research and Engineering teams for valuable feedback, and in particular Mathieu Baudet, Andrey Chursin, George Danezis, Zekun Li, and Dahlia Malkhi for discussions that shaped this work.

References

1. Abraham, I., Malkhi, D., Nayak, K., Ren, L., Yin, M.: Sync HotStuff: simple and practical synchronous state machine replication. In: 2020 IEEE Symposium on Security and Privacy (S&P), pp. 106–118 (2020)
2. Abraham, I., et al.: Communication complexity of byzantine agreement, revisited. In: Proceedings of the 2019 ACM Symposium on Principles of Distributed Computing (PODC), pp. 317–326 (2019)
3. Abraham, I., Jovanovic, P., Maller, M., Meiklejohn, S., Stern, G., Tomescu, A.: Reaching consensus for asynchronous distributed key generation. In: Proceedings of the 2021 ACM Symposium on Principles of Distributed Computing (PODC), pp. 363–373 (2021)
4. Abraham, I., Malkhi, D., Spiegelman, A.: Asymptotically optimal validated asynchronous byzantine agreement. In: Proceedings of the 2019 ACM Symposium on Principles of Distributed Computing (PODC), pp. 337–346 (2019)
5. Blum, E., Katz, J., Loss, J.: Network-agnostic state machine replication. arXiv preprint arXiv:2002.03437 (2020)

6. Buchman, E., Kwon, J., Milosevic, Z.: The latest gossip on BFT consensus. arXiv preprint arXiv:1807.04938 (2018)
7. Buterin, V., Griffith, V.: Casper the friendly finality gadget. arXiv preprint arXiv:1710.09437 (2017)
8. Castro, M., Liskov, B.: Practical byzantine fault tolerance. In: Proceedings of the third symposium on Operating Systems Design and Implementation (NSDI), pp. 173–186 (1999)
9. Das, S., Xiang, Z., Ren, L.: Asynchronous data dissemination and its applications. In: Proceedings of the 2021 ACM SIGSAC Conference on Computer and Communications Security (CCS), pp. 2705–2721 (2021)
10. Das, S., Yurek, T., Xiang, Z., Miller, A., Kokoris-Kogias, L., Ren, L.: Practical asynchronous distributed key generation. Cryptology ePrint Archive, Report 2021/1591 (2021)
11. Dwork, C., Lynch, N., Stockmeyer, L.: Consensus in the presence of partial synchrony. J. ACM (JACM) 35(2), 288–323 (1988)
12. Fischer, M.J., Lynch, N.A., Paterson, M.S.: Impossibility of distributed consensus with one faulty process. J. ACM (JACM) 32(2), 374–382 (1985)
13. Gągol, A., Leśniak, D., Straszak, D., Aleph, M.: Efficient atomic broadcast in asynchronous networks with byzantine nodes. In: Proceedings of the 1st ACM Conference on Advances in Financial Technologies (AFT), pp. 214–228 (2019)
14. Gelashvili, R., Kokoris-Kogias, L., Sonnino, A., Spiegelman, A., Xiang, Z.: Jolteon and ditto: network-adaptive efficient consensus with asynchronous fallback. arXiv preprint arXiv:2106.10362 (2021)
15. Gueta, G.G., et al.: SBFT: a scalable and decentralized trust infrastructure. In: 2019 49th Annual IEEE/IFIP International Conference on Dependable Systems and Networks (DSN), pp. 568–580. IEEE (2019)
16. Guo, B., Lu, Z., Tang, Q., Xu, J., Zhang, Z.: Dumbo: faster asynchronous BFT protocols. In: Proceedings of the 2020 ACM SIGSAC Conference on Computer and Communications Security (CCS), pp. 803–818 (2020)
17. Jalalzai, M.M., Niu, J., Feng, C., Gai, F.: Fast-HotStuff: a fast and resilient hotstuff protocol. arXiv preprint arXiv:2010.11454 (2020)
18. Keidar, I., Kokoris-Kogias, E., Naor, O., Spiegelman, A.: All you need is DAG. In: Proceedings of the 2021 ACM Symposium on Principles of Distributed Computing (PODC) (2021)
19. Kogias, E.K., Jovanovic, P., Gailly, N., Khoffi, I., Gasser, L., Ford, B.: Enhancing bitcoin security and performance with strong consistency via collective signing. In 25th Usenix Security Symposium, pp. 279–296 (2016)
20. Kogias, E.K., Malkhi, D., Spiegelman, A.: Asynchronous distributed key generation for computationally-secure randomness, consensus, and threshold signatures. In: Proceedings of the 2020 ACM SIGSAC Conference on Computer and Communications Security (CCS), pp. 1751–1767 (2020)
21. Kursawe, K., Shoup, V.: Optimistic asynchronous atomic broadcast. In: Caires, L., Italiano, G.F., Monteiro, L., Palamidessi, C., Yung, M. (eds.) ICALP 2005. LNCS, vol. 3580, pp. 204–215. Springer, Heidelberg (2005). https://doi.org/10.1007/11523468_17
22. Libert, B., Joye, M., Yung, M.: Born and raised distributively: fully distributed non-interactive adaptively-secure threshold signatures with short shares. Theoret. Comput. Sci. 645, 1–24 (2016)
23. Loss, J., Moran, T.: Combining asynchronous and synchronous byzantine agreement: the best of both worlds. Cryptology ePrint Archive, Report 2018/235 (2018)

24. Lu, Y., Lu, Z., Tang, Q.: Bolt-Dumbo transformer: asynchronous consensus as fast as pipelined BFT. arXiv preprint arXiv:2103.09425 (2021)

25. Lu, Y., Lu, Z., Tang, Q., Wang, G.: Dumbo-MVBA: optimal multi-valued validated asynchronous byzantine agreement, revisited. In: Proceedings of the 39th Symposium on Principles of Distributed Computing (PODC), pp. 129–138 (2020)

26. Miller, A., Xia, Y., Croman, K., Shi, E., Song, D.: The honey badger of BFT protocols. In: Proceedings of the 2016 ACM SIGSAC Conference on Computer and Communications Security (CCS), pp. 31–42 (2016)

27. Ramasamy, H.G.V., Cachin, C.: Parsimonious asynchronous byzantine-fault-tolerant atomic broadcast. In: Anderson, J.H., Prencipe, G., Wattenhofer, R. (eds.) OPODIS 2005. LNCS, vol. 3974, pp. 88–102. Springer, Heidelberg (2006). https://doi.org/10.1007/11795490_9

28. Rambaud, M.: Malicious security comes for free in consensus with leaders. IACR Cryptology ePrint Archive, Report 2020/1480 (2020)

29. Spiegelman, A.: In search for an optimal authenticated byzantine agreement. In: 35th International Symposium on Distributed Computing (DISC) (2021)

30. Spiegelman, A., Rinberg, A.: ACE: abstract consensus encapsulation for liveness boosting of state machine replication. In: 23rd International Conference on Principles of Distributed Systems (OPODIS) (2020)

31. The DiemBFT Team: State Machine Replication in the diem blockchain (2021). https://developers.diem.com/docs/technical-papers/state-machine-replication-paper/

32. Yin, M., Malkhi, D., Reiter, M.K., Gueta, G.G., Abraham, I.: HotStuff: BFT consensus with linearity and responsiveness. In: Proceedings of the 2019 ACM Symposium on Principles of Distributed Computing (PODC), pp. 347–356 (2019)

Quick Order Fairness

Christian Cachin⬤, Jovana Mićić(✉)⬤, Nathalie Steinhauer⬤,
and Luca Zanolini⬤

Institute of Computer Science, University of Bern, Bern, Switzerland
{christian.cachin,jovana.micic,nathalie.steinhauer,
luca.zanolini}@unibe.ch

Abstract. Leader-based protocols for consensus, i.e., atomic broadcast, allow some processes to unilaterally affect the final order of transactions. This has become a problem for blockchain networks and decentralized finance because it facilitates front-running and other attacks. To address this, *order fairness* for payload messages has be en introduced recently as a new safety property for atomic broadcast complementing traditional *agreement* and *liveness*. We relate order fairness to the standard validity notions for consensus protocols and highlight some limitations with the existing formalization. Based on this, we introduce a new *differential* order fairness property that fixes these issues. We also present the *quick order-fair atomic broadcast protocol* that guarantees payload message delivery in a differentially fair order and is much more efficient than existing order-fair consensus protocols. It works for asynchronous and for eventually synchronous networks with optimal resilience, tolerating corruptions of up to one third of the processes. Previous solutions required there to be less than one fourth of faults. Furthermore, our protocol incurs only quadratic cost, in terms of amortized message complexity per delivered payload.

Keywords: Consensus · Atomic broadcast · Decentralized finance · Front-running attacks · Differential order fairness

1 Introduction

The nascent field of *decentralized finance* (or simply *DeFi*) suffers from insider attacks: Malicious miners in permissionless blockchain networks or Byzantine leaders in permissioned atomic broadcast protocols have the power of selecting messages that go into the ledger and determining their final order. Selfish participants may also insert their own, fraudulent transactions and thereby extract value from the network and its innocent users. For instance, a decentralized exchange can be exploited by *front-running*, where a genuine message m carrying an exchange transaction is *sandwiched* between a message m_{before} and a message m_{after}. If m buys a particular asset, the insider acquires it as well using m_{before} and sells it again with m_{after}, typically at a higher price. Such front-running and other price-manipulation attacks represent a serious threat. They are prohibited in traditional finance systems with centralized oversight but must

ⓒ International Financial Cryptography Association 2022
I. Eyal and J. Garay (Eds.): FC 2022, LNCS 13411, pp. 316–333, 2022.
https://doi.org/10.1007/978-3-031-18283-9_15

be prevented technically in DeFi. Daian *et al.* [7] have coined the term *miner extractable value (MEV)* for the profit that can be gained from such arbitrage opportunities.

The traditional properties of *atomic broadcast*, often somewhat imprecisely called *consensus* as well, guarantee a total order: that all correct parties obtain the same sequence of messages and that any message submitted to the network by a client is delivered in a reasonable lapse of time. However, these properties do not further constrain *which* order is chosen, and malicious parties in the protocol may therefore manipulate the order or insert their own messages to their benefit. Kelkar *et al.* [14] have recently introduced the new safety property of *order fairness* that addresses this in the Byzantine model. Kursawe [15] and Zhang *et al.* [19] have formalized this problem as well and found different ways to tackle it, relying on somewhat stronger assumptions.

Intuitively, *order fairness* aims at ensuring that messages received by "many" parties are scheduled and delivered earlier than messages received by "few" parties. The *Condorcet paradox* demonstrates, however, that such preference votes can easily lead to cycles even if the individual votes of majorities are not circular. The solution offered through *order fairness* [14] may therefore output multiple messages *together as a set* (or batch), such that there is *no order* among all messages in the same set. Kelkar *et al.* [14] name this property *block-order fairness* but calling such a set a "block" may easily lead to confusion with the low-level blocks in mining-based protocols.

In this paper, we investigate order fairness in networks with n processes of which f are faulty, for asynchronous and eventually synchronous atomic broadcast. This covers the vast majority of relevant applications, since timed protocols that assume synchronous clocks and permanently bounded message delays have largely been abandoned in this space.

We first revisit the notion of block-order fairness [14]. In our interpretation, this requires that when n correct processes broadcast two payload messages m and m', and $\overline{\gamma}n$ of them broadcast m before m' for some $\overline{\gamma} > \frac{1}{2}$, then m' is not delivered by the protocol before m, although both messages may be output together. This guarantee is difficult to achieve in practice because Kelkar *et al.* [14] show that for the relevant values of $\overline{\gamma}$ approaching one half, the resilience of any protocol decreases. Tolerating only a small number of faulty parties seems prohibitive in realistic settings.

More importantly, we show that $\overline{\gamma}$ cannot be too close to $\frac{1}{2}$ because $\overline{\gamma} \geq \frac{1}{2} + \frac{f}{n-f}$ is necessary for any protocol. This result follows from establishing a link to the differential validity notion of consensus, formalized by Fitzi and Garay [10]. Notice that block-order fairness is a relative measure. We are convinced that a differential notion is better suited to address the problem. We, therefore, overcome this inherent limitation of relative order fairness by introducing *differential order fairness*: When the number of correct processes that broadcast a message m before a message m' exceeds the number that broadcast m' before m by more than $2f + \kappa$, for some $\kappa \geq 0$, then the protocol must *not* deliver m' before m (but they may be delivered together). This notion takes into account existing results on differential validity for consensus [10]. In particular, when the difference between how many processes prefer one of m and m' over the other is smaller than $2f$, then *no protocol exists* to deliver them in fair order.

Last but not least, we introduce a new protocol, called *quick order-fair atomic broadcast*, that implements differential order fairness and is much more efficient than the previously existing algorithms. In particular, it works with optimal resilience $n > 3f$, requires $O(n^2)$ messages to deliver one payload on average and needs $O(n^2L + n^3\lambda)$ bits of communication, with payloads of up to L bits and cryptographic λ-bit signatures. This holds for *any* order-fairness parameter κ. For comparison, the asynchronous Aequitas protocol [14] has resilience $n > 4f$ or worse, depending on its order-fairness parameter, and needs $O(n^4)$ messages.

To summarize, the contributions of this paper are as follows:

- It illustrates some *limitations* that are inherent in the notion of block-order fairness (Sect. 4.1).
- It introduces *differential order fairness* as a measure for defining fair order in atomic broadcast protocols (Sect. 4.2).
- It presents the *quick order-fair atomic broadcast protocol* for differentially order-fair Byzantine atomic broadcast with optimal resilience $n > 3f$ (Sect. 5).
- It demonstrates that the quick order-fairness protocol has quadratic amortized message complexity, which is an n^2-fold improvement compared to the most efficient previous protocol for the same task (Sect. 6).

For lack of space, some material, proofs and detailed protocol analysis are omitted here, but available in the full version [6].

2 Related Work

Over the last decades, extensive research efforts have explored the state-machine replication problem. A large number of papers refer to this problem, but only a few of them consider fairness in the order of delivered payload messages. In this section, we review the related work on fairness.

Kelkar *et al.* [14] introduce a new property called *transaction order-fairness* which prevents adversarial manipulation of the ordering of transactions, i.e., payload messages. They investigate assumptions needed for achieving this property in a permissioned setting and formulate a new class of consensus protocols, called Aequitas, that satisfy order fairness. A subsequent paper by Kelkar *et al.* [12] extends this approach to a permissionless setting. Recently, Kelkar *et al.* [13] presented another permissioned Byzantine atomic-broadcast protocol called Themis. It introduces a new technique called *deferred ordering*, which overcomes a liveness problem of the Aequitas protocols.

Kursawe [15] and Zhang *et al.* [19] have independently postulated alternative definitions of order fairness, called *timed order fairness* and *ordering linearizability*, respectively. Both notions are strictly weaker than order fairness of transactions, however [12]. Timed order fairness assumes that all processes have access to synchronized local clocks; it can ensure that if all correct processes saw message m to be ordered before m', then m is scheduled and delivered before m'. Similarly, ordering linearizability says that if the highest timestamp provided by any correct process for a message m is lower than the lowest timestamp provided by any correct process for a message m', then m will appear before m' in the output sequence. The implementation of ordering linearizability [19] uses a median computation, which can easily be manipulated by faulty processes [12].

The Hashgraph [3] consensus protocol also claims to achieve fairness. It uses gossip internally and all processes build a *hash graph* reflecting all of the gossip events. However, there is no formal definition of fairness and the presentation fails to recognize the impossibility of fair message-order resulting from the *Condorcet paradox*. Kelkar *et al.* [14] also show an attack that allows a malicious process to control the order of the messages delivered by Hashgraph.

A complementary measure to prevent message-reordering attacks relies on threshold cryptography [5,8,18]: clients encrypt their input (payload) messages under a key shared by the group of processes running the atomic broadcast protocol. They initially order the encrypted messages and subsequently collaborate for decrypting them. Hence, their contents become known only *after* the message order has been decided. For instance, the Helix protocol [2] implements this approach and additionally exploits in-protocol randomness for two additional goals: to elect the processes running the protocol from a larger group and to determine which messages among all available ones must be included by a process when proposing a block. This method provides resistance to censorship but still permits some order-manipulation attacks.

3   System Model and Preliminaries

System Model. We model our system as a set of n *processes* $\mathcal{P} = \{p_1, \ldots, p_n\}$, also called *parties*, that communicate with each other. Processes interact with each other by exchanging messages reliably in a network. A protocol for $\mathcal{P}$ consists of a collection of programs with instructions for all processes. Processes are computationally bounded and protocols may use cryptographic primitives, in particular, digital signature schemes.

In our model, we distinguish two types of processes. Processes that follow the protocol as expected are called *correct*. Contrary, the processes that deviate from the protocol specification or may crash are called *Byzantine*.

We assume that there exists a low-level mechanism for sending messages over reliable and authenticated point-to-point links between processes. In our protocol implementation, we describe this as "sending a message" and "receiving a message". Additionally, we assume *first-in first-out (FIFO) ordering* for the links. This ensures that messages broadcast by the same correct process are delivered in the order in which they were sent by a correct recipient.

This work considers two models, *asynchrony* and *partial synchrony*. Together they cover most scenarios used today in the context of secure distributed computing. In an *asynchronous* network, no physical clock is available to any process and the delivery of messages may be delayed arbitrarily. In such networks, it is only guaranteed that a message sent by a correct process will *eventually* arrive at its destination. One can define asynchronous time based on logical clocks. A *partially synchronous* network [9] operates asynchronously until some point in time (not known to the processes), after which it becomes stable. This means that processing times and message delays are bounded afterwards, but the maximal delays are not known to the protocol.

Broadcast and Consensus Primitives. The following primitives are important for our work: Byzantine FIFO consistent broadcast channel (BCCH), validated Byzantine consensus (VBC) and atomic broadcast.

BCCH allows the processes to deliver multiple payloads and ensures FIFO delivery and consistency despite Byzantine senders [4, Sect. 3.12]. BCCH provides two events: *bcch-broadcast(m)* and *bcch-deliver(p_j, l, m)*.

Definition 1 (Byzantine FIFO Consistent Broadcast Channel). *A Byzantine FIFO consistent broadcast channel satisfies the following properties:*

Validity: *If a correct process broadcasts a message m, then every correct process eventually delivers m.*

No Duplication: *For every process p_j and label l, every correct process delivers at most one message with label l and sender p_j.*

Integrity: *If some correct process delivers a message m with sender p_j and process p_j is correct, then m was previously broadcast by p_j.*

Consistency: *If some correct process delivers a message m with label l and sender p_j, and another correct process delivers a message m' with label l and sender p_j, then $m = m'$.*

FIFO Delivery: *If a correct process broadcasts some message m before it broadcasts a message m', then no correct process delivers m' unless it has already delivered m.*

VBC [5] defines an *external validity* condition. It requires that the consensus value is legal according to a global, efficiently computable predicate P, known to all processes. A consensus primitive is accessed through the events *vbc-propose(v)* and *vbc-decide(v)*.

Definition 2 (Validated Byzantine Consensus). *A protocol solves validated Byzantine consensus with validity predicate P if it satisfies the following conditions:*

Termination: *Every correct process eventually decides some value.*

Integrity: *No correct process decides twice.*

Agreement: *No two correct processes decide differently.*

External validity: *Every correct process only decides a value v such that $P(v) = $ TRUE. Moreover, if all processes are correct and propose v, then no correct process decides a value different from v.*

Atomic broadcast ensures that all processes deliver the same messages and that all messages are output in the same order. This is equivalent to the processes agreeing on one sequence of messages that they deliver. Processes may broadcast a message m by invoking a-$broadcast(m)$, and the protocol outputs messages through a-$deliver(m)$ events.

Definition 3 (Atomic Broadcast). *A protocol for atomic broadcast satisfies the following properties:*

Validity: *If a correct process* a-broadcasts *a message* m, *then every correct process eventually* a-delivers m.

No Duplication: *No message is* a-delivered *more than once.*

Agreement: *If a message* m *is* a-delivered *by some correct process, then* m *is eventually* a-delivered *by every correct process.*

Total Order: *Let* m *and* m' *be two messages such that* p_i *and* p_j *are correct processes that* a-deliver m *and* m'. *If* p_i a-delivers m *before* m', *then* p_j *also* a-delivers m *before* m'.

4 Revisiting Order Fairness

4.1 Limitations

Defining a fair order for atomic broadcast in asynchronous networks is not straightforward since the processes might locally receive messages for broadcasting in different orders. We assume here that a correct process receives a payload to be broadcast (e.g., from a client) at the same time when it a-*broadcasts* it. If a process broadcasts a payload message m before a payload message m', according to its local order, we denote this by $m \prec m'$.

Furthermore, we abandon the *validity* property above in the context of atomic broadcast with order fairness and assume now that every payload message is a-broadcast by all correct processes. This corresponds to the implicit assumption made for deploying order-fair broadcast.

Even if all processes are correct, it can be impossible to define a fair order among all messages. This is shown by a result from social science, known as the *Condorcet paradox*, which states that there exist situations that lead to nontransitive collective voting preferences even if the individual preferences are transitive. Kelkar *et al.* [14] apply this to atomic broadcast and show that delivering messages in a fair order is not always possible. Their example considers three correct processes p_1, p_2, and p_3 that receive three payload messages m_a, m_b, and m_c. While p_1 receives these payload messages in the order $m_a \prec m_b \prec m_c$, process p_2 receives them as $m_b \prec m_c \prec m_a$ and p_3 in the order $m_c \prec m_a \prec m_b$. Obviously, a majority of the processes received m_a before m_b, m_b before m_c, but also m_c before m_a, leading to a cyclic order. Consequently, a fair order cannot be specified even with only correct processes.

One way to handle situations with such cycles in the order is presented by Kelkar *et al.* [14] with *block-order fairness*: their protocol delivers a "block" of payload messages at once. Typically, a block will contain those payloads that are involved in a cyclic order. Their notion requires that if sufficiently many processes receive a payload m before another payload m', then no correct process delivers m after m', but they may both appear in the same block. Even though the order among the messages within a block remains unspecified, the notion of block-order fairness respects a fair order up to this limit.

Kelkar et al. [14] specify "sufficiently many" as a γ-fraction of all processes, where γ represents an order-fairness parameter such that $\frac{1}{2} < \gamma \leq 1$. More precisely, block-order fairness considers a number of processes η that all receive (and broadcast) two payload messages m and m'. Block-order fairness for atomic broadcast requires that whenever there are at least $\gamma\eta$ processes that receive m before m', then no correct process delivers m after m' (but they may deliver m and m' in the same block).

Kelkar et al. [14] explicitly count faulty processes for their definition. Notice that this immediately leads to problems: If $\gamma\eta < 2f$, for instance, the notion relies on a majority of faulty processes, but no guarantees are possible in this case. Therefore, we only count on events occurring at correct processes here and define a block-order fairness parameter $\overline{\gamma}$ to denote the fraction of *correct* processes that receive one message before the other.

Moreover, we assume w.l.o.g. that all correct processes eventually broadcast every payload, even if this is initially input by a single process only. This simplifies the treatment compared to original block-order fairness, which considers only processes that broadcast *both* payload messages, m and m' [14]. Our simplification means that a correct process that has received only one payload will receive the other payload as well later. This process should eventually include also the second payload for establishing a fair order. It corresponds to how atomic broadcast is used in practice; hence, we set $\eta = n - f$. In asynchronous networks, furthermore, one has to respect f additional correct processes that may be delayed. Their absence reduces the strength of the formal notion of block-order fairness in asynchronous networks even more.

In the following, we discuss the range of achievable values for $\overline{\gamma}$. Since we focus on models that allow asynchrony, we assume $n > 3f$ throughout this work. Fundamental results on validity notions for Byzantine consensus in asynchronous networks have been obtained by Fitzi and Garay [10]. Recall that a consensus protocol satisfies *termination*, *integrity*, and *agreement* according to Definition 2. *Standard consensus* additionally satisfies:

Validity: If all correct processes propose v, then all correct processes decide v.

Notice that this leaves the decision value completely open if only one correct process proposes something different. In their notion of *strong consensus*, however, the values proposed by correct processes must be better respected, under more circumstances:

Strong Validity: If a correct process decides v, then some correct process has proposed v.

Unfortunately, strong consensus is not suitable for practical purposes because Fitzi and Garay [10, Thm. 8] also show that if the proposal values are taken from a domain $\mathcal{V}$, then the resilience depends on $|\mathcal{V}|$. In particular, strong consensus is only possible if $n > |\mathcal{V}|f$.

Related to this, they also introduce δ-*differential consensus*, which respects how many times a value is proposed by the correct processes. This notion ensures, in short, that the decision value has been proposed by "sufficiently many" correct processes compared to how many processes proposed some different value. More precisely, for an execution of consensus and any value $v \in \mathcal{V}$, let $c(v)$ denote the number of correct processes that propose v:

δ-**Differential Validity:** If a correct process decides v, then every other value w proposed by some correct process satisfies $c(w) \leq c(v) + \delta$.

To summarize, whereas the standard notion of Byzantine consensus requires that *all* correct processes start with the same value in order to decide on one of the correct processes' input, strong consensus achieves this in any case. It requires that the decision value has been proposed by *some* correct process. However, it does not connect the decision value to how many correct processes have proposed it. Consequently, strong consensus may decide a value proposed by just one correct process. Differential consensus, finally, makes the initial plurality of the decision value explicit. For $\delta = 0$, in particular, the decision value must be one of the proposed values that is most common among the correct processes. More importantly, differential validity can be achieved under the usual assumption that $n > 3f$.

We now give another characterization of δ-differential validity. For a particular execution of some (asynchronous) Byzantine consensus protocol, let v^* be (one of) the value(s) proposed most often by correct processes, i.e., $v^* = \arg\max_v c(v)$.

Lemma 1. *A Byzantine consensus protocol satisfies δ-differential validity if and only if in every one of its executions, it never decides a value w with $c(w) < c(v^*) - \delta$.*

For consensus with a *binary* domain $\mathcal{V} = \{0, 1\}$, this means that a consensus protocol satisfies δ-differential validity if and only if in every one of its executions with, say, $c(0) > c(1) + \delta$, every correct process decides 0.

No asynchronous consensus algorithm for agreeing on the value proposed by a simple majority of correct processes exists, however. Fitzi and Garay [10, Thm. 11] prove that δ-differential consensus in asynchronous networks is *not possible* for $\delta < 2f$:

Theorem 1 ([10]). *In an asynchronous network, δ-differential consensus is achievable only if $\delta \geq 2f$.*

The above discussion already hints at issues with achieving fair order in asynchronous systems. Recall that Kelkar *et al.* [14] present atomic broadcast protocols with block-order fairness for the asynchronous setting with order-fairness parameter γ (whose definition includes faulty processes). The corruption bound is stated as $n > \frac{4f}{2\gamma - 1}$. For $\gamma = 1$, which ensures fairness only in the most clear cases, there are $n > 4f$ processes required. For values of γ close to $\frac{1}{2}$, the condition becomes prohibitive for practical solutions. In fact, even when using our interpretation, $\overline{\gamma}$ cannot be too close to $\frac{1}{2}$, as the following result shows. It rules out the existence of $\overline{\gamma}$-block-order-fair atomic broadcast in asynchronous or eventually synchronous networks for $\overline{\gamma} < \frac{1}{2} + \frac{f}{n-f}$.

Theorem 2. *In an asynchronous network with n processes and f faults, implementing atomic broadcast with $\overline{\gamma}$-fair block order is not possible unless $\overline{\gamma} \geq \frac{1}{2} + \frac{f}{n-f}$.*

Proof. Towards a contradiction, suppose there is an atomic broadcast protocol ensuring $\overline{\gamma}$-fair block order with $\frac{1}{2} < \overline{\gamma} < \frac{1}{2} + \frac{f}{n-f}$. We will transform this into a differential consensus protocol that violates Theorem 1.

The consensus protocol works like this. All processes initialize the atomic broadcast protocol. Upon *propose(v)* with some value v, a process simply a-broadcasts v. When the first value v' is *a-delivered* by atomic broadcast to a process, the process executes *decide(v')* and terminates.

Consider any execution of this protocol such that all correct processes propose one of two values, m or m'. Suppose w.l.o.g. that $c(m) = \overline{\gamma}(n - f)$ and $c(m') = (1-\overline{\gamma})(n-f)$, i.e., m is proposed $c(m)$ times by correct processes and more often than m', since $\overline{\gamma} > \frac{1}{2}$. It follows that $\overline{\gamma}(n - f)$ correct processes a-*broadcast* m before m' and $(1 - \overline{\gamma})(n - f)$ correct processes a-*broadcast* m' before m.

According to the properties of atomic broadcast all correct processes a-*deliver* the same value first in every execution. Moreover, the atomic broadcast protocol a-*delivers* m before m' by the $\overline{\gamma}$-fair block order property. This implies that the consensus protocol decides m in every execution and never m'. Since no further restrictions are placed on m and on m', this consensus protocol actually ensures δ-differential validity for some $\delta < c(m) - c(m')$ by Lemma 1.

However, the $c(m)$ and $c(m')$ satisfy, respectively,

$$c(m) = \overline{\gamma}(n - f) < \left(\tfrac{1}{2} + \tfrac{f}{n-f}\right)(n - f) = \tfrac{n+f}{2}$$
$$c(m') = (1 - \overline{\gamma})(n - f) > \left(1 - \tfrac{1}{2} - \tfrac{f}{n-f}\right)(n - f) = \tfrac{n-3f}{2}$$

and, therefore, $\delta < c(m) - c(m') < \frac{n+f}{2} - \frac{n-3f}{2} = 2f$. But δ-differential asynchronous consensus is only possible when $\delta \geq 2f$, a contradiction.

4.2   Differential Order-Fairness

The limitations discussed above have an influence on order fairness. The condition on δ to achieve δ-*differential consensus* directly impacts any measure of fairness. It becomes clear that a *relative* notion for block-order fairness, defined through a fraction like $\overline{\gamma}$, may not be expressive enough.

We now start to define our notion of *order-fair atomic broadcast*; it has almost the same interface as regular atomic broadcast. The primitive is accessed with *of-broadcast(m)* for broadcasting a payload message m and it outputs payload messages through *of-deliver(M)* events, where M is a *set* of payloads delivered at the same time; M corresponds the block of block-order fairness. We want to count the number of correct processes that *of-broadcast* a message m before another message m' and introduce a function $b : \mathcal{M} \times \mathcal{M} \to \mathbb{N}$ for all m and m' that were ever *of-broadcast* by correct processes. The value $b(m, m')$ denotes the *number of correct processes* that *of-broadcast* m before m' in an execution. As above we assume w.l.o.g. that a correct process will *of-broadcast* m and m' eventually and that, therefore, $b(m, m') + b(m', m) = n - f$.

Can we achieve that if $b(m, m') > b(m', m)$, i.e., when there are more correct processes that *of-broadcast* message m before m' than correct processes that *of-broadcast* m' before m, then no correct process will *of-deliver* m' before m? Using a reduction from δ-differential consensus, as in the previous result, we can show that this condition is too weak. The proof is provided in the full version [6].

Theorem 3. *Consider an atomic broadcast protocol that satisfies the following notion of order fairness for some $\mu \geq 0$:*

Weak Differential Order Fairness: *For any m and m', if $b(m, m') > b(m', m) + \mu$, then no correct process a-delivers m' before m.*

Then it must hold $\mu \geq 2f$.

On the basis of this result, we now formulate our notion of κ-*differentially order-fair atomic broadcast*, using a fairness parameter $\kappa \geq 0$ to express the strength of the fairness. Smaller values of κ ensure stronger fairness in the sense of how large the majority of processes that *of-broadcast* some m before m' must be to ensure that m will be *of-delivered* before m' and in a fair order.

Recall that throughout this work, we assume that if one correct process *of-broadcasts* some payload m, then every correct process eventually also *of-broadcasts* m. For reasons that are discussed in the full version [6], we use a weaker formal notion of validity, which considers executions with only correct processes.

Definition 4 (κ-Differentially Order-Fair Atomic Broadcast). *A protocol for κ-differentially order-fair atomic broadcast satisfies the properties* no duplication, agreement *and* total order *of atomic broadcast and additionally:*

Weak Validity: *If all processes are correct and of-broadcast a finite number of messages, then every correct process eventually of-delivers all of these of-broadcast messages.*

κ-Differential Order Fairness: *If $b(m, m') > b(m', m) + 2f + \kappa$, then no correct process of-delivers m' before m.*

Compared to the above notion of weak differential order fairness, we have $\kappa = \mu - 2f$. We show in the next section how to implement κ-differentially order-fair atomic broadcast.

5   Quick Order-Fair Atomic Broadcast Protocol

5.1   Overview

The protocol concurrently runs a Byzantine FIFO consistent broadcast channel (BCCH) and proceeds in rounds of consensus. BCCH allows processes to deliver multiple messages consistently. An incoming *of-broadcast* event with a payload message m triggers BCCH and *bcch -broadcasts* m to the network. Additionally, every process keeps a local vector clock that counts the payloads that have been *bcch -delivered* from each sending process. Every process also maintains an array of lists *msgs* such that *msgs*[i] records all *bcch -delivered* payloads from p_i.

When a process *bcch -delivers* the payload message m, it increments the corresponding vector-clock entry and appends m to the appropriate list in *msgs*. As soon as sufficiently many new payloads are found in *msgs*, a new round starts. Each process signs its vector clock and sends it to all others. The received vector clocks are collected in a matrix, and once $n - f$ valid vector clocks are recorded, a new validated Byzantine consensus (VBC) instance is triggered. The process proposes the matrix and the signatures for consensus, and VBC decides on a common matrix with valid signatures. This matrix defines a *cut*, which is a vector of indices, with one index per process, such that the index for p_j determines an entry in *msgs*[j] up to which payload messages are considered for creating the fair order in the round. It may be that the index points to messages that a process p_i does not store in *msgs*[j] because they have not been *bcch-delivered* yet. When the process detects such a missing payload, it asks all other processes to send the missing payload directly and in a verifiable way, such that every process will store all payloads up to the cut in *msgs*.

Once all processes received the payloads up to the cut, the algorithm starts to build a graph that represents the dependencies among messages that must be respected for a fair order. This graph resembles the one used in Aequitas [14], but its semantics and implementation differ. The vertices in the graph here are all *new* payload messages defined by the cut and an edge (m, m') indicates that m should at most be *of-delivered* before m'.

The graph results from two steps. In the first step, the process creates a vertex for every payload message that appears in a distinct lists in *msgs* and it is not yet *of-delivered*. In the second step, the algorithm builds a matrix M such that $M[m][m']$ counts how many times m appears before m' in *msgs* (up to the cut). $M[m][m']$ can be interpreted as *votes*, counting how many processes want to order m before m'. Notice that entries of M exist only for m and m' where at least one of $M[m][m']$ and $M[m'][m]$ is non-zero.

If the *difference* between entries $M[m][m']$ and $M[m'][m]$ is large enough, then the protocol adds a directed edge (m, m') to the graph. The edge indicates that m' must not be *of-delivered* before m. More precisely, assuming that messages m and m' have been observed by at least $n - f$ processes, such an edge is added for all m and m' with $M[m][m'] > M[m'][m] - f + \kappa$. The condition is explained through the following result.

Lemma 2. *If* $b(m, m') > b(m', m) + 2f + \kappa$, *then* $M[m][m'] > M[m'][m] - f + \kappa$.

In the discussion so far, we have assumed that the two messages m and m' were received by at least $n - f$ processes. Observe that every process can only contribute with 1 to either $M[m][m']$ or to $M[m'][m]$, but not to both. However, it may occur that only a few processes receive m and m' before the cut, which implies that $M[m][m']$ may be very small, for example. But that count might actually grow later and take on values up to $n - f - M[m'][m]$. For this reason, we extend the condition derived from Lemma 2 in the algorithm as follows: if $n - f - M[m'][m] > M[m'][m] - f + \kappa$ (which implies that $M[m'][m]$ is small, i.e., $M[m'][m] < \frac{n-\kappa}{2}$), we also add add an edge between m and m'. In summary, then, the algorithm adds an edge from m to m' whenever $\max\{M[m][m'], n - f - M[m'][m]\} > M[m'][m] - f + \kappa$. Creating the graph in this manner leads to a directed graph that represents constraints to be respected by a fair order. Notice that two messages may be connected by edges in both directions when the difference is small and $\kappa < f$, i.e., there may be a cycle (m, m') and (m', m). This means that the difference between the number of processes voting for one or the other order is too small to decide on a fair order. Longer cycles may also exist. All payload messages with circular dependencies among them will be *of-delivered* together as a set. For deriving this information, the algorithm repeatedly detects all strongly connected components in the graph and collapses them to a vertex. In other words, any two vertices m and m' are merged when there exists a path from m to m' and a path from m' to m. This technique also handles cases like those derived from the *Condorcet paradox*.

Finally, with the help of the collapsed graph, all payload messages defined by the cut are *of-delivered* in a fair order: First, all vertices without any incoming edges are selected. Secondly, these vertices are sorted in a deterministic way and the corresponding payloads are *of-delivered* one after the other. Then the processed vertices are removed from the graph and another iteration through the graph starts. As soon as there are no vertices left, i.e., all payload messages are *of-delivered*, the protocol proceeds to the next round.

Note that cycles may also extend beyond the cut, as shown by Kelkar *et al.* [13]. Therefore, the algorithm holds back payload messages and does not *of-deliver* them while they may still become part of a longer cycle. This is ensured by counting how many times a message appears in *msgs* up to the cut. In particular, let $C[m]$ count this number for a message m. We require that any message is only *of-delivered* when $C[m] \geq \frac{n+f-\kappa}{2}$, i.e., after m appears in *msgs* often enough such that it cannot become part of a cycle later or already be in a cycle that will grow later, e.g., through payloads that arrive after the cut.

5.2   Implementation

Algorithm 1–2 shows the *quick order-fair atomic broadcast protocol* for a process p_i. The protocol proceeds in rounds and maintains a round counter r (L1) and uses a boolean variable *inround*, which indicates whether the consensus phase of a round is executing (L2).

Every process maintains two hash maps: *msgs* (L3) and *vc* (L4). The process identifiers serve as keys in both hash maps. Hash map *msgs* contains ordered lists of *bcch-delivered* payload from each process in the system. Variable vc is a vector clock counting how many payload messages were *bcch-delivered* from each process.

Rounds. In each round, a matrix L (L5) and a list Σ (L6) are constructed as inputs for consensus. The matrix L will consist of vector clocks from the processes and Σ will contain the signatures of the processes. Additionally, every process maintains a list of values called *cut* (L7) that are calculated in every round. This cut represents an index for every list in *msgs* to determine the payload to be used for creating the fair order. Initially, all values are zero. Finally, all *of-delivered* payload messages are included in a set *delivered* (L8), to prevent a repeated delivery in future rounds.

The protocol starts when a client submits a payload message m using an *of-broadcast*(m) event. BCCH then broadcasts m to all processes in the network (L11). When m with label l from process p_j is *bcch* -delivered (L12), the vector clock vc for process p_j is incremented. The attached label l is not used by the algorithm and only serves to define that all correct processes *bcch* -deliver the same payload following Definition 1. Additionally, payload m is appended to the list *msgs*$[j]$ using an operation *append*(m) (L14). When the length of p_j's list in *msgs* exceeds the *cut* value for p_j, new payloads may have arrived that should be ordered (L15). This tells the protocol to initiate a new round. This condition can be adapted as described in the remarks at the end of this section.

The first step of round r is to set the flag *inround*. Secondly, the protocol digitally signs the vector clock vc and obtains a signature σ. The values r, σ, and vc are then sent in a STATUS message to all processes (L16–L18). When process p_i receives a STATUS message from p_j, it validates the contained signature σ' using *verify*(j, vc', σ') (L20). An additional security check is made by comparing the locally stored round number r with the round number r' from the message. If both conditions hold, the vector clock vc' is stored as row j in matrix L (L21) and σ' is stored in list Σ at index j (L22).

Defining a Cut. As soon as p_i has received $n - f$ valid STATUS-messages (L23), it invokes consensus (VBC, L24) for the round through *vbc-propose* with proposal (L, Σ). The predicate of VBC checks that a proposal consists of a matrix L and a vector Σ such that for at least $n - f$ values j, the entry $\Sigma[j]$ is a valid signature on row j of L. When the VBC protocol subsequently decides, it outputs a common matrix L' of vector clocks and a list Σ' of signatures (L26). The process then uses L' to calculate the cut, where *cut*$[j]$ is the largest value s such that at least $f + 1$ elements in column j in L' are bigger or equal than s (L29). In other words, *cut*$[j]$ represents how many payload messages from p_j were *bcch-delivered* by enough processes. This value is used as index into *msgs*$[j]$ to determine the payloads that will be considered for creating the order in this round.

The algorithm then makes sure that all processes will hold at least all those payloads in *msgs* that are defined by *cut*. Each process detects missing payload messages from sender p_j from any difference between $vc[j]$ and *cut*$[j]$ (L31); if there are any, the process broadcasts a MISSING-message to all others. When another process receives such a request from p_j and already has the requested payloads in *msgs*, it extracts them into a variable *resend* (L36). More precisely, it extracts a proof from the BCCH primitive with which any other process can verify that the payload from this particular sender is genuine. This is done by invoking *bcch-create-proof(resend)* (L37); the messages and the proof are then sent in a RESEND-message to the requesting process p_j (L38).

When process p_i receives a RESEND-message with a missing payload from p_k, it verifies the provided proof s' from the message by invoking *bcch-verify-proof(s')* function (L41). If the proof is valid, p_i extracts (L43) the payload messages through *bcch-get-messages(s')*, appends them to $msgs[k]$, and increments $vc[k]$ accordingly. The process repeats this until *msgs* contains all payloads included in the cut.

Ordering Messages. At this point, every process stores all payloads *msgs* that have been *bcch-delivered* up to the cut. The remaining operations of the round are deterministic and executed by all processes independently. The next step is to construct the directed *dependency graph* G that expresses the constraints on the fair order of the payload messages. Vertices (V) in G represent payload messages that may be *of-delivered* and edges (E) in G express constraints on the order among these payloads. First, all messages within the cut that are not yet delivered are added as vertices to the set V (L 45).

Then, for each pair of messages m and m' in V, the algorithm constructs M (L49) such that $M[m][m']$ counts how many times a payload m appears before payload m' in the cut. In the same loop, the algorithm counts how many times message m appears within the cut and stores this result in array C (L50). Finally, all entries $M[m][m']$ and $M[m'][m]$ are compared and if condition $max\{M[m][m'], n - f - M[m'][m]\} > M[m'][m] - f + \kappa$ holds, then a directed edge from m to m' is added (L51). This edge indicates that m must *not* be ordered *after* m', i.e., that m is *of-delivered* before m' or together with m'.

Any payloads that cannot be ordered with respect to each other now correspond to strongly connected components of G. A strongly connected component is a subgraph, which for each pair of vertices m and m' contains a path from m to m' and one from m' to m. In the next step, a graph $H = (W, F)$ is created and all strongly connected components in H are repeatedly collapsed until H contains no more cycles. This is done by contracting the edges in each connected component and merging all its vertices (L52–L54).

The algorithm further considers all vertices w without incoming edges and which satisfy condition $C[m] \geq \frac{n+f-\kappa}{2}$, checked in function *stable(w)* (L 63). All such w will be sorted in a deterministic way (L 53). Notice that w may correspond to a message from $\mathcal{M}$ or a recursive set of sets of messages. Therefore function *flatten(w)* (L 65) is used to extract payload messages and *of-deliver* them (L 57). All *of-delivered* payload messages are added to *delivered* (L58 to prevent a repeated processing. Finally, w is removed from H (L59), and a next pass of extracting vertices with no incoming edge follows. This is repeated until all vertices have been processed and *of-delivered*. The algorithm then initializes

Algorithm 1. Quick order-fair atomic broadcast (code for p_i).

State

1:     $r \leftarrow 1$: current round
2:     $inround \leftarrow$ FALSE
3:     $msgs \leftarrow []$: HashMap$[\{1, ..., n\} \rightarrow []]$: lists of $bcch$-$delivered$ messages
4:     $vc \leftarrow []$: HashMap$[\{1, ..., n\} \rightarrow \mathbb{N}]$: counters for $bcch$-delivered messages
5:     $L \leftarrow [0]^{n \times n}$: matrix of logical timestamps
6:     $\Sigma \leftarrow []^n$: list of signatures from STATUS messages
7:     $cut \leftarrow [0]^n$: the cut decided for the round
8:     $delivered \leftarrow \emptyset$: set of delivered messages

Initialization

9:     Byzantine FIFO consistent broadcast channel ($bcch$)

10: **upon** of-broadcast(m) **do**
11:     $bcch$-broadcast(m)

12: **upon** $bcch$-deliver(p_j, l, m) **do**
13:     $vc[j] \leftarrow vc[j] + 1$
14:     $msgs[j]$.append(m)

15: **upon** exists j such that $len(msgs[j]) > cut[j] \land \neg inround$ **do**
16:     $inround \leftarrow$ TRUE
17:     $\sigma \leftarrow sign(i, vc)$
18:     send message [STATUS, r, vc, σ] to all $p_j \in \mathcal{P}$

19: **upon** receiving message [STATUS, r', vc', σ'] from p_j
20:     such that $r' = r \land verify(j, vc', \sigma')$ **do**
21:         $L[j] \leftarrow vc'$
22:         $\Sigma[j] \leftarrow \sigma'$

23: **upon** $|\{p_j \in \mathcal{P} \mid \Sigma[j] \neq \perp\}| \geq n - f$ **do**
24:     vbc-propose((L, Σ)) for validated Byzantine consensus in round r
25:     $\Sigma \leftarrow []^n$

26: **upon** vbc-decide((L', Σ')) in round r **do**   // calculate cut
27:     **for** $j \in \{1, ..., n\}$ **do**   // for each row in L'
28:         // $cut[j]$ is largest s s.t. at least $f + 1$ el. in col. j in L' are at least s
29:         $cut[j] \leftarrow max\{s \mid |\{k \mid |\{L'[k][j] \geq s\}| > f\}\}$

30:     **for** $j \in \{1, ..., n\}$ **do**   // check for missing messages
31:         **if** $vc[j] < cut[j]$ **then**
32:             send message [MISSING, $r, j, vc[j]$] to all $p_k \in \mathcal{P}$

33: **upon** receiving message [MISSING, $r', k, index$] from p_j
34:     such that $r' = r$ **do**
35:         **if** $vc[k] \geq cut[k]$ **then**
36:             $resend \leftarrow msgs[k]$.get($index \ldots cut[k]$)   // copy messages from p_k
37:             $s \leftarrow bcch$-create-proof($resend$)
38:             send message [RESEND, r, k, s] to p_j // send missing messages

---

Algorithm 2. Quick order-fair atomic broadcast (code for p_i).

39: **upon** receiving message $[\text{RESEND}, r', k', s']$ from p_j
40:     **such that** $r' = r \wedge len(msgs[k]) < cut[k]$ **do**
41:         **if** bcch-verify-proof(s') **then**
42:             $vc[k] \leftarrow vc[k] + bcch\text{-}get\text{-}length(s')$
43:             $msgs[k].append(bcch\text{-}get\text{-}messages(s'))$

44: **upon** $len(msgs[j]) \geq cut[j]$ for all $j \in \{1, \ldots, n\}$ **do**
45:     $V \leftarrow \left(\bigcup_{j \in \{1, \ldots, n\}} msgs[j] \, [1 \ldots cut[k]] \right) \setminus delivered$
46:     $M \leftarrow [\,] : \text{HashMap}[\mathcal{M} \times \mathcal{M} \to \mathbb{N}]$
47:     $C \leftarrow [\,] : \text{HashMap}[\mathcal{M} \to \mathbb{N}]$
48:     **for** $m, m' \in V$ **do**
49:         $M[m][m'] \leftarrow \left| \{ j \in \{1, \ldots, n\} \mid m \text{ before } m' \text{ in } msgs[j] \, [1 \ldots cut[k]] \} \right|$
50:         $C[m] \leftarrow \left| \{ p_j \mid m \in msgs[j] \, [1 \ldots cut[k]] \} \right|$
51:     $E \leftarrow \left\{ (m, m') \; \middle| \; \max\{ M[m][m'], n - f - M[m'][m] \} > M[m'][m] - f + \kappa \right\}$
52:     $H \leftarrow (V, E)$ $// \, (V, E) = G$
53:     **while** H contains some strongly connected subgraph $\overline{H} = (\overline{W}, \overline{F}) \subseteq H$ **do**
54:         $H \leftarrow H / \overline{F}$ $//$ collapse vertices in $\overline{W}$ into a single vertex $\overline{w}$
55:     $// \, H = (W, F)$
56:     **while** $\exists w \in sort(W) : indegree(w) = 0 \wedge stable(w)$ **do**
                $//$ w may be a message or a (recursive) set of sets of messages
57:         of-deliver(flatten(w))
58:         $delivered \leftarrow delivered \cup flatten(w)$ $//$ keep track of delivered messages
59:         $W \leftarrow W \setminus \{w\}$
60:     $L \leftarrow [0]^{n \times n}$
61:     $inround \leftarrow \text{FALSE}$
62:     $r \leftarrow r + 1$ $//$ move to the next round

63: **function** stable(w)
64:     **return** $\left(w \in \mathcal{M} \wedge C[w] \geq \frac{n+f-\kappa}{2} \right) \vee \bigwedge_{w' \in w : w' \notin \mathcal{M}} stable(w')$

65: **function** flatten(w)
66:     **return** $\{ m \in w \mid m \in \mathcal{M} \} \cup \bigcup_{w' \in w : w' \notin \mathcal{M}} flatten(w')$

L, sets *inround* to FALSE, increments the round number r, and starts the next round (L60-L62).

6   Complexity

If the Byzantine FIFO consistent broadcast channel (BCCH) is implemented using "echo broadcast" [17], it takes $O(n)$ protocol messages per payload message. Since more than f processes *of-broadcast* each payload message and f is proportional to n, the overall message complexity of BCCH is $O(n^2)$. The cost of validated Byzantine consensus (VBC) depends on the assumptions used for implementing it. With a partially synchronous consensus protocol VBC uses $O(n)$ messages in the best case and $O(n^2)$ messages in the worst case. The total amortized cost of quick order-fair atomic broadcast per payload, therefore, is also $O(n^2)$ messages in this implementation. If digital signatures are of length λ and payload messages are at most L bits, the bit complexity of BCCH for one sender is $O(n^2 L + n^3 \lambda)$. Optimal asynchronous VBC protocols [1,16] have $O(nL + n^2\lambda)$ expected communication cost, for their payload length L. Since the proposals for VBC are $n \times n$ matrices, it follows that the amortized bit complexity of the algorithm per payload message is $O(n^2 L + n^3 \lambda)$.

Table 1 compares the cost of different order-fair atomic broadcast protocols. The asynchronous Aequitas protocol [14, Sec. 7] provides fair order using a *FIFO Broadcast primitive*, implemented by *OARcast* of Ho et al. [11]. Aequitas uses $\Omega(n^4)$ messages for delivering one payload, which exceeds the cost of quick order-fair broadcast at least by the factor n^2. The Pompē protocol cost is $O(n^2)$ messages and one instance of Byzantine consensus per payload message. The communication complexity of this protocol is $O(n^3 L)$ since each process broadcasts a SEQUENCE-message to all others with contents of length $O(nL)$. Themis [13] incurs a cost of $O(n)$ messages. The average communication complexity is $O(n^2 + nL)$ in the best case.

Table 1. Overview of different notions and their expected message and communication complexities.

Notion	Algorithm	Avg. messages	Avg. communication
Block-Order-Fairness [14]	Async. Aequitas [14]	$O(n^4)$	$O(n^4 L)$
Ordering linearizability [19]	Pompē* [19]	$O(n^2)$	$O(n^3 L)$
Block-Order-Fairness [13]	Themis [13]	$O(n)$	$O(n^2 + nL)$
Differential order fairness	Quick o.-f. broadcast	$O(n^2)$	$O(n^2 L + n^3 \lambda)$

7   Conclusion

The quick order-fair atomic broadcast protocol guarantees payload message delivery in a differentially fair order. It works both for asynchronous and eventually synchronous networks with optimal resilience, tolerating corruptions of up to one third of the processes. Compared to existing order-fair atomic broadcast protocols, our protocol is considerably more efficient and incurs only quadratic cost in terms of amortized message complexity per delivered payload.

Acknowledgments. We thank the anonymous reviewers for helpful suggestions and feedback. Special thanks go to Mahimna Kelkar, who pointed out a problem in an earlier version of this paper. This work has been funded by the Swiss National Science Foundation (SNSF) under grant agreement Nr . 200021_188443 (Advanced Consensus Protocols).

References

1. Abraham, I., Malkhi, D., Spiegelman, A.: Asymptotically optimal validated asynchronous byzantine agreement. In: PODC, pp. 337–346. ACM (2019)
2. Asayag, A., et al.: A fair consensus protocol for transaction ordering. In: ICNP, pp. 55–65. IEEE Computer Society (2018)
3. Baird, L.: The Swirlds hashgraph consensus algorithm: fair, fast, byzantine fault tolerance. Swirlds Tech Report, SWIRLDS-TR-2016-01 (2016). https://www.swirlds.com/downloads/SWIRLDS-TR-2016-01.pdf
4. Cachin, C., Guerraoui, R., Rodrigues, L.E.T.: Introduction to Reliable and Secure Distributed Programming, 2nd edn. Springer, Heidelberg (2011). https://doi.org/10.1007/978-3-642-15260-3
5. Cachin, C., Kursawe, K., Petzold, F., Shoup, V.: Secure and efficient asynchronous broadcast protocols. In: Kilian, J. (ed.) CRYPTO 2001. LNCS, vol. 2139, pp. 524–541. Springer, Heidelberg (2001). https://doi.org/10.1007/3-540-44647-8_31
6. Cachin, C., Mićić, J., Steinhauer, N.: Quick Order Fairness (2021). arXiv preprint arXiv:2112.06615
7. Daian, P., et al.: Flash boys 2.0: frontrunning in decentralized exchanges, miner extractable value, and consensus instability. In: IEEE Symposium on Security and Privacy, pp. 910–927. IEEE (2020)
8. Duan, S., Reiter, M.K., Zhang, H.: Secure causal atomic broadcast, revisited. In: DSN, pp. 61–72. IEEE Computer Society (2017)
9. Dwork, C., Lynch, N.A., Stockmeyer, L.J.: Consensus in the presence of partial synchrony. J. ACM **35**(2), 288–323 (1988)
10. Fitzi, M., Garay, J.A.: Efficient player-optimal protocols for strong and differential consensus. In: PODC, pp. 211–220. ACM (2003)
11. Ho, C., Dolev, D., van Renesse, R.: Making distributed applications robust. In: Tovar, E., Tsigas, P., Fouchal, H. (eds.) OPODIS 2007. LNCS, vol. 4878, pp. 232–246. Springer, Heidelberg (2007). https://doi.org/10.1007/978-3-540-77096-1_17
12. Kelkar, M., Deb, S., Kannan, S.: Order-fair consensus in the permissionless setting. IACR Cryptology ePrint Archive Paper 2021/139 (2021). https://eprint.iacr.org/2021/139
13. Kelkar, M., Deb, S., Long, S., Juels, A., Kannan, S.: Themis: fast, strong order-fairness in byzantine consensus. IACR Cryptology ePrint Archive Paper 2021/1465 (2021). https://eprint.iacr.org/2021/1465
14. Kelkar, M., Zhang, F., Goldfeder, S., Juels, A.: Order-fairness for byzantine consensus. In: Micciancio, D., Ristenpart, T. (eds.) CRYPTO 2020. LNCS, vol. 12172, pp. 451–480. Springer, Cham (2020). https://doi.org/10.1007/978-3-030-56877-1_16
15. Kursawe, K.: Wendy, the good little fairness widget: achieving order fairness for blockchains. In: AFT, pp. 25–36. ACM (2020)
16. Lu, Y., Lu, Z., Tang, Q., Wang, G.: Dumbo-MVBA: optimal multi-valued validated asynchronous byzantine agreement, revisited. In: PODC, pp. 129–138. ACM (2020)
17. Reiter, M.K.: Secure agreement protocols: reliable and atomic group multicast in rampart. In: CCS, pp. 68–80. ACM (1994)
18. Reiter, M.K., Birman, K.P.: How to securely replicate services. ACM Trans. Program. Lang. Syst. **16**(3), 986–1009 (1994)
19. Zhang, Y., Setty, S.T.V., Chen, Q., Zhou, L., Alvisi, L.: Byzantine ordered consensus without byzantine oligarchy. In: OSDI, pp. 633–649. USENIX Association (2020)

Mostly Payment Networks

Analysis and Probing of Parallel Channels in the Lightning Network

Alex Biryukov, Gleb Naumenko, and Sergei Tikhomirov$^{(\boxtimes)}$

University of Luxembourg, Esch-sur-Alzette, Luxembourg
alex.biryukov@uni.lu, gleb@thelab31.xyz, sergey.s.tikhomirov@gmail.com
http://www.thelab31.xyz

Abstract. Bitcoin can process only a few transactions per second, which is insufficient for a global payment network. The Lightning Network (LN) aims to address this challenge. The LN allows for low-latency bitcoin transfers through a network of payment channels. In contrast to regular Bitcoin transactions, payments in the LN are not globally broadcast. Thus it may improve not only Bitcoin's scalability but also privacy. However, the probing attack allows an adversary to discover channel balances, threatening users' privacy. Prior work on probing did not account for the possibility of multiple (parallel) channels between two nodes. Naive probing algorithms yield false results for parallel channels.

In this work, we develop a new probing model that accurately accounts for parallel channels. We describe jamming-enhanced probing that allows for full balance information extraction in multi-channel hops, which was impossible with earlier probing methods. We quantify the attacker's information gain and propose an optimized algorithm for choosing probe amounts for multi-channel hops. We demonstrate its efficiency based on real-world data using our own probing-focused LN simulator. Finally, we discuss countermeasures such as new forwarding strategies, intra-hop payment split, rebalancing, and unannounced channels.

Keywords: Lightning Network · Bitcoin · Payment channels · Privacy

1 Introduction

To ensure public verifiability on widely available hardware, the throughput of Bitcoin is limited by design [24]. Second-layer (L2) protocols [11] aim to address this issue. The most prominent L2 protocol for Bitcoin[1] is a payment channel network called the Lightning Network (LN) [30]. A payment channel is a trust-minimized two-party protocol for low-latency cryptocurrency payments [14] with minimal interaction with the underlying blockchain. A channel network allows for multi-hop payments between users who do not share a channel.

In contrast to Bitcoin transactions, which are public and provide very limited privacy [2,22], L2 payments are not globally broadcast. Hence the LN may be

---

[1] Similar protocols are possible for other cryptocurrencies.

© International Financial Cryptography Association 2022
I. Eyal and J. Garay (Eds.): FC 2022, LNCS 13411, pp. 337–357, 2022.
https://doi.org/10.1007/978-3-031-18283-9_16

seen as a privacy-enhancing technology. However, attacks on LN privacy have been described, including balance probing. Probing allows for cheaply revealing channel balances by sending fake payments (probes) [8,15,18,45]. It can be used as a building block to spy on payments or to deanonymize users.

The LN allows nodes to share multiple *parallel* channels. Alice, for instance, may want to open a new channel to Bob if all funds in their existing channel are on Bob's side, preventing her from sending further payments. That would allow Alice to send without losing the ability to receive through the older channel. Earlier probing algorithms assume at most one channel between each pair of nodes and may give false or incomplete results if parallel channels are present.[2]

Our Contributions. After providing the necessary background (Sect. 2), we introduce the probing model (Sect. 3) and propose an optimized amount selection method to maximize probing speed. We enhance the probing attack by combining it with jamming or fee targeting. Using simulations[3] based on a real-world data, we show that enhanced probing extracts full balance information in parallel channels, which was impossible with prior methods (Sect. 4). Moreover, optimized amount selection increases probing speed by up to 15%, compared to single-dimensional binary search. In Sect. 5, we discuss the limitations of our approach, attack cost and trade-offs, payment flow discovery, and countermeasures. We review related work in Sect. 6 and conclude in Sect. 7.

2 Background

To open a payment channel, Alice and Bob lock coins into a cooperatively owned address, establishing the initial channel state. To make a payment, the parties negotiate a new state, thereby provably invalidating the old one [11]. Any party can close the channel and withdraw their coins on-chain at any time. A penalty mechanism ensures security of channel state updates. If one party tries to cheat by closing the channel with an outdated state (claiming more funds than the latest state prescribes), the other party is granted a time window to withdraw all funds from the channel.

The total number of coins in a channel, constant throughout its lifetime, is called *capacity* (Fig. 1). The number of coins owned by each party is called its *balance* and changes as payments are made. We refer to a pair of adjacent nodes along with all (parallel) channels that they share as a *hop*. Parallel channels within one hop may have different fees and routing policies [5]. A node may disable a channel direction (e.g., before an expected loss of connectivity or channel settlement), making the channel *unidirectional*.[4]

---

[2] The paper [26] writes on probing in the presence of multiple channels between the same nodes: "Our tool failed to produce accurate results in this scenario [. . .] further research on how to deal with this complication would be highly appreciated.".

[3] The code is at https://github.com/s-tikhomirov/ln-probing-simulator.

[4] Not to be confused with an earlier unidirectional channel construction [14].

Fig. 1. A channel with capacity 5 and balances 3 and 2 for Alice and Bob, respectively

LN nodes and channels are identified by persistent IDs. Node IDs are random; channel IDs are derived from the parameters of the respective opening transactions. Nodes can (but do not have to) announce the availability, capacities, and policies of their channels in the P2P network.[5]

An LN user can send *multi-hop payments* without establishing a channel with the receiver. To initiate a payment, the receiver generates a *payment secret* and sends its hash (the *payment hash*) to the sender. The sender routes the payment along the *payment path* (an ordered list of *routing*[6] *nodes* chosen based on the sender's local view of the network). Routing nodes usually charge fees by forwarding a bit less than they receive. If an intermediary hop contains parallel channels, a routing node may use any of them (*non-strict forwarding*). Upon receiving a payment, the receiver propagates the payment secret along the path back to the sender. This ensures atomicity of balance shifts along the path as they all depend on the same secret being revealed.[7]

LN nodes are only aware of payments that they send, receive, or forward. Due to onion routing, intermediary nodes only know the previous and the next node in the path, but not the ultimate sender or receiver. Intermediaries do, however, learn the amounts of payments that they forward.

The forwarding ability of a channel is determined by its *balance* in the direction of the payment. However, the sender only knows the *capacities* of announced channels.[8] Therefore, multi-hop payments may fail due to low balance at an intermediary hop. In that case, the erring node notifies the sender which error has occurred and where. The sender may have to make multiple attempts using different paths until the payment succeeds.

The three major LN implementations (LND, CORE-LIGHTNING, and ECLAIR) use different channel selection strategies for multi-channel hops.[9] ECLAIR selects the channel with the lowest capacity (among the channels with the same capacity, it prefers the one with a lower balance).[10] LND chooses a random channel.[11] CORE-LIGHTNING does not support parallel channels.

---

[5] A 2020 study estimated that 28.7% of LN channels were unannounced [31].

[6] Routing nodes may also be referred to as *forwarding* or *intermediary* nodes. Alternative approaches are trampoline [42] and rendezvous routing [49].

[7] It may be argued though that the wormhole attack [21] violates atomicity.

[8] Obviously, nodes also know the balances of their own channels, even if unannounced.

[9] Path selection algorithms also differ [20].

[10] https://github.com/ACINQ/eclair/blob/5f9d0d/eclair-core/src/main/scala/fr/acinq/eclair/payment/relay/ChannelRelay.scala#L199.

[11] https://github.com/lightningnetwork/lnd/blob/f98a3c/htlcswitch/switch.go#L1091.

Fig. 2. A probing setup for a two-channel target hop: the attacker does not know which channel the probes go through.

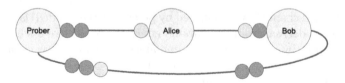

Fig. 3. Jamming attack: a jam (light-colored circle) is blocking other potential payments through the channel from Alice to Bob.

Attacks on Lightning

For our work, the most relevant attacks on the LN are probing and jamming.

Probing allows an attacker to reveal the balance of any forwarding channel (assuming no multi-channel hops) by sending probes through it [15,18,45]. A probe is a payment with amount a that contains a random value instead of a payment hash. A probe fails either at an intermediary node due to insufficient balance, or at the receiver because of the unknown hash preimage.[12] The location of the erring node within the path reveals whether the balance of the erring channel is above or below a. We say that a probe that reaches[13] the target hop *succeeds* if it goes through or that it *fails* if it does not. By sending probes with different amounts, the attacker can infer the balance in the target channel with high accuracy. Assuming uniform balance distribution, the best strategy for choosing probe amounts is binary search. If the target hop contains parallel channels, probing may provide incorrect results (Fig. 2).

Jamming is a family of denial-of-service attacks on LN channels [9,43]. An attacker initiates a payment (a *jam*) along a circular[14] path, which includes the target channel, and refuses to reveal the payment secret, locking up the funds along the path (Fig. 3). Shortly before timelocks expire, the attacker fails the payment to release their coins without paying routing fees. In *capacity-based jamming*, an attacker initiates payments of a given (presumably high) value [27]. In *slot-based jamming*, an attacker sends a series of small payments (each above a certain dust limit) to reach the limit of *payment slots* for in-flight payments (at most 483 in each direction; channel parties may set lower limits) [44]. Onion routing complicates protection against jamming: the victim does not know who is sending the jams.

---

[12] We do not consider other potential errors for simplicity.

[13] When probing via multi-hop paths, probes may fail before reaching the target hop.

[14] Alternatively, the path may terminate at a different node controlled by the attacker.

3   Probing Model

We assume the following threat model. The goal of the attacker is to reveal exact channel balances in target hops as quickly as possible.[15] The attacker only uses public knowledge about nodes and channels. The attacker can run multiple LN nodes, open channels, and maintain them for the duration of the attack.[16] The attacker can run modified software but has no control over other users' software.

We define channel direction as follows: $dir0$ is the direction from the node with the alphanumerically smaller ID to the other node; $dir1$ is the opposite direction. We define channel balance (in satoshis[17]) as the balance of the node with the alphanumerically smaller ID. Note that the $dir0/dir1$ notation depends neither on the payment direction nor on who opened the channel.

A hop with N channels is defined by channel capacities $C = (c_1, \ldots, c_N)$ and balances $B = (b_1, \ldots, b_N)$. Let E^d be the set of channels enabled in direction d, where $d \in \{dir0, dir1\}$. The forwarding ability of a hop is determined by the maximal balances among the channels enabled in a given direction, which we denote as h for $dir0$ and g for $dir1$:

$$h = \max_{i \in E^{dir0}} b_i \tag{1}$$

$$g = \max_{i \in E^{dir1}} (c_i - b_i) \tag{2}$$

In the general case, probes only give the attacker information about h or g, not about individual balances.[18] The attacker maintains the current lower and upper bounds[19] for h and g: $h^l < h \leq h^u$ and $g^l < g \leq g^u$, initially set to:

$$h^l = g^l = -1 \tag{3}$$

$$h^u = \max_{i \in E^{dir0}} c_i \tag{4}$$

$$g^u = \max_{i \in E^{dir1}} c_i \tag{5}$$

Let F be the set of all possible values of B, as per the attacker's current knowledge. $S(F)$ is the number of values F contains. Each probe cuts F in two parts, one of which is excluded from further consideration. Assuming uniform balance distribution, an optimal probe should cut F in half.

---

[15] We assume that all target channels are equally interesting for the attacker.

[16] Sending one probe normally takes a few seconds.

[17] 1 satoshi equals 10^{-8} BTC and is the smallest sub-unit of bitcoin. The LN operates with millisatoshi precision off-chain, but such amounts cannot be settled on-chain precisely. For simplicity, our model operates with satoshi-level precision.

[18] Enhanced probing techniques described in Sect. 3.4 overcome this limitation.

[19] Note that for lower bound is strict, and the upper bound is non-strict. If the probe of amount a in direction $dir0$ succeeds, h is *greater or equal* to a, but if the probe fails, it is *strictly less* than a, and analogously for g and $dir1$. Our definitions reflect this asymmetry and thus allow for uniform calculations when deriving Eq. (8).

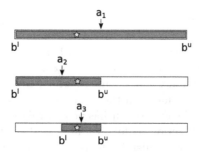

Fig. 4. Probing a one-channel hop with simple binary search. The star denotes the true balance. The colored rectangle represents the attacker's current estimates.

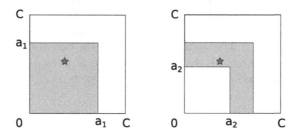

Fig. 5. A geometrical model for the first two probes of a two-channel target hop. The first probe (left) fails (upper bound); the second probe (right) succeeds (lower bound).

3.1   Examples

As the simplest example, consider a hop containing a single channel with capacity c (Fig. 4). Let b^l and b^u be the current lower (strict) and upper (non-strict) bounds for the true balance b, respectively.[20] Initially, $b^l = -1$ and $b^u = c$. $F = (b^l, b^u]$. For each next i^{th} probe, the attacker chooses the amount as:

$$a_i = (b^l + b^u + 1)/2 \qquad (6)$$

If the probe fails, b^u is updated to $a_i - 1$, otherwise b^l is updated to $a_i - 1$.

Next, consider a two-channel hop with equal capacities $c_1 = c_2 = c$ (Fig. 5). Initially, $S(F) = (c+1)^2$. The first probe amount should be:

$$a_1 = (c+1)/\sqrt{2} \qquad (7)$$

Note that $a_1 = (c+1)/2$ would divide $S(F)$ in the proportion $3 : 1$, not $1 : 1$.

The probe failing indicates that the balance is within a smaller area (the colored square in Fig. 5, left). The second probe divides that area in half (Fig. 5, right), and so on.

---

[20] The definition is asymmetric to maintain uniformity with the generalized model introduced later in Sect. 3.2.

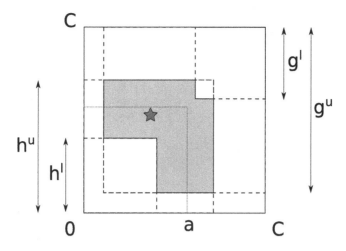

Fig. 6. A geometrical model for probing a two-channel hop

3.2 Generalized Geometrical Model

We can think of an N-channel hop as an N-dimensional (hyper-)rectangle R, with sides parallel to the axes.[21] Each side corresponds to one channel (some channels may be unidirectional). Along the ith dimension, R is defined by the coordinates $[0, c_i]$. The coordinates of each point within R correspond to a possible balance vector. One of the vertices of R is the origin point $(0, \ldots, 0)$.

A probe with amount a "cuts" an a-sided square either from the origin point (for *dir0*) or from the opposite vertex (for *dir1*). If the probe fails, all coordinates of B are lower than a (a new upper bound), otherwise at least one coordinate of B is greater than or equal to a (a new lower bound). If both directions have at least one channel enabled, the attacker may choose any direction for the probe.

Figure 6 illustrates a two-dimensional case with $c_1 = c_2 = c$. The attacker currently knows that the balance cannot be within the two smaller squares with sides h^l and g^l because the corresponding probes have succeeded. At the same time, the balance must be within the two larger squares with sides h^u and g^u because the corresponding probes have failed.

We can define F (colored) as the intersection of two L-shaped figures, reflecting the current bounds on h and g. F may take different shapes, depending on how the bounds relate to each other and to the hop configuration. The attacker chooses the next probe amount a to cut F in half.

Consider an illustrative probing of a two-channel hop with both channels enabled in both directions (Fig. 7). Note that in the final stages of probing F consists of two disjoint diagonally symmetric rectangles, reflecting the fact that channel balances can only be revealed up to permutation.

Let us denote $\bar{x} = x + 1$ and use subscript i for the ith coordinate. In the general case, we calculate $S(F)$ as follows. For full derivation, see [4].

---

[21] We continue using 2D-terms such as "rectangle" and "area" for clarity.

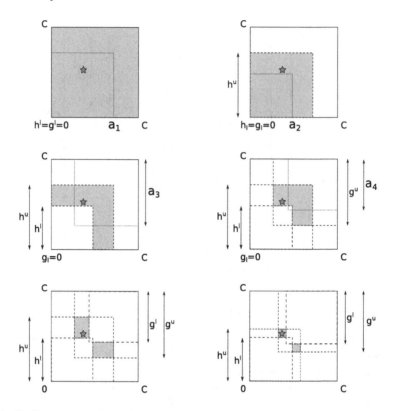

Fig. 7. Probing a two-channel hop step by step. Probing steps omitted between the bottom-left and the bottom-right (final) figures.

$$S(F) = \prod_{i=1}^{N}(\overline{h_i^u}+\overline{g_i^u}-\overline{c_i}) - \prod_{i=1}^{N}(\overline{h_i^l}+\overline{g_i^u}-\overline{c_i}) - \prod_{i=1}^{N}(\overline{h_i^u}+\overline{g_i^l}-\overline{c_i}) + \prod_{i=1}^{N}(\overline{h_i^l}+\overline{g_i^l}-\overline{c_i}) \quad (8)$$

In prior probing algorithms, each next amount a was chosen as the midpoint between the current bounds (*single-dimensional binary search*), which is suboptimal in the multi-dimensional case (Sect. 3.1). Instead, we propose an optimized amount choice algorithm to cut F in half. It works as follows. Initially, set $a^l = h^l + 1$, $a^u = h^u$, and consider a candidate value $a = (a^l + a^u)/2$. Let S_a be the area under the potential cut. If $S_a < S/2$, set $a^l = a$, else set $a^u = a$. Repeat until S_a is as close as possible[22] to $S/2$. For $N = 1$, the two methods are equivalent.

---

[22] It is usually impossible to cut F in half precisely: increasing a by 1 satoshi adds multiple points to $S(F)$ in multi-channel hops (depending on hop configuration).

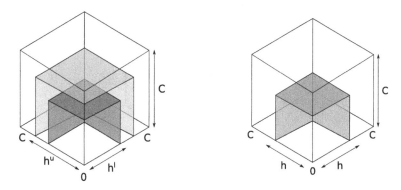

Fig. 8. Probing a 3-channel hop from direction $dir0$: in progress (left), finished (right)

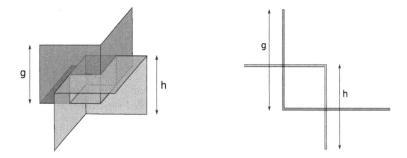

Fig. 9. The final result of probing a 3-channel hop (left) and a 2-channel hop (right). Exact balances in the 3-channel hop are unknown even after fully revealing h and g.

3.3   Challenge of Probing Multi-channel Hops

Hops with three channels or more cannot be fully probed due to dimensionality. Consider a three-channel hop with equal-capacity channels. Each probe in $dir0$ cuts an a-sided cube from the corner of the larger C-sided cube. Bounds on h are represented by two surfaces, each composed of three faces of the respective cube (Fig. 8, left). The smaller surface represents h^l, and the larger surface represents h^u. Each probe brings the two surfaces closer until they collapse into one surface representing the true value of h (Fig. 8, right). Analogously, probes in $dir1$ cut cubes from the opposite corner of the large cube.

Consider the final state of the attack when h and g have been fully revealed (Fig. 9, left). The true balance point lies at the intersection of two surfaces, each composed of three perpendicular squares. In the general case, this intersection is composed of six intervals and cannot be shrunk to single points. In contrast, in a 2-channel hop, exact balances are revealed (up to permutation) as an intersection of two L-shapes, i.e., two points (Fig. 9, right).

Another reason why fully probing multi-channel hops may be impossible is a vast difference in channel capacities, which allows larger channels to "mask" smaller ones. See [4] for details.

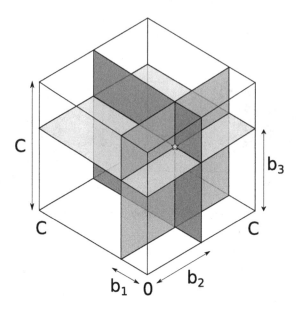

Fig. 10. A geometrical representation of jamming-enhanced probing for a 3-channel hop with equal capacities. The three balances are revealed separately.

3.4 Enhanced Probing

The only way for the attacker to gain more balance information for multi-channel hops would be to force probes to go through specific channels. The attacker cannot affect the channel choice strategy of a routing node. However, it is possible to reduce the set of *suitable* channels the routing node picks from.

We consider two probing enhancement techniques to achieve this goal. In *jamming-enhanced probing*, the attacker jams all channels in a target hop except one, and then probes the remaining channel. In geometrical terms, this allows for making cuts parallel to the axes, which ultimately leads to revealing the exact balance point as the intersection of three perpendicular planes (Fig. 10).

In *fee-aware probing* [32], the attacker sets the fee offered along with the probe such that the probe can only be forwarded through a subset of cheapest channels in the target hop. In the best case (for the attacker), fees for all channels in the target hop are different. In the worst case, all channels require equal fees, and fee-aware probing yields no advantage. Jamming-enhanced and fee-aware probing may be combined, which allows for probing individual channels inside one fee level. More generally, the prober may tune other parameters, such as timeouts, instead of or in addition to fee levels (*policy-aware probing*).

We used an isolated testing environment based on real LN implementations to confirm that enhanced probing indeed allows an attacker to infer individual balances of parallel channels. Setup details are provided in [4].

4 Evaluation

4.1 Data Source

We captured an LN snapshot on 2021-12-09 using our own CORE-LIGHTNING node. The snapshot contains 17068 nodes and 78076 channels[23] with a total capacity of 3370 BTC.[24] This is in line with public explorers such as the one operated by ACINQ[25] (the developers of ECLAIR), which on the same day reported 16977 nodes and 77906 channels. 63697 channels (82%) are enabled in both directions. Multi-channel hops hold a disproportionately large share of capacity (Table 1) and thus presumably play a more important role in routing than single-channel hops.

Table 1. Share of hops by the number of channels and by total capacity

Channels in a hop	Share of hops (%)	Share of capacity (%)
1	95.4	77.6
2	4.2	10.7
3	0.3	2.7
4	0.1	2.0
≥ 5	0.02	0.3

4.2 Metrics

The uncertainty U of a hop is the number of bits required to encode the position of B, given the current attacker's knowledge. It is calculated as $\log_2(S(F_i))$, where F_i is the set of all possible balance points after the ith probe. After P probes, U decreases from $U_{before} = \log_2(S(F_0))$ to $U_{after} = \log_2(S(F_P))$. For a set T of target hops, the final achieved information gain is:

$$I = 1 - \sum_{t \in T} U_{after}^t / \sum_{t \in T} U_{before}^t \tag{9}$$

Assuming m messages sent in total, the probing speed is defined as:

$$S = \frac{1}{m} \left(\sum_{t \in T} U_{before}^t - \sum_{t \in T} U_{after}^t \right) \tag{10}$$

Messages include probes and jams (for jamming-enhanced probing).

---

[23] We only consider the largest connected component, which contains 99.1% of nodes and 99.9% of channels.

[24] For an earlier version of this paper, we used a snapshot taken on 2021-09-09. Within three months between the snapshots, the number of nodes increased by 25%, the number of channels by 19%, and the total capacity by 35%.

[25] https://explorer.acinq.co/.

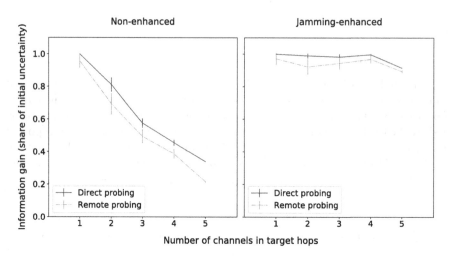

Fig. 11. Achieved information gain for non-enhanced and jamming-enhanced probing

4.3 Results

For each channel in the snapshot, we generate a balance uniformly at random between 0 and the channel capacity. We simulate probing attacks on target hops with 1 to 5 channels (hops with more channels are rare in the snapshot). We model two types of probing: direct and remote.

In *direct probing*, the attacker opens a channel to one of the parties of the target hop and sends probes via the 2-hop path. Direct probing is efficient (all probes reach the target) but requires paying on-chain fees for opening channels to each target hop. Moreover, it requires the victim to accept channel opening (though public nodes usually do so if the initiator fully funds it).

In *remote probing*, the attacker opens channels to a few well-connected nodes and sends probes through multi-hop paths. This approach allows for amortizing the on-chain cost of channel openings over multiple target hops. Another benefit is that remote probing yields information about intermediary hops in addition to the target hop. The main drawback of remote probing is that some probes do not reach the target hop due to low balance in an intermediary channel (this effect is more pronounced for larger amounts), although the attacker can decrease the number of such probes by using balance information from earlier probes.

We measure information gain and probing speed for two probing methods (non-enhanced and jamming-enhanced), two probe amount selection methods (optimized and non-optimized), and two types of probing (direct and remote). For each parameter combination, we average the results across 100 simulations. For each simulation, we probe 20 target hops chosen at random.

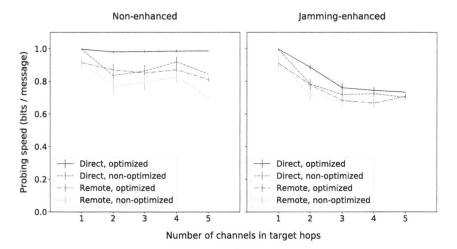

Fig. 12. Probing speed for non-enhanced and jamming-enhanced probing

Information gain decreases as N increases (Fig. 11) for non-enhanced probing. This is expected due to the dimensionality issue (Sect. 3.4). For example, 5-channel hops can only be probed to around 0.4 information gain. This applies to both direct and remote probing. In contrast, jamming-enhanced probing achieves high information gain (above 0.9) for all values of N, illustrating the advantage of such technique. A slight drop for $N = 5$ is caused by one atypical 5-channel hop in the snapshot that has most of its channels disabled. Lower information gain for remote probing compared to direct probing is explained by routing issues.

In terms of probing speed, the optimized amount selection method consistently outperforms the non-optimized method for all values of $N \geq 2$ (Fig. 12). (Information gain is the same for the two amount selection methods. The optimized method only allows for getting the same information faster rather than getting more information.) The speedup mostly decreases with increasing N, which is explained by the fact that the optimized method generally chooses higher amounts (for example, $1/2$ vs $1/\sqrt{2}$ in a two-channel hop with $c_1 = c_2 = 1$), which are more likely to fail. Direct probing is always faster than remote probing because all probes reach the target hop. Jamming-enhanced probing lowers the probing speed compared to non-enhanced probing as it implies sending jams in addition to probes. Finally, we note that the optimized method performs better than or similarly to the non-optimized one for all N in both direct and remote probing.

Additional simulations show how the capacity ratio in two-channel hops affects information gain (see [4]).

5   Discussion

The simulations have demonstrated that jamming-enhanced probing achieves nearly full balance information extraction, which is otherwise impossible for multi-channel hops in the general case. Moreover, optimized amount selection increases probing speed. The highest speedup is achieved for two-channel hops, which are the most prevalent multi-channel hops in the network.

5.1   Limitations

Our model does not provide theoretical guarantees on the performance of the attack. Simulation-based estimations may serve as rough upper bounds as they assume that remote nodes with sufficient balance always forward payments. In real-world scenarios, the result would depend on network topology, attacker's connectivity, routing policies of other nodes, and other factors.

Our model ignores regular LN activity. If a target hop is heavily used, balances may shift between probes, outdating attacker's estimations. This is one of the reasons why speeding up the attack is important for the attacker: it reduces the probability of interference with honest payments. Moreover, we do not model in-flight payments. Our model assumes that the two channel balances sum up to its capacity, which allows us to derive one balance from the other. In the real network, channel capacity is composed of the two balances and in-flight payments. We assume that in-flight payments resolve quickly enough to have no effect on probing results. We also do not account for routing fees.

We make some simplifying assumptions about jamming. First, we assume that the attacker can jam any hop. In practice, jamming requires additional liquidity and channel slots, which may be unavailable. Second, we assume that the attacker can jam a specific channel within a remote hop. In practice, routing nodes are free to choose which channel to forward the jam through in multi-channel hops (just like with regular payments). As a result, the attacker only knows how many channels are jammed but does not know which ones. Moreover, even if the attacker reveals N channel balances precisely, they are only known up to a permutation. Third, we assume that the attacker can jam channels in both directions. In practice, leaf hops can only be jammed in one direction.[26] Finally, channels disabled in both directions cannot be probed, even with jamming.

5.2   Attack Cost and Trade-Offs

Probing is relatively cheap. The attacker pays on-chain fees for opening and closing channels, but never pays routing fees, because probes never complete. There is a trade-off between direct and remote probing. Direct probing increases probing speed but requires more on-chain fees and locked-up capital. We leave the evaluation of this trade-off for future work.

---

[26] The attacker may still distinguish between parallel channels in leaf hops using fee-aware probing (see Sect. 3.4).

Jamming-enhanced probing brings additional costs. Capacity-based jamming requires at least one high-capacity channel. The amount of funds locked should be close to the aggregate balance of all parallel target channels. Slot-based jamming requires opening many low-capacity channels. The exact number of attacker's channels equals the number of channels to be jammed because the attacker's path is limited by the same number of slots.[27]

Jamming might be challenging for certain hop configurations. For example, it would be impossible to slot-jam more than one channel in a multi-channel target hop that is only connected to the rest of the network with a single channel. Similar limitations apply for capacity jamming.[28] To overcome this issue, the attacker needs to connect to the target hop via several disjoint paths.

5.3   Payment Flow Inference

Probing can be a building block for more advanced attacks, such as payment flow inference. Given a series of balance snapshots, the attacker can construct a balance difference graph where edges with non-zero value correspond to payments. The attacker can then discover the sender, the receiver, and the amount, as balances along the path are shifted by the same amount (modulo fees). Snapshots should be frequent because payments that pass through the same hop distort the picture. Prior work [18] has shown that 30-second snapshots allow revealing payments with 66% success rate, assuming low network usage (2000 payments per day). Obtaining a full network snapshot so quickly is challenging: each probe takes a few seconds. A more realistic goal could be to infer payment flows between given nodes by tracking balances in a few shortest paths between them. This looks feasible: the LN diameter is 6 hops [40], typical path lengths are 3–6 hops, and the target sub-network may be comprised of around 50 nodes.

5.4   Countermeasures

Probing is cheap because failed payment attempts are free. Proposals to limit the number of payment attempts a node can make, e.g., by demanding fees upfront, are being discussed [16,25]. Assuming no such changes to the LN protocol, we now discuss countermeasures that individual nodes can apply.

Alternative Forwarding Strategies. A routing node can try to obfuscate the state of its channels if probing is detected (e.g., if it notices a series of failed payments with amounts that follow the binary search pattern). In particular, routing nodes may select channels in a way that minimizes changes to h and g. A heavily used routing node could execute payments in batches. Within one batch, payments can be re-ordered so that they cancel each other out, at least partially. More generic flow concealment strategies are also possible.

---

[27] Assuming all channels have the same number of slots. The attacker may have higher limits than the victim, but no channel can have more than 483 slots per direction.

[28] Note that channels with sufficient capacity might be limited by slots.

Intra-hop Payment Split. A routing node can potentially divide a payment among parallel channels toward the next hop, optimizing hop bandwidth and hindering probing. This technique is being discussed as part of the future switch to a new type of channel construction [29,50]. From the prober's viewpoint, a multi-channel hop with intra-hop payment split is equivalent to a single-channel hop. The prober can reveal the sum of channel balances. Note the difference compared to multi-path[29] payments (MPP): in MPP, the sender fully determines how to split the payment [1], whereas in intra-hop split, such decisions are made locally by routing nodes.

Channel Rebalancing. Channel rebalancing [3,19] is a process by which an LN node initiates (presumably circular) payments to bring the ratio of its channel balance to channel capacity closer to some desirable value (e.g., 50%). Just-in-time (JIT) routing [28] is a form of rebalancing done while forwarding another payment. If a routing node is asked to forward a payment for which all its channels lack balance, it first moves some funds to the local side of one of its channels using a circular payment, and then proceeds with the forwarding. From a prober's standpoint, rebalancing changes the properties of a hop mid-probe, distorting the estimates. Without intra-hop splitting, a multi-channel hop between Alice and Bob with JIT routing becomes equivalent to a single-channel hop with balances equal to

$$
\min \left(\sum_{i \in E^{dir0}} b_i, \ \max_{i \in E^{dir0} \cap E^{dir1}} c_i \right) \tag{11}
$$

on the Alice's side and

$$
\min \left(\sum_{i \in E^{dir1}} (c_i - b_i), \ \max_{i \in E^{dir0} \cap E^{dir1}} c_i \right) \tag{12}
$$

on the Bob's side. Indeed, ignoring network topology, Alice can concentrate all her local balances in one channel, if the total does not exceed the capacity of the largest bidirectional channel. Note that for JIT routing to work, at least one channel must be enabled in both directions (i.e., $E^{dir0} \cap E^{dir1} \neq \emptyset$).

Unannounced Channels. To hide public channel balances, a node may open unannounced channels in parallel to announced ones. Depending on the relation between the balances of announced and unannounced channels, the attacker may still be able to discover unannounced channel balances (e.g., if the balance of the unannounced channel exceeds the balances of announced channels). Even in that case, the standard probing technique needs to be modified.

---

[29] Also referred to as multi-part payments.

6   Related Work

Attacks on the LN can be grouped into DoS-related [12,23,27,34,35,39,44,46], privacy-related [6,8,15,18,26,36,37,45], and incentive-related [47].

Prior work on channel probing introduced the general idea [15], suggested probing channels from both ends [8], controlling both the sender and the receiver of probes [18], and multi-hop probing [45]. Multiple LN simulators have been designed to analyze honest economic activity [6,7,48] or the cost of opening payment channels [10]. Rate-limiting has been proposed to mitigate issues like probing and jamming [17,25,33,43]. The fee structure [6,38] and the tension between privacy and utility of routing nodes [13,41] have also been discussed. Other relevant prior work focused on channel jamming [23,44], channel policy exploitation [32], and improved payment forwarding [50].

7   Conclusion

In this work, we have developed a comprehensive model for channel balance probing in the Lightning Network. Our model is the first one to account for parallel channels. We have introduced enhanced versions of the probing attack, combining it with channel jamming and fee targeting. Enhanced probing allows for nearly full extraction of balance information in multi-channel hops, which was impossible with prior methods. Moreover, we have proposed an optimized amount selection algorithm based on N-dimensional binary search that increases probing speed.

We have confirmed our findings experimentally in an isolated testing environment and using a new probing-focused Lightning simulator. The simulations based on a real-world network snapshot show that the optimized amount selection algorithm makes probing up to 15% faster compared to single-dimensional binary search (two-channel target hops, direct non-enhanced probing). The experiments also illustrate the trade-off between direct and multi-hop probing. Finally, we have outlined potential countermeasures and avenues for future work.

The Lightning Network promises to significantly improve Bitcoin's scalability and privacy. To fully realize its potential, Lightning should defend against attacks such as balance probing and channel jamming. We hope that this work helps improve the trade-offs between scalability, security, and privacy for Lightning, while preserving its permissionless nature.

Acknowledgments. We thank Antoine Riard for thoughtful feedback. This work was partially supported by the Luxembourg National Research Fund (FNR) project Fin-Crypt (C17/IS/11684537). Contributions of Gleb Naumenko were supported with a grant by 100x Group, the holding structure for the BitMEX platform. Contributions of Sergei Tikhomirov were partially supported by Chaincode Labs.

References

1. Multi-path payments in LND: Making channel balances add up (2020). https://lightning.engineering/posts/2020-05-07-mpp/

2. Androulaki, E., Karame, G.O., Roeschlin, M., Scherer, T., Capkun, S.: Evaluating user privacy in bitcoin. In: Sadeghi, A.-R. (ed.) FC 2013. LNCS, vol. 7859, pp. 34–51. Springer, Heidelberg (2013). https://doi.org/10.1007/978-3-642-39884-1_4

3. Awathare, N., Suraj, A., Ribeiro, V.J., Bellur, U.: REBAL: channel balancing for payment channel networks. In: 29th International Symposium on Modeling, Analysis, and Simulation of Computer and Telecommunication Systems, MASCOTS 2021, Houston, TX, USA, 3–5 November, 2021, pp. 1–8. IEEE (2021). https://doi.org/10.1109/MASCOTS53633.2021.9614304

4. Biryukov, A., Naumenko, G., Tikhomirov, S.: Analysis and probing of parallel channels in the lightning network. IACR Cryptol. ePrint Arch, p. 384 (2021). https://eprint.iacr.org/2021/384

5. BOLT: Lightning network specifications (2019). https://github.com/lightningnetwork/lightning-rfc

6. Béres, F., Seres, I.A., Benczúr, A.A.: A cryptoeconomic traffic analysis of Bitcoin's Lightning network. Cryptoeconomic Systems, 6 2020. https://cryptoeconomicsystems.pubpub.org/pub/b8rb0ywn

7. Conoscenti, M., Vetrò, A., Martin, J., Spini, F.: The CLoTH simulator for HTLC payment networks with introductory Lightning network performance results. Inf. **9**(9), 223 (2018)

8. van Dam, G., Kadir, R.A., Nohuddin, P.N.E., Zaman, H.B.: Improvements of the balance discovery attack on lightning network payment channels. In: Hölbl, M., Rannenberg, K., Welzer, T. (eds.) SEC 2020. IAICT, vol. 580, pp. 313–323. Springer, Cham (2020). https://doi.org/10.1007/978-3-030-58201-2_21

9. EmelyanenkoK: Payment channel congestion via spam-attack (2017). https://github.com/lightningnetwork/lightning-rfc/issues/182

10. Engelmann, F., Kopp, H., Kargl, F., Glaser, F., Weinhardt, C.: Towards an economic analysis of routing in payment channel networks. In: Proceedings of the 1st Workshop on Scalable and Resilient Infrastructures for Distributed Ledgers, December 2017. https://doi.org/10.1145/3152824.3152826,https://arxiv.org/abs/1711.02597

11. Gudgeon, L., Moreno-Sanchez, P., Roos, S., McCorry, P., Gervais, A.: SoK: layer-two blockchain protocols. In: Bonneau, J., Heninger, N. (eds.) FC 2020. LNCS, vol. 12059, pp. 201–226. Springer, Cham (2020). https://doi.org/10.1007/978-3-030-51280-4_12

12. Harris, J., Zohar, A.: Flood & loot: a systemic attack on the Lightning network. In: AFT '20: 2nd ACM Conference on Advances in Financial Technologies, New York, NY, USA, 21–23 October 2020, pp. 202–213. ACM (2020). https://doi.org/10.1145/3419614.3423248. https://arxiv.org/abs/2006.08513

13. Hase, T., Wallace, V.: Smarter autopilot, April 2019. https://blog.lightning.engineering/announcement/2019/04/23/mainnet-app.html

14. Hearn, M., Spilman, J.: Anti dos for tx replacement (2013). https://lists.linuxfoundation.org/pipermail/bitcoin-dev/2013-April/002417.html

15. Herrera-Joancomartí, J., Navarro-Arribas, G., Pedrosa, A.R., Pérez-Solà, C., García-Alfaro, J.: On the difficulty of hiding the balance of Lightning network channels. In: Galbraith, S.D., Russello, G., Susilo, W., Gollmann, D., Kirda, E., Liang, Z. (eds.) Proceedings of the 2019 ACM Asia Conference on Computer and Communications Security, AsiaCCS 2019, Auckland, New Zealand, 09–12 July, 2019. pp. 602–612. ACM (2019). https://doi.org/10.1145/3321705.3329812. https://eprint.iacr.org/2019/328

16. Jager, J.: A proposal for up-front payments (2020). https://lists.linuxfoundation.org/pipermail/lightning-dev/2020-March/002585.html

17. Jager, J.: Circuit breaker (2021). https://github.com/lightningequipment/circuitbreaker
18. Kappos, G., et al.: An empirical analysis of privacy in the lightning network. In: Borisov, N., Diaz, C. (eds.) FC 2021. LNCS, vol. 12674, pp. 167–186. Springer, Heidelberg (2021). https://doi.org/10.1007/978-3-662-64322-8_8
19. Khalil, R., Gervais, A.: Revive: Rebalancing off-blockchain payment networks. In: Thuraisingham, B.M., Evans, D., Malkin, T., Xu, D. (eds.) Proceedings of the 2017 ACM SIGSAC Conference on Computer and Communications Security, CCS 2017, Dallas, TX, USA, October 30 - November 03, 2017, pp. 439–453. ACM (2017). https://doi.org/10.1145/3133956.3134033. https://eprint.iacr.org/2017/823
20. Kumble, S.P., Roos, S.: Comparative analysis of lightning's routing clients. In: IEEE International Conference on Decentralized Applications and Infrastructures, DAPPS 2021, Online Event, 23–26 August, 2021, pp. 79–84. IEEE (2021). https://doi.org/10.1109/DAPPS52256.2021.00014
21. Malavolta, G., Moreno-Sanchez, P., Schneidewind, C., Kate, A., Maffei, M.: Anonymous multi-hop locks for blockchain scalability and interoperability. In: 26th Annual Network and Distributed System Security Symposium, NDSS 2019, San Diego, California, USA, February 24–27, 2019. The Internet Society (2019). https://eprint.iacr.org/2018/472
22. Meiklejohn, S., Pomarole, M., Jordan, G., Levchenko, K., McCoy, D., Voelker, G.M., Savage, S.: A fistful of bitcoins: Characterizing payments among men with no names. login Usenix Mag. **38**(6) (2013). https://www.usenix.org/publications/login/december-2013-volume-38-number-6/fistful-bitcoins-characterizing-payments-among
23. Mizrahi, A., Zohar, A.: Congestion attacks in payment channel networks. In: Borisov, N., Diaz, C. (eds.) FC 2021. LNCS, vol. 12675, pp. 170–188. Springer, Heidelberg (2021). https://doi.org/10.1007/978-3-662-64331-0_9
24. Nakamoto, S.: Bitcoin: A peer-to-peer electronic cash system (2008). https://bitcoin.org/bitcoin.pdf
25. Naumenko, G.: Preventing channel jamming (2021). https://blog.bitmex.com/preventing-channel-jamming/
26. Nisslmueller, U., Foerster, K., Schmid, S., Decker, C.: Toward active and passive confidentiality attacks on cryptocurrency off-chain networks. In: Furnell, S., Mori, P., Weippl, E.R., Camp, O. (eds.) Proceedings of the 6th International Conference on Information Systems Security and Privacy, ICISSP 2020, Valletta, Malta, 25–27 February 2020, pp. 7–14. SCITEPRESS (2020). https://doi.org/10.5220/0009429200070014,https://arxiv.org/abs/2003.00003
27. Pérez-Solà, C., Ranchal-Pedrosa, A., Herrera-Joancomartí, J., Navarro-Arribas, G., Garcia-Alfaro, J.: LockDown: balance availability attack against lightning network channels. In: Bonneau, J., Heninger, N. (eds.) FC 2020. LNCS, vol. 12059, pp. 245–263. Springer, Cham (2020). https://doi.org/10.1007/978-3-030-51280-4_14
28. Pickhardt, R.: Just in time routing (JIT-routing) and a channel rebalancing heuristic as an add on for improved routing success in BOLT 1.0 (2019). https://lists.linuxfoundation.org/pipermail/lightning-dev/2019-March/001891.html
29. Poelstra, A.: Lightning in scriptless scripts, March 2017. https://lists.launchpad.net/mimblewimble/msg00086.html
30. Poon, J., Dryja, T.: The Bitcoin Lightning network: Scalable off-chain instant payments. Technical report (2016)
31. Research, B.: Proportion of public vs private channels (2020). https://blog.bitmex.com/lightning-network-part-7-proportion-of-public-vs-private-channels/

32. Riard, A.: Route blinding, October 2020. https://github.com/lightningnetwork/lightning-rfc/pull/765#pullrequestreview-511147029
33. Riard, A., Naumenko, G.: Stake certificates (2020). https://thelab31.xyz/stake-certificates
34. Riard, A., Naumenko, G.: Time-dilation attacks on the Lightning network. Cryptoeconomic Systems 1(2), October 2021. https://doi.org/10.21428/58320208.6ac6960a.   https://cryptoeconomicsystems.pubpub.org/pub/riard-lightning-dilation
35. Rohrer, E., Malliaris, J., Tschorsch, F.: Discharged payment channels: Quantifying the Lightning network's resilience to topology-based attacks. In: 2019 IEEE European Symposium on Security and Privacy Workshops, EuroS&P Workshops 2019, Stockholm, Sweden, 17–19 June 2019, pp. 347–356. IEEE (2019). https://doi.org/10.1109/EuroSPW.2019.00045. https://arxiv.org/abs/1904.10253
36. Rohrer, E., Tschorsch, F.: Counting down thunder: timing attacks on privacy in payment channel networks. In: AFT '20: 2nd ACM Conference on Advances in Financial Technologies, New York, NY, USA, 21–23 October, 2020, pp. 214–227. ACM (2020). https://doi.org/10.1145/3419614.3423262. https://arxiv.org/abs/2006.12143
37. Romiti, M., Victor, F., Moreno-Sanchez, P., Nordholt, P.S., Haslhofer, B., Maffei, M.: Cross-layer deanonymization methods in the lightning protocol. In: Borisov, N., Diaz, C. (eds.) FC 2021. LNCS, vol. 12674, pp. 187–204. Springer, Heidelberg (2021). https://doi.org/10.1007/978-3-662-64322-8_9
38. Russel, R.: A proposal for up-front payments. https://lists.linuxfoundation.org/pipermail/lightning-dev/2019-November/002275.html
39. Russel, R.: Loop attack with onion routing, August 2015. https://lists.linuxfoundation.org/pipermail/lightning-dev/2015-August/000135.html
40. Seres, I.A., Gulyás, L., Nagy, D.A., Burcsi, P.: Topological analysis of Bitcoin's Lightning network. In: MARBLE, pp. 1–12. Springer (2019), https://arxiv.org/abs/1901.04972
41. Tang, W., Wang, W., Fanti, G.C., Oh, S.: Privacy-utility tradeoffs in routing cryptocurrency over payment channel networks. In: Yeh, E., Markopoulou, A., Tay, Y.C. (eds.) Abstracts of the 2020 SIGMETRICS/Performance Joint International Conference on Measurement and Modeling of Computer Systems, Boston, MA, USA, 8–12 June, 2020, pp. 81–82. ACM (2020). https://doi.org/10.1145/3393691.3394213. https://arxiv.org/abs/1909.02717
42. Teinturier, B.: Trampoline onion format (feature 24/25). https://github.com/lightningnetwork/lightning-rfc/pull/836
43. Teinturier, B.: Spamming the Lightning network, November 2020. https://github.com/t-bast/lightning-docs/blob/master/spam-prevention.md#costless-channel-probing
44. Tikhomirov, S., Moreno-Sanchez, P., Maffei, M.: A quantitative analysis of security, anonymity and scalability for the Lightning network. In: 2020 IEEE European Symposium on Security and Privacy Workshops, EuroS&P Workshops 2020, September, pp. 7–11, 2020. IEEE (2020). https://eprint.iacr.org/2020/303
45. Tikhomirov, S., Pickhardt, R., Biryukov, A., Nowostawski, M.: Probing channel balances in the Lightning network. CoRR abs/2004.00333 (2020). https://arxiv.org/abs/2004.00333
46. Tochner, S., Schmid, S., Zohar, A.: Hijacking routes in payment channel networks: a predictability tradeoff. CoRR abs/1909.06890 (2019). https://arxiv.org/abs/1909.06890

47. Tsabary, I., Yechieli, M., Manuskin, A., Eyal, I.: MAD-HTLC: because HTLC is crazy-cheap to attack. In: 42nd IEEE Symposium on Security and Privacy, SP 2021, San Francisco, CA, USA, 24–27 May 2021. pp. 1230–1248. IEEE (2021). https://doi.org/10.1109/SP40001.2021.00080. https://arxiv.org/abs/2006.12031
48. Zhang, Y., Yang, D., Xue, G.: Cheapay: an optimal algorithm for fee minimization in blockchain-based payment channel networks. In: ICC 2019–2019 IEEE International Conference on Communications (ICC), pp. 1–6 (2019). https://doi.org/10.1109/ICC.2019.8761804
49. ZmnSCPxj: Outsourcing route computation with trampoline payments (2019). https://lists.linuxfoundation.org/pipermail/lightning-dev/2019-April/001950.html
50. ZmnSCPxj: A payment point feature family, October 2019. https://lists.linuxfoundation.org/pipermail/lightning-dev/2019-October/002225.html

HIDE & SEEK: Privacy-Preserving Rebalancing on Payment Channel Networks

Zeta Avarikioti[1], Krzysztof Pietrzak[1], Iosif Salem[2], Stefan Schmid[2],

Samarth Tiwari[3(✉)], and Michelle Yeo[1]

[1] IST Austria, Klosterneuburg, Austria
{zetavar,krzysztof.pietrzak,michelle.yeo}@ist.ac.at
[2] Faculty of Computer Science, University of Vienna, Wien, Austria
{iosif.salem, stefan_schmid}@univie.ac.at
[3] Centrum Wiskunde & Informatica, Amsterdam, The Netherlands
samarth.tiwari@cwi.nl

Abstract. Payment channels effectively move the transaction load off-chain thereby successfully addressing the inherent scalability problem most cryptocurrencies face. A major drawback of payment channels is the need to "top up" funds on-chain when a channel is depleted. Rebalancing was proposed to alleviate this issue, where parties with depleting channels move their funds along a cycle to replenish their channels off-chain. Protocols for rebalancing so far either introduce local solutions or compromise privacy.

In this work, we present an opt-in rebalancing protocol that is both private and globally optimal, meaning our protocol maximizes the total amount of rebalanced funds. We study rebalancing from the framework of linear programming. To obtain full privacy guarantees, we leverage multi-party computation in solving the linear program, which is executed by selected participants to maintain efficiency. Finally, we efficiently decompose the rebalancing solution into incentive-compatible cycles which conserve user balances when executed atomically.

Keywords: Payment channel networks · Privacy · Rebalancing

1 Introduction

Cryptocurrencies are increasingly growing as an alternative payment method. By replacing a central trusted authority (e.g., a bank) with a decentralised ledger, i.e., a blockchain, mutually distrusting users now have the means to achieve consensus over

Supported by the Vienna Cybersecurity and Privacy Research Center (ViSP), funded by the Vienna business agency (Wirtschaftsagentur), 2020–2023.

Supported partially by the Austrian Science Fund (FWF) project "Design Framework for Self-Driving Networks" (ADVISE), I 4800-N, 2020–2023 and Vienna Cybersecurity and Privacy Research Center (ViSP), funded by the Vienna business agency (Wirtschaftsagentur), 2020–2023.

Supported partially by ERC Starting Grant QIP–805241, the Vienna Cybersecurity and Privacy Research Center (ViSP), funded by the Vienna business agency (Wirtschaftsagentur), 2020–2023, and by Harmony through the Research DAO.

I. Eyal and J. Garay (Eds.): FC 2022, LNCS 13411, pp. 358–373, 2022.
https://doi.org/10.1007/978-3-031-18283-9_17

transactions. However, achieving consensus on the blockchain is notoriously inefficient. Bitcoin, for instance, can only support at most 7 transactions per second on average [24]. This severely limits the scalability of blockchain solutions to every day life situations.

Payment channel networks (PCNs) aim to increase the efficiency and scalability of blockchains while maintaining the benefits of security and decentralisation. PCNs operate on top of blockchains introducing Layer 2 – the blockchain itself being Layer 1. As the name suggests, a PCN consists of several payment channels between pairs of users who wish to transact with each other. Users connected indirectly through a path of channels may route transactions through the network. To open a payment channel, two users create a funding transaction where they lock funds on-chain only to be used in this payment channel. Thereafter, each transaction on the payment channel is simply an exchange of a signed message that depicts the current balances between the two users; so it does not involve the blockchain at all. This can go on indefinitely until the users go back to the blockchain to close the channel. The process of closing a channel consists of one on-chain transaction optimistically, while in worst case of a small constant number of transactions (e.g., in Lightning closing a payment channel costs at most two on-chain transactions). Thus, with at most three blockchain transactions, any pair of users can in theory make an arbitrary number of costless transactions with each other.

A major drawback of payment channels is that users cannot simply "top up" their balance in the channel off-chain once it is depleted. Instead, they have to go on-chain to refund the payment channel. A solution to extend the lifetime of payment channels is *rebalancing*, which updates payment channels with the crucial condition that the overall balance of each node is unchanged. Although it is not possible to shift funds from one payment channel to another off-chain, the effect of rebalancing is precisely that: funds from well-funded payment channels transfer to depleted ones.

There are two predominant approaches to rebalancing. The first involves a local search of rebalancing cycles (i.e., transactions of a fixed amount that begin and end with the same user) initiated by a single user. This is the current rebalancing approach in the Lightning Network [1]. The second approach (introduced in [17]) is global instead of local: nodes looking to rebalance specify a maximum amount of rebalancing flow along each of their channels, where the rebalancing transactions are determined by a global evaluation of the state of the network.

A drawback of single-user based cycle finding is it overlooks other rebalancing requests across the network, leading to *local solutions*. Figure 1 illustrates one such consequence which we call the "cancelling out" effect. Suppose a user Charlie wants to move 10 coins from his channel with Bob to his channel with Alice. If Charlie utilises the cycle finding approach, he will only manage to rebalance 6 coins as depicted in the graph on the right. The channel between Bob and Alice would be ignored because of the lack of sufficient balance on Bob's end. In a globally optimal solution, however, the entire rebalancing in the graph on the left can be executed, as it takes into account that transactions in both directions can be above the capacity of a channel, as long as they "cancel out" and the resulting transaction is within the capacity.

Furthermore, users must check if the other users on the cycle are willing to forward the rebalancing transaction amount, even after finding rebalancing cycles. This could lead to a prolonged and laborious search for cycles with willing participants. Lastly,

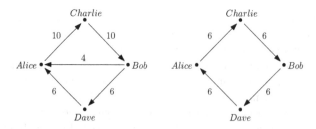

Fig. 1. The cancelling out effect. The weighted, directed edges on the graph on the left specifies the maximum coins a user can forward along the direction of the edge. The graph on the right shows the maximum rebalancing cycle Charlie can achieve using the cycle finding approach.

this approach requires users to have global knowledge of the network topology which can be unrealistic in terms of storage as the size of the network increases.

The second approach does not suffer from local limitations such as the cancelling out effect, and theoretically achieves the global optimal rebalancing. Revive [17] implemented this method by assigning a random delegate, either a trusted external third party or someone from the set of participants, to receive channel constraints and solve a linear program that models rebalancing. This is a serious *privacy loophole*, since the delegate now has information on the concerned payment channels. Moreover, the delegate has control over the rebalancing output; for instance, the delegate may compute the rebalancing transactions in a malicious or suboptimal way, favouring some transactions over others. Although the authors proposed a method for any participant to challenge the rebalancing transactions, the process is lengthy and requires giving the challenger access to the balances of all participants.

In this work, we present HIDE & SEEK, the first opt-in rebalancing protocol that is both *private* and achieves a *globally optimal rebalancing*. Each party that is interested in rebalancing specifies the maximum amount to be forwarded in each of the party's channel. We employ selected delegates that receive the maximum amounts per channel, calculate and share with each party the exact amount to be moved in each channel. We formulate our problem as a linear program and set our objective function to maximize the total amount of funds to be rebalanced in the network. Our protocol does not involve transaction fees.

On the other hand, we leverage multi-party computation to obtain a *fully private solution*. Specifically, the participants in HIDE & SEEK only learn the information they would have learned if a trusted third party computed the optimal rebalancing and returned to each participant the amount to be moved along each of their channel. No sensitive information such as the channel balances is leaked.

Finally, we guarantee the rebalancing can be securely and efficiently executed. We propose a simple way to decompose the optimal rebalancing circulation into a set of transaction cycles. As a result, the transactions of each cycle are easy to execute atomically using HTLCs. We note that atomicity is limited to each rebalancing cycle, therefore increasing the protocol's robustness; any cycle can be executed successfully regardless of the success of other cycles.

We highlight the advantages of our approach in Table 1.

Table 1. Summary of main approaches for rebalancing. Private solutions are solutions that do not leak balance information. Globally optimal refers to the optimality of the rebalancing solution. Opt-in refers to solutions where willing users choose to participate in the protocol and non-willing users are not involved at all. Network locality refers to solutions that only require local knowledge of the PCN.

	Private	Globally optimal	Opt-in	Network locality
Cycle finding solution	✓	✗	✗	✗
Revive	✗	✓	✓	✓
Our solution	✓	✓	✓	✓

Our Contributions. We introduce HIDE & SEEK, the first opt-in privacy-preserving and globally optimal rebalancing protocol that can be implemented in a secure and efficient manner. We acknowledge and discuss its limitations in terms of efficiency. We suggest several practical speed ups for the deployment of our solution, and outline possible extensions.

2 Preliminaries

2.1 Payment Channels Networks

Users u, v can open a payment channel between each other by locked some of their funds to be used only in this channel: if u locks a units and v locks b units, the state of the channel from u to v is modeled as a real number balance$(u, v) \in [-b, a]$, initialized as 0. The capacity of the channel refers to the sum $a + b$ of these funds. Once the channel is created, both users can send each other money by updating the channel balances in favour of the other party, as long as the state remains within the interval $[-b, a]$.

Users who are not directly connected by a channel in a PCN can still transact with each other if they are connected by a path of payment channels. The users along the transaction path which are not the sender or receiver typically charge a fee for forwarding the transaction that depends on the transaction amount. For a transaction to be successful, the sender has to first send enough money to cover both the desired payment amount and all the fees charged by each user on the payment path. That is, suppose user s wants to send x coins to user r along a payment path $p = \{(s, u_1), ..., (u_k, r)\}$. Then s must send $x + \sum_{i=1}^{k} \text{fee}(u_i)$. Secondly, the balance of each user along the path must be large enough to forward the payment amount together with fees. Then for each user u_i on p, balance$(u_i, u_{i+1}) \geq x + \sum_{j=i+1}^{k} \text{fee}(u_j)$. Although the channel capacities are typically public information, the individual balances on each end are private; so senders typically have to try different payment paths until one of them succeeds.

A desired guarantee for payment routing through a path in a PCN is atomicity, i.e., for all users along the path, either all of them update their balances or none of the balances in the path get updated. This is enforced in the Lightning Network using HTLCs [16]. An HTLC ($HTLC(u, v, x, h, t)$) is a smart contract between any two users u and v that locks some amount of coins x using a hash output h and a timelock t. To get the locked funds, v has to produce the preimage r to the hash $h = H(r)$ within time t, upon which the locked funds will be released to v. If v cannot do so within the time limit, u can claim the locked funds. Payment path atomicity is enforced using HTLCs for each channel on the path with the same hash value (determined using a secret chosen by the receiver on the path), but with decreasing timelock values from sender to receiver to guarantee the security of funds.

2.2 Network Flows

Consider a directed graph $G = (V, E)$ and the associated $|E|$-dimensional Euclidean space of non-negative flow along each edge. A circulation is a flow $\mathbf{f} = (f(u, v))_{(u,v) \in E}$ such that the net flow through each vertex is zero: $\sum_{v \in V} f(u, v) = \sum_{v \in V} f(v, u), \forall u \in V$. Two circulations $\mathbf{f}_1, \mathbf{f}_2$ can be added to get yet another circulation: $\mathbf{f}_1 + \mathbf{f}_2 = (f_1(u, v) + f_2(u, v))_{(u,v) \in E}$. A cycle is a sequence of vertices $v_1, v_2 \dots v_k$ such that $(v_i, v_{i+1}) \in E, \forall 1 \le i \le k - 1$ and $(v_k, v_1) \in E$ as well. We may equivalently refer to this cycle as $(e_1, e_2 \dots e_k)$ where $e_i = (v_i, v_{i+1}), \forall 1 \le i \le k - 1$ and $e_k = (v_k, v_1)$. We call k the length of this cycle. A cycle flow $\mathbf{f}$ of weight w on cycle C is a circulation where $f(e) = w, \forall e \in C$ and $f(e) = 0$ otherwise.

A standard result of network flow theory is that any circulation may be expressed as a sum of at most $|E|$ cycles. We refer the reader to the textbook of Ahuja, Magnanti and Orlin [3] for a detailed treatment.

3   Protocol Overview and Model

3.1 System Model

Payment Network Topology. We model the PCN as a graph $\tilde{G} = (\tilde{V}, \tilde{E})$, with a vertex for each node and an edge between u and v if there is a payment channel between them. Let $V \subset \tilde{V}$ be the users in the PCN that are interested in rebalancing and let $G = (V, E)$ be the subgraph of $\tilde{G}$ induced by V. We denote $|V| = n, |E| = m$. We assume each user u has only local knowledge of the PCN topology, i.e., only knows the capacities and balances on the edges incident to u.

Cryptographic Assumptions. We assume the existence of secure communications channels, hash functions and signatures. We follow [11] and assume the concept of an arithmetic black box for MPC $\mathcal{F}_{ABB}$, in particular with functionalities like secret sharing, storage, retrieval, addition, multiplication, and comparisons.

Blockchain & Network Model. We assume a synchronous network, i.e., there is known bounded message delay. We further assume the underlying blockchain satisfies persistence and liveness as defined in [14].

3.2 Protocol Overview

In a nutshell, our proposed protocol HIDE & SEEK consists of two phases: an exploration phase and an execution phase. Firstly, the goal of the exploration phase is to discover rebalancing cycles privately and efficiently. Then, the goal of the execution phase is to guarantee that the rebalancing transactions are executed in a secure manner. At the same time we want to maximise the efficacy of our protocol, that is, we want as many rebalancing cycles to go through as possible.

Exploration Phase. The exploration phase first formulates the rebalancing problem as a linear program. Then we randomly select k delegates out of the participants to perform an MPC protocol to jointly solve the linear program. Next, any set of participants that wish to participate in the rebalancing protocol prepares the shared inputs to the delegates. The output of the exploration phase is a rebalancing circulation.

Execution Phase. We first efficiently decompose the rebalancing circulation output of the exploration phase into a set of cycle flows. These cycle flows have the property that they are sign-consistent, i.e. they are consistent with the direction of the flows in the rebalancing circulation. This makes executing these cycles incentive-compatible, as no user would have to execute transactions which violate their specified rebalancing capacity and direction along channels. Once this is done, we enforce atomicity of these cycles by creating an HTLC for each cycle which ensures either transactions along the entire cycle goes through or none at all.

3.3 Desired Properties and Threat Model

In general, we assume a computationally bounded adversary, i.e., runs in probabilistic polynomial time. The properties HIDE & SEEK should guarantee are the following:

1. **Balance conservation (security):** The total balance of each node, which is the sum of the node's balances on each incident channel, must remain the same before and after HIDE & SEEK, even when *all other participants are corrupted* by the adversary.
2. **Privacy:** The information revealed during HIDE & SEEK should be not exceed the minimum required to execute rebalancing: (a) the participants must only learn the transaction amounts for each of their payment channels; (b) the delegates of MPC should not be able to determine private financial information of the participants. Both (a) and (b) should hold as long as *one of the delegates is not corrupted.*
3. **Optimality (completeness):** Assuming *every participant is honest*, the result should be optimal in that no other rebalancing yields greater total change over all payment channels.

4   The HIDE & SEEK Protocol

4.1 Exploration Phase

Linear Programming for Rebalancing. The practical problem of rebalancing has many facets, including keeping participants' financial information private and facilitating coordination. We overlook these considerations momentarily to present the underlying optimization problem of rebalancing.

For a payment channel between (u, v), the users would like to move the state balance(u, v) towards a desired state balance$^*(u, v)$. If balance$^*(u, v) <$ balance(u, v) then rebalancing would involve u transferring funds to v, and we model this as a directed edge from u to v with capacity $m(u, v) :=$ balance$(u, v) -$ balance$^*(u, v)$. If balance$^*(u, v) >$ balance(u, v) then there is a directed edge from v to u with capacity $m(v, u) :=$ balance$^*(u, v) -$ balance(u, v). Thus the graph G is transformed into a directed weighted graph.

The capacities $m(u, v)$ represent the most flow that can occur through each channel during rebalancing. If $m(u, v) = 0$ the edge from u to v is either non-existent or equivalently, a zero-capacity edge. We also enforce that if $m(u, v) > 0$, then necessarily $m(v, u) = 0$.

Let us denote a potential rebalancing by $\mathbf{f} \in \mathbb{R}^{|E|}$ on this directed graph, where $f(u, v)$ denote the flow from u to v. Since rebalancing should not result in a net financial gain or loss for any participant, we require $\mathbf{f}$ to be a circulation. Recall that it means the net flow through each vertex is zero:

$$\sum_{v:(u,v)\in E} f(u, v) = \sum_{v:(v,u)\in E} f(v, u).$$

Not only must the flows be non-negative, but they must also satisfy the capacity constraints as specified by participants:

$$0 \leq f(u, v) \leq m(u, v).$$

Thus, the set of valid rebalancings is a polytope in m-dimensional Euclidean space defined by $n + 2m$ linear constraints: n zero flow constraints for each vertex and m pairs of flow capacity constraints for each edge.

We wish to compute a rebalancing that maximizes the linear objective $\sum_{(u,v)\in E} f(u, v)$. We call the linear program so specified the rebalancing problem. This choice of objective function amounts to maximizing the total change in each payment channel's balance towards its desired state.

Solving the Rebalancing Problem. One can apply any linear programming algorithm of preference to solve the rebalancing, such as any from the family of simplex methods. In fact, the rebalancing problem can be reduced to the min-cost flow problem, a specialization of linear programming which can be solved more easily. For instance, the min-cost flow problem admits a strongly polynomial algorithm, meanwhile the corresponding question for linear programming is a major open problem in the field.

Appendix 9 illustrates how the rebalancing problem is equivalent to a min-cost flow problem with the same number of vertices and edges. Henceforth, we refer to the rebalancing problem as a min-cost flow problem.

Delegate Selection and Multi-party Computation. Delegate selection can be done using a simple version of cryptographic sortion as in [15]. Each of the k delegates involved in the MPC gets $n + 2m$ inputs which are shares of each of the n participant's

---

Algorithm 1: Depth-first Search Cycle Decomposition

---

    input : Circulation $\mathbf{f}$ on directed graph $G = (V, E)$
    output: A set of cycle flows $\mathcal{S}$ that sum to $\mathbf{f}$
1 initialize $i = 1$
2 initialize $R \longleftarrow \{e \in E : f(e) \neq 0\}$ set of active edges
3 **while** $R \neq \emptyset$ **do**
4   pick an edge $e_1 \in R$
5   run depth first search to find a cycle $C_i = (e_1, e_2, \ldots e_k)$ in R
6       $w_i \longleftarrow \min f(e), e \in C_i$
7   initialize $\mathbf{f}_i \longleftarrow 0$
8   **for** $e \in C_i$ **do**
9           $f_i(e) = w_i$
10          $f(e) \longleftarrow f(e) - f_i(e)$
11   **if** $f(e) = 0$ **then**
12   delete e from R

13       $i \longleftarrow i + 1$
14 **return** $\mathcal{S} = \{\mathbf{f}_1, \mathbf{f}_2 \ldots \mathbf{f}_i\}$

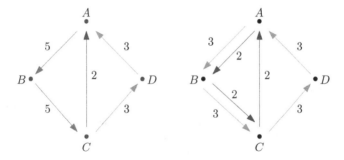

Fig. 2. The graph on the left depicts a circulation. The weight of each edge is the transaction amount to send along the edge. The cycles in the graph on the right is a sign consistent decomposition of the circulation.

zero flow constraints and the $2m$ rebalancing capacity constraint along the m directed edges (for each edge we have two constraints: one which specifies the maximum rebalancing flow in one direction, and another which specifies the flow has to be 0 in the other direction). The objective function is also shared and given as an input to the delegates. The delegates jointly compute the optimal solution to the rebalancing LP problem and each delegate outputs a share of the final flow on each edge at the end of the protocol.

4.2 Execution Phase

Cycle Decomposition. The exploration phase concludes with a solution to the rebalancing linear program obtained through multi-party computation. This solution $\mathbf{f}^*$ is in fact encoded as shared secrets, and, as observed in [29] (relevant passage), one can process the solution further before returning to individual participants. Instead of directly

---

Algorithm 2: HTLC creation for cycles

---

input : S set of directed cycles
1 **for** $c \in S$ **do**
2   select starting user u_c at random from users in c
3   timelock $t_c \longleftarrow len(c)$
4   u_c chooses random secret r_c and creates hash $h_c = H(r_c)$
5   **for** $e_c = (u, v) \in c$ *starting from* u_c **do**
6   u creates $HTLC(u, v, w_c, h_c, t_c)$
7   decrement t_c by 1

---

sending each $f^*(u, v)$ to u, we decompose the circulation into a sum of cycle flows. This makes the execution of rebalancing via HTLCs easier; instead of the entire network committing their funds to a large atomic rebalancing transaction, each cycle only requires coordination between nodes constituting the cycle.

As mentioned earlier, each circulation can be expressed as a sum of cycle flows. We briefly describe a standard algorithm to compute this decomposition efficiently. Algorithm 1 uses depth-first search as a subroutine to detect cycles and then induce cycle flows on them. Figure 2 depicts a circulation and its decomposition into cycle flows.

HTLC Commitments per Cycle. Given such a decomposition, we need to enforce atomicity of each cycle flow by creating an HTLC for each cycle c in the set. This can be done by first selecting a user in each cycle at random to initiate the cycle. This user has to choose a random secret r_c from some domain $\mathcal{X}$ and create a hash of the secret $h_c = H(r_c)$. The timelock for the initiator of the cycle and the next user is set equal to the length of the cycle. The transaction amount to send along each cycle is the weight of the cycle w_c. Every subsequent user in the cycle decrements the timelock value by 1 and looks up the next user in the cycle they should create an HTLC with (determined by the vertex order in the cycle). They then create an HTLC with that user with the decremented timelock value (lines 5–7 in Algorithm 2).

Finally we note that Algorithm 1 and Algorithm 2 can be computed privately using MPC. To prevent any two users on a cycle c from sharing their hash h_c with each other and thus finding out they are in the same cycle, one can use MAPPCN [30] to preserve user anonymity.

5 Analysis

Desired Properties. An execution of HIDE & SEEK satisfies the desired properties as stated in Sect. 3.3. Let us study each of the properties in order.

Balance Conservation. Suppose there is a node v that enjoys net financial gain through the execution of HIDE & SEEK under a malicious adversary. HIDE & SEEK specifies a set of cycle flows that the nodes may execute, and v must have participated in some subset of these. Note that by atomicity of cycle flows ensured through HTLCs, it is not possible for a cycle to be executed partially (even when parties act maliciously). If v's balance increased, that means there must be at least one cycle flow with net positive flow through v. But this contradicts the definition of cycle flows, since they must satisfy zero flow through each node:

$$\sum_{(u,v)\in E} f(u,v) = \sum_{(v,u)\in E} f(v,u) \quad \forall v \in V.$$

Privacy. The sensitive data used in the exploratory phase of HIDE & SEEK remains private as long as at least one delegate of the MPC is honest (inherited by the MPC). In the execution phase, users do not know the other users in their cycle except their predecessors and successors in their cycles as we use MAPPCN to preserve user anonymity.

Optimality. Assuming the delegates compute the solution correctly, the circulation returned by the min-cost flow algorithm maximizes the total flow through each edge. Under the same assumption, the cycle decomposition algorithm would result in an equivalent (and thus also optimal) set of cycle flows.

Efficiency. We break the analysis of the efficiency of HIDE & SEEK into three parts: (1) solving the rebalancing problem, (2) cycle decomposition, and (3) MPC.

Solving the Rebalancing Problem. Solving the underlying min-cost flow problem is the most computationally intensive aspect of HIDE & SEEK. Fortunately we can leverage the vast body of algorithms for this problem being asymptotically optimal in different parameter regimes. The complexity of these algorithms is analyzed in terms of n, m, the largest capacity U and the largest cost W of an edge. We may presently ignore the term W as each edge has identical cost 1. For the parameter regime of rebalancing, we recommend the double scaling algorithm of Ahuja, Goldberg, Orlin and Tarjan with computes the optimal solution in time $O(nm \log nW \log \log U)$ [4].

An alternative is to use a network simplex algorithm. This family of algorithms are excellent in practice, although theoretical analysis of their effectiveness is an active area of research in optimization. Simplex algorithms are also incredibly simple, and for this reason have they been recommended in Toft's framework for privately solving linear programs [29] despite the somewhat poorer theoretical guarantees. We recommend the network simplex algorithm of Orlin [22] for the rebalancing problem, which terminates in at most $O(nm \log n)$ pivots. Generally, the amortized cost per pivot is $O(n)$, but Orlin presents a modification with total runtime $O(nm \log n \log nW)$.

Cycle Decomposition. If the rebalancing circulation obtained by solving the min-cost flow contains n' vertices and m' edges, then the cycle decomposition algorithm as detailed in Algorithm 1 terminates in $O(n'm')$ time, which is $O(nm)$ at worst. Every loop iteration removes at least one edge, and each iteration visits at most n' vertices before finding a cycle. The pre-processing of G to obtain the subgraph induced by the circulation takes $O(n + m)$ time.

Also note that the timelocks used in the execution of a cycle flow are bounded by the length of the cycle.

MPC. Although MPC implementations of optimization algorithms incur a penalty in speed, there are multiple methods to speed up the implementation of HIDE & SEEK:

Firstly, the rebalancing problem, much like many other min-cost flow problems, satisfies the Hoffman-Gale conditions: the optimal solution, along with the vertices of the polytope, is guaranteed to be integral. This means the MPC can be performed over faster integer arithmetic rather than slower floating point arithmetic.

HIDE & SEEK can be implemented even faster by reducing the number of bits per variable. This quantity is governed by the maximum capacity per edge as well as the granularity of rebalancing, so that the number of bits required depends on the specific cryptocurrency. For instance, an implementation of HIDE & SEEK for Bitcoin with just 20 bits per variable may restrict all quantities to multiples of $2^{10} = 1024$ satoshis up to 2^{30} satoshis which is approximately 10 bitcoins.

The number of delegates chosen to compute the MPC also contributes to the communication cost during rounds, and here we note that HIDE & SEEK does not place any limitations on this number. In fact, it can be as low as two delegates as long as one of them is honest.

Finally, the efficiency of our protocol inherently depends on the MPC primitives used. This is a wide and active area of research, with a lot of new developments in making efficient MPC primitives [5, 8–10].

6   Limitations and Extensions

In this section, we identify the limitations of our protocol and discuss possible extensions.

Rational Participants. Participants in financial networks such as PCNs typically act selfishly, aiming to increase their financial gain. As a result, an interesting future study is the security of our scheme under rational participants. In the execution phase, the cycle decomposition ensures that participants always gain from executing a cycle because the cycles are sign-consistent. Nevertheless, HTLCs have been proven vulnerable to attacks where participants collude and act for-profit [20]. Regarding the exploration phase, it has been shown that when participants are rational (with respect to privacy) MPC is possible using randomized mechanisms with constant expected running time [2].

Weighted LP. The linear program of the rebalancing problem currently maximizes the total flow through each edge in the network. This is but an approximation of the practical objective, since in practice, flows through distinct edges are not necessarily equally important.

A more accurate model of rebalancing involved modifying the objective function from $\sum_{(u,v) \in E} f(u,v)$ to $\sum_{(u,v) \in E} w(u,v) f(u,v)$ for non-negative integral weights $w(u,v)$ supplied by u via secret sharing. Let W be the maximum possible weight that participants may specify.

This slight modification greatly enlarges the expressive power of participants, as they can now provide local preferences of one cycle over another. For instance, a user

u with one outgoing edge e_0 and three incoming edges e_1, e_2, e_3 wishes to rebalance e_0 desperately. u considers rebalancing along e_1 favorable but not urgent, is indifferent to rebalancing along e_2, and does not permit any flow through e_3. Knowing that outgoing flow through e_0 must be balanced by equal incoming flow, u may assign a weight $w(e_2) = 0$ to allow for flow through e_2 and then e_0 in order to rebalance e_0. This edge preference can be expressed by weights:

$$w(e_0) = W, \qquad w(e_1) = 1, \qquad w(e_2) = 0,$$

and by not including e_3 in the protocol at all.

The desired properties of HIDE & SEEK continue to hold after this modification. In terms of efficiency, the double scaling algorithm that we use runs in $O(nm \log nW \log \log U)$ time rather than $O(nm \log n \log \log U)$ [4].

The major drawback of this modification is game theoretic: although incorporating preferences is straightforward when users faithfully follow the protocol, it breaks under the assumption of rational participants. In particular, misreporting the weight of every edge as the maximum W is a dominant strategy, since that assigns the highest possible weight to every *cycle* that a user is part of. This reduces this modification to the original case of maximizing $\sum_{(u,v)\in E} f(u,v)$. An improved design of this mechanism, such as a clever budgeting of weights, could circumvent this problem, manage individual users' incentives, and let the weighted LP extension be used practically.

Optimality with Corrupted Participants. Participants' sensitive financial data, such as existence of a payment channel and its capacity for rebalancing, is not verified in the protocol, nor does our threat model consider falsification of this data with respect to optimality.

Unfortunately, this lack of verification can prevent any rebalancing to occur: an adversary with knowledge of the payment channel network can falsify edge data so that each cycle passes through one of their edges. The adversary can then refuse to participate in the execution phase and prevent others from rebalancing, even when cycle flows between honest parties exist.

To defend against such adversary, we propose that parties submit zero knowledge proof of validity along with their edge constraint data. Although one cannot force participants to participate in rebalancing cycles, this modification certainly increases the success rate of rebalancing cycles in HIDE & SEEK even under an active adversary.

7 Related Work

Rebalancing PCNs. There are several payment channel primitives proposed in literature [6,7,12,21,24,28]. Regardless of the primitive, a challenge all PCNs share is how to route transactions in the PCN while maintaining balanced channels for as long as possible. Classic routing studies in PCNs like SilentWhispers [19], SpeedyMurmurs [26], and others [25] ignore that channels may be slowly depleting. A promising approach to avoid channel depletion and prolong the network availability for transaction routing is to maintain balanced channels or occasionally perform rebalancing. But transaction routing is a challenging task on its own because the channel balances remain secret for privacy purposes [17,27,31], let alone avoiding channel depletion on-top.

Khalil and Gervais introduce the first channel rebalancing protocol, called Revive [17]. They formulate the problem as an LP, similarly to our work. Then, a delegate is elected to solve the LP and return the solution to the rebalancing participants. Although our work lies close to Revive, it also differs in several aspects. First, Revive considers rebalancing as an LP as well, but HIDE & SEEK employs faster and more specific min-cost flow algorithms. Second, Revive relies on a single delegate to compute the optimal rebalancing which leaks private information about balances to the delegate. In contrast, HIDE & SEEK uses MPC to achieve full privacy guarantees. Since HIDE & SEEK uses MPC, the speeds of the two protocols cannot be compared. We nevertheless expect Revive to also benefit from using our min-cost flow framework. Finally, atomic execution of the rebalancing transactions in Revive requires the transaction language of the underlying blockchain to be Turing-complete, and thus it is not suitable for Bitcoin. HIDE & SEEK avoids this issue by first decomposing the optimal rebalancing into cycles, and then executing these cycles atomically using HTLCs. The cycle decomposition in HIDE & SEEK also ensures that, as long as the channel is not part of all cycles, some rebalancing can still occur if individual HTLCs fail on a channel.

From a practical perspective, rebalancing in the Lightning Network currently utilises a brute force search for rebalancing cycles with sufficient capacity. An automated approach for doing so using the imbalance measure was proposed by [23]. Unlike HIDE & SEEK, these methods do not leverage other rebalancing requests to find the globally optimal rebalancing. These methods also require nodes to have global knowledge of the network whereas nodes in HIDE & SEEK only need to have local knowledge of the PCN.

Recently some works introduce routing protocols that attempt to maintain balanced channels. In particular, Spider [27] is a payment routing algorithm that maximizes the throughput while maintaining the original channel balances, without providing rebalancing however. Li et al. [18] propose to extend the lifetime of payments channels by estimating payment demand, and using this estimate to decide on the initial balance of channels. Engelshoven and Roos [13], on the other hand, leverage routing fees to incentivize the balanced use of payment channels. All these works are orthogonal and complementary to ours, as we introduce an opt-in rebalancing protocol.

Network Flows and MPC. The general problem of solving network flow problems via multi-party computation is considered in the comprehensive PhD thesis of Aly [5]. Various privacy preserving implementations of combinatorial optimization problems are presented. The author acknowledges that the cost for privacy is very high even for the simplest of problems. Roughly speaking, their MPC implementations must iterate for the theoretical worst-case number of iterations to maintain privacy. For the practical problem of rebalancing though, we do not choose to implement extra iterations. On the other hand, we believe that suboptimal rebalancing is better than no rebalancing, and recommend terminating the min-cost flow solution prematurely if needed. Both scaling algorithms and network simplex algorithms monotonically generate better solutions in each iteration, leaving the participants with a feasible solution if they stop early.

8   Conclusion and Future Work

In this work we study the rebalancing problem for PCNs. We present HIDE & SEEK, which is a secure opt-in rebalancing protocol, that is also private and finds the globally-optimal rebalancing. HIDE & SEEK achieves better efficiency by reducing the rebalancing problem to a min-cost flow problem. HIDE & SEEK also achieves better robustness by decomposing the solution into cycles and executing each cycle atomically, as opposed to executing the entire solution atomically.

An interesting direction for future work is to consider the transaction aggregation problem, which is similar to rebalancing but without the balance conservation property (for instance Alice's balance is not conserved if Alice wants to pay Bob 2 coins for a coffee). The main difficulty with transaction aggregation comes from the constraint that transactions may not be executed partially. In other words, where the optimization underlying rebalancing is a linear program (solvable in polynomial time), the problem underlying transaction aggregation is an integer program (which is NP-complete in general).

9   Appendix: Reduction of the Rebalancing Problem to Min-Cost Flow

Recall that the rebalancing problem consists of finding a circulation on a directed graph with maximum flow while also satisfying the capacity constraints. The related well-studied problem of min-cost circulation provides a cost to each edge as well as lower and upper bounds on the flow through each edge. Rebalancing can thus be seen as a circulation problem with negative costs with flow bounds given by 0 and capacity $m(u, v)$. Below, we provide a short reduction to the more fundamental min-cost flow problem on the same graph.

The reduction is a simple change of variables: define $\mathbf{f}' \in \mathbb{R}^m$ as $f'(v, u) := m(u, v) - f(u, v)$. Consider the reversed graph $G' = (V, E')$ where all directed edges from G are reversed $E' = \{e' = (v, u) : (u, v) \in E\}$. Rebalancing on G is equivalent to a min-cost flow problem on G'.

The constraints $0 \leq f(u, v) \leq m(u, v)$ transform into $0 \leq f'(v, u) \leq m'(v, u) = m(u, v)$. Finally, the zero flow constraints from the rebalancing problem

$$\sum_{(u,v)\in E} f(u, v) - \sum_{(v,u)\in E} f(v, u) = 0$$

transform into

$$\sum_{(v,u)\in E'} m(u, v) - f'(v, u) - \sum_{(u,v)\in E'} m(v, u) - f'(u, v) = 0,$$

or,

$$\sum_{(u,v)\in E'} f'(u, v) - \sum_{(v,u)\in E'} f'(v, u) = \sum_{(u,v)\in E} m(u, v) - \sum_{(v,u)\in E} m(v, u)$$

In other words, the sources and sinks can be defined by whether $\sum_{(u,v)\in E} m(u,v) - \sum_{(v,u)\in E} m(v,u)$ is positive or negative. By a standard technique, we can further reduce the problem to that containing a single source and single sink by appending so-called "super-source and super-sink" to G'.

Finally, we need to specify the cost to complete the problem description: if the objective of rebalancing is to maximise $\sum_{(u,v)\in E} c(u,v)f(u,v)$ then we specify the min-cost flow problem to minimize $\sum_{(u,v)\in E'} c(v,u)f'(u,v)$. In this way, not only are the feasible regions of both problems equivalent by the described change of variables, but so are the optimum solutions.

References

1. Rebalance plugin. https://github.com/lightningd/plugins/tree/master/rebalance
2. Abraham, I., Dolev, D., Gonen, R., Halpern, J.Y.: Distributed computing meets game theory: robust mechanisms for rational secret sharing and multiparty computation. In: PODC (2006). https://doi.org/10.1145/1146381.1146393
3. Ahuja, R., Magnanti, T., Orlin, J.: Network flows - theory, algorithms and applications (1993)
4. Ahuja, R., Goldberg, A., Orlin, J., Tarjan, R.: Finding minimum-cost flows by double scaling. Math. Program. **53**, 243–266 (1992). https://doi.org/10.1007/BF01585705
5. Aly, A.: Network flow problems with secure multiparty computation (2015)
6. Avarikioti, Z., Kogias, E.K., Wattenhofer, R., Zindros, D.: Brick: asynchronous incentive-compatible payment channels. In: FC (2021). https://fc21.ifca.ai/papers/168.pdf
7. Avarikioti, Z., Litos, O.S.T., Wattenhofer, R.: Cerberus channels: incentivizing watchtowers for bitcoin. In: FC (2020). https://doi.org/10.1007/978-3-030-51280-4_19
8. Baum, C., Orsini, E., Scholl, P., Soria-Vazquez, E.: Efficient constant-round MPC with identifiable abort and public verifiability. In: Micciancio, D., Ristenpart, T. (eds.) CRYPTO 2020. LNCS, vol. 12171, pp. 562–592. Springer, Cham (2020). https://doi.org/10.1007/978-3-030-56880-1_20
9. Catrina, O., de Hoogh, S.: Secure multiparty linear programming using fixed-point arithmetic. In: Gritzalis, D., Preneel, B., Theoharidou, M. (eds.) ESORICS 2010. LNCS, vol. 6345, pp. 134–150. Springer, Heidelberg (2010). https://doi.org/10.1007/978-3-642-15497-3_9
10. Cramer, R., Fehr, S., Ishai, Y., Kushilevitz, E.: Efficient multi-party computation over rings. In: Biham, E. (ed.) EUROCRYPT 2003. LNCS, vol. 2656, pp. 596–613. Springer, Heidelberg (2003). https://doi.org/10.1007/3-540-39200-9_37
11. Damgård, I., Nielsen, J.B.: Universally composable efficient multiparty computation from threshold homomorphic encryption. In: Boneh, D. (ed.) CRYPTO 2003. LNCS, vol. 2729, pp. 247–264. Springer, Heidelberg (2003). https://doi.org/10.1007/978-3-540-45146-4_15
12. Decker, C., Wattenhofer, R.: A fast and scalable payment network with bitcoin duplex micropayment channels. In: Stabilization, Safety, and Security of Distributed Systems (2015). https://doi.org/10.1007/978-3-319-21741-3_1
13. van Engelshoven, Y., Roos, S.: The merchant: avoiding payment channel depletion through incentives. CoRR abs/2012.10280 (2020). https://arxiv.org/abs/2012.10280
14. Garay, J., Kiayias, A., Leonardos, N.: The bitcoin backbone protocol: analysis and applications. In: Eurocrypt (2015). https://doi.org/10.1007/978-3-662-46803-6_10

15. Gilad, Y., Hemo, R., Micali, S., Vlachos, G., Zeldovich, N.: Algorand: scaling byzantine agreements for cryptocurrencies. In: SOSP (2017). https://doi.org/10.1145/3132747.3132757

16. Joseph Poon, T.D.: The bitcoin lightning network: Scalable off-chain instant payments. Technical report. https://lightning.network/lightning-network-paper.pdf

17. Khalil, R., Gervais, A.: Revive: rebalancing off-blockchain payment networks. In: CCS (2017). https://doi.org/10.1145/3133956.3134033

18. Li, P., Miyazaki, T., Zhou, W.: Secure balance planning of off-blockchain payment channel networks. In: IEEE INFOCOM 2020 - IEEE Conference on Computer Communications, pp. 1728–1737 (2020). https://doi.org/10.1109/INFOCOM41043.2020.9155375

19. Malavolta, G., Moreno-Sanchez, P., Kate, A., Maffei, M.: Silentwhispers: enforcing security and privacy in decentralized credit networks. In: NDSS (2017). https://doi.org/10.14722/ndss.2017.23448

20. Malavolta, G., Moreno-Sanchez, P., Schneidewind, C., Kate, A., Maffei, M.: Anonymous multi-hop locks for blockchain scalability and interoperability. In: NDSS (2019). https://doi.org/10.14722/ndss.2019.23330

21. Miller, A., Bentov, I., Bakshi, S., Kumaresan, R., McCorry, P.: Sprites and state channels: Payment networks that go faster than lightning. In: FC (2019). https://doi.org/10.1007/978-3-030-32101-7_30

22. Orlin, J.: A polynomial time primal network simplex algorithm for minimum cost flows. Math. Prog. **78**, 109–129 (1996). https://doi.org/10.1007/BF02614365

23. Pickhardt, R., Nowostawski, M.: Imbalance measure and proactive channel rebalancing algorithm for the lightning network. In: IEEE International Conference on Blockchain and Cryptocurrency, ICBC 2020, Toronto, ON, Canada, 2–6 May, 2020, pp. 1–5. IEEE (2020). https://doi.org/10.1109/ICBC48266.2020.9169456

24. Poon, J., Dryja, T.: The bitcoin lightning network: scalable off-chain instant payments (2015). https://lightning.network/lightning-network-paper.pdf

25. Prihodko, P., Zhigulin, S., Sahno, M., Ostrovskiy, A., Osuntokun, O.: Flare: an approach to routing in lightning network. shorturl.at/adrHP (2016)

26. Roos, S., Moreno-Sanchez, P., Kate, A., Goldberg, I.: Settling payments fast and private: efficient decentralized routing for path-based transactions. arXiv preprint arXiv:1709.05748 (2017)

27. Sivaraman, V., et al.: High throughput cryptocurrency routing in payment channel networks. In: 17th USENIX Symposium on Networked Systems Design and Implementation ({NSDI} 20), pp. 777–796 (2020)

28. Spilman, J.: Anti dos for tx replacement. https://lists.linuxfoundation.org/pipermail/bitcoin-dev/2013-April/002433.html. Accessed 22 Nov 2020

29. Toft, T.: Solving linear programs using multiparty computation. In: Dingledine, R., Golle, P. (eds.) FC 2009. LNCS, vol. 5628, pp. 90–107. Springer, Heidelberg (2009). https://doi.org/10.1007/978-3-642-03549-4_6

30. Tripathy, S., Mohanty, S.K.: MAPPCN: multi-hop anonymous and privacy-preserving payment channel network. In: Bernhard, M., et al. (eds.) FC 2020. LNCS, vol. 12063, pp. 481–495. Springer, Cham (2020). https://doi.org/10.1007/978-3-030-54455-3_34

31. Yu, R., Xue, G., Kilari, V.T., Yang, D., Tang, J.: Coinexpress: a fast payment routing mechanism in blockchain-based payment channel networks. In: 2018 27th International Conference on Computer Communication and Networks (ICCCN), pp. 1–9. IEEE (2018)

Short Paper: A Centrality Analysis
of the Lightning Network

Philipp Zabka[1]([✉]), Klaus-T. Foerster[2], Christian Decker[5],
and Stefan Schmid[1,3,4]

[1] Faculty of Computer Science, University of Vienna, Wien, Austria
philipp.zabka@univie.ac.at
[2] Technical University of Dortmund, Dortmund, Germany
[3] Faculty of Computer Science, Technical University of Berlin, Berlin, Germany
[4] Fraunhofer SIT, Darmstadt, Germany
[5] Blockstream, Zurich, Switzerland

Abstract. Payment channel networks (PCNs) such as the Lightning
Network offer an appealing solution to the scalability problem faced
by many cryptocurrencies operating on a blockchain such as Bitcoin.
However, PCNs also inherit the stringent dependability requirements of
blockchain. In particular, in order to mitigate liquidity bottlenecks as
well as on-path attacks, it is important that payment channel networks
maintain a high degree of decentralization. Motivated by this requirement, we conduct an empirical centrality analysis of the popular Lightning Network, and in particular, the betweenness centrality distribution
of the routing system. Based on our extensive data set (using several millions of channel update messages), we implemented a TimeMachine tool
which enables us to study the network evolution over time. We find that
although the network is generally fairly decentralized, a small number of
nodes can attract a significant fraction of the transactions, introducing
skew. Furthermore, our analysis suggests that over the last two years,
the centrality has increased significantly, e.g., the inequality (measured
by the Gini index) has increased by more than 10%.

1 Introduction

Blockchain, the technology which is currently revamping the financial sector
and which underlies cryptocurrencies such as Bitcoin and Ethereum, enables
mistrusting entities to cooperate without involving a trusted third party. However, with their quickly growing popularity, blockchain networks face a scalability
problem, and the requirement of performing repeated global consensus protocol
is known to limit the achievable transactions rate.

Payment channel networks (PCNs) are a promising solution to mitigate the
scalability issue, by allowing users to perform transactions *off-chain*. In particular, in a PCN, two users can establish so-called payment channels among each
other, in a peer-to-peer fashion. The set of channels can then be seen as a graph,
in which users are represented as nodes and channels are represented as edges.

© International Financial Cryptography Association 2022
I. Eyal and J. Garay (Eds.): FC 2022, LNCS 13411, pp. 374–385, 2022.
https://doi.org/10.1007/978-3-031-18283-9_18

Payments can then also be routed in a multi-hop manner across these channels (typically using source routing), with forwarding users typically charging a small fee. Nodes can discover the cheapest routes using a gossip mechanism. The scalability benefit comes from the fact that it is only when a channel is opened or closed, that changes have to be made to the blockchain.

By the nature of the service they provide, PCNs need to meet stringent dependability requirements. Interestingly, while over the last years, several interesting approaches to design and operate payment channel networks in an efficient and reliable manner have been proposed in the literature, relatively little is known about the properties of the actually deployed networks today.

We in this paper are particularly interested in the level of decentralization provided by PCNs: decentralization is generally one of the key features of blockchain, and also naturally required from off-chain solutions.

Indeed, it has recently been shown that skews in the routing system (e.g., due to exploits of the payment mechanism), can significantly harm the network performance, by depleting channels [1], or even lead to denial-of-service attacks [2] and privacy [3,4] and other security issues [5]. In order to gain a detailed understanding of Lightning, the most popular PCN, we monitored the network for several years, collecting millions of channel update and gossiping messages. To shed light on the network evolution, we further implemented tools which allow us to reconstruct the network at previous time stamps. In this paper, we present the main results of our study of the Lightning Network.

1.1   Our Contributions

Motivated by the increasing popularity of payment channel networks and the resulting performance and dependability requirements, we report on an extensive empirical study of the most popular PCN, Lightning. In particular, we study to which extent Lightning fulfills the premise of decentralized transaction routing.

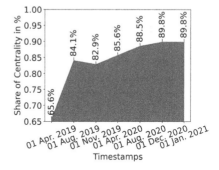

Fig. 1. Top 10% control over routes

We find that there is a trend of increasing centralization and a high level of inequality, where a small portion of the nodes participate on most transaction routes. We show that the level of centrality also depends on the transaction size, and we take a look at some of the highest ranked nodes according to centrality. We uncover that a fair share of nodes remained at the top over the examined period. To just give one example, our analysis shows that the top 10% of all nodes control a vast majority of all transaction routes, and that the controlled share increases over time, see Fig. 1.

For our study, we collected significant data from the live Lightning Network, over a time span of almost two years. This data includes over 400k node announcement messages, over 1m channel announcement messages, and over

6m channel update messages. We further developed *TimeMachine*, a tool which allows us to reconstruct the network at desired moments in time. We accomplish this with the help of the above mentioned gossip mechanism.

As a contribution to the research community, in order to ensure reproducibility as well as to support future research in this area, we make available all our code and experimental artifacts [6] together with this paper.

1.2 Related Work

Over the last years, many interesting approaches to design and operate payment channel networks have been proposed in the literature, often accounting for dependability aspects [7–12], and we refer the reader to [13–15] for an overview.

In this paper, we are particularly interested in issues related to centralization, a topic which has recently also received much attention in the context of Bitcoin in general [16–18]. In the context of PCNs, it has been shown that centralization of the routing system can harm performance [2,19], liquidity [1,20], security [5], and privacy aspects [3,4,21,22], especially when considering on-path adversaries.

Interestingly, relatively little is known about the empirical properties of deployed payment channel networks. The Lightning Network's topology has been analyzed by Seres et al. [23]. Their work studies the robustness of the network against random failures of nodes as well as attacks targeting nodes. A similar, but more in detail work has been carried out by Rohrer et al. [24]. Martinazzi et al. [25] analyzed the evolution of the Lightning Network over a period of one year, beginning on its launch on the Bitcoin mainnet in January 2018. Their work focuses on the topological robustness of the network, e.g., against attacks, where they also detect a high influence of a few nodes on the network. Next, a large scale empirical analysis on the client and geographical classification of nodes is performed by Zabka et al. [26,27], see also Mizrahi et al. [28]. Related to this, Scellato et al. [29] study how geographic distance affects social ties in a social network and Mislove et al. [30] examine geographical, gender and racial aspects of Twitter users to the U.S. population.

1.3 Organization

Organization. The remainder of this paper is organized as follows. Section 2 introduces some preliminaries and Sect. 3 describes our methodology, followed by the centrality analysis in Sect. 4. We subsequently conclude in Sect. 5.

2 Preliminaries

We now introduce some of the necessary basics of the Lightning Networks and some specific preliminaries for the remainder of the paper.

The Lightning Network. The Lightning Network is an off-chain solution to improve the scalability of cryptocurrencies such as Bitcoin. The network can be accessed via three clients, namely LND [31] implemented in Go, C-Lightning [32] implemented in C and Eclair [33] implemented in Scala. However, with an usage of more than 85%, LND is currently by far the most popular client [27]. The Lightning Network users are able to create bidirectional connections to other users, called channels. These channels can be used to send instant payments between two users, which do not need to be necessarily directly connected. If a payment is routed across multiple users, the users in between the route may demand fees for the routing process. The Lightning Network does not operate on the blockchain itself, however the first transaction called the funding transaction to create a channel needs to be propagated onto the blockchain. The same goes for the last transaction or closing transaction to end the connection between two users. All intermediary transactions are not propagated onto the blockchain and therefore can be processed in a much faster fashion.

Gossip Messages. As the name implies, gossip messages are propagated through the whole network to either announce a node or channel creation or an update. Therefore, all participants have an contemporary view of the network. This mechanism is especially important in the case that a node wants to route a payment to a node it is not directly connected with. In the following we will take a more in detail look at the three most important gossip messages, which are specified in the Basics of the Lightning Technology (BOLT) [41]:

- **node_announcement_message**: This message allows nodes to inform other participants about extra data associated with it, besides the node ID. It contains data such as the IP address, color, alias and timestamp as well as information for opting into higher level protocols.
- **channel_announcement_message**: If a channel is created between two nodes this message is propagated through the network. It contains information such as an short channel ID, which is an unique identifier for the channel, as well as both node IDs.
- **channel_update_message**: A channel is practically not usable until both sides announce their channel parameters. These parameters are announced in this message. As the Lightning Network is directed, both channel participants have to send a message. The parameters included in this message are among other things used to calculate the routing fees. Every time one side updates its channel parameters, this message is broadcast in the network.

Routing Fees. In the Lightning Network nodes along a routed path take a small fee for forwarding transactions. The parameters necessary for the calculation are *fee_base_msat* and *fee_proportional_millionths* which can be found in the *channel_update_message*. Hereby *fee_base_msat* denotes the constant fee a node will charge for a transfer and *fee_proportional_millionths* is the amount a node will charge for each transferred satoshi over their channel. Fees are calculated as follows, where transferred_amount denotes the transaction in millisatoshi:

fee_base_msat + (transferred_amount * fee_proportional_millionths/1000000)

Betweenness Centrality. The betweenness centrality represents a measure in a network based on shortest paths, a node's centrality is based on how many such paths traverse it. Formally, the betweenness centrality c_B of the nodes $v \in V$ is $c_B(v) = \sum_{s,t \in V} \sigma(s,t|v)/\sigma(s,t)$, with $\sigma(s,t)$ $[\sigma(s,t|v)]$ as # shortest st-paths [through v, $v \neq s,t$]. If $s = t$, $\sigma(s,t) = 1$, and if $v \in s,t$, $\sigma(s,t|v) = 0$ [34,35]. For every node pair in a connected unweighted graph, there exists at least one shortest path between these nodes such that the number of edges is minimized. For weighted graphs such as the Lightning Network, where channel routing fees represent edge weights, the sum of the edge weights is minimized.

Among several interesting alternatives [36,37], we focus on betweenness centrality as our main centrality measurement. Nodes with high betweenness centrality have a considerable amount of influence on a network by means of information control, since most of the network traffic will pass though them—in contrast to other centrality measures which represent a more local view, e.g., degree centrality, which counts the numbers of edges incident to a node.

A high betweenness centrality is a particular concern as nodes choose routing paths with the overall cheapest fees, and a skewed centrality indicates that routing paths are concentrated to a small subset of nodes. A skewed centrality may not only quickly deplete payment channels, but also makes the network vulnerable: many attacks recently reported in the literature are based on on-path adversaries [24,28]. Getting a significant amount of traffic can also raise privacy concerns, e.g., during route discovery.

3   Methodology

We next introduce the methods to obtain and process our data set.

TimeMachine. The Lightning Network TimeMachine [38] is a tool written in Python, which reconstructs the state at a prior point in time by replaying gathered gossip messages up to that point in time. We have deployed a number of C-Lightning nodes that collect and archive these messages, which are then deduplicated and ordered by their timestamp, in order to allow the TimeMachine to replay them in the correct order, and terminate once the desired point in time has been reached, leaving the view of the network close to what the public network would have looked like at that time. We utilized the TimeMachine to rebuild the network at seven different points in time, covering a time span of two years ranging from 01 Apr. 2019 to 01 Jan. 2021. We then used the Python library NetworkX [34] to further analyze the networks in regard to the betweenness distribution in different timestamps. With the help of our TimeMachine we were able to reconstruct the network as it was at the timestamps mentioned in Table 1. From now on we will reference the timestamps as T1–T7.

Data Set. Our data was collected with help of C-Lightning nodes, which synchronize their view of the network topology by listening and exchanging gossip messages. Internally C-Lightning will deduplicate messages, discard outdated *node_announcements* and *channel_updates*, and then apply them to the internal view. In order to persist the view across restarts, the node also writes the raw messages,

Table 1. Lightning network snapshots

Abbr.	Timestamp	Date	# Nodes
T1	1554112800	01 Apr. 2019	1362
T2	1564653600	01 Aug. 2019	4589
T3	1572606000	01 Nov. 2019	4699
T4	1585735200	01 Apr. 2020	5230
T5	1596276000	01 Aug. 2020	5905
T6	1606820400	01 Dec. 2020	6331
T7	1609498800	01 Jan. 2021	6629

along some internal messages, to a file called the *gossip_store*. The node compacts the *gossip_store* file from time to time in order to limit its growth. Compaction consists of rewriting the file, skipping messages that have been superceded in the meantime. Our data set is comprised of the three gossip messages discussed in the previous section. Our nodes have recorded more than 400 000 *node_announcement messages*, more than 1 000 000 *channel_announcement messages*, and over 6 400 000 million *channel_update messages*.

4 Centrality Analysis

This section reports our main results from the centrality analysis. We performed a detailed analysis where we measured the betweenness centrality, a major centrality measure, of the Lightning Network at different points in time and observed how it has developed over almost two years. More precisely, we took seven snapshots of the network, dating from 01 Apr. 2019 to 01 Jan. 2021. Based on the formula for calculating routing fees introduced in Sect. 2 we calculated the betweenness of each node based on three different realistic transaction sizes namely 10 000 000 Millisatoshi (0.0001 BTC), 1 000 000 000 Millisatoshi (0.01 BTC) and 10 000 000 000 Millisatoshi (0.1 BTC). The idea of calculating the betweenness with different transaction sizes was if we could detect significant changes.

4.1 Historic Betweenness Analysis of the Lightning Network

Evaluating the Lightning Network at different points in time in terms of the betweenness centrality can provide us with insights which allow us to better comprehend how it has developed until now e.g. has it become more centralized or the opposite and also make predictions in which direction it may develop in the future. We start by we examining our latest snapshot first.

Timestamp T7. We decided to use a logarithmic scale on the x-axis to better display the long range of centrality values (1–7 500 000). Further, we do not include nodes with a centrality value of 0, as they merely represent leafs in the graph. Also the amount of leaf nodes is astonishing high, up to 5520 nodes out of 6630 in T7, and would distort the graph.

In Fig. 2 (left) we can see that transaction size has indeed an influence on a node's centrality if the transaction amount is low or high enough. In the case of 0.1 BTC respectively 0.01 BTC there is almost no change in the centrality distribution among the nodes, however, in the case of 0.0001 BTC we can see a significant shift. A possible explanation for this shift in distribution we are experiencing is that for smaller transactions, different routes are calculated. The next noticeable observation is the high jump around the 4000 betweenness centrality mark for all three transaction sizes. For 0.0001 BTC roughly 100 nodes are affected and for 0.01 BTC or respectively 0.1 BTC roughly 80 nodes are concerned. A more in-depth analysis would be required to fully comprehend this phenomenon, but a possible cause can be that these nodes are all positioned on a specific shortest path and therefore share the same centrality.

Another interesting observation is that although the centrality of the majority of nodes is lower when calculated with the lowest transaction size, the centrality of the most central node is the highest of all three transaction sizes with 7 500 000. For comparison the centrality for 0.1 BTC and 0.01 BTC caps at 6 100 000.

Timestamp T4. In T4 we can make out only a few detailed changes 9 months prior to our latest timestamp T7. Observing Fig. 2 (middle) shows the centrality distribution for 1026 nodes out of 5231, so 4205 nodes remain leaf nodes with a centrality of 0. We can detect a similar jump at a centrality of approximately 3000 with 65 nodes having the exact same score. Another jump occurs at the 8000 mark with 48 nodes having the same value.

As was already the case in T7, the higher the centrality gets the more closer the share of nodes is that has a similar high centrality. However, this is due to the fact that only a few nodes share such a high betweenness centrality.

Timestamp T1. Figure 2 (right) depicts the centrality distribution for T1, which is 21 months prior to T7. At the first glance we can immediately detect that now all transaction sizes have a much more similar impact on the centrality distribution of the nodes in the network. However, this is most probably due to the overall lower amount of nodes in the network at that point in time and therefore limited amounts of paths that can be selected. According to our data, there are 1361 nodes in the network in T1 and only 347 out of them have a higher centrality than 0.

The graphs are rather similar, but jumps still occur. Betweenness values calculated with the transaction size of 0.0001 BTC experience the highest jumps. The first one starts at around 1000 and affects 0.3% of the nodes, the second one starts at around 1600 and affects 0.2% of the nodes. At last, compared to the most central node in T7, the most central node in T1 only reaches an centrality of 350 000. Even though the lower value is the result of fewer nodes in the network, one can not deny the rapid centralization of the network within the period of two years. We next further substantiate our observation of growing centrality.

4.2   Inequality in the Lightning Network

The Gini coefficient is an economic measure for the inequality within a nation or a social group. Similarly, we use this index in the context of payment channel

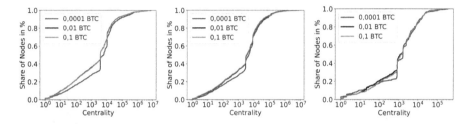

Fig. 2. Centrality distribution in timestamps T7 (left), T4 (middle) and T1 (right)

networks to shed light on the inequality and skew there exists in the network topology. In particular, an "unfair" distribution concentrates much control to a small set of nodes, which is problematic not only for the efficiency of the network but also raises security concerns. Many attacks in the literature are based on on-path adversaries [24, 28], which hence have significant control. This also generally goes against the idea of decentralization of finance.

Figure 3 (left and middle) depicts the Lorenz curves for T7 and T1. The Gini coefficient is equal to the area below the line of perfect equality minus the area below the Lorenz curve, divided by the area below the line of perfect equality. Looking at Fig. 3 (left) showing the latest snapshot of the network, we can see an excellent example of a perfectly unequal distribution, where 90% of the nodes only correspond to 10% of the cumulative betweenness of all nodes. Consequently, this indicates an extraordinarily high network centralization, where 90% of the shortest paths in the network lead through only a few highly centralized nodes. Next, looking at Fig. 3 (middle) we can observe that 90% of the nodes make up for slightly more than 30% of the betweenness, which is still not an ideal scenario. Subsequently, we can conclude from our observations that within 21 months the centralization has risen by 20%. Figure 3 (right) depicts the Gini coefficients for all seven timestamps. Here we observe an upward trend in the direction of inequality or centralization. The coefficient is slightly rising each timestamp, with the biggest jump with absolute 5% being between T1 and T2. Overall, we can deduce that the Lightning Network is highly centralized. Having only few, very influential nodes through which most paths are routed, is not beneficial for the robustness of the network. These nodes pose as significant targets for attacks and could disrupt the network in the case of failure. However not only attackers could exploit this situation, but also the nodes or rather the individuals controlling these nodes.

4.3   Analysis of the Top 10 Nodes

We lastly trace the performance of the most influential nodes, based on their centrality, in our latest and oldest timestamp, and briefly discuss our findings.

Figure 4 (left) depicts the top 10 nodes with the highest centrality in the latest timestamp T7 and their ranks in the earlier timestamps. We can see that most top nodes were also highly ranked in the past, e.g., N1 has always been in the Top 20—with some nodes starting to appear later, but then already at high rank, such as N3 (ACINQ [39], developer of Eclair).

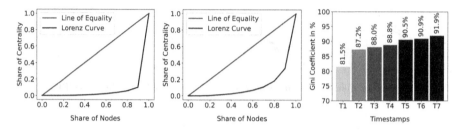

Fig. 3. Lorenz curves for the timestamps T7 (left) and T1 (middle). Gini Coefficients ranked according to all seven timestamps (right)

We now look the other way around to observe if a node could hold its central position in the network. Figure 4 (right) depicts the top 10 nodes in T1 our oldest snapshot and how the nodes performed from there on. For clarification the nodes depicted in this figure are partially not same as in Fig. 4 (left). Many nodes could not hold their position, the only nodes which stayed in the Top 10 through all timestamps are N3 [40] and N9 or respectively N7 and N8 in Fig. 4 (left).

Hence, we see that many powerful nodes of today were already highly influential in the past, respectively came in with a strong backing. Yet, a strong position in the past is not a guarantee, and many past top 10 nodes lost influence.

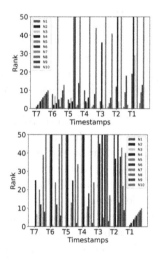

Fig. 4. Top ten influential node timelines, with latest left and oldest right

5   Future Work

We believe that our work opens several interesting directions for future research. In particular, it will be interesting to investigate other off-chain networks, further implications of centrality in cryptocurrency networks such as censorship concerns, and to develop mechanisms to foster more decentralization in payment channel networks. The latter includes the design of alternative, incentive-compatible routing mechanisms.

Acknowledgement. We thank our shepherd Karim Eldefrawy and the anonymous reviewers of Financial Cryptography and Data Security 2022 for their time and suggestions on how to improve the paper. This project has received funding from the Austrian

Science Fund (FWF) project ReactNet (P 33775-N), 2020–2024. This paper was also partially funded by Harmony through the Research DAO.

References

1. Khalil, R., Gervais, A.: Revive: Rebalancing off-blockchain payment networks. In: Proceedings of the ACM SIGSAC Conference on Computer and Communications Security (CCS), pp. 439–453 (2017)
2. Tochner, S., Zohar, A., Schmid, S.: Route hijacking and dos in off-chain networks. In: Proceedings of the ACM Conference on Advances in Financial Technologies (AFT) (2020)
3. Nisslmueller, U., Foerster, K.T., Schmid, S., Decker, C.: Toward active and passive confidentiality attacks on cryptocurrency off-chain networks. In: Proceedings of the 6th International Conference on Information Systems Security and Privacy (ICISSP) (2020)
4. Tang, W., Wang, W., Fanti, G., Oh, S.: Privacy-utility tradeoffs in routing cryptocurrency over payment channel networks. Proc. ACM Measur. Anal. Comput. Syst. **4**(2), 1–39 (2020)
5. Malavolta, G., Moreno-Sanchez, P., Schneidewind, C., Kate, A., Maffei, M.: Anonymous multi-hop locks for blockchain scalability and interoperability. In: 26th Annual Network and Distributed System Security Symposium (NDSS) (2019)
6. Zabka, P., Foerster, K.T., Schmid, S., Decker, C.: Data and other artifacts. https://github.com/philippzabka/fc22
7. Kappos, G., et al.: An Empirical Analysis of Privacy in the Lightning Network. arXiv:2003.12470 [cs], January 2021
8. Rohrer, E., Tschorsch, F.: Counting down thunder: timing attacks on privacy in payment channel networks. In: AFT, pp. 214–227. ACM (2020)
9. Romiti, M., et al.: Cross-Layer Deanonymization Methods in the Lightning Protocol. arXiv:2007.00764 [cs], February 2021
10. Harris, J., Zohar, A.: Flood & loot: a systemic attack on the lightning network. In: AFT, pp. 202–213. ACM (2020)
11. Moreno-Sanchez, P., Kate, A., Maffei, M., Pecina, K.: Privacy preserving payments in credit networks: enabling trust with privacy in online marketplaces. In: 22nd Annual Network and Distributed System Security Symposium, NDSS 2015, San Diego, California, USA, February 8–11, 2015. The Internet Society (2015)
12. Malavolta, G., Moreno-Sanchez, P., Schneidewind, C., Kate, A., Maffei, M.: Anonymous multi-hop locks for blockchain scalability and interoperability. In: 26th Annual Network and Distributed System Security Symposium, NDSS 2019, San Diego, California, USA, 24–27 February, 2019. The Internet Society (2019)
13. Dotan, M., Pignolet, Y.A., Schmid, S., Tochner, S., Zohar, A.: Survey on blockchain networking: context, state-of-the-art, challenges. ACM Comput. Surv. (CSUR) **54**(5), 1–34 (2021)
14. Gudgeon, L., Moreno-Sanchez, P., Roos, S., McCorry, P., Gervais, A.: SoK: layer-two blockchain protocols. In: Bonneau, J., Heninger, N. (eds.) FC 2020. LNCS, vol. 12059, pp. 201–226. Springer, Cham (2020). https://doi.org/10.1007/978-3-030-51280-4_12
15. Neudecker, T., Hartenstein, H.: Network layer aspects of permissionless blockchains. IEEE Commun. Surv. Tutorials **21**(1), 838–857 (2018)
16. Coindesk: Why china's crackdown may make bitcoin mining more centralized. In: online (2021)

17. Beikverdi, A., Song, J.: Trend of centralization in bitcoin's distributed network. In: 2015 IEEE/ACIS 16th International Conference on Software Engineering, Artificial Intelligence, Networking and Parallel/Distributed Computing (SNPD), pp. 1–6. IEEE (2015)
18. Forbes: Bitcoin mining centralization is 'quite alarming', but a solution is in the works. In: online (2019)
19. EmelyanenkoK: Payment channel congestion via spam-attack (2020). https://github.com/lightningnetwork/lightning-rfc/issues/182
20. Khamis, J., Schmid, S., Rottenstreich, O.: Demand matrix optimization for offchain payments in blockchain. In: 2021 IEEE International Conference on Blockchain and Cryptocurrency (ICBC). IEEE (2021)
21. Malavolta, G., Moreno-Sanchez, P., Kate, A., Maffei, M., Ravi, S.: Concurrency and privacy with payment-channel networks. In: Proceedings of the 2017 ACM SIGSAC Conference on Computer and Communications Security, pp. 455–471 (2017)
22. Tripathy, S., Mohanty, S.K.: MAPPCN: multi-hop anonymous and privacy-preserving payment channel network. In: Bernhard, M., et al. (eds.) FC 2020. LNCS, vol. 12063, pp. 481–495. Springer, Cham (2020). https://doi.org/10.1007/978-3-030-54455-3_34
23. Seres, I.A., Gulyás, L., Nagy, D.A., Burcsi, P.: Topological analysis of bitcoin's lightning network. In: Pardalos, P., Kotsireas, I., Guo, Y., Knottenbelt, W. (eds.) Mathematical Research for Blockchain Economy. SPBE, pp. 1–12. Springer, Cham (2020). https://doi.org/10.1007/978-3-030-37110-4_1
24. Rohrer, E., Malliaris, J., Tschorsch, F.: Discharged payment channels: quantifying the lightning network's resilience to topology-based attacks. In: EuroS&P Workshops, pp. 347–356. IEEE (2019)
25. Stefano Martinazzi, A.F.: The evolving topology of the lightning network: Centralization, efficiency, robustness, synchronization, and anonymity (2020)
26. Zabka, P., Foerster, K.T., Schmid, S., Decker, C.: Empirical evaluation of nodes and channels of the lightning network. Pervasive Mob. Comput. **83**, 101584 (2022)
27. Zabka, P., Förster, K., Schmid, S., Decker, C.: Node classification and geographical analysis of the lightning cryptocurrency network. In: ICDCN, pp. 126–135. ACM (2021)
28. Mizrahi, A., Zohar, A.: Congestion attacks in payment channel networks. arXiv:2002.06564v4 [cs], January 2021
29. Scellato, S., Mascolo, C., Musolesi, M., Latora, V.: Distance matters: Geo-social metrics for online social networks. In: WOSN. USENIX Association (2010)
30. Mislove, A., Lehmann, S., Ahn, Y., Onnela, J., Rosenquist, J.N.: Understanding the demographics of twitter users. In: ICWSM. The AAAI Press (2011)
31. LND GitHub Repository (2020). https://github.com/lightningnetwork/lnd. Accessed 15 July 2021
32. C-lightning GitHub Repository (2020). https://github.com/ElementsProject/lightning. Accessed 15 July 2021
33. Eclair GitHub Repository (2020). https://github.com/ACINQ/eclair. Accessed 15 July 2021
34. Hagberg, A.A., Schult, D.A., Swart, P.J.: Exploring network structure, dynamics, and function using networkx. In: Varoquaux, G., Vaught, T., Millman, J. (eds.) Proceedings of the 7th Python in Science Conference, pp. 11–15. Pasadena, CA USA (2008)
35. Brandes, U.: On variants of shortest-path betweenness centrality and their generic computation. Soc. Networks **30**(2), 136–145 (2008)

36. Liu, Y.Y., Slotine, J.J., Barabasi, A.L.: Controllability of complex networks. Nature **473**, 167–73 (2011). https://doi.org/10.1038/nature10011
37. Das, K., Samanta, S., Pal, M.: Study on centrality measures in social networks: a survey. Soc. Netw. Anal. Min. **8**(1), 1–11 (2018). https://doi.org/10.1007/s13278-018-0493-2
38. Decker, C.: Lightning network research; topology datasets. http://www.ithub.com/lnresearch/topology. https://doi.org/10.5281/zenodo.4088530. Accessed 01 Oct 2020
39. ACINQ Homepage (2021). https://acinq.co. Accessed 11 Sept 2021
40. Rompert.com (2021). https://rompert.com. Accessed 11 Sept 2021
41. Lightning Network: BOLT 7: P2P Node and Channel Discovery (2019). https://github.com/lightningnetwork/lightning-rfc/blob/master/07-routing-gossip.md. Accessed 15 July 2021

Resurrecting Address Clustering in Bitcoin

Malte Möser$^{(\boxtimes)}$ and Arvind Narayanan

Princeton University, Princeton, USA
mail@maltemoeser.de, arvindn@cs.princeton.edu

Abstract. Blockchain analysis is essential for understanding how cryptocurrencies like Bitcoin are used in practice, and address clustering is a cornerstone of blockchain analysis. However, current techniques rely on heuristics that have not been rigorously evaluated or optimized. In this paper, we tackle several challenges of change address identification and clustering. First, we build a ground truth set of transactions with known change from the Bitcoin blockchain that can be used to validate the efficacy of individual change address detection heuristics. Equipped with this data set, we develop new techniques to predict change outputs with low false positive rates. After applying our prediction model to the Bitcoin blockchain, we analyze the resulting clustering and develop ways to detect and prevent cluster collapse. Finally, we assess the impact our enhanced clustering has on two exemplary applications.

1 Introduction

Blockchain analysis techniques are essential for understanding how cryptocurrencies like Bitcoin are used in practice. A major challenge in analyzing blockchains is grouping transactions belonging to the same user. Users can create an unlimited amount of addresses to receive and send coins. As a result, their activity is often split among a multitude of such addresses. *Address clustering heuristics* aim to identify addresses under an individual user's control based on assumptions about how wallets create transactions. As the term *heuristic* suggests, address clustering today is more intuitive than rigorous; our overarching goal in this paper is to elevate it to a science.

There are at least four applications for which accurate address clustering is important. First, a law enforcement agency may be interested in evaluating the transactions of a specific entity. They may supplement their own investigation with a set of reliable heuristics to identify relevant transactions. Second, and conversely, the ability to accurately determine a user's transactions directly impacts their privacy. This tension between law enforcement needs and everyday users' privacy is inherent to cryptocurrencies due to their transparency and pseudonymity. Advocates from one side push for greater privacy and from the other side for stronger regulation. To better understand this tug-of-war, it is important to quantify how reliable change address heuristics are in practice.

© International Financial Cryptography Association 2022
I. Eyal and J. Garay (Eds.): FC 2022, LNCS 13411, pp. 386–403, 2022.
https://doi.org/10.1007/978-3-031-18283-9_19

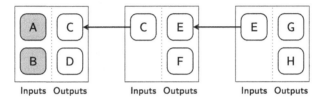

Fig. 1. The multi-input heuristic clusters addresses of inputs jointly spent in the same transaction. It does not cluster addresses that are never co-spent with other addresses (such as C and E).

Third, accurate grouping of transaction activity is important for aggregate analyses such as studying economic activity over time. This usually requires a full clustering of all addresses on the blockchain. Finally, the unique challenges of address clustering may be interesting for researchers outside of cryptocurrencies. For example, it may pose as an application domain for machine learning models and could be used as a benchmarking application.

The current state of address clustering techniques available to researchers is sub-optimal in multiple ways. The most common heuristic, *multi-input*, groups addresses that are jointly used in inputs of a transaction [26,27]. This heuristic is easy to apply, moderately effective in practice [12], and widely used. However, it misses addresses that are never co-spent with other addresses (cf. Figure 1).

Many of these addresses can be clustered using *change address* heuristics: as coins in Bitcoin cannot be spent partially, transactions return the surplus value back to the sender. Identifying the change output thus allows grouping the associated address with the inputs' addresses. However, as the Bitcoin protocol does not explicitly distinguish between change and spend outputs, heuristics need to be used to identify them.

While the importance of change address identification and clustering has been demonstrated empirically and through simulation [1,21], it remains difficult to assess how well it works in practice. A major issue is that researchers currently lack ground truth data on change outputs to assess the accuracy of individual heuristics. We are only aware of one prior study from 2015 that exploited weaknesses in a lightweight client [23], which allowed to extract the addresses of 37 585 wallets to assess four different clustering heuristics. Blockchain intelligence companies might possess manually curated and refined data sets and clusterings, but their techniques and data aren't openly available to researchers (or only shared in limited form, e.g., [11,32]). As a result, analyses of new heuristics often fall short of quantifying their accuracy and resort to analyzing the resulting clusterings only (e.g., [6,33]). Furthermore, clustering is applied inconsistently across studies: many forgo change address clustering entirely (e.g., [15,16,18,28]), whereas some simply apply a single change heuristic (e.g., [7,24]).

Considering this state of affairs, our goals in this paper are to address the lack of ground truth data and assessment methods, develop new techniques to apply heuristics to predict change and use them to create improved clusterings.

Contributions, Methods and Findings

1. **A new ground truth method and dataset:** We put forward a procedure to select and filter transactions for which the change output has been revealed on the blockchain. Our approach exploits that future transactions of users can reveal change outputs in past transactions. We extract a set of 35.26 million transactions, carefully filtered down from 53 million candidate transactions, that can be used as ground truth for validation and prediction (Sect. 2).
2. **Evaluating existing heuristics:** We've compiled and evaluate a set of 26 change address heuristics based on previous literature and community resources. Most heuristics individually produce few false positives at low to medium true positive rates. We find that due to changes in the protocol and usage patterns, heuristics wax and wane in their effectiveness over time, showing the need to use multiple heuristics and combine them in an adaptive way rather than rely on a fixed algorithm (Sect. 3.1).
3. **Improved prediction:** We use a random forest classifier to identify change outputs and compare it against a baseline: the majority vote of individual heuristics. While machine learning has been used to classify the type of entity behind a transaction (e.g., [2,11,13,15,17,31,32]), to the best of our knowledge our work is the first to apply it to change identification. Our random forest model outperforms the vote, correctly detecting twice as many change outputs for low false positive rates (Sects. 3.2 to 3.4).
4. **Preventing cluster collapse:** We find that a naive clustering of predicted change outputs leads to cluster collapse, despite using a high threshold to prevent false positives. We then apply constraints to the union-find algorithm underlying our clustering to prevent cluster collapse stemming from frequent, repeated interaction between entities. This prevents large-scale cluster collapse while still enhancing a majority of the involved clusters (Sect. 4).
5. **Assessing impact:** We assess the impact our enhanced clustering has on two exemplary applications: cash-out flows from darknet markets to exchanges and the velocity of bitcoins. We find that the results of such typical longitudinal analyses are off by at least 11% to 14% if they don't fully account for clustering (Sect. 5).

Limitations. Our results in this paper are limited by the availability of "real" (i.e. manually collected and validated) ground truth. As such, our analysis should be treated as a first step towards better understanding the feasibility of change address detection and clustering. However, we do not expect our high-level insights to change significantly in the light of minor corrections to our ground truth data set. We make our data set publicly available to allow other researchers to evaluate it using their own private ground truth or analysis techniques.

Our extraction mechanism relies on change outputs revealed by the multi-input heuristic. This heuristic is effective in practice [12] and widely used, but vulnerable to false positives from techniques like CoinJoin and PayJoin that are intentionally designed to break the heuristic (e.g., [8,19,20,22]). While we take measures to detect CoinJoin transactions and pre-existing cluster collapse, some

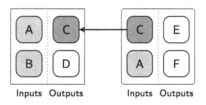

Fig. 2. The multi-input heuristic adds address C to the same cluster as addresses A and B, thereby revealing it as the change address of the first transaction.

errors can remain. Furthermore, entities that more effectively prevent address reuse are less likely to be included in our data set.

2   Building a Ground Truth Data Set

Core Assumption. We focus on the feasibility of detecting the change output in Bitcoin transactions with exactly two spendable outputs, by far the most common type of transaction as of June 2021 (75.8% of all transactions, see Fig. 3). Our core assumption is that one of these outputs is a payment, and the other output receives the change. We call this type of transaction a *standard* transaction, as they are created by typical end-user wallet software.[1]

For transactions with only one output there is no good indicator to directly and reliably determine whether the output belongs to the same user. The transaction may correspond to a user sweeping the balance of their wallet, but the destination address may not be under the same user's control (e.g., it could be managed by a cryptocurrency exchange).

Transactions with more than two outputs are less likely to originate from an ordinary wallet. They may belong to an exchange that batches payouts to multiple users, or correspond to a restructuring of their hot and cold wallets. Our assumption that exactly one of the outputs receives change may not hold here.

Method. Our approach leverages that change outputs are sometimes revealed by the multi-input heuristic at a later point in time due to address reuse. Figure 2 shows how such disclosure may unintentionally happen: a user spends coins at addresses A and B, their wallet directs the change to a new address C. Later, they spend the change at address C along with other coins at address A. At this point, the multi-input heuristic reveals that A, B and C belong to the same user, thus C is the change address in the first transaction. By identifying transactions that have their change revealed in this way, we can build a ground truth set of transactions with known change.

Comparison to Interactive Collection. In contrast to prior deanonymization studies (e.g., [21]) our primary interest is not in identifying address clusters of specific entities but to identify change outputs in their transactions. To achieve

---

[1] Our definition is unrelated to the `isStandard` test in the Bitcoin reference implementation that checks whether a transaction uses common script types.

this interactively, we would need to induce them to make a transaction to an address under our control. This would likely yield inferior ground truth:

- Heterogeneous ground truth requires transactions from a *variety of different use cases, entities and wallets*. We would only be able to directly interact with some types of intermediaries (such as exchanges). Our non-interactive method, instead, is not limited to a small set of intermediaries of our choosing.
- Interactive collection would be hard to *scale* beyond a few hundred transactions, as we would have to individually engage with the intermediaries. Our non-interactive approach instead yields a data set of millions of transactions.
- Interactive collection cannot be done retroactively and is therefore limited to a short, current *time frame*. The resulting data set wouldn't capture shifting patterns over different epochs of Bitcoin's history. Our non-interactive approach however can be applied to Bitcoin's entire history.

Our method has a few important limitations. First, because we extract ground truth data non-interactively from the blockchain, we are not able to fully verify its correctness. Second, our core assumption that exactly one of the outputs belongs to the user may not hold in every scenario. For example, a user sending funds to an address under their control could lead to ambiguous or incorrect labeling of change outputs. We take specific care to remove transactions likely to violate the core assumption in this way. Similarly, there could be instances where none of the outputs is a change output. As this would require a user to make a payment to two different entities using a perfectly matching set of inputs, we expect it to be rare. Third, our ground truth set could be biased towards entities or wallet implementations that are more prone to reuse and merge addresses.

2.1 Data Collection and Overview

We use and build upon BlockSci v0.7 [16], an open-source blockchain analysis framework that provides fast access to blockchain data upon which we implement custom heuristics and extraction procedures. We parse the Bitcoin blockchain until the end of June 2021 (block height 689 256) and create a *base clustering* using the multi-input heuristic (where we heuristically exclude CoinJoin transactions).

As of June 2021, the blockchain contains 91 million transactions with one output, 495 million with two outputs, and 67 million with three or more outputs (see Fig. 3).

We divide the transactions into mutually exclusive categories. Transactions with unspendable OP_RETURN outputs often signal the use of an overlay application that stores metadata in the blockchain [3]. Such transactions may follow unique rules for their construction, potentially making change detection unreliable. Transactions directly reusing an input address have their change output trivially revealed and applying change heuristics is not necessary. We thus focus on transactions where the change has been revealed by the multi-input heuristic and use them to construct our ground truth data set. For the remaining transactions, i.e. those with yet unknown change, we will later predict their change output.

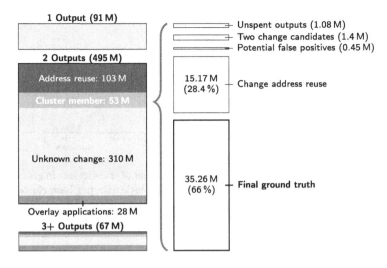

Fig. 3. Breakdown of different types of transactions in the Bitcoin blockchain until end of June 2021. Transactions with two outputs and change revealed through base cluster membership form the basis of our ground truth data, which we further refine to a final selection of 35.26 million transactions.

2.2   Refining the Candidate Set of Ground Truth Transactions

Our candidate set of ground truth transactions consists of transactions with two outputs (ignoring overlay transactions) where no input address is reused for change and where at least one output is in the same base cluster as the inputs. This yields a total of 53.41 million transactions. We further filter them as follows (see Fig. 3 for a visual breakdown).

1. We remove 1.08 million transactions with unspent outputs, as our subsequent analyses rely upon the spending transactions being known.
2. For 0.97 million transactions both outputs are in the same base cluster, violating our core assumption. We remove these transactions. As some base clusters appear to be more likely to produce such transactions, we exclude transactions from base clusters where more than 10% of transactions exhibit this behavior. This removes 0.48 million transactions in 9967 base clusters.
3. We check our base clustering for preexisting cluster collapse, which could create false positives. We remove 0.37 million transactions belonging to the Mt.Gox supercluster (cf. [12]) as well as 0.09 million transactions from one possible instance of cluster collapse detected using address tags from the website WalletExplorer.com.
4. We find many instances where the change address did not appear in the inputs, but had been used before and was known to be the change at the time the transaction was created through multi-input clustering. For example, there are 5.77 million transactions originating from the gambling service "SatoshiDice" that use only a total of 50 change addresses, and 1.27 million transactions from

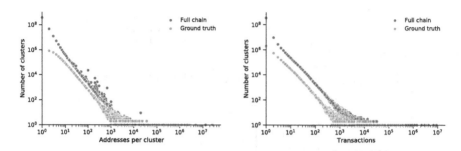

(a) Number of base clusters represented in our ground truth by total address count.

(b) Number of transactions in ground truth and full blockchain per base cluster.

Fig. 4. Address and transaction counts for base clusters in our ground truth.

"LuckyB.it" that use a single change address. For such transactions, applying change address heuristics is never necessary. We remove 15.17 million transactions where the change output was already known at the time the transaction was created.

2.3   Assessing the Final Set of Ground Truth Transactions

Scale and Time Frame. Our final ground truth set of 35.26 million transactions makes up about 7.6% of standard transactions and about 5.4% of all transactions. These percentages are relatively stable over time.

Variety of Included Clusters. Our ground truth includes transactions from 3.6 million base clusters. Figure 4a shows the distribution of address counts of base clusters that are represented with at least one transaction in our ground truth. Our ground truth contains transactions from base clusters of all sizes, giving us confidence that it can be representative of the blockchain overall.

Figure 4b shows the number of transactions per base cluster included in the ground truth compared to the total number of transactions per cluster, showing an overall similar distribution. The largest number of transactions from a single base cluster is 3.49 million, which has 28.85 million transactions in total. We did not find a label for it on WalletExplorer.com. The second highest number of transactions is 383 519, again from an unlabeled cluster.

Transaction Composition and Use of Protocol Features. Compared to standard transactions with yet unknown change, our ground truth transactions have more inputs (38.92% of transactions have three or more inputs, compared to 7.63% for the remaining transactions). This is an expected artifact of our selection method, which relies on transactions with more than one input to reveal change outputs. The share of transactions using SegWit serialization or allowing for fee bumping (RBF) is also higher in the set of remaining transactions.

2.4 Data Release

We make our ground truth data set publicly available to allow other researchers to evaluate it using their own tools and techniques.[2] We believe that making this data public does not create significant new privacy risks: all information necessary to recreate the data set is already publicly available on the Bitcoin blockchain and our method—extracting change outputs revealed by the multi-input heuristic—is easy to reproduce with open-source tools like BlockSci.

3   Predicting Change Outputs

The Bitcoin protocol does not explicitly distinguish between change and spend outputs. However, wallets create change outputs automatically to return surplus value when users make payments. This allows to guess the change using a variety of heuristics targeted at identifying specific wallet or user behavior.

In this paper we evaluate two general types of heuristics. *Universal* heuristics use characteristics of the transaction and change output to determine the change. For example, the address type of a change output is likely to match the address types of the inputs, and rounded output values may indicate spend amounts. *Fingerprint* heuristics determine change based on matching characteristics of the transactions spending the outputs. For example, if a transaction sets a positive locktime to prevent fee sniping [30] and only one of the outputs is spent in a transaction with the same behavior, it is likely the change. We are not aware of any prior work that has evaluated fingerprinting across the range of available protocol characteristics. In total, we use 9 variants of universal heuristics and 17 variants of fingerprinting heuristics (cf. Table 1). To prevent cluster collapse, we explicitly encode our constraint that only one output can be the potential change: if both outputs are change candidates, none is returned by our heuristics.

3.1   Assessing Individual Change Heuristics

In a first step we assess each of the heuristics using our ground truth data set. We find that most heuristics produce few false positives but often only apply to a small share of transactions (most heuristics have true positive rates between 10% to 30%). Figure 5 shows the average number of correct and incorrect predictions per transaction over time, grouped by the type of heuristic.

We see three important trends: first, the universal heuristics drop over time, likely due to rounded values becoming less common. Second, the consistent fingerprint heuristics see a steady uptick in the number of correct votes, enabled by the increasing variety of protocol features available in Bitcoin over time. Finally, there's an uptick in both correct and incorrect fingerprint votes starting in late 2017, when wallet implementations started to switch to SegWit serialization and address formats (e.g., [4, 29]).

---

[2] https://github.com/maltemoeser/address-clustering-data.

Table 1. Change heuristics proposed in the literature and used in this paper.

Heuristic	Notes and limitations	Used
Optimal change: There should be no unnecessary inputs: if one output is smaller than any of the (2+) inputs, it is likely the change. [23,25]	Only applies to transactions with 2+ inputs. We use two variants, one ignoring and one accounting for the fee	✓
Address type: The change likely uses the same address type as the inputs. [16,25]	False positives possible due to protocol upgrades or obfuscation	✓
Power of ten: As purchase amounts may be rounded, and change amounts depend on the input values and fee, it is more likely to have fewer trailing zeros. [16,25]	We use six different variants, which are partially redundant	✓
Shadow address: Many clients automatically generate fresh change addresses, whereas spend addresses may be more easily reused. [1,21]	Modern wallets discourage reuse of receiving addresses. We do not use the heuristic as our ground truth is filtered based on address freshness	x
Consistent fingerprint: The transaction spending a change output should share the same characteristics [5,25]. We use 17 variants based on the following characteristics: – input/output counts and order – version – locktime – serialization format (SegWit) – replace-by-fee (RBF) – transaction fee – input coin age (zero-conf) – address and script types	False positives are possible when a wallet implementation or the protocol change. We only consider characteristics after they are available in the protocol.	✓

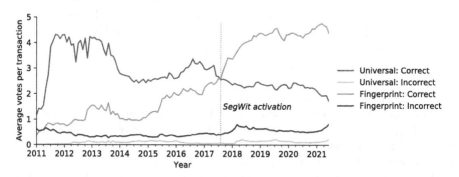

Fig. 5. Average number of correct and uncorrect votes per transaction and type of heuristic in the ground truth data set, over time

For 858 582 transactions no heuristic returned a change output, we remove these from the subsequent analyses. When we later predict change outputs for the remaining standard transactions, we will also exclude transactions where no heuristic determined a potential change output.

While most individual heuristics have high precision, they only cover a subset of transactions each. Furthermore, some heuristics may be more applicable during certain epochs of Bitcoin's history than others. Given the variety of heuristics available to us compared to previous studies (e.g., an evaluation of three change heuristics in [23]), we now consider new ways of combining them.

3.2 Threshold Vote

Figure 5 suggest that a majority of heuristics should generally identify the correct output. However, the number of heuristics returning an potential output varies among transactions, and individual heuristics could be incorrect. We thus compute a threshold vote: if at least t more heuristics vote for output a than for output b, then output a is considered the change. Increasing the threshold t thus allows the analyst to require higher degrees of confidence and thereby lower the risk of cluster collapse.

We apply the threshold vote to our ground truth data set and plot the resulting ROC curve in Fig. 6a (for comparison, we also show the FPR and TPR of each individual heuristic). We achieve an ROC AUC of 0.94, and, for example, a 37.0% true positive rate (TPR) below a false positive rate (FPR) of .1% with a threshold of $t = 7$.

Using a threshold vote may not be ideal as the individual heuristics have varying true positive and false positive rates, and some might be more or less reliable during different periods of Bitcoin's history. Rather, a specific subset of heuristics may provide better classification accuracy. Instead of manually trying different combinations, we opt to use a supervised learning classifier.

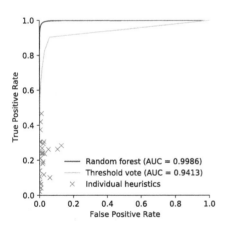
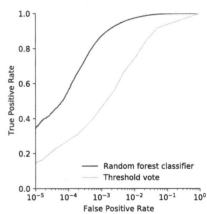

(a) The random forest classifier outperforms the threshold vote and the individual heuristics.

(b) The log scale highlights the difference between the classifiers for low false positive rates (on the same test set).

Fig. 6. ROC curves for predicting change in the ground truth data set using the threshold vote and the random forest classifier, compared to individual heuristics.

3.3   Random Forest Classifier

We decide to use a random forest classifier to predict a transaction's change output. A random forest is an ensemble classifier that trains and aggregates the results of individual decision trees. It is inherently well suited for our data set as it can divide it into homogeneous subsets, for example, based on protocol characteristics or time periods. In an initial comparison of supervised classifiers on our data it also achieved the highest ROC AUC score.

We model an output-based binary classification problem, where every output is either a change (1) or spend (0) output. An individual heuristic may produce one of three outcomes: vote for the output, against the output, or not be able to discern between the outputs. We further add characteristics about each output and corresponding transaction that may allow the random forest to differentiate between distinct types of transactions, or wallets.

As we consider an analyst who works with a static snapshot of the blockchain, we randomly split our data set into 80% training and 20% test set. We use the training set for hyperparameter tuning using 4-fold cross-validation, using the ROC AUC as our scoring metric. To account for the fact that transactions in the same base cluster may be highly similar, we explicitly ensure that all outputs of a base cluster remain in the same set and fold.

Applying the random forest model (RF-1) to the test set, we achieve an AUC of 0.9986 (Fig. 6a). The model is able to detect a higher share of outputs, especially at low false positive rates, compared to the threshold vote.

In Fig. 6b we show the ROC curves of both the threshold vote and the random forest on the same test set, log-transforming the x-axis to highlight the important difference in low false positive rates (to prevent cluster collapse). The random forest achieves much higher true positive rates at low false positive rates, meaning that it correctly identifies the change output in a larger number of transactions. For example, if we target a false positive rate below 0.1%, the threshold vote achieves a TPR of around 39% at a FPR of 0.06%. For the same FPR, the random forest achieves a TPR of 82%, more than twice as high.

We train a second random forest model (RF-2) without the fingerprint heuristics on transactions that contain predictions from the universal heuristics to later predict change in transactions with unspent outputs. Using a similar evaluation strategy as for the full model, the ROC AUC of this model is 0.9981.

To ensure that the performance of our model is not dependent on the particular split and to determine its variance, we repeatedly split our ground truth data set into 80% training and 20% test set 20 times and train the random forest classifier using the previously determined hyperparameters. The average ROC AUC score on the test sets is 0.9974 (SD = 0.0016) for RF-1, and 0.9965 (SD = 0.0036) for RF-2.

We note one caveat: because the base clustering is incomplete, grouping transactions by their base cluster may not fully prevent homogeneous transactions from the same entity to appear in both sets. Yet, some of the variability we see comes from unusual clusters that do not appear in the respective training sets. Other researchers with private, more heterogeneous ground truth may be able to evaluate the degree to which this affects the overall performance of the model.

3.4   Additional Model Validation

We use two data sets to assess the performance of the random forest model trained on the entire ground truth data. First, we use 16 764 transactions identified by Huang et al. [14] as ransom payments related to the Locky and Cerber ransomware. Those payments were identified through clustering, transaction graph analysis and known characteristics of the ransom amounts. After removing non-standard transactions and those with revealed change output, we predict the change output for 11 196 transactions and achieve an AUC of 0.996.

Our second data set is constructed using a GraphSense tagpack [10] that contains 382 tags for addresses of 273 distinct entities (such as exchanges or gambling services) extracted from WalletExplorer.com. We identify each associated cluster and then extract up to 1000 transactions occurring between the individual clusters, assuming that the output belonging to a different cluster is the spend output. After removing transactions with no predictions as well as those with revealed change output, we predict the change output for 268 774 transactions and achieve an AUC of 0.976.

4   Clustering Change Outputs

We now use our random forest models to enhance the base clustering by clustering change outputs. To this end, we predict the change outputs for 310 million standard transactions with yet unknown change. We exclude 10.5 million transactions where no individual heuristic identified a change output and use RF-2 for 19.3 million transactions with unspent outputs.

To keep the likelihood of false positives low, we use a conservative probability threshold of $p_{change} = 0.99$.[3] This gives us 155.56 million change outputs (for 50.24% of transactions). We then enhance the base clustering by merging the base cluster of the inputs with the base cluster of the change address in the order that the transactions appear on the blockchain.

4.1   Naive Merging Leads to Cluster Collapse

Naively clustering the identified change outputs reduces 184.3 million affected base clusters into 39.8 million enhanced clusters. However, it leads to severe cluster collapse: there is one large supercluster, containing the prior Mt. Gox

---

[3] This corresponds to a false positive rate of 0.044% for RF-1. We use a threshold of 0.997 for RF-2 to match the FPR.

supercluster, that contains 223.9 million addresses (a 1596% increase) and 108.2 million transactions (a 2500% increase). Inspecting the 273 clusters labeled by the Graphsense tag pack, we find that 113 have been merged into the supercluster.

4.2   Constraints Prevent Cluster Collapse

The majority of cluster merges involve address clusters from which only a single transaction originated. Here, the impact of a single misclassification is low unless a sequence of such merges collapses multiple larger clusters. At the same time, we observe a small number of merges that combine two large clusters. Imagine two large exchanges whose users frequently interact with each other. A single, misidentified change output could collapse their clusters.

Approach. We use this intuition to constrain which clusters we merge. While change outputs predicted by our model should be clustered, we can use predicted spend outputs to prevent cluster merges: the input cluster should not be clustered into the cluster of the spend. Given the probability p_i returned by the random forest model for output i, we define two thresholds p_{change} and p_{spend} such that if $p_i > p_{change}$ the clusters should be merged (as before), but if $p_i < p_{spend}$ then the clusters should not be merged. In many cases, these constraints will prevent the spend and change output of a transaction to end up in the same cluster (cf. Fig. 7).

This approach is comparable to that by Ermilov, Panov, and Yanovich [9] to use address tags in combination with a probabilistic model to reduce the number of conflicting tags in the final clustering. However, public sources of address tags contain information on a limited number of intermediaries only. Our approach, instead, potentially covers all clusters appearing in the 310 million standard transactions, including those that may be hard to interact with (and identify) manually. Due to the size of our data set we only consider the binary case of preventing any potential conflict, accepting that we may prevent some valid merges in the process.

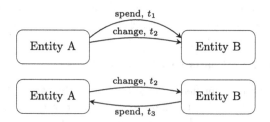

Fig. 7. In the pictured scenarios our constrained clustering prevents the merging of clusters A and B due to conflicting types of payments between them.

We implement a constrained union-find algorithm that prevents merging two clusters related by a predicted spend output. For every spend from cluster c_m to cluster c_n, predicted with $p_i < p_{spend}$, we add a constraint to cluster c_m that it must not be merged with cluster c_n. Before merging two clusters, we the check the constraints of both clusters and skip the merge if it would violate them.

Results. Using the same $p_{change} = 0.99$ and setting $p_{spend} = 0.01$, the constrained clustering prevents 413 608 merges that would have violated constraints and retains 231 340 more individual clusters than the unconstrained clustering.

We find that the constraints prevent the previously observed severe cluster collapse. For example, the constrained clustering does not produce the large Mt. Gox supercluster: the cluster contains only 4.4 million transactions (a 6% increase) and 14.5 million addresses (a 10% increase). Assessing the 273 labeled clusters, there are seven instances where two labeled clusters were merged. We suspect that unusual types of payouts from these services might have triggered the collapse.

The largest cluster in the constrained clustering contains 20.4 million transactions and 40.5 million addresses. Inspecting its composition, we find that it is the result of merging many small clusters (including 9 421 343 single-transaction clusters).

Overall, in at least 90% of merges the smaller cluster created at most one outgoing transaction, which highlights the usefulness of change address clustering to merge small clusters that are missed by multi-input clustering. The constrained clustering specifically prevents some of the largest merges observed in the naive clustering, thereby preventing cluster collapse.

Varying Thresholds. We chose conservative thresholds in order to reduce the possibility of cluster collapse. At the same time, this means that fewer change outputs are being clustered than with lower thresholds. To assess the impact of varying thresholds, we create two additional constrained clusterings, one with a threshold corresponding to a 0.1% FPR and one corresponding to a 1% FPR. At 0.1%, the number of collapsed clusters identified by the Graphsense tag pack increases to 12. At 1%, however, there are already 60 instances of cluster collapse. This highlights the importance of using conservative thresholds to prevent cluster collapse.

5   Impact on Blockchain Analyses

Address clustering is a common preprocessing step before analyzing activity of entities on the blockchain. Using different change heuristics (or none at all) thus affects the outcome of these analyses.

5.1   Increased Cashout Flows from Darknet Markets to Exchanges

We evaluate the impact of our enhanced clustering on analysing payment flows from darknet markets to exchanges. Such analyses are potentially relevant for cybercrime researchers, economists, regulators or law enforcement, highlighting the importance of address clustering for a variety of use cases. To identify relevant intermediaries, we use address tags in the GraphSense tag pack for 117 exchanges and 15 darknet markets.

We extract the value of all outputs in transactions initiated by a darknet market that are sending bitcoins to an exchange, comparing the transaction volume calculated using our base clustering to that of our enhanced clustering. The median increase in value sent across all 15 markets amounts to 11.5%. The total amount of bitcoins flowing from the darknet markets to exchanges increases from BTC 823 839 to BTC 937 330 (a 13.8% increase).

5.2   Improved Estimate of Velocity

We replicate the analysis of velocity conducted by Kalodner et al. [16], an example for a longitudinal analysis of economic activity occurring on the Bitcoin blockchain. For this analysis, clustering is used to remove self-payments of users (such as change outputs), which would artificially inflate estimates of economic activity. The better and more complete our clustering, the more self-payments are removed and hence the lower the estimate will be.

Our refined clustering reduces their estimate of bitcoins moved per day between January 2017 to June 2021 by about 11.9%. We notice that the magnitude is quite similar to the impact on cash-out flows.

5.3   Comparison to the Meiklejohn et al. Heuristic

Finally, we compare our clustering to one created naively using the address reuse-based heuristic presented by Meiklejohn et al. [21], which has subsequently been used in other studies (e.g., [7,24]). While the authors highlight the need for manual intervention to prevent cluster collapse, this is likely infeasible for analysts without in-depth domain knowledge or the right set of tools. The heuristic considers an output to be the change if its address has only been used a single time, based on common wallet behavior to not reuse change addresses.

Applying the heuristic to standard transactions with unknown change produces a supercluster containing 133.1 million transactions and 298.4 million addresses, with 177 tagged clusters ending up in the supercluster. The probability of two addresses being clustered together increases by a factor of 40 compared to our constrained clustering. Looking at the individual predictions, the heuristic differs on 1.9 million transactions out of an overlapping 81.1 million. The total pairwise difference in output values between those predictions amounts to BTC 4.1 million, or USD 38.7 billion, a significant difference in economic activity that might be misattributed due to clustering.

6   Conclusion

Address clustering is an important cornerstone of many blockchain analyses. In this paper, we've taken a first step towards building better models that allow analysts to identify change outputs in transactions, enabled by a new ground truth data set extracted from the Bitcoin blockchain. Evaluating this data set, we find that for most transactions identifying the change address is feasible with high precision. Crucially, our work is the first to apply machine learning to the problem of change identification. We find that our random forest model outperforms a baseline voting mechanism, detecting twice as many change outputs when targeting low false positive rates. Turning to the subsequent clustering of change addresses, we've demonstrated that constraints based on our model's predictions can prevent cluster collapse. Finally, we've explored the impact of our clustering on the outcome of economic analyses. We hope that our work will encourage and enable further research into address clustering.

Extended version: An extended version of this paper is available on arXiv.[4]

Acknowledgement. We thank Rainer Böhme and Kevin Lee for their feedback on an earlier draft of this paper. This work is supported by NSF Award CNS-1651938 and a grant from the Ripple University Blockchain Research Initiative.

References

1. Androulaki, E., Karame, G.O., Roeschlin, M., Scherer, T., Capkun, S.: Evaluating user privacy in bitcoin. In: Sadeghi, A.-R. (ed.) FC 2013. LNCS, vol. 7859, pp. 34–51. Springer, Heidelberg (2013). https://doi.org/10.1007/978-3-642-39884-1_4
2. Bartoletti, M., Pes, B., Serusi, S.: Data mining for detecting bitcoin Ponzi schemes. In: 2018 Crypto Valley Conference on Blockchain Technology (CVCBT), pp. 75–84. IEEE (2018)
3. Bartoletti, M., Pompianu, L.: An analysis of bitcoin OP_RETURN metadata. In: Brenner, M., et al. (eds.) FC 2017. LNCS, vol. 10323, pp. 218–230. Springer, Cham (2017). https://doi.org/10.1007/978-3-319-70278-0_14
4. Bitcoin core 0.16.0. https://bitcoincore.org/en/releases/0.16.0/
5. Blockchair.com API VOL 2.0.76 documentation: Privacy-o-meter. https://blockchair.com/api/docs#link_M6
6. Chang, T.-H., Svetinovic, D.: Improving bitcoin ownership identification using transaction patterns analysis. IEEE Trans. Syst. Man Cybern Syst. **50**(1), 9–20 (2018)
7. Conti, M., Gangwal, A., Ruj, S.: On the economic significance of ransomware campaigns: a bitcoin transactions perspective. Comput. Secur. **79**, 162–189 (2018)
8. Dorier, N.: A simple Payjoin proposal. https://github.com/bitcoin/bips/blob/master/bip-0078.mediawiki
9. Ermilov, D., Panov, M., Yanovich, Y.: Automatic bitcoin address clustering. In: 2017 16th IEEE International Conference on Machine Learning and Applications (ICMLA), pp. 461–466. IEEE (2017)

---

[4] https://arxiv.org/abs/2107.05749.

10. Graphsense public tagpacks. https://github.com/graphsense/graphsense-tagpacks
11. Harlev, M.A., Yin, H,S., Langenheldt, K.C., Mukkamala, R., Vatrapu, R.: Breaking bad: de-anonymising entity types on the bitcoin blockchain using supervised machine learning. In: Proceedings of the 51st Hawaii International Conference on System Sciences (2018)
12. Harrigan, M., Fretter, C.: The unreasonable effectiveness of address clustering. In: 2016 Intl IEEE Conferences on Ubiquitous Intelligence & Computing, Advanced and Trusted Computing, Scalable Computing and Communications, Cloud and Big Data Computing, Internet of People, and Smart World Congress (UIC/ATC/ScalCom/CBDCom/IoP/SmartWorld), pp. 368–373. IEEE (2016)
13. Hu, Y., Seneviratne, S., Thilakarathna, K., Fukuda, K., Seneviratne, A.: Characterizing and detecting money laundering activities on the bitcoin network. arXiv preprint arXiv:1912.12060 (2019)
14. Huang, D.Y., et al.: Tracking ransomware end-to-end. In: IEEE Symposium on Security and Privacy, pp. 618–631. IEEE (2018)
15. Jourdan, M., Blandin, S., Wynter, L., Deshpande, P.: Characterizing entities in the bitcoin blockchain. In: 2018 IEEE International Conference on Data Mining Workshops (ICDMW), pp. 55–62. IEEE (2018)
16. Kalodner, H., et al.: BlockSci: design and applications of a blockchain analysis platform. In: 29th USENIX Security Symposium, pp. 2721–2738 (2020)
17. Lin, Y.-J., Wu, P.-W., Hsu, C.-H., Tu, I.-P., Liao, S.: An evaluation of bitcoin address classification based on transaction history summarization. In: 2019 IEEE International Conference on Blockchain and Cryptocurrency (ICBC), pp. 302–310. IEEE (2019)
18. Di Francesco, D., Maesa, A.M., Ricci, L.: Data-driven analysis of bitcoin properties: exploiting the users graph. Int. J. Data Sci. Anal. 6(1), 63–80 (2018)
19. Maxwell, G.: CoinJoin: bitcoin Privacy for the Real World (2013). https://bitcointalk.org/index.php?topic=279249.0
20. Meiklejohn, S., Orlandi, C.: Privacy-enhancing overlays in bitcoin. In: Brenner, M., Christin, N., Johnson, B., Rohloff, K. (eds.) FC 2015. LNCS, vol. 8976, pp. 127–141. Springer, Heidelberg (2015). https://doi.org/10.1007/978-3-662-48051-9_10
21. Meiklejohn, S., et al.: A fistful of bitcoins: characterizing payments among men with no names. In: Internet Measurement Conference, pp. 127–140. ACM (2013)
22. Möser, M., Böhme, R.: The price of anonymity: empirical evidence from a market for bitcoin anonymization. J. Cybersecur. 3(2), 127–135 (2017)
23. Nick, J.D.: Data-driven de-anonymization in bitcoin (2015)
24. Parino, F., Beiró, M.G., Gauvin, L.: Analysis of the bitcoin blockchain: socioeconomic factors behind the adoption. EPJ Data Sci. 7(1), 38 (2018)
25. Privacy - bitcoin wiki. https://en.bitcoin.it/Privacy
26. Reid, F., Harrigan, M.: An analysis of anonymity in the Bitcoin system. In: Altshuler, Y., Elovici, Y., Cremers, A., Aharony, N., Pentland, A. (eds.) Security and Privacy in Social Networks. Springer, New York (2013). https://doi.org/10.1007/978-1-4614-4139-7_10
27. Ron, D., Shamir, A.: Quantitative analysis of the full bitcoin transaction graph. In: Sadeghi, A.-R. (ed.) FC 2013. LNCS, vol. 7859, pp. 6–24. Springer, Heidelberg (2013). https://doi.org/10.1007/978-3-642-39884-1_2
28. Schatzmann, J.E., Haslhofer, B.: Bitcoin trading is irrational! an analysis of the disposition effect in bitcoin. arXiv preprint arXiv:2010.12415 (2020)
29. SegWit FAQ. https://help.coinbase.com/en/pro/getting-started/general-crypto-education/segwit-faq

30. Todd, P.: Discourage fee sniping with nLockTime #2340 (2014). https://github. com/bitcoin/bitcoin/pull/2340
31. Toyoda, K., Ohtsuki, T., Mathiopoulos, P.T.: Multi-class bitcoin-enabled service identification based on transaction history summarization. In: 2018 IEEE International Conference on Internet of Things (iThings) and IEEE Green Computing and Communications (GreenCom) and IEEE Cyber, Physical and Social Computing (CPSCom) and IEEE Smart Data (SmartData), pp. 1153–1160. IEEE (2018)
32. Weber, M., et al.: Anti-money laundering in bitcoin: experimenting with graph convolutional networks for financial forensics. arXiv preprint arXiv:1908.02591 (2019)
33. Zhang, Y., Wang, J., Luo, J.: Heuristic-based address clustering in bitcoin. IEEE Access **8**, 210582–210591 (2020)

Incentives

ABSNFT: Securitization and Repurchase Scheme for Non-Fungible Tokens Based on Game Theoretical Analysis

Hongyin Chen[1], Yukun Cheng[2(✉)], Xiaotie Deng[1(✉)], Wenhan Huang[3], and Linxuan Rong[4]

[1] Center on Frontiers of Computing Studies, Peking University, Beijing, China
{chenhongyin,xiaotie}@pku.edu.cn
[2] Suzhou University of Science and Technology, Suzhou, China
ykcheng@amss.ac.cn
[3] Department of Computer Science, Shanghai Jiao Tong University, Shanghai, China
rowdark@sjtu.edu.cn
[4] Washington University in St. Louis, St. Louis, MO, USA
l.rong@wustl.edu

Abstract. The Non-Fungible Token (NFT) is viewed as one of the important applications of blockchain technology. Currently NFT has a large market scale and multiple practical standards, however several limitations of the existing mechanism in NFT markets still exist. This work proposes a novel securitization and repurchase scheme for NFT to overcome these limitations. We first provide an Asset-Backed Securities (ABS) solution to settle the limitations of non-fungibility of NFT. Our securitization design aims to enhance the liquidity of NFTs and enable Oracles and Automatic Market Makers (AMMs) for NFTs. Then we propose a novel repurchase protocol for a participant owing a portion of NFT to repurchase other shares to obtain the complete ownership. As the participants may strategically bid during the acquisition process, we formulate the repurchase process as a Stackelberg game to explore the equilibrium prices. We also provide solutions to handle difficulties at market such as budget constraints and lazy bidders.

Keywords: Non-Fungible Token · Asset-Backed Securities · Blockchain · Stackelberg game

1 Introduction

Ever since the birth of the first piece of Non-Fungible Token (NFT) [11,23], the world has witnessed an extraordinarily fast growth of its popularity. NFT markets, especially Opensea[1], have prospered with glamorous statistics of a total of over 80 million pieces of NFTs on the platform and a total transaction volume of over 10 billion US dollars.[2]

---

[1] Opensea Platform. https://opensea.io/.

[2] Data source from Opensea https://opensea.io/about.

© International Financial Cryptography Association 2022
I. Eyal and J. Garay (Eds.): FC 2022, LNCS 13411, pp. 407–425, 2022.
https://doi.org/10.1007/978-3-031-18283-9_20

NFT is a type of cryptocurrency that each token is non-fungible. The first standard of NFT, ERC-721 [10], gives support to a type of tokens that each has a unique identifier. The feature of uniqueness makes NFTs usually be tied to specific assets, such as digital artwork and electronic pets. Some researches also explore the application of NFT in patent, copyright and physical assets [5,20].

The technology of NFT has also advanced rapidly. Besides ERC-721, ERC-1155 [9] is also a popular standard of NFT. ERC-1155 is a flexible standard that supports multiple series of tokens, each series is a type of NFT or Fungible Token (FT). NFT protocols are usually derived by smart contracts in a permissionless blockchain, but there are now some NFT designs for permissioned blockchains [12].

Although NFT has a large market scale and multiple practical standards, there still exist several limitations in NFT market, one of which is the poor liquidity. The issue of liquidity is crucial in both De-fi and traditional finance. Usually, if assets have higher liquidity, they would have higher trading volume, and further have higher prices [2]. Particularly, in blockchain, the liquidity of Fungible Tokens, such as wBTC and ETH, has been enhanced by Oracles [17] and Automated Market Makers (AMMs) [3] like Uniswap and Sushiswap. However, the non-fungibility property of NFT leads to poor liquidity. For this reason, the existing NFT marketplace usually uses the English Auction or Dutch Auction to trade NFTs [14].

- Firstly, Non-Fungibility means indivisible. As the NFT series with the highest market value, CryptoPunks has an average trading price of 189 Eth[3], which is worth more than 790,000 U.S. dollars[4]. If bitcoins are expensive, we can trade 0.01 bitcoins, but we can't trade 0.01 CryptoPunks. As a result, the liquidity of CryptoPunks is significantly lower than other NFT series. Therefore, the liquidity for NFTs with high values is limited.
- Secondly, shared ownership is not allowed because of Non-Fungibility. Therefore, it's difficult to reduce risk and enhance the liquidity of NFTs through portfolios. What's more, Some NFT assets such as patents need financial support to foster the process of development. They would require a means to attract finance. The above two limitations also exist in traditional settings.
- Thirdly, the feature of non-fungible makes NFT unable to be directly applied in Oracles [17] and Automated Market Makers (AMMs) [3], which are important methods of pricing in the blockchain. This is because fungibility is the basis of Oracles and AMMs.

1.1 Main Contributions

We present ABSNFT, a securitization and repurchase scheme for NFT, which overcomes the above-mentioned limitations from the following three aspects.

---

[3] 90-day average before November 22, 2021. Data source from https://opensea.io/activity/cryptopunks.

[4] The price of Eth here refers to the data on November 22, 2021. https://etherscan.io/chart/etherprice.

- Firstly, we propose an Asset-Backed Securities (ABS) [4] solution to settle the limitations of non-fungibility of NFT. We design a smart contract including three parts: NFT Securitization Process, NFT Repurchase Process, and NFT Restruction Process. In our smart contract, a complete NFT can be securitized into fungible securities, and fungible securities can be reconstructed into a complete NFT.

  The securitization process manages to resolve the majority of issues the current NFT application is confronted with: the securities of NFT have lower values compared to the complete one before securitization, which increases market liquidity; securities could act as fungible tokens that can be applied in Oracles and AMMs; the investment risk is being reduced dramatically; financing is possible since securities can belong to different owners.
- Secondly, we design a novel repurchase process based on Stackelberg game [21], which provides a mechanism to repurchase NFT securities at a fair price. The NFT Repurchase Process can be triggered by the participant who owns more than half of the securities of the NFT. We analyze the Stackelberg Equilibrium (SE) in three different settings and get good theoretical results.
- Thirdly, we propose solutions to the budget constraints and lazy bidders, which make good use of the decentralization of blockchain. We propose a protocol that allows participants to accept financial support in the repurchase game to reduce the influence of budget constraints. We also propose two solutions for players that might not bid in the game, which prevent the game process from being blocked and protect the utility of lazy bidders.

1.2   Related Works

In financial research, there are two well-studied repurchase scenarios, repurchase agreement and stock repurchase.

Repurchase agreement is a short-term transaction between two parties in which one party borrows cash from the other by pledging a financial security as collateral [1]. The former party is called the security issuer, and the latter party is called the investors. To avoid the failure of liquidation, the security issuer needs to mortgage assets or credit. An instance of such work from the Federal Reserve Bank of New York Quarterly Review introduces and analyzes a repurchase agreement for federal funds [16]. The Quarterly Review describes the repurchase agreement as "involving little risk", as either parties' interests are been safeguarded.

Studies of repurchase agreement cannot be directly applied to our topic. The key point is that the problem we are studying is not to mortgage NFTs to obtain cash flow, but to securitize NFTs to overcome the restrictions of non-fungibility. What's more, the repurchase prices are usually derived from the market model. But the NFT market is not as mature as the financial market, which makes it hard to calculate a fair price through the market model.

Stock repurchase refers to the behavior that listed companies repurchase stocks from the stockholders at a certain price [8]. Usually, stock repurchase is adopted to release positive signals to the stock market and doesn't aim to repurchase all stocks. However, NFTs usually need to be complete without securities in cross-chain scenarios.

Oxygen [18] is a decentralized platform that supports repurchase agreement based on digital assets. In Oxygen, users can borrow cash flow or assets with good liquidity by pledging assets with poor liquidity. The repurchase prices and the evaluations of assets are provided by a decentralized exchange, Serum [19]. However, such pricing method is dangerous because decentralized exchanges are very vulnerable to attacks like flash loans [22].

ABSNFT is distinguished among all these works because it adapts well to the particularities of NFT market and blockchain.

– Firstly, the securities in ABSNFT represent property rights rather than creditor's rights. Investors do not need to worry that the cash flow or the mortgaged assets of the securities issuer may not cover the liquidation, which may be risky in a repurchase agreement. What's more, any investor can trigger a repurchase process as long as he owns more than half of the shares.
– Secondly, the repurchase process of ABSNFT doesn't depend on market models or exchanges. The repurchase price is decided by the bids given by participants, and every participant won't get negative utility if he bids truthfully.
– Thirdly, ABSNFT has well utilized the benefits of blockchain technology. The tradings of securities are driven by the smart contract. The operations of ABSNFT don't rely on centralized third-party and are available 24×7 for participants.

The rest of the paper is arranged as follows. Section 2 introduces the NFT securitization process. In Sect. 3 and Sect. 4, we study the two-player repurchase game in a single round and the repeated setting. In Sect. 5, we analyze the repurchase game with multiple leaders and one follower. In Sect. 6, we discuss the solution to the issues with budget constraints and lazy bidders in the blockchain setting. In the last section, we give a summary of ABSNFT and propose some future works.

2   NFT Securitization and Repurchase Scheme

In this section, we would like to introduce the general framework of the smart contract, denoted by C_{NFT}, which includes the securitization process, the trading process, repurchase process and restruction process for a given NFT.

2.1   Basic Setting of NFT Smart Contract

There are two kinds of NFTs discussed in this paper.

– **Complete NFT.** Complete NFTs are conventional non-fungible tokens, which appear in blockchain systems as a whole. Each complete NFT has a unique token ID. We use $CNFT(id)$ to denote one complete NFT with token ID of id.

– **Securitized NFT.** Securitized NFTs are the *Asset Based Securities* of complete NFTs. A complete NFT may be securitized into an amount of securitized units. All units of securitized NFTs from a complete NFT $CNFT(id)$ have the same ID, associated with the ID of $CNFT(id)$. Thus we denote the securitized NFT by $SNFT(id)$. In our smart contract, all securitized NFTs can be freely traded.

In our setting, all complete NFTs and securitized NFTs belong to one smart contract, denoted by C_{NFT}. Although the securitized NFTs are similar to the fungible tokens in ERC-1155 standard [9], our smart contract C_{NFT} is actually quite different from ERC-1155 standard. That is because all securitized NFTs in C_{NFT}, associated to one complete NFT, have the same ID, while different NFTs and different fungible tokens generally have different token IDs in ERC-1155 standard. Therefore, our C_{NFT} is based on ERC-721 standard [10], and the complete NFTs are just the NFTs defined in ERC-721. Table 1 lists all functions in C_{NFT}.

Table 1. The key functions of C_{NFT}

Function name	Function utility
$CNFTownerOf(id)$	Return the address of the owner of $CNFT(id)$
$CNFTtransferFrom$ $(addr1, addr2, id)$	Transfer the ownership of $CNFT(id)$ from address $addr1$ to address $addr2$. Only the owner of $CNFT(id)$ has the right to trigger this function
$SNFTtotalSupply(id)$	Return the total amount of $SNFT(id)$ in contract C_{NFT}
$SNFTbalanceOf(addr, id)$	Return the amount of $SNFT(id)$ owned by address $addr$
$SNFTtransferFrom$ $(addr1, addr2, id, amount)$	Transfer the ownership of $amout$ unit of $SNFT(id)$ from address $addr1$ to address $addr2$
$CNFTsecuritization$ $(addr, id, amount)$	Freeze $CNFT(id)$, and then transfer $amout$ units of $SNFT(id)$ to address $addr$. Only the owner of $CNFT(id)$ can trigger this function
$CNFTrestruction(addr, id)$	Burn all $SNFT(id)$, unfreeze $CNFT(id)$, and then transfer the ownership of $CNFT(id)$ to address $addr$. Only the one who owns all amounts of $SNFT(id)$ can trigger this function
$Repurchase(id)$	Start the repurchase process of $SNFT(id)$. Only the one who owns more than half amounts of $SNFT(id)$ can trigger this function

The task of smart contract C_{NFT} includes securitizing complete NFTs, trading the securitized NFTs among participants, and restructing complete NFT after repurchasing all securitized NFTs with the same ID. Because the transactions of securitized NFTs are similar to those of fungible tokens, we omit the trading process here and introduce NFT securitization process, NFT repurchase process and NFT restruction process in the subsequent three subsections respectively.

2.2 NFT Securitization Process

This subsection focuses on the issue of Asset-Backed Securities for Complete NFTs. We propose Algorithm 1 to demonstrate the NFT securitization process. To be specific, once $CNFTsecuritization(addr, id, amount)$ is triggered by the owner of $CNFT(id)$, the $amount$ units of securitized NFTs are generated and transferred to address $addr$ in Line 2–4; then the ownership of $CNFT(id)$ would be transferred to a fixed address $FrozenAddr$ in Line 5.

It is worth to note that if $Repurchase(id)$ has not been triggered, securitized NFTs can be freely traded in blockchain system.

Algorithm 1. NFT Securitization

1: **procedure** CNFTSECURITIZATION   ▷ Triggered by $sender$
2:     $require(sender == CNFTownerOf(id))$ ▷ $sender$ is the owner of $CNFT(id)$
3:     $totalSupply[id] \leftarrow amount$ ▷ Record the total amount of units of $SNFT(id)$
4:     $tokenBalance[id][addr] \leftarrow amount$ ▷ the $amount$ units $SNFT(id)$ are generated and transferred to address $addr$
5:     $CNFTtransferFrom(sender, FrozenAddr, id)$ ▷ Freeze $CNFT(id)$

2.3 NFT Repurchase Process

After the securitization process, a complete NFT $CNFT(id)$ is securitized into M units of $SNFT(id)$. Suppose that there are $k+1$ participants, $N = \{N_0, \cdots, N_k\}$, each owning m_i units of $SNFT(id)$. Thus $\sum_{i=0}^{k} m_i = M$. If there is one participant, denoted by N_0, owing more than half of $SNFT(id)$ (i.e. $m_0 > \frac{1}{2}M$), then he can trigger the repurchase process by trading with each N_i, $i = 1, \cdots, k$. Majority is a natural requirement for a participant to trigger a repurchase mechanism, and thus our repurchase mechanism sets the threshold as $\frac{1}{2}$. In addition, if the trigger condition is satisfied (i.e., someone holds more than half of shares), then there must be exactly one participant who can trigger the repurchase mechanism. This makes our mechanism easy to implement. Our mechanism also works well if the threshold is larger than $\frac{1}{2}$.

Let v_i be N_i's value estimate for one unit of $SNFT(id)$ and p_i be the bid provided by N_i, $i = 0, \cdots, k$, in a deal. Specially, our smart contract C_{NFT} requires each value $v_i \in \{1, \cdots\}$ and bid $p_i \in \{0, 1, \cdots\}$ to discretize our analysis. We assume that the estimation of v_i is private information of N_i, not known to others. The main reason is that most of NFT objects, such as digital art pieces, would be appreciated differently in different eyes. Participants may have different opinions about a same NFT, which makes each of them has a private value v_i. Without loss of generality, we assume that N_i's private value on the complete NFT is $M \cdot v_i$.

Mechanism 1 (Repurchase Mechanism). *Suppose participant N_0 owes more than half of $SNFT(id)$ and triggers the repurchase mechanism. For the repurchase between N_0 and N_i, $i = 1, \cdots, k$,*

- *if $p_0 \geq p_i$, then N_0 successfully repurchases m_i units of $SNFT(id)$ from N_i at the unit price of $\frac{p_0 + p_i}{2}$;*
- *if $p_0 \leq p_i - 1$, then N_0 fails to repurchase, and then he shall sell m_i units of $SNFT(id)$ to N_i. The unit price that N_i pays is $\frac{p_0 + p_i}{2}$, and N_0 obtains a discounted revenue $\frac{p_0 + p_i - 1}{2}$ for each unit of $SNFT(id)$.*

Mechanism 1 requires that the repurchase process only happens between N_0 and N_i, $i = 1, \cdots, k$. If $p_0 \geq p_i$, then N_0 successfully repurchases m_i units of $SNFT(id)$ from N_i, and the utilities of N_0 and N_i are

$$U_0^i(p_0, p_i) = m_i(v_0 - \frac{p_0 + p_i}{2}), \ U_i(p_0, p_i) = m_i(\frac{p_0 + p_i}{2} - v_i), \ if \ p_0 \geq p_i. \quad (1)$$

If $p_0 < p_i$, then N_0 fails to repurchase from N_i, and the utilities of N_0 and N_i are

$$U_0^i(p_0, p_i) = m_i(\frac{p_0 + p_i - 1}{2} - v_0), \ U_i(p_0, p_i) = m_i(v_i - \frac{p_0 + p_i}{2}), \ if \ p_0 \leq p_i - 1. \quad (2)$$

All participants must propose their bids rationally under Mechanism 1. If the bid p_0 is too low, N_0 would face the risk of repurchase failure. Thus, the securities of N_0 would be purchased by other participants at a low price, and N_0's utility may be negative. Similarly, if bid p_i of N_i, $i = 1, \cdots, k$, is too high, N_i would purchase securities with an extra high price and get negative utility. However, if a participant bids truthfully, he always obtains non-negative utility.

During the repurchase process, the key issue for each participant is how to bid p_i, $i = 0, \cdots, k$, based on its own value estimation. To solve this issue, we would model the repurchase process as a stackelberg game to explore the equilibrium pricing solution in the following Sects. 3 to 5.

2.4   NFT Restruction Process

Once one participant successfully repurchases all securitized NFTs, he has the right to trigger $CNFTrestruction(addr, id)$, shown in Algorithm 2, to burn these securitized NFTs in Line 3 to 4 and unfreeze $CNFT(id)$, such that the ownership of $CNFT(id)$ would be transferred from address $FrozenAddr$ to this participant's address $addr$ in Line 5.

After NFT restruction, all $SNFT(id)$ are burnt, and $CNFT(id)$ is unfrozen. The owner of $CNFT(id)$ has the right to securitize it or trade it as a whole.

3   Two-Player Repurchase Stackelberg Game

This section discusses the repurchase process for a two-player scenario. To be specific, in the two-player scenario, when a player owns more than half of $SNFT(id)$,

---

Algorithm 2. NFT Restruction

1: **procedure** CNFTRESTRUCTION   ▷ Triggered by *sender*
2:     $require(tokenBalance[id][sender] == totalSupply[id])$ ▷ *sender* should be the
       owner of all $SNFT(id)$
3:     $totalSupply[id] \leftarrow 0$ ▷ Burn all $SNFT(id)$
4:     $tokenBalance[id][sender] \leftarrow 0$ ▷ Burn all $SNFT(id)$
5:     $CNFTtransferFrom(FrozenAddr, addr, id)$ ▷ Unfreeze $CNFT(id)$

---

denoted by N_0, he will trigger the repurchase process with another player N_1. To explore the optimal bidding strategy for both players, we model the repurchase process as a two-stage Stackelberg game, in which N_1 acts as the leader to set its bid p_1 in Stage I, and N_0, as the follower, decides its bid p_0 in Stage II. Recall that all bids and all values are in $\{0, 1, \cdots\}$.

(1) N_0's *bidding strategy in Stage II:* Given the bid of p_1, set by N_1 in Stage I, N_0 decides its bid to maximize its utility, which is given as:

$$U_0(p_0, p_1) = \begin{cases} m_1(v_0 - \frac{p_0+p_1}{2}) & if\ p_0 \geq p_1; \\ m_1(\frac{p_0+p_1-1}{2} - v_0) & if\ p_0 \leq p_1 - 1. \end{cases} \tag{3}$$

(2) N_1's *bidding strategy in Stage I:* Once obtain the optimal bid $p_0^*(p_1)$ of N_0 in Stage II, which is dependent on p_1, N_1 goes to compute the optimal bid p_1^* by maximizing his utility function $max_{p_1} U_1(p_0^*(p_1), p_1)$, where

$$U_1(p_0, p_1) = \begin{cases} m_1(\frac{p_0+p_1}{2} - v_1) & if\ p_1 \leq p_0; \\ m_1(v_1 - \frac{p_0+p_1}{2}) & if\ p_1 \geq p_0 + 1. \end{cases} \tag{4}$$

3.1   Analysis Under Complete Information

(1) **Best response of N_0 in Stage II.** Given the bid p_1 provided by N_1, in Stage II, N_0 shall determine the best response $p_0^*(p_1)$ to maximize his utility.

Lemma 1. *In the two-stage Stackelberg game for repurchase process, if the bid p_1 is given in Stage I, the best response of N_0 in Stage II is*

$$p_0^*(p_1) = \begin{cases} p_1 - 1 & if\ p_1 \geq v_0 + 1 \\ p_1 & if\ p_1 \leq v_0 \end{cases} \tag{5}$$

Proof. According to (3), U_0 is monotonically increasing when $p_0 \leq p_1 - 1$ and monotonically decreasing when $p_0 \geq p_1$. So $p_0^*(p_1) \in \{p_1 - 1, p_1\}$. In addition, when $p_1 \geq v_0 + 1$, we have

$$U_0(p_0 = p_1, p_1) = m_1(v_0 - p_1) < 0 \leq m_1(p_1 - 1 - v_0) = U_0(p_0 = p_1 - 1, p_1).$$

It implies that the best response of N_0 is $p_0^*(p_1) = p_1 - 1$ if $p_1 \geq v_0 + 1$. When $p_1 \leq v_0$, we have

$$U_0(p_0 = p_1, p_1) = m_1(v_0 - p_1) \geq 0 > m_1(p_1 - 1 - v_0) = U_0(p_0 = p_1 - 1, p_1).$$

So under the situation of $p_0 \leq v_0$, the best response of N_0 is $p_0^*(p_1) = p_1$.   □

(2) **The optimal strategy of N_1 in Stage I.** The leader N_1 would like to optimize his bidding strategy to maximize his utility shown in (4).

Lemma 2. *In the two-stage Stackelberg game for repurchase process, the optimal bidding strategy for the leader N_1 is*

$$p_1^* = \begin{cases} v_0 & if \ v_1 \leq v_0 \\ v_0 + 1 & if \ v_1 \geq v_0 + 1. \end{cases} \tag{6}$$

Proof. Based on Lemma 1, we have

$$U_1(p_0^*(p_1), p_1) = \begin{cases} m_1(p_1 - v_1) & if \ p_1 \leq v_0; \\ m_1(v_1 - p_1 + \frac{1}{2}) & if \ p_1 \geq v_0 + 1. \end{cases}$$

Thus U_1 is monotonically increasing when $p_1 \leq v_0$ and monotonically decreasing when $p_1 \geq v_0 + 1$, indicating the optimal bidding strategy $p_1^* \in \{v_0, v_0 + 1\}$. In addition, for the case of $v_0 \geq v_1$, if $p_1 = v_0$, then $p_0^*(p_1) = p_1 = v_0$ by Lemma 1 and $U_1(v_0, v_0) = m_1(v_0 - v_1) \geq 0$. On the other hand, if $p_1 = v_0 + 1$, then $p_0^*(p_1) = p_1 - 1 = v_0$ by Lemma 1 and $U_1(v_0, v_0 + 1) = m_1(v_1 - v_0 - \frac{1}{2}) < 0$. Therefore, $U_1(v_0, v_0) > U_1(v_0, v_0 + 1)$, showing the optimal bidding strategy of N_1 is $p_1^* = v_0$ when $v_0 \geq v_1$. Similarly, for the case of $v_0 \leq v_1 - 1$, we can conclude that $p_1^* = v_0 + 1$. This lemma holds.   □

Combining Lemmas 1 and 2, the following theorem can be derived directly.

Theorem 1. *When $v_0 \geq v_1$, there is exactly one Stackelberg equilibrium where $p_1^* = p_0^* = v_0$. And when $v_0 \leq v_1 - 1$, there is exactly one Stackelberg equilibrium where $p_0^* = v_0$, $p_1^* = v_0 + 1$.*

Furthermore, the following theorem demonstrates the relation between Stackelberg equilibrium and Nash equilibrium, whose proof is shown in the full version [6] of this paper.

Theorem 2. *Each Stackelberg equilibrium in Theorem 1 is also a Nash equilibrium.*

3.2   Analysis of Bayesian Stackelberg Equilibrium

In the previous subsection, the Stackelberg equilibrium is deduced based on the complete information about the value estimate v_0 and v_1. However, the value estimates may be private in practice, which motivates us to study the Bayesian Stackelberg game with incomplete information. In this proposed game, although the value estimate v_i is not known to others, except for itself N_i, $i = 0, 1$, the probability distribution of each V_i is public to all. Here we use V_i to denote the random variable of value estimate. Based on the assumption that all V_i are integers, we continue to assume that each N_i's value estimate V_i has finite integer states, denoted by $v_i^1, v_i^2, \cdots, v_i^{k_i}$, and its discrete probability distribution is $Pro(V_i = v_i^l) = P_i^l$, $l = 1, \cdots, k_i$, and $\sum_{l=1}^{k_i} P_i^l = 1$, $i = 0, 1$.

(1) **Best response of N_0 in Stage II.** Because v_0 is deterministic to N_0, and p_1 is given by N_1 in Stage I, Lemma 1 still holds, so

$$p_0^*(p_1) = \begin{cases} p_1 - 1 & if \ p_1 \geq v_0 + 1; \\ p_1 & if \ p_1 \leq v_0. \end{cases}$$

(2) **Optimal bidding strategy of N_1 in Stage I.** By Lemma 1, we have

$$U_1(p_0^*(p_1), p_1) = \begin{cases} m_1(p_1 - v_1) & if \ p_1 \leq v_0; \\ m_1(v_1 - p_1 + \frac{1}{2}) & if \ p_1 \geq v_0 + 1. \end{cases}$$

Based on the probability distribution of V_0, the expected utility of U_1 is:

$$E_1(p_1) = \sum_{v_0^l \geq p_1} m_1(p_1 - v_1)P_0^l + \sum_{v_0^l \leq p_1 - 1} m_1(v_1 - p_1 + \frac{1}{2})P_0^l \quad (7)$$

To be specific, if $p_1 \geq v_0^{k_0} + 1$, then $E_1(p_1) = m_1(v_1 - p_1 + \frac{1}{2})$, and N_1 obtains his maximal expected utility at $p_1^* = v_0^{k_0} + 1$. If $p_1 \leq v_0^1$, then $E_1(p_1) = m_1(p_1 - v_1)$, and N_1 obtains his maximal expected utility at $p_1^* = v_0^1$. If there exists an index l, such that $v_0^{l-1} < p_1 \leq v_0^l$, $l = 2, \cdots, k_0$, then

$$E_1(p_1) = \sum_{h=1}^{l-1} m_1(v_1 - p_1 + \frac{1}{2})P_0^h + \sum_{h=l}^{k_0} m_1(p_1 - v_1)P_0^h.$$

Therefore, N_1 can obtain his maximal expected utility at $p_1^* = v_0^l$, when $\sum_{h=l}^{k_0} P_0^h \geq \sum_{h=1}^{l-1} P_0^h$. Otherwise, N_1's maximal expected utility is achieved at $p_1^* = v_0^{l-1} + 1$. Hence, the optimal bid $p_1^* \in \{v_0^l, v_0^l + 1\}_{l=1,\cdots,k_0}$.

Theorem 3. *There is a Stackelberg equilibrium in the Bayesian Stackelberg game.*

(1) If $p_1^* \leq v_0$, then $p_0 = p_1^*$ and $p_1 = p_1^*$ is a Stackelberg equilibrium.
(2) If $p_1^* \geq v_0 + 1$, then $p_0 = p_1^* - 1$ and $p_1 = p_1^*$ is a Stackelberg equilibrium.

4   Repeated Two-Player Stackelberg Game

This section would extend the study of the one-round Stackelberg game in the previous section to the repeated Stackelberg game. Before our discussion, we construct the basic model of a repeated two-player Stackelberg game by introducing the necessary notations.

Definition 1. *Repeated two-player Stackelberg repurchase game is given by a tuple $G_r = (M, N, V, S, L, P, U)$, where:*

- $N = \{N_0, N_1\}$ is the set of two participants. The role of being a leader or a follower may change in the whole repeated process.

- M is the total amount of $SNFT(id)$. W.l.o.g., we assume that M is odd, such that one of $\{N_0, N_1\}$ must have more than half of $SNFT(id)$.
- $V = \{v_0, v_1\}$ is the set of participants' value estimates. Let $v_i \in \{1, 2, 3, \cdots\}$ be an integer.
- $S = \{s^1, s^2, \cdots, s^t, z\}$ is the set of sequential states. $s^j = (m_0^j, m_1^j)$, in which $m_0^j, m_1^j > 0$ are integers, $m_0^j + m_1^j = M$, and $m_0^j \neq m_1^j$ because M is odd. $z \in Z = \{z_0, z_1\}$ represents the terminal state, where $z_0 = (M, 0), z_1 = (0, M)$. If the sequential states are infinity, then $t = +\infty$. Let us denote $(m_0^{t+1}, m_1^{t+1}) = z$.
- $L = \{l^1, l^2, \cdots, l^t\}$ is the set of sequential leaders, where l^j is the leader in the j-th round. To be specific, $l^j = N_1$, if $m_0^j > m_1^j$; otherwise, $l^j = N_0$. It shows the participant who triggers the repurchase process in each round should be the follower.
- $P_i = \{p_i^1, p_i^2, \cdots, p_i^t\}$ is the set of sequential prices bidded by N_i, $p_i^j \in \{0, 1, 2, \cdots\}$.
- $U_i : S \times P_0 \times P_1 \to R$ is the utility function of player N_i in a single round. The detailed expressions of U_i will be proposed later.

In practice, v_i, $i = 0, 1$, may not be common information. However, we can extract them from the historical interaction data of the repeated game by online learning [24] or reinforcement learning [15] methods. Therefore, we mainly discuss the case with complete information in this section.

Repeated Stackelberg Game Procedure. Repeated game G_r consists of several rounds, and each round contains two stages. In the j-th round,

- In **Stage I**, the leader provides a bid $p_i^j \in \{0, 1, \cdots\}$.
- In **Stage II**, the follower provides a bid $p_{1-i}^j \in \{0, 1, \cdots\}$.
- If $p_i^j \leq p_{1-i}^j$, N_{1-i} successfully purchased m_i^j units of $SNFT(id)$ from N_i at the unit price of $\frac{p_i^j + p_{1-i}^j}{2}$.
- If $p_i^j \geq p_{1-i}^j + 1$, N_i purchases m_i^j units of $SNFT(id)$ from N_{1-i} at the unit price of $\frac{p_i^j + p_{1-i}^j}{2}$. And N_{1-i} only obtains a discounted revenue $m_i^j \cdot \frac{p_i^j + p_{1-i}^j - 1}{2}$.

The whole game process is shown in Fig. 1. Based on the description for the j-th round of repeated game, the utilities of N_0 and N_1 are

$$U_0(m_0^j, m_1^j, p_0^j, p_1^j) = \begin{cases} (v_0 - (p_0^j + p_1^j)/2)m_1^j & \text{if } p_0^j \geq p_1^j, m_0^j > m_1^j; \\ ((p_0^j + p_1^j - 1)/2 - v_0)m_1^j & \text{if } p_0^j < p_1^j, m_0^j > m_1^j; \\ ((p_0^j + p_1^j)/2 - v_0)m_0^j & \text{if } p_1^j \geq p_0^j, m_0^j < m_1^j; \\ (v_0 - (p_1^j + p_0^j)/2)m_0^j & \text{if } p_1^j < p_0^j, m_0^j < m_1^j. \end{cases} \quad (8)$$

$$U_1(m_0^j, m_1^j, p_0^j, p_1^j) = \begin{cases} ((p_0^j + p_1^j)/2 - v_1)m_1^j & \text{if } p_0^j \geq p_1^j, m_0^j > m_1^j; \\ (v_1 - (p_0^j + p_1^j)/2)m_1^j & \text{if } p_0^j < p_1^j, m_0^j > m_1^j; \\ (v_1 - (p_0^j + p_1^j)/2)m_0^j & \text{if } p_1^j \geq p_0^j, m_0^j < m_1^j; \\ ((p_0^j + p_1^j - 1)/2 - v_1)m_0^j & \text{if } p_1^j < p_0^j, m_0^j < m_1^j. \end{cases} \quad (9)$$

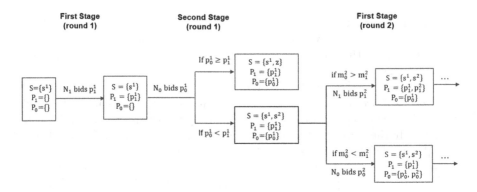

Fig. 1. Two-player repeated repurchase Stackelberg Game.

Both participants are interested in their total utilities in the whole process

$$U_i = \sum_{j \in \{1,2,\cdots,t\}} U_i(m_0^j, m_1^j, p_0^j, p_1^j).$$

Lemma 3. *For each participant* N_i, $i \in \{0,1\}$, *if his bid is set as* $p_i^j = v_i$ *in the* j-th round, $j \in \{1, 2, \cdots, t\}$, *then* $U_i(m_0^j, m_1^j, p_0^j, p_1^j) \geq 0$.

Lemma 3 can be directly deduced from (8) and (9).

Lemma 4. *If the repeated game goes through indefinitely, that is* $t = +\infty$, *then* $U_0 + U_1 = -\infty$.

Proof. For the j-th round, let $N_i = l^j$ be the leader and thus N_{1-i} is the follower. Since there are only two players, all $SNFT(id)$ will belong to one player, if the follower can successfully repurchase $SNFT(id)$ from the leader, and then the repeated game stops. It means that in the j-th round, m_i^j units of $SNFT(id)$ is bought by N_{1-i} from N_i and the game stops at the terminal state z_{1-i}. So if the repeated game goes through indefinitely, it must be that in each $j \in \{1, 2, \cdots\}$, $p_i^j > p_{1-i}^j$, and N_i buys m_i^j from N_{1-i}. Thus in the $j+1$-th round, $m_i^{j+1} = 2m_i^j$.

$$U_0(m_0^j, m_1^j, p_0^j, p_1^j) + U_1(m_0^j, m_1^j, p_0^j, p_1^j) =$$
$$\begin{cases} (v_0 - v_1)m_0^j - \frac{1}{2}m_0^j = (v_0 - v_1)(m_0^{j+1} - m_0^j) - \frac{1}{2}m_0^j & \text{if } N_0 \text{ is the leader;} \\ (v_1 - v_0)m_1^j - \frac{1}{2}m_1^j = (v_1 - v_0)(m_1^{j+1} - m_1^j) - \frac{1}{2}m_1^j & \text{if } N_1 \text{ is the leader;} \end{cases}$$
$$\leq (m_0^{j+1} - m_0^j)(v_0 - v_1) - \frac{1}{2}; \tag{10}$$

and

$$U_0 + U_1 = \lim_{t \to +\infty} \sum_{j=\{1,2,\cdots,t\}} U_0(m_0^j, m_1^j, p_0^j, p_1^j) + U_1(m_0^j, m_1^j, p_0^j, p_1^j)$$

$$\leq \lim_{t \to +\infty} \sum_{j=\{1,2,\cdots,t\}} \left[(m_0^{j+1} - m_0^j)(v_0 - v_1) - \frac{1}{2} \right]$$

$$= \lim_{t \to +\infty} \left[(m_0^{t+1} - m_0^1)(v_0 - v_1) - \frac{1}{2}t \right] \leq M|v_0 - v_1| - \lim_{t \to +\infty} \frac{1}{2}t = -\infty.$$

This result holds.   □

Combining Lemma 3 and Lemma 4, we have the following conclusion.

Lemma 5. *If there is a Stackelberg equilibrium in the two-player repeated Stackelberg game, then $U_0 + U_1 \geq 0$ in this Stackelberg equilibrium.*

Proof. Suppose to the contrary that $U_0 + U_1 < 0$ in this Stackelberg equilibrium, then there must exist $i \in \{0, 1\}$, such that $U_i < 0$. However, by Lemma 3, we know that if each player sets its price as $p_i^j = v_i$, then its utility $U_i^j \geq 0$. Hence N_i can obtain more utility by setting $p_i^j = v_i$, which is a contradiction that N_i doesn't give the best response in this Stackelberg equilibrium.   □

Combining Lemma 4 and Lemma 5, we have

Lemma 6. *If there is a Stackelberg equilibrium in the two-player repeated Stackelberg game, then the repeated game stops in a finite number of steps, meaning $t < +\infty$, in this Stackelberg equilibrium.*

The following theorem states that once a Stackelberg equilibrium exists and $v_i > v_{1-i}$, then this player N_i must buy all $SNFT(id)$ at last.

Theorem 4. *If $v_i > v_{1-i}$, $i = 0, 1$, and a Stackelberg equilibrium exists, then $z = z_i$, in all Stackelberg equilibria.*

Proof. By (8) and (9), we have

$$U_0(m_0^j, m_1^j, p_0^j, p_1^j) + U_1(m_0^j, m_1^j, p_0^j, p_1^j) \leq (m_0^{j+1} - m_0^j)(v_0 - v_1).$$

$$U_0 + U_1 \leq \sum_{j \in \{1,2,\cdots,t\}} U_0(m_0^j, m_1^j, p_0^j, p_1^j) + U_1(m_0^j, m_1^j, p_0^j, p_1^j)$$

$$\leq \sum_{j \in \{1,2,\cdots,t\}} (m_0^{j+1} - m_0^j)(v_0 - v_1) = (m_0^{t+1} - m_0^1)(v_0 - v_1).$$

If $v_0 > v_1$, then it must be $m_0^{t+1} > m_0^1$. Otherwise, $U_0 + U_1 < 0$, showing no Stackelberg equilibrium exists. This is a contradiction. Because the repeated game stops in a finite number of steps, $m_0^{t+1} \in \{0, M\}$. Combing the condition $m_0^{t+1} > m_0^1 > 0$, we have $m_0^{t+1} = M$. Therefore, at last $z = z_0$. Similarly, it is easy to deduce $z = z_1$ if $v_1 > v_0$.   □

Based on Theorem 4, we go to prove the existence of the Stackelberg equilibrium by proposing an equilibrium strategy in the following theorem. Its proof is provided in the full version [6] of this paper.

Theorem 5. *If $v_i > v_{1-i}$, $i = 0$, 1, the following strategy is a Stackelberg equilibrium:*

$$p_{1-i}^j = v_{1-i}; \quad p_i^j = \begin{cases} v_{1-i} + 1 & if \ l^j = i; \\ p_{1-i}^j & if \ l^j = 1 - i, \ p_{1-i}^j \le v_{1-i}; \\ p_{1-i}^j - 1 & if \ l^j = 1 - i, \ p_{1-i}^j > v_{1-i}. \end{cases} \tag{11}$$

5   Multi-player Repurchase Stackelberg Game

This section goes to extend the discussion for the multi-player scenario, in which N_0 has more than half of $SNFT(id)$, and $\{N_1, \cdots, N_k\}$ are repurchased participants. N_0 triggers the repurchase process, and asks all other repurchased participants to report their bids p_i at first, and N_0 decides his bid p_0 later. We also model the repurchase process of the multi-player scenario as a two-stage Stackelberg game, where $\{N_1, \cdots, N_k\}$ are the leaders to determine their bids in Stage I, and N_0 acts as the followers to decide his bid p_0 in Stage II. Different from the two-player scenario, N_0 shall trade with each N_i, $i = 1, \cdots, k$. Then each N_i, $i = 1, \cdots, k$, has his utility $U_i(p_0, p_i)$ as (1) and (2). But the utility of N_0 is the total utility from the trading with all N_i. That is

$$U_0(p_0, p_1, \cdots, p_k) = \sum_{i=1}^{k} U_0^i(p_0, p_i),$$

where $U_0^i(p_0, p_1)$ is defined as (1) and (2).

5.1   Analysis of Stackelberg Equilibrium

In the Stackelberg repurchase game for multi-player scenario, N_0 shall trade with each N_i, $i = 1, \cdots, k$. Inspired by the Stackelberg equilibrium in the two-player Stackelberg game, we first discuss the best response of N_0, if each N_i reports his bid as

$$p_i^* = \begin{cases} v_0 & if \ v_i \le v_0; \\ v_0 + 1 & if \ v_i \ge v_0 + 1. \end{cases} \tag{12}$$

Then we study the collusion from a group of repurchased players. Our task is to prove that once a group of repurchased participants deviate from the bidding strategy (12), then their total utility must be decreased. This guarantees that each participant would like to follow the bidding strategy (12).

Lemma 7. *In the Stackelberg repurchase game for the multi-player scenario, if all leaders set their bids $\{p_i^*\}$ as (12) in Stage I, then the best response of the follower N_0 in Stage II is $p_0^*(p_1^*, \cdots, p_n^*) = v_0$.*

Proof. For each trading between N_0 and N_i, $i = 1, \cdots, k$, Lemma 1 ensures that $v_0 = argmax_{p_0} U_0^i(p_0, p_i^*)$. Since each $U_0^i(p_0, p_i^*) \geq 0$, we have

$$p_0^*(p_1^*, \cdots, p_k^*) = \underset{p_0}{\operatorname{argmax}} \, U_0(p_0, p_1^*, \cdots, p_k^*) = \underset{p_0}{\operatorname{argmax}} \sum_{i=1}^{k} U_0^i(p_0, p_i^*) = v_0.$$

This lemma holds. $\square$

To study the collusion of repurchased participants, we partition the set of $\{N_1, \cdots, N_k\}$ into two disjoint subsets A and B, such that each $N_i \in A$ follows the bidding strategy (12), while each $N_i \in B$ does not. Thus given all bids provided by players, the bid profile $\mathbf{p} = (p_0, \{p_i^*\}_{N_i \in A}, \{p_i\}_{N_i \in B})$ can be equivalently expressed as $\mathbf{p} = (p_0, \mathbf{p}_A^*, \mathbf{p}_B)$. Here we are interested in the total utility of all players in B, and thus define

$$U_B(p_0, \mathbf{p}_A^*, \mathbf{p}_B) = \sum_{N_i \in B} U_i(p_0, p_i).$$

Following Lemma shows that once a group of participants deviate from the bidding strategy (12), then their total utility decreases. The proof is in the full version [6] of this paper.

Lemma 8. *Let $A = \{N_i | p_i = p_i^*\}$ and $B = \{N_i | p_i \neq p_i^*\}$. Then*

$$U_B(p_0^*(\mathbf{p}_A^*, \mathbf{p}_B), \mathbf{p}_A^*, \mathbf{p}_B) < U_B(v_0, p_1^*, p_2^*, \cdots, p_k^*).$$

Theorem 6. *In the multi-player Stackelberg repurchase game, the bid profile $(v_0, p_1^* \cdots, p_k^*)$ is a Stackelberg equilibrium, where p_i^* is set as (12).*

Proof. To simplify our discussion, we define the price profile $\mathbf{p}^* = (p_1^*, \cdots, p_k^*)$, and $\mathbf{p}_{-i}^*$ denotes the profile without the price of N_i. So $\mathbf{p}^* = (\mathbf{p}_{-i}^*, p_i^*)$. From Lemma 7, we have the best response of N_0 in Stage II is $p_0^*(\mathbf{p}^*) = v_0$. However, Lemma 8 indicates that no one would like to deviate from the pricing strategy (12), as $U_i(p_0^*(\mathbf{p}_{-i}^*, p_i), \mathbf{p}_{-i}^*, p_i) < U_i(v_0, \mathbf{p}_i^*)$. Thus given the price profile $\mathbf{p}^*$, nobody would like to change its strategy p_i^* unilaterally. Therefore, $(v_0, p_1^* \cdots, p_k^*)$ is a Stackelberg equilibrium. $\square$

From the perspective of cooperation, we can observe that no group of repurchased participants would like to collude to deviate from the bidding strategy (12) by Lemma 8. Thus we have the following corollary.

Corollary 1. *Given the Stackelberg equilibrium of $(v_0, p_1^* \cdots, p_k^*)$, no group of repurchased participants would like to deviate this equilibrium.*

In the case of incomplete information, the analysis of the Bayesian Stackelberg equilibrium becomes extremely complicated. As discussed in Sect. 3.2, in the case of the two-player Stackelberg game, the leader only needs to optimize the utility based on incomplete information. However, when there are multiple leaders, the strategies of leaders should reach a Bayesian Nash equilibrium, which is much more difficult to calculate. So we regard it as our future work to analyze the Bayesian Stackelberg equilibrium of the multi-player repurchase Stackelberg game.

6   Discussion

6.1   A Blockchain Solution to Budget Constraints

In the previous settings, we do not consider the budget constraints. However, this is a common problem for many newly proposed mechanisms. Therefore, we propose a solution scheme by blockchain for the setting with budget constraints.

Suppose N_0 owes more than half of $SNFT(id)$ and triggers the repurchase process. Our mechanism consists of two stages. All participants except for N_0 report their bids in Stage I, and N_0 gives his bid p_0 in Stage II. We assume N_0's budget is larger than $(M-m_0)p_0$, so that he can repurchase all other shares at his bid p_0. For N_i, $i \neq 0$, if $p_i > p_0$, N_i should pay $\frac{p_0+p_i}{2}m_i$. However, the payment of $\frac{p_0+p_i}{2}m_i$ may exceed his budget, such that N_i has not enough money to buy m_i units of $SNFT(id)$. Under this situation, we provide a blockchain solution for N_i to solve the problem of budget shortage. That is, we allow N_i to sell his option of buying m_i units of $SNFT(id)$ to anyone in the blockchain system. If nobody would like to buy N_i's repurchase option, then N_0 can repurchase N_i's shares at a lower price. Therefore, after reporting bids, additional four steps are needed to finish the payment procedure.

- Step 1. N_0 pays $\sum_{i \in \{1,2,\cdots,k\}, p_i \leq p_0} \frac{p_0+p_i}{2}m_i$. After the payment, N_0 gets $\sum_{i \in \{1,2,\cdots,k\}, p_i \leq p_0} m_i$ pieces of $SNFT(id)$. For each N_i with $p_i \leq p_0$, $i \in \{1, 2, \cdots, k\}$, he gets the revenue of $\frac{p_0+p_i}{2} \cdot m_i$ and loses m_i units of $SNFT(id)$.
- Step 2. For all $i \in \{1, 2, \cdots, k\}$ that $p_i > p_0$, N_i shall pay $\frac{p_0+p_i}{2} \cdot m_i$ to buy m_i units of $SNFT(id)$ from N_0. Once m_i units of $SNFT(id)$ of N_0 is sold to N_i, N_0 obtains a discounted revenue $\frac{p_0+p_i-1}{2} \cdot m_i$.
  If N_i would not like to repurchase $SNFT(id)$, then he can sell his repurchase option to others at a price of $\widetilde{p}_i \in \mathbb{Z}$. The price of repurchase option $\widetilde{p}_i$ could be negative, meaning that N_i shall pay $\widetilde{p}_i$ to another who accepts his chance. If N_i does nothing, we regard that N_i proposes $\widetilde{p}_i = 0$.
- Step 3. If a participant in the blockchain system accepts the price of $\widetilde{p}_i$, then he would propose a transaction to buy m_i units of $SNFT(id)$ from N_0. The total cost of this participant is $\widetilde{p}_i + \frac{p_0+p_i}{2} \cdot m_i$, in which $\widetilde{p}_i$ is paid to N_i and N_0 obtains a discounted revenue of $\frac{p_0+p_i-1}{2} \cdot m_i$. And m_i units of $SNFT(id)$ are transferred from N_0 to the participant who buys the repurchase option. At the end of this step, let C be the participant set, in which each participant's repurchase option hasn't been sold yet.
- Step 4. For each participant $N_i \in C$, N_0 repurchases m_i units of $SNFT(id)$ from N_i at a lower price of $2p_0 - p_i(< p_0)$. At the end of this step, N_0 obtains m_i units of $SNFT(id)$, and N_i obtains a revenue of $(2p_0 - p_i) \cdot m_i$.

6.2   A Blockchain Solution to Lazy Bidders

Under some circumstances, an $SNFT(id)$ holder might not bid in the repurchase process, who is named as a lazy bidder. This lazy behavior may block the repurchase process. To solve the problem caused by lazy bidders, we propose the following two schemes.

- **Custody Bidding.** NFT's smart contract supports the feature for the $SNFT(id)$ holders to assign administrators to report a bid when the holder is idle or fails to make a bid.
- **Value Predetermination.** Whenever a participant obtains any units of $SNFT(id)$, this participant is required to predetermine the value at which he is willing to bid, and this information is stored in the smart contract. At the beginning of the repurchase process, if a participant fails to make a bid within a certain amount of time, the smart contract automatically reports this participant's predetermined bid. This does not mean, however, that the participant has to bid at the predetermined price if he decides to make an active bid.

7 Conclusion

In this paper, we propose a novel securitization and repurchase scheme for NFT to overcome the restrictions in existing NFT markets. We model the NFT repurchase process as a Stackelberg game and analyze the Stackelberg equilibria under several scenarios. To be specific, in the setting of the two-player one-round game, we prove that in a Stackelberg equilibrium, N_0, the participant who triggers the repurchase process, shall give the bid equally to his own value estimate. In the two-player repeated game, all securities shall be finally owned by the participant who has a higher value estimate. In the setting of multiple players, cooperation among participants cannot bring higher utilities to them. What's more, each participant can get non-negative utility if he bids truthfully in our repurchase process.

How to securitize and repurchase NFT efficiently is a popular topic in the field of blockchain. Our work proposes a sound solution for this problem. In the future, we continue to refine our theoretical analysis. First, for the multi-player repurchase Stackelberg game, we will consider the case with incomplete information and explore the Bayesian Stackelberg equilibrium. Second, a model of blockchain economics will be constructed to analyze the payment procedure in Sect. 6.1. Furthermore, there exist some other interesting problems, including how to securitize and repurchase a common-valued NFT [13], how to host Complete NFTs or Securitized NFTs in decentralized custody protocols [7], whether ABSNFT can serve as a price Oracle, and so on.

Acknowledgment. This research was partially supported by the National Major Science and Technology Projects of China-"New Generation Artificial Intelligence" (No. 2018AAA0100901), the National Natural Science Foundation of China (No. 11871366), and Qing Lan Project of Jiangsu Province.

References

1. Acharya, V.V., Oncu, S.: The repurchase agreement (repo) market. Regulating Wall Street, pp. 319–350 (2011)
2. Amihud, Y., Mendelson, H.: Liquidity, asset prices and financial policy. Financ. Anal. J. **47**(6), 56–66 (1991)
3. Angeris, G., Chitra, T.: Improved price oracles: Constant function market makers. In: Proceedings of the 2nd ACM Conference on Advances in Financial Technologies. pp. 80–91 (2020)
4. Bhattacharya, A.K., Fabozzi, F.J.: Asset-backed securities, vol. 13. Wiley (1996)
5. Çağlayan Aksoy, P., Özkan Üner, Z.: Nfts and copyright: challenges and opportunities. J. Intellectual Property Law Practice (2021)
6. Chen, H., Cheng, Y., Deng, X., Huang, W., Rong, L.: Absnft: securitization and repurchase scheme for non-fungible tokens based on game theoretical analysis. arXiv preprint arXiv:2202.02199 (2022)
7. Chen, Z., Yang, G.: Decentralized custody scheme with game-theoretic security. arXiv preprint arXiv:2008.10895 (2020)
8. Constantinides, G.M., Grundy, B.D.: Optimal investment with stock repurchase and financing as signals. Rev. Financ. Stud. **2**(4), 445–465 (1989)
9. ERC-1155. https://erc1155.org/
10. ERC-721. https://erc721.org/
11. Fairfield, J.: Tokenized: The law of non-fungible tokens and unique digital property. Indiana Law J. Forthcoming (2021)
12. Hong, S., Noh, Y., Park, C.: Design of extensible non-fungible token model in hyperledger fabric. In: Proceedings of the 3rd Workshop on Scalable and Resilient Infrastructures for Distributed Ledgers, pp. 1–2 (2019)
13. Kagel, J.H., Levin, D.: Common value auctions and the winner's curse. Princeton University Press (2009)
14. Kong, D.R., Lin, T.C.: Alternative investments in the fintech era: The risk and return of non-fungible token (nft). SSRN 3914085 (2021)
15. Li, C., et al.: Latent dirichlet allocation for internet price war. In: Proceedings of the AAAI Conference on Artificial Intelligence. vol. 33, pp. 639–646 (2019)
16. Lucas, C.M., Jones, M.T., Thurston, T.B.: Federal funds and repurchase agreements. Federal Reserve Bank New York Quarterly Rev. **2**(2), 33–48 (1977)
17. Mammadzada, K., Iqbal, M., Milani, F., García-Bañuelos, L., Matulevičius, R.: Blockchain Oracles: a framework for blockchain-based applications. In: Asatiani, A., et al. (eds.) BPM 2020. LNBIP, vol. 393, pp. 19–34. Springer, Cham (2020). https://doi.org/10.1007/978-3-030-58779-6_2
18. Oxygen: Breathing new life into crypto assets. https://oxygen.trade/OXYGEN_White_paper_February.pdf
19. Serum. https://www.projectserum.com/
20. Valeonti, F., Bikakis, A., Terras, M., Speed, C., Hudson-Smith, A., Chalkias, K.: Crypto collectibles, museum funding and openglam: challenges, opportunities and the potential of non-fungible tokens (nfts). Appl. Sci. **11**(21), 9931 (2021)
21. Von Stackelberg, H.: Market structure and equilibrium. Springer Science & Business Media (2010)
22. Wang, D., et al.: Towards a first step to understand flash loan and its applications in defi ecosystem. In: Proceedings of the Ninth International Workshop on Security in Blockchain and Cloud Computing, pp. 23–28 (2021)

23. Wang, Q., Li, R., Wang, Q., Chen, S.: Non-fungible token (nft): overview, evaluation, opportunities and challenges. arXiv preprint arXiv:2105.07447 (2021)
24. Weed, J., Perchet, V., Rigollet, P.: Online learning in repeated auctions. In: Conference on Learning Theory, pp. 1562–1583. PMLR (2016)

Decentralisation Conscious Players and System Reliability

Sarah Azouvi[1(✉)] and Alexander Hicks[2]

[1] Protocol Labs, San Francisco, USA
sarah.azouvi@protocol.ai
[2] University College London, London, UK
alexander.hicks@ucl.ac.uk

Abstract. We propose a game-theoretic model of the reliability of decentralised systems based on Varian's model of system reliability [28], to which we add a new normalised total effort case that models *decentralisation conscious players* who prioritise decentralisation.

We derive the Nash equilibria in the normalised total effort game. In these equilibria, either one or two values are played by players that do not free ride. The speed at which players can adjust their contributions can determine how an equilibrium is reached and equilibrium values. The behaviour of decentralisation conscious players is robust to deviations by other players.

Our results highlight the role that decentralisation conscious players can play in maintaining decentralisation. They also highlight, however, that by supporting an equilibrium that requires an important contribution they cannot be expected to increase decentralisation as contributing the equilibrium value may still imply a loss for many players. We also discuss practical constraints on decentralisation in the context of our model.

Keywords: Decentralisation · Public goods · Free-riding · Reliability

1 Introduction

The reliability of a system captures the likelihood that it performs as intended. For a decentralised system, there are two important components to consider, the number of participants and the distribution of power between them [27]. Even if there is a high number of contributors, if one of them has significantly more control over the system, there will be no meaningful level of decentralisation. This presents a problem that has been hard to solve in practice. How can the effort put into a system grow while maintaining an acceptable level of decentralisation?

Participation rewards can incentivise an increase in the effort invested in a system but a greater total effort can also be more centralised. Certain protocol considerations may alleviate this effect, e.g., at the consensus level [8]. It is also sometimes assumed that a portion of players will behave altruistically, following protocol guidelines even when an a priori more profitable strategies exist.

© International Financial Cryptography Association 2022
I. Eyal and J. Garay (Eds.): FC 2022, LNCS 13411, pp. 426–443, 2022.
https://doi.org/10.1007/978-3-031-18283-9_21

An alternative assumption, which we consider here, is that players have an incentive to maintain decentralisation. Short-term profits may be outweighed by the possible long-term profits associated with maintaining a reliable system. For example, the value of a cryptocurrency that is vulnerable to hostile takeovers may decrease so miners have an incentive to maintain decentralisation and preserve the value of the tokens they hold and continue to receive.

Three observations support this assumption. First, the market price of a cryptocurrency is linked to its security [10]. Second, numerous flaws have been identified in the incentive structure of cryptocurrencies [12,22], yet attacks based on these have scarcely been observed [24]. Third, a mining pool has previously acted to avoid controlling more than half of Bitcoin's hash rate [21].

To further understand the rationality of maintaining decentralisation, this paper studies a game-theoretic model of decentralisation conscious players who prioritise decentralisation. With this model, we can analyse how such players will behave to ensure that a system remains decentralised, what effort they may contribute, and under which circumstances they will free-ride.

Our Contributions. The main contribution of this paper is the introduction and analysis of the normalised total effort game with decentralisation conscious players that extends Varian's system reliability model to decentralised systems.

We introduce our model based on the normalised total effort (NTE) function in the context of Varian's system reliability model [28] in Sect. 2. In Sect. 3, we derive the two types of Nash equilibria between decentralisation conscious players in which players contribute the same amount or two distinct amounts while others free ride. We also consider the social optimum, in which players contribute the same effort while minimising their costs to maximise decentralisation.

To understand how decentralisation conscious players will behave in real systems alongside selfish and Byzantine players, we study in Sect. 4 the robustness of the previously derived equilibria when (i) the number of players change, which does not always affect the equilibrium; (ii) players deviate from the equilibrium, which can lead to a new equilibrium where players (possibly fewer) contribute a greater effort. Non-myopic players may, therefore, be incentivised to deviate from an equilibrium to reach a new equilibrium with fewer contributing players and a greater share of rewards.

Finally, we discuss in Sect. 6 some practical constraints on decentralisation in relation to our model.

2 Modelling System Reliability and Normalised Total Effort

Varian's original model of system reliability (treated as a public good) considers three cases based on how the individual efforts x_i of players are factored in [28]. The weakest link case considers the minimal effort exerted by any one of the players i.e., $F(x_1, \ldots, x_n) = \min_i(x_i)$. The total effort case considers the sum of every player's efforts i.e., $F(x_1, \ldots, x_n) = \sum_{i=1}^{n} x_i$. The best shot case considers the maximal effort exerted by any one of the players i.e., $F(x_1, \ldots, x_n) = \max_i(x_i)$.

Reliability will usually depend on a combination of these cases. For example, in the case of software security, a program's correctness can depend on the weakest link (the developer that introduces bugs), vulnerability testing depends on the total effort of all the testers, and the contributions of a system architect maps to the best shot case [4].

For each case, the Nash equilibria can be computed with the expected pay-off u_i for a player i expressed as in Eq. 1, as can be the social optimum based on social pay-off SP expressed as in Eq. 2. The likelihood that the system operates successfully is captured by $P(F(x_1, \ldots, x_n))$, which is assumed to be differentiable, increasing, and concave. The parameter v_i is the value derived by player i of the system operating successfully, and $c_i x_i$ is the cost to player i where c_i is a constant. The choice of a linear cost function of the form $c_i x_i$ implicitly ignores more complex forms of cost and any fixed costs. This is a limitation but it is realistic in relevant cases e.g., the energy required to operate a computer may be valued at a fixed price per kilowatt-hours.

$$u_i = P(F(x_1, \ldots, x_n))v_i - c_i x_i \tag{1}$$

$$SP = P(F(x_1, \ldots, x_n)) \sum_{i=1}^{n} v_i - \sum_{i=1}^{n} c_i x_i \tag{2}$$

The equilibria can be used to determine when free-riding can be expected to occur based on the form of F. For example, in the total effort case, the equilibrium is for players to free ride on the player who has the highest benefit-cost ratio $\frac{v_i}{c_i}$. The social optimum, obtained by maximising the social pay-off rather than the player's utility functions, can also reveal how selfish behaviour from the players will lead to an outcome that is different from the social optimum. This is the case in the total effort case used as an example. Players free ride on the player with the highest benefit-cost ratio, which amounts to less total effort than in the social optimum, and the "wrong" players (those with the smallest benefit-cost ratio) can be found to contribute that effort.

The takeaway from Varian's results is that centralisation emerges even in the total effort case that involves everyone's contributions, and that rational behaviour can conflict with the social optimum i.e., selfish behaviour can lead to a weaker system – a concept known as *the price of anarchy* [25]. If decentralisation is desired, this means that an alternative model that produces individual and social outcomes that support a decentralised and stronger system is required.

To model decentralisation, the *relative* contribution of every player in the system must be taken into account because while the total effort should be as high as possible, the effort must also be as evenly distributed as possible. In practice, however, there are trade-offs between maximising total effort and distributing effort evenly. It is unlikely that every player will have the same capacity to contribute, so maximising the total effort is likely to come at the cost of a uniform distribution of effort, and vice versa.

With this in mind, we define in Eq. 3 the normalised total effort (NTE) function based on the total effort and the maximal contribution. If the total effort is high but the maximal effort is also high then the NTE may not be as high as when the total effort is high but the maximal effort is low.

$$F(x_1, \ldots, x_n) = \frac{\sum_{i=1}^{n} x_i}{\max_i(x_i)} \quad (3)$$

The normalised total effort function is scale invariant i.e., $F(\alpha x_1, \ldots, \alpha x_n) = F(x_1, \ldots, x_n)$ for any α. This is because we are modelling players who care about decentralisation over total effort. The goal is to capture the fact that in systems that are designed to be decentralised, it is not only the total effort (studied by Varian) that matters but the distribution of effort and, in particular, how much the maximal contribution by a single player is as a portion of the total effort, which our measure captures. Finding a measure that captures both this and the benefits of a higher total effort is an open problem, and measures similar to ours (e.g., the work of Kwon et al. [23]) suffer from the same limitation.

We show in Sect. 4 that contributions can still be expected to increase given that other players who prioritise maximising their share of rewards exist. Thus, much like in software security, a decentralised system's reliability depends on nodes that are primarily concerned with decentralisation (normalised total effort) and nodes that are primarily concerned with higher contributions (and higher rewards) that increase the best shot and total effort. Because the best shot and total effort case have already been studied by Varian, our focus in this paper is the normalised total effort case.

3   Equilibria Between Decentralisation Conscious Players

We begin by studying the Nash equilibria of the NTE game defined below.

Definition 1 (Normalised Total Effort Game). *We call the normalised total effort game (NTEG) the game consisting of n players with costs $(c_1, \ldots, c_n) \in (\mathbb{R}_+^*)^n$, valuations $(v_1, \ldots, v_n) \in (\mathbb{R}_+^*)^n$, contributions $(x_1, \ldots, x_n) \in (\mathbb{R}_+)^n$, utility functions defined by Eqs. 3 and 1, benefit-cost ratios $\beta_i = \frac{v_i}{c_i}$ such that $\beta_1 < \ldots < \beta_n$, and where we assume a logarithmic reliability function $P(F(x_1, \ldots, x_n)) = \ln\left(\frac{\sum_{i=1}^{n} x_i}{\max_i(x_i)}\right)$ for $\max_i(x_i) > 0$. By convention we have $P(F(0, \ldots, 0)) = 0$ i.e., a system with no contributions does not function.*

$$F(x_1, \ldots, x_n) = \frac{\sum_{i=1}^{n} x_i}{\max_i(x_i)} \quad (3)$$

$$u_i = v_i P(F(x_1, \ldots, x_n)) - c_i x_i \quad (1)$$

Two-Player Case. We start by considering the simple case of a two-player game and the following theorem, The proof is left for the long version of the paper [7].

Theorem 1. *In a two-player NTEG, the Nash equilibria are for both players to contribute the same effort $x_1 = x_2 = x_{eq}$ such that $x_{eq} \leq \frac{1}{2} \min(\beta_1, \beta_2)$.*

Both players contribute the same effort when the equilibrium is played, which is the only possible "decentralised" solution.

Multiplayer Case. For $n > 2$ players, we prove the following in the full version the paper [7].

Theorem 2. *In a $n > 2$ player NTEG, there exist two types of equilibrium.*

1. *(1-value equilibria) players $i+1$ to n (for $1 \leq i < n$) contribute x_{eq} subject to the constraint expressed by Inequality 4 and players 1 to i with the smallest benefit-cost ratio free ride on them.*

$$\frac{1}{n-i}\beta_i \leq x_{eq} \leq \frac{1}{n-i}\beta_{i+1} \tag{4}$$

2. *(2-value equilibria) player i contributes x_m , players $(i+1$ to $n)$ contribute x_M, where $x_m < x_M$, subject to the constraints in Inequality 5 and Eq. 6 and players 1 to $i-1$ free ride, for $1 \leq i \leq n$ (with no players free riding if $i = 1$).*

$$\frac{1}{n-i+1}\beta_i < x_M < \frac{1}{n-i}\beta_i \tag{5}$$

$$x_m = \beta_i - (n-i)x_M \tag{6}$$

We highlight Lemma 1 (proven as part of the proof) that we will reuse later.

Lemma 1. *If there exist two contributing rational players whose contributions are strictly less than $\max_i(x_i)$ and who play their best strategy, then those players must have the same benefit-cost ratio.*

Unless specified otherwise, we denote by x_{eq} the value played by the players or bulk of players in the 1-value or 2-value equilibrium, respectively. For both types of equilibrium, the lower x_{eq} is the more decentralised the system is, as more players can contribute and the less free-riding there is.

The fact that one equilibrium is for all players to contribute the same amount of effort makes sense as the NTE function encodes the social goal of maximising decentralisation. It also prevents the perverse effects of any feedback loops that enable some players to contribute increasingly more than other players.

The 2-value equilibrium is less expected. It shows that, even if some players cannot match the other players' contributions (due to their own costs or valuation), they may still be incentivised to contribute.

3.1   The Impact of a Reward

The equilibria we have derived above include the case where everyone contributes no effort. Adding a reward function $R_i(x_1, \ldots, x_n)$ to the utility function, as in Eq. 7. (e.g., cryptocurrency mining rewards) is a way of explicitly incentivising non-zero contributions, particularly from new players.

$$u_i = P(F(x_1, \ldots, x_n))v_i - c_i x_i + R_i(x_1, \ldots, x_n) \tag{7}$$

A reward separate from the valuation v models the compensation for the effort invested in the system rather than the benefit derived from being able to use the system. In practice, it may be a constant R that can be won by players with a probability proportional to the effort they contribute. Under certain conditions, this is an optimal allocation rule [15] so we restrict ourselves to this case.

$$R_i(x_1, \ldots, x_n) = \begin{cases} R\frac{x_i}{\sum_{j=1}^{n} x_j}, & \text{if } \max(x_1, \ldots, x_n) > 0 \\ 0, & \text{if } \max(x_1, \ldots, x_n) = 0 \end{cases} \tag{8}$$

This removes the $x_{eq} = 0$ equilibrium without significantly affecting other equilibria. In the two-player case, an equilibrium still involves the two players contributing the same value x subject to different constraints and under the additional assumptions that $R < \min(v_1, v_2)$. This expresses the fact that the player's valuations of the system must be at least greater than the value of the reward – it would make little sense to gain a reward that is greater than the value of the system functioning. We prove the following theorem in the full version the paper [7].

Theorem 3. *In a two player NTEG with reward $R < \min(v_1, v_2)$ there exist infinite Nash equilibria where both players contribute the same value x such that*

$$\begin{cases} \frac{c_1}{4R}((R\frac{1-\sqrt{\Delta_1'}}{2c_1})^2 - \beta_1^2) < x < \frac{c_1}{4R}((R\frac{1+\sqrt{\Delta_1'}}{2c_1})^2 - \beta_1^2) \\ \frac{c_2}{4R}((R\frac{1-\sqrt{\Delta_2'}}{2c_2})^2 - \beta_2^2) < x < \frac{c_2}{4R}((R\frac{1+\sqrt{\Delta_2'}}{2c_2})^2 - \beta_2^2) \end{cases} \tag{9}$$

with $\Delta_1' = 1 + 4\frac{c_1}{R}(\frac{v_1^2 c_1}{R} + \frac{v_1}{c_1})$ and $\Delta_2' = 1 + 4\frac{c_2}{R}(\frac{v_2^2 c_2}{R} + \frac{v_2}{c_2})$.

We leave the multiplayer analysis as future work.

3.2   Social Optimum

An insight from Varian's work is that the equilibria and social optima are not necessarily the same e.g., the total effort social optimum involves players contributing much more than in the Nash equilibrium [28].

In the NTE case, the social optimum is for players to contribute the smallest non-zero amount possible as this maximises the level of decentralisation while minimising their costs. If all contributions are equal then in most cases it is also a Nash equilibrium. This convenient outcome is expected from our choice of NTE that reflects a desire to ensure that the social goal of decentralisation is met, so the NTE function is well defined in that sense. The only exception is when the benefit-cost ratio of some players is too low as they then free-ride.

Figuring out an acceptable minimal contribution can be straightforward when it is possible to impose a minimum contribution. Ethereum's implementation of proof-of-stake does this, but not all systems impose a minimum contribution.

4   Robustness of Decentralisation Conscious Players to Variations by Others

In practice, players may leave or join the game, as well as increase or decrease their contributions because of selfish behaviour or, more generally, Byzantine faults. Thus, it is important to analyse how decentralisation conscious players tolerate variations in the actions of other players. We do this by studying how the equilibria for the NTEG change after such events.

In the analysis that follows we will be using a result derived in the proof of Theorem 2, which is that for each player j the best response to (fixed) contributions of other players is as follows.

1. if $\sum_{i \neq j} x_i < \beta_j$, contribute $\min(\max_{i \neq j}(x_i), \beta_j - \sum_{i \neq j} x_i)$
2. if $\sum_{i \neq j} x_i \geq \beta_j$, contribute zero.

Equivalently, player's j best response can be written as in Eq. 10.

$$\max\{0, \min(\max_{i \neq j}(x_i), \beta_j - \sum_{i \neq j} x_i)\} \tag{10}$$

In this section, we note n the number of contributing players.

4.1   Change in Number of Players

New Player Joining.

1-value Equilibrium. We first consider the case where the players play the 1-value equilibrium described in Theorem 2. If one player joins the game, the robustness of the equilibrium depends both on x_{eq} and on the benefit-cost ratio β of the new player. From Condition 4, we have that $x_{eq} \leq \frac{1}{n}\beta_j$, $\forall 1 \leq j \leq n$.

We proceed as follows. For different values of x_{eq} we study what would be the new player's best response x_{new} and whether they would join the game i.e., contribute a non-zero effort. We then look at whether the introduction of a new player playing x_{new} disrupts the equilibrium for the rest of the players i.e., whether having n players play x_{eq} and one player play x_{new} is still an equilibrium. We find that the original n players change their contributions if and only if $\beta > \beta_1$ and $\frac{1}{n+1}\beta_1 < x_{eq} < \frac{1}{n}\beta$. We prove this result in the full version the paper [7].

Theorem 4. *In a NTEG that is in a state of 1-value equilibrium with n players contributing x_{eq}, the introduction of a new player with benefit-cost ratio β changes the value played by the other players if and only if $\beta > \beta_1$ and $\frac{1}{n+1}\beta_1 < x_{eq} < \frac{1}{n}\beta$.*

2-value equilibrium In the case where the players were initially in a 2-value equilibrium, we have the following theorem, which we prove in the full version the paper [7].

Theorem 5. *In a NTEG that is in a state of 2-value equilibrium with player 1 playing x_1 and the other $n - 1$ players playing x_{eq}, the introduction of a new player with benefit-cost ratio β does not change the value played by the other players unless $\sum_{i=1}^{n} x_i < \beta$ or $\beta_1 < \beta$.*

We now consider how the utility of each player changes following the introduction of a new player. If the new player contributes a strictly positive effort and the value played at equilibrium stays unchanged for the other players it is clear that the introduction of a new player increases everyone's utility as it increases the reliability of the system without changing anyone's cost. When the equilibrium is changed, if only one player (player 1) leaves the system, then this is simply a player replacement and the reliability of the system stays the same. Player 1 increases their utility in this case as the reliability of the system is the same as before but their cost is now zero.

However, from the proof of Theorem 4 we have that a new player could potentially incentivise more than one player to decrease their contribution. Lemma 1 tells us that this means that the players would potentially need many iterations before reaching a new equilibrium if they reach one, where only one or two values are played. Although it could be presumed that a new player joining should increase the reliability of the system, this result shows that if one or more players have to decrease their contributions then it is not clear that the final reliability of the system will be higher with $n + 1$ player than with the original n players. We study simulations of equilibrium disruption in Sect. 5 and leave a rigorous study of the outcome of the new game as an open problem.

Player Leaving the Game. In the case where a player leaves the game, we have the following theorems, which we prove in the full version the paper [7].

Theorem 6. *In the NTEG, if the n players are playing a $1-value$ Nash equilibrium, the removal of a new player with benefit-cost ratio β_i does not change the value played by the other players.*

Theorem 7. *In the NTEG with n players playing a 2-value equilibrium where players 2 to n play the same value x_{eq} at the equilibrium, the removal of a new player with benefit-cost ratio β_i changes the value played by the other players unless in the specific case where player 1 is leaving the game.*

If other contributions stay unchanged, a player leaving the system decreases the reliability of the system as it renders it more centralised. The utilities of the remaining players will therefore always decrease in this case.

4.2   Deviation from an Equilibrium

We now consider the case where one player (player k) deviates from the equilibrium and changes their contribution to x_{k_0}. We are concerned with the response of the $n-1$ other players and what new equilibrium is reached, regardless of whether it will be the best strategy for player k to keep their value x_{k_0} in the new equilibrium (i.e., player k may be irrational). We prove the following theorem in the full version the paper [7].

Theorem 8. *In the NTEG with n players contributing the same value x_{eq} at the equilibrium, the deviation of player k with benefit-cost ratio β_k to a new value x_{k_0} does not change the value played by the other players unless $x_{k_0} > x_{eq}$.*

In the 2-value equilibrium, the results are very similar. We prove the following theorem in the full version the paper [7].

Theorem 9. *In the NTEG with n players playing a 2-value equilibrium where players 2 to n play the same value x_{eq} at the equilibrium, the deviation of player k with benefit-cost ratio β_k to a new value x_{k_0} changes the value played by the other players unless in the specific case where player 1 is deviating to a new value $x_{k_0} \neq x_1$ and for all $2 \leq j \leq n$ we have (1) $x_{k_0} < x_{eq}$ (2) $\beta_j > (n-2)x_{eq} + x_{k_0} + \max(x_{eq}, x_{k_0})$ and (3) $(n-2)x_{k_0} + x_{k_0} < \beta_2$.*

In the case where the players do not change their equilibrium after an irrational player deviates (i.e., $x_{k_0} < x_{eq}$) the utility of players will decrease as reliability will be lower for the same costs and contributions.

In the other case, before the other players can adjust their contribution, their utility will also decrease, and in some realistic cases, players may not be able to change their contribution as we discuss in Sect. 6. This is an undesirable effect defined as *immunity* by Abraham et al. [2] in the context of distributed systems where one or more irrational players can negatively impact the utility of rational players. If players can change their contributions, the reliability functions could go up or down depending on the new value x_{eq} and the benefit-cost of other players (i.e., whether they will free ride).

After the deviation from player k, we have from Condition 10 that each player i such that $x_{k_0} \geq \frac{\beta_i - (n-2)x_{eq}}{2}$ changes their contribution to $x_{i,\text{new}} = \beta_i - x_{k_0} - (n-2)x_{eq}$ or zero if that value is negative, and each player i such that $x_{k_0} \leq \frac{\beta_i - (n-2)x_{eq}}{2}$ changes their contribution to x_{k_0}.

In Lemma 1, we showed that if there exists two contributing rational players whose contributions are strictly less than $\max_j(x_j)$, then those players must have the same benefit-cost ratio. This is true regardless of the existence of an irrational player. Since we assume that all the benefit-cost ratios are different, this means that there can be at most one rational player playing strictly less than the maximum value x_M. According to the strategy defined in Condition 10, no rational player is incentivised to play more than $\max_j(x_j)$. Thus, even after players adjust their contributions we will still have $\max_j(x_j) = x_{k_0}$ and, following the deviation, the bulk of the players will align with the deviating players or free ride, except for one rational player. By setting x_{k_0} high enough, the deviating player could ensure that many players switch to free-riding, which could pose a threat to the system if it facilitates one party taking control of the system (e.g., a 51% attack).

4.3 Non-myopic Players

Motivated by Brünjes et al. [14], we consider *non-myopic players* deviating from the equilibrium. The utility function of such players accounts for the effects an action will have on the other players, unlike Nash equilibria that consider the best response of players given that the other players' strategies are fixed.

In the previous section, we have seen that a player deviating from the equilibrium may disrupt the best response of the other players and lead to a new equilibrium. In a Nash equilibrium, assuming that other players keep their contribution unchanged, deviating means that one's utility is reduced, but this does not account for the possibility of a new equilibrium being reached. A new equilibrium (if reached) may be a better equilibrium for the deviating player if their utility is higher in the new equilibrium.

Does a non-myopic player have incentives to deviate from the equilibria we have derived? We have established that a condition to disrupt the equilibrium is to change one's contribution to a value $x_{k_0} > x_{eq}$. We have also observed that by setting this value high enough, the deviating player can cause some players to free ride. In a NTEG without a reward, the new equilibrium would, therefore, have fewer contributing players with greater contributions. In a 1-value equilibrium, this would mean we have $F(x_1, \ldots, x_n) = n_{\text{new}} < n$ where n_{new} is the new number of contributing players. However, because $x_{k_0} > x_{eq}$, the cost will be higher and this strategy is therefore not rational as the new equilibrium results in less utility for the deviating player and the other players.

In a NTEG with reward, however, fewer players implies a greater share of rewards. Thus a non-myopic player may be incentivised to deviate from an existing equilibrium to reach a new one with fewer contributing players.

This suggests that a fixed proportional reward may increase centralisation. Designing a protocol with a variable reward such that players would earn similar revenue regardless of the number of players is an open problem due to the pseudonymous nature of systems like cryptocurrencies. Another alternative is to rely on a fixed reward but design the system such that it is not possible to increase one's contribution, as in proof-of-personhood schemes [13].

4.4 Coalition-Resistance

A group of miners may decide to form a coalition if this increases their expected gain, even if doing so centralises the system. In this case a coalition is equivalent to having one player contributing $X = \sum_{i \in [i_1, \ldots, i_c]} x_i$ for all the players $(i_1, \ldots, i_c)$ in the coalition instead of having each contributing separately. Because the sum of the efforts stay the same but the maximum effort potentially

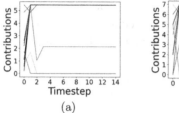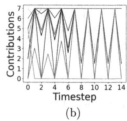

(a)   (b)

Fig. 1. Without constraints on contribution changes players can reach an equilibrium (Fig. 1a) but may also oscillate indefinitely (Fig. 1).

increases, $F(x_1, \ldots, x_{i_1}, \ldots, x_{i_c}, \ldots, x_n) \geq F(x_1, \ldots, X, \ldots, x_n)$. Thus, the utility of decentralisation conscious players decreases when they form a coalition i.e., they are not incentivised to create coalitions.

5   Dynamics of Decentralisation Conscious Players

As we have shown, there are many possible equilibria, each corresponding to different equilibrium values. How an equilibrium is reached i.e., how quickly and how many players reach it, as well as which equilibrium value is reached could depend on several factors that we look at in this section.

Methodology. Using a Python script, we simulate the NTEG where each player computes their best strategy at each time unit. By iterating over multiple time units we observe how players (simultaneously) re-evaluate their contributions based on the effort of other players in the previous time unit. The scenarios we simulate are not exhaustive but highlight interesting behaviour, the benefit-cost ratios were chosen randomly within a range.

Random Initial Values. To observe how an equilibrium is reached, we initialise a NTEG with 10 players to which we assign random initial values (contributions, costs, benefits) and look at how they change their contributions until an equilibrium is reached. (The same initial contributions and benefit-cost ratios are used for every simulation.) According to the strategy defined by Eq. 10, no decentralisation conscious player is incentivised to contribute more than other players hence the player that has the maximum contribution in step 1 of the game (set by nature's move) will be reducing their contribution in the next step. On the other hand, other players with a high enough benefit-cost ratio will be incentivised to increase their contributions to the maximum value in step two of the game.

Under ideal conditions i.e., when the maximum contribution $x_{\max}$ is such that $n x_{\max} < \min_i \beta_i$, the equilibrium is reached after a few steps. Players with the greatest benefit-cost ratios align their contributions to the maximum value

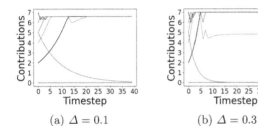
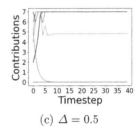

(a) $\Delta = 0.1$ (b) $\Delta = 0.3$ (c) $\Delta = 0.5$

Fig. 2. Oscillations disappear with constraints on contribution changes. The speed at which equilibria are reached depends on the constraints (slower with $\Delta = 0.1$, faster with $\Delta = 0.5$), as do the type of equilibria (1-value with $\Delta = 0.1$, 2-value $\Delta = 0.3$ or 0.5) and equilibrium value (greater with $\Delta = 0.3$ or 0.5).

(except perhaps for one of them, resulting in a 2-value equilibrium) while the remaining players free ride, as shown in Fig. 1a.

In other cases, as shown in Fig. 1b, some players may keep oscillating indefinitely. For these players, it must be the case that $\beta_j < nx_{eq}$, else playing x_{eq} at the same time as other players will be their best strategy and an equilibrium will be reached. Thus whenever everyone is playing x_{eq} at one time unit, they decrease their contributions to $\beta_j - nx_{eq}$ in the next step. However, after other oscillating players have also decreased their contributions, it is now the best strategy to go back to x_{eq}, and so on. This is due to players being myopic, not anticipating that other players will increase their contributions at the same time as them.

Constraints on the Rate of Change of Contributions. To avoid the unrealistic case where players oscillate forever we constrain the change in each player's contribution from one time unit to another by a factor Δ. This dampens the oscillations and allows players to converge to an equilibrium.

Because Δ affects how quickly players can converge to an equilibrium, the equilibrium that is reached varies with Δ. For example, in the case where $\Delta = 0.1$ participants are allowed to change their contributions by at most 10% from one time unit to another and a 1-value equilibrium is reached, as shown in Fig. 2a. When $\Delta = 0.3$ or $\Delta = 0.5$, a 2-value equilibrium is reached, as shown in Figs. 2b and c. Keeping this in mind we will, however, stick to the $\Delta = 0.1$ case in most of the simulations that follow for simplicity as the overall player behaviours i.e., players increasing their contribution or free-riding are the same although the final equilibrium differs.

We have also computed the different values of the reliability in each case but did not observe any clear pattern. Whether there is a pattern that is not clearly observable is left as an open problem.

Not only is a constraint on the change in the effort of players useful for them to efficiently converge to an equilibrium, it is also realistic. Players in real life are likely to understand the adverse effects of over correcting and are also likely to have constraints on how much they can change their effort (at least upwards)

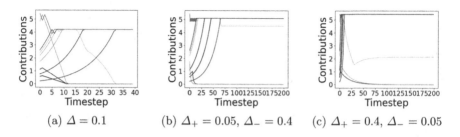

Fig. 3. Constraining the total effort can increase free-riding and reduce equilibrium values (Fig. 2a), as can reductions in contributions being easier than increases (Figs. 3b and c).

due to the cost of doing so. We discuss this constraint further in the next section, in relation to resource scarcity.

Moreover, every player updating their contributions at the same time is not a realistic assumption either. Bounding the change of contribution of each player from one step to another also helps get closer to a continuous time model.

Constraints on Total Effort. Another constraint that can be implemented is a limit on the overall change in the effort of all players i.e., the total effort. This models the constraint that the stock of resources used to contribute effort (e.g., new hardware) may be limited at any point in time. Figure 3a shows that in this case, some players may not be able to change their contribution enough to converge to the equilibrium and, therefore, switch to free riding.

Since it is usually easier to reduce one's contribution than to increase it, we also simulate the game with different constraints on the increase and the decrease of contributions from one step to another. We see in Figs. 3b and c that a 2-value equilibrium is reached, although the relative constraints on increasing and decreasing contributions result in different equilibrium values. The value played by the bulk of the player x_{eq} is higher when there is a greater constraint on the increase of contributions than on the decrease. This is because players can more rapidly reach the new maximum value. As a consequence, the second value played at the equilibrium is smaller.

Disruptions to an Equilibrium. A new player joining the game when it is in a 1-value equilibrium (which happens according to the conditions defined in Theorem 4) can lead to a new equilibrium being reached after a few steps, as shown in Fig. 4a in the case of a strong constraint.

When an equilibrium is disrupted by a player deviating from the equilibrium, players that increase their contribution to contribute more effort than the equilibrium value incentivise other decentralisation conscious players to free ride or increase their effort to reach a new equilibrium value if it is allowed by their benefit-cost ratio. This is shown in Fig. 4b, in the case of a strong constraint.

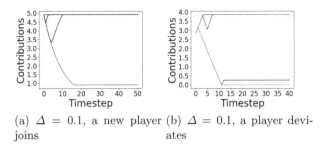

(a) $\Delta = 0.1$, a new player joins

(b) $\Delta = 0.1$, a player deviates

Fig. 4. Disruptions to an equilibrium due to a new player joining or a player deviating lead to new equilibriums.

6   Discussion

6.1   The Role of Decentralisation Conscious Players

Our model and choice of NTE function shows that decentralisation conscious players can help maintain a decentralised system. However, as Theorems 8 and 9 show, decentralisation conscious players only ever increase their effort in response to another player increasing their contribution at the cost of decentralisation. They maintain decentralisation within the constraints of their benefit-cost ratio but ignore players that free ride after their benefit-cost ratio no longer allows them to contribute.

Because decentralisation conscious players can only maintain a pre-existing level of decentralisation and can be leveraged by selfish players to implement a minimum benefit-cost ratio that acts as a form of gate-keeping against players with lower benefit-cost ratios, there is a distinction between decentralisation conscious players and *altruistic* players that operate regardless of their benefit-cost ratio. This suggests that new mechanisms dictating how effort is contributed or rewarded may be needed for players to have rational ways of increasing decentralisation outside of purely altruistic behaviour.

6.2   Modelling Constraints

Resource Scarcity. Players contribute based on their benefit-cost ratios and, as we have seen in Sect. 5, equilibria depend on the rate of change of contributions. An implicit assumption made by our model is that a player can contribute more (at a cost) should they wish to do so but this may not be possible. For example, cryptocurrency mining hardware has suffered from shortages that forced buyers to obtain hardware at significant premiums and logistical difficulties [29]. When resources are unobtainable, it can become impossible to contribute more or continue contributing the same amount (if resources must be replaced), causing involuntary deviations from otherwise rational strategies.

If it is impossible to acquire the resources to contribute, the system will rely on players having a high valuation of the system. Contributors to systems like Tor [26] operating nodes at a loss may demonstrate this but in the case of cryptocurrencies new miners are less likely to have a high valuation of the system because they are unlikely to have a stake in it, unlike miners that have accumulated rewards. Miners in cryptocurrencies that are more centralised due to the high practical costs of mining can, therefore, form an effective oligopoly [5,17].

Can we avoid issues of resource scarcity? One way of avoiding the problematic reliance on resources with variable stock (e.g., stake, hardware) is to opt for mechanisms like proof-of-personhood [13], which is equally distributed ("1 person = 1 vote") and maximises the NTE, although this has other issues to overcome.

Geographical and Political Decentralisation. Because players contribute based on their benefit-cost ratios so the geographical distribution of players will matter if costs vary with location. For example, cryptocurrency mining is concentrated in the few areas where mining is most profitable.

Markets are also affected by political power and changes in regulations. China controlled 65% of Bitcoin's hashpower in 2019 [18] but following new Chinese regulations [9] the share of hashpower in the US has grown due to political stability with respect to Bitcoin mining [3]. The impact of markets and political power on decentralisation adds complexity and uncertainty in models, which may motivate decentralised systems less reliant on other markets e.g., proof-of-stake (based on the cryptocurrency's native tokens) or proof-of-personhood may be easier to reason about than proof-of-work (energy and hardware markets).

Incomplete and Unequal Information. Our model has assumed perfect information at each step with players changing their contributions based on this information, but players could hide information such as the stock of unused resources they have at their disposal. Attacks such as selfish mining in proof-of-work cryptocurrencies [16] are based on abusing information asymmetry, as are hostile takeovers which use previously unused but available mining capacity [11]. There is also an inherent delay in information propagating through a network. This may result in different equilibria as players adapt their contributions based on the information they receive at a point where it may no longer be accurate.

How much this matters is hard to determine. Attacks such as selfish mining have seldom been observed, and effort rarely varies across short time periods. (See the Bitcoin hashrate distribution over short time periods, even if the larger trend is growth [1].) This may be due to issues like acquiring the additional resources needed to contribute more effort, but it may also be to maintain a level of decentralisation as our model suggests miners might do.

6.3   Related Work

There is an important literature on modelling incentives in cryptocurrencies through refinements of Nash Equilibria that has been systematised [6]. Although the types of players and games considered vary across papers, none of the papers surveyed (except Varian's paper [28]) consider the reliability of the system.

Varian's system reliability paper [28] has previously been extended by Grossklags et al. [19] in the context of investments in security and insurance. Grossklags et al. [20] have also applied Varian's model to study the difference between expert and naive players in security games to quantify the impact of information. In this work, we have instead focused on decentralisation and introduced the NTEG, which extends Varian's model in another direction.

7   Conclusion

We have proposed a model for decentralisation conscious players based on the NTE function we have introduced. The Nash equilibria show what could be expected from such players. Using simulations we have also considered how players may reach an equilibrium, including after disruptions. There is a variety of possibilities for future work and opportunities to apply our model to specific cases. This includes cases with valuations of the system which are hard to precisely define e.g., ideological commitment, as well as cases with very explicit valuations and dependencies on rewards but complex financial optimisation such as cryptocurrencies. Protocol designers who wish to incorporate rational players, as opposed to honest players, but also wish to incorporate the reliability of the system in addition to short-term rewards could use the NTE function.

Acknowledgment. Alexander Hicks was partially supported by Protocol Labs for this work.

References

1. Pools-timeseries. https://www.blockchain.com/charts/pools-timeseries
2. Abraham, I., Dolev, D., Gonen, R., Halpern, J.: Distributed computing meets game theory: robust mechanisms for rational secret sharing and multiparty computation. In: Proceedings of the Twenty-Fifth Annual ACM Symposium on Principles of Distributed Computing, pp. 53–62 (2006)
3. Allison, I.: Long in China's shadow, the US is becoming a Bitcoin mining power again (2020). https://www.coindesk.com/us-becoming-bitcoin-mining-power-again
4. Anderson, R.: Security engineering: a guide to building dependable distributed systems. John Wiley & Sons (2020)
5. Arnosti, N., Weinberg, S.M.: Bitcoin: a natural oligopoly. arXiv preprint arXiv:1811.08572 (2018)
6. Azouvi, S., Hicks, A.: SoK: tools for game theoretic models of security for cryptocurrencies. arXiv preprint arXiv:1905.08595 (2019)
7. Azouvi, S., Hicks, A.: Decentralisation conscious players and system reliability. arXiv preprint arXiv:2204.11980 (2022)
8. Bano, S., et al.: SoK: consensus in the age of blockchains. In: Proceedings of the 1st ACM Conference on Advances in Financial Technologies, pp. 183–198 (2019)
9. Baydakova, A.: China's crypto miners struggle to pay power bills as regulators clamp down on OTC desks (2020). https://www.coindesk.com/chinese-miners-struggle-to-pay-for-electricity

10. Bissias, G., Böhme, R., Thibodeau, D., Levine, B.N.: Pricing security in proof-of-work systems. arXiv preprint arXiv:2012.03706 (2020)
11. Bonneau, J.: Hostile blockchain takeovers (short paper). In: Zohar, A., et al. (eds.) FC 2018. LNCS, vol. 10958, pp. 92–100. Springer, Heidelberg (2019). https://doi.org/10.1007/978-3-662-58820-8_7
12. Bonneau, J., Miller, A., Clark, J., Narayanan, A., Kroll, J.A., Felten, E.W.: SoK: research perspectives and challenges for Bitcoin and cryptocurrencies. In: 2015 IEEE symposium on security and privacy, pp. 104–121. IEEE (2015)
13. Borge, M., Kokoris-Kogias, E., Jovanovic, P., Gasser, L., Gailly, N., Ford, B.: Proof-of-personhood: Redemocratizing permissionless cryptocurrencies. In: 2017 IEEE European Symposium on Security and Privacy Workshops (EuroS&PW), pp. 23–26. IEEE (2017)
14. Brünjes, L., Kiayias, A., Koutsoupias, E., Stouka, A.P.: Reward sharing schemes for stake pools. arXiv preprint arXiv:1807.11218 (2018)
15. Chen, X., Papadimitriou, C., Roughgarden, T.: An axiomatic approach to block rewards. In: Proceedings of the 1st ACM Conference on Advances in Financial Technologies, pp. 124–131 (2019)
16. Eyal, I., Sirer, E.G.: Majority is not enough: bitcoin mining is vulnerable. In: Christin, N., Safavi-Naini, R. (eds.) FC 2014. LNCS, vol. 8437, pp. 436–454. Springer, Heidelberg (2014). https://doi.org/10.1007/978-3-662-45472-5_28
17. Gencer, A.E., Basu, S., Eyal, I., van Renesse, R., Sirer, E.G.: Decentralization in bitcoin and ethereum networks. In: Meiklejohn, S., Sako, K. (eds.) FC 2018. LNCS, vol. 10957, pp. 439–457. Springer, Heidelberg (2018). https://doi.org/10.1007/978-3-662-58387-6_24
18. Godbole, O.: Highest in 2 years: 65% of Bitcoin hash power is in China, report finds (2019). https://www.coindesk.com/highest-in-2-years-65-of-bitcoin-hash-power-is-in-china-report-finds
19. Grossklags, J., Christin, N., Chuang, J.: Secure or insure? a game-theoretic analysis of information security games. In: Proceedings of the 17th International Conference on World Wide Web, pp. 209–218 (2008)
20. Grossklags, J., Johnson, B., Christin, N.: When information improves information security. In: Sion, R. (ed.) FC 2010. LNCS, vol. 6052, pp. 416–423. Springer, Heidelberg (2010). https://doi.org/10.1007/978-3-642-14577-3_37
21. Hajdarbegovic, N.: Bitcoin miners ditch ghash.io pool over fears of 51% attack (2014). https://www.coindesk.com/bitcoin-miners-ditch-ghash-io-pool-51-attack
22. Judmayer, A., et al.: Pay-to-win: incentive attacks on proof-of-work cryptocurrencies. IACR Cryptology ePrint Archive Paper 2019/775 (2019)
23. Kwon, Y., Liu, J., Kim, M., Song, D., Kim, Y.: Impossibility of full decentralization in permissionless blockchains. In: Proceedings of the 1st ACM Conference on Advances in Financial Technologies, pp. 110–123. AFT 2019, ACM, New York, NY, USA (2019). https://doi.org/10.1145/3318041.3355463
24. Neudecker, T., Hartenstein, H.: Short paper: an empirical analysis of blockchain forks in bitcoin. In: Goldberg, I., Moore, T. (eds.) FC 2019. LNCS, vol. 11598, pp. 84–92. Springer, Cham (2019). https://doi.org/10.1007/978-3-030-32101-7_6
25. Roughgarden, T.: Selfish routing and the price of anarchy, vol. 174. MIT press Cambridge (2005)
26. Syverson, P., Dingledine, R., Mathewson, N.: Tor: the second generation onion router. In: Usenix Security, pp. 303–320 (2004)
27. Troncoso, C., Isaakidis, M., Danezis, G., Halpin, H.: Systematizing decentralization and privacy: lessons from 15 years of research and deployments. Proc. Priv. Enhancing Technol. **2017**(4), 404–426 (2017)

28. Varian, H.: System reliability and free riding. In: Camp, L.J., Lewis, S. (eds.) EIS. AIS, vol. 12, pp. 1–15. Springer, Boston (2004). https://doi.org/10.1007/1-4020-8090-5_1

29. Wong, J.I.: Ethereum miners are renting Boeing 747s to ship graphics cards and AMD shares are soaring (2017). https://qz.com/1039809/amd-shares-are-soaring-ethereum-miners-are-renting-boeing-747s-to-ship-graphics-cards-to-mines/

Towards Overcoming the Undercutting Problem

Tiantian Gong[1]([✉]) [ID], Mohsen Minaei[2], Wenhai Sun[1], and Aniket Kate[1]

[1] Purdue University, West Lafayette, USA
{tg,sun841,aniket}@purdue.edu
[2] Visa Research, Palo Alto, USA
mominaei@visa.com

Abstract. Mining processes of Bitcoin and similar cryptocurrencies are currently incentivized with voluntary transaction fees and fixed block rewards which will halve gradually to zero. In the setting where optional and arbitrary transaction fee becomes the prominent/remaining incentive, Carlsten et al. [CCS 2016] find that an undercutting attack can become the equilibrium strategy for miners. In undercutting, the attacker deliberately forks an existing chain by leaving wealthy transactions unclaimed to attract petty complaint miners to its fork. We observe that two simplifying assumptions in [CCS 2016] of fees arriving at fixed rates and miners collecting *all* accumulated fees regardless of block size limit are often infeasible in practice and find that they are inaccurately inflating the profitability of undercutting. Studying Bitcoin and Monero blockchain data, we find that the fees deliberately left out by an undercutter may not be attractive to other miners (hence to the attacker itself): the deliberately left out transactions may not fit into a new block without "squeezing out" some other to-be transactions, and thus claimable fees in the next round cannot be raised arbitrarily.

This work views undercutting and shifting among chains rationally as mining strategies of rational miners. We model profitability of undercutting strategy with block size limit present, which bounds the claimable fees in a round and gives rise to a pending (cushion) transaction set. In the proposed model, we first identify the conditions necessary to make undercutting profitable. We then present an easy-to-deploy defense against undercutting by selectively assembling transactions into the new block to invalidate the identified conditions. Indeed, under a typical setting with undercutters present, applying this avoidance technique is a Nash Equilibrium. Finally, we complement the above analytical results with an experimental analysis using both artificial data of normally distributed fee rates and actual transactions in Bitcoin and Monero.

Keywords: Bitcoin incentive · Transaction fee · Undercutting · Undercutting avoidance

M. Minaei—Part of this work was done while the author was at Purdue University.

I. Eyal and J. Garay (Eds.): FC 2022, LNCS 13411, pp. 444–463, 2022.
https://doi.org/10.1007/978-3-031-18283-9_22

1 Introduction

Bitcoin network [19] and several cryptocurrencies rely on nodes participating in transaction verification, ordering and execution, and mining new blocks for their security and performance. Specifically, with honest majority, Byzantine-fault tolerant consensus is possible with Proof of Work (PoW) assuming network synchrony. With honest majority, attacks like double spending [23] are also harder to implement in practice. Additionally, with more honest computing peers, liveness is provided with a higher probability. A proper incentive design helps attract more honest parties to join. Bitcoin currently incentivizes nodes (or miners) with fixed block rewards and voluntary transaction fees. Historically, the block reward has been the dominating source of miners' revenues. However, for Bitcoin, it is a system parameter that halves approximately every four years.[1] Its domination is expected to vanish due to the deteriorating nature and transaction fees will then become the major mining revenue generator.

With a stable reward, a miner's expected revenues rely mostly on its probability of finding a block, which itself is contingent on the miner's hash power. However, in the fee-based incentive system, the revenues additionally depend on the fee amount inside a block, which further relies on users' offerings and miners' transaction selections. The total fees inside blocks are market-dependent and time-variant because (i) transaction arrival can be arbitrary; (ii) transaction fees are voluntary under the current mechanism, so they can be arbitrary (even 0) and the threshold fee rates for faster confirmation change with supply and demand in the block space market; (iii) miners have the freedom of sampling transactions to form new blocks. As a result, the fair sharing of revenue based on hashing power may not be maintained. For example, consider two miners A and B in the system with the same mining power. If A mines blocks each with total fees of 1 BTC and B always encounters wealthy transactions and mines blocks each with 2 BTC total fees, B's revenue is twice A's revenue.

In particular, the fee-based incentivization framework nurtures a possible new deviating mining strategy called undercutting [4]. In undercutting, the attacker intentionally forks an existing chain by leaving wealthier transactions out in its new block to attract other (petty compliant) miners to join the fork. Unlike honest miners, who follow the longest chain that appears first, petty compliant (PC) miners break ties by selecting the chain that leaves out the most fees. In [4], fees accumulate at a fixed rate and miners claim *all* accumulated fees when creating a new block. Thus, a miner undercuts another miner's block because it receives 0 of the fees in the target block but expects nonzero returns via forking. Similarly, PC miners join the fork because the undercutter leaves out more fees unclaimed (and they can claim *all* fees in the next block). Carlsten et al. find that undercutting can become the equilibrium strategy for miners, thus making the system unstable as miners undercut each other.

However, this result is based on a setting disregarding the block size limit. If the fees claimable in the next block are bounded and a pending transaction

---
[1] The next halving event to 3.125 BTC is scheduled for May 2024 [10].

set exists due to the block size cap, PC miners may not join the fork and undercutting may not be more profitable than extending the current chain head. The intuition is that the extra claimable fees are bounded, and the fork does not win with absolute probability, while the main chain may provide slightly fewer fees but extends with probability 1 when there's no attack. We give an illustrative example below where undercutting is not rational when we consider the limit. Let there be 33% honest, 17% undercutter, and 50% PC mining power, 100 total token fees with 20 claimable in each block. As we elaborate in the full version of this report [9], the undercutter expects 3.4 token returns by extending the chain head. Suppose it instead undercuts and claims half of the tokens in the target block, 10 tokens, in its first forking block (as in [4]). If PC miners do not shift, they expect 10 tokens from the next main-chain block; if they follow the fork, they expect to gain 10 tokens. But, shifting is not rational for the owner of the undercutting target block and may not be rational for others as they have started mining the main chain for some time. Even if they shift, we find the undercutter's expected return to be $1.717 < 3.4$.

Towards modeling undercutting attacks more realistically and generally, we construct a new model to capture rational behaviors related to and performance of the undercutting strategy. Miners in our model are either honest or rational. A rational miner may **undercut** or **arbitrarily shift among chains** as long as the action maximizes its returns. Fees in our model arrive with transactions. By sorting transactions in the unconfirmed transaction set and packing at most a block size limit of transactions, we obtain the maximum claimable fees at a certain timestamp. Miners can choose to claim no more than this maximum fee.

Essentially, when undercutting, the rational miner's goal is to earn more than what it can potentially gain not undercutting. The attacker needs to first (i) attract other rational miners to join its fork if necessary, and second (ii) avoid being undercut by others. If it leaves out too many fees, it may end up being worse off undercutting. If it claims more than necessary, other rational miners may undercut its fork, annihilating its efforts. Then how many fees should an undercutter take to achieve both goals simultaneously? And can others make it not possible to do so? We seek to first locate such a feasible area for an undercutter to secure its premiums and next, uncover defenses against this attack. Note that undercutting is not desired because it hurts the expected profits for honest miners. Successful undercutting also harms users who attach high fee rates to have their transactions processed faster.

1.1   Contributions

We define an analytical model that captures behaviors that are "rational" but not necessarily "honest" like undercutting and shifting rationally. This can be used to analyze other rational deviating strategies in a fee-based incentive system. The key is to pinpoint reward distributions and probabilities of earning the rewards.

Specifically for undercutting and as a key contribution, we offer **closed-form conditions on the unconfirmed transaction set to make undercutting**

profitable. The key quantity is the ratio (γ) between the maximum claimable fees in the next block (w.r.t. block size limit) and the fees in the current block. For clarity, let the mining power fraction of the undercutter be β_u and that of the honest miner be β_h, remaining rational miner be β_r. **(i)** In the best case for the undercutter in our model, the undercutter forgoes the fork after being one block behind instead of hanging on longer. **(ii)** When $\gamma < \frac{a\beta_r + \beta_u}{1 - \beta_u}$, the attacker can expect to earn a premium by proper undercutting. It should carefully craft the first block on its fork (deciding parameter a) in such a way that rational miners can be attracted to join the fork when needed but not tempted to undercut it again. We provide more details in Sect. 4. The conditions for the case where the undercutter holds on for one more block (Appendix A) are stricter, as noted in (i) and the overall expected returns are fewer.

As a side-product and naturally, we provide an **alternative transaction selection rule** to counter undercutting, other than fitting all available transactions into a block. Once we have identified effective conditions for profitable undercutting, we work backward to proactively check the conditions before creating a new block. By making the conditions no longer satisfied, potential undercutters are no longer motivated to undercut. Applying the defense technique is Nash equilibrium in a typical setting. In the equilibrium, we additionally calculate the price of anarchy (PoA) to capture the inefficiency a strong undercutter brings or the advantage it has in a system. To make the system more stable, we can either strengthen the second potential undercutter or weaken the strongest undercutter through decentralization.

We **experiment with real-world data** from Bitcoin and Monero blockchains to evaluate the profitability of undercutting and the effectiveness of avoidance techniques. We decide on the two systems because Bitcoin is representative of swamped blockchains and Monero typically has a small unconfirmed transaction set. **(i)** In Bitcoin, for a 17.6% undercutter, the average return is 17.9%. For a hypothetical 49.9% attacker, the average revenue is 60.8%. In Monero, we observe a profit increase of around 8% points from fair shares for a 35% attacker. **(ii)** After enabling defense, undercutting generates around a fair share for Monero 35% undercutter where the two strongest rational miners possess the same mining powers. We test a strong undercutter's advantage in Bitcoin (49.9%, 20%), which gives the 49.9% attacker around 63.5% of the total returns.

1.2 Related Work

Carlsten et al. [4] introduce the undercutting mining strategy to show the instability of the future Bitcoin fee-based incentivization system because undercutting can become the equilibrium strategy. There, transaction fees accumulate at a constant rate and miners can include all fees when creating a new block. But fees essentially are *not* independent of transactions. If we dive into the transaction level and account for the block size limit, the fees one can claim are restricted and there can potentially be a large pending transaction set, which can cushion or even annihilate the effects of undercutting. Based on this intuition, we construct the new model focusing on transaction selection rules, which determine fees claimed and left out. Further, both undercutting and hopping among chains are modeled more generally as actions of rational miners instead of separately as two types of miners as in [4]. This helps quantify the profit margin and brings about opportunities for mitigation.

Together with Other Non-compliant Mining Strategies. There have already been rigorous discussions on attacks related to mining strategies. Most notable attacks are selfish mining [7,20,26], block withholding [5,6,16,17,22], and fork after withholding [13]. Defenses against these game-theoretic attacks have also been studied [11,14,15,21,28]. It is possible to combine undercutting with other mining strategies like selfish mining and block withholding. For the latter, because undercutters prefer larger mining power, the two attacks have opposite goals, so one needs to balance the computation resource allocation. Selfish mining purposely hides discovered blocks, while undercutting intends to publish a block and attract other miners. They do not share the same rationale, but we can schedule the two strategies and apply the one with higher expected returns at a certain time. In this work, we put our focus on the profitability and mitigation of undercutting, which affects the undercutting part of the strategy scheduler.

Lemon Market. Another angle to look at the problem on a higher level is through the market for "lemons" [2], the brand-new car that becomes defective the minute one bought it. In the Bitcoin block space market, users are bidders, and miners are sellers. Users decide prices to pay based on their observation of the relationship between confirmation time and fee rates. They attach fee rates corresponding to the desired waiting time. If undercutting is prevailing, users who attach high fee rates but are ghosted are provided with "lemons" instead of "peaches" – fast confirmation. This can result in a decrease in the overall fee rates, diminishing the profitability of undercutting.

2   Preliminaries

Mempool. Mempool [3] is an unconfirmed transaction set maintained by miners locally. When a transaction is announced to the network, it enters into miners' mempools. Miners select transactions from their mempools to form new blocks. Usually, a miner chooses the bandwidth set (Definition 1) with respect to the local mempool and global block size limit. An undercutting miner intentionally leaves out wealthy transactions when forming blocks to attract other rational miners. Wealthy transactions are those with high fee rates. When a new block is published, miners verify the block and then update their local mempools to exclude transactions included in the newly published block.

Definition 1 (Bandwidth Set). *Given block size limit B and an unconfirmed transaction set $\mathbb{T}$ comprising N transactions, $S^* \in P(\mathbb{T})$ is a bandwidth set of $\mathbb{T}$ with respect to B if $S^*.size \leq B$ and $\forall S_i \in P(\mathbb{T})$ with $S_i.size \leq B, S^*.fee \geq S_i.fee$, where $P(\mathbb{T})$ is the power set of $\mathbb{T}$.*

Remark 1. A bandwidth set is a set of transactions in a miner's mempool providing the most fees a miner claimable in one block. If the unconfirmed transaction set is of size $\leq B$, then the bandwidth set is the memory pool itself. Note that the bandwidth set is not necessarily unique.

Definition 2 (Safe margin). *When a chain C^* is D block(s) ahead of competing chains, a miner with safe margin parameter D always extends C^*.*

Remark 2. Honest miners apply the longest chain rule and always have $D = 1$.[2] For rational miners, $D \geq 1$. When the length discrepancy between competing chains is within D, they select the chain with the most expected returns.

3   Mining Game Featuring Undercutting Strategy

In this section, we model the mining game involving the undercutting strategy. We consider honest miners, who follow the default protocol specifications, and rational miners. The latter are addressed as undercutters when they undercut.

Game Definition. We define the mining game $G = \langle M, A, R \rangle$ as follows:

- n Players $M = \{M_0, M_1, ..., M_{n-1}\}$: without loss of generality, we label a subset of the miners that have a total of β_h mining power as honest; we label a miner with β_u mining power as the current undercutter under discussion; we label the remaining miners as (currently) non-undercutting rational miners and their total mining power is denoted as $\beta_r = 1 - \beta_h - \beta_u$. Honest miners are treated as one because they follow the same mining rules, and we assume they are informed the same way.
- Actions $A = \{undercut(\cdot), stay(\cdot), shift(\cdot)\}$: we index chains during a game according to their timestamps after the branching point, e.g. the original (main) chain with index $Chain_0$, abbreviated as C_0. Honest miners always honest mine and may choose to stay or shift depending on circumstances. Rational miners may choose to undercut an existing chain and start a new chain, stay on a working chain, or shift among existing chains.
- Utility functions $U = \{u_i\}_{M_i \in M}$: we let $u_i = R_i - c_i$, where R_i is the total transaction fees it receives and c_i is the cost. We treat the cost c_i as fixed and reduce the problem of maximizing utility to maximization of obtained fees.

---

[2] When there is a tie, they choose the chain with the oldest timestamp. If timestamps should be the same, they select a chain at random.

Threat Model. We allow no miner to own more than 50% mining power (i.e., $\beta_u \leq 0.5$). We let miners publish their discovered blocks immediately to attract other miners to join. We assume the best case for the undercutter and let the mempool be the same for miners on the same chain. Because undercutting is not practical or meaningful if miners have distinct mempools, since wealthy transactions an attacker left unclaimed may not exist in others' mempools in the first place. This assumption makes the attacker stronger, and we intend to uncover what the attacker can obtain in advantageous environment settings.

We let miners know of other miners' types (e.g. honest or rational) after sufficient observations. We assume miners can approximate the amount of mining power concentrated on a chain based on the block generation time on that chain.

Solution Concept. We solve for Nash Equilibrium (NE) in the mining game with undercutting mining strategy. In a Nash Equilibrium, players do not earn extra utility by unilaterally deviating from the equilibrium strategy.

3.1 Miner's Winning Probability

A miner's expected returns from mining equal the product of its winning probability of a block and the fees residing in that block. Firstly, miner M_i's winning probability of a block is simply its mining power when there is only one chain. In the case of competing chains, we need to additionally quantify a chain's winning probability when working in systems where only one chain survives.

A Chain's Winning Probability. In undercutting, the attacker forks an existing chain by leaving out wealthy transactions. In the following discussions, we refer to the undercutting chain as C_1 and the current main chain as C_0. C_0 might not be on the main chain eventually if C_1 wins the race. The effective height of a chain is the number of blocks it has accumulated after the forking point. These competing blocks are called effective blocks in the game analysis.

Overall, the process proceeds as follows. The undercutter sees a new block is appended to C_0 by another miner. It starts to work on a forking block that excludes wealthy transactions appearing in the current chain head. With some probability, it can create the fork faster than the next block appearing on C_0. When the undercutter publishes its block, some rational miners consider shifting to C_1 because there are more high fee rate transactions that they can benefit from. To model this procedure, we screenshot the state of the system as a tuple that we denote as $\vec{S} = (m_0, m_1, \vec{F^0}, \vec{F^1}, O, \delta, \lambda_0, \lambda_1)$, where m_0 and m_1 are respectively the effective height of C_0 and C_1; $\vec{F^0}$ and $\vec{F^1}$ are the list of transaction fee total in effective blocks on C_0 and C_1; O is the mining power currently working on C_1, which updates upon new block appending events; $\delta \in (-1, 1)$ is the mining power shifting from the source chain to the destination chain, which is defined to be positive if miners are shifting to C_1 and negative if they are shifting to C_0; λ_0 and λ_1 are block generation rates for C_0 and C_1.

To obtain the winning probability measure for a chain from state $\vec{S}$, we view the block generation event as a Poisson process and use a random variable to represent the waiting time between block occurrence events. We denote waiting time for C_0 as X and C_1 as Y. They both follow exponential distribution but with different rates. The rate parameters depend on the mining power distribution. Given the state $\vec{S}$, we obtain the block occurrence rate as: $\lambda_0 = \frac{1-O}{I}$; and $\lambda_1 = \frac{O}{I}$, where I is block generation interval (e.g. 10 min for Bitcoin). This is derived from the thinning theorem of the Poisson point process. The main idea is that independent sub-processes of a Poisson process are still Poisson processes with individual rates. With this property, we can determine the time interval for the next block to appear on a chain. Then, the key is the mining power concentrated on a chain, and further is whether honest and rational miners shift.

For $D = 1$, there is only one state that the currently non-undercutting rational miners β_r need to make a decision, when the undercutter extends C_1 before the C_0 extends by one. The two competing chains are in a tie with relative height difference $\tilde{D} = 0$. The probability that C_1 wins is simply $p = \Pr[C_1 \ Wins] = \Pr[Y < X] = O + \delta$.

For $D = 2$, there is an infinite number of states where flexible rational miners need to make decisions about shifting. We let $\tilde{D} = m_1 - m_0 < D$, denoting the number of blocks by which C_1 leads C_0. For example, when $\tilde{D} = -1$, C_1 is one block behind C_0. Then C_1 wins if it creates 3 blocks before C_0 extends by 1, or discovers 4 blocks before C_0 extends by 2, and so on. Thus, we have $p = \sum_{i=0}^{\infty} \Pr[(D - \tilde{D} + i)Y < (i+1)X]$.

(i) **When $\tilde{D} = -1$**, C_1 is behind C_0. For C_1 to win, we need $p = \sum_{i=0}^{\infty} \Pr[(3 + i)Y < (1 + i)X] = \sum_{i=0}^{\infty} (\beta_u + \delta)^{3+i}(1 - \beta_u - \delta)^i$.

(ii) **When $\tilde{D} = 0$**, there is a tie between C_1 and C_0. In this case, $p = \sum_{i=0}^{\infty} \Pr[(2 + i)Y < (1 + i)X] = \sum_{i=0}^{\infty} (\beta_u + \delta)^{2+i}(1 - \beta_u - \delta)^i$.

(iii) **When $\tilde{D} = 1$**, C_1 is leading. We have $p = \sum_{i=0}^{\infty} \Pr[(1 + i)Y < (1 + i)X] = \sum_{i=0}^{\infty} (\beta_u + \delta)^{1+i}(1 - \beta_u - \delta)^i$.

A Miner's Probability of Winning a Block. Suppose a miner M_i with β_{M_i} mining power is mining on a chain C_j with β_{C_j} accumulated total mining power which has winning probability p_{C_j}. Then M_i's winning probability is $\frac{\beta_{M_i}}{\beta_{C_j}} p_{C_j}$.

4   Game Analysis

We analyze the profitability of the undercutting strategy with parameter $D = 1$ in
this section and continue the discussion with
$D = 2$ in the full report, for which a summary
resides in Appendix A. The latter generates
fewer profits. We differentiate between scenarios with "abundant" and "limited" amounts
of fees. The extreme case where there are
only negligible fees claimable for a long period
("drought") is described in the full report.

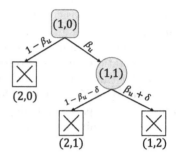

Fig. 1. State transition for $D = 1$.
"X" Boxes are terminal states. For
non-terminal states, circles indicate ties. Every left branch means
C_0 extends by one and every right
branch refers to C_1 creating a new
block. The quantity on the arrow is
the probability of state transition.

4.1   Giving Up if One Block Behind

We use the abbreviated state $S^* = (m_0, m_1)$
in discussion. We denote the transaction fees
inside the first two blocks of C_0 as F_1^0 and
F_2^0, the transaction fees inside blocks of C_1 as
F_1^1 and F_2^1, the expected returns for flexible
rational miners β_r as R_r and the expected returns for the undercutter as R_u.
When there is no undercutting, we denote their respective expected return as
R_r' and $R_{\overline{u}}$.

For $D = 1$, rational miners only need to decide whether to shift at state
$S^* = (1, 1)$ when undercutting becomes visible as shown in Fig. 1. Suppose they
shift x of their mining power β_r to C_1. They can decide x that gives max $E[R_r]$:

$$\underset{x \in [0,1]}{\arg\max} \left(\mathbb{1}_{owner} \cdot (1-p) \cdot F_1^0 + \frac{(1-x)\beta_r}{\beta_h + (1-x)\beta_r}(1-p) \cdot F_2^0 + \frac{x\beta_r}{x\beta_r + \beta_u}p \cdot F_2^1 \right) \quad (1)$$

where p is the probability of C_1 winning and $\mathbb{1}_{owner}$ indicates whether a rational
miner is the owner of the first block on chain 0. The shift can then be calculated as
$\delta = x\beta_r$. Observe that the optimization problem involves fees inside succeeding
blocks after the forking point. We represent fees in a relative way for general
interpretability: we let $F_1^0 = 1$ and have fee total in other blocks measured
relative to it. Now we discuss two different mempool conditions.

Mempools with Limited Bandwidth Set. By "limited" we mean the current
bandwidth set on C_0 has a small enough transaction fee total ($< \frac{\beta_u}{1-\beta_u}F_1^0$). We
provide more details concerning this threshold as we proceed. WLOG, we assume
$F_1^0 = 1$, $F_2^0 = \gamma \geq 0$ (s.t. $\frac{F_2^0}{F_1^0} = \gamma$), $F_1^1 = a$ and $F_2^1 = b$ where $a \in [0,1]$. We
can let $b = 1 + \gamma - a$, assuming the best case for the undercutter that it can
compose the first block on C_1 in such a way that the second block can claim all
unclaimed fees within one block. If a rational miner decides to undercut, with
probability β_u, the undercutter can create a new chain and the game is started.

In the remaining game, with probability $p = \beta_u + \delta$, C_1 wins and with probability $(1 - p)$, C_0 wins. The expected profit of the undercutter is

$$E[R_u] = \beta_u(\beta_u + \delta) \cdot (1 \cdot a + \frac{\beta_u}{\beta_u + \delta} \cdot (1 + \gamma - a))$$

The expected return for the rational miner if it does not undercut is $E[R_{\bar{u}}] = \beta_u \gamma$. The miner will undercut only if $E[R_{\bar{u}}] < E[R_u]$. Then

$$\gamma < \frac{\delta a + \beta_u}{1 - \beta_u} \tag{2}$$

With $\gamma < \frac{\beta_u}{1-\beta_u}$, $E[R_{\bar{u}}] < E[R_u]$ even when $\delta = 0$. That is, even no rational miner shifts to C_1, there are so few fees left in the mempool that the attacker is always better off by forking C_0 compared with extending it.

One extreme case is when there are no transactions left or the bandwidth set has negligible fees and $F_2^0 = 0$. The rational miner will fork because originally there is nothing left on C_0 and $E[R_{\bar{u}}] = 0$. One detail is that the attacker needs to craft the first block (determine a) it generates to avoid being undercut again. Suppose when $\gamma < T$ ($T = \frac{\beta_u}{1-\beta_u}$ in our current context), a potential undercutter initiates the attack. Then by choosing a in such a way that $\frac{1+\gamma-a}{a} \geq T_2$ ($T_2 = \frac{\beta_{u_2}}{1-\beta_{u_2}}$ in the current context), the undercutter can avoid being undercut again. Note that here when an undercutter decides a, it is picturing a potential undercutter β_{u_2} other than itself. We will revisit the choice of a after complete the discussion for $\gamma > \frac{\beta_u}{1-\beta_u}$ case.

In conclusion, for $D = 1$, when the attacker is stronger (β_u is larger), the requirements on the mempool bandwidth set fee total for undercutting to be profitable regardless of rational miners' actions is looser. When β_u approximates 0.5, the threshold ratio approaches 1, which occurs with high frequency. For $\beta_u = 0.2$, the upper bound is 0.25, where the current bandwidth set is 1/4 of the fees inside the chain head of C_0.

Mempools with Sufficient Bandwidth Set. By "sufficient" we mean the current bandwidth set in the mempool has more than "limited" transaction fee total ($\geq \frac{\beta_u}{1-\beta_u} F_1^0$). In this case, the undercutter needs to attract some rational miners at state (1,1) (make $\delta > 0$). It's straightforward to verify that the owner of the undercutting target block is better off by staying on C_0. We treat this miner as honest in the following calculations and only make decisions for the remaining rational players. To decide whether to shift to C_1, rational miners solve for x in

$$\arg\max_{x \in [0,1]} E[R_r] = \arg\max_{x \in [0,1]} \left(\frac{(1-x)\beta_r}{\beta_h + (1-x)\beta_r}(1-p)\gamma + \frac{x\beta_r}{x\beta_r + \beta_u}p(1+\gamma-a) \right)$$

Here $p = O + \delta = \beta_u + x\beta_r$. One observation is that the rational miners either move to C_1 with all their mining power or none (function is linear in x after simplification). When $x = 1$, we have $E[R_{r|x=1}] = \beta_r(1 + \gamma - a)$. Similarly, in setting $x = 0$, we obtain $E[R_{r|x=0}] = \beta_r \gamma$. To encourage shifting of rational miners, we need $E[R_{r|x=1}] > E[R_{r|x=0}]$, which means $a < 1$. To avoid being undercut, the undercutter additionally needs to pick an a such that this condition is not satisfied for the first block on its C_1. This is to say the undercutter can profitably undercut C_0 in expectation, but others do not expect to attack its C_1 successfully. As previously touched on, we need

$$a \le \frac{1 + \bar{\gamma}}{1 + T} = \frac{1 + \bar{\gamma}}{1 + \frac{a_2 \beta_{r_2} + \beta_{u_2}}{1 - \beta_{u_2}}}, a_2 \le \frac{1 + \bar{\gamma}'}{1 + \frac{a\beta_r + \beta_u}{1 - \beta_u}} \tag{3}$$

where β_{u_2} is the mining power of the strongest potential undercutter for this attacker, a_2 is what this opponent would claim in the first block if he forks the undercutter's chain and β_{r_2}, β_{h_2} is the remaining flexible rational mining power and honest mining power in that case. Here, $\bar{\gamma}, \bar{\gamma}'$ are the fee totals in the respective next bandwidth set measured relative to the respective current bandwidth set, when the strongest and second strongest undercutters are making the attack decisions. We can easily solve for a and a' numerically given assignments for mining power distributions and the mempool (for computing $\bar{\gamma}, \bar{\gamma}'$ from bandwidth sets). A program for this task can be found here [18].

In conclusion, for $D = 1$, the undercutter sets a, the fees to claim in the first block (measured relative to the fees in the target block), properly and undercut if $\gamma < \frac{a\beta_r + \beta_u}{1 - \beta_u}$ for a potentially profitable attack. We say "potentially" because new transactions may arrive and change the bandwidth set, resulting in uncertainties in implementing undercutting. We summarize below the algorithm for $D = 1$.

(Part 1) A potential **undercutter** decides whether to undercut: Compute a numerically according to Inequalities 3 that maximizes $E[R_u]$ and check if $\gamma < \frac{a\beta_r + \beta_u}{1 - \beta_u}$. If Yes, start undercutting.

(Part 2) Flexible rational miners decide mining resource distribution: Solve for x (proportion of resources to shift to the chain) in Eq. 1.

(Part 3) Miners avoid being undercut: Calculate the attack condition $T(= \frac{a\beta_r + \beta_u}{1 - \beta_u})$ for the strongest undercutter a miner is defending against. Check if the current $\bar{\gamma} < T$. If Yes, include in the current block $< \frac{1 + \bar{\gamma}}{1 + T}$ of the fees in the bandwidth set; otherwise, use the bandwidth set.

Treating Rational Miners as a Whole. In the above analysis, rational miners make decisions from a collective perspective by maximizing $E[R_r]$ instead of the expected returns for a specific rational miner. This can give rise to coordination problems. Fortunately, rational miners either move all their mining power or stay on their current chain. There is one scenario in practice when a rational miner may not be flexible, which is when this miner owns the current chain head of C_0. When a rational miner is not flexible, as mentioned in the above analysis, we treat it like honest miners. Since miners are aware of other miners' types across time, they will be able to adjust their reasoning process.

When to Apply Undercutting Avoidance. Suppose the current bandwidth set contains fees of 1 and the remaining next bandwidth set contains fees of γ. The mempool is always sorted so $\gamma \leq 1$ (except when no transaction exists and γ is not well-defined). Suppose we have computed the corresponding threshold attacking condition T for a rational attacker and $\gamma < T$. Then this attacker undercuts if a miner simply assembles the current bandwidth set into a block or claims $\geq \frac{1+\gamma}{1+T}$ of the fees in the bandwidth set. We state the following theorem.

Theorem 1. *In setting $D = 1$, each miner applying avoidance procedure when creating a new block is NE.*

Proof. Let $M_i \in M$ be a miner with mining power β_{M_i} and M_i calculates $T = \frac{a\beta_r + \beta_u}{1 - \beta_u}$. When $\gamma \geq T$, M_i proceeds as normal. Therefore, we only need to show that for M_i, when $\gamma < T$, M_i is better off by claiming $a < \frac{1+\gamma}{1+T}$ of the fees in bandwidth set. The key element here is that the decision of how many fees to claim in a block is decided before one successfully generates the proof of work. Let the current bandwidth set BS_0 have a fee total of 1, and we measure the expected returns relative to it. We denote M_i's expected return from not applying avoidance as $E[R_{M_i}]$ and applying avoidance as $E[R_{M_i,avoid}]$.

It's straightforward to see that $E[R_{M_i,avoid}] = 1 \cdot \beta_{M_i} = \beta_{M_i}$ because the strongest and other rational miners do not undercut. M_i can claim fees in the current bandwidth set BS_0 in different rounds. Each time, M_i generates a successful proof of work with probability β_{M_i}.

If M_i does not apply avoidance and claim all fees in BS_0, at least the strongest rational miner is incentivized to undercut given that $\gamma < T$. From previous analysis (see Fig. 1 for a quick reference), we know that the undercutter wins with probability $\beta_u(\beta_u + \delta)$ where $0 \leq \delta \leq \beta_r - \beta_u$. Thus, M_i can expect to gain profits $E[R_{M_i}] = 1 \cdot \beta_{M_i}(1 - \beta_u(\beta_u + \delta)) < E[R_{M_i,avoid}]$.

By unilaterally deviating from avoidance when γ satisfies undercutting conditions of a potential undercutter, M_i receives smaller expected returns. $\qquad\square$

There are two special cases worth noting: (1) all miners are honest ($\beta_h = 1$) so that $T = 0$. We know that $\gamma \geq 0$. No effective avoidance is ever needed in this case; (2) M_i is the only rational miner ($\beta_r = 0$) so that $T = 0$ for itself. M_i does not need to apply avoidance since $\gamma \geq 0$.

Quantifying Strong Undercutter's Advantage. Let the strongest undercutter have mining power β_u and the second strongest undercutter have mining power β_{u_2}. We know from the previous discussion that a miner should always apply avoidance techniques to avoid being undercut in our current setting. For miners other than the strongest undercutter β_u, they need to defend against β_u while β_u itself only needs to defend against β_{u_2}. Let T, T' be the threshold ratio computed for β_u and β_{u_2} respectively. We can capture its advantage with the ratio $\frac{1+T}{1+T'}$. For example, if $\beta_u = 0.5, \beta_{u_2} = 0.2, \beta_h = 0, \frac{1+T}{1+T'} = 4$, which means that the strongest undercutter can claim 4 times than what the other miners are collecting each time. When the discrepancy between β_u, β_{u_2} approaches 0, $\frac{1+T}{1+T'}$ approaches 1. More formally, we capture this inefficiency brought by selfish behavior with the price of anarchy (PoA) [12].

Corollary 1 (Price of Anarchy). *In setting $D = 1, \beta_h < 1, \beta_r > 0$, with the strongest and the second-strongest undercutters respectively having mining power β_u, β_{u_2}, the Price of Anarchy is $PoA = \frac{1+T}{(T-T')\beta_u + 1 + T'}$, where T, T' are as defined above.*

This follows from the above analysis. When all miners stay honest, the "undercutter" is expected to earn a fair share β_u. When miners apply avoidance, the strongest undercutter claims $\frac{1+\gamma}{1+T'}$ each time while others claim $\frac{1+\gamma}{1+T}$. We can obtain its share $\frac{\beta_u \frac{1+\gamma}{1+T'}}{\beta_u \frac{1+\gamma}{1+T'} + (1-\beta_u)\frac{1+\gamma}{1+T}}$. Then we can calculate the PoA as the ratio between the strongest undercutter's shares in its optimal situation (the worst-case NE for the system) and in its worst case (the optimal all honest outcome). We do not include other miners' returns in the calculation because the total shares always sum up to 1 regardless of the outcome and our focus is on capturing the advantage of the undercutter. To give a demonstrative example, let $\beta_u = 0.499, \beta_{u_2} = 0.176$ and $\beta_h \in \{0, 0.05, 0.10, \ldots, 0.30\}$, on average (over β_h) $T = 1.30, T' = 0.29$ and $PoA = 1.29$. This means that for β_u, the mean revenue proportion from undercutting is $0.499 \times 1.29 = 0.63$.

One observation is that when β_u and $T - T'$ are large, PoA is large. To move it towards 1 (a more stable system), we can either strengthen the second potential undercutter or downsize β_u through further decentralization.

5   System Evaluation

In this section, we evaluate the profitability of undercutting using data obtained from Bitcoin and Monero, along with artificial transactions generated from normal distributions. Bitcoin is a typical example of congested blockchains, and Monero is a more available one. The simulation codes and a sample data set have been made open source [18]. In the previous analysis, we let the undercutter be aware of future transaction flows in and out of the mempool. In reality, there is more uncertainty involved. Another difference is that now mining powers are discrete, and we model each miner individually.

5.1   Data Collection and Experiment Setup

Transactions. We obtain the blocks from height $630, 457$ (May 15th, 2020 after the Bitcoin's block reward halving) to $634, 928$ (June 15th, 2020) from the Bitcoin blockchain using the API provided by blockchain.com [24], comprising $9, 167, 040$ transactions. The Monero blockchain data are collected using a similar API from xmrchain.net. In total, we acquire $1, 482, 296$ transactions from block height $2,100,000$ (May 17th, 2020) to $2,191,000$ (Sept 20th, 2020). For each of these transactions, we extract the size, fee, and timestamp attributes. Note that transactions that appeared during the sample period but not in any of the collected blocks are not included. Thus, the memory pools reconstructed are not the exact mempools miners were faced with. We also create artificial transaction data sets with normally distributed fee rates.

Miners. To mimic the actual Bitcoin network, we follow the mining power distribution of miners published by blockchain.com [25] on July 30th, 2020. We make the strongest miner with 17.6% mining power the undercutting miner. We additionally consider a hypothetical undercutter with 49.9% mining power. This is to uncover the profitability of undercutting for a strong attacker and its advantage over other miners when avoidance techniques are adopted by all. For the Monero network, we follow the mining power distributions published by exodus [27] and moneropool.com [1]. The strongest pool with 35% mining power is made the undercutting miner.

Setup. We model the blockchain system as event-based, with new block creation being the event. Parameters and states of the system are updated upon a new block creation event that we denote as B_i for the remaining of this section. Miners have the same view of the network and the same latency in propagating the blocks and transactions. So miners working on the same chain see the same mempool. We initialize the time of the system to the earliest transaction timestamp. As shown in Algorithm 1, new block creation first happens (lines 2–4). Then chains, miners, and mempools are updated in lines 5–7. We include more details for chain and miner updating routines in Algorithm 2. Detailed descriptions for each routine can be found in the full report.

Simulation Run. In a normal run, we repeat the above steps until we exhaust all transactions. In an avoidance-enabled simulation run, we repeat the procedure but with all miners actively defending against undercutting in line 4, according to the two summarized algorithms in Sect. 4.1 and Appendix A.

5.2   Experiment Results

Normal Runs. Overall in a normal run, a strong undercutter can expect to earn more than fair shares by conditional undercutting as shown in Figs. 2b and 2d. **(i)** In Bitcoin runs, the 17.6% undercutter receives on average (for $D = 1$) 17.9% shares for 0–50% honest mining power (Fig. 2a). The strong 49.9% undercutter receives a greater profit of 60.8% of the shares (Fig. 2b). **(ii)** In runs with artificial transactions, the profits for $D = 1, 2$ bear a wider gap than with actual Bitcoin transactions (Fig. 2c). **(iii)** In Monero runs, the 35% undercutter obtains 43.2% of the profit on average (for $D = 1, 2$) for different honest miner portions (Fig. 2d). Undercutting is especially efficient in Monero because of its small mempools, which provide limited cushion effects.

Algorithm 1: Simulation Overview

```
   input : txSet, minerSet, chainsTime
1: while txSet not empty do
2:      extChain ← nextChainToExtend(chainsTime);
3:      m ← selectNextBlockMiner(extChain);
4:      nextBlock ← publishBlock(m);
5:      updateChains(extChain, nextBlock);
6:      updateMiners(extChain);
7:      updateMempool(extChain);
```

Algorithm 2: Chain and Miner Updates

```
 1: Function updateChains(extChain, nextBlock):
 2:      extChain.append(nextBlock);
 3:      foreach chain in chainsTime do
 4:       |  remove from chainsTime if it is non-wining
 5:      t ← NextBlockCreationTime(extChain);
 6:      update chainsTime with tuple (extChain, t);

 7: Function updateMiners(extChain):
 8:      foreach miner in minerSet do
 9:          if miner = undercutter then
10:              decide to fork or not and craft the new block as described in Part 1 of the
                 D = 1 algorithm in 4.1, the D = 2 algorithm in Appendix A;
11:          if miner = honest then
12:              if extChain longest chain then
13:               |  switch to extChain;
14:          if miner = rational then
15:              decide to switch to extChain or stay on current chain as described in Part
                 2 of the D = 1 algorithm in 4.1, the D = 2 algorithm in Appendix A;
```

With Undercutting Avoidance. As noted by PoA, the attacker has an advantage over others in equilibrium. The predicted average revenue proportion (adjusted for rounds where the undercutter mines a block and attacking is unnecessary) for the 49.9% attacker is around 63%. **(i)** In Bitcoin actual and artificial data runs, the return proportion is close to this predicted average. Avoidance runs can result in better revenues for the undercutter if the attack *cannot* be carried out to its ideal extent. That is because a large mempool along with continual incoming transactions lowers the profitability of undercutting. The implication is that if undercutting cannot be implemented ideally, avoidance can be relaxed from the exact extent. **(ii)** For Monero, we observe profit reduction for attackers in both margins after enabling avoidance, as shown in Fig. 2d. **(iii)** Monero runs and Bitcoin runs for 17.6% undercutter provide more straightforward results, compared to Bitcoin runs with 49.9% attacker. Because the second undercutter in Monero has 35% mining power, which equals the strongest undercutter's mining power and in Bitcoin, the configuration is that the second-strongest mining power is 15.3% for 17.6% attacker and 20% for 49.9% attacker.

Minor Changes to Bitcoin Core Codebase. We provide discussions concerning undercutting avoidance implementation and other possible defenses in the full report. We note that only light code changes in the Bitcoin core codebase are needed, which we demonstrate in this source [8].

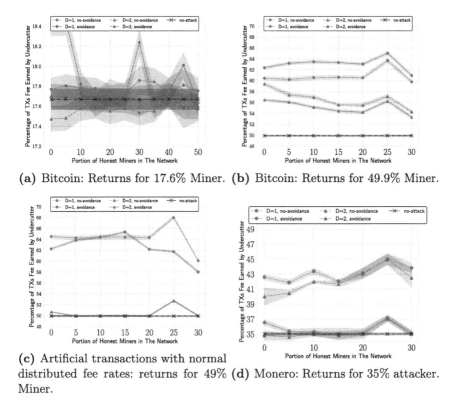

(a) Bitcoin: Returns for 17.6% Miner. **(b)** Bitcoin: Returns for 49.9% Miner.

(c) Artificial transactions with normal distributed fee rates: returns for 49% Miner. **(d)** Monero: Returns for 35% attacker.

Fig. 2. Undercutting returns: normal runs (dashed lines) and runs with avoidance feature enabled (solid lines). The shadowed band is statistics' 95% confidence interval.

6   Conclusion

We study the profitability of the undercutting mining strategy with the block size limit present. The intentional balancing of undercutting others and avoiding one's fork being undercut again demands specific conditions on the unconfirmed transaction set at the time of decision-making. Once conditions are met, an attacker can expect positive premiums. However, because such conditions are not easy to satisfy, are time-dependent (can be invalidated if new transactions arrive), and can be manipulated, it opens a door for mitigation. By applying an avoidance technique to invalidate the aforementioned conditions, miners can avoid being undercut. Avoidance encourages miners to claim fewer fees if the current bandwidth set is sufficiently wealthier than the next bandwidth set. As a result, the competition of undercutting can involuntarily promote the fair sharing of fees even in a time-variant fee system. Nevertheless, in a one-sided competition where the mining power discrepancy between the first and second strongest undercutters is large, the stronger undercutter has a natural advantage over others because it only has to defend against the weaker.

Acknowledgement. We would like to thank our shepherd Marko Vukolic and anonymous reviewers for their valuable comments. We thank Dankrad Feist for his feedback in the early stage of this project. This work has been partially supported by the National Science Foundation under grant CNS-1846316.

A   Giving Up After Two Blocks Behind

We present major steps for analyzing the $D = 2$ case and the complete analysis can be found in the full report. Rational miners now make decisions at states $S^* = \{(1,1), (1,2), (2,1), (2,2), ...\}$. The winning probabilities now comprise infinite series. Without loss of generality, we let $F_1^0 = 1$, $F_2^0 = F_3^0 = \gamma$, $F_1^1 = a, F_2^1 = b$ and $F_3^1 = 1 + 2\gamma - a - b$ (where $a \in [0,1], \gamma \geq 0$). F_2^0, F_3^0 can be of different values in reality but here we use the same value to highlight the wealthiness of F_1^0. Suppose eventually we derive an attacking condition T for setting $D = 2$ as well, then the undercutter would want to set a and b to satisfy $\frac{1+\gamma-a}{a} > T$ and $\frac{1+2\gamma-a-b}{b} > T$ to avoid being undercut.

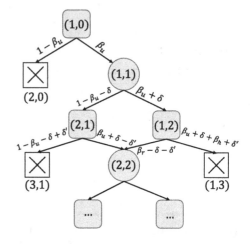

Fig. 3. State transition for $D = 2$. Notations are the same as Fig. 1. Now we have infinite state transitions. δ' and δ'' are the amount of rational mining power shifting from one chain to another.

We take the same route as in the $D = 1$ case. We know that if there is no attack, the undercutter expects to receive $E[R_{\overline{u}}] = 2\beta_u\gamma$. If it starts the attack, its expected return from the right branches (shown in Fig. 3) when the undercutter succeeds and no rational miners assist is

$$E[R_u] = \beta_u(2\gamma + 1) \sum_{i=0}^{\infty} \beta_u^{i+2}(1 - \beta_u)^i = \frac{\beta_u^3(2\gamma + 1)}{1 - \beta_u(1 - \beta_u)}$$

The limited bandwidth set condition, $\gamma < \frac{\beta_u^2}{2(1-\beta_u)}$, is more demanding than the one for $D = 1$. For $\beta_u = 0.5$, the upper bound is now 0.25 instead of 1. For $\beta_u = 0.2$, the bound is 0.025 instead of 0.25. Overall, for weak attackers, the condition is way more demanding than before.

Next, we consider $\gamma \geq \frac{\beta_u^2}{2(1-\beta_u)}$ (with sufficient bandwidth set) and the undercutter needs rational miners to join C_1. Same as before, rational miners allocate their mining power among the two chains to maximize their expected returns:

$$\underset{x\in[0,1]}{\arg\max}\, E[R_r] = \underset{x\in[0,1]}{\arg\max}\left(\mathbb{1}_{owner}\cdot p_0 + \frac{(1-x)\beta_r}{\beta_h + (1-x)\beta_r}p_0\cdot 2\gamma\right.$$

$$\left. + \frac{x\beta_r}{x\beta_r + \beta_u}p_1\cdot b + \frac{x\beta_r}{x\beta_r + \beta_u + \beta_h}p_1\cdot(1+2\gamma-a-b)\right) \quad (4)$$

where $p_0 \le (1-\beta_u - x\beta_r)^2$ is the probability of C_0 leading by 2 blocks first and $p_1 \ge (\beta_u + x\beta_r)(\beta_u + x\beta_r + \beta_h)$ is the probability of C_1 leading by 2 blocks first. Here we only consider the leftmost and rightmost branch in Fig. 3 because they are the two most significant paths. We can observe that the objective function is convex. By Jensen's inequality, the expected returns reach maximum at either of the two ends. Again we let $E[R_{r|x=0}] < E[R_{r|x=1}]$ and obtain

$$2(1-\beta_u)\gamma < b + (\beta_u + \beta_r)(1+2\gamma-a-b) \overset{\beta_h \ge \beta_u}{\Rightarrow} \gamma < \tfrac{(\beta_u+\beta_r)(1-a)+\beta_h b}{2(\beta_h - \beta_u)}$$

When $\beta_h \le \beta_u$, flexible rational miners move to the fork if $b > 0$. With rational miners joining, the expected return for undercutter on the rightmost branch is now $E[R_u] = \left(a + \frac{\beta_u}{\beta_u+\beta_r}b + \beta_u(1+2\gamma-a-b)\right)\cdot\beta_u(\beta_u + \beta_r)$. We let $E[R_u] > E[R_{\overline{u}}]$ and obtain the condition on γ for profitable undercutting:

$$\gamma < \min\{\frac{(\beta_u + \beta_r)a + \beta_u b + \beta_u(\beta_u + \beta_r)(1-a-b)}{2(1-\beta_u(\beta_u + \beta_r))},$$

$$\mathbb{1}^*_{\beta_h > \beta_u}\frac{(\beta_u + \beta_r)(1-a) + \beta_h b}{2(\beta_h - \beta_u)}\} \quad (5)$$

where $\mathbb{1}^*_{\beta_h > \beta_u} = \infty$ if $\beta_h \le \beta_u$ and 1 otherwise. Same as before, we denote the right-hand side condition as T and solve for a and b numerically by considering the strongest potential undercutter the attacker is facing.

$$a \le \frac{1+\tilde{\gamma}}{1+T}, a_2 \le \frac{1+\tilde{\gamma}'}{1+T'}, b \le \frac{1+2\tilde{\gamma}-a}{1+T}, b_2 \le \frac{1+2\tilde{\gamma}'-a}{1+T'} \quad (6)$$

where T and T' are the attack conditions for the undercutter under discussion and its strongest opponent. Here, $\tilde{\gamma}, \tilde{\gamma}'$ are the fee totals in the respective third bandwidth set measured relative to the respective next bandwidth set. We present the algorithm for $D = 2$ below.

(Part 1) A potential **undercutter** decides whether to undercut: Compute a, b numerically according to Inequalities 6 that maximizes $E[R_u]$ and check if γ satisfies Inequality 5. If Yes, start undercutting.
(Part 2) Flexible rational miners decide mining resource distribution: Solve for x in a generalized Eq. 4 (explicitly given in the full report).
(Part 3) Miners avoid being undercut: Calculate the attack condition T (right-hand side of Inequality 5) for the strongest undercutter a miner is defending against. Check if current $\tilde{\gamma} < T$. If Yes, include in the current block $< \frac{1+\tilde{\gamma}}{1+T}$ of the fees in the bandwidth set; otherwise, use the bandwidth set.

References

1. Monero pools since 2016 (2020). http://moneropools.com/
2. Akerlof, G.A.: The market for "lemons": quality uncertainty and the market mechanism. In: Uncertainty in Economics, pp. 235–251. Elsevier (1978)
3. Bitcoin.org: Memory pool. https://developer.bitcoin.org/devguide/p2p_network.html#memory-pool
4. Carlsten, M., Kalodner, H., Weinberg, S.M., Narayanan, A.: On the instability of bitcoin without the block reward. In: Proceedings of the 2016 ACM SIGSAC Conference on Computer and Communications Security, pp. 154–167. ACM (2016)
5. Courtois, N.T., Bahack, L.: On subversive miner strategies and block withholding attack in bitcoin digital currency. arXiv preprint arXiv:1402.1718 (2014)
6. Eyal, I.: The Miner's dilemma. In: 2015 IEEE Symposium on Security and Privacy, pp. 89–103. IEEE (2015)
7. Abdolmaleki, B., Baghery, K., Lipmaa, H., Siim, J., Zajac, M.: UC-secure CRS generation for SNARKs. In: Buchmann, J., Nitaj, A., Rachidi, T. (eds.) AFRICACRYPT 2019. LNCS, vol. 11627, pp. 99–117. Springer, Cham (2019). https://doi.org/10.1007/978-3-030-23696-0_6
8. Gong, T.: Bitcoin core source code updated to account for undercutting avoidance. https://github.com/haas256/bitcoin
9. Gong, T., Minaei, M., Sun, W., Kate, A.: Towards overcoming the undercutting problem. arXiv preprint arXiv:2007.11480 (2020)
10. Half, B.B.: Bitcoin halving 2024 (2020). https://www.bitcoinblockhalf.com/. Accessed 22 July 2020
11. Heilman, E.: One weird trick to stop selfish miners: fresh bitcoins, a solution for the honest miner (Poster Abstract). In: Böhme, R., Brenner, M., Moore, T., Smith, M. (eds.) FC 2014. LNCS, vol. 8438, pp. 161–162. Springer, Heidelberg (2014). https://doi.org/10.1007/978-3-662-44774-1_12
12. Koutsoupias, E., Papadimitriou, C.: Worst-case equilibria. In: Meinel, C., Tison, S. (eds.) STACS 1999. LNCS, vol. 1563, pp. 404–413. Springer, Heidelberg (1999). https://doi.org/10.1007/3-540-49116-3_38
13. Kwon, Y., Kim, D., Son, Y., Vasserman, E., Kim, Y.: Be selfish and avoid dilemmas: fork after withholding (FAW) attacks on bitcoin. In: Proceedings of the 2017 ACM SIGSAC Conference on Computer and Communications Security, pp. 195–209. ACM (2017)
14. Kwon, Y., Kim, H., Yi, Y., Kim, Y.: An eye for an eye: economics of retaliation in mining pools. In: Proceedings of the 1st ACM Conference on Advances in Financial Technologies, pp. 169–182 (2019)
15. Lavi, R., Sattath, O., Zohar, A.: Redesigning bitcoin's fee market. In: The World Wide Web Conference, pp. 2950–2956. ACM (2019)
16. Luu, L., Saha, R., Parameshwaran, I., Saxena, P., Hobor, A.: On power splitting games in distributed computation: the case of bitcoin pooled mining. In: 2015 IEEE 28th Computer Security Foundations Symposium, pp. 397–411. IEEE (2015)
17. Luu, L., Teutsch, J., Kulkarni, R., Saxena, P.: Demystifying incentives in the consensus computer. In: Proceedings of the 22nd ACM SIGSAC Conference on Computer and Communications Security, pp. 706–719 (2015)
18. Minaei, M., Gong, T.: Source code of the blockchain simulation and undercutting experiments. https://github.com/haas256/UP
19. Nakamoto, S.: Bitcoin: a peer-to-peer electronic cash system (2008)

20. Nayak, K., Kumar, S., Miller, A., Shi, E.: Stubborn mining: generalizing selfish mining and combining with an eclipse attack. In: 2016 IEEE European Symposium on Security and Privacy (EuroS&P), pp. 305–320. IEEE (2016)
21. Pass, R., Shi, E.: FruitChains: a fair blockchain. In: Proceedings of the ACM Symposium on Principles of Distributed Computing, pp. 315–324. ACM (2017)
22. Rosenfeld, M.: Analysis of bitcoin pooled mining reward systems. arXiv preprint arXiv:1112.4980 (2011)
23. Rosenfeld, M.: Analysis of hashrate-based double spending. arXiv preprint arXiv:1402.2009 (2014)
24. Blockchain Luxembourg S.A.: Bitcoin blockchain API (2020). https://www.blockchain.com/api. Accessed 26 Sept 2022
25. Blockchain Luxembourg S.A.: Bitcoin miners mining power (2020). https://www.blockchain.com/en/pools. Accessed 27 Feb 2020
26. Sapirshtein, A., Sompolinsky, Y., Zohar, A.: Optimal selfish mining strategies in bitcoin. In: Grosslags, J., Preneel, B. (eds.) FC 2016. LNCS, vol. 9603, pp. 515–532. Springer, Heidelberg (2017). https://doi.org/10.1007/978-3-662-54970-4_30
27. Won, D.: 2020's best monero pools (2020). https://www.exodus.io/blog/best-monero-pools/
28. Zhang, R., Preneel, B.: Publish or perish: a backward-compatible defense against selfish mining in bitcoin. In: Handschuh, H. (ed.) CT-RSA 2017. LNCS, vol. 10159, pp. 277–292. Springer, Cham (2017). https://doi.org/10.1007/978-3-319-52153-4_16

Arbitrage Attack: Miners of the World, Unite!

Yuheng Wang[1], Jiliang Li[1(⊠)], Zhou Su[1], and Yuyi Wang[2(⊠)]

[1] School of Cyber Science and Engineering, Xi'an Jiaotong University, Xi'an, China
wangdahu1211@stu.xjtu.edu.cn, jiliang.li@xjtu.edu.cn, zhousu@ieee.org
[2] ETH Zürich, Zürich, Switzerland
yuyiwang920@gmail.com

Abstract. Blockchain oracles are introduced to mitigate the gap between blockchain-based applications and real-world information. To solve the centralization problem of current oracle systems, many decentralized protocols have been designed. In this paper, we define the basic model for decentralized oracles that rely on unencrypted transactions for verification and adjustment tasks. Furthermore, we introduce Arbitrage attack against such decentralized oracles carried out by rational miners and mining pools. We analyze the attack based on game-theoretic methods. Moreover, we briefly discuss the price of anarchy to demonstrate the characteristic of attackers' cooperation union under different circumstances.

Keywords: Blockchain · Decentralized price oracle · Nash equilibrium · Price of anarchy (PoA)

1 Introduction

If we take a look at all the impressive events that happened in 2021, the epic "Gamestop (GME) Short Squeeze" war that happened among the union of retail investors, certain hedge funds as well as short-sellers at the very beginning of this year can't avoid discussion [28]. Gamestop is an offline game retailer company selling games, game consoles, and accessories. Under the influence of e-commerce, the revenue of Gamestop had been greatly impacted. Therefore many hedge funds and short-sellers believe that the stock price is going to drop and took the opportunity to short sell Gamestop's stock. However, many Gamestop's loyal customers as well as some speculators, on the contrary, started to buy in Gamestop's stock in order to hinder venture capital firms' plan. Due to the internet propaganda, more and more retail investors and even some famous investors also participated in and started to buy in the stock. Consequently, Gamestop's stock price had surprisingly risen a lot, which caused many venture capital firms great loss [31].

The important reason for this great victory is that a large number of independent retail investors, who even don't know each other before, take the same action and manage to "change" and "manipulate" the price of Gamestop's stock price together. From the view of a bystander, it seems that these retail investors

© International Financial Cryptography Association 2022
I. Eyal and J. Garay (Eds.): FC 2022, LNCS 13411, pp. 464–487, 2022.
https://doi.org/10.1007/978-3-031-18283-9_23

form a temporary union to achieve this goal. So will this kind of temporary union appear in other fields? Currently, there have been extensive discussions about possible applications of blockchain technology, and decentralized finance (DeFi) has become a main driver of blockchain adoption. Compared with the traditional finance industry, DeFi uses transparent and immutable on-chain smart contracts to realize trading activity instead of centralized custodians, banks, and brokers. So will a temporary union appears in the DeFi system and "manipulate" the DeFi market price to obtain high profit?

Noted that, most of DeFi projects rely on smart contracts to perform trading operations, and these smart contracts need an oracle (also known as data feed) to carry the real-world information (e.g., the current market price of Bitcoin) to the blockchain as evidence to trigger execution. This is because smart contracts are only able to use on-chain information, to guarantee the safety of blockchain systems. Most of the oracle systems currently being used are centralized oracles that depend on trusted third-party facilities or platforms (e.g., Town Criers [8]) to fetch outside information, and later the information will be given to the customer through a transaction proposed by the oracle's on-chain account.

Although such a method is effective, the deployment of centralized oracles brings back the problem of centralization. To mitigate the problem, decentralized oracles protocols have been proposed. Decentralized oracles (e.g., the NEST protocol [18]) try to avoid the centralization problem by letting different users propose opinions after hearing a query task and make decisions for the final output together. Consequently, some inaccurate and malicious personal opinions might inevitably be brought in. Therefore verification and adjustment methods will be the only guarantee of decentralized oracle's reliability. And in most cases, procedures of opinion proposition, verification as well as adjustment are realized in the form of on-chain transactions.

Most studies about decentralized oracles only take opinion proposers' influence into consideration and neglect miners as well as mining pools. It is well known that miners, especially mining pools, have considerable influence on the publishing of transactions, which can also cause damage to the reliability and accuracy of decentralized oracles. However, to our notice there have been very few decentralized oracle studies considering the power of miners and mining pools, especially when tampering with the publishing of certain transactions will benefit them more. We believe that under such circumstances, the miners and mining pools can form a temporary union just like retail investors in "Gamestop Short Squeeze" event to manipulate the output of decentralized oracles and obtain greater profit. So in this paper, we introduce the Arbitrage attack, an attack against decentralized oracles by the union of miners and mining pools, and carry out further analysis based on game theory.

1.1 Related Work

Oracles have been a very hot research topic these days due to the prosperous applications based on smart contracts. Different kinds of oracle protocols have been proposed. In general, oracles can be classified into two different types: centralized and decentralized.

For centralized oracles, there is always a third party involved in the information transportation task. Zhang et al. presented a very famous and widely used centralized oracle model, Town Crier (TC) [8]. TC guarantees reliability and confidentiality by using Software Guard Extensions (SGX). Each user's query request is executed by codes running in SGX, and corresponding information is fetched from corresponding official websites. Similarly, the Provable oracle in [29] directly fetches information from data sources and uses TLSNotary to prove the integrity. And the PriceGeth oracle from [30] continuously sends fetched data through the oracle's smart contract. However, the implementation of centralized oracles like the ones mentioned above brings centralized problems back to the blockchain system. Since safety, confidentiality, and reliability are once again dependent on a third party that needs to be trusted.

Therefore, various decentralized oracle protocols have been proposed to mitigate the shortcomings of centralized oracles [10]. In Augur, proposed by Peterson et al. [15], all users can vote on the possible outputs given by the oracle system, and each vote weights differently based on users' reputation. Adler et al. designed an oracle protocol ASTRAEA [14] which outputs results proposed and certified also by the votes of users. However, such an oracle can only report data in the form of Boolean propositions, each user will vote for agreement or disagreement for query questions e.g., today's weather is sunny. Similarly, in Witnet oracle, designed by de Pedro et al. [16], information is retrieved and attested by different users based on their reputation.

The rational mining pool is another important question attracting many researchers' attention. In [20], Eyal et al. analyze the feasibility and effect for mining pools to carry out selfish mining attack, which shows the power of mining pools in the blockchain system. Besides, there are other kinds of attacks due to the rationality of mining pools like bribing [24,25], and front-running [26,27] that may tamper with blockchain-based applications.

1.2   Our Contributions

In this paper, we first provide a basic model for decentralized oracles that depend on unencrypted transactions to realize adjustment and verification like NEST protocol [18]. This model contains the necessary procedures for a decentralized oracle of this type to form a reliable output.

Based on the proposed decentralized oracle model, we introduce the Arbitrage attack which is carried out by rational miners and mining pools. We argue that it is possible for rational miners and mining pools to maliciously manipulate the decentralized oracle's output by taking the same actions together like a temporary union in order to obtain more profit.

We further conduct a game-theoretic analysis on this attack. We use a multi-stage static game of perfect information to model the whole attack procedure and analyze each participant's Nash equilibrium strategies during the game to depict the progress of the whole attack under different circumstances. When possible. We also compute the price of anarchy, the ratio of the social costs of the worst Nash equilibrium, and the social optimum, to represent the influence when the attack union is lacking cooperation.

2 Preliminaries

In the following, we outline the required background of blockchains and decentralized oracles for our proposed Arbitrage attack.

2.1 Blockchains

Smart Contract and DeFi. Currently, many blockchain platforms like Ethereum have supported smart contracts, which are based on pseudo-Turing complete programs to manage cryptocurrency assets. Thanks to the flexibility of smart contracts, blockchain network users are able to do more complex tradings besides transferring to accounts, e.g., lend and borrow assets [2], margin trade [3], short and long trading [3] and derivative assets creation [2], and all these complex tradings constitute the foundation of Decentralized Finance (DeFi).

Mining Pool. A mining pool refers to a group of miners that gather their computational power together to solve the POW problem and divide the revenue for the creation of a new block according to each miner's contribution [5]. The chance of solving the cryptography puzzles is prominently increased by forming mining pools. Hence, miners' revenue becomes higher and more stable. At present, nearly 80% hashrate of Bitcoin belong to less than 8 mining pools and less than 3 mining pools controls 60% of Ethereum's total hashrate [6]. Although miners' revenue is guaranteed because of the emergence of the mining pool, the problem of centralization has appeared again. To be more specific, each mining pool has a pool server connecting to an on-chain account to gather the latest transaction information, construct a block template, and send it to pool miners. In this case, the pool server can decide which transactions will be selected [7] in the block template.

2.2 Oracle

Most blockchain applications, especially in DeFi projects, rely on certain information to trigger the execution of smart contracts, but only on-chain information can be reached by smart contracts because blockchain systems are isolated from the outside world to guarantee safety [10]. Although information like the latest trading price in Uniswap can be used, these kinds of on-chain information sources are unreliable due to the lack of variety and stability. To be more specific, in Uniswap, there may only be one or two transactions about two niche digital assets at a certain time, which is not convincing enough. Besides, the price of these transactions could be proposed by the same person, which means the price might be malicious. Therefore, oracles that carry information from the outside world back to the blockchain are designed to solve this problem [11,12]. Up till now, many oracles being used bring back the problem of centralization since a trusted third party is always required for transporting information to blockchain systems from the real world [8,13]. Consequently, decentralized oracles, whose output information is decided by different users is currently a hot research spot with many problems that need to be solved [14–16].

3   Decentralized Oracle Model

In this section, we propose the basic model of decentralized oracles relying on unencrypted transactions based on the NEST protocol [18], which is a currently widely used decentralized oracle.

3.1   Participants

A decentralized oracle can accomplish basic query tasks generally based on four different kinds of participants: customer, oracle platform, contributors: proposers & verifiers, and information sources.

Customer. Decentralized oracles' customers could be any blockchain network user or smart contract that needs information from the outside world. They can send transactions to oracle platforms to submit an information query task, and certain fees are required for each query which constitutes the main income source of oracle platforms.

Oracle Platform. Oracle platform, which usually exists in the form of smart contracts and on-chain accounts, acts as a portal that collects query tasks and outputs required information. Oracle platform is also responsible for managing collected enquiry fees, distributing rewards, and adjusting the oracle protocol's parameters.

Contributors: Proposer & Verifier. According to the definition of the decentralized oracle, each oracle's output can actually be considered as the consensus of different users, who are also noted as Contributors. To reach consensus, contributors who first propose their opinions are called Proposers, and those who verify and make adjustments to these proposed opinions are called Verifiers. Noted that all messages from both two kinds of contributors are unencrypted, therefore can be viewed by any blockchain user without limitations. For instance, assuming that a decentralized oracle accepts a request to search Bitcoin's current market price. Proposers will propose their opinions about the current price based on the information sources they subscribed to. However, these personal opinions may be inaccurate due to narrow information resources or delays, and some may even be malicious. Therefore, verifiers are required or incentivized to make adjustments or verification based on their information sources to these personal propositions, and finally form a final oracle output at last.

Information Sources. Decentralized oracles' outputs are formed based on users' personal opinions, and these users can form an opinion based on their freely chosen information sources like official websites as well as the latest on-chain transactions like mentioned in Sect. 2.2. As a result, the choice of information resources is not limited compared with centralized oracles and only using on-chain information, which makes the oracles' outputs more convincing.

3.2   Enquiry Process

Consider a decentralized oracle platform O, a customer C, a set of n contributors $Con = \{Con_1, Con_2, \cdots, Con_n\}$ and m different information sources $I = \{I_1, I_2, \cdots, I_m\}$. To finish a query task Q proposed by C, all of the participants of decentralized oracles should carry out following procedures as shown in Fig. 1:

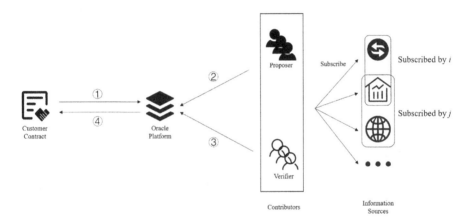

Fig. 1. Decentralized oracle model and necessary procedures for a query task proposed by a customer smart contract.

1. **Propose query request.** The customer C propose a query task Q with required query fees to decentralized oracle platform O through a transaction.
2. **Form and propose personal opinions.** After noticing a new query task, contributor Con_i will form a personal opinion p_i about the query based on personal subscribed information sources set $I_{Con_i} \subseteq I$. Noted that different personal information source sets I_{Con_i} and I_{Con_j} could be the same, totally different, or partly overlapped since there is no limitation for choosing information sources. After that, some of the contributors (proposers) will propose their personal opinion to O.

3. **Verification and adjustment.** For each of the proposed personal opinions, some of the rest of the contributors, except the one who proposes this opinion, will be verifiers and may choose to make an adjustment to these personal opinions or propose verification for valid opinions. Such verification process may last for a limited time, e.g., after s blocks are mined.
4. **Deliver output.** The opinion after adjustment and verification will be the final output of O and given to C also in the form of transaction. Some encryption methods may be applied here to protect the customer's privacy and interest.

Note that in some decentralized oracle protocols, there may only be opinion proposers and no contributor specially dedicated as a verifier to propose adjustment and verification transactions. Instead, mechanisms or algorithms like reputation or voting are used by the oracle platform itself to adjust proposed opinions. Assume there are total n opinion transactions been proposed to the oracle platform for a query task, and if we set a specific transaction as the target opinion, then among the rest $n-1$ transactions, those opinions that are against the target opinions' will therefore be regarded as adjustment and verification opinions. The contributors who propose these transactions can relatively be considered as verifiers. In that case, the decentralized oracle model we proposed above can still apply to these kinds of decentralized oracle protocols. Besides, we also believe that the Arbitrage attack introduced in the following sections will also be feasible in these decentralized oracle protocols.

4 Arbitrage Attack

In this section, we propose a possible attack against the decentralized oracle model mentioned before, which is carried out by rational mining pools.

4.1 Mining Pools' Influence on Decentralized Oracle

As mentioned before, mining pools with overwhelming hashrate nearly have the right to decide which transactions would be added to the chain as well as the corresponding order. The accuracy of decentralized oracles' outputs can also be influenced by mining pools since in most cases, oracles' main procedures are also carried out through on-chain transactions sent by contributors. Therefore, if some transactions are delayed or ignored because of mining pools' intervention, then the oracle's outputs might be seriously affected.

Due to the negative influence of mining pools, many mitigation methods have been implemented in the updates of the existing blockchain system. Besides, many mining pools cut their hashrate voluntarily, since the negative influence of their dominating hashrate may do damage to the blockchain system and further cause a loss to their assets in the blockchain system. Consequently, the dominating mining pools have gradually been replaced by several different mining pools with less hashrate. In that case, the capacity of mining pools is greatly weakened and transactions will be less likely to be blocked or delayed because of one or two mining pools' willingness.

What can go wrong?

Because of the distribution of total hashrate, divergence may appear among mining pools, since decisions will only be made based on each one's own benefits. However, once their target overlaps during a time period, a temporary union may appear, which is similar to retail investors in the Gamestop event. When it comes to decentralized oracles, different mining pools may take the same action and cooperate to block contributors' certain transactions to manipulate oracles' outputs and arbitrage later. This is what we called the Arbitrage attack that may happen in a decentralized oracle.

4.2   Arbitrage Attack Model

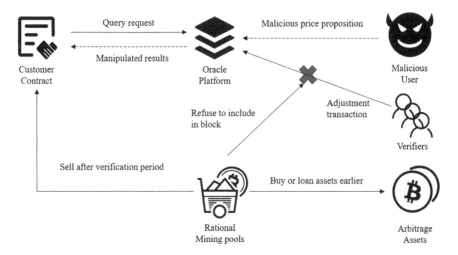

Fig. 2. Procedures of the whole Arbitrage attack. The customer contract will be caused huge damage due to the rationality of mining pools

Assuming that there are n rational mining pools in the blockchain network and search for high profit in the blockchain network (i.e., individual miners can be considered as mining pools with lower hashrate). And there is a decentralized oracle O that outputs the current price of Bitcoin, for instance, to all its consumers in the blockchain network.

When a malicious user wants to intervene in the oracle's output, it will first propose a malicious price quotation through transaction t_m which is greatly deviated from the real market price, much higher for example. According to the mechanism of O, an honest verifier may notice the difference during the verification procedure and propose an adjustment transaction t_a with gas fee. Generally, mining pools would be willing to include t_a into the next block they are currently mining and win normal profit A, which is the reward for following the protocol. However, after noticing the malicious transaction t_m, rational mining pools may hesitate because t_m represents an arbitrage opportunity for higher profit than A.

As a result, instead of simply including t_a, a rational mining pool may choose to buy or loan a large amount of Bitcoin as soon as they see the price quotation t_m, and prepare a set of arbitrage transactions to propose after the attack succeeds. Noted that these transactions are all against customer contracts of oracle O. Later they will together ignore any adjustment transactions that want to amend the quotation together like a union, since these transactions are also unencrypted and therefore can be distinguished easily. Finally, they can sell out all the Bitcoin they have by proposing a newly mined block containing arbitrage transactions set t_{arb} they want to make after the quotation t_m becomes valid. By doing so, mining pools are able to obtain higher arbitrage profit B. Consequently, customers using O as their information source will be severely influenced because of these arbitrage transactions. The whole attack process is shown in Fig. 2. It is worth to be noted that, the detailed expressions and calculated methods of profit A and B should be uncertain and depend on specific decentralized oracle protocol. But generally speaking, the arbitrage profit B will always be higher than the normal profit A.

4.3   Attack Feasibility

The profit of a successful Arbitrage attack is usually attractive and irresistible. Intuitively, it seems that mining pools will definitely choose to attack when B is larger than the normal profits A. However, not all of the rational mining pools will obtain B at last. Currently, most cryptocurrency transactions are based on AMM DEXs (automated market maker decentralized exchanges), like Uniswap. For AMM DEXs, an exchange with a large scale will cause a great slippage, which means the second user who wants to arbitrage will gain no profit [4]. To simplify the analysis, we propose the following assumption:

Assumption 1. *Each mining pool has sufficient property to propose large enough transactions to every victim smart contracts using oracle O.*

The assumption above is reasonable since the current prosperous DeFi system allows users to borrow specific crypto assets through services like Flash Loan [23]. Besides, what we mean by a transaction is "large enough" here is that the transaction will cause a great slippage. And based on Assumption 1 we can propose the following theorem:

Theorem 1. *There can be only one winner to obtain profit for the Arbitrage attack no matter success or not.*

On the one hand, Theorem 1 shows that the final arbitrage profit B could be tremendous compared to the normal transaction fee A, and rational mining pools are fully incentivized to carry out this attack. On the other hand, since there can be only one winner, some rational mining pools may give up before the oracle's output is changed (i.e. before the attack succeeds) and decide to obtain the normal transaction fee A, especially for those mining pools with less hashrate. However, even though a mining pool with less hashrate decides to stop the attack and break the union by publishing a block containing transaction t_a, the possibility of success is based on its hashrate which is also very low.

Consequently, a key question that needs to be figured out is that whether this temporary union of rational mining pools trying to manipulate the oracle's output will maintain during the whole oracle's adjustment period until the final decisive output. In the following section, we will analyze this question based on game-theoretical analysis.

5   Game Theory Analysis

5.1   Game Model Forming

Before formal analysis, we first use the following assumption to restrict the ability of mining pools:

Assumption 2. *A mining pool can only decide not to include certain transactions in the block building by itself, but will not ignore or block valid blocks containing certain transactions proposed by others.*

What assumption 2 guarantees is that mining pools can leave the attack union by publishing a new block containing the adjustment transactions. And we will not consider the situations like blockchain forking in this paper.

Assuming that there are n mining pools in the network denoted by $[n]$ and they are all rational, searching for high profits. w.l.o.g., the hashrate satisfy $P_1 > P_2 > ... > P_n$ and $\sum_{j=1}^{n} P_j = 1$. Noted that in reality, mining pools may use part of hashrate for selfish mining [20], which won't contribute to the attack. However such a situation will not have a fundamental effect on the following analysis, so we only consider the hashrate assumption mentioned above for simplicity. We also assume that these mining pools know each other's hashrate ratio:

Assumption 3. *Rational mining pools are all aware of each other's hashrate proportion.*

According to the attack model mentioned in Sect. 4.2, consider a malicious proposition t_m arrives in block b_0 and an adjustment transaction t_a is broadcast to the entire blockchain network at the very moment after b_0 is published (in the real scenario, there might be a longer period of time between the appearance of these two transactions), and $[n]$ rational mining pools will simultaneously notice this arbitrage opportunity. During the verification period which lasts for s blocks, if the adjustment transaction t_a is included in block $b_i, b_0 + 1 \leq b_i \leq b_0 + s$, the malicious proposition t_m will become invalid and the Arbitrage attack will fail, the mining pool which publish block b_i will be the only winner and obtain normal profit A. On the contrary, if no adjustment appeared during s blocks, then the rational mining pool that successfully mines the block with arbitrage transactions set t_{arb} in block $b_0 + s + 1$ will obtain the arbitrage profit B. And the possibility for a rational mining pool to mine a block approximately equal to its hashrate ratio P_i.

Consequently, when mining blocks between b_0 and $b_0 + s + 1$, each rational mining pool need to decide whether include the adjustment transaction t_a and t_{arb} into the next block it is mining right now (t_{arb} is only decided for block b_0+s+1). Therefore, we can denote the whole Arbitrage attack into a multi-stage static game, and according to Assumption 3, the game is of perfect information since mining pools know each others' hashrate ratio and the revenue for this attack. There are at most $s + 1$ static games of perfect information during the whole attack. From game 1 to game s, mining pools need to decide whether include transaction t_a in the block they are mining, and in game $s + 1$ mining pools will decide whether include arbitrage transactions set t_{arb}. The multi-stage game will end if a block with t_a is successfully mined. During the attack, after block $b_0 + i - 1$ has been added to the chain, $[n]$ rational mining pools' strategy for forming template of block $b_0 + i$, which is also game i, can be denoted as

$$T_i = (T1_i, T2_i, ..., Tn_i)$$

where

$$T j_i = \begin{cases} Y & \text{include transaction } t_a \text{ in block } b_0 + i \\ N & \text{not include transaction } t_a \text{ in block } b_0 + i \end{cases}$$

$T j_i*$ represent the Nash equilibrium strategy and the utility function for each mining pool's strategy is

$$U(T_i) = (U_1(T_i), U_2(T_i), ..., U_n(T_i))$$

For simplicity, in the following part we will use i block ($1 \le i \le s + 1$) to represent block $b_0 + i$.

5.2   Nash Equilibrium Strategy

Based on the multi-stage static game of the perfect information model mentioned above, we can easily get the following conclusion

Theorem 2. *For a rational mining pool j, its strategy for block i should be the Nash equilibrium strategy for game i.*

Theorem 2 shows that it is necessary to analyze each stage game's Nash equilibrium strategy T_i^*. It is already known that the expression of the utility function of strategy for each stage game is crucial to finding the Nash equilibrium strategy. However, things are really complicated if we sequentially analyze the problem from game 1 to game $s+1$, since the utility function will be complex due to a large number of potential strategy combinations. Therefore, we need to find another method to obtain the Nash equilibrium strategy of each game. Intuitively, it is obvious that at block $s+1$ every rational mining pools' strategy will be the same Y, for they will have no chance to gain profit at last. Conclusively, we can learn from the idea of reverse induction and start to analyze the Nash equilibrium strategy at $s+1$ block, then infer the Nash equilibrium strategy for previous blocks.

Block $s+1$ After publishing s block, which doesn't include t_a, all rational mining pools need to decide whether include the arbitrage transactions set t_{arb} into the $s+1$ block they are building. Apparently, we can easily obtain the Nash equilibrium strategy for this final game by comparing the utility function:

Theorem 3. *The Nash equilibrium strategy for block $s+1$ is*

$$T_{s+1} = \underbrace{(Y, Y, ..., Y)}_{n}$$

Block s Since all rational mining pools' Nash equilibrium strategies when deciding the $s+1$ block are determinate, it will be practical to obtain mining pool j's utility function for block s:

$$U_j(T_s) = \begin{cases} P_j A + P_{Ns}(j) P_j B & Tj_s = Y \\ (P_{Ns}(j) + P_j) P_j B & Tj_s = N \end{cases}$$

where P_{Ns} represent the sum of hashrate of mining pools whose strategy is N, except mining pool j, $P_{Ns} = \sum_{k \in \{k | Tk_s = N, k \neq j\}} P_k$. We use P_{Ns}^* to represent the situation for Nash equilibrium strategy.

By comparing those two different utility functions, the Nash equilibrium strategy Tj_s^* should be related to the ratio of two different profits and the hashrate:

$$Tj_s^* = \begin{cases} Y & \frac{B}{A} < \frac{1}{P_j} \\ N & \frac{B}{A} > \frac{1}{P_j} \end{cases}$$

We can therefore consider Nash equilibrium strategies in three different scenarios:

Proposition 1. *When $\frac{B}{A} > \frac{1}{P_n} > ... > \frac{1}{P_1}$, for a random mining pool j, $Tj_s^* = N$, $T_s^* = \underbrace{(N, N, ..., N)}_{n}$ and $U_j(Tj_s^*) = P_j B$*

Proposition 2. *When $\frac{B}{A} < \frac{1}{P_1} < ... < \frac{1}{P_n}$, for a random mining pool j, $Tj_s^* = Y$, $T_s^* = \underbrace{(Y, Y, ..., Y)}_{n}$ and $U_j(Tj_s^*) = P_j A$*

Proposition 3. *When* $\frac{1}{P_1} < \frac{B}{A} < \frac{1}{P_n}$, *w.l.o.g.* $\frac{1}{P_1} < ... < \frac{1}{P_R} < \frac{B}{A} < \frac{1}{P_{R+1}} <$ *... $< \frac{1}{P_n}$. Then for a random mining pool j, Nash equilibrium strategy should be*

$$Tj_s{}^* = \begin{cases} Y & j \geq R+1 \\ N & j \leq R \end{cases}$$

and the utility function should be:

$$U_j(Tj_s{}^*) = \begin{cases} P_j A + P_{Ns}(j)^* P_j B & Tj_s^* = Y \\ (P_{Ns}(j)^* + P_j) P_j B & Tj_s^* = N \end{cases}$$

Propositions above show that the ratio of two different kinds of profit will influence the Nash equilibrium strategies for game s. If B greatly exceeds the normal transaction fee profit A, then more mining pools will persist in the attack, which fits our intuition. Based on the analysis of $s+1$ and s blocks, we can extend our analysis method to the more general scenarios like the Nash equilibrium strategies for i $(0 \leq i < s)$ block.

Block i Similar to s block, a random mining pool j's utility function at i block should be related to its Nash equilibrium utility function in $i+1$ block:

$$U_j(T_i) = \begin{cases} P_j A + P_{Ni}(j) U_j(Tj_{i+1}{}^*) & Tj_i = Y \\ (P_{Ni}(j) + P_j) U_j(Tj_{i+1}{}^*) & Tj_i = N \end{cases}$$

and therefore the Nash equilibrium strategy should be

$$Tj_i{}^* = \begin{cases} Y & U_j(Tj_{i+1}{}^*) < A \\ N & U_j(Tj_{i+1}{}^*) > A \end{cases}$$

Similar to the analysis for the s block, we also consider the Nash equilibrium strategies in three different scenarios.

Proposition 4. *When* $\frac{B}{A} > \frac{1}{P_n} > ... > \frac{1}{P_1}$, *for a random mining pool j,* $U_j(Tj_s{}^*) = P_j B > A$*holds. By mathematical induction, the Nash equilibrium strategy for game i should be* $T_i{}^* = (\underbrace{N, N, ..., N}_{n})$

Proposition 5. *When* $\frac{B}{A} < \frac{1}{P_1} < ... < \frac{1}{P_n}$, *for a random mining pool j,* $U_j(Tj_s{}^*) = P_j B < A$*holds. By mathematical induction, the Nash equilibrium strategy for game i should be* $T_i{}^* = (\underbrace{Y, Y, ..., Y}_{n})$

When $\frac{1}{P_1} < \frac{B}{A} < \frac{1}{P_n}$, divergence will appear in the attack union compared to the two other conditions mentioned above, it is worthwhile to figure out the change of Nash equilibrium strategies of each mining pool during the whole attack process.

In order to depict the change of Nash equilibrium strategy for different stage game, here we also assume that $\frac{1}{P_1} < ... < \frac{1}{P_R} < \frac{B}{A} < \frac{1}{P_{R+1}} < ... < \frac{1}{P_n}$, we first give following theorem:

Theorem 4. *For a random mining pool j, if its Nash equilibrium strategy for block $i+1$ is Y, then the Nash equilibrium strategy for block i is also Y.*

From Theorem 4 we can conclude that

Corollary 1. *For a mining pool j, it is impossible that the Nash equilibrium strategy for game i is N and Y for game $i+1$.*

Corollary 2. *$P_{Ni}(j)^*$ should increase with i increase to s.*

Have these corollaries in mind, we only need to consider mining pool j's Nash equilibrium strategy for game i when the equilibrium strategy for game $i+1$ is N.

Theorem 5. *For a mining pool j, if its Nash equilibrium strategy for game $i+1$ is N and Y for j. Then for any mining pool h with $P_h < P_j$, there should be $Th_i^* = Y$.*

From Theorem 5 we can get the following results:

Corollary 3. *With block number i increases, mining pools with more hashrate will change their strategy from Y to N more sooner than mining pools with less hashrate.*

Corollary 4. *There won't be a Nash equilibrium strategy T_i^* for game i where $Th_i^* = N, Tj_i^* = Y$ $(P_h < P_j)$.*

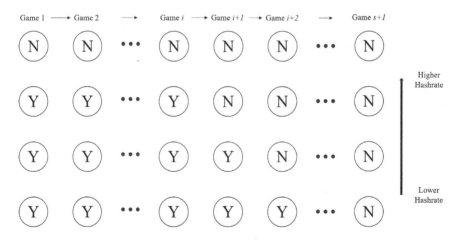

Fig. 3. Example of four different mining pool's Nash equilibrium strategies' changes during the whole attack.

Combine Theorem 4 and 5 as well as corollaries above we can depict the change of Nash equilibrium strategy for mining pool j at game i $(0 \leq i \leq s)$ when $\frac{1}{P_1} < \frac{B}{A} < \frac{1}{P_n}$, Fig. 3 shows an example with four different mining pools:

- If j's Nash equilibrium strategy is Y at game $i + 1$, for any other game $g, g < i + 1$, mining pool j's Nash equilibrium strategy will also be Y.
- If j's Nash equilibrium strategy is N at game $i + 1$. Then Nash equilibrium strategy at game i will be Y if $P_j B \prod_{k=i}^{s} (P_N k(j) + P_j) < A$, else the Nash equilibrium strategy will be N.

With the Nash equilibrium strategy change under different circumstances mentioned above, each mining pool is able to decide their strategies for each block they are building with the attack proceeding. The whole process for a rational mining pool to decide the final strategy is described as an algorithm pseudo-code in Appendix B.

5.3 Price of Anarchy

The ratio between the worst Nash equilibrium and the social optimum is the price of anarchy (PoA), the formal definition can be denoted as:

$$PoA = \frac{min_{t \in N} profit(t)}{max_{t \in T_{all}} profit(t)}$$

where N is the set of Nash equilibrium strategies and T_{all} is the set of all possible strategies during the process of attack. $profit(t)$ represents the expected profit for the union of rational mining pools when the attack ends, no matter successful or not.

The price of anarchy provides an insight into the effects of lack of corporation. To be more specific, PoA represents the gap between system performance when players all behave selfishly and follow central coordination. When the price of anarchy is close to 1, selfish players don't severely influence the union's total profit, which means the union is stable. In contrast, the low price of anarchy shows that the union is loose.

Since the ratio of two kinds of profit B and A will influence the Nash equilibrium strategies, we can determine the price of anarchy in different situations.

Corollary 5. *When* $\frac{B}{A} > \frac{1}{P_n} > ... > \frac{1}{P_1}$, *the price of anarchy is* $PoA = 1$.

Corollary 6. *When* $\frac{B}{A} < \frac{1}{P_1} < ... < \frac{1}{P_n}$, *the price of anarchy is* $PoA = \frac{A}{B}$.

Corollary 7. *When* $\frac{1}{P_1} < \frac{B}{A} < \frac{1}{P_n}$, *the price of anarchy is*

$$PoA = \frac{(1 - \prod_{i=1}^{s} P_{Ni}) A + \prod_{i=1}^{s} P_{Ni} B}{B}.$$

6   Conclusion, Limitations and Extensions

In this paper, we introduce an Arbitrage attack against decentralized oracles carried out by rational mining pools. We show that when potential arbitrage profit weights far more than regular profits, different mining pools will take the same actions to delay or block transactions like a temporary union to carry on the attack. And as the attack progresses, the union becomes more and more stable. In the parts below, we will further discuss the limitations and possible extensions of this paper.

Generality. As mentioned before, the attack discussed in this paper is against decentralized oracles that depend on transactions to make adjustments and verification, therefore a very promising topic to discuss is whether this attack will be feasible to a more general decentralized oracle model.

And in another aspect, this attack may be feasible to not only decentralized oracles. To be more specific, similar to decentralized oracles, many other blockchain applications also realized certain functions based on proposing different transactions. Therefore, we believe that the temporary union in Arbitrage attack may happen in other blockchain applications. For instance, consider a DAO managing the parameters of a transaction pool of two kinds of digital assets like Curve [19], members of DAO are supposed to vote to decide the specific parameters like the exchange rate of these two assets for the next several days. Assume that all members need to vote by proposing transactions to DAO's official voting account, and the voting period will last for several blocks for example. In that case, the rational mining pools may take the same actions in Arbitrage attacks by blocking or delaying voting transactions against their will during the voting period, to manipulate the final decision. Consequently, although efficient incentive mechanisms are applied to guarantee DAO's rational members to vote honestly, the final decision still can be influenced because of the power of mining pools.

Game Theory Analysis. The game theory analysis in this paper can become more complete. For one thing, in this paper, we only depict the possible process during the attack when the two revenue A and B are stable. However, in reality, the revenue A and B could be dynamic, since the number of adjustment transactions could increase which will makes A increase during the process. By considering changes of A may help to depict the whole attack process more dynamically. Similarly, the attack revenue B could also change due to the price fluctuation of the digital assets associated with the attack. For the other, even a mining pool becomes the final winner of the attack, the negative social influence of the attack may also cause the winner a great loss. Such a potential loss may exert influence on mining pools' strategy during the attack. However, such kind of loss is difficult to describe, which also makes the game theory analysis pretty challenging.

Forking. In Assumption 2, we make some restrictions about mining pools' ability since the attack is closely related to the forking problem. Without the restriction, mining pools that wish to continue the attack can choose to fork and ignore the block containing adjustment transactions published by mining pool that chooses to give up the attack. Besides, at the end of the attack, loser mining pools can even call for forking by claiming that the only winner is the "evil attacker" in order to make the winner unable to obtain the revenue. These kinds of problems are complicated but deserve further discussion.

Mitigation Methods. Detailed mitigation methods are not given in this paper, and we plan to do further exploration about feasible solutions to this attack. So far, we believe there may be two practical ways to solve the problem. One is to adjust the time of the verification process s. Intuitively, longer s will make the attack less likely to succeed. But longer verification time will also make the oracle's outputs less time-sensitive, which could be a deadly drawback for oracles designed for scenarios like the high-frequency trading market. Therefore the optimal verification time or period can only be obtained by detailed analysis. The other possible solution is to bring in cryptography methods like "secret ballots" [32] in the internet voting system. The mining pools will be unable to distinguish transactions with adjustments information if transactions' contents are encrypted. But the detailed procedure needs to be well designed to ensure safety.

A   Proofs

Theorem 1. *There can be only one winner for the Arbitrage attack no matter success or not.*

Proof. In the case of failure, since there can be only one block containing adjustment transaction t_a, therefore this block's publisher should be the only winner with normal profit A.

In the case of success, each rational mining pool can publish a smart contract in the blockchain including all the transaction it would like to make after the oracle's output is manipulated. This smart contract has enough time to become valid during the oracle's verification period. After the output has been changed, the mining pool can propose a newly mined block containing arbitrage transactions set t_{arb} and exploit all arbitrage opportunities.   □

Theorem 2. *For a rational mining pool j, its strategy for block i should be the Nash equilibrium strategy for game i.*

Proof. The Nash equilibrium strategy at game i for mining pool j should satisfy

$$U_1(T_i^*) \geq U_1(\overline{T_i^*})$$

where T_i^* represents the equilibrium strategy and $\overline{T_i^*}$ represents other strategies. Thus a rational mining pool will choose the equilibrium strategy while making decision for block i.   □

Theorem 3. *The Nash equilibrium strategy for block $s + 1$ is*

$$T_{s+1} = \underbrace{(Y, Y, ..., Y)}_{n}$$

Proof. According to the attack model, all the rational mining pools will try to mine their own block containing the arbitrage transactions set t_{arb}, so the utility function for a mining pool j can be easily denoted as:

$$U_j(T_{s+1}) = \begin{cases} P_j B & Tj_{s+1} = Y \\ 0 & Tj_{s+1} = N \end{cases}$$

Where P_j is the hashrate ratio of mining pool j. Therefore, all the rational mining pools will choose to add the transaction to the block. □

Proposition 1. *When $\frac{B}{A} > \frac{1}{P_n} > ... > \frac{1}{P_1}$, for a random mining pool j, $Tj_s{}^* = N$, $T_s{}^* = \underbrace{(N, N, ..., N)}_{n}$ and $U_j(Tj_s{}^*) = P_j B$.*

Proof. For all rational mining pools that participated in the attack, the profit ratio $\frac{B}{A}$ is larger than the reciprocal of any mining pool's hashrate. As a result, according to the utility function of two different actions, every mining pool's Nash equilibrium strategy will be N, which will guarantee the attack will succeed and game $s+1$ will be conducted, therefore the utility will be $P_j B$ for a random mining pool j. □

Proposition 2. *When $\frac{B}{A} < \frac{1}{P_1} < ... < \frac{1}{P_n}$, for a random mining pool j, $Tj_s{}^* = Y$, $T_s^* = \underbrace{(Y, Y, ..., Y)}_{n}$ and $U_j(Tj_s{}^*) = P_j A$.*

Proof. For all rational mining pools that participated in the attack, the profit ratio $\frac{B}{A}$ is less than the reciprocal of any mining pool's hashrate. Similarly, according to the utility function of two different actions, every mining pool's Nash equilibrium strategy will be Y, which will guarantee the attack will fail and game $s + 1$ will be not conducted, therefore the utility will be $P_j A$ for a random mining pool j. □

Proposition 3. *When $\frac{1}{P_1} < \frac{B}{A} < \frac{1}{P_n}$, w.l.o.g. $\frac{1}{P_1} < ... < \frac{1}{P_R} < \frac{B}{A} < \frac{1}{P_{R+1}} < ... < \frac{1}{P_n}$. Then for a random mining pool j, Nash equilibrium strategy should be*

$$Tj_s{}^* = \begin{cases} Y & j \geq R+1 \\ N & j \leq R \end{cases}$$

and the utility function should be:

$$U_j(Tj_s{}^*) = \begin{cases} P_j A + P_{Ns}(j)^* P_j B & Tj_s^* = Y \\ (P_{Ns}(j)^* + P_j) P_j B & Tj_s^* = N \end{cases}$$

Proof. According to the utility function, mining pools whose hashrate ratio's reciprocal is higher than $\frac{B}{A}$ will choose Y and N for the rest of the mining pools, and the utility can be easily obtained based on their Nash equilibrium strategies. □

Proposition 4. When $\frac{B}{A} > \frac{1}{P_n} > \dots > \frac{1}{P_1}$, for a random mining pool j, $U_j(Tj_s{}^*) = P_j B > A$ holds. By mathematical induction, the Nash equilibrium strategy for game i should be $T_i{}^* = \underbrace{(N, N, \dots, N)}_{n}$.

Proof. According to Theorem 1, for a random mining pool j, $U_j(Tj_s{}^*) = P_j B > A$ holds. Therefore, for game $s-1$, the Nash equilibrium strategy and corresponding utility can be easily obtained:

$$T_{s-1}{}^* = \underbrace{(N, N, \dots, N)}_{n}$$

$$U_j(Tj_{s-1}{}^*) = P_j B > A$$

Then by mathematical induction, rational mining pools' Nash equilibrium strategy for every game should be $\underbrace{(N, N, \dots, N)}_{n}$. $\qquad \square$

Proposition 5. When $\frac{B}{A} < \frac{1}{P_1} < \dots < \frac{1}{P_n}$, for a random mining pool j, $U_j(Tj_s{}^*) = P_j B < A$ holds. By mathematical induction, the Nash equilibrium strategy for game i should be $T_i{}^* = \underbrace{(Y, Y, \dots, Y)}_{n}$.

Proof. According to Theorem 2, for a random mining pool j, $U_j(Tj_s{}^*) = P_j A < A$ holds. Therefore, for game $s - 1$, the Nash equilibrium strategy and corresponding utility can be easily obtained:

$$T_{s-1}{}^* = \underbrace{(Y, Y, \dots, Y)}_{n}$$

$$U_j(Tj_{s-1}{}^*) = P_j A < A$$

Then by mathematical induction, rational mining pools' Nash equilibrium strategy for every game should be $\underbrace{(Y, Y, \dots, Y)}_{n}$. $\qquad \square$

Theorem 4. For a random mining pool j, if its Nash equilibrium strategy for block $i + 1$ is Y, then the Nash equilibrium strategy for block i is also Y.

Proof. Assuming that mining pool j's Nash equilibrium strategy for block $i + 1$ is Y, then

$$U_j(T_{i+2}^*) < A$$

Therefore

$$U_j(Tj_{i+2}{}^*) < A$$
$$U_j(Tj_{i+1}{}^*) = P_j A + P_{N(i+1)}(j)^* U_j(Tj_{i+2}{}^*)$$
$$< (P_j + P_{N(i+1)}(j)^*) A \leq A$$
$$\Rightarrow U_j(Tj_{i+1}{}^*) < A$$

The Theorem is therefore proved. $\qquad \square$

Corollary 1. *For a mining pool j, it is impossible that the Nash equilibrium strategy for game i is N and Y for game $i + 1$.*

Proof. According to Theorem 4, a mining pool's Nash equilibrium strategy for game i can only be Y, if its Nash equilibrium strategy for game $i + 1$ is Y. ☐

Corollary 2. $P_{Ni}(j)^*$ *will not decrease with i increase to s.*

Proof. According to Corollary , once a mining pool's Nash equilibrium strategy is N for a game, then its Nash equilibrium strategy will not change to Y in later games. Instead, it is possible for mining pools with Y as Nash equilibrium strategy to change in later games. Therefore, the total hashrate of mining pools with Nash equilibrium strategy N will not decrease with the process of the whole attack. ☐

Theorem 5. *For a mining pool j, if its Nash equilibrium strategy for game $i+1$ is N and Y for i. Then for any mining pool h with $P_h < P_j$, there should be $Th_i{}^* = Y$.*

Proof. We can prove the theorem with contradiction. Assuming that there is a mining pool h with $P_h < P_j$, and its Nash equilibrium strategy for game i is N.

According to Theorem 4, mining pool h's Nash equilibrium strategy for game $i+1$ should be N, therefore $U_h(Th_{i+1}{}^*) = P_h b \prod_{k=i+1}^{s}(P_N k(h) + P_h)$ should be greater than A

$$U_h(Th_{i+1}{}^*) > A$$

However, for mining pool j

$$U_j(T_{i+1}^*) = P_j B \prod_{k=i+1}^{s}(P_N k(j) + P_j) < A$$

since the Nash equilibrium strategy changes to Y. Notice that

$$U_h(Th_{i+1}{}^*) < U_j(T_{i+1}^*)$$

because $P_h < P_j$. Then a contradiction happens. ☐

Corollary 3. *With block number i increases, mining pools with more hashrate will change their strategy from Y to N more sooner than mining pools with less hashrate.*

Proof. According to Theorem 5, if a mining pool j's Nash equilibrium strategy is N for game $i+1$ and Y for i, then in game i the Nash equilibrium strategy for all the mining pools with less hashrate will also be Y, which will not change for the game before i according to Theorem 4. Consequently, with block number i increase, mining pool j's Nash equilibrium strategy will change from Y to N before the mining pools with less hashrate. ☐

Corollary 4. *There won't be a Nash equilibrium strategy T_i^* for game i where $Th_i^* = N, Tj_i^* = Y(P_h < P_j)$.*

Proof. Corollary 3 shows that with block number i increases, mining pools with higher hashrate will change its strategy from Y to N sooner, besides it is not possible to change from N to Y. Conclusively, there won't be a Nash equilibrium strategy T_i^* for game i where $Th_i^* = N, Tj_i^* = Y(P_h < P_j)$. □

Corollary 5. *When $\frac{B}{A} > \frac{1}{P_n} > ... > \frac{1}{P_1}$, the price of anarchy is $PoA = 1$.*

Proof. According to Proposition 4, all rational mining pools will choose N during the whole s blocks period, then

$$PoA = \frac{profit(N\text{for all})}{profit(N\text{for all}}$$
$$= \frac{B}{B}$$
$$= 1$$

□

Corollary 6. *When $\frac{B}{A} < \frac{1}{P_1} < ... < \frac{1}{P_n}$, the price of anarchy is $PoA = \frac{A}{B}$.*

Proof. According to Proposition 5, all rational mining pools will choose Y during the whole s blocks period, then

$$PoA = \frac{profit(Y\text{for all})}{profit(N\text{for all})}$$
$$= \frac{A}{B}$$

□

Corollary 7. *When $\frac{1}{P_1} < \frac{B}{A} < \frac{1}{P_n}$, the price of anarchy is*

$$PoA = \frac{(1 - \prod_{i=1}^{s} P_{Ni})A + \prod_{i=1}^{s} P_{Ni}B}{B}.$$

Proof. When $\frac{1}{P_1} < \frac{B}{A} < \frac{1}{P_n}$, since there will always be mining pools that decide to publish the adjustment contract t_a during the s blocks and gain profit A, the only situation to obtain profit B is when mining pools whose Nash equilibrium strategy is N successfully mine the block   □

B   Algorithm

Algorithm 1. Mining pool q's Nash equilibrium strategy for block k

---

Input: Pool q's hashrate ratio P_q, block number for verification period s, mining
    pools' total number n, target block number k, profit A, B, mining pools' hashrate
    sequence $P = (P_1, P_2, P_3...P_n)$ //*in descending order*

Output: Strategy T //*T = Y represents including adjustment transaction in block k*
    template, $T = N$ represents not including.

1: ArrayN=[ ]; //*array for mining pools with strategy N*
2: ArrayT=[$Y, Y...Y$]; //*strategy array*
3: **for** $j = 1, i = 1; j \leq n; j + +$ **do**
4:     **if** $\frac{1}{P_j} < \frac{B}{A}$ **then**
5:         ArrayN[i++]=P_j;
6:         ArrayT[j]=N;
7:     **end if**
8: **end for**
9: **if** len(ArrayN)==n **then** //*Nash equilibrium strategy for every block is N*
10:     **return** N;
11: **end if**
12: **if** len(ArrayN)==0 **then** //*Nash equilibrium strategy for every block is Y*
13:     **return** Y;
14: **end if**
15: **if** q $\notin$ ArrayN **then** //*Nash equilibrium strategy for block s is Y, return Y*
16:     **return** Y;
17: **end if**
18: **for** $i = s - 1; i \geq k + 1; i - -$ **do**
19:     COMPARE($A, U(Tq_{i+1}^*)$) //*compare the utility with A to decide final strategy*
20:     **if** A is larger **then**
21:         **return** Y
22:     **end if**
23:     **for** $q \in$ ArrayN **do**
24:         **if** $A > U(Tj_{i+1}^*)$ **then**
25:             POP(ArrayN,j) //*delete mining pools whose strategy changes*
26:         **end if**
27:     **end for**
28:     $U(Tq_i^*)$=SUM(ArrayN)*$U(Tq_{i+1}^*)$
29: **end for**
30: **return** N

References

1. Zheng, Z., et al.: An overview on smart contracts: challenges, advances and platforms. Futur. Gener. Comput. Syst. **105**, 475–491 (2020)
2. Finance, C.: Compound finance (2021). https://compound.finance/
3. bZx network: bzx network (2021). https://bzx.network/
4. Zhou, L., Qin, K., Torres, C.F., Le, D.V., Gervais, A.: High-frequency trading on decentralized on-chain exchanges. arXiv preprint arXiv:2009.14021 (2020)

5. Apostolaki, M., Zohar, A., Vanbever, L.: Hijacking bitcoin: routing attacks on cryptocurrencies. In: 2017 IEEE Symposium on Security and Privacy (SP), pp. 375–392. IEEE (2017)
6. Shi, H., Wang, S., Hu, Q., Cheng, X., Zhang, J., Yu, J.: Fee-free pooled mining for countering pool-hopping attack in blockchain. IEEE Trans. Depend. Secur. Comput. **18**, 1580–1590 (2020)
7. Antonopoulos, A.M.: Mastering Bitcoin (2019)
8. Zhang, F., Cecchetti, E., Croman, K., Juels, A., Shi, E.: Town crier: an authenticated data feed for smart contracts. In: Proceedings of the 2016 ACM SIGSAC Conference on Computer and Communications Security, pp. 270–282 (2016)
9. Yamashita, K., Nomura, Y., Zhou, E., Pi, B., Jun, S.: Potential risks of hyperledger fabric smart contracts. In: 2019 IEEE International Workshop on Blockchain Oriented Software Engineering (IWBOSE), IEEE, pp. 1–10 (2019)
10. Al-Breiki, H., Rehman, M.H.U., Salah, K., Svetinovic, S.: Trustworthy blockchain oracles: review, comparison, and open research challenges. IEEE Access **8**, pp. 85 675–85 685 (2020)
11. Xu, X., et al.: The blockchain as a software connector. In: 2016 13th Working IEEE/IFIP Conference on Software Architecture (WICSA). pp. 182–191. IEEE (2016)
12. Moudoud, H., Cherkaoui, S., Khoukh, L.: An IoT blockchain architecture using oracles and smart contracts: the use-case of a food supply chain. In: 2019 IEEE 30th Annual International Symposium on Personal, Indoor and Mobile Radio Communications (PIMRC), pp. 1–6. IEEE (2019)
13. Cloud, G.: Building hybrid blockchain/cloud applications with ethereum and google cloud (2021). https://cloud.google.com/blog/products/data-analytics/building-hybrid-blockchain-cloud-applications-with-ethereum-and-google-cloud
14. Adler, J., Berryhill, R., Veneris, Z. Poulos, A., Veira, N., Kastania, A.: Astraea: a decentralized blockchain oracle. In: 2018 IEEE International Conference on Internet of Things (IThings) and IEEE Green Computing and Communications (GreenCom) and IEEE cyber, Physical and Social Computing (CPSCom) and IEEE Smart Data (SmartData), pp. 1145–1152, IEEE (2018)
15. Peterson, J., Krug, J., Zoltu, M., Williams, A.K., Alexander, S.: Augur: a decentralized oracle and prediction market platform. arXiv preprint arXiv:1501.01042 (2015)
16. de Pedro, A.S., Levi, D., Cuende, L.I.: WitNet: a decentralized oracle network protocol. arXiv preprint arXiv:1711.09756 (2017)
17. Wang, S., et al.: Decentralized autonomous organizations: concept, model, and applications. IEEE Trans. Comput. Soc. Syst. **6**(5), 870–878 (2019)
18. NEST Protoco: The NEST protocol (2021). https://nestprotocol.org/
19. Curve finance (2021). https://curve.fi/
20. Eyal, I., Sirer, E.G.: Majority is not enough: bitcoin mining is vulnerable. In: Christin, N., Safavi-Naini, R. (eds.) FC 2014. LNCS, vol. 8437, pp. 436–454. Springer, Heidelberg (2014). https://doi.org/10.1007/978-3-662-45472-5_28
21. Zhou, L., Qin, K., Ferreira Torres, C., Gervais, A., et al.: High-frequency trading on decentralized on-chain exchanges. In: IEEE Symposium on Security and Privacy, pp. 23–27 May 2021
22. Nakamoto, S.: Bitcoin: a peer-to-peer electronic cash systemBitcoin: a peer-to-peer electronic cash system. Decent. Bus. Rev. 21260 (2008)
23. Wang, D., et al.: Towards a first step to understand flash loan and its applications in DEFI ecosystem. In: Proceedings of the Ninth International Workshop on Security in Blockchain and Cloud Computing, pp. 23–28 (2011)

24. Liao, K., Katz, J.: Incentivizing blockchain forks via whale transactions. In: Brenner, M., et al. (eds.) FC 2017. LNCS, vol. 10323, pp. 264–279. Springer, Cham (2017). https://doi.org/10.1007/978-3-319-70278-0_17

25. McCorry, P., Hicks, A., Meiklejohn, S.: Smart contracts for bribing miners. In: Zohar, A., et al. (eds.) FC 2018. LNCS, vol. 10958, pp. 3–18. Springer, Heidelberg (2019). https://doi.org/10.1007/978-3-662-58820-8_1

26. Daian, P., et al.: Flash boys 2.0: Frontrunning in decentralized exchanges, miner extractable value, and consensus instability. In: 2020 IEEE Symposium on Security and Privacy (SP), pp. 910–927. IEEE (2020)

27. Eskandari, S., Moosavi, S., Clark, J.: SoK: transparent dishonesty: front-running attacks on blockchain. In: Bracciali, A., Clark, J., Pintore, F., Rønne, P.B., Sala, M. (eds.) FC 2019. LNCS, vol. 11599, pp. 170–189. Springer, Cham (2020). https://doi.org/10.1007/978-3-030-43725-1_13

28. Chohan, U.W.: Counter-Hegemonic Finance: The Gamestop Short Squeeze. SSRN (2021)

29. provable: Provable documentation (2021). https://docs.provable.xyz

30. Eskandari, S., Clark, J., Sundaresan, V., Adham, M.: On the feasibility of decentralized derivatives markets. In: Brenner, M., et al. (eds.) FC 2017. LNCS, vol. 10323, pp. 553–567. Springer, Cham (2017). https://doi.org/10.1007/978-3-319-70278-0_35

31. Anand, A., Pathak, J.: WallStreetBets against wall street: the role of reddit in the GameStop short squeeze. IIM Bangalore Research Paper, no. 644 (2021)

32. Wu, H., Vora, P.L., Zagórski, F.: PrivApollo-secret ballot E2E-V Internet voting. In: Financial Cryptography Workshops, pp. 299–313 (2019)

Suborn Channels:
Incentives Against Timelock Bribes

Zeta Avarikioti[1] and Orfeas Stefanos Thyfronitis Litos[2(✉)]

[1] TU Wien, Vienna, Austria
georgia.avarikioti@tuwien.ac.at
[2] Technical University of Darmstadt, Darmstadt, Germany
orfeas.thyfronitis@tu-darmstadt.de

Abstract. As the Bitcoin mining landscape becomes more competitive, analyzing potential attacks under the assumption of rational miners becomes increasingly relevant. In the rational setting, blockchain users can bribe miners to reap an unfair benefit. Established protocols such as Duplex Micropayment Channels and Lightning Channels are susceptible to bribery, which upends their financial guarantees. Indeed, we prove that in a two-party contract in which the honest party can spend an output right away, whereas the malicious can only spend the same output after a timelock, the latter party can promise a high fee to the miners, who then intentionally ignore the transaction of the honest party in anticipation of the higher fee. This effectively prevents a valid transaction from ever entering the blockchain, resulting in potentially severe financial losses for the honest and considerable gains for the malicious party.

We expand previous results on timelock bribes to more realistic blockchains, proving that a general class of contracts are susceptible. We then apply our results to Duplex Micropayment Channels and Lightning Channels, providing exact bounds on their safe operating region. Furthermore, we enhance the Bitcoin Script of Duplex Micropayment Channels so that the coins of a party that attempts to bribe are given to the miners as fees, therefore effectively disincentivizing bribes. Our solution, named SUBORN channels, is implemented as a proof-of-concept. We also propose a small change to Lightning Channels that achieves a similar effect. Moreover, we formally express the exact circumstances under which our two proposals ensure alignment of miner incentives with the prescribed protocol outcome.

Keywords: Bitcoin · Security · Layer 2 · Payment channels · Lightning network · Incentives · Bribing

1 Introduction

Blockchains like Bitcoin [23] and Ethereum [28] reformed the financial landscape. Nevertheless, blockchains scale poorly in comparison to conventional centralized

O.S. Thyfronitis Litos—Work done while the author was at the University of Edinburgh.

I. Eyal and J. Garay (Eds.): FC 2022, LNCS 13411, pp. 488–511, 2022.
https://doi.org/10.1007/978-3-031-18283-9_24

payment systems [9]. One of the major approaches to alleviate the scalability issue of blockchains is *payment channel networks* (PCNs).

Payment channels allow two parties to lock funds on the blockchain and thereafter securely transact off-chain. A number of PCN proposals exist [2–8, 10–15, 17, 21, 24, 25], each improving on previous designs, exploiting features of different blockchains or balancing various trade-offs differently. Two of the earliest PCNs are the *Lightning Network* (LN) [24] and the *Duplex Micropayment Channels* (DMC) [11], both applicable on Bitcoin.

As Bitcoin implements a (crypto-)currency, financial incentives are critical to the security of the protocol. These financial incentives naturally transfer to the off-chain network operating on top of Bitcoin, e.g., DMC or LN, since the off-chain network also involves locked cryptocurrency funds. As a result, several bribing attacks have been proposed on PCNs [22, 26, 27]. In this work, we focus on a specific type of bribing attacks, the so-called *timelocked bribes*: a briber pays the miners to include the briber's transaction which will only be valid in the future, and *not* include a conflicting but currently valid transaction from an honest party. This attack affects directly the security of most PCNs.

The success of a timelock bribing attack is conditional on several variables. Determining those variables and therefore the parameter regions in which parties can transact securely against a briber is a challenging task. Furthermore, we ask whether expanding these safe regions is possible, as this would imply a wider functioning area for payment channels. In this work, we take up these challenges.

Our Contributions. We first formally describe the dynamics governing miners' choices on whether to mine a future transaction with a high fee or a currently spendable but conflicting transaction with a smaller fee. To this end, we perform a game-theoretic analysis in Sect. 3. We then formulate and prove in Theorem 1 under which circumstances it is a *strictly dominant strategy* for miners to ignore the currently spendable transaction in favor of the future one. This theorem generalizes the incentive analysis performed in [26] to blockchains with more than 1 transaction per block and to a more generic smart contract than HTLC [11]. At a high level, miners prefer the future transaction if it offers a very high fee (a.k.a. bribe) compared to the currently spendable transaction. The exact bound depends also on the fees paid by ordinary transactions and the mining power of the weakest miner but, somewhat surprisingly, is independent of the length of the timelock for large enough bribes.

In Sect. 4 we apply our theorem to DMC, providing exact bounds on the cases in which a timelock bribe is possible. Subsequently, we modify the DMC protocol and propose a new scheme which we term SUBORN channels in order to greatly expand those bounds. The core idea is that SUBORN channels allow miners to claim the coins the briber owns in the channel when the honest party proves the briber cheated. The exact script for SUBORN channels is provided as well, along with its proof of concept implementation[1].

---

[1] https://gitlab.com/fc22-submission-69/suborn.

Lastly, we apply our theorem to LN, characterizing exactly when a timelock bribe is beneficial. We then propose a straightforward change to the protocol that completely nullifies timelock bribes; we simply increase the transaction fees to include the coins owned by the briber. We further analyze the circumstances under which our proposal would not cost money to the honest party and recommend how the honest party can avoid cost-inducing situations entirely. We note that no change in LN Script is necessary for implementing our proposal.

2   Background and Notation

2.1   Bitcoin

Bitcoin users publish *transactions*, which are temporarily stored by miners. Each miner composes a *block* that consists of valid transactions. Miners compete with each other in a lottery which periodically selects a winner with probability proportional to their *mining power* – a quantity that we assume is constant and common knowledge among participants. *Mining* is a resource-intensive process that each miner performs locally. The winning miner gets their block included in the blockchain and gains a (constant) *block reward* plus the sum of the fees of all included transactions; thus rational miners attempt to maximize their received fees. Then miners verify that all transactions in the new block are valid, compose a new block compatible with all past ones (including the new valid block they just received) and attempt to win the next lottery. In case a miner receives two or more conflicting blocks of the same *height* (a.k.a. when they encounter a *fork*), they can mine on top of any one. With high probability one of the forks will eventually overtake the others by accumulating more blocks, so all miners will switch to the longest chain, dropping the other forks and resolving the conflict.

Smart Contracts. Blockchains like Bitcoin [23] and Ethereum [28] enable *smart contracts*, i.e., programmable scripts that attach a wide variety of rules which must be satisfied in order to spend coins. In Bitcoin, coins are attached to *transaction outputs*, which in turn are locked with a specific script. Bitcoin smart contracts commonly employ the use of multisignatures, timelocks, and hashlocks.

The most commonly used smart contract requires a single *signature* from a specific public key: such a contract ensures that the coins of interest are exclusively owned by whoever knows the associated private key. An m-of-n *multisignature* is a contract that demands at least m signatures which correspond to any m of the n predefined public keys.

Hashlocks are another type of contract, available also in Bitcoin Script. If a transaction output is hashlocked, it requires the pre-image of the specific hash to become valid and thus spendable. For instance, suppose $h(s)$ denotes the hash of a secret s. If an output is hashlocked with $h(s)$, it is valid only if the secret s is revealed.

Timelocked outputs can only be spent after a specified time in the future. One of the simplest practical smart contracts that uses timelocks is the *conditional timelock*, which allows the associated output to be spent either with the signature of party P_1 right away, or with the signature of party P_2 after a timelock – possibly additional requirements encumber one or both spending methods, e.g. hashlocks or multisigs.

2.2 Payment Channels

The core idea behind payment channels is the same across different constructions: two parties may lock coins on an escrow on the blockchain, or a so-called channel, and then perform arbitrarily many transactions off-chain. Each off-chain transaction is a signed message that depicts the current balance of coins between the parties. Any party can close the channel at any time, either in collaboration with the counterparty, or unilaterally by publishing the last message signed by both parties. Therefore, the blockchain is only used to open and close the channel, and to resolve potential conflicts between parties. The conflict resolution mechanism differs significantly among channel constructions. Please see [29] for a survey of PCNs.

In this work, after establishing a general result for conditionally timelocked contracts, we apply our results to two specific PCNs: DMC [11] and LN [24]. We now describe these constructions, excluding their HTLCs.

DMC Overview. At a high level, a DMC between parties P_1 and P_2 works as follows: At first the parties agree on a *setup* transaction, which spends their initial coins and moves them to an output locked with a 2-*of*-2 *multisig*. They then establish a series of *opt-in* transactions. These transactions form a chain of a pre-agreed length and are all timelocked until a common pre-agreed future time $T_{\max}$. The first transaction consumes the setup transaction output and provides a similar 2-of-2 multisig output. Each subsequent transaction consumes the output of the previous opt-in transaction and provides a similar 2-of-2 multisig output, with the exception of the last one. This opt-in transaction has *two* 2-of-2 multisig outputs instead, each carrying coins equal to one party's initial coins.

Each of the two last outputs constitutes the *setup output* for a *simple micropayment channel* (not to be confused with the setup transaction of the DMC itself). A simple channel can only facilitate payments in *one direction*, so there is one channel for each direction. We here explain briefly how the channel in which P_2 pays P_1 functions; the other one is symmetric. The channel starts off with P_1 and P_2 agreeing on a *refund* transaction that is timelocked until $T_{\max}$, spends the setup output and provides one output that carries P_2's initial coins that are spendable by P_2 alone. Once both parties know the relevant opt-in and refund transactions along with the necessary signatures by their counterparty, they only need to put the DMC setup transaction on-chain to open the DMC. When P_2 holds c_2 and wants to pay δ coins to P_1, who holds c_1 coins, P_2 signs and sends to P_1 an *update* transaction which has no timelock, spends the setup output and has one output per party; P_1's output carries $c_1 + \delta$ and P_2's carries $c_2 - \delta$ coins. The balances c_1, c_2 are as in the last update transaction if any, otherwise as in the refund. Note that P_1 can put on-chain any update transaction if needed, so he prefers the latest update transaction in which he has most coins – this mechanism is called *replace by incentive*.

Due to their unidirectional nature, one of the two simple channels may eventually get depleted. In such a case, the parties *invalidate* them along with the last opt-in transaction by creating a new competing opt-in transaction with a lower timelock. This opt-in transaction provides two new simple micropayment channels, each initially containing the sum of the payer's coins in the just invalidated simple channels. In case the timelock of the new opt-in transaction is smaller than a pre-agreed value T_{min}, the two parties replace the last two opt-in transactions instead. Both new opt-in transactions use the same timelock, which is lower than the timelock of the second-last opt-in transaction in the old chain. The same replacement logic, called *replace by timelock*, can be extended backwards to the entire length of the opt-in transactions' chain. This way, an *invalidation tree* is created that consists of opt-in transactions as non-leaf nodes and pairs of simple micropayment channels as leaves.

When an invalidation tree is itself depleted, cooperative parties can *refresh* their DMC and obtain a new invalidation tree with a single on-chain transaction. Similarly, cooperative parties can close their channel with a single on-chain *teardown* transaction.

The above construction depicted in Fig. 1, ensures that an honest party can always retrieve its coins unilaterally by publishing the opt-in transactions of the latest branch when their timelock expires, even if the counterparty stops cooperating in arbitrary ways. This security guarantee holds only if a transaction with a lower timelock is always included on-chain when competing only with transactions with a higher timelock. As we see in this work however, this assumption does not always hold.

LN Overview. LN bases its functionality on an entirely different construction. A central premise is that, in contrast to DMC, not all of the transactions stored locally by the two parties are the same: some have differing scripts.

The two parties first negotiate the *funding* output, which carries all of the channel's coins in a 2-of-2 multisig. They then build a pair of *commitment* transactions, one for each party, each of which can spend the funding output. P_1's commitment transaction is signed by P_2 and has two outputs. One carries P_2's initial coins and can be spent with a simple signature by P_2. The other carries P_1's initial coins and can be spent in one of two ways: either with a signature by P_1 after a pre-agreed timelock (the *honest* spending method), or with a signature by a special *revocation* key that is generated by the two parties cooperatively (the *punishment* spending method). The latter private key has the unusual property that it can remain unknown to both parties while allowing the corresponding public key to be computed cooperatively: Each party has a *secret share*, from which it can generate a *public share*. The two secret shares combine to the private key, whereas the two public ones combine to the public key, thus the two parties can cooperatively derive the public key without disclosing their secret shares. This construction is formalized and proved secure in [18]. P_2's commitment transaction is symmetric. Once each party holds its first commitment transaction, they can put the funding output on-chain to open the channel.

Conceptually, an off-chain payment is performed in two steps. First, the two parties generate and sign a new pair of commitment transactions of which the outputs pay out the newly agreed coins to each party. New revocation keys are used. Second, each party sends to its counterparty the secret share of the revocation key used in the previous commitment transaction, revoking the latter. This way, if a party publishes an old commitment transaction, the counterparty can take all coins in the channel as punishment as long as it uses the punishment spending method before the timelock of the honest spending method expires. Note that the actual update procedure is slightly more complicated than in this simplified, but morally correct, description.

Lastly, the two parties can cooperatively close the channel by building a single *closing* transaction that spends the funding output and gives each party its coins without a timelock.

The LN construction ensures that an honest party which checks the blockchain periodically can always unilaterally retrieve its coins or more, either by publishing its latest commitment transaction and waiting for its timelock to expire or by punishing its counterparty in case the latter published a revoked commitment transaction. This guarantee though holds only under the assumption that a non-timelocked transaction which competes only with a timelocked one can always go on-chain. As we mentioned however, this assumption is violated under certain circumstances. The LN construction is illustrated in Fig. 2.

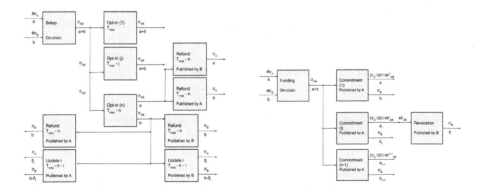

Fig. 1. Duplex micropayment channels   **Fig. 2.** Lightning channels

3   Incentive Analysis

3.1   Model

As in [26], we assume that all $n \geq 2$ miners are rational and each has a proportion $0 < \lambda_i < 1$ of the total mining power, constant throughout the execution.

Block rewards are ignored to simplify the analysis, but would not change our results as long as they remain constant throughout the time frame of interest. Let $\lambda_{\min} = \min_{i \in [n]} \lambda_i$. We assume that each block is comprised of a fixed number of transactions N (as opposed to, e.g., a fixed block size like Bitcoin or a fixed gas limit like Ethereum). The game evolves in rounds. At the beginning of each round, each miner decides on a set of transactions to include in her block. Subsequently a single miner is chosen at random according to the mining power distribution, her block is appended to the blockchain, the included transaction consumes its designated UTXO(s) and potentially provides one or more new unspent outputs, the winning miner obtains the fee of the transaction and all miners learn who won. This completes the round and miners attempt to mine a new block.

The utility of each miner u_i is equal to the sum of fees she obtains over all game rounds – we restrict our attention to games with a finite number of rounds, say T. All transactions that may be included in a block are publicly known and carry a constant fee f, unless stated otherwise. The mining power distribution along with the rest of the model discussed above is common knowledge.

In each round $k \in [T]$, the i-th miner employs a *strategy* σ_i^k that takes values in the set Σ_i^k, which consists of the transactions that the miner chooses for its block at round k. A *strategy profile* for round k is the tuple of the strategies of all miners for round k and is denoted with $\sigma^k = (\sigma_1^k, \ldots, \sigma_n^k) \in \Sigma^k$. A strategy profile for rounds from k_1 to k_2 is the concatenation of the strategy profiles of rounds k_1 to k_2 and is denoted with $\sigma^{k_1 \ldots k_2} = \sigma^{k_1} \ldots \sigma^{k_2} \in \Sigma^{k_1 \ldots k_2}$. The Nash equilibrium strategy profile for rounds from k_1 to k_2 is denoted with $\overline{\sigma}^{k_1 \ldots k_2}$. Note that the latter constitutes a slight abuse of notation since the strategy profiles in rounds after k_2 may in principle influence what is the Nash equilibrium of rounds up to k_2, but in our games of interest every future round has exactly one Nash equilibrium that is also the unique strictly dominant strategy profile (ignoring inclusion of a different set of transactions unrelated to the conditionally timelocked output O of interest, c.f. Definition 1, as such differences do not change the utility), thus no problem arises. A strategy profile for all rounds is denoted with $\sigma = \sigma^{1 \ldots T} \in \Sigma$. The Nash equilibrium strategy profile for all rounds is denoted with $\overline{\sigma}$. We denote the tuple of all miners' strategies apart from that of the i-th miner with $\sigma_{-i} \in \Sigma_{-i}$, and we may add a superscript to denote one or more rounds as above. Note that our notation cannot represent games in which there are multiple Nash equilibria. This is not a concern, as we will not come across such games.

3.2   Conditionally Timelocked Game and Analysis

In this section, we define a game that captures the race between two transactions tx_1 and tx_2 that spend the same unspent output but under different conditions. On the one hand, tx_1 allows the output to be spent immediately, while tx_2 bounds the output to a timelock. On the other hand, tx_1 pays the miner a fee f_1, while tx_2 pays a fee f_2. Both $f_1, f_2 > f$, f the fee of ordinary transactions.

Naturally, if $f_1 > f_2$ any rational miner will immediately include $\mathtt{tx}_1$. We are therefore interested in the case where $f_2 > f_1$. For this case, we determine the exact conditions under which all rational miners will wait out the timelock and include $\mathtt{tx}_2$ (irrespective of the timelock). We observe that these conditions depend solely on the two fees f_1, f_2, the minimum mining power λ_{min}, and the number of necessary bribing transactions m (e.g., 2 for DMC and 1 for LN).

Definition 1 (Conditionally timelocked output). *A* conditionally time-locked output *is an on-chain transaction output with spending condition* $\mathtt{cond}_1 \vee \mathtt{cond}_2$ *such that* $\mathtt{cond}_1$ *is not encumbered with any timelock and* $\mathtt{cond}_2$ *is encumbered with a timelock that expires* T *blocks after block with height* T_0.

Definition 2 (Conditionally timelocked game). *A* conditionally timelocked game *is a game that consists of* T *rounds, starting from a blockchain of height* T_0 *which includes an unspent conditionally timelocked output* $O = (\cdot, \mathtt{cond}_1 \vee \mathtt{cond}_2)$. *From the onset of the game, miners are aware of a set of transactions* $\mathtt{txs}_1$ *that fits in a single block.* $\mathtt{txs}_1$ *contains a transaction* $\mathtt{tx}_1$ *which spends* O *by satisfying* $\mathtt{cond}_1$. *All other transactions in* $\mathtt{txs}_1$ *spend at least one output of* $\mathtt{tx}_1$ *or of another transaction in* $\mathtt{txs}_1$. *Miners are also aware of another set of transactions* $\mathtt{txs}_2$ *that fits in a single block as well.* $\mathtt{txs}_2$ *contains a transaction* $\mathtt{tx}_2$ *that spends* O *by satisfying* $\mathtt{cond}_2$. *All other transactions in* $\mathtt{txs}_2$ *spend at least one output of* $\mathtt{tx}_2$ *or of another transaction in* $\mathtt{txs}_2$. *Furthermore, there are at every round enough valid, "unrelated" transactions to fill a block that do not spend* O *or any output spent or produced by any transaction in* $\mathtt{txs}_1 \cup \mathtt{txs}_2$, *and each offers fee* f. *We denote any set of unrelated transactions with* $\mathtt{txs}_u$.

Let $m = \max\{|\mathtt{txs}_1|, |\mathtt{txs}_2|\}$. *For* $i \in \{1, 2\}$, *we denote by* f_i *the maximum value a miner can extract (as fees or outputs that can be spent by anyone) by including in her block an m-sized set of transactions that includes* $\mathtt{tx}_i$ *and by* $\mathtt{txs}_i^*$ *any such set of transactions.*

Additionally, for $k \in [T]$ *we denote with* Γ_k *the subgame of* Γ *at the beginning of the k-th round with* O *still unspent. Likewise we denote with* Γ_k^* *the subgame of* Γ *at the beginning of the k-th round with* O *having already been spent.*

We note the following in the context of a conditionally timelocked game:

- $\mathtt{tx}_1$ is an ancestor of all other transactions in $\mathtt{txs}_1$,
- $\mathtt{tx}_2$ is an ancestor of all other transactions in $\mathtt{txs}_2$,
- $\mathtt{tx}_1$ and $\mathtt{tx}_2$ are mutually exclusive, therefore no pair of transactions from $\mathtt{txs}_1$ and $\mathtt{txs}_2$ respectively can coexist in the blockchain.
- For $i \in \{1, 2\}$, a set of transactions $\mathtt{txs}_i^*$ that extracts value f_i for the miner may contain anywhere from 1 to m transactions from $\mathtt{txs}_i$. The remaining transactions in $\mathtt{txs}_i^*$, as well as the rest of the transactions in the block, are unrelated transactions.
- If O is unspent at a round before T, a miner cannot mine $\mathtt{tx}_2$.
- If O is unspent at round T, a miner may mine either of $\mathtt{tx}_1, \mathtt{tx}_2$.
- If O is spent, a miner cannot mine either of $\mathtt{tx}_1, \mathtt{tx}_2$.
- We ignore games in which O is initially spent, as they provide no opportunity to bribe.

- Since $\Gamma_1 = \Gamma$ and O is initially unspent, there is no Γ_1^* game.
- The notation $\mathtt{txs}_u$ does not clarify the exact size of the set, but it will always be clear from context, keeping in mind that each block must contain exactly N transactions.

Intuitively, $\mathtt{txs}_1$ represent honest and $\mathtt{txs}_2$ represent bribing sets of transactions. Looking forward, the reason we consider sets of transactions (as opposed to just a single transaction) is because in Lightning a briber cannot offer the bribe just with $\mathtt{tx}_2$ (i.e. "HTLC-Timeout" [1]), since the fee of this transaction is agreed upon by both protocol parties; the briber has to publish one more transaction instead, which would spend HTLC-Timeout and offer the bribing fee. This observation renders the analysis of [26] technically inapplicable to Lightning. Our model generalizes that of [26] to cover such situations. Furthermore, our approach applies to bribing scenarios in protocols that do not include hashlocks, such as DMC.

Lemma 1. *Consider a conditionally timelocked game Γ. If $mf > f_1$, then attempting to mine $\mathtt{tx}_1$ at any round is a strictly dominated strategy for all miners.*

Proofs to all lemmas and theorems can be found in Appendix B.

Lemma 2. *Consider a conditionally timelocked subgame Γ_k^* in which O has been spent. $\forall \sigma \in \Sigma, \forall i \in [n]$, it is $u_i(\sigma, \Gamma_k^*) = \lambda_i(T - k + 1)Nf$.*

Theorem 1. *Consider a conditionally timelocked game Γ. If $f_2 > \frac{f_1 - mf}{\lambda_{\min}} + mf > f_1$, then the unique Nash Equilibrium is for every miner to attempt to mine only $\mathtt{txs}_u$ at each round before T and attempt to mine $\mathtt{txs}_2^* \cup \mathtt{txs}_u$ at round T, in other words that $\overline{\sigma} = \underbrace{(\mathtt{txs}_u, \ldots, \mathtt{txs}_u)}_{n}^{T-1} \underbrace{(\mathtt{txs}_2^* \cup \mathtt{txs}_u, \ldots, \mathtt{txs}_2^* \cup \mathtt{txs}_u)}_{n}.$*

Intuitively, Theorem 1 asserts that for a big enough bribe, every miner is incentivized to ignore the honest transactions, wait instead for the timelock to expire and then mine the bribing transactions, thus ensuring the success of the bribing attempt. The minimum required size of the bribe is proportional to the fees of the honest transactions, inversely proportional to the minimum mining power and independent of the timelock length.

4   Timelock Bribe Analysis

In this section, we leverage the analysis of Sect. 3 to examine the race between a briber that publishes an old transaction alongside with a bribe, and an honest party that follows the protocol specification; meaning that the honest party attempts to include on-chain the last update transaction or the revocation transaction in DMC and Lightning channels respectively. As explained in Sect. 2, the old transaction is timelocked but typically offers a bribe, while the honest transaction can be spent immediately but typically pays the miner less coins.

We first determine the parameter region under which the DMC channels are susceptible to such bribing attacks. Then, we modify the DMC channels, and propose a novel scheme, which we term SUBORN channels, to limit the bribing region. The core idea is that, if a party tries to bribe, its coins in the last agreed transaction are awarded to the miners by-design, in addition to the transaction fee. We note that a rational briber will at most bribe the miners with its gain between the two competing transactions. For instance, suppose the cheating transaction awards 7 coins to the briber and 3 coins to the honest party, while the last agreed transaction awards 4 and 6 respectively. Then, the 4 coins (of the briber in the last state) can be claimed by the miner that mines the honest party's transaction, while the briber can only profitably bribe for less than $7 - 4 = 3$ coins, clearly losing the race. Our construction thus limits the parameter region in which timelock bribes are effective.

Thereafter, we identify the parameter region in which bribes are effective in LN. Finally, we propose the use of an increased fee in the revocation transaction, depending on the value of each transaction, to expand the aforementioned parameter region with similar effects to SUBORN channels.

4.1   Timelock Bribe

Now, let P_1 be an honest party and P_2 a rational party which tries to maximize its coins like the miners. We assume that both parties have no mining power.

Definition 3 (Timelock Bribe). *Consider parties P_1, P_2 and a publicly known transaction tx with one output O that can be either spent by P_1 with a transaction tx_1, possibly after a timelock, such that tx_1 offers miners a value f_1, or by P_2 with a transaction tx_2 which has a timelock that is strictly greater than that of tx_1 (if the latter has any). Consider a set of transactions txs_2, $|txs_2| = m$, that contains tx_2, offers total value f_2 to miners and all transactions in txs_2 apart from tx_2 spend at least one output of tx_2 or another transaction in txs_2. We say that P_2 offers a* timelock bribe *if P_2 publishes all txs_2 before the timelock of tx_2 has expired and $f_2 > \frac{f_1 - mf}{\lambda_{\min}} + mf$.*

Theorem 1 implies that the excessive fee paid by P_2 intends to discourage miners from including P_1's transaction before P_2's timelock expires and eventually include P_2's transaction instead. We now prove that the briber prefers to use the fewer (bribing) transactions possible (denoted by m).

Lemma 3.

$$\forall m \in [N - 1], \frac{f_1 - mf}{\lambda_{\min}} + mf < \frac{(f_1 + f) - (m + 1)f}{\lambda_{\min}} + (m + 1)f$$

Note that the $(f_1 + f)$ in the numerator of the right-hand side of the inequality stems from the fact that an additional unrelated transaction has to be added to txs_1^* if the number of briber's transactions txs_2 are increased by 1 while it is already $|txs_2| \geq |txs_1|$. In other words, Lemma 3 states the following: *Given* *that briber's transactions are more than the honest party's transactions, timelock bribes involving fewer transactions are cheaper for the briber.* This holds because a lower number of bribe transactions means that the briber has to surpass a lower minimum bribe in order to incentivize miners in her favor.

4.2   Timelock Bribe in DMC

Let parties P_1 and P_2 that have a DMC channel and consider one of the two latest transactions, i.e., the only two non-invalidated, refund transactions gives $c_{r,1}$ to P_1, $c_{r,2}$ to P_2 and offers fee f_r, whereas the latest corresponding update transaction gives $c_{u,1}$ to P_1, $c_{u,2}$ to P_2 and offers fee f_u. Note that the update transaction is not timelocked, whereas the refund transaction is, and that the two transactions are mutually exclusive. Assume $c_{r,2} > c_{u,2}$. Then in this simple micropayment channel payments flow from P_2 to P_1, thus it is in the benefit of P_2 if the refund transaction is put on-chain instead of any of the replacement update transactions. Furthermore assume that all the timelocks of the opt-in transactions of the branch of interest have expired and that P_1 has published them along with the latest update transaction of the simple micropayment channel under discussion, but no child transaction that spends its $c_{u,1}$ coins – this is honest behavior according to the DMC protocol. Note that in the other simple micropayment channel of the current branch, payments flow from P_1 to P_2, therefore P_2 prefers the latest update transaction to the refund transaction in that channel and would not attempt to timelock bribe there.

The result intended by the DMC construction is for the update transaction, and not the refund transaction, to be included on-chain. Unfortunately, under the assumption of rational miners, there are cases in which this expectation is violated. In particular, P_2 can offer a timelock bribe and turn the inclusion of the refund transaction into a strictly dominant strategy profile for the miners. We identify the parameter region for which this is possible.

Theorem 2. *A DMC bribe is possible if $c_{r,2} - c_{u,2} > \frac{f_u - 2f}{\lambda_{\min}} + 2f - f_r$, where $c_{r,2}, c_{u,2}$ are P_2's coins in the refund and update transactions respectively, and f_r, f_u are the fees of the refund and updated transactions.*

P_1 should therefore take care to avoid such a situation by invalidating the current refund transaction before such a state is reached. Note that due to Lemma 3 it does not make sense for P_2 to attempt to bribe using more transactions than just the refund transaction and tx_b, lest she wants to pay a higher bribe. Also note that it is essentially risk-free for P_2 to attempt a timelock bribe, since if it fails the latest update transaction will be mined and P_2 will receive her fair share without any punishment. Due to symmetry between the two parties, the analysis above holds with the roles of P_1 and P_2 reversed.

Observe that in practice parties have the ability to locally re-estimate the value of $\lambda_{\min}$ on the fly and act accordingly: if a change to apparent mining power distribution makes one of the two parties decide that the current balance is reaching risky values, it can ask its counterparty to invalidate the current leaf and refuse to do any further payments until this is done.

4.3   Improving DMC Incentives: Simple Suborn Channels

Simple Suborn Channel Design. Our goal is to drastically reduce the effectiveness of timelock bribing in DMC. To that end, we propose the following changes. Remember that the only valid state of a DMC channel is essentially two unidirectional channels. We denote with $(1 \rightarrow 2)$ the channel in which P_1 pays P_2, and with $(2 \rightarrow 1)$ the reverse; this notation is also used as a superscript.

Each party locally stores a different refund transaction (instead of having identical ones). In channel $(2 \rightarrow 1)$, P_2's refund transaction has two outputs: (a) an output with P_1's coins, spendable just with P_1's signature, (b) an output with P_2's coins, spendable with P_2's signature and the preimage of a specified hash. P_1's refund transaction in $(2 \rightarrow 1)$ is as in DMC (only signatures required).

The update transaction of channel $(2 \rightarrow 1)$ (held by P_1) is changed as follows. (a) P_1's output can be spent with P_1's signature, whereas (b) P_2's output has two spending methods: either with P_2's signature, *or* with the preimage of the aforementioned hash (same as the refund transaction) *without any signature*. Channel $(1 \rightarrow 2)$ is symmetric. The changes are depicted in Fig. 3.

To establish a channel, each party generates a secret preimage and sends to the counterparty its hash. Upon receiving the hash, the party sends to the counterparty its signature on the refund transaction. To perform a payment, the payer signs and sends the new update transaction to the counterparty. The closing of a simple SUBORN channel is similar to DMC (collaboratively, or unilaterally with a refund or update transaction).

When P_2 attempts to spend her $c_{r,2}^{2 \rightarrow 1}$ coins in her own refund transaction, she has to reveal the preimage. This secret can be used by a miner to claim P_2's coins from P_1's update transaction. This effectively increases the fee of P_1's update transaction using P_2's coins. The miner only knows the preimage if P_2 attempts to timelock bribe (disclosing the secret in the process) while neither the refund nor the update transaction is on-chain.

Note that this change does not jeopardize P_2's ability to use her refund transaction honestly. In case the timelock of P_2's refund transaction expires, she can publish it, wait for it to be confirmed deep enough in the blockchain, and only then publish a transaction that spends her $c_{r,2}$ coins. At that moment it is safe for P_2 to reveal the preimage, since the update transaction cannot be included on-chain anymore.

Analysis. In order to determine the exact bounds within which our technique prevents timelock bribes, we perform a similar analysis as for the original DMC.

Theorem 3. *A bribe in the simple* SUBORN *channels is possible if* $c_{r,2} - c_{u,2}(1 + \frac{1}{\lambda_{\min}}) > \frac{f_u - 2f}{\lambda_{\min}} + 2f - f_r$, *where* $c_{r,2}, c_{u,2}$ *are* P_2*'s coins in the refund and update transactions respectively, and* f_r, f_u *are the fees of the refund and updated transactions.*

We see that the bounds of balances within which timelock bribes may take place is much smaller than in the DMC construction. For example, if $\lambda_{\min} = 0.02$

(as estimated in [22]), then $c_{u,2}$ may become 51 times smaller than in plain DMC before a bribing opportunity arises. Unfortunately, these bounds are still tighter than the ones originally recommended in DMC, which allowed simple micropayment channels to be completely depleted before moving on to a new branch – as we showed, this would risk a timelock bribe opportunity. Once again, Lemma 3 precludes a case where it is in the benefit of P_2 to bribe using more transactions. Note that this change exposes P_2 to some risk if she attempts a timelock bribe even if the Nash equilibrium for the miners is to ignore P_1's update transaction. In case any winning miner is irrational and chooses to mine P_1's update and take P_2's coins, P_2 is *punished* and takes no coins. The analysis for P_1 is symmetric.

Overhead Over DMC. When opening the channel, each party has to generate a single preimage (32 bytes), send its hash (32 bytes) to the counterparty, receive and store the counterparty's hash. This has to be done only once for the entire lifetime of the channel. No additional communication rounds are needed, as the hashes can be appended to existing messages. When closing the channel, if a refund transaction is used, then the on-chain overhead is a hash (33 bytes, the extra byte specifies the length of the hash), its preimage (33 bytes as well) and the corresponding opcodes for its verification (OP_SHA256 & OP_EQUAL, 1 byte each, c.f. Appendix A), adding 68 bytes. If one party publishes its update transaction and its counterparty is honest, then the on-chain overhead is the branch with the hashlock in the counterparty's output, which adds a hash and 4 opcodes (OP_IF & OP_ELSE & OP_ENDIF, c.f. Appendix A), adding 38 bytes. The overhead of the update transaction can be eliminated if the taproot[2] optimization is used.

4.4   Incentivizing DMC Across Branches: Suborn Channels

Suborn Channel Design. The previous technique can be extended to discourage cross-branch bribes. Suppose the briber attempts to incentivize miners to ignore the valid branch of the invalidation tree altogether in favor of an invalidated branch, i.e., one which is encumbered with a longer timelock than the valid one. Now the briber may instead use an old update transaction to cheat. To address this issue, we require update transactions to include a hashlock as well. More specifically, the output of P_2, both in the refund and in the update transactions of P_2, should require the preimage of the hash along with P_2's signature. The changes are mirrored for the other party. This way all avenues for bribing are encumbered with preimage revelation. The two hashes (one per party) must remain the same across branches in all update and refund transactions. This way bribing in an old branch can be punished in the last branch. See Appendix A for the exact Script, and Fig. 3 for an illustration of SUBORN channels.

In our scheme, to decide whether our balance is within safe bounds, we must consider all past update and refund transactions. This must be taken into account

---

[2] https://github.com/bitcoin/bips/blob/master/bip-0341.mediawiki.

in the parameter region analysis. Note that in every simple channel the payer only stores the refund transaction, whereas the payee stores both the refund and the update transactions. The payee always prefers the update to the refund transaction, as simple channels are unidirectional.

Let $k_l \in \mathbb{N}$ be the total number of leaves – the only valid leaf is the k_l-th. Let $k \in [k_l - 1]$. Furthermore, assume that branches k_l and k have j distinct opt-in transactions. The coins held in the outputs of the two last update transactions of the k-th branch that belong to P_2 are denoted with $c_{k,u,2}^{1 \rightarrow 2}$ and $c_{k,u,2}^{2 \rightarrow 1}$. Analogous notation is used for the refund transactions and P_1's coins. Let f_b be the necessary bribe given by $\mathtt{tx}_b$ to incentivize miners to ignore the latest leaf – P_2 may only have $\mathtt{tx}_b$ consume her $c_{k,r,2}^{2 \rightarrow 1}$ and optionally in addition her $c_{k,u,2}^{1 \rightarrow 2}$ coins, as all opt-in transactions only include multisig outputs that can only be spent according to the protocol. All opt-in, update and refund transactions have a fee f_o, f_u and f_r respectively.

Theorem 4. *A bribe in* SUBORN *channels is possible if* $\forall k \in [k_l - 1], c_{k,u,2}^{1 \rightarrow 2} + c_{k,r,2}^{2 \rightarrow 1} - (c_{k_l,u,2}^{1 \rightarrow 2} + c_{k_l,u,2}^{2 \rightarrow 1})(1 + \frac{1}{\lambda_{\min}}) < \frac{1}{\lambda_{\min}}(jf_o + 2f_u - (j+3)f) + (j+3)f - jf_o - f_r - f_u.$

Before every payment P_1 must ensure that Theorem 4 will still hold to prevent a timelock bribe from P_2. Otherwise P_1 should refuse to facilitate the payment and propose creating a new branch instead. Lemma 3 ensures that it is in the benefit of P_2 to bribe with only one additional transaction $\mathtt{tx}_b$. Similarly to the previous subsection, P_2 is exposed to some risk if it attempts a timelock bribe even when the Nash equilibrium is in her favor, since there may be a winning irrational miner that chooses to mine P_1's transaction and punish P_2. The analysis for P_1 is symmetric.

Overhead over Simple Suborn Channels. The only additional overhead compared to Subsect. 4.3 is a hash, a preimage and 2 opcodes, for a total of 68 bytes, when the party that publishes an update transaction spends its own output.

4.5   Timelock Bribe in LN

LN is also susceptible to timelock bribes. P_2 can timelock bribe by publishing an old, revoked commitment transaction together with a bribing transaction $\mathtt{tx}_b$. $\mathtt{tx}_b$ spends P_2's output of the commitment transaction, offers fee f_b and pays the rest to P_2. For big enough f_b, this incentivizes miners to ignore P_1's revocation transaction, which carries a fee f_r; the revocation transaction gives all P_2's coins to P_1 (without a timelock) as a punishment for publishing an old commitment transaction. Let c_{old} and c_{new} be P_2's coins in the old and new commitment transactions respectively.

Theorem 5. *A bribe in LN channels is possible if* $c_{\mathrm{old}} - c_{\mathrm{new}} > \frac{f_r - f}{\lambda_{\min}} + 2f.$

Therefore, in order to avoid a timelock bribe, P_1 must not allow the channel balance to reach the condition of Theorem 5 for any old channel state. Lemma 3 ensures that it is not in P_2's benefit to attempt to bribe with more than one transaction. The analysis for P_1 is symmetric.

4.6 Fixing LN Incentives

In order to shrink the bounds in which a timelock bribe is possible in LN, we propose the following change: Instead of having revocation transactions only offer fee f_r, they would instead offer a higher fee f_r', such that bribes are not possible (reversing the inequality of Theorem 5). Note that we only consider countermeasures where the honest party does not lose coins. Figure 4 demonstrates the proposed modification to the lightning channel construction.

Theorem 6. *A bribe in modified LN channels is not possible if* $f_r' \geq f + \lambda_{\min}(c_{\text{old}} - c_{\text{new}} - 2f)$ *and* $\lambda_{\min} \leq \frac{c_{\text{new}} - f}{c_{\text{old}} - c_{\text{new}} - 2f}$, *where* c_{old} *are the maximum coins* P_2 *owned in any old channel state and* c_{new} *the coins* P_2 *currently owns.*

Before each payment, P_1 should ensure that Theorem 6 holds for the new balance. To do so, P_1 substitutes the values $\lambda_{\min}$, f, c_{old} and c_{new} – the latter is P_2's coins after the prospective update.

The maximum possible $\lambda_{\min}$ occurs when there are exactly two equal miners, meaning that $\lambda_{\min} = 0.5$. Then, $\frac{c_{\text{new}} - f}{c_{\text{old}} - c_{\text{new}} - 2f} \geq 0.5 \Leftrightarrow 2(c_{\text{new}} - f) \geq c_{\text{old}} - c_{\text{new}} - 2f \Leftrightarrow 3c_{\text{new}} \geq c_{\text{old}}$, meaning that P_1 can always nullify P_2's bribes if $3c_{\text{new}} \geq c_{\text{old}}$. For any lower $\lambda_{\min}$, the safe region is even larger.

Conveniently for P_1, the fee f_r' does not have to be determined in advance; it can be directly calculated and applied only if P_2 attempts to timelock bribe. Indeed, the revocation transaction can be built unilaterally by P_1 when it is needed and with the desired fee, as the punishment path of a commitment transaction is locked with a single key (namely "revocationpubkey" [1]) and P_1 knows the corresponding private key (namely "revocationprivkey" [1]). Moreover, f_r' does not need to be applied at all in case P_2 publishes an old commitment transaction without bribing. *No change in Script is necessary, just a suitable increase in the fee of revocation transactions*, as discussed above. The analysis for P_1 is symmetric.

Overhead Over LN. Since our solution does not change any of the data exchanged neither adds outputs nor complicates scripts, its only overhead is the calculation of the new fee f_r', a local computation that in practice is negligible.

5   Related Work

Bribing attacks on blockchains with Nakamoto-style consensus have been identified in the past, initially ones that incentivize miners to double-spend transactions [19]. Accepting such bribes carries an associated risk for the miner. Specifically, while the honest miners extend the longest chain, the bribed miner would

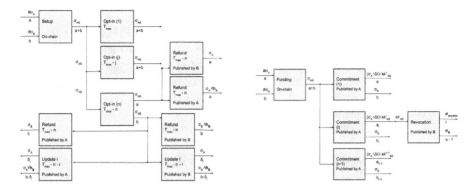

Fig. 3. Suborn channels   **Fig. 4.** Modified lightning channels

have to ignore the last block and instead mine enough new blocks on top of an older block to catch up with the last block – a high risk/high returns strategy. Furthermore, attempts to fork the blockchain are often publicly visible and attributable, and could lead to damaged miner reputation.

On the other hand, accepting a timelock bribe is risk-free for the miner, as it does not involve creating a fork; it simply has the miner ignore a particular transaction when forming a block and then mining on top of the longest chain. Previous analyses [22,26,27] of timelock bribes cover slightly different scenarios with distinct approaches and thus arrive to varying conclusions.

In particular, [22] focuses on the resilience of the HTLC smart contract under a timelock bribe, which is analyzed in the context of LN and *Cross-Chain Atomic Swaps* [16] under the assumption of rational miners and for all possible ranges of bribe values. A simple utility function is used, as it only considers the miners' payouts of the competing bribing and honest transactions, not taking into account fees offered by candidate unrelated transactions that could be included instead in a block. Modulo these differences, the subset of their analysis that treats the same bribe ranges as ours is indeed compatible with the results of the current work. For smaller bribes, the authors conclude that no opportunity for bribery exists given that the timelock is long enough – its exact length depends on the honest transaction fee, the bribe and the mining power distribution. Given the results of their analysis, the authors provide recommendations on safe parameters for LN and Atomic Swaps.

In [27] three different bribery mechanisms are presented and analyzed for a general setting of transaction censorship attacks. Fees from unrelated transactions are taken into account in the miners' utility function. The first attack involves paying out a separate bribe to each miner if it succeeds, not just to the winner of the last round. The second attack pays out bribes throughout the execution to each winning miner as long as the honest transactions are ignored. This attack can be cheaper than the first, but cannot, to the best of our knowledge, be implemented in Bitcoin Script without explicit cooperation by the honest party. The last attack is inspired by *feather forks* [20]: It bribes a miner with enough mining power to commit to ignoring blocks with undesired transactions, effectively threatening other miners to orphan their blocks if they act honestly. If the committed miner defects, she loses a deposit. This attack is cheaper than the other two, but needs a miner that is willing to publicly commit to a malicious strategy. Due to incompatible assumptions on the setting, particularly on the payout schedule of the honest transactions, the results of [27] and the current work are not directly comparable.

Lastly in [26] bribing attacks against standard HTLC contracts are analyzed, bribing ranges beyond which the attack succeeds are provided, an extension to the Bitcoin Core code that allows miners to specify arbitrary strategies is implemented and a collateral-based modification of HTLC that provably withstands bribing attacks is built. Our incentive analysis constitutes a generalization of the approach of [26]. We further apply our analysis to both DMC and LN. We also provide an alternative method to discourage bribes, which does not employ collateral.

6   Conclusion and Future Work

6.1   Future Work

In the context of a conditionally timelocked output, another direction of interest is to formally analyze miner incentives when $\frac{f_h - mf}{\lambda_{\min}} + mf > f_b > f_h$, where f_h is the fee of the timelock-free transaction and f_b is the bribe. Such a study would highlight opportunities for cheaper bribing, formulate the effects of the transition of the bribe value from one regimen to the other in a unified framework, and examine the effectiveness of our proposals against such lower bribe values. Ideally it would also unify the settings of [22, 26, 27] and the current work.

HTLCs, which are used both in DMC and LN for multi-hop atomic payments, leverage timelocks for their functionality. The methodology used in this work can be extended to techniques for mitigating timelock bribing for HTLCs as well.

6.2   Conclusion

In this work, we analyzed the circumstances under which a general form of timelock bribes may be carried out by a rational participant of a two-party protocol, assuming rational miners. We further applied our findings to provide bounds on the applicability of timelock bribes in DMC [11] and LN [24]. Subsequently, using specially tailored novel techniques that allow the honest party to use the rational party's funds to counter-bribe the miners, we reduced the opportunities for timelock bribes compared to the original constructions and effectively expanded their safe operating region.

A   Suborn Transactions Script for Incentivized DMC

(Figs. 7, 8 and 9)

```
OP_IF
    <remote_pubkey>
    OP_CHECKSIG
OP_ELSE                              OP_SHA256
    OP_SHA256                        <local_hash>
    <remote_hash>                    OP_EQUALVERIFY
    OP_EQUAL                         <local_pubkey>
OP_ENDIF                             OP_CHECKSIG
```

Fig. 5. Script for P_{3-i}'s output of P_i's update transactions, $i \in \{1, 2\}$

Fig. 6. Script for P_i's output in P_i's refund and update transactions, $i \in \{1, 2\}$

```
    1                                    <preimage>
    <remote_sig>                         <local_sig>
```

Fig. 7. Witness script spending honest ("IF") branch of Fig. 5 script

Fig. 8. Witness script spending Fig. 6 script

```
                    0
                    <preimage>
```

Fig. 9. Witness script spending punishment ("ELSE") branch of Fig. 5 script

B   Omitted Proofs

Proof of Lemma 1. For round $k \in [T]$, the game is either Γ_k or Γ_k^*. If a miner attempts to mine $\mathtt{tx_1}$ in round k, the maximum value she can extract is if she chooses to mine $\mathtt{txs_1^*}$ and fill the remaining $N - m$ slots with unrelated transactions. There is no benefit to be gained in this or later rounds if a different way of including $\mathtt{tx_1}$ is chosen, so we ignore such other options. The expected fee she gains from this round is $\lambda_i(f_1 + (N - m)f)$ in the first case and 0 in the second (as her block would be invalid). If instead she attempts to mine only unrelated transactions, her expected gains from this round are $\lambda_i N f$. It is $mf > f_1 \Leftrightarrow Nf > f_1 + (N - m)f \Leftrightarrow \lambda_i N f > \lambda_i(f_1 + (N - m)f)$ and $\lambda_i N f > 0$, so attempting to mine only unrelated transactions offers higher value in both cases. Since the expected utility is the sum of the expected gains of all rounds, attempting to mine $\texttt{txs}_1^*$ in any round is strictly dominated by attempting to mine $\texttt{txs}_u$ in their place. □

Proof of Lemma 2. Since O is spent, all remaining valid transactions offer fee f. Therefore the i-th miner has a probability λ_i to obtain fee Nf for each of the remaining $T - k + 1$ rounds, for a total expected utility $u_i(\sigma, \Gamma) = \lambda_i(T - k + 1)Nf$. □

Proof of Theorem 1. We will prove the theorem using induction and iterated elimination of strictly dominated strategies.

First of all, we note that

$$f_2 > f_1 > mf \ . \tag{1}$$

The first inequality stems directly from the theorem precondition, whereas the second arises when we solve $\frac{f_1 - mf}{\lambda_{\min}} + mf > f_1$ for f_1 while keeping in mind that $0 < \lambda_{\min} < 1$.

Consider now the i-th miner, $i \in [n]$ when she decides which transaction to include for the last round, T. If O is unspent, then

$$\forall \sigma_{-i}^T \in \Sigma_{-i}^T \text{ it is}$$
$$u_i(\sigma_{-i}^T; \sigma_i^T = \texttt{txs}_u, \Gamma_T) = \lambda_i Nf \ ,$$
$$u_i(\sigma_{-i}^T; \sigma_i^T = (\texttt{txs}_1^* \cup \texttt{txs}_u), \Gamma_T) = \lambda_i(f_1 + (N - m)f) \ ,$$
$$u_i(\sigma_{-i}^T; \sigma_i^T = (\texttt{txs}_2^* \cup \texttt{txs}_u), \Gamma_T) = \lambda_i(f_2 + (N - m)f) \ .$$

From inequalities (1) we deduce that $\sigma_i^T = \texttt{txs}_2^* \cup \texttt{txs}_u$ is a strictly dominant strategy for any $i \in [n]$, so $\overline{\sigma}^T = (\underbrace{(\texttt{txs}_2^* \cup \texttt{txs}_u), \ldots, (\texttt{txs}_2^* \cup \texttt{txs}_u)}_{n})$ in subgame

Γ_T with $u_i(\overline{\sigma}^T, \Gamma_T) = \lambda_i(f_2 + (N - m)f)$.

We will now prove via induction that $\overline{\sigma}^{1 \ldots T-1} = (\underbrace{\texttt{txs}_u, \ldots, \texttt{txs}_u}_{n})^{T-1}$ for

subgame Γ_k, in other words that the Nash equilibrium in all rounds prior to the last one in which O is unspent is for all players to attempt to mine only unrelated transactions.

The base of the induction is $k = T - 1$. For $i \in [n]$, it is either $\sigma_i^{T-1} = \texttt{txs}_1^* \cup \texttt{txs}_u$ or $\sigma_i^{T-1} = \texttt{txs}_u$ (as in the proof of Lemma 1, we ignore all configurations that include $\texttt{tx}_1$ except for $\texttt{txs}_1^*$). Let $\sigma_{-i}^{T-1} \in \Sigma_{-i}^{T-1}$ and λ_u the sum of mining power of miners who try to mine only unrelated transactions in round $T - 1$, excluding the i-th miner. If $\texttt{tx}_1$ is mined, then the last round is Γ_T^* and by Lemma 2 the utility obtained by the i-th miner at the last round is $\lambda_i Nf$. It is

$$u_i((\sigma_{-i}^{T-1}; \sigma_i^{T-1} = \mathtt{txs}_u)\overline{\sigma}^T, \Gamma_{T-1})$$
$$= \lambda_i(Nf + u_i(\overline{\sigma}^T, \Gamma_T)) + \lambda_u u_i(\overline{\sigma}^T, \Gamma_T) + (1 - \lambda_u - \lambda_i)\lambda_i Nf$$
$$= \lambda_i(Nf + \lambda_i(f_2 + (N - m)f)) + \lambda_u \lambda_i(f_2 + (N - m)f) + (1 - \lambda_u - \lambda_i)\lambda_i Nf,$$
$$u_i((\sigma_{-i}^{T-1}; \sigma_i^{T-1} = (\mathtt{txs}_1^* \cup \mathtt{txs}_u))\overline{\sigma}^T, \Gamma_{T-1})$$
$$= \lambda_i((f_1 + (N - m)f) + \lambda_i Nf) + \lambda_u u_i(\overline{\sigma}^T, \Gamma_T) + (1 - \lambda_u - \lambda_i)\lambda_i Nf$$
$$= \lambda_i((f_1 + (N - m)f) + \lambda_i Nf) + \lambda_u \lambda_i(f_2 + (N - m)f) + (1 - \lambda_u - \lambda_i)\lambda_i Nf.$$

It is

$$u_i((\sigma_{-i}^{T-1}; \sigma_i^{T-1} = \mathtt{txs}_u)\overline{\sigma}^T, \Gamma_{T-1}) > u_i((\sigma_{-i}^{T-1}; \sigma_i^{T-1} = \mathtt{txs}_1^* \cup \mathtt{txs}_u)\overline{\sigma}^T, \Gamma_{T-1})$$
$$\Leftrightarrow \lambda_i(Nf + \lambda_i(f_2 + (N - m)f)) > \lambda_i((f_1 + (N - m)f) + \lambda_i Nf)$$
$$\Leftrightarrow f_2 > \frac{f_1 - mf}{\lambda_i} + mf.$$

It is $\frac{f_1 - mf}{\lambda_i} + mf \le \frac{f_1 - mf}{\lambda_{\min}} + mf$ so the above is true. Therefore $\overline{\sigma}^{T-1} = \underbrace{(\mathtt{txs}_u, \ldots, \mathtt{txs}_u)}_{n}$, thus $\lambda_u = 1 - \lambda_i$ and $u_i(\overline{\sigma}^{T-1...T}, \Gamma_{T-1}) = \lambda_i(Nf + \lambda_i(f_2 + (N - m)f) + (1 - \lambda_i)\lambda_i(f_2 + (N - m)f) = \lambda_i((2N - m)f + f_2)$.

Let $k \in [T - 2]$. The inductive assumption for $k + 1$ is firstly that $\overline{\sigma}^{k+1} = \underbrace{(\mathtt{txs}_u, \ldots, \mathtt{txs}_u)}_{n}$ and secondly $u_i(\overline{\sigma}^{k+1...T}, \Gamma_{k+1}) = \lambda_i((T - k)Nf + f_2 - mf)$.

For the inductive step, let once again $i \in [n]$. It is either $\sigma_i^k = \mathtt{txs}_1^* \cup \mathtt{txs}_u$ or $\sigma_i^k = \mathtt{txs}_u$ (again ignoring suboptimal transaction sets that include $\mathtt{tx}_1$ but are not $\mathtt{txs}_1^*$). Let $\sigma_{-i}^k \in \Sigma_{-i}^k$ and λ_u the sum of mining power of miners who try to mine only unrelated transactions in round k, excluding the i-th miner. If $\mathtt{tx}_1$ is mined, then the next round is Γ_{k+1}^* and by Lemma 2 the utility obtained by the i-th miner from all rounds after k is $\lambda_i(T - k)Nf$. It is

$$u_i((\sigma_{-i}^k; \sigma_i^k = \mathtt{txs}_u)\overline{\sigma}^{k+1...T}, \Gamma_k)$$
$$= \lambda_i(Nf + u_i(\overline{\sigma}^{k+1...T}, \Gamma_{k+1})) + \lambda_u u_i(\overline{\sigma}^{k+1...T}, \Gamma_{k+1}) + (1 - \lambda_u - \lambda_i)\lambda_i(T - k)Nf$$
$$= \lambda_i(Nf + \lambda_i((T - k)Nf + f_2 - mf))$$
$$+ \lambda_u \lambda_i((T - k)Nf + f_2 - mf) + (1 - \lambda_u - \lambda_i)\lambda_i(T - k)Nf,$$
$$u_i((\sigma_{-i}^k; \sigma_i^k = \mathtt{txs}_1^* \cup \mathtt{txs}_u)\overline{\sigma}^{k+1...T}, \Gamma_k)$$
$$= \lambda_i(f_1 + (N - m)f + \lambda_i(T - k)Nf)$$
$$+ \lambda_u u_i(\overline{\sigma}^{k+1...T}, \Gamma_{k+1}) + (1 - \lambda_u - \lambda_i)\lambda_i(T - k)Nf$$
$$= \lambda_i(f_1 + (N - m)f + \lambda_i(T - k)Nf)$$
$$+ \lambda_u \lambda_i((T - k)Nf + f_2 - mf) + (1 - \lambda_u - \lambda_i)\lambda_i(T - k)Nf.$$

It is

$$u_i((\sigma_{-i}^k; \sigma_i^k = \mathbf{txs}_u)\overline{\sigma}^{k+1...T}, \Gamma_k) > u_i((\sigma_{-i}^k; \sigma_i^k = \mathbf{txs}_1^* \cup \mathbf{txs}_u)\overline{\sigma}^{k+1...T}, \Gamma_k)$$

$$\Leftrightarrow \lambda_i(Nf + \lambda_i((T-k)Nf + f_2 - mf)) > \lambda_i(f_1 + (N-m)f + \lambda_i(T-k)Nf)$$

$$\Leftrightarrow f_2 > \frac{f_1 - mf}{\lambda_i} + mf \ .$$

Like in the induction base, it is $\frac{f_1-mf}{\lambda_i} + mf \le \frac{f_1-mf}{\lambda_{\min}} + mf$ so the above is true. Therefore $\overline{\sigma}^k = \underbrace{(\mathbf{txs}_u, \ldots, \mathbf{txs}_u)}_{n}$, thus $\lambda_u = 1 - \lambda_i$ and

$$u_i(\overline{\sigma}^{k...T}, \Gamma_k)$$
$$= \lambda_i(Nf + \lambda_i((T-k)Nf + f_2 - mf)) + (1 - \lambda_i)\lambda_i((T-k)Nf + f_2 - mf)$$
$$= \lambda_i((T-k+1)Nf + f_2 - mf).$$

We have proven that $\forall k \in [T-1]$ it is $\overline{\sigma}^k = \underbrace{(\mathbf{txs}_u, \ldots, \mathbf{txs}_u)}_{n}$ thus we deduce

that $\overline{\sigma} = \underbrace{(\mathbf{txs}_u, \ldots, \mathbf{txs}_u)}_{n}^{T-1}\underbrace{(\mathbf{txs}_2^* \cup \mathbf{txs}_u, \ldots, \mathbf{txs}_2^* \cup \mathbf{txs}_u)}_{n}$. $\qquad\square$

Proof of Lemma 3. Let $m \in [N-1]$.

$$\frac{f_1 - mf}{\lambda_{\min}} + mf < \frac{(f_1 + f) - (m+1)f}{\lambda_{\min}} + (m+1)f$$

$$\Leftrightarrow \frac{f_1 - mf}{\lambda_{\min}} < \frac{f_1 - mf}{\lambda_{\min}} + f \Leftrightarrow 0 < f$$

The latter is true, thus the proof is complete. $\qquad\square$

Proof of Theorem 2. P_2 publishes the refund transaction, along with a transaction $\mathbf{tx}_b$ that spends her $c_{r,2}$ coins, transferring some of them to a new address that belongs to P_2 and offering the rest as fee f_b, such that $f_r + f_b > \frac{f_u - 2f}{\lambda_{\min}} + 2f$. Due to Theorem 1, miners will ignore the update transaction, wait for the timelock of the refund transaction to expire and mine it along with $\mathbf{tx}_b$. In order for this timelock bribe to be beneficial to P_2, it must hold that $c_{r,2} - f_b > c_{u,2} \Leftrightarrow c_{r,2} - c_{u,2} > f_b$. Therefore, a suitable f_b exists if $c_{r,2} - c_{u,2} > \frac{f_u - 2f}{\lambda_{\min}} + 2f - f_r$. $\qquad\square$

Proof of Theorem 3. More specifically, consider P_2 evaluating whether to timelock bribe. Publishing the refund transaction and $\mathbf{tx}_b$ offers to miners a total fee $f_r + f_b$, of which f_b is taken from $c_{r,2}$, therefore bribing makes sense only if $c_{r,2} - f_b > c_{u,2} \Leftrightarrow c_{r,2} - c_{u,2} > f_b$. In that case the published update transaction offers an effective fee of $f_u + c_{u,2}$. Leveraging Theorem 1, we deduce that miners will accept the bribe if $f_r + f_b > \frac{f_u + c_{u,2} - 2f}{\lambda_{\min}} + 2f \Leftrightarrow f_b > \frac{f_u + c_{u,2} - 2f}{\lambda_{\min}} + 2f - f_r$. Therefore, a suitable f_b exists if and only if $c_{r,2} - c_{u,2} > \frac{f_u + c_{u,2} - 2f}{\lambda_{\min}} + 2f - f_r \Leftrightarrow c_{r,2} - c_{u,2}(1 + \frac{1}{\lambda_{\min}}) > \frac{f_u - 2f}{\lambda_{\min}} + 2f - f_r$. $\qquad\square$

Proof of Theorem 4. For each $k \in [k_l - 1]$, P_2 prefers the update transaction of $(1 \rightarrow 2)$ and the refund transaction of $(2 \rightarrow 1)$ k-th leaf to the update transactions of the currently valid leaf if $c_{k,u,2}^{1 \rightarrow 2} + c_{k,r,2}^{2 \rightarrow 1} - f_b > c_{k_l,u,2}^{1 \rightarrow 2} + c_{k_l,u,2}^{2 \rightarrow 1} \Leftrightarrow c_{k,u,2}^{1 \rightarrow 2} + c_{k,r,2}^{2 \rightarrow 1} - (c_{k_l,u,2}^{1 \rightarrow 2} + c_{k_l,u,2}^{2 \rightarrow 1}) > f_b$. Since branches k and k_l have j distinct opt-in transactions, then $j + 3$ transactions are implicated in the bribe. Thus, according to Theorem 1 miners will choose the bribe if $jf_o + f_r + f_u + f_b > \frac{1}{\lambda_{\min}}(jf_o + 2f_u + c_{k_l,u,2}^{2 \rightarrow 1} + c_{k_l,u,2}^{1 \rightarrow 2} - (j+3)f) + (j+3)f \Leftrightarrow f_b > \frac{1}{\lambda_{\min}}(jf_o + 2f_u + c_{k_l,u,2}^{2 \rightarrow 1} + c_{k_l,u,2}^{1 \rightarrow 2} - (j+3)f) + (j+3)f - jf_o - f_r - f_u$. Therefore, a compatible fee f_b exists if $c_{k,u,2}^{1 \rightarrow 2} + c_{k,r,2}^{2 \rightarrow 1} - (c_{k_l,u,2}^{1 \rightarrow 2} + c_{k_l,u,2}^{2 \rightarrow 1}) > \frac{1}{\lambda_{\min}}(jf_o + 2f_u + c_{k_l,u,2}^{2 \rightarrow 1} + c_{k_l,u,2}^{1 \rightarrow 2} - (j+3)f) + (j+3)f - jf_o - f_r - f_u$. □

Proof of Theorem 5. For the bribe to be profitable for P_2, it must be $c_{\text{old}} - f_b > c_{\text{new}} - f \Leftrightarrow c_{\text{old}} - c_{\text{new}} - f > f_b$ – the fee f is included because this is the minimum fee P_2 would have to pay anyway in order to use its c_{new} coins. By applying Theorem 1, we deduce that miners will accept the bribe if $f_b > \frac{f_r - f}{\lambda_{\min}} + f$, therefore a suitable f_b exists if and only if $c_{\text{old}} - c_{\text{new}} - f > \frac{f_r - f}{\lambda_{\min}} + f \Leftrightarrow c_{\text{old}} - c_{\text{new}} > \frac{f_r - f}{\lambda_{\min}} + 2f$. □

Proof of Theorem 6. To discourage bribes, from Theorem 5, the fee of the honest party should satisfy the following: $c_{\text{old}} - c_{\text{new}} \leq \frac{f_r' - f}{\lambda_{\min}} + 2f$. This means that $f_r' \geq f + \lambda_{\min}(c_{\text{old}} - c_{\text{new}} - 2f)$. We will now ensure that this f_r' does not lead to loss of coins for P_1. Let c be the total channel value, which stays constant throughout the channel lifetime. P_1 has to own enough coins in the old state, so that their sum with the counterparty's coins minus the fee f_r' exceeds or matches P_1's coins in the latest state. Formally, $c - c_{\text{old}} + c_{\text{old}} - f_r' \geq c - c_{\text{new}} \Leftrightarrow c_{\text{new}} \geq f_r'$. Combining the above, it has to be $c_{\text{new}} \geq f + \lambda_{\min}(c_{\text{old}} - c_{\text{new}} - 2f) \Leftrightarrow \lambda_{\min} \leq \frac{c_{\text{new}} - f}{c_{\text{old}} - c_{\text{new}} - 2f}$. The last step is valid since $c_{\text{old}} - c_{\text{new}} - 2f > 0$. This is true since, as we saw above, P_2 only attempts to bribe if $c_{\text{old}} - c_{\text{new}} - f > f_b$ and we know that $f_b \geq f$. □

References

1. Lightning network specification, BOLT #3: bitcoin transaction and script formats. https://github.com/lightning/bolts/blob/master/03-transactions.md
2. Aumayr, L., et al.: Generalized bitcoin-compatible channels. Cryptology ePrint Archive, Report 2020/476 (2020). https://eprint.iacr.org/2020/476
3. Aumayr, L., et al.: Bitcoin-compatible virtual channels. In: IEEE Symposium on Security and Privacy, Oakland, USA, 23 May 2021–27 May (2021). https://eprint.iacr.org/2020/554.pdf
4. Aumayr, L., Moreno-Sanchez, P., Kate, A., Maffei, M.: Donner: utxo-based virtual channels across multiple hops. Cryptology ePrint Archive, Report 2021/855 (2021). https://eprint.iacr.org/2021/855
5. Avarikioti, Z., Kogias, E.K., Wattenhofer, R., Zindros, D.: Brick: asynchronous incentive-compatible payment channels. In: International Conference on Financial Cryptography and Data Security (2021)

6. Avarikioti, Z., Thyfronitis Litos, O.S., Wattenhofer, R.: CERBERUS channels: incentivizing watchtowers for bitcoin. In: Bonneau, J., Heninger, N. (eds.) FC 2020. LNCS, vol. 12059, pp. 346–366. Springer, Cham (2020). https://doi.org/10.1007/978-3-030-51280-4_19
7. Burchert, C., Decker, C., Wattenhofer, R.: Scalable funding of bitcoin micropayment channel networks. In: The Royal Society (2018)
8. Chakravarty, M.M.T., et al.: Hydra: fast isomorphic state channels. Cryptology ePrint Archive, Report 2020/299 (2020). https://eprint.iacr.org/2020/299
9. Croman, K., et al.: On scaling decentralized blockchains. In: Clark, J., Meiklejohn, S., Ryan, P.Y.A., Wallach, D., Brenner, M., Rohloff, K. (eds.) FC 2016. LNCS, vol. 9604, pp. 106–125. Springer, Heidelberg (2016). https://doi.org/10.1007/978-3-662-53357-4_8
10. Decker, C., Russell, R., Osuntokun, O.: eltoo: a simple layer2 protocol for bitcoin. https://blockstream.com/eltoo.pdf
11. Decker, C., Wattenhofer, R.: A fast and scalable payment network with bitcoin duplex micropayment channels. In: Pelc, A., Schwarzmann, A.A. (eds.) SSS 2015. LNCS, vol. 9212, pp. 3–18. Springer, Cham (2015). https://doi.org/10.1007/978-3-319-21741-3_1
12. Dong, M., Liang, Q., Li, X., Liu, J.: Celer network: bring internet scale to every blockchain (2018)
13. Dziembowski, S., Eckey, L., Faust, S., Malinowski, D.: Perun: virtual payment hubs over cryptocurrencies. In: 2019 2019 IEEE Symposium on Security and Privacy (SP), pp. 344–361, Los Alamitos, CA, USA, IEEE Computer Society, May 2019
14. Dziembowski, S., Faust, S., Hostáková, K.: General state channel networks. In: Proceedings of the 2018 ACM SIGSAC Conference on Computer and Communications Security, CCS 2018, Toronto, ON, Canada, 15–19 October 2018, pp. 949–966 (2018)
15. Egger, C., Moreno-Sanchez, P., Maffei, M.: Atomic multi-channel updates with constant collateral in bitcoin-compatible payment-channel networks. In: Proceedings of the 2019 ACM SIGSAC Conference on Computer and Communications Security, CCS 2019, pp. 801–815, New York, Association for Computing Machinery (2019)
16. Herlihy, M.: Atomic cross-chain swaps. In: Proceedings of the 2018 ACM Symposium on Principles of Distributed Computing, PODC 2018, Egham, United Kingdom, 23–27 July 2018, pp. 245–254 (2018)
17. Jourenko, M., Larangeira, M., Tanaka, K.: Lightweight virtual payment channels. In: Krenn, S., Shulman, H., Vaudenay, S. (eds.) CANS 2020. LNCS, vol. 12579, pp. 365–384. Springer, Cham (2020). https://doi.org/10.1007/978-3-030-65411-5_18
18. Kiayias, A., Thyfronitis Litos, O.S.: A composable security treatment of the lightning network. In: 33rd IEEE Computer Security Foundations Symposium, pp. 334–349. IEEE (2020)
19. Liao, K., Katz, J.: Incentivizing blockchain forks via whale transactions. In: Brenner, M., et al. (eds.) FC 2017. LNCS, vol. 10323, pp. 264–279. Springer, Cham (2017). https://doi.org/10.1007/978-3-319-70278-0_17
20. Miller, A.: Feather-forks: enforcing a blacklist with sub-50% hash power. https://bitcointalk.org/index.php?topic=312668.0. Accessed 22 Nov 2020
21. Miller, A., Bentov, I., Kumaresan, R., Cordi, C., McCorry, P.: Sprites and state channels: payment networks that go faster than lightning. arXiv preprint arXiv:1702.05812 (2017)
22. Nadahalli, T., Khabbazian, M., Wattenhofer, R.: Timelocked bribing. In: Borisov, N., Diaz, C. (eds.) FC 2021. LNCS, vol. 12674, pp. 53–72. Springer, Heidelberg (2021). https://doi.org/10.1007/978-3-662-64322-8_3

23. Nakamoto, S.: Bitcoin: a peer-to-peer electronic cash system (2008)
24. Poon, J., Dryja, T.: The bitcoin lightning network: scalable off-chain instant payments, January 2016. https://lightning.network/lightning-network-paper.pdf
25. Spilman, J.: Anti dos for tx replacement. https://lists.linuxfoundation.org/pipermail/bitcoin-dev/2013-April/002433.html. Accessed 22 Nov 2020
26. Tsabary, I., Yechieli, M., Eyal, I.: MAD-HTLC: because HTLC is crazy-cheap to attack. In: IEEE S&P (2021)
27. Winzer, F., Herd, B., Faust, S.: Temporary censorship attacks in the presence of rational miners. In: 2019 IEEE European Symposium on Security and Privacy Workshops (EuroS & PW), pp. 357–366. IEEE (2019)
28. Wood, G.: Ethereum: a secure decentralised generalised transaction ledger. Ethereum Project Yellow Paper (2014)
29. Zhao, L., et al.: Sok: hardware security support for trustworthy execution (2019)

Sliding Window Challenge Process
for Congestion Detection

Ayelet Lotem[1]([✉])(ID), Sarah Azouvi[2](ID), Patrick McCorry[3], and Aviv Zohar[1](ID)

[1] The Hebrew University of Jerusalem, Jerusalem, Israel
{ayelem02,avivz}@cs.huji.ac.il
[2] Protocol Labs, London, UK
sarah.azouvi@protocol.ai
[3] Infura, London, UK

Abstract. Many prominent smart contract applications such as payment channels, auctions, and voting systems often involve a mechanism in which some party must respond to a challenge or appeal some action within a fixed time limit. This pattern of challenge-response mechanisms poses great risks if, during periods of high transaction volume, the network becomes congested. In this case, fee market competition can prevent the inclusion of the response in blocks, causing great harm. As a result, responders are allowed long periods to submit their response and overpay in fees. To overcome these problems and improve challenge-response protocols, we suggest a secure mechanism that detects congestion in blocks and adjusts the deadline of the response accordingly. The responder is thus guaranteed a deadline extension should congestion arise. We lay theoretical foundations for congestion signals in blockchains and then proceed to analyze and discuss possible attacks on the mechanism and evaluate its robustness. Our results show that in Ethereum, using short response deadlines as low as 3 h, the protocol has >99% defense rate from attacks even by miners with up to 33% of the computational power. Using shorter deadlines such as one hour is also possible with a similar defense rate for attackers with up to 27% of the power.

Keywords: Congestion · Challenge-response

1 Introduction

DeFi platforms constructed over blockchains such as Ethereum have seen a recent boom of activity and interest. Their growing ecosystem allows for increasingly complex financial interactions executed in a fully decentralized manner. The main building blocks used to construct these platforms are the smart contracts that define the rules of interaction in code.

Smart contracts enable a wide range of applications, such as auctions, voting systems, and second layer protocols (e.g., payment channels) that operate above the blockchain layer. They typically provide rules that allow them to act as an automated adjudicator in case conflicts between participants arise.

© International Financial Cryptography Association 2022
I. Eyal and J. Garay (Eds.): FC 2022, LNCS 13411, pp. 512–530, 2022.
https://doi.org/10.1007/978-3-031-18283-9_25

For many applications, interactions with smart contracts are time dependent and are even subject to deadlines, meaning that in some cases, transactions added after a specific moment will effectively be rejected. For example in the case of auctions, a bid must be received before the end of the auction otherwise it is not valid. Another example appears in the context of payment channels [12] where participants have a limited interval of time to dispute the division of funds if they disagree with their peers.

A major weakness of such deadlines is that in cases where the blockchain is congested, users that submit transactions will not have them included in blocks in time. In fact, several attacks and failures can be attributed directly to this weakness (we provide some examples below). One mitigation often employed by participants is to offer higher fees for transactions with deadlines which means users are usually overpaying. Another is to extend the deadlines which greatly delays processing and settlement within the context of the relevant smart contract. In many cases, transaction fees and deadlines are decided upon in advance, before the exact conditions that will prevail when the transaction is actually transmitted are known, which causes participants to take wider safety margins and increases costs further. Due to the well-known scalability issues of blockchains [1], we expect congested periods to become increasingly more common, which will directly impact the design of time-sensitive smart contracts.

Our Contributions. In this work we present a mechanism aimed at solving these issues. We propose to set short deadlines that are automatically extended if congestion occurs. We lay the theoretical foundations of congestion monitoring in blockchains and formalize the notion of challenge-response protocols in this context. We then propose two different protocols to detect congestion over multiple blocks: the 'L Consecutive Blocks' protocol defines uncongestion by the existence of L consecutive uncongested blocks; its generalization, the 'Sliding Window (K-out-of-N)' protocol, defines uncongestion by the existence of N consecutive uncongested blocks with K uncongested blocks among them. We show that the Sliding Window protocol is more resilient to attacks than the L Consecutive Blocks protocol when attacked by miners. Furthermore, we propose a new opcode for Ethereum that will provide the required functionality; we also provide an implementation (not requiring new opcodes) in Solidity, using opcodes introduced by Ethereum Improvement Proposal 1559 (EIP 1559) [5].

Examples of Congestion Attacks and Related Failures. A recent well-known example of congestion-related failure took place on *Crypto Black Thursday* (March 12th, 2020) when the price of Ethereum dropped by more than 50% in less than 24 h [11]. This led to a panic-sale of coins and increased congestion. At the peak, during a 2–3 h window, the Ethereum blockchain's fees climbed to $1.65 on average, more than 10 times their cost on previous days.

The drop in ETH price triggered many MakerDAO auctions to liquidate collateral (typically collateral on short positions must be sold if prices fluctuate too much). The tokens to be sold were purchased at almost no cost due to the inability of many bidders to send transactions and participate. This has, allegedly, been leveraged by one user to gain \$8.3 million worth of ETH [3].

Several studies [10,13] deal with different types of attacks designed to prevent a party from responding on time to a challenge [10]. Harris and Zohar [13] present an attack where the attacker forces many victims at once to flood the blockchain with claims for their funds. The ensuing congestion allows the attacker to steal the funds that cannot be claimed before the deadline. Our protocol will prevent these issues by extending the deadlines until the congestion passes.

2   Related Work

Congestion is a real-world problem faced by the most prominent cryptocurrencies. In addition to the popular examples of Crypto Black Thursday or Cryptokitties, widely discussed online [3,6,11], Sokolov [18] examined periods of congestion caused by ransomware.

One way to deal with congestion is to improve the scalability of the underlying consensus protocol [7,9,19–21] or to introduce higher-level layers that help to scale. Solutions ranging from sharding [23], off-chain payment channels [12] or layer-zero optimization [22] (i.e., network-level optimization) have been considered. All these solutions improve the number of transactions per second that the network can process, but congestion may still occur even at higher rates.

Other methods that help to ensure that time-sensitive transactions are processed are rather ad-hoc. For example, the *replace by fee* [4] and *child pays for parent* [2] mechanisms allow users to add or change the fees of their transactions. Bitcoin's fee mechanism—equivalent to a first-price auction—is sub-optimal and often results in users paying more than what is necessary. EIP 1559 was made to change this mechanism in Ethereum [5,17]. EIP 1559 implements a *base fee* that is burned. This base fee can be seen as an indication of the level of congestion in recent blocks, and we utilize this in our implementation.

Another line of research that could potentially prevent transaction fees from spiking considers order-fairness consensus protocols [14,15]. The idea is to ensure that transactions are ordered in the blockchain in the same order they arrived in. This also helps to avoid problems such as front-running [8].

3   Preliminaries and Definitions

3.1   Challenge-Response Protocols

A challenge-response protocol is an implementation of a pattern in which some party must respond to a challenge within a fixed time limit. This pattern consists of a challenge that takes effect at time T_c and a response deadline T_{rd} which is the latest time by which response to the challenge will be accepted. We call the time period between T_c and T_{rd} the challenge window. Responding to the challenge during the challenge window yields different results compared to responding *after* the deadline. The protocol we propose inspects the challenge window period and extends it (by extending T_{rd}) as long as the blockchain stays congested.

3.2   Blockchain Congestion

Our protocol has two components. First it relies on a mechanism to define what it means for a block to be congested. We then use this definition to define an uncongested *period*. Intuitively, a period will be (un)congested if some threshold of blocks is (un)congested. We start by defining block congestion before moving on to presenting different period congestion definitions and choosing one that meets our requirements.

Blocks and Transactions. A block $\mathbf{B} = \{\mathsf{tx}_1, \cdots, \mathsf{tx}_n\}$ is as a set of transactions (we ignore the order of transactions in the block as well as other data—such as nonce—as they are irrelevant to our problem). Transactions pending to be included in a block are kept locally by each node in their *mempool* until they are included in the chain. Each transaction tx has a size $w(tx)$, and a fee density $\phi(tx)$. The fee paid by the transaction is therefore $w(tx) \cdot \phi(tx)$. We define the total weight of transactions in a block $\mathbf{B}$ with a fee density above θ as $\mathcal{W}_{\mathbf{B}}(\theta) := \sum_{tx \in B: \ \phi(tx) \geq \theta} w(tx)$.

Blocks can contain transactions with total size bounded by $\mathcal{B}$, i.e., $\mathcal{W}_{\mathbf{B}}(0) \leq \mathcal{B}$. For simplicity, we treat every block as *full*, i.e., for any *block* $\mathcal{W}_{\mathbf{B}}(0) = \mathcal{B}$ (if necessary, we fill them artificially with transactions with a fee of 0).

The total amount of fees collected from a block by the miner is $\mathcal{U}_{\mathbf{B}} := \sum_{tx \in B} w(tx) \cdot \phi(tx)$. If the size of the mempool is bigger than the maximum block size $\mathcal{W}_{\mathbf{B}}(0)$, we assume that honest miners choose the transactions in a way to maximize the fees they get.

Period. A period $Pe = (b_1, b_2, ..., b_n)$ in the blockchain is a non-empty sequence of **consecutive** blocks. We denote the length (number of blocks) of the period by $|Pe| = n$, and write for $i \in \{1, ..., n\}$: $Pe[i] = b_i \in Pe$. For a period P_2, we say that period P_1 is included in P_2 and note $P_1 \subseteq P_2$ if every block in P_1 is included in P_2.

In this work, we want to capture the notion of congestion: a phenomenon where there's a spike in the number of transactions waiting in the mempool. Since the mempool is not part of the blockchain, we instead rely on the data in the blocks in order to define congestion. We propose the following definition for *block congestion*.

Definition 1 ((θ, γ)-congestion).   *We say that a single block* $\mathbf{B}$ *is* (θ, γ)-*conges-ted if* $\mathcal{W}_{\mathbf{B}}(\theta) \geq \gamma \cdot \mathcal{B}$ *and denote* $\mathcal{C}_{\theta, \gamma}(\mathbf{B}) = 1$, *where* $\mathcal{C}_{\theta, \gamma}$ *is the corresponding indicator function.*

Per this definition, all transactions above fee density θ are examined and required to make up at least a γ-fraction of the block in terms of size. Intuitively, for $\gamma = 1$ the definition captures that if a block is $(\theta, 1)$-congested, a transaction needs to have a fee density that is at least θ in order to have a better chance of being included. In other words, we use the price of entering a transaction to the blockchain as a reliable signal for congestion.

For a block $\mathbf{B}$ and a fee density $\theta \geq 0$, we define the θ-*weight threshold* $\gamma_{\mathbf{B}}(\theta)$ as the maximum fraction of the block weight under which the block is (θ, γ)-congested. From Definition 1 it is clear that $\gamma_{\mathbf{B}}(\theta) = \frac{\mathcal{W}_{\mathbf{B}}(\theta)}{\mathcal{B}}$. Similarly, for a block $\mathbf{B}$ and a fraction $\gamma \geq 0$, we define the γ-*fee density threshold* $\theta_{\mathbf{B}}(\gamma)$ as the maximum fee density under which the block is (θ, γ)-congested ($\theta_{\mathbf{B}}(\gamma) := \max\{\theta \mid \mathcal{C}_{\theta,\gamma}(\mathbf{B}) = 1\}$).

Block Manipulation. One of the key measures we are interested in is when is an adversary able to manipulate blocks' congestion signals. When a miner mines a block, they can choose to include transactions from their mempool or to add dummy transactions that move money between their accounts and pay a fee (to themselves), making the fees appear different than they ought to be. However, miners cannot manipulate blocks at arbitrary heights, and doing so would incur a cost. The miner's chance of mining a new block depends on its relative computational power. Therefore, as is standard, we denote the computational power of an adversary by α. Each block has a probability α to be mined by the adversary, and $1 - \alpha$ to be mined by the other miners. Furthermore, giving up mempool transactions means missing out their fees and hence induces a loss that we compute in the next two propositions.

Proposition 1. *An adversary manipulating a block $\mathbf{B}$ to make it (θ_1, γ_1)-conges-ted when it is not, will lose a potential profit of at-least $\mathcal{B} \cdot \int_{1-(\gamma_1 - \gamma_{\mathbf{B}}(\theta_1))}^{1} \theta_{\mathbf{B}}(\gamma) \, d\gamma$.*

Proposition 2. *An adversary manipulating a block $\mathbf{B}$ to reverse its signal from (θ_1, γ_1)-congested to not congested will lose a potential profit of at-least $\mathcal{B} \cdot \int_{\gamma_1}^{\gamma_{\mathbf{B}}(\theta_1)} (\theta_{\mathbf{B}}(\gamma) - \theta_1) \, d\gamma$.*

The proofs for both propositions can be found in the full version of the paper [16].

Before moving on to define period congestion, we note that there exist other ways in which block congestion could be defined. For example, in Sect. 5, we take the EIP 1559 *base fee* as a measure of congestion and use it to implement our suggested protocol. We include several other examples that are less efficient in the full version of the paper [16].

Congestion Vector of a Period. To determine whether a period Pe is uncongested we will refer to the congestion vector $Pe^c := (\mathcal{C}(Pe[i]))_{i=1}^{n} \in \{0,1\}^n$ which consists of the congestion signal of its blocks. Intuitively, if most of the blocks in the period are congested then the period is congested and vice-versa. However, we must also account for the fact that an adversary may be able to change the congestion signal of some of the blocks, as already discussed. We will consider different protocols to define period uncongestion, a situation in which the period is considered not congested. An uncongestion period protocol is a function that we denote by $\mathsf{UCP}:\{0,1\}^* \to \{0,1\}$. This function takes as input a binary series representing the congestion signal of the blocks in the examined time period.

It will return 0 if the period is congested and 1 otherwise. This function can furthermore be extended to also provide auxiliary information such as a proof π in the case where the period is uncongested. For the efficiency of the protocol, we will strive for a definition that can provide a compact and easy-to-verify proof. Throughout the rest of the paper, we use $B(n, p)$ to denote the binomial distribution with parameters n and p.

Definition 2 (Period Manipulation). *For a period Pe and an adversary with a fraction α of the total computational power, we associate a manipulated period $\hat{Pe}$ defined as follows. For $i \in \{1, \ldots, |Pe|\}$ the adversary can replace $Pe[i]$ with probability α, with a block that has a congestion signal of their choice. We denote by $\overline{m} = m_{|Pe|}(\alpha) \sim B(|Pe|, \alpha)$ the vector that indicates which of the blocks in the given period the adversary controls, meaning the adversary can replace the $Pe[i]$ block's congestion signal iff $\overline{m}[i] = 1$. We then define the adversary's manipulation set $S_{\overline{m}, Pe} := \{\hat{Pe}^c \in \{0, 1\}^{|Pe|} \mid \forall 1 \leq i \leq |Pe| : \overline{m}[i] = 0 \Rightarrow \hat{Pe}^c[i] = Pe^c[i]\}$. Intuitively, $S_{\overline{m}, Pe}$ corresponds to the set of possible congestion vectors that the adversary could create by changing the signal of the blocks that it controls.*

In a real world setting, even if there is a long period of uncongestion, it could be the case that one or more of the blocks are fuller than the others due to some randomness in the transactions' arrival time (e.g., there was a temporary high transaction volume). To account for this randomness, we make a simplifying assumption that blocks are congested independently with probability p and say that the blockchain is $p-congested$. We note that, in reality, congestion is often changing and is usually correlated when considering several consecutive blocks. We leave more complex models of congestion for future work. In our case, the congestion vector of a period Pe chosen at random has a binomial distribution: $Pe^c \sim B(n, p)$. When studying attacks where the adversary tries to convert a congested period to an uncongested one, we will assume that p is close to one (i.e., most of the blocks are congested), whereas when studying the opposite case, we will consider p to be close to zero.

Our protocol consists in extending the deadline of challenge-response in the event of a congestion period. However, to avoid an edge case where the deadline is extended indefinitely, we define $\hat{M}$, an upper bound on the total length of the extended period.

Definition 3 ($\hat{M}$-maximum Extension). *Given a challenge-response protocol in a $p-congested$ blockchain where the challenge starts at block height h, we say that $\hat{M}$ is the maximum extension of the challenge if the deadline cannot be extended further than height $h + \hat{M}$.*

3.3 Desirable Properties of Protocols

In this section, we define some properties that we aim for our protocol to achieve.

In the rest of the paper we use the notation $D \leftarrow s$ to denote that s was selected randomly from the distribution D. We start by describing the two types of attack that we will consider—a congestion attack and an uncongestion attack—before defining the *robustness* of the protocol, which captures the security of the protocol against either attack.

Definition 4 (Congestion/Uncongestion Attack on Pe). *Given a period Pe, chosen at random in a p-congested blockchain, we say that the adversary wins a congestion, resp. uncongestion, attack on Pe if it can manipulate Pe into an congested, resp. uncongested, period.*

Definition 5 ((α, p, q, n)-congestion Robustness). *We say an uncongestion period protocol $UCP:\{0,1\}^* \to \{0,1\}$ is (α, p, q, n)-congestion robust if, given an adversary with a relative computational power α, his probability of winning a congestion attack, i.e., of successfully manipulating a period Pe of n blocks into a congested period $\hat{Pe}$, is less than q.*

$$B(n,p) \leftarrow Pe \ : \ P_r(\exists \hat{Pe} \in S_{\overline{m},Pe} \ s.t. \ UCP(\hat{Pe}) = 0) \leq q.$$

Definition 6 ((α, p, q, n)-uncongestion Robustness). *We say an uncongestion period protocol $UCP:\{0,1\}^* \to \{0,1\}$ is (α, p, q, n)-uncongestion robust if, given an adversary with a relative computational power α, his probability of winning an uncongestion attack, i.e., of successfully manipulating a period Pe of n blocks into an uncongested period $\hat{Pe}$, is less than q.*

$$B(n,p) \leftarrow Pe \ : \ P_r(\exists \hat{Pe} \in S_{\overline{m},Pe} \ s.t. \ UCP(\hat{Pe}) = 1) \leq q.$$

Definition 7 (Monotonicity). *A congestion protocol is **monotone** if for every two periods Pe_1 and Pe_2, if $Pe_1 \subseteq Pe_2$ and Pe_1 is considered uncongested, then so is Pe_2, i.e., $\forall Pe_1 \subseteq Pe_2 : UCP(Pe_1^c) = 1 \to UCP(Pe_2^c) = 1$.*

A monotone protocol is easier to verify as the prover only needs to select a portion of blocks from the time period Pe in order to prove uncongestion. Furthermore, a monotone protocol requires only sporadic access to the blockchain. A prover can go offline and prove uncongestion when they come back online by choosing any uncongested period from the time they were offline. In the case of a non-monotonic protocol, if the prover is offline during an uncongested period, they cannot prove the uncongestion of the longer period, after they came back online, they missed the uncongested period.

Efficiency Properties. We define two properties that capture the efficiency of the protocol.

- **Concise proof size** The evidence needed to prove uncongestion of a period should be as concise as possible.
- **Concise refresh information** The extra information needed to be kept when checking the congestion signal of a period that has already been extended due to congestion should be as concise as possible. Ideally, when we extend a period from Pe_1 to Pe_2 in order to check Pe_2 for congestion, we should not have to recheck every block in Pe_1 but, rather, aggregate this information.

In the next section we will discuss different period congestion protocols with the goal of finding one that will be proof efficient and robust against an attacker with reasonable hash rate with high probability.

4   Uncongested Period Protocols

In this section, we examine different protocols that fit the definition of congestion of a period Pe. We start by presenting "naive" protocols and discuss why they are not good enough, i.e., why they lack the desirable properties defined in Sect. 3.3.

4.1   Strawman Protocols

Definition 8 (Cumulative M). *Period Pe is uncongested if there exists M blocks which are uncongested:* $\mathsf{UCP}_{CM}(Pe^c) = 1 \leftrightarrow \left(\sum_{b \in Pe} (1 - \mathcal{C}(b)) \geq M \right)$.

This protocol is monotonic but is not sufficiently robust to adversarial attacks: if we wait long enough, the probability of the adversary controlling M blocks becomes overwhelming (even if α is small). We solve this in the next strawman by considering the percentage of blocks instead of a fixed number.

Definition 9 (Percentage). *A period Pe is uncongested if $x\%$ of its blocks are not congested:* $\mathsf{UCP}_{PC}(Pe^c) = 1 \leftrightarrow \left(\sum_{b \in Pe} (1 - \mathcal{C}(b)) \geq \frac{x}{100} \cdot |Pe| \right)$.

This protocol is much more robust but has the drawback of not being monotonic. For example, if all blocks are uncongested during the first part of the period and congestion begins in the second part, then the beginning of the period is uncongested while the whole period may not be.

We now suggest the following monotonic rule:

Definition 10 (L Consecutive Blocks). *A period Pe is uncongested if there exists at least L consecutive uncongested blocks included in it:* $\mathsf{UCP}_L(Pe^c) = 1 \leftrightarrow (\exists\, 1 \leq i \leq |Pe| - L + 1 \text{ s.t. } \forall\, 0 \leq j \leq L - 1 : Pe^c[i + j] = 0)$.

We show that this protocol is monotonic and inspect its efficiency in the full version of the paper [16]. We now evaluate its robustness.

Evaluation of the Robustness of the L Consecutive Blocks Protocol. We examine situations where the adversary attempts to manipulate the congestion signal for a given period. We separate this into two attacks: uncongestion and congestion attacks (as in Definition 4). We strive to achieve a high defense rate against both attacks, meaning finding a value L that will give a low probability for an adversary to succeed in each of the attacks separately.

Evaluation of the Uncongestion Attack. In order to compute the probability of an attacker to successfully manipulate Pe into an uncongested period, we define the following matrix $T_{(L+1)\times(L+1)}$:

$$\forall\, 0 \le i,j \le L: \quad T_{i,j} = \begin{cases} (1-\alpha)\cdot p & \text{if } j = 0 \wedge i \ne L \\ \alpha + (1-\alpha)\cdot(1-p) & \text{if } j = i+1 \\ 1 & \text{if } i = j = L \\ 0 & \text{otherwise} \end{cases} \tag{1}$$

and denote by e_i the ith unit vector of dimension $L+1$ (i.e., e_i has a 1 in the ith coordinate and 0's elsewhere).

Theorem 1. *The probability of an attacker with a relative computational power α to successfully manipulate Pe into an uncongested period in a p-congested network equals $e_1 \cdot T^n \cdot e_{L+1}^t$.*

Proof. We note that, at each block, the attacker has a probability α to mine the next block, which allows them to decide its congestion level. In this context, this means setting the block to be uncongested. In addition, the congestion signal of a block not mined by the attacker depends on the prevailing congestion state which is expressed by p. The probability of an honest block being congested, resp. uncongested, is hence equal to $(1-\alpha)\cdot p$, resp. $\alpha + (1-\alpha)\cdot(1-p)$. We define the following Markov chain that describes a random walk on Pe's blocks and whose states represent the number of consecutive blocks that are uncongested at a point in time.

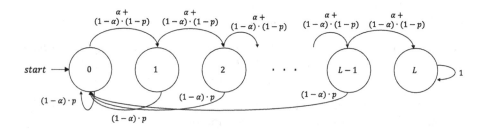

The initial state is 0 since it corresponds to the 0 consecutive uncongested blocks at the beginning of the walk. With each step, we move from state i to state $i+1$, for $i < L$, if the block is uncongested, and return to state 0 if it is not. If we reach state L, we stay there since it means the adversary has reached the goal of L consecutive uncongested blocks in Pe and can manipulate it to an uncongested period.

T is the corresponding transition matrix; hence the probability of reaching state L in $|Pe| = n$ steps is expressed by $e_1 \cdot T^n \cdot e_{L+1}^t$. □

Evaluation of the Congestion Attack. For the attack in the opposite direction we define $\hat{T}_{(L+1)\times(L+1)}$ as follows:

$$\forall\, 0 \le i,j \le L: \quad \hat{T}_{i,j} = \begin{cases} \alpha + (1-\alpha)\cdot p & \text{if } j = 0 \wedge i \ne L \\ (1-\alpha)\cdot(1-p) & \text{if } j = i+1 \\ 1 & \text{if } i = j = L \\ 0 & \text{otherwise} \end{cases} \tag{2}$$

Theorem 2. *The probability of an attacker with a relative computational power α to successfully manipulate Pe into a congested period, in a p-congested network equals $1 - e_1 \cdot \hat{T}^n \cdot e_{L+1}^t$.*

Proof. This time, if the attacker succeeds in mining a block, they will make it congested. Therefore the probability for a block to be uncongested is $(1-\alpha) \cdot (1-p)$. As before, we define the following Markov chain whose states represent the number of consecutive blocks that are uncongested at a point in time in Pe:

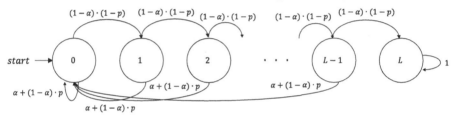

$\hat{T}$ is the corresponding transition matrix. Therefore, the probability for the adversary to succeed in the congestion attack is equivalent to the probability that the rest of the miners will not reach the L state in n steps, which is expressed by: $1 - e_1 \cdot \hat{T}^n \cdot e_{L+1}^t$. □

Now that we have the attacks' success rates, we examine the robustness of the protocol against both attacks for different values of L.

Although attacks are potentially expensive for the adversary (who needs to change the contents of its block and, hence, loses transaction fees), we still desire a low success probability for the attack even for strong attackers. We assume in the following evaluations that the attacker controls 33% of the computational power.

Given that congestion may cause period extension, we need a value for L that gives protection also against attacks over longer periods. We examine the behavior of the protocol for periods as long as $\hat{M}$ using different values for L.

The value p should represent realistic network conditions. For our analysis we pick $p = 0.85$ when studying the congestion attack, to simulate more congested settings, or $p = 0.15$ when studying the uncongestion attack, to simulate relatively uncongested settings. Other values can be plugged in, if needed, for other conditions. We start by examining the robustness of the protocol for a period of 1 day.

Figures 1a–1b present the probability of success in both attacks for two different period lengths: 6450 blocks in Fig. 1a and 144 blocks in Fig. 1b. These periods correspond, roughly, to a single day in Ethereum and a single day in Bitcoin. The red curves correspond to the congestion attack and the blue curves to the uncongestion attack. We compute these probabilities for different values of L.

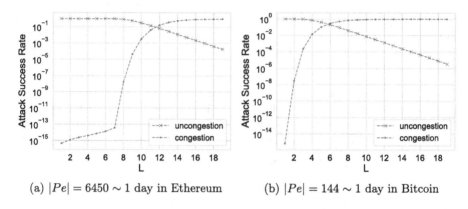

(a) $|Pe| = 6450 \sim 1$ day in Ethereum   (b) $|Pe| = 144 \sim 1$ day in Bitcoin

Fig. 1. Attack success rate as a function of L, for $\alpha = 0.33$

The results in both figures show there is no value L that gives a probability of success less than 1% for both attacks. Formally, it shows that the L Consecutive Blocks protocol cannot be simultaneously $(0.33, 0.15, 0.01, 1 \, day)$-congestion robust and $(0.33, 0.85, 0.01, 1 \, day)$-uncongestion robust. Therefore, we find the L Consecutive Blocks protocol not sufficiently secure. Intuitively, this is because more robust estimates of congestion are typically obtained over longer observation windows. The L Consecutive Blocks protocol obtains longer observations if L is increased, but then the requirement for consecutive blocks to be uncongested is too strict and is not robust. As a result of this insight, we propose a new protocol that generalizes the L Consecutive Blocks protocol and allows for longer observation windows with a relaxed condition for uncongestion.

4.2   Sliding Window (K-out-of-N) Protocol

Definition 11 (K-out-of-N Sliding Window). *A period Pe is uncongested if there exists a period $\hat{P}e$ of length N included in it in which at least K blocks are uncongested.*

$$UCP_{SW}(Pe^c) = 1 \leftrightarrow \left(\exists \, \hat{P}e \subseteq Pe : |\hat{P}e| = N \land \left(\sum_{b \in \hat{P}e} (1 - C(b)) \geq K \right) \right)$$

We note that the L Consecutive Blocks protocol is a special case in which $L = N = K$.

Proposition 4. *The Sliding Window protocol is monotonic.*

Proof. Given an uncongested period Pe_1, according to the Sliding Window protocol, which is included in period Pe_2:

$$\mathsf{UCP}_{SW}(Pe_1^c) = 1 \Rightarrow \left(\exists \, \hat{P}e \subseteq Pe_1 : |\hat{P}e| = N \wedge \left(\sum_{b \in \hat{P}e} \mathcal{C}(b) \geq K \right) \right)$$

$$Pe_1 \subseteq Pe_2 \Rightarrow \left(\hat{P}e \subseteq Pe_2 \right) \wedge \left(\sum_{b \in \hat{P}e} \mathcal{C}(b) \geq K \right)$$

$$\Rightarrow \mathsf{UCP}_{SW}(Pe_2^c) = 1$$

$\square$

We now evaluate its efficiency.

Proof Size. In order to provide evidence for the uncongestion of a period Pe of size n, it is enough to point to a window in which uncongestion occurs. Formally, to present $\pi = i \in \{1, ..., n - K + 1\}$ s.t. $\sum_{l=i}^{i+N}(1 - \mathcal{C}(Pe[l])) \geq K$.

Refresh Information. Given a congested period Pe, and $\hat{P}e$ that extends it, in order to determine the congestion level of the extended period $\mathsf{UCP}_{SW}(\hat{P}e^c)$, it is enough to check only windows that overlap blocks in $\hat{P}e \setminus Pe$.

Evaluation of the Sliding Window Protocol's Robustness. We consider the two attacks in Definition 4. We first note that the two attacks may differ in their consequences. While the congestion attack can cause a delay in the response deadline (i.e., a deadline will be extended even if it is not really needed), the uncongestion attack might lead participants to miss the chance to respond on time, as the deadline will not be extended even if the network is congested. The damage in each case depends on the particular use case. For example, in the case of payment channels, not responding in time is more severe and may lead to financial losses. We strive to achieve a high level of security against both types of attack, i.e., to find values for parameters (N, K) that will yield a low probability of success for both.

We begin by presenting upper bounds on the probabilities of success in each of the attacks.

Theorem 3. *The probability of an attacker with a relative computational power α to successfully manipulate Pe into an uncongested period, in a p-congested network, is bounded above by $(n - N + 1) \cdot \sum_{j=K}^{N} \binom{N}{j} \cdot q^j \cdot (1 - q)^{N-j}$, for $q = \alpha + (1 - p) \cdot (1 - \alpha)$.*

Proof. The probability for a block to be uncongested during this attack is $q = \alpha + (1 - p) \cdot (1 - \alpha)$. In a period of size n, there are $n - N + 1$ different sliding windows. We denote by A_i the event in which there are K out of N uncongested blocks in the ith sliding window. Therefore, the probability of a single sliding window being uncongested is $P(A_i) = \sum_{j=K}^{N} \binom{N}{j} \cdot q^j \cdot (1-q)^{N-j}$. To succeed in the uncongestion attack, at least one of the sliding windows has to be uncongested, which is expressed by $P(\cup_{i=1}^{n-N+1} A_i)$. We use the union bound to bound this probability and get:

$$P(\cup_{i=1}^{n-N+1} A_i) \leq \sum_{i=1}^{n-N+1} P(A_i) = (n - N + 1) \cdot \sum_{j=K}^{N} \binom{N}{j} \cdot q^j \cdot (1 - q)^{N-j} \quad \square$$

Theorem 4. *The probability of an attacker with a relative computational power α to successfully manipulate Pe into a congested period, in a p-congested network is bounded above by $(\sum_{j=0}^{K-1} \binom{N}{j} \cdot q^j \cdot (1 - q)^{N-j})^{\lfloor \frac{n}{N} \rfloor}$, for $q = (1 - p) \cdot (1 - \alpha)$.*

Proof. The probability for a block to be uncongested is $q = (1 - p) \cdot (1 - \alpha)$. We denote by B_i the event in which there are less than K uncongested blocks in the ith sliding window. The probability of a single sliding window being congested is $P(B_i) = \sum_{j=0}^{K-1} \binom{N}{j} \cdot q^j \cdot (1 - q)^{N-j}$. To succeed in the congestion attack, all sliding windows in the period must be congested, which is expressed by $P(\cap_{i=1}^{n-N+1} B_i)$. We bound this probability by $P(\cap_{i=1}^{\lfloor \frac{n}{N} \rfloor} B_{N \cdot (i-1)+1})$, i.e., we consider a subset of events B_i that are independent from each other (removing overlapping windows). We compute the intersection of the pairwise independent events and get: $P(\cap_{i=1}^{n-N+1} B_i) \leq P(\cap_{i=1}^{\lfloor \frac{n}{N} \rfloor} B_{N \cdot (i-1)+1}) = \prod_{i=1}^{\lfloor \frac{n}{N} \rfloor} P(B_{N \cdot (i-1)+1}) = (\sum_{j=0}^{K-1} \binom{N}{j} \cdot q^j \cdot (1 - q)^{N-j})^{\lfloor \frac{n}{N} \rfloor}$. $\quad \square$

We would like to compute the robustness of the protocol for 1 day to 1 h sliding windows. We examine the situation where a period Pe of size n is chosen at random and the blockchain is $p - congested$ for values of $p = 0.85$ (relatively congested) and $p = 0.15$ (relatively uncongested) against an attacker with computational power $\alpha \leq 0.33$. In the evaluation, we allow periods to be extended up to two weeks, a reasonable time for congestion to pass. We set the $\hat{M}$-maximum extension (see Definition 3) accordingly (90300 blocks in Ethereum and 2016 blocks in Bitcoin).

We first evaluate the attack over Ethereum, computing the above bounds for different sliding window sizes. We begin with a sliding window of 1 day ($N = 6450$), setting $K = \frac{N}{2} = 3225$. Figure 2 presents the two upper bounds for the different possible period lengths $N \leq n \leq \hat{M}$. For the protocol to be considered secure, we need low values in both curves for the different period lengths (since periods might be extended). As can be seen, the probabilities in the graph are extremely low, showing the protocol to be very secure. We emphasize that the blue curve is not horizontal, as shown in the graph; all of its values are smaller than 10^{-323}. Note that these are only upper bounds; the actual probabilities are even lower.

We evaluate the attack for smaller sliding windows. The following table summarizes our results:

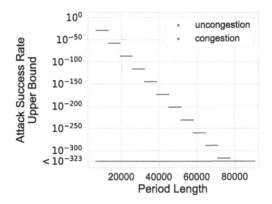

Fig. 2. Upper bounds on the attacks' success rates as a function of the period length, for $\hat{M} = 90300, N = 6450, K = 3225, \alpha = 0.33$

N	K	Uncongestion	Congestion
6450 (1 day)	3225	$< 10^{-323}$	1.44×10^{-29}
3225 (12 h)	1612	1.26×10^{-10}	8.06×10^{-16}
1612 (6 h)	815	7.14×10^{-5}	1.08×10^{-7}
806 (3 h)	421	8.87×10^{-3}	3.16×10^{-3}

The wider the sliding window is, the greater the protection. For smaller sliding windows, such as 1 h ($N = 269$), we can achieve a 99% defense rate against each attack if we lower the attackers' computation power to $\alpha \leq 0.27$ (instead of 0.33). We provide examples of N, K values and the level of protection they provide (an upper bound), but these are configurable and subject to the user's discretion. One can choose to increase the level of protection from one attack at the expense of the other, or to set a larger initial period length ($>N$) to increase the protection.

Next, we want to know what happens with smaller periods such as in Bitcoin, which has longer block intervals. To do so, we set $\hat{M} = 2016$ and begin with a sliding window of 1 day ($N = 144$).

We use a simulation to draw 100,000 samples $Pe^c \sim B(\hat{M}, p)$ of congestion vectors and to compute the success rates of both attacks among the samples (Figs. 3a,c,d). We use error plots to plot the standard error of the data; however, the errors are very small and therefore are almost invisible in the graphs.

Figure 3a presents the probability of success in each of the attacks for different K values. As the graph shows, choosing $K = 89$ gives protection against both attacks. We compute the upper bounds (from Theorems 3–4) for this value of K in Fig. 3b. The presented bounds as they appear in the graph are loose compared to the simulation results and afford a low level of defense, especially against the congestion attack. These bounds give us useful, but non-tight, upper bounds on the results for periods that are of longer length, for which the probability is extremely small. To get more precise results, we use more simulations to

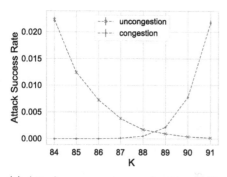

(a) Attack success rate as a function of K, for $n = 2016, N = 144, \alpha = 0.33$

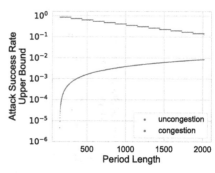

(b) Upper bounds on the attacks' success rates as a function of the period length, for $N = 144, K = 89, \alpha = 0.33$

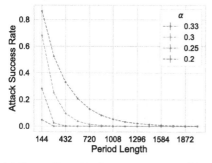

(c) Congestion attack success rate as a function of the period length, for $N = 144, K = 89$

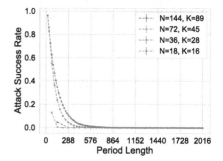

(d) Congestion attack success rate as a function of the period length, for $\alpha = 0.2$

Fig. 3. Evaluation of the attacks' success rates for $\hat{M} = 2016$ (2 weeks in Bitcoin)

compute the congestion attacks' success rate for different period lengths and present the results in Fig. 3c. Each curve corresponds to a different value of α, the computational power of the attacker. The defense rate against congestion attacks is extremely low for short periods. For $\alpha = 0.33$, we reach a $>99\%$ defense rate only for periods of ~ 11 days or more. Lowering the computational power of the adversary naturally improves these results. For example, considering an attacker with computational power $\alpha = 0.2$ results in an above 0.9995 defense rate for period lengths starting from 2 days.

Finally, in Fig. 3d we consider an attacker with a computational power $\alpha = 0.2$ and show the congestion attack success rate for different choices of N, K correspondig to sliding windows of lengths $24/12/6/3$ h. We do not present the uncongestion attack results which had above 99% defense rate for any $N \le n \le \hat{M} = 2016$.

We conclude that the longer the periods are, the higher and more effective the protection against attacks is. In Ethereum, we obtained very high defense rates even when choosing short sliding window sizes and against strong attackers. In

Bitcoin, on the other hand, we need to compromise on the window size and on the attackers' power to achieve higher defense.

We defined uncongested period protocols and suggested a concrete one, the Sliding Window protocol, which meets our requirements (as defined in Sect. 3.3). In the next section, we will describe how to use an uncongested period protocol to adjust the challenge-response protocol to deal with congested periods.

4.3 Application to Challenge-Response Protocols

A challenge-response protocol consists of a challenge that takes effect at time T_c and a response deadline T_{rd} (see Sect. 3.1). We link T_c and T_{rd} to their corresponding block height and denote by $b(T)$ the block at height T.

The parties involved in the challenge decide in advance on an uncongestion period protocol UCP to use. We recall that $\mathsf{UCP}:\{0,1\}^* \rightarrow \{0,1\}$ accepts a congestion vector (a binary series representing the congestion signal of blocks in a period) and returns 1 if the period is congested and 0 otherwise. To apply the uncongestion period protocol, the parties adjust T_{rd} to a short deadline that gives them a reasonable time to respond to the challenge assuming an optimal case with no congestion.

The response deadline T_{rd} is applied only in the event that the challenge window $Pe = (b(T_c), b(T_c + 1), ..., b(T_{rd}))$ is uncongested. In the case where the challenge window is congested, we repeatedly extend T_{rd}, 1 block at a time, as long as it remains congested. To avoid an edge case where the deadline is extended indefinitely, we define $\hat{T}_{rd} = T_c + \hat{M}$, an upper bound on the deadline (see Definition 3). The challenge-response protocol adjustment is summarized in the algorithm below.

$T_c \leftarrow init$
$T_{rd} \leftarrow init$
$Pe = (b(T_c), b(T_c + 1), ..., b(T_{rd}))$
$Pe^c \leftarrow congestion\_vector(Pe)$
while $UCP(Pe^c) = 0$ *and* $T_{rd} < \hat{T}_{rd}$ **do**
$\quad \mid \quad T_{rd} \leftarrow T_{rd} + 1$
$\quad \mid \quad Pe = (b(T_c), b(T_c + 1), ..., b(T_{rd}))$

We emphasize that the extension of the deadline is not necessarily carried out at the exact moment of the deadline (since smart contract actions need to be triggered by a transaction to the contract). Instead, a transaction that is submitted afterwards is determined to be either before or after the deadline given any possible extensions that are due. The uncongestion period protocol is specified in advance in the smart contract, and the deadline calculation is triggered either by a late response to the challenge or by the challenger that claims that a response did not arrive in time.

5   Implementation

We provide an implementation of the Sliding Window protocol as an Ethereum smart contract using the EIP 1559 *base fee* to determine block congestion. EIP 1559 implements a *base fee* that is adjusted up and down by the protocol according to how congested the network is. The EVM supports fetching the *base fee* of the highest (current) block. We suggest extending this to fetch the *base fee* of any block, and to add an opcode that checks whether a block is congested (without such opcodes, it is not possible to fully implement the mechanisms put forward in this paper). This opcode will receive as inputs a block and a maximum base fee (chosen by a user) and will return whether the maximum base fee exceeds the block's base fee.

In the implementation, we set the sliding window size equal to the initial deadline of the examined period (before being granted any extension).

The full github[1] repository includes the smart contracts, the new opcode, and the tests.

6   Conclusion

In this paper, we tackled a problem that arises when challenge-response protocols face congested periods. When the network experiences congestion, users will often miss the response deadline, which can lead to serious issues including financial loss. We formalized the problem and proposed a new protocol called the Sliding Window as a solution. Our protocol defines a reliable way to detect congested periods by looking only at the data available on-chain. We then used this to extend the challenge-response deadline when congestion occurs. We studied the security of the protocol for different parameters. Our results showed that it is possible to decrease the time settlement (deadline) of challenge-response protocols significantly, while expanding the security of the protocol to deal with cases of congestion.

For future work, it would be interesting to evaluate and optimize this protocol and its security analysis for more realistic congestion settings—in particular, settings in which congestion is correlated between consecutive blocks—and to provide more experimental analysis of these settings. Is is also of interest to explore whether Ethereum's proposed base fee can be used as a sufficiently robust congestion signal.

Acknowledgments. Ayelet Lotem and Aviv Zohar are partially supported by grants from the Israel Science Foundation (grants 1504/17 & 1443/21) and by a grant from the HUJI Cyber Security Research Center in conjunction with the Israel National Cyber Bureau.

---

[1] https://github.com/stonecoldpat/slidingwindow.

References

1. Bano, S., et al.: SoK: consensus in the age of blockchains. In: AFT 2019: Proceedings of the 1st ACM Conference on Advances in Financial Technologies, pp. 183–198 (2019)
2. Bitcoin Optech: Child pays for parent (CPFP). https://bitcoinops.org/en/topics/cpfp
3. Mempool manipulation enabled theft of $8m in MakerDAO collateral on Black Thursday: Report. https://www.coindesk.com/tech/2020/07/22/mempool-manipulation-enabled-theft-of-8m-in-makerdao-collateral-on-black-thursday-report/
4. Bitcoin wiki: Replace by fee. https://en.bitcoin.it/wiki/Replace_by_fee
5. Buterin, V., Conner, E., Dudley, R., Slipper, M., Norden, I., Bakhta, A.: EIP-1559: Fee market change for ETH 1.0 chain. https://eips.ethereum.org/EIPS/eip-1559 (2019)
6. ConsenSys: The inside story of the CryptoKitties congestion crisis, February 2018. https://consensys.net/blog/news/the-inside-story-of-the-cryptokitties-congestion-crisis/
7. Croman, K., et al.: On scaling decentralized blockchains. In: International conference on financial cryptography and data security, pp. 106–125. Springer (2016). https://doi.org/10.1007/978-3-662-53357-4_8
8. Daian, P., et al.: Flash boys 2.0: frontrunning, transaction reordering, and consensus instability in decentralized exchanges. arXiv preprint arXiv:1904.05234 (2019)
9. Eyal, I., Gencer, A.E., Sirer, E.G., Van Renesse, R.: Bitcoin-NG: a scalable blockchain protocol. In: 13th {USENIX} symposium on networked systems design and implementation ({NSDI} 16), pp. 45–59 (2016)
10. Felten, E.: Fighting censorship attacks on smart contracts. https://medium.com/offchainlabs/fighting-censorship-attacks-on-smart-contracts-c026a7c0ff02 (2020)
11. Frangella, E.: Crypto Black Thursday: the good, the bad, and the ugly. https://medium.com/aave/crypto-black-thursday-the-good-the-bad-and-the-ugly-7f2acebf2b83. Accessed 31 Aug 2021
12. Gudgeon, L., Moreno-Sanchez, P., Roos, S., McCorry, P., Gervais, A.: SoK: layer-two blockchain protocols. In: International Conference on Financial Cryptography and Data Security, pp. 201–226. Springer (2020). https://doi.org/10.1007/978-3-030-51280-4_12
13. Harris, J., Zohar, A.: Flood & loot: a systemic attack on the lightning network. In: AFT 2020: Proceedings of the 2nd ACM Conference on Advances in Financial Technologies, pp. 202–213 (2020)
14. Kelkar, M., Zhang, F., Goldfeder, S., Juels, A.: Order-fairness for byzantine consensus. In: Annual International Cryptology Conference, pp. 451–480. Springer (2020). https://doi.org/10.1007/978-3-030-56877-1_16
15. Kursawe, K.: Wendy, the good little fairness widget: achieving order fairness for blockchains. In: AFT 2020: Proceedings of the 2nd ACM Conference on Advances in Financial Technologies, pp. 25–36 (2020)
16. Lotem, A., Azouvi, S., McCorry, P., Zohar, A.: Sliding window challenge process for congestion detection. arXiv preprint arXiv:2201.09009 (2022)
17. Roughgarden, T.: Transaction fee mechanism design for the Ethereum blockchain: an economic analysis of EIP-1559. Department of Computer Science, Columbia University, Technical report (2020)

18. Sokolov, K.: Ransomware activity and blockchain congestion. J. Finan. Econom. **141**, 771–782 (2021)
19. Sompolinsky, Y., Lewenberg, Y., Zohar, A.: SPECTRE: a fast and scalable cryptocurrency protocol. IACR Cryptology ePrint Archive, Report 2016/1159 (2016)
20. Sompolinsky, Y., Wyborski, S., Zohar, A.: PHANTOM and GHOSTDAG: A scalable generalization of Nakamoto consensus. IACR Cryptology ePrint Archive, Report 2018/104 (2018)
21. Sompolinsky, Y., Zohar, A.: Secure high-rate transaction processing in bitcoin. In: International Conference on Financial Cryptography and Data Security, pp. 507–527. Springer (2015). https://doi.org/10.1007/978-3-662-47854-7_32
22. Tanana, D.: Avalanche blockchain protocol for distributed computing security. In: 2019 IEEE International Black Sea Conference on Communications and Networking (BlackSeaCom), pp. 1–3. IEEE, New York (2019)
23. Wang, G., Shi, Z.J., Nixon, M., Han, S.: SoK: sharding on blockchain. In: AFT 2019: Proceedings of the 1st ACM Conference on Advances in Financial Technologies, pp. 41–61 (2019)

Short Paper: On Game-Theoretically-Fair Leader Election

Rati Gelashvili, Guy Goren$^{(\boxtimes)}$, and Alexander Spiegelman

Novi Research, Novi, USA
`sgoren@campus.technion.ac.il`

Abstract. This work studies the problem of game-theoretically-fair leader election. That is, provide fairness in the strong sense that the probability of any player being elected cannot be reduced even when facing an adversarial coalition of all other players. We extend a recent lower bound by [8] that shows that the tournament-tree protocol (based on Blum [5]) is optimal in the number of rounds, among the protocols that are restricted to immediately open the cryptographic commitments.

Our argument works even if commitments can be opened at arbitrary times, which is an open question left by [8]. To this end, we make two technical assumptions, one of which is weaker than the prior restriction and both of which are satisfied by the tournament-tree protocol, even if all players commit to their randomness for the entire execution in the beginning. The resulting proof is simple and streamlined, which we hope facilitates further research into an unconditional lower bound (or a new upper bound).

1 Introduction

Leader election is a fundamental task in distributed computing [16]. A natural predicate to compute in a multiparty setting, it provides the symmetry breaking power of a designated leader that often plays a key role in efficient distributed protocols for complex problems.

Leader election is closely related to *shared-coin* [4], another important distributed task of generating a shared value with guarantees about its distribution, based on the local randomness of protocol participants. Since an honest leader can toss a coin locally and share the outcome, the problem can be reduced to electing an honest leader. Leader election can also be viewed as an n-way shared coin-toss, and in fact, shared-coin is a commonly used building block for randomized distributed protocols [19].

There is a vast research spanning over four decades into the resilience of coin-flipping protocols against adversarial corruptions, e.g. [10,11,13,20]. The classic lower bound by Cleve [10] shows that a strong version of fairness called *unbiasability*, isn't achievable in the presence of a corrupt majority. A simple,

G. Goren—The work of Guy Goren was partly supported by a grant from the Technion Hiroshi Fujiwara cyber security research center and by the Israel Science Foundation under grant 2061/19.

I. Eyal and J. Garay (Eds.): FC 2022, LNCS 13411, pp. 531–538, 2022.
https://doi.org/10.1007/978-3-031-18283-9_26

well-known protocol of Blum [5], however, allows two participants to achieve a weaker, *game-theoretic* notion of fairness via leader election. Participants first commit to binary values, then they open the commitments, and the XOR of the values determines the leader (who determines the shared-coin value). The result can only be biased by deviating from the protocol and not revealing the commitment. In this case, the other participant becomes the leader, hence an adversarial participant can't improve the likelihood of its desired outcome.

Recent papers [9,21] have characterized the computational landscape of game-theoretic fairness and incentive compatibility of n-party shared-coin protocols. The impossibility results established for large coalitions of participants contrast with a tournament-tree generalization (standard construction akin [1,3,17]) of Blum's 2-party protocol, which maintains game-theoretic fairness even against coalitions of size $n - 1$. In particular, adversarial behavior can never decrease the chance of any honest participant becoming the leader as compared to the system where all participants behave honestly.

The leader-driven nature of consensus in state machine replication [6,7,14, 15], with the emerging economics and incentives in blockchain systems [18], further motivates exploring fair leader election protocols. The tournament tree protocol requires $O(\log n)$ rounds of communication. Chung, Chan, Wen and Shi [8] showed a clever lower bound argument that $\Omega(\log n)$ rounds are required for game-theoretically fair leader election in the standard broadcast model with a perfect commitment scheme, albeit when committed values must be opened immediately after they are broadcast (a restriction that still includes Blum's protocol and a variant of the tournament tree generalization). This is a foundational result, and in general, proving tight logarithmic lower bounds for similar tournament-based leader election protocols is notoriously difficult [1,2].

Not requiring commitments to be immediately opened significantly weakens the adversary controlling the coalition and complicates lower bound arguments, as the corrupted participants can no longer determine their messages based on the actual execution (*adaptive* adversary), but only based on the distribution of all possible executions (*oblivious* adversary). To contrast the adversarial power, note that in standard asynchronous shared memory with crash failures, a protocol with $O(\log^\star n)$ step complexity exists against the oblivious adversary [12], while the best known protocol against the adaptive adversary is the $O(\log n)$ tournament-tree of [1]. The authors in [8] emphasize the important dependency of their lower bound on immediately opening the commitments, and the need for more sophisticated techniques to overcome these in the context of their proof.

We take a step in better understanding this dependency on opening commitments and adversarial power for the problem of game-theoretically fair leader election. We remove the restriction on the commitment scheme in [8] but our lower bound also makes two assumptions about the protocol. Our lower bound applies to a different set of protocols, including the tournament-based protocol even if all commitments are made in the beginning of the protocol.

Our first assumption is that in any sub-protocol (a protocol that can be reached by rounds of honest execution), any player that has an overall positive probability to win when all players are honest, also has a chance to win regardless of the set of messages of the other players (in the first round of the sub-protocol). On the other hand, immediately opening commitments restriction in [8] implies that all sub-protocols are also game-theoretically fair, which in turn implies a stronger version of our assumption (that, in addition, the positive probabilities against fixed message vectors of other players are all equal to each other).

Our second assumption is more technical and captures the idea of an essential inductive ingredient in the previous proof of [8]. While we cannot claim that this assumption is weaker or follows from the previous commitment requirement, it is trivially satisfied by the tournament-tree protocol and leads to a simple, streamlined argument. Proving an unconditional lower bound (or a better upper bound) is an important open problem, and having a proof based on a different set of assumptions could help gain intuition about the general problem.

2   Model

We strive to remain close to the structure and notation of [8]. Therefore, we consider a standard synchronous round-based broadcast model with n participants that will be called *players* that communicate via a broadcast channel. As in [8], we restrict our attention to the case when the set of messages that a player i may send in each round is finite—denoted by M_i—to avoid non-measurable and other technical issues. Without loss of generality, we restrict to the case when in each round, an honest player i uniformly samples a message to send from M_i. Also like in [8], we assume that the $|M_i|$ is the same in every round. This is justified since we can construct equivalent protocols by sampling over multiple copies of every message.

In [8], it was assumed that a protocol could use a perfect commitment scheme to make the adversary commit to its randomness. However, the adversary could determine the message in a round based on the transcript of all previous rounds. This corresponds to the restriction on the protocol to immediately open every commitment. Without this restriction, the adversary must determine the messages of corrupted players ahead of time, and can only rely on the distribution of possible executions as opposed to the actual execution unfolding. This is a known, major distinction between the *adaptive* and *oblivious* randomized adversarial models.

In our setting, a round consists of each (non-crashed) player attempting to broadcast a message, while the adversary can *rush* to *crash*: it observes the messages and decides which players to crash[1]. After this, the messages of all non-crashed players appear on the broadcast channel. A crashed player remains crashed in all subsequent rounds, with its messages treated as $\perp$. Finally, notice that we assumed that a corrupted player j always sends a message from M_j. This is without loss of generality since otherwise, the corruption would be detectable on the broadcast channel, so the adversary could instead just crash the player j.

---

[1] Intuitively, this corresponds to not opening a commitment.

2.1   Coalition Resistant Protocols

A 0-round leader election protocol must elect a unique, single winner among n players (without any communication). An r-round protocol is defined recursively, where processes engage in a round of communication, and proceed to an $(r-1)$-round leader election protocol.

Given a leader election protocol φ, let $p_i(\varphi)$ be the probability of player i winning over all failure-free executions. We call $p(\varphi) \in [0,1]^n$ the *winning probability distribution* of φ. We simply write p (or p_i) whenever the parameter φ is clear from the context. Since the adversary may choose not to corrupt any players, p_i upper bounds the minimum probability of player i winning against the adversary that can corrupt all players except i. We call a protocol φ *coalition resistant* if player i's probability of winning is p_i regardless of any adversarial strategy, which may control coalitions of size up to $n-1$.

For any multi-round protocol φ, we say φ' is a *sub-protocol* of φ if it can be reached by a finite number of rounds in which all players act honestly according to φ. Since a sub-protocol φ' is reachable by an all-honest execution, we can define the winning probability distribution p'_i for φ' analogous to the definition of p_i for φ (i.e., considering failure-free executions only). For a sub-protocol φ, let $S(\varphi)$ denote the support of the winning probability distribution of φ. Formally, for a probability distribution $p(\varphi) \in [0,1]^n$, we have $S(\varphi) := \{i \in [n] : p_i > 0\}$. For any vector μ of possible messages for all n players, let $\varphi(\mu)$ denote the sub-protocol reached by one round of φ in which each player sends the corresponding message.

We will use the notation $\varphi(X_1 \leftarrow x_1, \ldots, X_k \leftarrow x_k)$ when $X_1, \ldots, X_k$ is a partition of all players and x_i is a vector of messages sent by players in X_i. I.e., this is the same as $\varphi(\mu)$ for a μ determined by $x_1, \ldots, x_k$.

For any sub-protocol φ', we call a subset $A \subseteq S(\varphi')$ of players a *winning subset* of φ' if for any possible vector a' of the non-A players, there exists a vector of messages a for the players in A, such that $S(\varphi'(A \leftarrow a, [n] \setminus A \leftarrow a')) \subseteq A$, and in addition, for some a' there exists an a such that $S(\varphi'(A \leftarrow a, [n] \setminus A \leftarrow a')) = A$. In other words, players in A always have messages that eliminate all other players from contention (regardless of the messages of non-A players), and there is at least one possibility that all players in A maintain a chance to win.

Our lower bound applies to any coalition resistant protocol φ that satisfies the following two conditions.

Assumption 1. *For any sub-protocol φ' of φ, any player $i \in S(\varphi')$, and any possible vector x of messages for the non-$\{i\}$ players $X = [n] \setminus \{i\}$, there exists a message m_i of player i such that $i \in S(\varphi'(X \leftarrow x, \{i\} \leftarrow m_i))$.*

In other words, if player i had a positive probability of winning, there is no possible combination of messages that the other players may send such that i can no longer win after one round. As noted in the introduction, this requirement is weaker than having the sub-protocol φ' being also coalition resistant (as is implied by the immediately opening every commitment constraint in [8]).

Assumption 2. *For any sub-protocol φ' of φ with a support size $|S(\varphi')| > 1$, we can find two disjoint winning subsets of players $A, B \subset S(\varphi')$.*

Note that the tournament-tree based protocol satisfies these assumptions regardless of whether the players commit to messages at each round or at the beginning of the protocol. A sub-protocol is just a level in the tournament tree consisting of pairs of players engaging in 2-player Blum mechanism. For each of these pairs, we can place one player in subset A and the other in B, satisfying Assumption 2.

3   Lower Bound

Let φ be a coalition resistant protocol that satisfies Assumptions 1 and Assumption 2. We prove by induction that for any r-round sub-protocol φ' of φ (consisting of the last r rounds of φ), it holds that $S(\varphi') \leq 2^r$. Consequently, a protocol that elects one out of n possible leaders requires at least $\log n$ rounds. Clearly, 0-round sub-protocols do not send any messages so there is just one possible execution and since the protocol must elect a unique winner, the induction base is satisfied for $r = 0$.

For the induction step, let us consider any $(r + 1)$-round sub-protocol φ' and define subsets $A, B \subset S(\varphi')$ satisfying Assumption 2. By the induction hypothesis and the definition of a winning subset, $|A| \leq 2^r$ and $|B| \leq 2^r$. To complete the argument, we show that $A \cup B = S(\varphi')$, which will give $S(\varphi') = |A| + |B| \leq 2^{r+1}$ as desired.

Suppose for contradiction that disjoint subsets A and B do not include all players in $S(\varphi')$, and let i be some player among the rest of the players (in $S(\varphi') \setminus (A \cup B)$). Let D be the (possibly empty) set of all remaining players (in $S(\varphi') \setminus (A \cup B \cup \{i\})$)—for these players we will set a vector of messages d throughout the following argument.

Let $M(A, B)$ be a set of pairs of vectors (a, b) of messages for players in A and B, that allow only players in A or only players in B to retain a chance to win. Formally, $(a, b) \in M(A, B)$ iff there exists m with $S(\varphi'(A \leftarrow a, B \leftarrow b, \{i\} \leftarrow m, D \leftarrow d)) \subseteq A$ or $S(\varphi'(A \leftarrow a, B \leftarrow b, \{i\} \leftarrow m, D \leftarrow d)) \subseteq B$. A (and B) are winning subsets by Assumption 2, thus, $M(A, B)$ is non-empty.

We assign a *valency* to each element $(a, b) \in M(A, B)$, defined as the number of different messages m_i for player i, such that i retains a chance to win, i.e. $i \in S(\varphi'(A \leftarrow a, B \leftarrow b, \{i\} \leftarrow m_i, D \leftarrow d))$. For the rest of the argument, let (a, b) be the element in $M(A, B)$ with the minimum valency. Suppose, without loss of generality that there exists i's message m_A such that only players in A retain a chance to win, i.e. $S(\varphi'(A \leftarrow a, B \leftarrow b, \{i\} \leftarrow m_A, D \leftarrow d)) \subseteq A$ (the case for B is symmetrical, and one of these cases hold by the definition of $M(A, B)$).

First, we prove that for any message m' of i for which i does not retain a chance to win in $\varphi'(A \leftarrow a, B \leftarrow b, \{i\} \leftarrow m', D \leftarrow d)$, only players in A retain a chance to win.

Lemma 1. *For m' with $i \notin S(\varphi'(A \leftarrow a, B \leftarrow b, \{i\} \leftarrow m', D \leftarrow d))$, we have $S(\varphi'(A \leftarrow a, B \leftarrow b, \{i\} \leftarrow m', D \leftarrow d)) \subseteq A$.*

Proof. Suppose for contradiction that m' allows a player $j \neq i$ that is not in A to retain a chance to win, i.e. $j \in S(\varphi'(A \leftarrow a, B \leftarrow b, \{i\} \leftarrow m', D \leftarrow d))$.

We show an adversary that contradicts the coalition resistance of protocol φ. The adversary acts as follows in sub-protocol φ': it observes the messages of all players once revealed, and then it might choose to crash player i so that its message is not delivered.

Let p_A be the winning probability distribution of $\varphi'(A \leftarrow a, B \leftarrow b, \{i\} \leftarrow m_A, D \leftarrow d)$ and let p' be the winning probability distribution of $\varphi'(A \leftarrow a, B \leftarrow b, \{i\} \leftarrow m', D \leftarrow d)$. Recall that, by definition of m_A and the lemma assumption on m', player i has probability 0 both in p_A and p'. Moreover, the probabilities of players in A sum to 1 in p_A, and player j has a non-zero probability in p'. Hence, the probabilities of A-players in p_A summed with the probability of j in p_j is larger than 1 and cannot be a probability vector. To determine the precise adversarial strategy, we consider a winning probability distribution $p_\perp$ for sub-protocol $\varphi'(A \leftarrow a, B \leftarrow b, \{i\} \leftarrow \perp, D \leftarrow d)$, where player i crashes.

In $p_\perp$, either player j has lower probability than in p', or some player in A has a lower probability than in p_A. In the first case, the adversary crashes player i when it observes messages $A \leftarrow a, B \leftarrow b, \{i\} \leftarrow m', D \leftarrow d$, reducing the probability of player j winning. Otherwise, the adversary crashes player i when it observes $A \leftarrow a, B \leftarrow b, \{i\} \leftarrow m_A, D \leftarrow d$, reducing the probability of a player in A winning.

This contradicts the fact that φ' is a sub-protocol of a coalition resistant protocol φ. The adversary only crashes player i when an all-honest execution reaches sub-protocol φ', which by definition of a sub-protocol occurs by a positive probability. This still reduces the overall winning probability of some honest player in the original protocol, giving the desired contradiction. □

Let m_i be a message for which player i retains a chance to win in $\varphi'(A \leftarrow a, B \leftarrow b, \{i\} \leftarrow m_i, D \leftarrow d)$. By Assumption 1, all valencies are positive, so such an m_i exists. Because by Assumption 2 B is a winning subset, there exists a vector b' of messages for B-players such that $S(\varphi'(A \leftarrow a, B \leftarrow b', \{i\} \leftarrow m_i, D \leftarrow d)) \subseteq B$.

Next, we prove that

Lemma 2. $i \in S(\varphi'(A \leftarrow a, B \leftarrow b', \{i\} \leftarrow m_i, D \leftarrow d))$.

Proof. We start by showing that for any m' that satisfies $S(\varphi'(A \leftarrow a, B \leftarrow b, \{i\} \leftarrow m', D \leftarrow d)) \subseteq A$, we have $i \notin S(\varphi'(A \leftarrow a, B \leftarrow b', \{i\} \leftarrow m', D \leftarrow d))$. For contradiction, assume $S(\varphi'(A \leftarrow a, B \leftarrow b, \{i\} \leftarrow m', D \leftarrow d)) \subseteq A$ and $i \in S(\varphi'(A \leftarrow a, B \leftarrow b', \{i\} \leftarrow m', D \leftarrow d))$ for some message m'. However, the same adversarial strategy as in the proof of Lemma 1 but by replacing the role of player j in the previous lemma by player i in this lemma and crashing players in B (in the current lemma) instead of player i (in the previous lemma), contradicts the coalition-resistance of the protocol φ.

Applying Lemma 1, we get that for any m' such that $i \notin S(\varphi'(A \leftarrow a, B \leftarrow b, \{i\} \leftarrow m', D \leftarrow d))$, we have $i \notin S(\varphi'(A \leftarrow a, B \leftarrow b', \{i\} \leftarrow m', D \leftarrow d))$.

Note that (a, b') is in $M(A, B)$ by definition of b'. By the choice of (a, b) with the minimum valency, the valency of (a, b') is at least as large as the valency of (a, b). Since player i always sends one out of the same number of possible messages, the valency of (a, b) and (a, b') are the same. Moreover the set of messages for which the valency is counted is also the same. In particular, since for m_i we have $i \in S(\varphi'(A \leftarrow a, B \leftarrow b, \{i\} \leftarrow m_i, D \leftarrow d))$ we also get that $i \in S(\varphi'(A \leftarrow a, B \leftarrow b', \{i\} \leftarrow m_i, D \leftarrow d))$. $\square$

However, since $S(\varphi'(A \leftarrow a, B \leftarrow b', \{i\} \leftarrow m_i, D \leftarrow d)) \subseteq B$ and $i \notin B$ we get the desired contradiction and complete the induction.

4 Conclusion

The elegant proof by [8] that showed a lower bound of $\log n$ rounds for coalition-resistant leader election, left open a question of relaxing a restriction on the protocols to immediately open all cryptographic commitments.

We take a step in this direction by removing this restriction. In particular, our lower bound captures the standard tournament-tree protocol even if all message commitments are made in the beginning ("static" adversarial behavior). However, we require a new assumption for our proof that may help viewing the open problem of the unconditional round complexity of coalition-resistant leader election in a different light - i.e. when attempting to circumvent this assumption by a clever algorithm or a stronger lower bound.

References

1. Afek, Y., Gafni, E., Tromp, J., Vitányi, P.M.B.: Wait-free test-and-set (extended abstract). In: Proceedings of the 6th International Workshop on Distributed Algorithms, WDAG 1992, pp. 85–94 (1992)
2. Alistarh, D., Gelashvili, R., Nadiradze, G.: Lower bounds for shared-memory leader election under bounded write contention. In: Proceedings of the 35th International Symposium on Distributed Computing, DISC 2021 (2021)
3. Bartoletti, M., Zunino, R.: Constant-deposit multiparty lotteries on bitcoin. In: International Conference on Financial Cryptography and Data Security, pp. 231–247 (2017)
4. Ben-Or, M., Linial, N.: Collective coin flipping, robust voting schemes and minima of banzhaf values. In: Proceedings of the 26th Symposium on Foundations of Computer Science, FOCS 1985, pp. 408–416 (1985)
5. Blum, M.: Coin flipping by telephone a protocol for solving impossible problems. ACM SIGACT News 15(1), 23–27 (1983)
6. Castro, M., Liskov, B.: Practical byzantine fault tolerance. In: Proceedings of the 3rd Symposium on Operating Systems Design and Implementation, OSDI 1999, pp. 173–186 (1999)

7. Chan, B.Y., Shi, E.: Streamlet: textbook streamlined blockchains. In: Proceedings of the 2nd Conference on Advances in Financial Technologies, AFT 2020, pp. 1–11 (2020)
8. Chung, K.-M., Chan, T.-H.H., Wen, T., Shi, E.: Game-theoretic fairness meets multi-party protocols: the case of leader election. In: Annual International Cryptology Conference, pp. 3–32 (2021)
9. Chung, K.-M., Guo, Y., Lin, W.-K., Pass, R., Shi, E.: Game theoretic notions of fairness in multi-party coin toss. In: Theory of Cryptography Conference, pp. 563–596 (2018)
10. Cleve, R.: Limits on the security of coin flips when half the processors are faulty. In: Proceedings of the 18th ACM symposium on Theory of Computing, STOC 1986, pp. 364–369 (1986)
11. Feige, U.: Noncryptographic selection protocols. In: Proceedings of the 40th Symposium on Foundations of Computer Science, FOCS 1999, pp. 142–152 (1999)
12. Giakkoupis, G., Woelfel, P.: Efficient randomized test-and-set implementations. Distrib. Comput. **32**(6), 565–586 (2019). https://doi.org/10.1007/s00446-019-00349-z
13. Haitner, I., Karidi-Heller, Y.: A tight lower bound on adaptively secure full-information coin flip. In: Proceedings of the 61st Symposium on Foundations of Computer Science, FOCS 2020, pp. 1268–1276 (2020)
14. Kotla, R., Alvisi, L., Dahlin, M., Clement, A., Wong, E.: Zyzzyva: speculative byzantine fault tolerance. In: Proceedings of Twenty-First ACM SIGOPS Symposium on Operating Systems Principles, pp. 45–58 (2007)
15. Lamport, L.: Paxos made simple. ACM SIGACT News **32**(4), 18–25 (2001)
16. Lynch, N.A.: Distributed algorithms. Elsevier (1996)
17. Miller, A., Bentov, I.: Zero-collateral lotteries in bitcoin and ethereum. In: EuroS&PW Workshop, pp. 4–13 (2017)
18. Nakamoto, S.: Bitcoin: a peer-to-peer electronic cash system. Decentralized Business Review, 21260 (2008)
19. Rabin, M.: Randomized byzantine generals. In: Proceedings of the 24th Symposium on Foundations of Computer Science, FOCS 1983, pp. 403–409 (1983)
20. Russell, A., Saks, M., Zuckerman, D.: Lower bounds for leader election and collective coin-flipping in the perfect information model. SIAM J. Comput. **31**(6), 1645–1662 (2002)
21. Wu, K., Asharov, G., Shi, E.: A complete characterization of game-theoretically fair, multi-party coin toss. https://eprint.iacr.org/2021/748 (2021)

Not Proof of Work

The Availability-Accountability Dilemma and Its Resolution via Accountability Gadgets

Joachim Neu⬤, Ertem Nusret Tas$^{(\boxtimes)}$⬤, and David Tse⬤

Stanford University, Stanford, USA
{jneu,nusret,dntse}@stanford.edu

Abstract. For applications of Byzantine fault tolerant (BFT) consensus protocols where the participants are economic agents, recent works highlighted the importance of *accountability*: the ability to identify participants who provably violate the protocol. At the same time, being able to reach consensus under dynamic levels of participation is desirable for censorship resistance. We identify an *availability-accountability dilemma*: in an environment with dynamic participation, no protocol can simultaneously be accountably-safe and live. We provide a resolution to this dilemma by constructing a provably secure optimally-resilient accountability gadget to checkpoint a longest chain protocol, such that the full ledger is live under dynamic participation and the checkpointed prefix ledger is accountable. Our accountability gadget construction is black-box and can use any BFT protocol which is accountable under static participation. Using HotStuff as the black box, we implemented our construction as a protocol for the Ethereum 2.0 beacon chain, and our Internet-scale experiments with more than 4,000 nodes show that the protocol achieves the required scalability and has better latency than the current solution Gasper, which was shown insecure by recent attacks.

1 Introduction

1.1 Accountability and Dynamic Participation

Safety and liveness are the two fundamental security properties of consensus protocols. A protocol run by a distributed set of nodes is safe if the ledgers generated by the protocol are consistent across nodes and across time. It is live if all honest transactions eventually enter into the ledger. Traditionally, consensus protocols are developed for fault-tolerant distributed computing, where a set of distributed computing devices aims to emulate a reliable centralized computer. In modern decentralized applications such as cryptocurrencies, consensus nodes are no longer just disinterested computing devices but are agents acting based on economic and other rationales. To provide the proper incentives to encourage nodes to follow the protocol, it is important that they can be held accountable for their protocol-violating behavior. This point of view is advocated by Buterin

---

Extended version [29]: The authors contributed equally and are listed alphabetically.

© International Financial Cryptography Association 2022
I. Eyal and J. Garay (Eds.): FC 2022, LNCS 13411, pp. 541–559, 2022.
https://doi.org/10.1007/978-3-031-18283-9_27

and Griffith [4] in the context of their effort to add accountability (among other things) to Ethereum's Proof-of-Work (PoW) longest chain protocol, and is also central to the design of Gasper [5], the protocol running Ethereum 2.0's Proof-of-Stake (PoS) beacon chain. In these protocols, accountability is used to incentivize proper behavior by slashing the stake of protocol-violating agents.

PoW protocols like Bitcoin [24] or Ethereum 1.0 do not assign identities to miners, and hence cannot be expected to provide accountability. Even Nakamoto-style PoS protocols such as Cardano's Ouroboros family [2,12,20] lack accountability. On the other hand, protocols that are designed to provide accountability include Polygraph [10] and Tendermint [3], and a recent comprehensive work [37] shows that accountability can be added on top of many (but not all) 'traditional' propose-and-vote-style Byzantine fault tolerant (BFT) protocols, such as HotStuff [40], PBFT [6], or Streamlet [7,27]. There is, however, another crucial difference between Nakamoto-style and propose-and-vote-style protocols. While protocols from the first group do not provide accountability, they tolerate dynamic participation, a sought after feature of public permissionless blockchains not only for censorship resistance. In Bitcoin, *e.g.*, the total hash rate varies over many orders of magnitude over the years. Yet, the blockchains remain continuously *available*, *i.e.*, live. Protocols from the second group, oppositely, provide accountability but do not tolerate dynamic participation.[1] Why is there no protocol that both supports accountability and tolerates dynamic participation?

1.2 Availability-Accountability Dilemma and Resolution via Accountability Gadgets

Our first result says that it is impossible to support accountability for *dynamically available* protocols, *i.e.*, protocols that are live under dynamic participation (*cf.* Theorem 1). We call this the *availability-accountability dilemma*.

Our second contribution is to provide a resolution to the dilemma. As no *single* ledger protocol can simultaneously be available and accountable, we design and implement an accountability gadget which, when applied to a longest chain protocol, generates a dynamically available ledger $\mathsf{LOG}_{\mathrm{da}}$ and a checkpointed prefix ledger $\mathsf{LOG}_{\mathrm{acc}}$ with provably optimal security properties.

Consider a network with a total of n permissioned nodes, and an environment where the network may partition and the nodes may go online and offline.

1. **(P1: Accountability)** The accountable ledger $\mathsf{LOG}_{\mathrm{acc}}$ can provide an accountable safety resilience of $n/3$ at all times (*i.e.*, identify that many protocol violators in case of a safety violation), and it is live after a possible partition heals and greater than $2n/3$ honest nodes come online.
2. **(P2: Dynamic Availability)** The available ledger $\mathsf{LOG}_{\mathrm{da}}$ is guaranteed to be safe after a possible network partition and live at all times, provided that fewer than $1/2$ of the online nodes are adversarial.

---

[1] For completeness, there are also protocols which neither provide accountability nor tolerate dynamic participation, *e.g.*, Algorand [9].

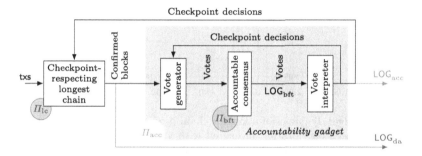

Fig. 1. We construct an accountability gadget Π_{acc} from any accountable BFT protocol Π_{bft} and apply it to a longest-chain-type protocol Π_{lc} as follows: The fork choice rule of Π_{lc} is modified to respect the latest checkpoint decision. Blocks confirmed by Π_{lc} are output as available ledger LOG_{da}. They are also the basis on which nodes generate a proposal and vote for the next checkpoint. To ensure that all nodes reach the same checkpoint decision, consensus is reached on which votes to count using Π_{bft}. Checkpoint decisions are output as accountable ledger LOG_{acc} and fed back into the protocol to ensure consistency of future block production in Π_{lc} and future checkpoints with previous checkpoints.

Note that while the checkpointed ledger is by definition always a prefix of the full available ledger, the above result says that the checkpointed ledger will catch up with the available ledger when the network heals and a sufficient number of honest nodes come online. Users can choose individually whether to resolve the dilemma in favor of availability or accountability. For example, under exceptional circumstances, a coffee shop might rather tolerate payments reverting than stalling, while a car dealer might prefer stalling over reverting payments.

The achieved resiliences are optimal, which can be seen by comparing this result with [37, Theorem B.1] (for P1) and [32, Theorem 3] (for P2). The checkpointed ledger LOG_{acc} cannot achieve better accountable safety resilience than $n/3$; it in fact achieves exactly that. The dynamically available ledger LOG_{da} cannot achieve a better resilience than $1/2$; the ledger in fact achieves it. Moreover, even if the network was synchronous at all times, no protocol could have generated an accountable ledger with better resilience (Theorem 1). So we are getting partition-tolerance for free, even though accountability is the goal.

The accountability gadget construction is shown in Fig. 1. It is built on top of any existing longest chain protocol modified to respect the checkpoints. That is, new blocks are proposed and the ledger of confirmed transactions is determined based on the longest chain among all the chains containing the latest checkpointed block. This gives the available full ledger LOG_{da}. Periodically, nodes vote on the next checkpoint (following a randomly selected leader's proposal). To ensure that when tallying votes all nodes base their decision for the next checkpoint on the same set of votes, any accountable BFT protocol designed for a fixed level of participation can be used (entirely as a black box) to reach consensus on the votes. The chain up to the latest checkpoint constitutes the

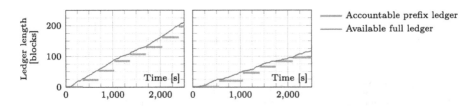

Fig. 2. Left: Ledger dynamics of a longest chain protocol outfitted with our accountability gadget based on HotStuff, measured with 4,100 nodes distributed around the world. No attack. The available full ledger grows steadily. The accountable prefix periodically catches up whenever a new block is checkpointed. **Right:** Even in the presence of a $\beta = 25\%$ adversary who mines selfishly in Π_{lc} and boycotts leader duty in Π_{bft} and Π_{acc}, $\mathrm{LOG_{da}}$ grows steadily and $\mathrm{LOG_{acc}}$ periodically catches up with $\mathrm{LOG_{da}}$. Under attack, the growth rate of $\mathrm{LOG_{da}}$ is reduced (due to selfish mining) and $\mathrm{LOG_{acc}}$'s catching up is occasionally slightly delayed due to leader timeouts. (Parameters $n = 4100$, $T_{\mathrm{cp}} = 5\,\mathrm{min}$, $T_{\mathrm{to}} = 1\,\mathrm{min}$, $T_{\mathrm{hs}} = 20\,\mathrm{s}$, $k_{\mathrm{cp}} = k = 6$, all nodes online; *cf.* Sects. 4.1, 5)

accountable prefix ledger $\mathrm{LOG_{acc}}$. The gadget ensures that block production and confirmation in Π_{lc} and future checkpoints honor established checkpoints. When instantiated with an accountable BFT protocol that is secure under network partitions, $\mathrm{LOG_{acc}}$ inherits its partition-tolerance.

Since there are many accountable BFT protocols [37], we have a lot of implementation choices. Due to its maturity and the availability of a high quality open-source implementation which we could employ practically as a black box, we decided to implement a prototype of our accountability gadget using the HotStuff protocol [40]. Taking the Ethereum 2.0's beacon chain as a target application and matching its key performance characteristics such as latency and block size, we performed Internet-scale experiments to demonstrate that our solution can meet the target specification with over 4,000 participants (see Fig. 2(l)). In particular, for the chosen parameterization and even before taking reduction measures, the peak bandwidth required for a node to participate does not exceed 1.5 MB/s (with a long-term average of 78 KB/s) and hence is feasible even for many consumer-grade Internet connections. At the same time, our prototype provides 5× better average latency of $\mathrm{LOG_{acc}}$ compared to the instantiation of Gasper currently used for Ethereum 2's beacon chain.

1.3   Related Work

Accountability. Accountability in distributed protocols has been studied in earlier works. [18] designed a system, PeerReview, which detects faults. [19] classifies faults into different types and studies their detectability. Casper [4] focuses on accountability and fault detection when there is violation of safety, and led to the notion of accountable safety resilience we use in this work. Polygraph [10] is a partially synchronous BFT protocol which is secure when there are less than $n/3$ adversarial nodes, and when there is a safety violation, at least $n/3$

Table 1. Accountability gadgets provide security, accountability, and predictable validity, which are not found conjoint in any one of the previous works [5, 27, 30, 35].

	Gasper [5]	Checkp. LC [35]	Snap&Chat [27, 30]	Acc. gadgets (This work)
Provable security	✗	✓	✓	✓
Accountability	✓	✗	✓	✓
Predictable validity	✓	✓	✗	✓

nodes can be held accountable. [34] builds upon [10] to create a blockchain which can exclude Byzantine nodes that were found to have violated the protocol.

Many of these previous works focus on studying the accountability of *specific* protocols and think of accountability as an add-on feature in addition to the basic security properties of the protocol. [37] follows this spirit but broadens the investigation to formulate a framework to study the accountability of many existing BFT protocols. More specifically, their framework augments the traditional resilience metric with accountable safety resilience (which they call forensic support). The present work is more in the spirit of [4] where accountability is a central design goal, not just an add-on feature. To formalize this spirit, we split traditional resilience into safety and liveness resiliences, upgrade safety resilience to accountable safety resilience, and formulate accountable security as a tradeoff between liveness resilience and accountable safety resilience. Further, we broaden the study to the important dynamic participation environment, where we discovered the availability-accountability dilemma (Theorem 1). While at its heart the impossibility result Theorem B.1 of [37] is really about the tradeoff between liveness and accountable safety resiliences, although not stated as such, and it is indeed applicable very generally, when applied to the dynamic participation setting it would give a loose result and would not have been able to demonstrate the availability-accountability dilemma.

Availability-Finality Dilemma and Finality Gadgets. The *availability-finality dilemma* [17, 21, 30] states that no protocol can provide both finality, *i.e.*, safety under network partitions, and availability, *i.e.*, liveness under dynamic participation. The *availability-accountability dilemma* states that no protocol can provide both accountable safety and liveness under dynamic participation. Although they are different, it turns out that some, but not all, protocols that resolve the availability-finality dilemma can be used to resolve the availability-accountability dilemma. Casper [4] and Gasper [5] pioneered resolution of the dilemmata but lacked a specification of the desired security properties and suffered from attacks [25, 26, 28, 30, 31, 36]. Specifically, Gasper is insecure [26, 28, 30, 36] (Table 1). The first provably secure resolution of the availability-finality dilemma is the class of snap-and-chat protocols [30], which combines a longest chain protocol with a partially synchronous BFT protocol in a black box manner to provide finality. If the partially synchronous BFT protocol is accountable, it is not too difficult to show [27] that the resulting snap-and-chat protocol would also provide a resolution to the availability-accountability dilemma. On the other hand, checkpointed longest chain [35], another resolution of the availability-finality dilemma, is not accountable [29, Appendix G] (Table 1).

A strength of snap-and-chat protocols is its black box nature which gives it flexibility to provide additional features. A drawback is that the protocol may reorder the blocks from the longest chain protocol to form the final ledger [27]. This means that when a proposer proposes a block on the longest chain, it cannot predict the ledger state and check the validity of transactions by just looking at the earlier blocks in the longest chain. This lack of *predictable validity* (Table 1) opens the protocol up to spamming and prohibits the use of standard techniques for sharding and light client support. Checkpointed longest chain builds upon a line of work called finality gadgets [4,5,13,38] and overcomes this limitation of snap-and-chat protocols because the longest chain protocol is modified to respect the checkpoints so that the order of blocks can be preserved. However, checkpointed longest chain's finality gadget is not black box, but specifically uses Algorand BA [8], which is not accountable [37]. It is not readily apparent if and how Algorand BA could be replaced with any accountable BFT protocol.

The accountability gadget we design combines structural elements from snap-and-chat protocols and from the checkpointed longest chain to uniquely achieve the best of both worlds. It builds on the checkpointed longest chain and earlier (not provably secure) finality gadgets in that it complements a longest chain protocol with a checkpointing mechanism and thus achieves predictable validity. Like snap-and-chat protocols, it allows the use of any BFT protocol as a black box for checkpointing, retaining simplicity and flexibility and, when an accountable BFT protocol like HotStuff is used, the checkpointed ledger is accountable. Our accountability gadget provides security, accountability, and predictable validity (Table 1), which are not found conjoint in any one of the prior works.

1.4 Outline

We introduce in Sect. 2 the notation and model for the proof of the availability-accountability dilemma in Sect. 3 and the construction and security proof of accountability gadgets in Sect. 4. Finally, we discuss details of a prototype implementation and experimental performance results in Sect. 5.

2 Model

In the client-server model of state machine replication (SMR), *nodes* take inputs called *transactions* and enable clients to agree on a single sequence of transactions, called the *ledger* and denoted by LOG, that produced the state evolution. For this purpose, nodes exchange messages, *e.g.*, blocks or votes, and each node i records its view of the protocol by time t in an execution transcript T_i^t. To obtain the ledger at time t, clients query the nodes running the protocol. When a node i is queried at time t, it produces *evidence* w_i^t by applying an *evidence generation function* $\mathcal{W}$ to its current transcript: $\mathsf{w}_i^t \triangleq \mathcal{W}(\mathsf{T}_i^t)$. Upon collecting evidences from some subset S of the nodes, each client applies the *confirmation rule* $\mathcal{C}$ to this set of evidences to obtain the ledger: $\mathsf{LOG} \triangleq \mathcal{C}(\{\mathsf{w}_i^t\}_{i \in S})$. Protocols typically require to query a subset S containing at least one honest node.

Environment and Adversary: We assume that transactions are input to nodes by the environment $\mathcal{Z}$. There exists a public-key infrastructure and each of the n nodes is equipped with a unique cryptographic identity. A random oracle serves as a common source of randomness. Time is slotted and the nodes have synchronized local clocks. *Corruption:* Adversary $\mathcal{A}$ is a probabilistic poly-time algorithm. Before the protocol execution starts, $\mathcal{A}$ gets to corrupt (up to) f nodes, then called *adversarial* nodes. Adversarial nodes surrender their internal state to the adversary and can deviate from the protocol arbitrarily (Byzantine faults) under the adversary's control. The remaining $(n-f)$ nodes are called *honest* and follow the protocol as specified. *Networking:* Nodes can send each other messages. Before a *global stabilization time* GST, $\mathcal{A}$ can delay network messages arbitrarily. After GST, $\mathcal{A}$ is required to deliver all messages sent between honest nodes within a known upper bound of Δ slots. GST is chosen by $\mathcal{A}$, unknown to the honest nodes, and can be a causal function of the randomness in the protocol. *Sleeping:* To model dynamic participation, we adopt the concept of *sleepiness* [33]. Before a *global awake time*[2] GAT, $\mathcal{A}$ chooses, for every time slot and honest node, whether it is *awake* (*i.e.*, online) or *asleep* (*i.e.*, offline). After GAT, all honest nodes are awake. An awake honest node executes the protocol faithfully. An asleep honest node does not execute the protocol, and messages that would have arrived in that slot are queued and delivered in the first slot in which the node is awake again. Adversarial nodes are always awake. We define β as the maximum fraction of adversarial nodes among awake nodes throughout the execution of the protocol. GAT, just like GST, is chosen by the adversary, unknown to the honest nodes and can be a causal function of the randomness. But, while GST needs to happen eventually (GST $< \infty$), GAT may be infinite.

Given above definition of a partially synchronous network with dynamic participation $(\mathcal{A}_{\mathrm{pda}}, \mathcal{Z}_{\mathrm{pda}})$, we model a synchronous network $(\mathcal{A}_{\mathrm{s}}, \mathcal{Z}_{\mathrm{s}})$, a partially synchronous network $(\mathcal{A}_{\mathrm{p}}, \mathcal{Z}_{\mathrm{p}})$, and a synchronous network with dynamic participation $(\mathcal{A}_{\mathrm{da}}, \mathcal{Z}_{\mathrm{da}})$ as special cases with GST = GAT = 0, GAT = 0, and GST = 0, respectively. Subsequently, we specify for every theorem under which of the above four $(\mathcal{A}_{...}, \mathcal{Z}_{...})$ it holds. Examples of Nakamoto-style and propose-and-vote-style BFT protocols framed in the above model are given in [29, Appendix H].

Safety and Liveness Resiliences: Safety and liveness are defined as the traditional security properties of SMR protocols:

Definition 1. *Let T_{confirm} be a polynomial function of the security parameter σ of an SMR protocol Π. We say that Π with a confirmation rule $\mathcal{C}$ is secure and has transaction confirmation time T_{confirm} if ledgers output by $\mathcal{C}$ satisfy:*

---

[2] Node operators are rewarded and incur little expenses for protocol participation. Thus, one naturally expects frequent periods of (near) full participation. GAT models the time when participation stabilizes, analogous to the GST of network delays.

– **Safety:** *For any time slots t, t' and sets of nodes S, S' satisfying the requirements stipulated by the protocol, either* $\mathsf{LOG} \triangleq \mathcal{C}(\{\mathsf{w}_i^t\}_{i \in S})$ *is a prefix of* $\mathsf{LOG}' \triangleq \mathcal{C}(\{\mathsf{w}_i^{t'}\}_{i \in S'})$ *or vice versa.*

– **Liveness:** *If $\mathcal{Z}$ inputs a transaction to an awake honest node at some time t, then, for any time slot $t' \geq \max(t, \mathsf{GST}, \mathsf{GAT}) + T_{\mathrm{confirm}}$ and any set of nodes S satisfying the requirements stipulated by the protocol, the transaction is included in* $\mathsf{LOG} \triangleq \mathcal{C}(\{\mathsf{w}_i^{t'}\}_{i \in S})$.

Definition 2. *For static (dynamic) participation, safety resilience of a protocol is the maximum number f of adversarial nodes (maximum fraction β of adversarial nodes among awake nodes) such that the protocol satisfies safety. Such a protocol provides f-safety (β-safety).*

Definition 3. *For static (dynamic) participation, liveness resilience of a protocol is the maximum number f of adversarial nodes (maximum fraction β of adversarial nodes among awake nodes) such that the protocol satisfies liveness. Such a protocol provides f-liveness (β-liveness).*

Accountable Safety Resilience: To formalize the concept of accountable safety resilience, we define an *adjudication function* $\mathcal{J}$, similar to the forensic protocol defined in [37], as follows:

Definition 4. *An adjudication function $\mathcal{J}$ takes as input two sets of evidences W and W' with conflicting ledgers $\mathsf{LOG} \triangleq \mathcal{C}(W)$ and $\mathsf{LOG}' \triangleq \mathcal{C}(W')$, and outputs a set of nodes that have provably violated the protocol rules.*

So, $\mathcal{J}$ never outputs an honest node. When the clients observe a safety violation, *i.e.*, at least two sets of evidences W and W' such that $\mathsf{LOG} \triangleq \mathcal{C}(W)$ and $\mathsf{LOG}' \triangleq \mathcal{C}(W')$ conflict with each other, they call $\mathcal{J}$ on these evidences to identify nodes that have violated the protocol. Note that $\mathsf{LOG} \triangleq \mathcal{C}(\{\mathsf{w}_i^t\}_{i \in S})$ may satisfy safety/liveness only if the evidences come from a set S of nodes that satisfies some assumptions stipulated by the protocol, *e.g.*, that S contains one honest node. On the other hand, $\mathcal{J}$ should only output nodes that have undoubtedly violated protocol, without the verdict being conditional on any presumption.

Accountable safety resilience builds on the concept of *α-accountable-safety* first introduced in [4]:

Definition 5. *For static (dynamic) participation, accountable safety resilience of a protocol is the minimum number f of nodes (minimum fraction β of nodes among awake nodes) output by $\mathcal{J}$ in the event of a safety violation. Such a protocol provides f-accountable-safety (β-accountable-safety).*

Note that β-accountable-safety implies β-safety of the protocol (and the same for f) since $\mathcal{J}$ outputs only adversarial nodes.

3 The Availability-Accountability Dilemma

We observe that the strictest tradeoff between the liveness and accountable safety resilience occurs for dynamically available protocols under $(\mathcal{A}_{\mathrm{da}}, \mathcal{Z}_{\mathrm{da}})$, a result which was named the availability-accountability dilemma in Sect. 1.2:

Theorem 1. *No SMR protocol provides both β_a-accountable-safety and β_l-liveness for any $\beta_\mathrm{a}, \beta_\mathrm{l} > 0$ under $(\mathcal{A}_\mathrm{da}, \mathcal{Z}_\mathrm{da})$.*

Theorem 1 states that under dynamic participation it is impossible for an SMR protocol to provide both positive accountable safety resilience and positive liveness resilience. In light of this result, protocol designers are compelled to choose between protocols that maintain liveness under fluctuating participation, and protocols that can enforce the desired incentive mechanisms highlighted in Sect. 1.1 via accountability. Since both of the above features are desirable properties for Internet-scale consensus protocols, the availability-accountability dilemma presents a serious obstacle in the effort to obtain an incentive-compatible and robustly live protocol for applications such as cryptocurrencies.

To build intuition for the proof of Theorem 1, let us consider a permissioned longest chain protocol under $(\mathcal{A}_\mathrm{da}, \mathcal{Z}_\mathrm{da})$ where half of nodes are adversarial. Adversarial nodes avoid all communication with honest nodes and build a private chain that conflicts with the chain built collectively by the honest nodes. Such diverging chains mean the possibility of an (ostensible) safety violation. Think of an honest client towards whom adversarial nodes pretend to be asleep and who confirms a ledger based solely on the longest chain provided by the honest evidences; and a co-conspirator of the adversary who pretends to not have received any evidences from honest nodes and to have confirmed a ledger based solely on the longest chain provided by the adversarial evidences. Indeed, both would obtain non-empty ledgers, because the longest chain is dynamically available, but these two ledgers would conflict. Yet, based on the two sets of evidences, the judge $\mathcal{J}$ can neither distinguish who is honest client and who is co-conspirator, nor tell which nodes are honest or adversarial. So none of the adversarial nodes can be held accountable (without risking to falsely convict an honest node).

Formal proof of Theorem 1 [29, Appendix A] relies on the fact that in a dynamically available protocol, adversarial nodes, by private execution, can always create a set of evidences that yields a conflicting ledger through the confirmation rule $\mathcal{C}$. This is because dynamically available protocols cannot set a lower bound on the number of evidences eligible to generate a non-empty ledger through $\mathcal{C}$, and thus are forced to output ledgers for evidences from any number of nodes.

Theorem 1 is also related to a contemporaneous result [22] which shows that dynamically available protocols cannot produce certificates of confirmation, where such a certificate guarantees that there cannot be a conflicting confirmation so long as stipulated constraints on the adversary hold.

4   Accountability Gadgets

In this section, we formalize and prove the security properties **P1** and **P2** of Sect. 1.2 for accountability gadgets based on *permissioned* LC protocols [2,12, 20,33]. (For an extension of the security analysis to Proof-of-Work and Proof-of-Space LC protocols, see [29, Appendix F].)

Like the checkpointed longest chain [35], accountability gadgets output a prefix ledger safe under partial synchrony along with a full ledger live under dynamic

Algorithm 1. Checkpoint vote generator (helper functions: see [29, Appendix E])

```
1:  lastCp, props ← ⊥, {c : ⊥ | c = 0, 1, ...}          ▷ Last checkpoint, proposals
2:  for currIter ← 0, 1, ...                            ▷ Loop over checkpoint iterations
3:      if lastCp ≠ ⊥
4:          while waiting T_cp time                    ▷ Wait T_cp time after new checkpoint decision
5:              PERFORMBOOKKEEPING
6:      if CpLeaderOfIter(currIter) = myself  ▷ Broadcast proposal if leader of current iteration
7:          BROADCAST(⟨propose, currIter, GETCURRPROPOSALTIP()⟩_myself)
8:      while waiting T_to time                        ▷ Wait T_to for timeout of checkpoint iteration
9:          PERFORMBOOKKEEPING
10:         on props[currIter] ≠ ⊥, but at most once    ▷ Act on the first proposal received from
            authorized leader before end of T_cp-wait and T_to-timeout
11:             if ISVALIDPROPOSAL(props[currIter])   ▷ Valid proposal is consistent with current
                checkpoint-respecting LC
12:                 SUBMITVOTE(⟨accept, currIter, props[currIter]⟩_myself)
13:             else
14:                 SUBMITVOTE(⟨reject, currIter⟩_myself)        ▷ Reject invalid proposal
15:     SUBMITVOTE(⟨reject, currIter⟩_myself)                    ▷ Reject due to timeout
16:     wait on Checkpoint(c, b) from checkpoint vote interpreter (Algorithm 2) with c = currIter
17:     lastCp ← b                                ▷ Keep track of checkpoint decision
18: macro PERFORMBOOKKEEPING
19:     on receiving Checkpoint(c, b) from checkpoint vote interpreter (Algorithm 2) with c =
        currIter
20:         goto 17                              ▷ Jump to conclusion of current iteration
21:     on receiving Proposal(c, b) from checkpoint leader of iteration c with props[c] = ⊥
22:         props[c] ← b    ▷ Keep track of first proposal from authorized leader per iteration c
```

participation. For this purpose, both protocols are deployed as overlays on top of a dynamically available longest chain protocol and periodically checkpoint its output to protect against reversals under network partition. Accountability gadgets can be instantiated from any partially synchronous BFT SMR protocol, which is used as a black box for checkpointing. If the selected protocol provides accountability, then adversarial nodes can be held to account should there ever be a reversal of a checkpoint. In contrast, the checkpointed longest chain is interwoven with a variant of a particular protocol, Algorand BA [8], which does not provide accountability [37] [29, Appendix G]. Furthermore, it is not readily apparent how to use another protocol instead. As a result, the checkpointed longest chain cannot provide a resolution to the availability-accountability dilemma, whereas accountability gadgets can.

4.1 Protocol Description

Accountability gadgets, denoted by Π_{acc}, can be used in conjunction with any dynamically available longest chain (LC) protocol Π_{lc} such as Nakamoto's PoW LC protocol [24], Sleepy [33], Ouroboros [2,12,20] and Chia [11] (Fig. 1). Subsequently, we focus on permissioned/PoS LC protocols. PoW and Proof-of-Space are discussed in [29, Appendix F]. The protocol Π_{lc} then follows a modified chain selection rule where honest nodes build on the tip of the LC that contains all of the *checkpoints* they have observed.[3] We call such chains *checkpoint-respecting*

---

[3] There are no conflicting checkpoints unless a safety violation has already occurred. Upon detecting a safety violation, honest nodes stop participating in the protocol. Punishment of parties identified by the accountability mechanism as malicious and system recovery are handled by mechanisms external to the protocol.

Algorithm 2. Checkpoint vote interpreter (helper functions: see [29, Appendix E])

1: **for** currIter ← 0, 1, ...	
2: currVotes ← {(pk, ⊥) | pk ∈ committee}	▷ *Latest vote of each node*
3: **while** true	▷ *Go through votes as ordered by Π_{bft}*
4: vote ← GETNEXTVERIFIEDVOTEFROMBFT()	▷ *Verify signature*
5: **if** vote = ⟨accept, c, b⟩$_{\mathrm{pk}}$ **with** c = currIter	
6: currVotes[pk] ← Accept(b)	▷ *Count accept vote for block b*
7: **else if** vote = ⟨reject, c⟩$_{\mathrm{pk}}$ **with** c = currIter	
8: currVotes[pk] ← Reject	▷ *Count reject vote*
9: **if** ∃b : |{pk | currVotes[pk] = Accept(b)}| ≥ 2n/3	
10: OUTPUTCP(Checkpoint(currIter, b))	▷ *New checkpoint decision*
11: **break**	
12: **else if** |{pk | currVotes[pk] = Reject}| ≥ n/3	
13: OUTPUTCP(Checkpoint(currIter, ⊥))	▷ *Abort current iteration*
14: **break**	

LCs. At each time slot t, each honest node i outputs the k-deep prefix of the checkpoint-respecting LC (or the prefix of the latest checkpoint, whichever is longer) in its view as $\mathsf{LOG}_{\mathrm{da},i}^{t}$.

The accountability gadget Π_{acc} has three main components as shown on Fig. 1: a checkpoint vote generator (Algorithm 1) issues checkpoint proposals and votes, an accountable SMR protocol Π_{bft} is used to reach consensus on which votes to count for the checkpoint decision, and a checkpoint vote interpreter (Algorithm 2) outputs checkpoint decisions computed deterministically from the checkpoint votes sequenced by Π_{bft}. The protocol Π_{bft} can be instantiated with any accountable BFT protocol, *e.g.*, Streamlet [7], LibraBFT [23], or HotStuff [40]. It is used as a black box ordering service within Π_{acc} and is assumed to have confirmation time T_{confirm}. We denote the ledger output by Π_{bft} as $\mathsf{LOG}_{\mathrm{bft}}$, and emphasize that it is internal to Π_{acc}. Checkpoint vote generator and interpreter are run locally by each node and interact with Π_{bft} and $\mathsf{LOG}_{\mathrm{bft}}$. Hence, when we refer to $\mathsf{LOG}_{\mathrm{bft}}$ in the following, we mean the ledger in the view of a specific node.

The accountability gadget Π_{acc} proceeds in *checkpoint iterations* denoted by c, each of which attempts to checkpoint a block in Π_{lc}. The checkpoint vote generator produces requests which can be of three forms: ⟨propose, c, b⟩$_i$ proposes block b for checkpointing in iteration c, ⟨accept, c, b⟩$_i$ votes in favor of block b in iteration c, ⟨reject, c⟩$_i$ votes to reject iteration c. Here, ⟨...⟩$_i$ denotes a message signed by node i. Each iteration c has a publicly verifiable and unique random leader $\mathsf{L}^{(c)}$. The leader obtains the k_{cp}-deep block b on its checkpoint-respecting LC and broadcasts it to all other nodes as the checkpoint proposal for c (Algorithm 1, l. 7). Nodes receive checkpoint proposals (signed by the legitimate leader $\mathsf{L}^{(c)}$) from the network, and order them with respect to their checkpoint iteration (Algorithm 1, l. 21). A proposal is *valid* in view of node i if the proposed block is within i's checkpoint-respecting LC and extends all previous checkpoints observed by i. During an iteration c, each node i checks if the proposal received for c is valid (Algorithm 1, l. 11). If it has received a valid proposal with block

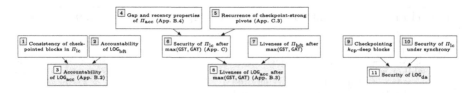

Fig. 3. Dependency of the security properties of $\mathsf{LOG}_{\mathrm{acc}}$ and $\mathsf{LOG}_{\mathrm{da}}$ on the properties of Π_{acc}, Π_{lc} and Π_{bft}.

b, it votes $\langle \mathsf{accept}, c, b \rangle_i$ (Algorithm 1, l. 12). Otherwise, if i does not receive any valid proposal for a timeout period T_{to}, i votes $\langle \mathsf{reject}, c \rangle_i$ (Algorithm 1, l. 14, 15). Votes are input as payload to Π_{bft}, which sequences them into ledger $\mathsf{LOG}_{\mathrm{bft}}$. Thus, nodes reach consensus on which votes to count for checkpoint decision of the given iteration.

The checkpoint vote interpreter (Algorithm 2) processes the sequence of votes in $\mathsf{LOG}_{\mathrm{bft}}$ to produce checkpoint decisions. Each node processes verified votes (*i.e.*, with valid signature) in the order they appear on $\mathsf{LOG}_{\mathrm{bft}}$ (Algorithm 2, l. 4). Upon observing $2n/3$ unique $\langle \mathsf{accept}, c, b \rangle_i$ votes for a block b and the current iteration c, each node outputs b as the *checkpoint* for c (Algorithm 2, l. 10). The checkpointed blocks output over time, together with their respective prefixes, constitute $\mathsf{LOG}_{\mathrm{acc},i}^t$. Furthermore, checkpoint decisions are fed back to Π_{lc} and the checkpoint vote generator to ensure consistency of future block production in Π_{lc} and of checkpoint proposals with prior checkpoints. Oppositely, upon observing $n/3$ unique $\langle \mathsf{reject}, c \rangle_i$ votes for the current iteration c, each node outputs $\perp$ as the checkpoint decision for c (Algorithm 2, l. 13) to signal that c was aborted with no new checkpointed block. This happens if honest nodes reject because they have not seen progress for too long. Once a node outputs a decision for current iteration c, the checkpoint vote interpreter proceeds to $c+1$; thus, only a single decision is output per iteration.

Upon receiving a new checkpoint for the current iteration c, nodes leave c of the checkpoint vote generator and enter $c + 1$ (Algorithm 1, l. 20). If the checkpoint decision was for $b \neq \perp$, nodes wait for T_{cp} time (*checkpoint interval*) before considering checkpoint proposals for $c+1$. As will become clear in the analysis, the checkpoint interval is crucial to ensure that Π_{lc}'s chain dynamics are 'not disturbed too much' by accommodating and respecting checkpoints. Note that throughout the execution there is only a single instantiation Π_{bft}, since the votes for different checkpoint iterations can still be ordered into a single sequence.

4.2 Security Properties

In this section, we formalize and prove the security properties **P1** and **P2** of Sect. 1.2 for accountability gadgets based on *permissioned* LC protocols [2,12,20, 33]. (For an extension of the security analysis to Proof-of-Work and Proof-of-Space LC protocols, see [29, Appendix F].)

For the worst case, we first fix $f = \lceil n/3 \rceil - 1$ and consider an accountability gadget Π_{acc} instantiated with a partially synchronous BFT protocol Π_{bft} that provides $(n - 2f)$-accountable-safety at all times, and f-liveness under partial synchrony after the network partition heals and sufficiently many honest nodes are awake. (An example Π_{bft} is HotStuff [40] with a quorum size $(n - f)$.)

Let λ and σ denote the security parameters associated with the employed cryptographic primitives and the LC protocol Π_{lc}, respectively. Then, the security properties of $\mathsf{LOG}_{\mathrm{acc}}$ and $\mathsf{LOG}_{\mathrm{da}}$ output by the accountability gadget Π_{acc} and the LC protocol Π_{lc} (modified to be checkpoint-respecting) are:

Theorem 2. *For any λ, σ, and $T_{\mathrm{confirm}}, k, k_{\mathrm{cp}}$ linear in σ:*

1. *(**P1: Accountability**) Under $(\mathcal{A}_{\mathrm{pda}}, \mathcal{Z}_{\mathrm{pda}})$, the accountable ledger $\mathsf{LOG}_{\mathrm{acc}}$ provides $(n - 2f)$-accountable-safety at all times (except with probability $\mathrm{negl}(\lambda)$), and there exists a constant $\mathbf{C}$ such that $\mathsf{LOG}_{\mathrm{acc}}$ provides f-liveness with confirmation time T_{confirm} after $\mathbf{C}\max(\mathsf{GST}, \mathsf{GAT})$ (except with probability $\mathrm{negl}(\sigma)$).*
2. *(**P2: Dynamic Availability**) Under $(\mathcal{A}_{\mathrm{da}}, \mathcal{Z}_{\mathrm{da}})$, the available ledger $\mathsf{LOG}_{\mathrm{da}}$ provides $1/2$-safety and $1/2$-liveness at all times (except with probability $\mathrm{negl}(\sigma) + \mathrm{negl}(\lambda)$).*
3. *(**Prefix**) $\mathsf{LOG}_{\mathrm{acc}}$ is always a prefix of $\mathsf{LOG}_{\mathrm{da}}$.*

Here, $\mathrm{negl}(.)$ denotes a negligible function that decays faster than all polynomials. To prove Theorem 2, we first focus on the security of $\mathsf{LOG}_{\mathrm{da}}$ under $(\mathcal{A}_{\mathrm{da}}, \mathcal{Z}_{\mathrm{da}})$, synchronous network with dynamic availability (⑪ of Fig. 3). We know from [2,12,20,33] that Π_{lc} is safe and live with some security parameter σ under the original LC rule when $\beta < 1/2$ (⑩). Hence, if k_{cp} is selected as an appropriate linear function of σ, once a block becomes k_{cp}-deep at time s in the LC held by an honest node, it stays on the LCs held by all honest nodes forever. Since there are at least $n - f > f$ accept votes for any block checkpointed by an honest node at time s, there is at least one honest node that voted accept for any such block. As honest nodes accept only proposals that are at least k_{cp}-deep in their LCs, (⑨), checkpointed blocks are already part of the LCs held by every other honest node at time s under $(\mathcal{A}_{\mathrm{da}}, \mathcal{Z}_{\mathrm{da}})$. Thus, new checkpoints can only appear in the common prefix of the honest nodes' LCs and do not affect the security of the LC protocol.

Next accountability and liveness of $\mathsf{LOG}_{\mathrm{acc}}$ under $(\mathcal{A}_{\mathrm{pda}}, \mathcal{Z}_{\mathrm{pda}})$ (③, ⑧). The pseudocode of Π_{acc} stipulates that honest nodes accept only proposals that are consistent with previous checkpoints (①), and a new checkpoint requires $(n - f)$ accept votes (l. 9 of Algorithm 2). Thus, in the event of a safety violation, either there are two inconsistent ledgers $\mathsf{LOG}_{\mathrm{bft}}$ held by honest nodes, or $(n - 2f)$

nodes have voted for inconsistent checkpoints. In both cases, $(n-2f)$ adversarial nodes are identified as violators by invoking either $(n-2f)$-accountable-safety of $\mathsf{LOG_{bft}}$ (②) or the consistency requirement for checkpoints (①), implying $(n-2f)$-accountable-safety of $\mathsf{LOG_{acc}}$. Detailed proof in [29, Appendix B.2].

Liveness of $\mathsf{LOG_{acc}}$ (⑧) requires the existence of iterations after $\max(\mathsf{GST}, \mathsf{GAT})$ where all honest nodes accept honest proposals. This, in turn, depends on whether the proposals by honest leaders are consistent with the checkpoint-respecting LCs at honest nodes after $\max(\mathsf{GST}, \mathsf{GAT})$. To show this, we prove that Π_{lc} recovers its security after $\max(\mathsf{GST}, \mathsf{GAT})$ (⑥). We first observe that with checkpoints, honest nodes abandon their LC if a new checkpoint appears on another (possibly shorter) chain. Then, some honest blocks produced meanwhile may not contribute to chain growth. This feature of checkpoint-respecting LCs violates a core assumption of the standard proof techniques [15, 20, 33] for LC protocols. To bound the number of abandoned honest blocks and demonstrate the *self-healing* property of checkpoint respecting LCs, we follow an approach introduced in [35]. We first observe the *gap* and *recency* properties for Π_{acc} ([29, Appendix B.4]) which are necessary conditions for any checkpointing mechanism to ensure self-healing of Π_{lc} (④). The gap property states that T_{cp} has to be sufficiently longer than the time it takes for a proposal to get checkpointed. The recency property requires that newly checkpointed blocks were held in the checkpoint-respecting LC of at least one honest node within a short time interval before the checkpoint decision.

Using the gap and recency properties, we next extend the analysis of [35] to permissioned protocols by introducing the concept of *checkpoint-strong pivots*, a generalization of strong pivots [33]. Whereas strong pivots count honest and adversarial blocks to claim convergence of the LC in the view of different honest nodes, checkpoint-strong pivots consider only honest blocks that are guaranteed to extend the checkpoint-respecting LC, thus resolving non-monotonicity for these chains. Recurrence of checkpoint-strong pivots after $\max(\mathsf{GST}, \mathsf{GAT})$ (⑤) along with the gap and recency properties lead to security of Π_{lc} after $\max(\mathsf{GST}, \mathsf{GAT})$. Details in [29, Appendix C]. Given self-healing of Π_{lc}, liveness of $\mathsf{LOG_{acc}}$ follows from liveness of Π_{bft} after $\max(\mathsf{GST}, \mathsf{GAT})$ (⑦). Full proof in [29, Appendix B.3].

Finally, the prefix property follows readily from the way in which both $\mathsf{LOG_{da}}$ and $\mathsf{LOG_{acc}}$ are derived from the checkpoint-respecting LC.

5   Experimental Evaluation

To evaluate whether the protocol of Sect. 4.1 can be a drop-in replacement for the Ethereum 2 beacon chain, we have implemented a prototype[4]. Our protocol incurs average required bandwidth comparable to Gasper at reduced latency of $\mathsf{LOG_{acc}}$. Gasper's resilience decreases as the number of nodes increases, for

---

[4] Source code: https://github.com/tse-group/accountability-gadget-prototype.

fixed latency of LOG_{acc}, due to a new attack [28], whereas our protocol is provably secure. Supplemental material of experimental evaluation is given in [29, Appendix D].

A diagram of the different components of our prototype and their interactions is provided in Fig. 4. We use a longest chain protocol modified to respect latest checkpoints as Π_{lc}, with a permissioned block production lottery; and a variant of HotStuff[5] as Π_{bft}. All communication (including HotStuff's) takes place in a broadcast fashion via libp2p's Gossipsub protocol[6], mimicking Ethereum 2 [1]. The parameters of our protocol match the number of validators ($n = 4096$), average block inter-arrival time (12 s) and block payload size (22 KBytes) of the Ethereum 2 beacon chain. We chose $k_{cp} = 6$ so that an honest checkpoint proposal is likely accepted by honest nodes, and $k = 6$ for swift 72 s average latency of LOG_{da}. Setting $T_{hs} = 20$ s and $T_{to} = 1$ min avoids HotStuff timeouts escalating into checkpoint timeouts unnecessarily. Finally, to target 5× improvement in average LOG_{acc} latency over Gasper (*cf.* Fig. 7, we set $T_{cp} = 5$ min.

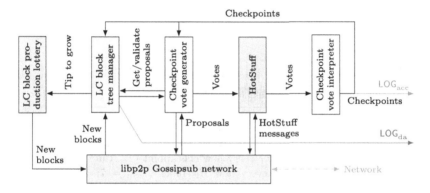

Fig. 4. Components and their interactions in implementation of Fig. 1. Gray: off the shelf components used as black boxes. Blue: taken from Π_{lc} without modification. Green: taken from Π_{lc}, modified to respect checkpoints. (Color figure online)

Adversarial nodes in the experiment boycott leader duty in Π_{bft} and mine selfishly [14] in Π_{lc}. We ran our prototype (a) with no adversary (Fig. 2(l)), and (b) with $\beta = 25\%$ adversary (Fig. 2(r)), each for 2500 s on five AWS EC2 c5a.8xlarge instances in each of ten AWS regions with 82 nodes per machine, for a total of 4100 nodes. Each honest (adversarial) node connected to 15 (15 honest, 15 adversarial) randomly selected peers for the peer-to-peer network. Both without (Fig. 2(l)) and under attack (Fig. 2(r)) LOG_{da} (——) grows steadily, albeit under attack slower due to selfish mining. In both cases, LOG_{acc} (——) periodically catches up with LOG_{da}. Timeouts cause minor delayed catch-up.

---

[5] We used this Rust implementation: https://github.com/asonnino/hotstuff [16].
[6] We used this Rust implementation: https://github.com/libp2p/rust-libp2p [39].

Network traffic (Figs. 5, 6 *for an exemplary AWS instance, i.e.*, for 82 nodes) shows frequent small spikes for Π_{lc} blocks and infrequent wide spikes for Π_{acc} votes and Π_{bft} blocks and votes. Traffic increases slightly under attack (per node: avg. $78\,\mathrm{KB/s}$ vs. $56\,\mathrm{KB/s}$, peak $1.5\,\mathrm{MB/s}$ vs. $1.34\,\mathrm{MB/s}$) because inactive adversarial leaders cause more iterations in Π_{acc} and Π_{bft}. The bandwidth requirement does not limit participation using consumer-grade Internet access. Note that our prototype does not employ bandwidth reduction techniques that are orthogonal to the consensus problem, such as aggregate and short signatures or spreading the vote out over time. Figure 7 corroborates that even if voting was artificially rate-limited and thus spread out over time (as is the case in Gasper), bandwidth and latency comparable to Gasper could be achieved.

Figure 7 compares bandwidth and latency of $\mathsf{LOG}_{\mathrm{acc}}$ for varying parameters and $\beta = 0, \Delta = 0$. Gasper transmits $2 \cdot \frac{n}{C}$ votes per $12\,\mathrm{s}$, with C the number of slots per epoch, our protocol transmits $5 \cdot n$ votes per T_{cp} time. A transaction takes on average $\frac{1}{2}+2$ epochs to enter into $\mathsf{LOG}_{\mathrm{acc}}$ for Gasper, and $k_{\mathrm{cp}} \cdot 12\,\mathrm{s}+\frac{1}{2} \cdot T_{\mathrm{cp}}$ time to enter $\mathsf{LOG}_{\mathrm{acc}}$ for our protocol. Our protocol offers slightly improved

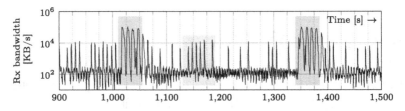

Fig. 5. Setting of Fig. 2(l): The network traffic for each AWS instance (i.e., 82 nodes) shows four marked spikes (red) for every new checkpoint (T_{cp} time = 5 min interval) and smaller spikes (orange) for every new Π_{lc} block (T_{slot} = 7:5 s interval). (Color figure online)

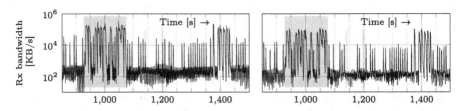

Fig. 6. Setting of Fig. 2(r): Leader timeouts in Π_{bft} and Π_{acc} can delay new checkpoints (red). *E.g.*, after the end of a checkpoint interval ($t \approx 870\,\mathrm{s}$), and subsequent Π_{acc} leader timeout ($t \approx 930\,\mathrm{s}$), honest nodes vote to reject the current checkpoint iteration, but the decision is delayed by another Π_{bft} leader timeout. The next checkpoint iteration has an honest leader, but a decision is again delayed by a Π_{bft} leader timeout, until a new checkpoint is finally reached ($t \approx 1070\,\mathrm{s}$). Traffic at honest nodes (**right**) lacks some of the small spikes (orange) of traffic at adversarial nodes (**left**), since the adversary temporarily withholds some of its blocks from honest nodes due to selfish mining. (Color figure online)

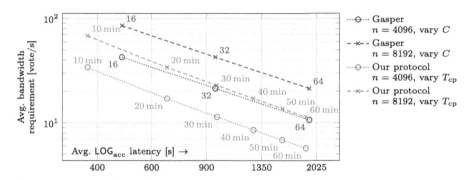

Fig. 7. For fixed n, the average latency of $\mathsf{LOG}_{\mathrm{acc}}$ for Gasper and our protocol (here for $k_{\mathrm{cp}} = 6$) increases with the number C of slots per epoch and with T_{cp}, respectively, while the bandwidth required for votes reduces proportionally. Our protocol offers a better tradeoff and can tolerate twice the n at comparable latency and bandwidth (our protocol for $n = 8192, T_{\mathrm{cp}} = 30\,\mathrm{min}$ vs. Gasper for $n = 4096, C = 32$).

latency at comparable bandwidth, or comparable bandwidth and latency but for a larger number of nodes.

Acknowledgment. JN, ENT, and DT are supported by the Reed-Hodgson Stanford Graduate Fellowship, the Stanford Center for Blockchain Research, and the Center for Science of Information (CSoI), an NSF Science and Technology Center under grant agreement CCF-0939370, respectively.

References

1. Ethereum 2.0 networking specification (2021). https://github.com/ethereum/eth2. 0-specs/blob/dev/specs/phase0/p2p-interface.md
2. Badertscher, C., Gaži, P., Kiayias, A., Russell, A., Zikas, V.: Ouroboros genesis: composable proof-of-stake blockchains with dynamic availability. In: Conference on Computer and Communications Security, CCS 2018, pp. 913–930. ACM (2018)
3. Buchman, E., Kwon, J., Milosevic, Z.: The latest gossip on BFT consensus. arXiv:1807.04938 (2018)
4. Buterin, V., Griffith, V.: Casper the friendly finality gadget. arXiv:1710.09437 (2019)
5. Buterin, V., et al.: Combining GHOST and Casper. arXiv:2003.03052 (2020)
6. Castro, M., Liskov, B.: Practical byzantine fault tolerance. In: Symposium on Operating Systems Design and Implementation, OSDI 1999, pp. 173–186. USENIX Association (1999)
7. Chan, B.Y., Shi, E.: Streamlet: textbook streamlined blockchains. In: Advances in Financial Technologies, AFT 2020, pp. 1–11. ACM (2020)
8. Chen, J., Gorbunov, S., Micali, S., Vlachos, G.: ALGORAND AGREEMENT: Super fast and partition resilient Byzantine agreement. IACR Cryptology ePrint Archive, Report 2018/377 (2018)
9. Chen, J., Micali, S.: Algorand: a secure and efficient distributed ledger. Theoret. Comput. Sci. **777**, 155–183 (2019)

10. Civit, P., Gilbert, S., Gramoli, V.: Polygraph: accountable Byzantine agreement. In: ICDCS, pp. 403–413. IEEE (2021)
11. Cohen, B., Pietrzak, K.: The Chia Network blockchain (2019). www.chia.net/assets/ChiaGreenPaper.pdf
12. David, B., Gaži, P., Kiayias, A., Russell, A.: Ouroboros Praos: an adaptively-secure, semi-synchronous proof-of-stake blockchain. In: Nielsen, J.B., Rijmen, V. (eds.) EUROCRYPT 2018. LNCS, vol. 10821, pp. 66–98. Springer, Cham (2018). https://doi.org/10.1007/978-3-319-78375-8_3
13. Dinsdale-Young, T., Magri, B., Matt, C., Nielsen, J., Tschudi, D.: Afgjort: a partially synchronous finality layer for blockchains. In: Conference on Security and Cryptography for Networks, SCN 2020, pp. 24–44. (2020)
14. Eyal, I., Sirer, E.G.: Majority is not enough: Bitcoin mining is vulnerable. Commun. ACM 61(7), 95–102 (2018)
15. Garay, J., Kiayias, A., Leonardos, N.: The Bitcoin backbone protocol: analysis and applications. In: Oswald, E., Fischlin, M. (eds.) EUROCRYPT 2015. LNCS, vol. 9057, pp. 281–310. Springer, Heidelberg (2015). https://doi.org/10.1007/978-3-662-46803-6_10
16. Gelashvili, R., Kokoris-Kogias, L., Sonnino, A., Spiegelman, A., Xiang, Z.: Jolteon and Ditto: network-adaptive efficient consensus with asynchronous fallback. In: Financial Cryptography and Data Security. FC 2022 (2022)
17. Guo, Y., Pass, R., Shi, E.: Synchronous, with a chance of partition tolerance. In: Boldyreva, A., Micciancio, D. (eds.) CRYPTO 2019. LNCS, vol. 11692, pp. 499–529. Springer, Cham (2019). https://doi.org/10.1007/978-3-030-26948-7_18
18. Haeberlen, A., Kouznetsov, P., Druschel, P.: PeerReview: Practical accountability for distributed systems. SIGOPS Oper. Syst. Rev. 41(6), 175–188 (2007)
19. Haeberlen, A., Kuznetsov, P.: The Fault Detection Problem. In: International Conference on Principles of Distributed Systems. OPODIS 2009 (2009)
20. Kiayias, A., Russell, A., David, B., Oliynykov, R.: Ouroboros: a provably secure proof-of-stake blockchain protocol. In: Katz, J., Shacham, H. (eds.) CRYPTO 2017. LNCS, vol. 10401, pp. 357–388. Springer, Cham (2017). https://doi.org/10.1007/978-3-319-63688-7_12
21. Lewis-Pye, A., Roughgarden, T.: Resource pools and the CAP theorem. arXiv:2006.10698 (2020)
22. Lewis-Pye, A., Roughgarden, T.: How does blockchain security dictate blockchain implementation? In: CCS, pp. 1006–1019. ACM (2021)
23. Libra Association: Libra white paper (2020). https://www.libra.org/en-US/white-paper/
24. Nakamoto, S.: Bitcoin: a peer-to-peer electronic cash system (2008). https://bitcoin.org/bitcoin.pdf
25. Nakamura, R.: Analysis of bouncing attack on FFG (2019). http://ethresear.ch/t/analysis-of-bouncing-attack-on-ffg/6113
26. Neu, J., Tas, E.N., Tse, D.: A balancing attack on Gasper, the current candidate for Eth2's beacon chain (2020). https://ethresear.ch/t/a-balancing-attack-on-gasper-the-current-candidate-for-eth2s-beacon-chain/8079
27. Neu, J., Tas, E.N., Tse, D.: Snap-and-chat protocols: system aspects. arXiv:2010.10447 (2020)
28. Neu, J., Tas, E.N., Tse, D.: Attacking Gasper without adversarial network delay (2021). https://ethresear.ch/t/attacking-gasper-without-adversarial-network-delay/10187
29. Neu, J., Tas, E.N., Tse, D.: The availability-accountability dilemma and its resolution via accountability gadgets. arXiv:2105.06075 (2021)

30. Neu, J., Tas, E.N., Tse, D.: Ebb-and-flow protocols: a resolution of the availability-finality dilemma. In: IEEE Symposium on Security and Privacy, pp. 446–465. IEEE (2021)
31. Neu, J., Tas, E.N., Tse, D.: Two attacks on proof-of-stake GHOST/Ethereum. arXiv:2203.01315 (2022)
32. Pass, R., Shi, E.: Rethinking large-scale consensus. In: Computer Security Foundations Symposium, CSF 2017, pp. 115–129. IEEE (2017)
33. Pass, R., Shi, E.: The sleepy model of consensus. In: Takagi, T., Peyrin, T. (eds.) ASIACRYPT 2017. LNCS, vol. 10625, pp. 380–409. Springer, Cham (2017). https://doi.org/10.1007/978-3-319-70697-9_14
34. Ranchal-Pedrosa, A., Gramoli, V.: Blockchain is dead, long live blockchain! accountable state machine replication for longlasting blockchain. arXiv:2007.10541 (2020)
35. Sankagiri, S., Wang, X., Kannan, S., Viswanath, P.: Blockchain CAP theorem allows user-dependent adaptivity and finality. In: Borisov, N., Diaz, C. (eds.) FC 2021. LNCS, vol. 12675, pp. 84–103. Springer, Heidelberg (2021). https://doi.org/10.1007/978-3-662-64331-0_5
36. Schwarz-Schilling, C., Neu, J., Monnot, B., Asgaonkar, A., Tas, E.N., Tse, D.: Three attacks on proof-of-stake Ethereum. In: Financial Cryptography and Data Security. FC 2022 (2022)
37. Sheng, P., Wang, G., Nayak, K., Kannan, S., Viswanath, P.: BFT protocol forensics. In: CCS, pp. 1722–1743. ACM (2021)
38. Stewart, A., Kokoris-Kogia, E.: GRANDPA: a Byzantine finality gadget. arXiv:2007.01560 (2020)
39. Vyzovitis, D., Napora, Y., McCormick, D., Dias, D., Psaras, Y.: GossipSub: attack-resilient message propagation in the Filecoin and ETH2.0 networks. arXiv:2007.02754 (2020)
40. Yin, M., Malkhi, D., Reiter, M.K., Gueta, G.G., Abraham, I.: HotStuff: BFT consensus with linearity and responsiveness. In: Symposium on Principles of Distributed Computing, PODC 2019, pp. 347–356. ACM (2019)

Three Attacks on Proof-of-Stake Ethereum

Caspar Schwarz-Schilling[1] , Joachim Neu[2] , Barnabé Monnot[1] ,
Aditya Asgaonkar[1], Ertem Nusret Tas[2](✉) , and David Tse[2]

[1] Ethereum Foundation, Berlin, Germany
{caspar.schwarz-schilling,barnabe.monnot,aditya.asgaonkar}@ethereum.org
[2] Stanford University, Stanford, USA
{jneu,nusret,dntse}@stanford.edu

Abstract. Recently, two attacks were presented against Proof-of-Stake
(PoS) Ethereum: one where short-range reorganizations of the underlying consensus chain are used to increase individual validators' profits and delay consensus decisions, and one where adversarial network
delay is leveraged to stall consensus decisions indefinitely. We provide
refined variants of these attacks, considerably relaxing the requirements
on adversarial stake and network timing, and thus rendering the attacks
more severe. Combining techniques from both refined attacks, we obtain
a third attack which allows an adversary with vanishingly small fraction
of stake and no control over network message propagation (assuming
instead probabilistic message propagation) to cause even long-range consensus chain reorganizations. Honest-but-rational or ideologically motivated validators could use this attack to increase their profits or stall the
protocol, threatening incentive alignment and security of PoS Ethereum.
The attack can also lead to destabilization of consensus from congestion
in vote processing.

1 Introduction

The Proof-of-Stake (PoS) Ethereum consensus protocol [1,2,4] is constructed by
applying the finality gadget Casper FFG [6] on top of the fork choice rule LMD
GHOST, a flavor of the Greedy Heaviest-Observed Sub-Tree (GHOST) [20] rule
which considers only each participant's most recent vote (Latest Message Driven,
LMD). Participants with stake that allows them to vote as part of the protocol
are called *validators*. A slightly simplified and analytically more tractable variant
of PoS Ethereum is given by the Gasper protocol [7].

Recent works [16,18,19] have presented two attacks on Gasper and PoS
Ethereum. The first attack [19] uses short-range reorganizations (*reorgs*) of the
blockchain stipulating consensus to delay finality of consensus decisions. Such
short-range reorgs also allow validators to increase their earnings from participating in the protocol (*e.g.*, from Maximal Extractable Value, MEV [10]). As a
result, honest-but-rational validators will deviate from the protocol, threatening
the assumptions underlying the security arguments for it. In the second attack

© International Financial Cryptography Association 2022
I. Eyal and J. Garay (Eds.): FC 2022, LNCS 13411, pp. 560–576, 2022.
https://doi.org/10.1007/978-3-031-18283-9_28

[16,18], the adversary exploits adversarial network delay and strategic voting by a vanishing fraction of adversarial validators to stall the protocol indefinitely.

Our Contributions. In this paper we present enhanced variants of the above two attacks [18,19]. First, we reduce the number of validators necessary to launch a short-range reorg. An adversary who could perform a reorg of k blocks (k-*reorg*) using the old strategy [19] is now able to perform a $(k+1)$-reorg using our new strategy. In particular, an adversary with 0.09% of total stake is in a position to execute a 1-reorg for any given day with 99.6% probability. Second, we considerably relax the network assumption under which the adversary can stall PoS Ethereum using techniques similar to [16,18]: we show that the adversary does not need to exert control over message propagation delays, but that merely stationary *probabilistic* network delay, as is commonly assumed to model networks under normal operation, together with a still vanishingly small (albeit slightly larger than before) fraction of adversarial validators suffices for the adversary to be able to effectively stall the protocol. We then combine techniques from both refined attacks to devise a long-range reorg attack which requires only an extremely small number of adversarial validators and no adversarial (but only probabilistic) network delay.

This third attack is particularly severe for PoS Ethereum for three reasons: 1. Honest-but-rational validators might adopt the strategy as they can use it to increase their payouts from MEV and transaction fees. The resulting protocol deviations destabilize consensus on both the fork choice and the finality gadget level because the blockchain does not grow steadily anymore. 2. Reorgs lead to uncertainty and delay in block confirmation, impacting user experience and quality of service, and undermining users' trust in the protocol. 3. Reorgs can reduce the throughput of the consensus layer to the point where not enough votes can be processed timely, reducing resilience against adversarial validators and jeopardizing proper functioning of PoS Ethereum.

Related Work. In both selfish mining [11] and our attacks the adversary withholds blocks to displace honest blocks from the chain. Unlike selfish mining however, our attacks do not lead to an increased block production reward. Undercutting attacks [12] showcase how consensus instability can arise from reorgs incentivized by large variance in block rewards. In fact, this concern will be aggravated by diminishing block rewards in Bitcoin in the future [9]. Timebandit attacks [10] point out that MEV earned in past blocks can incentivize and subsidize reorgs and other attacks in the future, *e.g.*, for renting hash power or bribing validators.

Outline. PoS Ethereum and its network model are reviewed in Sect. 2. Sections 3 and 4 each first introduce a recent attack and then describe our refined variant thereof. Combining techniques from our refined attacks, we devise a long-range reorg attack in Sect. 5. We discuss in Sect. 6 the impact of the presented long-range reorg attack on various aspects of PoS Ethereum.

2   Proof-of-Stake Ethereum: The Gasper Protocol

We provide a concise summary of the PoS Ethereum/Gasper protocol and the network environment it is designed for. The exposition is slightly idealized and streamlined for ease of comprehension. For all details, refer to the paper [7] of Gasper and the PoS Ethereum beacon chain protocol specifications [1, 2, 4].

2.1   Model

We assume a static pool of N protocol participants (called *validators* or *nodes*), each with unit stake. This corresponds to consensus in a *permissioned* setting. Network communication among validators is synchronous, *i.e.*, network delay is under adversarial control, up to a known delay upper bound Δ. Clocks across nodes are synchronized. This amounts to a *synchronous network* [13]. There is an external shared source of randomness which can be used by the protocol to sample a group (of predetermined size) of validators in a uniform manner without replacement. Validators follow the protocol as prescribed, except for a fraction β which are under adversarial control and can deviate from the protocol in arbitrary and coordinated fashion (*Byzantine faults*).

In its basic version, the state machine replication (SMR) formulation of consensus asks for a protocol that can be run among the N protocol participants to obtain a linear ordering of *transactions* input by the environment to participants, into a shared *ledger* (*i.e.*, to implement an ordering service) with the following security properties:

- *Liveness:* If some honest validator becomes aware of a transaction, then not too long thereafter that transaction will have entered the ledger as output by any honest validator (*i.e.*, 'good things do happen', 'transactions enter the ledger').
- *Safety:* The ledgers output by different honest validators at different points in time are consistent. In other words, it does not happen that a transaction, which has once entered the ledger in some honest validator's view at some time, disappears later (*i.e.*, 'bad things do not happen', 'if a transaction enters the ledger, then it will not leave it').

Given an SMR protocol, we seek to understand for which adversarial fractions β the ledger output by that protocol is both safe and live (and hence *secure*).

2.2   Protocol

Being a composite with the LMD GHOST fork choice rule as the basis and Casper FFG as a finality gadget on top, PoS Ethereum consensus proceeds roughly in two stages and on two time scales.

First, on the smaller time scale where LMD GHOST operates, time proceeds in synchronized slots of duration 2Δ. For each slot, one *block proposer* and a *committee* of W validators is drawn uniformly at random from the N validators.

The following LMD GHOST rule is used to determine a canonical block (and its prefix of blocks as a canonical chain) in a node's view in slot t: "Starting at the highest block b_0 'justified' by Casper FFG (see below), sum for each child block b the number of unique (i.e., one per slot and slot's committee member, breaking ties adversarially) valid (i.e., only from earlier than the current slot, and no voting on future blocks) votes for that block and its descendants; count for every validator only its most recently cast vote (LMD). Pick the child block b^* with highest weight (GHOST) (breaking ties adversarially). Recurse ($b_0 \leftarrow b^*$), until reaching a leaf block. Output that leaf block." At the beginning of each slot, the slot's proposer determines a block using LMD GHOST and extends it with a new proposal. Half way into each slot (i.e., Δ time after the proposal and after the beginning of the slot), the slot's committee members determine a block using LMD GHOST in their view and vote for it (votes are also called *attestations*). (At the same time they also cast a Casper FFG vote, as described later.) An exact confirmation rule of LMD GHOST/Gasper is not specified.

Second, on the larger time scale where Casper FFG operates, time proceeds in epochs comprised of 32 slots. On a high level, Casper FFG is a two-phase traditional propose-and-vote-style Byzantine fault tolerant (BFT) consensus protocol (cast as a blockchain protocol into the chained framework, like Chained HotStuff [22]), except there is no leader in charge of assembling proposals. Instead, the proposals are supposed to be generated consistently across honest nodes by the LMD GHOST fork choice layer. Casper FFG proceeds as follows: Blocks first become justified if a super-majority ($2N/3$) votes 'for them', and subsequently become finalized, roughly when a super-majority votes 'from them' for a subsequent block. The genesis block is justified and finalized by definition. The blocks among which validators cast their votes during an epoch are the so-called epoch boundary blocks, which are those blocks that are leaf blocks after truncating the block tree to only those blocks that came from the previous epoch. Validators vote for the highest epoch boundary block that is consistent with the highest justified block they have observed, which in turn extends the latest finalized block they have observed. Due to the super-majority required to advance a proposal, as well as the two-phase confirmation (called *finalization*), Casper FFG remains safe even under temporary network partition. The confirmation rule on the Casper FFG level is to output the latest finalized block and its prefix.

3 A Refined Reorg Attack

3.1 Motivation

Previous work [19] described a malicious, low-cost reorg attack. In particular, the attack leverages strategic timing of broadcasting blocks and attestations, as opposed to honestly releasing them when supposed to. In a nutshell, in the strategy of [19], an adversarial block proposer in slot n keeps its proposal hidden. The honest block proposer in slot $n+1$ will then propose a competing block. The adversary can now use its committee members' votes from both slots n and $n+1$ to vote for the withheld block of slot n in an attempt to outnumber honest votes

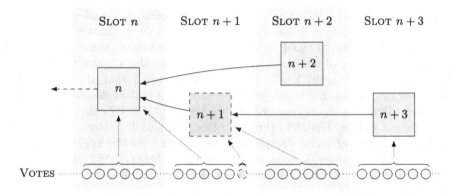

Fig. 1. Example of a one-block reorg attack using the refined strategy: In slot $n+1$ the adversary privately creates block $n+1$ on block n and attests to it. Honest validators of slot $n+1$ do not see any block and thus attest to block n as head of the chain. In the next slot, an honest proposer publishes block $n+2$ building on block n, which is the current head in their view. Simultaneously, the adversary finally publishes block $n+1$ and the attestation voting for block $n+1$. All honest validators of slot $n+2$ attest to block $n+1$ as head of the chain, because it has more weight than block $n+2$. In the next slot block $n+3$ is proposed building on block $n+1$. Block $n+2$ is reorged out.

on the proposal of slot $n+1$. As a result, blocks proposed by honest validators may end up orphaned, *i.e.*, they are displaced out of the chain chosen by LMD GHOST. In [19] this reorg strategy is part of a bigger scheme to delay consensus.

We show how the attack of [19] can be modified such that the number of adversary validators required is significantly reduced, from a set of size linear in the total number of validators to a constant-size set – indeed for a one-block reorg as little as one adversarial validator is sufficient. Note that similar to [19] the adversarial strategy does not involve any slashable behavior[1] and is therefore relatively cheap. In Sect. 5, we further improve upon this refined reorg attack, combining strategies from both this section and Sect. 4.

3.2 Refined Reorg Strategy

Consider Fig. 1, which shows the adversary being the proposer of slot $n+1$ as well as controlling a committee member in slot $n+1$. We describe the adversarial strategy to perform a 1-reorg:

1. At the beginning of slot $n+1$ the adversary privately creates block $n+1$ on block n and privately attests to it. Honest validators do not see block $n+1$ and so they attest to the previous head of the chain, block n.
2. At the beginning of the next slot, an honest validator proposes block $n+2$. Assuming zero network latency for now, the adversary finally publishes the

---

[1] Some provably protocol-violating validator actions are *slashable* in the sense that the responsible validator's deposit may get confiscated to deter from such behavior.

private block and attestation from slot $n+1$ at the same time as block $n+2$ is released. Honest validators now see both block $n+1$ (and its one attestation) as well as block $n+2$. These blocks are conflicting because they share the same parent, block n. Another result of sharing the same parent is that block $n+1$ inherits all the weight of block n, in particular the honest attestations from slot $n+1$ voting for block n also count in favor of it.

3. Hence, in slot $n+2$ all honest validators vote for block $n+1$ as head of the chain, because it has more weight due to the single adversarial attestation from slot $n+1$.

4. Finally, at the beginning of slot $n+3$, an honest validator proposes block $n+3$ pointing to block $n+1$ as its parent. This effectively orphans block $n+2$ and brings the reorg attack to its conclusion.

The above strategy shows that a block proposer which controls a single committee member of the same slot can successfully perform a 1-reorg. Naturally, the logic of this strategy can be extended to reorg attacks of arbitrary length k. Let the number of honest validators in any given committee be $W_{\text{honest}} \approx (1-\beta)W \leq W$. Then, for a successful reorg attack of length $k > 1$, the proposing adversary needs to control $W_{\text{honest}}(k-1) + 1$ validators, since it offsets honest committee members' votes in the first $(k-1)$ slots and uses the above refined attack strategy in the last slot.

The refined reorg attacked described here improves on the strategy proposed in [19] by removing the need for the adversary to compete with the committee of slot $n+k+1$. While the improvement for long-range reorg attacks may not be as significant, short reorg attacks are considerably more feasible using the above refined strategy. In particular, 1-reorg attacks are effectively always possible for large enough parties. With currently 230,000 active validators[2] and 32 slots per epoch, an adversary controlling 200 validators (which amounts to 0.09% of total stake) has a 99.8% chance of being selected block proposer at least once per any given day, and once selected as block proposer in a particular slot controls at least one committee member validator in that slot with probability 99.8%. So with more than 99.6% probability, an adversary with 0.09% of total stake is in a position to execute a 1-reorg for any given day.

We will now relax the assumption of zero network latency. PoS Ethereum's fork choice rule only considers attestations that are at least one slot old [2] (so votes from slot $n+2$ do not count in the fork choice for slot $n+2$). Further, a committee member is supposed to attest if "(a) the validator has received a valid block from the expected block proposer for the assigned slot or (b) one-third of the slot has transpired [...] - whichever comes first"[3] [4]. After block $n+2$ is broadcasted to the network, honest validators immediately attest to it upon reception (unless by that time they see another chain as leading in fork choice). Thus, the adversary must ensure that a majority of validators of slot $n+2$ see block $n+1$ and the adversary's attestation voting for block $n+1$ (from slot

---

[2] https://beaconcha.in/validators. Accessed: 2021-10-09.

[3] Regarding attestation timing, PoS Ethereum practice slightly deviates from Gasper.

$n + 1$) before they see block $n + 2$, but after block $n + 2$ was proposed (to ensure it extends block n). This proves to be a non-trivial but practically feasible issue.

Suppose the adversary controls a number of nodes at different 'locations' in the topology of the peer-to-peer gossip network [3] (these nodes might still be physically collocated). This is possible without greater difficulty because the gossip network has no defenses against such Sybil attacks. Then, some adversarial node will likely receive the new proposal block $n + 2$ relatively early on in its dissemination process. The adversary can then release the private block and attestation in a coordinated fashion from all the different locations in the peer-to-peer topology where the adversary controls nodes. Due to the superior number of sources of the adversarial block and attestation it is likely that these arrive earlier than the proposal block $n + 2$ at enough (a majority of) honest nodes to ultimately orphan block $n + 2$.

4   A Refined Liveness Attack

4.1   Motivation

Earlier works [8,14–16,18] have described balancing-type attacks against variants of the GHOST fork choice rule used in PoS Ethereum as modelled in the Gasper protocol [7]. In particular, the attack described in [16,18] uses adversarial network delay to show that PoS Ethereum is not secure in traditional (partially) synchronous networks. While adversarial network delay (up to some delay bound) is a widely employed assumption in the consensus literature, there is disagreement whether it is appropriate for Internet-scale open-participation consensus. As a result, past attacks are often seen as impractical and have not been mitigated: "Note that this attack does depend on networking assumptions that are highly contrived in practice (the attacker having fine-grained control over latencies of individual validators), [...]" [5]

We show how the attack of [16,18] can be modified and implemented [17] so that an adversary controlling 15% of stake can stall PoS Ethereum *without requiring adversarial network delay*. (For ever larger numbers of validators, ever smaller fractions of adversarial stake suffice.) To this end, we show through experiments that aggregate properties of many individually random message propagation processes (*e.g.*, 'within time T this transmission is received by fraction x of nodes') in real-world Internet-scale peer-to-peer gossip networks [3,21] are sufficiently predictable to give the adversary the required control over how many validators see which adversarial messages when. None of the adversarial actions are slashable protocol violations.

4.2   High-Level Idea

Recall that the *balancing attack* [16,18] consists of two steps: First, adversarial block proposers initiate two competing chains – call them Left and Right. Then,

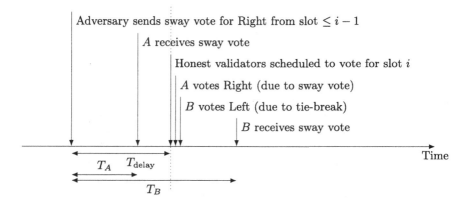

Fig. 2. Assuming a tie between two chains Left and Right, with tie-break favoring Left. The adversary releases a sway vote for Right from a slot $< i$ at time T_{delay} before the point in time at which honest validators vote in slot i according to the protocol. The parameter T_{delay} is chosen such that roughly half of honest validators (such as A) receive the sway vote *before* they submit their vote (and hence vote Right, as Right *now* has more votes *in their view*), and the other half of honest validators (such as B) receive the sway vote *after* they submit their vote for (and hence vote Left, as the tie-break *still* favors Left *in their view*).

a handful of adversarial votes per slot, released under carefully chosen circumstances, suffice to steer honest validators' votes so as to keep the system in a tie between the two chains and consequently stall consensus.

Assume, w.l.o.g., that when viewing Left and Right with equal number of votes, the protocol's tie-break favors Left over Right. If the adversary manages to deliver a withheld adversarial vote for Right from an earlier slot to roughly one half of honest validators for the current slot i, before validators submit their votes for slot i, while the other half does not receive said vote before casting their votes, then roughly half of honest validators (those who have received the sway vote 'in time') see Right as leading and will vote for it in slot i, while the other half (those who see the sway vote 'late' and hence at the time of voting see a tie which they break in favor of Left) will vote for Left in slot i (see Fig. 2).

Idealizing the above as voting according to a coin flip for each validator, roughly $W_{\text{honest}}/2$ of W_{honest} honest validators per slot would vote Left and Right, respectively, with a gap of $O(\sqrt{W_{\text{honest}}})$ (*cf.* variance of a binomially distributed random variable). So, $O(1/\sqrt{W_{\text{honest}}})$ adversarial fraction of stake would suffice to rebalance the vote to a tie and keep the system in limbo. In Sect. 4.4 we provide evidence from real-world propagation delay measurements in a replica of Ethereum 2's gossip network [3] to support the hypothesis that the adversary can indeed reliably determine the time T_{delay} it takes for approximately half of nodes to receive a message broadcast by the adversary.

4.3   Detailed Description

First we describe the attack for a given T_{delay}, then we describe how to obtain T_{delay}. Our simulation[4] using the gossip network propagation model obtained in Sect. 4.4 provides further details.

First, the adversary waits for an opportune epoch to launch the attack. An epoch is opportune if the block proposers in slot 0 and 1 are adversarial (this can be strengthened). Due to the random committee selection in PoS Ethereum, this happens with probability β^2 for any given epoch, so that the adversary needs to wait on average $1/\beta^2$ epochs until it can launch the attack. In the following, assume epoch 0 is opportune. The adversarial proposers of slots 0 and 1 propose conflicting new chains 'Left' and 'Right', respectively. Note that this is not a slashable protocol violation. Both withhold their proposals so that none of slot 0 or 1 honest validators vote for either block. The adversary releases the blocks after slot 1. We assume w.l.o.g. that the tie between Left and Right (recall that no vote has been cast for either so far) is broken in favor of Left.

Time T_{delay} before honest validators in slot 2 vote, the adversary releases a vote for Right from an adversarial committee member of slot 1 (so called *sway vote*, see Fig. 2). If T_{delay} is tuned well to the network propagation behavior *at large*, then roughly one half of honest committee members of slot 2 see the sway vote before they cast their vote, and thus view Right as leading (due to the sway vote) and will vote for it; and the other half see the sway vote only after they cast their vote, and thus view Left as leading (due to the tie-break) at the time of voting and will vote for it. Once the adversary has observed the outcome of the vote, which now should be a split up to an $O(\sqrt{W_{\text{honest}}})$ gap, the adversary uses its slot 2 committee members (which stipulates the adversarial fraction $O(1/\sqrt{W_{\text{honest}}})$ required for this attack) as well as slot 0 and 1 committee members to rebalance the vote to a tie. As the tie is restored, the adversary can use the same strategy in the following slot, and so forth.

Note that the adversary can observe the outcome of a vote and learns how many honest committee members saw Left and Right leading, respectively. The adversary can use this information to improve its estimate of T_{delay}. We show in Sect. 4.4 that the optimal T_{delay} can be reliably localized using grid search.

4.4   Experimental Evaluation

To understand whether the network propagation delay distribution is sufficiently well-behaved for an adversary to reproducibly broadcast messages so that they arrive at roughly half of nodes by a fixed deadline, we replicated the gossip network of Ethereum 2 [3] and measured the network propagation delay of test 'ping' packets from a designated sender to all nodes. The implementation in the Rust programming language used libp2p's Gossipsub protocol and implementation, as is used in Ethereum 2 [3].

The gossip network comprised 750 nodes, each on an AWS EC2 m6g.medium instance (with 50 instances each in all 15 AWS regions that supported

---

[4] Source code: https://github.com/tse-group/gasper-gossip-attack.

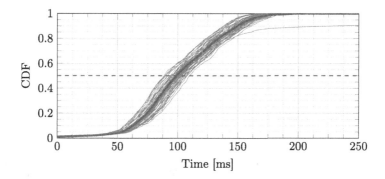

Fig. 3. Fraction of participants in the peer-to-peer gossip network who have received a message broadcast by node 0 at time 0 by the given time (50 sample messages in gray, mean over all samples in blue). Median (dashed red) at ≈ 100 ms.

m6g.medium as of 21-April-2021). Each node initiated a connection with ten randomly chosen peers. The five nodes with lowest instance ID were designated as senders and continuously broadcasted beacon messages with inter-transmission times uniformly distributed between zero and five seconds over a period of 20 minutes, logging the time when each message was broadcast. All nodes logged the time when a message was first received.

The network propagation delay was determined for each message and each receiving node. The respective CDFs, *i.e.*, what fraction of nodes have received a given message by a certain delay, is plotted as an example for a sample of messages from the first designated sender (node 0) in Fig. 3 (together with the average CDF of all messages originating at node 0). (CDFs for the other four designated senders are omitted for brevity here. They show similar behavior, just slightly shifted in time.) It is apparent from the CDFs that depending on the location of the node (nodes 0, 1, 2, 3, 4 happened to be located in us-east-2, ap-northeast-1, us-east-1, ap-northeast-1, ap-northeast-2, respectively) both geographically as well as within the peer-to-peer network topology, the median of the average CDF varies, but considering messages originating at a fixed sender, the fraction of validators reached by the median of the average CDF is fairly concentrated around 1/2. This suggests that the adversary can indeed determine T_{delay} so that with little dispersion honest validators get split in two halves.

We simulated the attack for $\beta = 0.15, m = 128$, using the network propagation delay samples as a model for random network delay.[5] Assigning the simulated adversary to one of the five designated senders for all of the attack, whenever the adversary broadcasts a sway vote, the propagation delays to the honest committee members of the given slot are sampled (without replacement) from the delays of one randomly drawn message of that designated sender.

---

[5] Source code: https://github.com/tse-group/gasper-gossip-attack.

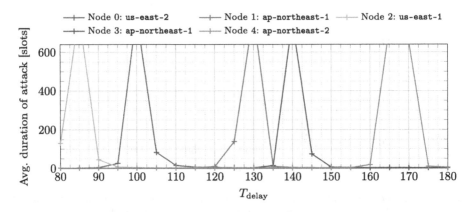

Fig. 4. Using the propagation delay measurements to model network propagation, we simulated our attack for fixed $\beta = 0.15$, varying T_{delay}, and five different positions of the adversary in the network, and plot the resulting average duration of the liveness interruption (cut off at 800 slots horizon). Observe that the peak for node 0 fits well to the median observed in Fig. 3. The curves are smooth and allow for easy and reliable localization of the optimal T_{delay}.

To determine the optimal T_{delay}, we performed grid search (with 5 ms step size) and for each T_{delay} simulated ten attacks in opportune epochs and recorded (see Fig. 4) how long the adversary was able to stall liveness (terminating at a horizon of 800 slots corresponding to 160 minutes). It is apparent that for the adversary in the position of each of the five designated senders of the measurement experiment, different T_{delay} are optimal. The optimal T_{delay} correspond well with the median of the average CDF (*cf.* Fig. 3). As the curves are smooth and have a single distinct peak of width ≈ 5 ms, the adversary can locate the optimal T_{delay} well. In particular, even with T_{delay} approximating the optimal value only up to 10 ms, the adversary can stall liveness for dozens of slots. Recall that none of the adversarial actions are slashable protocol violations, so the adversary can refine T_{delay} iteratively and launch this attack over and over.

5 Reorg Attack Using Probabilistic Network Delay

5.1 Motivation

In Sect. 3 we describe how an adversary might execute a 1-reorg with only a single adversarial committee member's vote. In Sect. 4 we show how an adversary can stall consensus and thus delay finality without adversarial control over network delay. By combining ideas from both attacks, we now describe an attack in which the adversary can execute a long-range reorg with vanishingly small stake and without control over network delay.

On a high level, the adversary avoids competing directly with honest validators of $(k-1)$ committees, as done in the reorg attack described in Sect. 3.

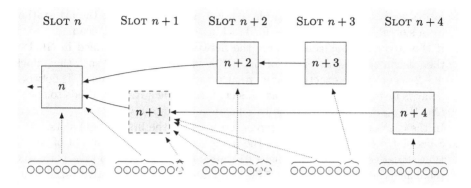

Fig. 5. Example of a 2-reorg combining refined reorgs and balancing strategies: In slot $n+1$ the adversary privately creates block $n+1$ on block n and withholds adversarial votes on it. Honest validators of slot $n+1$ attest to block n. In slot $n+2$, an honest proposer builds block $n+2$ on block n. The adversary releases block $n+1$ and one of the withheld votes in such a way that roughly half of honest committee members vote for blocks $n+1$ and $n+2$, respectively. If the adversary has tight control over network delays, they can effect that block $n+2$ has one more vote than block $n+1$. Without adversarial control of delays, a vanishing fraction of adversarial votes still suffices to rebalance accordingly. In slot $n+3$, the honest proposer views block $n+2$ leading and proposes block $n+3$ off it. The adversary releases two votes voting for block $n+1$ in such a way that a majority of honest committee members vote for block $n+1$, breaking the tie and completing the 2-reorg which orphaned blocks $n+2$ and $n+3$ in slot $n+4$.

Instead, the adversary uses the technique of Sect. 4 to keep honest committee members split roughly in half by ensuring they have different views on what the current head of the chain is. This way, honest nodes work against each other and maintain a tie which the adversary can tip to their liking at any point using only a few votes.

5.2 Refined Strategy Using Probabilistic Network Delay

Consider Fig. 5, in which the adversary is the proposer of slot $n+1$. We describe the strategy where the adversary executes a 2-reorg and analyze how many validators the adversary needs to control, depending on our assumption on the adversary's control over the network:

1. First, in slot $n+1$ the adversary privately builds block $n+1$ on top of the current head of the chain, block n. Further, the adversary privately votes for block $n+1$ using an attestation from slot $n+1$.
2. In the next slot, the proposer of block $n+2$ builds on block n because they have not seen block $n+1$. Before honest validators in slot $n+2$ attest, the adversary releases block $n+1$, along with the withheld attestation, in such a way that roughly half of honest committee members of slot $n+2$ attest before they see the sway vote (and thus vote for block $n+2$ as the current

head), and the other half sees block $n+1$ as leading due to the attestation from slot $n+1$ and thus votes for block $n+1$ as the current head.

If the adversary has control over the network delay, as assumed in [16,18], then it can target the release of the withheld block and vote such that block $n+2$ accumulates exactly one more attestation than block $n+1$. If network delay is instead probabilistic, as in Sect. 4, then the adversary needs to spend $O(\sqrt{W_{\text{honest}}})$ adversarial votes to rebalance the gap in votes.

In the case of a k-reorg, this step is repeated for the first $(k-1)$ slots.

3. Since slot $n+3$ is the last slot of the reorg attack, we use the insight of Sect. 3 that the adversary does not have to wait for honest votes to take place and rebalance them, but instead can sway validators towards the adversarial chain as soon as the honest proposal for this slot was created. So, in slot $n+3$, the current proposer views block $n+2$ as leading and thus builds block $n+3$ on it. Finally, the adversary releases two withheld attestations such that a majority of honest committee members of slot $n+3$ views them before attesting. Thus, a majority of validators votes for block $n+1$ as head of the chain. Remember that the fork choice rule only considers attestations at least one slot old.

4. Lastly, in slot $n+4$ the proposer views block $n+1$ as leading and thus builds block $n+4$ on block $n+1$. This completes the 2-reorg and orphans blocks $n+2$ and $n+3$.

For 1-reorg the adversary needs to control a single validator in the same slot they propose their block. For reorg lengths $k>1$, the number of adversarial validators required depends on the level of control over network delays. If delays are under adversarial control, then $(2k-1)$ adversarial validators suffice for a k-reorg, an amount linear in the reorg length only, but independent of the size of the validator set. If instead network delay is probabilistic rather than under adversarial control, a vanishingly small fraction $O(1/\sqrt{W_{\text{honest}}})$ of adversarial validators suffices to perform the necessary rebalancing to maintain the tie throughout the first $(k-1)$ slots of the k-reorg, leading to an overall requirement of $O(k\sqrt{W_{\text{honest}}})$ adversarial votes. Thus, large stakers can easily execute long-range reorg attacks. To illustrate the severe reduction of attacking conditions, consider the following: Under adversarial network delay, an adversary can perform a 10-reorg by merely controlling 19 validators.

6   Discussion

6.1   Ex Ante vs Ex Post Reorgs

Typically reorgs refer to an attack in which the adversary observes a block that they subsequently attempt to fork out. We call this an *ex post* reorg attack. The reorg attacks we describe are different in nature. Here, the adversary attempts to fork out a future block that is unknown to the adversary at the start of the attack. We call this an *ex ante* reorg attack.

In an ex post reorg attack, the adversary typically targets a block with abnormally large rewards that the adversary seeks to capture for themselves. In the context of Bitcoin it could be a block that contains transactions paying extraordinary amounts of fees, also referred to as 'whale transactions' [12]. In the context of Ethereum it could be blocks containing large MEV opportunities. Upon observing a lucrative block, the adversary attempts to capture it retrospectively. In PoS Ethereum this proves to be exceptionally difficult for non-majority actors due to the fact that the block the adversary wishes to orphan quickly accrues attestations from committee members in parallel. Each attestation adds weight to the block in question, which in turn is considered by the fork-choice rule LMD GHOST to determine the head of the chain. In short, no technique is known for non-majority adversaries to perform ex post reorg attacks reliably.

In contrast, ex ante reorg attacks are currently very much possible in PoS Ethereum, as this paper shows. The adversary overcomes the 'power of many parallel attestations' by exploiting LMD GHOST as described in Sects. 3 and 5. Intuitively, this is enabled by tricking honest validators into contrary views of the chain such that a handful of adversary validators are sufficient to tip the chain to their favor and thus successfully perform reorgs of sizable length. As a consequence of the different nature of the attack, the adversary's motivations to attack are different. In an ex ante reorg the adversary cannot observe valuable blocks and orphan them ex post, but must find other strategies to extract more value from it than it could from making an honest proposal, one of which is discussed in Sect. 6.2.

6.2   Reaping Higher Fees and MEV via the Attack

Maximal Extractable Value (MEV, formerly Miner Extractable Value [10]) represents a third source of profits for block producers, along with the proposer and attester rewards as well as transaction fees. MEV in PoS Ethereum captures the block proposer's action space to extract value by strategically including and ordering transactions in a given block. Common MEV opportunities include arbitraging a trade, frontrunning it to earn greater profits, or tailing liquidation events to buy the collateralized assets backing the defaulting position.

MEV opportunities grow with an increasing amount of pending transactions since more possible transaction order combinations exist. At the same time, the adversary is able to choose from a larger set of pending transactions those earning them the highest fees. More time between blocks then implies weakly more extractable MEV and transaction fees, which in turn implies more profits for the block proposer. The reorg attacks described in this paper can be interpreted as buying the adversary more time to construct their block.

With k-reorgs, it is possible for the malicious proposer to extend their listening period to up to $12k$ s (refined reorg strategy from Sect. 3), the 12 s elapsed between the previous block produced and their own slot, as well as $12(k-1)$ more seconds until the next honest block is included in the canonical chain. (The 2Δ duration introduced in Sect. 2.2 is set to 12 s in the PoS Ethereum implementation.) With k-reorgs in less idealized scenarios, as described in Sect. 5, the adversary only gains an additional 12 s of listening time (24 s in total). This is due to the fact that in the refined strategy using probabilistic network delay the adversary always releases the private block early (irrespective of reorg length k) to split honest committees roughly in half.

Further, the adversary may listen to honest blocks they wish to orpahn, and capture their MEV should they find better opportunities than the adversary themselves. Interestingly, the adversary may also simply release their block late, without attempting a reorg, to increase their listening time and ultimately rewards.

6.3   Reorgs Cause Attestation Overflow

While reorg attacks weakly benefit those who launch them, consensus degradation may be obtained as an unintended side-effect of the reorg.

Validators in a slot committee are distributed among a number of subcommittees. With a target subcommittee size of 128 and currently 230,000 active validators, ≈ 57 subcommittees are formed per slot. In the current implementation of PoS Ethereum, all identical votes from the same subcommittee may be aggregated into one 'summary' vote, lightening the block size. A block may include up to 128 such aggregates. Ideally, with all validators voting correctly and on time, the next block need only feature 57 aggregates, one per subcommittee. In practice, we observe such a number of large aggregates (summarizing many votes) in the block, with most validators voting identically, along with some aggregates summarizing other votes from validators who may have suffered from latency issues and voted identically, albeit wrongly. Suboptimal packing of the aggregates or adversarial voting behavior may also contribute to filling up the available slots for aggregates in the block. In the case of a reorg, deconfirmed aggregates return into the mempool and need to be included in future blocks. Even for short-range reorgs this can lead to congestion in the sense that many more aggregates wait to be included than there is space available in blocks.

Votes state their view of the current target of the FFG mechanism. A target vote is valid only if it is included in a block no later than 32 slots after the attesting slot. By reorging blocks, an attacker strains the capacity of the chain to include these valid votes. In the worst case, finalization is fully delayed whenever more than $1/3 - \beta$ of valid honest votes do not manage to be included.

6.4   Delaying Finality

Our attacks also enable *a priori* malign actors, perhaps ideologically motivated, to delay and in some cases outright stall consensus decisions. The refined attack of Sect. 4.2 gives the adversary a tool to do just that, even if the adversary cannot control message propagation delays (which instead are assumed to be probabilistic). Furthermore, in the regime of many validators, a vanishing fraction of adversarial stake suffices to mount the attack.

The attack of Sect. 5 enables long-range reorgs of the chain constituting consensus. The consequences are two-fold. Readily, transaction confirmation in the

LMD GHOST part of the protocol gets delayed. Transactions might enter/leave the LMD GHOST chain multiple times before eventually settling. This causes uncertainty and delay for users who consider a transaction confirmed once it has stabilized in the LMD GHOST chain. Furthermore, the adversary can use reorgs, as proposed in [19], to destabilize epoch boundary blocks. No epoch boundary block might then get the necessary number of FFG votes to become justified, which delays finality by at least an epoch and thus creates delay for users who rely on the finalized ledger.

Acknowledgment. JN, ENT and DT are supported by a gift from the Ethereum Foundation. JN is supported by the Reed-Hodgson Stanford Graduate Fellowship. ENT is supported by the Stanford Center for Blockchain Research.

References

1. Ethereum 2.0 phase 0 - the beacon chain. http://github.com/ethereum/eth2.0-specs/blob/dev/specs/phase0/beacon-chain.md
2. Ethereum 2.0 phase 0 - beacon chain fork choice (2020). http://github.com/ethereum/eth2.0-specs/blob/dev/specs/phase0/fork-choice.md
3. Ethereum 2.0 networking specification (2021). http://github.com/ethereum/eth2.0-specs/blob/dev/specs/phase0/p2p-interface.md'
4. Ethereum 2.0 phase 0 - honest validator (2021). http://github.com/ethereum/eth2.0-specs/blob/dev/specs/phase0/validator.md'
5. Buterin, V.: Proposal for mitigation against balancing attacks to LMD GHOST (2020). https://notes.ethereum.org/@vbuterin/lmd_ghost_mitigation
6. Buterin, V., Griffith, V.: Casper the friendly finality gadget. arXiv:1710.09437 [cs.CR] (2019)
7. Buterin, V., et al.: Combining GHOST and Casperar arXiv:2003.03052 [cs.CR] (2020)
8. Buterin, V., Stewart, A.: Beacon chain Casper mini-spec (comments #17, #19) (2018). http://ethresear.ch/t/beacon-chain-casper-mini-spec/2760/17
9. Carlsten, M., Kalodner, H., Weinberg, S.M., Narayanan, A.: On the instability of Bitcoin without the block reward. In: Proceedings of the 2016 ACM SIGSAC Conference on Computer and Communications Security, pp. 154–167 (2016)
10. Daian, P., et al.: Flash boys 2.0: Frontrunning in decentralized exchanges, miner extractable value, and consensus instability. In: IEEE Symposium on Security and Privacy, pp. 910–927. IEEE (2020)
11. Eyal, I., Sirer, E.G.: Majority is not enough: Bitcoin mining is vulnerable. Commun. ACM **61**(7), 95–102 (2018)
12. Liao, K., Katz, J.: Incentivizing blockchain forks via whale transactions. In: Brenner, M., et al. (eds.) FC 2017. LNCS, vol. 10323, pp. 264–279. Springer, Cham (2017). https://doi.org/10.1007/978-3-319-70278-0_17
13. Lynch, N.A.: Distributed Algorithms. Morgan Kaufmann Publishers Inc., San Francisco (1996)
14. Nakamura, R.: Analysis of bouncing attack on FFG (2019). http://ethresear.ch/t/analysis-of-bouncing-attack-on-ffg/6113
15. Nakamura, R.: Prevention of bouncing attack on FFG (2019). http://ethresear.ch/t/prevention-of-bouncing-attack-on-ffg/6114

16. Neu, J., Tas, E.N., Tse, D.: A balancing attack on Gasper, the current candidate for Eth2's beacon chain (2020). http://ethresear.ch/t/a-balancing-attack-on-gasper-the-current-candidate-for-eth2s-beacon-chain/8079

17. Neu, J., Tas, E.N., Tse, D.: Attacking Gasper without adversarial network delay (2021). http://ethresear.ch/t/attacking-gasper-without-adversarial-network-delay/10187

18. Neu, J., Tas, E.N., Tse, D.: Ebb-and-flow protocols: a resolution of the availability-finality dilemma. In: IEEE Symposium on Security and Privacy, pp. 446–465. IEEE (2021)

19. Neuder, M., Moroz, D.J., Rao, R., Parkes, D.C.: Low-cost attacks on Ethereum 2.0 by sub-1/3 stakeholders. arXiv:2102.02247 [cs.CR] (2021)

20. Sompolinsky, Y., Zohar, A.: Secure high-rate transaction processing in Bitcoin. In: Böhme, R., Okamoto, T. (eds.) FC 2015. LNCS, vol. 8975, pp. 507–527. Springer, Heidelberg (2015). https://doi.org/10.1007/978-3-662-47854-7_32

21. Vyzovitis, D., Napora, Y., McCormick, D., Dias, D., Psaras, Y.: GossipSub: attack-resilient message propagation in the Filecoin and ETH2.0 networks. arXiv:2007.02754 [cs.NI] (2020)

22. Yin, M., Malkhi, D., Reiter, M.K., Gueta, G.G., Abraham, I.: HotStuff: BFT consensus with linearity and responsiveness. In: Symposium on Principles of Distributed Computing, PODC 2019, pp. 347–356. ACM (2019)

Permissionless Consensus in the Resource Model

Benjamin Terner[(✉)]

UC Irvine, Irvine, USA
bterner@uci.edu

Abstract. This paper introduces a new model that abstracts resource-restricted distributed computation and permits simpler reasoning about consensus protocols in the resource-restricted regime. Our model introduces a simple abstraction – simply called "resources" – to capture a resource-restricted primitive which is general enough to capture most Proof of X such as Proof of Work and Proof of Stake. The supply of such resources is scarce, and a single resource allows a party to send a single message with elevated protocol status. For example, every puzzle solution in Proof of Work or Proof of Stake is a resource; the message associated with each resource is the payload of the puzzle. We show the power of resources for the problem of consensus, in which participants attempt to agree on a function of their inputs. We prove that given few additional assumptions, resources are sufficient to achieve consensus in the permissionless regime, even in the presence of a full-information adversary that can choose which parties get resources and when they get them. In the resource model, the participants do not need to know a bound on network delay, they do not need clocks, and they can join and leave the execution arbitrarily, even after sending only a single message. We require only a known upperbound on the rate at which resources enter the system, relative to the maximum network delay (without needing to know the network delay), and that over the long term, a majority of resources are acquired by honest participants. Our protocol for consensus follows from a protocol for graph consensus, which we define as a generalization of blockchains. Our graph consensus works even when resources enter the system at high rates, but the required honest majority increases with the rate. We show how to modify the protocol slightly to achieve one-bit consensus. We also show that for every graph consensus protocol that outputs a majority of honest vertices there exists a one-bit consensus protocol.

Keywords: Consensus · Blockchain · Permissionless · Full information model

1 Introduction

The distributed system problem of *consensus*, in which participants in the protocol communicate over a network in an attempt to agree on a single bit or an append-only log based on their inputs, has been studied for decades since

© International Financial Cryptography Association 2022
I. Eyal and J. Garay (Eds.): FC 2022, LNCS 13411, pp. 577–593, 2022.
https://doi.org/10.1007/978-3-031-18283-9_29

the seminal works of [18,24]. The advent of Bitcoin [21] ushered in renewed interest in consensus protocols by introducing the *permissionless* regime. The permissionless regime models internet-scale protocols in which participation is *dynamic*, meaning participants can join and leave an execution arbitrarily, the number of active participants may be in constant flux, the identities of the participants at any point in time are unknowable, and the adversary may control arbitrarily many parties.

Consensus protocols for the permissionless regime have proliferated since Bitcoin [5,13] as new approaches have focused on the resource-restricted model. The resource-restricted model changes the basis of security from the proportion of honest participants in a system to the physical resources that they control. In Eurocrypt 2020, Garay et al. [12] formalized a randomized resource-restricted model and showed that by restricting the ability of parties to send messages, it is possible to bypass known bounds for both Byzantine Agreement and MPC. Bitcoin famously requires participants to solve Proof of Work to participate [2,10,21]. In response to Proof of Work's wasteful computation, many Proof of X (PoX) variants have been proposed (see [5]), the most popular being Proof of Stake [3,8,16] (PoS).

Resources: A Unifying Abstraction for a New Model. To better understand the permissionless regime and the power of PoX, we ask:

> Is there a unifying abstraction for PoX that implies consensus in the permissionless regime? If so, under what assumptions does it imply consensus?

In this work, we model a unifying abstraction of PoX which we simply call *resources*. We use resources to cast permissionless protocols into a *new model* in which a subset of messages are given special elite status, and the supply of these messages are constrained. We model the "competition process" for resources implicitly (and more generally) by deferring it to the environment. This allows us to decouple the resource-producing process (usually, but not limited to, mining) from the resource-consuming process (in our case, a graph protocol). We then isolate a few properties of resources, and show that any arbitrarily bad resource-producing process (implemented by the environment, or forwarded to our protocol by the environment) allows us to achieve consensus, as long as resources satisfy the properties we present. We show that it is possible to achieve consensus if (a) a majority of resources are received by honest parties over the long term, and (b) an upper bound on the rate at which resources enter the system is known.

Our novel protocol requires weaker synchronization assumptions than current practice; this shows that we may weaken the assumptions required for consensus by building PoX from weaker synchronization assumptions. To date, all other works we know for the permissionless model require either knowledge of the network delay [7,8,11] or (weakly synchronized) clocks [3,4,9,16], plus some assumption about the number of active participants. In our model, parties have no way to synchronize, they may join and leave an execution arbitrarily, and there is no bound on the number of parties in an execution.

Specifically, we make the following contributions:

1. We provide a simple abstraction of PoX called *resources* with very few properties. A resource is a black-box generalization of a puzzle solution, which holds a string chosen by the party that "discovers" the resource.
2. We show that our abstraction implies consensus while requiring weaker assumptions and facing a stronger adversary than existing constructions.
3. We argue that the uses of PoX for consensus (that we know of) implement our abstraction, and that our model generalizes current designs.

Generalizing Resource Generation. Resources can be implemented in many ways that are not limited to cryptographic puzzles; any process that achieves the properties we describe can be used to achieve consensus. As a thought experiment, we consider that before a protocol execution, some setup may select specific parties to be designated as "leaders" at specific points in the execution. (For example, an execution could be divided into epochs, and during each epoch a small set of leaders may be chosen.) During the execution, those parties are informed that they are leaders and permitted to send a single message to all other parties, along with a certificate that they have been selected as a leader at that moment. (Looking ahead, we will show that this leader selection can even be determined adaptively by the adversary.) We defer a discussion of generalized resource generation to the full version [25].

1.1   Overview of Our Model

The Permissionless Regime. We give a short overview of our model here, and a full syntactic framework in the full version [25]. An execution proceeds in rounds and is directed by the environment, which serves as the adversary. Participation is dynamic (meaning parties can join and leave the execution arbitrarily), and completely controlled by the adversary; in every round, the adversary controls which parties send and receive messages, and which are completely inactive. Parties that send or receive messages in a round are considered *active* in that round. The maximum network delay Δ is unknown and participants do not have clocks. The number of participants is unknown to the parties *and may be unbounded.* Moreover, the adversary has *full information* about the states of all honest parties; it can corrupt parties adaptively; and it chooses which parties receive resources and when they receive them. (Note that in the full information model, we do not have digital signatures; this work shows that given resources, we do not additionally need signatures to imply consensus.) Communication occurs over peer-to-peer channels or via multicast. Honest parties cannot tell whether a message was sent over a peer-to-peer link or over multicast (this allows corrupt parties to selectively send messages to some parties but not to others).

Any protocol that is secure in our model must achieve consensus even when every honest participant sends *at most one message* before it leaves the execution, and even when every honest participant is only active for a (very) short period of time from the moment it joins to the moment it leaves. (In the extreme, just long enough to receive the state of the system and send a single message.)

The Properties of Resources. Recall that in our model, the environment both directs the execution and abstracts the resource-producing process. Therefore, rather than requiring participants to solve a PoX puzzle, we say that participants are *allocated* resources from the environment, and our protocols show how participants use the resources they receive. We express properties of resources that mimic PoX via a syntactic model, in which the properties of resources are expressed as constraints on an execution transcript. The full model is in the full version [25]; we overview the syntactic model and properties here.

We model resources as a set of symbols Ψ, and require that a protocol specify how parties respond when they receive resources. When a resource $\psi \in \Psi$ is allocated by the environment to a party p, a special event called a *resource allocation* is recorded in the transcript, which states that p receives ψ. The following rules govern how these symbols may appear in the transcript.

1. **Unforgeability.** No participant can "fake" the fact that it has a resource. In practice, PoX schemes enforce this requirement by requiring that PoX solutions must be found by solving some puzzle, and the solutions are verifiable by other participants. Formally, a transcript satisfies *resource unforgeability* if no resource appears in the transcript before its allocation event. This enforces that parties are constrained to obtaining resources *only* by receiving them from the environment, which abstracts the resource-producing process.

2. **Binding.** Each resource can be *bound* with one and only one string, which gives the resource semantics. The string must be chosen at the moment that the resource is generated. This models that in PoX schemes, parties attempt to solve puzzles with respect to a specific message they wish to send. (In some implementations, this message includes a public key that boostraps special status to future messages signed with that key.) Formally, a string m bound to a resource ψ is encoded as $\psi||m||\psi^1$, where $||$ denotes concatenation. A transcript satisfies *resource binding* if for any two encodings $\psi||m||\psi$ and $\psi'||m'||\psi'$: $\psi = \psi'$ implies $m = m'$.

Constraining the Supply of Resources. We model constraints on resources which mimic the assumptions common to PoX mechanisms:

1. **Long Term Honest Majority.** Over any period of time in which n resources are allocated, we require that $\alpha n - \varepsilon$ are allocated to honest participants and at most $\beta n + \varepsilon$ are allocated to corrupt participants, where $\beta = 1 - \alpha$. When $\alpha > \beta$, we say that honest participants receive a *long term* majority of resources. ε represents a short-term corrupt advantage, which models an adversary which pools its physical resources in order to achieve a short "burst" of resources.

2. **Rate Limit.** We let ρ upperbound the number of resources that may be generated per Δ time, where Δ is the (unknown) maximum network delay.

---

[1] This is a standard encoding technique. By encompassing the message with its resource, it is clear where the string bound to the resource begins and ends.

In the full version [25], we give a full treatment explaining how Proof of Work and Proof of Stake implement resources, including what constitutes a resource for each scheme. We stress that in most designs, *every solution of a cryptographic puzzle is a resource*. We additionally explain how the model captures other cryptographic and non-cryptographic PoX.

1.2   Main Results

One-Bit Consensus. Our main result is that resources imply consensus in our new model. In the consensus problem, all parties have an input $b \in \{0,1\}$, and they must output some value $v \in \{0,1\}$ subject to the following constraints. By *agreement*, all parties must output the same bit. By *nontriviality*, if every honest party has the same input, then they must output that bit. By *termination*, the protocol must terminate after a finite number of resources have been allocated. We show that resources imply consensus assuming only knowledge of ρ, which upperbounds the rate at which resources are allocated relative to the (unknown) maximum network delay, and that honest parties receive a (large enough) majority of resources in the long term.

Theorem 1 (Informal). *Let $c = O(\rho + \varepsilon)$. For all $\alpha > \rho c(1 - \alpha)$, there exists a one-bit consensus protocol in the permissionless regime with resources.*

Graph Consensus. We build one-bit consensus from resources using a technique reminiscent of so-called blockchains. We define a problem called graph consensus in which honest participants maintain local graphs and propose vertices to be included in each other's graphs. The security goals of a graph consensus protocol are generalizations of those proposed by [6,14,22]. A graph consensus protocol should achieve two properties. *Consistency* requires that for any two graphs output by honest participants, one participant's output must be a subgraph of the other. *Liveness* requires that honest participants may not trivially output empty graphs, but that their outputs grow over time.

Theorem 2 (Informal). *Let $c = O(\rho + \varepsilon)$. For all $\alpha > \rho c(1 - \alpha)$, there exists a graph consensus protocol in the permissionless regime with resources.*

Notably, we show that it is possible to achieve graph consensus when $\rho > 1$, i.e. more than 1 resource may allocated per Δ time. However, interestingly, our protocol requires that α grow with $O(\rho^2(1 - \alpha))$ in order to maintain security.

Necessity of Assumptions. For completeness, we additionally show the necessity of our assumptions. The proof of the following theorem follows from standard techniques, and the discussion is deferred to the full version [25].

Theorem 3 (Informal). *There is no consensus protocol in the permissionless model that does not require both a long-term majority of resources and a constraint on the network delay.*

The Parameter Regime. The parameter regimes for which our protocols are secure are not competitive with existing designs. For example, the protocols are secure for $\alpha = 0.865, \epsilon = 1, \rho = 1$, or $\alpha = 0.954, \epsilon = 2, \rho = 2$, but these are not comparable to the best parameters for protocols which make stronger assumptions. Nevertheless, we provide feasibility results in the presence of a very strong adversary. Our regime is overly restrictive, as we comment below that no longest-chain protocol can be proven secure for nontrivial rates ($\rho > 1$). However, the fact that consensus is achievable even in such a difficult regime is a stronger statement to the power of resources.

1.3   Technical Overview

Our technique to build consensus builds directly on our graph consensus protocol. We show that given a long-term majority of resources and a bound on the rate, honest participants can use the properties of resources to build a directed acyclic graph (DAG) which captures the (partial) ordering in which they receive their resources. Importantly, every vertex in the global DAG is associated with a resource (much like every vertex in a blockchain is associated with a PoX). The unforgeability and binding properties of resources enforce that corrupt participants cannot manipulate the graph structure. The honest participants embed structure into the graph that can be used to infer when corrupt parties attempt to cheat by "withholding" their resources, i.e. not immediately multicasting a vertex they have added to the graph.

In our graph protocol, we use the long term honest advantage in resources similarly to many longest-chain blockchains. We define the depth of a vertex in a DAG to be the length of the longest path from the root to that vertex (where the DAG grows from a root with no indegree to the leaves with no outdegree). We then require that the honest participants can build deeper branches on the DAG than the corrupt participants.

The structure that honest participants build into the global DAG is *reachability*. Every honest vertex which is added to the global DAG is guaranteed to gain an honest successor, and to always be a predecessor of one of the deepest vertices in the global DAG. However, corrupt vertices are not guaranteed to become predecessors of any honest vertices. If honest participants can build longer paths in the global DAG over time than corrupt participants, then if corrupt participants withhold their vertices for too long, their withheld branches will eventually fall behind the depth of the global DAG. Honest participants extract their outputs by selecting vertices in their local views of the global DAG which are predecessors of the deepest vertices in their views, excising all corrupt vertices on branches which have fallen short. Our technical challenge is to compute how long it takes – measured in depth – for a withheld branch to fall short of the honest parties' branch.

One-bit consensus follows from any graph consensus protocol which guarantees that for any sufficiently large output graph, a majority of the vertices must be associated with resources allocated to honest participants.

Why Chain Protocols Fail: Pathological Chain Structures. In our model, *no longest-chain or heaviest-chain protocol can be proven secure* at non-trivial resource rates ($\rho > 1$). Consider an execution of a chain protocol in which a fork develops at the root and is never resolved. Because in our model, when $\rho > 1$ the adversary can always allocate multiple resources concurrently, forks in chain protocols can be perpetuated indefinitely. Therefore, although a party's local graph grows as a function of the number of resources that have been allocated, consistency requires that no party can ever output either branch of the fork. In this case, liveness fails because no party ever outputs any vertices. Note that this may happen even if the corrupt participants receive no resources. In comparison, in a random model, the random distribution of resource arrivals implies that forks will be resolved eventually, which allows participants to eventually output one branch. The perpetual fork attack is also discussed in [17].

1.4   Related Work

Comprehensive overviews of the blockchain literature can be found in the systemizations of knowledge by [5,13], and [26] (who introduced the term PoX). Here we describe only works we know about that address the properties of resource-like objects; in the full version [25] we give extended related work on the permissionless model and consensus protocols.

Generalizing Resource-Constrained Results. This work generalizes the findings of other works, surprisingly showing that impossibility results that depend on strong assumptions need not hold if another system parameter can be bounded. The work of Lewis-Pye and Roughgarden [19], which originally appeared online after this work but has related themes, proves a CAP-style theorem that a protocol cannot be secure in the partially synchronous setting when the size of the resource pool is unknown. Similarly, Pass and Shi [7,23] prove that for protocols which require mining, if the maximum network delay is unknown then the number of participants must be known within a factor of 2, even when participants are synchronous and have clocks. Intuitively, the number of participants are proxy for the mining rate; in the attack, the adversary splits the execution into two groups, and delivers messages within each group quickly but between groups slowly. These works implicitly assume that the mining rate cannot be bounded without the assumptions in their models. Our work show that *an upperbound on the rate* of resources relative to the network delay (in the above cases, puzzle solutions) is a sufficient network assumption; if this can be approximated without granular knowledge of the above required system parameters, consensus is still possible. Therefore, we show that is possible to achieve consensus in an expanded set of environments where the resource rate can be upperbounded. (For discussions on deferring resource generation to the environment, and on why a known upper bound on the rate is a weaker assumption than previously studied, refer to the full version [25]).

Properties of PoX. As far as we know, no other works present the common qualities of PoX via a single abstraction. However, Miller et al. [20] model Proof of Work as scratch-off-puzzles, showing a number of desirable properties for Proof of Work objects. Alwen and Tackman [1] model desirable properties for moderately hard puzzles. Garay et al. [15] model the sufficient properties of PoW to yield consensus. Garay et al. [12] further abstract the properties of PoW to a randomized resource-restricted model.

1.5   Paper Organization

In Sect. 2 we define graph consensus in our model. In Sect. 3 we present our main protocol, our main theorem, and an overview of the proof. In the full version [25], we include the following discussions: We discuss how several popular forms of PoX implement resources. We discuss our modeling choices and frame our results with respect to other models; we include discussions of whether it is reasonable to know the resource rate, and why knowing an upper bound on the rate is weaker than knowing the network delay. We provide our full formal model based on a syntactic framework for resources. We prove security of our graph consensus protocol. We define one-bit consensus in our model, provide a protocol that achieves it, and provide a generic transformation from graph consensus to one-bit consensus. We prove that honest majority and some bound on the network are necessary for consensus in the permissionless regime.

2   Graph Consensus Problem

2.1   Preliminaries for Graphs

A graph $G = (V, E)$ is a set of vertices and a set of edges between vertices. For a graph G, we denote the set of its vertices as $G.V$ and its edges as $G.E$. In this work we consider only directed acyclic graphs (DAGs); we therefore use term graph to refer to a DAG. A *root vertex* in a graph is a vertex with in-degree 0. In this work, every graph which we consider has exactly one root vertex, which in cryptocurrencies is also called a genesis vertex.

We define depth of a vertex and depth of a graph in a non-standard way:

Definition 1 (Depth of a Vertex, Depth of a Graph). *Let* root *be the root vertex of a graph G. The* depth *of a vertex v in G is defined as the length of the longest* path from root *to v. The* depth *of G is defined as the depth of its deepest vertex.*

We use $\mathsf{D}(G)$ to denote the depth of a graph G, and use $\mathsf{D}_G(v)$ to denote the depth of a vertex v in G. When the graph is implied from context, we simply write $\mathsf{D}(v)$. The depth of a root vertex is always 0. We use $G\big|_d$ to denote the subgraph of G including only vertices with depth $\leq d$. Figure 1 illustrates the depths of vertices in a simple graph. We denote a path from vertices v to u as $v \to u$. A path $v \to u$ *spans d depth* if $\mathsf{D}(u) - \mathsf{D}(v) = d$. We say $u \in G.V$ is

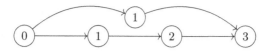

Fig. 1. An example graph in which each vertex is labeled with its depth. The root vertex has depth 0 by definition, and every other vertex's depth is defined by the longest path from the root to the vertex.

reachable from $v \in G.V$ if there is a path $v \to u$. For a vertex $v \in G.V$, the *predecessor graph* of v is the subgraph of G containing v and every vertex and edge on every path from root to v. We use $\cup$ to denote graph union and $\subseteq$ to denote a subgraph. We let indegree(v) denote the indegree of a vertex v and outdegree(v) denote its outdegree. (In the full version [25], a vertex may have a "payload" string that gives semantics to the vertex.)

2.2 Graph Consensus Protocol

In an execution of a graph consensus protocol, participants have no input. Each participant p maintains a local graph G_p based on the messages it has received so far and the protocol specification. A graph consensus protocol specifies how participants generate new vertices, and how to propose that other participants include the new vertices in their local graphs. It also specifies how a participant determines whether a new vertex, which it receives in a proposal from another participant, should be included in its local graph. For a participant p active at time t, we denote by $G_p^{(t)}$ its local graph after all vertices are added at t. Each participant p additionally maintains an output graph G_p^*, which it outputs whenever it is active. The protocol must specify a deterministic way for each p to compute G_p^* as a function of its local graph G_p. We denote by $G_p^{*(t)}$ the output of p at time t.

An execution of graph consensus may continue indefinitely. The goal of a protocol is for the participants' outputs to obey consistency and liveness properties across time. Graph consistency requires that if participants p active at t and q active at t', output $G_p^{*(t)}$ and $G_q^{*(t')}$, then one output graph must be a subgraph of the other.

Definition 2 (Graph Consistency). *An execution satisfies* graph consistency *if for all times t and t', and for all honest p and q active at t and t', respectively:* $G_p^{*(t)} \nsubseteq G_q^{*(t')} \implies G_q^{*(t')} \subseteq G_p^{*(t)}$.

A protocol can trivially satisfy graph consistency if participants always output the empty graph. We therefore define liveness to require that each participant p's output G_p^* grows as a function of the number of resources which have been allocated up to some point in time, as follows:

Definition 3 (f-Liveness). *Let $f : \mathbb{N} \to \mathbb{N}$. An execution satisfies f-liveness if for every time t and honest participant p active at t: if the environment has allocated N resources by time t, then $|G_p^{*(t)}.V| \geq f(N)$.*

When $f = 0$, liveness is trivial because parties may always output the empty graph. When f is nontrivial we require a nontrivial protocol. Our protocols satisfy liveness for nontrivial f. We remark that unlike other definitions of liveness, ours does not require that a party's output graph grow as a function of time. Rather, we require that a party's output grow as a function of the number of resources allocated by the environment. Looking ahead, consider that a protocol which depends on resources should not need to make progress if there are no resources allocated. In our model, the fact that resources are produced depends on the environment, and we do not assume a lowerbound on the resource rate; however, only when the environment delivers sufficiently many resources are our protocols required to produce output.

In some applications, it is desirable to show that some proportion of the vertices in an honest participant's output must be generated by honest participants. If a vertex is generated by an honest participant, we call it an honest vertex; otherwise, we call it a corrupt vertex. We let $\mathsf{hon}(G.V)$ denote the honest vertices in G. We define h-honest-vertex liveness to quantify the guaranteed proportion of honest vertices in a participant's output graph.

Definition 4 (h-Honest-Vertex Liveness). *Let $h\colon \mathbb{N} \to \mathbb{N}$. An execution satisfies h-honest-vertex liveness if for every time t and honest participant p active at t:* $|\mathsf{hon}(G_p^{*(t)}.V)| \geq h(|G_p^{(t)}.V|)$.

In the rest of the paper, we refer to f-liveness and h-honest-vertex liveness together by f,h-liveness to say that a protocol satisfies both f-liveness and h-honest-vertex liveness.

3   Main Protocol

3.1   Protocol Description

Protocol Π^G, presented in Fig. 2, is a graph consensus protocol. It is parameterized by α and ε, which describe the proportion of honest resources which are allocated, and the maximum rate of resource allocation ρ.

Each participant p maintains a local DAG G_p in which every vertex except the root is a resource. The graph G_p is initialized to $(\{\mathsf{root}\}, \emptyset)$, and grows from the root toward high depths throughout the execution as participants are allocated resources and receive messages. Whenever p is allocated a resource, it adds the resource to its graph as a new vertex, and then immediately multicasts its local graph including the new vertex to all honest participants. When an honest participant receives a message containing a graph, it updates its local graph to include new vertices and edges not previously in its local graph. We must show how a participant p chooses the predecessors of each vertex that it adds to its graph, and p computes its output G_p^* from its local graph G_p.

We describe resources as vertices as follows. When any participant is allocated resource ψ, we let v_ψ denote the vertex corresponding to ψ. When describing an arbitrary vertex, we denote it as v or u, eliding its respective resource.

When any honest participant p adds a new vertex to its graph, it adds the vertex to its graph as the new deepest vertex. Specifically, when p is allocated a resource ψ and adds vertex v_ψ to its local graph G_p, p adds an inbound edge to v_ψ from every vertex u in G_p which (a) has no outbound edges in G_p, and (b) is close in depth to G_p. When p is allocated ψ, it must also choose v_ψ's edges *immediately*, as p must bind the inbound edges of v_ψ to ψ. Because each vertex's inbound edges are bound to the vertex's respective resource, it may not gain additional predecessors.

Over time, some vertices will gain successors and some vertices may be "orphaned" and stop gaining successors. Each participant computes its output G_p^* as a subgraph of its G_p consisting of vertices which are both far from the end of its graph (measured in the difference in depth between the vertex and the graph) and are still gaining successors.

Encoding a Graph Using Resources. We model a resource as a black box object which is *bound to a string* that conveys its semantics *at the moment* it is allocated. In Π^G, the string bound to each resources encodes the direct predecessors of its respective vertex; when a participant is allocated a resource ψ, it binds to ψ the encoding of each vertex which has an outbound edge to v_ψ. If no edges are bound to ψ, then v_ψ is defined to have an edge from root. In this way, each vertex is uniquely committed to its predecessors at the moment it is allocated. A participant multicasts its local graph by sending all of the bound resources which encode the vertices and edges in its local graph.

Event Responses. We now detail how participants respond when they are allocated resources and when they receive messages, and we explain how participants compute their outputs from their local graphs.

On Resource Allocation. When an honest participant p is allocated a resource ψ, we say that it *generates* a vertex v_ψ that it adds to its local graph G_p. Participant p chooses the inbound edges of v_ψ based on its current graph G_p by adding an edge to v_ψ from each vertex u in G_p for which both $\mathsf{outdegree}(u) = 0$ and $\mathsf{D}(G_p) - \mathsf{D}(u) < c$, where c is a constant computed from the protocol parameters and is the maximum depth spanned by an honestly chosen edge. Immediately after generating v_ψ, p multicasts its entire local graph containing v_ψ and its inbound edges.

On Receipt of a Message. Every message sent between participants is an encoding of a graph. (Any other message is ignored.) When a participant p receives a graph G' in a message, it verifies that G' is a valid graph. If G' is valid, then p updates its local graph as $G_p \leftarrow G_p \cup G'$. If G' is not valid, then p ignores G'.

G' may be invalid in two ways. First, G' may contain an edge (v, u) which spans more than c depth. Second, G' may be "missing a vertex," meaning there is a vertex v in $G'.V$ for which not all of v's predecessors are in $G'.V$. (This means the graph G is incomplete in the party's view.)

Protocol 1 DAG Protocol for Graph Consensus $\Pi^G(\alpha, \varepsilon, \rho)$

Parameters: $\alpha, \varepsilon, \rho$

Derived Constants:

1. $\beta = 1 - \alpha$
2. $\gamma = (1 + \beta)\rho + \varepsilon + \frac{\varepsilon}{\rho} + 1$
3. $c = \gamma + \rho + \frac{\varepsilon}{\alpha}$
4. $\ell_1 = \gamma + \rho$

5. $\ell_2 = c(\varepsilon + 1) + \rho + \frac{c\beta}{\frac{\alpha}{\rho} - c\beta}(c(\varepsilon + 1) + (2 + \beta)\rho + \frac{\varepsilon}{\alpha} + 2\frac{\varepsilon}{\rho} + 2)$
6. $\ell^* = \ell_1 + \ell_2$

Internal Variables:

1. $G_p = (V_p, E_p)$ is a participant's local state. Initially, $G_p = (\{\text{root}\}, \emptyset)$
2. $G_p^* = (V_p^*, E_p^*)$ is a participant's output graph. Initially, $G_p^* = (\emptyset, \emptyset)$

Event Responses:

1. On Receiving a Graph (G')
   - $G_p \leftarrow G_p \cup \text{validateGraph}(G')$
   - $G_p^* \leftarrow \text{extract}(G_p)|_{\mathsf{D}(G_p) - \ell^*}$

2. On Being Allocated a Resource ψ
   - $G_p \leftarrow \text{addVert}(G_p, \psi)$
   - multicast G_p
   - $G_p^* \leftarrow \text{extract}(G_p)|_{\mathsf{D}(G_i) - \ell^*}$

Internal Functions:

1. $\text{addVert}(G, \psi)$:
   - $V' \leftarrow \{u \in G.V : \mathsf{D}(G) - \mathsf{D}(u) < c \text{ and } \text{outdegree}(u) = 0\}$
   - return new graph G' such that
     - $G'.V \leftarrow G.V \cup \{v_\psi\}$
     - $G'.E \leftarrow G.E \cup \{(u, v_\psi) : u \in V'\}$
2. $\text{extract}(G)$:
   - $S \leftarrow \{v \in G.V : \mathsf{D}(G) - \mathsf{D}(v) \leq c + \rho\}$ // "starting vertices"
   - return $S \cup \{v \in G.V : \exists u \in S \text{ such that } u \text{ is reachable from } v\}$
3. $\text{validateGraph}(G')$:
   - if
     (a) $\exists (u, v) \in G'.E$ such that $\mathsf{D}(u) - \mathsf{D}(v) > c$, or
     (b) $\exists (u, v) \in G'.E$ such that $u \notin G'.V$
     then return $(\emptyset, \emptyset)$
   - return G'

Fig. 2. Protocol Π^G for graph consensus

Computing Output. An honest participant p computes its output G_p^* from its local graph G_p by first extracting a subgraph of G_p into an intermediate graph, and then outputting all but the deepest vertices in the intermediate graph. More precisely, p extracts a subgraph of G_p using the procedure $\text{extract}(G_p)$, as follows. First, p selects a set of "starting vertices" as the set $S = \{v \in G_p : \mathsf{D}(G_p) - \mathsf{D}(v) < c + \rho\}$. Next, p extracts every starting vertex and every vertex from which any starting vertex is reachable. Finally, p outputs $G_p^* \leftarrow \text{extract}(G_p)|_{\mathsf{D}(G_p) - \ell^*}$, which contains all the vertices in its extracted subgraph with depth less than $\mathsf{D}(G_p) - \ell^*$, where ℓ^* is derived from the protocol parameters.

Remark 1 (Sending a Whole Graph). Whenever a participant generates a new vertex, it multicasts its entire graph. We admit it is unrealistic in practice to multicast an entire local graph. Our protocol should be considered only theoretical. It remains future work to show that participants need not multicast their entire graphs whenever they generate a new vertex.

3.2 Theorem Statement

We now state our main theorem, which is that protocol Π^G satisfies graph consensus for appropriate parameters.

Theorem 4. *For all N, all ρ, and all ε, and for all $\alpha > \rho(1-\alpha)((3-\alpha)\rho + \frac{\varepsilon}{\alpha} + \frac{\varepsilon}{\rho} + \varepsilon + 1)$ every (α, ε)-honest, ρ-rate-limited, admissible execution of $\Pi^G(\alpha, \varepsilon, \rho)$ satisfies graph consistency and f, h-liveness for $f(N) = h(N) = \alpha N - \varepsilon - \rho(\ell^* + 1)$, where ℓ^* is a derived constant defined as in the protocol.*

Recall that in Π^G, each participant computes its output by extracting a subgraph from its local graph and then chopping off the deepest vertices in the extracted subgraph, where the chop-off threshold is the derived constant ℓ^*. Intuitively, liveness follows from the fact that as a participant's local graph increases in depth, the depth of the graph which it outputs also increases. The main objective of the proof is to show that the protocol achieves graph consistency.

The main desideratum of the proof of graph consistency follows:

Proposition 1. *Let $c = (3-\alpha)\rho + \frac{\varepsilon}{\alpha} + \frac{\varepsilon}{\rho} + \varepsilon + 1$ (as in Protocol Π^G). If $\alpha > \rho\beta c$, then for all k, times t and t', and honest participants p and q active at t and t', respectively, if $\mathsf{D}(G_p^{(t)}) > k + \ell^*$ and $\mathsf{D}(G_q^{(t')}) > k + \ell^*$, then $\mathsf{extract}(G_p^{(t)})|_k = \mathsf{extract}(G_q^{(t')})|_k$.*

where c and ℓ^* are defined as in the protocol.

Graph consistency follows directly from assigning $G_p^* \leftarrow \mathsf{extract}(G_p)|_{\mathsf{D}(G_p)-\ell^*}$, since when two honest participants output graphs, then the less deep output graph must always be a subgraph of the deeper (if the output graphs have the same depth, then they must be the same graph).

3.3 Proof Overview

We now overview the proof of Proposition 1. The full proofs of Proposition 1 and Theorem 4 are in the full version [25].

Building a Virtual Global Graph. We consider that the participants collectively build a virtual global graph $\mathbb{G}$ throughout an execution. When the execution begins, $\mathbb{G}$ is initialized to a graph with only a root vertex. Whenever *any* participant is allocated a resource, the vertex that it generates is immediately added to $\mathbb{G}$. In particular, even if a corrupt participant generates a vertex and "withholds" the vertex by not sending it to any honest participant, the vertex is still added to $\mathbb{G}$ at the moment that it is generated. We denote by $\mathbb{G}^{(t)}$ the state of $\mathbb{G}$ after all vertices are added at time t.

$\mathbb{G}$ represents the global state of the execution. Consider that $G_p^{(t)}$ is p's its local view of $\mathbb{G}^{(t)}$, and it is easy to see that $G_p^{(t)}$ must be a subgraph of $\mathbb{G}^{(t)}$. Moreover, for every vertex $v \in \mathbb{G}^{(t)}.V$, if v is in $G_p^{(t)}$, then $\mathsf{D}_{\mathbb{G}^{(t)}}(v) = \mathsf{D}_{G_p^{(t)}}(v)$. Henceforth, when we refer to the depth of a vertex, we simply write $\mathsf{D}(v)$ because its depth is uniquely defined.

Outputting Predecessors and Omitting Orphans. Recall that an honest participant p active at time t outputs a vertex v from its local graph $G_p^{(t)}$ if and only
if $v \in \text{extract}(G_p^{(t)})|_{\mathsf{D}(G_p^{(t)})-\ell^*}$. By applying $\text{extract}()$ and chopping off the deep-
est vertices, the protocol enforces two requirements in order to output a vertex.
First v must be far from the end of a participant's graph $(\mathsf{D}(G_p^{(t)}) > \mathsf{D}(v) + \ell^*)$.
Second, v must be a predecessor of one of the starting vertices in $G_p^{(t)}$.

Intuitively, one can consider that every participant p decides whether each
vertex v in its view should be output or not. However, p "waits" before making
a decision until v is sufficiently far from the end of its graph. At that point, p
does not output v only if v has been "orphaned." A vertex is "orphaned" if it is
more than ℓ^* depth from the end of a graph but not a predecessor of one of the
graph's starting vertices.

To achieve graph consistency, p must make the same decision on v as every
other honest participant. We show that by the time the depth of G_p exceeds ℓ^*
more than the depth of v, v's status as an orphan or not an orphan has been
determined in $\mathbb{G}$ and will not change; moreover, v's orphan status in G_p must
mirror its status in $\mathbb{G}$. If v is not a predecessor of one of the starting vertices
in G_p, then v will never be a predecessor of a starting vertex in any honest
participant's local graph which is deep enough to decide on v. However, if v is a
predecessor of one of the starting vertices in G_p, then v will never be orphaned
in any honest participant's local graph.

Consistency of Honest Vertices. We first show consistency of the honest
vertices which honest participants output. We do so by showing that no honest
vertex is ever orphaned, and therefore *all* honest vertices are eventually output
by honest participants. Our high-level lemma towards this statement actually
says something stronger. It says that every honest vertex in $\mathbb{G}$ which is more
than $\ell_1 < \ell^*$ distance from the end of an honest participant's graph must be
extracted from the graph when it computes its output from its local graph.

Lemma 1 (Honest Vertex Extraction). *For every time t, honest partici-
pant p active at t, and honest vertex $v \in \mathbb{G}^{(t)}$: $\mathsf{D}(G_p^{(t)}) - \mathsf{D}(v) > \ell_1 \implies v \in$*
$\text{extract}(G_p^{(t)})$.

Lemma 1, consistency of honest vertices in participants' outputs, follows
trivially from composition of Lemmas 2 and 3, described below. Lemma 2 shows
that by the time $\mathsf{D}(G_p) > \mathsf{D}(v) + \ell_1$ for any honest participant's graph G_p and
honest vertex v, enough time must have passed since v was originally multicast
that v is in G_p. Lemma 3 shows that every such honest vertex in an honest
participant's graph must be a predecessor of a starting vertex in the graph.

Consistency of Honest Vertices in Honest Views. For the first step, we show
that if an honest participant's local graph G_p is deeper than an honest vertex v
by more than a fixed distance ℓ_1, then $v \in G_p$.

Lemma 2 (Depth-Based Indicator for Honest Vertices). *For all t, honest p active at t, and honest vertex $v \in \mathbb{G}^{(t)}$: $\mathsf{D}(G_p^{(t)}) - \mathsf{D}(v) > \ell_1 \implies v \in G_p^{(t)}$.*

Intuitively, ℓ_1 is derived as follows. Let t_v be the time that some honest vertex v is generated by honest participant q. Naively, one would like to claim that if $\mathsf{D}(G_p^{(t)}) - \mathsf{D}(v) > \rho$, then ρ vertices must have been generated after v, and it follows from the rate limit on resource allocations that $t > t_v + \Delta$. However, the naive attempt makes the unfounded assumption that at t_v, v must be the deepest vertex in $\mathbb{G}^{(t_v)}$. Instead, we derive a constant γ that gives the maximum difference between $\mathbb{G}^{(t)}$ and an honest view $G_p^{(t)}$ at any time t. We then derive $\ell_1 = \gamma + \rho$ and show that if $\mathsf{D}(G_p^{(t)}) - \mathsf{D}(v) > \ell_1$, then Δ time must have elapsed since v was generated and multicast. It follows that $v \in G_p^{(t)}$.

Extracting Every Honest Vertex. Recall that an honest participant extracts the starting vertices in its graph and all their predecessors, and then outputs only the vertices which are far from the end of its graph. We show that an honest participant always extracts *every* honest vertex in its graph.

Lemma 3 (Extracting All Honest Vertices in a Local Graph). *For every time t, honest participant p active at t, and honest vertex $v \in \mathbb{G}^{(t)}$: $v \in G_p^{(t)} \implies v \in \mathsf{extract}(G_p^{(t)})$.*

The lemma follows by showing that every honest vertex v eventually gains at least one honest successor which is not too far from v, measured in terms of depth. Intuitively, after an honest vertex v is generated, the first vertex generated by an honest participant with v in its view must be a successor of v. It follows that for every honest vertex v which is not a starting vertex in an honest participant's graph, there must be a path from v to a starting vertex in the graph.

Consistency of Corrupt Vertices. We show that consistency of corrupt vertices follows from consistency of their honest successors (or lack thereof). If every vertex is honestly generated and immediately multicast, then no vertex is ever orphaned. Only if a corrupt participant withholds a vertex can the vertex be orphaned. We show that after a corrupt vertex is generated, there is a limited time during which it must gain an honest successor or it will be orphaned. Imagine that starting at some time in an execution, corrupt participants use all of their resources to build a "withheld branch" B of $\mathbb{G}$ which includes no honest vertices, while honest participants continue to build $\mathbb{G}$ as per the protocol. Intuitively, if $\frac{\alpha}{\rho} > \beta$ (as we require), then the corrupt participants cannot keep pace with the honest participants, and eventually B will fall behind the depth of $\mathbb{G}$. We can compute for how long a withheld branch B can remain close in depth to $\mathbb{G}$. We derive a constant ℓ_2 for which any vertex which is ℓ_2 depth from the end of an honest participant's local graph and is a predecessor of a starting vertex must have an honest successor.

Lemma 4 (Honest Reachability Requirement for Extraction). *For all t, participant p active at t, and vertex $v \in \mathsf{extract}(G_p^{(t)})$: $\mathsf{D}(G_p^{(t)}) - \mathsf{D}(v) > \ell_2$ implies there exists an honest vertex u reachable from v such that $\mathsf{D}(u) - \mathsf{D}(v) \leq \ell_2$.*

Recall that an honest participant decides whether to output a vertex v only once v is $\ell^* = \ell_1 + \ell_2$ depth from the end of its local graph. If v is a predecessor of a starting vertex, then it must have an honest successor which is more than ℓ_1 depth from the end of the graph. This honest successor must be in every honest participant's local graph with depth sufficient to output v; therefore, because u must be extracted from every honest view in which it exists, every honest participant with local graph deep enough to output v must do so.

References

1. Alwen, J., Tackmann, B.: Moderately hard functions: definition, instantiations, and applications. In: Kalai, Y., Reyzin, L. (eds.) TCC 2017. LNCS, vol. 10677, pp. 493–526. Springer, Cham (2017). https://doi.org/10.1007/978-3-319-70500-2_17
2. Back, A., et al.: Hashcash-a denial of service counter-measure (2002)
3. Badertscher, C., Gazi, P., Kiayias, A., Russell, A., Zikas, V.: Ouroboros genesis: composable proof-of-stake blockchains with dynamic availability. In: ACM Conference on Computer and Communications Security, pp. 913–930. ACM (2018)
4. Badertscher, C., Maurer, U., Tschudi, D., Zikas, V.: Bitcoin as a transaction ledger: a composable treatment. In: Katz, J., Shacham, H. (eds.) CRYPTO 2017. LNCS, vol. 10401, pp. 324–356. Springer, Cham (2017). https://doi.org/10.1007/978-3-319-63688-7_11
5. Bano, S., et al.: Consensus in the age of blockchains. CoRR, abs/1711.03936 (2017)
6. Bentov, I., Hubácek, P., Moran, T., Nadler, A.: Tortoise and hares consensus: the meshcash framework for incentive-compatible, scalable cryptocurrencies. IACR Cryptology ePrint Archive, 2017:300 (2017)
7. Bentov, I., Pass, R., Shi, E.: The sleepy model of consensus. IACR Cryptology ePrint Archive, 2016:918 (2016)
8. Bentov, I., Pass, R., Shi, E.: Snow white: provably secure proofs of stake. IACR Cryptology ePrint Archive, 2016:919 (2016)
9. David, B., Ga, P., Kiayias, A., Russell, A.: Ouroboros praos: an adaptively-secure, semi-synchronous proof-of-stake protocol. Technical report, Cryptology ePrint Archive, Report 2017/573 (2017). http://eprint.iacr.org/2017/573
10. Dwork, C., Naor, M.: Pricing via processing or combatting junk mail. In: Brickell, E.F. (ed.) CRYPTO 1992. LNCS, vol. 740, pp. 139–147. Springer, Heidelberg (1993). https://doi.org/10.1007/3-540-48071-4_10
11. Eckey, L., Faust, S., Loss, J.: Efficient algorithms for broadcast and consensus based on proofs of work. IACR Cryptology ePrint Archive, 2017:915 (2017)
12. Garay, J., Kiayias, A., Ostrovsky, R., Panagiotakos, G., Zikas, V.: Resource-restricted cryptography: revisiting MPC bounds in the proof-of-work era. Cryptology ePrint Archive, Report 2019/1264 (2019). https://eprint.iacr.org/2019/1264
13. Garay, J.A., Kiayias, A.: SoK: a consensus taxonomy in the blockchain era. IACR Cryptology ePrint Archive, 2018:754 (2018)
14. Garay, J., Kiayias, A., Leonardos, N.: The bitcoin backbone protocol: analysis and applications. In: Oswald, E., Fischlin, M. (eds.) EUROCRYPT 2015. LNCS, vol. 9057, pp. 281–310. Springer, Heidelberg (2015). https://doi.org/10.1007/978-3-662-46803-6_10

15. Garay, J.A., Kiayias, A., Panagiotakos, G.: Consensus from signatures of work. Cryptology ePrint Archive, Report 2017/775 (2017). https://eprint.iacr.org/2017/775

16. Gilad, Y., Hemo, R., Micali, S., Vlachos, G., Zeldovich, N.: Algorand: scaling byzantine agreements for cryptocurrencies. Cryptology ePrint Archive, Report 2017/454 (2017). https://eprint.iacr.org/2017/454

17. Kiffer, L., Rajaraman, R., Shelat, A.: A better method to analyze blockchain consistency. In: Proceedings of the 2018 ACM SIGSAC Conference on Computer and Communications Security, CCS 2018, pp. 729–744. Association for Computing Machinery, New York (2018)

18. Lamport, L., Shostak, R., Pease, M.: The byzantine generals problem. ACM Trans. Program. Lang. Syst. (TOPLAS) **4**(3), 382–401 (1982)

19. Lewis-Pye, A., Roughgarden, T.: A general framework for the security analysis of blockchain protocols. CoRR, abs/2009.09480 (2020)

20. Miller, A., Kosba, A., Katz, J., Shi, E.: Nonoutsourceable scratch-off puzzles to discourage bitcoin mining coalitions. In: Proceedings of the 22nd ACM SIGSAC Conference on Computer and Communications Security, pp. 680–691. ACM (2015)

21. Nakamoto, S.: Bitcoin: a peer-to-peer electronic cash system (2008)

22. Pass, R., Seeman, L., Shelat, A.: Analysis of the blockchain protocol in asynchronous networks. IACR Cryptology ePrint Archive, 2016:454 (2016)

23. Pass, R., Shi, E.: Rethinking large-scale consensus. In: 2017 IEEE 30th Computer Security Foundations Symposium (CSF), pp. 115–129. IEEE (2017)

24. Pease, M., Shostak, R., Lamport, L.: Reaching agreement in the presence of faults. J. ACM (JACM) **27**(2), 228–234 (1980)

25. Terner, B.: Permissionless consensus in the resource model. Cryptology ePrint Archive, Report 2020/355 (2020). https://ia.cr/2020/355

26. Tschorsch, F., Scheuermann, B.: Bitcoin and beyond: a technical survey on decentralized digital currencies. Cryptology ePrint Archive, Report 2015/464 (2015). https://eprint.iacr.org/2015/464

Performance

Plumo: An Ultralight Blockchain Client

Psi Vesely[1,2], Kobi Gurkan[2,3], Michael Straka[2], Ariel Gabizon[4],
Philipp Jovanovic[2,5(✉)], Georgios Konstantopoulos[6], Asa Oines[2],
Marek Olszewski[2], and Eran Tromer[2,7,8]

[1] University of California San Diego, San Diego, USA
psi@ucsd.edu
[2] cLabs, Berlin, Germany
{kobi,a,m,mstraka}@clabs.co
[3] Ethereum Foundation, Berlin, Germany
[4] AZTEC Protocol, London, UK
ariel@aztecprotocol.com
[5] University College London, London, UK
p.jovanovic@ucl.ac.uk
[6] Paradigm, San Francisco, USA
me@gakonst.com
[7] Columbia University, New York, USA
[8] Tel Aviv University, Tel Aviv, Israel
tromer@cs.tau.ac.il

Abstract. Syncing the latest state of a blockchain can be a resource-intensive task, driving (especially mobile) end users towards centralized services offering instant access. To expand full decentralized access to anyone with a mobile phone, we introduce a consensus-agnostic compiler for constructing *ultralight clients*, providing secure and highly efficient blockchain syncing via a sequence of SNARK-based state transition proofs, and prove its security formally. Instantiating this, we present *Plumo*, an ultralight client for the Celo blockchain capable of syncing the latest network state summary in just a few seconds even on a low-end mobile phone. In Plumo, each transition proof covers four months of blockchain history and can be produced for just $25 USD of compute. Plumo achieves this level of efficiency thanks to two new SNARK-friendly constructions, which may also be of independent interest: a new BLS-based offline aggregate multisignature scheme in which signers do not have to know the members of their multisignature group in advance, and a new composite algebraic-symmetric cryptographic hash function.

Keywords: Ultralight clients · SNARKs · Aggregate multisignatures

1 Introduction

Among numerous obstacles to widespread adoption of blockchain technologies, scalability has been identified as a major hurdle [33]. Recent years have seen major improvements to throughput and latency via new proof-of-stake (PoS)

© International Financial Cryptography Association 2022
I. Eyal and J. Garay (Eds.): FC 2022, LNCS 13411, pp. 597–614, 2022.
https://doi.org/10.1007/978-3-031-18283-9_30

protocols [3,38], sharding [1,30], and payment channels [26,31]. This work tackles another scalability challenge: high participation costs for end users.

To securely interact with a blockchain without trusting a centralized party, a node must first download and verify the blockchain. The requisite data, storage, and computation resources are unavailable to many potential participants. For example, as of August 2021, the Ethereum blockchain is over 900 GB (in non-archival mode). Even in light sync mode, 6.5 GB of header metadata must be downloaded and verified, exceeding the bandwidth and storage available to many mobile users. Participation cost concerns for end users also apply in the context of cross-blockchain interoperability protocols, where smart contract code running on one chain (with high storage and computation costs) needs to verify the state of another chain.

High participation costs motivate the need for *ultralight* clients (UCs), which verify succinct proofs of valid blockchain data leading up to the current state. Prior attempts [13,16,18,35] have various restrictions and drawbacks, including specificity to Proof-of-Work (PoW), implementation complexity, unsuitability for smart contract blockchains, and significant blockchain performance hits outside the UC context. Some of these relative drawbacks are outlined in Table 1.

We introduce the PLUMO system, an efficient UC protocol, which overcomes these drawbacks and achieves nearly-instant ultralight client synchronization. It is based on succinct transition proofs, using two new SNARK-friendly constructions.

A Brief History of Ultralight Clients. To contextualize, we first describe previous works in more detail, and then describe how our techniques overcome prior drawbacks.

Kiayias et al. introduced NIPoWPoWs in [28], a PoW-specific proof of SPV that relies on statistical properties of hashes to make probabilistic guarantees about the amount of work a chain contains. Bünz et al. extended this result in Flyclient [16], the first NIPoPoW-based UC, guaranteeing unconditional succinctness with $O(\log^2 n)$ sized proofs[1] and supporting variable mining difficulty. It is integrated into chains by adding Merkle Mountain Range (MMR) commitment to the transaction roots of the entire blockchain to each header. Given the latest block header containing a MMR commitment, the verifier hashes it to obtain challenge block heights pseudorandomly; they accept if also provided MMR-inclusion and subtree equality-proofs that verify with respect to those challenges and the MMR commitment. Smart contracts are supported, since miners are trusted to have verified all consensus rules. However, this approach does not extend to PoS blockchains, or to full verification of a PoW blockchain, since these require checking every pertinent state transition.

Chiesa and Tromer proposed PCD, a primitive permitting distributed computations between mutually distrustful parties that run indefinitely [20]. Its first practical construction by Ben-Sasson et al. used recursive composition of fully

---

[1] The NIPowPow protocol of Kiayias et al. is forced to revert to the SPV light client protocol in the presence of bribing and selfish mining attacks.

Table 1. Comparison of UCs. App curve bits denotes the size of the curve used for most network activity including making transactions; prover curve bits refers to the curve used to produce and verify UC proofs. Estimates for both [18] and Flyclient proof sizes are taken from [18] and are for a "barebones" (scriptless) Bitcoin. The Flyclient paper reports slightly larger proof sizes for Ethereum due to the difference in header size. Since block times for Celo are about 120× shorter than for Bitcoin, we compare UC proof sizes by time since the genesis block. Halo 2 and Pickles are both proposed network upgrades to ZCash and Mina, resp., exact proof sizes are not yet available. NIPoWPoWs are restricted to PoW networks and in particular SPV; recursive composition based PCD as used by Mina and [18] requires a trusted setup; otherwise consensus, simplifying assumptions (SA), programmability, and trusted setup should be seen as implementation choices rather than limitations of a proof type. Some proof types also impose curve requirements (see below).

UC	Proof type	Consensus	SA	Programmability	Trusted setup	App/prover curve bits	Proof sizes (days)			Verifier time
							347	694	1,736	
PLUMO	Transition	BFT	✓	✓	✓	377 → 761	1.2 KB	2.5 KB	6.4KB	$o(n)$
Flyclient	NIPoPoW	PoW	✓	✓	χ	256	135 KB	163 KB	204KB	$O(\log^2 n)$
[18]	Transition	PoW	χ	χ	✓	753 ↻ 753	7.4 KB	10 KB	18KB	$o(n)$
[18]	PCD	PoW	χ	χ	✓	753 ↻ 753	0.4 KB			$O(1)$
Mina	PCD	Ouroboros	χ	χ	✓	753 ↻ 753	7.1 KB			$O(1)$
Halo 2/Pickles	PCD	PoW/Ouroboros	χ		χ	255 ↻ 255	$O(1)$			$O(1)$

succinct SNARKs over cycles of elliptic curves in [6]. Building on this PCD construction, Bonneau et al. proposed Mina (formerly known as Coda) [13], the first fully succinct (i.e., constant-sized) blockchain whose state at any time can be verified in constant time. While this results in an ideal situation for the UC verifier, these techniques impose a large performance overhead on the part of the protocol being proved (all of consensus in the case of Mina) and the heavy cryptographic machinery required imposes high development costs.

Foremost, both the UC prover and verifier, and all of the consensus verified by the UC protocol must be set over a cycle of quite inefficient pairing-friendly curves at 753 bits[2] where, e.g., it was found Groth16 verification takes roughly 15× longer than on BLS12-381 [18]. Additionally, a trusted setup is required for each curve and these setups must be computed sequentially[3].

Recent developments in PCD constructions allow compatibility with transparent SNARKs and cycles of non-pairing friendly curves, which can provide 100-bits security at just 255 bits. Bowe et al. introduced Halo [14], later formalized as an atomic accumulation scheme by Bünz et al. in [17]. Halo amortizes the cost of proof system verification based on *interactive oracle proofs* (IOPs) [5] and *algebraic holographic proofs* (AHPs) [21] via lazy batch verification of polynomial commitment openings, recursively verifying just the comparatively cheap

---

[2] MNT4-753/MNT6-753 is the most efficient known pairing-friendly cycle at 128-bits security. Evidence suggests the nonexistence of significantly better options [19].

[3] Subsequent work introducing fully succinct SNARKs with universal SRSs [32] allow parallel setups, but performance lags behind circuit-specific SNARKs [21].

arithmetic checks on the evaluations. ZCash is currently working on a refinement of these techniques with "Halo 2," and Mina is introducing a "Pickles" network upgrade that will also use atomic accumulation based PCD. These advantages come at the loss of pairing-based cryptography, which powers efficiency and non-interactivity otherwise not afforded[4].

Simplifying Assumptions. Using simplifying assumptions (SAs) provides weaker security guarantees for light clients than proving consensus in full. Adversarial control of the majority of mining power or a dishonest supermajority on a BFT committee can result in a light client being convinced of an invalid state. Under these conditions full nodes can still be convinced of an alternate history, though transactions in the malicious fork have to follow consensus rules, which can still enable a great deal of fraud and theft. The violation of such assumptions, however, would still render the blockchain insecure for full nodes, despite enabling even worse attacks for light clients. This justifies their use in practice.

Proving a light client protocol has several advantages over proving all of consensus. First, there's simply much less to prove, especially so for networks offering programmability; indeed, only Flyclient and PLUMO support programmable blockchains. Even without programmability, a single prover cannot keep up with the 1tx/s Mina blockchain, and to deal with this they incentivize "SNARK workers" to compete to provide proofs for different parts of a PCD recursion tree (allowing parallelization of prover work). Second, to efficiently prove all of consensus, all of consensus must be optimized to this end. However, optimizing for SNARK arithmetization can negatively impact performance outside the context of the SNARK prover, e.g., while the BHP-BLAKE2s cryptographic hash we introduce in Sect. 5 is SNARK-efficient, it is much less efficient than symmetric-flavor hashes like SHA3 on conventional von Neumann computer architecture.

Transition Proofs. PLUMO is the first UC to use transition proofs, allowing a client hardcoded with the genesis state s_0 to sync to some later state s_n via a chain of sequential intermediate SNARKs. We believe the use of a SA is not just justified, but essential to our approach[5]; together with heavy optimization of just the small part of consensus our light client protocol encapsulates, our SA allows each SNARK to attest to four months of blockchain history.

---

[4] E.g., non-interactive multisignatures, used often in BFT consensus and multisignature wallets, are only possible with pairings; for consensus naive $O(n^2)$ communication can be avoided with CoSi [29], but higher latency persists, and multisignature wallet spends would require participants to all be online concurrently. Pairing-based cryptography will also power Celo's forthcoming ARKE private contact discovery system (see https://celo.org/papers/future-of-digital-currencies).

[5] We believe the estimates of subsequent work [18] for a transition-based UC proving full consensus of a barebones Bitcoin network to be off by an order of magnitude even assuming a circuit an order of magnitude greater than PLUMO's (which required coordinating a historically large 2^{28} powers-of-τ trusted setup ceremony), and hashing with SNARK-optimized Poseidon [25]. Such circumstances would allow proofs to cover about a week, but Flyclient would offer much faster verifier time with only slightly larger proofs given the relative costs of SNARK verification and hashing.

Our design also allows us to keep the full Celo consensus on the efficient pairing-friendly BLS12-377 curve. To get around the problem that proving signatures over the same curve they were created on is not possible without highly expensive non-native arithmetic, we borrow the approach of using a two-chain of elliptic curves introduced by Bowe et al. in Zexe [15], thus avoiding the need to run consensus over a costly pairing-friendly cycle.

Contributions. This paper presents the following contributions:

- A formal model of UCs general enough to capture all aforementioned UCs, while at the same time remaining quite simple.
- A compiler theorem capturing our simple and efficient approach to building secure UCs with transition proofs.
- BBSGLRY, a new BLS-based aggregate multisignature scheme that improves on state-of-the-art AMSP-PoP [10] by removing the need to know and append the aggregate public key of one's multisignature group before signing.
- A framework for building composite algebraic-symmetric cryptographic hashes, which improve on the SNARK-efficiency of symmetric hash functions while maintaining their more well-established security guarantees, and our proposed instantiation BHP-BLAKE2s.
- A Rust implementation of Plumo showing that for $25/day USD of compute on modern cloud infrastructure an untrusted prover can provide proofs for the whole Celo network, and that a Plumo client can sync and verify a summary of the latest blockchain state in seconds even on a low-end mobile phone.

Organization. The rest of the paper is organized as follows. Section 2 gives an overview of the Plumo architecture. Section 3 describes our threat model. Section 4 presents a formalization of ultralight clients, our compiler, and then Plumo as an instantiation. Section 5 presents our aggregate multisignature scheme and framework for composite algebraic-symmetric SNARK-friendly hashes, which we instantiate with Bowe-Hopwood-Pedersen and BLAKE2s. Section 6 presents benchmarks for our Plumo Rust implementation and details numerous optimizations.

2   Overview

The Celo blockchain uses the Istanbul BFT consensus [34]. We observe that in order to verify the latest block header in BFT networks a client only needs the public keys of the current committee. As long as no committee has had a dishonest supermajority, a client who verifies a chain of committee hand-off messages certifying the PoS election results, known as *epoch messages*, does not need to check each block or even the headers of each block. Instead, to make (or verify a recent) transaction, the client simply asks for the latest (or otherwise relevant) block header, and verifies that it has been signed by a supermajority of the current committee. This constitutes the simplifying assumption (SA) and light client protocol proved by Plumo (formally, Assumption 1).

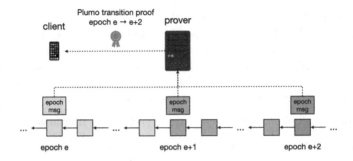

Fig. 1. Plumo architecture overview. In practice, our proofs cover 120 epochs.

Since Celo has 5s block times, this means transition proofs skip 17,280 blocks for every epoch message they verify. Further, it reduces the task of optimizing the transition proof SNARK circuit to just optimizing the epoch messages and their associated signatures (Fig. 1).

In our circuit, we verify 120 sequential epoch messages, each signed by a potentially different group of roughly 67–100 validators. A multisignature is already computed over each epoch message as part of our light client protocol; compounding this efficiency, the PLUMO prover aggregates these multisignatures into a single aggregate multisignature, which costs half the constraints to verify for our BBSGLRY signature scheme. To further reduce the circuit size, instead of passing in the list of public keys that signed each epoch message, we pass in a bitmap indicating who signed, where the canonical ordering is given by the preceding epoch message listing the committee public keys. The Hamming weight is first verified to be sufficient, and then the bitmap is used to compute the aggregate public key corresponding to each epoch message.

As cryptographic hashes that perform many bitwise operations are particularly expensive inside SNARKs, for epoch messages we instantiate BBSGLRY with a new composite cryptographic hash built from the collision-resistant Bowe-Hopwood-Pedersen hash [27] and the symmetric-flavor BLAKE2s cryptographic hash [4]. While lookup tables make it possible to at least avoid scalar multiplications, Bowe-Hopwood-Pedersen still requires many group additions, and while efficient in SNARKs is slow on conventional von Neumann computer architecture. By instantiating BBSGLRY with BLAKE2s for signing block headers, the vast majority of consensus is unaffected by this inefficiency, simultaneously ensuring ultralight clients (UCs) can efficiently verify block headers after syncing the current committee's public keys.

Aggregate Multisignatures. The BBSGLRY aggregate multisignature scheme takes the Boneh-Lynn-Shacham (BLS) signature [11] as its starting point and combines various extensions from [9,12,36]. Its most similar to the AMSP-PoP aggregate multisignature scheme presented by Boneh et al. in [10]. AMSP-PoP requires signers who create a multisignature know the group of signers in advance. In particular, signers must compute the aggregate public key apk of the signer group and then prepend it to the message before hashing and signing in the normal way: $\mathsf{Sign}(\mathsf{sk}, \mathsf{apk}, m) = \mathsf{H_s}(\mathsf{apk}\|m)^{\mathsf{sk}}$. For one, this expands the size of our circuit by adding more data to hash. Further, this forces BFT consensus to restart if a node who participates honestly in earlier rounds goes Byzantine and fails to produce their contribution to the multisignature.

BBSGLRY overcomes these limitations as follows. We observe that in the definitions used by [10] that proofs-of-possession are checked by the key aggregation algorithm KeyAgg. The adversary is permitted to output both a set of aggregate public keys and a set of pairs of public keys and PoPs. Since KeyAgg is not run on the aggregate public keys, an aggregate public key must be prepended when signing to prevent rogue key attacks. We believe their definitions do not reflect the usage of PoPs in production systems, including Celo. We thus provide new definitions where every public key the adversary outputs must be accompanied by a valid PoP (see the full version of the paper [37]). Working from these definitions, we are able to prove security of BBSGLRY, where signing is identical to BLS: $\mathsf{Sign}(\mathsf{sk}, m) = \mathsf{H_s}(m)^{\mathsf{sk}}$.

SNARK-Friendly Hashing. When representing an arithmetic circuit in R1CS, addition gates are essentially free, while multiplication gates are not. Only recently have we seen the introduction of low-multiplication cryptographic hash functions, such as MiMC [2] and Poseidon [25]. While such hash functions are a promising development, we believe there has so far been insufficient time for cryptanalysis of these designs. As an alternative, we formalize a folklore technique of first "shrinking" a long message with an algebraic collision-resistant hash (CRH) requiring far fewer constraints per message bit, and then call the compression function of a "symmetric-flavor" cryptographic hash function on its output. Our compiler in Sect. 5.2 formalizes this approach and provides a security reduction appropriate for use when instantiating a random oracle (as in necessary for BBSGLRY). We instantiate our compiler with the Bowe-Hopwood-Pedersen hash and with the BLAKE2s compression function to produce the BHP-BLAKE2s cryptographic hash we use for epoch messages.

A Two-Chain of Elliptic Curves. A SNARK arithmetic circuit is defined in the scalar field $\mathbb{F}_p$ of an elliptic curve. This presents a problem when verifying authenticated data computed over that same field, where verification (such as of BBSGLRY signatures) generally involves $\mathbb{F}_q$ operations. To avoid performing costly non-native arithmetic, which blows up circuit size, or moving to an expensive pairing-friendly cycle, we use a two-chain of elliptic curves, where the scalar field of the second curve is the same size as the base field of the first. In particular, we use the BLS12-377/BW6-761 two-chain, where the first (inner) curve is the same as in the original two-chain by Bowe et al. [15], and the second (outer) was introduced by Housni and Guillevic [22] as more efficient replacement for the outer curve of Bowe et al. This allows all of consensus to be carried out over an efficient pairing-friendly curve, while only the UC prover and UC verifier when syncing use the slower second curve.

3   Threat Model

In addition to a number of cryptographic hardness assumptions, PLUMO makes the following security assumptions with respect to network participants:

Assumption 1. *For each epoch it holds $n > \lceil f/3 \rceil$, where n and f are the number of total and dishonest validators.*

Assumption 2. *There is at least a single honest participant in the multi-party computation (MPC) for the SNARK trusted setup.*

For background on proof-of-stake and the Istanbul Byzantine fault tolerant consensus Celo uses, we refer the reader to the full version of the paper [37]. There we discuss the impacts of *long-range attacks* and *future committee attacks*, a new related attack on PoS consensus that we identify and propose a simple defense for. For more information on the multiparty computation used for our SNARK trusted setup ceremony, including optimizations that have made it faster to carry out and verify than past public ceremonies please see [37].

4   Ultralight Clients

We distinguish between full nodes, which use a state transition function S to incrementally compute the full state s corresponding to a blockchain $\boldsymbol{b} = [b_i]_{i=1}^n$ as new blocks $b_{n+1}, b_{n+2}, \ldots$ arrive, and light clients, which use the summary update function $\hat{S}$ to incrementally compute a summary $\hat{s}$ of the blockchain as they receive new trimmings $\hat{b}_{n+1}, \hat{b}_{n+2}, \ldots$. A trimming is a chunk of blockchain data (e.g., block headers for PoW blockchains or epoch messages for BFT consensus) belonging to a trimming language $\mathcal{L}_{\hat{C}}$ representing local checks such as syntax and signature verifications. A blockchain summary belongs to the summary language $\mathcal{L}_{\hat{s}}$ and is a commitment to the full state of the blockchain, enabling verification of specific transactions and full state values via succinct inclusion proofs.

Ultralight Clients. Informally, we define an ultralight client (UC) to be one that receives succinct arguments of knowledge (AoKs) of trimmings. For $n \in \mathbb{Z}^+$ and $\hat{\boldsymbol{b}}$ of length n, an UC receives proofs of the *summary relation*:

$$\mathcal{R}_{\hat{s}}^{(n)} = \left\{ (\hat{s} \in \mathcal{L}_{\hat{s}};\ \hat{\boldsymbol{b}} \in \mathcal{L}_{\hat{C}})\ :\ \hat{s} = \hat{S}(\hat{s}_g, \hat{\boldsymbol{b}}) \right\} .$$

An UC starts with a hardcoded genesis summary $\hat{s}_g$. It can verify $\hat{s}$ is the valid summary of the blockchain n trimmings later by verifying a succinct proof of $\mathcal{R}_{\hat{s}}^{(n)}$. The argument of knowledge property guarantees that a valid trimmed blockchain $\hat{\boldsymbol{b}} \in \mathcal{L}_{\hat{C}}$ corresponding to $\hat{s}$ can always be extracted from the proofs.

Incremental Provers. Since prover resources are finite, for sufficiently high n it becomes impractical to prove $\mathcal{R}_{\hat{s}}^{(n)}$. An UC prover thus needs to be able to create such proofs incrementally and re-use work in some way. We model this by incrementally giving the prover one or more new trimmings each time it is invoked to create a new proof for the latest summary. The prover locally stores an auxiliary state ω to help it create the new proof. The growth of ω necessarily must be significantly sublinear in the size of the trimmed blockchain for this approach to remain concretely efficient long-term.

PCD based UCs address this by recursively verifying the previous state transition proof together with the new blocks or trimmings. Avoiding various drawbacks of this approach elaborated on in Sect. 1, we opt for the simpler approach of transition proofs, i.e., prove $\mathcal{R}_{\hat{s}}^{(n)}$ for any n by producing $\lceil n/m \rceil$ SNARK proofs of

$$\mathcal{R}_{\hat{s}}^{(m)} = \left\{ (\hat{s}_{i-1}, \hat{s}_i \in \mathcal{L}_{\hat{s}};\ \hat{\boldsymbol{b}} \in \mathcal{L}_{\hat{b}}^m)\ :\ \hat{s}_i = \hat{S}(\hat{s}_{i-1}, \hat{\boldsymbol{b}}) \right\}\ , \tag{1}$$

for $i \in \lceil n/m \rceil$. For sufficiently large n (e.g., 4 months in the case of PLUMO), the concrete proof length and verification time of this sublinear approach can be on par with asymptotically better (but more complex) approaches for years out, as illustrated by our results Table 1.

Extraction in the Presence of Oracles. A summary relation often must some authenticated data (e.g., validator signatures). Unfortunately, standard AoK definitions fail to guarantee extraction when the adversary is granted access to additional oracles such as signature oracles. This problem has been first and foremost studied by Fiore and Nitulescu, who developed the notion of an O-SNARK and produced the first results regarding their existence [23]. We adapt their knowledge soundness definition to our UC interface.

4.1 Ultralight Clients

An ultralight client (UC) Π_{UC} is defined by a triple of efficient non-interactive algorithms (Setup, ProveUpdate, VerifyUpdate) working as follows

- Setup$(1^\lambda) \to$ pp: a randomized setup algorithm run by one or more parties that, input a security parameter λ (in unary), outputs a set of public parameters pp.
- ProveUpdate$(\mathsf{pp}, \hat{s}, \omega, \hat{s}', \hat{\boldsymbol{b}}) \to (\pi', \omega')$: an untrusted light client acts as the prover that, input public parameters pp, previous summary $\hat{s} \in \mathcal{L}_{\hat{s}}$ with auxiliary state ω, and current summary $\hat{s}'$ with corresponding new trimmings $\hat{\boldsymbol{b}} \in \mathcal{L}_{\hat{b}}^n$, outputs a new proof π and auxiliary state ω'.
- VerifyUpdate$(\mathsf{pp}, \hat{s}, \pi) \to \{0, 1\}$: an UC verifier that, given a summary $\hat{s}$ and proof π, outputs 0 (reject) or 1 (accept).

and satisfying *succinctness*, *perfect completeness*, and *adaptive security*, as defined below. Assuming a strict total order $\leq$ on summaries, if presented with more than one valid $(\hat{s}, \pi)$ pair, an UC can efficiently determine and accept the greater as the current summary.

Succinctness. Let $\|\hat{\boldsymbol{b}}\|$ be the length of the description of $\hat{\boldsymbol{b}}$ (as opposed to the number of trimmings $|\hat{\boldsymbol{b}}|$). Succinctness is captured by the set of properties that

(1) $|\pi|$ grows sublinearly in $||\hat{\boldsymbol{b}}||$, (2) VerifyUpdate runs in time sublinear in $||\hat{\boldsymbol{b}}||$, and (3) $|\omega|$ grows sublinearly in $||\hat{\boldsymbol{b}}||$.

Completeness. An UC $\Pi_{\mathsf{UC}} = (\mathsf{Setup}, \mathsf{ProveUpdate}, \mathsf{VerifyUpdate})$ is *perfectly complete* if for every adversary $\mathcal{A}$ it holds that

$$\Pr\left[\begin{array}{c} \hat{\boldsymbol{b}}_1 || \cdots || \hat{\boldsymbol{b}}_m \in \mathcal{L}_{\hat{C}} \\ \wedge \\ \exists i \in [m] : \\ \mathsf{VerifyUpdate}(\mathsf{pp}, \hat{s}_i, \pi_i) \neq 1 \end{array} \middle| \begin{array}{l} \mathsf{pp} \leftarrow \mathsf{Setup}(1^\lambda) \\ [\hat{\boldsymbol{b}}_i]_{i=1}^m \leftarrow \mathcal{A}(\mathsf{pp}) \\ \text{For } i \in [m] : \\ \quad \hat{s}_i \leftarrow \hat{S}(\hat{s}_{i-1}, \hat{\boldsymbol{b}}_i) \\ \quad (\pi_i, \omega_i) \leftarrow \mathsf{ProveUpdate}(\mathsf{pp}, \hat{s}_{i-1}, \omega_{i-1}, \hat{s}_i, \hat{\boldsymbol{b}}) \end{array}\right] = 0,$$

where $\hat{s}_0 \leftarrow \hat{s}_g$, $\pi_0 \leftarrow \perp$, and $\omega_0 \leftarrow \perp$, and the probability is taken over choice of pp and any random coins used by $\mathcal{A}$.

Adaptive Security. An UC is adaptively secure if it satisfies the definition of a $\mathcal{Z}$-auxiliary input O-SNARK for $\mathbb{O}$ (see [37]) for $\mathcal{R} = \mathcal{R}_{\hat{s}}^{(*)}$ and the appropriate auxiliary input generator and oracle families, and where $(\mathrm{x}, \mathrm{w}) = (\hat{s}, \hat{\boldsymbol{b}})$ and Verify = VerifyUpdate.

Flexibility of Our Definition. We illustrate the flexibility of our definitions by showing how they can capture PCD and NIPoWPoW based UCs as well. A trimmed blockchain can be modeled as a DAG where the current summary is the sink. Starting with the edge leaving the sole source, labeled $\hat{s}_g$, each edge $e = (\hat{s}, \hat{s}')$ is labeled with a consecutive trimming $\hat{b}$ taking the state from $\hat{s}$ to $\hat{s}' = \hat{S}(\hat{s}, \hat{b})$. Then depending on the construction of PCD used, we have $\omega = (\pi, x)$ where x is additional auxiliary information such as state tree roots and π is the proof generated by a S/NARK and/or succinct accumulator.

Next consider Flyclient [16], where the summary is a Merkle Mountain Range commitment to the block headers, which themselves form the trimmed blockchain. Here the UC prover must store the entire trimmed blockchain on disk, but only needs to open the commitment by reading from disk block headers at a logarithmic number of heights; thus we define $|\omega|$ to be logarithmic. Here proofs, composed of leaf inclusion and subtree equality proofs, are distinct from auxiliary state, but also logarithmic in $|\hat{\boldsymbol{b}}|$.

4.2 An Ultralight Client Compiler

We introduce a compiler that outputs a secure UC given a summary relation $\mathcal{R}_{\hat{s}}^{(m)}$ for a fixed $m \in \mathbb{Z}^+$ and O-SNARK Π_{OS} for the oracles corresponding to the authenticated data verified in $\mathcal{R}_{\hat{s}}$[6].

---

[6] We note that proofs of $\mathcal{R}_{\hat{s}}^{(m')}$ for $1 \leq m' \leq m$ are called for by our construction as well. With transparent and universal setup SNARKs this can be achieved just by making m circuits, but for SNARKs with circuit-specific setups adding support for padding in $\mathcal{R}_{\hat{s}}^{(m)}$ can avoid the need for m distinct trusted setups.

Construction 1. *Given a $\mathcal{Z}$-auxiliary input O-SNARK $\Pi_{OS} = $ (Gen, Prove, Verify) for $\mathcal{R}_{\hat{s}}^{(m)}$ and for the oracle families corresponding to all data computed using a secret state verified in $\mathcal{R}_{\hat{s}}^{(m)}$, we construct an ultralight client $\Pi_{UC} = $ (Setup, ProveUpdate, VerifyUpdate) as follows:*

Setup$(1^\lambda) \to$ pp :	VerifyUpdate(pp, $\hat{s}, \pi$) :
1. Output pp $\leftarrow$ Gen(1^λ)	1. Parse $([\hat{s}]_{i=1}^{k-1}, [\pi_i]_{i=1}^k) \leftarrow \pi$
	2. Set $\hat{s}_0 \leftarrow \hat{s}_g$ and $\hat{s}_k \leftarrow \hat{s}$.
	3. Output $b \leftarrow \wedge_{i=1}^k$Verify(crs, $\hat{s}_{i-1}, \hat{s}_i, \pi_i$)

ProveUpdate(pp, $\hat{s}, \omega, \hat{s}', \hat{b}$)

1. *If $\hat{s}$ corresponds to a trimmed blockchain of n trimmings, then ω will contain $r \equiv n \mod m$ "remainder" trimmings $\hat{b}_r$, $k = \lceil n/m \rceil$ SNARK proofs $\boldsymbol{\pi} = [\pi_i]_{i=1}^k$, and $k-1$ intermediate summaries $\hat{\boldsymbol{s}} = [\hat{s}_i]_{i=1}^{k-1}$.*
2. *If $r = 0$ reset $\hat{\boldsymbol{s}} \leftarrow \hat{\boldsymbol{s}} \| \hat{s}$, else reset $\boldsymbol{\pi} \leftarrow [\pi_i]_{i=1}^{k-1}$ as the last proof covers only $r < m$ trimmings.*
3. *Set $\hat{\boldsymbol{b}}_1' \| \cdots \| \hat{\boldsymbol{b}}_t' \leftarrow \hat{\boldsymbol{b}}_r \| \hat{\boldsymbol{b}}$ where partitions $[\hat{\boldsymbol{b}}_i']_{i=1}^{t-1}$ each contain m trimmings and*

$$|\hat{\boldsymbol{b}}_t'| = r' = n + |\hat{\boldsymbol{b}}| \pmod m \ \vee \ m \ .$$

4. *If $r' < m$ then set $\hat{\boldsymbol{b}}_{r'} \leftarrow \hat{\boldsymbol{b}}_t'$, else set $\hat{\boldsymbol{b}}_{r'} \leftarrow \perp$.*
5. *Generate new intermediate states and proofs for $i \in [t]$:*
$$\hat{s}_i' \leftarrow \hat{S}(\hat{s}_{i-1}', \hat{\boldsymbol{b}}_i') \qquad \hat{\pi}_i \leftarrow \text{Prove(crs, } \hat{s}_{i-1}', \hat{s}_i'; \ \hat{\boldsymbol{b}}_i')$$
where $\hat{s}_0'$ is the last intermediate summary in $\hat{\boldsymbol{s}}$.
6. *Let $\boldsymbol{\pi}' \leftarrow \boldsymbol{\pi} \| \boldsymbol{\pi}'$, $\hat{\boldsymbol{s}}' \leftarrow \hat{\boldsymbol{s}} \| [\hat{s}_i']_{i=1}^{t-1}$, and $\omega' \leftarrow (\hat{\boldsymbol{b}}_{r'}, \boldsymbol{\pi}', \hat{\boldsymbol{s}}')$. Output $(\boldsymbol{\pi}', \omega')$.*

Theorem 1. *If $\Pi_{OS} = $ (Gen, Prove, Verify) is an adaptively secure SNARK for relation $\mathcal{R}_{\hat{s}}$, auxiliary input generator $\mathcal{Z}$, and oracle family $\mathbb{O}$, then the UC Π_{UC} output by Construction 1 is adaptively secure (Sect. 4.1) for $\mathcal{R}_{\hat{s}}$, $\mathcal{Z}$, and $\mathbb{O}$.*

We refer to the full version of the paper [37] that presents the proof of the above theorem.

4.3 The PLUMO Ultralight Client

We make a few simplifications for clarity of exposition in this section; we present a full specification of our circuit in the full version of the paper [37]. Celo uses the Istanbul BFT consensus algorithm [34]. We observe that by taking Assumption 1 as our simplifying assumption (SA), a light client only needs verify a valid chain of epoch messages delegating authority from committee to the next in order to learn the current committee public key set. From there, they can download the most recent block header, verify its multisignature, and learn the latest state roots (and also easily check their balance, make a transaction, etc.). The most recent Celo epoch message is the current summary. In addition to the current committee public key set, the summary contains the epoch index, the *current and parent entropy* (to mitigate future committee attacks [37]), and the signer threshold[7]. The standard operator $\leq$ over the epoch index of each summary defines the required total order $\leq$ over summaries (a strict total order under our simplifying assumption). The summary update relation checks there exists a sequence of epoch messages where each successive message (1) is signed by at least the signer threshold number of validators, (2) increases the epoch index by 1, and (3) has parent entropy matching the previous current entropy. Then it verifies an aggregate multisignature over the result. PLUMO instantiates the compiler from the previous section using the Groth16 proof system, which was proven to be knowledge sound in the AGM under the q-DLOG assumption in [24]. For PLUMO, we must additionally require Groth16 is an O-SNARK with respect to BBSGLRY signing oracles. We also assume that the auxiliary input our adversary receives is "benign"[8]. We note here that there have been few prior results on extraction in the presence of auxiliary inputs and/or oracles [8,23], none of which apply to our construction[9].

Theorem 2. *Let $\mathcal{H} : \{0,1\}^* \to \mathbb{G}_1$ be a hash family modeled as a random oracle and let $\mathsf{BBSGLRY}_{\mathcal{H}}$ be the $\mathsf{BBSGLRY}$ signature scheme (Sect. 5.1) instantiated with $\mathcal{H}$, and let $\mathcal{Z}$ be a benign auxiliary input generator. Assume the Groth16 SNARK is an adaptive argument of knowledge for $(\mathcal{O}_{\mathcal{H}}, \mathcal{O}_{\mathsf{BBSGLRY}_{\mathcal{H}}})$ and $\mathcal{Z}$. Then PLUMO is an adaptively secure UC for $\mathcal{R}_{\hat{s}}$, $\mathcal{Z}$, $\mathcal{O}_{\mathcal{H}}$, and $\mathcal{O}_{\mathsf{BBSGLRY}_{\mathcal{H}}}$.*

Proof. This follows directly from the compiler Theorem 1. $\square$

5   SNARK-Friendly Signatures and Hashing

5.1   BBSGLRY: Non-interactive Aggregate Multisignatures

BBSGLRY is an offline aggregate multisignature scheme providing non-interactive key and signature aggregation, and not requiring signers know the multisignature group in advance.

Construction 2 (BBSGLRY aggregate multisignature scheme). *Given a type 3 bilinear group sampler $\mathsf{SampleGrp}_3$ and two hash families $\mathcal{H}_s : \{0,1\}^* \to \mathbb{G}_1$ and $\mathcal{H}_p : \mathbb{G}_2 \to \mathbb{G}_1$, our aggregate multisignature scheme $\mathsf{BBSGLRY}$ is defined by an 8-tuple of efficient algorithms ($\mathsf{Setup}, \mathsf{KeyGen}, \mathsf{VPoP}, \mathsf{Sign}, \mathsf{KeyAgg}, \mathsf{MultiSign}, \mathsf{AggSign}, \mathsf{Verify}$), working as follows:*

– $\mathsf{Setup}(1^\lambda) \to \mathsf{pp}$: *sample a type 3 bilinear group $\langle\mathsf{group}\rangle \leftarrow \mathsf{SampleGrp}_3(1^\lambda)$ and two hash functions $(\mathsf{H_p}, \mathsf{H_s}) \xleftarrow{\$} \mathsf{H}_\lambda$. Return $\mathsf{pp} \leftarrow (\langle\mathsf{group}\rangle, \mathsf{H_p}, \mathsf{H_s})$.*

---

[7] Our PoS election occasionally elects $n<100$ committee members. Rather than compute $\lceil 2n/3 \rceil + 1$ in the circuit, we piggyback on our SA, including it in the epoch message.

[8] A benign distribution supplies negligible advantage to any adversary against any construction (e.g., the uniform distribution is conjectured benign [7]).

[9] Results for hash-then-sign signatures in [23] require modifying the signer to sample and prepend a random nonce to each message they sign—currently no UCs which prove verification of signatures are doing this.

- KeyGen(pp) $\rightarrow$ (pk, sk, π): *choose a secret key* sk $\xleftarrow{\$}$ $\mathbb{F}$ *and set the public key* pk $\leftarrow G_2^{sk} \in \mathbb{G}_2$. *Create the PoP* $\pi \leftarrow H_p(pk)^{sk} \in \mathbb{G}_1$. *Return* (pk, sk, π).
- VPoP(pp, pk, π): *given public key* pk $\in \mathbb{G}_2$ *and PoP* $\pi \in \mathbb{G}_1$, *return* 1 *if* $e(\pi, G_2) = e(H_p(pk), pk)$, *else* 0.
- Sign(pp, sk, m) $\rightarrow$ σ: *given a secret key* sk $\in \mathbb{F}$ *and message* $m \in \{0,1\}^*$, *return a signature* $\sigma \leftarrow H_s(m)^{sk} \in \mathbb{G}_1$.
- KeyAgg(pp, $\{pk_i\}_{i=1}^n$) $\rightarrow$ apk: *given* n *distinct public keys* $\{pk_i\}_{i=1}^n \in \mathbb{G}_2^n$, *return aggregate public key* apk $\leftarrow \prod_{i=1}^n pk_i \in \mathbb{G}_2$.
- MultiSign(pp, $\{\sigma_i\}_{i=1}^n$) $\rightarrow$ σ: *given* n *signatures* $\{\sigma_i\}_{i=1}^n \in \mathbb{G}_1^n$ *under distinct public keys for the same message, return multisignature* $\sigma \leftarrow \prod_{i=1}^n \sigma_i \in \mathbb{G}_1$.
- AggSign(pp, $[\sigma_i]_{i=1}^n$) $\rightarrow$ Σ : *given a list of* n *multisignatures* $[\sigma_i]_{i=1}^n \in \mathbb{G}_1^n$, *return aggregate multisignature* $\Sigma \leftarrow \prod_{i \in [n]} \sigma_i \in \mathbb{G}_1$.
- Verify(pp, $[(apk_i, m_i)]_{i=1}^n, \Sigma$) $\rightarrow$ $\{0,1\}$: *given a list of* n *aggregate public key and message pairs* $[(apk_i, m_i)]_{i=1}^n$ *and an aggregate multisignature* Σ, *return* 1 *if* $e(\Sigma, G_2) = \prod_{i=1}^n e(H_s(m_i), apk_i)$; *else return* 0.

In the full version of the paper [37] we prove the following unforgeability theorem.

Theorem 3. BBSGLRY *is a computationally unforgeable aggregate multisignature under* ψ-co-CDH *when instantiated with random oracles* H_s, H_p.

5.2 Composite Algebraic-Symmetric Hash Functions

BHP-BLAKE2s is a cryptographic hash function that first "shrinks" its input using the SNARK-optimized Bowe-Hopwood-Pedersen (BHP) collision-resistant hash [27], then runs the BLAKE2s compression function [4] on the result. We prove security via instantiating the following construction.

Construction 3. *Given collision-resistant hash* CRH : $\{0,1\}^* \rightarrow \mathcal{B}$, *injective encoding* Encode : $\mathcal{B} \rightarrow \{0,1\}^{b-t}$, *and random oracle* $\mathcal{O}$: $\{0,1\}^b \rightarrow \{0,1\}^c$ *for positive integers* ℓ *and* $t \geq \lceil \log_2(\lceil \ell/c \rceil + 1) \rceil$, *we construct a composite hash function* H : $\{0,1\}^* \rightarrow \{0,1\}^\ell$ *as follows. Let* $k \leftarrow \lceil \ell/c \rceil$, *and for integers* $0 \leq x \leq 2^t - 1$ *denote by* xut *the* t-*bit unsigned binary representation of* x. *On input* $m \in \mathcal{M}$:

1. *Shrink the message to obtain the intermediate hash* $h' \leftarrow$ CRH(m).
2. *Compute the binary encoding of the intermediate hash* $h'_{enc} \leftarrow$ Encode(h').
3. *Output the first* ℓ *bits of* $\mathcal{O}(0ut\|h'_{enc})\|\mathcal{O}(1ut\|h'_{enc})\| \dots \|\mathcal{O}(kut\|h'_{enc})$.

In the full version of the paper [37] we prove the following indistinguishability theorem.

Theorem 4. *If* CRH *is computationally collision-resistant* Encode *is injective, and* $\mathcal{O}$ *is a random oracle, then the hash function* H *is computationally indistinguishable from a random oracle.*

In BHP, presented below, input messages are split into segments m_i, then further divided into 3-bit chunks $m_{i,j}$. The maximum number of chunks in a segment, denoted C_{max}, depends on the curve. A formula to derive it is given in [27].

$$\frac{\text{BHP.Setup}(1^\lambda, s) \to \text{pp}}{(\mathbb{G}, q) \leftarrow \text{SampleGroup}(1^\lambda)} \quad \frac{\text{BHP.Eval}(\text{pp}, m \in \{0,1\}^n) \to h}{\text{Divide } m \text{ into segments } m_i \text{ of size } C_{\text{max}}}$$

$$[g_i]_{i=1}^s \leftarrow \mathbb{G}^s \qquad\qquad \text{Divide each } m_i \text{ into 3-bit chunks } m_{i,j}$$

$$\text{pp} \leftarrow (\mathbb{G}, q, [g_i]_{i=1}^s) \qquad h \leftarrow \sum_{i,j} g_i^{2^{4i}(1+m_{i,j}[0]+2\cdot m_{i,j}[1])(1-2\cdot m_{i,j}[2])}$$

We refer the reader to [4] for a description of the BLAKE2s.

6 Implementation

PLUMO was implemented in Rust[10] using the arkworks libraries.

6.1 Optimizations

Try-and-Increment Hashing. Since constant-time hashing is not important to the security of PLUMO, we opt for a more efficient hash-to-group by using a variant of "try-and-increment" [11]. For a Weierstrass form curve, let q be the order of the base field and $\ell = \lceil \log_2(q) \rceil$. Given a hash function $\mathsf{H} : \{0,1\} \to \{0,1\}^{\ell+1}$ and input m, we can hash to $\mathbb{G}_1$ using rejection sampling as follows. Try each sequential nonce η in $0, \ldots, 2^c - 1$ encoded as c-bit string (for some completeness parameter c) until the first ℓ bits of $h \leftarrow \mathsf{H}(\eta \| m)$ is less than q. To obtain a prime-order group point from h, clear the cofactors from the first ℓ bits of h to obtain an x-coordinate. If the last bit of h is 0 (1) choose the smaller (larger) corresponding y-coordinate. We crucially observe that it is not necessary to increment inside the SNARK, and that the nonce can be included as a private input. Indeed, if we write the message of any signature scheme as $\mathcal{M} = \{0,1\}^c \times \mathcal{M}'$, where $\mathcal{M}'$ is considered the meaningful part, then the unforgeability of a signature on any message in $\mathcal{M}$ implies the unforgeability of a signature on any message in $\mathcal{M}'$. In the ROM, the probability of succeeding on each try is $q/2^\ell$, and thus an expected $2^\ell/q$ tries will be required to hash each message. The chance a given message cannot be hashed is given by $(1 - q/2^\ell)^c$. For our concrete parameters, BLS12-377 and $c = 8$, this gives an exceedingly small probability of 2^{-677}.

Computing BHP over a Birationally Equivalent Curve. Following [27], we compute the Bowe-Hopwood-Pedersen hash over the birationally equivalent Montgomery form of the twisted Edwards curve $E_{\text{Ed}/\text{BW6}}$ curve (of equal order to BW6-761) in a way that guarantees the incomplete addition formulas (which cost 3 constraints instead of 6) are sufficient.

Reducing Verifier Time and Proof Sizes. Verification of Groth16 requires computing a $\mathbb{G}_1$ multi-exponentiation of size $\ell = |\mathbf{x}|$. If the initial and m-epochs-later epoch messages were directly encoded as the instance, ℓ would be approaching 1,000. Instead, the verifier hashes the input and output epoch messages using

---

[10] See https://github.com/celo-org/celo-bls-snark-rs and https://github.com/celo-org/snark-setup.

a hash-to-field built with BLAKE2s, producing an input and output hash, which is the instance of size $\ell = 2$ for the Groth16 verification circuit. The circuit has to be modified to prove knowledge of openings of these two hashes, and then the usual checks are made on these openings. This unfortunately increases the size of the circuit, but at least this cost is constant in the number of epochs being proved. This optimization gives us another for free. The ultralight client (UC) only needs to learn the most recent epoch message. When verifying multiple SNARK proofs the UC can simply download the intermediate summaries as hashes, thereby significantly reducing proof sizes.

6.2 Evaluation

We benchmarked our prover on a Google Cloud machine with 4 Intel Xeon E7-8880 v4 processors and $3,844$ GB of DDR4 RAM, which rents for \$25/h USD. Figure 2 shows the time and space efficiency of our prover, and Table 2 gives our circuit size as a function of the committee size and number of epochs spanned. Since proofs for 120 epochs are computable in less than an hour and epochs are approximately one day, maintaining up-to-date UC proofs for PLUMO is possible for \$25 worth of compute a day. In contrast to our powerful prover, we evaluated the performance of our verifier on a Motorola Moto X (2nd Gen), a 2014 mobile phone with 1 GB RAM and a 32-bit Quad-core 2.45 GHz Krait 400 processor. We used a directly cross-compiled, unoptimized implementation. The results show it is possible to verify such a proof in about 0.5 s.

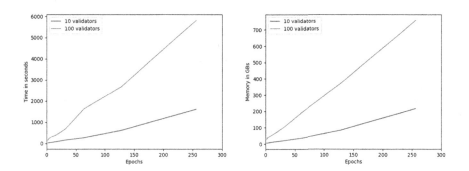

Fig. 2. Proving time and peak memory consumption over BW6-761.

Table 2. Constraints for our summary update transition proof circuit.

Epochs	10 validators	100 validators
32	2,787,485	20,465,083
64	4,753,568	34,097,470
128	8,685,734	61,362,244
256	16,550,063	115,891,789
512	32,278,721	224,950,879
1024	63,736,037	443,069,059

References

1. Al-Bassam, M., et al.: Chainspace: a sharded smart contracts platform. In: Proceedings of the 25th Network and Distributed System Security Symposium, NDSS 2018 (2018). https://eprint.iacr.org/2016/492.pdf

2. Albrecht, M., et al.: MiMC: efficient encryption and cryptographic hashing with minimal multiplicative complexity. In: 22nd International Conference on the Theory and Application of Cryptology and Information Security, pp. 191–219 (2016). https://eprint.iacr.org/2016/492.pdf

3. Amoussou-Guenou, Y., et al.: Correctness of tendermint-core blockchains. In: 22nd International Conference on Principles of Distributed Systems, OPODIS 2018, vol. 125, pp. 16:1–16:16 (2018). https://eprint.iacr.org/2018/574.pdf

4. Aumasson, J.-P., et al.: BLAKE2: simpler, smaller, fast as MD5. In: 11th International Conference of Applied Cryptography and Security, ACNS 2013 (2013). https://www.blake2.net/blake2_20130129.pdf

5. Ben-Sasson, E., Ciesa, A., Spooner, N.: Interactive oracle proofs. In: 14th Theory of Cryptography Conference, TCC 2016 (2016). https://www.iacr.org/archive/tcc2016b/99850156/99850156.pdf

6. Ben-Sasson, E., et al.: Scalable zero knowledge via cycles of elliptic curves. In: 34th Annual International Cryptology Conference, CRYPTO 2014, pp. 276–294 (2014). https://eprint.iacr.org/2014/595.pdf

7. Bitansky, N., et al.: Recursive composition and bootstrapping for SNARKs and proof-carrying data. In: 45th ACM Symposium on the Theory of Computing, STOC 2013, pp. 111–120 (2013). https://eprint.iacr.org/2012/095.pdf

8. Bitansky, N., et al.: On the existence of extractable one-way functions. SIAM J. Comput. **45**(5) (2016). Preliminary Version Appeared in STOC 2014, pp. 1910–1952. https://eprint.iacr.org/2014/402.pdf

9. Boldyreva, A.: Threshold signatures, multisignatures and blind signatures based on the gap-Diffie-Hellman-group signature scheme. In: 6th International Conference on Practice and Theory in Public Key Cryptography, PKC 2003, pp. 31–46 (2003). https://www.cc.gatech.edu/~aboldyre/papers/bold.pdf

10. Boneh, D., Drijvers, M., Neven, G.: Compact multi-signatures for smaller blockchains. In: 24th International Conference on the Theory and Application of Cryptology and Information Security, ASIACRYPT 2018, pp. 435–464 (2018). https://eprint.iacr.org/2018/483.pdf

11. Boneh, D., Lynn, B., Shacham, H.: Short signatures from the weil pairing. In: 7th International Conference on the Theory and Application of Cryptology and Information Security, ASIACRYPT 2001, pp. 514–532 (2001). https://www.iacr.org/archive/asiacrypt2001/22480516.pdf
12. Boneh, D., et al.: Aggregate and verifiably encrypted signatures from bilinear maps. In: 22nd Annual International Conference on the Theory and Applications of Cryptographic Techniques, EUROCRYPT 2003, pp. 416–432 (2003). https://crypto.stanford.edu/~dabo/pubs/papers/aggreg.pdf
13. Bonneau, J., et al.: Coda: Decentralized Cryptocurrency at Scale. Cryptology ePrint Archive, Report 2020/352 (2020). https://eprint.iacr.org/2020/352.pdf
14. Bowe, S., Grigg, J., Hopwood, D.: Recursive Proof Composition without a Trusted Setup. Cryptology ePrint Archive, Report 2019/1021 (2019). https://eprint.iacr.org/2019/1021.pdf
15. Bowe, S., et al.: Zexe: enabling decentralized private computation. In: 41st IEEE Symposium on Security and Privacy, S&P 2020, pp. 947–964 (2020). https://eprint.iacr.org/2018/962.pdf
16. Bünz, B., et al.: FlyClient: super-light clients for cryptocurrencies. In: 41st IEEE Symposium on Security and Privacy, S&P 2020, pp. 928–946 (2020). https://eprint.iacr.org/2019/226.pdf
17. Bünz, B., et al.: Recursive proof composition from accumulation schemes. In: 18th Theory of Cryptography Conference, TCC 2020, vol. 2, pp. 1–18 (2020). https://eprint.iacr.org/2020/499.pdf
18. Chen, W., et al.: Reducing Participation Costs via Incremental Verification for Ledger Systems. Cryptology ePrint Archive, Report 2020/1522 (2020). https://eprint.iacr.org/2020/1522.pdf
19. Chiesa, A., Chua, L., Weidner, M.: On cycles of pairing-friendly elliptic curves. SIAM J. Appl. Algebra Geom. 3(2), 175–192 (2019). https://arxiv.org/pdf/1803.02067.pdf
20. Chiesa, A., Tromer, E.: Proof-carrying data and hearsay arguments from signature cards. In: 1st Conference on Innovations in Computer Science, ICS 2010, pp. 310–331 (2010). http://people.eecs.berkeley.edu/~alexch/docs/CT10.pdf
21. Chiesa, A., et al.: Marlin: preprocessing zkSNARKS with universal and updatable SRS. In: 39th Annual International Conference on the Theory and Applications of Cryptographic Techniques, EUROCRYPT 2020, pp. 738–768 (2020). https://eprint.iacr.org/2019/1047.pdf
22. El Housni, Y., Guillevic, A.: Optimized and secure pairing-friendly elliptic curves suitable for one layer proof composition. Cryptology ePrint Archive, Report 2020/351 (2020)
23. Fiore, D., Nitulescu, A.: On the (in)security of SNARKs in the presence of oracles. In: 14th International Conference on the Theory of Cryptography, TCC 2016, pp. 108–138 (2016). https://eprint.iacr.org/2016/112.pdf
24. Fuchsbauer, G., Kiltz, E., Loss, J.: The algebraic group model and its applications. In: 38th Annual International Cryptology Conference, CRYPTO 2018, pp. 33–62 (2018). https://eprint.iacr.org/2017/620.pdf
25. Grassi, L., et al.: Starkad and Poseidon: New Hash Functions for Zero Knowledge Proof Systems (2019). https://eprint.iacr.org/2019/458.pdf
26. Gudgeon, L., et al.: SoK: off the chain transactions. Cryptology ePrint Archive, Report 2019/360 (2019). https://eprint.iacr.org/2019/360.pdf
27. Hopwood, D., et al.: Zcash Protocol Specification [Overwinter+Sapling] (2021). https://raw.githubusercontent.com/zcash/zips/master/protocol/sapling.pdf

28. Kiayias, A., Miller, A., Zindros, D.: Non-interactive proofs of proof-of-work. In: 24th International Conference on Financial Cryptography and Data Security, FC 2020, pp. 505–522 (2020). https://eprint.iacr.org/2017/963.pdf

29. Kokoris-Kogias, E., et al.: Enhancing bitcoin security and performance with strong consistency via collective signing. In: 25th USENIX Conference on Security Symposium, USENIX Security 2016, pp. 279–296 (2016). https://arxiv.org/pdf/1602.06997.pdf

30. Kokoris-Kogias, E., et al.: OmniLedger: a secure, scale-out, decentralized ledger via sharding. In: 39th IEEE Symposium on Security and Privacy, S&P 2018, pp. 583–598 (2018). https://eprint.iacr.org/2017/406.pdf

31. Malavolta, G., et al.: Concurrency and privacy with payment-channel networks. In: 2017 ACM SIGSAC Conference on Computer and Communications Security, CCS 2017, pp. 455–471. Association for Computing Machinery (2017). https://eprint.iacr.org/2017/820.pdf

32. Maller, M., et al.: Sonic: zero-knowledge SNARKs from linear-size universal and updateable structured reference strings. In: 26th ACM Conference on Computer and Communications Security, CS 2019, pp. 2111–2128 (2019). https://eprint.iacr.org/2019/099.pdf

33. Meiklejohn, S.: Top ten obstacles along distributed ledgers path to adoption. IEEE Secur. Priv. **16**(4), 13–19 (2018). https://discovery.ucl.ac.uk/id/eprint/10057035/1/accepted-topten.pdf

34. Moniz, H.: The Istanbul BFT Consensus Algorithm. arXiv abs/2002.03613. https://arxiv.org/pdf/2002.03613.pdf

35. Nikitin, K., et al.: CHAINIAC: proactive software-update transparency via collectively signed skipchains and verified builds. In: 26th USENIX Security Symposium, USENIX Security 2014, pp. 1271–1287 (2017). https://eprint.iacr.org/2017/648.pdf

36. Ristenpart, T., Yilek, S.: The power of proofs-of-possession: securing multiparty signatures against rogue-key attacks. In: 26th Annual International Conference on the Theory and Applications of Cryptographic Techniques, EUROCRYPT 2007, pp. 228–245 (2007). https://www.iacr.org/archive/eurocrypt2007/45150228/45150228.pdf

37. Vesely, P., et al.: Plumo: An ultralight blockchain client. Cryptology ePrint Archive, Paper 2021/1361 (2021). https://eprint.iacr.org/2021/1361

38. Yin, M., et al.: HotStuff: BFT consensus with linearity and responsiveness. In: ACM Symposium on Principles of Distributed Computing 2019, PODC 2019, pp. 347–356 (2019). https://arxiv.org/pdf/1803.05069.pdf

SoK: Blockchain Light Clients

Panagiotis Chatzigiannis[1]([✉]), Foteini Baldimtsi[1], and Konstantinos Chalkias[2]

[1] George Mason University, Fairfax, VA, USA
{pchatzig,foteini}@gmu.edu
[2] Mysten Labs, Palo Alto, CA, USA
kostas@mystenlabs.com

Abstract. Blockchain systems, as append-only ledgers, are typically associated with linearly growing participation costs. Therefore, for a blockchain client to interact with the system (query or submit a transaction), it can either pay these costs by downloading, storing and verifying the blockchain history, or forfeit blockchain security guarantees and place its trust on third party intermediary servers.

With this problem becoming apparent from early works in the blockchain space, the concept of a *light client* has been proposed, where a resource-constrained client such as a browser or mobile device can participate in the system by querying and/or submitting transactions without holding the full blockchain but while still inheriting the blockchain's security guarantees. A plethora of blockchain systems with different light client frameworks and implementations have been proposed, each with different functionalities, assumptions and efficiencies. In this work we provide a systematization of such light client designs. We unify the space by providing a set of definitions on their properties in terms of provided functionality, efficiency and security, and provide future research directions based on our findings.

Keywords: Blockchain · Light clients · Consensus · Long range attacks

1 Introduction

Blockchain-based, systems such as Bitcoin and Ethereum, typically include three types of participants: *consensus nodes* (also known as miners or validators), who run a consensus protocol to reach a common agreement on the current blockchain state, *full nodes* who store and communicate blockchain data, and *clients* which submit queries or transactions. Full nodes are considered to have relatively sufficient resources to perform their tasks, which involve communicating with each other through a gossip protocol in a peer-to-peer fashion, storing and communicating unconfirmed transactions, maintaining the entire blockchain history and

---

Panagiotis Chatzigiannis did part of this work during an internship at Novi Financial/Facebook Research. Konstantinos Chalkias did part of this work at Novi Financial/Facebook Research.

I. Eyal and J. Garay (Eds.): FC 2022, LNCS 13411, pp. 615–641, 2022.
https://doi.org/10.1007/978-3-031-18283-9_31

replying to queries. To perform transactions (e.g. in cryptocurrencies such as Bitcoin and Ethereum), clients first need to verify that the underlying blockchain is valid. Naively, this implies downloading and verifying all blocks, an operation that could take hours or days, and require gigabytes of bandwidth and storage. Therefore, the only remaining option for resource-constrained clients (such as mobile devices or browsers) is to place their trust on full nodes which will serve as intermediary servers, provide clients a view of the blockchain based on client queries, and forward submitted transactions on the client's behalf.

Nevertheless, in the early days of Bitcoin, the three roles mentioned were not necessarily distinct. For example, the Bitcoin core software [3] served as a common frontend to solve the Proof of Work puzzle as part of the consensus protocol, run a full node and submit queries and transactions. However, it quickly became necessary to decouple the client functionality to ensure less powerful clients can interact with the system while preserving as many security guarantees possible, which was mainly done through the Simplified Payment Verification (SPV) protocol [86]. Interestingly, while SPV required much less resources compared to a full node, it was still not lightweight enough to support resource-constrained environments with very low computational, storage and communication capabilities such as a mobile or browser-based client, while the introduction of more complex blockchain systems such as Ethereum made this gap even wider. In addition, SPV introduced additional trust assumptions and attack vectors, as in many implementations all communication and queries are executed through a small set of servers.

More recently, several implementations and academic works were proposed as "light clients" or "light-client friendly", either tailored to specific blockchain systems, or even as entirely new systems. However, every proposal provides different properties, definitions and goals for a light client, either implicitly or explicitly, while there are still many different interpretations for a "light client" in the blockchain space, even after a decade of evolution of cryptocurrencies. As a result, existing implementations approach the problem from a different angle, and no complete solution exists that makes a mobile client possible while maintaining all of the strong security guarantees of the underlying blockchain system.

Our Contributions. In this paper, we unify the diverse conception of light clients in the blockchain world by providing definitions for light client properties in terms of functionalities, efficiency and security, and provide a common list of assumptions for such clients. Then, we provide a systematization of prominent existing works based on our defined properties. Finally, through our systematization, we provide a series of insights and gaps serving as exciting future research directions, including considerations regarding long range attacks due to validator re-configurations, and light clients for privacy preserving blockchains or as smart contracts to allow for native interoperability between independent ledgers.

1.1   What is a Light Client?

We begin by providing an informal definition of a standard (non-light) client, which is the generic protocol that directly interacts with the blockchain system. This interaction includes at least one of the following functionalities:

- Perform queries (e.g. the balance of an account or the state of a transaction, with a specific time or block number as optional parameters). Such queries are typically accompanied by proofs verifiable by the client protocol (created by other entities in the system such as consensus participants or full nodes), in order to preserve security and prevent the client from being manipulated by malicious actors.
- Hold secret information (e.g. account private keys) and submit transactions to the blockchain system. This functionality is often referred to as a *wallet*.

Note that the terms *clients* and *wallets* are often considered equivalent and used interchangeably in the blockchain space, with the term "wallet" typically associated with a specific software implementation. However, based on the above informal definition, we make an explicit distinction between these terms: In a nutshell, a *wallet* is the software implementation of the *client* protocol that holds secret information used to submit transactions to the blockchain. As an example, Bitcoin Core [3] is Bitcoin's standard client which includes both wallet *and* full node functionalities, as discussed previously.

Starting again from the cryptocurrency community, a "light client" mostly refers to the wallet software running a "more" lightweight client implementation in its back-end compared to the standard client. This software usually interacts with the blockchain through a fully synchronized node, which in turn submits the transactions on the client's behalf (e.g. by placing them on a "mempool" and broadcasting them to other nodes and miners through a gossip protocol). The goal of such a client is to be more compatible with resource-constrained environments such as mobile devices or browsers, where the system's fully-fledged client might be prohibitive to work. Also, another goal of the light client might be to reduce the costs of the initial joining process, without requiring to download the full blockchain history (which for a standard client is typically in the order of gigabytes). The trade-off however for the efficiency of such clients is usually security; for instance they might need to trust the full node they are interacting with, they do not verify the consensus process, do not store and communicate ledger information themselves, and therefore do not contribute to decentralization, one of the blockchain's main goals.

However, in some implementations (e.g. Ethereum or Polkadot), a "light client" refers to a "lighter" version of a full node (i.e. with faster setup and synchronization time and lower computational/storage requirements), which only stores block headers but still directly interacts with the blockchain network in a peer-to-peer fashion, and therefore does not need to introduce all of the trust assumptions discussed above [29]. However this type of client is still not suitable to run in very constrained environments such as mobile devices, and is still above the bar in terms of such requirements.

Towards the "light client" goal, some systems have adopted additional cryptographic primitives or techniques, for instance succinct proofs to maintain a "compact" representation of the blockchain with fast verification [40].

Based on the above, we can envision an "ideal" light client as a client having very low computation, storage, communication and initial setup requirements (making such a client feasible even in mobile devices or browsers). However, the light client should retain the security guarantees without introducing additional trust assumptions. Therefore, it still needs to act as the verifier of *efficient* cryptographic proofs, which will convince the client on the received query replies (e.g. on an account's balance or the state of a transaction). These proofs would be created by entities in the blockchain in the *prover* role (e.g. miners or full nodes), ideally without introducing a significant overhead. In Sect. 3.1, we provide informal definitions of the above desired properties that we consider in our work.

1.2   Light Client Implementations in Major Blockchain Systems

We now overview how a light client is perceived and implemented in prominent blockchain systems.

Bitcoin: As discussed previously, the earliest and most well known concept of light client is the Simplified Payment Verification (SPV) client in Bitcoin [86]. An SPV light client only verifies the chain of Proof of Work solutions through the block headers, and requests Merkle proofs on-demand from a full node to verify if a specific transaction is valid (e.g. for transactions that are associated with a wallet address). This approach, while popular even by today's wallets, is not consistent with "decentralization", and introduces additional security assumptions as well as privacy concerns. Satoshi's whitepaper proposed "pruning" as a method to downsize the blockchain (and therefore make it practical for light clients) by discarding spent transaction outputs in each block. However, this method a) requires clients to make a full synchronization even before performing pruning, and b) as of today, it has not been implemented because of security concerns. [4,5,22,28]. We also note some early proposals to store Bitcoin's UTXO set in a Merkle tree for fast bootstrapping [26].

Ethereum: Being an account-based system, Ethereum has the following three types of nodes: a) *full* nodes (most common), which cryptographically verify all account states at all times, but can *prune* account state tries older than 1024 blocks to save space [14], b) *archival* nodes, which always keep the full blockchain history without pruning, and c) *light* nodes which only store block headers to reduce resource requirements. Note that pruning can potentially hurt past transaction or account state querying (and therefore auditability) if there are no archival nodes available to provide a query reply along with a proof (e.g. a Merkle path). Also, Ethereum node software implementations include client and wallet functionalities, therefore the terms clients and nodes are used interchangeably [15].

In contrast with Bitcoin, there is no single node/client software implementation but several different open-source clients written in different programming languages. Geth, written in Go, is the most commonly used [17], and recently introduced a new "snapshot" functionality for full node synchronization in order to improve read disk access speeds, by including a "flattened" version of all account states as well. However, no Ethereum node/client is light-client friendly even in light mode [1,11]. In practice, considering a Raspberry Pi 4 as a "light client" platform (which is still more powerful compared to mobile devices, especially in terms of energy resources), a geth full node with the new snapshot features can barely run on in, as it still needs a great amount of fast read-write disk storage (i.e. at least 1TB SSD). A geth light node comes without that storage requirement but it still requires a slow, communication-intensive setup phase, which is also required when the node desynchronizes (e.g. in periods of power-off, sleep or disconnections) and is prone to database corruptions.

All Ethereum node types rely on an initial peer discovery algorithm based on the Kademlia Distributed Hash Table (DHT) protocol to connect to other nodes. This is in contrast with Bitcoin core software (the official standard node/client for Bitcoin), which relies on a hardcoded DNS list feed. Lastly, Ethereum plans to implement light clients in its Proof of Stake version (Ethereum 2.0) by introducing "sync committees" to help minimize bootstrapping costs [13], however at the time of writing, details for these committees have not yet been released.

Algorand: Implementing an SPV client in a Proof of Stake blockchain such as Algorand is not straightforward, since block headers are not enough to securely verify the chain [27] (i.e. the client also needs the voters' balances for each block, also discussed in Sect. 4.1). Vault [80], a recent work approach based on Algorand's Proof of Stake protocol, "skips" blocks in each verification step, essentially compressing the block history, while also compressing the voter certificates themselves by using a smaller committee size, but requires a larger percentage of the committee members to vote in order to preserve the validity of the certificate. Vault is discussed in detail in the next section.

Diem: Clients in Diem interact with the blockchain through a full node's JSON-RPC endpoint [9,23], however the client API at the time of writing simply provides answers to queries, without accompanying proofs to provide the client verification capabilities. A client with full verifying functionalities is work in progress [10], and a recent work includes a framework to make client implementations in Diem lightweight [51].

Mina - Coda: Mina inherently supports light clients (full-nodes) through recursive SNARK compositions, which enable maintaining a constant-sized (20KB) blockchain that can be efficiently verified by a client with limited resources. It utilizes a variant of Ouroboros proof-of-stake algorithm to preserve consensus security properties. However Mina, while being light-client oriented, still requires a heavy amount of work for the Block producers, who are in the prover role [20,21,40] (its testnet has a 8-core processor and 16 GB of RAM as minimum requirements).

ZCash: ZIP 221 [16,19] implements Flyclient [45], an efficient block header verification method for light clients. Based on Non-Interactive Proofs of Proof-of-Work (NIPoPoWs) [75], it compresses blockchain transaction histories for light clients by only needing to download a small subset of all block headers, which correspond to blocks with higher difficulty target. We discuss both NIPoPoWs and Flyclient in the next section and consider them in our systematization.

Cardano: Although Cardano currently has naive light client implementations that need to place their trust on a full node, it plans to utilize recent work (Mithril) [48] to enable secure and fast boostrapping of light clients in Proof of Stake using a novel primitive, "stake-based threshold multisignatures".

Cosmos - InterBlockchain Communication (IBC): Using the Tendermint BFT Proof of Stake consensus [44], Cosmos' InterBlockchain Communication (IBC) [62] proposes a decentralized protocol for making blockchains communicate with each other, even when these ledgers have fundamentally different underlying architectures. IBC has explicit light client support tailored to its consensus algorithm [42], which only requires to download block headers after a trusted period, which contain sufficient validator signatures proving correctness of validator evolution up to that period. State proofs are then provided to light clients through a full node.

Binance: A light client in Binance chain [24], which uses a Proof of Stake consensus variant (Proof of Authority) [8], is simply implemented by querying a full node, seemingly with a trust model that resembles SPV.

1.3 Related Systematization of Knowledge Works

A recent work [71] provides a taxonomy for cryptocurrency wallets, however its scope is more narrow, focusing on existing wallet implementations (recall the distiction we provided in Sect. 1.1). Still, this work provides some brief insights on (super-)light clients, as well as definitions for the "light" property and its security compared to a full client.

[67] provided a survey on existing blockchain scalability solutions. These include sharding approaches such as OmniLedger [78], layer-2 blockchain protocols [66] or other direct modifications to the blockchain protocol such as increasing block size or replacing the chain structure entirely. At first glance, such scalability solutions might seem related to the light client problem. However, their end goal is different, which is to increase the blockchain's transaction throughput and latency, and not necessary to better support light clients.

2   Cryptographic Building Blocks

In this section we briefly discuss common cryptographic building blocks used by light clients.

2.1 Succinct Set Representation and Proofs

Cryptographic Accumulators enable a succinct and binding representation of a set of elements S and support constant-size proofs of membership (or non-membership) on S. An accumulator typically consists of algorithms to add an element x to it, create a membership proof π that x is contained in the accumulator, verify π, and later update a proof to π' after an element x' has been added to the accumulator. Sub-categories of accumulators are defined if an accumulator manager is needed, if trapdoor information exists and if it supports additional operations like removing elements or creating proofs of non-membership. We point the reader to [35] for formal accumulator definitions and properties. **Merkle Trees** [85] are a specific construction of accumulators, where each element x is represented in a tree of hashes.

Vector commitments [47] enable committing to a vector of elements $[x_i]_{i=1}^n$, and later open the commitment at any position i of the vector. While a VC might not be necessarily hiding as a standard commitment, it needs to be *position binding* instead of just binding.

SNARKs (succinct non-interactive arguments of knowledge) are proof systems that are succinct (i.e. have very small proof size compared to that of the statement or the witness) and do not require interaction between the prover and the verifier. zk-SNARKs are a special type of SNARKS augmented with the zero-knowledge property, i.e. constructing a verifiable proof without revealing any information about the witness [88]. In addition, zk-SNARK verification typically requires much less computation than constructing the proof itself. We refer the reader to [65,88] for relevant definitions and sample constructions.

2.2 Hash Functions and Signatures

Aggregate signatures are a special type of digital signatures, where from a set of users U with each user having a signing keypair (pk_u, sk_u) and a subset of signatures $[\sigma_u]$ and corresponding messages $[m_u]$, an aggregator can combine them into a single aggregate signature σ [38,39,74].

Threshold signatures [48,91] enable a subset of k out of n valid signers to generate a signature, but does not allow to create a valid signature with fewer than k of those signers.

Chameleon hashes [79] are collision-resistant hash functions, that have additional properties associated with public-private key pairs compared to standard hash functions. While anyone can compute the output of the chameleon hash function using the public key, the private key serves as trapdoor information to easily find collisions for a specific input.

3 Definitions

3.1 Light Client Properties

Given the plethora of light-client definitions and implementations that exist in the blockchain space, there is a need to unify and standardize their functional, efficiency and security properties. We informally discuss these properties below, assuming a blockchain B which contains transactions tx and accounts acc, with participating light clients C, consensus participants CN and full nodes N. By B_1 we define the genesis block which we assume that holds all the system parameters and will be used for verifiable bootstrapping.

Functional Properties. As discussed in Sect. 1.1, the system needs to support the following protocols which all run between a client C and a set of full nodes N who always keep B as an input and serve as intermediaries:

- $\mathsf{Init}(B_1) \rightarrow (\mathsf{st}, \pi)$: The client on input the genesis block B_1, bootstraps/initializes its state st by running an interactive protocol with a full node and receives a proof π of correct initialization.
- $\mathsf{Upd}(\mathsf{st}) \rightarrow (\mathsf{st}', \pi)$: The client updates its state from st to st' to reflect the newest view of B via an interactive protocol with a full node.
- $\mathsf{VrfySt}(\mathsf{st}, \mathsf{st}', \pi) \rightarrow b$: The client verifies π that st' is a correct transition from st (or B_1) and outputs $b \in \{0, 1\}$.
- $\mathsf{Q}(\mathsf{st}, data) \rightarrow (\mathsf{r}, \pi)$: The client makes a query for *data* where $data = \mathsf{tx}$ (e.g. timestamp or block height) or $data = \mathsf{acc}$ (e.g. an account's address). We also assume that *data* includes the type of query, i.e. current balance of an account, sender/receiver/value of a transaction, etc. The client receives a reply r and a proof π. If $data \notin B$, Q typically returns error $\bot$, however *optionally*, it can still provide a proof of non-existence as $(\bot, \pi)$.
- $\mathsf{Vrfy}(\mathsf{st}, r, \pi) \rightarrow b$ Client verifies π for r and outputs $b \in \{0, 1\}$.
- $\mathsf{S}(\mathsf{st}, \mathsf{tx}, \mathsf{acc}, \mathsf{sk}) \rightarrow (\mathsf{st}')$ (optional wallet functionality): Submit a transaction tx to B on behalf of acc with secret information sk.

Security Properties. We list the required security properties that correspond to threats relevant to the operation of the light client.

- *Secure bootstrapping and synchronizing:* This property implies that given a publicly known genesis block B_1, an adversarial full node $\mathcal{A}$ should not be able to convince an honest client C to accept a forged blockchain state B^* (for any B^*) and therefore accept queries on it.

$$\Pr \left[\begin{array}{l} B_1; \\ \mathcal{A}(B^*) \text{ and C run } \mathsf{Init}(B_1), \mathsf{Upd}(\mathsf{st}): \\ (B^* \neq B) \wedge \mathsf{VrfySt}(B_1, \mathsf{st}, \pi) \rightarrow 1 \end{array} \right] \leq negl(\lambda)$$

- *Secure querying:* After bootstrapping, a malicious adversary $\mathcal{A}$ should not be able to convince a light client C to accept a forged transaction or account state. For instance, the adversary should not be able to convince the client that an unverified or forged transaction exists in the blockchain or accept an incorrect account balance. Secure querying also includes the case where $\mathcal{A}$ falsely convinces C the that an accepted transaction or existing account is not part of the blockchain history (i.e. forged proof of non-existence), which is omitted for brevity from our definition.

$$\Pr \begin{bmatrix} \mathsf{B}_1; \\ \mathcal{A}, \mathsf{Init}(), \mathsf{Upd}(), \mathsf{Q}(), \mathsf{S}() : \\ \exists data \notin \mathsf{B} \wedge \mathsf{Q}(data, \mathsf{st}) \rightarrow (\mathsf{r}, \pi) \wedge \mathsf{Vrfy}(r, \pi) \rightarrow 1 \end{bmatrix} \leq negl(\lambda)$$

Efficiency Properties. We identify the following efficiency properties in terms of storage, computation and communication costs ($|\mathsf{B}|$ denotes blockchain size, or number of blocks). We focus on the operations that happen on the light client side.

- *Efficient bootstrapping and synchronizing:* $\mathsf{Init}()$ and $\mathsf{Upd}()$ computation and communication are sublinear to $|\mathsf{B}|$.
- *Efficient storage:* storage costs (i.e. state size) for light clients, is sublinear to $|\mathsf{B}|$.
- *Efficient communication:* $\mathsf{Q}()$ and $\mathsf{S}()$ (if applicable) require communication costs sublinear to $|\mathsf{B}|$, where communication happens between C and N.
- *Efficient client computation:* $\mathsf{Q}()$ and $\mathsf{S}()$ (if applicable) require client computation costs sublinear to $|\mathsf{B}|$.
- $\mathsf{Vrfy}()$ requires computational costs sublinear to $|\mathsf{B}|$.

Overall, the overhead for B, CN and N in order to support light clients should be minimal compared to the equivalent system that does not provide such support. That said, the full nodes supporting the light clients, might already perform work linear to B.

3.2 Underlying Assumptions

While the variety of light clients operate under different threat models and assumptions depending on the underlying system properties (i.e. PoW or PoS based consensus), we identify a set of common assumptions that we list below.

Basic Light Client Assumptions. To the best of our knowledge, all light client designs implicitly make the following assumptions:

- Trusted genesis block (note that [59] discusses the presence of adversarial pre-computed genesis blocks).
- Reliable consensus (i.e. safety and liveness).
- Secure underlying cryptographic primitives.
- Weak synchrony, i.e. no long network partitions. We do not consider Eclipse network level attacks.

Additional Assumptions. Depending on their design, some systems impose additional assumptions.

- Trusted setup phase for the underlying cryptographic primitives (i.e. zk-SNARKs setup).

- Network-level assumptions: we assume that a client receives and relays information in a peer-to-peer fashion (i.e. distributed networking). This is generally preferred over communicating with a single full node which could act
maliciously by relaying a forged view of B to C or prevent it from completing
Init() or Upd() (i.e. DoS attack).
- Game-theoretic assumptions, i.e. that participants behave in a rational model.
- Special assumptions e.g. fixed Proof of Work difficulty or certain blockchain
participants performing specific operations (e.g. accounts needing to restore
other accounts not included in the bootstrapped state).

4   Generic Techniques to Build Light Clients

In this section we provide an overview of several generic techniques and protocols
that can be used towards designing blockchain light clients and list examples of
light client implementations that are based on each technique.

4.1   Header Verification and Consensus Evolution

A common approach when designing bootstrapping and synchronizing for light
clients is to only have them verify the block headers and skip verification of
transactions or account states (as opposed to standard clients who verify the full
blockchain history). This popular technique is adopted by SPV [86], Ethereum
[17] and many others.

In Proof of Work consensus, block header verification is straightforward, as
the client only needs to verify the proofs of work based on block hashes and
nonces. However, additional considerations must be made in Proof of Stake or
BFT consensus blockchains to preserve security. For instance, in Proof of Stake,
normally the client also needs to verify account states and balances in the whole
blockchain history, or consider the risk of long range attacks [6]. In short, the
client needs to be convinced that the blockchain consensus has evolved correctly
and honestly throughout the history, and no malicious majority was ever present.
For BFT-consensus, there is an additional challenge: BFT validators can join and
leave, and a client needs to verify the consensus evolution through all validator
signatures. A common technique to shorten the client's work is by storing intermediate checkpoints [30] so that clients are not referring to the genesis block
each time they verify the current validator set. On the other hand, validator set
re-configurations, known as "epochs", present additional considerations as we
discuss later in our paper.

4.2   Compressing the State

Being append-only immutable ledgers, the issue of ever-growing storage requirements in blockchains was implied even in the original Bitcoin whitepaper [86],
which considered pruning old, spent transaction information (although never

adopted from the community due to security concerns). However, securely pruning "obsolete" data from a blockchain is a direct step towards client efficient bootstrapping and synchronizing as previously discussed in Sect. 3.1. As an example, Ethanos [77] uses a form of "temporary" pruning in the account-based model.

We note that *redacting* is a relevant but stronger notion, with the main goal being to make the blockchain conditionally mutable rather than just reclaiming storage [31,32,61]. This "mutable" blockchain approach mainly relies on the *chameleon hash* primitive discussed in Sect. 2.

As another method of compressing the state, aggregate signatures, such as Schnorr and pairing-based BLS signatures [38,39], can compress many signatures (even under different keys) into a single signature, which in case of BLS, is constant-sized. However in the blockchain setting, aggregate signatures are vulnerable to "rogue key" attacks, where an adversary can produce an aggregated signature for arbitrary public keys, and typically requires a zero-knowledge proof (ZKP) of correct public key computation. Non-interactive EdDSA half aggregation [49] provides ways of compressing multiple Schnorr/EdDSA signatures to a single signature with half the size of the original signatures. One could also consider aggregating signatures using zero knowledge proofs [74]. Overall, aggregate signatures, already used by Plumo [58], is a promising primitive towards light client implementations, as it is estimated to save a significant portion of the needed bandwidth and storage. Another potential option is for the validators to engage into some interactive protocol in advance as part of the consensus committee protocol, using threshold signatures [46,60].

In Appendix A we briefly mention some additional proposals and works whose main goal is to compress the blockchain state. Although these works are not standalone light client implementations, they can serve as examples towards implementing light clients. However, we do not explicitly consider them in our systematization in the later Sections.

4.3   Removing the State

Taking it one step further, *stateless* blockchains aim to only keep a succinct and verifiable representation of the entire state at all times. Compacting a blockchain in this manner is light-client friendly[1], as the bootstrapping and syncing costs would be minimal, and the "stateless" blockchain approach used by Coda-Mina [40], Edrax [54] and others, is also becoming popular. However this can potentially hurt security guarantees, for example the consensus algorithm should be able to securely handle forks, which can happen at any point; there is either a significant share of malicious consensus participants, or simply a network partition. Some works [41] claim that stateless Proof of Stake blockchains are impossible, while others [34,52] introduce special consensus considerations to maintain security.

---

[1] This approach is sometimes referenced in the literature as "extremely light clients".

Several works point towards the stateless blockchain direction. For instance, Vector Commitments and Subvector Commitments [93] (a special category of Vector commitments), can be used to build a stateless cryptocurrency by committing to key-value maps. Pointproofs [63] further improved this idea by enabling aggregation of individual subvector commitment proofs into a single proof by anyone, as well as cross-commitment proof aggregation (i.e. from multiple subvector commitments) while also ensuring the hiding property (which vector commitments do not necessarily guarantee). Hyperproofs [92] are tree-based data structures that are aggregateable and homomorphic, which are very useful properties for implementing stateless blockchains, and have polynomial commitments [72] as their underlying primitive. Although efficient in their aggregation and update operations, hyperproofs require a trusted setup and have a public parameter size linear to the number of the proofs (i.e. the tree leaves). Finally, SNARKs seem to be a natural tool for implementing stateless or succinct blockchains, while also requiring very low computation for verification; however to be practical, ZKP friendly cryptographic primitives are recommended.

4.4   Leveraging Game-Theoretic Assumptions

In a unique approach as shown by [81], light clients can be built on top of a smart contract interacting with the client and a set of full nodes, thus offloading all blockchain queries and replies to those nodes, with the client themselves performing minimal computational work. In this setting, all participants (i.e. client and full nodes) need to lock funds in an "arbiter" contract as collateral to discourage dishonest behavior. Therefore, rational full nodes are incentivized to provide correct replies to the client's queries or risk being penalized. Such an approach naturally requires a blockchain that is augmented with smart-contract capabilities, but is otherwise agnostic to its other properties.

5   Systematization Methodology

The design of light clients has always been a vibrant topic of discussion in the community. A number of proposals have been given ranging from simple forum or blog posts to rigorous theoretical works and actual deployed systems. In our systematization, we only consider works that represent a distinct light client proposal (i.e. not generic techniques as discussed in Sect. 4), and include at least some form of security discussion. Our systematization is performed over the axes corresponding to the light client properties provided in Sect. 3.1.

In particular, we first consider the **functional and basic operation** axis, where we categorize light client proposals based on their functional properties. These include their compatibility on existing systems (which is preferred), if they require modifications or if they propose a new standalone system. We also note if they are designed for a specific consensus algorithm, and the cryptographic primitives they use. Table 1 shows our findings. We observe that verifiable queries of non-existence are neglected by light client protocols and therefore omitted from the table. Also note that while clients should always be able to make verifiable queries, wallet functionality is not always included in each one of them. However, we omit a reference to this functionality from our table, as adding it to an existing client protocol or implementation is usually trivial.

The **efficiency** axis, includes several aspects of light client efficiency characteristics, in line with the properties discussed in Sect. 3.1. Note that our systematization is not meant to be used as a direct asymptotic comparison between different light client proposals and protocols. Such a comparison is impossible as the clients operate on top of different underlying schemes. In Table 2, we provide a coarse categorization based on their performance in each efficiency category, indicated with a "good" or "bad" practice icon (thumbs up and down icons respectively). In general, a sublinear cost with respect to the number of blocks is treated as good practice, however, in some cases we deviate from this rule to take concrete costs into account - we mark those with a "*" in the Table. For storage efficiency, we consider both the prover and verifier, where a thumbs up icon denotes good practice for both. Communication efficiency denotes the requirements for proof size, while bootstrapping efficiency denotes the initial cost of client joining the system as well as the syncing maintenance cost.

Finally we consider **security** as the third systematization axis and present our findings in Table 3. We start by listing any required assumptions (i.e. beyond the Basic Assumptions listed in Sect. 3.2) that each light client proposal needs, "-" means that no additional assumptions are made. Then, for each required security property (secure bootstrapping and querying), we indicate whether the light client scheme satisfies the property (✔) or a known vulnerability exists (✗)[2]. In cases where a security guarantee of a light client has not been proven via a security (or sketch) of proof, we denote this by the exclamation mark symbol "!". In Table 3, we also consider the network-level assumption separately, as it is more secure for the light client to communicate with the blockchain in a distributed fashion. Therefore we mark schemes with ✔ that communicate independently (e.g. peer-to-peer) with the blockchain system, while schemes marked with ✗ rely on a centralized server or full node.

In all of our Tables, we group the schemes into two main categories based on their design. The first group follows the "stateless blockchain" approach for constructing efficient light clients, while the second group follows the "efficient bootstrapping - synchronization" approach. We keep the game theoretic-based work as a third separate category.

6   Existing Light Client Constructions: Insights and Gaps

In this section we discuss the works listed in our Tables in more detail, and present a series of interesting insights and gaps. We organize our discussion in a similar way to our scheme grouping for each table, by first analyzing schemes

---

[2] To mark that a system satisfies a property, we do not necessarily require a formal security proof, but we do require at least some relevant informal discussion.

Table 1. Light client functional properties overview.

System - client	Consensus	Compatibility	Crypto primitives
Mina [40]	PoS	New system	SNARKs
Plumo [58]	BFT	Modification	SNARKs, BLS signatures
PoNW [73]	PoW	New system or Modification	SNARKs
Chen et al. [52]	Not specified	Modification	SNARKs (trusted or universal)
Batched accumulators [37]	Not specified	New system or Modification	Batched RSA accumulator
Edrax [54]	Not specified	New system	Sparse MT, Distributed VC, zkSNARKs
SPV [86]	Any	Yes	
Geth light mode [17]	PoW	Yes	
Vault [80]	PoS	New system	Stamping certificates
Ethanos [77]	PoW	Modification	
NiPoPoW [75]	PoW	Modification	NiPoPoWs [75]
Flyclient [45]	PoW	Modification	MMR commitments
Diem [10]	BFT	Yes	
Cosmos IBC [62]	BFT - PoS	New system	
Binance [24]	PoS variant	New system	
Cardano [48]	PoS	Modification	Stake-based threshold multisignatures
Lu et al. [81]	Any	Yes	

Table 2. Light client efficiency overview.

System - client	Bootstrapping	Storage	Communication	Prover Computation*	Client Computation
Mina [40]	👍	👍	👍	👎	👍
Plumo [58]	👍*	👎 (prover)	👍	👎 (long intervals)	👍
PoNW [73]	👍	👎 (prover)	👍	👍 (embedded in PoW puzzle)	👍
Chen et al. [52]	👍	👍	👍	👎	👍
Batched accumulators [37]	👎	👍	👍	👎	👎
Edrax [54]	👎	👍	👍	👎	👍
SPV [86]	👍*	👍	👍	👍	👍
Geth light mode [17]	👎	👎*	👎*	👍	👍
Vault [80]	👍	👎	👎	👎	👎*
Ethanos [77]	👍*	👎	👎	👍	👍*
NiPoPoW [75]	👍	👍	👍	👍	👍
Flyclient [45]	👍	👍	👍	👎	👍
Diem (verifying) [10]	👍	👍	👍	👍	👍
Cosmos IBC [62]	👍	👍	👍	👎	👍
Binance [24]	👍	👍	👎*	👍	👍
Cardano [48]	👍	👍	👍	👍	👍
Lu et al. [81]	👍	👍	👍	👍	👍

Table 3. Light client schemes security properties.

System - client	Assumptions	Bootstrapping	Querying	Distributed networking
Mina [40]	Trusted setup	✔	✔	✔
Plumo [58]	Trusted setup	✔	✔	✗
PoNW [73]	Trusted setup	!	!	✗
Chen et al. [52]	-	!	!	✗
Batched accumulators [37]	Trusted setup or class groups	✔	✔	!
Edrax [54]	-	✔	✔	!
SPV [86]	-	✗	✗	✗
Geth [17]	-	✔	✔	✔
Vault [80]	Weak synchrony	✔	✔	✔
Ethanos [77]	Active account availability	✔	✔	✔
NiPoPoW [75]	Fixed difficulty	✔	✔	✗
Flyclient [45]	-	✔	✔	✗
Diem [10]	-	✔	✔	✗
Cosmos IBC [62]	-	!	!	✗
Binance [24]	-	!	!	✗
Cardano [48]	-	✔	!	✗
Lu et al. [81]	Rational behavior	!	✔	!

that follow the stateless blockchain approach, then schemes which have efficient bootstrapping and synchronization as their main goal.

6.1 Stateless Blockchains for Light Clients

Here we consider schemes that enable a stateless blockchain design, namely a blockchain with a succinct and verifiable representation of its entire state, as previously discussed in Sect. 4.3.

SNARKs are an effective tool for implementing a stateless blockchain, with Coda-Mina [40] using them in an recursive fashion, chaining them together, eventually having a single SNARK to verify the whole blockchain state. As discussed in Sect. 1.2, it utilizes a variant of the Ouroboros Genesis Proof of Stake algorithm [34] to preserve consensus properties in a stateless setting. Essentially, SNARKS are used as a tool to implement "incremental" verification of recursively-composed proofs, and follow-up works [52,73] improved this paradigm. However, SNARKs typically imply a significant burden on the prover. Plumo [58] uses SNARKs for proving transitions in the consensus committee, enabling fast synchronization of light clients through "checkpoints", thus only needing to fetch data after the most recent checkpoint. These checkpoints also include periodic proofs of BFT consensus evolution to preserve consensus properties, efficiently verifiable by light clients such as resource-constrained mobile phones. [73] also uses SNARKs and incremental verification, in addition to a Proof-or-Work variant (Proof of Necessary Work) to take advantage of the computation performed by the consensus layer, while Chen et al. [52] in a more extensive study of incremental verification in blockchains, provide a framework to make an existing system incrementally verifiable using a "compatible" consensus algorithm. This work is also the first to provide directions for implementing this paradigm in the context of privacy-preserving blockchains like Zcash [36] by applying incremental verification combined with ZKPs on the public state of the system (which for the case of Zcash is the set of serial numbers and coin commitments). Still, it leaves many questions open, such as which entities will be responsible for providing the proofs, or the overhead on the system which is already not among the most efficient ones.

Gap 1. *Is a complete and efficient light-client scheme possible that is compatible with privacy-preserving systems?*

We should also mention that zk-SNARKs were used in zk-rollups [18]: a layer-2 scalability solution to move data and computation off-chain. However, except for [52], none of the SNARK-based approaches seem to consider the prover's substantial overhead, which in a blockchain system would be the consensus participants or the full nodes. Beyond the prover costs, most SNARK approaches come with additional assumptions such as a trusted setup phase. That leads us to the following Gap:

Gap 2. *Can we design a light-client scheme that satisfies all the security properties while being efficient and practical for the client with a minimal overhead to the consensus participants or full nodes?*

As an intermediate solution, additional financial incentives for entities producing such proofs could alleviate the extra computational requirements, however this is only applicable to blockchains that implement or contain a cryptocurrency.

Improving on the Vector Commitment approach discussed in Sect. 4.3, Boneh et al. [37] introduced techniques for efficiently batching various operations in RSA accumulators (e.g. additions, deletions and witness creation), all of which can potentially utilized for implementing stateless blockchains (e.g. committing to the UTXO set as an accumulator state). RSA accumulators are used by MiniLedger [50] as an alternative model to Merkle trees discussed above. Since RSA Accumulators involve a trusted setup (or novel but more expensive class groups), hash-based accumulators were proposed by [57], however with a different goal, to reduces storage for a fully validating node. An additional concern in the RSA accumulator approach is the extra overhead of maintaining the accumulator (which depending on the implementation, would be paid either by consensus participants or full nodes).

Edrax [54] proposed a cryptocurrency where validators only need to verify a commitment of the most recent state. Edrax implemented this approach in the UTXO model by utilizing sparse Merkle trees to represent the UTXO set, and also in account model by utilizing distributed vector commitments. In the UTXO-based case, validators first verify if a transaction's input belongs in the set, and then simply remove that input and add the output in the set. In the account-based case, they utilize distributed vector commitments to still make transactions possible without requiring interaction between the sender and receiver. However, clients need to constantly synchronize their local proofs with respect to those commitments, and will have to pay a significant synchronization cost after an offline period. Although Edrax proposes an additional untrusted entity to provide synchronization proofs on behalf of the client, this nevertheless introduces a significant overhead overall in the system.

Insight 1. *Redactable blockchains have not been explored as a solution towards implementing light clients.*

Blockchain redaction, discussed in Sect. 4.2, has the potential to be utilized in several ways, for instance, a series of blocks can be replaced by a single block containing compressed information. An interesting direction might be to execute redaction operations at the consensus layer.

6.2   Reducing Bootstrapping and Synchronization Costs

An important property of light clients is the requirement for an efficient way to initialize itself and join the system; downloading gigabytes of data and performing heavy verification operations on millions of transactions is prohibitive for a mobile or browser-based client. This is also important if the client is disconnected for some periods of time and needs to reconnect, or even just to maintain a synchronization with the current state of the blockchain.

Gap 3. *No light client approach or implementation explicitly considers frequent offline phases, where the client needs to re-sync with the current system state.*

As discussed in Sect. 1.2, SPV follows the Header verification approach, which while generally efficient for a light client, suffers from potential security issues (especially in Proof of Stake and BFT consnensus), and relies on the availability and honesty of a small set of servers, while also exposing its privacy to the chosen server(s) from that set [7,12]. Ethereum's native light client also follows this paradigm without relying on a chosen server or full node, however its concrete bootstrapping, storage and communication requirements are practically prohibitive for a light client implementation.

Vault [80] is a prominent example of a standalone system designed for significantly decreasing bootstrapping and participation costs. It is based on Algorand's proof of stake protocol, however it works in an account based model using sparse Merkle trees similar to Ethereum. Vault introduces techniques such as decoupling double-spend detection from account balances by making transactions valid only for a parameterized block window, while also pruning accounts with no balance, sharding the account state tree across participants, and using additional "stamping" certificates to convince new joining clients on block validity, which have reduced size by trading off liveness while still preserving safety. Although Vault (as a standalone cryptocurrency) was not designed with light clients in mind (e.g. a client needs to constantly perform an update operation while its transaction is pending), its techniques which seem to decrease bootstrapping costs by one or two orders of magnitude, can serve as a guideline for implementing light clients on top of existing systems.

In another approach, Ethanos [77] chooses to reduce the bootstrapping costs on Ethereum by not downloading "inactive" accounts, and invoking a "restore" transaction when such an account needs to reactivate itself. This special transaction type has the inherent limitation of needing to be submitted by another "active" address, and is essentially a Merkle proof of the last known account state (or checkpoint), along with void proofs that no more recent checkpoint exists (paired with a Bloom filter for space efficiency). In this manner, Ethanos reduces bootstrapping costs by a constant factor of 2.

Non-Interactive Proofs of Proof-of-Work (NIPoPoWs) [75] further improve the notion of SPV client by introducing a new primitive under the same name. This primitive, designed for Proof of Work blockchains, constructs a multi-layer chain of blocks from the basic chain, where each layer is essentially a skip list of blocks that satisfy a lower target (i.e. higher difficulty) in the PoW puzzle. In this way, a new client can avoid fetching the entire chain of block headers as in SPV, which translates to logarithmic asymptotic costs (or a few hundred kilobytes proof) making an even more efficient light client. While NIPoPoWs assumed static difficulty across the chain, Flyclient [45] uses an efficiently-updatable Merkle tree variant (Merkle Mountain Range commitments) as underlying primitive for compatibility with variable-difficulty PoW chains.

We also mention some works further improving NIPoPoWs and FlyClient. Kiayias et al. [76] discuss how to securely implement them on top of existing systems through a "velvet" fork, i.e. without requiring a soft or hard fork but only through a minority of the miners. TxChain [96] extends NIPoPoWs and Fly-Client to efficiently handle a large number of transaction verifications distributed across several blocks, by introducing a new transaction type ("contingent" transaction), serving as a single reference to other transactions and replacing the need to provide transaction and block inclusion proofs for the skipped blocks (which potentially can be more expensive even than a naive SPV client).

Diem's verifying light client [10] (as discussed in Sect. 1.2) fully relies on a full node to receive query replies and proofs (in contrast, Binance light client [24] which also relies on a full node, does not explicitly verifies any proofs). As Diem utilizes a BFT consensus, it also needs to receive "epoch proofs", which prove to the client correctness of evolution of validator signatures, which is the approach discussed in Sect. 4.1. In addition, recent work [51] suggest to further compress epoch proofs by an *epoch skipping* technique, without however addressing long range attacks. Also as discussed in Sect. 1.2, Tendermint [42] (used in Cosmos IBC) proposes a similar technique based on the latest block height which ensures that at least one validator is honest based on validator intersection and the byzantine threshold. Plumo's proofs of BFT consensus evolution [58] also aim to reduce client synchronization load as discussed previously.

Insight 2. *Light clients in BFT-based consensus blockchains can be implemented through full nodes, where clients make queries and full nodes provide verifiable proofs alongside with epoch proofs.*

Insight 3. *In BFT-based consensus blockchains, aggregate signatures (e.g. BLS signatures or ZK-friendly signatures) can be used to compress not only transactions, but also validator signatures, leading to further reduced bootstrapping and synchronization costs for light clients.*

An alternative approach to Diem and Plumo is used by Dfinity's Internet computer [68], a blockchain-based protocol that creates a network of decentralized data centers running smart contracts, inspired by Ethereum. Dfinity utilizes key re-sharing within a threshold signature scheme to accommodate validators joining or leaving, aiming at circumventing the need for tracking their key evolution by a client [64]. However, it is unclear whether this approach guarantees BFT security at all times, as it assumes that validators will delete their old shares afterwards. For instance, suppose the consensus system has 7 honest validators from a quorum of 10 validators, which guarantees the $2f + 1$ consensus security properties. Still, if 12 validators join afterwards, which now implies a tolerance of 7 Byzantine validators, this can potentially compromise consensus, as the previous 7 "honest" validators might not have deleted their key shares. In addition, Aumasson and Shlomovits [33] highlighted the possibility of an adversary corrupting the key re-sharing process in some threshold signature schemes, which could potentially hurt consensus liveness.

Insight 4. *For blockchains based on BFT consensus, frequent validator reconfigurations (e.g. joining, leaving or key rotations) usually imply additional work for clients.*

While the insight above is not applicable to off-chain reconfiguration approaches such as Dfinity [64], such approaches are typically prone to long range attacks as we discussed previously.

Gap 4. *A light client of a BFT-based consensus blockchain normally needs to verify the evolution of validator signatures using "epoch proofs" to prevent long range attacks. Is it possible to design a secure protocol for BFT consensus that either compress these proofs or circumvents this requirement entirely?*

More recently, Chaidos and Kiayias [48] proposed a new primitive, called stake-based threshold multisignatures. This primitive enables a client's bootstrapping through header verification in Proof of Stake systems like Cardano, in a similar way to SPV, without however needing to verify the participant's stake history (as discussed in Sect. 4.1) and without the need of any modifications to the Proof of Stake consensus as in Mina [40].

6.3 Smart-Contract Based Approaches and Blockchain Interoperability

We briefly discuss implementing light clients by querying full nodes though a smart contract, and assuming "rational" behavior from the client and the full nodes after the required collateral deposits to participate, similar to the work by Lu et al. [81]. This approach can potentially address many of the previously discussed gaps, as the rational behavior assumption can circumvent technical difficulties or limitations which rise from complex cryptographic primitives. For instance, as [81] showed, a light client can make a query of non-existence, and assuming full node rational behavior, will get a correct reply (i.e. inclusion proof if queried data exists, or a negative reply in case such data does not exist, which can be challenged if another node presents an inclusion proof thus penalizing a false non-existence claim). However there are several caveats to such an approach: First it naturally requires a smart-contract, which implies a time delay until it received the reply to its query, incompatibility with blockchains without a smart contract, and additional monetary costs for the contract's "gas" fees which can be potentially very high. Also, the client might merely receive an answer to its query (e.g. a simple "♯" reply if answer to query does not exist) without a cryptographic proof (as defined in Sect. 3.1 as an optional functional property), which leaves this problem still open. Finally, the game-theoretic model might not capture cases where the client is considered a "high value target", where a full node (or a coalition of them) might choose to actually behave "irrationally" and intentionally risk being penalized in hope for other (not necessary monetary) gains.

Gap 5. *Can we design a light client protocol compatible with queries of transaction or account state non-existence proofs?*

From the above approach we observe however that it is trivial to implement an efficient light client that makes and receives queries to a "trusted oracle" (which in the above case were the rational full nodes following the protocol), without needing to make verifications, even if such an oracle is decentralized. This implies that such a client would be possible to exist even in extremely resource-constrained environments such as a smart contract *itself*:

Insight 5. *Interoperability: Ideally, light clients should be implemented as a smart contract without the use of trusted oracles. This would allow for verifying transactions of a blockchain A inside a contract of blockchain B.*

Gap 6. *Implementing reasonably efficient light clients inside smart contracts might be impractical for many non zero-knowledge proof friendly blockchains or ledgers without succinct fraud proof in optimistic settings [18].*

Although Cosmos makes a first step towards building a light client compatible with several blockchain systems (including those with smart contracts), it is still not known if we can also utilize previous techniques or primitives to implement such clients in pure smart-contract based blockchains, e.g. Ethereum.

7   Conclusion

The blockchain community is witnessing a continuous effort towards implementing efficient light clients, suitable for resource-constrained devices or environments like browsers or mobile phones, while maintaining the underlying blockchain's security guarantees, and without introducing additional trust assumptions. As we observe different perceptions of light client properties across blockchain systems, we first provide a categorization of the most important light client properties. Then, we present a systematization of proposed light clients across three axes derived from our property categorization. Our systemization helps to identify a number of exciting open problems on implementing light clients which we summarize below.

We first observe that light clients satisfying our properties, and compatible with privacy preserving systems have not yet been implemented (Gap 1), with recent works providing preliminary directions [52]. In addition, no current scheme seems to satisfy all of our functional, efficiency and security properties together (Gap 2). Also, existing works seem to neglect the case of frequent light client offline phases, which might be inefficient even for clients with efficient bootstrapping protocols (Gap 3). Distributing prover's work among the main blockchain participants (consensus layer or full nodes) along with providing incentives are possible directions.

Furthermore, it is not yet known if light clients can be efficient enough, such that they can be run from smart contracts across different blockchains (Gap 6). SNARKs seem to be a promising primitive towards this, although this still need to be shown in practice. Also there seems to be room for improvement for light clients implemented on BFT-consensus blockchains (Gap 4) by leveraging primitives such as key re-sharing and threshold signatures in off-chain protocols, while however considering Byzantine nodes in special cases. Finally, proofs of non-existence, a desired property in blockchain systems, is still missing from all current light client implementations (Gap 5). We hope our work will provide research directions for the community towards usable and secure light clients for blockchain systems.

Acknowledgements. Foteini Baldimtsi and Panagiotis Chatzigiannis were supported by NSF #1717067, NSA #204761 and a Facebook Research Award. Panagiotis Chatzigiannis was partially supported by Harmony through the Research DAO. The authors would like to thank Matthew Zipkin for the constructive feedback.

A   Towards the Light Client Goal

A number of works and proposals exist towards improving efficiency in state representation. Merkle trees were initially proposed to store Bitcoin's UTXO set (which represents the blockchain state) for fast bootstrapping [26], with a $O(\lg n)$ algorithm for updating and re-balancing the tree across blocks (i.e. updating values, insertions and deletions of accounts). Then [89] further optimized the re-balancing algorithm using AVL trees. MiniLedger [50] also used Merkle trees to represent the history of transactions per participant. Meanwhile, Ethereum used tries as a more efficient method to represent the account-balance state [95].

In addition, Karakostas et al. [70] proposed a modification of storing the UTXO set which represents the blockchain state in UTXO-model cryptocurrencies by incentivizing constructing "state-friendly" transactions, while [94] proposes a modification on Bitcoin to represent transactions with a trie-based authenticated data structure to enable efficient membership and non-membership proofs. Stateless clients have also been considered in Ethereum using asynchronous accumulators [25,90].

Aiming exclusively for faster client bootstrapping, [2] suggested to distribute the state through external file sharing protocols (e.g. Bittorrent). Then [53] proposed a modification designed for Proof-of-Work blockchains that stores a constant number of state snapshots, in a similar fashion to Ethereum. Similarly, [83] proposes a state-based synchronization based on Bitcoin (i.e. snapshot-based approach), forming a side-chain linked to the main chain, and claiming to reduce blockchain size by 93%. Which however required modifications to Bitcoin, since blocks with invalid attached states should be rejected.

Works that include blockchain pruning include [43], which replaces a UTXO set with an account tree that is cryptographically tied to each mined block, and [87], which proposes a pruning algorithm for permissioned blockchains, executed by each participant separately, using predicate functions to remove spent transactions. Matzutt et al. [84] proposed a pruning scheme for Bitcoin that makes snapshots of the Bitcoin state for efficient bootstrapping of new clients, and also includes a qualitative comparison of related work to pruning and efficient bootstrapping. In addition, Corda [69] can aggregate (and then prune) previous transactions into a single new, reissued transaction.

In the context of blockchain redaction, in addition to preliminary works as [32], we mention [82] designed for "execute-order-validate blockchains" such as Hyperledger Fabric, however with a goal to improve privacy rather efficiency. Also [56] and [55] consider "policy-based" blockchain redaction, which can also serve as a useful tool towards light client implementations.

References

1. Ask about geth: snapshot acceleration. https://blog.ethereum.org/2020/07/17/ask-about-geth-snapshot-acceleration/
2. Bitcoin blockchain data torrent. https://bitcointalk.org/index.php?topic=145386.0
3. Bitcoin core client. https://bitcoin.org/en/bitcoin-core/
4. Bitcoin wiki - clients. https://en.bitcoin.it/wiki/Clients
5. Bitcoin wiki - scalability. https://en.bitcoin.it/wiki/Scalability#Simplified_payment_verification
6. Blockchain light client. https://medium.com/codechain/blockchain-light-client-1171dfa1269a
7. Breadwallet SPV bitcoin C library. https://github.com/breadwallet/breadwallet-core

8. Consensus engine of binance smart chain. https://docs.binance.org/smart-chain/guides/concepts/consensus.html
9. Diem client SDKs. https://github.com/diem/client-sdks
10. Diem verifying client. https://github.com/diem/diem/blob/main/sdk/client/src/verifying_client.rs
11. Dodging a bullet: Ethereum state problems. https://blog.ethereum.org/2021/05/18/eth_state_problems/
12. Electrum docs - frequently asked questions. https://electrum.readthedocs.io/en/latest/faq.html
13. Eth 2.0 specs - minimal light client. https://github.com/ethereum/eth2.0-specs/blob/dev/specs/altair/sync-protocol.md
14. The ethereum-blockchain size will not exceed 1TB anytime soon. https://dev.to/5chdn/the-ethereum-blockchain-size-will-not-exceed-1tb-anytime-soon-58a
15. Ethereum nodes and clients. https://ethereum.org/en/developers/docs/nodes-and-clients/
16. Explaining flyclient. https://electriccoin.co/blog/explaining-flyclient/
17. How to run a light node with geth. https://ethereum.org/en/developers/tutorials/run-light-node-geth/
18. An incomplete guide to rollups. https://vitalik.ca/general/2021/01/05/rollup.html
19. Introducing heartwood. https://electriccoin.co/blog/introducing-heartwood/
20. Mina documentation. https://docs.minaprotocol.com/en
21. Mina protocol - a succinct blockchain. https://masked.medium.com/the-coda-protocol-bbcb4b212b13
22. Nakamoto: a new bitcoin light-client. https://cloudhead.io/nakamoto/
23. The official diem client SDK for python. https://github.com/diem/client-sdk-python
24. Run a light client to join binance chain. https://docs.binance.org/light-client.html
25. The stateless client concept. https://ethresear.ch/t/the-stateless-client-concept/172
26. Storing UTXOs in a balanced Merkle tree. https://bitcointalk.org/index.php?topic=101734.msg1117428
27. A suggestion for a light-client wallet (like the BTC SPV wallet with Merkle tree). https://forum.algorand.org/t/a-suggestion-for-a-light-client-wallet-like-the-btc-spv-wallet-with-merkle-tree/1092/4
28. Ultimate blockchain compression w/ trust-free lite nodes. https://bitcointalk.org/index.php?topic=88208.0/
29. What is a light client and why you should care? https://www.parity.io/blog/what-is-a-light-client/
30. Amsden, Z., et al.: The libra blockchain (2019). https://developers.libra.org/docs/assets/papers/the-libra-blockchain.pdf
31. Ashritha, K., Sindhu, M., Lakshmy, K.: Redactable blockchain using enhanced chameleon hash function. In: 2019 5th International Conference on Advanced Computing Communication Systems (ICACCS), pp. 323–328 (2019). https://doi.org/10.1109/ICACCS.2019.8728524
32. Ateniese, G., Magri, B., Venturi, D., Andrade, E.R.: Redactable blockchain - or - rewriting history in bitcoin and friends. In: 2017 IEEE European Symposium on Security and Privacy, EuroS&P 2017, Paris, France, 26–28 April 2017, pp. 111–126. IEEE (2017). https://doi.org/10.1109/EuroSP.2017.37
33. Aumasson, J.P., Shlomovits, O.: Attacking threshold wallets. Cryptology ePrint Archive, Report 2020/1052 (2020). https://eprint.iacr.org/2020/1052

34. Badertscher, C., Gazi, P., Kiayias, A., Russell, A., Zikas, V.: Ouroboros genesis: composable proof-of-stake blockchains with dynamic availability. In: Lie, D., Mannan, M., Backes, M., Wang, X. (eds.) ACM CCS 2018, pp. 913–930. ACM Press, October 2018. https://doi.org/10.1145/3243734.3243848

35. Baldimtsi, F., et al.: Accumulators with applications to anonymity-preserving revocation. In: 2017 IEEE European Symposium on Security and Privacy, EuroS&P 2017, Paris, France, 26–28 April 2017, pp. 301–315. IEEE (2017). https://doi.org/10.1109/EuroSP.2017.13

36. Ben-Sasson, E., et al.: Zerocash: decentralized anonymous payments from bitcoin. In: 2014 IEEE Symposium on Security and Privacy, pp. 459–474. IEEE Computer Society Press, May 2014. https://doi.org/10.1109/SP.2014.36

37. Boneh, D., Bünz, B., Fisch, B.: Batching techniques for accumulators with applications to IOPs and stateless blockchains. In: Boldyreva, A., Micciancio, D. (eds.) CRYPTO 2019, Part I. LNCS, vol. 11692, pp. 561–586. Springer, Cham (2019). https://doi.org/10.1007/978-3-030-26948-7_20

38. Boneh, D., Gentry, C., Lynn, B., Shacham, H.: Aggregate and verifiably encrypted signatures from bilinear maps. In: Biham, E. (ed.) EUROCRYPT 2003. LNCS, vol. 2656, pp. 416–432. Springer, Heidelberg (2003). https://doi.org/10.1007/3-540-39200-9_26

39. Boneh, D., Lynn, B., Shacham, H.: Short signatures from the weil pairing. In: Boyd, C. (ed.) ASIACRYPT 2001. LNCS, vol. 2248, pp. 514–532. Springer, Heidelberg (2001). https://doi.org/10.1007/3-540-45682-1_30

40. Bonneau, J., Meckler, I., Rao, V., Shapiro, E.: Coda: decentralized cryptocurrency at scale. Cryptology ePrint Archive, Report 2020/352 (2020). https://eprint.iacr.org/2020/352

41. Bonnet, F., Bramas, Q., Défago, X.: Stateless distributed ledgers. In: Georgiou, C., Majumdar, R. (eds.) NETYS 2020. LNCS, vol. 12129, pp. 349–354. Springer, Cham (2021). https://doi.org/10.1007/978-3-030-67087-0_22

42. Braithwaite, S., et al.: A tendermint light client. CoRR abs/2010.07031 (2020). https://arxiv.org/abs/2010.07031

43. Bruce, J.: The mini-blockchain scheme (2017). https://cryptonite.info/files/mbc-scheme-rev3.pdf

44. Buchman, E., Kwon, J., Milosevic, Z.: The latest gossip on BFT consensus. CoRR abs/1807.04938 (2018). https://arxiv.org/abs/1807.04938

45. Bünz, B., Kiffer, L., Luu, L., Zamani, M.: FlyClient: super-light clients for cryptocurrencies. In: 2020 IEEE Symposium on Security and Privacy, pp. 928–946. IEEE Computer Society Press, May 2020. https://doi.org/10.1109/SP40000.2020.00049

46. Canetti, R., Gennaro, R., Goldfeder, S., Makriyannis, N., Peled, U.: UC non-interactive, proactive, threshold ECDSA with identifiable aborts. In: Proceedings of the 2020 ACM SIGSAC Conference on Computer and Communications Security, pp. 1769–1787 (2020)

47. Catalano, D., Fiore, D.: Vector commitments and their applications. In: Kurosawa, K., Hanaoka, G. (eds.) PKC 2013. LNCS, vol. 7778, pp. 55–72. Springer, Heidelberg (2013). https://doi.org/10.1007/978-3-642-36362-7_5

48. Chaidos, P., Kiayias, A.: Mithril: stake-based threshold multisignatures. Cryptology ePrint Archive, Report 2021/916 (2021). https://ia.cr/2021/916

49. Chalkias, K., Garillot, F., Kondi, Y., Nikolaenko, V.: Non-interactive half-aggregation of EdDSA and variants of schnorr signatures. In: Paterson, K.G. (ed.) CT-RSA 2021. LNCS, vol. 12704, pp. 577–608. Springer, Cham (2021). https://doi.org/10.1007/978-3-030-75539-3_24

50. Chatzigiannis, P., Baldimtsi, F.: Miniledger: compact-sized anonymous and auditable distributed payments. Cryptology ePrint Archive, Report 2021/869 (2021). https://eprint.iacr.org/2021/869

51. Chatzigiannis, P., Chalkias, K.: Proof of assets in the diem blockchain. Cryptology ePrint Archive, Report 2021/598 (2021). https://eprint.iacr.org/2021/598

52. Chen, W., Chiesa, A., Dauterman, E., Ward, N.P.: Reducing participation costs via incremental verification for ledger systems. Cryptology ePrint Archive, Report 2020/1522 (2020). https://ia.cr/2020/1522

53. Chepurnoy, A., Larangeira, M., Ojiganov, A.: Rollerchain, a blockchain with safely pruneable full blocks (2016)

54. Chepurnoy, A., Papamanthou, C., Zhang, Y.: Edrax: a cryptocurrency with stateless transaction validation. Cryptology ePrint Archive, Report 2018/968 (2018). https://eprint.iacr.org/2018/968

55. Derler, D., Samelin, K., Slamanig, D., Striecks, C.: Fine-grained and controlled rewriting in blockchains: chameleon-hashing gone attribute-based. In: NDSS 2019. The Internet Society, February 2019

56. Deuber, D., Magri, B., Thyagarajan, S.A.K.: Redactable blockchain in the permissionless setting. In: 2019 IEEE Symposium on Security and Privacy, pp. 124–138. IEEE Computer Society Press, May 2019. https://doi.org/10.1109/SP.2019.00039

57. Dryja, T.: Utreexo: a dynamic hash-based accumulator optimized for the bitcoin UTXO set. Cryptology ePrint Archive, Report 2019/611 (2019). https://eprint.iacr.org/2019/611

58. Gabizon, A., et al.: Plumo: towards scalable interoperable blockchains using ultra light validation systems (2020)

59. Garay, J.A., Kiayias, A., Leonardos, N., Panagiotakos, G.: Bootstrapping the blockchain, with applications to consensus and fast PKI setup. In: Abdalla, M., Dahab, R. (eds.) PKC 2018, Part II. LNCS, vol. 10770, pp. 465–495. Springer, Cham (2018). https://doi.org/10.1007/978-3-319-76581-5_16

60. Garillot, F., Kondi, Y., Mohassel, P., Nikolaenko, V.: Threshold schnorr with stateless deterministic signing from standard assumptions. In: Malkin, T., Peikert, C. (eds.) CRYPTO 2021. LNCS, vol. 12825, pp. 127–156. Springer, Cham (2021). https://doi.org/10.1007/978-3-030-84242-0_6

61. Gligor, V.D., Woo, S.L.M.: Establishing software root of trust unconditionally. In: NDSS 2019. The Internet Society, February 2019

62. Goes, C.: The interblockchain communication protocol: an overview. CoRR abs/2006.15918 (2020). https://arxiv.org/abs/2006.15918

63. Gorbunov, S., Reyzin, L., Wee, H., Zhang, Z.: Pointproofs: aggregating proofs for multiple vector commitments. In: Ligatti, J., Ou, X., Katz, J., Vigna, G. (eds.) ACM CCS 2020, pp. 2007–2023. ACM Press, November 2020. https://doi.org/10.1145/3372297.3417244

64. Groth, J.: Introducing noninteractive distributed key generation. https://medium.com/dfinity/applied-crypto-one-public-key-for-the-internet-computer-ni-dkg-4af800db869d

65. Groth, J.: On the size of pairing-based non-interactive arguments. In: Fischlin, M., Coron, J.-S. (eds.) EUROCRYPT 2016, Part II. LNCS, vol. 9666, pp. 305–326. Springer, Heidelberg (2016). https://doi.org/10.1007/978-3-662-49896-5_11

66. Gudgeon, L., Moreno-Sanchez, P., Roos, S., McCorry, P., Gervais, A.: SoK: layer-two blockchain protocols. In: Bonneau, J., Heninger, N. (eds.) FC 2020. LNCS, vol. 12059, pp. 201–226. Springer, Cham (2020). https://doi.org/10.1007/978-3-030-51280-4_12

67. Hafid, A., Hafid, A.S., Samih, M.: Scaling blockchains: a comprehensive survey. IEEE Access **8**, 125244–125262 (2020). https://doi.org/10.1109/ACCESS.2020.3007251

68. Hanke, T., Movahedi, M., Williams, D.: Dfinity technology overview series, consensus system (2018)

69. Hearn, M., Brown, R.G.: Corda: a distributed ledger (2019). https://www.corda.net/wp-content/uploads/2019/08/corda-technical-whitepaper-August-29-2019.pdf

70. Karakostas, D., Karayannidis, N., Kiayias, A.: Efficient state management in distributed ledgers. Cryptology ePrint Archive, Report 2021/183 (2021). https://eprint.iacr.org/2021/183

71. Karantias, K.: SoK: a taxonomy of cryptocurrency wallets. Cryptology ePrint Archive, Report 2020/868 (2020). https://eprint.iacr.org/2020/868

72. Kate, A., Zaverucha, G.M., Goldberg, I.: Constant-size commitments to polynomials and their applications. In: Abe, M. (ed.) ASIACRYPT 2010. LNCS, vol. 6477, pp. 177–194. Springer, Heidelberg (2010). https://doi.org/10.1007/978-3-642-17373-8_11

73. Kattis, A., Bonneau, J.: Proof of necessary work: succinct state verification with fairness guarantees. Cryptology ePrint Archive, Report 2020/190 (2020). https://eprint.iacr.org/2020/190

74. Khaburzaniya, I., Chalkias, K., Lewi, K., Malvai, H.: Aggregating hash-based signatures using starks. Cryptology ePrint Archive, Report 2021/1048 (2021). https://ia.cr/2021/1048

75. Kiayias, A., Miller, A., Zindros, D.: Non-interactive proofs of proof-of-work. In: Bonneau, J., Heninger, N. (eds.) FC 2020. LNCS, vol. 12059, pp. 505–522. Springer, Cham (2020). https://doi.org/10.1007/978-3-030-51280-4_27

76. Kiayias, A., Polydouri, A., Zindros, D.: The velvet path to superlight blockchain clients. Cryptology ePrint Archive, Report 2020/1122 (2020). https://eprint.iacr.org/2020/1122

77. Kim, J., Lee, J., Koo, Y., Park, S., Moon, S.: Ethanos: efficient bootstrapping for full nodes on account-based blockchain. In: Barbalace, A., Bhatotia, P., Alvisi, L., Cadar, C. (eds.) EuroSys 2021: Sixteenth European Conference on Computer Systems, Online Event, United Kingdom, 26–28 April 2021, pp. 99–113. ACM (2021). https://doi.org/10.1145/3447786.3456231

78. Kokoris-Kogias, E., Jovanovic, P., Gasser, L., Gailly, N., Syta, E., Ford, B.: OmniLedger: a secure, scale-out, decentralized ledger via sharding. In: 2018 IEEE Symposium on Security and Privacy, pp. 583–598. IEEE Computer Society Press, May 2018. https://doi.org/10.1109/SP.2018.000-5

79. Krawczyk, H., Rabin, T.: Chameleon hashing and signatures. Cryptology ePrint Archive, Report 1998/010 (1998). https://eprint.iacr.org/1998/010

80. Leung, D., Suhl, A., Gilad, Y., Zeldovich, N.: Vault: fast bootstrapping for the algorand cryptocurrency. In: NDSS 2019. The Internet Society, February 2019

81. Lu, Y., Tang, Q., Wang, G.: Generic superlight client for permissionless blockchains. In: Chen, L., Li, N., Liang, K., Schneider, S. (eds.) ESORICS 2020, Part II. LNCS, vol. 12309, pp. 713–733. Springer, Cham (2020). https://doi.org/10.1007/978-3-030-59013-0_35

82. Manevich, Y., Barger, A., Assa, G.: Redacting transactions from execute-order-validate blockchains. In: IEEE International Conference on Blockchain and Cryptocurrency, ICBC 2021, Sydney, Australia, 3–6 May 2021, pp. 1–9. IEEE (2021). https://doi.org/10.1109/ICBC51069.2021.9461093

83. Marsalek, A., Zefferer, T., Fasllija, E., Ziegler, D.: Tackling data inefficiency: compressing the bitcoin blockchain. In: 2019 18th IEEE International Conference on Trust, Security and Privacy in Computing and Communications/13th IEEE International Conference on Big Data Science and Engineering (TrustCom/BigDataSE), pp. 626–633 (2019). https://doi.org/10.1109/TrustCom/BigDataSE.2019.00089

84. Matzutt, R., Kalde, B., Pennekamp, J., Drichel, A., Henze, M., Wehrle, K.: How to securely prune bitcoin's blockchain. In: 2020 IFIP Networking Conference, Networking 2020, Paris, France, 22–26 June 2020, pp. 298–306. IEEE (2020). https://ieeexplore.ieee.org/document/9142720

85. Merkle, R.C.: A digital signature based on a conventional encryption function. In: Pomerance, C. (ed.) CRYPTO 1987. LNCS, vol. 293, pp. 369–378. Springer, Heidelberg (1988). https://doi.org/10.1007/3-540-48184-2_32

86. Nakamoto, S.: Bitcoin: a peer-to-peer electronic cash system (2009). https://bitcoin.org/bitcoin.pdf

87. Palm, E., Schelén, O., Bodin, U.: Selective blockchain transaction pruning and state derivability. In: Crypto Valley Conference on Blockchain Technology, CVCBT 2018, Zug, Switzerland, 20–22 June 2018, pp. 31–40. IEEE (2018). https://doi.org/10.1109/CVCBT.2018.00009

88. Parno, B., Howell, J., Gentry, C., Raykova, M.: Pinocchio: nearly practical verifiable computation. In: 2013 IEEE Symposium on Security and Privacy, pp. 238–252. IEEE Computer Society Press, May 2013. https://doi.org/10.1109/SP.2013.47

89. Reyzin, L., Meshkov, D., Chepurnoy, A., Ivanov, S.: Improving authenticated dynamic dictionaries, with applications to cryptocurrencies. In: Kiayias, A. (ed.) FC 2017. LNCS, vol. 10322, pp. 376–392. Springer, Cham (2017). https://doi.org/10.1007/978-3-319-70972-7_21

90. Reyzin, L., Yakoubov, S.: Efficient asynchronous accumulators for distributed PKI. In: Zikas, V., De Prisco, R. (eds.) SCN 2016. LNCS, vol. 9841, pp. 292–309. Springer, Cham (2016). https://doi.org/10.1007/978-3-319-44618-9_16

91. Shoup, V.: Practical threshold signatures. In: Preneel, B. (ed.) EUROCRYPT 2000. LNCS, vol. 1807, pp. 207–220. Springer, Heidelberg (2000). https://doi.org/10.1007/3-540-45539-6_15

92. Srinivasan, S., Chepurnoy, A., Papamanthou, C., Tomescu, A., Zhang, Y.: Hyperproofs: aggregating and maintaining proofs in vector commitments. Cryptology ePrint Archive, Report 2021/599 (2021). https://eprint.iacr.org/2021/599

93. Tomescu, A., Abraham, I., Buterin, V., Drake, J., Feist, D., Khovratovich, D.: Aggregatable subvector commitments for stateless cryptocurrencies. In: Galdi, C., Kolesnikov, V. (eds.) SCN 2020. LNCS, vol. 12238, pp. 45–64. Springer, Cham (2020). https://doi.org/10.1007/978-3-030-57990-6_3

94. White, B.: A theory for lightweight cryptocurrency ledgers (2015). https://raw.githubusercontent.com/input-output-hk/qeditas-ledgertheory/master/lightcrypto.pdf

95. Wood, G.: Ethereum: A secure decentralized generalised transaction ledger (2021). https://ethereum.github.io/yellowpaper/paper.pdf. Accessed 14 Feb 2021

96. Zamyatin, A., Avarikioti, Z., Perez, D., Knottenbelt, W.J.: TxChain: efficient cryptocurrency light clients via contingent transaction aggregation. Cryptology ePrint Archive, Report 2020/580 (2020). https://eprint.iacr.org/2020/580

Achieving Almost All Blockchain Functionalities with Polylogarithmic Storage

Parikshit Hegde[1]($\boxtimes$), Robert Streit[1], Yanni Georghiades[1], Chaya Ganesh[2], and Sriram Vishwanath[1]

[1] The University of Texas at Austin, Texas, USA
{hegde,rpstreit,yanni.georghiades,sriram}@utexas.edu
[2] Indian Institute of Science, Karnataka, India
chaya@iisc.ac.in

Abstract. In current blockchain systems, full nodes that perform all of the available functionalities need to store the entire blockchain. In addition to the blockchain, full nodes also store a blockchain-summary, called the *state*, which is used to efficiently verify transactions. With the size of popular blockchains and their states growing rapidly, full nodes require massive storage resources in order to keep up with the scaling. This leads to a tug-of-war between scaling and decentralization since fewer entities can afford expensive resources. We present *hybrid nodes* for proof-of-work (PoW) cryptocurrencies which can validate transactions, validate blocks, validate states, mine, select the main chain, bootstrap new hybrid nodes, and verify payment proofs. With the use of a protocol called *trimming*, hybrid nodes only retain polylogarithmic number of blocks in the chain length in order to represent the proof-of-work of the blockchain. Hybrid nodes are also optimized for the storage of the state with the use of *stateless blockchain* protocols. The lowered storage requirements should enable more entities to join as hybrid nodes and improve the decentralization of the system. We define novel theoretical security models for hybrid nodes and show that they are provably secure. We also show that the storage requirement of hybrid nodes is near-optimal with respect to our security definitions.

Keywords: Blockchains · Cryptocurrency · Storage · NIPoPoW · Hybrid nodes · Trimming

1 Introduction

Blockchains enable a group of untrusting parties to securely maintain a distributed ledger without relying on a trusted third party. Instead, the power to decide what is recorded in the blockchain is distributed amongst a set of decentralized nodes. This property is desirable for applications used by a set of mutually distrustful parties, such as a digital currency. For this reason, *cryptocurrencies* are a fundamental application of blockchains and are increasingly

© International Financial Cryptography Association 2022
I. Eyal and J. Garay (Eds.): FC 2022, LNCS 13411, pp. 642–660, 2022.
https://doi.org/10.1007/978-3-031-18283-9_32

growing in popularity. In this paper, we focus on cryptocurrencies built on top of a proof-of-work (PoW) blockchain employing the longest chain rule. A blockchain node for a cryptocurrency typically has the following functionalities:

1. *Transaction validation*: When the node receives a new transaction, it checks if the transaction is valid with respect to the transactions already confirmed in the blockchain.
2. *Block validation*: When the node receives a new block, it verifies that the block hash is valid, all the transactions in the block are valid, and the block otherwise follows all of the conventions imposed by the protocol.
3. *State Validation*: Given a summary of currency ownership in the system, called the *state*, the node verifies that the state is consistent with the blockchain.
4. *Mining*: The node can append a block to the blockchain by verifying its contents and producing a PoW for the block. A node which does not mine blocks is assumed to have mining power 0.
5. *Chain Selection*: Given a set of conflicting chains, the node can choose the main chain which has the most PoW. Any two honest nodes which receive the same set of conflicting chains in the same order must select the same main chain.
6. *Bootstrapping new nodes to the blockchain*: A node can provide new nodes entering the system with the blockchain.
7. *Serving payment proofs*: Given a transaction tx, the node can provide a *proof* of tx's inclusion in the blockchain.
8. *Verification of payment proofs*: Given a proof of transaction tx's inclusion in the blockchain, the node can verify the correctness of the proof.

In order to have all of the functionalities above, a node must verify and store the entire blockchain. We will refer to such nodes as *full nodes*. Popular systems like Bitcoin and Ethereum also allow for other types of nodes with more limited functionalities [16, 20]. For instance, *pruned nodes* initially download the entire blockchain and verify it. However, they later *prune* the blockchain, meaning that they discard block data and only retain block headers for blocks older than the most recent k blocks in the blockchain. By retaining a summary of the blockchain called the *state*, they can still perform all desired functionalities except for serving proofs of payment and bootstrapping new nodes. *Lightweight nodes* only download the block-headers, and their only functionality is to verify payment proofs provided by full nodes. Importantly, full nodes are necessary to bootstrap both pruned and lightweight nodes into the blockchain.

Since full nodes need to store the entire blockchain, their resource requirements can be high. This is an entry barrier that makes fewer nodes participate, which leads to a centralization of trust. In this paper, we optimize storage requirements in order to lower this entry barrier. In deference to the storage capabilities of modern computational hardware, we divide storage into two categories. The first is *cold storage*, which is accessed infrequently and is stored on disk. This includes older blocks that are deep inside the blockchain. The second is *hot storage*, which is accessed frequently and is stored in memory. Naturally, the blockchain state used to validate blocks and transactions is kept in hot storage.

In this paper, we propose a new class called *hybrid nodes*. Hybrid nodes have all of the above functionalities except for the ability to provide payment proofs. Importantly, hybrid nodes can bootstrap new hybrid nodes into the system, meaning they do not depend on any other type of nodes, including full nodes. Moreover, if B is the length of the blockchain, hybrid nodes only require $polylog(B)$ cold storage to represent the PoW of the chain. This is achieved by a process we call *trimming*, an extension of non-interactive-proofs-of-proof-of-work [14] (henceforth, NIPoPoW). NIPoPoW is a protocol that enables a prover (which is most often a full node) to provide payment proofs of $polylog(B)$ size rather than the traditional B size, but NIPoPoW still requires the prover to store the entire blockchain. We extend these techniques further in our trimming protocol to securely remove blocks and reduce storage.

We now comment on the *practical implications* of our proposed protocols for hybrid nodes. There are two main components of a blockchain with significant storage requirements for hybrid nodes. First is the storage required to represent the PoW of the chain, which is used by the consensus protocol. In traditional systems, since the entire chain of block-headers must be stored, the storage requirements for this component at the time of writing could be in the order of 100s of megabytes for systems such as Bitcoin and Ethereum. Our trimming protocols for hybrid nodes can decrease this requirement to the order of 100s of kilobytes. While 100MB might not seem large, if one wishes to run a number of blockchains on a single device then the storage requirement can quickly multiply into the gigabytes range if methods such as *trimming* are not employed. Moreover, since hybrid nodes only store $polylog(B)$ number of block headers, their storage requirement grows slower with time too. The second component that requires storage is the blockchain state (UTXO or account-based for cryptocurrencies). For instance, the size of Bitcoin's UTXO set is roughly 4 GB [3]. However, some novel stateless blockchain protocols reduce this storage requirement to the order of kilobytes by requiring clients to provide payment proofs [1]. In Sect. 7, we show that hybrid nodes can employ stateless blockchain protocols, thus optimizing both their PoW and state storage.

Previous works, specifically CoinPrune and SecurePrune [15,18], achieve the same functionalities as hybrid nodes with lower storage requirements than full nodes. They achieve this by storing a commitment to the blockchain-state in the blocks and pruning blocks that are deep in the blockchain. However, their storage requirement still scales linearly with blockchain length. Moreover, these works provide a largely qualitative analysis of their respective protocols. In contrast, we perform a rigorous security analysis and provide proofs that hybrid nodes are secure.

Concurrent with the initial submission of our work, we were made aware of an independent work that uses a modification of NIPoPoWs to obtain polylogarithmic storage [13]. Although both protocols are similarly motivated, we believe that our security definitions and the corresponding analysis are novel and crucial to this area. Of particular note, we believe that security against a trim-attack (see Sect. 5), is crucial for the operation of hybrid nodes. Unlike our protocol,

[13] claim to not require *optimism* for *succinctness* (see further in Theorem 3 and Remark 1). However, we note that it doesn't seem economically viable for an adversary to expend resources to simply hurt the succinctness of hybrid nodes.

We now summarize our results and outline the organization of the paper. In Sect. 2, we introduce the basic model and notation. In Sect. 3, we summarize CoinPrune and NIPoPoW, which are building blocks for our protocol. In Sect. 4, we explain the properties of the hybrid node's chain and describe the trimming protocol, chain selection and state verification protocols. In Sect. 5, we introduce novel security definitions for hybrid nodes, including trim-attacked, congruence, state-attacked, and bootstrap-attacked. In Sect. 6, we show that hybrid nodes satisfy all the security properties with high probability, and we also discuss the polylogarithmic storage requirement and the lower bound on the storage requirement. For brevity, formal proofs for these results are omitted. In Sect. 7, we illustrate that when combined with stateless blockchain protocols, hybrid nodes are optimized both in terms of cold and hot storage. And, we examine directions for future work in Sect. 8.

Our primary contributions are the protocols associated with the hybrid nodes and the novel security definitions and their associated theorems. These are in Sects. 4, 5 and 6.

2   Model and Notation

In this work, we consider a set of nodes running a PoW blockchain. We model the system using continuous time, which accurately models systems with high hash-rates such as Bitcoin Ethereum [2,8]. In this section, we restrict the model description to the essentials required to describe our protocol.

Several communication models are considered in the literature. The simplest is the *synchronous* model where a block broadcast by a node at a certain time is received by all other nodes immediately [9,10]. Since time is continuous, no more than one block is mined at any given time, implying only one block could be in communication at any given time. More complicated communication models with communication delays are also considered in the literature [17,21]. For the sake of simplicity, we consider the synchronous model in this paper and leave it to future work to transfer our results to more complicated communication models. Note that because of synchronous communication, all honest nodes have knowledge of the same set of blocks at any given time.

Basic Blockchain Notation. The honest (longest-)chain at time t is represented by $\mathcal{C}_t$. The number of blocks in $\mathcal{C}_t$ is called the chain-length and is denoted as B_t. When the time t is clear from context, we may drop the subscript and refer to it as just $\mathcal{C}$. Blocks in $\mathcal{C}$ are indexed as an array in a similar convention to the Python programming language, meaning that $\mathcal{C}[i]$ is denoted as block i. Since it is convenient, we refer to a block by its index i and not its contents. $\mathcal{C}[0]$ is called the *genesis block*. $\mathcal{C}[i_1 : i_2]$ represents the segment of the chain from block i_1 to block $(i_2 - 1)$. If at any time an honest node hears of another chain $\mathcal{D}$ which is longer than $\mathcal{C}_t$, then it adopts $\mathcal{D}$ as the honest chain (i.e., $\mathcal{C}_{t^+} = \mathcal{D}$, where t^+

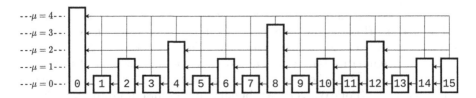

Fig. 1. An example of the interlink structure (inspired by Fig. 1 of [6]). At the bottom of each block is its index, and the block's height signifies its superblock level. Each block has a link to the closest ancestor at every level, which is shown by the arrows linking blocks to ancestors. Notice all the blocks are contained in level 0, and only the genesis block is in level 4.

indicates the time incrementally after t). The last common block between two chains C and D is called the *latest common ancestor* (LCA), and is denoted as $b = \mathsf{LCA}(C, D)$. Specifically, $C_t[: b+1] = D[: b+1]$, and $C_t[b+1 :] \cap D[b+1 :] = \emptyset$. When a new block $\bar{b}$ is appended to C, we denote the extended chain as $C\,\bar{b}$.

In our model, hybrid nodes do not store the entire chain C_t, but instead store a trimmed version which contains fewer blocks than C_t. The trimming protocol and its associated notation is described in Sect. 4.

Blockchain State. When a new transaction is submitted, a node must check if it is "valid" with respect to the chain C_t. This could be accomplished by parsing through the complete log of transactions in C_t. However, due to the rapidly increasing size of C_t, it is far more efficient for a node to validate transactions against a summary of the chain called the state, and denoted as $\mathsf{state}(C_t)$. Equivalently, we may refer to the state as $\mathsf{state}(B_t)$, where B_t is the length of the chain C_t. Validating a transaction against C_t is equivalent to validating it with respect to $\mathsf{state}(C_t)$, so using $\mathsf{state}(C_t)$ is preferred due to its smaller hot storage requirement. After a new block $\bar{b}$ is added to the chain, the new state is computed as $\mathsf{state}(C_t\,\bar{b}) = F(\mathsf{state}(C_t), \bar{b})$, where $F()$ is a function that applies the transactions in $\bar{b}$ to $\mathsf{state}(C_t)$. When the new block is clear from context, we denote the function simply as $F(\mathsf{state}(C_t))$, and when the function is applied on n sequential new blocks, we denote the operation as $\mathsf{state}(C_t\, b_1 b_2 \ldots b_n) = F^n(C_t)$. Two types of states are popular: 1) *UTXO-based State*: this stands for unspent transaction output, and is used by Bitcoin. The UTXO state consists of a list of unspent coins. A new transaction is valid with respect to the state, if it consumes one or more of these coins, and creates new coins whose total value is no larger than the consumed coins; 2) *Account Based State:* This is used in Ethereum. An account-based state consists of a vector of key-value mappings, with one mapping corresponding to each user. The key establishes the user's identity, and the value establishes the balance in the user's account. A user can issue a transaction that transfers a part of his account's balance to another user.

Interlinks. In traditional blockchains like Bitcoin, each block contains a link (using a hash) to the previous block in the chain. To enable hybrid nodes to store the blockchain in a succinct way, we employ a clever link structure called the *interlink*. Interlinks were introduced in [12] and further developed in [14].

In the interlink model, a block contains the following information: 1) transactions in the block; 2) the Merkle root x of all the transactions in the block; 3) the Merkle root y ($\mathsf{state}(B_t)$) of the corresponding blockchain state; 4) the block index i; 5) the *interlink*, which contains hash links to several previous blocks and is described in detail in the following paragraphs; 6) the random nonce η; and 7) the block hash $\mathsf{id} = H(\eta, x, y, i, \mathsf{interlink})$, where $H()$ is a hash function. For a block to be valid, id must contain at least T leading 0's. Equivalently, we say that $\mathsf{id} \leq 2^{-T}$. All the information in the block *except* the list of transactions is referred to as the *block-header*. Observe that the id of the block can be verified given just the block-header.

To describe the interlink, we first need to define *superblocks*. A level-μ superblock is a block with $\mathsf{id} \leq 2^{-(T+\mu)}$. Since a valid block satisfies $\mathsf{id} \leq 2^{-T}$, all valid blocks are level-0 superblocks. The genesis block is defined to be a superblock of every level from 0 to ∞. And, a level-μ superblock is also a level-μ' superblock for all $0 \leq \mu' \leq \mu$, since $2^{-(T+\mu)} \leq 2^{-(T+\mu')}$.

The `interlink` data-structure in a block contains a link to the previous superblock of level μ for every level μ that is in the chain $\mathcal{C}_t$ up to that block. Since the previous block will always be a superblock of level at least 0, the interlink always contains a link to the previous block (thus, without any further modification, the security properties of the blockchain are unaffected). Also, since the genesis block is of all possible levels, a link to the genesis block is always included. A pictorial example of this is shown in Fig. 1.

Using interlinks, it is possible to "skip" over blocks when traversing the blockchain. To be more specific, it is useful to define notation for "traversing the blockchain at level-μ". For any given chain $\mathcal{C}$, the level-μ *upchain*, denoted $\mathcal{C} \uparrow^{\mu}$, is the sequence of all level-μ superblocks in $\mathcal{C}$. That is,

$$\mathcal{C} \uparrow^{\mu} \triangleq \left\{ b : b \in \mathcal{C}, \text{ and } \mathsf{id}(b) \leq 2^{-(T+\mu)} \right\}. \tag{1}$$

Note that although it is convenient to use set-notation to define it, $\mathcal{C} \uparrow^{\mu}$ is a sequence with the order of its blocks being the same as they are in $\mathcal{C}$. From the definition of the interlink, each block in the upchain $\mathcal{C} \uparrow^{\mu}$ contains a reference to the previous block in the upchain. Therefore, it is possible to traverse through $\mathcal{C} \uparrow^{\mu}$. Additionally, a chain $\mathcal{C}'$ is called a level-μ *superchain* if all its blocks are level-μ superblocks. That is, if the underlying chain of $\mathcal{C}'$ is $\mathcal{C}$, then $\mathcal{C}' \subseteq \mathcal{C} \uparrow^{\mu}$.

We use square-brackets to index $\mathcal{C} \uparrow^{\mu}$, similar to a python array. However, at times it is useful to refer to blocks in $\mathcal{C} \uparrow^{\mu}$ according to the block's index in $\mathcal{C}$. In this case, we use curly-braces to index $\mathcal{C} \uparrow^{\mu}$. This is best illustrated using an example. Consider, $\mathcal{C} = \{0, 1, 2, 3, 4, 5, 6, 7, 8, 9, 10\}$, and let $\mathcal{C} \uparrow^{\mu} = \{0, 3, 4, 7, 10\}$. In this case, $\mathcal{C} \uparrow^{\mu} [3:] = \{7, 10\}$, but $\mathcal{C} \uparrow^{\mu} \{3:\} = \{3, 4, 7, 10\}$. As a further illustration of the upchain notation, in the blockchain in Fig. 1, $\mathcal{C} \uparrow^2 = \{0, 4, 8, 12\}$.

3   Preliminaries

Before describing our protocol, we summarize CoinPrune [15] and NIPoPoW [14]. Our protocol builds upon both of these protocols.

CoinPrune. In CoinPrune, similar to our model, blocks contain commitments to the blockchain-state. The protocol selects a *pruning point* k blocks from the tip of the chain. All blocks after the pruning point are retained completely, while only block headers are retained prior to the pruning point. The state of the blockchain at the pruning point is also stored. Then, the PoW in the chain can be established since the block headers for the entire chain are preserved. Furthermore, since the state at the pruning point is preserved and a commitment to it is stored in the blocks, the state corresponding to each block after the pruning point can be recovered. Refer to Fig. 2 for a visual description.

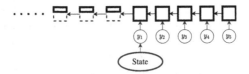

Fig. 2. An instance of CoinPrune. Complete square-boxes indicate the complete blocks after the pruning point, and incomplete boxes indicate block-headers of blocks before the pruning point. The variables y_i are the state-commitments of the respective states stored in the block headers. They are shown separately from the block only for emphasis. The state at the pruning point is stored, and its validity is confirmed by the state-commitments y_i's.

While our method for establishing the state of the blockchain is similar to CoinPrune, we deviate in the way we establish the PoW of the chain. We note that although CoinPrune improves storage compared to full nodes, they still store the entire block-header chain prior to the pruning point. Thus, their storage requirement still scales linearly in the length of the chain, albeit the multiplicative constant may be very small. In contrast, we retain only a subset of the block headers, leading to sublinear storage requirement in the number of blocks in the blockchain. To accomplish this, we take inspiration from NIPoPoW.

NIPoPoW. NIPoPoW is a protocol that is used to provide succinct proofs of payments to lightweight clients. Payment proofs have two components. First, the proof needs to establish the amount of PoW in the blockchain, and second, it needs to contain a proof of inclusion of the payment in the chain. Traditionally, the PoW of the chain is established by sending the entire chain of block headers to the lightweight client. NIPoPoWs optimize this step by making the following observation. Informally, by the property of concentration around the means, the μ-upchain $\mathcal{C} \uparrow^{\mu}$ of an underlying chain $\mathcal{C}$ is such that $2^{\mu}|\mathcal{C} \uparrow^{\mu}| \approx |\mathcal{C}|$ (as an illustration, in Fig. 1, superblocks of level-2 appear roughly every $2^2 = 4$ blocks).

Recall that a level-μ superblock is 2^μ times harder to find than a regular block (i.e., a level-0 superblock). Therefore, if $2^\mu |\mathcal{C} \uparrow^\mu| \approx |\mathcal{C}|$, then it is as hard for an adversary to create a fork around $\mathcal{C} \uparrow^\mu$ with level-μ superblocks as it is to create a fork around $\mathcal{C}$ with level-0 superblocks. Therefore, it is sufficient to just provide $\mathcal{C} \uparrow^\mu$ as a proof of the PoW of the chain. For a large enough level μ, $\mathcal{C} \uparrow^\mu$ is much smaller in size than the underlying chain $\mathcal{C}$, thus making NIPoPoWs much faster than traditional protocols.

Our protocol differs from NIPoPoWs in several ways. First, the goal of our protocol is to optimize a hybrid node's storage while retaining almost all of a full node's functionalities, while the goal of NIPoPoWs is to provide succinct payment proofs. Second, NIPoPoWs do not optimize the prover's storage since the prover must still store the entire blockchain. Third, NIPoPoWs are one-time proofs of payment, meaning they need to be generated afresh for every new proof request, whereas our protocol proceeds in an iterative manner throughout the blockchain's execution. In particular, we employ different *level ranges* (elaborated in the next section) in order to optimize storage throughout time, whereas NIPoPoW only uses a single level range. Fourth, since our end goal is different, our security requirements are different from NIPoPoWs. Lastly, we note that since our security models are different, we use vastly different parameters in our protocol compared to NIPoPoW, and also do novel analysis.

4 Trimming Protocol

In this section we describe our protocol to trim the blockchain. Other associated protocols that compare trimmed-chains to select the main chain are also explained briefly.

First, we start with an intuitive description of the trimmed chain which is best understood by referring to the example in Fig. 3. Similar to NIPoPoWs, the high-level idea in our approach is to retain only a subset of (super)blocks in order to represent the proof of work of the chain. Let the trimmed chain be denoted by $\mathcal{P}_t$ (subscript t may be omitted when time is clear from context). $\mathcal{P}$ is a subset of the complete blockchain $\mathcal{C}$, i.e., $\mathcal{P} \subseteq \mathcal{C}$. And, it has an associated number B_t' called the *trimming point*. All blocks to the right of B_t' are retained, including their data and block headers. That is, $\mathcal{P}\{B' :\} = \mathcal{C}[B' :]$. We refer to $\mathcal{P}\{B' :\}$ as the *untrimmed tail*. Blocks to the left of B' may be trimmed, meaning $\mathcal{P}\{: B'\} \subseteq \mathcal{C}[: B']$. Only the block-headers of the blocks in $\mathcal{P}\{: B'\}$ are retained. The blocks that are not in $\mathcal{P}\{: B'\}$ are permanently deleted by the hybrid node. Here is where we differ from pruning. In pruning, all the block headers are retained. In trimming, blocks are completely deleted, including their headers.

The trimmed section of $\mathcal{P}$ is further partitioned into *level-ranges*, each level-range corresponding to a unique level μ. A level-range is spread contiguously over a region of the blockchain, and each level range begins at the point its predecessor ends. We denote the starts and ends of level ranges by *level-range functions* $L_f : \mathbb{Z}^+ \rightarrow \mathbb{Z}^+$ and $L_l : \mathbb{Z}^+ \rightarrow \mathbb{Z}^+$. We define $L_f(\mu)$ as the index of the

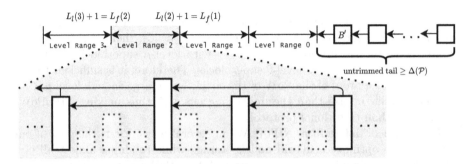

Fig. 3. An example of a trimmed chain at an honest node. Notice how it is partitioned into distinct level ranges, each beginning once its predecessor ends. We show a portion of the second level range, $\mathcal{P}\{L_f(2) : L_l(2)\}$. The greyed blocks with dashed outlines represents blocks that have been trimmed. Like Fig. 1, the height of the (super)block is its highest level. Furthermore, after the trimming point, B', is the untrimmed tail where all the blocks are retained.

first block in level-range μ. Similarly, $L_l(\mu)$ is the last block in the level-range μ. Beyond a certain level μ_h, called the highest level, the level-range functions are 0: $L_f(\mu) = L_l(\mu) = 0$ for $\mu > \mu_h$. Also, below a certain level $\mu < \mu_l$, called the lowest level, we have $L_f(\mu) = L_l(\mu) = B' - 1$. Notice then that for $\mu_l \leq \mu < \mu_h$, we have $L_l(\mu + 1) + 1 = L_f(\mu)$. The level ranges are also pictorially shown in the example in Fig. 3.

At level-range μ, we are primarily interested in level-μ superblocks. As explained with the intuition of NIPoPoW, we need to weigh level-μ superblocks by 2^μ. In order to avoid confusion with PoW, which traditionally does not look at super-levels, we call this notion of weighted PoW simply as the *weight* at level-μ. For the level-range μ, we denote the weight-function $W(\mathcal{P}, \mu)$ as,

$$W(\mathcal{P}, \mu) = 2^\mu |\mathcal{P}\{L_f(\mu) : L_l(\mu) + 1\} \uparrow^\mu|.$$

Our trimming protocol in Algorithm 1 ensures that a higher level-range precedes a lower-level range (as illustrated in Fig. 3). Therefore, we can compute the sum of work from the genesis block up to and including level range μ by, $S(\mathcal{P}, \mu) = \sum_{\mu \leq \mu' \leq \mu_h} W(\mathcal{P}, \mu')$.

Since hybrid nodes do not have access to the underlying chain, $S(\mathcal{P}, \mu)$ can be interpreted as their estimate of the PoW up to block $L_l(\mu)$. Note that $W(\mathcal{P}, \mu)$ and $S(\mathcal{P}, \mu)$ are functions of the level-range functions as well. However, we assume that the level-range functions are implicitly defined by $\mathcal{P}$ in order to keep the notation minimal.

The trimming procedure is detailed in Algorithm 1. We briefly describe it here. Trimming is attempted every time the chain grows by Q blocks (line 1). We call Q the trimming interval. The trimming point is set by the required chain-tail length (line 2). Given that μ_h is the highest level-range in the current trimmed chain, we attempt to trim it further to level $\mu_h + 1$. If trimming to that level is not possible, we try to do it to one level lower and so on (line 3).

Algorithm 1: Trimming Protocol

---

     input   : $\mathcal{P}$ :: My (trimmed) chain
                              Q :: The trimming interval
                              μ_h :: Highest level-range in $\mathcal{P}$
                              $L_f(), L_l()$ :: Level-Range functions
                              $g(), f(), \Delta()$ :: Protocol parameter-functions
                              $\mathbf{good}_{\delta,g}()$ :: Good-Superchain function)

1 **on event** $\mathcal{P}$ *has grown by* Q *blocks since the last trimming attempt*:
2      $B' = \mathcal{P}[-1] - \Delta(\mathcal{P})$
3   **for** μ *from* $\mu_h + 1$ *down to 1* **do**
4          $g \leftarrow g(\mathcal{P}, \mu)$
5          $f \leftarrow f(\mathcal{P}, \mu)$
6   **if** $|\mathcal{P}\{L_f(\mu) : B'\} \uparrow^{\mu}| \geq f$ *and* $\mathbf{good}_{\delta,g}(\mathcal{P}\{L_f(\mu) : B'\} \uparrow^{\mu}, \mu)$ **then**
7              $\mathcal{P}, L_f, L_l, \text{success} \leftarrow \texttt{trim}(\mathcal{P}, L_f, L_l, B', \mu, g, f)$
8   **if** success$=1$ **then**
9   **break**
10   **return**
11
12 **func** $\texttt{trim}(\mathcal{D}, L_f, L_l, B', \mu, g, f)$:
13      $\mathcal{E} \leftarrow \mathcal{D}\{L_f(\mu) : B'\} \uparrow^{\mu}$
14      $A \leftarrow \mathcal{E}[-f]$
15
16   **for** μ' *from* $\mu - 1$ *to 0* **do**
17          $\alpha \leftarrow \mathcal{D}\{A : B'\} \uparrow^{\mu'}$
18          $\mathcal{E} \leftarrow \mathcal{E} \cup \alpha$
19
20   **if** $|\alpha| \geq f$ *and* $\mathbf{good}_{\delta,g}(\alpha, \mu')$ **then**
21              $A \leftarrow \alpha[-f]$
22
23   **if** $|\alpha| \geq f$ *and* $\mathbf{good}_{\delta,g}(\alpha, \mu')$ **then**
24          $L_f(\mu'), L_l(\mu') \leftarrow B' - 1$, for all $\mu < \mu'$
25          $L_l(\mu) \leftarrow B' - 1$
26          $\mathcal{D} \leftarrow \mathcal{D}\{: L_f(\mu)\} \cup \mathcal{E} \cup \mathcal{D}\{B' :\}$
27   **return** $\mathcal{D}, L_f, L_l, 1$
28   **else**
29   **return** $\mathcal{D}, L_f, L_l, 0$

Trimming to a level μ can be attempted if the specified range of blocks contains enough level-μ superblocks, and if the corresponding μ-upchain is good (line 6). Roughly, a μ-upchain $\mathcal{C} \uparrow^{\mu}$ is good if its weight represents the weight of the other level upchains ($|\mathcal{C} \uparrow^{\mu}| \approx 2^{(\mu-\mu')}|\mathcal{C} \uparrow^{\mu'}|$, $\mu' < \mu$). Given condition on line 6 is satisfied, the trim function is called for level μ (line 7).

The trim function is very similar to the goodness-aware Prove algorithm of the NIPoPoW protocol [14, Algorithm 8]. In the trim function, the μ-upchain is obtained first (line 13). Next, the $(\mu - 1)$-level upchain under the last f blocks of the μ-level upchain is also added (lines 17 and 18). If the $(\mu-1)$-level upchain is good, then the $(\mu - 2)$-level upchain under its last f blocks is added (lines 20 and 21). Otherwise, the $(\mu - 2)$-level upchain under the last f blocks of the μ-upchain are added. This procedure continues until level 0.

At the end, the trim function checks if the trimming was a "success" by checking if level 0 of the trimmed chain is good. The trim being a success means that it is at least as hard for an adversary to create a longer fork around the trimmed chain, as it would be to do so around the complete chain. Intuitively, this is because the necessary levels of the upchains in this range are good, meaning that they represent the PoW of their corresponding downchains.

In case the trim is a success, the trim function along with the new level range functions are returned (lines 23 to 27) indicating that the trim can be used. Otherwise, the old trimmed chain and level range functions are returned (lines 28 and 29).

Chain Selection. Hybrid nodes need to have a protocol, Compare($\mathcal{C}^{(1)}, \mathcal{C}^{(2)}$), to chose the main chain given two conflicting chains, $\mathcal{C}^{(1)}$ and $\mathcal{C}^{(2)}$. Full nodes (that store the entire blockchain) simply choose the longer of the two chains as the main chain. The chain selection protocol for hybrid nodes is a little more complicated since they do not store the entire chain. At a high level, they use the sum of the cumulative weight, $S(\mathcal{P}, 0)$, of the trimmed portion of a chain and the length of untrimmed section of the chain as a proxy for the chain length.

State Verification. Similar to CoinPrune [15], a short commitment to the state at the block is stored in every block. Therefore, a hybrid node can verify the correctness of the blockchain's state by comparing it to the corresponding state commitment. The protocol will be called state $-$ verify.

Hybrid Node's Functionalities. Here, we describe how a hybrid-node employing the trimming algorithm has the functionalities claimed in Sect. 1. Since a hybrid node stores the state of the blockchain at its tip, it can perform transaction validation, block validation and state validation. Using the Compare($\cdot, \cdot$) protocol, a hybrid node can select the main chain given competing chains. As a consequence, the node can perform mining as well.

A new node joining the system can choose the main chain using the Compare($\cdot, \cdot$) protocol, and verify the state using the state-verify protocol. Thus, hybrid nodes can bootstrap other hybrid nodes into the system.

The hybrid node verifies payment proofs as follows. In traditional systems like Bitcoin, the prover provides the chain of block-headers in order to establish the PoW, and then provides a short proof for the transaction's inclusion (inclusion-proof) in the chain. In NIPoPoWs the prover provides a superchain (which is logarithmic in the size of the underlying chain) in order to establish the PoW. In either case, the hybrid node can use the Compare($\cdot, \cdot$) protocol to compare the given chain (superchain) to its own trimmed chain. If the two chains only differ near the tail and the inclusion-proof is consistent with the provided chain, then the hybrid node approves the prover's payment proof. Otherwise, it returns false.

5   Security Definitions

Security from Trim Attack. Consider the dangerous attack scenario depicted in Fig. 4, where the adversary provides a trimmed-chain $\mathcal{P}^{(2)}$ which is "longer" than the honest chain $\mathcal{P}^{(1)}$ (i.e. $\mathsf{Compare}(\mathcal{P}^{(1)}, \mathcal{P}^{(2)}) = \mathcal{P}^{(2)}$) and the LCA between the two chains precedes the honest chain's trimming point: $b = \mathsf{LCA}(\mathcal{P}^{(1)}, \mathcal{P}^{(2)}) < B'^{(1)}$. Denote b_1 to be the (super)block after b in $\mathcal{P}^{(2)}$. The honest node cannot verify the state transition from b to b_1. This is because the honest node only has access to block headers and not the full state, meaning they can only verify the validity of the block headers, but not of the state transition between the blocks. Moreover, even if the honest node had access to the state at those blocks, there may be a number of blocks between b and b_1 that were skipped during the trimming.

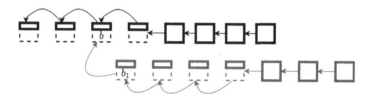

Fig. 4. A trim-attack. The honest chain is shown in black, and adversary's chain in red. Complete square-boxes indicate the complete blocks beyond the trimming point, and incomplete boxes indicate block-headers of blocks before the trimming point. Curved arrows indicate that the corresponding blocks may not be subsequent blocks. (Color figure online)

Therefore, if at any time the adversary is able to create a fork as in Fig. 4, they could arbitrarily alter the state of the chain to their advantage. For instance, the adversary could transfer all of the chain's cryptocurrency into their own accounts. One approach to circumventing this problem is to have the hybrid node re-download the blockchain from a full node in case it encounters a fork preceding its trimming point. However, in that case the security of the system would again rely on the small number of full nodes. We require that hybrid nodes can work independently from full nodes to keep the system as decentralized as possible. To accomplish this, we ensure that there exists no time when an adversary is able to create a fork from beyond a hybrid node's trimming point.

Definition 1 (Attack on the trimmed Chain). *Let ω be the fixed randomness[1]. Let $\mathcal{P}_{t,\omega}^{(1)}$ be the honest trimmed chain at some honest node at time t. Let $\mathcal{P}_{t,\omega}^{(2)}$ be the adversary's trimmed chain. Let $B'(\mathcal{P}^{(1)})$ and $B'(\mathcal{P}^{(2)})$ be their respective trimming points. Let $b_{t,\omega}$ be the LCA block between them: $b_{t,\omega} = \mathsf{LCA}(\mathcal{P}_{t,\omega}^{(1)}, \mathcal{P}_{t,\omega}^{(2)})$. Then, we say that the system is* **trim-attacked** *if there exists a time t such that the adversarial trimmed chain is declared to be longer than the honest trimmed chain and the LCA block is before the honest node's trimming point. That is,*

$$\mathsf{trim\text{-}attacked} = \{\omega : \exists t \ s.t. \ b_{t,\omega} < B'(\mathcal{P}_{t,\omega}^{(1)}), \ and \ \mathsf{Compare}(\mathcal{P}_{t,\omega}^{(1)}, \mathcal{P}_{t,\omega}^{(2)}) = \mathcal{P}_{t,\omega}^{(2)}\}.$$

Congruence. Since hybrid nodes only have access to trimmed chains $\mathcal{P}$, we need that the selection of the main trimmed-chain made according to $\mathsf{Compare}(\cdot, \cdot)$ is in agreement with the underlying complete chains. We formalize this by a property called *congruence*.

Definition 2 (Congruence). *Given any two (complete) chains $\mathcal{C}^{(1)}$ and $\mathcal{C}^{(2)}$ with corresponding trimmed chains $\mathcal{P}^{(1)}$ and $\mathcal{P}^{(2)}$, they are said to be congruent with each other if, $|\mathcal{C}^{(1)}| > |\mathcal{C}^{(2)}| \implies \mathsf{Compare}\left(\mathcal{P}^{(1)}, \mathcal{P}^{(2)}\right) = \mathcal{P}^{(1)}$.*

State Security. Hybrid nodes do not have access to transaction history preceding their trimming point. Instead, they rely on the state at the trimming point, $\mathsf{state}(B'_t)$, to compute state at the tip of the chain. State is verified using $\mathsf{state\text{-}verify}$. Firstly, if the adversary launches a trimming attack (Definition 1), then they could change the state of the blockchain arbitrarily. Additionally, the state of the hybrid node is also attacked if at any point the adversary can create a different state, state', that also passes through $\mathsf{state\text{-}verify}$.

Definition 3 (Attack on the State). *Let ω be the fixed randomness. At some time t, let the trimming point of an honest chain $\mathcal{P}_{t,\omega}^{(1)}$ be $B'^{(1)}_{t,\omega}$, and let its associated state be $\mathsf{state}^{(1)}(B'^{(1)}_{t,\omega})$. Let the trimming point of the adversary's chain $\mathcal{P}_{t,\omega}^{(2)}$ be $B'^{(2)}_{t,\omega}$, and let its claimed state be $\mathsf{state}_{t,\omega}^{(2)}$. The state of the honest node is said to be attacked, denoted by* **state-attacked**, *if there is either a trim-attack or there exists a time t such that, $\mathsf{state}_{t,\omega}^{(2)} \neq \mathsf{state}^{(1)}(B'_{t,\omega})$, such that it verifies against the chain. Denoting, $\mathcal{P}_{t,\omega} = \mathsf{Compare}(\mathcal{P}_{t,\omega}^{(1)}, \mathcal{P}_{t,\omega}^{(2)})$, we define,*

$$\mathsf{state\text{-}attacked} = \{\omega : \omega \in \mathsf{trim\text{-}attacked}\}$$
$$\bigcup \{\omega : \exists t \ such \ that \ \mathsf{state\text{-}verify}(\mathsf{state}_{t,\omega}^{(2)}, \mathcal{P}_{t,\omega}) = 1\}.$$

---

[1] Randomness is w.r.t., a stochastic model for the blockchain. Details are in the full version of the paper.

Bootstrapping Security. When a new (honest) node joins the system, it downloads (possibly trimmed) copies of the blockchain from a number of other hybrid or full nodes. It then chooses the main chain using the Compare$(\cdot, \cdot)$ protocol and then downloads and verifies the state using the state-verify protocol. In order to show that it adopts the honest trimmed chain and the honest state, we define bootstrapping security below.

Definition 4 (Bootstrapping Security). *A joining node is said to be securely bootstrapped into the system if, at the point of it joining, it adopts a trimmed chain that is not* trim-attacked *with respect to the system's honest chain, and it adopts a state which is not* state-attacked *with respect to the system's honest state. Otherwise, the node is said to be* bootstrap-attacked.

In our system model, we assume that the mining rate of the honest parties and the adversary remains constant. This might seem to be counter-factual to Definition 4 because it assumes that nodes can join the system. We remark that we make the constant mining rate assumption to make the rigorous security analysis tractable. Practically, we conjecture that if the rate of nodes joining and leaving the system is nearly equal and small enough, then the constant mining rate assumption is a good model for the system.

6   Security Results for Hybrid Nodes

The protocol has security parameters $k, k' \in \mathbb{N}$, $a, c \in \mathbb{R}^+$, and $\delta \in (0, 1)$. Referring to the protocol parameter-functions from Alogrithm 1 are defined as: $\Delta(\mathcal{P}) = k' + a \log \left(S(\mathcal{P}, 0) + |\mathcal{P}\{B' :\}| \right)$, $g(\mathcal{P}, \mu) = k + a \log S(\mathcal{P}, \mu)$, and $f(\mathcal{P}, \mu) = c \cdot g(\mathcal{P}, \mu)$. We simply state the results here without proof due to lack of space.

First, we show if the honest nodes have the majority of mining power, we can choose security parameters such that our protocol is secure against a trim-attack.

Theorem 1 (Security of the trimmed Chain). *Assume an honest majority, $\lambda_h > \lambda_a$, where λ_h and λ_a are the mining rates of the honest and adversarial nodes respectively. Let the trimming algorithm (Algorithm 1) parameters k, k', c, a, δ satisfy,*

$$k' = k - a \log \left(((1 + \delta^2) + \delta)/\delta \right), \quad 1 < (1 - \delta)^3 \frac{\lambda_h}{\lambda_a} \frac{c' - 1}{c'} \frac{c - 1 - c'}{c},$$

$$1 < (1 - \delta)^5 \frac{\lambda_h}{\lambda_a} \frac{c - 1}{c}, \quad a \geq \frac{8}{\delta^2},$$

where $2 < c' < c$ is some constant. Then[2], $\mathbb{P}(\text{trim-attacked}) = \mathsf{negl}(k)$.

As a corollary to the above theorem, we can conclude the chain-selection made by hybrid-nodes is consistent with underlying chain lengths.

---

[2] In our work, $\mathsf{negl}(k) = e^{-\Omega(k)} < \frac{1}{\mathrm{poly}(k)}$.

Corollary 1. *The congruence property holds except with probability* negl(k).

Theorem 2 (State Security). *Assuming honest majority,* $\lambda_h > \lambda_a$, *and that the security parameters are as in Theorem 1, then,* $\mathbb{P}(\text{state-attacked}) = \text{negl}(k)$.

Corollary 2 (Bootstrapping Security). *Assume the arrival process of new nodes is independent of the randomness of the blockchain system. If we further assume that a new node contacts at least one honest node and that there is honest mining majority, then* bootstrap-attacked *occurs with probability* negl(k).

In the next theorem, we provide an upper bound on the cold-storage required to store the trimmed chain. This theorem relies on the assumption that a particular kind of adversary is absent. We further comment on this in Remark 1. Additionally, we also note that the following theorem doesn't account for the storage required to store the state at the trimming point. We discuss optimizing the storage for the state using stateless blockchains in Sect. 7.

Theorem 3 (Optimistic Succinctness). *Assuming that all the nodes are honest, the cold-storage requirements for a hybrid node to store the trimmed-chain* $\mathcal{P}$ *is* $O(\log^4 B)$ *with high probability in* k. *Here,* B *is the length of the underlying chain* $\mathcal{C}$.

Remark 1 (Need of Optimism for Succinctness). Since our protocol is an extension of NIPoPoWs, we need to rely on optimism for succinctness as well. In particular, note that when trimming we need to ensure that the level ranges are "good". We have also shown that under honest behaviour, the sizes of the different upchains concentrate around the mean, thus leading to good level-ranges with high probability. However, an adversary with a small mining power could launch an attack which hampers the concentrations around the means and thus makes good-superchains more unlikely. This attack is formally described in [14]. We note that, just like in NIPoPoWs, the adversary can only hurt the succinctness of our model, but not its security. Although the economics of launching an attack on the hybrid node's succinctness is yet to be studied formally, we venture to guess that such an attack wouldn't be economically viable to the adversary.

Clearly, the size of the untrimmed tail is a lower bound on the cold-storage required. In the next theorem we prove that the length of the chain tail has to be at least $\log B$ in order to protect a hybrid node against a trim-attack. This implies that our protocol is near-optimal in terms of cold storage, since it only requires $polylog(B)$ storage.

Theorem 4 (Vulnerability of Short Tails). *Let the blockchain length be* B_t *at time* t, *and the trimming point be* B'_t. *If at all times* t, $\mathbb{P}\left(B_t - B'_t = o(\log B_t)\right) > \epsilon$, *for some* $\epsilon > 0$, *then there exists an adversary with small mining power,* $\lambda_a < \lambda_h$, *such that* $\mathbb{P}(\text{trim-attacked}) = 1$.

7 Optimizing State Storage with Stateless Blockchains

Our trimming protocol optimizes the amount of cold storage required to represent the PoW in the blockchain. In this section, we outline how our work can interface with methods optimizing the storage of the *state*. In hybrid nodes, states need to be stored in cold and hot storage. Along with the length of the blockchain, the size of the blockchain-state is rapidly increasing with time. For instance, at the time of writing Bitcoin's UTXO state is almost 4GB in size, which motivates lessening high storage and verification time by extending our work to optimize both the state's cold-storage at the trimming point, and its hot-storage at the chain tip.

We described that storing state-commitments in the blocks enables one to securely establish the state of a trimmed chain, by use of the state-verify protocol. In a different line of work, called *stateless blockchains*, state-commitments are used to reduce the amount of hot-storage required for transaction validation, thus speeding up validation. We claim that when hybrid nodes are used in stateless-blockchains, then state commitments can serve a dual purpose: 1) they can be used to establish the state of the trimmed chain; 2) and, they can be used to perform stateless transaction validation.

Stateless validation, first proposed by Todd [22], is a scheme where nodes validating transactions store a short cryptographic state-commitment rather than the entire state. A client then provides a membership proof that the node can verify against the commitment. Recently, several constructions have been developed to perform stateless validation in both the UTXO and account-based state models using various cryptographic primitives [1,4,5,7,11,19,23].

Stateless blockchains optimize hot-storage by obviating the need to store the state at the tip of the chain in the RAM. At this point, the state at the trimming point is still stored in the cold storage. We can use this to provide an interface from trimming to stateless blockchains: First, if the proof for some client becomes outdated past the trimming point because it was offline for a long time, then the client can recompute its latest proof by querying a hybrid node for $\mathsf{state}(B'_t)$ and the untrimmed chain tail. Second, if a fork in the chain makes the proofs of several clients invalid, they can all recompute their proofs by contacting the hybrid node similarly.

Now, we describe a way to optimize the cold-storage of the state at the trimming point as well. In order to do this, we need to make an assumption on the clients. At every point, the client needs to store its membership proof corresponding to every block in the untrimmed tail of hybrid nodes. This enforces a couple of constraints on clients. First, the storage requirements of a client would scale logarithmically in the length of the blockchain as well, since the length of the chain-tail grows logarithmically. Second, the clients need to be online very often so that their proofs never get outdated. If this is too cumbersome, clients can alternatively delegate the job of saving and updating proofs to proof-serving nodes [5]. In this case, the hybrid node need not store the entire state at the trimming point either. This is because, even in the event that a fork is created in the untrimmed-tail, all the clients would have their proofs corresponding to the forking point. In this case, a joining hybrid node would no longer need to use the state-verify protocol, since just the state commitment suffices. The rest of the hybrid node's protocols proceed as before.

8 Future Directions

In this paper, we presented hybrid nodes which use trimming to optimize the cold-storage required to represent the PoW in the chain. When used in conjunction with stateless blockchains, we illustrated that hybrid nodes are optimized both in terms of cold and hot storage. In this section, we lay out some directions for future work.

We assume that there is honest majority, $\lambda_h > \lambda_a$, throughout the execution of the blockchain protocol. Given that we use novel security models, it will be interesting to study if it is economically viable for an adversary to acquire massive resources in order to attain a majority mining power temporarily, and launch an attack such as a trim − attack. Similarly, it will be interesting to study the economics of an adversary who simply attempts to hurt the succinctness of hybrid nodes. In hurting the succinctness, fewer nodes would join as hybrid nodes. Thus, an adversary could attempt to take advantage of the reduced decentralization.

We have proved in Theorem 4, that our protocol is near-optimal in terms of the storage it requires to represent a blockchain's PoW if it is to be secure against a trim − attack. However, it is at the moment unclear if further storage optimization in terms of storing the state is possible for a node that needs to have all the functionalities of a hybrid node (without assuming properties on the clients as we do in Sect. 7).

In our analysis, we assume that the block id's have a constant difficulty target throughout the blockchain's execution. It may be useful to relax this assumption in order to make our model closer to practical systems.

Finally, our work in this paper has mainly focused on theoretical analysis. An interesting line of work would be to implement the protocol and study the practical gains of using hybrid nodes.

References

1. Agrawal, S., Raghuraman, S.: KVaC: key-value commitments for blockchains and beyond. In: Moriai, S., Wang, H. (eds.) ASIACRYPT 2020. LNCS, vol. 12493, pp. 839–869. Springer, Cham (2020). https://doi.org/10.1007/978-3-030-64840-4_28
2. Bitcoin hash rate. https://www.coinwarz.com/mining/bitcoin/hashrate-chart. (Accessed 29 Apr 2021)
3. Bitcoin utxo size. https://tinyurl.com/cr7w2ep5. (Accessed 13 Sep 2021)

4. Boneh, D., Bünz, B., Fisch, B.: Batching techniques for accumulators with applications to IOPs and stateless blockchains. In: Boldyreva, A., Micciancio, D. (eds.) CRYPTO 2019. LNCS, vol. 11692, pp. 561–586. Springer, Cham (2019). https://doi.org/10.1007/978-3-030-26948-7_20

5. Chepurnoy, A., Papamanthou, C., Zhang, Y.: Edrax: A cryptocurrency with stateless transaction validation. IACR Cryptol. ePrint Arch. **2018**, 968 (2018)

6. Daveas, S., Karantias, K., Kiayias, A., Zindros, D.: A gas-efficient superlight bitcoin client in solidity. In: Proceedings of the 2nd ACM Conference on Advances in Financial Technologies, AFT 2020, pp. 132–144. Association for Computing Machinery (2020). https://doi.org/10.1145/3419614.3423255. ISBN 9781450381390

7. Dryja, T.: Utreexo: A dynamic hash-based accumulator optimized for the bitcoin utxo set. IACR Cryptol. ePrint Arch. **2019**, 611 (2019)

8. Ethereum hash rate. https://www.coinwarz.com/mining/ethereum/hashrate-chart. (Accessed 29 Apr 2021)

9. Eyal, I., Sirer, E.G.: Majority is not enough: Bitcoin mining is vulnerable. In: Christin, N., Safavi-Naini, R. (eds.) FC 2014. LNCS, vol. 8437, pp. 436–454. Springer, Heidelberg (2014). https://doi.org/10.1007/978-3-662-45472-5_28

10. Garay, J., Kiayias, A., Leonardos, N.: The bitcoin backbone protocol: Analysis and applications. In: Oswald, E., Fischlin, M. (eds.) EUROCRYPT 2015. LNCS, vol. 9057, pp. 281–310. Springer, Heidelberg (2015). https://doi.org/10.1007/978-3-662-46803-6_10

11. Gorbunov, S., Reyzin, L., Wee, H., Zhang, Z.: Pointproofs: aggregating proofs for multiple vector commitments. In: Proceedings of the 2020 ACM SIGSAC Conference on Computer and Communications Security, pp. 2007–2023 (2020)

12. Kiayias, A., Lamprou, N., Stouka, A.-P.: Proofs of proofs of work with sublinear complexity. In: Clark, J., Meiklejohn, S., Ryan, P.Y.A., Wallach, D., Brenner, M., Rohloff, K. (eds.) FC 2016. LNCS, vol. 9604, pp. 61–78. Springer, Heidelberg (2016). https://doi.org/10.1007/978-3-662-53357-4_5

13. Kiayias, A., Leonardos, N., Zindros, D.: Mining in logarithmic space. Cryptology ePrint Archive, Report 2021/623 (2021). https://ia.cr/2021/623

14. Kiayias, A., Miller, A., Zindros, D.: Non-interactive proofs of proof-of-work. In: Bonneau, J., Heninger, N. (eds.) FC 2020. LNCS, vol. 12059, pp. 505–522. Springer, Cham (2020). https://doi.org/10.1007/978-3-030-51280-4_27

15. Matzutt, R., Kalde, B., Pennekamp, J., Drichel, A., Henze, M., Wehrle, K.: How to securely prune bitcoin's blockchain. In: 2020 IFIP Networking Conference (Networking), pp. 298–306. IEEE (2020)

16. Nodes and clients. https://ethereum.org/en/developers/docs/nodes-and-clients/. (20 May 2021)

17. Pass, R., Seeman, L., Shelat, A.: Analysis of the blockchain protocol in asynchronous networks. In: Coron, J.-S., Nielsen, J.B. (eds.) EUROCRYPT 2017. LNCS, vol. 10211, pp. 643–673. Springer, Cham (2017). https://doi.org/10.1007/978-3-319-56614-6_22

18. Reddy, B.: secureprune: Secure block pruning in utxo based blockchains using accumulators. In: 2021 International Conference on COMmunication Systems & NETworkS (COMSNETS), pp. 174–178. IEEE (2021)

19. Reyzin, L., Meshkov, D., Chepurnoy, A., Ivanov, S.: Improving authenticated dynamic dictionaries, with applications to cryptocurrencies. In: Kiayias, A. (ed.) FC 2017. LNCS, vol. 10322, pp. 376–392. Springer, Cham (2017). https://doi.org/10.1007/978-3-319-70972-7_21

20. Running a full node. https://bitcoin.org/en/full-node (Accessed 20 May 2021)
21. Sankagiri, S., Gandlur, S., Hajek, B.: The longest-chain protocol under random delays. arXiv preprint arXiv:2102.00973 (2021)
22. Todd, P.: Making utxo set growth irrelevant with low-latency delayed txo commitments. https://petertodd.org/2016/delayed-txo-commitments (Accessed 24 May 2021)
23. Tomescu, A., Abraham, I., Buterin, V., Drake, J., Feist, D., Khovratovich, D.: Aggregatable subvector commitments for stateless cryptocurrencies. In: Galdi, C., Kolesnikov, V. (eds.) SCN 2020. LNCS, vol. 12238, pp. 45–64. Springer, Cham (2020). https://doi.org/10.1007/978-3-030-57990-6_3

Measurements

Short Paper: On the Claims of Weak Block Synchronization in Bitcoin

Seungjin Baek[1], Hocheol Nam[1], Yongwoo Oh[1], Muoi Tran[2],
and Min Suk Kang[1(✉)]

[1] KAIST, Daejeon, South Korea
{seungjinb,hcnam,yongwoo95,minsukk}@kaist.ac.kr
[2] National University of Singapore, Singapore, Singapore
muoitran@comp.nus.edu.sg

Abstract. Recent Bitcoin attacks [15,17,18] commonly exploit the phenomenon of so-called weak block synchronization in Bitcoin. The attacks use two independently-operated Bitcoin monitors — i.e., `Bitnodes` and a system of customized supernodes — to confirm that block propagation in Bitcoin is surprisingly slow. In particular, `Bitnodes` constantly reports that around 30% of nodes are 3 blocks (or more) behind the blockchain tip and the supernodes show that on average more than 60% of nodes do not receive the latest block even after waiting for 10 min. In this paper, we carefully re-evaluate these controversial claims with our own experiments in the live Bitcoin network and show that block propagation in Bitcoin is, in fact, fast enough (e.g., most peers we monitor receive new blocks in about 4 s) for its safety property. We identify several limitations and bugs of the two monitors, which have led to these inaccurate claims about the Bitcoin block synchronization. We finally ask several open-ended questions regarding the technical and ethical issues around monitoring blockchain networks.

1 Introduction

Timely propagation of blocks in Bitcoin is critical to ensure its safe consensus operations [10]. Indeed, recent partitioning [15,18] and double-spending [17] attacks against Bitcoin have exploited the phenomenon of so-called *weak block synchronization* — i.e., a large fraction of nodes (e.g., 60%) do not have the up-to-date blockchain even after an extended time (e.g., 10 min). This surprisingly slow block propagation is measured and confirmed by two independent sources: (1) `Bitnodes` monitor [20], a long-running and highly-cited third-party Bitcoin network crawler, and (2) `RPC-based` monitor [15], a data collector that interacts with a few Bitcoin supernodes via RPC calls. Recently, Saad et al. [16] further conjecture that weak block synchronization can be possibly caused by the increased network size and churn rate in Bitcoin. Yet, slow block propagation is a controversial claim because several anecdotal evidence from past studies and measurements from other Bitcoin monitors have suggested otherwise. In 2013,

---

S. Baek and H. Nam—Co-leading authors.

© International Financial Cryptography Association 2022
I. Eyal and J. Garay (Eds.): FC 2022, LNCS 13411, pp. 663–671, 2022.
https://doi.org/10.1007/978-3-031-18283-9_33

Decker et al. [5] report that a new block reaches the majority of peers in less than a few tens of seconds. In 2016, a technique called Compact Block Relay [4] was introduced as the default block relaying scheme in Bitcoin to further reduce the block propagation time. Besides, DSN Bitcoin Monitoring [7], a closed-source crawler developed for academic studies, independently reports that in 2021 Bitcoin blocks take only 10 s or less to reach 90% of nodes.

In this paper, we carefully evaluate the claims of the weak block synchronization in Bitcoin and attempt to give a more accurate account of the current state of block propagation. In particular, we challenge the accuracy of the two (i.e., Bitnodes and RPC-based) Bitcoin monitors that have been the main sources of supporting evidence for these claims. We first show that both monitors do not successfully capture the accurate block synchronization status of several live nodes that we deploy and control in the Bitcoin network. Next, we investigate their publicly available codebase and discover a number of problems that may have caused measurement errors. Some of them are architectural limitations; e.g., the polling-based block data collection in the Bitnodes monitor always offers outdated block information. Some are protocol-level bugs; e.g., the RPC-based monitor mistakenly alters the block propagation of its peers and eventually misses a significant portion of block information. We then conduct large-scale measurements of the block propagation in the Bitcoin network with our fixed RPC-based monitor, showing that the network is well-synchronized (e.g., 90% of peers receive new blocks in less than 4 s). Lastly, we re-confirm the fast block propagation in a realistic controlled network in which blocks with various sizes (e.g., 0.5–1.6 MB) are propagated through up to 10 hops of globally distributed nodes.

The paper is organized as follows: Sect. 2 provides the necessary background. Section 3 presents our measurements and analysis on the claims of weak block synchronization. In Sect. 4, we discuss several future research directions before we conclude the paper in Sect. 5.

2   Background

In this section, we briefly introduce the block propagation protocol logic in Bitcoin (§2.1) and then describe the high-level operations of Bitnodes and RPC-based Bitcoin monitors (§2.2).

2.1   Block Propagation in Bitcoin

In Bitcoin [13], several thousands of distributed nodes independently validate and store the *blockchain*, a public ledger containing the historical transactions of all users. Transactions are written to the blockchain via a process called mining, in which specialized nodes, commonly known as miners, compete to extend the blockchain by finding a new block that includes validated transactions and the hash of the previous block. Every 10 min on average, a miner generates and sends a new block to all other nodes in the system so they can validate it and update their blockchain accordingly. Block data is propagated via a permissionless peer-to-peer network between nodes, in which each of them typically establishes up to 10 outgoing connections to *reachable* nodes that have publicly routable IP addresses and accept incoming connections. Upon receiving a new block, nodes validate and relay it immediately to their peers until the entire network is synchronized with the latest block. Since 2016, Bitcoin protocol allows compact block relaying that requires less data transmission and, hence, potentially reduces the block propagation latency [4]. Desired to receive and send block data as fast as possible, some Bitcoin miners are believed to use additional overlay techniques to accelerate their block propagation, such as using a separate block relay network (e.g., FIBRE [8], bloXRoute [2]).

2.2   Bitcoin Network Monitors

Since measuring the required time for all nodes to receive the latest block is crucial for evaluating the efficiency and safety of the Bitcoin network, there have existed several network monitors in Bitcoin. These network monitors connect to the reachable nodes and monitor their block update information but not unreachable nodes since they do not accept incoming connections. Here, we briefly describe two notable Bitcoin monitors, that is, `Bitnodes` [20], a popular online service, and an `RPC-based` crawler that is recently proposed in a peer-reviewed paper [15]. Among other Bitcoin network monitors (e.g., DSN Bitcoin Monitoring [7], Coin Dance [3]), the `Bitnodes` and `RPC-based` monitors are the only two monitors that have source code available and record the block propagation delay. Recent studies also use the block propagation measurements directly from these two monitors to motivate several new Bitcoin attacks [15,17,18].

Bitnodes Monitor. `Bitnodes` is a Python-based lightweight crawler [19] designed to estimate the number of reachable Bitcoin nodes. `Bitnodes` operates continuously in rounds approximately every 4 min, attempting to establish connections to all reachable nodes. During the connection handshake with the reachable nodes, the `Bitnodes` monitor extracts their latest block heights from their `version` messages. After each round, `Bitnodes` monitor dumps the list of reachable nodes and their block heights into snapshots and publishes them. Recent `Bitnodes` snapshots show that there are usually around 30% of nodes that are 3 blocks (or more) behind the latest blockchain tip.

RPC-based Monitor. The `RPC-based` monitor is particularly designed to measure the block synchronization performance of Bitcoin [15] and it consists of a data collector and a few supernodes, i.e., Bitcoin clients that increase the connection limit so that they can connect to thousands of reachable IPs concurrently. Periodically, the data collector issues RPC calls to the supernodes to retrieve the block heights of their peers. In particular, the collector uses the `getpeerinfo` RPC call that returns the list of peers connected by a supernode and their `synced_blocks` values indicating their latest block heights known by the supernode. The measurements collected by the `RPC-based` monitor show that only 40% of nodes have the latest block after about 10 min [15].

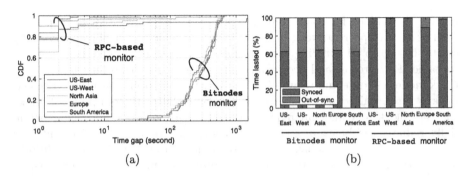

Fig. 1. Evidence of inaccurate measurements of the two monitors. (a) Cumulative distribution of the time taken by the two monitors to publish the up-to-date blockchain of our five full nodes. (b) Percentage of lasted time of each synchronization status measured by the two monitors.

3   Our Measurements and Analysis

In this section, we evaluate the claims of weak block synchronization in four following steps. First, we present empirical evidence that both Bitnodes and RPC-based monitors fail to report the synchronization status of our own live Bitcoin nodes promptly (§3.1). Second, we report several limitations and bugs that we found in the two monitors, which have incorrectly led to the slow block propagation conclusions (§3.2). Third, we independently measure and show the fast block propagation in today's Bitcoin network (§3.3). Fourth, we conduct a controlled block propagation experiment to confirm that propagating Bitcoin blocks through multiple (e.g., 10) hops of peers only requires a few seconds of delay (§3.4). Finally, we discuss some ethical considerations of our measurements (§3.5).

3.1   Empirical Evidence of Inaccurate Measurements

To verify the block synchronization reported by the Bitnodes and RPC-based monitors, we use the ground truth data recorded at our live Bitcoin nodes. We run five Bitcoin Core clients with version 0.21.1 in five geographic regions of Amazon EC2 (i.e., US-East, US-West, South America, Europe, and North Asia) for 12 h on September 9, 2021. Since the original RPC-based monitor [15] is not operating as of this writing, we download and run it too. For each of the 60 blocks our nodes receive in this experiment, we report the exact timestamps when our nodes receive it, the timestamps of the Bitnodes snapshots reporting our nodes with the updated height, and the timestamps when the RPC-based monitor observes our nodes updating their synced_blocks values.

We found that the Bitnodes monitor frequently exhibits significant delays in publishing the latest block heights of our nodes. Figure 1a shows that in 50% of cases, the Bitnodes monitor takes more than 4 min to include the up-to-date block heights of our nodes in a snapshot and the delay can be as high as 10 min in some worst cases. The `RPC-based` monitor reports most of the block heights of our nodes within 10 s except a few outliers with one notable case in which the height update of our node in Europe is delayed for 25 min. As a result, the `Bitnodes` monitor incorrectly concludes that our nodes are out-of-sync for about 35% of the time while the `RPC-based` monitor incorrectly reports that our node in Europe is out-of-sync for about 10% of the time; see the orange bars in Fig. 1b. These incorrect block synchronization measurements of only five nodes suggest that the large-scale measurements (e.g., covering all 10K reachable nodes) made by the `Bitnodes` and `RPC-based` monitors can be seriously misleading.

3.2 Discovered Problems in Two Monitors

We now investigate the publicly available codebase of the `Bitnodes` [19] and `RPC-based` [1] monitors to identify the root causes of their inaccurate block synchronization measurements.

Bitnodes Monitor. We identify two inherent limitations of the `Bitnodes` monitor. The first limitation stems from its polling-based monitoring architecture, that is, `Bitnodes` crawls reachable IPs from the Bitcoin network in 4-min cycles. In each crawling cycle, `Bitnodes` connects to other nodes at random timestamps, records their `version` messages, and exports them into a snapshot when the cycle ends. When a node receives a new block after sending

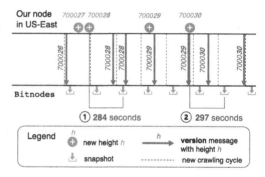

Fig. 2. Block height updates in a Bitcoin full node and the `Bitnodes` monitor.

its `version` message in a crawling cycle, it has to wait for the next cycle to update its new block height, which can be up to 8 min of delay. We also note an additional delay of at least 30 s for exporting a snapshot at the end of each cycle. In Fig. 2, we illustrate how the `Bitnodes` monitor is delayed in updating the latest block height of our node in the US-East region in a 30-min interval. For example, in ①, our node receives block **700028** after notifying `Bitnodes` with a `version` message carrying the height **700026**. Therefore, our node must wait for 284 s until its block height of **700028** is reflected in a snapshot. Similarly, in ②, the `Bitnodes` monitor publishes the block height **700030** of our node with 297 s of delay.

Another limitation stems from some buggy block height reports frequently observed in the `Bitnodes` snapshots. That is, in all the `Bitnodes` snapshots we analyze, there exist thousands (about 15% of the entire set) of reachable nodes with a zero block height. Interestingly, the vast majority (e.g., 80%) of these nodes are `.onion` addresses, accounting for about 50% of all connected Bitcoin-over-Tor nodes. We separately investigate these nodes with zero block height and

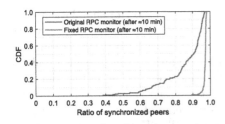
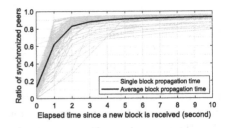

Fig. 3. Cumulative distribution of the ratio of synchronized peers measured by the original and fixed RPC-based monitors.

Fig. 4. Synchronization of peers in the first 10 s since a new block is received by our monitor. We show 100 blocks starting with height **699860**.

confirm in our experiment (see §3.3) that they are all regularly updated with the latest blockchain. According to the Bitnodes source code [19], the block height 0 of a node indicates that either the version messages sent by the node are corrupted or the internal database fails to record the actual height. From this, we conjecture that some unreliable interactions between Bitnodes database and .onion addresses might be the root cause of these nodes with zero block height. We leave further investigations for future work.

RPC-based Monitor. Unlike the Bitnodes monitor, which is deployed to estimate the network size, the RPC-based monitor is specifically designed to monitor the block synchronization. Unfortunately, we identify one subtle yet critical problem in it that contaminates its measurement results. In particular, the RPC-based monitor mistakenly propagates a new block hash to all other peers that have not relayed it to the monitor. The synced_blocks value of a peer is, however, updated *only* when the peer sends a new block hash to the RPC-based monitor. When a peer receives a new block hash from the monitor before it sends the same hash to the monitor, it is considered by the RPC-based monitor as *unsynchronized* at least until the next block is generated.

To confirm this bug and its impact on the block synchronization measurement, we run two versions of the RPC-based monitor for 24 h and compare their results. The two versions include the original open-source RPC-based monitor [1] and a *fixed* RPC-based monitor that disables block information forwarding (i.e., preventing inv, headers, and cmpctblock message types from being sent in the PushMessage function in net.cpp [1]). We also make our best effort to provide the same or improved experiment setup as in the original paper [15], such as issuing getpeerinfo calls every second, load balancing the crawling task using 10 servers. Since the exact locations and configurations of the original RPC-based monitors are unknown, we reasonably use 20 t2.xlarge instances in the US-West region of Amazon EC2 in this experiment. Our original and fixed RPC-based monitors connect to about 9.2K and 9.1K reachable peers, respectively, showing that our experiment successfully covers the vast majority of reachable peers in the Bitcoin network.

We show the cumulative distribution of the percentage of "synchronized" peers reported by two RPC-based monitors in Fig. 3. The definition of being synchronized is borrowed from the original paper [15]; that is, a peer is said to be synchronized when it receives the latest block anytime before the next block is received by the monitors (e.g., after ≈ 10 min). Figure 3 shows that the original (i.e., inaccurate) RPC-based monitor reports that Bitcoin is weakly synchronized; that is, a significant portion (about 10% in the median case and 35% in the worst 10th percentile case) of reachable peers are not synchronized even after about 10 min. In contrast, our fixed RPC-based monitor reports a drastically different result; that is, 95% or more Bitcoin reachable peers are almost always synchronized in less than 10 min. This comparison confirms that (1) the mistake of relaying block information to peers found in the RPC-based monitor is indeed a source of critical measurement errors and (2) the current Bitcoin is pretty well synchronized in practice!

3.3   Block Propagation Measured by Our Fixed RPC-based Monitor

We monitor how quickly a new block propagates through the network of reachable nodes using our fixed RPC-based monitor. In Fig. 4, we highlight the network-wide synchronization status in the first 10 s since a new block is sent to our monitor and we show this for 100 consecutive blocks. First, it is evident that new block information is propagated to 90% of peers in the network in about 4 s on average. Second, once a new block propagates to the majority (e.g., about 90%) of reachable peers, its propagation quickly tapers off. Note that this result shows a stark difference from the same experiments made with the original RPC-based monitor [15], which shows that blocks take 76 s and 140 s to reach 90% of reachable peers in two examples.

3.4   Justification of Fast Block Propagation

Our measurements in this section so far strongly suggest that blocks propagate through the Bitcoin network with much faster speed than reported by the two monitors [15,20]. We now re-confirm that Bitcoin blocks indeed traverse multiple hops of nodes within a few seconds through a simple, fully-controlled experiment in a Bitcoin regtest network. We run 11 Bitcoin nodes in different cities around the world using Amazon EC2 t2.large instances. These 11 nodes are

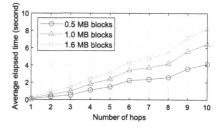

Fig. 5. Average elapsed time of multi-hop block propagation.

connected to each other to form a private network with a line topology of 10 hops. We note that the number of 10 hops is chosen conservatively since the network diameter of Bitcoin is unknown. We generate blocks with different sizes (i.e., 0.5 MB, 1.0 MB, 1.6 MB) at the first node and measure the elapsed time for the blocks to be fully received by other nodes. We repeat the same experiment 100 times and take note of the averaged propagation time. Figure 5 shows that larger blocks require more time to be propagated and all blocks need less than 10 s to propagate through 10 hops. We note that the application delay in Bitcoin Core nodes in the live network can be slightly higher since they would have more peers to relay blocks to (e.g., up to 125 for reachable nodes and 10 nodes for unreachable nodes). These results re-confirm the fast block propagation in Bitcoin.

3.5 Ethical Considerations

Throughout our experiments, we operate a few Bitcoin nodes that differ from the default client in only some additional logging messages. Our `Bitnodes`, original, and fixed `RPC-based` monitors unavoidably occupy 1–3 out of 115 incoming slots of most reachable nodes. Hence, we run them in a very short period of time (e.g., from a few hours to one day) and minimize their disturbance to the Bitcoin network. In Sect. 4, we discuss the risks of allowing monitoring nodes in Bitcoin and envision a better approach for Bitcoin network monitoring with little to no ethical concerns.

4 Future Work

As we criticize the limitations and bugs found in the two monitors, we fix some of them (e.g., disabling block information forwarding) to obtain a more accurate measurement; yet, some others deserve more in-depth studies. For example, it is still unclear why `Bitnodes` frequently fails to capture the block heights of nodes with `.onion` addresses.

Another future work would be the re-evaluation of several recent Bitcoin attacks [15,17,18] that rely on the inaccurate synchronization measurements in Bitcoin. It is unclear whether the claims in these offensive security research work would still hold when Bitcoin is much better synchronized in practice.

A longer-term future work would be a clean-slate design of Bitcoin network monitors. Monitoring peer-to-peer networks has never been a designed feature of blockchain protocols and thus it always relies on running supernodes [5,14] and/or exploiting protocol side channels [6,12]. Particularly, running monitor supernodes in blockchains is a fundamentally dangerous approach because it either changes the network states (i.e., observer effect) or degrades the network performance (e.g., supernodes damage the network connectivity to some extent), creating ethical concerns. We believe that accurate yet safe network monitoring, like existing proposals for Tor performance measurements [9,11], is desired as an integrated feature of Bitcoin and other blockchains.

5 Conclusion

Network measurement is known to be tricky and error-prone when dealing with a live distributed system, comprised of heterogeneous software/hardware components, whose states are constantly changing. This paper attempts to identify and correct some errors in recent Bitcoin network monitoring projects. Since accurate measurement of blockchain networks is evidently critical for ensuring their safety property, it is highly desirable to have more reliable and effective network monitoring primitives embedded in the blockchain protocols.

Acknowledgements. This work was supported by Electronics and Telecommunications Research Institute (ETRI) grant funded by the Korean Government (22ZR1330, Research on Intelligent Cyber Security and Trust Infra).

References

1. Bitcoin Lockstep Synchronous (2021). https://anonymous.4open.science/r/56e77487-0470-4e10-b634-b13e939863c0
2. bloxroute (2021). https://bloxroute.com/
3. Coin Dance: Bitcoin Nodes Summary (2021). https://coin.dance/nodes
4. Corallo, M.: BIP 152: Compact Block Relay (2016)
5. Decker, C., Wattenhofer, R.: Information propagation in the Bitcoin network. In: Proceedings of IEEE P2P (2013)
6. Delgado-Segura, S., et al.: TxProbe: Discovering Bitcoin's network topology Using orphan transactions. In: Proceedings of FC (2019)
7. DSN Bitcoin Monitoring (2021). https://www.dsn.kastel.kit.edu/bitcoin/
8. FIBRE: Fast Internet Bitcoin Relay Engine (2021). https://bitcoinfibre.org/
9. Jansen, R., Johnson, A.: Safely measuring Tor. In: Proceedings of ACM CCS (2016)
10. Kiffer, L., Rajaraman, R., Shelat, A.: A better method to analyze blockchain consistency. In: Proceedings of ACM CCS (2018)
11. Mani, A., Wilson-Brown, T., Jansen, R., Johnson, A., Sherr, M.: Understanding Tor usage with privacy-preserving measurement. In: Proceedings of ACM IMC (2018)
12. Miller, A., et al.: Discovering Bitcoin's Public Topology and Influential Nodes (2015)
13. Nakamoto, S.: Bitcoin: A Peer-to-Peer Electronic Cash System (2009)
14. Neudecker, T., Andelfinger, P., Hartenstein, H.: Timing analysis for inferring the topology of the Bitcoin peer-to-peer network. In: IEEE ATC (2016)
15. Saad, M., Anwar, A., Ravi, S., Mohaisen, D.: Revisiting nakamoto onsensus in asynchronous networks: a comprehensive analysis of Bitcoin safety and chain quality. In: ACM CCS (2021)
16. Saad, M., Chen, S., Mohaisen, D.: Root cause analyses for the deteriorating bitcoin network synchronization. In: Proceedings of IEEE ICDCS (2019)
17. Saad, M., Chen, S., Mohaisen, D.: SyncAttack: double-spending in Bitcoin without mining power. In: ACM CCS (2021)
18. Saad, M., Cook, V., Nguyen, L., Thai, M.T., Mohaisen, A.: Partitioning attacks on Bitcoin: colliding space, time, and logic. In: Proceedings of IEEE ICDCS (2019)
19. Yeow, A.: Bitnodes source code (2021). https://github.com/ayeowch/bitnodes
20. Yeow, A.: Global Bitcoin nodes distribution (2021). https://bitnodes.io/

India's "Aadhaar" Biometric ID: Structure, Security, and Vulnerabilities

Pratyush Ranjan Tiwari[1]($\boxtimes$), Dhruv Agarwal[2], Prakhar Jain[3], Swagam Dasgupta[4], Preetha Datta[5], Vineet Reddy[6], and Debayan Gupta[7]

[1] Johns Hopkins University, Baltimore, USA
pratyush@cs.jhu.edu
[2] Microsoft Research, Bengaluru, India
t-dhaga@microsoft.com
[3] Fractal Analytics, New York, USA
[4] Bastion Media, Bengaluru, India
[5] Aalto University, Espoo, Finland
[6] Northeastern University, Boston, USA
[7] Ashoka University, Sonepat, India

Abstract. India's Aadhaar is the largest biometric identity system in history, designed to help deliver subsidies, benefits, and services to India's 1.4 billion residents. The Unique Identification Authority of India (UIDAI) is responsible for providing each resident (not each citizen) with a distinct identity—a 12-digit Aadhaar number—using their biometric and demographic details. We provide the first comprehensive description of the Aadhaar infrastructure, collating information across thousands of pages of public documents and releases, as well as direct discussions with Aadhaar developers. Critically, we describe the first known cryptographic issue within the system, and discuss how a workaround prevents it from being exploitable at scale. Further, we categorize and rate various security and privacy limitations and the corresponding threat actors, examine the legitimacy of alleged security breaches, and discuss improvements and mitigation strategies.

Keywords: Resident identification · Biometric · Security & privacy

1 Introduction

Resident identification systems are pervasive in the world today, with many using biometrics [15]. These systems hold and mediate vast amounts of private data, which in many cases is also used to facilitate welfare schemes and other public programs. Aadhaar is a 12-digit unique ID issued by the Indian government to each Indian resident (not citizen), using their demographic and biometric information. To date, over 1.3 billion residents have been enrolled [34]: it is the largest biometric identity system ever built and is linked to bank a counts, income tax numbers, social security schemes, etc. And while Aadhaar is technically not

---

P. R. Tiwari and D. Agarwal—Equal contribution.

© International Financial Cryptography Association 2022
I. Eyal and J. Garay (Eds.): FC 2022, LNCS 13411, pp. 672–693, 2022.
https://doi.org/10.1007/978-3-031-18283-9_34

required for many things (such as getting a new cellular connection), its ubiquity has rendered it the default form of identification in India.

Though public trust in Aadhaar is crucial, the system has been relatively opaque, leading to much confusion and speculation. Civil activists [4] and media outlets [41] have alleged that Aadhaar is vulnerable to numerous types of breaches; corroborating these claims is difficult as there exists no comprehensive resource detailing Aadhaar's system and security architecture. Public documentation about Aadhaar is outdated or ambiguous, and *no unified description of the infrastructure exists*. As a result, one has to collate information from multiple (often unreliable) sources. We present the first comprehensive description of Aadhaar, analyze all reported privacy or security breaches, and assess defenses against future attacks. We also report the first known[1] cryptographic issue (fortunately *not* exploitable at scale under current conditions) in the system.

Contributions. *Comprehensive snapshot:* We outline the journey of an individual's data through the Aadhaar system and the entities involved (for data collection, processing, storage, and usage), covering the entire body of publicly available information on Aadhaar. Previous work has looked at authentication or verification, etc. [4,30], but none have covered the whole infrastructure.

Security Flaws: We analyze all documentation made public by UIDAI—trawling through thousands of pages over time—as well as all alleged attacks to compile and analyze possible security issues. We find that the way Aadhaar generates IVs for AES (it uses AES-GCM) opens up the possibility to mount an identity forgery attack and steal data. We note that *the attack is not currently deployable*: we have made sure that this is not exploitable before publishing. However, any batching of queries or capture of multiple messages within the same second may still render the system insecure. Specifically, one could forge the identity of any individual whose Aadhaar number is available[2].

1.1   Paper Overview

Section 2 provides a brief background and discusses related work. A list of all abbreviations, in order of appearance, is provided in Appendix B. Section 3 describes Aadhaar's infrastructure in detail (along with data privacy and security policies)[3] This snapshot is divided into the following main sections: the Enrollment Ecosystem (Sect. 3.1), the Authentication Ecosystem (Sect. 3.2), the Central Identities Data Repository or CIDR (Sect. 3.3). Section 4 details the security of different endpoints at which an individual's data is vulnerable to attacks.

---

[1] Media reports have alleged flaws in associated organizations, or engineering/policy flaws (e.g., software bugs), but a cryptographic flaw within the Aadhaar infrastructure itself has never been discussed.

[2] Collections of Aadhaar numbers have been leaked at various times by multiple organizations, though never by UIDAI itself.

[3] We collate information from myriad technical reports, policy documents, Memoranda of Understanding (MoUs), and circulars published and signed by UIDAI and other organizations in Aadhaar infrastructure. We archive these reports here.

Section 5 discusses information security in Aadhaar, using standard benchmarks. We define the threat model and discuss a cryptographic flaw we identified and its mitigation strategies (Sect. 5.2). We use the threat model along with the snapshot, in Sect. 6, to filter legitimate attacks from our database of media allegations (Sect. 6). We discuss possible attacks, categorize the feasibility of these breaches based on the threat actor involved, cost (time and resources) and the level of security provided by Aadhaar (Sect. 6). Section 6 discusses technical and structural mitigation strategies for each type of breach. A study of alleged attacks is provided in supplementary analysis Appendix C.

2   Background

The Unique Identification Authority of India (UIDAI) was established in January 2009. Its mission was to issue a unique identification (UID) number, an "Aadhaar Number," to every resident of the country. The UID's purpose was to be a one-stop identification that is eventually linked to every social service to make the disbursement of welfare services effective and efficient (by reducing leakages). The bill that provides legal backing to Aadhaar is called the "Aadhaar (Targeted Delivery of Financial and other Subsidies, benefits and services) Act." Apart from providing Indian residents with a unique identity (an Aadhaar number), the UIDAI is also responsible for providing a platform for residents to authenticate their physical presence [63] at a point of service. Aadhaar's policies regarding its vision, ethical implications, data security, and privacy have been under intense scrutiny [20].

This becomes all the more important with Aadhaar's ubiquity. It is different from login.gov [5,11], for example. It is not merely a single point of contact system for welfare. Aadhaar is what you can use to get on a plane, to open a bank account, to get a phone connection. Getting tested or vaccinated for COVID-19? Aadhaar. It is MOSIP [40] on steroids: closed-source, universal, and practically (although not officially) mandatory.

2.1   Related Work

National identification projects of many countries have attracted considerable academic research—Jamaica's attempt [33], Nepal's National Identity Project (NIDP) [3], UAE's ID system [6], Europe's e-ID systems [9], United States' Social Security Number [18], etc. Being the world's largest biometric ID system, India's Aadhaar has been an active research topic in the areas of ICTD, HCI, security, and privacy. Singh and Jackson [35] perform an ethnographic study of Aadhaar. They find exclusion of people in various phases: during enrollment, while authenticating, and while linking ("seeding") their Aadhaar numbers with existing public welfare databases (like the Public Distribution System database). Srinivasan and Johri [36] draw similarities between the legitimization and support tactics of Aadhaar and previously successful infrastructure projects like railroads in British India and dams in post-Independence India.

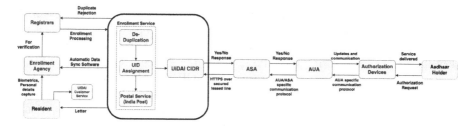

Fig. 1. Flowchart of Aadhaar's architecture. Yellow cells depict entry points into the enrollment (left) and authentication (right) ecosystems. Enrollment starts with the resident visiting the Enrollment Agency which uses an enrollment software provided by the Enrollment Service. The data is then sent to the Registrars for verification. If de-duplication succeeds, the data is stored in the CIDR and the user is enrolled. The authentication procedure starts with the Aadhaar holder's information reaching the CIDR via AUA and ASA. The biometric data is captured by the authorization devices, sent to the CIDR through AUA and ASA. The response is sent back by the CIDR via the same route. (Color figure online)

Prior security and privacy works have recommended using a Trust and Role-Based Access Control Model for internal Aadhaar processes and using cryptography to prevent illegal tracking and profiling [30]. Rajput and Gopinath [31] have analyzed the privacy of authentication workflows offered by Aadhaar and recommended new ones. The work of Agrawal, Banerjee and Sharma [4], though relatively informal, is the closest to ours. It provides a broad analysis of Aadhaar's vulnerabilities like faking biometrics, identification without consent, and illegal tracking by collation of data across service providers. Our work differs from these: we present a detailed overview of the system and do not assume the correctness of media allegations and activism (which are essential in their own right). Instead, we analyze Aadhaar's security and allegations against it based on an extensive study of available documentation.

3 Snapshot: Aadhaar System Design

Aadhaar has three primary components: (1) the *Enrollment* ecosystem, (2) the *Authentication* ecosystem, and (3) the *CIDR* (Central Identities Data Repository). Enrollment handles onboarding and assigning of unique identity numbers. Authentication provides verification services when residents want to prove their identity. CIDR is a database that stores the collected biometric and demographic data. We provide an overview of a typical resident's interaction with the Aadhaar system and then discuss its usability and the three components. An overview of the entire architecture is available in Fig. 1.

Usability of Aadhaar. The entire process assumes significant privilege: that a resident can read and speak fluently, has a phone (for many services, a smartphone), access to the internet, etc. Also, during the COVID pandemic, many centers are either fully or partially shut down: simple tasks such as linking a mobile number to one's Aadhaar for the first time have turned herculean. If one's Aadhaar number is lost (e.g., loss of card), there is no way to recover it for someone without a mobile phone (or an unlinked phone). This can result in loss of welfare [7], and restoring the UID is incredibly difficult. On the other hand, there is no way to remove one's data from the CIDR if the citizen wants/needs this (e.g., changing residency to another country). There are also on-ground issues like the prevalent use of the Aadhaar "card" or a photocopy as a visual proof of identity without biometric validation (e.g., at airports).

3.1 Enrollment Ecosystem

The Enrollment ecosystem (Fig. 2) handles onboarding of residents into Aadhaar with the objective of providing each resident with a unique ID (UID). It also handles updating of demographic and biometric details of existing UID holders. Residents enroll only once but may request updates. The ecosystem is designed to work offline to allow enrollment of residents from areas that lack connectivity. There are two major actors: Registrars and Enrollment Agencies (EAs). UIDAI appoints Registrars, and each Registrar appoints EAs under it.

Registrar: UIDAI partners with various ministries, banks, public sector organizations, and other agencies that interact with Indian residents [61,66] to facilitate issuing Aadhaar numbers by enrolling residents and validating resident data during enrollment and updation. Registrars must take special measures to enroll women, children, persons with disabilities, unskilled workers, nomadic tribes, and people belonging to marginalized groups who cannot produce a valid Proof of Identity (PoI) and/or Proof of Address (PoA) [61]. "Introducers" are individuals (such as Registrar employees, members of local administrative and elected bodies, etc.) recognized by Registrars to confirm resident data without PoI or PoA. Registrars must follow protocols and standards prescribed by the UIDAI. They usually outsource these tasks to EAs. While they are responsible for the correct functioning of these EAs, there is no mention of Registrars having to inform UIDAI about the EAs. A Registrar uses a UIDAI developed Enrollment Client to enroll residents, and must follow the Demographic Data Standards and Verification Procedure (DDSVP) [43].

Security (Policy and Logs). The MoUs between Registrars and UIDAI specify that UIDAI periodically audits the Registrars and EAs (frequency not specified). Although the standard penalties are nowhere specified, if a Registrar fails to follow the security mandates, UIDAI will only make "reasonable attempts" [66] to discuss and resolve difficulties with the Registrar. Organizations have been penalized in the past: UIDAI terminated a Registrar's contract citing "enormous number of complaints of corruption and enrollment process violations against Aadhaar Enrollment/Update Centres under CSC e-Gov" [37].

Enrollment Agency. Registrars employ third-party vendors called Enrollment Agencies (EA) to carry out enrollment services using tools and procedures [59] prescribed by the UIDAI. Sometimes, Registrars double up EAs instead of employing external EAs. For example, a bank may use its branches as EAs. In such cases, "Enrollment Agency" and "Enrollment Centre" become synonymous. As this is pervasive, we use these terms interchangeably in this paper. EAs are the on-ground functional arm of the Enrollment ecosystem and are responsible for providing operators and supervisors for each Enrollment Centre [60]. These Enrollment Operators (EOs) collect demographic and biometric data for enrollment or updation using UIDAI-approved equipment [53]. Before enrollment, EAs must verify the resident's PoA and PoI documents and ensure that the details entered in the Aadhaar Enrollment Client match. This verification is done by duly appointed officers at the EA called Verifiers [62].

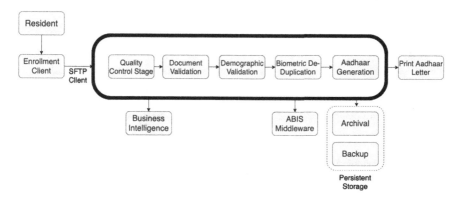

Fig. 2. Flowchart of the Aadhaar Enrollment Ecosystem. The resident's data is captured by the Enrollment Client and sent via the SFTP client for de-duplication. After multiple validity checks, an Aadhaar identity is generated and a physical card is printed.

Security (Technical). **Enrollment Equipment** – UIDAI mandates Registrars to follow guidelines to set up the enrollment environment. Only certified equipment is allowed [49]. The Enrollment Client is equipped to work under "Indian conditions", which we assume means low lighting, lack of internet connectivity, dusty environments, etc. [26]. **Data Validation** – The resident's PoI and PoA documents are verified by the Verifier, and details are entered into the Enrollment Client by the EO, followed by biometric data capture and validation by the resident. Most onboarding happens offline—data is periodically synced with CIDR [53]. **Operator Activity Tracking** – Every EO using the Enrollment Client must sign each enrollment and update with their own biometrics. EO login involves a username, password, and the EO's biometrics [53].

Security (Policy and Logs). When a Registrar hires an EA, the EOs working there need training and certification. The UIDAI provides a questionnaire [44] and a presentation to ensure basic training. The "Training, Testing and Certification" team designs lessons to ensure that EOs can recognize the necessary documents for the first check [65]. Periodically, "Mega Training and Certification Programs" [50] are organized to facilitate mass onboarding of operators when there is high demand. Refresher courses are also organized.

3.2   Authentication Ecosystem

The Authentication ecosystem (Fig. 3) provides paperless identity verification: **Authentication** – Uses an Aadhaar number and a one-time password (or biometrics) as a second factor to authenticate an individual. The CIDR returns a signed Yes/No [57]. **e-KYC** – identity verification via a signed and encrypted demographic record (name, age, address, etc.) from the CIDR.

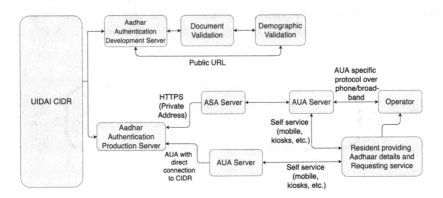

Fig. 3. Flowchart of Aadhaar's Authentication Ecosystem. We start at bottom right with a resident requesting a service. Aadhaar details are sent to the CIDR either through an AUA Server directly to the Production Server or via an ASA server. The CIDR then authenticates this information and returns the results via the same route.

AUAs and KUAs: A requesting entity is an agency that uses Aadhaar authentication and e-KYC facilities to provide services such as opening bank accounts, LPG connections, purchasing mobile SIMs, etc. [57]. There are two types of requesting entities [51,52]: an Authentication User Agency (AUA) uses only the authentication service, while a Know-Your-Customer User Agency (KUA) *also* uses the e-KYC service. When serving an individual, an AUA submits their Aadhaar number and demographic/biometric information to the CIDR for authentication [27]. An AUA connects to the CIDR through an Authentication Service Agency (ASA), which owns a secure connection to the CIDR. In response, the AUA receives a digitally signed response from the CIDR. A *sub-AUA* uses Aadhaar authentication to enable its services by contracting the services of an AUA. A KUA, *in addition to being an AUA*, uses e-KYC authentication facility to retrieve a resident's personal information from the CIDR. When an Aadhaar holder wants to submit their KYC details to a KUA, they download a copy of their e-KYC in XML or QR Code format from the Aadhaar website. This is encrypted with a "Share Code" set by the user. To verify the submitted file, a request is sent to CIDR through a KSA. The KUA receives a "digitally signed [machine readable XML] e-KYC authentication response with encrypted e-KYC data [58]." The KUA uses this copy of the holder's KYC data retrieved from UIDAI to verify the offline copy the resident submitted. The encrypted XML file contains the resident name, download reference number, address, photo, gender, DoB/YoB, hash of mobile number, hash of email.

Security (Technical). Aadhaar numbers collected by an AUA/KUA are encrypted and stored locally in an "Aadhaar Data Vault" [13]. The encryption keys must be stored in a Hardware Security Module (HSM). The UIDAI does not mandate audits nor specifies repercussions if the vault stores plaintext. The implementation of the Data Vault is usually outsourced, and many third-party vendors [22] offer their own variants. An AUA/KUA can transmit biometric information over a network only after creating an encrypted Personal Identity Data (PID) block in accordance with UIDAI specifications [47]. The encrypted PID block cannot be stored except for buffered authentication (for up to 24 h, after which it must be deleted from local storage) [25]. AUA/KUAs send authentication and e-KYC requests to ASAs/KSAs (who relay them to the CIDR) via secure private lines or a secure channel (SSL, VPN) [42].

Security (Policy and Logs). Access to the application, audit logs, source code etc. is only given to authorized personnel [25]. The basis on which a person becomes authorized and the extent of access are unknown. AUAs/KUAs are required to maintain online logs of each authentication transaction for two years, for grievance and dispute redressal. After this, logs are archived offline for five more years and then deleted (unless required in a pending dispute). The logs record the Aadhaar number, auth request, CIDR's response, information disclosed upon authentication, and the person's consent for authentication [25, p. 12]. Logs do not store PID information. No encryption/safety standards are specified; we discuss the resultant privacy issues in Sect. 5.3. Aadhaar holders can self-generate Virtual IDs (VID) for privacy. VIDs are temporary, revocable 16-digit random numbers that are one-way mapped from the Aadhaar number [64]. This mapping should be secret and the Aadhaar number should not be recoverable from it. The algorithm used for generating VIDs is not specified.

AUAs/KUAs are required to ensure that their operations are audited, including information security controls and technical testing like vulnerability assessment, penetration tests, etc., especially for new technologies introduced [25]. This audit must be done by a recognised body (presumably government empanelled auditors [12]) annually and on a need basis [25, p. 46] or by UIDAI itself to ensure compliance. Although UIDAI states that only authorized personnel can access the audit trails, selection criteria and security policies are unspecified.

ASAs and KSAs: Authentication/KYC Service Agencies (ASAs/KSAs) are public and private agencies that have an "established secure leased line connectivity with the CIDR" [57] in accordance with UIDAI's standards and specifications [25]. Only they can interact directly with the CIDR in the Authentication ecosystem. ASAs provide secure CIDR access to AUAs for authentication; KSAs are ASAs with additional e-KYC permissions and therefore serve KUAs. Hence, ASAs/KSAs act as enabling intermediaries between an AUA/KUA and the CIDR as shown in Figs. 1 and 3. There are 27 live ASAs/KSAs [56].

Security (Technical). Servers used by ASAs to connect to the CIDR must be located within India. ASA/KSA server host must be within a segregated network segment. It should be isolated from the rest of the network of the ASA/KSA. The ASA/KSA server host is solely dedicated to Aadhaar authentication. The PID block includes the keys generated by the ASAs/KSAs (sensitive and must never be stored). ASAs perform key generation, distribution, and storage.

Security (Policy and Logs). Access control, communication policies, log maintenance and expiration, and audit protocols are the same as those of AUAs/KUAs (Refer to Sect. 3.2). The logs can be accessed by UIDAI or the requesting entity solely for grievance and dispute redressal and contain the following information: identity of the requesting entity, parameters of authentication request submitted, and parameters received as authentication response.

3.3   CIDR (Central Identities Data Repository)

The Central Identities Data Repository (CIDR) is a centralized database that stores all Aadhaar numbers and corresponding demographic and biometric data. Maintained by UIDAI and distributed across multiple servers throughout India, CIDR is the core of Aadhaar and interacts with both the Enrollment and Authentication ecosystems. CIDR is also (indirectly) responsible for deduplication as deduplication servers access biometric data residing in the CIDR to check for matches before enrolling a new resident. Post-enrollment access to the CIDR comprises mainly authentication and e-KYC requests (see Sect. 3.2).

Security (Technical). **Enrollment Client**: The connection between the CIDR and the Enrollment Client is protected using SSL. The enrollment data (XML) is POSTed to the CIDR [26,45]. To ensure only certified operators and Enrollment Clients connect to the CIDR, each time an operator logs into the client, an XML document containing the machine identifier, enrollment agency code, and station number is sent to the CIDR for validation. The CIDR then sends back a security token, which is used to send subsequent enrollment data. The XML document containing the enrollment data is sent in the form of packets to the CIDR, *each* of which is encrypted using a public key published by UIDAI, and signed by the sender (to avoid wasting resources on extracting packets without a valid signature [26]). This packet encryption phase is handled by the Client Security module of the Enrollment Client, which also stores certificates and manages keys. The key management uses public-key style encryption where *two* sets of public keys are maintained – one for data exchange between the Enrollment Client and the CIDR, and another for data exchange between the Registrar and the CIDR. The CIDR is classified as a Protected System under the IT Act, and the link between the CIDR and the Enrollment Client is encrypted using 2048 bit PKI. **Deduplication**: Deduplication at the billion scale has never been previously attempted [26]. For risk mitigation, UIDAI has *three* independent ABIS (Automatic Biometric Identification System) providers performing biometric deduplication. At enrollment, Aadhaar first does a demographic and reduced biometric check for matches. The Aadhaar enrollment server integrates the ABIS solutions using an ABIS API and dynamically allocates deduplication requests to the 3 ABIS servers. Then, ABIS deduplication servers are sent packages of size 3–5 MB. The enrollment packet (containing all demographic, biometric, and metadata) is encrypted at the client side and then sent to CIDR; the CIDR interacts with the ABIS servers and sends them these packages. Only the Enrollment Server (maintained by CIDR) can decrypt the enrollment packet. It does this in memory; the decrypted packet is **never** sent to storage. Original biometric data is archived and sent to offline storage and is not available on an online network. 2048-bit PKI is used throughout. See supplementary analysis Appendix C for more details. When a registered device is called, it captures, processes, and encodes the digitally signed biometric record. The biometric data received by the CIDR is essentially a Base-64 of the DSA signature of a hash (SHA-256) of the biometric data and a timestamp, device code, and device private key.

4 Security Landscape

We consider the security of different endpoints at which an individual's data could be vulnerable and the steps Aadhaar takes to prevent any attacks.

4.1 Hardware Security and Certification

Biometric data is first collected during registration, and subsequently used to verify that individual's identity. These biometric devices, therefore, are a critical component of Aadhaar. The official documentation [49] specifies two types of devices. *Public Devices* are biometric capture devices that can be attached to the Aadhaar application provided to AUA/Sub-AUA to capture Aadhaar compliant biometric data. The application then encrypts the data before authentication. *Registered Devices* (RD) have three key additional features over public devices. Each RD has a unique device identifier, biometric data is signed with the device key to ensure liveness and encrypted on-device rather than on the host application, and lastly, the RD service is certified regardless of the device provider. "RD service" refers to the process of capturing biometrics, signing them, and forming a personal identity data (PID) block before returning to the application.

Device Compliance Levels. The RD service is certified over two levels. *Level 0 Compliance* ensures that the implementation of signing and encryption of biometrics is within the software zone at host's OS level. This includes ensuring that the associated private keys are not compromised through access via any external applications within the OS, and the biometric data can not be injected maliciously. *Level 1 Compliance* enhances security by ensuring that the signing and encryption take place within a Trusted Execution Environment (TEE). The private keys and the biometrics are stored in, and accessed via, the TEE.

Pre-certified Hardware: Any provider of an L1 compliant device needs to supply "Pre-certified" Hardware (PCH) and accompanying system software. This must protect against Hardware Cloning, Hardware Tampering (Physical, voltage, frequency, temperature attacks on crypto blocks), Differential Power analysis, Probing, Memory segregation of cryptographic operations, Cryptography implementation vulnerability, Attacks against Secure Boot and Secure Upgrade and TEE, and Secure processor OS attacks.

Certification: The agencies responsible for the certification are UIDAI and Standardization Testing and Quality Certification (STQC) Directorate (which is an attached office of the Ministry of Electronics and Information Technology). The certification process is exhaustive and combines testing over multiple, widely regarded industry and government standards like NIST's FIPS [38] for the security of cryptographic modules, PCI PTS [29] and PED for physical and software tampering, GlobalPlatform certification for the TEE, and other dedicated hardware for L1, like secure boot, secure upgrade, etc. More details are available in [49]. UIDAI and STQC also check for tamper responsiveness: these devices can detect box-open tampering, chemical tampering, etc. and destroy sensitive data upon detection. However, a small part of hardware and system software is vendor self-certified. We were unable to find any reasoning for this; it is unclear how a vendor can verifiably self-certify a lack of backdoors!

4.2   Key Management and Device Registration

Each device provider must register and obtain a device provider ID via UIDAI. UIDAI then signs a public-key certificate procured by the device provider from a certificate authority(CA) licensed by the Govt. of India's Controller of Certifying Authorities (CCA). These certificates are X.509 v3 compliant. Furthermore, the UIDAI policy specifies time periods after which device keys have to be rotated.

L1 compliant devices store their signing and encryption keys in PCH. There exists a hardware key-store in these devices. The certificate issued for the device, called the *Chip Identity Certificate*, is stored therein and must be non-clonable. The signing and encrypting key-pair generation and the cryptographic operations happen within this hardware key-store. However, L0 compliant devices have a software-based key-store provided by the OS. Common software security practices are specified and required for this key-store in [49]. All accesses to this key-store are logged. The private key is not extractable in any format, and the key-store is cleared and zeroed if the RD service is deleted. The key-store password is auto-generated using some random data, user credentials, and device identities of hardware like hard disk serial number, processor ID, and other device IDs. This key derivation is not public and obfuscated to prevent attacks. *We note that this can be dangerous.* Historically, security by obscurity has been a terrible idea [39], and has meant that bad security went uncriticized.

4.3   Biometric Deduplication and Locking

Since Aadhaar has the face, fingerprint, and iris biometrics for enrolled residents, it can combine these for de-duplication upon enrollment. With ten fingerprints and a facial image, a 95% de-duplication rate could be achieved over a population of 50 million. To increase the de-duplication rate to 99%, usage of iris biometrics was proposed. However, there is *no documentation* about the matching algorithms running at the ABIS and how well they perform. The accuracy listed above implies that authentication for valid Aadhaar numbers and corresponding residents might fail for a small fraction of requests. While UIDAI has not released any documentation about the de-duplication process, we discovered the following information from our interviews of Aadhaar personnel: The de-duplication problem is viewed and solved as a multi-class classification problem where there are as many classes as there are individuals in the Aadhaar database. Using deep learning techniques, the set consisting of Aadhaar IDs, ten fingerprints, iris and face biometric data is pre-processed before classification. Since this is a huge dataset, this process is optimized by reducing some features. If candidate duplicates are discovered, they are checked using some more features along with a combination of manual assistance. The biometric algorithms used were described as standard ones from the works of Jain et al. [21,67]

5   Security, Privacy and Attacks

Defining "security" and "privacy" in the context of Aadhaar is nontrivial. It's easy to provide stringent requirements, but those would almost certainly result in the exclusion of large sections of marginalized people in India, who may not have much documentation—precisely those we want to help. Many Indians also routinely use different spellings for their names (and other data) and may need to update the same without requiring a complicated court process (names in various Indian languages can be anglicized in multiple ways). Therefore, any realistic treatment of security (and attacks) cannot be too broad; we detail our Aadhaar-specific interpretations of the CIA (Confidentiality, Integrity, and Availability) information security triad in this section. We also explicitly list a variety of threat actors and their abilities (see supplementary analysis Appendix C).

Classifying Attacks. We use the CIA standard for information security. Any attack must violate one or more of: **Confidentiality** – Access to a resident's data (demographic or biometric) collected at the time of enrollment or updation is granted only to authorized individuals within UIDAI and its partner organizations. **Integrity** – A resident's information within the CIDR or during transmission is not modified or lost in an unauthorized manner. **Availability** – A resident's data is available to authorized entities within UIDAI and its partner organizations when required.

5.1   Threat Actors

We conduct a threat actor analysis to identify possible threats as an individual's data travels through the system. In the attached report in the Appendix C, we classify threat actors based on their *capability, motivation*, and *damage caused* and give low/medium/high ratings for each. The threat actors we identified are described below.

Rogue Enrollment Operator: The first barrier an individual's information has to the central repository is the enrollment operator, which has the responsibility of asking the individual their information and verifying its authenticity. A rogue agent can possibly enroll the individual with faulty data or, worse, make a copy of their data and enroll a fake resident instead.

Rogue Agency Seeking AUA/ASA Services: AUA/ASA provide services to agencies seeking to become requesting entities for authentication. Aadhaar specifies the criteria for such agencies [46]. However, in some cases, the authentication devices are operator-assisted: a service might be provided without authentication or based on identity forgery. E.g., an operator at a cellular agency could authenticate twice by using Anita's Aadhaar details (when she applies for a new SIM) and keep one connection for themselves.

Rogue Enrollment Agent: A rogue enrollment agent can help generate fake Aadhaar cards; in practice, there is little oversight in place.

Rogue UIDAI Official: The access privileges of a high-ranking UIDAI official, if misused, can result in identity theft, fake voter IDs, and more.

External Parties: Governments, IT companies, and curious residents could try to access confidential Aadhaar information for varying motives. The resources possessed by all these external parties can vary quite a bit.

5.2   Forbidden Attack: A Cryptographic Challenge

We describe a possible cryptographic attack on Aadhaar; note that carrying out such an attack would be illegal, as Aadhaar is classified as a "protected system" under Section 70 of the Indian IT Act, 2000 [1]. We reported this attack to UIDAI, which validated its correctness and ensured its mitigation.

Aadhaar's API security document [54, p. 29] details that packaged biometrics are sent for authentication as a Pid (Personal Identity Data) element, which is a base-64 encoded block. Before base-64 encoding, the Pid blocks are encrypted with a dynamic session key using AES-256 symmetric algorithm, using the Galois Counter Mode (GCM). Refer Appendix A for details about GCM. One major issue discussed by Antoine Joux in his comments to NIST on GCM [8] is *A forbidden attack with repeated IV*. If an adversary sees two different messages encrypted with the same IV, it can inject malicious content into the communication channel. One such attack is demonstrated in detail by Böck et al. [10].

The document [54] describes exactly how Aadhaar instantiates AES GCM: *"The last 12 bytes of the* ts *(string formatted date) is used as the IV or nonce."* The ts attribute (timestamp) is described as follows [54, p. 15]: *"Timestamp at the time of capture of authentication input. This is in the format YYYY-MM-DDThh:mm:ss (derived from ISO 8601)."*

The implementation available on the Github repo [24] and the old Aadhaar developer portal [48], and our interviews with Aadhaar officials confirm this timestamp format. So, suppose the timestamp is 2020-06-22T19:47:30. Then last 12 bytes are -22T19:47:30 and the string used as IV for AES GCM comprises just the day-of-month and the time. Trivially, the IV is reused if multiple messages are sent within the same second, or if messages are buffered or batched. Further, the IV -22T19:47:30 repeats at time 19:47:30 on the 22 date of each month, leading to monthly IV reuse. We describe this forbidden attack formally in Appendix A. Briefly: an adversary can exchange their invalid biometrics with valid data and still authenticate. (They cannot recover keys, but we want to protect the data, not just the keys.) Authentication requests can be altered over the channel due to IV reuse. As a consequence, a malicious party can open a bank account, fly domestically, get a SIM card, etc. —all in someone else's name.

Benchmarking. Using data published by the Govt. of India [55], we estimate how many times AES-GCM is used for encrypting requests. One source of such requests is the Authentication API; the other is e-KYC, which also uses AES-GCM in the exact same way [45]. Between October 2016 to September 2019, 7.9 billion requests were made for e-KYC; on average, the IV was reused ~ 83 times per second. Consequently, the malleability of the encrypted plaintext becomes a major security issue, and hence, all chosen ciphertext attacks become feasible.

Mitigation. The IV for AES-GCM is 96-bits (12 bytes) and we need to prevent IV reuse. Currently, the IV is of the form -22T19:47:30 (day-of-month and time). In this format, the IV takes $< \sim 2^{22}$ different values (since the dates vary in range 1–31, range of hours is 0–23 and minutes and seconds are in range 0–59 each). Instead, if a simple counter is utilized, it would take values in the whole 2^{96} range space (as IV length is 96 bits). However, the communication complexity of a synchronized task across 30 million devices is infeasible: maintaining it proved impractical and so the Aadhaar team decided[4] to use timestamps as IVs due to the availability of this information across all devices. *To mitigate this attack, all AES-GCM communications now occur over secure channels with unique session keys. This prevents the attack from being exploitable.* Note that the UIDAI encrypts all communications and storage across Aadhaar. UIDAI policy is to use RSA [32] with 2048 bit keys for public key and AES with 256-bit keys for symmetric key encryption [47].

5.3   Privacy Issues

Aadhaar's policy for logging requests and responses creates two issues. (1) the privacy of registered individuals in the event of a breach; and (2) the possibility of surveillance. The logs are rich spatio-temporal data on almost everyone in India. Obviously, a leak would be catastrophic if the data is not anonymized; but even "anonymized" spatio-temporal data can be used to uniquely identify a very large fraction of the individuals, as demonstrated by de Montjoye et al. [28]. Therefore, the use of virtual IDs (see Sect. 3.2) is essential. However, existing documentation is ambiguous as to whether virtual IDs are used by default for authentication

---

[4] This was discussed during our interviews of Aadhaar personnel.

requests. Further, while all communication of Aadhaar's biometric templates is end-to-end encrypted, they remain vulnerable to social engineering attacks and the like at ECs; the privacy loss inherent in the storage of biometric templates for a national ID is beyond the scope of this work.

Non-KYC operations should not reveal anything beyond verification (yes/no). If an entity has knowledge of $a_1, a_2, ...a_k$ columns of a person's Aadhaar information, they should not be able to gain knowledge of the a_{k+1}^{th} column, including brute-forcing by checking against the same column multiple times (given someone's name and phone number, an entity should not be able to query multiple times with different dates of birth). Services using aggregated data must be differentially private. The work of Wilson et al. [68] focuses on this approach and provides extensive theoretical and practical analysis. This gives a scalable method which is generic enough to apply to all national ID systems including Aadhaar. Extensive data logging for almost a decade means that such a system can very easily be used to track registered individuals. Differentially private (DP) anonymized logs can be used to protect against such tracking. While such logs and streams have been studied in some detail [16, 23], it remains to be seen if such proposals would be feasible at this scale (see Sect. 5.2). The closest (in scale) DP system is the recent work of the US Census Bureau [17] which shows that DP is not a one-size fits-all solution [19]. Aadhaar is meant to ensure the targeted delivery of benefits and services to Indian citizens. Verification of a resident's existence to receive a service must not leak personally identifiable information. Another solution to mitigate privacy concerns is via brokered identification [11]. Here, a centralized hub mediates communication between an identity authority and a user with identity credentials. The US FCCX [2] and GOV.UK Verify proposed using this, but were unable to ensure all the properties required (see [11]). Using such a mechanism would mitigate the possibility of surveillance using Aadhaar authentication requests.

6   Media Allegations Analysis

Filtering Legitimate Breaches. Our primary database of media allegations consists of 36 reports from various news outlets. We filter breaches that are "legitimate" based on our knowledge of the Aadhaar infrastructure and our definitions of security and privacy. This yielded 17 legitimate security breaches and 10 privacy breaches, which were further analyzed. (Security and privacy breaches are not mutually exclusive.) Additionally, for each legitimate security breach, we ascertain whether or not there was a breach of Confidentiality, Integrity, or Availability of data in the Aadhaar infrastructure. (See Table C in supplementary material Appendix C.) According to our analysis, the prevalent breach is of **confidentiality**; this usually entails a subset of Aadhaar data being made public. Prevention goes back to ensuring that data is secured in encrypted "data vaults" and access is limited. Breach of **integrity** is also common. It compromises the quality of the central database. They typically occur at an individual level, involving a small set of rogue insider-agents or the hacking of individual accounts. This is easily detected if performed repeatedly, while for a specific use-case like introducing certain individuals into the database, the breach is virtually undetectable. OTP-based security, standardized punishments, and closing some known structural gaps could mitigate this. Breaches of **availability** are rare and occurs only in cases of insider attacks. The CIDR repository itself is reasonably secure, and removing/editing information is hard to do illegally. Internal attacks can be mitigated by using a decentralized system of checks and balances where no individual can commit edits [14]. For example, all operations by high-level employees could require approval by randomly chosen officers (anonymously).

Attack Analysis. We define three broad classes of attacks: **(1) Server compromise:** Hacking of the UIDAI or Partner software/database. **(2) Infrastructural loopholes**: Access via legitimate UIDAI channels. **(3) Sub-par hardware**: UIDAI hardware tricked into approving false biometrics as genuine due to flaws or backdoors. We analyze the feasibility of attacks based on the cost (time and resources used) and the effort required to protect against it. We then suggest mitigation strategies to ensure robust security. A detailed breakdown of our examination is provided in Appendix C. Aadhaar is predominantly vulnerable to "Infrastructure Loopholes." These breaches exploit the general negligence to set or adhere to security protocols. As discussed, agents of Aadhaar, such as and especially EOs, can effectively be a threat to the security of the database if their credentials are not stored properly (multiple instances of this have occurred). This is a breach that is detected often, but measures taken to curb it are seemingly nonexistent. Complimentary and robust security standards like OTPs and Iris scans for these Aadhaar agents may be effective in ensuring accountability. The CIDR Database is secure and there exist no reports of it being hacked, but data in UIDAI's partner organizations are regularly stored insecurely. We recommend that the UIDAI sets stricter standards and enforce them across the board. No one should store any Aadhaar data except the CIDR. Any queries to the database should go through the CIDR, and local copies should not be stored.

Privacy Breach Analysis. Listing the various allegations of Aadhaar privacy breaches, we find that limited access to the database and illegal or insecure storage of Aadhaar information are common. These are primarily due to improper or inefficient handling of data by UIDAI's partner organizations. We summarize the number and type of privacy breaches in the attached supplementary material Appendix C. In either case, the pivotal issue is that an individual can be identified, resulting in the misuse of their data by malicious actors. This can include surveillance, profiling, or creating new services (without consent) by the state or other private actors. Most security breaches happen within the Enrollment Ecosystem; privacy breaches largely appear in the Authentication Ecosystem. For Aadhaar to be effective in the targeted delivery of subsidies, it needs to ensure that resident data is private beyond enrollment. If organizations require Aadhaar data to analyze aggregated trends, we strongly recommend differentially private systems be used.

7 Conclusion

We analyze Aadhaar, the world's largest digital biometric identification system, and provide the first detailed, unified description of the infrastructure. We conclude that the framework does not have glaring security flaws of the kind suggested by media reports. Almost all the issues we found were due to a set of challenges unique to a system at Aadhaar's scale. While we discussed mitigations for any flaws we found, we did not make any policy recommendations in this paper: if we had to make one, it would be for the system to be *significantly more transparent and open-source*. Throughout its lifetime, Aadhaar has been subject to multiple allegations that have made national headlines in India. We list, analyze, and classify these allegations to allow for a more balanced view of Aadhaar, identifying which ones are likely to be legitimate. (We note that most of the alleged attacks are now infeasible.)

We emphasize that our focus remained on the strengths and vulnerabilities of the technology, structure, and policy behind Aadhaar, and not issues with large-scale biometric ID schemes in general.

Acknowledgements. The first author is supported in part by the Office of Naval Research under awards N00014-19-1-2294 and N00014-19-1-2292 and by the NSF under award CNS-1814919.

A   Background

AES-GCM. AES GCM (Galois/Counter Mode) is a block-cipher mode of operation which encrypts the plaintext by using the counter mode. For authentication, a hash function called GHASH is used, which computes over the Galois Field $GF(2^{128})$. For a comprehensive description of AES GCM we suggest referring to the work of Böck et al. [10].

Forbidden Attack. Consider a passive adversary $\mathcal{A}$ which only sees ciphertext data, including initialization vector (IV), associated data, and authentication tag. The authentication key is $H = \mathsf{Enc}_k(0^{128})$ where k is the secret key for encryption. The authentication tag t is the evaluation of a polynomial g at the authentication key H. The coefficients of polynomial g depend on the ciphertext blocks and the constant coefficient is the nonce. Suppose that $\mathcal{A}$ finds two messages m_1 and m_2 encrypted using the same IV. $\mathcal{A}$ now has two polynomials with known coefficients (the ciphertext is public) and the same constant coefficient. Let these polynomials be $g_1(\cdot)$ and $g_2(\cdot)$. For the two authentication tags, t_1 and t_2

$$g_1(H) = t_1, g_2(H) = t_2$$

The adversary $\mathcal{A}$ now knows two polynomials $g_1(x) - t_1$ and $g_2(x) - t_2$ with a common root H, and they can recover a short list of candidates for the authentication key. In theory, this list could be as long as the degree of the polynomial, but is relatively short in practice. The GCD of the two polynomials gives $\mathcal{A}$

a polynomial of small degree with H as a root. Similarly, by finding more IV reuses, the possible number of candidate H keeps reducing, and eventually, H is found. **Now that H is known, $\mathcal{A}$ can substitute any information they like and replace a valid ciphertext.** For a more detailed analysis and description of the attack we refer readers to the work of Joux [8] and Böck et al. [10].

B   Abbreviations

See Table 1 for a list of abbreviations used in the paper.

Table 1. Summary of abbreviations used in the paper (in order of appearance)

Abbreviation	Full form
UIDAI	Unique Identification Authority of India
MoUs	Memoranda of Understanding
CIDR	Central Identities Data Repository
UID	Unique Identification
KYC	Know Your Customer
EA	Enrollment Agency
EO	Enrollment Officer
AUA	Authentication User Agency
KUA	KYC User Agency
SSUP	Self Service Update Portal
PoI	Proof of Identity
PoA	Proof of Address
DDSVP	Demographic Data Standards and Verification Procedure
HSM	Hardware Security Module
PID	Personal Identity Data
VID	Virtual ID
ABIS	Automatic Biometric Identification System
GCM	Galois Counter Mode
RD	Registered Devices
TEE	Trusted Execution Environment
PCH	Pre-Certified Hardware
STQC	Standardization Testing and Quality Certification
CA	Certificate Authority
CCA	Controller of Certifying Authorities
EC	Enrollment Center
DP	Differentially Private
OTP	One-Time Password
CIA	Confidentiality, Integrity, Availability

C   Supplementary Material

This work summarizes a long ongoing effort to provide the most comprehensive view of Aadhaar. The full version of this work (accessed at http://ia.cr/2022/481) explains are methodology for Aadhaar's security breach analysis and threat actor analysis pertaining to the security breach. A complete analysis of media allegations can be accessed at http://pratyush.site/files/AadhaarAnalysis.pdf.

References

1. Information technology ACT, 2000. https://www.meity.gov.in/writereaddata/files/act2000n_0.doc
2. Fccx briefing (2014). https://csrc.nist.gov/csrc/media/events/ispab-june-2014-meeting/documents/ispab_jun2014_fccx-briefing_glair.pdf
3. Adhikari, G.P.: National ID project of Nepal: future challenges. In: Proceedings of the 5th International Conference on Theory and Practice of Electronic Governance, ICEGOV 2011, pp. 379–380. Association for Computing Machinery, New York (2011). https://doi.org/10.1145/2072069.2072151
4. Agrawal, S., Banerjee, S., Sharma, S.: Privacy and security of Aadhaar: a computer science perspective. Econ. Polit. Wkly **52**, 93–102 (2017)
5. Aiemworawutikul, W., Datla, M.V., Lee, J.C.S., Wen, T., Zhang, Y.: Vulnerability assessment in national identity services (2019)
6. Al-Khouri, A.M.: Facing the challenge of enrolment in national id schemes. In: Brömme, A., Busch, C. (eds.) BIOSIG 2010: Biometrics and Electronic Signatures. Proceedings of the Special Interest Group on Biometrics and Electronic Signatures, pp. 13–28. Gesellschaft für Informatik e.V., Bonn (2010)
7. Anil, V., Dreze, J.: Without Aadhaar, without identity (2021). https://indianexpress.com/article/opinion/columns/flaw-in-aadhaar-architecture-uidai-card-enrolment-7389133/
8. Joux, A.: Authentication Failures in NIST version of GCM (2006). http://csrc.nist.gov/csrc/media/projects/block-cipher-techniques/documents/bcm/joux_comments.pdf
9. Arora, S.: National e-ID card schemes: a European overview. Inf. Secur. Tech. Rep. **13**(2), 46–53 (2008). https://doi.org/10.1016/j.istr.2008.08.002. http://www.sciencedirect.com/science/article/pii/S1363412708000241
10. Böck, H., Zauner, A., Devlin, S., Somorovsky, J., Jovanovic, P.: Nonce-disrespecting adversaries: practical forgery attacks on GCM in TLS. In: 10th USENIX Workshop on Offensive Technologies, WOOT 2016, Austin, TX, USA, 8–9 August 2016. USENIX Association (2016)
11. Brandão, L.T., Christin, N., Danezis, G., et al.: Toward mending two nation-scale brokered identification systems. Proc. Priv. Enh. Technol. **2015**(2), 135–155 (2015)
12. CERT-In: Empanelled Information Security Auditing Organizations (2018). https://www.cert-in.org.in/PDF/Empanel_org.pdf
13. Compliance Uncovered: Aadhaar Data Vault - To whom it applies, September 2018. https://complianceuncovered.com/2018/09/03/aadhar-data-vault-to-whom-it-applies/
14. Cybersecurity and Infrastructure Security Agency: Insider threat mitigation (2019). https://www.dhs.gov/cisa/insider-threat-mitigation

15. Electronic Frontier Foundation: Mandatory national IDs and biometric databases (2021). https://www.eff.org/issues/national-ids
16. Elkoumy, G., Pankova, A., Dumas, M.: Mine me but don't single me out: differentially private event logs for process mining. In: ICPM 2021, pp. 80–87 (2021)
17. Garfinkel, S.: Implementing differential privacy for the 2020 census. USENIX Association (2021)
18. Garfinkel, S.L.: Risks of social security numbers (1995)
19. Garfinkel, S.L., Abowd, J.M., Powazek, S.: Issues encountered deploying differential privacy (2018)
20. Goel, V.: 'Big Brother' in India Requires Fingerprint Scans for Food, Phones and Finances, April 2018. https://www.nytimes.com/2018/04/07/technology/india-id-aadhaar.html
21. Jain, A.K., Flynn, P.J., Ross, A.A.: Handbook of Biometrics. Springer, New York (2010). https://doi.org/10.1007/978-0-387-71041-9
22. JISA Softech Pvt Ltd: Aadhaar Data Vault (2018). https://www.jisasoftech.com/aadhaar-data-vault/
23. Kellaris, G., Papadopoulos, S., Xiao, X., Papadias, D.: Differentially private event sequences over infinite streams. Proc. VLDB Endow. **7**(12), 1155–1166 (2014)
24. Geodesic Limited: Source code for Aadhaar v1.6 (2011). https://github.com/GeoAmida/AadhaarAuth1.6. Accessed 19 Jan 2021
25. MeitY and UIDAI: Compendium of Regulations, Circulars & Guidelines For ASA and AUA (2018). https://uidai.gov.in/images/resource/compendium_auth_19042018.pdf
26. Ministry of Electronics and Information Technology: Aadhaar technology & architecture (2014). https://archive.org/details/Aadhaar-Technology-Architecture/page/n2
27. Ministry of Law and Justice and Government of India: The Aadhaar (Targeted Delivery of Financial and Other Subsidies, Benefits and Services) Act, 2016 (2016). https://uidai.gov.in/images/targeted_delivery_of_financial_and_other_subsidies_benefits_and_services_13072016.pdf
28. de Montjoye, Y.A.A., Hidalgo, C.D., Verleysen, M., Blondel, V.: Unique in the crowd: the privacy bounds of human mobility (2013). https://www.nature.com/articles/srep01376
29. PCI: Payment Card Industry PTS POI Security Requirements v4.0, June 2013. https://nvlpubs.nist.gov/nistpubs/FIPS/NIST.FIPS.140-2.pdf
30. Rajput, A., Gopinath, K.: Towards a more secure Aadhaar. In: Proceedings of Information Systems Security - 13th International Conference, ICISS 2017, Mumbai, India, 16–20 December 2017, pp. 283–300 (2017)
31. Rajput, A., Gopinath, K.: Analysis of newer Aadhaar privacy models. In: Proceedings of Information Systems Security - 14th International Conference, ICISS 2018, Bangalore, India, 17–19 December 2018, pp. 386–404 (2018)
32. Rivest, R.L., Shamir, A., Adleman, L.M.: A method for obtaining digital signatures and public-key cryptosystems (reprint). Commun. ACM **26**(1), 96–99 (1983)
33. Dunn, H.S.: Risking identity: a case study of Jamaica's short-lived national id system. J. Inf. Commun. Ethics Soc. **18**(3), 329–338 (2020). https://doi.org/10.1108/JICES-04-2020-0040
34. Indo-Asian News Service: 125 Crore Aadhaar Cards Issued Since 2009: Centre, December 2019. https://www.ndtv.com/india-news/centre-says-125-crore-aadhaar-cards-issued-till-date-2155184

35. Singh, R., Jackson, S.J.: From Margins to Seams: Imbrication, Inclusion, and Torque in the Aadhaar Identification Project, pp. 4776–4824. Association for Computing Machinery, New York (2017). https://doi.org/10.1145/3025453.3025910
36. Srinivasan, J., Johri, A.: Creating machine readable men: legitimizing the "Aadhaar" mega e-infrastructure project in India. In: Proceedings of the Sixth International Conference on Information and Communication Technologies and Development: Full Papers, ICTD 2013, vol. 1, pp. 101–112. Association for Computing Machinery, New York (2013). https://doi.org/10.1145/2516604.2516625
37. Srivas, A.: Millions of Rural Indians May be Hit as UIDAI Ends Contract With CSC Network For Aadhaar Enrolment, February 2018. https://thewire.in/tech/millions-may-affected-uidai-centres-csc-network-clash-renewal-aadhaar-services-contract
38. National Institute of Standards and Technology: FIPS 140-2: Security Requirements for Cryptographic Modules, May 2001. https://nvlpubs.nist.gov/nistpubs/FIPS/NIST.FIPS.140-2.pdf
39. Swire, P.P.: A theory of disclosure for security and competitive reasons: open source, proprietary software, and government systems. Hous. L. Rev. **42**, 1333 (2005)
40. Modular Open Source Identity Platform (MOSIP) Documentation (2021). https://docs.mosip.io/platform/. Accessed 19 Jan 2021
41. Tech2News Staff: Aadhaar Security Breaches: Here are the major untoward incidents that have happened with Aadhaar and what was actually affected, September 2018. https://www.firstpost.com/tech/news-analysis/aadhaar-security-breaches-here-are-the-major-untoward-incidents-that-have.-happened-with-aadhaar-and-what-was-actually-affected-4300349.html
42. Thales: Complying with UIDAI's AADHAAR Number Regulations (2018). https://go.thalesesecurity.com/rs/480-LWA-970/images/Thales-UIDAI-AADHAAR-cb.pdf
43. UIDAI: Demographic Data Standards and Verification procedure (DDSVP) Committee Report (2009). https://uidai.gov.in/images/UID_DDSVP_Committee_Report_v1.0.pdf
44. UIDAI: Questionnaire - UIDAI Operators (2011). https://uidai.gov.in/images/training-2019/QuestionBank-Operator-510/English_510QB_24012019.pdf
45. UIDAI: Aadhaar E-KYC Specification - Version 2.0 (2016). https://uidai.gov.in/images/aadhaar_ekyc_api_2_0.pdf
46. UIDAI: Eligibility criteria for appointment as requesting entities (2016). https://uidai.gov.in/images/resource/eligibility_criteria_for_aua_kua_17122016.pdf
47. UIDAI: Aadhaar Authentication API Specification - Version 2.0 (2017). https://uidai.gov.in/images/FrontPageUpdates/aadhaar_authentication_api_2_0.pdf
48. UIDAI: Aadhaar Developer Portal (2017). https://web.archive.org/web/20170326113654/authportal.uidai.gov.in/web/uidai/developer. Accessed 26 Mar 2017
49. UIDAI: Aadhaar Registered Devices - Technical Specification, vol. 2.0. MeitY, New Delhi, Delhi, 1 edn (2017). https://uidai.gov.in/images/resource/aadhaar_registered_devices_2_0_09112016.pdf
50. UIDAI: Request for Empanelment of Enrolment Agencies. Empanelment of Enrolling Agencies, MeitY, New Delhi, India (2017). https://uidai.gov.in/images/RFE_SEPT_Final_11092017.pdf
51. UIDAI: List of Live Authentication User Agencies (AUAs), August 2018. https://uidai.gov.in/images/list_of_live_aua.pdf

52. UIDAI: List of Live KUAs, August 2018. https://uidai.gov.in/images/list_of_live_kua.pdf

53. UIDAI: Setting up and Managing an Enrolment Centre (2018). https://www.nictcsc.com/images/AadhaarProjectTrainingModule/EnglishTrainingModule/module_3a_settingup_managing_enrolment_centre17122012.pdf

54. UIDAI: Aadhaar Authentication API Specification - Version 2.5 (2019). https://uidai.gov.in/images/resource/aadhaar_authentication_api_2_5.pdf

55. UIDAI: Aadhaar Authentication Service Questions at Lok Sabha (Unstarred 2600) (2019). https://uidai.gov.in/images/loksabha/LSPQ_2600_Unstarred.pdf

56. UIDAI: List of Live Authentication Service Agencies (ASAs) (2019). https://uidai.gov.in/images/list_of_live_asa.pdf

57. UIDAI: Authentication Requesting Agency (Live). https://uidai.gov.in/ecosystem/authentication-ecosystem/authentication-requesting-agency.html

58. UIDAI: Operation Model (Live). https://uidai.gov.in/ecosystem/authentication-ecosystem/operation-model.html

59. UIDAI: Aadhaar FAQ (Live web page). https://www.uidai.gov.in/298-faqs/enrolment-update/enrolment-partners-ecosystem-partners/2014-what-are-the-fifteen-commandments-that-an-operator-must-remember.-during-resident-enrolment.html

60. UIDAI: Enrolment Agencies (Live web page). https://uidai.gov.in/ecosystem/enrolment-ecosystem/enrolment-agencies.html

61. UIDAI: Registrars - Enrolment Ecosystem (Live web page). https://uidai.gov.in/ecosystem/enrolment-ecosystem/registrars.html

62. UIDAI: Roles and Responsibilities of Verifier and Introducer (Live web page). https://www.uidai.gov.in/images/training_nov_17/Roles_Responsibility_Verifier_Introducer_05122017.pdf

63. UIDAI: Vision & Mission (Live web page). https://uidai.gov.in/about-uidai/unique-identification-authority-of-india/vision-mission.html

64. UIDAI and MeitY: Circular No. 1 of 2018: Enhancing Privacy of Aadhaar holders - Implementation of Virtual ID, UID Token and Limited KYC (2018). https://uidai.gov.in/images/resource/UIDAI_Circular_11012018.pdf

65. UIDAI and MeitY: Training, Testing and Certification (2019). https://uidai.gov.in/aadhaar-eco-system/training-testing-certification-ecosystem.html

66. UIDAI, IDBI Bank: Memorandum of Understanding - UIDAI and IDBI Bank (2011). https://uidai.gov.in/images/mou/partners/mou_idbi.pdf

67. Wayman, J., Jain, A.K., Maltoni, D., Maio, D.: Biometric Systems: Technology, Design and Performance Evaluation. Springer, London (2005)

68. Wilson, R.J., Zhang, C.Y., Lam, W., Desfontaines, D., Simmons-Marengo, D., Gipson, B.: Differentially private SQL with bounded user contribution. Proc. Priv. Enh. Technol. (2020)

Short Paper: What Peer Announcements Tell Us About the Size of the Bitcoin P2P Network

Matthias Grundmann[(⊠)] [iD], Hedwig Amberg, Max Baumstark,
and Hannes Hartenstein [iD]

KASTEL Security Research Labs, Karlsruhe Institute of Technology (KIT),
Karlsruhe, Germany
{matthias.grundmann,hannes.hartenstein}@kit.edu

Abstract. Bitcoin is based on a P2P network of which only a few quantities are publicly known. While the number of peers that disseminate transactions and blocks is relevant for the robustness of the network, only the number of reachable peers is so far being measured. However, there exists an unknown number of unreachable peers in the network, that is, peers that do not accept incoming connections but typically also disseminate transactions and blocks. We propose the Passive Announcement Listening (PAL) method that gives an estimate of the number of unreachable peers by observing peer announcements in ADDR messages. We use the PAL method to analyze data from a long-term measurement of the Bitcoin P2P network from 2015 to 2022. The PAL estimate shows that since 2018 the number of unreachable peers is at least three times higher than the number of reachable peers. An empirical validation indicates that about 76% of all unreachable peers announce their address and the PAL approach finds about 94% of these unreachable peers. Thus, we estimate the total number of unreachable peers in May 2022 to be around 34,000. We also report on a spam wave of ADDR messages that shows that peer announcements 'leak' even more information than the size of the network.

1 Introduction

Bitcoin [17] is based on a peer-to-peer (P2P) network that is used to disseminate transactions and blocks of the blockchain. For reasons of robustness, the P2P network should disseminate blocks quickly and transactions efficiently [8]. As the number of peers in the network influences the dissemination of transactions and blocks [22], the number of peers needs to be known to understand the P2P network and to build realistic models used for the development and evaluation of protocol mechanisms. By design, the Bitcoin protocol does not implement a method to collect such quantities about the P2P network and, thus, these quantities can only be estimated or inferred from observations. In 2014 and 2015, some methods to infer the topology of the P2P network based on Bitcoin Core's handling of peer announcements were discussed [1,13,16]. However, these methods showed a high complexity or were impeded by subsequent updates in

© International Financial Cryptography Association 2022
I. Eyal and J. Garay (Eds.): FC 2022, LNCS 13411, pp. 694–704, 2022.
https://doi.org/10.1007/978-3-031-18283-9_35

the implementation of Bitcoin Core. In this paper, we present a novel approach based on observations of peer announcements to estimate the number of peers that disseminate transactions and blocks.

To form the P2P network, each peer creates outgoing connections to other peers. Not every peer, however, is able or willing to accept incoming connections, either because a peer is behind a NAT or a firewall or because of a deliberate policy choice. Thus, peers can be categorized into reachable peers that accept incoming connections and unreachable peers that do not accept incoming connections [4]. Categorizing peers into reachable and unreachable peers is not trivial because reachability depends on the vantage point. A first approach might be to define a peer as unreachable if all other peers cannot initiate a connection to that peer. However, a peer might accept incoming connections from one group of peers but refuse incoming connections from other peers. Thus, one could use the following definition: A peer p is called unreachable if the majority of other peers cannot initiate a connection to p. While this definition clarifies the set of unreachable peers, one cannot practically measure it. Thus, we will follow a 'relativistic' approach for our measurements by categorizing peers based on our given vantage point. In [9], we further discuss the challenges of defining unreachability.

The number of unreachable peers that disseminate transactions and blocks (*disseminating peers*) is relevant for the robustness of the P2P network on the one hand because unreachable disseminating peers support dissemination just as reachable peers but are harder to attack precisely because they are unreachable, and on the other hand because anomalies in the number of unreachable peers can indicate attacks on the P2P network. Some projects [6,25] continuously measure the number of reachable peers. However, unreachable peers are harder to detect because one cannot connect to them. One way to get an estimate of the number of unreachable peers is to observe a fraction of unreachable peers and extrapolate the whole number of unreachable peers, e.g., by running a reachable peer that accepts connections from unreachable peers (see [24]). Another way is to observe effects that are caused by unreachable peers and infer their number from these observations.

In this paper, we follow the latter approach of 'observing effects' and present the Passive Announcement Listening (PAL) method to estimate the number of unreachable peers. This approach relies on observing peer announcements that are propagated by peers in the network. The PAL method uses a passive monitor node that connects to all reachable peers and waits for unsolicited ADDR messages. The rationale behind the PAL method is that if the monitor receives an address in an unsolicited ADDR message, one can conclude – based on how Bitcoin Core propagates peer announcements – that less than ten minutes ago there was a peer at this address. Because peers regularly announce their address, collecting all unsolicitedly sent addresses during one day gives an estimate of the set of peers having existed during this day. By filtering out reachable peers, we obtain an estimate of the set of unreachable peers.

Previous work has estimated the number of unreachable peers to be around 16,000 peers [19], 54,000 peers [18], 90,000 peers [1], and 155,000 peers [24].

The wide range of estimations comes not only from different measuring times and methods but also from the fact that the number of unreachable peers at a certain point in time differs from the number of unreachable peers measured over a time interval. In this work, we consider the problem of estimating the number of unreachable peers during time intervals. Using a model for churn (see [12]), this number can be used to estimate how many unreachable peers existed at a given point in time.

We will give an overview of related work in Sect. 2. In Sect. 3, background on the peer behavior of the most common Bitcoin implementation is provided. Then, in Sect. 4, we present the PAL method and the results of applying the method to data collected from the Bitcoin P2P network. As there is no ground truth available, we validate our approach in Sect. 5 by verifying our assumptions and by comparing the results of our approach to an observation of a fraction of unreachable peers. In Sect. 6 we describe how a recent spam wave of ADDR messages helped to estimate the number of neighbors of reachable peers and to find peers with multiple addresses. We conclude in Sect. 7.

2   Related Work

The number of *reachable* peers has been analyzed by previous research [5, 21] and is continuously measured by different projects [6, 25]. These projects share the basic approach of recursively searching the network for reachable peers. As an example, we explain the approach of Bitnodes [25] which is similar to that of Donet et al. [5] and Park et al. [21]: The software starts with an initial set of peers, connects to each peer and requests addresses from each peer using a GETADDR message. This message is replied to by an ADDR message that contains up to 1,000 entries from the sending peer's database of which some addresses might be outdated and not belong to a peer anymore. On receiving the ADDR message as a reply, the software tries to connect to each of the addresses in the reply and, for each successfully opened connection, addresses are requested over this new connection. The set of peers that a connection has been established to is regarded as the set of reachable peers. In case a connection to an address cannot be established, it is unknown whether there is an unreachable peer at this address or the address is outdated and there is no peer at this address. Consequently, this approach is not capable of measuring the number of unreachable peers.

Only few attempts have been made to estimate the number of *unreachable* peers. In May 2017, Wang and Pustogarov [24] ran 102 reachable peers as probes for seven days and logged all incoming connections and associated information. For each peer that connected to one of the probes, they tested whether it was reachable by trying to open a connection to that peer's address. They observed on average about 10,000 unique unreachable addresses in a six-hour interval and estimate without a detailed explanation that there were at least 155,000 unreachable peers in each six-hour interval. Bitcoin developer Luke-Jr runs a website [15] that lists about 50,000 unreachable peers and 5,500 reachable peers at the time of writing (May 2022). The methodology behind the website is not publicly documented, but, in the absence of other reference points, we also compare our measurements to the numbers obtained from this website. The role of unreachable peers in the Bitcoin P2P network has only been studied to a very limited degree. Franzoni and Daza [7] recently showed how the robustness and efficiency of the P2P network can be improved by giving unreachable peers a special role in the dissemination of transactions.

3   Background on Bitcoin Peers

We refer to an implementation of a client for the Bitcoin protocol as Bitcoin software. We define a *peer* as a running instance of a Bitcoin software that is connected to at least one other running instance of a Bitcoin software. We expect most peers to be connected to multiple peers in order to reduce chances of being eclipsed [11]. A Bitcoin P2P network consists of peers that are directly or indirectly connected to each other. In this paper, we consider only peers in the Bitcoin P2P network that is referred to as the "Bitcoin mainnet" [3].

Peers are identified by their addresses. A peer can have multiple addresses (in the most common case an IPv4 address and an IPv6 address) and multiple peers can share an address (e.g., an IPv4 address because they are behind the same NAT). We will make the simplifying assumption that each peer has exactly one address. If we simply use the term address, then it refers to any type of address being used in the Bitcoin protocol, e.g., IPv4, IPv6, or Tor address (see [14]).

In the following, we describe the protocol for peers in the Bitcoin P2P network [2] and the behavior of Bitcoin Core, the software that is run by the majority of peers [25]. Peers need to know the addresses of other peers to be able to connect to them. To this end, addresses are exchanged between peers using ADDR messages that contain between one and 1,000 entries. Each entry consists of an address, a port, a timestamp, and service flags. The service flags describe the services offered and extensions implemented by the peer running at the address. A peer unsolicitedly sends a *self announcement* of its address to a connected peer once a connection has been established and then on average every 24 h. The self announcement contains the announcing peer's service flags and the timestamp of the self announcement is set to the time of sending. If the announced address is routable, i.e. not from an IP address range that is reserved for private use, and the service flags contained in the self announcement include certain required flags (the NODE_WITNESS flag and the NODE_NETWORK or NODE_NETWORK_LIMITED flag), then the address is propagated in the network together with the associated timestamp and service flags until the timestamp is older than ten minutes. In Bitcoin Core, the sending of ADDR messages per connection is limited to two messages per minute (on average), and addresses received in multiple incoming ADDR messages might be batched in one outgoing ADDR message. If an incoming ADDR message contains ten or fewer entries, Bitcoin Core considers the addresses in the ADDR message as a batch of self announcements originally sent unsolicitedly and, therefore, for propagation. In the remainder of this paper, we only consider such unsolicited ADDR messages that contain up to ten entries.

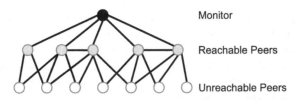

Fig. 1. Setup overview. The monitor node that collects the data for the PAL method is connected to all reachable peers but not to unreachable peers.

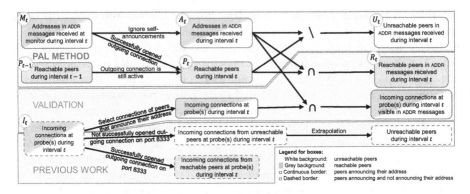

Fig. 2. Data flow of the PAL method, validation, and previous work [24]. The sets M_t and I_t are collected during measurements and the arrows show filters and operations to derive more specific sets during the analysis. The border of each box indicates whether the respective set contains only peers that set the flags required for address propagation or also those peers that do not set these flags. The background colors indicate whether the respective sets contain reachable and/or unreachable peers. (Color figure online)

4   PAL Method and Results

In this section, we present the PAL method's setup for data collection, the methodology for analyzing the data and the resulting findings.

Data Collection. The monitor node [20] connects to all known reachable peers in the network (see Fig. 1) and does not send any ADDR messages. The only messages the monitor sends are VERSION messages during connection establishment and GETADDR messages. The solicited ADDR messages that are received in reply to GETADDR messages are ignored for the PAL method but are used to learn about reachable peers. The monitor tries to connect to each received address (rate-limited per address to once every six hours). The monitor logs all received ADDR messages, VERSION messages and the time when a connection to another peer is established or closed.

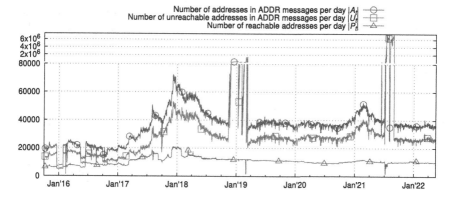

Fig. 3. Number of addresses observed in ADDR messages compared to reachable addresses per day. Note that the upper part uses a different scale than the lower part.

Data Analysis. We analyze the logs created by the monitor to learn the number of peers in the network. This process is depicted in the upper part of Fig. 2. For each day t, we collect all unsolicited addresses that were received by the monitor (M_t in Fig. 2). We define the set A_t by ignoring the self announcements of (reachable) peers, i.e. entries of an ADDR message that equal the address of the sender of this ADDR message. The set A_t includes addresses of reachable and unreachable peers that were announced on day t. To determine the set P_t of all addresses that the monitor node was connected to on day t, we collect all addresses that the monitor already was connected to at the beginning of day t or a connection was established and a VERSION message received during day t. We consider this set P_t as the set of all reachable peers at day t. Our estimate of the set of unreachable peers U_t for day t is $U_t = A_t \setminus P_t$.

Limitations. The PAL method cannot distinguish whether an unreachable peer existed only for a short moment on a day or the whole day. Also, the addresses and associated information in ADDR messages are not authenticated. Therefore, the approach can be disturbed by flooding the network with bogus addresses.

Measurements. We applied the method to data collected from 2015 to 2022 by a monitor node hosted in the network of KIT (AS 34878). Figure 3 shows $|A_t|$, the number of addresses received in ADDR messages for each day t and the number $|U_t|$ of addresses that were unreachable. In each set, an address is counted only once if it is received multiple times during t. On the majority of days in the observation range, between 20,000 and 60,000 addresses were received in ADDR messages. Most noticeably, the plot shows a high number of addresses at the end of 2018 and in July 2021 which we will discuss later. The remaining plot shows that the number of addresses varied over the years and had local maxima in December 2017 (72,000 addresses) and in February 2021 (51,000 addresses). The number of unreachable peers $|U_t|$ is on average about 73% of the number of all addresses $|A_t|$. In May 2022, the number of unreachable peers $|U_t|$ equals about 26,000 peers. A comparison with the number of reachable peers $|P_t|$ shows that since 2018 the number of unreachable peers in ADDR messages was about three times the number of reachable peers and had a similar development.

The peak at the end of the year 2018 seems like many unreachable peers joined the network within a few days. An alternative explanation would be that bogus addresses were distributed that do not actually belong to peers. We examined the addresses that were received only during this time and did not find any irregularities with regard to their distribution in the IP address space, autonomous system, or country of autonomous system. However, for the highest peak in March 2019, we found that this peak was caused by many IP addresses from the same /8 subnet. As IP addresses from this subnet were only very rarely observed before and after March 2019, we assume that this effect was caused by unknown actions of one party that flooded the network with these IP addresses. Examples of such actions might be the explanations we find for the recent peak in July and August 2021 that we discuss in Sect. 6.

5   Validation

Reachable Peers. Validating the PAL method is difficult because we do not have a reliable ground-truth to compare our results to. However, while the goal of the PAL method is to find unreachable peers, it can also be used to find reachable peers. As we know the set of reachable peers quite accurately, we can validate whether reachable peers can be found in ADDR messages during each day. Putting this into the context of Fig. 2, this means that, if the PAL method works perfectly, we expect that set R_t equals set P_t. We evaluate this for the data collected during the year 2020 and find that on average 95.4% of the addresses of reachable peers on a day were received in an ADDR message on the same day (excluding self-announcements). Increasing the length of the interval t from one day to five days increases the share of observed reachable peers to 96.1% while with an interval length of one hour only on average 84.9% of the addresses of reachable peers were received in an ADDR message in the same hour. This indicates that reachable peers are consistently found by the PAL method and that the interval length of one day is a reasonable trade-off.

Unreachable Peer. To validate our assumption that an unreachable peer is being found by the PAL method, we permanently ran an unreachable peer from December 2020 to June 2021. The monitor received the unreachable peer's address on 200 of 212 days which means that on each day the probability for the peer to be detected was 94%.

Second Monitor. For further validation with another vantage point, we have run a second monitor node since 2019. The second monitor node is set up as described above for the first monitor node but runs in a different location and a different autonomous system. If the measurement method is reproducible, the addresses received by the two monitor nodes should largely overlap. We analyzed the addresses received by both monitors since 2019 and find that 96% of the addresses overlap. This indicates that the measurement is reproducible and that the view of our monitor node is not subjective to the specific instance of the monitor.

Validation with Incoming Connections. The approach of Wang and Pustogarov [24] is to run many reachable peers and wait for unreachable peers to connect to them. This approach can only find a fraction of unreachable peers and it is unclear how to reliably extrapolate from this fraction to the whole network. However, the approach can collect reliable information about the observed fraction of unreachable peers because they are directly connected. For further validation, we use a similar approach and run two additional peers p_I and p_R that accept incoming connections. After running these peers for two years, we find that 24.1% of the unreachable peers that connected to p_I and p_R did not announce their address. We conjecture that these are peers that are explicitly configured to be unreachable and, thus, do not announce their address and are not detectable by the PAL method. To quantify how well the detectable unreachable peers are found by the PAL method, we consider for our validation only unreachable peers seen by p_I and p_R that announced their address to p_I or p_R. We find that the PAL method detected on average 94% of peers that connected to p_I or p_R and announced their address. We conclude that peers that announce their address are detected by the PAL method with high probability.

Comparison to Previous Measurements. There is no ground truth that we could compare the PAL method's results to but we can compare it to previous estimations and measurements. Neudecker et al. [19] simulated the Bitcoin P2P network in 2016 and estimated from the simulated propagation behavior that the P2P network had about 16,000 unreachable disseminating peers. The PAL method calculates about 14,000 unreachable peers per day averaged over the year 2016. As the results of Neudecker et al. are for one point in time and the PAL method estimates the number of unreachable peers during one day, we would rather expect that the PAL method would find *more* unreachable peers. The lower number of unreachable peers detected by the PAL method might be caused by peers not announcing their address.

A measurement of unreachable peers was conducted by Wang and Pustogarov [24] in 2017 (see Sect. 2). Based on their observation of a fraction of unreachable peers, they estimated at least 155,000 unreachable peers to be active in each six-hour interval. They report that 93.9% of all connections lasted shorter than one minute and 80% of unreachable peers were mobile peers. We assume that these peers either did not announce their addresses or that they did not provide services required for address propagation. In this case, they would be invisible to the PAL method which explains why the estimate by Wang and Pustogarov is higher than the results obtained through the PAL method.

The measurement by Luke-Jr [15] gives an estimate of the number of reachable and unreachable peers over a time span similar to our measurements. The number of unreachable peers in the data from Luke-Jr is higher compared to the estimation using the PAL method. This is probably accounted for again by the fact that not all unreachable peers announce their address.

6 Observation of ADDR Spam in July and August 2021

The number of unique addresses in ADDR messages increased significantly in July 2021 (see Fig. 3) from about 40,000 unique addresses per day to about 6,000,000 unique addresses per day. This increase was caused by an unknown party sending many spam addresses into the Bitcoin P2P network. Observations of the propagation of the spam addresses show that more than the number of unreachable peers can be learned from observing peer announcements (see [10]): We analyzed the behavior of the spamming peers and found that our observations of the propagated spam addresses could be used to estimate the node degree (number of neighbors) of reachable peers based on an idea that dates back to 2014 [1, Section 10.1]. Further, we found that the observed propagation of spam addresses could be used to map multiple addresses to the same reachable peers when the same spam addresses are forwarded to our monitors from different IP addresses. In August 2021, our monitor nodes were connected to 8,647 reachable addresses per day on average. From the obtained mapping from addresses to actual peers, we infer that the monitor nodes were connected to only 7,518 peers per day on average. This shows that estimating the number of reachable peers by counting reachable addresses overestimates their number by 15% [10].

7 Conclusion

Unreachable peers contribute to the Bitcoin P2P network by disseminating blocks and transactions, but are inherently hard to detect and count. We have presented the PAL method that analyzes peer announcements to estimate the number of unreachable peers. Our observed number of unreachable peers in May 2022 is about 26,000 peers which, as indicated by our validation, might correspond to about 76% of all unreachable peers. We estimate by extrapolation that there could actually be about 34,000 unreachable peers which corresponds to three to four times the number of reachable peers. In contrast to the costly approach of running many reachable peers to find unreachable peers, the PAL method is deployable as a continuously running project. We will continue to monitor and publish the updated data and results [6].

Acknowledgements. The authors would like to thank Till Neudecker and the anonymous reviewers for their feedback. The authors acknowledge support by the State of Baden-Württemberg through bwHPC. This work was supported by funding from the topic Engineering Secure Systems of the Helmholtz Association (HGF) and by KASTEL Security Research Labs.

References

1. Biryukov, A., Khovratovich, D., Pustogarov, I.: Deanonymisation of Clients in Bitcoin P2P Network. In: Proceedings of the 2014 ACM SIGSAC Conference on Computer and Communications Security, pp. 15–29. CCS 2014, Association for Computing Machinery, New York, NY, USA, November 2014. https://doi.org/10.1145/2660267.2660379

2. Bitcoin-Developers: Bitcoin Reference (2019). https://developer.bitcoin.org/reference/index.html

3. Bitcoin-Developers: Bitcoin Glossary (2020). https://developer.bitcoin.org/glossary.html

4. Delgado-Segura, S., Pérez-Solà, C., Herrera-Joancomartí, J., Navarro-Arribas, G., Borrell, J.: Cryptocurrency Networks: A New P2P Paradigm. Mob. Inf. Syst. **2018**(3), 1–16 (2018). https://doi.org/10.1155/2018/2159082

5. Donet Donet, J.A., Pérez-Solà, C., Herrera-Joancomartí, J.: The Bitcoin P2P network. In: Böhme, R., Brenner, M., Moore, T., Smith, M. (eds.) FC 2014. LNCS, vol. 8438, pp. 87–102. Springer, Heidelberg (2014). https://doi.org/10.1007/978-3-662-44774-1_7

6. DSN: Bitcoin Network Monitoring (2021). https://dsn.kastel.kit.edu/bitcoin/

7. Franzoni, F., Daza, V.: Improving Bitcoin Transaction Propagation by Leveraging Unreachable Nodes. In: 2020 IEEE International Conference on Blockchain (Blockchain), pp. 196–203 (2020). https://doi.org/10.1109/Blockchain50366.2020.00031

8. Garay, J., Kiayias, A., Leonardos, N.: The Bitcoin backbone protocol: analysis and applications. In: Oswald, E., Fischlin, M. (eds.) EUROCRYPT 2015. LNCS, vol. 9057, pp. 281–310. Springer, Heidelberg (2015). https://doi.org/10.1007/978-3-662-46803-6_10

9. Grundmann, M., Amberg, H., Hartenstein, H.: On the estimation of the number of unreachable peers in the Bitcoin P2P network by observation of peer announcements. arXiv preprint arXiv:2102.12774 (2021)

10. Grundmann, M., Baumstark, M., Hartenstein, H.: On the peer degree distribution of the Bitcoin P2P network. In: 2022 IEEE International Conference on Blockchain and Cryptocurrency (ICBC), pp. 1–5 (2022). https://doi.org/10.1109/ICBC54727.2022.9805511

11. Heilman, E., Kendler, A., Zohar, A., Goldberg, S.: Eclipse attacks on Bitcoin's peer-to-peer network. In: Proceedings of the 24th USENIX Conference on Security Symposium, pp. 129–144. SEC2015, USENIX Association, USA (2015)

12. Imtiaz, M.A., Starobinski, D., Trachtenberg, A., Younis, N.: Churn in the Bitcoin Network. IEEE Trans. Netw. Serv. Manage. **18**(2), 1598–1615 (2021). https://doi.org/10.1109/TNSM.2021.3050428

13. Nick, J.: Guessing Bitcoin's P2P Connections (2015). https://jonasnick.github.io/blog/2015/03/06/guessing-bitcoins-p2p-connections/

14. van der Laan, W.J.: BIP 155: addrv2 message (2019). https://github.com/bitcoin/bips/blob/master/bip-0155.mediawiki

15. Luke-Jr: Bitcoin Node Count History (2021). https://luke.dashjr.org/programs/bitcoin/files/charts/historical.html

16. Miller, A., et al.: Discovering Bitcoin's Public Topology and Influential Nodes (2015)

17. Nakamoto, S.: Bitcoin: A Peer-to-Peer Electronic Cash System. Tech. rep. (2008)

18. Naumenko, G., Maxwell, G., Wuille, P., Fedorova, A., Beschastnikh, I.: Erlay: efficient transaction relay for Bitcoin. In: Proceedings of the 2019 ACM SIGSAC Conference on Computer and Communications Security - CCS 2019, pp. 817–831. ACM Press, London, United Kingdom (2019). https://doi.org/10.1145/3319535.3354237
19. Neudecker, T., Andelfinger, P., Hartenstein, H.: Timing Analysis for Inferring the Topology of the Bitcoin Peer-to-Peer Network. In: Proceedings of the 13th IEEE International Conference on Advanced and Trusted Computing, pp. 358–367 (2016). https://doi.org/10.1109/UIC-ATC-ScalCom-CBDCom-IoP-SmartWorld.2016.0070
20. Neudecker, T.: Characterization of the Bitcoin Peer-to-Peer Network (2015–2018) (2019). https://doi.org/10.5445/IR/1000091933
21. Park, S., Im, S., Seol, Y., Paek, J.: Nodes in the Bitcoin network: comparative measurement study and survey. IEEE Access **7**, 57009–57022 (2019). https://doi.org/10.1109/ACCESS.2019.2914098
22. Shahsavari, Y., Zhang, K., Talhi, C.: A theoretical model for block propagation analysis in Bitcoin network. IEEE Trans. Eng. Manage. **PP**(99), 1–18 (2020). https://doi.org/10.1109/TEM.2020.2989170
23. Tange, O.: GNU Parallel 20200522 ('Kraftwerk') (2020). https://doi.org/10.5281/zenodo.3841377
24. Wang, L., Pustogarov, I.: Towards Better Understanding of Bitcoin Unreachable Peers. arXiv preprint arXiv:1709.06837 (2017)
25. Yeow, A.: Bitnodes (2021). https://bitnodes.io

An Empirical Study of Two Bitcoin Artifacts Through Deep Learning

Richard Tindell, Alex Mitchell, Nathan Sprague, and Xunhua Wang[✉]

James Madison University, Harrisonburg, VA 22807, USA
{tindelrj,mitch5aj}@dukes.jmu.edu, {spragunr,wangxx}@jmu.edu

Abstract. Human artifacts like technical papers and computer programs often carry the individual styles of their creators. If retrieved properly, such style information from the artifacts can be used to categorize the artifacts, compare the relative "similarities" among artifacts, and may even be used for tracing the authorship of a new artifact.

Bitcoin is a peer-to-peer cryptocurrency and its author(s) goes/go by the pseudonym of Satoshi Nakamoto. In this article, we use deep learning to study the styles of two Bitcoin artifacts: the first version of Bitcoin's source code, v0.1.0, which was released in early 2009, and the original Bitcoin white paper, which is dated Oct. 2008. Both studies use the deep learning technique, which first utilizes extensive computing power to generate a neural network model from labelled training data and then uses the model to predict the authorship of unknown data. For the Bitcoin source code artifact, the data set is a set of cryptography software that were built around 2008/2009 and it has 16 known labels. Our model achieves 89.1% validation accuracy and our prediction results show that the Bitcoin source code is likely produced by multiple authors and Hal Finney is *not* one of them. For the Bitcoin white paper, we compiled a second data set of financial cryptography papers that are in the same knowledge domain. This data set has 436 known labels. Our model achieves 55.1% validation accuracy and it has identified four technical papers that are "similar" to the Bitcoin white paper.

Keywords: Financial cryptography · Bitcoin · Deep learning · Anonymity · Authorship attribution · Code stylometry

1 Introduction

Bitcoin is a peer-to-peer cryptography currency that does *not* require a trusted central bank to create digital money or detect counterfeit & double-spending. Unlike various digital currencies before it, Bitcoin gained wide public acceptance quickly, has sustained several waves of rise and fall, and will likely stay active in the foreseeable future. Bitcoin's design was published as a white paper, under the name of Satoshi Nakamoto, in Oct. 2008 at a web site [31] and Satoshi Nakamoto is obviously a pseudonym. Bitcoin's initial implementation, version *0.1.0*, was released, also under the name of Satoshi Nakamoto, in Jan. 2009 and

© International Financial Cryptography Association 2022
I. Eyal and J. Garay (Eds.): FC 2022, LNCS 13411, pp. 705–724, 2022.
https://doi.org/10.1007/978-3-031-18283-9_36

it includes both a binary executable and some source code files in C++. Satoshi Nakamoto communicated with the outside world in email and posted to technical forums, but often took caution to use non-identity-revealing pseudonyms, for example with email addresses like *satoshi@vistomail.com* and *satoshin@gmx.com* and online pseudonyms like *satoshi* at bitcointalk.org. (It remains a question whether these "satoshi" are the same person(s); there are claims that Satoshi's email accounts and social media accounts have been hacked.)

Naturally, the true identity of Satoshi has aroused much public interests. In March 2014, Newsweek published an investigative report [19], claiming that Satoshi Nakamoto is Dorian Nakamoto, a Californian who subsequently vehemently denied the claim. So did Satoshi in an anonymous post after the Newsweek publication [32]. On 2 May 2016, the BBC and The Economist published an article [40], in which Craig Wright, an Australian, self-revealed to be Satoshi Nakamoto. As a companion proof [43], Wright provided a digital signature on a message which can be verified by a public key that Satoshi has left in the public block chain. Since only Satoshi has his/her/their private key, only Satoshi is capable of generating a digital signature on a new message. However, later, it has been revealed that the digitally signed message that Wright provided can be extracted from an existing Bitcoin transaction in the public block chain and thus cannot be used to prove the identity of Satoshi [25]. In April 2019, Wright successfully registered US copyright in both the Bitcoin white paper [31] and the code for Bitcoin 0.1, to which the US Copyright Office further clarified that "In a case in which a work is registered under a pseudonym, the Copyright Office does not investigate whether there is a provable connection between the claimant and the pseudonymous author" [41].

This leads to the following questions: Is Wright really Satoshi Nakamoto? Can the author(s) of Bitcoin be traced at all, since there are claims that Satoshi's email accounts were hacked and so were likely Satoshi's social media accounts? Can we find out who Satoshi is purely through the public traces, such as the white paper and the Bitcoin computer programs, left by Satoshi?[1] Can we mine these artifacts to answer the above questions? In addition to the above claims on Satoshi Nakamoto, there have been some other speculations on Bitcoin's authorship. For example, Hal Finney, a cryptography engineer who exchanged public discussions with Satoshi in the early stage of Bitcoin, is considered by many as Satoshi Nakamoto [37]. Is this claim accurate?

Deep learning [1,9,21,26] in recent years has seen big success in multiple applications such as computer vision, speech recognition, auto-piloting, and fraud detection in credit card transactions. Multiple open-source deep learning tools, including scikit-learn, Keras, PyTorch, and TensorFlow, are available. Can these tools be applied to Satoshi's artifacts for authorship tracing?

The Bitcoin white paper is written in English, a natural language. English word-based deep learning has seen wide application and has also been used, in

---

[1] A public web site called the Satoshi Nakamoto Institute [29] has archived the email messages from Satoshi, posts to public forums claimed from Satoshi, and the earlier versions of the Bitcoin software.

a couple of earlier efforts, for tracing the author(s) of the Bitcoin white paper; more on this later in Sect. 2.2. The Bitcoin computer program source code, on the other hand, is written in C++ (a formal programming language), has its peculiar characteristics, and needs its own treatment in data mining. There have been multiple studies on source-code-based authorship attribution over a controlled data set [2,7] (more on this later in Sect. 2.1 and Sect. 6) and to our best knowledge, this study is the first reported result on using language-agnostic deep learning on Bitcoin source code with a real-world data set.

In this application-driven research, we explored using existing deep learning techniques for Bitcoin authorship attribution in two ways. Our first attribution is based on the Bitcoin v0.1.0 source code. As a cryptocurrency, the Bitcoin v0.1.0 implementation heavily depends on cryptographic techniques and it uses the OpenSSL library v0.9.8h. It is not unreasonable to assume the Bitcoin developer might be among the developers of the cryptographic libraries. We started by building a source code data set of cryptographic libraries with preselected known authors. To avoid the potential trap of evolving coding style, care was taken to use those cryptographic libraries that were developed at roughly the same time as Bitcoin v0.1.0. For those authors with too few source code samples, mutants were generated so that the data set is balanced for deep learning. We next used this data set to train a neural network. From this trained model authorship predictions for the Bitcoin source code were made. This data set does include code from Hal Finney but not code from Craig Wright, due to its unavailability. Our results show that contrary to one popular belief [37], the relative similarity between Bitcoin code and Finney's code is *not* smaller than other similarities in the data set, showing that Finney is not particularly likely Satoshi. We wish this will settle the Finney argument once and for all. Our results also show that the Bitcoin software 0.1.0 was likely produced by multiple authors, instead of single person.

Our second study followed the Bitcoin technical paper [31], which was first published in Oct. 2008 and then officially in Mar. 2009. This technical paper describes, among other things, the high-level design of Bitcoin, including Bitcoin *transaction, block, proof-of-work*, and *incentives*. These concepts fall well in the domain of financial cryptography. As a result, the author(s) of the Bitcoin technical paper may well be among the authors of the proceedings of the financial cryptography conferences and related papers. To follow this lead, we compiled a second data set of technical papers, with 436 known labels/author-combinations, from several sources, including most papers in financial cryptography 1997 through financial cryptography 2012, and the technical writings of Hal Finney [12–15,17], Wei Dai [11], Adam Back [3], and Craig Wright [43].

We next used this data set to train a neural network model. From this trained model authorship predictions for the Bitcoin technical paper were made. Our results show that the Bitcoin white paper has styles "similar" to four papers.

The remainder of this article is organized as follows. In Sect. 2, we review priori work related to this research. Section 3 gives a high-level description of our research approach. In Sect. 4, we present the details of our study on the Bitcoin source code, including the data collection, balancing, the deep learning model, the results, and their interpretation. Similar details for the Bitcoin white paper are given in Sect. 5. In Sect. 6, we further discuss the results and implications of this research. A summary of this research is given in Sect. 7.

2   Related Work

Stylometry aims to find the author(s) of a novel, a poem, a music piece, or a paint, through identifying styles and patterns in them. Previous stylometry examples include the successful identification of the authors for The Federalist Papers [30] and for confirming the collaboration between William Shakespear and Fletcher and Christopher Marlowe [27,28]. Existing techniques for stylometry include *lexical analysis* to count frequencies of terms and words, more complex *statistics* such as Gaussian statistics, and *neural networks*.

2.1   Code Stylometry

Stylometry has also been extended to textual computer programs such as C/C++ source code [2,7,22,35]. It has been observed that just like novelists, painters, and music composers, software developers leave their footprints in source code and this can be used for authorship tracing.

There are two studies with best reported results in this line. Both studies aim for large dataset with thousands of authors and high accuracy. Caliskan-Islam et al. [7] takes a language-dependent approach and it first extracts *layout*, *lexical*, and *abstract syntax tree-based syntactic* features from C/C++ source code. Next, it uses a random forest classifier to de-anonymize C/C++ source code. This research defines 120,000 layout-based, lexical, and syntactic features but only sends a small subset of features to the random forest classifier. On the Google Code Jam (GCJ) dataset with 1600 programmers, this approach reports 92.83% accuracy. Among the 928 important features identified in [7], 1% are layout (i.e. *shallow*, human-friendly) features, 55% are lexical (i.e. *intermediate-level*) features, and 44% are syntactic (i.e. *deep*, more machine-oriented) features.

Abuhamad et al. [2] takes a language-agnostic approach and uses deep learning based on multiple recurrent natural networks (RNN) layers to extract machine-oriented, statistical features. Next, it sends these features to a random forest classifier for authorship attribution. Like [7], Abuhamad et al. [2] uses the Google Code Jam dataset with 1600 authors, with seven files per author, and reports an accuracy of 96%. Abuhamad et al. [2] also tests their approach on chosen real-world code samples from 1987 public repositories on GitHub, with 745 C programmers and 10 samples per author; this research reports 94.38% accuracy.

Both studies report results on the GCJ controlled data set, which may be very different from real-world data sets; see Sect. 6 for more details on this. Also, the aforementioned code stylometry techniques work on normal computer code by general programmers, who when writing code typically do not take measures to hide their identities. This can be considered as a *benign* situation for source code authorship attribution.

However, in some situations, a software developer may deliberately take measures to hide their identities, for example, with pseudonyms, no identity-revealing comments, or no comments at all. Such examples include TrueCrypt and Bitcoin. Even worse, a computer program may be developed to transform source code in a semantics-preserving manner to defeat authorship attribution [38]. Quiring et al. [38] considers an adversary who has a black-box access to the machine learning-based attribution method. In this powerful attack, the adversary does not know the training data or the algorithm of the attribution method but it can send any source code to the attribution method and get both the prediction result and the corresponding prediction score back. Under this attack, Quiring et al. [38] shows that a Monte-Carlo tree-based computer program can be developed to effectively defeat the authorship attribution methods of both [7] and [2], two of the best authorship attribution studies.

It is our belief that the Bitcoin authorship attribution problem does *not* completely fall within this worst-case scenario and is more likely somewhere between the benign case and the worst-case scenario. Both the Bitcoin software v0.1.0 and the technical paper [31] were developed, in 2008/2009, before deep-learning became popular [26].

2.2 Text-Based Bitcoin Authorship Attribution

There has never been lack of interest in tracing the Bitcoin author(s). In addition to the events in Sect. 1, earlier efforts in tracing the authorship of the Bitcoin white paper include [4–6, 10, 23, 24, 39, 42].

Chon [10] built a data set of 27 technical papers by 5 known authors and used support vector machine, random forest, and Gaussian Naive Bayes to trace the author(s) of the Bitcoin white paper. Hubbs [24] compiled a data set of writings, including blogs, papers, and published articles, by 7 known authors and used multiple classifiers to trace the author(s) of the Bitcoin white paper. Ramesh and Watson [39] built a data set of write-ups by 7 known authors and used bidirectional LSTM to trace the author(s) of the Bitcoin white paper.

In a different line, Grey [23] studied and compared the human-friendly linguistic features, instead of machine-oriented features, in the Bitcoin white paper and Nick Szabo's writing. Also in this line is a study by Watson [42], which uses a computer program to perform unique word analysis on the Bitcoin white paper and potential candidates' write-ups.

Our work in Sect. 5 belongs to the camp of machine learning and uses a much bigger data set, with 436 known labels, of more structured and formal texts extracted from peer-reviewed articles.

3 Deep Learning for Bitcoin Artifacts

Both the Bitcoin software v0.1.0 source code and the Bitcoin technical paper, after text extraction from the PDF file, can be considered as *text*, defined as a sequence of *characters* or mostly English *words*. Text has been processed and classified by neural network-based deep learning very well with recurrent neural network (RNN), such as the Long Short-Term Memory (LSTM) and Gated Recurrent Units (GRU), and one-dimensional convolutional neural networks (1D convnets) [9, chap 6]. Deep learning works by first training a neural network model with large amount of known raw data, without much human intervention, and then using the model for prediction for unknown raw data. Deep learning techniques are good at taking raw data/text and automatically producing discriminating statistical features for classification.

In this research, we will apply existing deep learning techniques to both Bitcoin artifacts for their authorship tracing. The texts in those two Bitcoin artifacts are in different subcategories. The source code in the Bitcoin software v0.1.0 was written in C++. Typical C++ source code files contain the code itself, as character strings, and some companion comments, both of which may contain information for authorship tracing. The source code files may also contain additional *lexical and layout features* that could be informational for authorship identification [7]. Example lexical features include the keyword length, comment length, token length, and line length; example layout features include tab length, space length, and empty length.

In contrast, the Bitcoin white paper is a PDF file generated by *PDF-XChange (PDFTools4.exe v4.0.0201.0000)*. Due to the PDF generation process, lexical and layout information in the original source document could have been lost in the PDF file. As a result, the most personal identifiable information in the Bitcoin white paper PDF file probably lies in its content as words.

To study the two Bitcoin artifacts with deep learning, we will need to build a data set for each first. From a data set, a neural network may retrieve multiple types of *discriminators* for classification, including the direct content of the data, such as programming language keywords or English words, and the styles of the authors in the data set. *Not* all such classification discriminators are appropriate for authorship attribution. For example, two technical papers, one about Bitcoin by Alice (called label A) and the other not about Bitcoin by Bob (called label B), can be used to train a neural network. The Bitcoin subject may be chosen by the neural network as a classification discriminator. When a new article of unknown author about Bitcoin is sent to the resulting model for prediction, it may be classified as A but the new article could be written by Bob, hence a wrong authorship attribution. However, when an appropriate data set is used, such as one with items in the same subject category and in sufficient amount, the deep learning-based classifier will discover internal representations that are useful for discriminating between artifacts and these discriminators are more likely about the stylistic similarity of the artifact authors.

In the next two sections, we shall describe how our data sets are chosen, balanced, and processed. Our computer programs to generate neural network models are based on TensorFlow [1] and are written in Python. TensorFlow was chosen over other deep learning libraries in this research for its availability to us and *not* for any particular technical reasons.

4   Source Code Tracing: Tracing the Authorship of Bitcoin V0.1.0

In this section, we shall investigate how to use deep learning techniques to trace the author(s) of the Bitcoin software v0.1.0. We start by building a set of source code libraries with known authors that are the potential developers for Bitcoin v0.1.0. We then develop methods to balance this data set and make sure that each known author has enough *samples*. Next, we use this data set to train a deep learning model and in the end use the trained model for prediction.

4.1   Data Collection

Bitcoin software v0.1.0 was built on the top of several software libraries, including OpenSSL, Berkeley DB, Boost, and wxWidgets. It bases its cryptographic functions, such as *elliptic-curve key pair generation, digital signing, signature verification*, and *cryptographic hashing*, on OpenSSL. Bitcoin v0.1.0 also includes explicit instructions to exclude encryption routines from OpenSSL, as Bitcoin does not use encryption. For elliptic-curve digital signature algorithm (ECDSA) [34], it does not use the default parameters in the ECDSA standard. Instead, it uses the Standards for Efficient Cryptography (SEC) parameter *secp256k1* [8]. For cryptographic hashing, it uses both SHA256 [33] and RIPEMD160.

All these point to the fact that the Bitcoin v0.1.0 developers have significant knowledge in cryptography, might have contributed to public cryptographic libraries, or are in the league of these library developers. For Bitcoin v0.1.0 authorship attribution, we collected a set of public cryptographic libraries developed in C/C++ around the time frame of 2008/2009, the time that Bitcoin v0.1.0 was released, as shown in Table 1.

In Table 1, Hal Finney was chosen because his early involvement in email discussions with Satoshi Nakamoto. Until today, Finney has been believed by many to be Satoshi [37]. However, public code by Finney was not common and the only code, as a single file, attributed to him is found at Github as *bc_key*, which is indeed related to Bitcoin.

Some cryptographic libraries such as OpenSSL and Cryptlib are products of multiple authors. Fortunately, the files in these libraries are well marked with author names and thus separated into different data items in Table 1.

Two libraries, *libgcrypt* and *gnupg*, were developed by the same author Werner Koch. Also, the library NSS was ostensibly developed by multiple authors and deserve attention. The author(s) of the TrueCrypt library deliberately masks their/his/her identities. We tried but failed to find the source code of any computer programs written by Craig Wright.

For these chosen libraries, extra steps have been taken to clean them up for duplicate source code files.

4.2   Data Balancing with Mutants

Figure 6 of the Appendix section gives the total numbers of *.c, .h, .cpp, or .hpp* source files in the *original* libraries of Table 1. These numbers are very

Table 1. A list of existing cryptographic libraries when Bitcoin was first released

Package Name	Author(s)	Chosen version	Release date	Notes
Bitcoin	unknown	0.1.0	Jan. 2009	
bc_key	Hal Finney		Feb. 9, 2011	from Github
CryptoPP	Wei Dai	5.6.0	Mar. 15, 2009	
Cryptlib	Peter Gutmann	3.4.5	Oct. 6, 2010	
	Brian Gladman		≈ Jan. 31, 2006	From cryptlib
OpenSSL	Eric Young	0.9.7m	Feb. 23, 2007	Files are separated in terms of authors
	Stephen Henson			
	Ben Laurie			
	Richard Levitte			
	Geoff Thorpe			
Libgcrypt	Werner Koch	1.4.3	≈ Jan. 22, 2009	
Libmcrypt	Nikos Mavroyanopoulos	2.5.8	Feb. 19, 2007	
Botan	Jack Lloyd	1.8.0	Dec. 08, 2008	
NSS	Group	3.9.2	≈ Apr. 21, 2008	
TrueCrypt	Anonymous, group	6.1	Oct. 31, 2008	
LUKS	Clemens Fruhwirth	1.1.1	Aug. 12, 2008	
Gnupg	Werner Koch	2.0.9	Mar. 26, 2008	

imbalanced. More specifically, *bc_key* by Hal Finney has only one file; within OpenSSL, 4 files were attributed to Ben Laurie, 9 for Richard Levitte, and 9 for Geoff Thorpe. On the other hand, the CryptoPP package has 243 source files (for Wei Dai), Cryptlib has 246 files for Peter Gutmann and 12 files for Brian Gladman, Botan has 586 files (for Jack Lloyd); inside OpenSSL, there are 550 files for Eric Young and 111 files for Stephen Henson.

These files, if not further processed before sending to a machine learning model for training, will inevitably skew the model to be trained toward labels/authors with more files and hence also skew the prediction results. Enforcing a simple threshold (such as 7, as done in [2]) on known authors and dropping those who with smaller files does not work either, as this threshold is likely larger than 1 and thus disqualify labels such as that of *bc_key*, which carries non-trivial weight in Bitcoin source code authorship attribution.

For those known labels/authors with too few samples, one way to overcome the above dilemma is to generate, from the small number of files available, more mutant files that have programming styles very close to the sample files and use the mutant files in model training and validation.

C/C++ .c and .cpp source files may include a section of the *#include* preprocessor directive, a section of the *#define* preprocessor directive for constants and/or macros, some struct definitions, global and static variables, some function declarations, and some function definitions. Not all of these sections appear in a single C/C++ source file. A mutant can be generated by switching the internal order of multiple #include lines/statements, the internal order of multiple functions, or both. When not enough functions or include statements are available, the internal order of constant/macro definitions can be switched. We believe that mutants generated this way are natural and have a programming style very close to the original files, as they have very close layout-based, lexical, and syntactic features.

Care must be used in dealing with conditional compilation directives in C/C++ source files. Conditional compilation directives may group together multiple #include statements, function definitions, or even a block of statements within a function into different compilation cases (for example, for different hardware platforms). Such conditional compilation directives may appear almost everywhere in a source code file. Switching the internal order of multiple #include statements in the same compilation case may be fine but cross-case switching could be problematic, as the resulting code may not compile or function correctly, is unnatural, and thus should be avoided. In our mutant generation, only the multiple #include statements within the innermost conditional compilations and the multiple function definitions within the innermost conditional compilations are permuted to generate mutants.

Often, given a source file, multiple mutants can be generated through statement permutation and they could be just a subset of all possible mutants. As a whole, each such mutant file is a *different* sequence of characters. However, whenever possible, a mutant should have maximal differences from other chosen mutants from the same source file. In this way, even when a mutant is split into multiple segments in model training and validation, the differences among segments will likely be very different, which helps model training and improves the soundness of model validation results.

It is also worth noting that this mutant generation strategy only works for files that have enough information. It is our estimate that the original files for each label in the data set of Table 1 does have enough information and even the single file bc_key.c, which has 17 functions. After mutation generation, each label/author of Table 1 has at least 100 source files.

4.3 Data Preprocessing, Modeling, and Validation

Content-wise, a C/C++ source file comprises of comments, including copyright notice, and the source code. Both comments and source code are a sequence of characters but they differ in one important way: comments are often in a natural language while source code is in a formal language. Comments and pure code, together with the layout and lexical characteristics of the file, could form three relatively independent inputs to a deep learning model.

However, for the data set of Table 1, not all these three inputs have the same significance in training a deep learning model. Through extensive testing, we observed that comments and lexical/layout features play a very small role compared to the source code in deep learning training and validation. As a result, we adopted a model solely on the pure character-based source code, as shown in Fig. 1.

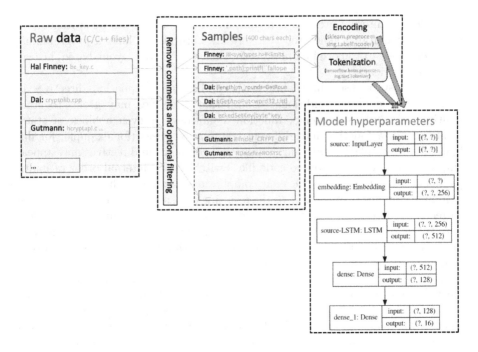

Fig. 1. Deep learning model based on pure source code

In Fig. 1, on the left are the raw data in the format of C/C++ files and they are balanced through mutants, as described in Sect. 4.2, so that each label has at least 100 files. Next, each raw file is preprocessed in a series of steps, first by removing the comment lines, filtering out C/C++ language keywords such as "*break, case, include, public, private, protected, int, long, float,*" and then splitting into smaller *samples* (for example, each with 400 characters). For each label, 1500 *unique* samples are chosen and they are sent to the deep learning model, with 80% of the selected samples are randomly chosen for model training and the rest are used for model validation.

On the right of Fig. 1 is the neural network, which includes one Long Short-Term Memory (LSTM) layer with a dimensionality of 512 for the output space and two dense layers, with 128 and 16 as their dimensionality of the output space respectively. (There are 16 known authors in Table 1.) A softmax activation function is applied to the output layer and the network is trained using cross-entropy loss. These hyperparameters are chosen after repeated train-and-validation trials.

From the input samples, we randomly select 80% of the samples for training and the rest for validation. Each training/validation generates a model. Since the network weights are initialized randomly, the final behavior of the models will differ somewhat from one training run to the next. On the same set of samples we ran the process 81 times. The average training accuracy of these runs reaches 96.9%, with a standard deviation of 0.01; the average validation accuracy is 89.1%, with a standard deviation of 0.018. An early stopping policy, with $1e-2$ min delta and patience of 3, was used. The average epoch number of these runs is 25.67, with a standard deviation of 2.43.

As one example of these 81 runs, the train and validation accuracies and losses are given in Fig. 2 and Fig. 3 respectively.

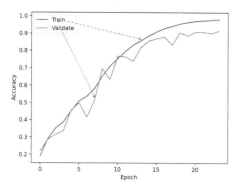

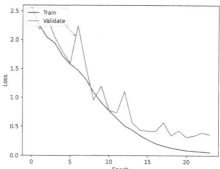

Fig. 2. Example code model accuracy   **Fig. 3.** Example model loss

4.4   Prediction Results and Interpretation

For each of the 24 source files in Bitcoin software v0.1.0, the 81 models described in Sect. 4.3 were used to predict its authorship. The prediction probability of each file by each model is above 90%. However, there is variation among the predictions by different models. Table 2 gives the most frequent attribution along with the percentage of models that made that attribution[2].

Care needs to be taken in interpreting the results of Table 2. In this study, we are essentially using the created neural network models to measure the relative "similarities" between the Bitcoin source code v0.1.0 and those 16 libraries in Table 1.

The results in Table 2 show that

1. None of the reported Bitcoin authorship is Hal Finney. In other words, the relative similarities between the source files of Bitcoin v0.1.0 and Hal Finney's code are not smaller than those between Bitcoin v0.1.0 and other libraries in Table 1. Compared to other authors in Table 1, Hal Finney is much less likely to be the developer or one of the developers of Bitcoin source code v0.1.0. This conclusion contradicts a popular belief that Finney is Satoshi.

---

[2] The data set and the corresponding computer programs for this part are available at https://github.com/wangxx2016/source-code-stylometry.

Table 2. Bitcoin source code authorship attribution over 81 runs

File Name	Reported Attribution	File Name	Reported Attribution
base58.h	CryptoPP (51%) TrueCrypt (49%)	*net.cpp*	TrueCrypt (52%) CryptoPP (48%)
bignum.h	CryptoPP (40%) TrueCrypt (41%) Botan (28%)	*net.h*	TrueCrypt (67%) CryptoPP (32%)
db.cpp	CryptoPP (70%) TrueCrypt (19%)	*script.cpp*	CryptoPP (54%) TrueCrypt (47%)
db.h	CryptoPP (53%) TrueCrypt (47%)	*script.h*	TrueCrypt (54%) CryptoPP (32%)
headers.h	TrueCrypt (54%) CryptoPP (44%)	*serialize.h*	TrueCrypt (77%)
irc.cpp	TrueCrypt (53%) CryptoPP (43%)	*ui.cpp*	TrueCrypt (36%) Botan (36%) CryptoPP (27%)
irc.h	TrueCrypt (75%)	*ui.h*	Botan (47%) TrueCrypt (25%)
keys.h	Botan (44%) TrueCrypt (40%)	*uibase.cpp*	CryptoPP (43%) TrueCrypt (41%)
main.cpp	CryptoPP (65%) TrueCrypt (35%)	*uibase.h*	CryptoPP (43%) TrueCrypt (41%)
main.h	TrueCrypt (80%) CryptoPP (20%)	*u256int.h*	TrueCrypt (84%)
market.cpp	TrueCrypt (57%) CryptoPP (43%)	*util.cpp*	TrueCrypt (85%)
market.h	TrueCrypt (94%)	*util.h*	TrueCrypt (85%)

2. Two source files, *db.cpp* and *main.cpp*, have the largest similarity to CryptoPP.
3. Eight source files, *irc.h*, *main.h*, *market.h*, *net.h*, *serialize.h*, *u256int.h*, *util.cpp*, and *util.h*, have the largest similarity to TrueCrypt.
4. TrueCrypt was developed by anonymous author(s). If TrueCrypt was *not* developed by the author of CryptoPP, Wei Dai, then there are multiple programming styles in Bitcoin v0.1.0 and it is likely that multiple developers have contributed to Bitcoin v0.1.0.

5 Document Tracing: Tracing the Authorship of the Bitcoin White Paper

In this section we shall use deep learning to trace the author(s) of another Bitcoin artifact, the Bitcoin white paper [31]. The Bitcoin white paper describes the high-level design of the Bitcoin cryptocurrency. However, there is *no* guarantee that the Bitcoin white paper author(s) is/are the same person(s) as the author(s) of the Bitcoin source code.

5.1 Data Collection

As a peer-to-peer cryptocurrency, Bitcoin is more than just a set of cryptographic techniques. Unlike the numerous cryptocurrencies before it, Bitcoin takes into considerations financial incentives for human beings through its *peer-to-peer* characteristic and the concept of *proof of work*. It more or less falls within the category of financial cryptography. Based on this observation, we chose the data set to include the following technical papers in English: Wei Dai's *b-money* [11], Adam Back's *hashcash* [3], Hal Finney's write-ups [12–17], and most papers from the proceedings of Financial Cryptography, between 1997 and 2012, organized by International Financial Cryptography Association (IFCA). A semi-technical writeup, Craig Wright's write-up [43], is also included.

In this data set, there are 436 unique known *author combinations*. An author combination can be either a single author or a combination of multiple authors. Two different author combinations may share one or more but not all authors. It is assumed that each author combination has its unique and distinguishable style. There is at least one technical paper, as a digital file, for each author combination. Most files are in the format of PDF and their textual content was extracted through optical character recognition. A further grammar check was conducted on the extracted texts to clean them up before they were sent to a neural network.

5.2 Data Modeling

Unlike the *character*-based computer source code of Sect. 4.3, the raw data of this part is based on English *words*. As shown in Fig. 4, the raw English word sequences are partitioned into fixed-size, 100-word *samples*. Each of the 436 labels has 40 samples. If the raw word sequence of a label is not long enough, overlapping samples are generated from the word sequence. This preprocessing step guarantees the balance of the training samples.

To take advantage of the nature of English words, as shown in Fig. 4, in the neural network model, Glove, the Global vectors for word presentation [36], is used in the untrainable embedding layer to reduce training time.

In the model of Fig. 4, a 1024 dimensional bidirectional LSTM is used, which is followed by a 256-dimensional Dense layer.

From the input samples the neural network randomly picks 80% of the samples for training and the rest for validation. Each training/validation generates

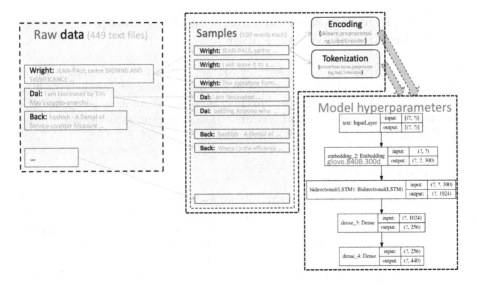

Fig. 4. Deep learning model for text

a model. This process is kind of probabilistic. On the same set of samples we ran the process 100 times. The average *training* accuracy of these runs reaches 96.6%, with a standard deviation of 0.008; the average *validation* accuracy is 55.1%, with a standard deviation of 0.014. The average epoch number of these runs is 14.66, with a standard deviation of 0.956. It should be noted that the 55.1% validation accuracy is achieved over the 436 labels, compared to 89.1% over 16 labels in Sect. 4.3.

As one example of these 100 runs, the train and validation accuracies and losses are given in Fig. 7 and Fig. 8 in the Appendix section respectively.

5.3   Prediction Results and Interpretation

For the Bitcoin white paper, the 100 models described in Sect. 5.2 were used to predict its authorship. While the prediction probability by each model is 97.5% on average (with a standard deviation of 0.028), there are variation among the predictions by different models. Figure 5 gives the attribution results, along with the percentage of models that made that attribution[3]. The *x*-axis is the *predicted labels* (i.e., attribution results), each of which consists of a unique number, the year of financial cryptography proceeding, the ordinal number of the article in the proceeding, and the last names of the author(s), all separated with a hyphen. The *y*-axis of Fig. 5 is the percentage of models that made that prediction.

---

[3] For this part, the computer programs and a part of the data, with copyrighted materials removed, are available at https://github.com/wangxx2016/text-stylometry/.

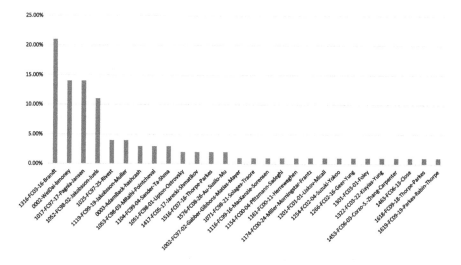

Fig. 5. Bitcoin white paper authorship attribution results

Figure 5 shows that

1. Among the 436 known labels, the Bitcoin white paper [31] is more similar, in style, to four papers (the leftmost four in Fig. 5), each supported by 21%, 14%, 14%, and 11% of the 100 models respectively;
2. Craig Wright's write-up [43] is *not* among the predicted labels;
3. Hal Finney's write-ups [12–17] are *not* among the predicted labels;

6   Discussions

Deep learning is an effective tool for classification and has big potential for both text and source code-based authorship identification. Several points warrant further discussions in using it for real-world authorship identification, especially in tracing the authorship of computer program source code.

It is worth noting that there are multiple differences between a controlled data set and a real-world data set. The source code in a controlled data set such as the Google Code Jam (GCJ) [20] is developed to solve the same set of problems and as a result, the authorship discriminators in it might be more identifiable than in other real-world data.

Second, in a controlled data set, there are a minimal number of files (for example, seven or ten [2]) for each author and this may not be true in many real-world applications. Often, as shown in Sect. 4.2, steps are needed to generate mutants for balancing real-world training data.

Third, authorship attribution on a controlled data set is a closed-set classification, where the target author is assumed/known to be in a given set of authors. This is *not* necessarily true for applications like Bitcoin, as it is hard to tell whether Satoshi is among any given set of authors. The Bitcoin authorship attribution is an open-set classification problem [18]. As a result, as shown in Sect. 4.4 and Sect. 5.3, the deep learning classification results can help us evaluate negative statements such as Finney did not write the Bitcoin software; in the open-set setting, they cannot help us evaluate positive statements like Wright has developed the Bitcoin software.

Another point in using deep learning classification for authorship attribution is that the attribution results depend heavily on the chosen data set. This is also true in our studies of the Bitcoin source code in Sect. 4 and the Bitcoin white paper in Sect. 5. The current selections of the cryptographic libraries in our first data set and the structured technical papers in our second data set are intuitive and can be expanded in future work, for example, to include less structured writings such as blog and discussion forum posts.

7 Summary

Despite having become a household name, the identities of Bitcoin's creator(s) are not known. To trace the author(s) of the Bitcoin source code and Bitcoin white paper, we compiled two data sets, developed computer programs based on deep learning techniques, used the programs to train models on the two data sets, and then used the models to predict the authors of Bitcoin. The first data set has 16 known labels, the model validation accuracy reaches 89.1%, and the prediction results of our models contradict one popular belief that Hal Finney is Satoshi; the prediction results also indicate that there might be multiple contributors to the code. The second data set has 436 labels, the model validation accuracy reaches 55.1%, and the prediction results on the Bitcoin white paper have identified four technical papers that are more similar than others to the Bitcoin white paper.

Our first data set also provides a useful tool for identifying/excluding possible Satoshi and will be shared so that others may find better ways to leverage the data.

Acknowledgments. The authors wish to thank the anonymous reviewers for their insightful comments and the shepherd for the pointed guidance. We also thank Jason Brake and Sam Martins for setting up the environment in the early stage of the project. This work is supported in part by the state of Virginia's Commonwealth Cyber Initiative (CCI) through its Northern Virginia node.

Appendix

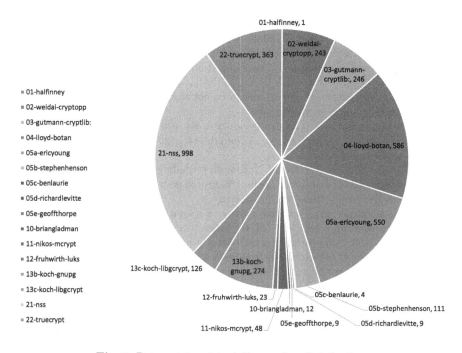

Fig. 6. Data set 1: original file number distribution

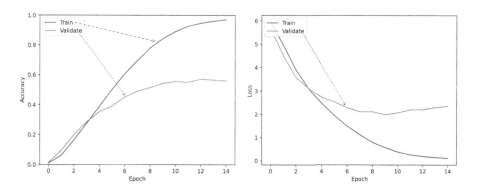

Fig. 7. Example text model accuracy   **Fig. 8.** Example text model loss

References

1. Abadi, M.: TensorFlow: a system for large-scale machine learning. In: Proceedings of the 12th USENIX Conference on Operating Systems Design and Implementation (OSDI'16), pp. 265–283 (2016)

2. Abuhamad, M., AbuHmed, T., Mohaisen, A., Nyang, D.: Large-scale and language-oblivious code authorship identification. In: Proceedings of the 2018 ACM SIGSAC Conference on Computer and Communications Security (CCS '18), pp. 101–114 (2018)

3. Back, A.: Hashcash - a denial of service counter-measure (2002). http://www.hashcash.org/papers/hashcash.pdf

4. bit(bit@ungeared.com). The strange story of Satoshi Nakamoto's spelling choices, 31 Dec 2020. https://ungeared.com/the-strange-story-of-satoshi-nakamotos-spelling-choices-part-1/

5. bit(bit@ungeared.com). Satoshi Nakamoto's spelling paradox solved: everything was by design, 11 Jan 2021. https://ungeared.com/satoshi-nakamotos-spelling-paradox-solved-everything-was-by-design/

6. bit(bit@ungeared.com). Authorship dispute resolution method applied to uncover Satoshi Nakamoto, 18 Jan 2021. https://ungeared.com/authorship-dispute-resolution-method-applied-to-uncover-satoshi-nakamoto/

7. Caliskan-Islam, A., et al.: De-anonymizing programmers via code stylometry. In: Proceedings of the 24th USENIX Security Symposium, pp. 255–270(August), pp. 12–14, 2015. https://www.usenix.org/conference/usenixsecurity15/technical-sessions/presentation/caliskan-islam

8. Certicom Research. Sec 2: Recommended elliptic curve domain parameters version 2.0. Standards for Efficient Cryptography, 27 Jan 2010. http://www.secg.org/sec2-v2.pdf

9. Chollet, F.: Deep Learning with Python. Manning (2017). ISBN 9781617294433

10. Chon, M.: Stylometric analysis: Satoshi Nakamoto, 26 Dec 2017. https://towardsdatascience.com/stylometric-analysis-satoshi-nakamoto-294926cdf995

11. Dai, W.: b-money (1998). http://www.weidai.com/bmoney.txt

12. Finney, H.: Digital cash & privacy, 19 Aug 1993. http://fennetic.net/irc/finney.org/hal/dig_cash_priv.html

13. Finney, H.: Detecting double spending, 15 Oct 1993. https://nakamotoinstitute.org/detecting-double-spending/

14. Finney, H.: PGP web of trust misconceptions, 30 Mar 1994. http://fennetic.net/irc/finney.org/hal/web_of_trust.html

15. Finney, H.: RPOW - reusable proofs of work, 15 Aug 2004. https://cryptome.org/rpow.htm

16. Finney, H.: Dying outside, 4th Oct 2009. https://www.lesswrong.com/posts/bshZiaLefDejvPKuS/dying-outside

17. Finney, H.: Bitcoin and me, 19 March 2013. https://bitcointalk.org/index.php?topic=155054.0

18. Geng, C., Huang, S.J., Chen, S.: Recent advances in open set recognition: a survey. In: IEEE transactions on pattern analysis and machine intelligence, Mar 18 (2020)

19. Goodman, L.: The face behind bitcoin. Newsweek, 6 March 2014. http://www.newsweek.com/2014/03/14/face-behind-bitcoin-247957.html

20. Google. Google code jam. https://codingcompetitions.withgoogle.com/codejam

21. Google. TensorFlow: an end-to-end open source machine learning platform. https://www.tensorflow.org/

22. Gray, A., Sallis, P., MacDonell, S.: IDENTIFIED (integrated dictionary-based extraction of non-language dependent token information for forensic identification, examination, and discrimination): a dictionary-based system for extracting source code metrics for software forensics. In Proceedings of the 1998 International Conference Software Engineering: Education and Practice, 29 Jan 1998

23. Grey, S.: Satoshi Nakamoto is (probably) Nick Szabo, 1 Dec 2013. https://likeinamirror.wordpress.com/2013/12/01/satoshi-nakamoto-is-probably-nick-szabo/

24. Hubbs, C.: Can machine learning unmask Satoshi Nakamoto? Sept 2017. https://www.datahubbs.com/can-machine-learning-unmask-satoshi-nakamoto/

25. Kaminsky, D.: Validating Satoshi (or not), 2 May 2016. https://dankaminsky.com/2016/05/02/validating-satoshi-or-not/

26. LeCun, Y., Bengio, Y., Hinton, G.: Deep learning. Nature **521**, 436–444 (2015)

27. Robert, A., Matthews, J., Thomas, V., Merriam, N.: Neural omputation in stylometry I: an application to the works of shakespeare and fletcher. Literary and Linguistic Computing, 8 (4), 203–209 (1993)

28. Thomas, V., Merriam, N., Robert, A., Matthews, J.: Neural computation in stylometry II: An application to the works of shakespeare and marlowe merriam. Literary Linguist. Comput. **9**(1), 1–6 (1994)

29. michael@bitstein.org. The complete Satoshi. https://satoshi.nakamotoinstitute.org/

30. Mosteller, F., Wallace D.L.: Applied Bayesian and classical inference: the case of the federalist papers. Springer, New York (1984). https://doi.org/10.1007/978-1-4612-5256-6

31. Nakamoto, S.: Bitcoin: a peer-to-peer electronic cash system. First released to the cryptography mailing list on October 31, 2008 at https://www.metzdowd.com/pipermail/cryptography/2008-October/014810.html; however, the commonly seen PDF file carries a creation timestamp of March 24, 2009, (2008). http://bitcoin.org/bitcoin.pdf

32. Nakamoto, S.: I am not Dorian Nakamoto, 7 March 2014. http://p2pfoundation.ning.com/forum/topics/bitcoin-open-source?commentId=2003008

33. National Institute of Standards and Technology. Secure hash standard (SHS). FIPS PUB 180-4, March 2012. http://csrc.nist.gov/publications/fips/fips180-4/fips-180-4.pdf

34. National Institute of Standards and Technology. Digital signature standard (DSS). FIPS PUB 186-4 July 2013. http://nvlpubs.nist.gov/nistpubs/FIPS/NIST.FIPS.186-4.pdf

35. Oman, P.W., Cook, C.R.: Typographic style is more than cosmetic. Commun. ACM **33**(5), 506–519 (1990)

36. Pennington, J., Socher, R., Manning, C.D.: Glove: global vectors for word representation. In: Empirical Methods in Natural Language Processing (EMNLP), pp. 1532–1543 (2014). http://www.aclweb.org/anthology/D14-1162

37. Protos. Finney 'most likely' bitcoin's Nakamoto, say researchers, 18 Jan 2021. https://protos.com/bitcoin-creator-satoshi-nakamoto-candidates-analysis-hal-finney/

38. Quiring, E., Maier, A., Rieck, K.: Misleading authorship attribution of source code using adversarial learning. In: Proceedings of the 28th USENIX Security Symposium, August 14–16 2019. https://www.usenix.org/system/files/sec19-quiring.pdf

39. Ramesh, V., Watson, J.L.: Shakespeare and Satoshi - de-anonymizing writing using BiLSTMs with attention, 31 Dec 2018. https://web.stanford.edu/class/archive/cs/cs224n/cs224n.1184/reports/6858026.pdf

40. The Economist. Craig Wright reveals himself as Satoshi Nakamoto. The Economist, 2nd May 2016. https://www.economist.com/briefing/2016/05/02/craig-wright-reveals-himself-as-satoshi-nakamoto

41. The U.S. Copyright Office. Questions about certain bitcoin registrations, 22 May 2019. https://www.copyright.gov/press-media-info/press-updates.html

42. Watson, T.: A fascinating discovery uncovers Satoshi Nakamoto's identity, 26 May 2021. https://zycrypto.com/exclusive-a-fascinating-discovery-uncovers-satoshi-nakamotos-identity/

43. Wright, C.: Jean-Paul Sartre, signing and significance, 02 May 2016. https://craigwright.net/blog/math/jean-paul-sartre-signing-and-significance/

Author Index